THE

PUBLIC GENERAL ACTS

AND GENERAL SYNOD MEASURES

2010

[IN FOUR PARTS]

PART II

(Chapters 8-15)

with

Lists of the Public General Acts

Local Acts and General Synod Measures

information & publishing solutions

Published by TSO (The Stationery Office) and available from:

Online
www.tsoshop.co.uk

Mail, Telephone, Fax & E-mail
TSO
PO Box 29, Norwich NR3 1GN
General enquiries: 0870 600 5522
Order through the Parliamentary Hotline *Lo-call* 0845 7 023474
Fax orders: 0870 600 5533
Email: customer.services@tso.co.uk
Textphone: 0870 240 3701

The Parliamentary Bookshop
12 Bridge Street, Parliament Square
London SW1A 2JX
Telephone orders: 020 7219 3890
General enquiries: 020 7219 3890
Fax orders: 020 7219 3866
Email: bookshop@parliament.uk
Internet: http://www.bookshop.parliament.uk

TSO@Blackwell and other Accredited Agents

ISBN 9780118405133

LONDON BOROUGH OF
BARKING & DAGENHAM

REFERENCE

LIBRARIES

THIS PUBLICATION

relates to

the Public General Acts
and General Synod Measures
which received the Royal Assent in 2010
in which year ended the FIFTY-EIGHTH YEAR
and began the FIFTY-NINTH YEAR
of the Reign of HER MAJESTY
QUEEN ELIZABETH THE SECOND
and
ended the Fifth Session
of the Fifty-Fourth Parliament
and began the First Session of the Fifty-Fifth Parliament
of the United Kingdom of Great Britain
and Northern Ireland

The Table of Effect of Legislation has been prepared for the Queen's
Printer of Acts of Parliament by Justis Publishing Ltd.

First published 2011
Printed in the UK by The Stationery Office Limited under the authority
and superintendence of Carol Tullo, Controller of Her Majesty's
Stationery Office and Queen's Printer of Acts of Parliament.

CONTENTS

TABLE I
Alphabetical List of
the Public General Acts of 2010

TABLE II
Chronological List of
the Public General Acts of 2010

TABLE III
Alphabetical List of
the Local and Personal Acts of 2010

TABLE IV
Chronological List of
the General Synod Measures of 2010

Taxation (International and Other Provisions) Act 2010

CHAPTER 8

CONTENTS

CHAPTER 2

DOUBLE TAXATION RELIEF BY WAY OF CREDIT

Effect to be given to credit for foreign tax allowed against UK tax

Interpretation of Chapter

Credits where same income charged to income tax in more than one tax year

Cases in which credit not allowed

Exceptions to requirement to be UK resident

Calculating income or gains in respect of which credit is allowed

Limits on credit: general rules

Limit on, and reduction of, credit against income tax

CHAPTER 3

MISCELLANEOUS PROVISIONS

PART 3

DOUBLE TAXATION RELIEF FOR SPECIAL WITHHOLDING TAX

PART 4

TRANSFER PRICING

CHAPTER 1

BASIC TRANSFER-PRICING RULE

CHAPTER 2

KEY INTERPRETATIVE PROVISIONS

Meaning of certain expressions that first appear in section 147

"Direct participation" in management, control or capital of a person

"Indirect participation" in management, control or capital of a person

Application of OECD principles

CHAPTER 3

EXEMPTIONS FROM BASIC RULE

CHAPTER 4

POSITION, IF ONLY ONE AFFECTED PERSON POTENTIALLY ADVANTAGED, OF OTHER AFFECTED PERSON

Claim by affected person who is not advantaged

Claims: special cases

Alternative way of claiming if a security is involved

Notification to persons who may be disadvantaged

Treatment of interest where claim made

Adjustment of double taxation relief where claim made

Interpretation of Chapter

CHAPTER 5

POSITION OF GUARANTOR OF AFFECTED PERSON'S LIABILITIES UNDER A SECURITY ISSUED BY THE PERSON

PART 7

TAX TREATMENT OF FINANCING COSTS AND INCOME

CHAPTER 1

INTRODUCTION

CHAPTER 2

APPLICATION OF PART

CHAPTER 3

DISALLOWANCE OF DEDUCTIONS

CHAPTER 4

EXEMPTION OF FINANCING INCOME

CHAPTER 5

INTRA-GROUP FINANCING INCOME WHERE PAYER DENIED DEDUCTION

CHAPTER 6

TAX AVOIDANCE

CHAPTER 7

"FINANCING EXPENSE AMOUNT" AND "FINANCING INCOME AMOUNT"

CHAPTER 8

"TESTED EXPENSE AMOUNT" AND "TESTED INCOME AMOUNT"

CHAPTER 9

"AVAILABLE AMOUNT"

CHAPTER 10

OTHER INTERPRETATIVE PROVISIONS

PART 8

OFFSHORE FUNDS

Tax treatment of participants in offshore funds

Supplementary

PART 9

AMENDMENTS TO RELOCATE PROVISIONS OF TAX LEGISLATION

PART 10

GENERAL PROVISIONS

Subordinate legislation

Interpretation

Final provisions

Taxation (International and Other Provisions) Act 2010

2010 CHAPTER 8

An Act to restate, with minor changes, certain enactments relating to tax; to make provision for purposes connected with the restatement of enactments by other tax law rewrite Acts; and for connected purposes.

[18th March 2010]

B E IT ENACTED by the Queen's most Excellent Majesty, by and with the advice and consent of the Lords Spiritual and Temporal, and Commons, in this present Parliament assembled, and by the authority of the same, as follows: —

PART 1

OVERVIEW

1   Overview of Act

(1)   The following Parts contain provisions relating to international aspects of taxation—

    (a)   Parts 2 and 3 (double taxation relief),

    (b)   Parts 4 and 5 (transfer pricing and advance pricing agreements),

    (c)   Part 6 (tax arbitrage),

    (d)   Part 7 (tax treatment of financing costs and income), and

    (e)   Part 8 (offshore funds).

(2)   Part 9 contains amendments of tax legislation to relocate enactments to appropriate places.

(3)   In particular, Part 9 contains amendments of TCGA 1992, ITTOIA 2005 and ITA 2007 that insert provisions relating to—

    (a)   oil activities (see section 364 and Schedule 1),

    (b)   alternative finance arrangements (see section 365 and Schedule 2),

(c)   leasing arrangements involving finance leases or loans (see section 367 and Schedule 3),

(d)   sale and lease-back etc (see section 368 and Schedule 4),

(e)   factoring of income etc (see section 369 and Schedule 5), and

(f)   UK representatives of non-UK residents (see section 370 and Schedule 6).

(4)   Part 10 contains provisions of general application (including definitions for the purposes of the Act).

(5)   For abbreviations used in this Act see section 373, and for defined expressions used in Parts 2 to 8 see Schedule 11.

PART 2

DOUBLE TAXATION RELIEF

CHAPTER 1

DOUBLE TAXATION ARRANGEMENTS AND UNILATERAL RELIEF ARRANGEMENTS

Double taxation arrangements

2   Giving effect to arrangements made in relation to other territories

(1)   If Her Majesty by Order in Council declares —

(a)   that arrangements specified in the Order have been made in relation to any territory outside the United Kingdom with a view to affording relief from double taxation in relation to taxes within subsection (3), and

(b)   that it is expedient that those arrangements should have effect,

those arrangements have effect.

(2)   If arrangements have effect under subsection (1), they have effect in accordance with section 6.

(3)   The taxes are —

(a)   income tax,

(b)   corporation tax,

(c)   capital gains tax,

(d)   petroleum revenue tax, and

(e)   any taxes imposed by the law of the territory that are of a similar character to taxes within paragraphs (a) to (d).

(4)   In this Part "double taxation arrangements" means arrangements that have effect under subsection (1).

3   Arrangements may include retrospective or supplementary provision

(1)   Section 2(1) gives effect to arrangements even if the arrangements include —

(a)   provision for relief from tax for periods before the passing of this Act, or

(b)   provision for relief from tax for periods before the making of the arrangements.

Taxation (International and Other Provisions) Act 2010 (c. 8)   895
Part 2 — Double taxation relief
Chapter 1 — Double taxation arrangements and unilateral relief arrangements

(2) Section 2(1) gives effect to arrangements even if the arrangements include—

    (a) provision as to income that is not subject to double taxation,

    (b) provision as to chargeable gains that are not subject to double taxation, or

    (c) provision as to foreign-field consideration that is not subject to double taxation.

(3) In subsection (2)(c) "foreign-field consideration" means consideration brought into charge to tax under section 12 of the Oil Taxation Act 1983 (charge to petroleum revenue tax on consideration in respect of United Kingdom use of a foreign field asset).

4 Meaning of "double taxation" in sections 2 and 3

(1) For the purposes of sections 2 and 3, any amount within subsection (2) is to be treated as having been payable.

(2) An amount is within this subsection if it is an amount of tax that would have been payable under the law of a territory outside the United Kingdom but for a relief—

    (a) given under the law of the territory with a view to promoting industrial, commercial, scientific, educational or other development in a territory outside the United Kingdom, and

    (b) about which provision is made in double taxation arrangements.

(3) References in sections 2 and 3 to double taxation are to be read in accordance with subsection (1).

5 Orders under section 2: contents and procedure

(1) If an Order under section 2 ("the later Order") revokes an earlier Order under that section, the later Order may contain transitional provisions that appear to Her Majesty to be necessary or expedient.

(2) An Order under section 2 is not to be submitted to Her Majesty in Council unless a draft of the Order has been laid before and approved by a resolution of the House of Commons.

6 The effect given by section 2 to double taxation arrangements

(1) Subject to this Part and Part 18 of ICTA, double taxation arrangements have effect in accordance with subsections (2) to (4) despite anything in any enactment.

(2) Double taxation arrangements have effect in relation to income tax and corporation tax so far as the arrangements provide—

    (a) for relief from income tax or corporation tax,

    (b) for taxing income of non-UK resident persons that arises from sources in the United Kingdom,

    (c) for taxing chargeable gains accruing to non-UK resident persons on the disposal of assets in the United Kingdom,

    (d) for determining the income or chargeable gains to be attributed to non-UK resident persons,

896

Taxation (International and Other Provisions) Act 2010 (c. 8)
Part 2 — Double taxation relief
Chapter 1 — Double taxation arrangements and unilateral relief arrangements

   (e)   for determining the income or chargeable gains to be attributed to agencies, branches or establishments in the United Kingdom of non-UK resident persons,

   (f)   for determining the income or chargeable gains to be attributed to UK resident persons who have special relationships with non-UK resident persons, or

   (g)   for conferring on non-UK resident persons the right to a tax credit under section 397(1) of ITTOIA 2005 in respect of qualifying distributions made to them by UK resident companies.

(3)   Double taxation arrangements have effect in relation to capital gains tax so far as the arrangements provide —

   (a)   for relief from capital gains tax,

   (b)   for taxing capital gains accruing to non-UK resident persons on the disposal of assets in the United Kingdom,

   (c)   for determining the capital gains to be attributed to non-UK resident persons,

   (d)   for determining the capital gains to be attributed to agencies, branches or establishments in the United Kingdom of non-UK resident persons, or

   (e)   for determining the capital gains to be attributed to UK resident persons who have special relationships with non-UK resident persons.

(4)   Double taxation arrangements have effect in relation to petroleum revenue tax so far as the arrangements provide for relief from petroleum revenue tax charged under section 12 of the Oil Taxation Act 1983 (charge to petroleum revenue tax on consideration in respect of United Kingdom use of a foreign field asset).

(5)   In the case of relief under this Chapter that is not also relief under Chapter 2, the relief is not available in respect of special withholding tax (a corresponding rule applies in relation to relief under Chapter 2 as a result of the definition of foreign tax given by section 21).

(6)   Relief under subsection (2)(a), (3)(a) or (4) requires a claim.

(7)   In subsection (3) "UK resident person" and "non-UK resident person" have the meaning given by section 989 of ITA 2007.

(8)   In subsection (5) "special withholding tax" has the same meaning as in Part 3 (see section 136).

7   General regulations

(1)   The Commissioners for Her Majesty's Revenue and Customs may make regulations generally for carrying out the provisions of the treaty sections or any double taxation arrangements.

(2)   Regulations under subsection (1) may in particular provide for securing that relief from taxation imposed by the law of the territory to which any double taxation arrangements relate does not enure for the benefit of persons not entitled to that relief.

(3)   Subsection (4) applies to tax if —

   (a)   the tax is deductible from a payment but, in order to comply with double taxation arrangements, has not been deducted, and

Taxation (International and Other Provisions) Act 2010 (c. 8)   897
Part 2 — Double taxation relief
Chapter 1 — Double taxation arrangements and unilateral relief arrangements

     (b)   it is discovered that the arrangements did not apply to that payment.

(4)   Regulations under subsection (1) may in particular provide for authorising recovery of tax to which this subsection applies —

     (a)   by assessment on the person entitled to the payment from which the tax is not deducted, or

     (b)   by deduction from subsequent payments.

(5)   In subsection (1) "the treaty sections" means —

       sections 2 to 6,

       section 134(1), and

       section 134(3) to (6) so far as relating to section 134(1).

(6)   This section does not apply in relation to —

     (a)   petroleum revenue tax, or

     (b)   taxes imposed by the law of a territory outside the United Kingdom that—

        (i)   are of a similar character to petroleum revenue tax, and

        (ii)   are not of a similar character to income tax, corporation tax or capital gains tax.

Unilateral relief arrangements

8   Interpretation: "unilateral relief arrangements" means rules 1 to 9, etc

(1)   In this Part "unilateral relief arrangements", in relation to a territory outside the United Kingdom, means the rules set out in sections 9 to 17.

(2)   In sections 11 to 17, and in Chapter 2 (except section 29) in its application to relief under unilateral relief arrangements, references to tax payable or paid under the law of a territory outside the United Kingdom include only —

     (a)   taxes which are charged on income and which correspond to income tax,

     (b)   taxes which are charged on income or chargeable gains and which correspond to corporation tax, and

     (c)   taxes which are charged on capital gains and which correspond to capital gains tax.

(3)   For the purposes of subsection (2), tax may correspond to income tax, corporation tax or capital gains tax even though it —

     (a)   is payable under the law of a province, state or other part of a country, or

     (b)   is levied by or on behalf of a municipality or other local body.

9   Rule 1: the unilateral entitlement to credit for non-UK tax

(1)   Credit for tax —

     (a)   paid under the law of the territory,

     (b)   calculated by reference to income arising, or any chargeable gain accruing, in the territory, and

     (c)   corresponding to UK tax,

is to be allowed against any income tax or corporation tax calculated by reference to that income or gain.

898   *Taxation (International and Other Provisions) Act 2010 (c. 8)*
Part 2 — Double taxation relief
Chapter 1 — Double taxation arrangements and unilateral relief arrangements

(2) Credit for tax —

    (a)   paid under the law of the territory,

    (b)   calculated by reference to any capital gain accruing in the territory, and

    (c)   corresponding to UK tax,

is to be allowed against any capital gains tax calculated by reference to that gain.

(3) For the purposes of subsection (1), profits from, or remuneration for, personal or professional services performed in the territory are to be treated as income arising in the territory.

(4) For the purposes of subsection (1)(c), tax corresponds to UK tax if —

    (a)   it is charged on income and corresponds to income tax, or

    (b)   it is charged on income or chargeable gains and corresponds to corporation tax.

(5) For the purposes of subsection (2)(c), tax corresponds to UK tax if it is charged on capital gains and corresponds to capital gains tax.

(6) For the purposes of subsections (4) and (5), tax may correspond to income tax, corporation tax or capital gains tax even though it —

    (a)   is payable under the law of a province, state or other part of a country, or

    (b)   is levied by or on behalf of a municipality or other local body.

(7) If the territory is the Isle of Man or any of the Channel Islands, subsections (1)(b) and (2)(b) have effect with the omission of "in the territory".

(8) Subsections (1) and (2) are subject to sections 11 and 12.

10   Rule 2: accrued income profits

(1) Subsection (2) applies if —

    (a)   a person is treated under section 628(5) of ITA 2007 as making accrued income profits in an interest period,

    (b)   the person would, were the person to become entitled in the relevant tax year to any interest on the securities concerned, be liable in respect of the interest to tax chargeable under ITTOIA 2005 on relevant foreign income, and

    (c)   the person is liable under the law of the territory to tax in respect of interest payable on the securities at the end of the interest period or the person would be so liable if the person were entitled to that interest.

(2) Credit is to be allowed against income tax calculated by reference to the accrued income profits.

(3) The amount of the credit allowed under subsection (2) is given by —

$$AIP \times FTR$$

where —

     AIP is the amount of the accrued income profits, and

     FTR is the rate of tax to which the person is or would be liable as mentioned in subsection (1)(c).

(4) Subsection (2) is subject to section 11.

Taxation (International and Other Provisions) Act 2010 (c. 8)
Part 2 – Double taxation relief
Chapter 1 – Double taxation arrangements and unilateral relief arrangements

899

(5) In subsection (1)(b) "the relevant tax year" means the tax year in which, under section 617(2) of ITA 2007, the accrued income profits are treated as made.

(6) Expressions used in this section and in Chapter 2 of Part 12 of ITA 2007 (accrued income profits) have the same meaning as in that Chapter.

11   Rule 3: interaction between double taxation arrangements and rules 1 and 2

(1) Credit for tax paid under the law of the territory is not allowed under section 9 or 10 in the case of any income or gains if any credit for that tax is allowable in respect of that income or those gains under double taxation arrangements made in relation to the territory.

(2) If credit in respect of an amount of tax may be allowed under double taxation arrangements made in relation to the territory, credit is not allowed under section 9 or 10 in respect of that tax.

(3) If double taxation arrangements made in relation to the territory contain express provision to the effect that relief by way of credit is not to be given under the arrangements in cases or circumstances specified or described in the arrangements, credit is not allowed under section 9 or 10 in those cases or circumstances.

12   Rule 4: cases in which, and calculation of, credit allowed for tax on dividends

(1) Credit under section 9 for overseas tax on a dividend paid by a company ("P") resident in the territory is allowed only if section 13, 14, 15 or 16 so provides.

(2) If credit is allowed in principle as a result of at least one of sections 14, 15 and 16, any tax in respect of P's profits that is paid by P under the law of the territory is to be taken into account in considering whether any, and (if so) what, credit is in fact to be allowed under section 9 in respect of the dividend.

(3) If credit is allowed in principle as a result of at least one of sections 15 and 16, there is to be taken into account, as if it were tax payable under the law of the territory, any tax that would be so taken into account under section 63(5) if the recipient of the dividend—

 (a) directly or indirectly controlled, or

 (b) were a subsidiary of a company that directly or indirectly controlled,

at least 10% of the voting power in P.

(4) For the purposes of subsection (3), the recipient is a subsidiary of another company if the other company controls, directly or indirectly, at least 50% of the voting power in the recipient.

13   Rule 5: credit for tax charged directly on dividend

(1) This section applies for the purposes of section 12(1).

(2) Credit under section 9 for overseas tax on a dividend paid by a company ("P") resident in the territory is allowed if—

 (a) the overseas tax is charged directly on the dividend (whether by charge to tax, deduction of tax at source or otherwise), and

 (b) neither P nor the recipient of the dividend would have borne any of that tax if the dividend had not been paid.

900   *Taxation (International and Other Provisions) Act 2010 (c. 8)*
Part 2 – Double taxation relief
Chapter 1 – Double taxation arrangements and unilateral relief arrangements

14   **Rule 6: credit for underlying tax on dividend paid to 10% associate of payer**

(1)   This section applies for the purposes of section 12(1).

(2)   Credit under section 9 for overseas tax on a dividend paid by a company ("P") resident in the territory is allowed if conditions A and B are met.

(3)   Condition A is that—

    (a)   the recipient of the dividend is a company resident in the United Kingdom, or

    (b)   the recipient is a company resident outside the United Kingdom but the dividend forms part of the profits of a permanent establishment of the recipient in the United Kingdom.

(4)   Condition B is that the recipient—

    (a)   directly or indirectly controls, or

    (b)   is a subsidiary of a company which directly or indirectly controls,

at least 10% of the voting power in P.

(5)   For the purposes of subsection (4), the recipient is a subsidiary of another company if the other company controls, directly or indirectly, at least 50% of the voting power in the recipient.

15   **Rule 7: credit for underlying tax on dividend paid to sub-10% associate**

(1)   This section applies for the purposes of section 12(1).

(2)   Credit under section 9 for overseas tax on a dividend paid by a company ("P") resident in the territory is allowed if each of conditions A to C is met.

(3)   Condition A is that—

    (a)   the recipient of the dividend is a company resident in the United Kingdom, or

    (b)   the recipient is a company resident outside the United Kingdom but the dividend forms part of the profits of a permanent establishment of the recipient in the United Kingdom.

(4)   Condition B is that the recipient—

    (a)   directly or indirectly controls, or

    (b)   is a subsidiary of a company which directly or indirectly controls,

less than 10% of the voting power in P.

(5)   If condition B is met, in subsection (6) "the held percentage" means the voting power in P which is directly or indirectly controlled by—

    (a)   the recipient, or

    (b)   a company of which the recipient is a subsidiary.

(6)   Condition C is that—

    (a)   the held percentage has been reduced below 10%,

    (b)   the recipient shows that the reduction below the 10% limit (and any further reduction)—

        (i)   could not have been prevented by any reasonable endeavours on the part of the recipient, a parent or an associate, and

        (ii)   was due to a cause or causes not reasonably foreseeable by the recipient, a parent or an associate when control of the relevant voting power was acquired, and

Taxation (International and Other Provisions) Act 2010 (c. 8)   901
Part 2 — Double taxation relief
Chapter 1 — Double taxation arrangements and unilateral relief arrangements

    (c)   the recipient shows that no reasonable endeavours on the part of the recipient, a parent or an associate could have restored, or (as the case may be) increased, the held percentage to at least 10%.

(7)   For the purposes of subsection (6) a company is an "associate" if —

    (a)   the company is neither the recipient nor a parent,

    (b)   before the reduction, the voting power in P that is in question was controlled otherwise than directly by the recipient, and

    (c)   the company is relevant for determining whether, before the reduction, the recipient —

        (i)   indirectly controlled, or

        (ii)   was a subsidiary of a company which directly or indirectly controlled,

    at least 10% of the voting power in P.

(8)   In subsections (6) and (7) "parent" means a company of which the recipient is a subsidiary.

(9)   In subsection (6) "the relevant voting power" means —

    (a)   the voting power in P as a result of which relief was due under section 14 before the reduction, or

    (b)   if control of the whole of that voting power was not acquired at the same time, that part of the voting power of which control was last acquired.

(10)   For the purposes of this section, the recipient is a subsidiary of another company if the other company controls, directly or indirectly, at least 50% of the voting power in the recipient.

16   Rule 8: credit for underlying tax on dividend paid by exchanged associate

(1)   This section applies for the purposes of section 12(1).

(2)   Credit under section 9 for overseas tax on a dividend paid by a company ("P") resident in the territory is allowed if each of conditions A to C is met.

(3)   Condition A is that —

    (a)   the recipient of the dividend is a company resident in the United Kingdom, or

    (b)   the recipient is a company resident outside the United Kingdom but the dividend forms part of the profits of a permanent establishment of the recipient in the United Kingdom.

(4)   Condition B is that the recipient —

    (a)   directly or indirectly controls, or

    (b)   is a subsidiary of a company which directly or indirectly controls,

    less than 10% of the voting power in P.

(5)   If condition B is met, in subsection (6) "the held percentage" means the voting power in P which is directly or indirectly controlled by —

    (a)   the recipient, or

    (b)   a company of which the recipient is a subsidiary.

(6)   Condition C is that —

902   *Taxation (International and Other Provisions) Act 2010 (c. 8)*
Part 2 — Double taxation relief
Chapter 1 — Double taxation arrangements and unilateral relief arrangements

    (a)   the held percentage has been acquired in exchange for voting power in another company ("X"),

    (b)   before the exchange, the recipient—

        (i)   directly or indirectly controlled, or

        (ii)   was a subsidiary of a company which directly or indirectly controlled,

    at least 10% of the voting power in X,

    (c)   the recipient shows that the exchange (and any reduction after the exchange)—

        (i)   could not have been prevented by any reasonable endeavours on the part of the recipient, a parent or an associate, and

        (ii)   was due to a cause or causes not reasonably foreseeable by the recipient, a parent or an associate when control of the relevant voting power was acquired, and

    (d)   the recipient shows that no reasonable endeavours on the part of the recipient, a parent or an associate could have restored, or (as the case may be) increased, the held percentage to at least 10%.

(7)   For the purposes of subsection (6) a company is an "associate" if—

    (a)   the company is neither the recipient nor a parent,

    (b)   before the exchange, the voting power in X that is in question was controlled otherwise than directly by the recipient, and

    (c)   the company is relevant for determining whether, before the exchange, the recipient—

        (i)   indirectly controlled, or

        (ii)   was a subsidiary of a company which directly or indirectly controlled,

    at least 10% of the voting power in X.

(8)   In subsections (6) and (7) "parent" means a company of which the recipient is a subsidiary.

(9)   In subsection (6) "the relevant voting power" means—

    (a)   the voting power in X as a result of which relief was due under section 14 before the exchange, or

    (b)   if control of the whole of that voting power was not acquired at the same time, that part of the voting power of which control was last acquired.

(10)   For the purposes of this section, the recipient is a subsidiary of another company if the other company controls, directly or indirectly, at least 50% of the voting power in the recipient.

17   Rule 9: credit in relation to dividends for spared tax

(1)   Subsection (2) applies if—

    (a)   under the law of the territory, an amount of tax ("the spared tax") would, but for a relief, have been payable by a company resident in the territory ("company A") in respect of any of its profits,

    (b)   company A pays a dividend out of those profits to another company resident in the territory ("company B"),

Taxation (International and Other Provisions) Act 2010 (c. 8)   903
Part 2 – Double taxation relief
Chapter 1 – Double taxation arrangements and unilateral relief arrangements

      (c)   company B, out of profits which consist of or include the whole or part of that dividend, pays a dividend to a company resident in the United Kingdom ("company C"), and

      (d)   the circumstances are such that, had company B been resident in the United Kingdom, it would have been entitled, as a result of the operation of section 20(2) in relation to double taxation arrangements made in relation to the territory, to treat the spared tax for the purposes of Chapter 2 as having been payable.

(2)   The spared tax is to be taken into account —

      (a)   for the purposes of sections 9 to 16, and

      (b)   subject to section 31(4), for the purposes of Chapter 2 in its application to relief under these rules in relation to the dividend paid to company C,

as if it had been payable and paid.

(3)   References in these rules and that Chapter —

      (a)   to tax payable or chargeable, or

      (b)   to tax not chargeable directly or by deduction,

are to be read in accordance with subsection (2).

(4)   Except as provided by subsection (2), in relation to any dividend paid —

      (a)   by a company resident in the territory,

      (b)   to a company resident in the United Kingdom,

credit as a result of these rules is not to be given under section 63(5) in respect of tax which would have been payable under the law of the territory, or under the law of any other territory outside the United Kingdom, but for a relief.

(5)   Subsection (4) has effect despite any double taxation arrangements —

      (a)   made in relation to the territory, or

      (b)   made in relation to any other territory outside the United Kingdom,

which make provision about a relief given, under the law of the territory in relation to which the arrangements are made, with a view to promoting industrial, commercial, scientific, educational or other development in a territory outside the United Kingdom.

(6)   In this section "these rules" means sections 9 to 16 and this section.

CHAPTER 2

DOUBLE TAXATION RELIEF BY WAY OF CREDIT

Effect to be given to credit for foreign tax allowed against UK tax

18   Entitlement to credit for foreign tax reduces UK tax by amount of the credit

(1)   Subsection (2) applies if —

      (a)   under double taxation arrangements, or

      (b)   under unilateral relief arrangements for a territory outside the United Kingdom,

credit is to be allowed against any income tax, corporation tax or capital gains tax chargeable in respect of any income or chargeable gain.

904   *Taxation (International and Other Provisions) Act 2010 (c. 8)*
Part 2 – Double taxation relief
Chapter 2 – Double taxation relief by way of credit

(2) The amount of those taxes chargeable in respect of the income or gain is to be reduced by the amount of the credit.

(3) In subsection (1) "credit"—

    (a) in relation to double taxation arrangements, means credit for tax payable under the law of the territory in relation to which the arrangements are made, and

    (b) in relation to unilateral relief arrangements for a territory outside the United Kingdom, means credit for tax payable under the law of that territory,

but see sections 12(3) and 63(5) (dividends: certain tax payable otherwise than under the law of a territory treated as payable under that law).

(4) Subsection (2) applies subject to—

    (a) the following provisions of this Chapter,

    (b) section 106 (Chapter 1 and this Chapter operate for capital gains tax purposes separately from their operation for the purposes of other United Kingdom taxes), and

    (c) Chapter 2 of Part 18 of ICTA (double taxation relief: pooling of foreign dividends paid before 1 July 2009).

(5) Credit is allowed under subsection (2) against any tax only if, under the arrangements concerned, credit is allowable against that tax.

(6) Credit against income tax is given effect at Step 6 of the calculation in section 23 of ITA 2007.

19 Time limits for claims for relief under section 18(2)

(1) Subsections (2) and (3) apply to a claim for relief under section 18(2).

(2) If the claim is for credit for foreign tax in respect of any income or chargeable gain charged to income tax or capital gains tax for a tax year, the claim must be made on or before—

    (a) the fourth anniversary of the end of that tax year, or

    (b) if later, the 31 January following the tax year in which the foreign tax is paid.

(3) If the claim is for credit for foreign tax in respect of any income or chargeable gain charged to corporation tax for an accounting period, the claim must be made not more than—

    (a) four years after the end of that accounting period, or

    (b) if later, one year after the end of the accounting period in which the foreign tax is paid.

20 Foreign tax includes tax spared because of international development relief

(1) Subsections (2) and (4) apply if the arrangements are double taxation arrangements.

(2) For the purposes of this Chapter, any amount within subsection (3) is to be treated as having been payable.

(3) An amount is within this subsection if it is an amount of tax that would have been payable under the law of a territory outside the United Kingdom but for a relief—

Taxation (International and Other Provisions) Act 2010 (c. 8)   905
Part 2 – Double taxation relief
Chapter 2 – Double taxation relief by way of credit

      (a)   given under the law of that territory with a view to promoting industrial, commercial, scientific, educational or other development in a territory outside the United Kingdom, and

      (b)   about which provision is made in double taxation arrangements.

(4)   References in this Chapter –

      (a)   to tax payable or chargeable, or

      (b)   to tax not chargeable directly or by deduction,

    are to be read in accordance with subsection (2).

(5)   Subsections (2) and (4) have effect subject to –

      (a)   subsection (6), and

      (b)   sections 31(4) and 32(5) (income and gains not to be increased in calculations under section 31 or 32 by amounts treated by this section as having been payable).

(6)   If section 63(5) applies because conditions A and B in section 63 are met, relief is not given in accordance with section 63(5) (relief for certain tax underlying dividends paid between related companies) because of this section unless double taxation arrangements make express provision for the relief.

(7)   Subsection (6) does not affect the operation of section 17(2) (treatment, for purposes of unilateral relief, of dividend paid by foreign company that has received dividends from a company benefiting from tax-sparing relief).

Interpretation of Chapter

21   Meaning of "the arrangements", "the non-UK territory", "foreign tax" etc

(1)   In this Chapter (except section 18) –

      "the arrangements" means the arrangements mentioned in section 18(1),

      "the non-UK territory" means the territory mentioned in section 18(3),

      "foreign tax" means tax chargeable under the law of the non-UK territory –

          (a)   for which credit may be allowed under the arrangements, and

          (b)   which is not special withholding tax, and

      "underlying tax" means, in relation to any dividend, tax which is not chargeable in respect of that dividend directly or by deduction.

(2)   In subsection (1) "special withholding tax" has the same meaning as in Part 3 (see section 136).

(3)   The definitions in subsection (1) are to be read with sections 17(3) and 20(4) (meaning of references to tax payable or chargeable, and of references to tax not chargeable directly or by deduction).

(4)   See also section 8(2) (meaning of references to tax payable or paid under the law of a territory outside the United Kingdom).

906   *Taxation (International and Other Provisions) Act 2010 (c. 8)*
Part 2 – Double taxation relief
Chapter 2 – Double taxation relief by way of credit

Credits where same income charged to income tax in more than one tax year

22   Credit for foreign tax on overlap profit if credit for that tax already allowed

(1)   Subsection (2) applies in relation to foreign tax ("FT") paid in respect of any income if—

     (a)   the income is overlap profit, and

     (b)   credit for FT would have been allowed under section 18(2) against income tax chargeable for a tax year ("year L") in respect of the income but for the fact that credit for FT had been allowed against income tax chargeable in respect of the income for a previous tax year.

(2)   Credit for FT is allowed against income tax chargeable for year L in respect of the income.

(3)   The amount of credit allowed for year L under subsection (2) in respect of the income must not exceed the difference between—

     (a)   T, and

     (b)   the amount of credit which was in fact allowed, under subsection (2) or section 18(2), in respect of the income for any earlier tax year or years.

(4)   For the purposes of subsection (3)(a), T is the amount ("A") of the foreign tax charged on the income, but this is subject to subsections (5) to (7).

(5)   If Y exceeds FP—

$$T = \frac{Y}{FP} \times A$$

where—

     Y is the number of tax years for which credit is allowed, under subsection (2) or section 18(2), against income tax in respect of the income, and

     FP is the number of foreign periods of assessment.

(6)   For the purposes of subsection (5), a tax year or foreign period of assessment for which part only of the income is charged to tax is counted not as one year or period but as a fraction of a year or period, the fraction being—

$$\frac{P}{W}$$

where—

     P is that part of the income, and

     W is the whole of the income.

(7)   If the same income is charged to different foreign taxes for different foreign periods of assessment—

     (a)   subsection (5) (read with subsection (6)) is to be applied separately to each of those taxes, and

     (b)   T is the sum of those taxes after subsection (5) has been applied to them in accordance with paragraph (a).

(8)   In this section—

     "overlap profit" has the same meaning as in Chapter 15 of Part 2 of ITTOIA 2005 (see section 204 of that Act), and

     "foreign period of assessment", in relation to any income, means a period for which the income is, under the law of the non-UK territory, charged to the foreign tax concerned.

Taxation (International and Other Provisions) Act 2010 (c. 8)
Part 2 — Double taxation relief
Chapter 2 — Double taxation relief by way of credit

907

23   Time limits for claims for relief under section 22(2)

(1)   Relief under section 22(2) requires a claim.

(2)   Any claim for relief by way of credit under section 22(2) against income tax for any tax year must be made on or before the fifth anniversary of the 31 January following that tax year, subject to subsection (3).

(3)   If there is more than one tax year in respect of which such relief may be given, any claim for the relief must be made on or before the fifth anniversary of the 31 January following the later of those tax years.

24   Claw-back of relief under section 22(2)

(1)   Subsections (4) and (5) apply if —
    (a)   credit against income tax for any tax year is allowed under section 22(2) in respect of any income ("the original income"), and
    (b)   the original income, or any part of it, contributes to an amount which, under section 205 or 220 of ITTOIA 2005, is deducted in calculating profits of a later tax year ("the later year").

(2)   For the purposes of subsections (4) and (5), amount A is the difference between —
    (a)   the amount of the credit which, as a result of the application of sections 18(2) and 22(2) and subsection (5) of this section, has been allowed against income tax in respect of so much of the original income as contributes as mentioned in subsection (1), and
    (b)   the amount of the credit which, ignoring sections 22 and 23 and this section, would have been allowed under section 18(2) against income tax in respect of so much of the original income as contributes as mentioned in subsection (1).

(3)   For the purposes of subsections (4) and (5), amount B is the amount of credit which, on the assumption that no amount were deducted under section 205 or 220 of ITTOIA 2005, would be allowable under section 18(2) against income tax in respect of income arising in the later year from the same source as the original income.

(4)   If amount A exceeds amount B —
    (a)   no credit is allowed for income arising from that source in the later year,
    (b)   an amount of income tax equal to the excess is charged for the later year, and
    (c)   the liable person is liable for the tax.

(5)   If amount B exceeds amount A, the liable person is allowed for the later year an amount of credit equal to the excess.

(6)   In subsections (4) and (5) "the liable person" means the person liable for income tax charged on the income (if any) arising in the later year from the same source as the original income.

(7)   For the purposes of subsections (1) to (6), it is to be assumed that, where an amount is deducted under section 220 of ITTOIA 2005, each of the overlap profits added together at Step 1 of the calculation in subsection (3) of that section contributes to that amount in the proportion which that overlap profit bears to the total that is the result of that Step.

908

Taxation (International and Other Provisions) Act 2010 (c. 8)
Part 2 – Double taxation relief
Chapter 2 – Double taxation relief by way of credit

(8)　In this section—

　　(a)　"overlap profit" has the same meaning as in Chapter 15 of Part 2 of ITTOIA 2005 (see section 204 of that Act), and

　　(b)　references to income arising in any year include income received in the year that is income on which income tax is to be calculated by reference to the amount of income received in the United Kingdom.

Cases in which credit not allowed

25　Credit not allowed if relief allowed against overseas tax

(1)　Subsection (2) applies if relief may be allowed—

　　(a)　under the arrangements, or

　　(b)　under the law of the non-UK territory in consequence of the arrangements,

in respect of an amount of tax that would, but for the relief, be payable under the law of that territory.

(2)　Credit under section 18(2) is not allowed in respect of that tax, whether or not the relief has been used.

26　Credit not allowed under arrangements unless taxpayer is UK resident

(1)　Credit under section 18(2) against income tax, corporation tax or capital gains tax for a chargeable period is not allowed unless the person in respect of whose income or chargeable gains the tax is chargeable is UK resident for that period.

(2)　Sections 28 to 30 (credit under unilateral relief arrangements allowed to some non-UK resident persons) contain exceptions to subsection (1).

(3)　In subsection (1) so far as it relates to capital gains tax "chargeable period" means tax year (see section 288(1ZA) of TCGA 1992).

(4)　In subsection (1) so far as it relates to capital gains tax "UK resident" has the meaning given by section 989 of ITA 2007.

27　Credit not allowed if person elects against credit

Credit under section 18(2) against income tax, corporation tax or capital gains tax charged on any income or chargeable gains of a person is not allowed if the person elects for credit not to be allowed in respect of that income or those gains.

Exceptions to requirement to be UK resident

28　Unilateral relief for Isle of Man or Channel Islands tax

(1)　Subsection (2) applies if the arrangements—

　　(a)　are unilateral relief arrangements for a territory outside the United Kingdom, and

　　(b)　provide for credit to be allowed for tax paid under the law of the Isle of Man ("the Isle of Man tax").

Taxation (International and Other Provisions) Act 2010 (c. 8)
Part 2 – Double taxation relief
Chapter 2 – Double taxation relief by way of credit

909

(2) Credit under section 18(2) against any of the UK taxes for a chargeable period may be allowed for the Isle of Man tax if the person in respect of whose income or chargeable gains the UK tax is payable is—

    (a) resident for that period in the United Kingdom, or

    (b) resident for that period in the Isle of Man.

(3) Subsection (4) applies if the arrangements—

    (a) are unilateral relief arrangements for a territory outside the United Kingdom, and

    (b) provide for credit to be allowed for tax paid under the law of any of the Channel Islands ("the Channel Islands tax").

(4) Credit under section 18(2) against any of the UK taxes for a chargeable period may be allowed for the Channel Islands tax if the person in respect of whose income or chargeable gains the UK tax is payable is—

    (a) resident for that period in the United Kingdom, or

    (b) resident for that period in any of the Channel Islands.

(5) Each of the following is a UK tax for the purposes of this section—

    (a) income tax,

    (b) corporation tax, and

    (c) capital gains tax.

(6) In subsections (2) and (4) so far as they relate to capital gains tax "chargeable period" means tax year (see section 288(1ZA) of TCGA 1992).

29 Unilateral relief for tax on income from employment or office

(1) Subsection (3) applies if the arrangements are unilateral relief arrangements for a territory outside the United Kingdom.

(2) In subsection (3) "overseas tax" means tax—

    (a) paid under the law of the territory,

    (b) charged on income and corresponding to income tax or to corporation tax, and

    (c) calculated by reference to income from an office or employment the duties of which are performed wholly or mainly in the territory.

(3) Credit for overseas tax may be allowed under section 18(2) against income tax for a tax year—

    (a) calculated by reference to that income, and

    (b) charged on employment income,

if the person performing the duties is resident in the United Kingdom, or resident in the territory, for that year.

(4) For the purposes of subsection (2)(b) tax may correspond to income tax or corporation tax even though it—

    (a) is payable under the law of a province, state or other part of a country, or

    (b) is levied by or on behalf of a municipality or other local body.

910

Taxation (International and Other Provisions) Act 2010 (c. 8)
Part 2 — Double taxation relief
Chapter 2 — Double taxation relief by way of credit

30   Unilateral relief for non-UK tax on non-resident's UK branch or agency etc

(1)   Subsection (2) applies if the arrangements are unilateral relief arrangements for a territory outside the United Kingdom.

(2)   Credit for tax within subsection (3) or (4) may be allowed under section 18(2) against any of the UK taxes if the territory is not one in which the person or company concerned is liable to tax by reason of domicile, residence or place of management.

(3)   Tax is within this subsection if the arrangements provide for credit for it to be allowed against income tax or corporation tax, and it is paid under the law of the territory in respect of the income or chargeable gains—

(a)   of a branch or agency in the United Kingdom of a non-UK resident person who is not a company, or

(b)   of a permanent establishment in the United Kingdom of a non-UK resident company.

(4)   Tax is within this subsection if the arrangements provide for credit for it to be allowed against capital gains tax, and it is paid under the law of the territory in respect of the capital gains—

(a)   of a branch or agency in the United Kingdom of a non-UK resident person who is not a company, or

(b)   of a permanent establishment in the United Kingdom of a non-UK resident company.

(5)   Relief under subsection (2) may not exceed the relief which would have been available if—

(a)   the branch or agency, or permanent establishment, had been a UK resident person, and

(b)   the income or gains had been income or gains of that person.

(6)   Each of the following is a UK tax for the purposes of subsection (2)—

(a)   income tax,

(b)   corporation tax, and

(c)   capital gains tax.

(7)   In this section so far as it relates to capital gains tax—

"branch or agency" has the meaning given by section 10(6) of TCGA 1992,

"company" has the same meaning as in TCGA 1992 (see section 288 of that Act),

"permanent establishment", in relation to a company, has the meaning given by Chapter 2 of Part 24 of CTA 2010, and

"UK resident" or "non-UK resident", in relation to a company or other person, has the meaning given by section 989 of ITA 2007.

Calculating income or gains in respect of which credit is allowed

31   Calculation of income or gain where remittance basis does not apply

(1)   Subsection (2) applies if—

(a)   under the arrangements, credit is to be allowed for foreign tax in respect of any income or gain, and

Taxation (International and Other Provisions) Act 2010 (c. 8)
Part 2 — Double taxation relief
Chapter 2 — Double taxation relief by way of credit

911

    (b)   section 32(2) (cases where UK tax payable by reference to amount received in UK) does not apply.

(2)   In calculating the amount of the income or gain for the purposes of income tax, corporation tax or capital gains tax —

    (a)   no deduction is to be made for foreign tax or special withholding tax, whether in respect of the same or any other income or gain, and

    (b)   if the credit is for foreign tax in respect of a dividend, the amount of the dividend is to be treated as increased by any underlying tax within subsection (3).

(3)   In relation to a dividend, underlying tax is within this subsection if —

    (a)   under the arrangements it is to be taken into account in considering whether any, and (if so) what, credit is to be allowed in respect of the dividend,

    (b)   because the amount given by Step 2 of the calculation under section 58 is more than the amount given by Step 3 of that calculation, it is not to be taken into account in considering the questions mentioned in paragraph (a), or

    (c)   under section 60(3) it is not to be taken into account in considering those questions.

(4)   The amount of any income or gain is not to be increased under subsection (2)(b) by reference to any foreign tax which, although not payable, is treated by section 20(2) as having been payable.

(5)   Subsections (1) to (4) have effect for the purposes of corporation tax despite —

    (a)   section 464(1) of CTA 2009 (matters to be brought into account in the case of loan relationships only under Part 5 of that Act), and

    (b)   section 906(1) of CTA 2009 (matters to be brought into account in respect of intangible fixed assets only under Part 8 of that Act).

(6)   In this section "special withholding tax" means special withholding tax —

    (a)   within the meaning of Part 3 (see section 136), and

    (b)   in respect of which a claim has been made under that Part.

32   Calculation of amount received where UK tax charged on remittance basis

(1)   Subsection (2) applies if —

    (a)   under the arrangements, credit is to be allowed for foreign tax in respect of any income or capital gain, and

    (b)   income tax or capital gains tax is payable by reference to the amount received in the United Kingdom.

(2)   For the purposes of whichever of income tax and capital gains tax is payable as mentioned in subsection (1)(b), the amount received is to be treated as increased —

    (a)   by the amount of the foreign tax in respect of the income or gain,

    (b)   by the amount of any special withholding tax levied in respect of the income or gain, but see subsection (4), and

    (c)   if the credit is for foreign tax in respect of a dividend, by any underlying tax that under the arrangements is to be taken into account in considering whether any, and (if so) what, credit is to be allowed in respect of the dividend.

912　　　　　　　　　　　　　　*Taxation (International and Other Provisions) Act 2010 (c. 8)*
Part 2 – Double taxation relief
Chapter 2 – Double taxation relief by way of credit

(3) For the purposes of subsection (4), a gain is a "special gain" if—

    (a) it is a chargeable gain that accrues to a person on a disposal by the person of assets,

    (b) the consideration for the disposal consists of or includes an amount of savings income, and

    (c) special withholding tax is levied in respect of the whole or any part of the consideration for the disposal.

(4) If the credit is for foreign tax in respect of a gain that is a special gain, the amount of the increase under subsection (2)(b) is given by—

$$AWT \times \frac{GUK}{SG - AWT}$$

where—

    AWT is the amount of special withholding tax levied in respect of the whole or the part of the consideration for the disposal concerned,

    GUK is the amount of the gain received in the United Kingdom, and

    SG is the amount of the gain.

(5) The amount of any income or gain is not to be increased under this section by reference to any foreign tax which, although not payable, is treated by section 20(2) as having been payable.

(6) In this section—

    "savings income" has the same meaning as in Part 3 (see section 136), and

    "special withholding tax" means special withholding tax—

        (a) within the meaning of Part 3 (see section 136), and

        (b) in respect of which a claim has been made under that Part.

Limits on credit: general rules

33 Limit on credit: minimisation of the foreign tax

(1) The credit under section 18(2) must not exceed the credit which would be allowed had all reasonable steps been taken—

    (a) under the law of the non-UK territory, and

    (b) under double taxation arrangements made in relation to that territory,

to minimise the amount of tax payable in that territory.

(2) The steps mentioned in subsection (1) include—

    (a) claiming, or otherwise securing the benefit of, reliefs, deductions, reductions or allowances, and

    (b) making elections for tax purposes.

(3) For the purposes of subsection (1), any question as to the steps which it would have been reasonable for a person to take is to be determined on the basis of what the person might reasonably be expected to have done in the absence of relief under this Part.

34 Reduction in credit: payment by reference to foreign tax

(1) Subsection (2) applies if—

    (a) credit for foreign tax is to be allowed to a person ("P") under the arrangements, and

Taxation (International and Other Provisions) Act 2010 (c. 8)
Part 2 — Double taxation relief
Chapter 2 — Double taxation relief by way of credit

913

    (b)   a payment is made by a tax authority to P, or any person connected with P, by reference to the foreign tax.

(2)   The amount of that credit is to be reduced by an amount equal to that payment.

(3)   Whether a person is connected with P is determined in accordance with section 1122 of CTA 2010.

35   Disallowed credit: use as a deduction

(1)   Subsection (2) applies if the application of section 36(2) or 42(2) prevents an amount of credit for foreign tax from being allowable against income tax or corporation tax.

(2)   The taxpayer's income is to be treated as reduced by the amount of the disallowed credit.

(3)   Subsection (4) applies if the application of section 40(2) prevents an amount of credit for foreign tax from being allowable against capital gains tax.

(4)   The taxpayer's chargeable gains are to be treated as reduced by the amount of the disallowed credit.

(5)   Subsection (2) or (4) applies only so far as the amount of disallowed credit does not exceed the amount of any loss attributable to the income or gain in respect of which the foreign tax was paid.

(6)   For the purposes of subsection (5), payment of the foreign tax is to be taken into account despite section 31(2).

Limit on, and reduction of, credit against income tax

36   Amount of limit

(1)   This section is about the amount of credit allowed under section 18(2) against a person's income tax for any tax year.

(2)   The amount of credit in respect of income from any particular source must not exceed the difference between—
    (a)   the amount of income tax to which the person would be liable for the tax year if the person were charged to income tax on—
$$TI - X,$$
    and
    (b)   the amount of income tax to which the person would be liable for the tax year if the person were charged to income tax on—
$$TI - (X + C).$$

(3)   If credit is allowed (whether or not under the same tax-relief arrangements) in respect of income from more than one source, apply subsection (2) successively to the income from each source, taking the sources in the order which will result in the greatest reduction in the person's income tax liability for the tax year.

(4)   In subsection (2)—
    TI is the person's total income for the tax year,

914   Taxation (International and Other Provisions) Act 2010 (c. 8)
Part 2 — Double taxation relief
Chapter 2 — Double taxation relief by way of credit

X is the income (if any) to which subsection (2) has already been applied, and

C is the income in respect of which the credit is to be allowed.

(5) The rules for calculating an amount of income tax under subsection (2) are—

    (a) the calculation is to be made in accordance with sections 31 and 32, and

    (b) no credit is to be allowed for foreign tax, and

    (c) no reduction is to be made under section 26 of FA 2005 (trusts for the benefit of a vulnerable beneficiary), but

    (d) any other income tax reduction under the Income Tax Acts is to be made.

(6) See section 29(2) and (3) of ITA 2007 (tax reductions limited by reference to tax liability) for further limits on the total amount of credit for foreign tax to be allowed to a person against income tax.

(7) For the purposes of subsection (3) the following are "tax-relief arrangements"—

    (a) double taxation arrangements, and

    (b) unilateral relief arrangements for a territory outside the United Kingdom.

37   Credit against tax on trade income: further rules

(1) Apply section 36(2) in accordance with subsections (2) to (5) if the tax against which the credit is to be allowed is income tax on trade income.

(2) Treat the reference to income from any particular source as a reference to trade income arising out of a transaction, arrangement or asset.

(3) C is the income arising out of the transaction, arrangement or asset in connection with which the credit arises.

(4) In calculating an amount of income tax under section 36(2) deduct, from the income arising out of the transaction, arrangement or asset in connection with which the credit arises, deductions which would be allowed in a calculation of the taxpayer's liability in respect of that income.

(5) Treat section 36(3) as referring—

    (a) to trade income instead of income, and

    (b) to a transaction, arrangement or asset instead of a source.

(6) In subsection (4) "deductions" includes a just and reasonable apportionment of deductions that relate—

    (a) partly to the income arising out of the transaction, arrangement or asset in connection with which the credit arises, and

    (b) partly to other matters.

(7) In this section "trade income" means income chargeable to tax under—

    (a) Chapter 2 or 18 of Part 2 of ITTOIA 2005 (trade profits and post-cessation receipts), or

    (b) Chapter 3 or 10 of Part 3 of ITTOIA 2005 (profits of property businesses and post-cessation receipts).

Taxation (International and Other Provisions) Act 2010 (c. 8)   915
Part 2 — Double taxation relief
Chapter 2 — Double taxation relief by way of credit

38   Credit against tax on royalties: further rules

(1)   Subsection (2) applies if —

     (a)   the arrangements are double taxation arrangements, and

     (b)   royalties, as defined in the arrangements, are paid in respect of an asset in more than one foreign jurisdiction.

(2)   For the purposes of section 36(2) —

     (a)   royalty income arising in more than one foreign jurisdiction in a tax year in respect of the asset is to be treated as a single item of income, and

     (b)   credits available for foreign tax in respect of the royalty income are to be aggregated accordingly.

(3)   In this section "foreign jurisdiction" means a jurisdiction outside the United Kingdom.

39   Credit reduced by reference to accrued income losses

(1)   Subsection (5) applies if each of conditions A to C is met.

(2)   Condition A is that a person is entitled under section 18(2) to credit against income tax.

(3)   Condition B is that the income tax is calculated by reference to income consisting of interest in respect of which the person is entitled under section 679 of ITA 2007 (no income tax on interest so far as matched by accrued income losses) to an exemption from liability to income tax.

(4)   Condition C is that —

     (a)   the arrangements are unilateral relief arrangements for a territory outside the United Kingdom and the credit is allowed as a result of section 9, or

     (b)   the arrangements are double taxation arrangements and the credit is allowed as a result of the inclusion in the arrangements of any provision corresponding to that section.

(5)   The amount of the credit is to be reduced to the amount given by —

$$\frac{I-E}{I} \times C$$

where —

     I is the amount of the interest,

     E is the amount of the exemption, and

     C is the amount the credit would be apart from this subsection.

(6)   Expressions used in this section and in Chapter 2 of Part 12 of ITA 2007 (accrued income profits) have the same meaning in this section as in that Chapter.

Limit on credit against capital gains tax

40   Amount of limit

(1)   This section is about the amount of credit allowed under section 18(2) against a person's capital gains tax for any tax year.

916   *Taxation (International and Other Provisions) Act 2010 (c. 8)*
Part 2 — Double taxation relief
Chapter 2 — Double taxation relief by way of credit

(2)   The amount of credit in respect of any particular capital gain must not exceed the difference between—

    (a)   the amount of capital gains tax to which the person would be liable for the tax year if the person were charged to capital gains tax on—

$$TG - X,$$

    and

    (b)   the amount of capital gains tax to which the person would be liable for the tax year if the person were charged to capital gains tax on—

$$TG - (X + C).$$

(3)   If credit is allowed (whether or not under the same tax-relief arrangements) in respect of more than one capital gain, apply subsection (2) successively to each capital gain, taking the gains in the order which will result in the greatest reduction in the person's capital gains tax liability for the tax year.

(4)   In subsection (2)—

    TG is the total amount of the chargeable gains accruing to the person in the tax year,

    X is the total amount of the gains (if any) to which subsection (2) has already been applied, and

    C is the amount of the gain in respect of which the credit is to be allowed.

(5)   The rules for calculating an amount of capital gains tax under subsection (2) are—

    (a)   the calculation is to be made in accordance with sections 31 and 32, and

    (b)   no credit is to be allowed for foreign tax.

(6)   For the purposes of subsection (3) the following are "tax-relief arrangements"—

    (a)   double taxation arrangements, and

    (b)   unilateral relief arrangements for a territory outside the United Kingdom.

Limit on total credit against income tax and capital gains tax

41   Amount of limit

(1)   In subsection (2) "the total credit" means—

$$F + G$$

where—

    F is the total credit, under all tax-relief arrangements, allowed under section 18(2) against a person's income tax for any tax year, and

    G is the total credit, under all tax-relief arrangements, allowed under section 18(2) against the person's capital gains tax for that tax year.

(2)   The total credit is not to be more than—

$$I + C - A$$

where—

    I is the total income tax payable by the person for the tax year,

    C is the total capital gains tax payable by the person for the tax year, and

    A is the total amount of the tax treated under section 414 of ITA 2007 (gift aid) as deducted from gifts made by the person in the tax year.

(3) In calculating I and C for the purposes of subsection (2), no reduction is to be made for credit under section 18(2).

(4) Subsection (2) applies in addition to sections 36 and 40.

(5) For the purposes of subsection (1) the following are "tax-relief arrangements"—

    (a) double taxation arrangements, and

    (b) unilateral relief arrangements for a territory outside the United Kingdom.

Limit on credit against corporation tax

42   Amount of limit

(1) Subsection (2) is about the amount of credit allowed under section 18(2) against corporation tax to which a company is liable in respect of any income or chargeable gain.

(2) The credit must not exceed—

$$R \times IG$$

where—

R is the rate of corporation tax payable by the company, before any credit under this Part, on the company's income or chargeable gains for the accounting period in which the income arises or the gain accrues, and

IG is the amount of the income or gain (but see subsection (3)).

(3) For the purposes of applying subsection (2), IG is reduced (or extinguished) by any amount allocated to it under—

section 52(2) (general deductions),

section 53(2) (earlier years' deficits on loan relationships),

section 54(2) or (4) (debits on loan relationships),

section 55(5) (current year's deficits on loan relationships), or

section 56(2) (debits on intangible fixed assets).

(4) Subsection (2) is to be read with—

section 43, which, if the company has a permanent establishment outside the United Kingdom, is about attributing profits to the establishment for the purposes of applying subsection (2),

sections 44 to 49, which modify how subsection (2) applies in connection with allowing credit against tax on trade income (as defined in section 44), and

sections 50 and 51, which require subsection (2) to be applied as if corporation tax were charged in a modified way on profits of the company for the period from loan relationships and intangible fixed assets.

43   Profits attributable to permanent establishment for purposes of section 42(2)

(1) The permanent-establishment provisions apply with the necessary modifications in determining for the purposes of section 42(2) how much of a UK resident company's chargeable profits is attributable to a permanent establishment of the company outside the United Kingdom.

918   *Taxation (International and Other Provisions) Act 2010 (c. 8)*
Part 2 – Double taxation relief
Chapter 2 – Double taxation relief by way of credit

(2)   In subsection (1) –

     "chargeable profits" means profits on which corporation tax is chargeable, and

     "the permanent-establishment provisions" means –

        (a)   Chapter 4 of Part 2 of CTA 2009 (profits attributable to permanent establishment), and

        (b)   any regulations made under section 24 of CTA 2009 (application to insurance companies).

44   Credit against tax on trade income

(1)   Apply section 42(2) in accordance with subsections (2) and (3) if the tax against which the credit is to be allowed is corporation tax on income that is trade income.

(2)   The amount of the credit must not exceed the corporation tax attributable to the income arising out of the transaction, arrangement or asset in connection with which the credit arises.

(3)   In calculating the amount of corporation tax attributable to any income, take into account –

        (a)   deductions which would be allowed in calculating the company's liability, and

        (b)   expenses of a company connected with the company, so far as reasonably attributable to the income,

     but see section 49 (restriction if company is a bank or is connected with a bank).

(4)   In subsection (3)(a) "deductions" includes a just and reasonable apportionment of deductions that relate –

        (a)   partly to the transaction, arrangement or asset from which the income arises, and

        (b)   partly to other matters.

(5)   Section 1122 of CTA 2010 (meaning of "connected") applies for the purposes of subsection (3)(b).

(6)   In this section "trade income" means –

        (a)   income chargeable to tax under Chapter 2 or 15 of Part 3 of CTA 2009 (trade profits and post-cessation receipts),

        (b)   income chargeable to tax under Chapter 3 or 9 of Part 4 of CTA 2009 (profits of property businesses and post-cessation receipts),

        (c)   income which arises from a source outside the United Kingdom and is chargeable to tax under section 979 of CTA 2009 (charge to tax on income not otherwise charged), and

        (d)   any other income or profits which by a provision of ICTA is or are –

            (i)   chargeable to tax under Chapter 2 of Part 3 of CTA 2009, or

            (ii)   calculated in the same way as the profits of a trade,

     but does not include income to which section 99 of this Act (insurance companies) applies.

(7)   In subsection (6) the references –

        (a)   to income chargeable under Chapter 15 of Part 3 of CTA 2009, and

        (b)   to income chargeable under Chapter 9 of Part 4 of CTA 2009,

Taxation (International and Other Provisions) Act 2010 (c. 8)
Part 2 — *Double taxation relief*
Chapter 2 — *Double taxation relief by way of credit*

919

do not include income that would, but for the repeal by CTA 2009 of section 103 of ICTA (post-cessation receipts where pre-cessation profits calculated on an earnings basis and other post-cessation receipts that become due or are ascertained after cessation), have been chargeable to corporation tax under that section.

45 Credit against tax on trade income: anti-avoidance rules

(1) If a company ("A") carrying on a trade giving rise to trade income enters into a scheme or arrangement with another person ("B") a main purpose of which is to alter the effect of section 44(2) and (3) in relation to A, income received in pursuance of the scheme or arrangement is to be treated for the purposes of section 44(2) and (3) as trade income of B (and not as income of A).

(2) Income of a person ("D") is to be treated for the purposes of section 44 as trade income (if it is not otherwise trade income) of D if—

    (a) the income is received by D as part of a scheme or arrangement entered into by D and a connected person ("C"),

    (b) had C received the income, it would be reasonable to assume that it would be trade income of C, and

    (c) a main purpose of the scheme or arrangement is to produce the result that section 44(2) and (3) will not have effect in relation to the income because it is received by D.

(3) For the purposes of subsection (2)(b) it is to be assumed that, in the case of any relevant transaction to which a relevant person is a party, C were that party to the transaction.

(4) In subsection (3) —
    "relevant person" means—
        (a) D, or
        (b) any other connected person who is a party to the scheme or arrangement mentioned in subsection (2), and
    "relevant transaction" means any of the transactions giving rise to the income mentioned in subsection (2)(b).

(5) In subsections (2) to (4) "connected person" means a person with whom D is connected.

(6) Section 1122 of CTA 2010 (meaning of "connected") applies for the purposes of subsection (5).

(7) In this section "trade income" has the same meaning as in section 44.

46 Applying section 44(2): asset in hedging relationship with derivative contract

(1) If an asset is in a hedging relationship with a derivative contract, section 44(2) applies in relation to the asset as if the income arising from the asset is the income arising from the asset and the contract taken together, subject to subsection (2).

(2) Take account of the income or loss from the derivative contract only so far as reasonably attributable to the hedging relationship.

(3) For the purposes of subsection (1), an asset is in a hedging relationship with a derivative contract if—

920   *Taxation (International and Other Provisions) Act 2010 (c. 8)*
Part 2 – Double taxation relief
Chapter 2 – Double taxation relief by way of credit

(a) the asset is acquired as a hedge of risk in connection with the contract, or

(b) the contract is entered into as a hedge of risk in connection with the asset.

(4) If an asset or a contract is wholly or partly designated as a hedge for the purposes of a person's accounts, that is conclusive for the purposes of subsection (3).

47 Applying section 44(2): royalty income

(1) Subsection (2) applies if—
   (a) the arrangements are double taxation arrangements, and
   (b) royalties, as defined in the arrangements, are paid in respect of an asset in more than one foreign jurisdiction.

(2) For the purposes of section 44(2)—
   (a) royalty income arising in more than one foreign jurisdiction in an accounting period in respect of the asset is to be treated as income arising from a single asset, and
   (b) credits available for foreign tax in respect of the royalty income are to be aggregated accordingly.

(3) In this section "foreign jurisdiction" means a jurisdiction outside the United Kingdom.

48 Applying section 44(2): "portfolio" of transactions, arrangements or assets

(1) Subsection (5) applies if each of conditions A to C is met.

(2) Condition A is that transactions, arrangements or assets are treated by a taxpayer as a series or group ("the portfolio").

(3) Condition B is that credits for foreign tax arise in respect of the portfolio.

(4) Condition C is that—
   (a) it is not reasonably practicable to prepare a separate calculation of income for the purposes of section 44(2) in respect of each transaction, arrangement or asset, or
   (b) a separate calculation of income in respect of each transaction, arrangement or asset for the purposes of section 44(2) would not, compared with an aggregated calculation, make a material difference to the amount of credit for foreign tax which is allowable.

(5) The income arising from the portfolio, or part of the portfolio, may be aggregated and apportioned for the purposes of section 44(2) in a just and reasonable manner.

49 Restricting section 44(3) if company is a bank or connected with a bank

(1) Section 44(3) is subject to subsection (2) of this section if—
   (a) the company is a bank or is connected with a bank, and
   (b) the amount of the included funding costs is significantly less than the amount of the notional funding costs.

Taxation (International and Other Provisions) Act 2010 (c. 8)
Part 2 — Double taxation relief
Chapter 2 — Double taxation relief by way of credit

921

(2) The amount of the notional funding costs is to be included in the amount to be taken into account under section 44(3), but only so far as it exceeds the amount of the included funding costs.

(3) In this section—
   "the company" means the company mentioned in section 44(3)(a),
   "included funding costs" means the total of the funding costs that are—
   (a) incurred by the company, or any company connected with the company, in respect of capital used to fund the relevant transaction, and
   (b) included in the amount to be taken into account under section 44(3) before the application of subsection (2) of this section,
   "notional funding costs" means the funding costs that the relevant bank would incur (on the basis of its average funding costs) in respect of the capital that would be needed to wholly fund the relevant transaction if that transaction were funded in that way,
   "the relevant bank" means the bank that is the company, or with which the company is connected, and
   "the relevant transaction" means the transaction, arrangement or asset from which the income mentioned in section 44(1) arises.

(4) The following provisions apply for the purposes of this section—
   section 1120 of CTA 2010 (meaning of "bank"), and
   section 1122 of CTA 2010 (meaning of "connected").

Calculating tax for purposes of section 42(2)

50   Tax for period on loan relationships

(1) Subsection (2) applies for the purposes of section 42(2) if the company has at least one non-trading credit for the period that is eligible for double taxation relief.

(2) Assume that the charge to corporation tax on income, as applied by section 299 of CTA 2009, is charged on TNTC, not on the non-trading profits that the company has for the period in respect of its loan relationships.

(3) For the purposes of subsection (1), a non-trading credit relating to an item is "eligible for double taxation relief" if there is in respect of that item an amount of foreign tax for which, under the arrangements, credit is allowable against United Kingdom tax calculated by reference to that item.

(4) In this section—
   "non-trading credit" means a non-trading credit for the purposes of Part 5 of CTA 2009 (loan relationships), and
   "TNTC" is the total amount of the company's non-trading credits for the period.

51   Tax for period on intangible fixed assets

(1) Subsection (2) applies for the purposes of section 42(2) if the company has at least one non-trading credit for the period that is eligible for double taxation relief.

922

Taxation (International and Other Provisions) Act 2010 (c. 8)
Part 2 — Double taxation relief
Chapter 2 — Double taxation relief by way of credit

(2) Assume that the charge to corporation tax on income, as applied by section 752 of CTA 2009, is charged on TNTC, not on the non-trading gains arising to the company in the period on intangible fixed assets.

(3) For the purposes of subsection (1), a non-trading credit relating to an item is "eligible for double taxation relief" if there is in respect of that item an amount of foreign tax for which, under the arrangements, credit is allowable against United Kingdom tax calculated by reference to that item.

(4) In this section—

"non-trading credit" means a non-trading credit for the purposes of Part 8 of CTA 2009 (intangible fixed assets), and

"TNTC" is the total amount of the company's non-trading credits for the period.

Allocation of deductions etc to profits for purposes of section 42

52 General deductions

(1) Subsection (2) applies for the purposes of section 42 if in the accounting period there is any amount ("the deduction") that for corporation tax purposes is deductible from, or otherwise allowable against, profits of more than one description.

(2) The company may allocate the deduction in such amounts, and to such of its profits for the period, as it thinks fit.

53 Earlier years' non-trading deficits on loan relationships

(1) Subsection (2) applies for the purposes of section 42 if an amount ("the deficit") is carried forward to the period under section 457(1) of CTA 2009 (non-trading deficits on loan relationships set against profits of subsequent years).

(2) The deficit can be allocated only to the company's non-trading profits for the period, but the company may allocate the deficit to such of those profits, and in such amounts, as the company thinks fit.

(3) In this section "non-trading profits" has the meaning given by section 457(5) of CTA 2009.

54 Non-trading debits on loan relationships

(1) Subsection (2) applies for the purposes of section 42 if the company has at least one non-trading credit for the period that is eligible for double taxation relief.

(2) That much of the company's non-trading debits for the period as is given by the formula—

$$TNTD - (CB + CF + GR)$$

may be allocated by the company to such of its profits for the period, and in such amounts, as the company thinks fit, but this is subject to subsection (4).

(3) Subsection (4) applies for the purposes of section 42 if—

(a) the company has at least one non-trading credit for the period that is eligible for double taxation relief, and

Taxation (International and Other Provisions) Act 2010 (c. 8)
Part 2 — Double taxation relief
Chapter 2 — Double taxation relief by way of credit

923

     (b)   the company sets the whole or part of XS against profits of the period in pursuance of a current-year provision or claim.

(4)   So much of the company's non-trading debits as is equal to that amount of XS must be allocated to the profits against which that amount of XS is set in pursuance of the current-year provision or claim.

(5)   In this section, if the company has a non-trading deficit ("D") on its loan relationships for the period —

        CB is so much of D as is the subject of a carry-back claim,

        CF is so much of D as is carried forward to a subsequent accounting period in accordance with a carry-forward provision,

        GR is so much of D as is surrendered as group relief under section 99 of CTA 2010, and

        if $D > CB + CF + GR$ then XS is so much of D as is given by the formula —

$$D - (CB + CF + GR)$$

(6)   For the purposes of subsections (1) and (3), a non-trading credit relating to an item is "eligible for double taxation relief" if there is in respect of that item an amount of foreign tax for which, under the arrangements, credit is allowable against United Kingdom tax calculated by reference to that item.

(7)   In this section —

        "carry-back claim" means a claim —

            (a)   under section 389(1) of CTA 2009 (insurance companies: carry-back, to earlier accounting periods, of non-trading deficit on loan relationships), or

            (b)   under section 459(1)(b) of CTA 2009 (carry-back: other companies),

        "carry-forward provision" means —

            (a)   section 391 of CTA 2009 (insurance companies), or

            (b)   section 457(1) of CTA 2009 (other companies),

        "current-year provision or claim" means —

            (a)   section 388(1) of CTA 2009 (insurance companies: non-trading deficit on loan relationships set against current year's profits), or

            (b)   a claim under section 459(1)(a) of CTA 2009 (other companies: setting of deficit against current year's profits),

        "non-trading credit" means a non-trading credit for the purposes of Part 5 of CTA 2009 (loan relationships),

        "non-trading debit" means a non-trading debit for the purposes of that Part, and

        "TNTD" is the total amount of the company's non-trading debits for the period.

55   Current year's non-trading deficits on loan relationships

(1)   Subsection (5) applies for the purposes of section 42 if conditions A and B are met.

(2)   Condition A is that the company —

        (a)   has no non-trading credits for the period, or

924

Taxation (International and Other Provisions) Act 2010 (c. 8)
Part 2 – Double taxation relief
Chapter 2 – Double taxation relief by way of credit

    (b)   has non-trading credits for the period but none of those credits is eligible for double taxation relief.

(3)   For the purposes of subsection (2)(b), a non-trading credit relating to an item is "eligible for double taxation relief" if there is in respect of that item an amount of foreign tax for which, under the arrangements, credit is allowable against United Kingdom tax calculated by reference to that item.

(4)   Condition B is that an amount ("the deficit") is set against any of the company's profits for the period—

    (a)   under section 388(1) of CTA 2009 (insurance company's non-trading deficit on loan relationships set against current year's profits), or

    (b)   under section 459(1)(a) of CTA 2009 (other company's non-trading deficit on loan relationships set against current year's profits).

(5)   The deficit can be allocated only to profits against which the deficit is set under section 388(1) or 459(1)(a) of CTA 2009.

(6)   In this section "non-trading credit" means a non-trading credit for the purposes of Part 5 of CTA 2009 (loan relationships).

56 Non-trading debits on intangible fixed assets

(1)   Subsection (2) applies for the purposes of section 42 if the company has at least one non-trading credit for the period that is eligible for double taxation relief.

(2)   That much of the company's non-trading debits for the period as is given by the formula—

$$TNTD - CF$$

may be allocated by the company to such of its profits for the period, and in such amounts, as the company thinks fit.

(3)   In subsection (2)—

    TNTD is the total amount of the company's non-trading debits for the period, and

    CF is the amount (if any) carried forward to the next accounting period under section 753(3) of CTA 2009 (carry forward of non-trading loss so far as neither subject to a claim to set it against profits of current period nor surrendered by way of group relief).

(4)   For the purposes of subsection (1), a non-trading credit relating to an item is "eligible for double taxation relief" if there is in respect of that item an amount of foreign tax for which, under the arrangements, credit is allowable against United Kingdom tax calculated by reference to that item.

(5)   In this section—

    "non-trading credit" means a non-trading credit for the purposes of Part 8 of CTA 2009 (intangible fixed assets), and

    "non-trading debit" means a non-trading debit for the purposes of that Part.

Taxation (International and Other Provisions) Act 2010 (c. 8)
Part 2 – *Double taxation relief*
Chapter 2 – *Double taxation relief by way of credit*

925

Taking account of foreign tax underlying dividends

57 Credit in respect of dividend: taking account of underlying tax

(1) Subsections (2) and (3) apply if, as a result of provision made by the arrangements, underlying tax is to be taken into account in considering whether any and (if so) what credit is to be allowed against corporation tax, income tax or capital gains tax in respect of a dividend.

(2) The amount of underlying tax to be taken into account as a result of the provision is to be calculated —

    (a) under section 58 if the dividend is one paid by a company resident outside the United Kingdom to a company resident in the United Kingdom, and

    (b) under section 61 if the dividend is not one paid by a company resident outside the United Kingdom to a company resident in the United Kingdom.

(3) No underlying tax is to be taken into account as a result of the provision if, under the law of any territory outside the United Kingdom, a deduction is allowed to a resident of the territory in respect of an amount determined by reference to the dividend.

(4) See also —

    (a) section 63 (underlying tax paid in the United Kingdom, or otherwise outside the non-UK territory, treated in some cases as underlying tax paid in the non-UK territory), and

    (b) section 65 (underlying tax paid in respect of profits of a company which pays a dividend treated in some cases as underlying tax paid in respect of profits of company to which dividend is paid).

58 Calculation if dividend paid by non-resident company to resident company

(1) A calculation under this section (see section 57(2)(a)) is as follows —

Step 1

Calculate the amount of the foreign tax borne on the relevant profits by the company paying the dividend.

Step 2

Calculate how much of that amount is properly attributable to the proportion of the relevant profits represented by the dividend.

Step 3

Calculate the amount given by —

$$(D + PA) \times M$$

where —

    D is the amount of the dividend,

    PA is the amount given by the calculation at Step 2, and

    M is the rate of corporation tax applicable to profits of the recipient for the accounting period in which the dividend is received or, if there is more than one such rate, the average rate over the whole of that accounting period.

Step 4

If under the law of the non-UK territory the dividend has been increased for tax purposes by an amount to be —

926

Taxation (International and Other Provisions) Act 2010 (c. 8)
Part 2 – Double taxation relief
Chapter 2 – Double taxation relief by way of credit

(a) set off against the recipient's own tax under that law, or

(b) paid to the recipient so far as it exceeds the recipient's own tax under that law,

calculate the amount of the increase.

Step 5

If the amount given by the calculation at Step 2 is less than the amount given by the calculation at Step 3, UT is the amount given by the calculation at Step 2 but reduced by any amount calculated at Step 4.

Step 6

If the amount given by the calculation at Step 2 is equal to or more than the amount given by the calculation at Step 3, UT is the amount given by the calculation at Step 3 but reduced by any amount calculated at Step 4.

(2) In this section "UT" means the amount of underlying tax to be taken into account as a result of the provision mentioned in section 57(1).

59 Meaning of "relevant profits" in section 58

(1) This section applies for the purposes of section 58.

(2) "Relevant profits", if the dividend is within subsection (3), means the profits in respect of which the dividend is treated as paid for the purposes of section 931H of CTA 2009 (dividends derived from transactions not designed to reduce tax).

(3) A dividend is within this subsection if—

(a) it is received in an accounting period of the recipient in which the recipient is not a small company for the purposes of Part 9A of CTA 2009 (company distributions: see section 931S of that Act), and

(b) for the purposes of section 931H of that Act, it is treated as paid in respect of profits other than relevant profits (see subsection (4) of that section).

(4) "Relevant profits", if the dividend is not within subsection (3) but is paid for a specified period, means—

(a) the distributable profits of that period, plus

(b) if the total dividend exceeds those profits, so much of the distributable profits of preceding periods as is equal to the excess.

(5) "Relevant profits", if the dividend is not within subsection (3) and is not paid for a specified period, means—

(a) the distributable profits of the last period for which accounts of the company were made up which ended before the dividend became payable, plus

(b) if the total dividend exceeds those profits, so much of the distributable profits of preceding periods as is equal to the excess.

(6) In subsection (4)(b) or (5)(b), the reference to distributable profits of preceding periods does not include—

(a) profits previously distributed, or

(b) profits previously treated as relevant profits for the purposes of section 58, section 799 of ICTA or section 506 of the Income and Corporation Taxes Act 1970.

Taxation (International and Other Provisions) Act 2010 (c. 8)
Part 2 – *Double taxation relief*
Chapter 2 – *Double taxation relief by way of credit*

927

(7) For the purposes of subsection (4)(b) or (5)(b), the profits of the most recent preceding period are to be taken into account first, then the profits of the next most recent preceding period, and so on.

(8) In this section "distributable profits", in relation to a company, means the profits available for distribution as shown in accounts relating to the company –

    (a) drawn up in accordance with the law of the country or territory under whose law the company is incorporated or formed, and

    (b) making no provision for reserves, bad debts, impairment losses or contingencies other than such as is required to be made under the law of that country or territory.

(9) The reference in subsection (6)(b) to section 799 of ICTA is without prejudice to the generality of paragraph 4(1) of Schedule 9 (references to rewritten provisions include references to superseded provisions).

60 Underlying tax to be left out of account on claim to that effect

(1) Subsection (2) applies if –

    (a) under the arrangements a company resident in the United Kingdom makes a claim for an allowance by way of credit in accordance with this Chapter, and

    (b) the claim relates to a dividend paid to the company by a company resident outside the United Kingdom.

(2) The claim may be framed so as to exclude amounts of underlying tax specified for the purpose in the claim.

(3) Any amounts of underlying tax so excluded are to be left out of account for the purposes of section 57.

61 Calculation if section 58 does not apply

A calculation under this section (see section 57(2)(b)) is as follows –

Step 1

Calculate the amount of the foreign tax borne on the relevant profits by the body corporate paying the dividend.

Step 2

Calculate how much of that amount is properly attributable to the proportion of the relevant profits represented by the dividend.

Step 3

If under the law of the non-UK territory the dividend has been increased for tax purposes by an amount to be –

    set off against the recipient's own tax under that law, or

    paid to the recipient so far as it exceeds the recipient's own tax under that law,

calculate the amount of the increase.

Step 4

The amount of underlying tax to be taken into account as a result of the provision mentioned in section 57(1) is the amount given by the calculation at Step 2 but reduced by any amount calculated at Step 3.

928   *Taxation (International and Other Provisions) Act 2010 (c. 8)*
Part 2 — Double taxation relief
Chapter 2 — Double taxation relief by way of credit

62 Meaning of "relevant profits" in section 61

(1) This section applies for the purposes of section 61.

(2) "Relevant profits", if the dividend is paid for a specified period, means—

    (a) the profits of that period, plus

    (b) if the total dividend exceeds the distributable profits of that period, so much of the distributable profits of preceding periods as is equal to the excess.

(3) "Relevant profits", if the dividend is not paid for a specified period but is paid out of specified profits, means those profits.

(4) "Relevant profits", if the dividend is paid neither for a specified period nor out of specified profits, means—

    (a) the profits of the last period for which accounts of the body corporate paying the dividend were made up which ended before the dividend became payable, plus

    (b) if the total dividend exceeds the distributable profits of that period, so much of the distributable profits of preceding periods as is equal to the excess.

(5) In subsection (2)(b) or (4)(b), the reference to distributable profits of preceding periods does not include—

    (a) profits previously distributed, or

    (b) profits previously treated as relevant profits for the purposes of section 61, section 799 of ICTA or section 506 of the Income and Corporation Taxes Act 1970.

(6) For the purposes of subsection (2)(b) or (4)(b), the profits of the most recent preceding period are first to be taken into account, then the profits of the next most recent preceding period, and so on.

(7) In this section "distributable profits", in relation to a period, means profits available for distribution of the period.

(8) The reference in subsection (5)(b) to section 799 of ICTA is without prejudice to the generality of paragraph 4(1) of Schedule 9 (references to rewritten provisions include references to superseded provisions).

Taking account of tax underlying dividends that is not foreign tax

63 Non-UK company dividend paid to 10% investor: relief for UK and other tax

(1) If condition A is met, and one of conditions B and C is met, subsection (5) applies for the purpose of allowing, under the arrangements, credit against corporation tax in respect of a dividend paid by a company resident outside the United Kingdom ("the overseas company") to another company ("the recipient company").

(2) Condition A is that the recipient company—

    (a) controls directly or indirectly, or

    (b) is a subsidiary of a company which controls directly or indirectly,

at least 10% of the voting power in the overseas company.

(3) Condition B is that the recipient company is resident in the United Kingdom.

Taxation (International and Other Provisions) Act 2010 (c. 8)
Part 2 – Double taxation relief
Chapter 2 – Double taxation relief by way of credit

929

(4) Condition C is that—

    (a) the recipient company is resident outside the United Kingdom, but

    (b) the dividend forms part of the profits of a permanent establishment of the recipient company in the United Kingdom.

(5) There is to be taken into account, as if it were tax payable under the law of the territory ("territory R") in which the overseas company is resident—

    (a) any income tax or corporation tax payable by the overseas company in respect of its profits, and

    (b) any tax which, under the law of any territory outside the United Kingdom other than territory R, is payable by the overseas company in respect of its profits.

(6) For the purposes of subsection (2), one company ("S") is a subsidiary of another company ("P") if P controls, directly or indirectly, at least 50% of the voting power in S.

Tax underlying dividend treated as underlying tax paid by dividend's recipient

64 Meaning of "dividend-paying chain" of companies

(1) For the purposes of sections 65, 67 and 70 there is a dividend-paying chain if—

    (a) condition A is met, and

    (b) one of conditions B to D is met.

(2) Condition A is that a company ("the second company") pays a dividend to another company ("the first company").

(3) Condition B is that there is a third company which is a 10% associate of, and pays a dividend to, the second company.

(4) Condition C is that there is a succession of companies consisting of—

    (a) a third company which is a 10% associate of, and pays a dividend to, the second company, and

    (b) a fourth company which is a 10% associate of, and pays a dividend to, the third company.

(5) Condition D is that there is a succession of companies consisting of—

    (a) a third company which is a 10% associate of, and pays a dividend to, the second company, and

    (b) two or more companies (the fourth and fifth companies, and so on) each of which is a 10% associate of, and pays a dividend to, the company above it in the succession.

(6) For the purposes of this section, a company ("X") is a 10% associate of another company ("H") if H—

    (a) controls directly or indirectly, or

    (b) is a subsidiary of a company which controls directly or indirectly,

at least 10% of the voting power in X or at least 10% of the ordinary share capital of X.

(7) For the purposes of subsection (6), a company ("S") is a subsidiary of another company ("P") if P controls, directly or indirectly, at least 50% of the voting power in S.

930   *Taxation (International and Other Provisions) Act 2010 (c. 8)*
Part 2 – Double taxation relief
Chapter 2 – Double taxation relief by way of credit

65   Relief for underlying tax paid by company lower in dividend-paying chain

(1)   Subsection (4) applies if conditions E and F are met.

(2)   Condition E is that there is a dividend-paying chain (see section 64) in which—

    (a)   the first company is the recipient company mentioned in section 63, and

    (b)   the second company is the overseas company mentioned in that section.

(3)   Condition F is that there is underlying tax, payable by a company ("L") lower in the chain than the second company, that would be taken into account under this Part if—

    (a)   the dividend paid by L to the company ("K") above L in the chain had been paid—

        (i)   by a company resident outside the United Kingdom to a company resident in the United Kingdom, and

        (ii)   at the time when the dividend paid by the second company is received by the first company, and

    (b)   double taxation arrangements had provided for the underlying tax to be taken into account.

(4)   The underlying tax is to be treated—

    (a)   for the purposes of section 63(5), and

    (b)   for the purposes of subsection (3),

as tax paid by K in respect of its profits, but see section 66 (limitations).

(5)   In applying section 63 for the purpose of deciding whether condition F is met, read section 63(2) as if ", or at least 10% of the ordinary share capital of," were inserted after "at least 10% of the voting power in".

(6)   Section 58 (first method of calculating amount of underlying tax to be taken into account) does not apply for the purposes of subsections (3) and (4) unless the company referred to in subsection (2)(a) is resident in the United Kingdom and, even if that company is resident in the United Kingdom, section 58 applies for those purposes only—

    (a)   if K and L are not resident in the same territory, or

    (b)   in such other cases as may be prescribed by regulations made by the Treasury.

(7)   Section 61 (second method of calculation) applies for the purposes of subsections (3) and (4) if section 58 does not apply for those purposes.

66   Limitations on section 65(4)

(1)   Section 65(4) is subject to the limitations set out in subsections (2) and (3).

(2)   No tax is to be taken into account in respect of a dividend paid by a company resident in the United Kingdom except—

    (a)   corporation tax, and

    (b)   any tax for which the company is entitled to credit under this Part.

(3)   No tax is to be taken into account in respect of a dividend paid by a company resident outside the United Kingdom to another such company unless it could have been taken into account, under the provisions of this Part other than section 65(4), had the other company been resident in the United Kingdom.

Taxation (International and Other Provisions) Act 2010 (c. 8)
Part 2 — Double taxation relief
Chapter 2 — Double taxation relief by way of credit

931

Tax underlying dividends: restriction of relief, and particular cases

67 Restriction of relief if underlying tax at rate higher than rate of corporation tax

(1) Subsection (6) applies if —

    (a) conditions A and B are met, and

    (b) one of conditions C and D is met.

(2) Condition A is that a company ("the claimant company") makes a claim for an allowance by way of credit in accordance with this Part.

(3) Condition B is that the claim relates to underlying tax on a dividend paid to the claimant company by a company resident outside the United Kingdom ("the overseas company").

(4) Condition C is that the underlying tax is, or includes, an amount in respect of tax payable at a high rate by the overseas company and —

    (a) that amount would not be, or would not be included in, the underlying tax, or

    (b) any part of that amount would not be included in the underlying tax,

but for the existence of, or but for there having been, an avoidance scheme (see section 68).

(5) Condition D is that —

    (a) there is a dividend-paying chain (see section 64) in which —

        (i) the first company is the claimant company, and

        (ii) the second company is the overseas company, and

    (b) the underlying tax is, or includes, an amount in respect of tax payable at a high rate by a company lower in the chain than the overseas company and —

        (i) that amount would not be, or would not be included in, the underlying tax, or

        (ii) any part of that amount would not be included in the underlying tax,

but for the existence of, or but for there having been, an avoidance scheme (see section 68).

(6) The amount of credit to which the claimant company is entitled on the claim is to be determined as if the tax payable at a high rate had instead been tax at the relievable rate.

(7) For the purposes of this section, tax payable by a company is "tax payable at a high rate" so far as the amount payable exceeds the amount that would represent tax at the relievable rate on the profits of the company which, for the purposes of this Part, are taken to bear the payable tax.

(8) In this section "the relievable rate" means the rate of corporation tax in force when the dividend mentioned in subsection (3) was paid.

68 Meaning of "avoidance scheme" in section 67

(1) In section 67 "avoidance scheme" means any scheme or arrangement in respect of which each of conditions A to C is met.

932   *Taxation (International and Other Provisions) Act 2010 (c. 8)*
Part 2 — Double taxation relief
Chapter 2 — Double taxation relief by way of credit

(2)   Condition A is that the purpose, or one of the main purposes, of the scheme or arrangement is to have an amount of underlying tax taken into account on a claim for an allowance by way of credit in accordance with this Part.

(3)   Condition B is that the parties to the scheme or arrangement include—

       (a)   the company which is the claimant company for the purposes of section 67,

       (b)   a company related to the claimant company, or

       (c)   a person connected with the claimant company.

(4)   Condition C is that the parties to the scheme or arrangement include a person who was not under the control of the claimant company at any time before the doing of anything as part of, or in pursuance of, the scheme or arrangement.

(5)   For the purposes of subsection (3)(b), a company ("R") is related to the claimant company if the claimant company—

       (a)   controls directly or indirectly, or

       (b)   is a subsidiary of a company which controls directly or indirectly,

     at least 10% of the voting power in R.

(6)   For the purposes of subsection (3)(c), whether a person is connected with another is determined in accordance with section 1122 of CTA 2010.

(7)   For the purposes of subsection (4), a person who is a party to a scheme or arrangement is to be taken to have been under the control of the claimant company at all the following times—

       (a)   any time when the claimant company would have been taken (in accordance with sections 450 and 451 of CTA 2010) to have had control of the person for the purposes of Part 10 of CTA 2010 (close companies),

       (b)   any time when the claimant company would have been so taken if sections 450 and 451 of CTA 2010 applied (with the necessary modifications) in the case of partnerships and unincorporated associations as they apply in the case of companies, and

       (c)   any time when the person acted in relation to the scheme or arrangement, or any proposal for it, either directly or indirectly under the direction of the claimant company.

(8)   For the purposes of subsection (5), the claimant company is a subsidiary of another company ("P") if P controls, directly or indirectly, at least 50% of the voting power in the claimant company.

(9)   In this section "arrangement" means an arrangement of any kind, whether in writing or not.

69   Dividends paid out of transferred profits

(1)   This section applies if—

       (a)   a company resident outside the United Kingdom ("company A") has paid tax under the law of a territory outside the United Kingdom in respect of any of its profits,

       (b)   some or all of those profits become profits of another company resident outside the United Kingdom ("company B") otherwise than as a result of the payment of a dividend to company B, and

       (c)   company B pays a dividend out of those profits to another company, wherever resident.

Taxation (International and Other Provisions) Act 2010 (c. 8)
Part 2 — Double taxation relief
Chapter 2 — Double taxation relief by way of credit

933

(2) If this section applies, this Part has effect, so far as relating to the determination of underlying tax in relation to any dividend paid —

    (a) by any company resident outside the United Kingdom (whether or not company B),

    (b) to a company resident in the United Kingdom,

as if company B had paid the tax paid by company A in respect of those profits of company A which have become profits of company B as mentioned in subsection (1)(b).

(3) But the amount of relief under this Part which is allowable to a company resident in the United Kingdom is not to exceed the amount which would have been allowable to that company had those profits become profits of company B as a result of the payment of a dividend by company A to company B.

70   Underlying tax reflecting interest on loans

(1) Subsection (2) applies if —

    (a) a bank, or a company connected with a bank, makes a claim for an allowance by way of credit in accordance with this Chapter,

    (b) there is a dividend-paying chain (see section 64) in which —

        (i) the first company is the claimant, and

        (ii) the second company is a company resident outside the United Kingdom,

    (c) the claimant —

        (i) controls directly or indirectly, or

        (ii) is a subsidiary of a company which controls directly or indirectly,

    at least 10% of the voting power in the second company,

    (d) the claim relates to underlying tax on a dividend paid by the second company,

    (e) that underlying tax is, or includes, tax payable under the law of a territory outside the United Kingdom on, or by reference to, interest or dividends earned or received in the course of its business by a company ("the receiving company") which is —

        (i) the second company, or

        (ii) a company lower in the chain than the second company, and

    (f) section 44 would have applied to the receiving company had it been resident in the United Kingdom.

(2) The amount of the credit for the tax mentioned in subsection (1)(e) ("the non-UK tax") is not to exceed the sum equal to corporation tax, at the rate in force at the time the non-UK tax was chargeable, on —

$$ID - E$$

where —

    ID is the amount of the interest or dividends mentioned in subsection (1)(e), and

    E is the amount of the receiving company's expenditure which is properly attributable to the earning of that interest or those dividends.

(3) For the purposes of subsection (1)(a) —

934   *Taxation (International and Other Provisions) Act 2010 (c. 8)*
Part 2 − Double taxation relief
Chapter 2 − Double taxation relief by way of credit

    (a)   "bank" means a company carrying on, in the United Kingdom or elsewhere, any trade which includes the receipt of interest or dividends, and

    (b)   whether a company is connected with a bank is determined in accordance with section 1122 of CTA 2010.

(4)   For the purposes of subsection (1)(c), the claimant is a subsidiary of another company ("P") if P controls, directly or indirectly, at least 50% of the voting power in the claimant.

71   Foreign taxation of group as single entity

(1)   Subsections (2) and (3) apply in relation to a claim for credit in respect of underlying tax in relation to a dividend paid by a company resident outside the United Kingdom to a company resident in the United Kingdom if, under the law of a territory outside the United Kingdom, tax is payable by any one company resident in the territory ("the responsible company") in respect of the aggregate profits, or aggregate profits and aggregate gains, of —

    (a)   that company and another company resident in the territory, or

    (b)   that company and two or more other companies resident in the territory,

taken together as a single taxable entity.

(2)   This Part, so far as relating to the determination of underlying tax in relation to any dividend paid by any of the companies mentioned in subsection (1)(a) or (b) (the "non-resident companies") to another company ("the payee company"), has effect as if —

    (a)   the non-resident companies, taken together, were a single company,

    (b)   anything done by or in relation to any of the non-resident companies (including the payment of the dividend) were done by or in relation to that single company, and

    (c)   that single company were related to the payee company if the company which actually pays the dividend is related to the payee company.

(3)   In particular, this Part has effect as if —

    (a)   the relevant profits for the purposes of section 58 is a single aggregate figure in respect of that single company, and

    (b)   the tax paid in the territory by the responsible company is tax paid in the territory by that single company.

(4)   For the purposes of this section, a company ("X") is related to another company ("H") if H —

    (a)   controls directly or indirectly, or

    (b)   is a subsidiary of a company which controls directly or indirectly,

at least 10% of the voting power in X.

(5)   For the purposes of subsection (4), H is a subsidiary of another company ("P") if P controls, directly or indirectly, at least 50% of the voting power in H.

Taxation (International and Other Provisions) Act 2010 (c. 8)
Part 2 – Double taxation relief
Chapter 2 – Double taxation relief by way of credit

935

Unrelieved foreign tax on profits of overseas permanent establishment

72 Application of section 73(1)

(1) Section 73(1) applies if, in an accounting period of a company resident in the United Kingdom—

   (a) the amount of the credit for foreign tax which under the arrangements would, if section 42 were ignored, be allowable against corporation tax in respect of the company's qualifying income from an overseas permanent establishment, exceeds

   (b) the amount of the credit for foreign tax which under the arrangements is allowed against corporation tax in respect of the company's qualifying income from that overseas permanent establishment.

(2) For the purposes of subsection (1) and section 73(1), the company's qualifying income from an overseas permanent establishment is the profits of the overseas permanent establishment which are—

   (a) profits, chargeable under Chapter 2 of Part 3 of CTA 2009, of a trade carried on partly, but not wholly, outside the United Kingdom, or

   (b) included in the profits of a gross roll-up business chargeable under section 436A of ICTA.

(3) In sections 73 to 78—

   "the company" means the company mentioned in subsection (1),

   "the excess" means the excess referred to in that subsection,

   "the PE" means the overseas permanent establishment mentioned in that subsection, and

   "period A" means the accounting period mentioned in that subsection.

73 Carry-forward and carry-back of unrelieved foreign tax

(1) For the purposes of allowing credit relief under this Part, the excess is to be treated—

   (a) as if it were foreign tax paid in respect of, and calculated by reference to, the company's qualifying income from the PE in the accounting period after period A (whether or not the company in fact has any qualifying income from that source in the accounting period after period A), or

   (b) in accordance with the rules in section 74, as if it were foreign tax paid in respect of, and calculated by reference to, the company's qualifying income from the PE in one or more of the recent periods, or

   (c) partly as mentioned in paragraph (a) and partly as mentioned in paragraph (b).

(2) If in period A the company ceases to have the PE, the excess, so far as it is not treated as mentioned in subsection (1)(b), is to be reduced to nil (so that none of the excess is to be treated as mentioned in subsection (1)(a)).

(3) If an amount is treated as mentioned in subsection (1)(b) it is not to be so treated for the purpose of any further application of subsection (1).

(4) In subsection (1)(b) "recent period" means an accounting period which is earlier than period A but begins not more than 3 years before period A.

936

Taxation (International and Other Provisions) Act 2010 (c. 8)
Part 2 – Double taxation relief
Chapter 2 – Double taxation relief by way of credit

74   Rules for carrying back unrelieved foreign tax

(1)   This section sets out the rules mentioned in section 73(1)(b).

(2)   The first rule is that—

    (a)   credit for the excess, or for any remaining balance of the excess, is allowed against corporation tax in respect of a later recent period, before

    (b)   credit for any of the excess is allowed against corporation tax in respect of any earlier recent period.

(3)   The second rule is that, before allowing credit for any of the excess against corporation tax in respect of income of any particular accounting period ("period P"), credit for foreign tax is allowed—

    (a)   first for foreign tax in respect of the income of period P, other than amounts which are foreign tax as a result of applying section 73(1) to an excess from an accounting period other than period P, and

    (b)   then for amounts which are foreign tax as a result of applying section 73(1) to an excess from an accounting period before period P.

(4)   In subsection (2) "recent period" means an accounting period which is earlier than period A but begins not more than 3 years before period A.

75   Two or more establishments treated as a single establishment

(1)   Subsection (2) applies if, under the law of a territory outside the United Kingdom, tax is charged in respect of the profits of two or more overseas permanent establishments in that territory, taken together.

(2)   For the purposes of the provisions of sections 72 to 78 other than the excepted provisions, those overseas permanent establishments are to be treated as if they together constituted a single overseas permanent establishment.

(3)   In subsection (2) "the excepted provisions" means section 73(2), this section and section 77.

76   Former and subsequent establishments regarded as distinct establishments

(1)   If the company—

    (a)   at any time ceases to have a particular overseas permanent establishment in a particular territory ("the old establishment"), but

    (b)   subsequently again has an overseas permanent establishment in that territory ("the new establishment"),

the old establishment and the new establishment are, for the purposes of the provisions of sections 72 to 78 other than the excepted provisions, to be regarded as different overseas permanent establishments.

(2)   In subsection (1) "the excepted provisions" means sections 73(2), 75 and 77.

77   Claims for relief under section 73(1)

(1)   The excess is to be treated as mentioned in section 73(1) only on a claim.

(2)   A claim under subsection (1) must specify—

    (a)   the amount (if any) of the excess which is to be treated as mentioned in section 73(1)(a), and

Taxation (International and Other Provisions) Act 2010 (c. 8)
Part 2 — Double taxation relief
Chapter 2 — Double taxation relief by way of credit

937

      (b)   the amount (if any) of the excess which is to be treated as mentioned in section 73(1)(b).

(3)   A claim under subsection (1) must be made not more than—
      (a)   4 years after the end of period A, or
      (b)   if later, 1 year after the end of the accounting period in which the foreign tax concerned is paid.

78 Meaning of "overseas permanent establishment"

(1)   For the purposes of sections 72 to 76 "overseas permanent establishment" means a permanent establishment through which the company carries on a trade in a territory outside the United Kingdom.

(2)   In subsection (1) "permanent establishment"—
      (a)   if the arrangements are double taxation arrangements and define the expression, has the meaning given by the arrangements, and
      (b)   if the arrangements are double taxation arrangements but do not define the expression, or if the arrangements are unilateral relief arrangements for a territory outside the United Kingdom, is to be read in accordance with Chapter 2 of Part 24 of CTA 2010.

Action after adjustment of amount payable by way of UK or foreign tax

79 Time limits for action if tax adjustment makes credit excessive or insufficient

(1)   Subsection (2) applies to a claim or assessment if—
      (a)   the amount of any credit given under the arrangements is reduced under section 34, or becomes excessive or insufficient by reason of any adjustment of the amount of any tax payable either in the United Kingdom or under the law of any other territory,
      (b)   the reduction or adjustment gives rise to the claim or assessment, and
      (c)   the claim or assessment is made not later than 6 years from the time when all material determinations have been made, whether in the United Kingdom or elsewhere.

(2)   Nothing in—
      (a)   the Tax Acts, and
      (b)   the enactments relating to capital gains tax,
    limiting the time for the making of assessments, or limiting the time for the making of claims for relief, applies to the assessment or claim.

(3)   In subsection (1)(c) "material determination" means an assessment, reduction, adjustment or other determination that is material in determining whether any, and (if so) what, credit is to be given.

80 Duty to give notice that adjustment has rendered credit excessive

(1)   This section applies if—
      (a)   any credit for foreign tax has been allowed to a person under the arrangements,

938

Taxation (International and Other Provisions) Act 2010 (c. 8)
Part 2 – Double taxation relief
Chapter 2 – Double taxation relief by way of credit

(b)   later, the amount of that credit is reduced under section 34, or becomes excessive as a result of an adjustment of the amount of any tax payable under the law of a territory outside the United Kingdom, and

(c)   the reduction or adjustment is not a Lloyd's adjustment (see subsection (5)).

(2)   The person must give notice that a reduction has been made or that the amount of the credit has become excessive as a result of the making of an adjustment.

(3)   Notice under subsection (2) is to be given—

(a)   to an officer of Revenue and Customs, and

(b)   within one year from when the reduction or adjustment is made.

(4)   If the person fails to comply with the requirements imposed by subsections (2) and (3), the person is liable to a penalty not greater than the amount by which the credit has been reduced or has become excessive as a result of the adjustment.

(5)   For the purposes of subsection (1)(c), the reduction or adjustment is a "Lloyd's adjustment" if the consequences of the reduction or adjustment in relation to the credit are to be given effect in accordance with regulations under—

(a)   section 182(1) of FA 1993 (regulations about individual members of Lloyd's), or

(b)   section 229 of FA 1994 (regulations relating to corporate members of Lloyd's).

(6)   In this section so far as it relates to capital gains tax "notice" means notice in writing.

Schemes and arrangements designed to increase relief: anti-avoidance

81   Giving a counteraction notice

(1)   Subsection (2) applies if an officer of Revenue and Customs considers, on reasonable grounds, that each of conditions A to D of section 82 is or may be met in relation to a person.

(2)   The officer may give the person a notice which—

(a)   informs the person of the officer's view under subsection (1),

(b)   specifies the chargeable period in relation to which the officer formed that view,

(c)   specifies, if the amount of foreign tax considered by the officer to meet condition B of section 82 is an amount of underlying tax, the body corporate whose payment of foreign tax is relevant to that underlying tax, and

(d)   informs the person that, as a result of the giving of the notice, section 90(2) will apply in relation to the person's tax return for the chargeable period specified if each of conditions A to D of section 82 is met in relation to that period.

(3)   Section 92 (when notice may be given after tax return made) imposes limits on when the power under subsection (2) is exercisable.

(4)   In this section "foreign tax" includes any tax which for the purpose of allowing credit under the arrangements against corporation tax is treated by section 63(5) as if it were tax payable under the law of the non-UK territory.

Taxation (International and Other Provisions) Act 2010 (c. 8)
Part 2 – Double taxation relief
Chapter 2 – Double taxation relief by way of credit

939

(5)   In this section so far as it relates to capital gains tax—

"chargeable period" means tax year (see section 288(1ZA) of TCGA 1992), and

"notice" means notice in writing.

82   Conditions for the purposes of section 81(1)

(1)   Conditions A to D are the conditions mentioned in section 81(1).

(2)   Condition A is that, in respect of any income or chargeable gain—

(a)   taken into account for the purposes of determining a person's liability to UK tax in a chargeable period, or

(b)   to be taken into account for the purposes of determining a person's liability to UK tax in a chargeable period,

there is an amount of foreign tax for which, under the arrangements, credit is allowable against UK tax for the period.

(3)   Condition B is that there is a scheme or arrangement the main purpose of which, or one of the main purposes of which, is to cause an amount of foreign tax to be taken into account in the person's case for the period.

(4)   Condition C is that the scheme or arrangement is within section 83.

(5)   Condition D is that T is more than a minimal amount, where T is the sum of—

(a)   the total amount of the claims for credit that the person has made, or is in a position to make, for the period ("the counteraction period"), and

(b)   the total amount of all connected-person claims.

(6)   In subsection (5) "connected-person claim" means a claim that any person connected to the person has made, or is in a position to make, for any chargeable period that overlaps the counteraction period by at least one day.

(7)   In this section—

"chargeable period", in relation to capital gains tax, means tax year (see section 288(1ZA) of TCGA 1992),

"foreign tax" includes any tax which for the purpose of allowing credit under the arrangements against corporation tax is treated by section 63(5) as if it were tax payable under the law of the non-UK territory, and

"UK tax" means income tax, corporation tax or capital gains tax.

(8)   Section 286 of TCGA 1992 (meaning of "connected") applies for the purposes of subsection (6) so far as applying in relation to capital gains tax.

83   Schemes and arrangements referred to in section 82(4)

(1)   For the purposes of section 82(4), a scheme or arrangement is within this section if it is within subsection (2) or (4).

(2)   A scheme or arrangement is within this subsection if—

(a)   it is not an underlying-tax scheme or arrangement, and

(b)   one or more of sections 84 to 88 apply to it.

(3)   For the purposes of this section, a scheme or arrangement is an "underlying-tax" scheme or arrangement if its main purpose, or one of its main purposes, is to cause an amount of underlying tax allowable in respect of a dividend paid

940

Taxation (International and Other Provisions) Act 2010 (c. 8)
Part 2 – Double taxation relief
Chapter 2 – Double taxation relief by way of credit

by an overseas-resident body corporate to be taken into account in a person's case.

(4) A scheme or arrangement is within this subsection if—

    (a) it is an underlying-tax scheme or arrangement, and

    (b) one or more of sections 84 to 88 would, on the assumption in subsection (5), apply to it.

(5) The assumption is that the body corporate is resident in the United Kingdom.

(6) Nothing in subsection (5) requires it to be assumed that there is any change in the place or places at which the body corporate carries on its activities.

(7) In subsection (3) "overseas-resident" means resident in a territory outside the United Kingdom.

84 Section 83(2) and (4): schemes enabling attribution of foreign tax

(1) This section applies to a scheme or arrangement if—

    (a) the scheme or arrangement enables a participant to pay, in respect of a source of income or chargeable gain, an amount of foreign tax, and

    (b) all or part of that amount of foreign tax is properly attributable to another source of income or chargeable gain.

(2) In subsection (1) "participant" means a person who is party to, or concerned in, the scheme or arrangement.

85 Section 83(2) and (4): schemes about effect of paying foreign tax

(1) This section applies to a scheme or arrangement if, under the scheme or arrangement, the condition in subsection (2) is met in relation to a person ("C") who for a chargeable period has claimed, or is in a position to claim, any credit that under the arrangements is to be allowed for foreign tax.

(2) The condition is that—

    (a) C pays an amount of foreign tax ("the FT amount"), and

    (b) when C entered into the scheme or arrangement, it could reasonably be expected that the effect of the payment of the FT amount on the foreign-tax total would be to increase that total by less than amount X.

(3) In subsection (2)(b)—

    "the foreign-tax total" means the amount found by—

        (a) totalling the amounts of foreign tax paid or payable by the participants in respect of the transaction or transactions forming part of the scheme or arrangement, and

        (b) taking into account any reliefs that arise to the participants, including any reliefs arising to any one or more of the participants as a consequence of the payment by C of the FT amount, and

    "amount X" means the amount allowable to C as a credit in respect of the payment of the FT amount.

(4) In subsection (3)—

    "participant" means a person who is party to, or concerned in, the scheme or arrangement, and

Taxation (International and Other Provisions) Act 2010 (c. 8)
Part 2 – Double taxation relief
Chapter 2 – Double taxation relief by way of credit

941

"reliefs" means reliefs, deductions, reductions or allowances against or in respect of any tax.

(5) In subsection (1) so far as it relates to capital gains tax "chargeable period" means tax year (see section 288(1ZA) of TCGA 1992).

86 Section 83(2) and (4): schemes about claims or elections etc

(1) This section applies to a scheme or arrangement if under the scheme or arrangement—
  (a) a step is taken by a participant, or
  (b) a step that could have been taken by a participant is not taken,
  and that action or failure to act has the effect of increasing, or giving rise to, a claim by a participant for an allowance by way of credit under this Part.

(2) The steps mentioned in subsection (1) are steps that may be taken—
  (a) under the law of any territory, or
  (b) under double taxation arrangements made in relation to any territory.

(3) The steps mentioned in subsection (1) include—
  (a) claiming, or otherwise securing the benefit of, reliefs, deductions, reductions or allowances, and
  (b) making elections for tax purposes.

(4) In subsection (1) "participant" means a person who is party to, or concerned in, the scheme or arrangement.

87 Section 83(2) and (4): schemes that would reduce a person's tax liability

(1) This section applies to a scheme or arrangement if, under the scheme or arrangement, the condition in subsection (2) is met in relation to a person who for a chargeable period has claimed, or is in a position to claim, any credit that under the arrangements is to be allowed for foreign tax.

(2) The condition is that amount A is less than amount B.

(3) Amount A is the amount of UK tax payable by the person in respect of income and chargeable gains arising in the chargeable period.

(4) Amount B is the amount of UK tax that would be payable by the person in respect of income and chargeable gains arising in the chargeable period if, in determining that amount, the transactions forming part of the scheme or arrangement were disregarded.

(5) In this section "UK tax" means income tax, corporation tax and capital gains tax.

(6) In this section so far as it relates to capital gains tax "chargeable period" means tax year (see section 288(1ZA) of TCGA 1992).

88 Section 83(2) and (4): schemes involving tax-deductible payments

(1) This section applies to a scheme or arrangement if the scheme or arrangement includes—
  (a) the making by a person ("P") of a relevant payment or payments, and

942   *Taxation (International and Other Provisions) Act 2010 (c. 8)*
Part 2 – Double taxation relief
Chapter 2 – Double taxation relief by way of credit

      (b)   the giving, in respect of the payment or payments, of qualifying consideration.

(2)   For the purposes of subsection (1), a payment is a "relevant payment" if all or part of it may be brought into account—

      (a)   in calculating P's income for the purposes of income tax or corporation tax, or

      (b)   in calculating P's chargeable gains for the purposes of capital gains tax.

(3)   For the purposes of subsection (1), consideration is "qualifying consideration" if—

      (a)   all or part of it consists of a payment made to P or a person connected with P, and

      (b)   tax is chargeable in respect of the payment under the law of a territory outside the United Kingdom.

(4)   In this section "payment" includes a transfer of money's worth.

(5)   For the purposes of this section, whether a person is connected with another is determined in accordance with section 1122 of CTA 2010.

89   Contents of counteraction notice

(1)   Subsections (2) and (3) apply if an officer of Revenue and Customs gives a person a counteraction notice.

(2)   The notice may specify the adjustments that, in the view of the officer, section 90 requires the person to make.

(3)   If the notice specifies under section 81(2)(c) a body corporate resident outside the United Kingdom, the adjustments specified may include treating the body as having paid, or being liable to pay, only so much foreign tax as would have been allowed to it as a credit if—

      (a)   it were resident in the United Kingdom, and

      (b)   a counteraction notice had been given to it as regards an amount of foreign tax.

(4)   In this section "foreign tax" includes any tax which for the purpose of allowing credit under the arrangements against corporation tax is treated by section 63(5) as if it were tax payable under the law of the non-UK territory.

90   Consequences of counteraction notices

(1)   If—

      (a)   a counteraction notice has been given to a person in respect of a chargeable period specified in the notice, and

      (b)   that chargeable period is a chargeable period in relation to which each of conditions A to D of section 82 is met,

subsection (2) applies to the person's tax return for the period.

(2)   The person must in the return make, or must amend the return so as to make, such adjustments as are necessary for counteracting the effects of the scheme or arrangement in that period that are referable to the purpose referred to in condition B of section 82.

Taxation (International and Other Provisions) Act 2010 (c. 8)
Part 2 — Double taxation relief
Chapter 2 — Double taxation relief by way of credit

943

91 Counteraction notices given before tax return made

(1) Subsection (2) applies if —

    (a) an officer of Revenue and Customs gives a counteraction notice to a person before the person has made the person's tax return for the chargeable period specified in the notice, and

    (b) the person makes a tax return for that period before the end of the 90 days beginning with the day on which the notice is given.

(2) The person may —

    (a) make a tax return that disregards the notice, and

    (b) at any time after making the return and before the end of the 90 days, amend the return for the purpose of complying with the provision referred to in the notice.

(3) Subsection (2)(b) does not prevent the return becoming incorrect if the return —

    (a) is not amended in accordance with subsection (2)(b) for the purpose of complying with the provision referred to in the notice, but

    (b) ought to have been so amended.

92 Counteraction notices given after tax return made

(1) This section applies if —

    (a) a person has made a tax return for a chargeable period, and

    (b) ignoring the restrictions imposed by this section, an officer of Revenue and Customs has power to give the person a counteraction notice in relation to the period.

(2) The officer may give the person a counteraction notice in relation to the period only if a notice of enquiry has been given to the person in respect of the return.

(3) After any enquiries into the return have been completed, the officer may give the person a counteraction notice in relation to the period only if conditions E and F are met.

(4) Condition E is that, at the time the enquiries were completed, no officer of Revenue and Customs could have been reasonably expected, on the basis of the information made available to Her Majesty's Revenue and Customs before that time, to have been aware that the circumstances were such that a counteraction notice could have been given to the person in relation to the period.

(5) Condition F is that —

    (a) the person was requested to provide information during an enquiry into the return, and

    (b) if the person had duly complied with the request, an officer of Revenue and Customs could have been reasonably expected to give the person a counteraction notice in relation to the period.

(6) Section 94 sets out the circumstances in which, for the purposes of condition E, information is made available.

93 Amendment, closure notices and discovery assessments in section 92 cases

(1) This section applies if a person is given a counteraction notice in relation to a chargeable period after having made a tax return for the period.

944
Taxation (International and Other Provisions) Act 2010 (c. 8)
Part 2 – Double taxation relief
Chapter 2 – Double taxation relief by way of credit

(2) The person may amend the return for the purpose of complying with the provision referred to in the notice at any time before the end of the 90 days beginning with the day on which the notice is given.

(3) If the counteraction notice is given after the person has been given a notice of enquiry in relation to the return, no closure notice may be given in relation to the return before the deadline.

(4) If the counteraction notice is given after any enquiries into the return are completed, no discovery assessment may be made as regards the income or chargeable gain to which the counteraction notice relates before the deadline.

(5) In subsections (3) and (4) "the deadline" means—
   (a) the end of the 90 days beginning with the day on which the counteraction notice is given, or
   (b) if earlier, the amendment of the return for the purpose of complying with the provision referred to in the counteraction notice.

(6) Subsection (2) does not prevent the return becoming incorrect if the return—
   (a) is not amended in accordance with subsection (2) for the purpose of complying with the provision referred to in the counteraction notice, but
   (b) ought to have been so amended.

94   Information made available for the purposes of section 92(4)

(1) This section applies for the purposes of section 92(4), and in this section—
   "the period",
   "the person", and
   "the return",
   mean (respectively) the chargeable period, the person and the tax return mentioned in section 92(1).

(2) Information is made available to Her Majesty's Revenue and Customs if the return is under section 8 or 8A of TMA 1970 (personal or trustee's return) and the information—
   (a) is contained in the return,
   (b) is contained in the person's return under that section for either of the two immediately preceding tax years,
   (c) is contained in documents accompanying a return within paragraph (a) or (b), or
   (d) is, or is contained in documents which are, produced or provided by or on behalf of the person to an officer of Revenue and Customs for the purposes of any enquiries into a return within paragraph (a) or (b).

(3) Information is made available to Her Majesty's Revenue and Customs if the return is under section 8 of TMA 1970 (personal return), the person carries on a trade, profession or business in partnership and the information—
   (a) is contained in a return under section 12AA of TMA 1970 (partnership return) with respect to the partnership for the period,
   (b) is contained in a return under section 12AA of TMA 1970 with respect to the partnership for either of the two immediately preceding tax years,

Taxation (International and Other Provisions) Act 2010 (c. 8)   945
Part 2 — Double taxation relief
Chapter 2 — Double taxation relief by way of credit

(c) is contained in documents accompanying a return within paragraph (a) or (b), or

(d) is, or is contained in documents which are, produced or provided by or on behalf of the person to an officer of Revenue and Customs for the purposes of any enquiries into a return within paragraph (a) or (b).

(4) Information is made available to Her Majesty's Revenue and Customs if the return is a company tax return and the information —

(a) is contained in the return,

(b) is contained in the person's company tax return for either of the two immediately preceding accounting periods,

(c) is contained in documents accompanying a return within paragraph (a) or (b), or

(d) is, or is contained in documents which are, produced or provided by the person to an officer of Revenue and Customs for the purposes of any enquiries into a return within paragraph (a) or (b).

(5) Information is made available to Her Majesty's Revenue and Customs if the return is under section 8 or 8A of TMA 1970 and the information —

(a) is contained in any claim made as regards the period by, or on behalf of, the person acting in the same capacity as that in which the person made the return,

(b) is contained in any documents accompanying such a claim, or

(c) is, or is contained in documents which are, produced or provided by or on behalf of the person to an officer of Revenue and Customs for the purposes of any enquiries into such a claim.

(6) Information is made available to Her Majesty's Revenue and Customs if the return is a company tax return and the information —

(a) is contained in a claim made by or on behalf of the person as regards the period,

(b) is contained in an application under section 751A of ICTA (applications relating to controlled foreign companies) made by or on behalf of the person which affects the return,

(c) is contained in any documents accompanying such a claim or application, or

(d) is, or is contained in documents which are, produced or provided by the person to an officer of Revenue and Customs for the purposes of any enquiries into such a claim or application.

(7) Information is made available to Her Majesty's Revenue and Customs if the existence of the information, and the relevance of the information as regards exercise of power to give the person a counteraction notice in relation to the period —

(a) could reasonably be expected to be inferred by an officer of Revenue and Customs from information falling within subsections (2) to (6), or

(b) are notified in writing by or on behalf of the person to an officer of Revenue and Customs.

95   Interpretation of sections 89 to 94

(1) This section applies for the purposes of sections 89 to 94, and subsection (4) applies also for the purposes of subsection (8).

946   *Taxation (International and Other Provisions) Act 2010 (c. 8)*
Part 2 — Double taxation relief
Chapter 2 — Double taxation relief by way of credit

(2) "Chargeable period", in relation to capital gains tax, means tax year (see section 288(1ZA) of TCGA 1992).

(3) "Closure notice" means a notice under —
   (a) section 28A or 28B of TMA 1970 (completion of enquiry into personal, trustee's or partnership return), or
   (b) paragraph 32 of Schedule 18 to FA 1998 (completion of enquiry into company return).

(4) "Company tax return" means the return required to be delivered pursuant to a notice under paragraph 3 of Schedule 18 to FA 1998, as read with paragraph 4 of that Schedule (company returns).

(5) "Counteraction notice" means a notice under section 81(2).

(6) "Discovery assessment" means an assessment under —
   (a) section 29 of TMA 1970 (assessment to income tax or capital gains tax), or
   (b) paragraph 41 of Schedule 18 to FA 1998 (assessment on company).

(7) "Notice of enquiry" means a notice under —
   (a) section 9A or 12AC of TMA 1970 (enquiry into personal, trustee's or partnership return), or
   (b) paragraph 24 of Schedule 18 to FA 1998 (enquiry into company return).

(8) "Tax return" means —
   (a) a return under section 8, 8A or 12AA of TMA 1970 (personal return, trustee's return or partnership return), or
   (b) a company tax return.

Insurance companies

96   Companies with overseas branches: restriction of credit

(1) Subsection (4) applies if credit for foreign tax —
   (a) which is payable in respect of insurance business carried on by a company through a permanent establishment in the non-UK territory, and
   (b) which is calculated otherwise than wholly by reference to profits arising in the non-UK territory,

   is to be allowed (in accordance with this Part) against corporation tax charged under section 35 of CTA 2009 or section 436A of ICTA in respect of the profits, calculated in accordance with the provisions applicable for the purposes of section 35 of CTA 2009, of life assurance business or gross roll-up business carried on by the company in an accounting period (in this section called "the relevant UK-taxable profits").

(2) For the purposes of subsection (1)(b), the cases in which foreign tax is "calculated otherwise than wholly by reference to profits arising in the non-UK territory" are those cases in which the charge to tax in the non-UK territory is within subsection (3).

(3) A charge to tax is within this subsection if it is such a charge made otherwise than by reference to profits as (by disallowing their deduction in calculating the amount chargeable) to require sums payable and other liabilities arising

Taxation (International and Other Provisions) Act 2010 (c. 8)   947
Part 2 — Double taxation relief
Chapter 2 — Double taxation relief by way of credit

under policies to be treated as sums or liabilities falling to be met out of amounts subject to tax in the hands of the company.

(4)   If this subsection applies, the amount of the credit is not to exceed the greater of —

    (a)   any such part of the foreign tax as is charged by reference to profits arising in the non-UK territory, and

    (b)   the shareholders' share of the foreign tax.

(5)   For the purposes of subsection (4), the shareholders' share of the foreign tax is so much of that tax as is represented by the fraction —

$$\frac{A}{B}$$

where —

    A is an amount equal to the amount of the relevant UK-taxable profits before making any deduction authorised by subsection (7), and

    B is an amount equal to the excess of —

        (a)   the amount taken into account as receipts of the company in calculating those profits, apart from premiums and sums received by virtue of a claim under a reinsurance contract, over

        (b)   the amount taken into account as expenses in calculating those profits.

(6)   If there is no such excess, or if the profits are greater than any excess, the whole of the foreign tax is the shareholders' share; and, subject to that, if there are no profits, none of the foreign tax is the shareholders' share.

(7)   If, by virtue of this section, the credit for any foreign tax is less than it otherwise would be, section 31(2)(a) does not prevent a deduction being made for the difference in calculating the relevant UK-taxable profits.

97   Companies with more than one category of business: restriction of credit

(1)   Subsection (2) has effect if —

    (a)   an insurance company carries on more than one category of long-term business in an accounting period, and

    (b)   there arises to the company in that period any income or gain ("the relevant income") in respect of which credit for foreign tax is to be allowed under the arrangements.

(2)   The amount of the credit for foreign tax which, under the arrangements, is allowable against corporation tax in respect of so much of the relevant income as is referable (in accordance with the provisions of sections 432ZA to 432E of ICTA) to a particular category of business must not exceed the fraction of the foreign tax which, in accordance with the following provisions of this section and with the provisions of section 98, is attributable to that category of business.

(3)   If the relevant income arises from an asset which is linked solely to a category of business, the whole of the foreign tax is attributable to that category of business, unless section 98(3) applies.

(4)   If the relevant income arises from foreign business assets, the whole of the foreign tax is attributable to gross roll-up business, unless section 98(3) applies.

(5)   If subsection (3) does not apply and the category of business in question is —

948   *Taxation (International and Other Provisions) Act 2010 (c. 8)*
Part 2 — Double taxation relief
Chapter 2 — Double taxation relief by way of credit

      (a)   basic life assurance and general annuity business, or

      (b)   PHI business,

the fraction of the foreign tax that is attributable to that category of business is the fraction given by—

$$\frac{\text{The referable part of the relevant income}}{\text{The whole of the relevant income}}$$

where "the referable part" of the relevant income is the part of the relevant income which is referable to that category of business by virtue of any provision of section 432A of ICTA.

(6)   Section 98(2) and (3) apply if the category of business in question is gross roll-up business.

(7)   No part of the foreign tax is attributable to any category of business except as provided by subsections (3) to (6) and section 98(2) and (3).

(8)   If under this section or section 98(2) and (3) an amount of foreign tax is for the purposes of this section attributable to gross roll-up business, credit in respect of the foreign tax so attributable is allowed only against corporation tax in respect of profits charged under section 436A of ICTA (charge on profits from gross roll-up business).

98   Attribution for section 97 purposes if category is gross roll-up business

(1)   Subsections (2) and (3) apply for the purposes of section 97 in accordance with section 97(6), and in this section "the relevant income" has the meaning given by section 97(1).

(2)   If—

      (a)   section 97(3) does not apply, and

      (b)   some or all of the relevant income is taken into account in accordance with section 83 of FA 1989 in an account in relation to which the provisions of section 432C of ICTA apply,

the fraction of the foreign tax that is attributable to gross roll-up business is the fraction given by—

$$\frac{\text{The referable part of the relevant income}}{\text{The whole of the relevant income}}$$

where "the referable part" of the relevant income is the part of the relevant income which is referable to gross roll-up business by virtue of any provision of section 432C of ICTA.

(3)   If some or all of the relevant income falls to be taken into account in determining in accordance with section 83(2) of FA 1989 the amount referred to in section 432E(1) of ICTA as the net amount, the fraction of the foreign tax that is attributable to gross roll-up business is the fraction given by—

$$\frac{\text{The referable part of INV}}{\text{The whole of INV}}$$

where—

      "INV" is the investment income taken into account in that determination, and

      "the referable part" of INV is the part of INV which would be referable to gross roll-up business by virtue of section 432E of ICTA if INV were the only amount included in the net amount.

Taxation (International and Other Provisions) Act 2010 (c. 8)
Part 2 — *Double taxation relief*
Chapter 2 — *Double taxation relief by way of credit*

949

(4) The Treasury may by regulations amend subsection (3); and the regulations may include amendments having effect in accounting periods during which they are made.

99   Allocation of expenses etc in calculations under section 35 of CTA 2009

(1) Subsection (2) has effect if—

    (a) an insurance company carries on any category of insurance business in a period of account,

    (b) a calculation in accordance with the provisions applicable for the purposes of section 35 of CTA 2009 (charge on trade profits) falls to be made in relation to that category of business for that period, and

    (c) there arises to the company in that period any income or gain in respect of which credit for foreign tax is to be allowed under the arrangements.

(2) The amount of the credit for foreign tax which, under the arrangements, is to be allowed against corporation tax in respect of so much of that income or gain as is referable to the category of business concerned ("the relevant income") is to be limited by treating the amount of the relevant income as reduced in accordance with sections 100 and 101.

(3) In determining the amount of credit for foreign tax which is to be allowed as mentioned in subsection (2), the relevant income is not to be reduced except in accordance with that subsection.

(4) If a 75% subsidiary of an insurance company is acting in accordance with a scheme or arrangement and—

    (a) the purpose, or one of the main purposes, of the scheme or arrangement is to prevent or restrict the application of subsection (2) to the insurance company, and

    (b) the subsidiary does not carry on insurance business of any description,

the amount of corporation tax attributable (apart from this subsection) to any item of income or gain arising to the subsidiary is to be found by setting off against that item the amount of expenses that would be attributable to it under section 100(1) if that item had arisen directly to the insurance company.

(5) If the credit allowed for any foreign tax is, by virtue of subsection (2), less than it would be if the relevant income were not treated as reduced in accordance with that subsection, section 31(2)(a) does not prevent a deduction being made for the difference in calculating the profits of the category of business concerned.

(6) If, by virtue of subsection (4), the credit allowed for any foreign tax is less than it would be apart from that subsection, section 31(2)(a) does not prevent a deduction being made for the difference in calculating the income of the 75% subsidiary.

(7) For the purposes of the operation of this section in relation to any income or gain in respect of which credit is to be allowed under the arrangements, the amount of the income or gain that is referable to a category of insurance business is the same fraction of the income or gain as the fraction of the foreign tax that is attributable to that category of business in accordance with sections 97 and 98.

950

Taxation (International and Other Provisions) Act 2010 (c. 8)
Part 2 – Double taxation relief
Chapter 2 – Double taxation relief by way of credit

100   First limitation for purposes of section 99(2)

(1)   The first limitation for the purposes of section 99(2) is to treat the amount of the relevant income as reduced (but not below nil) for the purposes of this Chapter by the amount of expenses (if any) attributable to the relevant income.

(2)   For the purposes of subsection (1), the amount of expenses attributable to the relevant income is the appropriate fraction of the total relevant expenses of the category of business concerned for the period of account in question.

(3)   In subsection (2) "the appropriate fraction" means the fraction given by —

$$\frac{RI}{TI}$$

where —
    RI is the amount of the relevant income before any reduction in accordance with section 99(2), and
    TI is the total income of the category of business concerned for the period of account in question, but if that would result in TI being nil, TI is instead the amount described in subsection (4).

(4)   That amount is so much in total of the income and gains —
    (a)   which arise to the company in the period of account in question, and
    (b)   in respect of which credit for foreign tax is to be allowed under any double taxation arrangements or under unilateral relief arrangements for any territory outside the United Kingdom,
as are referable to the category of business concerned (before any reduction in accordance with section 99(2)).

(5)   Subsection (4) is to be read with section 104 (determining how much of any income or gain is referable to a category of business).

(6)   In this section "the relevant income" has the meaning given by section 99(2).

101   Second limitation for purposes of section 99(2)

(1)   If —
    (a)   the amount of the relevant income after any reduction under section 100(1),
exceeds —
    (b)   the relevant fraction of the profits of the category of business concerned for the period of account in question which are chargeable to corporation tax,
the second limitation is to treat the relevant income as further reduced (but not below nil) for the purposes of this Chapter to an amount equal to that fraction of those profits.

(2)   In subsection (1) "the relevant fraction" means the fraction given by —

$$\frac{RI}{\text{The referable share of total relievable income and gains}}$$

where —
    "RI" is the amount of the relevant income before any reduction in accordance with section 99(2), and
    "the referable share of total relievable income and gains" is so much in total of the income and gains —

Taxation (International and Other Provisions) Act 2010 (c. 8) 951
Part 2 — Double taxation relief
Chapter 2 — Double taxation relief by way of credit

    (a)   which arise to the company in the period of account in question, and

    (b)   in respect of which credit for foreign tax is to be allowed under any double taxation arrangements or under unilateral relief arrangements for any territory outside the United Kingdom,

as are referable to the category of business concerned (before any reduction in accordance with section 99(2)).

(3)   In subsection (1), any reference to the profits of a category of business is a reference to those profits after the set off of any losses of that category of business which have arisen in any previous accounting period.

(4)   Subsection (2) is to be read with section 104 (determining how much of any income or gain is referable to a category of business).

(5)   In this section "the relevant income" has the meaning given by section 99(2).

102   Interpreting sections 99 to 101 for life assurance or gross roll-up business

(1)   This section has effect for the interpretation of sections 99 to 101 if the category of business concerned —

    (a)   is life assurance business, or

    (b)   is gross roll-up business.

(2)   The "total income" of the category of business concerned for the period of account in question is the amount (if any) by which —

    (a)   so much of the total income shown in the revenue account in the periodical return of the company concerned for that period as is referable to that category of business,

exceeds —

    (b)   so much of any commissions payable and any expenses of management incurred in connection with the acquisition of the business, as shown in that return, as is referable to that category of business.

(3)   If any amounts are to be brought into account in accordance with section 83 of FA 1989, the amounts that are referable to the category of business concerned are to be determined for the purposes of subsection (2) in accordance with sections 432B to 432G of ICTA.

(4)   The "total relevant expenses" of the category of business concerned for any period of account is the amount of the claims incurred —

    (a)   increased by any increase in the liabilities of the company, or

    (b)   reduced (but not below nil) by any decrease in the liabilities of the company.

(5)   For the purposes of subsection (4), the amounts to be taken into account in the case of any period of account are the amounts as shown in the company's periodical return for the period so far as referable to the category of business concerned.

103   Interpreting sections 99 to 101 for other insurance business

(1)   This section has effect for the interpretation of sections 99 to 101 if the category of business concerned —

    (a)   is not life assurance business, and

952   *Taxation (International and Other Provisions) Act 2010 (c. 8)*
Part 2 – Double taxation relief
Chapter 2 – Double taxation relief by way of credit

        (b)   is not gross roll-up business.

(2)   The "total income" of the category of business concerned for any period of account is the amount (if any) by which —

        (a)   the sum of the amounts specified in subsection (3),

    exceeds —

        (b)   the sum of the amounts specified in subsection (4).

(3)   The amounts mentioned in subsection (2)(a) are —

        (a)   earned premiums, net of reinsurance,

        (b)   investment income and gains, and

        (c)   other technical income, net of reinsurance.

(4)   The amounts mentioned in subsection (2)(b) are —

        (a)   acquisition costs,

        (b)   the change in deferred acquisition costs, and

        (c)   losses on investments.

(5)   The "total relevant expenses" of the category of business concerned for any period of account is the sum of —

        (a)   the claims incurred, net of reinsurance,

        (b)   the changes in other technical provisions, net of reinsurance,

        (c)   the change in the equalisation provision, and

        (d)   investment management expenses,

    unless that sum is a negative amount, in which case the total relevant expenses is to be taken to be nil.

(6)   The amounts to be taken into account for the purposes of the paragraphs of subsections (3) to (5) are the amounts taken into account for the purposes of corporation tax.

(7)   Expressions used —

        (a)   in the paragraphs of subsections (3) to (5), and

        (b)   in the provisions of section B of Part 1 of Schedule 3 to the Large and Medium-sized Companies and Groups (Accounts and Reports) Regulations 2008 (S.I. 2008/410) which relate to the profit and loss account format (within the meaning of paragraph 1(1) and (2) of that Schedule),

    have the same meaning in those paragraphs as they have in those provisions.

104   Interpreting sections 100 and 101: amounts referable to category of business

(1)   This section applies for the purposes of the operation of sections 100 and 101 in relation to any income or gain in respect of which credit is to be allowed under any double taxation arrangements or under unilateral relief arrangements for a territory outside the United Kingdom.

(2)   The amount of the income or gain that is referable to a category of insurance business is the same fraction of the income or gain as the fraction found under subsection (3).

(3)   Apply sections 97 and 98 in relation to —

        (a)   that category of business,

        (b)   the income or gain, and

Taxation (International and Other Provisions) Act 2010 (c. 8)
Part 2 — Double taxation relief
Chapter 2 — Double taxation relief by way of credit

953

(c)   the double taxation arrangements, or unilateral relief arrangements, mentioned in subsection (1),

in order to find the fraction of the foreign tax that is attributable to that category of business.

CHAPTER 3

MISCELLANEOUS PROVISIONS

Application of Part for capital gains tax purposes

105   Meaning of "chargeable gain"

In this Part so far as it relates to capital gains tax "chargeable gain" has the same meaning as in TCGA 1992 (see, in particular, section 15(2) of that Act).

106   Chapters 1 and 2 apply to capital gains tax separately from other taxes

(1)   Subsection (2) applies if foreign gains tax may be brought into account under Chapters 1 and 2 so far as they apply for capital gains tax purposes.

(2)   The foreign gains tax is not to be taken into account under those Chapters so far as they apply otherwise than for capital gains tax purposes.

(3)   Subsection (2) applies whether or not relief in respect of the foreign gains tax is given under those Chapters so far as they apply for capital gains tax purposes.

(4)   Foreign non-gains tax is not be taken into account under those Chapters so far as they apply for capital gains tax purposes.

(5)   In this section—
   "foreign gains tax" means any tax which—
   (a)   is imposed by the law of a territory outside the United Kingdom, and
   (b)   is of a similar character to capital gains tax, and
   "foreign non-gains tax" means tax which—
   (a)   is imposed by the law of a territory outside the United Kingdom, and
   (b)   is not foreign gains tax.

When foreign tax disregarded in applying Part for corporation tax purposes

107   Disregard of foreign tax referable to derivative contract

(1)   In applying this Part for corporation tax purposes in relation to a company, disregard tax within subsection (2).

(2)   Tax is within this subsection in relation to a company so far as the tax—
   (a)   is tax under the law of a territory outside the United Kingdom, and
   (b)   is attributable, on a just and reasonable apportionment, to so much of a notional interest payment as, on such an apportionment, is attributable to a time when the company is not a party to the derivative contract concerned.

954   *Taxation (International and Other Provisions) Act 2010 (c. 8)*
Part 2 – Double taxation relief
Chapter 3 – Miscellaneous provisions

(3)   For the purposes of this section, a payment is a "notional interest payment" if —

    (a)   a derivative contract specifies —

        (i)   a notional principal amount,

        (ii)   a period, and

        (iii) a rate of interest,

    (b)   the amount of the payment is determined (wholly or mainly) by applying a rate to the specified notional principal amount for the specified period, and

    (c)   the value of the rate is the same at all times as that of the specified rate of interest.

108   Disregard of foreign tax attributable to interest under a loan relationship

(1)   In applying this Part for corporation tax purposes in relation to a company, disregard tax within subsection (2).

(2)   Tax is within this subsection in relation to a company so far as the tax —

    (a)   is tax under the law of a territory outside the United Kingdom, and

    (b)   is attributable, on a just and reasonable apportionment, to interest accruing under a loan relationship at a time when the company is not a party to the relationship.

(3)   Tax within subsection (2) is not to be disregarded under subsection (1) if the tax is also within section 109 or 110.

109   Repo cases in which no disregard under section 108

(1)   Tax attributable to interest accruing to a company under a loan relationship is within this section if —

    (a)   at the time when the interest accrues, the company has ceased to be a party to the relationship by reason of having made the initial sale under or in accordance with any debtor repo relating to the relationship, and

    (b)   that time is in the period for which the repo has effect.

(2)   In this section —

    "debtor repo" has the meaning given by the repo-definition section,

    "the initial sale", in relation to a debtor repo, means the sale mentioned in condition C in the repo-definition section, and

    "the repo-definition section" means section 548 of CTA 2009.

(3)   In this section, a reference to the period for which a debtor repo has effect is to the period from the making of the initial sale until the earlier of —

    (a)   the time when the subsequent purchase mentioned in condition D in the repo-definition section takes place, and

    (b)   the time when it becomes apparent that that subsequent purchase will not take place.

110   Stock-lending cases in which no disregard under section 108

(1)   Tax attributable to interest accruing to a company under a loan relationship is within this section if —

    (a)   at the time when the interest accrues, the company has ceased to be a party to the relationship by reason of having made the initial transfer

Taxation (International and Other Provisions) Act 2010 (c. 8)
Part 2 — Double taxation relief
Chapter 3 — Miscellaneous provisions

955

      under or in accordance with any stock lending arrangement relating to that relationship, and

    (b)   that time is in the period for which the arrangement has effect.

(2)   In this section—

      "the initial transfer", in relation to a stock lending arrangement, means the transfer mentioned in section 263B(1)(a) of TCGA 1992, and

      "stock lending arrangement" has the meaning given by section 263B of TCGA 1992.

(3)   In this section, a reference to the period for which a stock lending arrangement has effect is to the period from the making of the initial transfer until the earlier of—

    (a)   the time when the transfer mentioned in section 263B(1)(b) of TCGA 1992 takes place, and

    (b)   the time when it becomes apparent that that transfer will not take place.

Special rules for discretionary trusts

111   When payment to beneficiary treated as arising from foreign source

(1)   Subsection (6) applies if each of conditions A to D is met.

(2)   Condition A is that a payment is made by trustees of a settlement.

(3)   Condition B is that income tax is treated under section 494 of ITA 2007 (treatment of discretionary payments by trustees) as having been paid in relation to the payment.

(4)   Condition C is that the income arising under the settlement includes taxed overseas income.

(5)   Condition D is that the trustees certify—

    (a)   that the payment is one made out of income consisting of, or including, taxed overseas income of an amount, and from a source, stated in the certificate, and

    (b)   that that amount of taxed overseas income arose to the trustees not earlier than 6 years before the end of the tax year in which the payment is made.

(6)   The person to whom the payment is made may claim that the payment, up to the certified amount, is to be treated for the purposes of this Part as income received by the person—

    (a)   from the certified source, and

    (b)   in the tax year in which the payment is made.

(7)   In this section "taxed overseas income", in relation to a settlement, means income in respect of which the trustees are entitled to credit under this Part for tax under the law of a territory outside the United Kingdom.

956   *Taxation (International and Other Provisions) Act 2010 (c. 8)*
Part 2 – Double taxation relief
Chapter 3 – Miscellaneous provisions

Deduction for foreign tax where no credit allowed

112   Deduction from income for foreign tax (instead of credit against UK tax)

(1)   The amount of any income arising in any place outside the United Kingdom is reduced for the purposes of the Tax Acts—

    (a)   by any amount which has been paid in respect of non-UK tax on that income in the place where the income arose, or

    (b)   if subsection (2) applies, by the lesser amount mentioned in that subsection.

(2)   This subsection applies if credit would, were it allowable in respect of the income, be reduced under section 39 (reduction by reference to accrued income losses) to the lesser amount given by section 39(5).

(3)   If—

    (a)   income of any person ("P") is reduced under subsection (1) by an amount paid in respect of tax on that income in the place where the income arose, and

    (b)   a payment is made by a tax authority to P, or any person connected with P, by reference to that tax,

the amount of P's income is increased by the amount of the payment.

(4)   Subsection (1)—

    (a)   has effect subject to section 31(2)(a) (no deduction for foreign tax if credit allowed and UK tax calculated otherwise than by reference to the amount received in the United Kingdom),

    (b)   has effect subject to section 143(5) and (6) (no deduction for special withholding tax if UK tax calculated otherwise than by reference to the amount received in the United Kingdom),

    (c)   does not apply to income the tax on which is to be calculated by reference to the amount of income received in the United Kingdom, and

    (d)   does not require any income to be reduced by an amount of underlying tax which, under section 60(3), is to be left out of account for the purposes of section 57.

(5)   Subsection (1) has effect for corporation tax purposes despite—

    (a)   section 464(1) of CTA 2009 (matters to be brought into account in the case of loan relationships only under Part 5 of that Act), and

    (b)   section 906(1) of that Act (matters to be brought into account in respect of intangible fixed assets only under Part 8 of that Act).

(6)   In subsection (1) "non-UK tax" means tax under the law of a territory outside the United Kingdom.

(7)   For the purposes of subsection (3), whether a person is connected with P is determined in accordance with section 1122 of CTA 2010.

113   Deduction from capital gain for foreign tax (instead of credit against UK tax)

(1)   Subsection (2) applies to tax if it is—

    (a)   chargeable under the law of any territory outside the United Kingdom on the disposal of an asset, and

    (b)   borne by the person making the disposal.

Taxation (International and Other Provisions) Act 2010 (c. 8)
Part 2 — Double taxation relief
Chapter 3 — Miscellaneous provisions

957

(2) The tax is allowable as a deduction in the calculation of the gain.

(3) Subsection (2) is subject to—

    (a) Chapters 1 and 2 so far as they apply for corporation tax purposes (see, in particular, section 31),

    (b) Chapters 1 and 2 so far as they apply for capital gains tax purposes (see, in particular, section 31), and

    (c) section 143 (which includes provision about taking account of special withholding tax when calculating a gain for capital gains tax purposes).

(4) In subsection (1) "asset" and "disposal" have the same meaning as in TCGA 1992 (see, in particular, section 21 and the following provisions of TCGA 1992).

114 Time limits for action if tax adjustment makes reduction too large or too small

(1) Subsection (2) applies to a claim or assessment if—

    (a) the amount of any reduction under section 112(1) or 113(2) becomes excessive or insufficient by reason of any adjustment of the amount of any tax payable either in the United Kingdom or under the law of any territory outside the United Kingdom, or a person's income is increased under section 112(3),

    (b) the adjustment or increase gives rise to the claim or assessment, and

    (c) the claim or assessment is made not later than 6 years from the time when all material determinations have been made, whether in the United Kingdom or elsewhere.

(2) No time-limit rule applies to the assessment or claim.

(3) In subsection (1)(c) "material determination" means (as the case may be)—

    (a) an assessment, adjustment, increase or other determination that is material in determining whether any, and (if so) what, reduction is to be made under section 112(1) or increase is to be made under section 112(3), or

    (b) an assessment, adjustment or other determination that is material in determining whether any, and (if so) what, reduction is to be made under section 113(2).

(4) In subsection (2) "time-limit rule" means anything—

    (a) in TMA 1970,

    (b) in ICTA,

    (c) in TCGA 1992, or

    (d) in any other provision of the Tax Acts,

limiting the time for the making of assessments or limiting the time for the making of claims for relief.

115 Duty to give notice that adjustment has rendered reduction too large

(1) This section applies if—

    (a) the amount of any of a person's income is reduced under section 112(1),

    (b) that reduction ("the original reduction") later becomes excessive as a result of an adjustment of the amount of any tax payable under the law of a territory outside the United Kingdom or an increase under section 112(3), and

    (c) the adjustment or increase is not a Lloyd's adjustment.

958   *Taxation (International and Other Provisions) Act 2010 (c. 8)*
Part 2 – Double taxation relief
Chapter 3 – Miscellaneous provisions

(2)   This section also applies if —

    (a)   a deduction is allowed under section 113(2) in the case of a person making a disposal, and

    (b)   that deduction ("the original reduction") later becomes excessive as a result of an adjustment of the amount of any tax payable under the law of a territory outside the United Kingdom.

(3)   The person must give notice that the original reduction has become excessive as a result of the making of an adjustment or increase.

(4)   Notice under subsection (3) is to be given —

    (a)   to an officer of Revenue and Customs, and

    (b)   within one year from when the adjustment or increase was made.

(5)   If the person fails to comply with the requirements imposed by subsections (3) and (4), the person is liable to a penalty not greater than the amount given by —

$$A - B$$

where —

    A is the amount of tax payable by the person for the reduction period after giving effect to the reduction that ought to be made under section 112(1) or (as the case may be) under section 113(2), and

    B is the amount that would have been the tax payable by the person for that period after giving effect instead to the original reduction.

(6)   In subsection (5) "the reduction period" means the tax year, or accounting period of a company for corporation tax purposes, for which the original reduction was made.

(7)   For the purposes of subsection (1)(c), the adjustment or increase is a "Lloyd's adjustment" if the consequences of the adjustment or increase in relation to the reduction are to be given effect in accordance with regulations under —

    (a)   section 182(1) of FA 1993 (regulations about individual members of Lloyd's), or

    (b)   section 229 of FA 1994 (regulations relating to corporate members of Lloyd's).

(8)   In subsection (2) "disposal" has the same meaning as in TCGA 1992 (see, in particular, section 21(2) and the following provisions of TCGA 1992).

(9)   In this section so far as it relates to capital gains tax "notice" means notice in writing.

European cross-border transfers of business

116   Introduction to section 117

(1)   Subject to subsections (4) to (6), section 117 applies if condition A or B is met.

(2)   Condition A is that —

    (a)   a company resident in the United Kingdom transfers to a company resident in another member State the whole or part of a business which immediately before the transfer the transferor carried on in a member State other than the United Kingdom through a permanent establishment, and

    (b)   the transfer includes —

Taxation (International and Other Provisions) Act 2010 (c. 8)   959
Part 2 – Double taxation relief
Chapter 3 – Miscellaneous provisions

      (i)   the transfer of an asset or liability representing a loan relationship,

      (ii)   the transfer of rights and liabilities under a derivative contract, or

      (iii) the transfer of intangible fixed assets that are chargeable intangible assets in relation to the transferor immediately before the transfer and in the case of one or more of which the proceeds of realisation exceed the costs recognised for tax purposes.

(3)   Condition B is that—

    (a)   a company resident in the United Kingdom transfers part of its business to one or more companies,

    (b)   the part of the transferor's business which is transferred was carried on immediately before the transfer in a member State other than the United Kingdom through a permanent establishment,

    (c)   at least one transferee is resident in a member State other than the United Kingdom,

    (d)   the transferor continues to carry on a business after the transfer,

    (e)   the condition in subsection (2)(b) is met, and

    (f)   the transfer—

      (i)   is made in exchange for the issue of shares in or debentures of each transferee to each person holding shares in or debentures of the transferor, or

      (ii)   is not so made only because, and only so far as, a transferee is prevented from so issuing such shares or debentures by section 658 of the Companies Act 2006 (general rule against limited company acquiring own shares) or by a corresponding provision of the law of another member State preventing such an issue.

(4)   If a transfer that meets condition A or B includes such a transfer as is mentioned in subsection (2)(b)(i), section 117—

    (a)   only applies as respects the transfer so mentioned as a result of the transfer meeting condition A if the transfer is wholly or partly in exchange for shares or debentures issued by the transferee to the transferor, and

    (b)   only applies as respects the transfer so mentioned as a result of the transfer meeting condition B if each transferee is resident in a member State, but not necessarily the same one.

(5)   If a transfer that meets condition A or B includes such a transfer as is mentioned in subsection (2)(b)(ii), section 117—

    (a)   only applies as respects the transfer so mentioned as a result of the transfer meeting condition A if the transfer is wholly or partly in exchange for shares or debentures issued by the transferee to the transferor or to the persons holding shares in or debentures of the transferor,

    (b)   only applies as respects the transfer so mentioned as a result of the transfer meeting condition B if each transferee is resident in a member State, but not necessarily the same one, and

    (c)   only applies as respects the transfer so mentioned if the transferor makes a claim under this section in respect of it.

960   *Taxation (International and Other Provisions) Act 2010 (c. 8)*
Part 2 – Double taxation relief
Chapter 3 – Miscellaneous provisions

(6)   If a transfer that meets condition A or B includes such a transfer as is mentioned in subsection (2)(b)(iii), section 117 –

     (a)   only applies as respects the transfer so mentioned as a result of the transfer meeting condition A if –

         (i)   the companies mentioned in subsection (2)(a) are companies incorporated under the law of a member State, and

         (ii)   the transfer is wholly or partly in exchange for shares or other securities issued by the transferee to the transferor,

     (b)   only applies as respects the transfer so mentioned as a result of the transfer meeting condition B if –

         (i)   the transferor and at least one of the transferees mentioned in subsection (3)(a) is a company so incorporated, and

         (ii)   the transfer is in exchange for shares or debentures issued by the transferee to the persons holding shares in or debentures of the transferor, and

     (c)   only applies as respects the transfer so mentioned if –

         (i)   the transfer includes the whole of the assets of the transferor used for the purposes of the business or part, or the whole of those assets other than cash, and

         (ii)   the transferor makes a claim under this section in respect of the transfer so mentioned.

(7)   No claim may be made under subsection (6) in respect of a transfer in relation to which a claim is made under section 827 of CTA 2009 (claims to postpone charge on transfer of assets to non-UK resident company).

(8)   For the purposes of this section, a company is resident in a member State if –

     (a)   it is within a charge to tax under the law of the State as being resident for that purpose, and

     (b)   it is not regarded, for the purpose of any double taxation relief arrangements to which the State is a party, as resident in a territory not within a member State.

117   Tax treated as chargeable in respect of transfer of loan relationship, derivative contract or intangible fixed assets

(1)   If tax would have been chargeable under the law of one or more other member States in respect of the transfer mentioned in section 116(2)(b)(i), (ii) or (iii) but for the Mergers Directive, this Part applies, and any double taxation arrangements apply, as if that tax had been chargeable.

(2)   In calculating tax notionally chargeable under subsection (1), it is to be assumed –

     (a)   that, to the extent permitted by the law of the other member State, losses arising on the transfer mentioned in section 116(2)(b)(i), (ii) or (iii) are set against gains arising on that transfer, and

     (b)   that any relief due to the transferor under that law is claimed.

(3)   Subsection (1) does not apply if –

     (a)   the transfer of business mentioned in section 116(2)(a) or (3)(a) is not effected for genuine commercial reasons, or

     (b)   that transfer of business forms part of a scheme or arrangements of which the main purpose, or one of the main purposes, is avoiding liability to corporation tax, capital gains tax or income tax.

Taxation (International and Other Provisions) Act 2010 (c. 8)   **961**
Part 2 – Double taxation relief
Chapter 3 – Miscellaneous provisions

(4) But subsection (3) does not prevent subsection (1) from applying if before the transfer—

    (a) the appropriate applicant has applied to the Commissioners for Her Majesty's Revenue and Customs, and

    (b) the Commissioners have notified the appropriate applicant that they are satisfied subsection (3) will not have that effect.

(5) In subsection (4) "the appropriate applicant" means—

    (a) in a case where tax chargeable in respect of such a transfer as is mentioned in section 116(2)(b)(i) or (ii) is concerned, the companies mentioned in section 116(2)(a) or (3)(a), and

    (b) in a case where tax chargeable in respect of such a transfer as is mentioned in section 116(2)(b)(iii) is concerned, the transferor.

(6) Sections 427 and 428 of CTA 2009 (procedure and decisions on applications for clearance) have effect in relation to subsection (4) as in relation to section 426(2) of that Act, taking the references in section 428 to section 426(2)(b) as references to subsection (4)(b) of this section.

European cross-border mergers

118 Introduction to section 119

(1) Section 119 applies if each of conditions A to E is met and—

    (a) in the case of a merger within subsection (2)(a) or (b), condition F is met,

    (b) in the case of a merger within subsection (2)(c), conditions F and G are met, and

    (c) in the case of a merger within subsection (2)(d), condition G is met.

(2) Condition A is that—

    (a) an SE is formed by the merger of two or more companies in accordance with Articles 2(1) and 17(2)(a) or (b) of Council Regulation (EC) No. 2157/2001 on the Statute for a European company (Societas Europaea),

    (b) an SCE is formed by the merger of two or more co-operative societies, at least one of which is a society registered under the Industrial and Provident Societies Act 1965, in accordance with Articles 2(1) and 19 of Council Regulation (EC) No. 1435/2003 on the Statute for a European Co-operative Society (SCE),

    (c) a merger is effected by the transfer by one or more companies of all their assets and liabilities to a single existing company, or

    (d) a merger is effected by the transfer by two or more companies of all their assets and liabilities to a single new company (other than an SE or an SCE) in exchange for the issue by the transferee, to each person holding shares in or debentures of a transferor, of shares or debentures.

(3) Condition B is that each merging company is resident in a member State.

(4) Condition C is that the merging companies are not all resident in the same State.

(5) Condition D is that in the course of the merger a company resident in the United Kingdom ("company A") transfers to a company resident in another member State all assets and liabilities relating to a business which company A carried on in a member State other than the United Kingdom through a permanent establishment (but see subsection (9)).

962   *Taxation (International and Other Provisions) Act 2010 (c. 8)*
Part 2 — Double taxation relief
Chapter 3 — Miscellaneous provisions

(6) Condition E is that the transfer mentioned in subsection (5) includes—

    (a) the transfer of an asset or liability representing a loan relationship,

    (b) the transfer of rights and liabilities under a derivative contract, or

    (c) the transfer of intangible fixed assets—

        (i) that are chargeable intangible assets in relation to company A immediately before the transfer, and

        (ii) in the case of one or more of which the proceeds of realisation exceed the cost recognised for tax purposes.

(7) Condition F is that—

    (a) the transfer of assets and liabilities to the transferee in the course of the merger is made in exchange for the issue of shares or debentures by the transferee to each person holding shares in or debentures of a transferor, or

    (b) paragraph (a) is not met in relation to the transfer of those assets and liabilities only because, and only so far as, the transferee is prevented from so issuing such shares or debentures by section 658 of the Companies Act 2006 (general rule against limited company acquiring own shares) or by a corresponding provision of the law of another member State preventing such an issue.

(8) Condition G is that in the course of the merger each transferor ceases to exist without being in liquidation (within the meaning given by section 247 of the Insolvency Act 1986).

(9) In the case of a merger within subsection (2)(a) or (b), in determining whether section 119 applies in respect of such a transfer as is mentioned in subsection (6)(c), condition D is regarded as met even if all liabilities relating to the business which company A carried on are not transferred as mentioned in subsection (5).

(10) For the purposes of this section, a company is resident in a member State if—

    (a) it is within a charge to tax under the law of the State as being resident for that purpose, and

    (b) it is not regarded, for the purpose of any double taxation relief arrangements to which the State is a party, as resident in a territory not within a member State.

(11) In this section—

    "co-operative society" means a society registered under the Industrial and Provident Societies Act 1965 or a similar society governed by the law of a member State other than the United Kingdom,

    "SE" and "SCE" have the same meaning as in CTA 2009 (see section 1319 of that Act),

    "the transferee" means—

        (a) in relation to a merger within subsection (2)(a), the SE,

        (b) in relation to a merger within subsection (2)(b), the SCE, and

        (c) in relation to a merger within subsection (2)(c) or (d), the company to which assets and liabilities are transferred, and

    "transferor" means—

        (a) in relation to a merger within subsection (2)(a), a company merging to form the SE,

        (b) in relation to a merger within subsection (2)(b), a co-operative society merging to form the SCE, and

Taxation (International and Other Provisions) Act 2010 (c. 8)
Part 2 – Double taxation relief
Chapter 3 – Miscellaneous provisions

963

(c)   in relation to a merger within subsection (2)(c) or (d), a company transferring all of its assets and liabilities.

119   Tax treated as chargeable in respect of transfer of loan relationship, derivative contract or intangible fixed assets

(1)   If tax would have been chargeable under the law of one or more other member States in respect of the transfer mentioned in section 118(6)(a), (b) or (c) but for the Mergers Directive, this Part applies, and any double taxation arrangements apply, as if that tax had been chargeable.

(2)   In calculating tax notionally chargeable under subsection (1) in respect of the transfer mentioned in section 118(6)(a) or (b), it is to be assumed—

(a)   that, to the extent permitted by the law of the other member State, losses arising on that transfer are set against gains arising on that transfer, and

(b)   that any relief due to company A under that law is claimed.

(3)   Subsection (1) does not apply if—

(a)   the merger is not effected for genuine commercial reasons, or

(b)   the merger forms part of a scheme or arrangements of which the main purpose, or one of the main purposes, is avoiding liability to corporation tax, capital gains tax or income tax.

(4)   But subsection (3) does not prevent subsection (1) from applying if before the merger—

(a)   any of the merging companies has applied to the Commissioners for Her Majesty's Revenue and Customs, and

(b)   the Commissioners have notified the merging companies that they are satisfied subsection (3) will not have that effect.

(5)   Sections 427 and 428 of CTA 2009 (procedure and decisions on applications for clearance) have effect in relation to subsection (4) as in relation to section 426(2) of that Act, taking the references in section 428 to section 426(2)(b) as references to subsection (4)(b) of this section.

(6)   In this section "company A", "the merger" and "the merging companies" have the same meaning as in section 118.

Transparent entities involved in cross-border transfers and mergers

120   Introduction to section 121

(1)   Section 121 applies if, as a result of—

(a)   a relevant loan relationship transaction,

(b)   a relevant derivative contracts transaction, or

(c)   a relevant intangible fixed assets transaction,

tax would have been chargeable under the law of a member State other than the United Kingdom in respect of a relevant profit but for the Mergers Directive.

(2)   In this section "relevant loan relationship transaction" means—

(a)   a transfer of a kind which meets condition A or B in section 421 of CTA 2009 or would meet one of those conditions if—

964   *Taxation (International and Other Provisions) Act 2010 (c. 8)*
Part 2 – Double taxation relief
Chapter 3 – Miscellaneous provisions

          (i)   the business or part of the business transferred were carried on by the transferor in the United Kingdom, and

          (ii)   the condition in section 421(3)(c) or (4)(f) of that Act were met,

and in relation to which the transferor or transferee or one of the transferees is a transparent entity, or

    (b)   a merger of a kind mentioned in section 431(2) of that Act which meets —

          (i)   conditions B to D in section 431,

          (ii)   in the case of a merger within section 431(3)(a), (b) or (c), condition E in section 431, and

          (iii) in the case of a merger within section 431(3)(c) or (d), condition F in section 431,

and in relation to which one or more of the merging companies is a transparent entity.

(3)   In this section "relevant derivative contracts transaction" means —

    (a)   a transfer of a kind which meets condition A or B in section 674 of CTA 2009 or would meet one of those conditions if —

          (i)   the business or part of the business transferred were carried on by the transferor in the United Kingdom, and

          (ii)   the condition in section 674(2)(c) or (3)(f) of that Act were met,

and in relation to which the transferor is a transparent entity, or

    (b)   a merger of a kind mentioned in section 682(2) of that Act which meets —

          (i)   conditions B to D in section 682,

          (ii)   in the case of a merger within section 682(2)(a), (b) or (c), condition E in section 682, and

          (iii) in the case of a merger within section 682(2)(c) or (d), condition F in section 682,

and in relation to which one or more of the merging companies is a transparent entity.

(4)   In this section "relevant intangible fixed assets transaction" means —

    (a)   a transfer —

          (i)   which is of a kind which meets condition A or B in section 819 of CTA 2009, or would meet one of those conditions if the business or part of the business transferred were carried on by the transferor in the United Kingdom, and

          (ii)   in relation to which the transferor or transferee or one of the transferees is a transparent entity, or

    (b)   a merger —

          (i)   which is of a kind mentioned in section 821(2) of that Act,

          (ii)   which meets conditions B and C in section 821,

          (iii) which, if it is a merger within section 821(2)(a), (b) or (c), meets condition D in section 821,

          (iv) which, if it is a merger within section 821(2)(c) or (d), meets condition E in section 821,

          (v)   in the course of which no qualifying assets are transferred to which section 818 of that Act (company reconstruction involving transfer of business) applies, and

Taxation (International and Other Provisions) Act 2010 (c. 8)
Part 2 — Double taxation relief
Chapter 3 — Miscellaneous provisions

965

       (vi)   in relation to which one or more of the merging companies is a transparent entity.

(5)   In this section "relevant profit" means—

    (a)   in the case of a transfer within subsection (2)(a), a profit accruing to a transparent entity in respect of a loan relationship (or which would be treated as accruing if it were not transparent) because of the transfer of assets or liabilities representing a loan relationship by the transparent entity to the transferee,

    (b)   in the case of a merger within subsection (2)(b), a profit accruing to a transparent entity in respect of a loan relationship (or which would be treated as accruing if it were not transparent) because of the transfer of assets or liabilities representing a loan relationship by the transparent entity to another company in the course of the merger,

    (c)   in the case of a transfer within subsection (3)(a), a profit accruing to a transparent entity in respect of a derivative contract (or which would be treated as accruing if it were not transparent) because of the transfer of rights and liabilities under the derivative contract by the transparent entity to the transferee,

    (d)   in the case of a merger within subsection (3)(b), a profit accruing to a transparent entity in respect of a derivative contract (or which would be treated as accruing if it were not transparent) because of the transfer of rights and liabilities under the derivative contract by the transparent entity to another company in the course of the merger,

    (e)   in the case of a transfer within subsection (4)(a), a profit which would be treated as accruing to a transparent entity in respect of an intangible fixed asset, because of the transfer of intangible fixed assets by the transparent entity, if it were not transparent, and

    (f)   in the case of a merger within subsection (4)(b), a profit which would be treated as accruing to a transparent entity in respect of an intangible fixed asset, because of the transfer of intangible fixed assets by the transparent entity in the course of the merger, if it were not transparent.

(6)   In this section "transparent entity" means a company which is resident in a member State other than the United Kingdom and does not have an ordinary share capital.

121   Tax treated as chargeable in respect of relevant transactions

(1)   This Part applies, and any double taxation arrangements apply, as if the tax that would have been chargeable as mentioned in section 120(1) had been chargeable.

(2)   In calculating tax notionally chargeable under subsection (1), it is to be assumed—

    (a)   that, to the extent permitted by the law of the other member State mentioned in section 120(1), losses arising on the relevant transfer are set against profits arising on it, and

    (b)   that any relief available under that law is claimed.

(3)   In this section "the relevant transfer" means—

    (a)   the transfer of assets or liabilities mentioned in section 120(5)(a) or (b),

    (b)   the transfer of rights and liabilities mentioned in section 120(5)(c) or (d), or

966   Taxation (International and Other Provisions) Act 2010 (c. 8)
                                                      Part 2 – Double taxation relief
                                                  Chapter 3 – Miscellaneous provisions

    (c)   the transfer of intangible fixed assets mentioned in section 120(5)(e) or (f).

Cross-border transfers and mergers: chargeable gains

122   Tax treated as chargeable in respect of gains on transfer of non-UK business

(1)   Subsection (3) applies if—

    (a)   section 140C or 140F of TCGA 1992 applies, and

    (b)   gains accruing to company A on the transfer would have been chargeable to tax under the law of the host State but for the Mergers Directive.

(2)   In this section—

    "company A"—

        (a)   means the transferor within the meaning given by subsection (1) or (1A) of section 140C of TCGA 1992 if that subsection applies, and

        (b)   has the meaning given by section 140F(2) of TCGA 1992 if it applies,

    "the host State" means the member State (other than the United Kingdom) mentioned, in whichever of the transfer subsections applies, as the location in which company A carries on a business or part of a business,

    "the transfer" means the transfer made by company A that is mentioned in whichever of the transfer subsections applies, and

    "the transfer subsections" means—

        (a)   section 140C(1) of TCGA 1992 (transfer, of non-UK business or part, by UK resident "company" to one resident in another member State),

        (b)   section 140C(1A) of TCGA 1992 (transfer, of part of non-UK business, by UK resident "company" to transferees including a "company" resident in another member State), and

        (c)   section 140F(2) of TCGA 1992 (transfer of assets and liabilities of non-UK business, by UK resident "company" or co-operative society to one resident in another member State, as part of genuine merger of two or more "companies" or societies).

(3)   This Part applies, and any double taxation arrangements apply, as if the tax mentioned in subsection (4) were tax payable under the law of the host State.

(4)   That tax is the tax, calculated on the required basis, which but for the Mergers Directive would have been payable under the law of the host State in respect of the gains.

(5)   For the purposes of subsection (4) "the required basis" is that—

    (a)   so far as permitted under the law of the host State, any losses arising on the transfer are set against any gains arising on the transfer, and

    (b)   any relief available to company A under the law of the host State has been duly claimed.

Taxation (International and Other Provisions) Act 2010 (c. 8)
Part 2 — Double taxation relief
Chapter 3 — Miscellaneous provisions

967

Interpretation of sections related to the Mergers Directive

123 Interpretation of sections 116 to 122

In sections 116 to 122 and this section—

"company" means any entity listed as a company in the Annex to the Mergers Directive,

"derivative contract" has the same meaning as in Part 7 of CTA 2009,

"intangible fixed assets" and "chargeable intangible assets", in relation to any person, have the same meaning as in Part 8 of CTA 2009,

"loan relationship" has the same meaning as in Part 5 of CTA 2009,

"the Mergers Directive" means Council Directive 90/434/EEC of 23 July 1990 on the common system of taxation applicable to mergers, divisions, partial divisions, transfers of assets and exchanges of shares concerning companies of different member States and to the transfer of the registered office, of an SE or SCE, between member States,

"proceeds of realisation", in relation to intangible fixed assets, has the meaning given in section 739 of CTA 2009, and

"recognised for tax purposes" has the same meaning as in Part 8 of CTA 2009.

Cases about being taxed otherwise than in accordance with double taxation arrangements

124 Giving effect to solutions to cases and mutual agreements resolving cases

(1) Subsections (2) and (4) apply if under, and for the purposes of, double taxation arrangements made in relation to a territory outside the United Kingdom—

　(a) a person presents, to the Commissioners for Her Majesty's Revenue and Customs or to an authority in the territory, a case concerning the person's being taxed (whether in the United Kingdom or the territory) otherwise than in accordance with the arrangements, and

　(b) the Commissioners arrive at a solution to the case or make a mutual agreement with an authority in the territory for the resolution of the case.

(2) The Commissioners are to give effect to the solution or mutual agreement despite anything in any enactment, and any such adjustment as is appropriate in consequence may be made.

(3) An adjustment under subsection (2) may be made by way of discharge or repayment of tax, the allowance of credit against tax payable in the United Kingdom, the making of an assessment or otherwise.

(4) A claim for relief under any provision of—

　(a) the Tax Acts,

　(b) the enactments relating to capital gains tax, or

　(c) the enactments relating to petroleum revenue tax,

may be made in pursuance of the solution or mutual agreement at any time before the end of the period of 12 months following the notification of the solution or mutual agreement to the person affected, even if that involves making the claim after a deadline imposed by another enactment.

968   *Taxation (International and Other Provisions) Act 2010 (c. 8)*
Part 2 – Double taxation relief
Chapter 3 – Miscellaneous provisions

125   Effect of, and deadline for, presenting a case

(1)   This section applies if double taxation arrangements include provision for a person to present a case —

    (a)   to the Commissioners for Her Majesty's Revenue and Customs, or

    (b)   to an officer of Revenue and Customs,

concerning the person's being taxed otherwise than in accordance with the arrangements.

(2)   The presentation of any such case under and in accordance with the arrangements —

    (a)   does not constitute a claim for relief under the Tax Acts, the enactments relating to capital gains tax or the enactments relating to petroleum revenue tax, and

    (b)   is accordingly not subject to section 42 of TMA 1970 or any other enactment relating to the making of such claims.

(3)   Any such case must be presented before the end of —

    (a)   the period of 6 years following the end of the chargeable period to which the case relates, or

    (b)   such longer period as may be specified in the arrangements.

The Arbitration Convention

126   Meaning of "the Arbitration Convention"

In sections 127 and 128 "the Arbitration Convention" means the Convention, on the elimination of double taxation in connection with the adjustment of profits of associated enterprises, concluded on 23 July 1990 by the parties to the treaty establishing the European Economic Community (90/436/EEC).

127   Giving effect to agreements, decisions and opinions under the Convention

(1)   In this section "Convention determination" means —

    (a)   an agreement or decision, made under the Arbitration Convention by the Commissioners for Her Majesty's Revenue and Customs (or their authorised representative) and any other competent authority, on the elimination of double taxation, or

    (b)   an opinion, delivered by an advisory commission set up under the Arbitration Convention, on the elimination of double taxation.

(2)   Subsection (3) applies if the Arbitration Convention requires the Commissioners to give effect to a Convention determination.

(3)   The Commissioners are to give effect to the Convention determination despite anything in any enactment, and any such adjustment as is appropriate in consequence may be made.

(4)   An adjustment under subsection (3) may be made by way of discharge or repayment of tax, the allowance of credit against tax payable in the United Kingdom, the making of an assessment or otherwise.

(5)   An enactment which imposes deadlines for the making of claims for relief under any provision of the Tax Acts does not apply to a claim made in pursuance of a Convention determination.

Taxation (International and Other Provisions) Act 2010 (c. 8)
Part 2 — Double taxation relief
Chapter 3 — Miscellaneous provisions

969

128 Disclosure under the Convention

(1) The obligation as to secrecy imposed by any enactment does not prevent—
    (a) the Commissioners for Her Majesty's Revenue and Customs, or
    (b) any authorised Revenue and Customs official,
    from disclosing information required to be disclosed under the Arbitration Convention in pursuance of a request made by an advisory commission set up under the Convention.

(2) In this section "Revenue and Customs official" means any person who is or was—
    (a) a Commissioner for Her Majesty's Revenue and Customs,
    (b) an officer of Revenue and Customs,
    (c) a person acting on behalf of the Commissioners for Her Majesty's Revenue and Customs,
    (d) a person acting on behalf of an officer of Revenue and Customs, or
    (e) a member of a committee established by the Commissioners for Her Majesty's Revenue and Customs.

Disclosure of information

129 Disclosure where relief given overseas for tax paid in the United Kingdom

(1) Subsection (2) applies if the law of a territory outside the United Kingdom makes provision allowing, in respect of the payment of—
    (a) income tax,
    (b) corporation tax,
    (c) capital gains tax, or
    (d) petroleum revenue tax,
    relief from tax payable under that law.

(2) The obligation as to secrecy imposed upon Revenue and Customs officials by—
    (a) the Tax Acts,
    (b) the enactments relating to capital gains tax, and
    (c) the enactments relating to petroleum revenue tax,
    does not prevent disclosure, to the authorised officer of the authorities of the territory, of such facts as may be necessary to enable the proper relief to be given under the law of the territory.

(3) The reference in subsection (1) to tax payable under the law of the territory includes only—
    (a) taxes which are charged on income and which correspond to income tax,
    (b) taxes which are charged on income or chargeable gains and which correspond to corporation tax,
    (c) taxes which are charged on capital gains and which correspond to capital gains tax, and
    (d) taxes which—
        (i) are charged on amounts corresponding to amounts on which petroleum revenue tax is charged, and
        (ii) correspond to petroleum revenue tax.

970

Taxation (International and Other Provisions) Act 2010 (c. 8)
Part 2 – Double taxation relief
Chapter 3 – Miscellaneous provisions

(4) For the purposes of subsection (3), tax may correspond to income tax, corporation tax, capital gains tax or petroleum revenue tax even though it—

    (a) is payable under the law of a province, state or other part of a country, or

    (b) is levied by or on behalf of a municipality or other local body.

(5) In this section "Revenue and Customs official" means any person who is or was—

    (a) a Commissioner for Her Majesty's Revenue and Customs,

    (b) an officer of Revenue and Customs,

    (c) a person acting on behalf of the Commissioners for Her Majesty's Revenue and Customs,

    (d) a person acting on behalf of an officer of Revenue and Customs, or

    (e) a member of a committee established by the Commissioners for Her Majesty's Revenue and Customs.

Interpretation of double taxation arrangements

130 Interpreting provision about UK taxation of profits of foreign enterprises

(1) Subsection (4) applies if double taxation arrangements make the provision, however expressed, mentioned in subsection (2).

(2) The provision is that the profits of an enterprise within subsection (3) are not to be subject to United Kingdom tax except so far as they are attributable to a permanent establishment of the enterprise in the United Kingdom.

(3) An enterprise is within this subsection if the enterprise—

    (a) is resident outside the United Kingdom, or

    (b) carries on a trade, or profession or business, the control or management of which is situated outside the United Kingdom.

(4) The provision does not prevent income of a person resident in the United Kingdom being chargeable to income tax or corporation tax.

(5) Subsection (4)—

    (a) does not apply in relation to income of a person resident in the United Kingdom if section 858 of ITTOIA 2005 (UK resident partner is taxable on share of firm's income despite any double taxation arrangements) applies to the income, and

    (b) does not apply in relation to income of a company resident in the United Kingdom if section 1266(2) of CTA 2009 (UK resident company that is partner in a firm is taxable on share of firm's income despite any double taxation arrangements) applies to the income.

(6) A person is resident in the United Kingdom for the purposes of this section if the person is resident in the United Kingdom for the purposes of the double taxation arrangements.

131 Interpreting provision about interest influenced by special relationship

(1) Subsections (3) and (6) apply if double taxation arrangements—

    (a) make provision, whether for relief or otherwise, in relation to interest (as defined in the arrangements), and

Taxation (International and Other Provisions) Act 2010 (c. 8)
Part 2 — Double taxation relief
Chapter 3 — Miscellaneous provisions

971

    (b)   contain a special relationship rule.

(2)   A "special relationship rule" is provision that —

    (a)   applies if the amount of the interest paid is, because of a special relationship, greater than the amount ("the ordinary amount") that would have been paid in the absence of the relationship, and

    (b)   has the effect that the provision mentioned in subsection (1)(a) is to apply only to the ordinary amount.

(3)   The special relationship rule is to be read as requiring account to be taken of all factors, including —

    (a)   the question whether the loan would have been made at all in the absence of the special relationship,

    (b)   the amount which the loan would have been in the absence of the special relationship, and

    (c)   the rate of interest, and the other terms, which would have been agreed in the absence of the special relationship.

(4)   Subsection (3) does not apply if the special relationship rule expressly requires regard to be had to the debt on which interest is paid in determining the excess interest (and accordingly expressly limits the factors to be taken into account).

(5)   If —

    (a)   a company ("L") makes a loan to another company with which it has a special relationship, and

    (b)   it is not part of L's business to make loans generally,

the fact that it is not part of L's business to make loans generally is to be disregarded in applying subsection (3).

(6)   The special relationship rule is to be read as requiring the taxpayer —

    (a)   to show that there is no special relationship, or

    (b)   if there is a special relationship, to show the amount of interest that would have been paid in the absence of the relationship.

132   Interpreting provision about royalties influenced by special relationship

(1)   Subsection (3) and section 133 apply if double taxation arrangements —

    (a)   make provision, whether for relief or otherwise, in relation to royalties (as defined in the arrangements), and

    (b)   contain a special relationship rule.

(2)   A "special relationship rule" is provision that —

    (a)   applies if the amount of the royalties paid is, because of a special relationship, greater than the amount ("the ordinary amount") that would have been paid in the absence of the relationship, and

    (b)   has the effect that the provision mentioned in subsection (1)(a) is to apply only to the ordinary amount.

(3)   The special relationship rule is to be read as requiring account to be taken of all factors, including —

    (a)   the question whether the agreement under which the royalties are paid would have been made at all in the absence of the special relationship,

    (b)   the rate or amounts of royalties, and the other terms, which would have been agreed in the absence of the special relationship, and

972

Taxation (International and Other Provisions) Act 2010 (c. 8)
Part 2 – Double taxation relief
Chapter 3 – Miscellaneous provisions

    (c)   if subsection (4) applies, the factors specified in subsection (5).

(4)   This subsection applies if the asset in respect of which the royalties are paid, or any asset which that asset represents or from which it is derived, has previously been in the beneficial ownership of—

    (a)   the person ("PR") who is liable to pay the royalties,

    (b)   a person who is, or has at any time been, an associate of PR,

    (c)   a person who has at any time carried on a business which, at the time when the liability to pay the royalties arises, is being carried on in whole or in part by PR, or

    (d)   a person who is, or has at any time been, an associate of a person within paragraph (c).

(5)   The factors mentioned in subsection (3)(c) are—

    (a)   the amounts which were paid under the transaction, or under each of the transactions in a series of transactions, as a result of which the asset has come to be an asset of the beneficial owner for the time being,

    (b)   the amounts which would have been paid under that transaction, or under each of those transactions, in the absence of a special relationship, and

    (c)   the question whether the transaction, or series of transactions, would have taken place in the absence of a special relationship.

(6)   Subsection (3) does not apply if the special relationship rule expressly requires regard to be had to the use, right or information for which royalties are paid in determining the excess royalties (and accordingly expressly limits the factors to be taken into account).

(7)   For the purposes of this section, a person ("A") is an associate of another person ("B") at a given time if—

    (a)   A was directly or indirectly participating in the management, control or capital of B at that time, or

    (b)   the same person was, or the same persons were, directly or indirectly participating in the management, control or capital of A and B at that time.

(8)   For the interpretation of subsection (7), see sections 157(1), 158(4), 159(1) and 160(1) (which have the effect that references in subsection (7) to direct or indirect participation are to be read in accordance with provisions of Chapter 2 of Part 4).

133   Special relationship rule for royalties: matters to be shown by taxpayer

(1)   If this section applies (as to which, see section 132(1)), the special relationship rule is to be read as requiring the taxpayer to show—

    (a)   the absence of any special relationship, or

    (b)   as the case may be, the rate or amounts of royalties that would have been payable in the absence of the special relationship.

(2)   The requirement under subsection (1)(a) includes whichever is applicable of the following requirements.

(3)   The first of those requirements is—

Taxation (International and Other Provisions) Act 2010 (c. 8)
Part 2 – Double taxation relief
Chapter 3 – Miscellaneous provisions

973

      (a) to show that no person of any of the descriptions in section 132(4)(a) to (d) has previously been the beneficial owner of the asset in respect of which the royalties are paid, and

      (b) to show that no person of any of those descriptions has previously been the beneficial owner of any asset which that asset represents or from which it is derived.

(4) The second of those requirements is –

      (a) to show that the transaction, or series of transactions, mentioned in section 132(5)(a) would have taken place in the absence of a special relationship, and

      (b) to show the amounts which would have been paid under the transaction, or under each of the transactions in the series of transactions, in the absence of a special relationship.

Assessments

134 Correcting assessments where relief is available

(1) Subsections (5) and (6) apply if –

      (a) under double taxation arrangements, relief may be given in the United Kingdom, or in the territory in relation to which the arrangements are made, in respect of any income or any chargeable gain, and

      (b) condition A or B is met.

(2) Subsections (5) and (6) also apply if –

      (a) under unilateral relief arrangements for a territory outside the United Kingdom, relief may be given in respect of any income or any chargeable gain, and

      (b) condition A or B is met.

(3) Condition A is that it appears that the assessment –

      (a) to income tax or corporation tax made in respect of the income, or

      (b) to corporation tax or capital gains tax made in respect of the gain,

is not made in respect of the full amount of the income or gain.

(4) Condition B is that it appears that the assessment –

      (a) to income tax or corporation tax made in respect of the income, or

      (b) to corporation tax or capital gains tax made in respect of the gain,

is incorrect having regard to the credit, if any, to be given under the arrangements.

(5) Assessments may be made that are necessary to ensure –

      (a) that the full amount of the income or gain is assessed, and

      (b) that the proper credit, if any, is given.

(6) If the income is entrusted to any person in the United Kingdom for payment, an assessment under subsection (5) may be made on the recipient of the income.

(7) An officer of Revenue and Customs may make amendments –

      (a) of assessments or determinations, or

      (b) of decisions on claims,

974   *Taxation (International and Other Provisions) Act 2010 (c. 8)*
Part 2 – Double taxation relief
Chapter 3 – Miscellaneous provisions

that are necessary in consequence of Chapter 1 so far as it applies for petroleum revenue tax purposes.

PART 3

DOUBLE TAXATION RELIEF FOR SPECIAL WITHHOLDING TAX

Introductory

135   Relief under this Part: introductory

(1)   This Part (except sections 144 and 145) applies for the purpose of giving relief from double taxation in respect of special withholding tax.

(2)   Relief under this Part—
- (a)   is given by set-off against income tax or capital gains tax, and
- (b)   so far as it cannot be given by set-off against income tax or capital gains tax, is given by repayment.

136   Interpretation of Part

(1)   Subsections (2) to (7) have effect for the purposes of this Part.

(2)   "Double taxation arrangements" means arrangements that have effect under section 2(1) (double taxation relief by agreement with territories outside the United Kingdom).

(3)   "International arrangements", in relation to a territory, means arrangements made in relation to that territory with a view to ensuring the effective taxation of savings income—
- (a)   under the law of the United Kingdom, or
- (b)   under that law and the law of the territory.

(4)   "The Savings Directive" means Council Directive 2003/48/EC of 3 June 2003 on taxation of savings income in the form of interest payments.

(5)   "Savings income"—
- (a)   in the case of special withholding tax levied under the law of a member State, has the same meaning as the expression "interest payment" has for the purposes of the Savings Directive (see Articles 6 and 15 of the Directive), and
- (b)   in the case of special withholding tax levied under the law of a territory other than a member State, has the same meaning as the corresponding expression has for the purposes of the international arrangements concerned.

(6)   "Special withholding tax" means a withholding tax (however described) levied under the law of a territory outside the United Kingdom implementing—
- (a)   in the case of a member State, Article 11 of the Savings Directive (withholding tax to be levied in Belgium, Luxembourg and Austria for the period described in the Directive), or
- (b)   in the case of a territory other than a member State, any corresponding provision of international arrangements (whatever the period for which the provision is to have effect).

(7) In the application of this Part in relation to capital gains tax, expressions used in this Part and in TCGA 1992 have the same meaning in this Part as in TCGA 1992.

Credit etc for special withholding tax

137 Income tax credit etc for special withholding tax

(1) Subsection (5) applies if each of conditions A to C is met.

(2) Condition A is that a person—
   (a) is liable to income tax for a tax year in respect of a payment of savings income, or
   (b) would be liable to income tax for a tax year in respect of a payment of savings income but for any exemption or relief.

(3) Condition B is that special withholding tax is levied in respect of the payment.

(4) Condition C is that the person is UK resident for the tax year.

(5) On the making of a claim, income tax ("the deemed tax") is to be treated as having been—
   (a) paid by or on behalf of the person for the tax year, and
   (b) deducted at source for the tax year for the purposes of the provisions listed in subsection (7).

(6) The amount of the deemed tax is given by section 138.

(7) The provisions mentioned in subsection (5)(b) are—
   section 7 of TMA 1970 (notice of liability to income tax and capital gains tax),
   section 8 of TMA 1970 (personal return),
   section 8A of TMA 1970 (trustee's return),
   section 9 of TMA 1970 (returns to include self-assessment),
   section 59A of TMA 1970 (payments on account of income tax),
   section 59B of TMA 1970 (payments of income tax and capital gains tax), and
   section 824(3) of ICTA (repayment supplements: determination of relevant time).

138 Amount and application of the deemed tax under section 137

(1) For the purposes of section 137, the amount of the deemed tax is—
   (a) the amount of the special withholding tax levied (see section 137(3)), less
   (b) any amounts of that tax that are within subsection (2).

(2) An amount of special withholding tax levied is within this subsection if—
   (a) the person has obtained relief from double taxation in respect of that special withholding tax under the law of a territory outside the United Kingdom, and
   (b) the person was resident in that territory, or was under any double taxation arrangements treated as being resident in that territory, in the tax year mentioned in section 137(2).

(3)   Subsection (4) applies if the amount of the deemed tax exceeds the amount (which may be nil) of income tax for which the person is liable for that tax year (before any set-off for the deemed tax).

(4)   So far as it would not otherwise be the case –

    (a)   the excess is to be set against any capital gains tax for which the person is liable for that tax year, and

    (b)   the person is entitled to a repayment of income tax in respect of any remaining balance of the excess.

139   Capital gains tax credit etc for special withholding tax

(1)   Subsection (6) applies if each of conditions A to D is met.

(2)   Condition A is that a person makes a disposal of assets in a tax year.

(3)   Condition B is that if a chargeable gain were to accrue on the disposal –

    (a)   the gain would accrue to the person, and

    (b)   the person would be chargeable to capital gains tax in respect of the gain.

(4)   Condition C is that –

    (a)   the consideration for the disposal consists of, or includes, an amount of savings income, and

    (b)   special withholding tax is levied in respect of the whole, or any part, of the consideration.

(5)   Condition D is that the person is resident in the United Kingdom for the tax year.

(6)   On the making of a claim, capital gains tax ("the deemed tax") is to be –

    (a)   treated as having been paid by or on behalf of the person for the tax year, and

    (b)   treated for the purposes of section 283(2) of TCGA 1992 (repayment supplements: determination of relevant time) as having been paid on the 31 January following the tax year.

(7)   The amount of the deemed tax is given by section 140.

(8)   For the purposes of subsection (3)(b), disregard –

    (a)   any deductions that are to be made from the total amount referred to in section 2(2) of TCGA 1992 (deductions for allowable losses), and

    (b)   section 3 of TCGA 1992 (annual exempt amount).

140   Provisions about the deemed tax under section 139

(1)   For the purposes of section 139, the amount of the deemed tax is –

    (a)   the amount of the special withholding tax levied (see section 139(4)(b)), less

    (b)   any amounts of that tax that are within subsection (2) or (3).

(2)   An amount of special withholding tax levied is within this subsection if –

    (a)   the person has obtained relief from double taxation in respect of that special withholding tax under the law of a territory outside the United Kingdom, and

Taxation (International and Other Provisions) Act 2010 (c. 8)
Part 3 — Double taxation relief for special withholding tax

977

      (b)   the person was resident in that territory, or was under any double taxation arrangements treated as being resident in that territory, in the tax year mentioned in section 139(2).

(3)   An amount of special withholding tax levied is within this subsection if by reference to that amount of that tax —

      (a)   there is that amount of deemed tax under section 137(5), or

      (b)   there would be that amount of deemed tax under section 137(5) on the making of a claim.

(4)   Subsection (5) applies if the amount of the deemed tax exceeds the amount (which may be nil) of capital gains tax for which the person is liable for that tax year (before any set-off for the deemed tax).

(5)   So far as it would not otherwise be the case —

      (a)   the excess is to be set against any income tax for which the person is liable for that tax year, and

      (b)   the person is entitled to a repayment of capital gains tax in respect of any remaining balance of the excess.

(6)   For the purposes of the provisions listed in subsection (7) in relation to the person for that tax year, references in those provisions to income tax deducted at source for that tax year include the deemed tax.

(7)   Those provisions are —

        section 7 of TMA 1970 (notice of liability to income tax and capital gains tax),

        section 8 of TMA 1970 (personal return),

        section 8A of TMA 1970 (trustee's return),

        section 9 of TMA 1970 (returns to include self-assessment), and

        section 59B of TMA 1970 (payments of income tax and capital gains tax).

141   Credit under Chapter 2 of Part 2 to be allowed first

(1)   Any credit for foreign tax allowed under Chapter 2 of Part 2 against income tax or capital gains tax is to be allowed before effect is given to sections 137 to 140.

(2)   In this section "foreign tax" has the same meaning as in that Chapter (see section 21).

Calculation of income or gain on remittance basis where special withholding tax levied

142   Conditions for purposes of section 143

(1)   This section applies for the purposes of section 143.

(2)   Condition A is that —

      (a)   a person is liable to income tax in respect of a payment of savings income, or

      (b)   a chargeable gain accrues to a person on a disposal by the person of assets in circumstances where the consideration for the disposal consists of, or includes, an amount of savings income.

(3)   Condition B is that special withholding tax is levied in respect of —

      (a)   the payment of savings income, or

       (b)   the whole or any part of the consideration for the disposal.

(4)   Condition C is that a claim under this Part has been made in respect of the special withholding tax.

(5)   Condition D is that no credit for foreign tax in respect of the savings income or chargeable gain concerned is allowed under Chapter 2 of Part 2 (so that sections 31(2) and 32(2), which make provision similar to section 143, do not apply).

143   Taking account of special withholding tax in calculating income or gains

(1)   Subsection (2) applies if —
      (a)   each of conditions A to D of section 142 is met, and
      (b)   income tax is payable by reference to the amount of the savings income received in the United Kingdom.

(2)   For income tax purposes, the amount received is increased by the amount of special withholding tax —
      (a)   levied in respect of it, and
      (b)   in respect of which a claim under this Part has been made.

(3)   Subsection (4) applies if —
      (a)   each of conditions A to D of section 142 is met, and
      (b)   capital gains tax is payable by reference to the amount of the chargeable gain received in the United Kingdom.

(4)   For capital gains tax purposes, the amount received is increased by the amount given by —

$$SWT \times \frac{GUK}{G - SWT}$$

where —
       SWT is the amount of special withholding tax —
         (a)   levied in respect of the whole or the part of the consideration for the disposal, and
         (b)   in respect of which a claim has been made under this Part,
       GUK is the amount of the chargeable gain received in the United Kingdom, and
       G is the amount of the chargeable gain accruing to the person on the disposal.

(5)   Subsection (6) applies if —
      (a)   each of conditions A to D of section 142 is met, and
      (b)   neither subsection (2) nor subsection (4) applies.

(6)   In calculating —
      (a)   the amount of the income for income tax purposes, or
      (b)   the amount of any chargeable gain for capital gains tax purposes,
no deduction is to be made for special withholding tax in respect of which a claim has been made under this Part (whether special withholding tax in respect of the same, or any other, income or in respect of the same, or any other, chargeable gains).

Taxation (International and Other Provisions) Act 2010 (c. 8)
Part 3 — Double taxation relief for special withholding tax

979

Certificates to avoid levy of special withholding tax

144 Issue of certificate

(1) This section enables officers of Revenue and Customs to issue certificates to be used under the law of a territory outside the United Kingdom implementing —

   (a) in the case of a member State, Article 13(1)(b) of the Savings Directive (procedure to avoid levy of special withholding tax where beneficial owner presents to the paying agent a certificate drawn up by a competent authority in the beneficial owner's member State of residence for tax purposes), or

   (b) in the case of a territory other than a member State, any corresponding provision of international arrangements (whatever the period for which the provision is to have effect).

(2) If, on the written application of a person, an officer is satisfied that the applicant has provided an officer with —

   (a) the required information, and

   (b) the documents (if any) required by an officer to verify that information,

an officer must issue a certificate to the applicant.

(3) In subsection (2) "the required information" means —

   (a) the applicant's name and address,

   (b) the applicant's National Insurance number or, if the applicant does not have one, the applicant's date, town and country of birth,

   (c) the number of the account which is to, or may, give rise to payments of savings income to or for the applicant or, if there is no such number, a statement identifying the debt, instrument or arrangement which is to, or may, give rise to payments of savings income,

   (d) the name and address of the paying agent who is to make the payments of savings income to, or to secure the payments of savings income for, the applicant, and

   (e) the period, not exceeding 3 years, for which the applicant would like the certificate to be valid.

(4) A certificate under this section must be in writing and must state —

   (a) the information mentioned in subsection (3)(a) to (d), and

   (b) the period of validity of the certificate (which must not exceed 3 years).

(5) A certificate under this section must be issued no later than the end of the period of 2 months beginning with the date on which the applicant provides the information and documents required by or under subsection (2).

(6) If the requirements of —

   (a) Article 13(2) of the Savings Directive (requirements in relation to issue of certificates for purposes of Article 13(1)(b) procedure), and

   (b) any corresponding provision of any international arrangements,

differ to any extent, subsections (3) to (5) have effect, in their application in relation to the international arrangements, with such modifications as may be required because of those arrangements.

145   Refusal to issue certificate and appeal against refusal

(1)   This section applies if, on an application for a certificate under section 144, an officer of Revenue and Customs ("the decision officer") is not satisfied that the applicant has provided an officer with the information and documents required by or under section 144(2).

(2)   An officer must give written notice ("the refusal notice") to the applicant of the decision officer's refusal to issue a certificate.

(3)   The refusal notice must specify the reasons for the refusal.

(4)   The applicant may by written notice ("the appeal notice") appeal against the refusal.

(5)   The appeal notice must be given to an officer within 30 days of the date of the refusal notice.

(6)   Part 5 of TMA 1970 (appeals and other proceedings) is to apply in relation to an appeal under this section.

(7)   On an appeal that is notified to the tribunal, the tribunal may—

     (a)   confirm the refusal notice, or

     (b)   quash it and require an officer to issue a certificate.

(8)   In this section "the tribunal" means the First-tier Tribunal or, where determined by or under Tribunal Procedure Rules, the Upper Tribunal.

PART 4

TRANSFER PRICING

CHAPTER 1

BASIC TRANSFER-PRICING RULE

146   Application of this Part

This Part applies for—

     (a)   corporation tax purposes, and

     (b)   income tax purposes.

147   Tax calculations to be based on arm's length, not actual, provision

(1)   For the purposes of this section "the basic pre-condition" is that—

     (a)   provision ("the actual provision") has been made or imposed as between any two persons ("the affected persons") by means of a transaction or series of transactions,

     (b)   the participation condition is met (see section 148),

     (c)   the actual provision is not within subsection (7) (oil transactions), and

     (d)   the actual provision differs from the provision ("the arm's length provision") which would have been made as between independent enterprises.

(2)   Subsection (3) applies if—

     (a)   the basic pre-condition is met, and

Taxation (International and Other Provisions) Act 2010 (c. 8)
Part 4 — Transfer pricing
Chapter 1 — Basic transfer-pricing rule

981

      (b)   the actual provision confers a potential advantage in relation to United Kingdom taxation on one of the affected persons.

(3)   The profits and losses of the potentially advantaged person are to be calculated for tax purposes as if the arm's length provision had been made or imposed instead of the actual provision.

(4)   Subsection (5) applies if—

      (a)   the basic pre-condition is met, and

      (b)   the actual provision confers a potential advantage in relation to United Kingdom taxation (whether or not the same advantage) on each of the affected persons.

(5)   The profits and losses of each of the affected persons are to be calculated for tax purposes as if the arm's length provision had been made or imposed instead of the actual provision.

(6)   Subsections (3) and (5) have effect subject to—

      (a)   section 165 (exemption for dormant companies),

      (b)   section 166 (exemption for small and medium-sized enterprises),

      (c)   section 213 (this Part generally does not affect calculation of capital allowances),

      (d)   section 214 (this Part generally does not affect calculation of chargeable gains),

      (e)   section 447(5) and (6) of CTA 2009 (this Part generally does not affect how exchange gains or losses from loan relationships are accounted for), and

      (f)   section 694(8) and (9) of CTA 2009 (this Part generally does not affect how exchange gains or losses from derivative contracts are accounted for).

(7)   The actual provision is within this subsection if it is made or imposed by means of any transaction or deemed transaction in the case of which the price or consideration is determined in accordance with any of sections 225F to 225J of ITTOIA 2005 or any of sections 281 to 285 of CTA 2010 (transactions and deemed transactions involving oil treated as made at market value).

148   The "participation condition"

(1)   For the purposes of section 147(1)(b), the participation condition is met if—

      (a)   condition A is met in relation to the actual provision so far as the actual provision is provision relating to financing arrangements, and

      (b)   condition B is met in relation to the actual provision so far as the actual provision is not provision relating to financing arrangements.

(2)   Condition A is that, at the time of the making or imposition of the actual provision or within the period of six months beginning with the day on which the actual provision was made or imposed—

      (a)   one of the affected persons was directly or indirectly participating in the management, control or capital of the other, or

      (b)   the same person or persons was or were directly or indirectly participating in the management, control or capital of each of the affected persons.

982   *Taxation (International and Other Provisions) Act 2010 (c. 8)*
Part 4 – Transfer pricing
Chapter 1 – Basic transfer-pricing rule

(3) Condition B is that, at the time of the making or imposition of the actual provision—

  (a) one of the affected persons was directly or indirectly participating in the management, control or capital of the other, or

  (b) the same person or persons was or were directly or indirectly participating in the management, control or capital of each of the affected persons.

(4) In this section "financing arrangements" means arrangements made for providing or guaranteeing, or otherwise in connection with, any debt, capital or other form of finance.

(5) For the interpretation of subsections (2) and (3) see sections 157 to 163.

CHAPTER 2

KEY INTERPRETATIVE PROVISIONS

Meaning of certain expressions that first appear in section 147

149 "Actual provision" and "affected persons"

(1) In this Part—

  "the actual provision", and

  "the affected persons",

have the meaning given by section 147(1).

(2) Subsection (1) does not apply if Chapters 1 and 3 to 6 apply in accordance with section 205(2) to (4) (oil-related ring-fence trades) but, in that event, in this Part—

  "the actual provision" means the provision mentioned in section 205(1)(b), and

  "the affected persons" means the two persons mentioned in section 205(2).

(3) Subsections (1) and (2) are subject to subsection (4).

(4) If the participation condition (see section 148) would not be met but for section 161 or 162 (cases in which actual provision relates, to any extent, to financing arrangements), then in section 147(1)(d), (2)(b), (3), (4)(b) and (5) "the actual provision" is a reference to the actual provision so far as relating to the financing arrangements concerned.

150 "Transaction" and "series of transactions"

(1) In this Part "transaction" includes arrangements, understandings and mutual practices (whether or not they are, or are intended to be, legally enforceable).

(2) References in this Part to a series of transactions include references to a number of transactions each entered into (whether or not one after the other) in pursuance of, or in relation to, the same arrangement.

(3) A series of transactions is not prevented by reason only of one or more of the matters mentioned in subsection (4) from being regarded for the purposes of this Part as a series of transactions by means of which provision has been made or imposed as between any two persons.

Taxation (International and Other Provisions) Act 2010 (c. 8)   **983**
Part 4 – Transfer pricing
Chapter 2 – Key interpretative provisions

(4) Those matters are —

    (a) that there is no transaction in the series to which both those persons are parties,

    (b) that the parties to any arrangement in pursuance of which the transactions in the series are entered into do not include one or both of those persons, and

    (c) that there is one or more transactions in the series to which neither of those persons is a party.

(5) In this section "arrangement" means any scheme or arrangement of any kind (whether or not it is, or is intended to be, legally enforceable).

151   "Arm's length provision"

(1) In this Part "the arm's length provision" has the meaning given by section 147(1).

(2) For the purposes of this Part, the cases in which provision made or imposed as between any two persons is to be taken to differ from the provision that would have been made as between independent enterprises include the case in which provision is made or imposed as between two persons but no provision would have been made as between independent enterprises; and references in this Part to the arm's length provision are to be read accordingly.

152   Arm's length provision where actual provision relates to securities

(1) This section applies where —

    (a) both of the affected persons are companies, and

    (b) the actual provision is provision in relation to a security issued by one of those companies ("the issuing company").

(2) Section 147(1)(d) is to be read as requiring account to be taken of all factors, including —

    (a) the question whether the loan would have been made at all in the absence of the special relationship,

    (b) the amount which the loan would have been in the absence of the special relationship, and

    (c) the rate of interest and other terms which would have been agreed in the absence of the special relationship.

(3) Subsection (2) has effect subject to subsections (4) and (5).

(4) If —

    (a) a company ("L") makes a loan to another company with which it has a special relationship, and

    (b) it is not part of L's business to make loans generally,

the fact that it is not part of L's business to make loans generally is to be disregarded in applying subsection (2).

(5) Section 147(1)(d) is to be read as requiring that, in the determination of any of the matters mentioned in subsection (6), no account is to be taken of (or of any inference capable of being drawn from) any guarantee provided by a company with which the issuing company has a participatory relationship.

(6) The matters are —

984   *Taxation (International and Other Provisions) Act 2010 (c. 8)*
Part 4 — Transfer pricing
Chapter 2 — Key interpretative provisions

    (a)   the appropriate level or extent of the issuing company's overall indebtedness,

    (b)   whether it might be expected that the issuing company and a particular person would have become parties to a transaction involving —

        (i)   the issue of a security by the issuing company, or

        (ii)   the making of a loan, or a loan of a particular amount, to the issuing company, and

    (c)   the rate of interest and other terms that might be expected to be applicable in any particular case to such a transaction.

153 Arm's length provision where security issued and guarantee given

(1)   This section applies where the actual provision is made or imposed by means of a series of transactions which include —

    (a)   the issuing of a security by a company which is one of the affected persons ("the issuing company"), and

    (b)   the provision of a guarantee by a company which is the other affected person.

(2)   Section 147(1)(d) is to be read as requiring account to be taken of all factors, including —

    (a)   the question whether the guarantee would have been provided at all in the absence of the special relationship,

    (b)   the amount that would have been guaranteed in the absence of the special relationship, and

    (c)   the consideration for the guarantee and other terms which would have been agreed in the absence of the special relationship.

(3)   Subsection (2) has effect subject to subsections (4) and (5).

(4)   If —

    (a)   a company ("G") provides a guarantee in respect of another company with which it has a special relationship, and

    (b)   it is not part of G's business to provide guarantees generally,

the fact that it is not part of G's business to provide guarantees generally is to be disregarded in applying subsection (2).

(5)   Section 147(1)(d) is to be read as requiring that, in the determination of any of the matters mentioned in subsection (6), no account is to be taken of (or of any inference capable of being drawn from) any guarantee provided by a company with which the issuing company has a participatory relationship.

(6)   The matters are —

    (a)   the appropriate level or extent of the issuing company's overall indebtedness,

    (b)   whether it might be expected that the issuing company and a particular person would have become parties to a transaction involving —

        (i)   the issue of a security by the issuing company, or

        (ii)   the making of a loan, or a loan of a particular amount, to the issuing company, and

    (c)   the rate of interest and other terms that might be expected to be applicable in any particular case to such a transaction.

Taxation (International and Other Provisions) Act 2010 (c. 8)
Part 4 – Transfer pricing
Chapter 2 – Key interpretative provisions

985

154   Interpretation of sections 152 and 153

(1)   Subsections (3) to (7) apply for the purposes of sections 152 and 153.

(2)   Subsection (6) applies also for the purposes of subsection (7)(a).

(3)   "Special relationship" means any relationship by virtue of which the participation condition is met (see section 148) in the case of the affected persons concerned.

(4)   Any reference to a guarantee includes –
    (a)   a reference to a surety, and
    (b)   a reference to any other relationship, arrangements, connection or understanding (whether formal or informal) such that the person making the loan to the issuing company has a reasonable expectation that in the event of a default by the issuing company the person will be paid by, or out of the assets of, one or more companies.

(5)   One company ("A") has a "participatory relationship" with another ("B") if –
    (a)   one of A and B is directly or indirectly participating in the management, control or capital of the other, or
    (b)   the same person or persons is or are directly or indirectly participating in the management, control or capital of each of A and B.

(6)   "Security" includes securities not creating or evidencing a charge on assets.

(7)   Any –
    (a)   interest payable by a company on money advanced without the issue of a security for the advance, or
    (b)   other consideration given by a company for the use of money so advanced,
is to be treated as if payable or given in respect of a security issued for the advance by the company, and references to a security are to be read accordingly.

155   "Potential advantage" in relation to United Kingdom taxation

(1)   Subsection (2) applies for the purposes of this Part.

(2)   The actual provision confers a potential advantage on a person in relation to United Kingdom taxation wherever, disregarding this Part, the effect of making or imposing the actual provision, instead of the arm's length provision, would be one or both of Effects A and B.

(3)   Effect A is that a smaller amount (which may be nil) would be taken for tax purposes to be the amount of the person's profits for any chargeable period.

(4)   Effect B is that a larger amount (or, if there would not otherwise have been losses, any amount of more than nil) would be taken for tax purposes to be the amount for any chargeable period of any losses of the person.

(5)   In determining for the purposes of subsection (3) or (4) the amount that would be taken for tax purposes to be the amount of the profits or losses for a year of assessment in the case of a non-UK resident, there is to be left out of account any income of that person which is –
    (a)   disregarded income within the meaning given by section 813 of ITA 2007 (limits on liability to income tax of non-UK residents), or

986

Taxation (International and Other Provisions) Act 2010 (c. 8)
Part 4 — Transfer pricing
Chapter 2 — Key interpretative provisions

(b) disregarded company income within the meaning given by section 816 of that Act.

(6) For the purposes of subsections (2) to (4) —

(a) Part 7 (tax treatment of financing costs and income), and

(b) paragraph E of the list in section 1000(1) of CTA 2010 (excessive interest etc treated as a distribution),

are to be disregarded.

156 "Losses" and "profits"

(1) In this Part "losses" includes amounts which are not losses but in respect of which relief may be given in accordance with —

(a) section 57 of ITTOIA 2005 (pre-trading expenses),

(b) section 88 of ITA 2007 (carry forward of certain interest),

(c) section 61 of CTA 2009 (pre-trading expenses),

(d) sections 387 to 391 of CTA 2009 (insurance companies: non-trading deficits on loan relationships),

(e) Chapter 16 of Part 5 of CTA 2009 (non-trading deficits on loan relationships),

(f) section 1223 of CTA 2009 (excess of management expenses), or

(g) Part 5 of CTA 2010 (group relief).

(2) In this Part "profits" includes income.

"Direct participation" in management, control or capital of a person

157 Direct participation

(1) Subsection (2) applies for the purposes of —

(a) this Part,

(b) in Part 2, section 132(7), and

(c) in Part 5, section 219(2).

(2) A person is directly participating in the management, control or capital of another person at a particular time if (and only if) that other person is at that time —

(a) a body corporate or a firm, and

(b) controlled by the first person.

"Indirect participation" in management, control or capital of a person

158 Indirect participation: defined by sections 159 to 162

(1) This section is about how to read the references, in this Part and in some other provisions of this Act, to indirect participation.

(2) For the purposes of sections 148(2)(a) and (3)(a) and 175(2)(a), a person is indirectly participating in the management, control or capital of another person only if section 159, 160 or 161 so provides.

Taxation (International and Other Provisions) Act 2010 (c. 8)
Part 4 – Transfer pricing
Chapter 2 – Key interpretative provisions

987

(3) For the purposes of sections 148(2)(b) and (3)(b) and 175(2)(b), a person is indirectly participating in the management, control or capital of another person only if section 159, 160 or 162 so provides.

(4) For the purposes of —

    (a) sections 154(5) and 204(4),

    (b) in Part 2, section 132(7), and

    (c) in Part 5, section 219(2),

a person is indirectly participating in the management, control or capital of another person only if section 159 or 160 so provides.

159 Indirect participation: potential direct participant

(1) Subsection (2) applies for the purposes of —

    (a) sections 148(2) and (3), 154(5), 175(2) and 204(4),

    (b) in Part 2, section 132(7), and

    (c) in Part 5, section 219(2).

(2) A person ("P") is indirectly participating in the management, control or capital of another person ("A") at a particular time if P would be directly participating in the management, control or capital of A at that time if the rights and powers attributed to P included all the rights and powers mentioned in subsection (3) that are not already attributed to P for the purpose of deciding under section 157 whether P is directly participating in the management, control or capital of A.

(3) The rights and powers referred to in subsection (2) are —

    (a) rights and powers which P is entitled to acquire at a future date,

    (b) rights and powers which P will, at a future date, become entitled to acquire,

    (c) rights and powers of persons other than P so far as they are rights or powers falling within subsection (4),

    (d) rights and powers of any person with whom P is connected (see section 163), and

    (e) rights and powers which would be attributed by subsection (2) to a person with whom P is connected were it being decided under that subsection whether that connected person is indirectly participating in the management, control or capital of A.

(4) Rights and powers fall within this subsection so far as they —

    (a) are required, or may be required, to be exercised in any one or more of the following ways —

        (i) on behalf of P,

        (ii) under the direction of P, or

        (iii) for the benefit of P, and

    (b) are not confined, in a case where a loan has been made by one person to another, to rights and powers conferred in relation to property of the borrower by the terms of any security relating to the loan.

(5) In subsections (3)(c) to (e) and (4), the references to a person's rights and powers include references to any rights or powers which the person either —

    (a) is entitled to acquire at a future date, or

    (b) will, at a future date, become entitled to acquire.

988   *Taxation (International and Other Provisions) Act 2010 (c. 8)*
Part 4 — Transfer pricing
Chapter 2 — Key interpretative provisions

(6) In paragraph (e) of subsection (3), the reference to rights and powers which would be attributed to a connected person includes a reference to rights and powers which, by applying that paragraph wherever one person is connected with another, would be so attributed to the connected person through a number of persons each of whom is connected with at least one of the others.

(7) References in this section—

    (a) to rights and powers of a person, or

    (b) to rights and powers which a person is or will become entitled to acquire,

include references to rights or powers which are exercisable by that person, or (when acquired by that person) will be exercisable, only jointly with one or more other persons.

160   Indirect participation: one of several major participants

(1) Subsection (2) applies for the purposes of—

    (a) sections 148(2) and (3), 154(5), 175(2) and 204(4),

    (b) in Part 2, section 132(7), and

    (c) in Part 5, section 219(2).

(2) A person is indirectly participating in the management, control or capital of another person at a particular time if the first person is, at that time, one of a number of major participants in that other person's enterprise.

(3) For the purposes of this section, a person ("A") is a major participant in another person's enterprise at a particular time if at that time—

    (a) that other person ("the subordinate") is a body corporate or firm, and

    (b) the 40% test is met in the case of each of two persons—

        (i)   who, taken together, control the subordinate, and

        (ii) of whom one is A.

(4) For the purposes of this section, the 40% test is met in the case of each of two persons wherever each of them has interests, rights and powers representing at least 40% of the holdings, rights and powers in respect of which the pair of them fall to be taken as controlling the subordinate.

(5) For the purposes of this section—

    (a) the question whether a person is controlled by any two or more persons taken together, and

    (b) any question whether the 40% test is met in the case of a person who is one of two persons,

is to be determined after attributing to each of the persons all the rights and powers which would be attributed by section 159(2) to a person were it being decided under section 159(2) whether that person is indirectly participating in the management, control or capital of another person.

(6) References in this section—

    (a) to rights and powers of a person, or

    (b) to rights and powers which a person is or will become entitled to acquire,

include references to rights or powers which are exercisable by that person, or (when acquired by that person) will be exercisable, only jointly with one or more other persons.

Taxation (International and Other Provisions) Act 2010 (c. 8)   989
Part 4 — Transfer pricing
Chapter 2 — Key interpretative provisions

161   Indirect participation: sections 148 and 175: financing cases

(1)   Subsection (2) applies for the purposes of sections 148(2)(a) and (3)(a) and 175(2)(a).

(2)   A person ("P") is indirectly participating in the management, control or capital of another ("A") at the time of the making or imposition of the actual provision if —

    (a)   the actual provision relates, to any extent, to financing arrangements for A,

    (b)   A is a body corporate or firm,

    (c)   P and other persons acted together in relation to the financing arrangements, and

    (d)   P would be taken to have control of A if, at any relevant time, there were attributed to P the rights and powers of each of the other persons mentioned in paragraph (c).

(3)   It is immaterial for the purposes of subsection (2)(c) whether P and the other persons acting together in relation to the financing arrangements did so at the time of the making or imposition of the actual provision or at some earlier time.

(4)   In subsection (2)(d) "relevant time" means —

    (a)   a time when P and the other persons were acting together in relation to the financing arrangements, or

    (b)   a time in the period of six months beginning with the day on which they ceased so to act.

(5)   In determining for the purposes of subsection (2)(d) whether P would be taken to have control of another person ("A"), the rights and powers of any person (and not just P) are to be taken to include those that would be attributed to that person by section 159(2) were it being decided under section 159(2) whether that person is indirectly participating in the management, control or capital of A.

(6)   In this section "financing arrangements" means arrangements made for providing or guaranteeing, or otherwise in connection with, any debt, capital or other form of finance.

162   Indirect participation: sections 148 and 175: further financing cases

(1)   Subsection (2) applies for the purposes of sections 148(2)(b) and (3)(b) and 175(2)(b).

(2)   A person ("Q") is indirectly participating in the management, control or capital of each of the affected persons at the time of the making or imposition of the actual provision if —

    (a)   the actual provision relates, to any extent, to financing arrangements for one of the affected persons ("B"),

    (b)   B is a body corporate or firm,

    (c)   Q and other persons acted together in relation to the financing arrangements, and

    (d)   Q would be taken to have control of both B and the other affected person if, at any relevant time, there were attributed to Q the rights and powers of each of the other persons mentioned in paragraph (c).

990   *Taxation (International and Other Provisions) Act 2010 (c. 8)*
Part 4 — Transfer pricing
Chapter 2 — Key interpretative provisions

(3) It is immaterial for the purposes of subsection (2)(c) whether Q and the other persons acting together in relation to the financing arrangements did so at the time of the making or imposition of the actual provision or at some earlier time.

(4) In subsection (2)(d) "relevant time" means —

  (a) a time when Q and the other persons were acting together in relation to the financing arrangements, or

  (b) a time in the period of six months beginning with the day on which they ceased so to act.

(5) In determining for the purposes of subsection (2)(d) whether Q would be taken to have control of another person ("A"), the rights and powers of any person (and not just Q) are to be taken to include those that would be attributed to that person by section 159(2) were it being decided under section 159(2) whether that person is indirectly participating in the management, control or capital of A.

(6) In this section "financing arrangements" means arrangements made for providing or guaranteeing, or otherwise in connection with, any debt, capital or other form of finance.

163 Meaning of "connected" in section 159

(1) Subsections (2) and (3) apply for the purposes of section 159 and this section.

(2) Two persons are connected with each other if one of them is an individual and the other is —

  (a) the individual's spouse or civil partner,

  (b) a relative of the individual,

  (c) a relative of the individual's spouse or civil partner, or

  (d) the spouse, or civil partner, of a person within paragraph (b) or (c).

(3) Two persons are connected with each other if one of them is a trustee of a settlement and the other is —

  (a) a person who in relation to that settlement is a settlor, or

  (b) a person who is connected with a person within paragraph (a).

(4) In this section —

  "relative" means brother, sister, ancestor or lineal descendant, and

  "settlement" and "settlor" have the same meaning as in section 620 of ITTOIA 2005.

Application of OECD principles

164 Part to be interpreted in accordance with OECD principles

(1) This Part is to be read in such manner as best secures consistency between —

  (a) the effect given to sections 147(1)(a), (b) and (d) and (2) to (6), 148 and 151(2), and

  (b) the effect which, in accordance with the transfer pricing guidelines, is to be given, in cases where double taxation arrangements incorporate the whole or any part of the OECD model, to so much of the arrangements as does so.

(2) Subsection (1) has effect subject to —

Taxation (International and Other Provisions) Act 2010 (c. 8)
Part 4 — Transfer pricing
Chapter 2 — Key interpretative provisions

991

section 147(1)(c) and (7) (oil-related provision to which Part does not apply),

sections 205 and 206 (rules for oil-related ring-fence trades),

section 217(3) to (7) (provision for sales of oil),

section 447(5) and (6) of CTA 2009 (this Part generally does not affect how exchange gains or losses from loan relationships are accounted for), and

section 694(8) and (9) of CTA 2009 (this Part generally does not affect how exchange gains or losses from derivative contracts are accounted for).

(3) In this section "the OECD model" means —

(a) the rules which, at the passing of ICTA (which occurred on 9 February 1988), were contained in Article 9 of the Model Tax Convention on Income and on Capital published by the Organisation for Economic Co-operation and Development, or

(b) any rules in the same or equivalent terms.

(4) In this section "the transfer pricing guidelines" means —

(a) all the documents published by the Organisation for Economic Co-operation and Development, at any time before 1 May 1998, as part of their Transfer Pricing Guidelines for Multinational Enterprises and Tax Administrations, and

(b) such documents published by that Organisation on or after that date as may for the purposes of this Part be designated, by an order made by the Treasury, as comprised in the transfer pricing guidelines.

(5) In this section "double taxation arrangements" means arrangements that have effect under section 2(1) (double taxation relief by agreement with territories outside the United Kingdom).

CHAPTER 3

EXEMPTIONS FROM BASIC RULE

165 Exemption for dormant companies

(1) Section 147(3) and (5) do not apply in calculating for any chargeable period the profits and losses of a potentially advantaged person if that person is a company which meets the condition in subsection (2).

(2) The condition is that —

(a) the company was dormant throughout the pre-qualifying period, and

(b) apart from section 147, the company has continued to be dormant at all times since the end of the pre-qualifying period.

(3) In subsection (2) "the pre-qualifying period" means —

(a) if there is an accounting period of the company that ends on 31 March 2004, that accounting period, or

(b) if there is no such accounting period, the period of 3 months ending with that date.

(4) In this section "dormant" has the meaning given by section 1169 of the Companies Act 2006.

992

Taxation (International and Other Provisions) Act 2010 (c. 8)
Part 4 — Transfer pricing
Chapter 3 — Exemptions from basic rule

166 Exemption for small and medium-sized enterprises

(1) Section 147(3) and (5) do not apply in calculating for any chargeable period the profits and losses of a potentially advantaged person if that person is a small or medium-sized enterprise for that chargeable period (see section 172).

(2) Exceptions to subsection (1) are provided —
   (a) in the case of a small enterprise, by section 167, and
   (b) in the case of a medium-sized enterprise, by sections 167 and 168.

167 Small and medium-sized enterprises: exceptions from exemption

(1) Subsections (2) and (3) set out exceptions to section 166(1).

(2) The first exception is if the small or medium-sized enterprise elects for section 166(1) not to apply in relation to the chargeable period.
   Any such election is irrevocable.

(3) The second exception is if —
   (a) the other affected person, or
   (b) a party to a relevant transaction,
   is, at the time when the actual provision is or was made or imposed, a resident of a non-qualifying territory (whether or not that person is also a resident of a qualifying territory).

(4) For the purposes of subsection (3) —
   (a) a "party to a relevant transaction" is a person who, if the actual provision is or was imposed by means of a series of transactions, is or was a party to one or more of those transactions, and
   (b) "qualifying territory" and "non-qualifying territory" are defined in section 173.

(5) In subsection (3) "resident", in relation to a territory —
   (a) means a person who, under the law of that territory, is liable to tax there by reason of the person's domicile, residence or place of management, but
   (b) does not include a person who is liable to tax in that territory in respect only of income from sources in that territory or capital situated there.

168 Medium-sized enterprises: exception from exemption: transfer pricing notice

(1) Section 166(1) does not apply in relation to any provision made or imposed if —
   (a) the potentially advantaged person is a medium-sized enterprise for the chargeable period, and
   (b) the Commissioners for Her Majesty's Revenue and Customs give that person a notice requiring the person to calculate the profits and losses of that chargeable period in accordance with section 147(3) or (5) in the case of that provision.

(2) A notice under subsection (1) is referred to in this Chapter as a transfer pricing notice.

169 Giving of transfer pricing notices

(1) This section applies to a transfer pricing notice given to a person.

Taxation (International and Other Provisions) Act 2010 (c. 8)   993
Part 4 — Transfer pricing
Chapter 3 — Exemptions from basic rule

(2)   The notice may be given in relation to —

    (a)   any provision specified, or of a description specified, in the notice, or

    (b)   every provision in relation to which one or other of the assumptions in section 147(3) and (5) would, apart from section 166(1), be required to be made when calculating the person's profits and losses for tax purposes.

(3)   The notice may be given only after a notice of enquiry has been given to the person in relation to the person's tax return for the chargeable period concerned.

(4)   The notice must identify the officer of Revenue and Customs to whom any notice of appeal under section 170 is to be given.

(5)   In subsection (3) "notice of enquiry" means a notice under —

    (a)   section 9A or 12AC of TMA 1970, or

    (b)   paragraph 24 of Schedule 18 to FA 1998.

170   Appeals against transfer pricing notices

(1)   A person to whom a transfer pricing notice is given may appeal against the decision to give the notice, but only on the ground that the condition in section 168(1)(a) is not met.

(2)   Any such appeal must be brought by giving written notice of appeal to the officer of Revenue and Customs identified in the notice in accordance with section 169(4).

(3)   The notice of appeal must be given before the end of the period of 30 days beginning with the day on which the transfer pricing notice is given.

171   Tax returns where transfer pricing notice given

(1)   If a transfer pricing notice is given to a person ("T"), T may amend T's tax return for the purpose of complying with the notice at any time before the end of the period of 90 days beginning with —

    (a)   the day on which the notice is given, or

    (b)   if T appeals under section 170 against the decision to give the notice, the day on which the appeal is finally determined or abandoned.

(2)   If a transfer pricing notice is given in the case of any tax return, no closure notice may be given in relation to that tax return until —

    (a)   the end of the period of 90 days specified in subsection (1), or

    (b)   the earlier amendment of the tax return for the purpose of complying with the notice.

(3)   So far as relating to any provision made or imposed by or in relation to a person —

    (a)   who is a medium-sized enterprise for a chargeable period,

    (b)   who does not make an election under section 167(2) for that period, and

    (c)   who is not excepted from section 166(1) in relation to that provision for that period because of section 167(3),

the tax return required to be made for that period is a return that disregards section 147(3) and (5).

994   *Taxation (International and Other Provisions) Act 2010 (c. 8)*
Part 4 — Transfer pricing
Chapter 3 — Exemptions from basic rule

(4) Subsection (3) does not prevent a tax return for a period becoming incorrect if in the case of any provision made or imposed —

  (a) a transfer pricing notice is given which has effect in relation to that provision for that period,

  (b) the return is not amended in accordance with subsection (1) for the purpose of complying with the notice, and

  (c) the return ought to have been so amended.

(5) In this section —

  "closure notice" means a notice under —

    (a) section 28A or 28B of TMA 1970, or

    (b) paragraph 32 of Schedule 18 to FA 1998,

  "company tax return" means the return required to be delivered pursuant to a notice under paragraph 3 of Schedule 18 to FA 1998, as read with paragraph 4 of that Schedule, and

  "tax return" means —

    (a) a return under section 8, 8A or 12AA of TMA 1970, or

    (b) a company tax return.

172 Meaning of "small enterprise" and "medium-sized enterprise"

(1) In this Chapter —

  (a) "small enterprise" means a small enterprise as defined in the Annex, and

  (b) "medium-sized enterprise" means an enterprise which —

    (i) falls within the category of micro, small and medium-sized enterprises as defined in the Annex, and

    (ii) is not a small enterprise as defined in the Annex.

(2) For the purposes of subsection (1), the Annex has effect with the modifications set out in subsections (4) to (7).

(3) In this section "the Annex" means the Annex to Commission Recommendation 2003/361/EC of 6 May 2003 (concerning the definition of micro, small and medium-sized businesses).

(4) Where any enterprise is in liquidation or administration, the rights of the liquidator or administrator (in that capacity) are to be left out of account when applying Article 3(3)(b) of the Annex in determining for the purposes of this Part whether —

  (a) that enterprise, or

  (b) any other enterprise (including that of the liquidator or administrator),

is a small or medium-sized enterprise.

(5) Article 3 of the Annex has effect with the omission of paragraph 5 (declaration in good faith where control cannot be determined etc).

(6) The first sentence of Article 4(1) of the Annex has effect as if the data to apply to —

  (a) the headcount of staff, and

  (b) the financial amounts,

were the data relating to the chargeable period referred to in section 166(1) (instead of the period described in that sentence) and calculated on an annual basis.

Taxation (International and Other Provisions) Act 2010 (c. 8)   995
Part 4 — Transfer pricing
Chapter 3 — Exemptions from basic rule

(7)   Article 4 of the Annex has effect with the omission of the following provisions —

    (a)   the second sentence of paragraph 1 (data to be taken into account from date of closure of accounts),

    (b)   paragraph 2 (no change of status unless ceilings exceeded for two consecutive periods), and

    (c)   paragraph 3 (genuine estimate in case of newly established enterprise).

173   Meaning of "qualifying territory" and "non-qualifying territory"

(1)   In section 167(3) —

    "non-qualifying territory" means any territory which is not a qualifying territory, and

    "qualifying territory" means —

        (a)   the United Kingdom, or

        (b)   any territory in relation to which condition A or condition B is met.

(2)   Condition A is that —

    (a)   double taxation arrangements have been made in relation to the territory,

    (b)   the arrangements include a non-discrimination provision, and

    (c)   the territory is not designated as a non-qualifying territory for the purposes of this subsection in regulations made by the Treasury.

(3)   Condition B is that —

    (a)   double taxation arrangements have been made in relation to the territory, and

    (b)   the territory is designated as a qualifying territory for the purposes of this subsection in regulations made by the Treasury.

(4)   For the purposes of subsection (2)(b) a "non-discrimination provision", in relation to any double taxation arrangements, is a provision to the effect that nationals of a state which is a party to those arrangements (a "contracting state") are not to be subject in any other contracting state to —

    (a)   any taxation, or

    (b)   any requirement connected with taxation,

which is other or more burdensome than the taxation and connected requirements to which nationals of that other state in the same circumstances (in particular with respect to residence) are or may be subjected.

(5)   In subsection (4) "national", in relation to a state, includes —

    (a)   any individual possessing the nationality or citizenship of the state, and

    (b)   any legal person, partnership or association deriving its status as such from the law in force in that state.

(6)   In this section "double taxation arrangements" means arrangements that have effect under section 2(1) (double taxation relief by agreement with territories outside the United Kingdom).

(7)   Regulations under this section may only be made if a draft of the statutory instrument containing the regulations has been laid before and approved by a resolution of the House of Commons.

996   *Taxation (International and Other Provisions) Act 2010 (c. 8)*
Part 4 — Transfer pricing
Chapter 4 — Position, if only one affected person potentially advantaged, of other affected person

CHAPTER 4

POSITION, IF ONLY ONE AFFECTED PERSON POTENTIALLY ADVANTAGED, OF OTHER AFFECTED PERSON

Claim by affected person who is not advantaged

174   Claim by the affected person who is not potentially advantaged

(1)   Subsection (2) applies if —

    (a)   only one of the affected persons (in this Chapter called "the advantaged person") is a person on whom a potential advantage in relation to United Kingdom taxation is conferred by the actual provision, and

    (b)   the other affected person (in this Chapter called "the disadvantaged person") is within the charge to income tax or corporation tax in respect of profits arising from the relevant activities (see section 216).

(2)   On the making of a claim by the disadvantaged person —

    (a)   the profits and losses of the disadvantaged person are to be calculated for tax purposes as if the arm's length provision had been made or imposed instead of the actual provision, and

    (b)   despite any limit in the Tax Acts on the time within which any adjustment may be made, all such adjustments are to be made in the disadvantaged person's case as may be required to give effect to the assumption that the arm's length provision was made or imposed instead of the actual provision.

(3)   Provision about claims under this section is made by —

    section 175 (claim not allowed in some cases where actual provision relates to a security issued by one of the affected persons),

    section 176 (claim cannot be made unless advantaged person has made return on the basis that the arm's length provision applies),

    section 177 (when claim may be made or amended), and

    sections 181 to 184 (option to make claims in accordance with section 182 in some cases where actual provision relates to a security issued by one of the affected persons).

(4)   Subsection (2) has effect subject to —

    section 180 (closing trading stock and closing work in progress in a trade),

    sections 188 and 189 (effect of claims under this section on double taxation relief),

    Chapter 5 (provision, where liabilities of an affected person under securities issued by that person are guaranteed, for attribution to guarantor of things done by that affected person),

    section 447(5) and (6) of CTA 2009 (this Part generally does not affect how exchange gains or losses from loan relationships are accounted for), and

    section 694(8) and (9) of CTA 2009 (this Part generally does not affect how exchange gains or losses from derivative contracts are accounted for).

175   Claims under section 174 where actual provision relates to a security

(1)   A claim under section 174 may not be made if —

Taxation (International and Other Provisions) Act 2010 (c. 8)   997
Part 4 — Transfer pricing
Chapter 4 — Position, if only one affected person potentially advantaged, of other affected person

    (a)   the participation condition (see section 148) would not be satisfied but for section 161 or 162,

    (b)   the actual provision is provision in relation to a security issued by one of the affected persons ("the issuer"), and

    (c)   a guarantee is provided in relation to the security by a person with whom the issuer has a participatory relationship.

(2)   For the purposes of subsection (1), one person ("A") has a "participatory relationship" with another ("B") if —

    (a)   one of A and B is directly or indirectly participating in the management, control or capital of the other, or

    (b)   the same person or persons is or are directly or indirectly participating in the management, control or capital of each of A and B.

(3)   In subsections (1)(b) and (4)(a) "security" includes securities not creating or evidencing a charge on assets.

(4)   For the purposes of subsection (1)(b), any —

    (a)   interest payable by a company on money advanced without the issue of a security for the advance, or

    (b)   other consideration given by a company for the use of money so advanced,

is to be treated as if payable or given in respect of a security issued for the advance by the company, and references to a security are to be read accordingly.

(5)   The reference in subsection (1)(c) to a guarantee includes —

    (a)   a reference to a surety, and

    (b)   if the issuer is a company, a reference to any other relationship, arrangements, connection or understanding (whether formal or informal) such that the person making the loan to the issuer has a reasonable expectation that in the event of a default by the issuer the person will be paid by, or out of the assets of, one or more companies.

176   Claims under section 174: advantaged person must have made return

(1)   A claim may not be made under section 174 unless a calculation has been made in the case of the advantaged person on the basis that the arm's length provision was made or imposed instead of the actual provision.

(2)   A claim made under section 174 must be consistent with the calculation made on that basis in the case of the advantaged person.

(3)   For the purposes of subsections (1) and (2), a calculation is to be taken to have been made in the case of the advantaged person on the basis that the arm's length provision was made or imposed instead of the actual provision if (and only if) —

    (a)   the calculations made for the purposes of any return by the advantaged person have been made on that basis because of this Part, or

    (b)   a relevant notice (see section 190) given to the advantaged person takes account of a determination in pursuance of this Part of an amount to be brought into account for tax purposes on that basis.

998   *Taxation (International and Other Provisions) Act 2010 (c. 8)*
Part 4 — Transfer pricing
Chapter 4 — Position, if only one affected person potentially advantaged, of other affected person

177   Time for making, or amending, claim under section 174

(1)   A claim under section 174 can be made only in the period mentioned in subsection (2) or (3).

(2)   If a return has been made by the advantaged person on the basis mentioned in section 176(1), the period is the two years beginning with the day of the making of the return.

(3)   If a relevant notice (see section 190) taking account of such a determination as is mentioned in section 176(3)(b) has been given to the advantaged person, the period is the two years beginning with the day on which that notice was given.

(4)   Subsection (5) applies if—

    (a)   a claim under section 174 is made in relation to a return made on the basis mentioned in section 176(1), and

    (b)   a relevant notice taking account of such a determination as is mentioned in section 176(3)(b) is subsequently given to the advantaged person.

(5)   The disadvantaged person is entitled, within the period mentioned in subsection (3), to make any such amendment of the claim as may be appropriate in consequence of the determination contained in the relevant notice.

(6)   Subsections (1) and (5) have effect subject to section 186(3) (which provides for the extension of the period for making or amending a claim).

178   Meaning of "return" in sections 176 and 177

(1)   In sections 176 and 177 "return" means—

    (a)   any return required to be made under TMA 1970 or under Schedule 18 to FA 1998 for income tax or corporation tax purposes, or

    (b)   any voluntary amendment of a return within paragraph (a).

(2)   In subsection (1)(b) "voluntary amendment" means—

    (a)   an amendment under section 9ZA or 12ABA of TMA 1970 (amendment of personal, trustee or partnership return by taxpayer), or

    (b)   an amendment under Schedule 18 to FA 1998 other than one made in response to the giving of a relevant notice (see section 190).

Claims: special cases

179   Compensating payment if advantaged person is controlled foreign company

(1)   Subsection (2) applies if—

    (a)   the actual provision is provision made or imposed in relation to a controlled foreign company,

    (b)   in determining for the purposes of Chapter 4 of Part 17 of ICTA the amount of that company's chargeable profits for an accounting period, its profits and losses are to be calculated in accordance with section 147(3) or (5) in the case of that provision,

    (c)   the whole of those chargeable profits are to be apportioned under section 747(3) of ICTA to one or more companies resident in the United Kingdom, and

Taxation (International and Other Provisions) Act 2010 (c. 8) 999
Part 4 — Transfer pricing
Chapter 4 — Position, if only one affected person potentially advantaged, of other affected person

    (d)   tax is chargeable under section 747(4) of ICTA in respect of the whole of those chargeable profits, as so apportioned to those companies.

(2)   Sections 174 to 178 have effect as if the controlled foreign company were a person on whom a potential advantage in relation to United Kingdom taxation were conferred by the actual provision.

(3)   In applying sections 174 to 178 in a case in which they apply because of subsection (2) —

    (a)   references to the advantaged person in sections 176(3)(a) and (b) and 177(2), (3) and (4)(b) include a reference to any of the companies mentioned in subsection (1)(c), and

    (b)   references to corporation tax include a reference to tax chargeable under section 747(4) of ICTA.

(4)   In this section —

    "controlled foreign company" has the same meaning as in Chapter 4 of Part 17 of ICTA, and

    "accounting period", in relation to a controlled foreign company, has the same meaning as in that Chapter.

180   Application of section 174(2)(a) in relation to transfers of trading stock etc

(1)   Section 174(2)(a) does not affect the credits to be brought into account by the disadvantaged person in respect of —

    (a)   closing trading stock, or

    (b)   closing work in progress in a trade,

for accounting periods ending on or after the day given by subsection (2).

(2)   That day is the last day of the accounting period of the advantaged person in which the actual provision was made or imposed.

(3)   For the purposes of this section "trading stock", in relation to any trade, has the meaning given by —

    (a)   section 174 of ITTOIA 2005, or

    (b)   section 163 of CTA 2009.

Alternative way of claiming if a security is involved

181   Section 182 applies to claims where actual provision relates to a security

(1)   Subsection (2) applies if —

    (a)   both of the affected persons are companies, and

    (b)   the actual provision is provision in relation to a security issued by one of those companies.

(2)   A claim under section 174 may be made in accordance with section 182.

(3)   For the purposes of this Part, a "section 182 claim" is a claim under section 174 made in accordance with section 182.

(4)   In subsections (1)(b) and (5)(a) "security" includes securities not creating or evidencing a charge on assets.

(5)   For the purposes of subsection (1)(b), any —

1000

Taxation (International and Other Provisions) Act 2010 (c. 8)
Part 4 — Transfer pricing
Chapter 4 — Position, if only one affected person potentially advantaged, of other affected person

(a) interest payable by a company on money advanced without the issue of a security for the advance, or

(b) other consideration given by a company for the use of money so advanced,

is to be treated as if payable or given in respect of a security issued for the advance by the company, and references to a security are to be read accordingly.

182 Making of section 182 claims

(1) A section 182 claim may be made by —

    (a) the disadvantaged person, or

    (b) the advantaged person.

(2) A section 182 claim made by the advantaged person is to be taken to be made on behalf of the disadvantaged person.

(3) A section 182 claim may be made before or after a calculation within section 176(1) has been made.

(4) A section 182 claim must be made either —

    (a) at any time before the end of the period mentioned in section 177(2), or

    (b) within the period mentioned in section 177(3).

(5) Subsection (4) has effect subject to section 186(3) (which provides for the extension of the period for making a claim).

183 Giving effect to section 182 claims

(1) A section 182 claim is not a claim within paragraph 57 or 58 of Schedule 18 to FA 1998 (company tax returns, assessments and related matters).

(2) Accordingly, paragraph 59 of that Schedule (application of Schedule 1A to TMA 1970) has effect in relation to a section 182 claim.

(3) If —

    (a) a section 182 claim is made before a calculation within section 176(1) has been made,

    (b) such a calculation is subsequently made, and

    (c) the claim is not consistent with the calculation,

the affected persons are to be treated as if (instead of the claim actually made) a claim had been made that was consistent with the calculation.

(4) All such adjustments are to be made (including by the making of assessments) as are required to give effect to subsection (3).

(5) Subsection (4) has effect despite any limit on the time within which any adjustment may be made.

184 Amending a section 182 claim if it is followed by relevant notice

(1) Subsection (2) applies if —

    (a) a section 182 claim is made,

    (b) a return is subsequently made by the advantaged person on the basis mentioned in section 176(1), and

Taxation (International and Other Provisions) Act 2010 (c. 8)   **1001**
Part 4 — Transfer pricing
Chapter 4 — Position, if only one affected person potentially advantaged, of other affected person

    (c)   a relevant notice (see section 190) taking account of such a determination as is mentioned in section 176(3)(b) is subsequently given to the advantaged person.

(2)   If any amendment of the claim is appropriate in consequence of the determination contained in the relevant notice, the amendment may be made by—

    (a)   the disadvantaged person, or

    (b)   the advantaged person.

(3)   If an amendment under subsection (2) is made by the advantaged person it is to be taken to be made on behalf of the disadvantaged person.

(4)   Any amendment under subsection (2) must be made within the period mentioned in section 177(3).

(5)   Subsection (4) has effect subject to section 186(3) (which provides for the extension of the period for making an amendment).

Notification to persons who may be disadvantaged

185   Notice to potential claimants

(1)   Subsection (2) applies if—

    (a)   a relevant notice (see section 190) is given to any person,

    (b)   the notice, or anything contained in it, takes account of a transfer-pricing determination, and

    (c)   it appears to an officer that there is a person ("DP") who is or may be a disadvantaged person by reference to the subject-matter of the determination.

(2)   The officer must give to DP a notice containing particulars of the determination.

(3)   A contravention of subsection (2) does not affect the validity—

    (a)   of the relevant notice, or

    (b)   of any determination to which the notice relates.

(4)   For the purposes of this section, a person is a disadvantaged person by reference to the subject-matter of a transfer-pricing determination if (and only if) the person—

    (a)   is entitled, in consequence of the making of the determination, to make or amend a claim under section 174, or

    (b)   will be entitled, because of section 212(3), to be a party to any proceedings on an appeal relating to the determination.

(5)   In this section—

        "officer" means officer of Revenue and Customs, and

        "transfer-pricing determination" means a determination of an amount that is to be brought into account for tax purposes in respect of—

        (a)   any assumption made under section 147(3) or (5), or

        (b)   any advance-pricing-agreement assumptions (see section 222(6)).

1002   *Taxation (International and Other Provisions) Act 2010 (c. 8)*
Part 4 — Transfer pricing
Chapter 4 — Position, if only one affected person potentially advantaged, of other affected person

186   Extending claim period if notice under section 185 not given or given late

(1)   If there is a contravention of section 185(2), the Commissioners must consider whether, as a result of the contravention, any person has been prejudiced with respect to the making or amendment of a claim under section 174.

(2)   Subsection (3) applies if—

     (a)   there is a contravention of section 185(2), or

     (b)   a notice required by section 185(2) is given after the relevant notice concerned.

(3)   The Commissioners may, if they think fit, treat the period for the making or amendment of a claim under section 174 in the case concerned as extended by such further period as appears to them to be appropriate.

(4)   In this section "the Commissioners" means the Commissioners for Her Majesty's Revenue and Customs.

Treatment of interest where claim made

187   Tax treatment if actual interest exceeds arm's length interest

(1)   Subsection (6) applies if the following conditions are met.

(2)   Condition A is that interest is paid by any person under the actual provision.

(3)   Condition B is that section 147(3) or (5) applies in relation to the actual provision.

(4)   Condition C is—

     (a)   that the amount ("ALINT") of interest that would have been payable under the arm's length provision is less than the amount of interest paid under the actual provision, or

     (b)   that there would not have been any interest payable under the arm's length provision (so that ALINT is nil).

(5)   Condition D is that the person receiving the interest paid under the actual provision makes—

     (a)   a claim under section 174, or

     (b)   a section 182 claim.

(6)   The interest paid under the actual provision, so far as it exceeds ALINT—

     (a)   is not to be regarded as chargeable under Chapter 2 of Part 4 of ITTOIA 2005,

     (b)   is not subject to the provisions of Part 15 of ITA 2007 (deduction of income tax at source), and

     (c)   is not required to be brought into account under Part 5 of CTA 2009 (loan relationships) as a non-trading credit.

Adjustment of double taxation relief where claim made

188   Double taxation relief by way of credit for foreign tax

(1)   Subsection (2) applies if—

     (a)   a claim is made under section 174, and

Taxation (International and Other Provisions) Act 2010 (c. 8)
Part 4 — Transfer pricing
Chapter 4 — Position, if only one affected person potentially advantaged, of other affected person

1003

    (b)   the disadvantaged person ("DP") is entitled on that claim to make a calculation, or to have an adjustment made, on the basis that the arm's length provision was made or imposed instead of the actual provision.

(2)   Assumptions A and B are to be made in DP's case in relation to any credit for foreign tax which DP has been, or may be, given —

    (a)   under any double taxation arrangements, or

    (b)   under section 18(1)(b) and (2) (relief under unilateral relief arrangements).

(3)   Subsection (2) has effect subject to section 189(2).

(4)   Assumption A is that the foreign tax paid or payable by DP does not include any amount of foreign tax which would not be or have become payable were it to be assumed for the purposes of that tax that the arm's length provision had been made or imposed instead of the actual provision.

(5)   Assumption B is that the amount of DP's relevant profits in respect of which DP is given credit for foreign tax does not include the amount (if any) by which DP's relevant profits are treated as reduced in accordance with section 174.

(6)   If any adjustment is required to be made for the purpose of giving effect to any of the preceding provisions of this section —

    (a)   it may be made by setting the amount of the adjustment against any relief or repayment to which DP is entitled in pursuance of DP's claim under section 174, and

    (b)   nothing in the Tax Acts limiting the time within which any assessment is to be or may be made or amended prevents that adjustment from being so made.

(7)   In subsection (5) "DP's relevant profits" means the profits arising to DP from the carrying on of the relevant activities (see section 216).

(8)   In this section —

    "double taxation arrangements" means arrangements that have effect under section 2(1) (double taxation relief by agreement with territories outside the United Kingdom), and

    "foreign tax" means —

        (a)   any tax under the law of a territory outside the United Kingdom, or

        (b)   any amount that, for the purposes of any double taxation arrangements, is to be treated as if it were tax under the law of a territory outside the United Kingdom.

(9)   In determining for the purposes of this section whether a person is —

    (a)   under any double taxation arrangements, or

    (b)   under section 18(1)(b) and (2),

to be given credit for foreign tax, ignore any requirement that a claim is made before such a credit is given.

189 Double taxation relief by way of deduction for foreign tax

(1)   Subsection (2) applies if —

    (a)   a claim is made under section 174,

1004   *Taxation (International and Other Provisions) Act 2010 (c. 8)*
Part 4 — Transfer pricing
Chapter 4 — Position, if only one affected person potentially advantaged, of other affected person

    (b)   the disadvantaged person ("DP") is entitled on that claim to make a calculation, or to have an adjustment made, on the basis that the arm's length provision was made or imposed instead of the actual provision,

    (c)   the application of that basis in the calculation of DP's profits or losses for any chargeable period involves a reduction in the amount of any income, and

    (d)   that income is also income that is to be reduced in accordance with section 112(1) (deduction for foreign tax where no credit allowed).

  (2)   If this subsection applies—

    (a)   the reduction mentioned in subsection (1)(c) is to be treated as made before any reduction under section 112(1), and

    (b)   tax paid, in the place in which any income arises, on so much of that income as is represented by the amount of the reduction mentioned in subsection (1)(c) is to be disregarded for the purposes of section 112(1).

  (3)   If any adjustment is required to be made for the purpose of giving effect to any of the preceding provisions of this section—

    (a)   it may be made by setting the amount of the adjustment against any relief or repayment to which DP is entitled in pursuance of DP's claim under section 174, and

    (b)   nothing in the Tax Acts limiting the time within which any assessment is to be or may be made or amended prevents that adjustment from being so made.

Interpretation of Chapter

190   Meaning of "relevant notice"

In this Chapter "relevant notice" means—

    (a)   a closure notice under section 28A(1) of TMA 1970 in relation to an enquiry into a return under section 8 or 8A of TMA 1970,

    (b)   a closure notice under section 28B(1) of TMA 1970 in relation to an enquiry into a partnership return,

    (c)   a closure notice under paragraph 32 of Schedule 18 to FA 1998 in relation to an enquiry into a company tax return,

    (d)   a notice under section 30B(1) of TMA 1970 amending a partnership return,

    (e)   a notice of an assessment under section 29 of TMA 1970,

    (f)   a notice of a discovery assessment under paragraph 41 of Schedule 18 to FA 1998 (which includes a discovery assessment under that paragraph as applied by paragraph 52 of that Schedule), or

    (g)   a notice of a discovery determination under paragraph 41 of Schedule 18 to FA 1998.

Taxation (International and Other Provisions) Act 2010 (c. 8)
Part 4 — Transfer pricing
Chapter 5 — Position of guarantor of affected person's liabilities under a security issued by the person

1005

CHAPTER 5

POSITION OF GUARANTOR OF AFFECTED PERSON'S LIABILITIES UNDER A SECURITY ISSUED BY THE PERSON

191 When sections 192 to 194 apply

(1) Sections 192 to 194 apply if—

    (a) one of the affected persons ("the issuing company") is a company that has liabilities under a security issued by it,

    (b) those liabilities are to any extent the subject of a guarantee provided by a company ("the guarantor company"),

    (c) in calculating the profits and losses of the issuing company for tax purposes, the amounts to be deducted in respect of interest or other amounts payable under the security are required to be reduced (whether or not to nil) under section 147(3) or (5), and

    (d) that reduction is required because of section 153.

(2) In subsections (1)(a) and (3)(a) "security" includes securities not creating or evidencing a charge on assets.

(3) For the purposes of subsection (1)(a), any—

    (a) interest payable by a company on money advanced without the issue of a security for the advance, or

    (b) other consideration given by a company for the use of money so advanced,

is to be treated as if payable or given in respect of a security issued for the advance by the company, and the reference in subsection (1)(a) to a security is to be read accordingly.

(4) In subsection (1)(b) the reference to a guarantee includes—

    (a) a reference to a surety, and

    (b) a reference to any other relationship, arrangements, connection or understanding (whether formal or informal) such that the person making the loan to the issuing company has a reasonable expectation that in the event of a default by the issuing company the person will be paid by, or out of the assets of, one or more companies.

(5) In this Chapter—

    "the guarantor company" has the meaning given by subsection (1)(b),

    "the issuing company" has the meaning given by subsection (1)(a), and

    "the security" means the security mentioned in subsection (1)(a).

192 Attribution to guarantor company of things done by issuing company

(1) On the making of a claim, the guarantor company is, to the extent of the reduction mentioned in section 191(1)(c), to be treated for all purposes of the Taxes Acts as if it (and not the issuing company)—

    (a) had issued the security,

    (b) owed the liabilities under it, and

    (c) had paid any interest or other amounts paid under it by the issuing company.

(2) Subsection (1) is subject to subsection (3).

1006   *Taxation (International and Other Provisions) Act 2010 (c. 8)*
Part 4 — Transfer pricing
Chapter 5 — Position of guarantor of affected person's liabilities under a security issued by the person

(3) Where the issuing company's liabilities under the security are the subject of two or more guarantees (whether or not provided by the same person), TD must not exceed TR, where —

> TD is the total of the amounts brought into account by the guarantor companies because of subsection (1), and

> TR is the total amount of the reductions within section 191(1)(c).

(4) Provision about claims under subsection (1) is made by —

> section 193 (interaction between claims under subsection (1) and claims under section 174), and

> section 194 (general provision about claims under subsection (1)).

(5) In subsection (1) "the Taxes Acts" has the meaning given by section 118(1) of TMA 1970.

(6) In subsection (3) any reference to a guarantee includes —

    (a) a reference to a surety, and

    (b) a reference to any other relationship, arrangements, connection or understanding (whether formal or informal) such that the person making the loan to the issuing company has a reasonable expectation that in the event of a default by the issuing company the person will be paid by, or out of the assets of, one or more companies.

193   Interaction between claims under sections 174 and 192(1)

(1) In this section "the loan provision" means the actual provision made or imposed between —

    (a) the issuing company, and

    (b) another company ("the lending company"),

which is provision in relation to the security.

(2) Subsections (3) and (4) apply if —

    (a) the guarantor company makes a claim under section 192(1), and

    (b) the lending company makes a claim under section 174 in relation to the loan provision.

(3) In determining the arm's length provision for the purposes of section 174(2)(a) in relation to the lending company's claim, additional amounts are to be brought into account as credits corresponding to the debits that fall to be brought into account by the guarantor company because of section 192(1).

(4) If —

    (a) the lending company makes its claim under section 174 before the guarantor company makes its claim under section 192(1), and

    (b) the calculation on which the lending company's claim is based does not comply with subsection (3),

the guarantor company's claim is to be disallowed.

194   Claims under section 192(1): general provisions

(1) A claim under section 192(1) may be made —

    (a) by the guarantor company,

    (b) if there are two or more guarantor companies, by those companies acting together, or

Taxation (International and Other Provisions) Act 2010 (c. 8)   1007
Part 4 – Transfer pricing
Chapter 5 – Position of guarantor of affected person's liabilities under a security issued by the person

      (c)   by the issuing company.

(2)   A claim made under section 192(1) by the issuing company is to be taken to be made on behalf of the guarantor company or companies.

(3)   Sections 175 to 177 apply in relation to a claim under section 192(1) made by or on behalf of any person or persons as they apply in relation to a claim under section 174 made by the disadvantaged person, but taking—

      (a)   references in sections 176 and 177 to the advantaged person as references to the issuing company, and

      (b)   the reference in section 177 to the disadvantaged person as a reference to the guarantor company or companies.

CHAPTER 6

BALANCING PAYMENTS

195   Qualifying conditions for purposes of section 196

(1)   Conditions A to D are "the qualifying conditions" for the purposes of section 196.

(2)   Condition A is that only one of the affected persons ("the advantaged person") is a person on whom a potential advantage in relation to United Kingdom taxation is conferred by the actual provision.

(3)   Condition B is that the other affected person ("the disadvantaged person") is within the charge to income tax or corporation tax in respect of profits arising from the relevant activities (see section 216).

(4)   Condition C is that—

      (a)   a payment (the "balancing payment") is made, or

      (b)   two or more payments (the "balancing payments") are made,

    to the advantaged person by the disadvantaged person.

(5)   Condition D is that the sole or main reason for making that payment or those payments is that section 147(3) or (5) applies.

196   Balancing payments between affected persons: no charge to, or relief from, tax

(1)   If each of the qualifying conditions (see section 195) is met, subsection (2) applies—

      (a)   to the balancing payment if, or so far as, its amount does not exceed the available compensating adjustment, or

      (b)   to the balancing payments if, or so far as, their total amount does not exceed the available compensating adjustment.

(2)   Any payment to which this subsection applies—

      (a)   is not to be taken into account in calculating profits or losses of either of the affected persons for the purposes of income tax or corporation tax, and

      (b)   is not for any purpose of the Corporation Tax Acts to be regarded as a distribution.

(3)   In subsection (1) "the available compensating adjustment" means the difference between PL1 and PL2 where —

>   PL1 is the profits and losses of the disadvantaged person calculated for tax purposes on the basis of the actual provision, and
>
>   PL2 is the profits and losses of the disadvantaged person as (or as they would be) calculated for tax purposes on a claim under section 174.

(4)   For the purposes of subsection (3), take PL1 or PL2 —

>   (a)   as a positive amount if it is an amount of profits, and
>
>   (b)   as a negative amount if it is an amount of losses.

(5)   In this section, the following expressions have the meaning given by section 195 —

>   "the balancing payment" and "the balancing payments", and
>
>   "the disadvantaged person".

197   Qualifying conditions for purposes of section 198

(1)   Conditions A to F are the qualifying conditions for the purposes of section 198.

(2)   Condition A is that one of the affected persons ("the issuing company") is a company that has liabilities under a security issued by it.

(3)   Condition B is that those liabilities are to any extent the subject of a guarantee provided by a company ("the guarantor company").

(4)   Condition C is that, in calculating the profits and losses of the issuing company for tax purposes, the amounts to be deducted in respect of interest or other amounts payable under the security are required to be reduced (whether or not to nil) under section 147(3) or (5).

(5)   Condition D is that that reduction is required because of section 153.

(6)   Condition E is that —

>   (a)   a payment (the "balancing payment") is made, or
>
>   (b)   two or more payments (the "balancing payments") are made,

by the guarantor company to the issuing company.

(7)   Condition F is that the sole or main reasons for making that payment or those payments are —

>   (a)   that section 147(3) or (5) applies because of section 153, or
>
>   (b)   that sections 192 to 194 apply.

(8)   In subsections (2) and (9)(a) "security" includes securities not creating or evidencing a charge on assets.

(9)   For the purposes of subsection (2), any —

>   (a)   interest payable by a company on money advanced without the issue of a security for the advance, or
>
>   (b)   other consideration given by a company for the use of money so advanced,

is to be treated as if payable or given in respect of a security issued for the advance by the company, and the reference in subsection (2) to a security is to be read accordingly.

(10)   In subsection (3) the reference to a guarantee includes —

Taxation (International and Other Provisions) Act 2010 (c. 8)
Part 4 — Transfer pricing
Chapter 6 — Balancing payments

1009

    (a)   a reference to a surety, and

    (b)   a reference to any other relationship, arrangements, connection or understanding (whether formal or informal) such that the person making the loan to the issuing company has a reasonable expectation that in the event of a default by the issuing company the person will be paid by, or out of the assets of, one or more companies.

198   Balancing payments by guarantor to issuer: no charge to, or relief from, tax

(1)   If each of the qualifying conditions (see section 197) is met, subsection (2) applies to the balancing payments made by all of the guarantor companies if, or so far as, the total amount of those payments does not exceed the total amount of the reductions within section 197(4).

(2)   Payments to which this subsection applies —

    (a)   are not to be taken into account in calculating for the purposes of corporation tax the profits or losses of the guarantor company or companies or the issuing company, and

    (b)   are not for any purpose of the Corporation Tax Acts to be regarded as distributions.

(3)   In this section, the following expressions have the meaning given by section 197 —

        "the balancing payments",
        "the guarantor company", and
        "the issuing company".

199   Pre-conditions for making election under section 200

(1)   Conditions A to E are the pre-conditions for the purposes of section 200.

(2)   Condition A is that both of the affected persons are companies.

(3)   Condition B is that only one of the affected persons ("the advantaged person") is a person on whom a potential advantage in relation to United Kingdom taxation is conferred by the actual provision.

(4)   Condition C is that the other affected person ("the disadvantaged person") is within the charge to income tax or corporation tax in respect of profits arising from the relevant activities (see section 216).

(5)   Condition D is that the actual provision is provision in relation to a security (the "relevant security").

(6)   Condition E is that the capital market condition is met (see section 204).

(7)   In subsections (5) and (8)(a) "security" includes securities not creating or evidencing a charge on assets.

(8)   For the purposes of subsection (5), any —

    (a)   interest payable by a company on money advanced without the issue of a security for the advance, or

    (b)   other consideration given by a company for the use of money so advanced, is to be treated as if payable or given in respect of a security issued for the advance by the company, and the reference in subsection (5) to a security is to be read accordingly.

200   Election to pay tax rather than make balancing payments

(1)   If each of the pre-conditions (see section 199) is met, the disadvantaged person may make an election—

     (a)   to make no balancing payment within section 196 to the advantaged person in connection with section 147(3) or (5) applying because of section 152 in relation to the relevant security in a chargeable period, but

     (b)   instead, to undertake sole responsibility for discharging the advantaged person's liability to tax for that period so far as resulting from section 147(3) or (5) applying because of section 152 in relation to the relevant security.

(2)   Section 203 contains provision about the making and effect of elections under this section.

(3)   In this section, the following expressions have the meaning given by section 199—

     "the advantaged person",

     "the disadvantaged person", and

     "the relevant security".

201   Pre-conditions for making election under section 202

(1)   Conditions A to E are the pre-conditions for the purposes of section 202.

(2)   Condition A is that both of the affected persons are companies.

(3)   Condition B is that only one of the affected persons ("the advantaged person") is a person on whom a potential advantage in relation to United Kingdom taxation is conferred by the actual provision.

(4)   Condition C is that the other affected person ("the disadvantaged person") is within the charge to income tax or corporation tax in respect of profits arising from the relevant activities (see section 216).

(5)   Condition D is that the actual provision is made or imposed by means of a series of transactions which include—

     (a)   the issuing of a security ("the relevant security") by one of the affected persons ("the issuing company"), and

     (b)   the provision of a guarantee by the other affected person.

(6)   Condition E is that the capital market condition is met (see section 204).

(7)   In subsections (5) and (8)(a) "security" includes securities not creating or evidencing a charge on assets.

(8)   For the purposes of subsection (5), any—

     (a)   interest payable by a company on money advanced without the issue of a security for the advance, or

     (b)   other consideration given by a company for the use of money so advanced,

Taxation (International and Other Provisions) Act 2010 (c. 8)
Part 4 — Transfer pricing
Chapter 6 — Balancing payments

1011

is to be treated as if payable or given in respect of a security issued for the advance by the company, and the reference in subsection (5) to a security is to be read accordingly.

(9) In subsection (5) the reference to a guarantee includes —

    (a) a reference to a surety, and

    (b) a reference to any other relationship, arrangements, connection or understanding (whether formal or informal) such that the person making the loan to the issuing company has a reasonable expectation that in the event of a default by the issuing company the person will be paid by, or out of the assets of, one or more companies.

202 Election, in guarantee case, to pay tax rather than make balancing payments

(1) If each of the pre-conditions (see section 201) is met, the disadvantaged person may make an election —

    (a) to make no balancing payment within section 198 to the advantaged person in connection with section 147(3) or (5) applying because of section 153 in relation to the relevant security in a chargeable period, but

    (b) instead, to undertake sole responsibility for discharging the advantaged person's liability to tax for that period so far as resulting from section 147(3) or (5) applying because of section 153 in relation to the relevant security.

(2) Section 203 contains provision about the making and effect of elections under this section.

(3) In this section, the following expressions have the meaning given by section 201 —

    "the advantaged person",

    "the disadvantaged person", and

    "the relevant security".

203 Elections under section 200 or 202

(1) In this section "election" means election under section 200 or 202.

(2) An election must be made by being included (whether by amendment or otherwise) in the disadvantaged person's company tax return for the chargeable period in which the relevant security is issued.

(3) An election is irrevocable.

(4) An election has effect in relation to each of the affected persons for the chargeable period in which the relevant security is issued and all subsequent chargeable periods.

(5) An election is of no effect if the Commissioners for Her Majesty's Revenue and Customs give the disadvantaged person a notice refusing to accept the election.

(6) A notice under subsection (5) may be given only after a notice of enquiry in respect of the company tax return containing the election has been given to the disadvantaged person.

1012

Taxation (International and Other Provisions) Act 2010 (c. 8)
Part 4 — Transfer pricing
Chapter 6 — Balancing payments

(Paragraph 24 of Schedule 18 to FA 1998 makes provision about notices of enquiry in respect of company tax returns.)

(7) If an election has effect in relation to an accounting period of the advantaged person, the tax mentioned in subsection (1)(b) of the section under which the election is made—

    (a) is recoverable from the disadvantaged person as if it were an amount of corporation tax due and owing from that person, and

    (b) is not recoverable from the advantaged person.

(8) In this section—

"the advantaged person", "the disadvantaged person" and "the relevant security"—

    (a) in relation to an election under section 200, have the meaning given by section 199, and

    (b) in relation to an election under section 202, have the meaning given by section 201, and

"company tax return" means the return required to be delivered pursuant to a notice under paragraph 3 of Schedule 18 to FA 1998, as read with paragraph 4 of that Schedule.

(9) For the purposes of subsections (2) and (4), if the relevant security was issued in a chargeable period beginning before 1st April 2004 it is to be treated as if it had been issued in the chargeable period beginning on that date.

204 Meaning of "capital market condition" in sections 199 and 201

(1) For the purposes of section 199(6) or 201(6), the capital market condition is met if—

    (a) the actual provision forms part of a capital market arrangement,

    (b) the capital market arrangement involves the issue of a capital market investment,

    (c) the securities that represent the capital market investment are issued wholly or mainly to independent persons, and

    (d) the total value of the capital market investments made under the capital market arrangement is at least £50 million.

(2) In this section—

"capital market arrangement" has the same meaning as in section 72B(1) of the Insolvency Act 1986 (see paragraph 1 of Schedule 2A to that Act),

"capital market investment" has the same meaning as in section 72B(1) of the Insolvency Act 1986 (see paragraphs 2 and 3 of Schedule 2A to that Act), and

"independent person" means a person—

    (a) who is not the disadvantaged person, and

    (b) who does not have a participatory relationship with either of the affected persons.

(3) In subsection (2) "the disadvantaged person"—

    (a) for the purposes of the application of this section in relation to section 199(6) has the meaning given by section 199(4), and

    (b) for the purposes of the application of this section in relation to section 201(6) has the meaning given by section 201(4).

Taxation (International and Other Provisions) Act 2010 (c. 8)
Part 4 – Transfer pricing
Chapter 6 – Balancing payments

1013

(4) For the purposes of subsection (2), a person ("A") who is a company has a "participatory relationship" with one of the affected persons ("B") if—

    (a) one of A and B is directly or indirectly participating in the management, control or capital of the other, or

    (b) the same person or persons is or are directly or indirectly participating in the management, control or capital of each of A and B.

CHAPTER 7

OIL-RELATED RING-FENCE TRADES

205 Provision made or imposed between ring-fence trade and other activities

(1) Subsections (2) to (4) apply if—

    (a) a person carries on an oil-related ring-fence trade (see section 206), and

    (b) any provision is made or imposed by the person as between—

        (i) the oil-related ring-fence trade, and

        (ii) any other activities carried on by the person.

(2) Chapters 1 and 3 to 6 (read in accordance with Chapters 2 and 8) apply in relation to the provision as if—

    (a) the oil-related ring-fence trade, and the person's other activities, were carried on by two different persons,

    (b) the provision were made or imposed as between those two persons by means of a transaction,

    (c) those two persons were both controlled by the same person at the time when the provision was made or imposed, and

    (d) a potential advantage in relation to United Kingdom taxation were conferred by the provision on each of those two persons.

(3) Subsection (2) has effect subject to subsection (4).

(4) Chapters 1 and 3 to 6 apply in relation to the provision only if the effect of their applying is—

    (a) that a larger amount is taken for tax purposes to be the amount of the profits of the oil-related ring-fence trade for any chargeable period, or

    (b) that a smaller amount (including nil) is taken for tax purposes to be the amount for any chargeable period of any losses of the oil-related ring-fence trade.

(5) In subsection (4)(a), the reference to a larger amount includes, if there would not otherwise have been profits, an amount of more than nil.

206 Meaning of "oil-related ring-fence trade" in sections 205 and 218

(1) This section has effect for the interpretation of—

    (a) section 205, and

    (b) in Part 5, section 218(2)(f).

(2) Activities carried on by a person are an "oil-related ring-fence trade" carried on by that person if subsection (3) or (4) applies to the activities.

(3) This subsection applies to the activities if—

    (a) they are carried on by the person as part of a trade, and

1014

Taxation (International and Other Provisions) Act 2010 (c. 8)
Part 4 – Transfer pricing
Chapter 7 – Oil-related ring-fence trades

> (b) in accordance with section 16(1) of ITTOIA 2005 or section 279 of CTA 2010 (oil-related activities), they are treated for any tax purposes as a separate trade distinct from all other activities carried on by the person as part of the trade.

(4) This subsection applies to the activities if —

> (a) they are carried on by the person as a trade, and
>
> (b) in accordance with section 16(1) of ITTOIA 2005 or section 279 of CTA 2010 they would, if the person did carry on any other activities as part of the trade, be treated for any tax purposes as a separate trade distinct from all other activities carried on by the person as part of the trade.

CHAPTER 8

SUPPLEMENTARY PROVISIONS AND INTERPRETATION OF PART

Unit trusts

207 Application of Part to unit trusts

(1) This Part has effect as follows.

(2) As if a unit trust scheme were a company that is a body corporate.

(3) As if the rights of the unit holders under a unit trust scheme were shares in the company that the scheme is deemed to be.

(4) As if rights and powers of a person in the capacity of a person entitled to act for the purposes of a unit trust scheme were rights and powers of the scheme.

(5) As if provision made or imposed as between —

> (a) a person in the capacity of a person entitled to act for the purposes of a unit trust scheme, and
>
> (b) another person,

were made or imposed as between the scheme and that other person.

Determinations requiring Commissioners' sanction

208 The determinations which require the Commissioners' sanction

(1) A determination requires the Commissioners' sanction if it —

> (a) is a transfer-pricing determination made for any of the specified purposes, and
>
> (b) is not excepted by section 209 from the requirement for the Commissioners' sanction.

(2) In subsection (1) "transfer-pricing determination" means a determination of an amount to be brought into account for tax purposes in respect of any assumption made under section 147(3) or (5).

(3) For the purposes of subsection (1), each of the following is a specified purpose —

> (a) the giving of a closure notice under section 28A(1) of TMA 1970 in relation to an enquiry into a return under section 8 or 8A of TMA 1970,

Taxation (International and Other Provisions) Act 2010 (c. 8)
Part 4 — Transfer pricing
Chapter 8 — Supplementary provisions and interpretation of Part

1015

    (b)   the giving of a closure notice under section 28B(1) of TMA 1970 in relation to an enquiry into a partnership return,

    (c)   the giving of a closure notice under paragraph 32 of Schedule 18 to FA 1998 in relation to an enquiry into a company tax return,

    (d)   the giving of a notice under section 30B(1) of TMA 1970 amending a partnership return,

    (e)   the making of an assessment under section 29 of TMA 1970,

    (f)   the making of a discovery assessment under paragraph 41 of Schedule 18 to FA 1998 (which includes a discovery assessment under that paragraph as applied by paragraph 52 of that Schedule), and

    (g)   the making of a discovery determination under paragraph 41 of Schedule 18 to FA 1998.

(4)   In this section "the Commissioners" means the Commissioners for Her Majesty's Revenue and Customs.

209 Determinations exempt from requirement for Commissioners' sanction

(1)   A transfer-pricing determination made for a purpose specified in section 208(3) ("the specified purpose") does not require the Commissioners' sanction if —

    (a)   an agreement about the matters to which the determination relates has been made between an officer and the person in whose case the determination is made,

    (b)   the agreement is in force at the relevant time, and

    (c)   the matters to which the agreement relates include the amount determined by the transfer-pricing determination.

(2)   For the purposes of subsection (1)(b) —

    (a)   if the specified purpose is within section 208(3)(a) to (d), "the relevant time" is when the notice is given,

    (b)   if the specified purpose is within section 208(3)(e) or (f), "the relevant time" is when any notice of the assessment is given, and

    (c)   if the specified purpose is within section 208(3)(g), "the relevant time" is when any notice of the discovery determination is given.

(3)   For the purposes of subsection (1)(b), an agreement made between an officer and any person in relation to any matter is "in force" at any time if (and only if) —

    (a)   the agreement is one that has been made or confirmed in writing,

    (b)   that time is after the end of the cooling-off period, and

    (c)   the person has not, before the end of the cooling-off period, served a notice on an officer stating that the person is repudiating or resiling from the agreement.

(4)   In subsection (3) "the cooling-off period" means —

    (a)   if the agreement is made in writing, the 30 days beginning with the day when the agreement is made, and

    (b)   in any other case, the 30 days beginning with the day when the agreement is confirmed in writing.

(5)   For the purposes of subsections (3) and (4), an agreement made between an officer and any person is "confirmed in writing" if an officer serves on the person a notice in writing —

    (a)   stating that the agreement has been made, and

1016   *Taxation (International and Other Provisions) Act 2010 (c. 8)*
Part 4 – Transfer pricing
Chapter 8 – Supplementary provisions and interpretation of Part

(b)   setting out the terms of the agreement.

(6)   In this section—

"the Commissioners" means the Commissioners for Her Majesty's Revenue and Customs,

"officer" means officer of Revenue and Customs, and

"transfer-pricing determination" has the meaning given by section 208(2).

210   The requirement for the Commissioners' sanction

(1)   Subsection (2) applies in relation to a transfer-pricing determination made for a purpose specified in section 208(3)(a) to (d) if, under section 208(1), the determination requires the Commissioners' sanction.

(2)   If the closure notice, or notice under section 30B(1) of TMA 1970, is given to a person—

(a)   without the determination, so far as it is taken into account in the notice, having been approved by the Commissioners, or

(b)   without a copy of the Commissioners' approval having been served on the person at or before the time when the notice is given to the person,

the notice has effect as if given in the terms (if any) in which it would have been given had the determination not been taken into account.

(3)   Subsection (4) applies in relation to a transfer-pricing determination made for a purpose specified in section 208(3)(e) to (g) if, under section 208(1), the transfer-pricing determination requires the Commissioners' sanction.

(4)   If notice of the assessment, or notice of the discovery determination, is given to a person—

(a)   without the transfer-pricing determination, so far as it is taken into account in the assessment or discovery determination, having been approved by the Commissioners, or

(b)   without a copy of the Commissioners' approval having been served on the person at or before the time when the notice is given to the person,

the assessment or discovery determination has effect as if made (and notified) in the terms (if any) in which it would have been made had the transfer-pricing determination not been taken into account.

(5)   For the purposes of subsections (2) and (4), the Commissioners' approval of a transfer-pricing determination requiring their sanction—

(a)   must be given specifically in relation to the case concerned and must apply to the amount determined, but

(b)   subject to that, may be given by the Commissioners (either before or after the determination is made) in any such form or manner as the Commissioners may determine.

(6)   In this section "the Commissioners" means the Commissioners for Her Majesty's Revenue and Customs.

211   Restriction of right to appeal against Commissioners' approval

(1)   In subsection (2)—

"appeal" means an appeal by virtue of any provision of—

(a)   TMA 1970, or

Taxation (International and Other Provisions) Act 2010 (c. 8)   1017
Part 4 — Transfer pricing
Chapter 8 — Supplementary provisions and interpretation of Part

    (b)   Schedule 18 to FA 1998 (company tax returns and related matters), and

"approved determination" means a determination that, for the purposes of section 210(2) or (4), has been approved by the Commissioners.

(2)   The matters that may be questioned on so much of an appeal as relates to an approved determination do not include the Commissioners' approval.

(3)   Subsection (2) does not apply so far as the grounds for questioning the approval are the same as the grounds for questioning the determination.

(4)   In this section "the Commissioners" means the Commissioners for Her Majesty's Revenue and Customs.

Appeals

212   Appeals

(1)   The appeals within this subsection are—
    (a)   an appeal under section 31 of, or Schedule 1A to, TMA 1970,
    (b)   an appeal under paragraph 34(3) of Schedule 18 to FA 1998 against an amendment of a company's return, and
    (c)   an appeal under paragraph 48 of that Schedule against a discovery assessment or a discovery determination.

(2)   Subsection (3) applies so far as the question in dispute on an appeal within subsection (1)—
    (a)   is or involves a determination of whether this Part has effect, and
    (b)   relates to any provision made or imposed as between two persons each of whom is within the charge to income tax or corporation tax in respect of profits arising from the relevant activities (see section 216).

(3)   If this subsection applies—
    (a)   each of the persons as between whom the actual provision was made or imposed is entitled to be a party in any proceedings,
    (b)   the tribunal is to determine the question separately from any other question in the proceedings, and
    (c)   the tribunal's determination on the question has effect as if made in an appeal to which each of those persons was a party.

(4)   In subsection (1)(c)—
"discovery assessment" means a discovery assessment under paragraph 41 of Schedule 18 to FA 1998 (which includes a discovery assessment under that paragraph as applied by paragraph 52 that Schedule), and
"discovery determination" means a discovery determination under paragraph 41 of that Schedule.

Effect of Part on capital allowances and chargeable gains

213   Capital allowances

(1)   Nothing in this Part is to be read as affecting the calculation of the amount of any capital allowance or balancing charge made under CAA 2001.

1018
Taxation (International and Other Provisions) Act 2010 (c. 8)
Part 4 — Transfer pricing
Chapter 8 — Supplementary provisions and interpretation of Part

(2) Subsection (1) does not apply in relation to claims under section 174.

214 Chargeable gains

(1) Nothing in this Part is to be read as affecting the calculation in accordance with TCGA 1992 of the amount of any chargeable gain or allowable loss.

(2) Nothing in this Part requires the profits and losses of any person to be calculated for tax purposes as if, in the person's case, instead of income or losses to be brought into account in connection with the taxation of income, there were gains or losses to be brought into account in accordance with TCGA 1992.

(3) Subsections (1) and (2) do not apply in relation to claims under section 174.

Adjustments

215 Manner of making adjustments to give effect to Part

Any adjustments required to be made under this Part may be made by way of discharge or repayment of tax, by the modification of any assessment or otherwise.

Definitions

216 Meaning of "the relevant activities"

(1) In this Part "the relevant activities", in relation to a person ("A") who is one of the persons as between whom any provision is made or imposed, means activities that—
   (a) are within subsection (2), and
   (b) are not within subsection (3).

(2) The activities within this subsection are those of A's activities that comprise the activities in the course of which, or with respect to which, that provision is made or imposed.

(3) The activities within this subsection are any of A's activities carried on—
   (a) separately from the activities mentioned in subsection (2), or
   (b) for the purposes of a different part of A's business.

217 Meaning of "control" and "firm"

(1) References in this Part to a person controlling a body corporate or firm are to be read in accordance with section 1124 of CTA 2010.

(2) Subsection (1) has effect subject to subsection (4) and section 205(2).

(3) Subsection (4) applies if—
   (a) the actual provision is made or imposed by or in relation to a sale of oil,
   (b) the oil sold is oil which has been, or is to be, extracted under rights exercisable by a company ("the producer") which, although it may be the seller, is not the buyer, and

Taxation (International and Other Provisions) Act 2010 (c. 8)
Part 4 — Transfer pricing
Chapter 8 — Supplementary provisions and interpretation of Part

1019

    (c)   at the time of the completion of the sale or when possession of the oil passes, whichever is the earlier, at least 20% of the producer's ordinary share capital is owned directly or indirectly by one or more of the buyer and the companies (if any) that are linked to the buyer.

(4)   If this subsection applies, this Part has effect in relation to the actual provision as if —

    (a)   the buyer and the seller, and

    (b)   the producer, if it is not the seller,

were all controlled by the same person at the time of the making or imposition of the actual provision.

(5)   For the purposes of subsection (3)(c), two companies are "linked" if —

    (a)   one is under the control of the other, or

    (b)   both are under the control of the same person or persons.

(6)   For the purposes of subsection (3) —

    (a)   any question whether ordinary share capital is owned directly or indirectly by a company is to be decided as for Chapter 3 of Part 24 of CTA 2010, and

    (b)   rights to extract oil are to be taken to be exercisable by a company even if they are exercisable by that company only jointly with another company or two or more other companies.

(7)   In this section "oil" includes any mineral oil or relative hydrocarbon oil, as well as natural gas.

(8)   In this Part persons carrying on a trade, profession or other business in partnership are referred to collectively as a "firm".

PART 5

ADVANCE PRICING AGREEMENTS

218   Meaning of "advance pricing agreement"

(1)   In this Part "advance pricing agreement" means a written agreement that —

    (a)   is made by the Commissioners with any person ("A") as a consequence of an application by A under section 223,

    (b)   relates to one or more of the matters mentioned in subsection (2), and

    (c)   declares that it is an agreement made for the purposes of this section.

(2)   Those matters are —

    (a)   if A is not a company, the attribution of income to a branch or agency through which A has been carrying on a trade in the United Kingdom or is proposing to carry on a trade in the United Kingdom,

    (b)   if A is a company, the attribution of income to a permanent establishment through which A has been carrying on a trade in the United Kingdom or is proposing to carry on a trade in the United Kingdom,

    (c)   the attribution of income to any permanent establishment of A's, wherever situated, through which A has been carrying on, or is proposing to carry on, any business,

(d)   the extent to which income that has arisen or may arise to A is to be taken for any purpose to be income arising in a country or territory outside the United Kingdom,

(e)   the treatment for tax purposes of any provision made or imposed, whether before or after the date of the agreement, as between A and any associate (see section 219) of A's, and

(f)   the treatment for tax purposes of any provision made or imposed, whether before or after the date of the agreement, as between an oil-related ring-fence trade carried on by A (see section 206) and any other activities carried on by A.

219   Meaning of "associate" in section 218(2)(e)

(1)   This section applies for the purposes of section 218(2)(e).

(2)   Two persons are associates in relation to provision made or imposed as between them if at the time of the making or imposition of the provision—

     (a)   one of them is directly or indirectly participating in the management, control or capital of the other, or

     (b)   the same person or persons is or are directly or indirectly participating in the management, control or capital of each of the two persons.

(3)   Two persons are also associates in relation to any provision if section 217(4) (which applies to provision made or imposed in connection with sales of oil) requires the persons to be treated as controlled by the same person at the time of the making or imposition of that provision.

(4)   For the interpretation of subsection (2), see sections 157(1), 158(4), 159(1) and 160(1) (which have the effect that references in subsection (2) to direct or indirect participation are to be read in accordance with provisions of Chapter 2 of Part 4).

220   Effect of agreement on party to it

(1)   Subsection (2) applies if a chargeable period is one to which an advance pricing agreement relates.

(2)   The Tax Acts have effect in relation to the chargeable period as if, in the case of the person with whom the Commissioners made the agreement, questions relating to the matters mentioned in section 218(2) are to be determined—

     (a)   in accordance with the agreement, and

     (b)   without reference to the provisions in accordance with which they would otherwise be determined.

(3)   Subsection (2) is subject to—

     subsections (4) and (5), and

     section 221.

(4)   A question is to be determined as mentioned in subsection (2) only so far as the agreement provides for the question to be determined in that way.

(5)   In the case of so much of a question as—

     (a)   relates to any matter mentioned in paragraph (e) or (f) of section 218(2), and

(b) is not comprised in a question that relates to a matter within another paragraph of section 218(2),

reference to a provision is capable of being excluded under subsection (2) by an advance pricing agreement only if the provision is in Part 4.

221 Effect of revocation of agreement or breach of its conditions

(1) An advance pricing agreement does not have effect in accordance with section 220(2) in relation to any determination of a question if any of conditions A, B and C is met.

(2) Condition A is that a time to which the question relates is after a time as from which an officer has revoked the agreement in accordance with the agreement's terms.

(3) Condition B is that the question relates to a time after, or in relation to which, there has been a failure by a party to the agreement to comply with a significant provision of the agreement.

(4) Condition C is that the question relates to a matter as respects which a key condition has not been met or is no longer met.

(5) A provision of the agreement is "significant" for the purposes of subsection (3) if compliance with that provision is, under the terms of the agreement, to be a condition of the agreement's having effect.

(6) Any other condition that, under the terms of the agreement, is to be a condition of the agreement's having effect is a "key condition" for the purposes of subsection (4).

222 Effect of agreement on non-parties

(1) Subsections (2), (5) and (6) apply if —
    (a) an advance pricing agreement has effect in relation to any provision ("the actual provision") made or imposed as between any person ("A") and another ("B"), and
    (b) section 220(2) has the effect in A's case of requiring a question relating to the actual provision to be determined in accordance with the agreement rather than by reference to rules which would otherwise be applicable because of Part 4.

(2) The provisions mentioned in subsection (3) have effect in B's case on the assumption that any question within subsection (4) is to be determined, to the same extent as in A's case, by reference to the agreement.

(3) The provisions are —
    sections 174 to 178 (transfer pricing: claim by disadvantaged person), and
    sections 188 and 189 (transfer pricing: adjustment of double taxation relief if claim made).

(4) The questions are —
    (a) whether A is a person on whom a potential advantage in relation to United Kingdom taxation is conferred by the actual provision, and
    (b) what constitutes the arm's length provision in relation to the actual provision.

(5) Subsection (2) has effect subject to any advance pricing agreement made between the Commissioners and B.

(6) Any assumptions to be made because of the agreement are "advance-pricing-agreement assumptions" for the purposes of paragraph (b) of the definition in section 185(5) of "transfer-pricing determination".

223 Application for agreement

(1) For the purposes of section 218(1)(a), an application by a person ("A") is an application under this section if it complies with subsections (2) to (5).

(2) It must be an application to the Commissioners for the clarification by agreement of the effect in A's case of provisions by reference to which questions relating to any one or more of the matters mentioned in section 218(2) are to be, or might be, determined.

(3) It must set out A's understanding of what would in A's case be the effect, in the absence of any agreement, of the provisions in relation to which clarification is sought.

(4) It must set out the respects in which it appears to A that clarification is required in relation to those provisions.

(5) It must set out how A proposes that matters should be clarified in a manner consistent with the understanding mentioned in subsection (3).

224 Provision in agreement about years ended or begun before agreement made

(1) An advance pricing agreement may contain provision relating to chargeable periods ending before the agreement is made, subject to subsection (2).

(2) An advance pricing agreement may not contain provision relating to chargeable periods ending before 27 July 1999.

(3) If an advance pricing agreement—
   (a) relates to a chargeable period beginning or ending before the agreement is made, and
   (b) provides for the manner in which adjustments are to be made for tax purposes in consequence of the agreement,
   the adjustments are to be made for those purposes in the manner provided for in the agreement.

225 Modification and revocation of agreement

(1) Subsection (2) applies if an advance pricing agreement provides for the modification, or revocation, of the agreement—
   (a) by the Commissioners, or
   (b) by an officer.

(2) The agreement may provide for the modification or revocation to take effect as from such time as the Commissioners or officer may determine.

(3) A time determined under subsection (2) may be (but need not be) a time before the modification is made or the agreement is revoked.

226 Annulment of agreement for misrepresentation

(1) Subsection (6) applies if each of conditions A to D is met.

(2) Condition A is that the Commissioners and any person ("A") have at any time purported to enter into an advance pricing agreement.

(3) Condition B is that, before that time, A fraudulently or negligently provided the Commissioners with information which was false or misleading.

(4) Condition C is that the information was so provided —
    (a) for or in connection with the application to the Commissioners for the making of the agreement, or
    (b) otherwise in connection with the preparation of the agreement.

(5) Condition D is that the Commissioners have notified A that the agreement is nullified by reason of the misrepresentation.

(6) The agreement is to be treated as never made.

227 Penalty for misrepresentation in connection with agreement

A person is liable to a penalty of not more than £10,000 if the person fraudulently or negligently makes a false or misleading statement to the Commissioners or an officer —
    (a) for or in connection with any application to the Commissioners for them to enter into an advance pricing agreement, or
    (b) otherwise in connection with the preparation of an advance pricing agreement.

228 Party to agreement: duty to provide information

A party to an advance pricing agreement must provide the Commissioners from time to time with all reports and other information that the party may be required to provide —
    (a) under the agreement, or
    (b) as a result of a request made by an officer in accordance with the agreement.

229 Modifications of agreement for double taxation purposes

(1) Subsection (2) applies if a mutual agreement made under and for the purposes of any double taxation arrangements is not consistent with the terms of an advance pricing agreement.

(2) The Commissioners must ensure that the advance pricing agreement is modified so far as may be necessary for enabling effect to be given to the mutual agreement in relation to the subject-matter of the advance pricing agreement.

(3) The Commissioners may comply with subsection (2) by exercising powers conferred on them by the advance pricing agreement or otherwise.

(4) In this section "double taxation arrangements" means arrangements that have effect under section 2(1) (double taxation relief by agreement with territories outside the United Kingdom).

230   Interpretation of Part: meaning of "Commissioners" and "officer"

In this Part—

"the Commissioners" means the Commissioners for Her Majesty's Revenue and Customs, and

"officer" means an officer of Revenue and Customs.

PART 6

TAX ARBITRAGE

Introduction

231   Overview

(1)   This Part provides for the service on companies of two kinds of notice, as a result of which they must calculate or recalculate their income or chargeable gains or liability to corporation tax less advantageously.

(2)   Sections 232 to 248 deal with the first kind of notice ("deduction notices").

(3)   In particular—
    (a)   see sections 232 to 235 for provisions about the service of deduction notices,
    (b)   see sections 236 to 242 for the kinds of schemes ("deduction schemes") involved, and
    (c)   see sections 243 to 248 for the consequences of such notices.

(4)   Sections 249 to 254 deal with the second kind of notice ("receipt notices").

(5)   In particular—
    (a)   see sections 249 to 253 for provisions about the service of receipt notices, and
    (b)   see section 254 for their consequences.

(6)   Sections 255 to 257 contain general provisions about both kinds of notice.

(7)   For the meaning of "scheme" etc, see section 258 (schemes and series of transactions).

Deduction notices

232   Deduction notices

(1)   An officer of Revenue and Customs may give a company a notice under this section if—
    (a)   the company is within the charge to corporation tax, and
    (b)   the officer considers on reasonable grounds that each of the deduction scheme conditions is or may be met in relation to a transaction to which the company is party.

(2)   In this Part—
    (a)   a notice under this section is referred to as a "deduction notice", and
    (b)   "the deduction scheme conditions" means the conditions specified in section 233.

(3)   For the consequences of a deduction notice, see section 243.

233   The deduction scheme conditions

(1)   This section sets out the deduction scheme conditions.

(2)   Deduction scheme condition A is that the transaction to which the company is party forms part of a scheme that is a deduction scheme for the purposes of this Part (see sections 236 to 242).

(3)   Deduction scheme condition B is that the scheme is such that for corporation tax purposes the company —
   (a)   is in a position to claim, or has claimed, an amount by way of deduction in respect of the transaction, or
   (b)   is in a position to set off, or has set off, an amount relating to the transaction against profits in an accounting period.

(4)   Deduction scheme condition C is that the main purpose of the scheme, or one of its main purposes, is to achieve a UK tax advantage for the company.

(5)   Deduction scheme condition D is that the amount of the UK tax advantage is more than minimal.

234   Schemes achieving UK tax advantage for a company

(1)   For the purposes of section 233, a scheme achieves a UK tax advantage for a company if, in consequence of the scheme, the company is in a position to obtain, or has obtained —
   (a)   a relief or increased relief from corporation tax,
   (b)   a repayment or increased repayment of corporation tax, or
   (c)   the avoidance or reduction of a charge to corporation tax.

(2)   In subsection (1)(a) "relief from corporation tax" includes a tax credit under section 1109 of CTA 2010 (tax credits for certain recipients of qualifying distributions) for the purposes of corporation tax.

(3)   For the purposes of subsection (1)(c) avoidance or reduction may, in particular, be effected —
   (a)   by receipts accruing in such a way that the recipient does not pay or bear tax on them, or
   (b)   by a deduction in calculating profits or gains.

235   Further provisions about deduction notices

(1)   A deduction notice must specify the transaction in relation to which the officer of Revenue and Customs considers that each of the deduction scheme conditions is or may be met.

(2)   A deduction notice must specify the accounting period in relation to which the officer considers that deduction scheme condition B is or may be met in relation to the transaction.

(3)   A deduction notice must inform the company to which it is given that, as a result of the service of the notice, section 243(2) to (6) (consequences of a deduction notice) will apply if each of the deduction scheme conditions is met in relation to the transaction.

(4)   A deduction notice may relate to two or more transactions.

Deduction schemes

236   Schemes involving hybrid entities

(1)   A scheme is a deduction scheme if a party to a transaction forming part of the scheme meets conditions A and B.

(2)   Condition A is that the party is regarded as being a person under the tax law of any territory.

(3)   Condition B is that the party's profits or gains are treated, for the purposes of a relevant tax imposed under the law of any territory, as the profits or gains of a person or persons other than the person mentioned in condition A.

(4)   Condition B is not met just because the party's profits or gains are subject to a rule that—

    (a)   is similar to that in section 747(3) of ICTA (imputation of chargeable profits of controlled foreign company), and

    (b)   has effect under the tax law of any territory outside the United Kingdom.

(5)   For the purposes of this section, the following are relevant taxes—

    (a)   income tax,

    (b)   corporation tax, and

    (c)   any tax of a similar character to income tax or corporation tax that is imposed by the law of a territory outside the United Kingdom.

237   Instruments of alterable character

(1)   A scheme is a deduction scheme if one of the parties to the scheme is party to an instrument within subsection (2).

(2)   An instrument is within this subsection if under the law of a particular territory any party to the instrument may alter its tax characteristics.

(3)   The reference to altering an instrument's tax characteristics is to making an alteration which, under the law of a particular territory, has the effect of determining, for the tax purposes of that territory, whether the instrument is taken into account as giving rise—

    (a)   to income,

    (b)   to capital, or

    (c)   to neither.

(4)   An instrument is taken into account as giving rise to capital if any gain on the disposal of the instrument—

    (a)   would be a chargeable gain, or

    (b)   would be such a gain if the person making the disposal were UK resident.

238   Shares subject to conversion

(1)   A scheme is a deduction scheme if it includes—

    (a)   a company issuing shares subject to conversion, or

(b)   such an amendment of rights attaching to shares issued by a company that the shares become shares subject to conversion.

(2)   For the purposes of subsection (1)(a) a company's shares are shares subject to conversion if conditions A and B are met.

(3)   For the purposes of subsection (1)(b) a company's shares are shares subject to conversion if conditions A and C are met.

(4)   Condition A is that the rights attached to the shares include provision as a result of which a holder of such shares is entitled, on the occurrence of an event, to acquire securities in a company by conversion or exchange.

(5)   Condition B is that at the time when the shares are issued the company could reasonably expect that event to occur.

(6)   Condition C is that at the time when the rights attaching to the shares are amended as described in subsection (1)(b) the company could reasonably expect that event to occur.

239   Securities subject to conversion

(1)   A scheme is a deduction scheme if it includes—
    (a)   a company issuing securities subject to conversion, or
    (b)   such an amendment of rights attaching to securities issued by a company that the securities become securities subject to conversion.

(2)   For the purposes of subsection (1)(a) a company's securities are securities subject to conversion if conditions A and B are met.

(3)   For the purposes of subsection (1)(b) a company's securities are securities subject to conversion if conditions A and C are met.

(4)   Condition A is that the rights attached to the securities include provision as a result of which a holder of such securities is entitled, on the occurrence of an event, to acquire shares in a company by conversion or exchange.

(5)   Condition B is that at the time when the securities are issued the company could reasonably expect that event to occur.

(6)   Condition C is that at the time when the rights attaching to the securities are amended as described in subsection (1)(b) the company could reasonably expect that event to occur.

240   Debt instruments treated as equity

(1)   A scheme is a deduction scheme if it includes a debt instrument issued by a company that is treated as equity in the company under generally accepted accounting practice.

(2)   In this section "debt instrument" means an instrument issued by a company that—
    (a)   represents a loan relationship of the company, or
    (b)   would do so if the company were UK resident.

241   Scheme including issue of shares not conferring qualifying beneficial entitlement

(1)   A scheme is a deduction scheme if −

     (a)   it includes a company issuing shares to a connected person, and

     (b)   the shares do not meet conditions A, B and C.

(2)   Condition A is that on their issue the shares are ordinary shares that are fully paid-up.

(3)   Condition B is that when the issue takes place there is no arrangement or understanding under which the rights attaching to the shares may be amended.

(4)   Condition C is that, at all times in the accounting period of the company in which the issue takes place, each of the shares confers a beneficial entitlement to the appropriate proportion of −

     (a)   any profits available for distribution to equity holders of the company, and

     (b)   any assets of the company available for distribution to its equity holders on a winding-up.

(5)   For the purposes of subsection (4) the appropriate proportion, in relation to a share, is the same as the proportion of the issued share capital represented by that share.

(6)   Chapter 6 of Part 5 of CTA 2010 (equity holders and profits or assets available for distribution) applies for the purposes of subsection (4) as it applies for the purposes of the provisions specified in section 157(1) of that Act.

242   Scheme including transfer of rights under a security

(1)   A scheme is a deduction scheme if each of conditions A to D is met.

(2)   Condition A is that the scheme includes a transaction or a series of transactions under which a person ("the transferor") −

     (a)   transfers to one or more other persons rights to receive a payment under a security, or

     (b)   otherwise secures that one or more other persons are similarly benefited.

(3)   A person is similarly benefited for these purposes if the person receives a payment which, but for the transaction or series of transactions, would have arisen to the transferor.

(4)   Condition B is that −

     (a)   the transferor, and

     (b)   at least one of the persons to whom a transfer of rights is made or a similar benefit is secured,

are connected with each other.

(5)   Condition C is that, immediately after the transfer of rights or the securing of the similar benefit, two or more persons −

     (a)   hold rights to receive a payment under the security, or

     (b)   enjoy a similar benefit.

(6) Condition D is that, immediately after the transfer of rights or the securing of the similar benefit, the market value of all the relevant benefits of such of those persons as are connected equals or exceeds the market value of all other relevant benefits.

(7) In subsection (6) "relevant benefits" means —
  (a) rights to receive a payment under the security, and
  (b) similar benefits.

(8) In this section "security" includes an agreement under which a person receives an annuity or other annual payment (whether it is payable annually or at shorter or longer intervals) for a term which is not contingent on the duration of a human life or lives.

Consequences of deduction notices

243   Consequences of deduction notices

(1) This section applies in relation to a transaction if —
  (a) a deduction notice specifying the transaction is given to a company under section 232, and
  (b) when the notice is given, each of the deduction scheme conditions is met in relation to the transaction.

(2) The company must calculate (or recalculate) its income or chargeable gains for the purposes of corporation tax, or its liability to corporation tax, for —
  (a) the accounting period specified in the deduction notice, and
  (b) any later accounting period.

(3) That calculation (or recalculation) must be done in accordance with —
  (a) the rule in section 244 (the rule against double deduction), and
  (b) the rule in section 248 (the rule against deduction for untaxable payments) if it applies (see section 245).

(4) But the company is treated as having complied with subsections (2) and (3), so far as the scheme specified in the deduction notice is concerned, if the company incorporates the necessary relevant adjustments in its company tax return for the accounting period specified in the notice.

(5) For the purposes of subsection (4), adjustments are relevant if they —
  (a) treat all or part of a deduction allowable for corporation tax purposes as not being allowable, or
  (b) treat all or part of an amount that for corporation tax purposes may be set off against profits in an accounting period as not falling to be set off.

(6) For the purposes of subsection (4), relevant adjustments are the necessary adjustments if —
  (a) they are such adjustments as are necessary for counteracting those effects of the scheme that are referable to the purpose referred to in deduction scheme condition C (see section 233(4)), and
  (b) as a result of their incorporation in the return, the company counteracts those effects.

244   The rule against double deduction

(1)   The rule referred to in section 243(3)(a) is that, in respect of the transaction specified in the deduction notice, no amount is allowable as a deduction for the purposes of the Corporation Tax Acts so far as an amount is otherwise deductible or allowable in relation to the expense in question.

(2)   An amount is otherwise deductible or allowable if it may be otherwise deducted or allowed in calculating the income, profits or losses of any person for the purposes of any tax to which this subsection applies.

(3)   Subsection (2) applies to any tax (including any non-UK tax) other than—

     (a)   petroleum revenue tax, or

     (b)   the tax chargeable under section 330(1) of CTA 2010 (supplementary charge in respect of ring fence trades).

(4)   The reference in subsection (2) to an amount being able to be otherwise deducted or allowed as mentioned in that subsection includes a reference to an amount that would be able to be so deducted or allowed but for any tax rule that has the same effect as the rule in subsection (1).

(5)   In subsection (4) "tax rule" means—

     (a)   a provision of the Tax Acts, or

     (b)   a rule having effect under the tax law of any territory outside the United Kingdom.

(6)   In this section "non-UK tax" has the meaning given in section 187 of CTA 2010.

245   Application of the rule against deduction for untaxable payments

(1)   Section 248 (the rule against deduction for untaxable payments) applies if conditions A, B and C are met.

(2)   Condition A is that a transaction that forms part of the deduction scheme, or a series of transactions that forms part of the scheme, makes or imposes provision as a result of which—

     (a)   one person ("the payer") makes a payment, and

     (b)   another person ("the payee") receives, or becomes entitled to receive, a payment or payments.

(3)   Condition B is that, in respect of the payment by the payer, an amount may be deducted by, or otherwise allowed to—

     (a)   the payer, or

     (b)   another person who is party to, or concerned in, the scheme,

in calculating any profits or losses for tax purposes.

(4)   Condition C is that as a result of provision made or imposed by the deduction scheme—

     (a)   the payee is not liable to tax—

         (i)   in respect of the payment or payments that the payee receives or is entitled to receive as a result of the transaction or series of transactions, or

         (ii)   in respect of part of such payment or payments, or

     (b)   if the payee is so liable, the payee's liability to tax is reduced.

(5)   In this section—

      (a)   "the deduction scheme" means the scheme in relation to which the deduction scheme conditions are met, and

      (b)   "tax purposes" includes the purposes of any non-UK tax (within the meaning of section 187 of CTA 2010).

(6)   Sections 246 and 247 make further provision about condition C.

(7)   Expressions used in those sections or section 248 have the same meaning as in this section.

246 Cases where payee's non-liability treated as not a result of scheme

(1)   This section sets out two cases in which condition C in section 245(4) (which requires that as a result of the deduction scheme the payee is not liable to tax in respect of the whole or part of certain payments) is treated as not met.

(2)   The first case is where the reason why the payee is not liable to tax is that under the tax law of any territory the payee is not liable to tax on any income or gains received by the payee or received for the payee's benefit.

(3)   The second case is where, or to the extent that, the payee is not subject to tax because an exemption within subsection (4) applies.

(4)   An exemption is within this subsection if —

      (a)   it exempts a person from being liable to tax in respect of income or gains, without providing for that income or those gains to be treated as the income or gains of another person, and

      (b)   it is conferred by a provision contained in, or having the force of, an Act or by a provision of the tax law of any territory outside the United Kingdom.

247 Cases where payee treated as having reduced liability as a result of scheme

(1)   This section sets out two cases in which the payee's liability to tax in respect of the scheme payment is treated for the purposes of section 245(4)(b) as reduced as a result of provision made or imposed by the deduction scheme.

(2)   But that does not mean that there are no other cases in which that liability is so reduced.

(3)   In this section "the scheme payment" means the payment or payments that the payee receives or is entitled to receive as a result of the transaction or series of transactions referred to in section 245(2).

(4)   Case A is that an amount arising from —

      (a)   a transaction forming part of the scheme, or

      (b)   a series of such transactions,

falls to be deducted by, or otherwise allowed to, the payee in calculating for tax purposes any profits or losses arising from the scheme payment or the entitlement to receive it.

(5)   Case B is that an amount of relief arising from —

      (a)   a transaction forming part of the scheme, or

      (b)   a series of such transactions,

may be deducted from the amount of income or gains arising from the scheme payment or the entitlement to receive it.

248 The rule against deduction for untaxable payments

(1) The rule referred to in section 243(3)(b) is that the total deduction amount must be reduced.

(2) In this section "the total deduction amount" means the total of the amounts allowable as a deduction for the purposes of the Corporation Tax Acts in calculating any profits arising to the company from any transaction forming part of the deduction scheme.

(3) If the payee is not liable to tax for the purposes of section 245(4) in respect of the payment or payments that the payee receives or is entitled to receive, the total deduction amount must be reduced to nil.

(4) If the payee is liable to tax for those purposes in respect of part of that payment or those payments, the total deduction amount must be reduced by the same proportion of that amount as the proportion of the payment or payments on which the payee is not liable to tax.

(5) If the payee's liability to tax is reduced as described in section 245(4)(b), the total deduction amount must be reduced by the same proportion of that amount as the reduction in the payee's liability bears to that liability before reduction.

Receipt notices

249 Receipt notices

(1) An officer of Revenue and Customs may give a company a notice under this section if —
    (a) the company is UK resident, and
    (b) the officer considers on reasonable grounds that each of the receipt scheme conditions is or may be met in relation to the company.

(2) In this Part—
    (a) a notice under this section is referred to as a "receipt notice", and
    (b) "the receipt scheme conditions" means the conditions specified in section 250.

(3) For the consequences of a receipt notice, see section 254.

250 The receipt scheme conditions

(1) This section sets out the receipt scheme conditions.

(2) Receipt scheme condition A is that a scheme makes or imposes provision as between the company and another person ("the paying party") by means of a transaction or series of transactions.

(3) Receipt scheme condition B is that that provision includes the paying party making, by means of a transaction or series of transactions, a payment—
    (a) which is a qualifying payment in relation to the company, and
    (b) at least part of which is not an amount to which section 251 (amounts within corporation tax) applies.

(4)   A payment is a qualifying payment in relation to a company for the purposes of this section and sections 251 to 254 if it constitutes a contribution to the capital of the company.

(5)   Receipt scheme condition C is that on entering into the scheme the company and the paying party expected that a benefit would arise because at least part of the qualifying payment was not an amount to which section 251 applies.

(6)   Receipt scheme condition D is that there is an amount in relation to the qualifying payment that—

    (a)   is a deductible amount, and

    (b)   is not set against any scheme income arising to the paying party for income tax purposes or corporation tax purposes.

(7)   In subsection (6)—

    "deductible amount" means an amount that—

        (a)   is available as a deduction for the purposes of the Tax Acts, or

        (b)   may be deducted or otherwise allowed under the tax law of any territory outside the United Kingdom, and

    "scheme income" means income arising from the transaction or transactions forming part of the scheme.

(8)   Section 253 (exception for dealers) specifies a case where receipt scheme condition D is treated as not met.

251   Amounts within corporation tax

(1)   This section applies to an amount if it falls within subsection (2) or (4).

(2)   An amount is within this subsection if for the purposes of the Corporation Tax Acts it is—

    (a)   income or chargeable gains arising to the company in the accounting period in which the qualifying payment was made, or

    (b)   income arising to any other UK resident company in a corresponding accounting period.

(3)   For the purposes of this section, the accounting period of one company ("the first period") corresponds to the accounting period of another company ("the second period") if at least one day of the first period falls within the second period.

(4)   An amount is within this subsection if it is brought into account as a result of Chapter 2A or 6A of Part 6 of CTA 2009 (relationships treated as loan relationships: disguised interest, and shares accounted for as liabilities).

252   Further provisions about receipt notices

(1)   A receipt notice must inform the company to which it is given that the officer of Revenue and Customs giving it considers that each of the receipt scheme conditions is or may be met in relation to the company.

(2)   A receipt notice must specify the qualifying payment by reference to which the officer of Revenue and Customs considers receipt scheme conditions B, C and D are or may be met.

(3) A receipt notice must specify the accounting period of the company in which the qualifying payment is made.

(4) A receipt notice must inform the company that, as a result of the service of the notice, section 254(2) (rule for calculation or recalculation of income etc following receipt notice) will apply in relation to the payment if each of the receipt scheme conditions is met in relation to the company.

253 Exception for dealers

(1) Receipt scheme condition D (see section 250(6)) is treated as not met if—
   (a) the paying party ("P") is a dealer,
   (b) in the ordinary course of P's business, P incurs losses in respect of the transaction or transactions forming part of the scheme to which P is party, and
   (c) the amount by reference to which that condition would be met, but for this section, is an amount in respect of those losses.

(2) In subsection (1) "dealer" means a person who—
   (a) is charged to corporation tax under Part 3 of CTA 2009 (trading income) in respect of distributions of companies that are received in the course of a trade not consisting of insurance business, or
   (b) would be so charged if UK resident.

(3) In this section "the paying party" has the same meaning as in section 250.

254 Rule for calculation or recalculation of income etc following receipt notice

(1) This section applies in relation to a qualifying payment if—
   (a) a receipt notice specifying the payment is given to the company in relation to which it is a qualifying payment, and
   (b) when the notice is given, each of the receipt scheme conditions is met in relation to the company.

(2) The company must calculate (or recalculate)—
   (a) its income or chargeable gains for the purposes of corporation tax for the accounting period specified in the notice, or
   (b) its liability to corporation tax for that period,
   as if so much of the qualifying payment as falls within subsection (3) were a receipt of the company that is chargeable for that period under the charge to corporation tax on income.

(3) The qualifying payment falls within this subsection so far as—
   (a) receipt scheme condition D (see section 250(6)) is met in relation to it, and
   (b) it is not an amount to which section 251 (amounts within corporation tax) applies.

General provisions about deduction notices and receipt notices

255   Notices given before tax return made

(1)   This section applies if an officer of Revenue and Customs gives a company a deduction notice or a receipt notice before the company has made its company tax return for the accounting period specified in the notice.

(2)   If the company makes that return before the end of the period of 90 days beginning with the day on which the notice is given, it may —

    (a)   make a return that disregards the notice, and

    (b)   at any time after making the return and before the end of that 90 day period, amend the return for the purpose of complying with the provision referred to in the notice.

(3)   Subsection (2)(b) does not prevent a company tax return for a period becoming incorrect if —

    (a)   a deduction notice or a receipt notice is given to the company in relation to that period,

    (b)   the return is not amended in accordance with subsection (2)(b) for the purpose of complying with the provision referred to in the notice, and

    (c)   it ought to have been so amended.

256   Notices given after tax return made

(1)   If a company has made a company tax return for an accounting period, an officer of Revenue and Customs may only give the company a deduction notice or a receipt notice if a notice of enquiry has been given to the company in respect of the return.

(2)   After any enquiries into the return have been completed, an officer of Revenue and Customs may only give the company a deduction notice or a receipt notice if conditions A and B are met.

(3)   Condition A is that the officer could not have been reasonably expected to have been aware that the circumstances were such that a deduction notice or a receipt notice could have been given to the company in relation to the period.

(4)   Whether condition A is met must be determined on the basis of information made available to the Commissioners for Her Majesty's Revenue and Customs or an officer of Revenue and Customs before the time the enquiries into the return were completed.

(5)   Paragraph 44(2) and (3) of Schedule 18 to FA 1998 (information made available) applies for the purposes of subsection (4) as it applies for the purposes of paragraph 44(1) of that Schedule.

(6)   Condition B is that —

    (a)   the company was requested to provide information during an enquiry into the return, and

    (b)   if the company had duly complied with the request, an officer of Revenue and Customs could reasonably have been expected to give the company a deduction notice or a receipt notice in relation to the period.

257   Amendments, closure notices and discovery assessments where section 256 applies

(1)   Subsection (2) applies if, after having made a company tax return for an accounting period, a company is given a deduction notice or a receipt notice in relation to the period ("the Part 6 notice").

(2)   The company may amend the return for the purpose of complying with the provision referred to in the Part 6 notice at any time before the end of the period of 90 days beginning with the day on which the Part 6 notice is given ("the 90 day period").

(3)   Subsection (4) applies if the Part 6 notice is given to the company after it has been given a notice of enquiry in respect of the return.

(4)   No closure notice may be given in relation to the return until—

    (a)   the end of the 90 day period, or

    (b)   the earlier amendment of the return for the purpose of complying with the provision referred to in the Part 6 notice.

(5)   Subsection (6) applies if the Part 6 notice is given to the company after any enquiries into the return are completed.

(6)   No discovery assessment may be made in respect of the income or chargeable gain to which the Part 6 notice relates until—

    (a)   the end of the 90 day period, or

    (b)   the earlier amendment of the return for the purpose of complying with the provision referred to in the Part 6 notice.

(7)   Subsection (2) does not prevent a return for an accounting period becoming incorrect if—

    (a)   a deduction notice or receipt notice is given to the company in relation to the period,

    (b)   the return is not amended in accordance with subsection (2) for the purpose of complying with the provision referred to in the notice, and

    (c)   it ought to have been so amended.

Interpretation

258   Schemes and series of transactions

(1)   In this Part "scheme" means any scheme, arrangements or understanding of any kind whatever, whether or not legally enforceable, involving one or more transactions.

(2)   In determining whether any transactions have formed or will form part of a series of transactions or scheme for the purposes of this Part, it does not matter if the parties to one of the transactions are different from the parties to another of the transactions.

(3)   For the purposes of this Part, the cases in which any two or more transactions form, or form part of, a series of transactions or scheme include the cases where subsection (4) or (5) applies.

(4)   This subsection applies if it would be reasonable to assume that one or more of the transactions would not have been entered into independently of the other or others.

(5) This subsection applies if it would be reasonable to assume that one or more of the transactions would not have taken the same form or been on the same terms if entered into independently of the other or others.

259   Minor definitions

(1) In this Part—

"closure notice" means a notice under paragraph 32 of Schedule 18 to FA 1998,

"company tax return" means the return required to be delivered pursuant to a notice under paragraph 3 of that Schedule, as read with paragraph 4 of that Schedule,

"discovery assessment" means an assessment under paragraph 41 of that Schedule,

"notice of enquiry" means a notice under paragraph 24 of that Schedule, and

"security" has the meaning given in section 1117(1) of CTA 2010, but subject to section 242(8) of this Act.

(2) Section 1122 of CTA 2010 (meaning of "connected") applies for the purposes of this Part.

PART 7

TAX TREATMENT OF FINANCING COSTS AND INCOME

CHAPTER 1

INTRODUCTION

260   Introduction

(1) Chapter 2 contains provision for determining whether this Part applies in relation to any particular period of account of the worldwide group.

(2) Chapter 3 provides for the disallowance of certain financing expenses of relevant group companies arising in a period of account of the worldwide group to which this Part applies.

The total of the amounts disallowed is the amount by which the tested expense amount (defined in Chapter 8) exceeds the available amount (defined in Chapter 9).

(3) Chapter 4 provides for the exemption from the charge to corporation tax of certain financing income of UK group companies where financing expenses of relevant group companies have been disallowed under Chapter 3.

(4) Chapter 5 provides for the exemption from the charge to corporation tax of certain intra-group financing income of UK group companies where the paying company is denied a deduction for tax purposes otherwise than under this Part.

(5) Chapter 6 contains rules connected with tax avoidance.

(6) Chapter 7 defines a "financing expense amount" and "financing income amount" of a company for a period of account of the worldwide group, which

1038
Taxation (International and Other Provisions) Act 2010 (c. 8)
Part 7 – Tax treatment of financing costs and income
Chapter 1 – Introduction

are amounts that would, apart from this Part, be brought into account for the purposes of corporation tax.

(7) Chapter 8 defines the "tested expense amount" and the "tested income amount" of the worldwide group for a period of account of the group, which are totals deriving from the financing expense amounts and financing income amounts of certain group companies.

(8) Chapter 9 defines the "available amount" for a period of account of the worldwide group, which derives from certain financing costs disclosed in the group's consolidated financial statements.

(9) Chapter 10 contains further interpretative provisions.

CHAPTER 2

APPLICATION OF PART

261 Application of Part

(1) This Part applies to any period of account of the worldwide group for which—
   (a) the UK net debt of the group (see sections 262 and 263), exceeds
   (b) 75% of the worldwide gross debt of the group (see section 264).

(2) But a period of account that is within subsection (1) is not a period of account to which this Part applies if the worldwide group is a qualifying financial services group in that period (see section 266).

(3) The Treasury may by order amend subsection (1)(b) by substituting a higher or lower percentage for the percentage for the time being specified there.

(4) An order under subsection (3) may only be made if a draft of the statutory instrument containing the order has been laid before and approved by a resolution of the House of Commons.

(5) An order under subsection (3) may only have effect in relation to periods of account of the worldwide group beginning after the date on which the order is made.

262 UK net debt of worldwide group for period of account of worldwide group

(1) The reference in section 261 to the "UK net debt" of the worldwide group for a period of account of the group is to the sum of the net debt amounts of each company that was a relevant group company at any time during the period.

(2) In this section "net debt amount", in relation to a company, means the average of—
   (a) the net debt of the company as at that company's start date, and
   (b) the net debt of the company as at that company's end date.
   For the meaning of "net debt", see section 263.

(3) If the amount determined in accordance with subsection (2) is less than £3 million, the net debt amount of the company is nil.

(4) If a company is dormant (within the meaning given by section 1169 of the Companies Act 2006) at all times in the period beginning with that company's

Taxation (International and Other Provisions) Act 2010 (c. 8)
Part 7 – Tax treatment of financing costs and income
Chapter 2 – Application of Part

1039

start date and ending with that company's end date, the net debt amount of the company is nil.

(5) The Treasury may by order amend subsection (3) by substituting a higher or lower amount for the amount for the time being specified there.

(6) An order under subsection (5) may only be made if a draft of the statutory instrument containing the order has been laid before and approved by a resolution of the House of Commons.

(7) An order under subsection (5) may only have effect in relation to periods of account of the worldwide group beginning after the date on which the order is made.

(8) In this Chapter—

    (a) "the start date" of a company means the first day of the period of account of the worldwide group or, if later, the first day in the period on which the company was a relevant group company, and

    (b) "the end date" of a company means the last day of the period of account of the worldwide group or, if earlier, the last day in the period on which the company was a relevant group company.

263   Net debt of a company

(1) References in section 262 to the "net debt" of a company as at any date are to—

    (a) the sum of the company's relevant liabilities as at that date, less

    (b) the sum of the company's relevant assets as at that date.

(2) The amount determined in accordance with subsection (1) may be a negative amount.

(3) For the purposes of this section, a company's "relevant liabilities" as at any date are the amounts that are disclosed in the balance sheet of the company as at that date in respect of—

    (a) amounts borrowed (whether by way of overdraft or other short term or long term borrowing),

    (b) liabilities in respect of finance leases, or

    (c) amounts of such other description as may be specified in regulations made by the Commissioners.

(4) For the purposes of this section, a company's "relevant assets" as at any date are the amounts that are disclosed in the balance sheet of the company as at that date in respect of—

    (a) cash and cash equivalents,

    (b) amounts loaned (whether by way of overdraft or other short term or long term loan),

    (c) net investments, or net cash investments, in finance leases,

    (d) securities of Her Majesty's government or of the government of any other country or territory, or

    (e) amounts of such other description as may be specified in regulations made by the Commissioners.

(5) Expressions used in subsections (3)(a) and (b) and (4)(a) to (c) have the meaning for the time being given by generally accepted accounting practice.

1040
Taxation (International and Other Provisions) Act 2010 (c. 8)
Part 7 — Tax treatment of financing costs and income
Chapter 2 — Application of Part

264 Worldwide gross debt of worldwide group for period of account of the group

(1) The reference in section 261 to the "worldwide gross debt" of the worldwide group for a period of account of the group is to the average of—

    (a) the sum of the relevant liabilities of the group as at the day before the first day of the period, and

    (b) the sum of the relevant liabilities of the group as at the last day of the period.

(2) For the purposes of this section, the "relevant liabilities" of the worldwide group as at any date are the amounts that are disclosed in the balance sheet of the group as at that date in respect of—

    (a) amounts borrowed (whether by way of overdraft or other short term or long term borrowing),

    (b) liabilities in respect of finance leases, or

    (c) amounts of such other description as may be specified in regulations made by the Commissioners.

(3) Expressions used in subsection (2)(a) and (b) have the meaning for the time being given by the accounting standards in accordance with which the financial statements of the group are drawn up.

(4) For provision about references in this Part to financial statements of the worldwide group, and amounts disclosed in financial statements, see sections 346 to 349.

265 References to amounts disclosed in balance sheet of relevant group company

(1) This section applies for the purpose of construing references in section 263 to amounts disclosed in the balance sheet of a relevant group company as at any date ("the relevant date").

(2) If the company—

    (a) is not a foreign company, and

    (b) does not draw up a balance sheet as at the relevant date,

the references are to the amounts that would be disclosed in a balance sheet of the company as at that date, were one drawn up in accordance with generally accepted accounting practice.

(3) If the company—

    (a) is a foreign company, and

    (b) draws up a balance sheet ("a UK permanent establishment balance sheet") as at the relevant date in respect of the company's permanent establishment in the United Kingdom that treats the establishment as a distinct and separate enterprise,

the references are to amounts in that balance sheet.

(4) If the company—

    (a) is a foreign company, and

    (b) does not draw up a UK permanent establishment balance sheet as at the relevant date,

the references are to the amounts that would be disclosed in a UK permanent establishment balance sheet as at that date, were one drawn up in accordance with generally accepted accounting practice.

Taxation (International and Other Provisions) Act 2010 (c. 8)   **1041**
Part 7 — Tax treatment of financing costs and income
Chapter 2 — Application of Part

(5)   For the purposes of this section, a relevant group company is a "foreign company" if it is not resident in the United Kingdom and is carrying on a trade in the United Kingdom through a permanent establishment in the United Kingdom.

266   Qualifying financial services groups

(1)   The worldwide group is a qualifying financial services group in a period of account if the trading income condition —
  (a)   is met in relation to that period, or
  (b)   is not met in relation to that period, but only because of losses incurred by the group in respect of activities that are normally reported on a net basis in financial statements prepared in accordance with international accounting standards.

(2)   The trading income condition is met in relation to a period of account if —
  (a)   all or substantially all of the UK trading income of the worldwide group for that period, or
  (b)   all or substantially all of the worldwide trading income of the worldwide group for that period,
  is derived from qualifying activities (see section 267).

(3)   In this Chapter, in relation to a period of account of the worldwide group —
  "UK trading income" means the sum of the trading income for that period of each company that was a relevant group company at any time during that period (see section 271), and
  "worldwide trading income" means the trading income for that period of the worldwide group (see section 272).

267   Qualifying activities

In this Chapter "qualifying activities" means —
  (a)   lending activities and activities that are ancillary to lending activities (see section 268),
  (b)   insurance activities and insurance-related activities (see section 269), and
  (c)   relevant dealing in financial instruments (see section 270).

268   Lending activities and activities ancillary to lending activities

(1)   In this Chapter "lending activities" means any of the following activities —
  (a)   acceptance of deposits or other repayable funds,
  (b)   lending of money, including consumer credit, mortgage credit, factoring (with or without recourse) and financing of commercial transactions (including forfeiting),
  (c)   finance leasing (as lessor),
  (d)   issuing and administering means of payment,
  (e)   provision of guarantees or commitments to provide money,
  (f)   money transmission services,
  (g)   provision of alternative finance arrangements, and
  (h)   other activities carried out in connection with activities falling within any of paragraphs (a) to (g).

1042

Taxation (International and Other Provisions) Act 2010 (c. 8)
Part 7 — Tax treatment of financing costs and income
Chapter 2 — Application of Part

(2) Activities that are ancillary to lending activities are not qualifying activities for the purposes of this Chapter if the income derived from the ancillary activities forms a significant part of the total of —

    (a) that income, and

    (b) the income derived from lending activities of the worldwide group in the period of account.

(3) In subsection (2) "income" means the gross income or net income that would be taken into account for the purposes of section 266 in calculating the UK or worldwide trading income of the worldwide group for the period of account.

(4) The Commissioners may by order —

    (a) amend subsection (1), and

    (b) make other amendments of this section in consequence of any amendment of subsection (1).

(5) In subsection (1)(h), and in the references to ancillary activities in this section and section 267(a), "activities" includes buying, holding, managing and selling assets.

(6) In this section "alternative finance arrangements" has the same meaning as in Chapter 6 of Part 6 of CTA 2009.

269 Insurance activities and insurance-related activities

(1) In this Chapter "insurance activities" means —

    (a) the effecting or carrying out of contracts of insurance by a regulated insurer, and

    (b) investment business that arises directly from activities falling within paragraph (a).

(2) In this Chapter "insurance-related activities" means —

    (a) activities that are ancillary to insurance activities, and

    (b) activities that —

        (i) are of the same kind as activities carried out for the purposes of insurance activities,

        (ii) are not actually carried out for those purposes, and

        (iii) would not be carried out but for insurance activities being carried out.

(3) Subsection (2) is subject to subsection (4).

(4) Activities that fall within subsection (2)(a) or (b) ("the relevant activities") are not insurance-related activities if the income derived from the relevant activities forms a significant part of the total of —

    (a) that income, and

    (b) the income derived from insurance activities of the worldwide group in the period of account.

(5) In subsection (4) "income" means the gross income or net income that would be taken into account for the purposes of section 266 in calculating the UK or worldwide trading income of the worldwide group for the period of account.

(6) In this section —

    "activities" includes buying, holding, managing and selling assets,

Taxation (International and Other Provisions) Act 2010 (c. 8)
Part 7 — Tax treatment of financing costs and income
Chapter 2 — Application of Part

1043

> "contract of insurance" has the same meaning as in Chapter 1 of Part 12 of ICTA, and
>
> "regulated insurer" means a member of the worldwide group that—
>
> > (a) is authorised under the law of any territory to carry on insurance business, or
> >
> > (b) is a member of a body or organisation that is so authorised.

270 Relevant dealing in financial instruments

(1) In this Chapter "financial instrument" means anything that is a financial instrument for any purpose of the FSA Handbook.

(2) For the purposes of this Chapter, a dealing in a financial instrument is a "relevant dealing" if—

    (a) it is a dealing other than in the capacity of a broker, and

    (b) profits or losses on the dealing form part of the trading profits or losses of a business.

(3) In this section "broker" includes any person offering to sell securities to, or purchase securities from, members of the public generally.

271 UK trading income of the worldwide group

(1) This section applies in relation to section 266 for calculating the UK trading income of the worldwide group for a period of account.

(2) The trading income for that period of a relevant group company is the aggregate of—

    (a) the gross income calculated in accordance with subsection (3), and

    (b) the net income calculated in accordance with subsection (4).

(3) The income mentioned in subsection (2)(a) is the gross income—

    (a) arising from the activities of the relevant group company (other than net-basis activities), and

    (b) accounted for as such under generally accepted accounting practice,

without taking account of any deductions (whether for expenses or otherwise).

(4) The income mentioned in subsection (2)(b) is the net income arising from the net-basis activities of the relevant group company that—

    (a) is accounted for as such under generally accepted accounting practice, or

    (b) would be accounted for as such if income arising from such activities were accounted for under generally accepted accounting practice.

(5) Subsections (3) and (4) are subject to subsection (6).

(6) If a proportion of an accounting period of a relevant group company does not fall within the period of account of the worldwide group, the gross income or net income for that accounting period of the company is to be reduced, for the purposes of this section, by that proportion.

(7) Gross income or net income is to be disregarded for the purposes of subsection (2) if the income arises in respect of an amount payable by another member of the worldwide group that is either a UK group company or a relevant group company.

1044   Taxation (International and Other Provisions) Act 2010 (c. 8)
                                   Part 7 — Tax treatment of financing costs and income
                                                  Chapter 2 — Application of Part

(8)   In this section "net-basis activity" means activity that is normally reported on a net basis in financial statements prepared in accordance with generally accepted accounting practice.

272   Worldwide trading income of the worldwide group

(1)   This section applies in relation to section 266 for calculating the worldwide trading income of the worldwide group for a period of account.

(2)   The trading income for that period of the worldwide group is the aggregate of —
  (a)   the gross income calculated in accordance with subsection (3), and
  (b)   the net income calculated in accordance with subsection (4).

(3)   The income mentioned in subsection (2)(a) is the gross income —
  (a)   arising from the activities of the worldwide group (other than net-basis activities), and
  (b)   disclosed as such in the financial statements of the worldwide group,
without taking account of any deductions (whether for expenses or otherwise).

(4)   The income mentioned in subsection (2)(b) is the net income arising from the net-basis activities of the worldwide group that —
  (a)   is accounted for as such under international accounting standards, or
  (b)   would be accounted for as such if income arising from such activities were accounted for under international accounting standards.

(5)   In this section "net-basis activity" means activity that is normally reported on a net basis in financial statements prepared in accordance with international accounting standards.

(6)   For provision about references in this Part to financial statements of the worldwide group, and amounts disclosed in financial statements, see sections 346 to 349.

273   Foreign currency accounting

(1)   Subject to the following provisions of this section, references in this Chapter to an amount disclosed in a balance sheet of a relevant group company, or of the worldwide group, as at any date are, where the amount is expressed in a currency other than sterling, to that amount translated into its sterling equivalent by reference to the spot rate of exchange for that date.

(2)   Subsection (3) applies in relation to a period of account of the worldwide group if all the amounts disclosed in balance sheets (whether of relevant group companies, or of the worldwide group) that are relevant to a calculation under this Chapter in relation to that period are expressed in the same currency ("the relevant foreign currency") and that currency is not sterling.

(3)   If this subsection applies —
  (a)   references in this Part to an amount disclosed in a balance sheet of a relevant group company, or of the worldwide group, are to that amount expressed in the relevant foreign currency, and
  (b)   for the purposes of determining under section 262 the net debt amount of a company, subsection (3) of that section is to have effect as if the reference to the amount for the time being specified there ("the section 262(3) amount") were read as a reference to the relevant amount.

Taxation (International and Other Provisions) Act 2010 (c. 8)   **1045**
Part 7 — Tax treatment of financing costs and income
Chapter 2 — Application of Part

(4) For this purpose "the relevant amount" means the average of —

    (a) the section 262(3) amount expressed in the relevant foreign currency, translated by reference to the spot rate of exchange for the company's start date, and

    (b) the section 262(3) amount expressed in the relevant foreign currency, translated by reference to the spot rate of exchange for the company's end date.

CHAPTER 3

DISALLOWANCE OF DEDUCTIONS

274 Application of Chapter and meaning of "total disallowed amount"

(1) This Chapter applies if, for a period of account of the worldwide group to which this Part applies ("the relevant period of account") —

    (a) the tested expense amount (see Chapter 8), exceeds

    (b) the available amount (see Chapter 9).

(2) In this Chapter "the total disallowed amount" means the difference between the amounts mentioned in paragraphs (a) and (b) of subsection (1).

275 Meaning of "company to which this Chapter applies"

References in this Chapter to a company to which this Chapter applies are to a company that is a relevant group company at any time during the relevant period of account.

276 Appointment of authorised company for relevant period of account

(1) The companies to which this Chapter applies may appoint one of their number to exercise functions conferred under this Chapter on the reporting body in relation to the relevant period of account.

(2) An appointment under this section is of no effect unless it is signed on behalf of each company to which this Chapter applies by the appropriate person.

(3) The Commissioners may by regulations make further provision about an appointment under this section including, in particular, provision —

    (a) about the form and manner in which an appointment may be made,

    (b) about how an appointment may be revoked and the form and manner of such revocation,

    (c) requiring a person to notify HMRC of the making or revocation of an appointment and about the form and manner of such notification,

    (d) requiring a person to give information to HMRC in connection with the making or revocation of an appointment,

    (e) imposing time limits in relation to making or revoking an appointment,

    (f) providing that an appointment or its revocation is of no effect, or ceases to have effect, if time limits or other requirements under the regulations are not met, and

    (g) about cases where a company is not a relevant group company at all times during the relevant period of account.

(4) In this section "the appropriate person", in relation to a company, means —

1046   *Taxation (International and Other Provisions) Act 2010 (c. 8)*
Part 7 — Tax treatment of financing costs and income
Chapter 3 — Disallowance of deductions

    (a)   the proper officer of the company, or

    (b)   such other person as may for the time being have the express, implied or apparent authority of the company to act on its behalf for the purposes of this Part.

(5)   Subsections (3) and (4) of section 108 of TMA 1970 (responsibility of company officers: meaning of "proper officer") apply for the purposes of this section as they apply for the purposes of that section.

277   Meaning of "the reporting body"

In this Chapter "the reporting body" means—

    (a)   if an appointment under section 276 has effect in relation to the relevant period of account, the company appointed under that section, and

    (b)   if such an appointment does not have effect in relation to the relevant period of account, the companies to which this Chapter applies, acting jointly.

278   Statement of allocated disallowances: submission

(1)   The reporting body must submit a statement (a "statement of allocated disallowances") in relation to the relevant period of account to HMRC.

(2)   A statement submitted under this section must be received by HMRC within 12 months of the end of the relevant period of account.

(3)   A statement submitted under this section must comply with the requirements of section 280.

279   Statement of allocated disallowances: submission of revised statement

(1)   If the reporting body has submitted a statement of allocated disallowances under section 278 or this section, it may submit a revised statement to HMRC.

(2)   A statement submitted under this section must be received by HMRC within 36 months of the end of the relevant period of account.

(3)   A statement submitted under this section must comply with the requirements of section 280.

(4)   A statement submitted under this section—

    (a)   must indicate the respects in which it differs from the previous statement, and

    (b)   supersedes the previous statement.

280   Statement of allocated disallowances: requirements

(1)   This section applies in relation to a statement of allocated disallowances submitted under section 278 or 279.

(2)   The statement must be signed—

    (a)   if an appointment under section 276 has effect in relation to the relevant period of account, by the appropriate person in relation to the company appointed under that section, or

Taxation (International and Other Provisions) Act 2010 (c. 8)   **1047**
Part 7 – Tax treatment of financing costs and income
Chapter 3 – Disallowance of deductions

    (b)   if such an appointment does not have effect in relation to the relevant period of account, by the appropriate person in relation to each company to which this Chapter applies.

(3)   The statement must show –
    (a)   the tested expense amount,
    (b)   the available amount, and
    (c)   the total disallowed amount.

(4)   The statement must –
    (a)   list one or more companies to which this Chapter applies, and
    (b)   in relation to each listed company, specify one or more financing expense amounts for the relevant period of account that are to be disallowed, and give the relevant details in relation to each such amount.

(5)   For this purpose "the relevant details", in relation to a financing expense amount are –
    (a)   which of conditions A, B and C in section 313 is met in relation to the amount, and
    (b)   the relevant accounting period of the company in which the amount would, apart from this Part, be brought into account for the purposes of corporation tax.

(6)   The sum of the amounts specified under subsection (4)(b) must equal the total disallowed amount.

(7)   In this section "the appropriate person", in relation to a company, means –
    (a)   the proper officer of the company, or
    (b)   such other person as may for the time being have the express, implied or apparent authority of the company to act on its behalf for the purposes of this Part.

(8)   Subsections (3) and (4) of section 108 of TMA 1970 (responsibility of company officers: meaning of "proper officer") apply for the purposes of this section as they apply for the purposes of that section.

(9)   For the meaning of "financing expense amount", see Chapter 7.

281   Statement of allocated disallowances: effect

A financing expense amount of a company to which this Chapter applies that is specified in a statement of allocated disallowances under section 280(4)(b) is not to be brought into account by the company for the purposes of corporation tax.

282   Company tax returns

(1)   This section applies if –
    (a)   a company to which this Chapter applies has delivered a company tax return for a relevant accounting period, and
    (b)   as a result of the submission of a revised statement of allocated disallowances under section 279 –
        (i)   there is a change in the amount of profits on which corporation tax is chargeable for the period, or

1048

Taxation (International and Other Provisions) Act 2010 (c. 8)
Part 7 — Tax treatment of financing costs and income
Chapter 3 — Disallowance of deductions

(ii)   any other information contained in the return is incorrect.

(2)   The company is treated as having amended its company tax return for the accounting period so as to reflect the change mentioned in subsection (1)(b)(i) or to correct the information mentioned in subsection (1)(b)(ii).

283   Power to make regulations about statement of allocated disallowances

The Commissioners may by regulations make further provision about a statement of allocated disallowances including, in particular, provision —

(a)   about the form of a statement and the manner in which it is to be submitted,

(b)   requiring a person to give information to HMRC in connection with a statement,

(c)   as to circumstances in which a statement that is not received by the time specified in section 278(2) or 279(2) is to be treated as if it were so received, and

(d)   as to circumstances in which a statement that does not comply with the requirements of section 280 is to be treated as if it did so comply.

284   Failure of reporting body to submit statement of allocated disallowances

(1)   This section applies if no statement of allocated disallowances is submitted under section 278 that complies with the requirements of section 280.

(2)   Each company to which this Chapter applies that has a net financing deduction for the relevant period of account that is greater than nil must reduce the amounts that it brings into account in relevant accounting periods in respect of financing expense amounts.

(3)   The total of the reductions required to be made by a company because of subsection (2) is —

$$\frac{NFD}{TEA} \times TDA$$

where —

NFD is the net financing deduction of the company for the relevant period of account (see section 329(2)),

TEA is the tested expense amount for the relevant period of account (see section 329(1)), and

TDA is the total disallowed amount (see section 274(2)).

(4)   The particular financing expense amounts that must be reduced, and the amounts by which they must be reduced, must be determined in accordance with regulations made by the Commissioners.

(5)   Regulations under this section may, in particular, include any of the following —

(a)   provision conferring a discretion on a company required to make reductions under this section as to the particular financing expense amounts that are to be reduced,

(b)   provision requiring a company required to make reductions under this section to notify another relevant group company of the particular reductions made, and

Taxation (International and Other Provisions) Act 2010 (c. 8)
Part 7 — Tax treatment of financing costs and income
Chapter 3 — Disallowance of deductions

1049

(c)   provision as to the times by which such notices must be sent and as to information that must accompany such notices.

285   Powers to make regulations in relation to reductions under section 284

(1)   The Commissioners may by regulations make provision for the purpose of securing that a company required under section 284 to reduce the amounts that it brings into account in respect of financing expense amounts for the relevant period of account ("a company required to make default reductions") has sufficient information to determine their amount.

(2)   Provision that may be made in regulations under subsection (1) includes provision requiring one or more members of the worldwide group to send specified information to a company required to make default reductions.

(3)   The Commissioners may by regulations make provision about cases in which (whether as a result of non-compliance with regulations made under subsection (1) or otherwise) a company required to make default reductions does not possess specified information.

(4)   Provision that may be made in regulations under subsection (3) includes provision as to assumptions that may or must be made in determining the amount of a reduction under section 284 of a financing expense amount.

(5)   The Commissioners may by regulations make provision for determining a time later than that determined under paragraph 15(4) of Schedule 18 to FA 1998 (amendment of return by company) before which a company required to make default reductions may amend its company tax return so as to reflect a reduction under section 284.

(6)   In this section "specified" means specified in regulations under this section.

CHAPTER 4

EXEMPTION OF FINANCING INCOME

286   Application of Chapter and meaning of "total disallowed amount"

(1)   This Chapter applies if, for a period of account of the worldwide group to which this Part applies ("the relevant period of account") —
    (a)   the tested expense amount (see Chapter 8), exceeds
    (b)   the available amount (see Chapter 9).

(2)   In this Chapter the "total disallowed amount" means the difference between the amounts mentioned in paragraphs (a) and (b) of subsection (1).

287   Meaning of "company to which this Chapter applies"

References in this Chapter to a company to which this Chapter applies are to a company that is a UK group company at any time during the relevant period of account.

1050

Taxation (International and Other Provisions) Act 2010 (c. 8)
Part 7 — Tax treatment of financing costs and income
Chapter 4 — Exemption of financing income

288 Appointment of authorised company for relevant period of account

(1) The companies to which this Chapter applies may appoint one of their number to exercise functions conferred under this Chapter on the reporting body in relation to the relevant period of account.

(2) An appointment under this section is of no effect unless it is signed on behalf of each company to which this Chapter applies by the appropriate person.

(3) The Commissioners may by regulations make further provision about an appointment under this section including, in particular, provision—

   (a) about the form and manner in which an appointment may be made or revoked,

   (b) requiring a person to notify HMRC of the making or revocation of an appointment and about the form and manner of such notification,

   (c) requiring a person to give information to HMRC in connection with the making or revocation of an appointment,

   (d) imposing time limits in relation to making or revoking an appointment,

   (e) that an appointment or its revocation is of no effect, or ceases to have effect, if time limits or other requirements under the regulations are not met, and

   (f) about cases where a company does not meet condition A in section 345, or is not a member of the worldwide group, at all times during the relevant period of account.

(4) In this section "the appropriate person", in relation to a company, means—

   (a) the proper officer of the company, or

   (b) such other person as may for the time being have the express, implied or apparent authority of the company to act on its behalf for the purposes of this Part.

(5) Subsections (3) and (4) of section 108 of TMA 1970 (responsibility of company officers: meaning of "proper officer") apply for the purposes of this section as they apply for the purposes of that section.

289 Meaning of "the reporting body"

In this Chapter "the reporting body" means—

   (a) if an appointment under section 288 has effect in relation to the relevant period of account, the company appointed under that section, and

   (b) if such an appointment does not have effect in relation to the relevant period of account, the companies to which this Chapter applies, acting jointly.

290 Statement of allocated exemptions: submission

(1) The reporting body must submit a statement (a "statement of allocated exemptions") in relation to the relevant period of account to HMRC.

(2) A statement submitted under this section must be received by HMRC within 12 months of the end of the relevant period of account.

(3) A statement submitted under this section must comply with the requirements of section 292.

Taxation (International and Other Provisions) Act 2010 (c. 8)
Part 7 − Tax treatment of financing costs and income
Chapter 4 − Exemption of financing income

1051

291 Statement of allocated exemptions: submission of revised statement

(1) If the reporting body has submitted a statement of allocated exemptions under section 290 or this section, it may submit a revised statement to HMRC.

(2) A statement submitted under this section must be received by HMRC within 36 months of the end of the relevant period of account.

(3) A statement submitted under this section must comply with the requirements of section 292.

(4) A statement submitted under this section −

    (a) must indicate the respects in which it differs from the previous statement, and

    (b) supersedes the previous statement.

292 Statement of allocated exemptions: requirements

(1) This section applies in relation to a statement of allocated exemptions submitted under section 290 or 291.

(2) The statement must be signed −

    (a) if an appointment under section 288 has effect in relation to the relevant period of account, by the appropriate person in relation to the company appointed under that section, or

    (b) if such an appointment does not have effect in relation to the relevant period of account, by the appropriate person in relation to each company to which this Chapter applies.

(3) The statement must show −

    (a) the tested expense amount,

    (b) the available amount, and

    (c) the total disallowed amount.

(4) The statement must −

    (a) list one or more companies to which this Chapter applies, and

    (b) in relation to each listed company, specify one or more financing income amounts for the relevant period of account that are to be exempted, and give the relevant details in relation to each such amount.

(5) For this purpose "the relevant details" in relation to a financing income amount are −

    (a) which of conditions A, B and C in section 314 is met in relation to the amount, and

    (b) the relevant accounting period of the company in which the amount would, apart from this Part, be brought into account for the purposes of corporation tax.

(6) The sum of the amounts specified under subsection (4)(b) must not exceed the lower of −

    (a) the total disallowed amount, and

    (b) the tested income amount (see Chapter 8).

(7) In this section "the appropriate person", in relation to a company, means −

    (a) the proper officer of the company, or

1052   *Taxation (International and Other Provisions) Act 2010 (c. 8)*
Part 7 – Tax treatment of financing costs and income
Chapter 4 – Exemption of financing income

       (b)   such other person as may for the time being have the express, implied or apparent authority of the company to act on its behalf for the purposes of this Part.

  (8)   Subsections (3) and (4) of section 108 of TMA 1970 (responsibility of company officers: meaning of "proper officer") apply for the purposes of this section as they apply for the purposes of that section.

  (9)   For the meaning of "financing income amount", see Chapter 7.

293   Statement of allocated exemptions: effect

A financing income amount of a company to which this Chapter applies that is specified in a statement of allocated exemptions under section 292(4)(b) is not to be brought into account by the company for the purposes of corporation tax.

294   Company tax returns

  (1)   This section applies if –

       (a)   a company to which this Chapter applies has delivered a company tax return for a relevant accounting period, and

       (b)   as a result of the submission of a revised statement of allocated exemptions under section 291 –

           (i)   there is a change in the amount of profits on which corporation tax is chargeable for the period, or

           (ii)   any other information contained in the return is incorrect.

  (2)   The company is treated as having amended its company tax return for the accounting period so as to reflect the change mentioned in subsection (1)(b)(i) or to correct the information mentioned in subsection (1)(b)(ii).

295   Power to make regulations about statement of allocated exemptions

The Commissioners may by regulations make further provision about a statement of allocated exemptions including, in particular, provision –

       (a)   about the form of a statement and the manner in which it is to be submitted,

       (b)   requiring a person to give information to HMRC in connection with a statement,

       (c)   as to circumstances in which a statement that is not received by the time specified in section 290(2) or 291(2) is to be treated as if it were so received, and

       (d)   as to circumstances in which a statement that does not comply with the requirements of section 292 is to be treated as if it did so comply.

296   Failure of reporting body to submit statement of allocated exemptions

  (1)   This section applies if no statement of allocated exemptions is submitted under section 290 that complies with the requirements of section 292.

  (2)   Subject to the following provisions of this section, each financing income amount for the relevant period of account of each company to which this Chapter applies is to be reduced to nil.

Taxation (International and Other Provisions) Act 2010 (c. 8)
Part 7 – Tax treatment of financing costs and income
Chapter 4 – Exemption of financing income

1053

(3) In this section "unrestricted reduction" means a reduction of a financing income amount for the relevant period of account of a company to which this Chapter applies, determined in accordance with subsection (2).

(4) Subsection (5) applies if –
  (a) the total of the unrestricted reductions, exceeds
  (b) the lower of –
    (i) the total disallowed amount, and
    (ii) the tested income amount.

(5) Each unrestricted reduction is to be reduced by –

$$\frac{UR}{TUR} \times X$$

where –
  UR is the unrestricted reduction in question,
  TUR is the total of the unrestricted reductions, and
  X is the excess mentioned in subsection (4).

297 Power to make regulations in relation to reductions under section 296

(1) The Commissioners may by regulations make provision for the purpose of securing that a company required under section 296 to reduce the amounts that it brings into account in respect of financing income amounts for the relevant period of account ("a company required to make default reductions") has sufficient information to determine their amount.

(2) Provision that may be made in regulations under subsection (1) includes provision requiring one or more members of the worldwide group to send specified information to a company required to make default reductions.

(3) The Commissioners may by regulations make provision about cases in which (whether as a result of non-compliance with regulations made under subsection (1) or otherwise) a company required to make default reductions does not possess specified information.

(4) Provision that may be made in regulations under subsection (3) includes provision as to assumptions that may or must be made in determining the amount of a reduction under section 296 of a financing income amount.

(5) The Commissioners may by regulations make provision for determining a time later than that determined under paragraph 15(4) of Schedule 18 to FA 1998 (amendment of return by company) before which a company required to make default reductions may amend its company tax return so as to reflect a reduction under section 296.

(6) In this section "specified" means specified in regulations under this section.

298 Balancing payments between group companies: no tax charge or relief

(1) This section applies if –
  (a) one or more financing income amounts of a company ("company A") for the relevant period of account are –
    (i) because of section 293, not brought into account, or
    (ii) because of section 296, reduced,

1054

Taxation (International and Other Provisions) Act 2010 (c. 8)
Part 7 — Tax treatment of financing costs and income
Chapter 4 — Exemption of financing income

    (b)   one or more financing expense amounts of another company ("company B") for the relevant period of account are—

        (i)   because of section 281, not brought into account, or

        (ii)   because of section 284, reduced,

    (c)   company A makes one or more payments ("the balancing payments") to company B, and

    (d)   the sole or main reason for making the balancing payments is that the conditions in paragraphs (a) and (b) are met.

(2)   To the extent that the sum of the balancing payments does not exceed the amount specified in subsection (3), those payments—

    (a)   are not to be taken into account in computing profits or losses of either company A or company B for the purposes of corporation tax, and

    (b)   are not to be regarded as distributions for any of the purposes of the Corporation Tax Acts.

(3)   The amount mentioned in subsection (2) is the lower of—

    (a)   the sum of the financing income amounts mentioned in subsection (1)(a), and

    (b)   the sum of the financing expense amounts mentioned in subsection (1)(b).

CHAPTER 5

INTRA-GROUP FINANCING INCOME WHERE PAYER DENIED DEDUCTION

299   Tax exemption for certain financing income received from EEA companies

(1)   A financing income amount of a company that is a member of the worldwide group ("the recipient") is not to be brought into account for the purposes of corporation tax if—

    (a)   it arises as a result of a payment by another company that is a member of the worldwide group ("the payer"),

    (b)   the payment is received during a period of account of the worldwide group to which this Part applies, and

    (c)   conditions A, B and C are met.

(2)   Condition A is that, at the time the payment is received, the payer is a relevant associate of the recipient (see section 300).

(3)   Condition B is that, at the time the payment is received—

    (a)   the payer is tax-resident in an EEA territory (see section 301), and

    (b)   the payer is liable to a tax of that territory that is chargeable by reference to profits, income or gains arising to the payer.

(4)   Condition C is that—

    (a)   qualifying EEA tax relief for the payment is not available to the payer in the period in which the payment is made ("the current period") or any previous period (see section 302), and

    (b)   qualifying EEA tax relief for the payment is not available to the payer in any period after the current period (see section 303).

(5)   For the meaning of "financing income amount", see section 305.

Taxation (International and Other Provisions) Act 2010 (c. 8)
Part 7 − Tax treatment of financing costs and income
Chapter 5 − Intra-group financing income where payer denied deduction

1055

300 Meaning of "relevant associate"

For the purposes of this Chapter, the payer is a "relevant associate" of the recipient if −

   (a)   the payer is a parent of the recipient,

   (b)   the payer is a 75% subsidiary of the recipient, or

   (c)   the payer is a 75% subsidiary of a parent of the recipient.

301 Meaning of "tax-resident" and "EEA territory"

(1)   For the purposes of this Chapter, the payer is "tax-resident" in a territory if it is liable, under the law of that territory, to tax by reason of domicile, residence or place of management.

(2)   In this Chapter "EEA territory" means a territory outside the United Kingdom that is within the European Economic Area.

302 Qualifying EEA tax relief for payment in current or previous period

(1)   For the purposes of this Chapter, qualifying EEA tax relief for a payment is not available to the payer in the current period or a previous period if conditions A and B are met in relation to the payment.

(2)   Condition A is that no deduction calculated by reference to the payment can be taken into account in calculating any profits, income or gains that −

   (a)   arise to the payer in the current period or any previous period, and

   (b)   are chargeable to any tax of the United Kingdom or an EEA territory for the current period or any previous period.

(3)   Condition B is that no relief determined by reference to the payment can be given in the current period or any previous period for the purposes of any tax of the United Kingdom or an EEA territory by −

   (a)   the payment of a credit,

   (b)   the elimination or reduction of a tax liability, or

   (c)   any other means of any kind.

(4)   Conditions A and B are not met in relation to the payment unless every step is taken (whether by the payer or any other person) to secure that deductions are taken into account as mentioned in subsection (2) and reliefs are given as mentioned in subsection (3).

(5)   Conditions A and B are not met in relation to the payment unless they would be met disregarding a failure to obtain a deduction or relief as a result of −

   (a)   this Part, or

   (b)   provision made as a result of double taxation arrangements between any two territories (including provision sanctioned by associated enterprise rules contained in such arrangements).

(6)   For this purpose −

   (a)   arrangements are "double taxation arrangements" if they are arrangements made between any two territories with a view to affording relief from double taxation, and

   (b)   "associated enterprise rules" means −

      (i)   rules that, on the passing of FA 2009, were contained in Article 9 of the Model Tax Convention on Income and on Capital

1056   *Taxation (International and Other Provisions) Act 2010 (c. 8)*
Part 7 — Tax treatment of financing costs and income
Chapter 5 — Intra-group financing income where payer denied deduction

           published by the Organisation for Economic Co-operation and Development, or

    (ii)   any rules in the same or equivalent terms.

303   Qualifying EEA tax relief for payment in future period

(1)   For the purposes of this Chapter, qualifying EEA tax relief for a payment is not available to the payer in a period after the current period if conditions A and B are met in relation to the payment.

(2)   Condition A is that no deduction calculated by reference to the payment can be taken into account in calculating any profits, income or gains that—

    (a)   might arise to the payer in any period after the current period, and

    (b)   would, if they did so arise, be chargeable to any tax of the United Kingdom or an EEA territory for any period after the current period.

(3)   Condition B is that no relief determined by reference to the payment can be given in any period after the current period for the purposes of any tax of the United Kingdom or an EEA territory by—

    (a)   the payment of a credit,

    (b)   the elimination or reduction of a tax liability, or

    (c)   any other means of any kind.

(4)   The question whether a deduction can be taken into account as mentioned in subsection (2) or a relief can be given as mentioned in subsection (3) is to be determined by reference to the position immediately after the end of the current period.

(5)   Conditions A and B are not met in relation to the payment unless they would be met disregarding a failure to obtain a deduction or relief as a result of—

    (a)   this Part, or

    (b)   provision made as a result of double taxation arrangements between any two territories (including provision sanctioned by associated enterprise rules contained in such arrangements).

(6)   For this purpose—

    (a)   arrangements are "double taxation arrangements" if they are arrangements made between any two territories with a view to affording relief from double taxation, and

    (b)   "associated enterprise rules" means—

        (i)   rules that, on the passing of FA 2009, were contained in Article 9 of the Model Tax Convention on Income and on Capital published by the Organisation for Economic Co-operation and Development, or

        (ii)   any rules in the same or equivalent terms.

304   References to tax of a territory

(1)   References in this Chapter to a tax of the United Kingdom are to income tax or corporation tax.

(2)   References in this Chapter to a tax of a territory outside the United Kingdom are to a tax chargeable under the law of that territory that—

    (a)   is charged on income and corresponds to income tax, or

Taxation (International and Other Provisions) Act 2010 (c. 8)   **1057**
Part 7 — Tax treatment of financing costs and income
Chapter 5 — Intra-group financing income where payer denied deduction

      (b)   is charged on income or chargeable gains or both and corresponds to corporation tax.

(3)   For the purposes of this section, a tax chargeable under the law of a territory outside the United Kingdom does not fail to correspond to income tax or corporation tax just because —

      (a)   it is chargeable under the law of a province, state or other part of a country, or

      (b)   it is levied by or on behalf of a municipality or other local body.

305 Financing income amounts of a company

(1)   References in this Chapter to a "financing income amount" of a company are (subject to subsection (6)) to any amount that meets condition A, B or C.

(2)   Condition A is that the amount is a credit that —

      (a)   would, apart from this Chapter, be brought into account by the company for the purposes of corporation tax,

      (b)   would be so brought into account in respect of a loan relationship —

          (i)   under Part 3 of CTA 2009 as a result of section 297 of that Act (loan relationships for purposes of trade), or

         (ii)   under Part 5 of that Act (other loan relationships), and

      (c)   is not an excluded credit.

(3)   A credit is "excluded" if it is in respect of —

      (a)   the reversal of an impairment loss,

      (b)   an exchange gain, or

      (c)   a profit from a related transaction.

(4)   Condition B is that the amount is an amount that would, apart from this Chapter, be brought into account by the company for the purposes of corporation tax in respect of the financing income implicit in amounts received under finance leases.

(5)   Condition C is that the amount is an amount that would, apart from this Chapter, be brought into account by the company for the purposes of corporation tax in respect of the financing income receivable on debt factoring, or any similar transaction.

(6)   The provisions of Chapter 7 apply in relation to an amount that is a financing income amount of a company because of meeting condition A, B or C in this section as they apply in relation to an amount that is a financing income amount of a relevant group company because of meeting condition A, B or C in section 314.

CHAPTER 6

TAX AVOIDANCE

306 Schemes involving manipulation of rules in Chapter 2

(1)   A period of account of the worldwide group that, apart from this section, is not within section 261(1) is treated as within that provision if conditions A, B and C are met.

1058   *Taxation (International and Other Provisions) Act 2010 (c. 8)*
                                              Part 7 – Tax treatment of financing costs and income
                                                                     Chapter 6 – Tax avoidance

(2) Condition A is that—

    (a) at any time before the end of the period, a scheme is entered into, and

    (b) if the scheme had not been entered into, the period would have been within section 261(1).

(3) Condition B is that the main purpose, or one of the main purposes, of any party to the scheme on entering into the scheme is to secure that the period is not within section 261(1).

(4) Condition C is that the scheme is not an excluded scheme.

307 Schemes involving manipulation of rules in Chapters 3 and 4

(1) If conditions A, B and C are met in relation to a period of account of the worldwide group ("the relevant period of account"), the tested expense amount, the tested income amount and the available amount for the period are to be calculated in accordance with section 309.

(2) Condition A is that—

    (a) at any time before the end of the relevant period of account, a scheme is entered into, and

    (b) the main purpose, or one of the main purposes, of any party to the scheme on entering into it is to secure that the amount of the relevant net deduction (within the meaning given by section 308) is lower than it would be if that amount were calculated in accordance with section 309.

(3) Condition B is that a result of the scheme is that—

    (a) the sum of the profits of UK group companies that—

        (i) arise in relevant accounting periods, and

        (ii) are chargeable to corporation tax,

    is less than it would be if that sum were determined in accordance with section 309, or

    (b) the sum of the losses of UK group companies that—

        (i) arise in relevant accounting periods (other than any taken into account in calculating profits within paragraph (a)), and

        (ii) are capable of being a carried-back amount or a carried-forward amount (see section 310),

    is higher than it would be if that sum were determined in accordance with section 309.

(4) Condition C is that the scheme is not an excluded scheme.

(5) If—

    (a) a profit or loss arises in an accounting period of a UK group company, and

    (b) a proportion of that period does not fall within the relevant period of account,

the profit or loss is to be reduced, for the purposes of condition B, by the same proportion.

308 Meaning of "relevant net deduction"

(1) In section 307(2) the "relevant net deduction" means—

Taxation (International and Other Provisions) Act 2010 (c. 8)
Part 7 — Tax treatment of financing costs and income
Chapter 6 — Tax avoidance

1059

   (a)   the amount by which the total disallowed amount exceeds the tested income amount, or

   (b)   if the total disallowed amount does not exceed the tested income amount, nil.

(2)   In this section the "total disallowed amount" means—

   (a)   the amount by which the tested expense amount exceeds the available amount, or

   (b)   if the tested expense amount does not exceed the available amount, nil.

309   Calculation of amounts

(1)   References in section 307 to the calculation of any amount or sum in accordance with this section are to the calculation of that amount or sum on the following assumptions.

(2)   The assumptions are that—

   (a)   the scheme in question was not entered into, and

   (b)   instead, anything that it is more likely than not would have been done or not done had this Part not had effect in relation to the relevant period of account, was done or not done.

310   Meaning of "carried-back amount" and "carried-forward amount"

(1)   In section 307 "carried-back amount" means—

   (a)   an amount carried back under section 389(2) of CTA 2009 (deficits of insurance companies),

   (b)   an amount carried back as a result of a claim under section 459(1)(b) of CTA 2009 (non-trading deficits from loan relationships), or

   (c)   an amount carried back under section 37(3)(b) of CTA 2010 (relief for trade losses against total profits).

(2)   In section 307 "carried-forward amount" means—

   (a)   an amount carried forward under section 76(12) or (13) of ICTA (certain expenses of insurance companies),

   (b)   an amount carried forward under section 436A(4) of ICTA (insurance companies: losses from gross roll-up business),

   (c)   an amount carried forward under section 8(1)(b) of TCGA 1992 (allowable losses),

   (d)   an amount carried forward under section 391(2) of CTA 2009 (deficits of insurance companies),

   (e)   an amount carried forward under section 457(3) of CTA 2009 (non-trading deficits from loan relationships),

   (f)   an amount carried forward under section 753(3) of CTA 2009 (non-trading loss on intangible fixed assets),

   (g)   an amount carried forward under section 925(3) of CTA 2009 (patent income: relief for expenses),

   (h)   an amount carried forward under section 1223 of CTA 2009 (expenses of management and other amounts),

   (i)   an amount carried forward under section 45(4) of CTA 2010 (carry forward of trade loss against subsequent trade profit),

   (j)   an amount carried forward under section 62(5) of CTA 2010 (relief for losses made UK property business),

1060

Taxation (International and Other Provisions) Act 2010 (c. 8)
Part 7 — Tax treatment of financing costs and income
Chapter 6 — Tax avoidance

(k)   an amount carried forward under section 63(3) of CTA 2010 (company with investment business ceasing to carry on UK property business),

(l)   an amount carried forward under section 66(3) of CTA 2010 (relief for losses made in overseas property business), or

(m)   an amount carried forward under section 91(6) of CTA 2010 (relief for losses from miscellaneous transactions).

311   Schemes involving manipulation of rules in Chapter 5

(1)   This section applies to a financing income amount of a company received during a period of account of the worldwide group if—

    (a)   apart from this section, the financing income amount would, because of section 299, not be brought into account for the purposes of corporation tax, and

    (b)   conditions A, B and C are met.

(2)   Condition A is that, at any time before the financing income amount is received, a scheme is entered into that secures that any of the conditions in subsections (2) to (4) of section 299 ("the relevant section 299 condition") is met in relation to the amount.

(3)   Condition B is that the purpose, or one of the main purposes, of any party to the scheme on entering into the scheme is to secure that the relevant section 299 condition is met.

(4)   Condition C is that the scheme is not an excluded scheme.

(5)   If this section applies to a financing income amount, the relevant section 299 condition is treated as not met in relation to the amount.

(6)   Section 305 (meaning of references to a "financing income amount" of a company) applies for the purposes of this section.

312   Meaning of "scheme" and "excluded scheme"

(1)   For the purposes of this Chapter, "scheme" includes any scheme, arrangements or understanding of any kind whatever, whether or not legally enforceable, involving a single transaction or two or more transactions.

(2)   For the purposes of this Chapter, a scheme is "excluded" if it is of a description specified in regulations made by the Commissioners.

(3)   Regulations under subsection (2) may make different provision for different purposes.

CHAPTER 7

"FINANCING EXPENSE AMOUNT" AND "FINANCING INCOME AMOUNT"

313   The financing expense amounts of a company

(1)   References in this Part to a "financing expense amount" of a company for a period of account of the worldwide group are to any amount that meets condition A, B or C.

(2)   Condition A is that the amount is a debit that—

Taxation (International and Other Provisions) Act 2010 (c. 8)
Part 7 — Tax treatment of financing costs and income
Chapter 7 — "Financing expense amount" and "financing income amount"

1061

  (a) would, apart from this Part, be brought into account in a relevant accounting period of the company,

  (b) would be so brought into account in respect of a loan relationship—

    (i) under Part 3 of CTA 2009 as a result of section 297 of that Act (loan relationships for purposes of trade), or

    (ii) under Part 5 of that Act (other loan relationships), and

  (c) is not an excluded debit.

(3) A debit is "excluded" if it is in respect of —

  (a) an impairment loss,

  (b) an exchange loss, or

  (c) a related transaction.

(4) Condition B is that the amount is an amount that would, apart from this Part, be brought into account for the purposes of corporation tax in a relevant accounting period of the company in respect of the financing cost implicit in payments made under finance leases.

(5) Condition C is that the amount is an amount that would, apart from this Part, be brought into account for the purposes of corporation tax in a relevant accounting period of the company in respect of the financing cost payable on debt factoring, or any similar transaction.

(6) If—

  (a) a debit or other amount would, apart from this Part, be brought into account in an accounting period, and

  (b) a proportion of that period does not fall within the period of account of the worldwide group,

the debit or other amount is to be reduced, for the purposes of this section, by the same proportion.

(7) This section is subject to sections 316 to 327.

314 The financing income amounts of a company

(1) References in this Part (except in Chapter 5 and section 311) to a "financing income amount" of a company for a period of account of the worldwide group are to any amount that meets condition A, B or C.

(2) Condition A is that the amount is a credit that—

  (a) would, apart from this Part, be brought into account in a relevant accounting period of the company,

  (b) would be so brought into account in respect of a loan relationship—

    (i) under Part 3 of CTA 2009 as a result of section 297 of that Act (loan relationships for purposes of trade), or

    (ii) under Part 5 of that Act (other loan relationships), and

  (c) is not an excluded credit.

(3) A credit is "excluded" if it is in respect of—

  (a) the reversal of an impairment loss,

  (b) an exchange gain, or

  (c) a profit from a related transaction.

(4) Condition B is that the amount is an amount that would, apart from this Part, be brought into account for the purposes of corporation tax in a relevant

1062　　　　　　　　　　　　*Taxation (International and Other Provisions) Act 2010 (c. 8)*
Part 7 – Tax treatment of financing costs and income
Chapter 7 – "Financing expense amount" and "financing income amount"

accounting period of the company in respect of the financing income implicit in amounts received under finance leases.

(5) Condition C is that the amount is an amount that would, apart from this Part, be brought into account for the purposes of corporation tax in a relevant accounting period of the company in respect of the financing income receivable on debt factoring, or any similar transaction.

(6) If —

(a) a credit or other amount would, apart from this Part, be brought into account in an accounting period, and

(b) a proportion of that period does not fall within the period of account of the worldwide group,

the credit or other amount is to be reduced, for the purposes of this section, by the same proportion.

(7) This section is subject to sections 316 to 327.

315　Interpretation of sections 313 and 314

In sections 313 and 314 the following expressions have the same meaning as they have in Part 5 of CTA 2009 (loan relationships) —

"exchange gain" and "exchange loss",

"impairment",

"impairment loss", and

"related transaction".

316　Group treasury companies

(1) This section applies if, apart from this section, an amount ("the relevant amount") is —

(a) a financing expense amount of a group treasury company because of meeting condition A, B or C in section 313, or

(b) a financing income amount of a group treasury company because of meeting condition A, B or C in section 314.

(2) The relevant amount, and all other amounts that are relevant amounts in respect of the group treasury company and the relevant period, are treated as not being a financing expense amount or a financing income amount of the group treasury company, but only if that company makes an election for the purposes of this section in respect of the relevant period.

(3) An election under this section must be made within 3 years after the end of the relevant period.

(4) If two or more members of the worldwide group are group treasury companies in the relevant period, an election under this section made by any of them is not valid unless each of them makes such an election in respect of the relevant period before the end of the 3 year period mentioned in subsection (3).

(5) A company is a group treasury company in the relevant period if conditions 1, 2 and 3 are met.

(6) Condition 1 is that the company is a member of the worldwide group.

Taxation (International and Other Provisions) Act 2010 (c. 8)   1063
Part 7 — Tax treatment of financing costs and income
Chapter 7 — "Financing expense amount" and "financing income amount"

(7)   Condition 2 is that the company undertakes treasury activities for the worldwide group in the relevant period (whether or not it also undertakes other activities).

(8)   Condition 3 is that —

     (a)   if the company is the only company to meet conditions 1 and 2 in the relevant period, or the only other companies to meet those conditions are not UK group companies, at least 90% of the relevant income of the company for the relevant period is group treasury revenue, or

     (b)   if the company and one or more other companies each of which is a UK group company meet conditions 1 and 2 in the relevant period, at least 90% of the aggregate relevant income of those companies for the relevant period is group treasury revenue.

(9)   For the purposes of this section, a company undertakes treasury activities for the worldwide group in the relevant period if, in that period, it does one or more of the following things in relation to, or on behalf of, the worldwide group or any of its members —

     (a)   managing surplus deposits of money or overdrafts,

     (b)   making or receiving deposits of money,

     (c)   lending money,

     (d)   subscribing for or holding shares in another company which is a UK group company and a group treasury company,

     (e)   investing in debt securities, and

     (f)   hedging assets, liabilities, income or expenses.

(10)   For the purposes of this section "group treasury revenue", in relation to a company, means revenue —

     (a)   arising from the treasury activities that the company undertakes for the worldwide group, and

     (b)   accounted for as such under generally accepted accounting practice,

before any deduction (whether for expenses or otherwise).

(11)   But revenue consisting of a dividend or other distribution is not group treasury revenue unless it is a dividend or distribution from a company that is, in the relevant period —

     (a)   a UK group company, and

     (b)   a group treasury company.

(12)   In this section —

     "debt security" has the same meaning as in the FSA Handbook,

     "relevant income", in relation to a company, means income —

         (a)   arising from the activities of the company, and

         (b)   accounted for as such under generally accepted accounting practice,

     before any deduction (whether for expenses or otherwise), and

     "relevant period" means the period of account of the worldwide group to which the relevant amount relates.

317   Real estate investment trusts

(1)   This section applies if, apart from this section, an amount ("the relevant amount") is —

1064   *Taxation (International and Other Provisions) Act 2010 (c. 8)*
Part 7 – Tax treatment of financing costs and income
Chapter 7 – "Financing expense amount" and "financing income amount"

      (a)   a financing expense amount of a company because of meeting condition A in section 313, or

      (b)   a financing income amount of a company because of meeting condition A in section 314.

(2)   The relevant amount is treated as not being a financing expense amount or a financing income amount of the company if the finance arrangement is one to which section 211 of CTA 2009 does not apply because of section 599(3)(a) of CTA 2010.

318 Companies engaged in oil extraction activities

(1)   This section applies if, apart from this section, an amount ("the relevant amount") is—

      (a)   a financing expense amount of a company because of meeting condition A or condition B in section 313, or

      (b)   a financing income amount of a company because of meeting condition A or condition B in section 314.

(2)   The relevant amount is treated as not being a financing expense amount or a financing income amount of the company if conditions 1 and 2 are met.

(3)   Condition 1 is that the company is treated, in the accounting period in which the amount is brought into account, as carrying on a ring fence trade (see section 277 of CTA 2010).

(4)   Condition 2 is that the amount falls to be brought into account in calculating the profits of that trade for that accounting period.

319 Intra-group short-term finance: financing expense

(1)   This section applies if, apart from this section, an amount ("the relevant amount") is a financing expense amount of a company ("company A") because of meeting condition A in section 313.

(2)   The relevant amount is treated as not being a financing expense amount of company A, but only if an election is made for this purpose.

(3)   Such an election may not be made unless conditions 1 and 2 are met.

(4)   Condition 1 is that company A and the other party to the loan relationship ("company B") are both members of the worldwide group.

(5)   Condition 2 is that the finance arrangement is a short-term loan relationship as respects the period of account of the worldwide group.

(6)   An election under this section may only be made—

      (a)   jointly by company A and company B, and

      (b)   within 36 months of the end of the period of account of the worldwide group to which the relevant amount relates.

(7)   An election under this section is irrevocable.

(8)   In this section "short-term loan relationship" has the meaning given in section 321.

Taxation (International and Other Provisions) Act 2010 (c. 8)
Part 7 — Tax treatment of financing costs and income
Chapter 7 — "Financing expense amount" and "financing income amount"

1065

320 Intra-group short-term finance: financing income

(1) This section applies if —

    (a) under section 319, the relevant amount is treated as not being a financing expense amount of company A, and

    (b) apart from this section, the relevant amount is a financing income amount of company B because of meeting condition A in section 314.

(2) The relevant amount is treated as not being a financing income amount of company B.

(3) In this section "company A" and "company B" have the same meaning as in section 319.

321 Short-term loan relationships

(1) For the purposes of section 319, the finance arrangement is a short-term loan relationship as respects the period of account of the worldwide group ("the relevant period") if —

    (a) regulations made by the Commissioners provide for it to be so, or

    (b) condition A or B is met.

(2) Condition A is that the finance arrangement does not terminate during the relevant period and —

    (a) to the extent that the finance arrangement provides for the creation of money debt, its terms require all money debt created under it to be settled within 12 months of money debt first being created under it, and

    (b) to the extent that the finance arrangement is otherwise a loan relationship, its terms provide for it to terminate within 12 months of its coming into force.

(3) Condition B is that the finance arrangement terminates during, or after the end of, the relevant period and —

    (a) to the extent that the relationship provided for the creation of money debt, all money debt created under it was settled within 12 months of money debt first being created under it, and

    (b) to the extent that the relationship was otherwise a loan relationship, it terminated within 12 months of its coming into force.

(4) The Treasury may, by regulations, make provision about other circumstances in which the finance arrangement is to be taken not to be a short-term loan relationship as respects —

    (a) the relevant period, or

    (b) any part or parts of the relevant period.

(5) Regulations under subsection (4) may include provision for the finance arrangement to be taken never to have been a short-term loan relationship as respects the relevant period or the part or parts of it.

(6) Regulations under subsection (4) may only be made if a draft of the statutory instrument containing the regulations has been laid before and approved by a resolution of the House of Commons.

(7) The Commissioners may by regulations make provision (including provision conferring a discretion on the Commissioners) about circumstances in which

1066   *Taxation (International and Other Provisions) Act 2010 (c. 8)*
Part 7 – Tax treatment of financing costs and income
Chapter 7 – "Financing expense amount" and "financing income amount"

regulations under subsection (4) are not to apply in relation to the finance arrangements.

322   Stranded deficits in non-trading loan relationships: financing expense

(1)   This section applies if, apart from this section, an amount ("the relevant amount") is a financing expense amount of a company ("company A") because of meeting condition A in section 313.

(2)   The relevant amount is treated as not being a financing expense amount of company A, but only if an election is made for this purpose.

(3)   Such an election may not be made unless each of conditions 1 to 4 is met.

(4)   Condition 1 is that company A and the other party to the loan relationship ("company B") are both members of the worldwide group.

(5)   Condition 2 is that company B—
    (a)   is resident in the United Kingdom, or
    (b)   is not resident in the United Kingdom and is carrying on a trade in the United Kingdom through a permanent establishment in the United Kingdom.

(6)   Condition 3 is that, under section 457 of CTA 2009, company B carries forward an amount of non-trading deficit and sets it off against non-trading profits of an accounting period that falls wholly or partly within the period of account of the worldwide group.

(7)   Condition 4 is that the amount of non-trading deficit carried forward and set off is equal to, or greater than, the relevant amount.

(8)   An election under this section may only be made—
    (a)   jointly by company A and company B, and
    (b)   within 36 months of the end of the period of account of the worldwide group to which the relevant amount relates.

323   Stranded deficits in non-trading loan relationships: financing income

(1)   This section applies if—
    (a)   under section 322, the relevant amount is treated as not being a financing expense amount of company A, and
    (b)   apart from this section, the relevant amount is a financing income amount of company B because of meeting condition A in section 314.

(2)   The relevant amount is treated as not being a financing income amount of company B.

(3)   In this section "company A" and "company B" have the same meaning as in section 322.

324   Stranded management expenses in non-trading loan relationships: financing expense

(1)   This section applies if, apart from this section, an amount ("the relevant amount") is a financing expense amount of a company ("company A") because of meeting condition A in section 313.

Taxation (International and Other Provisions) Act 2010 (c. 8) 1067
Part 7 – Tax treatment of financing costs and income
Chapter 7 – "Financing expense amount" and "financing income amount"

(2) The relevant amount is treated as not being a financing expense amount of company A, but only if an election is made for this purpose.

(3) Such an election may not be made unless each of conditions 1 to 5 is met.

(4) Condition 1 is that company A and the other party to the finance arrangement ("company B") are both members of the worldwide group.

(5) Condition 2 is that company B is a company with investment business (within the meaning of Part 16 of CTA 2009) and –
   (a) is resident in the United Kingdom, or
   (b) is not resident in the United Kingdom and is carrying on a trade in the United Kingdom through a permanent establishment in the United Kingdom.

(6) Condition 3 is that company B is allowed a deduction under section 1219 of CTA 2009 (expenses of management of a company's investment business) in respect of an accounting period that falls wholly or partly within the period of account of the worldwide group ("the relevant period").

(7) Condition 4 is that the amount of the deduction allowed is equal to, or greater than, the relevant amount.

(8) Condition 5 is that the calculation of company B's total profits for the relevant period for the purposes of corporation tax results in a loss if company B's credit is not included in that calculation.

(9) An election under this section may only be made –
   (a) jointly by company A and company B, and
   (b) within 36 months of the end of the period of account of the worldwide group to which the relevant amount relates.

(10) In this section "company B's credit" means the credit to company B that arises from the debit to company A as a result of which condition A in section 313 is met.

325 Stranded management expenses in non-trading loan relationships: financing income

(1) This section applies if –
   (a) under section 324, the relevant amount is treated as not being a financing expense amount of company A, and
   (b) apart from this section, the relevant amount is a financing income amount of company B because of meeting condition A in section 314.

(2) The relevant amount is treated as not being a financing income amount of company B.

(3) In this section "company A" and "company B" have the same meaning as in section 324.

326 Charities

(1) This section applies if, apart from this section, an amount ("the relevant amount") is a financing expense amount of a company because of meeting condition A, B or C in section 313.

1068   *Taxation (International and Other Provisions) Act 2010 (c. 8)*
Part 7 — Tax treatment of financing costs and income
Chapter 7 — "Financing expense amount" and "financing income amount"

(2) The relevant amount is treated as not being a financing expense amount of the company if the creditor is a charity.

(3) In this section—

"charity" means any body of persons or trust established for charitable purposes only, and

"creditor" means—

    (a) if the relevant amount is a debit that meets condition A in section 313, the loan creditor who receives the payment in relation to which the relevant amount arises, and

    (b) if the relevant amount meets condition B or C in section 313, the recipient of the payment in relation to which the relevant amount arises.

327 Educational and public bodies

(1) This section applies if, apart from this section, an amount ("the relevant amount") is a financing expense amount of a company because of meeting condition A, B or C in section 313.

(2) The relevant amount is treated as not being a financing expense amount of the company if the creditor is—

    (a) a designated educational establishment,

    (b) a health service body,

    (c) a local authority, or

    (d) a person that is prescribed, or is of a description of persons prescribed, in an order made by the Commissioners for the purposes of this section.

(3) The Commissioners may not prescribe a person, or a description of persons, for the purposes of this section unless they are satisfied that the person, or each of the persons within the description, has functions some or all of which are of a public nature.

(4) In this section—

"creditor" means—

    (a) if the relevant amount is a debit that meets condition A in section 313, the loan creditor who receives the payment in relation to which the relevant amount arises, and

    (b) if the relevant amount meets condition B or C in section 313, the recipient of the payment in relation to which the relevant amount arises,

"designated educational establishment" has the same meaning as in section 105 of CTA 2009, and

"health service body" has the same meaning as in section 985 of CTA 2010.

328 Interpretation of sections 316 to 327

In sections 316 to 327 "finance arrangement" means—

    (a) in the case of an amount that is a debit or credit that meets the condition in section 313(2) or 314(2), the loan relationship to which the debit or credit relates,

    (b) in the case of an amount that meets the condition in section 313(4) or 314(4), the finance lease to which the amount relates, and

Taxation (International and Other Provisions) Act 2010 (c. 8)
Part 7 – Tax treatment of financing costs and income
Chapter 7 – "Financing expense amount" and "financing income amount"

1069

(c) in the case of an amount that meets the condition in section 313(5) or 314(5), the debt factoring or similar transaction to which the amount relates.

CHAPTER 8

"TESTED EXPENSE AMOUNT" AND "TESTED INCOME AMOUNT"

329 The tested expense amount

(1) References in this Part to the "tested expense amount" for a period of account of the worldwide group are to the sum of the net financing deductions of each relevant group company.

(2) References in this Part to the "net financing deduction" of a company for a period of account of the worldwide group are to—

    (a) the sum of the company's financing expense amounts for the period (see section 313), less

    (b) the sum of the company's financing income amounts for the period (see section 314).

(3) References in subsection (2) to a company's financing expense amounts or financing income amounts for a period of account of the worldwide group do not include any amount that arises as a result of a transaction that takes place at a time at which the company is not a relevant group company.

(4) If the amount determined in accordance with subsection (2) is negative, the net financing deduction of the company for the period is nil.

(5) If the amount determined in accordance with subsection (2) is small (see section 331), the net financing deduction of the company for the period is nil.

330 The tested income amount

(1) References in this Part to the "tested income amount" for a period of account of the worldwide group are to the sum of the net financing incomes of each UK group company.

(2) The reference in subsection (1) to the "net financing income" of a company for a period of account of the worldwide group is to—

    (a) the sum of the company's financing income amounts for the period (see section 314), less

    (b) the sum of the company's financing expense amounts for the period (see section 313).

(3) References in subsection (2) to a company's financing expense amounts or financing income amounts for a period of account of the worldwide group do not include any amount that arises as a result of a transaction that takes place at a time at which the company is not a UK group company.

(4) If the amount determined in accordance with subsection (2) is negative, the net financing income of the company for the period is nil.

(5) If the amount determined in accordance with subsection (2) is small (see section 331), the net financing income of the company for the period is nil.

1070   *Taxation (International and Other Provisions) Act 2010 (c. 8)*
Part 7 — Tax treatment of financing costs and income
Chapter 8 — "Tested expense amount" and "tested income amount"

331   Companies with net financing deduction or net financing income that is small

(1)   An amount determined in accordance with section 329(2) or 330(2) is "small" if it is less than £500,000.

(2)   The Treasury may by order amend subsection (1) by substituting a higher or lower amount for the amount for the time being specified there.

(3)   An order under subsection (2) may only be made if a draft of the statutory instrument containing the order has been laid before and approved by a resolution of the House of Commons.

(4)   An order under subsection (2) may only have effect in relation to periods of account of the worldwide group beginning after the date on which the order is made.

CHAPTER 9

"AVAILABLE AMOUNT"

332   The available amount

(1)   References in this Part to the "available amount" for a period of account of the worldwide group are to the sum of the amounts disclosed in the financial statements of the group for that period in respect of —

    (a)   interest payable on amounts borrowed,

    (b)   amortisation of discounts relating to amounts borrowed,

    (c)   amortisation of premiums relating to amounts borrowed,

    (d)   amortisation of ancillary costs relating to amounts borrowed,

    (e)   the financing cost implicit in payments made under finance leases,

    (f)   the financing cost relating to debt factoring, or

    (g)   matters of such other description as may be specified in regulations made by the Commissioners.

(2)   An amount that falls within any of paragraphs (a) to (g) of subsection (1) is to be disregarded for the purposes of that subsection to the extent that —

    (a)   the amount represents a dividend payable in respect of preference shares, and

    (b)   those shares are recognised as a liability in the financial statements of the group for the period.

333   Group members with income from oil extraction subject to particular tax treatment in UK

(1)   In calculating the available amount, an amount disclosed in the financial statements of the worldwide group ("the external finance amount") must be disregarded if conditions A and B are met.

(2)   Condition A is that a member of the worldwide group is treated in a relevant accounting period as carrying on a ring fence trade (see section 277 of CTA 2010).

(3)   Condition B is that the external finance amount falls to be brought into account for the purposes of corporation tax in calculating the profits of that trade for that accounting period.

Taxation (International and Other Provisions) Act 2010 (c. 8)
Part 7 — Tax treatment of financing costs and income
Chapter 9 — "Available amount"

1071

(4) In this section "relevant accounting period", in relation to a member of the worldwide group, means an accounting period of the member that falls wholly or partly within the period of account of the worldwide group.

334 Group members with income from shipping subject to particular tax treatment in UK

(1) In calculating the available amount, an amount disclosed in the financial statements of the worldwide group ("the external finance amount") must be disregarded if conditions A and B are met.

(2) Condition A is that a member of the worldwide group is, for a relevant accounting period, a tonnage tax company for the purposes of Schedule 22 to FA 2000.

(3) Condition B is that the external finance amount—
    (a) is taken into account in computing relevant shipping profits of that company for that accounting period, or
    (b) comprises deductible finance costs outside the ring fence, to the extent that they are adjusted under paragraph 61 or 62 of Schedule 22 to FA 2000.

(4) In this section—
    "relevant accounting period", in relation to a member of the worldwide group, means an accounting period of the member that falls wholly or partly within the period of account of the worldwide group, and
    "relevant shipping profits" has the same meaning as in Schedule 22 to FA 2000 (see Part 6 of that Schedule).

335 Group members with income from property rental subject to particular tax treatment in UK

(1) In calculating the available amount, an amount disclosed in the financial statements of the worldwide group ("the external finance amount") must be disregarded if conditions A and B are met.

(2) Condition A is that a member of the worldwide group is treated in a relevant accounting period as carrying on a separate business under section 541 of CTA 2010 (ring-fencing of property rental business).

(3) Condition B is that the external finance amount falls to be brought into account in calculating the profits arising from that business in that accounting period.

(4) In this section "relevant accounting period", in relation to a member of the worldwide group, means an accounting period of the member that falls wholly or partly within the period of account of the worldwide group.

336 Meaning of accounting expressions used in this Chapter

Subject to any provision to the contrary, expressions used in this Chapter have the meaning for the time being given by international accounting standards.

1072

Taxation (International and Other Provisions) Act 2010 (c. 8)
Part 7 − Tax treatment of financing costs and income
Chapter 10 − Other interpretative provisions

CHAPTER 10

OTHER INTERPRETATIVE PROVISIONS

337 The worldwide group

In this Part "the worldwide group" means any group of entities that−
   (a)   is large, and
   (b)   contains one or more relevant group companies.

338 Meaning of "group"

(1)   Subject to subsections (2) and (3), in this Part "group" has the meaning for the time being given by international accounting standards.

(2)   If a group would (apart from this subsection) contain more than one ultimate parent, each of those ultimate parents, together with its subsidiaries, is to be treated as a separate group.

(3)   An entity that is a parent of the ultimate parent of a group is to be treated as not being a member of the group.

(4)   Subsections (2) and (3) do not apply for the purposes of section 339.

339 Meaning of "ultimate parent"

(1)   For the purposes of this Part, "ultimate parent", in relation to a group, means an entity that−
   (a)   is a member of the group,
   (b)   is a corporate entity or a relevant non-corporate entity,
   (c)   is not a subsidiary (whether direct or indirect) of a corporate entity or a relevant non-corporate entity, and
   (d)   is not a collective investment scheme.

(2)   In this section "collective investment scheme" has the meaning given by section 235 of FISMA 2000.

340 Meaning of "corporate entity"

(1)   In this Part "corporate entity" means (subject to subsection (4))−
   (a)   a body corporate incorporated under the laws of any part of the United Kingdom or any other country or territory, or
   (b)   any other entity that meets conditions A and B.

(2)   Condition A is that the person or persons who have an interest in the entity hold shares in the entity, or interests corresponding to shares.

(3)   Condition B is that the amount of profits to which each person who has an interest in the entity is entitled depends upon a decision that−
   (a)   is taken by the entity or members of the entity, and
   (b)   is taken after the period in which the profits arise.

(4)   The following are not corporate entities for the purposes of this Part−
   (a)   the Crown,
   (b)   a Minister of the Crown,

Taxation (International and Other Provisions) Act 2010 (c. 8)
Part 7 – Tax treatment of financing costs and income
Chapter 10 – Other interpretative provisions

1073

    (c)   a government department,

    (d)   a Northern Ireland department, or

    (e)   a foreign sovereign power.

341   Meaning of "relevant non-corporate entity"

(1)   In this Part "relevant non-corporate entity" means an entity –

    (a)   that is not a corporate entity, and

    (b)   in relation to which conditions A and B are met.

(2)   Condition A is that shares or other interests in the entity are listed on a recognised stock exchange.

(3)   Condition B is that the shares or other interests in the entity are sufficiently widely held.

(4)   For this purpose shares or other interests in an entity are "sufficiently widely held" if no participator in the entity holds more than 10% by value of all the shares or other interests in the entity.

(5)   Section 454 of CTA 2010 (meaning of participator) applies for the purposes of this section.

(6)   In the application of that provision for those purposes, references to a company are to be treated as references to an entity.

342   Treatment of entities stapled to corporate, or relevant non-corporate, entities

(1)   If a corporate entity is stapled to another entity, the two entities are treated for the purposes of this Part as if –

    (a)   they were one entity, and

    (b)   that one entity were a corporate entity.

(2)   If a relevant non-corporate entity is stapled to another entity, the two entities are treated as if –

    (a)   they were one entity, and

    (b)   that one entity were a relevant non-corporate entity.

(3)   For the purposes of this section, an entity ("entity A") is "stapled" to another ("entity B") if, in consequence of the nature of the rights attaching to the shares or other interests in entity A (including any terms or conditions attaching to the right to transfer the interests), it is necessary or advantageous for a person who has, disposes of or acquires shares or other interests in entity A also to have, to dispose of or to acquire shares or other interests in entity B.

343   Treatment of business combinations

(1)   This section applies if two corporate entities –

    (a)   are not subsidiaries of the same entity, but

    (b)   are treated under international accounting standards as a single economic entity by reason of being a business combination achieved by contract.

(2)   The two entities are treated for the purposes of this Part as if –

    (a)   they were one entity, and

1074   *Taxation (International and Other Provisions) Act 2010 (c. 8)*
Part 7 — Tax treatment of financing costs and income
Chapter 10 — Other interpretative provisions

    (b)   that one entity were a corporate entity.

344 Meaning of "large" in relation to a group

(1) For the purposes of this Part, a group is "large" at any time if (and only if) any member of the group is not at that time within the category of micro, small and medium-sized enterprises as defined in the Annex to Commission Recommendation 2003/361/EC of 6 May 2003 ("the Annex").

(2) In its application as a result of subsection (1), the Annex has effect subject to the following qualifications.

(3) If a member of the group is in liquidation or administration, the rights of the liquidator or administrator (in that capacity) are to be left out of account when applying Article 3(3)(b).

(4) Article 3 has effect with the omission of paragraph (5) (declaration in good faith where control cannot be determined etc).

(5) The first sentence of Article 4(1) has effect as if the reference to the latest approved accounting period of a member of the group were to the current accounting period of that member.

(6) Article 4 has effect with the omission of —
    (a)   the second sentence of paragraph (1) (data to be taken into account from date of closure of accounts),
    (b)   paragraph (2) (no change of status unless ceilings exceeded for two consecutive periods), and
    (c)   paragraph (3) (estimate in case of newly established enterprise).

345 Meaning of "UK group company" and "relevant group company"

(1) This section applies for the purposes of this Part.

(2) A company is a "UK group company" if —
    (a)   it meets condition A, and
    (b)   it is a member of the worldwide group.

(3) A company is a "relevant group company" if —
    (a)   it meets condition A, and
    (b)   it meets condition B.

(4) Condition A is that the company —
    (a)   is resident in the United Kingdom, or
    (b)   is not resident in the United Kingdom and is carrying on a trade in the United Kingdom through a permanent establishment in the United Kingdom.

(5) Condition B is that the company is either —
    (a)   the ultimate parent of the worldwide group, or
    (b)   a relevant subsidiary of the ultimate parent of the worldwide group.

(6) A company is a "relevant subsidiary" of the ultimate parent of the worldwide group if the company is a member of the worldwide group and —
    (a)   the company is a 75% subsidiary of the ultimate parent,

Taxation (International and Other Provisions) Act 2010 (c. 8)
Part 7 – Tax treatment of financing costs and income
Chapter 10 – Other interpretative provisions

1075

  (b) the ultimate parent is beneficially entitled to at least 75% of any profits available for distribution to equity holders of the company, or

  (c) the ultimate parent would be beneficially entitled to at least 75% of any assets of the company available for distribution to its equity holders on a winding-up.

(7) Chapter 6 of Part 5 of CTA 2010 (equity holders and profits or assets available for distribution) applies for the purposes of subsection (6)(b) and (c) as it applies for the purposes of section 151(4) of that Act.

346 Financial statements of the worldwide group

(1) This section applies for the purposes of this Part.

(2) References to financial statements of the worldwide group are to consolidated financial statements of the ultimate parent and its subsidiaries; and references to a balance sheet of the worldwide group are to be read accordingly.

(3) References to a period of account of the worldwide group are to a period in respect of which financial statements of the worldwide group are drawn up.

347 Non-compliant financial statements of the worldwide group

(1) This section applies if —
  (a) financial statements of the worldwide group are drawn up in respect of a period,
  (b) those financial statements are not acceptable, and
  (c) the amounts disclosed in those financial statements are materially different from those that would be disclosed in IAS financial statements for the period.

(2) This Part (apart from this section) applies as if IAS financial statements had been drawn up in respect of the period.

(3) For the purposes of this section, financial statements are "acceptable" if —
  (a) they are drawn up in accordance with international accounting standards,
  (b) they meet such conditions relating to accounting standards, or accounting principles or practice, as may be specified in regulations made by the Commissioners, or
  (c) conditions A, B and C are met.

(4) Condition A is that —
  (a) the companies whose results are included in the financial statements, and
  (b) the companies whose results would be included in IAS financial statements of the worldwide group for the same period, were such statements drawn up,
  are the same.

(5) Condition B is that —
  (a) the transactions whose results are reflected in the amounts mentioned in section 332(1)(a) to (g) in the financial statements, and

1076

Taxation (International and Other Provisions) Act 2010 (c. 8)
Part 7 — Tax treatment of financing costs and income
Chapter 10 — Other interpretative provisions

(b)   the transactions whose results would be reflected in those amounts in IAS financial statements of the worldwide group for the same period, were such statements drawn up,

are the same.

(6)   Condition C is that the amounts mentioned in section 332(1)(a) to (d) in the financial statements are calculated using the effective interest method.

(7)   In this section, references to IAS financial statements of the worldwide group for a period are to financial statements of the group for the period drawn up in accordance with international accounting standards.

348   Non-existent financial statements of the worldwide group

(1)   This section applies if financial statements of the worldwide group are not drawn up in respect of a period ("the relevant period").

(2)   If the relevant period is 12 months or less, this Part (apart from this section) applies as if IAS financial statements had been drawn up in respect of the relevant period.

(3)   If the relevant period is more than 12 months, this Part (apart from this section) applies as if IAS financial statements had been drawn up in respect of each period to which subsection (4) applies.

(4)   This subsection applies to a period if —
    (a)   it is the first period of 12 months falling within the relevant period,
    (b)   it is a period of 12 months falling within the relevant period that begins immediately after the end of the period mentioned in paragraph (a), or immediately after the end of a period determined under this paragraph, or
    (c)   it is a period of less than 12 months that —
        (i)   begins immediately after the end of the period mentioned in paragraph (a) or after the end of a period determined under paragraph (b), and
        (ii)   ends at the end of the relevant period.

(5)   In this section, references to IAS financial statements of the worldwide group for a period are to financial statements of the group for the period drawn up in accordance with international accounting standards.

349   References to amounts disclosed in financial statements

(1)   References in this Part to amounts disclosed in financial statements include an amount comprised in an amount so disclosed.

(2)   References in this Part to amounts disclosed in financial statements do not include, in the case of an amount that —
    (a)   is an amount mentioned in section 332(1)(a) to (g), and
    (b)   has been capitalised and is accordingly included in the balance sheet comprised in the financial statements,

any part of that amount that was included in a balance sheet comprised in financial statements for an earlier period.

(3)   References in this Part to amounts disclosed in financial statements do not include —

Taxation (International and Other Provisions) Act 2010 (c. 8)
Part 7 — Tax treatment of financing costs and income
Chapter 10 — Other interpretative provisions

1077

(a)   any amount disclosed in respect of a group pension scheme, or

(b)   any amount disclosed in respect of any entity that is not a member of the group.

350   Translation of amounts disclosed in financial statements

(1)   References in this Part (except in Chapter 2) to an amount disclosed in financial statements for a period are, where the amount is expressed in a currency other than sterling, to that amount translated into its sterling equivalent.

(2)   The exchange rate by reference to which the amount is to be translated is the average rate of exchange for the period calculated from daily spot rates.

351   Expressions taking their meaning from international accounting standards

(1)   For the purposes of this Part, the following expressions have the meaning for the time being given by international accounting standards—

"effective interest method",

"entity",

"parent", and

"subsidiary".

(2)   The Commissioners may by order amend this section.

352   Meaning of "relevant accounting period"

For the purposes of this Part, a "relevant accounting period" of a company, in relation to a period of account of the worldwide group, means any accounting period that falls wholly or partly within the period of account of the worldwide group.

353   Other expressions

In this Part—

"the Commissioners" means the Commissioners for Her Majesty's Revenue and Customs,

"FISMA 2000" means the Financial Services and Markets Act 2000,

"FSA Handbook" means the Handbook made by the Financial Services Authority under FISMA 2000, and

"HMRC" means Her Majesty's Revenue and Customs.

PART 8

OFFSHORE FUNDS

Tax treatment of participants in offshore funds

354   Power to make regulations about tax treatment of participants

(1)   The Treasury may by regulations make provision about the treatment of participants in an offshore fund for the purposes of enactments relating to income tax, corporation tax or capital gains tax.

(2) Regulations under subsection (1) may, in particular, make special provision about the treatment of participants in an offshore fund comprising —

    (a) a part of umbrella arrangements (see section 360), or

    (b) arrangements relating to a class of interest in other arrangements (see section 361).

(3) Regulations under subsection (1) may, in particular —

    (a) make provision for an offshore fund, or a trustee or officer of an offshore fund, to make elections relating to the treatment of participants in the offshore fund for the purposes of income tax, corporation tax or capital gains tax,

    (b) make provision about the supply of information by offshore funds, or trustees or officers of offshore funds —

        (i) to Her Majesty's Revenue and Customs, or

        (ii) to participants,

    (c) make provision about the preparation of accounts and the keeping of records by offshore funds or trustees or officers of offshore funds, and

    (d) make other provision about the administration of offshore funds.

(4) Regulations under subsection (1) may, in particular, make provision consequential on the repeal by the Offshore Funds (Tax) Regulations 2009 (S.I. 2009/3001) of Chapter 5 of Part 17 of ICTA (offshore funds).

(5) Regulations under subsection (1) may, in particular —

    (a) provide for Her Majesty's Revenue and Customs to exercise a discretion in dealing with any matter,

    (b) make provision by reference to standards or other documents issued by any person,

    (c) modify an enactment (whenever passed or made),

    (d) make different provision for different cases or different purposes, and

    (e) make incidental, consequential, supplementary and transitional provision and savings.

(6) Regulations under subsection (1) may, in particular, provide for provisions to have effect in relation to the tax year, or accounting periods, current on the day on which the regulations are made.

(7) In this section —

    "enactment" includes subordinate legislation (within the meaning of the Interpretation Act 1978), and

    "modify" includes amend, repeal or revoke.

355 Meaning of "offshore fund"

(1) In section 354 "offshore fund" means —

    (a) a mutual fund constituted by a body corporate resident outside the United Kingdom,

    (b) a mutual fund under which property is held on trust for the participants where the trustees of the property are not resident in the United Kingdom, or

    (c) a mutual fund constituted by other arrangements that create rights in the nature of co-ownership where the arrangements take effect by virtue of the law of a territory outside the United Kingdom.

(2) Subsection (1)(c) does not include a mutual fund constituted by two or more persons carrying on a trade or business in partnership.

(3) In this section—

"body corporate" does not include a limited liability partnership, and

"co-ownership" is not restricted to the meaning of that term in the law of any part of the United Kingdom.

(4) See also section 151W(b) of TCGA 1992, section 564U(b) of ITA 2007 and section 519(4)(b) of CTA 2009 (which have the effect that investment bond arrangements are not an offshore fund for the purposes of section 354).

356 Meaning of "mutual fund"

(1) In section 355 "mutual fund" means arrangements with respect to property of any description (including money) that meet conditions A, B and C.

(2) Subsection (1) is subject—
   (a) to the exceptions made by or under sections 357 and 359, and
   (b) to sections 360 and 361.

(3) Condition A is that the purpose or effect of the arrangements is to enable the participants—
   (a) to participate in the acquisition, holding, management or disposal of the property, or
   (b) to receive profits or income arising from the acquisition, holding, management or disposal of the property or sums paid out of such profits or income.

(4) Condition B is that the participants do not have day-to-day control of the management of the property.

(5) For the purposes of condition B a participant does not have day-to-day control of the management of property by virtue of having a right to be consulted or to give directions.

(6) Condition C is that, under the terms of the arrangements, a reasonable investor participating in the arrangements would expect to be able to realise all or part of an investment in the arrangements on a basis calculated entirely, or almost entirely, by reference to—
   (a) the net asset value of the property that is the subject of the arrangements, or
   (b) an index of any description.

(7) The Treasury may by regulations amend condition C.

(8) Regulations under subsection (7) may only be made if a draft of the statutory instrument containing the regulations has been laid before and approved by a resolution of the House of Commons.

357 Exceptions to definition of "mutual fund"

(1) Arrangements are not a mutual fund for the purposes of section 355 if—
   (a) condition D is met, and
   (b) condition E or F is met.

(2) Condition D is that, under the terms of the arrangements, a reasonable investor participating in the arrangements would expect to be able to realise all or part of an investment in the arrangements on a basis mentioned in section 356(6) only in the event of the winding up, dissolution or termination of the arrangements.

(3) Condition E is that the arrangements are not designed to wind up, dissolve or terminate on a date stated in or determinable under the arrangements.

(4) Condition F is that—

    (a) the arrangements are designed to wind up, dissolve or terminate on a date stated in or determinable under the arrangements,

    (b) subsection (5), (6) or (7) applies, and

    (c) the arrangements are not designed to produce a return for participants that equates, in substance, to the return on an investment of money at interest.

(5) This subsection applies if none of the assets that are the subject of the arrangements is a relevant income-producing asset (see section 358).

(6) This subsection applies if, under the terms of the arrangements, the participants in the arrangements are not entitled to the income from the assets that are the subject of the arrangements or any benefit arising from such income.

(7) This subsection applies if—

    (a) under the terms of the arrangements, after deductions for reasonable expenses, any income produced by the assets that are the subject of the arrangements is required to be paid or credited to the participants, and

    (b) a participant who is an individual resident in the United Kingdom would be charged to income tax on the amounts paid or credited.

(8) For the purposes of this section the fact that arrangements provide for a vote or other action that may lead to the winding up, dissolution or termination of the arrangements does not, by itself, mean that the arrangements are designed to wind up, dissolve or terminate on a date stated in or determinable under the arrangements.

358 Meaning of "relevant income-producing asset"

(1) This section has effect for the purposes of section 357.

(2) An asset is a relevant income-producing asset if it produces income on which, if it were held directly by an individual resident in the United Kingdom, the individual would be charged to income tax (but see subsections (3) and (4)).

(3) An asset is not a relevant income-producing asset if the asset is hedged, provided that no income is expected to arise from—

    (a) the asset (taking account of the hedging), or

    (b) any product of the hedging arrangements.

(4) Cash awaiting investment is not a relevant income-producing asset, provided that the cash, and any income that it produces while awaiting investment, is invested as soon as reasonably practicable in assets that are not relevant income-producing assets (as defined by this section).

359 Power to make regulations about exceptions to definition of "mutual fund"

(1) The Treasury may by regulations amend or repeal any provision of section 357 or 358.

(2) The Treasury may by regulations provide that arrangements are not a mutual fund for the purposes of section 355 –
  (a) in specified circumstances, or
  (b) if they are of a specified description.

(3) Regulations under this section may include provision having effect in relation to the tax year, or accounting periods, current on the day on which the regulations are made.

(4) Regulations under subsection (1) may only be made if a draft of the statutory instrument containing the regulations has been laid before and approved by a resolution of the House of Commons.

Supplementary

360 Treatment of umbrella arrangements

(1) This section has effect for the purposes of this Part.

(2) In the case of umbrella arrangements (see section 363) –
  (a) each part of the umbrella arrangements is to be treated as separate arrangements, and
  (b) the umbrella arrangements are to be disregarded.

(3) Subsection (2)(a) is subject to section 361.

361 Treatment of arrangements comprising more than one class of interest

(1) This section has effect for the purposes of this Part.

(2) Where there is more than one class of interest in arrangements (the "main arrangements") –
  (a) the arrangements relating to each class of interest are to be treated as separate arrangements, and
  (b) the main arrangements are to be disregarded.

(3) In relation to umbrella arrangements, "class of interest" does not include a part of the umbrella arrangements (but there may be more than one class of interest in a part of umbrella arrangements).

362 Meaning of "participant" and "participation"

(1) In this Part references to "participant", in relation to arrangements (or a fund), are to a person taking part in the arrangements (or the arrangements constituting the fund), whether by becoming the owner of, or of any part of, the property that is the subject of the arrangements or otherwise.

(2) In this Part references (however expressed) to participation, in relation to arrangements (or a fund), are to be read in accordance with subsection (1).

363 Meaning of "umbrella arrangements" and "part of umbrella arrangements"

(1) In this Part "umbrella arrangements" means arrangements which provide for separate pooling of the contributions of the participants and the profits or income out of which payments are made to them.

(2) In this Part references to a part of umbrella arrangements are to the arrangements relating to a separate pool.

PART 9

AMENDMENTS TO RELOCATE PROVISIONS OF TAX LEGISLATION

364 Oil activities

Schedule 1, which inserts a new Chapter 16A (oil activities) in Part 2 (trading income) of ITTOIA 2005, has effect.

365 Alternative finance arrangements

Schedule 2, which—

    (a) inserts a new Part 10A in ITA 2007 (see Part 1 of the Schedule),

    (b) inserts a new Chapter 4 in Part 4 of TCGA 1992 (see Part 2 of the Schedule), and

    (c) makes other amendments (see Part 3 of the Schedule),

has effect.

366 Power to amend the alternative finance provisions

(1) The Treasury may by order amend the alternative finance provisions.

(2) The amendments which may be made by such an order include—

    (a) the variation of provision already included in the alternative finance provisions, and

    (b) the introduction into the alternative finance provisions of new provision relating to alternative finance arrangements.

(3) In subsection (2)(b) "alternative finance arrangements" means arrangements which in the Treasury's opinion—

    (a) equate in substance to a loan, deposit or other transaction of a kind that generally involves the payment of interest, but

    (b) achieve a similar effect without including provision for the payment of interest.

(4) An order under subsection (1) may, in particular—

    (a) make provision of a kind similar to provision already made by the alternative finance provisions,

    (b) make other provision about the treatment for the purposes of the Tax Acts of arrangements to which the order applies,

    (c) make provision generally or only in relation to specified cases or circumstances,

    (d) make different provision for different cases or circumstances, and

    (e) make incidental, supplemental, consequential and transitional provision and savings.

(5)   An order making consequential provision under subsection (4)(e) may, in particular, include provision amending a provision of the Tax Acts.

(6)   In this section "the alternative finance provisions" means—

   (a)   section 367A of ICTA,

   (b)   Chapter 4 of Part 4 of TCGA 1992,

   (c)   sections 372A to 372D, Part 10A and section 1005(2A) of ITA 2007,

   (d)   Chapter 6 of Part 6 of CTA 2009,

   (e)   sections 110, 256 to 259 and 1019 of CTA 2010.

(7)   An order under this section that—

   (a)   includes such amendments as are mentioned in subsection (2)(b), or

   (b)   amends an enactment not contained in the alternative finance provisions but contained in an Act,

may only be made if a draft of the statutory instrument containing the order has been laid before and approved by a resolution of the House of Commons.

367   Leasing arrangements: finance leases and loans

Schedule 3, which inserts—

   (a)   a new Part 11A in ITA 2007 (leasing arrangements: finance leases and loans), and

   (b)   a new section 37A in TCGA 1992 (consideration on disposal of certain leases),

has effect.

368   Sale and lease-back etc

Schedule 4, which inserts a new Part 12A in ITA 2007 (sale and lease-back etc), has effect.

369   Factoring of income etc

Schedule 5, which inserts new Chapters 5B and 5C (finance arrangements, and loan or credit transactions) in Part 13 of ITA 2007 (anti-avoidance), has effect.

370   UK representatives of non-UK residents

Schedule 6, which inserts—

   (a)   new Chapters 2B and 2C in Part 14 of ITA 2007 (income tax: UK representatives of non-UK residents), and

   (b)   a new Part 7A in TCGA 1992 (capital gains tax: UK representatives of non-UK residents),

has effect.

371   Miscellaneous relocations

Schedule 7 (amendments to relocate some miscellaneous tax enactments) has effect.

PART 10

GENERAL PROVISIONS

Subordinate legislation

372 Orders and regulations

(1) Any power of the Treasury or the Commissioners for Her Majesty's Revenue and Customs to make any order or regulations under this Act is exercisable by statutory instrument.

(2) Any statutory instrument containing any order or regulations made by the Treasury or the Commissioners for Her Majesty's Revenue and Customs under this Act is subject to annulment in pursuance of a resolution of the House of Commons.

(3) Subsection (2) does not apply —

    (a) in relation to regulations under section 7 (double taxation relief: general regulations),

    (b) in relation to regulations under section 354(1) or 359(2) (offshore funds) if a draft of the statutory instrument containing the regulations has been laid before and approved by a resolution of the House of Commons,

    (c) in relation to an order under section 377(2) (transitional or saving provision in connection with coming into force of this Act), or

    (d) if any other Parliamentary procedure is expressly provided to apply in relation to the order or regulations.

(4) Section 828 of ICTA (which includes provision about orders made before 1 April 2010 under provisions of the Corporation Tax Acts not contained in ICTA) does not apply in relation to an order made by the Treasury under this Act before 1 April 2010.

Interpretation

373 Abbreviated references to Acts

In this Act—

    "CAA 2001" means the Capital Allowances Act 2001,

    "CTA 2009" means the Corporation Tax Act 2009,

    "CTA 2010" means the Corporation Tax Act 2010,

    "FA", followed by a year, means the Finance Act of that year,

    "F(No.2)A", followed by a year, means the Finance (No. 2) Act of that year,

    "ICTA" means the Income and Corporation Taxes Act 1988,

    "ITA 2007" means the Income Tax Act 2007,

    "ITEPA 2003" means the Income Tax (Earnings and Pensions) Act 2003,

    "ITTOIA 2005" means the Income Tax (Trading and Other Income) Act 2005,

    "TCGA 1992" means the Taxation of Chargeable Gains Act 1992, and

    "TMA 1970" means the Taxes Management Act 1970.

Final provisions

374 Minor and consequential amendments

Schedule 8 (minor and consequential amendments, including amendments for purposes connected with other tax law rewrite Acts) has effect.

375 Power to make consequential provision

(1) The Treasury may by order make such provision as the Treasury consider appropriate in consequence of this Act.

(2) The power conferred by subsection (1) may not be exercised after 31 March 2013.

(3) An order under this section may amend, repeal or revoke any provision made by or under an Act.

(4) An order under this section may contain provision having retrospective effect.

(5) An order under this section may contain incidental, supplemental, consequential and transitional provision and savings.

(6) In subsection (3) "Act" includes an Act of the Scottish Parliament and Northern Ireland legislation.

376 Power to undo changes

(1) The Treasury may by order make provision, in relation to a case in which the Treasury consider that a provision of this Act changes the effect of the law, for the purpose of returning the effect of the law to what it would have been if this Act had not been passed.

(2) The power conferred by subsection (1) may not be exercised after 31 March 2013.

(3) An order under this section may amend, repeal or revoke any provision made by or under –
    (a) this Act, or
    (b) any other Act.

(4) An order under this section may contain provision having retrospective effect.

(5) An order under this section may contain incidental, supplemental, consequential and transitional provision and savings.

(6) In subsection (3)(b) "Act" includes an Act of the Scottish Parliament and Northern Ireland legislation.

377 Transitional provisions and savings

(1) Schedule 9 (transitional provisions and savings) has effect.

(2) The Treasury may by order make such transitional or saving provision as the Treasury consider appropriate in connection with the coming into force of this Act.

(3) An order under this section may contain provision having retrospective effect.

378 Repeals and revocations

(1) Schedule 10 (repeals and revocations, including of spent enactments and including repeals for purposes connected with other tax law rewrite Acts) has effect.

(2) If—

    (a) CTA 2010 repeals or revokes a provision and the repeal or revocation is for corporation tax purposes only (see section 1181(2) of that Act), and

    (b) this Act also repeals or revokes the provision,

the repeal or revocation of the provision by this Act is for all purposes other than corporation tax purposes.

379 Index of defined expressions

(1) Schedule 11 (index of defined expressions that apply for purposes of Parts 2 to 8) has effect.

(2) That Schedule lists the places where some of the expressions used in Parts 2 to 8 are defined or otherwise explained.

380 Extent

(1) This Act extends to England and Wales, Scotland and Northern Ireland (but see subsection (2)).

(2) An amendment, repeal or revocation contained in Schedule 7, 8 or 10 has the same extent as the provision amended, repealed or revoked.

381 Commencement

(1) This Act comes into force on 1 April 2010 and has effect—

    (a) for corporation tax purposes, for accounting periods ending on or after that day,

    (b) for income tax and capital gains tax purposes, for the tax year 2010-11 and subsequent tax years, and

    (c) for petroleum revenue tax purposes, for chargeable periods beginning on or after 1 July 2010.

(2) Subsection (1) does not apply to the following provisions (which therefore come into force on the day on which this Act is passed)—

    (a) section 372,

    (b) section 373,

    (c) the amendments in TCGA 1992 and ITA 2007 made by Part 13 of Schedule 8,

    (d) section 374 so far as relating to those amendments,

    (e) section 375,

    (f) section 376,

    (g) section 377(2) and (3),

    (h) section 380,

    (i) this section, and

    (j) section 382.

382 Short title

> This Act may be cited as the Taxation (International and Other Provisions) Act 2010.

SCHEDULES

SCHEDULE 1   Section 364

OIL ACTIVITIES: NEW CHAPTER 16A OF PART 2 OF ITTOIA 2005

1   ITTOIA 2005 is amended as follows.

2   After section 225 insert—

"CHAPTER 16A

OIL ACTIVITIES

Basic definitions

225A   Meaning of "oil extraction activities"

(1)   In this Chapter "oil extraction activities" means activities within any of subsections (2) to (5) (but see also section 225M(6)).

(2)   Activities of a person in searching for oil in the United Kingdom or a designated area or causing such searching to be carried out for that person.

(3)   Activities of a person in extracting, or causing to be extracted for that person, oil at any place in the United Kingdom or a designated area under rights which—
       (a)   authorise the extraction, and
       (b)   are held by that person.

(4)   Activities of a person in transporting, or causing to be transported for that person, oil extracted at any such place not on dry land under rights which—
       (a)   authorise the extraction, and
       (b)   are held by that person,
     if the transportation meets condition A or B (see subsections (6) and (7)).

(5)   Activities of a person in effecting, or causing to be effected for that person, the initial treatment or initial storage of oil won from any oil field under rights which—
       (a)   authorise its extraction, and
       (b)   are held by that person.

(6)   Condition A is that the transportation is to the place where the oil is first landed in the United Kingdom.

(7)   Condition B is that the transportation—

> (a) is to the place in the United Kingdom, or
>
> (b) in the case of oil first landed in another country, is to the place in that or any other country (other than the United Kingdom),
>
> at which the seller in a sale at arm's length could reasonably be expected to deliver it (or, if there is more than one such place, the one nearest to the place of extraction).

(8) The definition of "initial storage" in section 12(1) of OTA 1975 applies for the purposes of this section.

(9) But in its application for those purposes in relation to the person mentioned in subsection (5) and to oil won from any one oil field, that definition is to have effect as if the reference to the maximum daily production rate of oil for the field mentioned in that definition were to a share of that maximum daily production rate proportionate to that person's share of the oil won from that field.

(10) In this section "initial treatment" has the same meaning as in Part 1 of OTA 1975 (see section 12(1) of that Act).

225B Meaning of "oil rights"

In this Chapter "oil rights" means—

> (a) rights to oil to be extracted at any place in the United Kingdom or a designated area, or
>
> (b) rights to interests in or to the benefit of such oil.

225C Meaning of "ring fence income"

In this Chapter "ring fence income" means income arising from oil extraction activities or oil rights.

225D Meaning of "ring fence trade"

In this Chapter "ring fence trade" means activities which—

> (a) are within the definition of "oil-related activities" in section 16(2) (oil extraction and related activities), and
>
> (b) constitute a separate trade (whether because of section 16(1) or otherwise).

225E Other definitions

In this Chapter—

> "chargeable period" has the same meaning as in Part 1 of OTA 1975 (see section 1(3) of that Act),
>
> "designated area" means an area designated by Order in Council under section 1(7) of the Continental Shelf Act 1964,
>
> "oil" means any substance won or capable of being won under the authority of a licence granted under Part 1 of the Petroleum Act 1998 or the Petroleum (Production) Act (Northern Ireland) 1964 (c. 28 (N.I.)), other than methane gas won in the course of operations for making and keeping mines safe,
>
> "oil field" has the same meaning as in Part 1 of OTA 1975 (see section 12(1) of that Act),
>
> "OTA 1975" means the Oil Taxation Act 1975, and

"participator" has the same meaning as in Part 1 of OTA 1975 (see section 12(1) of that Act).

Oil valuation

225F Valuation where market value taken into account under section 2 of OTA 1975

(1) This section applies if a person disposes of oil in circumstances such that the market value of the oil —

    (a) falls to be taken into account under section 2 of OTA 1975, otherwise than by virtue of paragraph 6 of Schedule 3 to that Act, in calculating for petroleum revenue tax purposes the assessable profit or allowable loss accruing to that person in a chargeable period from an oil field, or

    (b) would so fall but for section 10 of that Act.

(2) For income tax purposes, the disposal of the oil, and its acquisition by the person to whom it was disposed of, are to be treated as having been for a consideration equal to the market value of the oil —

    (a) as so taken into account under section 2 of that Act, or

    (b) as would have been so taken into account under that section but for section 10 of that Act.

225G Valuation where disposal not sale at arm's length

(1) This section applies if conditions A, B and C are met.

(2) Condition A is that a person disposes of oil acquired by the person —

    (a) in the course of oil extraction activities carried on by the person, or

    (b) as a result of oil rights held by the person.

(3) Condition B is that the disposal is not a sale at arm's length (as defined in paragraph 1 of Schedule 3 to OTA 1975).

(4) Condition C is that section 225F does not apply in relation to the disposal.

(5) For income tax purposes, the disposal of the oil, and its acquisition by the person to whom it was disposed of, are to be treated as having been for a consideration equal to the market value of the oil.

(6) Paragraphs 2 and 3A of Schedule 3 to OTA 1975 (definition of market value of oil including light gases) apply for the purposes of this section as they apply for the purposes of Part 1 of that Act, but with the following modifications.

(7) Those modifications are that —

    (a) any reference in paragraph 2 to the notional delivery day for the actual oil is to be read as a reference to the day on which the oil is disposed of as mentioned in this section, and

    (b) paragraph 2(4) is to be treated as omitted.

225H Valuation where excess of nominated proceeds

(1) This section applies if an excess of nominated proceeds for a chargeable period —

(a) is taken into account in calculating a person's profits under section 2(5)(e) of OTA 1975, or

(b) would have been so taken into account if the person were chargeable to tax under OTA 1975 in respect of an oil field.

(2) For income tax purposes, the amount of the excess is to be added to the consideration which the person is treated as having received in respect of oil disposed of by that person in the period.

225I Valuation where relevant appropriation but no disposal

(1) This section applies if conditions A and B are met.

(2) Condition A is that a person makes a relevant appropriation of oil without disposing of it.

(3) Condition B is that the person does so in circumstances such that the market value of the oil —

(a) falls to be taken into account under section 2 of OTA 1975 in calculating for petroleum revenue tax purposes the assessable profit or allowable loss accruing to that person in a chargeable period from an oil field, or

(b) would so fall but for section 10 of that Act.

(4) For income tax purposes, the person is to be treated as having, at the time of the appropriation —

(a) sold the oil in the course of the separate trade consisting of activities falling within the definition of "oil-related activities" in section 16(2) (oil extraction and related activities), and

(b) purchased it in the course of the separate trade consisting of activities not so falling.

(5) For income tax purposes, that sale and purchase is to be treated as having been at a price equal to the market value of the oil —

(a) as so taken into account under section 2 of OTA 1975, or

(b) as would have been so taken into account under that section but for section 10 of that Act.

(6) In this section "relevant appropriation" has the meaning given by section 12(1) of OTA 1975.

225J Valuation where appropriation to refining etc

(1) This section applies if conditions A, B and C are met.

(2) Condition A is that a person appropriates oil acquired by the person —

(a) in the course of oil extraction activities carried on by the person, or

(b) as a result of oil rights held by the person.

(3) Condition B is that the oil is appropriated to refining or to any use except the production purposes of an oil field (as defined in section 12(1) of OTA 1975).

(4) Condition C is that section 225I does not apply in relation to the appropriation.

(5) For income tax purposes—

  (a) the person is to be treated as having, at the time of the appropriation, sold and purchased the oil as mentioned in section 225I(4)(a) and (b), and

  (b) that sale and purchase is to be treated as having been at a price equal to the market value of the oil.

(6) Paragraphs 2 and 3A of Schedule 3 to OTA 1975 (definition of market value of oil including light gases) apply for the purposes of this section as they apply for the purposes of Part 1 of that Act, but with the following modifications.

(7) Those modifications are that—

  (a) any reference in paragraph 2 to the notional delivery day for the actual oil is to be read as a reference to the day on which the oil is appropriated as mentioned in this section,

  (b) any reference in paragraphs 2 and 2A to oil being relevantly appropriated is to be read as a reference to its being appropriated as mentioned in this section, and

  (c) paragraph 2(4) is to be treated as omitted.

Regional development grants

225K Reduction of expenditure by reference to regional development grant

(1) This section applies if conditions A and B are met.

(2) Condition A is that a person has incurred expenditure (by way of purchase, rent or otherwise) on the acquisition of an asset in a transaction to which paragraph 2 of Schedule 4 to OTA 1975 applies (transactions between connected persons or otherwise than at arm's length).

(3) Condition B is that the expenditure incurred by the other person mentioned in that paragraph in acquiring, bringing into existence or enhancing the value of the asset as mentioned in that paragraph—

  (a) has been or is to be met by a regional development grant, and

  (b) falls (in whole or in part) to be taken into account under Part 2 or 6 of CAA 2001 (capital allowances relating to plant and machinery or research and development).

(4) Subsection (5) applies for the purposes of the charge to income tax on the income arising from the activities of the person mentioned in subsection (2) which are treated by section 16(1) (oil extraction and related activities) as a separate trade for those purposes.

(5) The expenditure mentioned in subsection (2) is to be reduced by the amount of the regional development grant mentioned in subsection (3).

(6) In this section "regional development grant" means a grant falling within section 534(1) of CAA 2001 (Northern Ireland regional development grant).

225L Adjustment as a result of regional development grant

(1) This section applies if conditions A, B and C are met.

(2) Condition A is that expenditure incurred by a person in relation to an asset in a tax year ("the initial period") has been or is to be met by a regional development grant.

(3) Condition B is that, despite the provisions of section 534(2) and (3) of CAA 2001 (Northern Ireland regional development grants) and section 225K of this Act, in determining that person's liability to income tax for the initial period, the whole or some part of that expenditure falls to be taken into account under Part 2 or 6 of CAA 2001.

(4) Condition C is that—

    (a) expenditure on the asset becomes allowable under section 3 or 4 of OTA 1975 in a tax year (an "adjustment period") subsequent to the initial period, or

    (b) the proportion of any such expenditure which is allowable in an adjustment period is different as compared with the initial period.

(5) There is to be redetermined for the purposes of subsections (7) and (8) the amount of the expenditure mentioned in subsection (2) which would have been taken into account as mentioned in subsection (3) if the circumstances mentioned in subsection (4) had existed in the initial period.

(6) According to whether the amount as so redetermined is greater or less than the amount actually taken into account as mentioned in subsection (3), the difference is referred to in subsections (7) and (8) as the increase or the reduction in the allowance.

(7) If there is an increase in the allowance, an amount of capital expenditure equal to the increase is to be treated, for the purposes of Part 2 or 6 of CAA 2001, as having been incurred by the person concerned in the adjustment period on an extension of, or addition to, the asset mentioned in subsection (2).

(8) If there is a reduction in the allowance, the person concerned is to be treated, for the purpose of determining that person's liability to income tax, as having received in the adjustment period, as income of the trade in connection with which the expenditure mentioned in subsection (2) was incurred, a sum equal to the amount of the reduction in the allowance.

(9) In this section "regional development grant" has the meaning given by section 225K(6).

Tariff receipts etc

225M Tariff receipts etc

(1) Subsection (5) applies to a sum which meets conditions A, B and C.

(2) Condition A is that the sum constitutes a tariff receipt or tax-exempt tariffing receipt of a person who is a participator in an oil field.

(3) Condition B is that the sum constitutes consideration in the nature of income rather than capital.

(4)   Condition C is that the sum would not, but for subsection (5), be treated as mentioned in that subsection.

(5)   The sum is to be treated as a receipt of the separate trade mentioned in section 16(1) (oil extraction and related activities).

(6)   So far as they would not otherwise be so treated, the activities—

    (a)   of a participator in an oil field, or

    (b)   of a person connected with the participator,

in making available an asset in a way which gives rise to tariff receipts or tax-exempt tariffing receipts of the participator are to be treated for the purposes of this Chapter as oil extraction activities.

(7)   In determining for the purposes of subsection (2) whether a sum constitutes a tariff receipt or tax-exempt tariffing receipt of a person who is a participator, no account may be taken of any sum which—

    (a)   is in fact received or receivable by a person connected with the participator, and

    (b)   constitutes a tariff receipt or tax-exempt tariffing receipt of the participator.

But in relation to the person by whom such a sum is actually received, subsection (2) has effect as if the person were a participator and as if condition A were met.

(8)   References in this section to a person connected with a participator include a person with whom the person is associated, within the meaning of paragraph 11 of Schedule 2 to the Oil Taxation Act 1983, but section 878(5) of this Act (application of definition of "connected" persons) does not apply for the purposes of this section.

(9)   In this section—

"tax-exempt tariffing receipt" has the meaning given by section 6A(2) of the Oil Taxation Act 1983, and

"tariff receipt" has the same meaning as in that Act.

Abandonment guarantees

225N Expenditure on and under abandonment guarantees

(1)   Subsection (2) applies if, as a result of section 3(1)(hh) of OTA 1975 (obtaining abandonment guarantee), expenditure incurred by a participator in an oil field is allowable (in whole or in part) for petroleum revenue tax purposes under section 3 of that Act.

(2)   So far as that expenditure is so allowable, it is to be allowed as a deduction in calculating the participator's ring fence income.

(3)   Subsection (4) applies if a payment is made by the guarantor under an abandonment guarantee.

(4)   So far as any expenditure for which the relevant participator is liable is met, directly or indirectly, out of the payment, the expenditure is not to be regarded for income tax purposes as having been incurred by the relevant participator or any other participator in the oil field concerned.

(5)   See also section 225P (payment under abandonment guarantee not immediately applied).

(6)   In this Chapter —

"abandonment guarantee" has the same meaning as it has for the purposes of section 105 of FA 1991 (see section 104 of that Act), and

"the guarantor" and "the relevant participator" have the same meaning as in section 104 of that Act.

225O Relief for reimbursement expenditure under abandonment guarantees

(1)   This section applies if —

(a)   a payment ("the guarantee payment") is made by the guarantor under an abandonment guarantee,

(b)   as a result of the making of the guarantee payment, the relevant participator becomes liable under the terms of the abandonment guarantee to pay any sum to the guarantor, and

(c)   expenditure is incurred, or consideration in money's worth is given, by the relevant participator in or towards meeting that liability.

(2)   In this section "reimbursement expenditure" means expenditure incurred as mentioned in subsection (1)(c) or consideration (or the value of consideration) given as so mentioned; and any reference to the incurring of reimbursement expenditure is to be read accordingly.

(3)   So much of any reimbursement expenditure as constitutes qualifying expenditure (see subsection (4)) is to be allowed as a deduction in calculating the relevant participator's ring fence income; and no part of the expenditure which is so allowed is to be otherwise deductible or allowable by way of relief for income tax purposes.

(4)   The amount of reimbursement expenditure incurred in any tax year by the relevant participator which constitutes qualifying expenditure is determined by the formula —

$$A \times \frac{B}{C}$$

where —

A is the reimbursement expenditure incurred in the tax year,

B is so much of the expenditure represented by the guarantee payment as, had it been incurred by the relevant participator, would have been taken into account (by way of capital allowance or a deduction) in calculating the relevant participator's ring fence income, and

C is the total of the sums which, at or before the end of the tax year, the relevant participator is or has become liable to pay to the guarantor as mentioned in subsection (1)(b).

But this is subject to subsection (5).

(5)   In relation to the guarantee payment, the total of the reimbursement expenditure (whenever incurred) which constitutes qualifying

expenditure may not exceed whichever is the less of B and C in subsection (4).

(6) Any limitation on qualifying expenditure under subsection (5) is to be applied to the expenditure of a later tax year in preference to an earlier one.

(7) For the purposes of this section, the expenditure represented by the guarantee payment is any expenditure—

    (a) for which the relevant participator is liable, and

    (b) which is met, directly or indirectly, out of the guarantee payment (and which, accordingly, because of section 225N(4) is not to be regarded as expenditure incurred by the relevant participator).

(8) See also—

    (a) section 225P (payment under abandonment guarantee not immediately applied), and

    (b) section 225Q which excludes amounts from subsection (1).

225P Payment under abandonment guarantee not immediately applied

(1) This section applies if—

    (a) a payment made by the guarantor under an abandonment guarantee is not immediately applied in meeting any expenditure,

    (b) the payment is for any period invested (either specifically or together with payments made by persons other than the guarantor) so as to be represented by, or by part of, the assets of a fund or account, and

    (c) at a subsequent time, any expenditure for which the relevant participator is liable is met out of the assets of the fund or account.

(2) The references in sections 225N(4) and 225O(7) to expenditure which is met, directly or indirectly, out of the payment are to be read as references to so much of the expenditure for which the relevant participator is liable as is met out of those assets of the fund or account which, at the subsequent time mentioned in subsection (1)(c), it is just and reasonable to attribute to the payment.

225Q Amounts excluded from section 225O(1)

(1) This section applies if—

    (a) the whole of the guarantee payment mentioned in section 225O, or of the assets which under section 225P are attributed to the guarantee payment, is not applied in meeting liabilities of the relevant participator so mentioned which fall within section 104(1)(a) and (b) of FA 1991, and

    (b) a sum representing the unapplied part of the guarantee payment or of those assets is repaid, directly or indirectly, to the guarantor so mentioned.

(2) Any liability of the relevant participator to repay that sum is to be excluded in determining the total liability of the relevant participator which falls within section 225O(1)(b).

(3) The repayment to the guarantor of that sum is not to be regarded as expenditure incurred by the relevant participator as mentioned in section 225O(1)(c).

Abandonment expenditure

225R Introduction to sections 225S and 225T

(1) Sections 225S and 225T apply if—

   (a) paragraph 2A of Schedule 5 to OTA 1975 applies, or would apply if a claim under paragraph 2A(2) of that Schedule were made, and

   (b) the default payment falls (in whole or part) to be attributed to the contributing participator under paragraph 2A(2) of that Schedule.

(2) In section 225S "the additional abandonment expenditure" means the amount which is attributed to the contributing participator as mentioned in subsection (1)(b) (whether representing the whole or only part of the default payment).

(3) In this Chapter "default payment", "the defaulter" and "contributing participator" have the same meaning as in paragraph 2A of Schedule 5 to OTA 1975.

225S Relief for expenditure incurred by a participator in meeting defaulter's abandonment expenditure

(1) Relief by way of capital allowance, or a deduction in calculating ring fence income, is to be available to the contributing participator in respect of the additional abandonment expenditure if any such relief or deduction would have been available to the defaulter if—

   (a) the defaulter had incurred the additional abandonment expenditure, and

   (b) at the time that that expenditure was incurred the defaulter continued to carry on a ring fence trade.

(2) The basis of qualification for or entitlement to any relief or deduction which is available to the contributing participator under this section is to be determined on the assumption that the conditions in subsection (1)(a) and (b) are met.

(3) But, subject to subsection (2), any such relief or deduction is to be available in the same way as if the additional abandonment expenditure had been incurred by the contributing participator for the purposes of the ring fence trade carried on by the contributing participator.

225T Reimbursement by defaulter in respect of certain abandonment expenditure

(1) This section applies if expenditure is incurred, or consideration in money's worth is given, by the defaulter in reimbursing the contributing participator in respect of, or otherwise making good to the contributing participator, the whole or any part of the default payment.

(2) In this section "reimbursement expenditure" means expenditure incurred as mentioned in subsection (1) or consideration (or the value of consideration) given as so mentioned; and any reference to the incurring of reimbursement expenditure is to be read accordingly.

(3) Reimbursement expenditure is to be allowed as a deduction in calculating the defaulter's ring fence income (but this is subject to subsection (6)).

(4) Reimbursement expenditure received by the contributing participator is to be treated as a receipt (in the nature of income) of the participator's ring fence trade for the relevant tax year (but this is subject to subsection (6)).

(5) Any additional assessment to income tax required in order to take account of the receipt of reimbursement expenditure by the contributing participator may be made at any time not later than 4 years after the end of the calendar year in which the reimbursement expenditure is so received.

(6) In relation to a particular default payment, reimbursement expenditure incurred at any time —

    (a) is to be allowed as mentioned in subsection (3), and

    (b) is to be taken into account as a result of subsection (4) in calculating the contributing participator's ring fence income,

only so far as, when aggregated with any reimbursement expenditure previously incurred in respect of that default payment, it does not exceed so much of the default payment as falls to be attributed to the contributing participator as mentioned in section 225R(1)(b).

(7) The incurring of reimbursement expenditure is not to be regarded, by virtue of section 532 of CAA 2001 (the general rule excluding contributions), as the meeting of the expenditure of the contributing participator in making the default payment.

(8) In subsection (4) "the relevant tax year" means —

    (a) the tax year in which the reimbursement expenditure is received by the contributing participator, or

    (b) if the contributing participator's ring fence trade is permanently discontinued before the receipt of the reimbursement expenditure, the last tax year in which that trade was carried on.

Interest on repayment of APRT

225U Interest on repayment of APRT

(1) Subsection (2) applies if interest is paid to a participator under paragraph 10(4) of Schedule 19 to FA 1982 (interest on advance petroleum revenue tax which becomes repayable).

(2) The interest paid is to be disregarded in calculating the participator's income for income tax purposes."

Taxation (International and Other Provisions) Act 2010 (c. 8)
Schedule 2 — Alternative finance arrangements
Part 1 — New Part 10A of ITA 2007

1099

SCHEDULE 2

ALTERNATIVE FINANCE ARRANGEMENTS

PART 1

NEW PART 10A OF ITA 2007

1   ITA 2007 is amended as follows.

2   After Part 10 insert —

"PART 10A

ALTERNATIVE FINANCE ARRANGEMENTS

Introduction

564A   Introduction

(1)   This Part —

(a)   contains provisions about the treatment as interest for certain income tax purposes of alternative finance return under alternative finance arrangements with financial institutions (see sections 564M to 564Q), and

(b)   contains some special provisions about the treatment of investment bond arrangements (see sections 564R to 564U) and some other rules about alternative finance arrangements (see sections 564V to 564Y).

(2)   In this Part "alternative finance arrangements" means —

(a)   purchase and resale arrangements,

(b)   diminishing shared ownership arrangements,

(c)   deposit arrangements,

(d)   profit share agency arrangements, and

(e)   investment bond arrangements.

(3)   In this Part —

(a)   "purchase and resale arrangements" means arrangements to which section 564C applies,

(b)   "diminishing shared ownership arrangements" means arrangements to which section 564D applies,

(c)   "deposit arrangements" means arrangements to which section 564E applies,

(d)   "profit share agency arrangements" means arrangements to which section 564F applies, and

(e)   "investment bond arrangements" means arrangements to which section 564G applies.

(4)   For the meaning of "alternative finance return", see sections 564I to 564L.

(5)   For the meaning of "financial institution", see section 564B.

1100

Taxation (International and Other Provisions) Act 2010 (c. 8)
Schedule 2 – Alternative finance arrangements
Part 1 – New Part 10A of ITA 2007

(6) Also, see section 366 of TIOPA 2010 (power to extend this Part and other provisions to other arrangements by order)."

3 After section 564A insert —

"564B Meaning of "financial institution"

(1) In this Part "financial institution" means —

    (a) a bank, as defined by section 991,

    (b) a building society,

    (c) a wholly-owned subsidiary —

        (i) of a bank within paragraph (a), or

        (ii) of a building society,

    (d) a person authorised by a licence under Part 3 of the Consumer Credit Act 1974 to carry on a consumer credit business or consumer hire business within the meaning of that Act,

    (e) a bond-issuer, within the meaning of section 564G, but only in relation to any bond assets which are rights under purchase and resale arrangements, diminishing shared ownership arrangements or profit share agency arrangements,

    (f) a person authorised in a jurisdiction outside the United Kingdom —

        (i) to receive deposits or other repayable funds from the public, and

        (ii) to grant credits for its own account,

    (g) an insurance company as defined in section 431(2) of ICTA, or

    (h) a person who is authorised in a jurisdiction outside the United Kingdom to carry on a business which consists of effecting or carrying out contracts of insurance or substantially similar business but not an insurance special purpose vehicle as defined in section 431(2) of ICTA.

(2) For the purposes of subsection (1)(c) a company is a wholly-owned subsidiary of a bank or building society ("the parent") if it has no members except —

    (a) the parent or persons acting on behalf of the parent, and

    (b) the parent's wholly-owned subsidiaries or persons acting on behalf of the parent's wholly-owned subsidiaries."

4 After section 564B insert —

"Arrangements that are alternative finance arrangements

564C Purchase and resale arrangements

(1) This section applies to arrangements if —

    (a) they are entered into between two persons ("the first purchaser" and "the second purchaser"), one or both of whom are financial institutions, and

    (b) under the arrangements —

Taxation (International and Other Provisions) Act 2010 (c. 8)
Schedule 2 — Alternative finance arrangements
Part 1 — New Part 10A of ITA 2007

1101

      (i)   the first purchaser purchases an asset and sells it to the second purchaser,

      (ii)   the sale occurs immediately after the purchase or in the circumstances mentioned in subsection (2),

      (iii)   all or part of the second purchase price is not required to be paid until a date later than that of the sale,

      (iv)   the second purchase price exceeds the first purchase price, and

      (v)   the excess equates, in substance, to the return on an investment of money at interest.

(2)   The circumstances are that—

    (a)   the first purchaser is a financial institution, and

    (b)   the asset referred to in subsection (1)(b)(i) was purchased by the first purchaser for the purpose of entering into arrangements within this section.

(3)   In this section—

      "the first purchase price" means the amount paid by the first purchaser in respect of the purchase, and

      "the second purchase price" means the amount payable by the second purchaser in respect of the sale.

(4)   This section is subject to section 564H (provision not at arm's length: exclusion of arrangements from this section and sections 564D to 564G)."

5   After section 564C insert—

"564D Diminishing shared ownership arrangements

(1)   This section applies to arrangements if under them—

    (a)   a financial institution ("the first owner") acquires a beneficial interest in an asset,

    (b)   another person ("the eventual owner") also acquires a beneficial interest in it,

    (c)   the eventual owner is to make payments to the first owner amounting in aggregate to the consideration paid for the acquisition of the first owner's beneficial interest (but subject to any adjustment required for such a reduction as is mentioned in subsection (5)),

    (d)   the eventual owner is to acquire the first owner's beneficial interest (whether or not in stages) as a result of those payments,

    (e)   the eventual owner is to make other payments to the first owner (whether under a lease forming part of the arrangements or otherwise),

    (f)   the eventual owner has the exclusive right to occupy or otherwise to use the asset, and

    (g)   the eventual owner is exclusively entitled to any income, profit or gain arising from or attributable to the asset (including, in particular, an increase in its value).

(2)   For the purposes of subsection (1)(a) it does not matter if—

1102
Taxation (International and Other Provisions) Act 2010 (c. 8)
Schedule 2 — Alternative finance arrangements
Part 1 — New Part 10A of ITA 2007

     (a)   the first owner acquires its beneficial interest from the eventual owner,

     (b)   the eventual owner, or another person who is not the first owner, also has a beneficial interest in the asset, or

     (c)   the first owner also has a legal interest in it.

(3)   Subsection (1)(f) does not prevent the eventual owner from granting an interest or right in relation to the asset if the conditions in subsection (4) are met.

(4)   The conditions are that—

     (a)   the grant is not to—

         (i)   the first owner,

         (ii)   a person controlled by the first owner, or

         (iii)   a person controlled by a person who also controls the first owner, and

     (b)   the grant is not required by the first owner or arrangements to which the first owner is a party.

(5)   Subsection (1)(g) does not prevent the first owner from—

     (a)   having responsibility for any reduction in the asset's value, or

     (b)   having a share in a loss arising out of any such reduction.

(6)   This section is subject to section 564H (provision not at arm's length: exclusion of arrangements from section 564C, this section and sections 564E to 564G)."

6   After section 564D insert—

"564E Deposit arrangements

(1)   This section applies to arrangements if under them—

     (a)   a person ("the depositor") deposits money with a financial institution,

     (b)   the money, together with money deposited with the institution by other persons, is used by it with a view to producing a profit,

     (c)   from time to time the institution makes or credits a payment to the depositor out of profit resulting from the use of the money,

     (d)   the payment is in proportion to the amount deposited by the depositor, and

     (e)   the payments so made or credited by the institution equate, in substance, to the return on an investment of money at interest.

(2)   This section is subject to section 564H (provision not at arm's length: exclusion of arrangements from sections 564C and 564D, this section and sections 564F and 564G)."

7   After section 564E insert—

"564F Profit share agency arrangements

(1)   This section applies to arrangements if under them—

Taxation (International and Other Provisions) Act 2010 (c. 8)   **1103**
Schedule 2 – Alternative finance arrangements
Part 1 – New Part 10A of ITA 2007

    (a)   a person ("the principal") appoints an agent,

    (b)   one or both of the principal and agent is a financial institution,

    (c)   the agent uses money provided by the principal with a view to producing a profit,

    (d)   the principal is entitled, to a specified extent, to profits resulting from the use of the money,

    (e)   the agent is entitled to any additional profits resulting from its use (and may also be entitled to a fee paid by the principal), and

    (f)   payments made because of the principal's entitlement to profits equate, in substance, to the return on an investment of money at interest.

(2)   This section is subject to section 564H (provision not at arm's length: exclusion of arrangements from sections 564C to 564E, this section and section 564G)."

8   After section 564F insert—

"564G Investment bond arrangements

(1)   This section applies to arrangements if—

    (a)   they provide for one person ("the bond-holder") to pay a sum of money ("the capital") to another ("the bond-issuer"),

    (b)   they identify assets, or a class of assets, which the bond-issuer will acquire for the purpose of generating income or gains directly or indirectly ("the bond assets"),

    (c)   they specify a period at the end of which they cease to have effect ("the bond term"),

    (d)   the bond-issuer undertakes under the arrangements—

        (i)   to dispose at the end of the bond term of any bond assets which are still in the bond-issuer's possession,

        (ii)   to make a repayment of the capital ("the redemption payment") to the bond-holder during or at the end of the bond-term (whether or not in instalments), and

        (iii)   to pay to the bond-holder other payments on one or more occasions during or at the end of the bond term ("additional payments"),

    (e)   the amount of the additional payments does not exceed an amount which would be a reasonable commercial return on a loan of the capital,

    (f)   under the arrangements the bond-issuer undertakes to arrange for the management of the bond assets with a view to generating income sufficient to pay the redemption payment and additional payments,

    (g)   the bond-holder is able to transfer the rights under the arrangements to another person (who becomes the bond-holder because of the transfer),

    (h)   the arrangements are a listed security on a recognised stock exchange, and

    (i)   the arrangements are wholly or partly treated in accordance with international accounting standards as a financial

1104   *Taxation (International and Other Provisions) Act 2010 (c. 8)*
Schedule 2 — Alternative finance arrangements
Part 1 — New Part 10A of ITA 2007

liability of the bond-issuer, or would be if the bond-issuer applied those standards.

(2) For the purposes of subsection (1) —

    (a) the bond-issuer may acquire bond assets before or after the arrangements take effect,

    (b) the bond assets may be property of any kind, including rights in relation to property owned by someone other than the bond-issuer,

    (c) the identification of the bond assets mentioned in subsection (1)(b) and the undertakings mentioned in subsection (1)(d) and (f) may (but need not) be described as, or accompanied by a document described as, a declaration of trust,

    (d) a reference to the management of assets includes a reference to disposal,

    (e) the bond-holder may (but need not) be entitled under the arrangements to terminate them, or participate in terminating them, before the end of the bond term,

    (f) the amount of the additional payments may be —

        (i) fixed at the beginning of the bond term,

        (ii) determined wholly or partly by reference to the value of or income generated by the bond assets, or

        (iii) determined in some other way,

    (g) if the amount of the additional payments is not fixed at the beginning of the bond term, the reference in subsection (1)(e) to the amount of the additional payments is a reference to the maximum amount of the additional payments,

    (h) the amount of the redemption payment may (but need not) be subject to reduction in the event of a fall in the value of the bond assets or in the rate of income generated by them, and

    (i) entitlement to the redemption payment may (but need not) be capable of being satisfied (whether or not at the option of the bond-issuer or the bond-holder) by the issue or transfer of shares or other securities.

(3) This section is subject to section 564H (provision not at arm's length: exclusion of arrangements from sections 564C to 564F and this section)."

9   After section 564G insert —

"564H Provision not at arm's length: exclusion of arrangements from sections 564C to 564G

(1) Arrangements to which this section applies are not —

    (a) purchase and resale arrangements,

    (b) diminishing shared ownership arrangements,

    (c) deposit arrangements,

    (d) profit share agency arrangements, or

    (e) investment bond arrangements.

(2) This section applies to arrangements if —

    (a) apart from this section they would be alternative finance arrangements,

Taxation (International and Other Provisions) Act 2010 (c. 8) **1105**
Schedule 2 – Alternative finance arrangements
Part 1 – New Part 10A of ITA 2007

      (b)   subsection (3) or (5) of section 147 of TIOPA 2010 (tax calculations to be based on arm's length, not actual, provision) requires the profits and losses of a person who is a party to the arrangements to be calculated for tax purposes as if the arm's length provision (within the meaning of that section) had been made or imposed rather than in accordance with the arrangements,

      (c)   any person who is an affected person for the purposes of Part 4 of that Act ("the affected person") is entitled to—

          (i)   relevant return in relation to the arrangements, or

          (ii)   an amount representing relevant return in relation to them, and

      (d)   the affected person is not subject—

          (i)   to income tax or corporation tax, or

          (ii)   to any corresponding tax under the law of a territory outside the United Kingdom,

on the relevant return or the amount representing it.

    (3)   In this section "relevant return", in relation to arrangements, means any amount which would be alternative finance return if the arrangements were alternative finance arrangements."

10   After section 564H insert—

"Meaning of "alternative finance return"

564I   Purchase and resale arrangements

    (1)   In the case of purchase and resale arrangements, so much of the second purchase price as is specified under the following provisions of this section is alternative finance return for the purposes of this Part.

    (2)   If under the arrangements the whole of the second purchase price is paid on one day, the alternative finance return equals the amount by which the second purchase price exceeds the first purchase price.

    (3)   If under the arrangements the second purchase price is paid by instalments, the alternative finance return in each instalment equals the appropriate amount.

    (4)   The appropriate amount is an amount equal to the interest which would have been included in the instalment on the assumptions in subsection (5).

    (5)   The assumptions are that—

      (a)   interest is payable on a loan by the first purchaser to the second purchaser of an amount equal to the first purchase price,

      (b)   the total interest payable on the loan is equal to the amount by which the second purchase price exceeds the first purchase price,

      (c)   the instalment is a part repayment of the principal of the loan with interest, and

1106

Taxation (International and Other Provisions) Act 2010 (c. 8)
Schedule 2 — Alternative finance arrangements
Part 1 — New Part 10A of ITA 2007

         (d)   the loan is made on arm's length terms and accounted for under generally accepted accounting practice.

    (6)   In this section expressions used in section 564C have the same meaning as in that section."

11   After section 564I insert—

"564J Purchase and resale arrangements where return in foreign currency

    (1)   If, in the case of purchase and resale arrangements, alternative finance return is paid in a currency other than sterling—

         (a)   by or to a person other than a company, and

         (b)   otherwise than for the purposes of a trade, profession or vocation or a property business,

subsections (2) and (3) apply as respects that person.

    (2)   The amount of the excess referred to in section 564I(2) and (5)(b) and the appropriate amount for the purposes of section 564I(3) and (4) are to be calculated in that other currency.

    (3)   The amount of each payment of alternative finance return is to be translated into sterling at a spot rate of exchange for the day on which the payment is made."

12   After section 564J insert—

"564K Diminishing shared ownership arrangements

    (1)   In the case of diminishing shared ownership arrangements, payments by the eventual owner under the arrangements are alternative finance return for the purposes of this Part, except so far as subsection (2) or (3) applies to them.

    (2)   This subsection applies to the payments so far as they amount to payments of the kind described in section 564D(1)(c) (payments to be made by the eventual owner to the institution, amounting to the consideration paid for the acquisition of the institution's beneficial interest).

    (3)   This subsection applies to the payments so far as they amount to payments in respect of any arrangement fee or legal or other expenses which the eventual owner is required under the arrangements to pay.

    (4)   In this section "the eventual owner" has the same meaning as in section 564D."

13   After section 564K insert—

"564L Other arrangements

    (1)   In the case of deposit arrangements, amounts paid or credited as mentioned in section 564E(1)(c) by a financial institution under the arrangements (payments to depositor out of profits resulting from use of money) are alternative finance return for the purposes of this Part.

    (2)   In the case of profit share agency arrangements, amounts paid or credited by a financial institution in accordance with such an

Taxation (International and Other Provisions) Act 2010 (c. 8)
Schedule 2 — Alternative finance arrangements
Part 1 — New Part 10A of ITA 2007

1107

entitlement as is mentioned in section 564F(1)(d) (principal's entitlement to profits under the arrangements) are alternative finance return for the purposes of this Part.

(3) In the case of investment bond arrangements, the additional payments under the arrangements are alternative finance return for the purposes of this Part, but subject to subsection (4).

(4) If any part of the additional payments in respect of investment bond arrangements equates in substance to discount, that part is not treated as alternative finance return for income tax purposes.

(5) In this section "additional payments" has the same meaning as in section 564G (see subsection (1)(d)(iii) of that section).

(6) For the treatment of the part of the additional payments to which subsection (4) applies, see section 564R (treatment of discount)."

14   After section 564L insert—

"Treatment of alternative finance return as interest etc

564M Treatment of alternative finance return as interest for ITTOIA 2005

(1) Alternative finance return is treated as interest for the purposes of ITTOIA 2005.

(2) References to interest in section 380 of that Act (funding bonds) include references to alternative finance return."

15   After section 564M insert—

"564N Alternative finance return under arrangements for trade or property business purposes

(1) This section applies so far as a person is a party to alternative finance arrangements for the purposes of—
    (a) a trade, profession or vocation carried on by that person, or
    (b) a property business of that person.

(2) Alternative finance return paid by that person is treated as an expense of the trade, profession, vocation or business.

(3) In section 58 of ITTOIA 2005—
    (a) references to a loan include references to alternative finance arrangements, and
    (b) references to interest include references to alternative finance return."

16   After section 564N insert—

"564O Relief for some alternative finance return under Chapter 1 of Part 8 etc

(1) Chapter 1 of Part 8 of this Act (interest payments) has effect as if—
    (a) purchase and resale arrangements involved the making of a loan, and
    (b) alternative finance return were interest.

(2) Section 412 (information) has effect accordingly."

1108

Taxation (International and Other Provisions) Act 2010 (c. 8)
Schedule 2 – Alternative finance arrangements
Part 1 – New Part 10A of ITA 2007

17   After section 564O insert—

"564P Tax relief schemes and arrangements

Section 809ZG (tax relief schemes and arrangements) applies to alternative finance return as it applies to interest."

18   After section 564P insert—

"564Q Deduction of income tax at source under Part 15

(1)   Chapter 2 of Part 15 (deduction of income tax at source: deduction by deposit-takers and building societies), and Chapter 19 of that Part so far as it has effect for the purposes of Chapter 2 of that Part, have effect as if—

    (a)   relevant alternative finance arrangements were a deposit,

    (b)   for the purposes of section 866(2)(a) such arrangements were a deposit consisting of a loan, and

    (c)   alternative finance return payable under such arrangements were interest.

(2)   For the purposes of subsection (1) alternative finance arrangements are relevant unless they are purchase and resale arrangements where the second purchaser is not a financial institution.

(3)   In subsection (2) "the second purchaser" has the same meaning as in section 564C.

(4)   In Chapter 12 of Part 15 (funding bonds) references to interest include references to alternative finance return.

(5)   Chapters 3 to 5 of Part 15, and Chapter 19 of that Part so far as it has effect for the purposes of those Chapters, apply to alternative finance return as they apply to interest."

19   After section 564Q insert—

"Special rules for investment bond arrangements

564R Treatment of discount

(1)   This section applies if any part of the additional payments in respect of investment bond arrangements is excluded from being alternative finance return by section 564L(4) because it equates in substance to discount.

(2)   That part is treated in accordance with section 381 of ITTOIA 2005 (discounts) unless subsection (3) applies.

(3)   If the arrangements are deeply discounted securities for the purposes of Chapter 8 of Part 4 of that Act (profits from deeply discounted securities), that part is treated in accordance with that Chapter.

(4)   In this section "additional payments" has the same meaning as in section 564G of this Act (see subsection (1)(d)(iii) of that section)."

Taxation (International and Other Provisions) Act 2010 (c. 8)
Schedule 2 — Alternative finance arrangements
Part 1 — New Part 10A of ITA 2007

1109

20   After section 564R insert—

"564S Treatment of bond-holder and bond-issuer

(1)   This section applies for the purposes of the Income Tax Acts and irrespective of the position for other purposes.

(2)   The bond-holder under investment bond arrangements is not treated as having a legal or beneficial interest in the bond assets.

(3)   The bond-issuer under such arrangements is not treated as a trustee of the bond assets.

(4)   Profits accruing to the bond-issuer in connection with the bond assets are profits of the bond-issuer and not of the bond-holder (and do not arise to the bond-issuer in a fiduciary or representative capacity).

(5)   Payments made by the bond-issuer by way of redemption payment or additional payment are not made in a fiduciary or representative capacity.

(6)   The bond-holder is not entitled to relief for capital expenditure in connection with the bond assets.

(7)   Expressions used in this section have the same meaning as in section 564G."

21   After section 564S insert—

"564T Treatment as securities

(1)   Investment bond arrangements are securities for the purposes of the Income Tax Acts (including Chapters 1 to 5 of Part 7 of ITEPA 2003).

(2)   For those purposes—
    (a)   a reference in an enactment to redemption is to be taken as a reference to making the redemption payment, and
    (b)   a reference in an enactment to interest is to be taken as a reference to alternative finance return.

(3)   In subsection (2) "the redemption payment" has the same meaning as in section 564G (see subsection (1)(d)(ii) of that section)."

22   After section 564T insert—

"564U Arrangements not unit trust scheme or offshore fund

Investment bond arrangements are not—
    (a)   a unit trust scheme for the purposes of section 1007 of this Act, or
    (b)   an offshore fund for the purposes of section 354 of TIOPA 2010 so far as relating to income tax."

1110

Taxation (International and Other Provisions) Act 2010 (c. 8)
Schedule 2 — Alternative finance arrangements
Part 1 — New Part 10A of ITA 2007

23   After section 564U insert—

"Other rules

564V   Exclusion of alternative finance return from consideration for sale of assets

(1)   If under purchase and resale arrangements an asset is sold by one party to the arrangements to the other party, the alternative finance return is excluded in determining the consideration for the sale and purchase of the asset for the purposes of the Income Tax Acts (apart from section 564C).

(2)   If under diminishing shared ownership arrangements an asset is sold by one party to the arrangements to the other party, the alternative finance return is excluded in determining the consideration for the sale and purchase of the asset for the purposes of the Income Tax Acts (apart from section 564D).

(3)   If under investment bond arrangements an asset is sold by one party to the arrangements to the other party, the alternative finance return is excluded in determining the consideration for the sale and purchase of the asset for the purposes of the Income Tax Acts (apart from section 564G).

(4)   Subsections (1) to (3) do not affect the operation of any provision of the Tax Acts or TCGA 1992 that provides that the consideration for a sale or purchase is taken for any purpose to be an amount other than the actual consideration."

24   After section 564V insert—

"564W Diminishing shared ownership arrangements not partnerships

Diminishing shared ownership arrangements are not treated as a partnership for the purposes of the Income Tax Acts."

25   After section 564W insert—

"564X Treatment of principal under profit share agency arrangements

(1)   The principal under profit share agency arrangements is not treated for the purposes of the Income Tax Acts as entitled to profits to which the agent is entitled in accordance with section 564F(1)(e).

(2)   And the agent under such arrangements is treated for those purposes as entitled to those profits and the profits specified in section 564F(1)(d).

(3)   In this section "the principal" and "the agent" are to be read in accordance with section 564F."

26   After section 564X insert—

"564Y Provision not at arm's length: relevant return

(1)   This section applies if arrangements to which section 564H (provision not at arm's length: exclusion of arrangements from sections 564C to 564G) applies would, but for that section, be alternative finance arrangements.

Taxation (International and Other Provisions) Act 2010 (c. 8)   **1111**
Schedule 2 — Alternative finance arrangements
Part 1 — New Part 10A of ITA 2007

(2) A person paying relevant return under the arrangements is not entitled to—

    (a) any deduction in respect of the relevant return in calculating profits or other income for income tax purposes, or

    (b) any deduction in respect of the relevant return in calculating net income.

(3) In this section "relevant return" has the same meaning as in section 564H (see subsection (3) of that section)."

PART 2

NEW CHAPTER 4 OF PART 4 OF TCGA 1992

27   TCGA 1992 is amended as follows.

28   After Chapter 3 of Part 4 insert—

"CHAPTER 4

ALTERNATIVE FINANCE ARRANGEMENTS

Introduction

151H Introduction

(1) This Chapter makes provision about the treatment of alternative finance arrangements with financial institutions and alternative finance return under such arrangements for the purposes of this Act (see sections 151T to 151Y).

(2) In this Chapter "alternative finance arrangements" means—

    (a) purchase and resale arrangements,

    (b) diminishing shared ownership arrangements,

    (c) deposit arrangements,

    (d) profit share agency arrangements, and

    (e) investment bond arrangements.

(3) In this Chapter—

    (a) "purchase and resale arrangements" means arrangements to which section 151J applies,

    (b) "diminishing shared ownership arrangements" means arrangements to which section 151K applies,

    (c) "deposit arrangements" means arrangements to which section 151L applies,

    (d) "profit share agency arrangements" means arrangements to which section 151M applies, and

    (e) "investment bond arrangements" means arrangements to which section 151N applies.

(4) For the meaning of "alternative finance return", see sections 151P to 151S.

(5) For the meaning of "financial institution", see section 151I.

(6) Also, see—

1112

Taxation (International and Other Provisions) Act 2010 (c. 8)
Schedule 2 — Alternative finance arrangements
Part 2 — New Chapter 4 of Part 4 of TCGA 1992

(a) section 366 of TIOPA 2010 (power to extend this Chapter and other provisions to other arrangements by order), and

(b) Schedule 61 to FA 2009 (alternative finance investment bonds) which makes further provision about the treatment of investment bond arrangements for the purposes of this Act."

29   After section 151H insert—

"151I Meaning of "financial institution"

(1)   In this Chapter "financial institution" means—

(a) a bank, as defined by section 1120 of CTA 2010,

(b) a building society,

(c) a wholly-owned subsidiary—

(i) of a bank within paragraph (a), or

(ii) of a building society,

(d) a person authorised by a licence under Part 3 of the Consumer Credit Act 1974 to carry on a consumer credit business or consumer hire business within the meaning of that Act,

(e) a bond-issuer, within the meaning of section 151N, but only in relation to any bond assets which are rights under purchase and resale arrangements, diminishing shared ownership arrangements or profit share agency arrangements,

(f) a person authorised in a jurisdiction outside the United Kingdom—

(i) to receive deposits or other repayable funds from the public, and

(ii) to grant credits for its own account,

(g) an insurance company as defined in section 431(2) of ICTA, or

(h) a person who is authorised in a jurisdiction outside the United Kingdom to carry on a business which consists of effecting or carrying out contracts of insurance or substantially similar business but not an insurance special purpose vehicle as defined in section 431(2) of ICTA.

(2)   For the purposes of subsection (1)(c) a company is a wholly-owned subsidiary of a bank or building society ("the parent") if it has no members except—

(a) the parent or persons acting on behalf of the parent, and

(b) the parent's wholly-owned subsidiaries or persons acting on behalf of the parent's wholly-owned subsidiaries."

30   After section 151I insert—

"Arrangements that are alternative finance arrangements

151J Purchase and resale arrangements

(1)   This section applies to arrangements if—

Taxation (International and Other Provisions) Act 2010 (c. 8)   **1113**
Schedule 2 — Alternative finance arrangements
Part 2 — New Chapter 4 of Part 4 of TCGA 1992

        (a)   they are entered into between two persons ("the first purchaser" and "the second purchaser"), one or both of whom are financial institutions, and

        (b)   under the arrangements —

            (i)   the first purchaser purchases an asset and sells it to the second purchaser,

            (ii)   the sale occurs immediately after the purchase or in the circumstances mentioned in subsection (2),

            (iii)   all or part of the second purchase price is not required to be paid until a date later than that of the sale,

            (iv)   the second purchase price exceeds the first purchase price, and

            (v)   the excess equates, in substance, to the return on an investment of money at interest.

(2)   The circumstances are that —

        (a)   the first purchaser is a financial institution, and

        (b)   the asset referred to in subsection (1)(b)(i) was purchased by the first purchaser for the purpose of entering into arrangements within this section.

(3)   In this section —

      "the first purchase price" means the amount paid by the first purchaser in respect of the purchase, and

      "the second purchase price" means the amount payable by the second purchaser in respect of the sale.

(4)   This section is subject to section 151O (provision not at arm's length: exclusion of arrangements from this section and sections 151K to 151N)."

31   After section 151J insert —

"151K Diminishing shared ownership arrangements

(1)   This section applies to arrangements if under them —

        (a)   a financial institution ("the first owner") acquires a beneficial interest in an asset,

        (b)   another person ("the eventual owner") also acquires a beneficial interest in it,

        (c)   the eventual owner is to make payments to the first owner amounting in aggregate to the consideration paid for the acquisition of the first owner's beneficial interest (but subject to any adjustment required for such a reduction as is mentioned in subsection (5)),

        (d)   the eventual owner is to acquire the first owner's beneficial interest (whether or not in stages) as a result of those payments,

        (e)   the eventual owner is to make other payments to the first owner (whether under a lease forming part of the arrangements or otherwise),

        (f)   the eventual owner has the exclusive right to occupy or otherwise to use the asset, and

1114   *Taxation (International and Other Provisions) Act 2010 (c. 8)*
Schedule 2 — Alternative finance arrangements
Part 2 — New Chapter 4 of Part 4 of TCGA 1992

  (g) the eventual owner is exclusively entitled to any income, profit or gain arising from or attributable to the asset (including, in particular, an increase in its value).

 (2) For the purposes of subsection (1)(a) it does not matter if—

  (a) the first owner acquires its beneficial interest from the eventual owner,

  (b) the eventual owner, or another person who is not the first owner, also has a beneficial interest in the asset, or

  (c) the first owner also has a legal interest in it.

 (3) Subsection (1)(f) does not prevent the eventual owner from granting an interest or right in relation to the asset if the conditions in subsection (4) are met.

 (4) The conditions are that—

  (a) the grant is not to—

   (i) the first owner,

   (ii) a person controlled by the first owner, or

   (iii) a person controlled by a person who also controls the first owner, and

  (b) the grant is not required by the first owner or arrangements to which the first owner is a party.

 (5) Subsection (1)(g) does not prevent the first owner from—

  (a) having responsibility for any reduction in the asset's value, or

  (b) having a share in a loss arising out of any such reduction.

 (6) Section 1124 of CTA 2010 (meaning of "control") applies for the purposes of this section.

 (7) This section is subject to section 151O (provision not at arm's length: exclusion of arrangements from section 151J, this section and sections 151L to 151N)."

32   After section 151K insert—

"151L Deposit arrangements

 (1) This section applies to arrangements if under them—

  (a) a person ("the depositor") deposits money with a financial institution,

  (b) the money, together with money deposited with the institution by other persons, is used by it with a view to producing a profit,

  (c) from time to time the institution makes or credits a payment to the depositor out of profit resulting from the use of the money,

  (d) the payment is in proportion to the amount deposited by the depositor, and

  (e) the payments so made or credited by the institution equate, in substance, to the return on an investment of money at interest.

Taxation (International and Other Provisions) Act 2010 (c. 8)   **1115**
Schedule 2 – Alternative finance arrangements
Part 2 – New Chapter 4 of Part 4 of TCGA 1992

(2)   This section is subject to section 151O (provision not at arm's length: exclusion of arrangements from sections 151J, 151K, this section and sections 151M and 151N)."

33   After section 151L insert—

"151M Profit share agency arrangements

(1)   This section applies to arrangements if under them—

(a)   a person ("the principal") appoints an agent,

(b)   one or both of the principal and agent is a financial institution,

(c)   the agent uses money provided by the principal with a view to producing a profit,

(d)   the principal is entitled, to a specified extent, to profits resulting from the use of the money,

(e)   the agent is entitled to any additional profits resulting from its use (and may also be entitled to a fee paid by the principal), and

(f)   payments made because of the principal's entitlement to profits equate, in substance, to the return on an investment of money at interest.

(2)   This section is subject to section 151O (provision not at arm's length: exclusion of arrangements from sections 151J to 151L, this section and section 151N)."

34   After section 151M insert—

"151N Investment bond arrangements

(1)   This section applies to arrangements if—

(a)   they provide for one person ("the bond-holder") to pay a sum of money ("the capital") to another ("the bond-issuer"),

(b)   they identify assets, or a class of assets, which the bond-issuer will acquire for the purpose of generating income or gains directly or indirectly ("the bond assets"),

(c)   they specify a period at the end of which they cease to have effect ("the bond term"),

(d)   the bond-issuer undertakes under the arrangements—

(i)   to dispose at the end of the bond term of any bond assets which are still in the bond-issuer's possession,

(ii)   to make a repayment of the capital ("the redemption payment") to the bond-holder during or at the end of the bond-term (whether or not in instalments), and

(iii)   to pay to the bond-holder other payments on one or more occasions during or at the end of the bond term ("additional payments"),

(e)   the amount of the additional payments does not exceed an amount which would be a reasonable commercial return on a loan of the capital,

(f)   under the arrangements the bond-issuer undertakes to arrange for the management of the bond assets with a view to generating income sufficient to pay the redemption payment and additional payments,

1116

Taxation (International and Other Provisions) Act 2010 (c. 8)
Schedule 2 — Alternative finance arrangements
Part 2 — New Chapter 4 of Part 4 of TCGA 1992

      (g)   the bond-holder is able to transfer the rights under the arrangements to another person (who becomes the bond-holder because of the transfer),

      (h)   the arrangements are a listed security on a recognised stock exchange, and

      (i)   the arrangements are wholly or partly treated in accordance with international accounting standards as a financial liability of the bond-issuer, or would be if the bond-issuer applied those standards.

(2)   For the purposes of subsection (1) —

      (a)   the bond-issuer may acquire bond assets before or after the arrangements take effect,

      (b)   the bond assets may be property of any kind, including rights in relation to property owned by someone other than the bond-issuer,

      (c)   the identification of the bond assets mentioned in subsection (1)(b) and the undertakings mentioned in subsection (1)(d) and (f) may (but need not) be described as, or accompanied by a document described as, a declaration of trust,

      (d)   a reference to the management of assets includes a reference to disposal,

      (e)   the bond-holder may (but need not) be entitled under the arrangements to terminate them, or participate in terminating them, before the end of the bond term,

      (f)   the amount of the additional payments may be —

           (i)   fixed at the beginning of the bond term,

           (ii)   determined wholly or partly by reference to the value of or income generated by the bond assets, or

           (iii)   determined in some other way,

      (g)   if the amount of the additional payments is not fixed at the beginning of the bond term, the reference in subsection (1)(e) to the amount of the additional payments is a reference to the maximum amount of the additional payments,

      (h)   the amount of the redemption payment may (but need not) be subject to reduction in the event of a fall in the value of the bond assets or in the rate of income generated by them, and

      (i)   entitlement to the redemption payment may (but need not) be capable of being satisfied (whether or not at the option of the bond-issuer or the bond-holder) by the issue or transfer of shares or other securities.

(3)   This section is subject to section 151O (provision not at arm's length: exclusion of arrangements from sections 151J to 151M and this section)."

35   After section 151N insert—

"151O Provision not at arm's length: exclusion of arrangements from sections 151J to 151N

(1)   Arrangements to which this section applies are not—

      (a)   purchase and resale arrangements,

      (b)   diminishing shared ownership arrangements,

Taxation (International and Other Provisions) Act 2010 (c. 8)
Schedule 2 — Alternative finance arrangements
Part 2 — New Chapter 4 of Part 4 of TCGA 1992

1117

      (c)   deposit arrangements,

      (d)   profit share agency arrangements, or

      (e)   investment bond arrangements.

(2)   This section applies to arrangements if—

      (a)   apart from this section they would be alternative finance arrangements,

      (b)   subsection (3) or (5) of section 147 of TIOPA 2010 (tax calculations to be based on arm's length, not actual, provision) requires the profits and losses of a person who is a party to the arrangements to be calculated for tax purposes as if the arm's length provision (within the meaning of that section) had been made or imposed rather than in accordance with the arrangements,

      (c)   any person who is an affected person for the purposes of Part 4 of that Act ("the affected person") is entitled to—

            (i)   relevant return in relation to the arrangements, or

            (ii)   an amount representing relevant return in relation to them, and

      (d)   the affected person is not subject—

            (i)   to income tax or corporation tax, or

            (ii)   to any corresponding tax under the law of a territory outside the United Kingdom,

    on the relevant return or the amount representing it.

(3)   In this section "relevant return", in relation to arrangements, means any amount which would be alternative finance return if the arrangements were alternative finance arrangements."

36   After section 151O insert—

"Meaning of "alternative finance return"

151P Purchase and resale arrangements

(1)   In the case of purchase and resale arrangements, so much of the second purchase price as is specified under the following provisions of this section is alternative finance return for the purposes of this Chapter.

(2)   If under the arrangements the whole of the second purchase price is paid on one day, the alternative finance return equals the amount by which the second purchase price exceeds the first purchase price.

(3)   If under the arrangements the second purchase price is paid by instalments, the alternative finance return in each instalment equals the appropriate amount.

(4)   The appropriate amount is an amount equal to the interest which would have been included in the instalment on the assumptions in subsection (5).

(5)   The assumptions are that—

      (a)   interest is payable on a loan by the first purchaser to the second purchaser of an amount equal to the first purchase price,

1118   *Taxation (International and Other Provisions) Act 2010 (c. 8)*
Schedule 2 — Alternative finance arrangements
Part 2 — New Chapter 4 of Part 4 of TCGA 1992

(b) the total interest payable on the loan is equal to the amount by which the second purchase price exceeds the first purchase price,

(c) the instalment is a part repayment of the principal of the loan with interest, and

(d) the loan is made on arm's length terms and accounted for under generally accepted accounting practice.

(6) In this section expressions used in section 151J have the same meaning as in that section."

37   After section 151P insert—

"151Q Purchase and resale arrangements where return in foreign currency

(1) If, in the case of purchase and resale arrangements, alternative finance return is paid in a currency other than sterling—

(a) by or to a person other than a company, and

(b) otherwise than for the purposes of a trade, profession or vocation or a property business,

subsections (2) and (3) apply as respects that person.

(2) The amount of the excess referred to in section 151P(2) and (5)(b) and the appropriate amount for the purposes of section 151P(3) and (4) are to be calculated in that other currency.

(3) The amount of each payment of alternative finance return is to be translated into sterling at a spot rate of exchange for the day on which the payment is made."

38   After section 151Q insert—

"151R Diminishing shared ownership arrangements

(1) In the case of diminishing shared ownership arrangements, payments by the eventual owner under the arrangements are alternative finance return for the purposes of this Chapter, except so far as subsection (2) or (3) applies to them.

(2) This subsection applies to the payments so far as they amount to payments of the kind described in section 151K(1)(c) (payments to be made by the eventual owner to the institution, amounting to the consideration paid for the acquisition of the institution's beneficial interest).

(3) This subsection applies to the payments so far as they amount to payments in respect of any arrangement fee or legal or other expenses which the eventual owner is required under the arrangements to pay.

(4) In this section "the eventual owner" has the same meaning as in section 151K."

39   After section 151R insert—

"151S Other arrangements

(1) In the case of deposit arrangements, amounts paid or credited as mentioned in section 151L(1)(c) by a financial institution under the

Taxation (International and Other Provisions) Act 2010 (c. 8)   **1119**
Schedule 2 – Alternative finance arrangements
Part 2 – New Chapter 4 of Part 4 of TCGA 1992

arrangements (payments to depositor out of profits resulting from use of money) are alternative finance return for the purposes of this Chapter.

(2) In the case of profit share agency arrangements, amounts paid or credited by a financial institution in accordance with such an entitlement as is mentioned in section 151M(1)(d) (principal's entitlement to profits under the arrangements) are alternative finance return for the purposes of this Chapter.

(3) In the case of investment bond arrangements, the additional payments under the arrangements are alternative finance return for the purposes of this Chapter.

(4) In this section "additional payments" has the same meaning as in section 151N (see subsection (1)(d)(iii) of that section)."

40   After section 151S insert—

"Special rules for investment bond arrangements

151T Investment bond arrangements are qualifying corporate bonds

(1) For the purposes of section 117, investment bond arrangements are a corporate bond, issued on the date on which the arrangements are entered into, if each of conditions A to D is met.

(2) Condition A is that the capital is expressed in sterling.

(3) Condition B is that the arrangements do not include provision for the redemption payment to be in a currency other than sterling.

(4) Condition C is that entitlement to the redemption payment is not capable of conversion (directly or indirectly) into an entitlement to the issue of securities apart from other arrangements to which section 151N applies.

(5) Condition D is that the additional payments are not determined wholly or partly by reference to the value of the bond assets.

(6) Section 117(2) applies for the purposes of this section as it applies for the purposes of section 117(1)."

41   After section 151T insert—

"151U Treatment of bond-holder and bond-issuer

(1) This section applies for the purposes of this Act and any other enactment about capital gains tax and irrespective of the position for other purposes.

(2) The bond-holder under investment bond arrangements is not treated as having a legal or beneficial interest in the bond assets.

(3) The bond-issuer under such arrangements is not treated as a trustee of the bond assets.

(4) Gains accruing to the bond-issuer in connection with the bond assets are gains of the bond-issuer and not of the bond-holder (and do not arise to the bond-issuer in a fiduciary or representative capacity).

1120

Taxation (International and Other Provisions) Act 2010 (c. 8)
Schedule 2 — Alternative finance arrangements
Part 2 — New Chapter 4 of Part 4 of TCGA 1992

(5) Payments made by the bond-issuer by way of redemption payment or additional payment are not made in a fiduciary or representative capacity.

(6) The bond-holder is not entitled to relief for capital expenditure in connection with the bond assets.

(7) Expressions used in this section have the same meaning as in section 151N."

42   After section 151U insert—

"151V Treatment as securities

(1) Investment bond arrangements are securities for the purposes of this Act and any other enactment about capital gains tax.

(2) For those purposes—

    (a) a reference in an enactment to redemption is to be taken as a reference to making the redemption payment, and

    (b) a reference in an enactment to interest is to be taken as a reference to alternative finance return.

(3) In subsection (2) "the redemption payment" has the same meaning as in section 151N (see subsection (1)(d)(ii) of that section)."

43   After section 151V insert—

"151W Investment bond arrangements not unit trust scheme or offshore fund

Investment bond arrangements are not—

    (a) a unit trust scheme for the purposes of this Act, or

    (b) an offshore fund for the purposes of section 354 of TIOPA 2010 so far as relating to capital gains tax."

44   After section 151W insert—

"Other rules

151X Exclusion of some alternative finance return from sale consideration

(1) If under purchase and resale arrangements an asset is sold by one party to the arrangements to the other party, the alternative finance return is excluded in determining the consideration for the sale and purchase of the asset for the purposes of this Act so far as it applies for capital gains tax (apart from section 151J).

(2) If under diminishing shared ownership arrangements an asset is sold by one party to the arrangements to the other party, the alternative finance return is excluded in determining the consideration for the sale and purchase of the asset for the purposes of this Act so far as it applies for capital gains tax (apart from section 151K).

(3) If under investment bond arrangements an asset is sold by one party to the arrangements to the other party, the alternative finance return is excluded in determining the consideration for the sale and

Taxation (International and Other Provisions) Act 2010 (c. 8)   **1121**
Schedule 2 – Alternative finance arrangements
Part 2 – New Chapter 4 of Part 4 of TCGA 1992

purchase of the asset for the purposes of this Act so far as it applies for capital gains tax (apart from section 151N).

(4) Subsections (1) to (3) do not affect the operation of any provision of this Act or the Tax Acts that provides that the consideration for a sale or purchase is taken for any purpose to be an amount other than the actual consideration."

45   After section 151X insert—

"151Y Diminishing shared ownership arrangements not partnerships

Diminishing shared ownership arrangements are not treated as a partnership for capital gains tax purposes."

PART 3

OTHER AMENDMENTS

Income and Corporation Taxes Act 1988 (c. 1)

46   ICTA is amended as follows.

47   After section 367 insert—

"367A Alternative finance arrangements

(1) Sections 353 and 365 have effect as if—
   (a) purchase and resale arrangements involved the making of a loan, and
   (b) alternative finance return were interest.

(2) Section 366 has effect accordingly.

(3) In this section—
   "alternative finance return" has the meaning given in sections 564I to 564L of ITA 2007, and
   "purchase and resale arrangements" means arrangements to which section 564C of ITA 2007 applies."

Income Tax (Earnings and Pensions) Act 2003 (c. 1)

48   ITEPA 2003 is amended as follows.

49   After section 173 (loans to which Chapter 7 of Part 3 (taxable benefits: loans) applies) insert—

"173A Alternative finance arrangements

(1) For the purposes of this Chapter a reference to a loan includes a reference to arrangements—
   (a) to which section 564C of ITA 2007 or section 503 of CTA 2009 (purchase and resale arrangements) applies (or would apply assuming one of the parties were a financial institution), or
   (b) to which section 564D of ITA 2007 or section 504 of CTA 2009 (diminishing shared ownership arrangements) applies (or would apply on that assumption).

1122

Taxation (International and Other Provisions) Act 2010 (c. 8)
Schedule 2 – Alternative finance arrangements
Part 3 – Other amendments

(2) In the application of this Chapter as a result of this section, a reference to interest is to be treated as including alternative finance return (or anything that would be such return on that assumption).

(3) In the application of this Chapter as a result of this section, a reference to the amount outstanding is to be taken—

    (a) in the case of arrangements within subsection (1)(a), as a reference to the purchase price minus such part of the aggregate payments made as does not represent alternative finance return (or anything that would be such return on that assumption),

    (b) in the case of arrangements to which section 564D of ITA 2007 or section 504 of CTA 2009 applies, as a reference to the amount of the financial institution's original beneficial interest minus such part of the aggregate payments made as does not represent alternative finance return, and

    (c) in the case of arrangements to which section 564D of ITA 2007 or section 504 of CTA 2009 would apply assuming one of the parties were a financial institution, as a reference to the amount of that party's original beneficial interest minus such part of the aggregate payments made as does not represent anything that would be alternative finance return on that assumption.

(4) In this section—

"alternative finance return" has the meaning given in sections 564I to 564L of ITA 2007 or sections 511 to 513 of CTA 2009, and

"financial institution" has the meaning given in section 564B of ITA 2007 or section 502 of CTA 2009.

(5) This section does not apply to arrangements entered into before 22 March 2006."

Income Tax Act 2007 (c. 3)

50 ITA 2007 is amended as follows.

51 At the beginning of Chapter 7 of Part 7 (Community Investment Tax Relief: supplementary and general) insert—

"Alternative finance arrangements

372A Meaning of "loan" and "interest"

(1) In this Part and regulations made under Chapter 2 of this Part—

    (a) references to a "loan" include references to alternative finance arrangements, and

    (b) references to "interest" include references to alternative finance return.

(2) In subsection (1)—

"alternative finance arrangements" means arrangements to which any of the following applies—

    (a) section 564C (purchase and resale arrangements),

Taxation (International and Other Provisions) Act 2010 (c. 8)   **1123**
Schedule 2 — Alternative finance arrangements
Part 3 — Other amendments

      (b)   section 564E (deposit arrangements), and

      (c)   section 564F (profit share agency arrangements), and

"alternative finance return" has the meaning given by section 564I and 564L(1) and (2).

  (3)   Subsection (1) needs to be read with—

      (a)   section 372B, in the case of arrangements to which section 564C applies,

      (b)   section 372C, in the case of arrangements to which section 564E applies, and

      (c)   section 372D, in the case of arrangements to which section 564F applies."

52   After section 372A insert—

"372B Purchase and resale arrangements

  (1)   This section applies if, under arrangements to which section 564C applies, a person ("the first purchaser") purchases an asset that is sold to another person ("the second purchaser").

  (2)   This Part and regulations made under Chapter 2 of this Part have effect in relation to the arrangements in accordance with subsections (3) to (9).

  (3)   The first purchaser is treated as making a loan to the second purchaser.

  (4)   The amount of the loan is treated as being equal to the first purchase price.

  (5)   If the arrangements provide that the first purchaser will transfer ownership of the asset to the second purchaser in instalments—

      (a)   references to the loan being drawn down over a period of time include references to the asset being transferred to the second purchaser in instalments,

      (b)   references to the date on which the first amount of the loan is drawn down include references to the date on which the first instalment is transferred to the second purchaser, and

      (c)   references to the amount drawn down at a given date include references to the value of the instalments transferred at that date.

  (6)   In calculating the amount of capital outstanding on the loan, each payment of the second purchase price (or part of the second purchase price), as reduced by any amount of alternative finance return included within each payment, is treated as repayment of the loan capital.

  (7)   References to the beneficial owner of the loan include references to the person beneficially entitled to payment of the second purchase price.

  (8)   References to the disposal of the whole or any part of the loan include references to the disposal of the right to receive payment of the whole or any part of the outstanding second purchase price.

1124　　　　　　　　*Taxation (International and Other Provisions) Act 2010 (c. 8)*
Schedule 2 − Alternative finance arrangements
Part 3 − Other amendments

(9) If arrangements to which section 564C applies are, as a result of this section, qualifying investments under Chapter 3 of this Part, paragraph (f) of section 366(1) is to be ignored in relation to the arrangements concerned.

(10) In this section "the first purchase price" and "the second purchase price" have the same meaning as in section 564C."

53　　　After section 372B insert—

"372C Deposit arrangements

(1) This section applies if, under arrangements to which section 564E applies, a person ("the depositor") deposits money with a financial institution.

(2) This Part and regulations made under Chapter 2 of this Part have effect in relation to the arrangements in accordance with subsections (3) to (9).

(3) The depositor is treated as making a loan to the financial institution.

(4) The amount of the loan is treated as being equal to the money deposited under the arrangements.

(5) If the arrangements provide that the depositor will deposit a sum of money with the financial institution in instalments—
  (a) references to the loan being drawn down over a period of time include references to the depositor depositing a sum of money with the financial institution in instalments,
  (b) references to the date on which the first amount of the loan is drawn down include references to the date on which the first instalment is deposited with the financial institution, and
  (c) references to the amount drawn down at a given date include references to the value of the instalments deposited with the financial institution at that date.

(6) The capital outstanding on the loan is treated as being equal to the balance of the repayable deposit.

(7) References to any repayment of the loan include references to any repayment of the deposit.

(8) References to the beneficial owner of the loan include references to the person beneficially entitled to repayment of the deposit.

(9) References to the disposal of the whole or any part of the loan include references to the disposal of the right to receive repayment of the whole or any part of the deposit.

(10) In this section "financial institution" has the same meaning as in Part 10A (see section 564B)."

54　　　After section 372C insert—

"372D Profit share agency arrangements

(1) This section applies if, under arrangements to which section 564F applies, a person ("the principal") appoints a financial institution as agent.

Taxation (International and Other Provisions) Act 2010 (c. 8)
Schedule 2 — Alternative finance arrangements
Part 3 — Other amendments

1125

(2) This Part and regulations made under Chapter 2 of this Part have effect in relation to the arrangements in accordance with subsections (3) to (9).

(3) The principal is treated as making a loan to the agent.

(4) The amount of the loan is treated as being equal to the money provided by the principal to the agent under the arrangements.

(5) If the arrangements provide that the principal will provide a sum of money to the agent in instalments—

   (a) references to the loan being drawn down over a period of time include references to the principal providing a sum of money to the agent in instalments,

   (b) references to the date on which the first amount of the loan is drawn down include references to the date on which the first instalment is provided to the agent, and

   (c) references to the amount drawn down at a given date include references to the value of the instalments provided to the agent at that date.

(6) The capital outstanding on the loan is treated as being equal to the balance of the repayable money provided to the agent.

(7) References to any repayment of the loan include references to any repayment of the money provided to the agent.

(8) References to the beneficial owner of the loan include references to the person beneficially entitled to repayment of the money provided to the agent.

(9) References to the disposal of the whole or any part of the loan include references to the disposal of the right to receive repayment of the whole or any part of the money provided to the agent.

(10) In subsection (1) "financial institution" has the same meaning as in Part 10A (see section 564B)."

55 In section 1005 (meaning of "recognised stock exchange" etc) after subsection (2) insert—

"(2A) An order under subsection (1) may designate a stock exchange for the purposes of this section in its application to section 564G of this Act, section 151N of TCGA 1992 and section 507 of CTA 2009 only."

SCHEDULE 3

Section 367

LEASING ARRANGEMENTS: FINANCE LEASES AND LOANS

PART 1

NEW PART 11A OF ITA 2007

1 ITA 2007 is amended as follows.

1126

Taxation (International and Other Provisions) Act 2010 (c. 8)
Schedule 3 — Leasing arrangements: finance leases and loans
Part 1 — New Part 11A of ITA 2007

2   After Part 11 insert—

"PART 11A

LEASING ARRANGEMENTS: FINANCE LEASES AND LOANS

CHAPTER 1

INTRODUCTION

Introduction

614A Overview of Part

(1)   This Part makes provision for the purposes of income tax about the taxation of leasing arrangements.

(2)   Chapter 2 makes provision in relation to certain arrangements involving the lease of assets where the conditions in section 614BC are or have been met, so far as the lease is not regarded as a long-funding lease for the purposes of Part 2 of CAA 2001 in accordance with Chapter 6A of that Part (see sections 614BB to 614BE).

(3)   Chapter 3 makes provision in relation to arrangements involving the lease of assets that are not within Chapter 2, so far as the lease is not so regarded (see sections 614C and 614CB).

(4)   The remaining provisions of this Chapter explain some expressions about rent for the purposes of this Part.

(5)   Chapter 4 contains further provisions supplementing this Part, including more about its interpretation.

Meaning of expressions about rent

614AA Normal rent

(1)   For the purposes of this Part, the "normal rent" in respect of a lease for a period of account of the lessor ("L") is the amount specified in subsection (2).

(2)   That amount is the amount that L would, apart from this Part, bring into account as rent from the lease that arises to L in that period of account for the purpose of determining L's liability to income tax for the related tax year or years.

(3)   For the meaning of "related tax year", see section 614DB(4).

614AB Accountancy rental earnings

(1)   For the purposes of this Part, the "accountancy rental earnings" in respect of a lease for a period of account of the lessor ("L") is the greatest of the amounts specified in subsection (2).

(2)   Those amounts are—

      (a)   the rental earnings for that period in respect of the lease in L's case,

Taxation (International and Other Provisions) Act 2010 (c. 8)
Schedule 3 — Leasing arrangements: finance leases and loans
Part 1 — New Part 11A of ITA 2007

1127

    (b)   the rental earnings for that period in respect of the lease in the case of a person connected with L, and

    (c)   the rental earnings for that period in respect of the lease for the purposes of consolidated group accounts of a group of companies of which L is a member.

(3)   For the meaning of "the rental earnings", see section 614AC.

614AC Rental earnings

(1)   In this Part "the rental earnings" for any period in respect of a lease of an asset in the case of any person or any consolidated group accounts is the amount specified in subsection (2).

(2)   That amount is the amount that falls for accounting purposes to be treated, in accordance with generally accepted accounting practice, as the gross return for that period on investment in respect of a finance lease or loan in respect of the leasing arrangements.

(3)   For the meaning of "for accounting purposes", see section 614DG."

3   After section 614AC insert—

"CHAPTER 2

FINANCE LEASES WITH RETURN IN CAPITAL FORM

Introduction

614B Arrangements to which this Chapter applies

(1)   This Chapter applies to arrangements involving the lease of an asset that meet conditions A and B.

(2)   Condition A is that in accordance with generally accepted accounting practice the arrangements fall to be treated as a finance lease or loan.

(3)   Condition B is that the effect of the arrangements is that some or all of the return on investment in respect of the finance lease or loan—

    (a)   is or may be in the form of a sum that is not rent, and

    (b)   would not, apart from this Part and Part 21 of CTA 2010, be wholly brought into account for tax purposes as rent from the lease of the asset.

(4)   It does not matter—

    (a)   when the arrangements are or have been entered into, or

    (b)   whether they are or have been entered into by companies or other persons.

614BA Purposes of this Chapter

(1)   This section sets out the main purposes of this Chapter where there are any arrangements to which this Chapter applies.

(2)   The first main purpose is to charge any person entitled to the lessor's interest under the lease of the asset to income tax on amounts of income determined as mentioned in subsections (3) and (4).

1128

Taxation (International and Other Provisions) Act 2010 (c. 8)
Schedule 3 — Leasing arrangements: finance leases and loans
Part 1 — New Part 11A of ITA 2007

(3) The amounts referred to in subsection (2) are determined by reference to the amounts that fall for accounting purposes to be treated, in accordance with generally accepted accounting practice, as the income return on and after 26 November 1996 on investment in respect of the finance lease or loan.

(4) The amounts referred to in subsection (2) are also determined taking into account the substance of the matter as a whole, including, in particular, the state of affairs —

(a) as between connected persons, or

(b) within a group of companies,

as reflected or falling to be reflected in accounts of any of those persons or in consolidated group accounts.

(5) The second main purpose of this Chapter is, if the sum mentioned in section 614B(3)(a) that is not rent falls due, to recover by reference to that sum the whole or any part of the capital expenditure reliefs.

(6) In subsection (5) "the capital expenditure reliefs" means any reliefs, allowances or deductions that are or have been allowed or made in respect of capital expenditure incurred in respect of the leased asset.

Leases to which this Chapter applies

614BB Application of this Chapter

(1) This Chapter applies if —

(a) a lease of an asset is or has been granted, and

(b) the conditions in section 614BC are or have been met in relation to the lease at some time in a period of account of the current lessor.

(2) But this Chapter does not apply so far as, in relation to the current lessor, the lease falls to be regarded as a long funding lease for the purposes of Part 2 of CAA 2001 (plant and machinery allowances) in accordance with Chapter 6A of that Part (interpretation of provisions about long funding leases) (see section 70G of that Act).

(3) If the conditions in section 614BC have been met at some time in a period of account of the person who was at that time the lessor, they are taken to continue to be met for the purposes of this Chapter unless and until one of the conditions in subsection (4) is met.

(4) The conditions are that —

(a) the asset ceases to be leased under the lease, or

(b) the lessor's interest under the lease is assigned to a person who is not connected with any of the persons specified in subsection (5).

(5) Those persons are —

(a) the assignor,

(b) any person who was the lessor at some time before the assignment, and

(c) any person who at some time after the assignment becomes the lessor pursuant to arrangements made by a person who

Taxation (International and Other Provisions) Act 2010 (c. 8)
Schedule 3 — *Leasing arrangements: finance leases and loans*
Part 1 — *New Part 11A of ITA 2007*

1129

was the lessor, or was connected with the lessor, at some time before the assignment.

(6) If at any time the person who was the lessor at that time was a person within the charge to corporation tax on income, the reference in subsection (3) to the conditions in section 614BC having been met at that time includes a reference to the conditions in section 902 of CTA 2010 having been so met.

(7) Nothing in subsection (3) prevents this Chapter from applying again in relation to the lease where the lessor's interest is assigned if the conditions for its application are met after the assignment.

614BC The conditions referred to in section 614BB(1)

(1) This section sets out the conditions required by section 614BB(1) to be met for this Chapter to apply (conditions A to E).

(2) Condition A is that at the relevant time—
    (a) the leasing arrangements fall for accounting purposes to be treated, in accordance with generally accepted accounting practice, as a finance lease or a loan, and
    (b) subsection (3) or (4) applies.

(3) This subsection applies if the lessor ("L"), or a person connected with L, falls for accounting purposes to be treated, in accordance with generally accepted accounting practice, as the finance lessor in relation to the finance lease or loan.

(4) This subsection applies if the finance lease or loan falls for accounting purposes to be treated, in accordance with generally accepted accounting practice, as subsisting for the purposes of consolidated group accounts of a group of companies of which L is a member.

(5) Condition B is that, under the leasing arrangements, there is or may be payable to L, or to a person connected with L, a sum (a "major lump sum") that is not rent but falls for accounting purposes to be treated, in accordance with generally accepted accounting practice—
    (a) as to part, as repayment of some or all of the investment in respect of a finance lease or loan, and
    (b) as to part, as a return on investment in respect of a finance lease or loan.

(6) Condition C is that not all of that part of the sum that falls within subsection (5)(b) would, apart from this Chapter, fall to be brought into account for income tax purposes in tax years ending with the relevant tax year as the normal rent from the lease for periods of account of L.

(7) Condition D is that, in relation to L at the relevant time—
    (a) the period of account of L in which the relevant time falls, or
    (b) an earlier period of account of L during which L was the lessor,
    is a period of account for which the accountancy rental earnings in respect of the lease exceed the normal rent for the period.

(8) Condition E is that at the relevant time—

1130

Taxation (International and Other Provisions) Act 2010 (c. 8)
Schedule 3 — Leasing arrangements: finance leases and loans
Part 1 — New Part 11A of ITA 2007

> (a) arrangements within section 614BE(1) exist, or
>
> (b) paragraph (a) does not apply and circumstances within section 614BE(3) exist.

(9) Section 614BD supplements this section.

614BD Provisions supplementing section 614BC

(1) In section 614BC —

"the relevant tax year", in relation to a major lump sum, means —

> (a) the tax year which is related to the period of account of the lessor ("L") in which the major lump sum is or may be payable in accordance with the leasing arrangements, or
>
> (b) if there are two or more such tax years, the latest of them, and

"the relevant time" means the time as at which it must be determined for the purposes of section 614BB(1) or (3) whether the conditions in section 614BC are or, as the case may be, were met.

(2) For the meaning of a tax year being related to a period of account, see section 614DB(4).

(3) Subsection (4) applies for determining the normal rent for a period of account for the purpose of determining whether condition D in section 614BC is met as respects L unless subsection (5) applies.

(4) Rent that falls to be brought into account for income tax purposes as it falls due is treated —

> (a) as accruing evenly throughout the period to which, in accordance with the terms of the lease, each payment falling due relates, and
>
> (b) as falling due as it so accrues.

(5) This subsection applies if any such payment as is mentioned in subsection (4)(a) falls due more than 12 months after the time at which any of the rent to which that payment relates is treated as accruing under subsection (4)(a).

614BE The arrangements and circumstances referred to in section 614BC(8)

(1) The arrangements referred to in section 614BC(8)(a) are arrangements under which —

> (a) the lessee or a person connected with the lessee may acquire, whether directly or indirectly, the leased asset or an asset representing the leased asset from the lessor or a person connected with the lessor, and
>
> (b) in connection with that acquisition, the lessor or a person connected with the lessor may receive, whether directly or indirectly, a qualifying lump sum from the lessee or a person connected with the lessee.

(2) In this section "qualifying lump sum" means any sum that is not rent but at least part of which would fall for accounting purposes to be

Taxation (International and Other Provisions) Act 2010 (c. 8)
Schedule 3 — Leasing arrangements: finance leases and loans
Part 1 — New Part 11A of ITA 2007

1131

treated, in accordance with generally accepted accounting practice, as a return on investment in respect of a finance lease or loan.

(3) The circumstances referred to in section 614BC(8)(b) are circumstances which make it more likely —

    (a) that the events described in subsection (4) will occur, than

    (b) that the event described in subsection (5) will occur.

(4) The events mentioned in subsection (3)(a) are —

    (a) that the lessee or a person connected with the lessee will acquire, whether directly or indirectly, the leased asset or an asset representing the leased asset from the lessor or a person connected with the lessor, and

    (b) that, in connection with that acquisition, the lessor or a person connected with the lessor will receive, whether directly or indirectly, a qualifying lump sum from the lessee or a person connected with the lessee.

(5) The event mentioned in subsection (3)(b) is that, before any such acquisition as is mentioned in subsection (4) takes place, the leased asset or, as the case may be, the asset representing the leased asset, will have been acquired, in a sale on the open market, by an independent third party.

(6) In subsection (5) "independent third party" means a person who —

    (a) is not the lessor or the lessee, and

    (b) is not connected with either of them.

(7) For the meaning of an asset representing the leased asset, see section 614DD.

Current lessor taxed by reference to accountancy rental earnings

614BF Current lessor taxed by reference to accountancy rental earnings

(1) This section applies if, in the case of any period of account of the current lessor ("L") —

    (a) this Chapter applies in relation to the lease, and

    (b) the accountancy rental earnings in respect of the lease for that period of account exceed the normal rent for that period.

(2) For income tax purposes, L is treated as if in that period of account L had been entitled to, and there had arisen to L, rent from the lease of an amount equal to those accountancy rental earnings (instead of the normal rent referred to in subsection (1)(b)).

(3) Such rent from the lease of an asset is treated for income tax purposes —

    (a) as if it had accrued at an even rate throughout so much of the period of account as falls within the period for which the asset is leased, and

    (b) as if L had become entitled to it as it accrued.

1132

Taxation (International and Other Provisions) Act 2010 (c. 8)
Schedule 3 — Leasing arrangements: finance leases and loans
Part 1 — New Part 11A of ITA 2007

Reduction of taxable rent by cumulative rental excesses

614BG Reduction of taxable rent by cumulative rental excesses: introduction

(1) This section and sections 614BH to 614BK provide for reductions of the taxable rent of a current lessor ("L") under a lease to which this Chapter applies.

(2) In this section and sections 614BH to 614BK "taxable rent", in relation to a period of account of L, means the amount that would, apart from those sections, be treated for income tax purposes as rent from the lease that arises to L in that period of account for the purpose of determining L's liability to tax for the related tax year or years.

(3) The reductions of taxable rent under sections 614BH to 614BK depend on there being —

    (a) a cumulative accountancy rental excess for the period of account of L in question, or

    (b) a cumulative normal rental excess for the period of account of L in question.

(4) For the meaning of "cumulative accountancy rental excess" and "cumulative normal rental excess", see sections 614BH and 614BJ respectively.

614BH Meaning of "accountancy rental excess" and "cumulative accountancy rental excess"

(1) For the purposes of this Chapter, there is an "accountancy rental excess" in relation to the lease for a period of account of the current lessor ("L") if the taxable rent in relation to the lease for the period is as a result of section 614BF (current lessor taxed by reference to accountancy rental earnings) an amount equal to the accountancy rental earnings.

(2) The amount of the accountancy rental excess for the period is equal to the difference between the accountancy rental earnings for the period and the normal rent for the period.

(3) But if the taxable rent for the period is reduced under section 614BK (reduction of taxable rent by the cumulative normal rental excess), there is only an accountancy rental excess for the period if —

    (a) the accountancy rental earnings, reduced by an amount equal to the reduction under that section, exceed

    (b) the normal rent.

(4) And in that case the amount of the accountancy rental excess for the period is equal to that excess.

(5) In this Chapter the "cumulative accountancy rental excess", in relation to the lease and a period of account of L, means so much of the total of the accountancy rental excesses for previous periods of account of L (as increased under section 614BM: recovery of bad debts following reduction under section 614BL) as has not been —

    (a) set off under section 614BI (reduction of taxable rent by the cumulative accountancy rental excess) against the taxable rent for any such previous period,

Taxation (International and Other Provisions) Act 2010 (c. 8)
Schedule 3 — Leasing arrangements: finance leases and loans
Part 1 — New Part 11A of ITA 2007

1133

(b) reduced under section 614BL (relief for bad debts: reduction of cumulative accountancy rental excess), or

(c) set off under section 37A of TCGA 1992 (consideration on disposal of certain leases) against the consideration for a disposal.

614BI Reduction of taxable rent by the cumulative accountancy rental excess

(1) This section applies if a period of account of the current lessor ("L") is one for which —

    (a) the normal rent in relation to the lease exceeds the accountancy rental earnings, and

    (b) there is a cumulative accountancy rental excess.

(2) The taxable rent for the period of account is reduced by setting against it the cumulative accountancy rental excess (but not so as to reduce that rent below the amount of the accountancy rental earnings).

(3) But see section 614BL(3) and (4) (under which the amount of the cumulative accountancy rental excess which may be set against the taxable rent is limited in some circumstances).

614BJ Meaning of "normal rental excess" and "cumulative normal rental excess"

(1) For the purposes of this Chapter, there is a "normal rental excess" in relation to a lease for any period of account of the current lessor ("L") throughout which the leasing arrangements fall for accounting purposes to be treated, in accordance with generally accepted accounting practice, as a finance lease or loan if —

    (a) the normal rent for the period, exceeds

    (b) the accountancy rental earnings for the period.

(2) The amount of the normal rental excess for that period is equal to that excess.

(3) But if the taxable rent for the period is reduced under section 614BI (reduction of taxable rent by the cumulative accountancy rental excess), there is only a normal rental excess for the period if —

    (a) the normal rent, reduced by an amount equal to the reduction under that section, exceeds

    (b) the accountancy rental earnings.

(4) And in that case the amount of the normal rental excess for the period is equal to that excess.

(5) In this Chapter "cumulative normal rental excess", in relation to the lease and a period of account of L, means so much of the total of the normal rental excesses for previous periods of account of L (as increased under section 614BO: recovery of bad debts following reduction under section 614BN) as has not been —

    (a) set off under section 614BK (reduction of taxable rent by the cumulative normal rental excess) against the taxable rent for any such previous period, or

    (b) reduced under section 614BN (relief for bad debts: reduction of cumulative normal rental excess).

1134

Taxation (International and Other Provisions) Act 2010 (c. 8)
Schedule 3 — Leasing arrangements: finance leases and loans
Part 1 — New Part 11A of ITA 2007

614BK Reduction of taxable rent by the cumulative normal rental excess

(1) This section applies if a period of account of the current lessor ("L") is one for which —

    (a) the taxable rent in relation to the lease is as a result of section 614BF (current lessor taxed by reference to accountancy rental earnings) an amount equal to the accountancy rental earnings, and

    (b) there is a cumulative normal rental excess.

(2) The taxable rent for the period of account is reduced by setting against it the cumulative normal rental excess (but not so as to reduce that rent below the amount of the normal rent).

(3) But see section 614BN(3) and (4) (under which the amount of the cumulative normal rental excess which may be set against the taxable rent is limited in some circumstances).

Relief for bad debts by reduction of cumulative rental excesses

614BL Relief for bad debts: reduction of cumulative accountancy rental excess

(1) This section applies if in relation to the lease for any period of account of the current lessor —

    (a) there is a cumulative accountancy rental excess, and

    (b) a bad debt deduction falls to be made in respect of rent from the lease.

(2) If for that period —

    (a) the accountancy rental earnings in relation to the lease exceed the normal rent, and

    (b) the amount of the bad debt deduction exceeds the amount of the accountancy rental earnings,

the cumulative accountancy rental excess for that period is reduced by the amount of the excess of that deduction over those earnings (but not so as to reduce the amount of that rental excess below nil).

(3) Subsections (4) and (5) apply if for that period the accountancy rental earnings in relation to the lease do not exceed the normal rent.

(4) The amount of the cumulative accountancy rental excess that may be set against the taxable rent for that period under section 614BI(2) (reduction of taxable rent by the cumulative accountancy rental excess) is limited to the amount (if any) by which the normal rent exceeds the bad debt deduction.

(5) If for that period the bad debt deduction exceeds the normal rent, the cumulative accountancy rental excess for that period is reduced by the amount of that excess (but not so as to reduce the amount of that rental excess below nil).

(6) In this section —

    "bad debt deduction", in relation to a period of account of the lessor, means the total of any sums falling within section 35(1)(a), (b) or (c) of ITTOIA 2005 in respect of amounts in

Taxation (International and Other Provisions) Act 2010 (c. 8)   **1135**
Schedule 3 — Leasing arrangements: finance leases and loans
Part 1 — New Part 11A of ITA 2007

respect of rents from the lease of the asset which are deductible as expenses for that period, and

"taxable rent" has the meaning given in section 614BG(2).

614BM Recovery of bad debts following reduction under section 614BL

(1) This section applies if in relation to the lease —

     (a) the cumulative accountancy rental excess for any period of account of the current lessor ("L") has been reduced under section 614BL(2) or (5) because of a bad debt deduction,

     (b) in a subsequent period of account of L, an amount ("the relevant credit") is recovered or credited in respect of the amount which constituted the bad debt deduction, and

     (c) there is a cumulative accountancy rental excess for that subsequent period.

(2) The cumulative accountancy rental excess for the subsequent period is increased.

(3) If the relevant credit does not exceed the total of the reductions under section 614BL(2) or (5), the increase is by the relevant credit.

(4) Otherwise, the increase is limited to that total.

(5) In this section "bad debt deduction" has the meaning given in section 614BL(6).

614BN Relief for bad debts: reduction of cumulative normal rental excess

(1) This section applies if in relation to the lease for any period of account of the current lessor —

     (a) there is a cumulative normal rental excess, and

     (b) a bad debt deduction falls to be made in respect of rent from the lease.

(2) If for that period —

     (a) the accountancy rental earnings in the case of the lease do not exceed the normal rent, and

     (b) the amount of the bad debt deduction exceeds the amount of that rent,

the cumulative normal rental excess for that period is reduced by the amount of the excess of that deduction over that rent (but not so as to reduce the amount of that rental excess below nil).

(3) Subsections (4) and (5) apply if for that period the accountancy rental earnings in relation to the lease exceed the normal rent.

(4) The amount of the cumulative normal rental excess that may be set against the taxable rent for that period under section 614BK (reduction of taxable rent by the cumulative normal rental excess) is limited to the amount (if any) by which the accountancy rental earnings exceed the bad debt deduction.

(5) If for that period the bad debt deduction exceeds the accountancy rental earnings, the cumulative normal rental excess for that period is reduced by the amount of the excess (but not so as to reduce the amount of that rental excess below nil).

1136

Taxation (International and Other Provisions) Act 2010 (c. 8)
Schedule 3 — Leasing arrangements: finance leases and loans
Part 1 — New Part 11A of ITA 2007

(6)   In this section, in relation to a period of account of the lessor —
        "bad debt deduction" has the meaning given in section 614BL(6), and
        "taxable rent" has the meaning given in section 614BG(2).

614BO Recovery of bad debts following reduction under section 614BN

(1)   This section applies if in relation to the lease —

    (a)   the cumulative normal rental excess for any period of account of the current lessor ("L") has been reduced under section 614BN(2) or (5) as a result of a bad debt deduction,

    (b)   in a subsequent period of account of L, an amount ("the relevant credit") is recovered or credited in respect of the amount which constituted the bad debt deduction, and

    (c)   there is a cumulative normal rental excess for that subsequent period.

(2)   The cumulative normal rental excess for the subsequent period is increased.

(3)   If the relevant credit does not exceed the total of the reductions under section 614BN(2) or (5), the increase is by the relevant credit.

(4)   Otherwise, the increase is limited to that total.

(5)   In this section "bad debt deduction" has the meaning given in section 614BL(6).

Effect of disposals

614BP Effect of disposals of leases: general

(1)   This section applies if the current lessor ("L") or a person connected with L disposes of —

    (a)   the lessor's interest under the lease,

    (b)   the leased asset, or

    (c)   an asset representing the leased asset (see section 614DD).

(2)   This Part has effect as if immediately before the disposal a period of account of L ended and another began.

(3)   If —

    (a)   two or more disposals within subsection (1) are made at the same time, and

    (b)   there is any cumulative accountancy rental excess for any period of account of L in which the disposal occurs,

    subsection (2) has effect in relation to those disposals as if they together constituted a single disposal.

(4)   In this section "dispose" and "disposal" are to be read in accordance with TCGA 1992.

(5)   In cases where there is any cumulative accountancy rental excess for L's period of account in which the disposal occurs, section 37A of that Act (consideration on disposal of certain leases) makes provision for the purposes of that Act about the reduction of the

Taxation (International and Other Provisions) Act 2010 (c. 8)   **1137**
Schedule 3 – Leasing arrangements: finance leases and loans
Part 1 – New Part 11A of ITA 2007

consideration for the disposal by that excess in determining if a gain has accrued.

614BQ Assignments on which neither a gain nor a loss accrues

(1) This section applies if—

    (a) the current lessor ("L") assigns the lessor's interest under the lease, and

    (b) the assignment is a disposal on which, as a result of any of the no gain/no loss provisions, neither a gain nor a loss accrues.

(2) This Part has effect as if—

    (a) a period of account of L ("L's period") ended with the assignment, and

    (b) a period of account of the assignee ("A's period") began with the assignment.

(3) Any cumulative accountancy rental excess for L's period becomes the cumulative accountancy rental excess for A's period.

(4) Any cumulative normal rental excess for L's period becomes the cumulative normal rental excess for A's period.

(5) If the assignee is a company subject to the charge to corporation tax on income, so far as this section relates to the assignee, it applies for the purposes of Part 21 of CTA 2010 as it would otherwise apply for the purposes of this Part.

(6) In this section "the no gain/no loss provisions" has the same meaning as in TCGA 1992 (see section 288(3A) of that Act).

Capital allowances: claw-back of major lump sum

614BR Effect of capital allowances: introduction

(1) This section and sections 614BS to 614BW apply if an occasion occurs on which a major lump sum falls to be paid in relation to the lease of the asset.

(2) In those sections the occasion is called "the relevant occasion".

614BS Cases where expenditure taken into account under Part 2, 5 or 8 of CAA 2001

(1) This section applies if capital expenditure incurred by the current lessor ("L") in respect of the leased asset is or has been taken into account for the purposes of any allowance or charge under—

    (a) Part 2 of CAA 2001 (plant and machinery allowances),

    (b) Part 5 of that Act (mineral extraction allowances), or

    (c) Part 8 of that Act (patent allowances).

(2) The Part of that Act in question ("the relevant Part") has effect as if the relevant occasion were an event ("the relevant event") as a result of which a disposal value is to be brought into account of an amount equal to the amount or value of the major lump sum (but subject to any applicable limiting provision).

1138   *Taxation (International and Other Provisions) Act 2010 (c. 8)*
Schedule 3 — Leasing arrangements: finance leases and loans
Part 1 — New Part 11A of ITA 2007

(3)   In this section "limiting provision" means a provision to the effect that the disposal value of the asset in question is not to exceed an amount ("the limit") described by reference to capital expenditure incurred in respect of the asset.

(4)   Subsection (5) applies if —

      (a)   as a result of subsection (2), a disposal value ("the relevant disposal value") falls or has fallen to be brought into account by a person in respect of the leased asset for the purposes of the relevant Part, and

      (b)   a limiting provision has effect in the case of that Part.

(5)   The limiting provision has effect (so far as it would not otherwise do so), in relation to the relevant disposal value and any simultaneous or later disposal value, as if —

      (a)   it did not limit any particular disposal value, but

      (b)   it limited the total amount of all the disposal values brought into account for the purposes of the relevant Part by L in respect of the leased asset.

(6)   In subsection (5) "simultaneous or later disposal value" means any disposal value which falls to be brought into account by L in respect of the leased asset as a result of any event occurring at the same time as, or later than, the relevant event.

614BT Cases where expenditure taken into account under other provisions of CAA 2001

(1)   This section applies if any allowance is or has been given in respect of capital expenditure incurred by the current lessor ("L") in respect of the leased asset under any provision of CAA 2001 other than —

      (a)   Part 2 of CAA 2001 (plant and machinery allowances),

      (b)   Part 5 of that Act (mineral extraction allowances), or

      (c)   Part 8 of that Act (patent allowances).

(2)   The amount specified in subsection (3) is treated, in relation to L, as if it were a balancing charge to be made on L for the chargeable period in which the relevant occasion falls.

(3)   That amount is an amount equal to —

      (a)   the total of the allowances given as mentioned in subsection (1) (so far as not previously recovered or withdrawn), or

      (b)   if it is less, the amount or value of the major lump sum.

(4)   In this section "chargeable period" has the meaning given by section 6 of CAA 2001.

614BU Capital allowances deductions: waste disposal and cemeteries

(1)   This section applies if any deduction is or has been allowed to the current lessor ("L") in respect of capital expenditure incurred in connection with the leased asset as a result of —

      (a)   section 165 or 168 of ITTOIA 2005 (preparation and restoration expenditure in relation to waste disposal site), or

      (b)   section 170 of that Act (cemeteries and crematoria: deduction for capital expenditure).

Taxation (International and Other Provisions) Act 2010 (c. 8)   **1139**
Schedule 3 – Leasing arrangements: finance leases and loans
Part 1 – New Part 11A of ITA 2007

(2)   L is treated as if trading receipts arose to L from the trade in question on the relevant occasion.

(3)   The amount of those receipts is equal to the lesser of —
    (a)   the amount or value of the major lump sum, and
    (b)   the deductions previously allowed.

614BV Capital allowances deductions: films and sound recordings

(1)   This section applies if —
    (a)   any relevant deduction has been allowed to the current lessor ("L") in respect of expenditure incurred in connection with the leased asset, and
    (b)   the amount or value of the major lump sum exceeds so much of that sum as was treated as receipts of a revenue nature under section 134(2) of ITTOIA 2005 (disposal proceeds of original master version of film or sound recording treated as receipt of a revenue nature).

(2)   In subsection (1) "relevant deduction" means any deduction as a result of —
    (a)   section 135 of ITTOIA 2005 (allocation of expenditure on master versions of films or sound recordings to periods), or
    (b)   section 138, 138A, 139 or 140 of that Act (relief for production or acquisition expenditure in respect of films).

(3)   L is treated as if receipts of a revenue nature arose to L from the trade or business in question on the relevant occasion.

(4)   The amount of those receipts is equal to the excess mentioned in subsection (1)(b).

614BW Contributors to capital expenditure

(1)   This section applies if —
    (a)   section 614BS or 614BT applies in relation to a leased asset,
    (b)   allowances are or have been made to a person ("the contributor") as a result of sections 537 to 542 of CAA 2001 (allowances in respect of contributions to capital expenditure), and
    (c)   those allowances are or were in respect of the contributor's contribution of a capital sum to expenditure on the provision of the leased asset.

(2)   Section 614BS or, as the case may be, section 614BT has effect in relation to the contributor and those allowances as it has effect in relation to the current lessor and allowances in respect of capital expenditure incurred by the current lessor in respect of the leased asset.

Schemes to which this Chapter does not at first apply

614BX Pre-26 November 1996 schemes where this Chapter does not at first apply

(1)   This section applies if —

1140   *Taxation (International and Other Provisions) Act 2010 (c. 8)*
Schedule 3 — Leasing arrangements: finance leases and loans
Part 1 — New Part 11A of ITA 2007

        (a)   the lease of an asset forms part of a pre-26 November 1996 scheme, but

        (b)   the conditions in section 614BC become met after 26 November 1996.

(2)   For the meaning of "forming part of a pre-26 November 1996 scheme", see section 614D.

(3)   This Part has effect as if —

        (a)   a period of account ("period 1") of the current lessor ("L") ended immediately before the time at which those conditions become met,

        (b)   another period of account of L ("period 2") began immediately before that time and ended immediately after that time, and

        (c)   another period of account of L began immediately after that time.

(4)   If, on the continuous application assumption (see subsection (9)), there would be an amount of cumulative accountancy rental excess for period 2, that amount is the cumulative accountancy rental excess for period 2.

(5)   If subsection (4) applies, L is treated for income tax purposes as if in period 1 L had been entitled to, and there had arisen to L, rent from the lease of an amount equal to that cumulative accountancy rental excess.

(6)   The amount of rent mentioned in subsection (5) —

        (a)   is in addition to any other rent from the lease for period 1, and

        (b)   is left out of account for the purposes of section 614BF (current lessor taxed by reference to accountancy rental earnings).

(7)   Rent within subsection (5) is treated for income tax purposes as if it had accrued and L had become entitled to it immediately before the end of period 1.

(8)   If, on the continuous application assumption, there would be an amount of cumulative normal rental excess for period 2, that amount is the cumulative normal rental excess for period 2.

(9)   In this section "the continuous application assumption" means the assumption that this Chapter (other than this section) had applied in the case of the lease at all times on or after 26 November 1996.

(10)   If at any time the person who was the lessor at that time was a person within the charge to corporation tax on income, the reference in subsection (9) to this Chapter (other than this section) includes a reference to Chapter 2 of Part 21 of CTA 2010 (other than section 923 of that Act).

614BY Post-25 November 1996 schemes to which Chapter 3 applied first

(1)   This section applies if —

        (a)   the conditions in section 614BC become met in the case of the lease of the asset, and

Taxation (International and Other Provisions) Act 2010 (c. 8)
Schedule 3 – Leasing arrangements: finance leases and loans
Part 1 – New Part 11A of ITA 2007

1141

    (b)   immediately before those conditions become met, Chapter 3 applied.

  (2) Subsection (3) applies for the purpose of determining—

    (a)   the cumulative accountancy rental excess for any period of account ending after those conditions become met, or

    (b)   the cumulative normal rental excess for any such period.

  (3) This Part has effect as if this Chapter had applied in relation to the lease at any time when Chapter 3 applied in relation to it.

  (4) If at any time the person who was the lessor at that time was a person within the charge to corporation tax on income—

    (a)   the reference in subsection (1)(a) to the conditions in section 614BC becoming met at that time includes a reference to the conditions in section 902 of CTA 2010 becoming so met,

    (b)   the reference in subsection (1)(b) to Chapter 3 applying immediately before that time includes a reference to Chapter 3 of Part 21 of that Act so applying, and

    (c)   the reference in subsection (3) to Chapter 3 applying at that time includes a reference to Chapter 3 of that Part so applying."

4   After section 614BY insert—

"CHAPTER 3

OTHER FINANCE LEASES

Introduction

614C Introduction to Chapter

  (1) This Chapter applies to arrangements involving the lease of an asset that—

    (a)   fall to be treated, in accordance with generally accepted accounting practice, as a finance lease or loan, but

    (b)   are not arrangements to which Chapter 2 applies.

  (2) It does not matter whether the arrangements are or have been entered into by companies or other persons.

614CA Purpose of this Chapter

  (1) The main purpose of this Chapter where there are arrangements to which this Chapter applies is to charge a person entitled to the lessor's interest under the lease of the asset to income tax on amounts of income determined as mentioned in subsection (2).

  (2) The amounts referred to in subsection (1) are determined by reference to the amounts that fall for accounting purposes to be treated, in accordance with generally accepted accounting practice, as the income return on and after 26 November 1996 on investment in respect of the finance lease or loan.

1142

Taxation (International and Other Provisions) Act 2010 (c. 8)
Schedule 3 — Leasing arrangements: finance leases and loans
Part 1 — New Part 11A of ITA 2007

(3)   The amounts referred to in subsection (1) are also determined taking into account the substance of the matter as a whole, including, in particular, the state of affairs—

    (a)   as between connected persons, or

    (b)   within a group of companies,

as reflected or falling to be reflected in accounts of any of those persons or in consolidated group accounts.

Leases to which this Chapter applies

614CB Leases to which this Chapter applies

(1)   This Chapter applies if—

    (a)   a lease of an asset is or has been granted on or after 26 November 1996,

    (b)   the lease forms part of a post-25 November 1996 scheme,

    (c)   condition A in section 614BC is or has been met at some time on or after 26 November 1996 in relation to the lease in a period of account of the current lessor ("L"), and

    (d)   Chapter 2 does not apply in relation to the lease because of the other conditions in that section not all being, or having been, met as mentioned in section 614BB.

(2)   For the meaning of "forming part of a post-25 November 1996 scheme", see section 614D.

(3)   This Chapter does not apply so far as, in relation to L, the lease falls to be regarded as a long funding lease for the purposes of Part 2 of CAA 2001 (plant and machinery allowances) in accordance with Chapter 6A of that Part (interpretation of provisions about long funding leases) (see section 70G of that Act).

(4)   If condition A in section 614BC has been met at any time on or after 26 November 1996 in a period of account of the person who was at that time the lessor, it is taken to continue to be met unless and until one of the conditions in subsection (5) is met.

(5)   The conditions are that—

    (a)   the asset ceases to be leased under the lease, or

    (b)   the lessor's interest under the lease is assigned to a person who is not connected with any of the persons specified in subsection (6).

(6)   Those persons are—

    (a)   the assignor,

    (b)   any person who was the lessor at some time before the assignment, and

    (c)   any person who at some time after the assignment becomes the lessor pursuant to arrangements made by a person who was the lessor, or was connected with the lessor, at some time before the assignment.

(7)   If at any time the person who was the lessor at that time was a person within the charge to corporation tax on income—

Taxation (International and Other Provisions) Act 2010 (c. 8) 1143
Schedule 3 — Leasing arrangements: finance leases and loans
Part 1 — New Part 11A of ITA 2007

    (a)   the reference in subsection (4) to condition A in section 614BC having been met at that time includes a reference to condition A in section 902 of CTA 2010 having been so met, and

    (b)   the reference in subsection (1)(d) to the other conditions in section 614BC not having been met as mentioned in section 614BB includes a reference to the other conditions in section 902 of that Act not having been met as mentioned in section 901 of that Act.

  (8)   Nothing in subsection (4) prevents this Chapter from applying again in relation to the lease where the lessor's interest is assigned if the conditions for its application are met after the assignment.

Current lessor taxed by reference to accountancy rental earnings

614CC Current lessor taxed by reference to accountancy rental earnings

  (1)   This section applies if, in the case of any period of account of the current lessor ("L") —

    (a)   this Chapter applies in relation to the lease, and

    (b)   the accountancy rental earnings in respect of the lease for that period of account exceed the normal rent for that period.

  (2)   For income tax purposes, L is treated as if in that period of account L had been entitled to, and there had arisen to L, rent from the lease of an amount equal to those accountancy rental earnings (instead of the normal rent referred to in subsection (1)(b)).

  (3)   Such rent from the lease of an asset is treated for income tax purposes —

    (a)   as if it had accrued at an even rate throughout so much of the period of account as falls within the period for which the asset is leased, and

    (b)   as if L had become entitled to it as it accrued.

Application of provisions of Chapter 2 for purposes of this Chapter

614CD Application of provisions of Chapter 2 for purposes of this Chapter

    Sections 614BG to 614BQ apply for the purposes of this Chapter as they apply for the purposes of Chapter 2, but taking the references in sections 614BH(1) and 614BK(1)(a) to section 614BF as references to section 614CC."

5   After section 614CD insert —

"CHAPTER 4

SUPPLEMENTARY PROVISIONS

614D Pre-26 November 1996 schemes and post-25 November 1996 schemes

  (1)   For the purposes of this Part, a lease of an asset —

    (a)   forms part of a pre-26 November 1996 scheme if (and only if) the conditions in subsection (2) or (3) are met, and

1144   *Taxation (International and Other Provisions) Act 2010 (c. 8)*
Schedule 3 — Leasing arrangements: finance leases and loans
Part 1 — New Part 11A of ITA 2007

      (b)   in any other case, forms part of a post-25 November 1996 scheme.

  (2)   The conditions in this subsection are that—

      (a)   a contract in writing for the lease of the asset was made before 26 November 1996,

      (b)   either—

            (i)   the contract was unconditional, or

            (ii)   if the contract was conditional, the conditions were met before that date, and

      (c)   no terms remain to be agreed on or after that date.

  (3)   The conditions in this subsection are that—

      (a)   a contract in writing for the lease of the asset was made before 26 November 1996,

      (b)   the condition in subsection (2)(b) or (c) was not met in the case of the contract,

      (c)   either—

            (i)   the contract was unconditional, or

            (ii)   if the contract was conditional, the conditions were met before the end of the finalisation period or within such further period as the Commissioners for Her Majesty's Revenue and Customs may allow in the particular case,

      (d)   no terms remain to be agreed after the end of the finalisation period or such further period as those Commissioners may so allow, and

      (e)   the contract in its final form was not materially different from the contract as it stood when it was made before 26 November 1996.

  (4)   In subsection (3) "the finalisation period" means the period which ended with the later of—

      (a)   31 January 1997, and

      (b)   the end of the period of six months beginning with the day after that on which the contract was made as mentioned in subsection (3)(a).

614DA Time apportionment where periods of account do not coincide

  (1)   Subsection (2) applies if a period of account of the lessor ("L") does not coincide with a period of account of a person connected with L.

  (2)   Any amount which falls for the purposes of this Part to be found for L's period of account but by reference to the connected person is found by making such apportionments as may be necessary between two or more periods of account of the connected person.

  (3)   Subsection (4) applies if a period of account of L does not coincide with a period for which consolidated group accounts of a group of companies of which L is a member fall to be prepared.

  (4)   Any amount which falls for the purposes of this Part to be found for L's period of account but by reference to the consolidated group accounts is found by making such apportionments as may be

Taxation (International and Other Provisions) Act 2010 (c. 8)　　　　　**1145**
Schedule 3 — Leasing arrangements: finance leases and loans
Part 1 — New Part 11A of ITA 2007

necessary between two or more periods for which consolidated group accounts of the group fall to be prepared.

(5)　Any apportionment under subsection (2) or (4) must be made in proportion to the number of days in the respective periods that fall within L's period of account.

614DB Periods of account and related periods of account and tax years

(1)　In this Part "period of account" means a period for which accounts are made up.

(2)　Except for the purposes of sections 614BB to 614BE and subsection (3), in this Part "period of account" does not include a period that begins before 26 November 1996.

(3)　But this Part applies in relation to a period of account that begins before 26 November 1996 and ends on or after that date as if—
　　(a)　so much of the period as falls before that date, and
　　(b)　so much of the period as falls on or after that date,
were separate periods of account.

(4)　For the purposes of this Part, a tax year is related to a period of account if the tax year consists of or includes the whole or any part of the period of account.

(5)　For the purposes of this Part a period of account is related to a tax year if the tax year is related to the period of account.

614DC Connected persons

(1)　For the purposes of this Part in its application as a result of any leasing arrangements, if a person ("A") is connected with another ("B") at some time during the relevant period A is treated as being connected with B throughout that period.

(2)　The relevant period is the period that—
　　(a)　begins at the earliest time at which any of the arrangements were made, and
　　(b)　ends when the current lessor finally ceases to have an interest in the asset or any arrangements relating to it.

614DD Assets which represent the leased asset

(1)　For the purposes of this Part, the assets described in subsection (2) are treated as representing the leased asset.

(2)　Those assets are—
　　(a)　any asset derived from the leased asset or created out of it,
　　(b)　any asset from which the leased asset was derived or out of which the leased asset was created,
　　(c)　any asset derived from or created out of an asset within paragraph (b), and
　　(d)　any asset that derives the whole or a substantial part of its value from the leased asset or an asset that itself represents the leased asset.

1146

Taxation (International and Other Provisions) Act 2010 (c. 8)
Schedule 3 — Leasing arrangements: finance leases and loans
Part 1 — New Part 11A of ITA 2007

614DE Parent undertakings and consolidated group accounts

(1) This Part has effect in relation to a body corporate that—

    (a) is a parent undertaking, but

    (b) for accounting purposes is not required to prepare consolidated group accounts in accordance with generally accepted accounting practice,

as if it were so required.

(2) For the purposes of subsection (1) it does not matter where the body corporate is incorporated.

(3) In subsection (1) "parent undertaking" is to be read in accordance with section 1162 of the Companies Act 2006.

614DF Assessments and adjustments

All such assessments and adjustments must be made as are necessary to give effect to this Part.

614DG Interpretation

In this Part, unless the context otherwise requires—

"accountancy rental earnings" has the meaning given by section 614AB(1),

"accountancy rental excess" is to be read—

    (a) for the purposes of Chapter 2, in accordance with section 614BH(1) to (4), and

    (b) for the purposes of Chapter 3, in accordance with section 614BH(1) to (4) as it has effect as a result of section 614CD,

"asset" means any form of property or rights,

"asset representing the leased asset" is to be read in accordance with section 614DD,

"cumulative accountancy rental excess" is to be read—

    (a) for the purposes of Chapter 2, in accordance with section 614BH(5), and

    (b) for the purposes of Chapter 3, in accordance with section 614BH(5) as it has effect as a result of section 614CD,

"cumulative normal rental excess" is to be read—

    (a) for the purposes of Chapter 2, in accordance with section 614BJ(5), and

    (b) for the purposes of Chapter 3, in accordance with section 614BJ(5) as it has effect as a result of section 614CD,

"the current lessor", in relation to a lease of an asset, means the person who is for the time being entitled to the lessor's interest under the lease,

"finance lessor" means a person who for accounting purposes is treated, in accordance with generally accepted accounting practice, as the person with—

    (a) the grantor's interest in relation to a finance lease, or

    (b) the lender's interest in relation to a loan,

Taxation (International and Other Provisions) Act 2010 (c. 8)   **1147**
Schedule 3 − Leasing arrangements: finance leases and loans
Part 1 − New Part 11A of ITA 2007

"for accounting purposes" means for the purposes of −

    (a)   accounts of companies incorporated in any part of the United Kingdom, or

    (b)   consolidated group accounts for groups all the members of which are companies so incorporated,

"lease" −

    (a)   in relation to land, includes an underlease, sublease, tenancy or licence, and any agreement for a lease, underlease, sublease, tenancy or licence and, in the case of land outside the United Kingdom, any interest corresponding to a lease as so defined, and

    (b)   in relation to any form of property or right other than land, means any kind of agreement or arrangement under which payments are made for the use of, or otherwise in respect of, an asset,

and "rent" is to be read accordingly,

"the leasing arrangements", in relation to a lease of an asset, means −

    (a)   the lease,

    (b)   any arrangements relating to or connected with the lease, and

    (c)   any other arrangements of which the lease forms part,

and includes a reference to any of the leasing arrangements,

"the lessee", in relation to a lease of an asset, means (except in the expression "the lessee's interest under the lease") the person entitled to the lessee's interest under the lease,

"the lessor", in relation to a lease of an asset, means (except in the expression "the lessor's interest under the lease") the person entitled to the lessor's interest under the lease,

"major lump sum" is to be read in accordance with section 614BC(5),

"normal rent" is to be read in accordance with section 614AA,

"normal rental excess" is to be read −

    (a)   for the purposes of Chapter 2, in accordance with section 614BJ(1) to (4), and

    (b)   for the purposes of Chapter 3, in accordance with section 614BJ(1) to (4) as it has effect as a result of section 614CD,

"period of account" is to be read in accordance with section 614DB(1) to (3),

"post-25 November 1996 scheme" is to be read in accordance with section 614D(1)(b),

"pre-26 November 1996 scheme" is to be read in accordance with section 614D(1)(a),

"related period of account" is to be read in accordance with section 614DB(5),

"related tax year" is to be read in accordance with section 614DB(4),

"the rental earnings", in relation to a lease of an asset and any period, has the meaning given by section 614AC, and

1148   *Taxation (International and Other Provisions) Act 2010 (c. 8)*
Schedule 3 — Leasing arrangements: finance leases and loans
Part 1 — New Part 11A of ITA 2007

"sum" includes any money or money's worth (and "pay" and related expressions are to be read accordingly)."

PART 2

NEW SECTION 37A OF TCGA 1992

6   TCGA 1992 is amended as follows.

7   After section 37 insert—

"37A   Consideration on disposal of certain leases

(1)   This section applies if—

     (a)   a disposal occurs that is within section 614BP of ITA 2007 (including that section as it has effect as a result of section 614CD of that Act), and

     (b)   for the purposes of Chapter 2 or 3 of Part 11A of that Act there is any cumulative accountancy rental excess in relation to the lease for the period of account of the current lessor in which the disposal takes place.

(2)   This section also applies if—

     (a)   a disposal occurs that is within section 915 of CTA 2010 (including that section as it has effect as a result of section 929 of that Act), and

     (b)   for the purposes of Chapter 2 or 3 of Part 21 of that Act there is any cumulative accountancy rental excess in relation to the lease for the period of account of the current lessor in which the disposal takes place.

(3)   In determining for the purposes of this Act the amount of any gain accruing to the person making the disposal, the consideration for the disposal is treated as reduced by setting against it that excess (but not so as to reduce the amount of that consideration below nil).

(4)   Subsection (3) only affects section 37 so far as subsection (5) provides.

(5)   Section 37 does not exclude any money or money's worth from the consideration for a disposal so far as it is represented by any such cumulative accountancy rental excess that, in accordance with subsection (3)—

     (a)   falls to be set against the consideration for the disposal, or

     (b)   has fallen to be set against the consideration for a previous disposal made by the person making the disposal in question or a person connected with that person.

(6)   Subsections (7) to (9) apply if the disposal mentioned in subsection (1) or (2) is a part disposal of the asset in question.

(7)   The cumulative accountancy rental excess mentioned in subsection (3) must be apportioned between—

     (a)   the property disposed of, and

     (b)   the property that remains undisposed of.

Taxation (International and Other Provisions) Act 2010 (c. 8)
Schedule 3 — Leasing arrangements: finance leases and loans
Part 2 — New section 37A of TCGA 1992

1149

(8) That apportionment must be made in the same proportions as those in which the sums that under section 38(1)(a) or (b) are attributable to the asset fall to be apportioned under section 42.

(9) Only so much of the cumulative accountancy rental excess as is so apportioned to the property disposed of is set against the consideration for the part disposal in accordance with subsection (3).

(10) If subsection (3) applies in a case where two or more disposals within subsection (1) or (2) are made at the same time, the cumulative accountancy rental excess mentioned in subsection (3) must be apportioned, subject to subsections (7) to (9), between the disposals in such proportions as are just and reasonable.

(11) Section 614DC of ITA 2007 (connected persons) applies for the purposes of this section in its application as a result of any leasing arrangements (within the meaning of that section) as it applies for the purposes mentioned in that section."

SCHEDULE 4

Section 368

SALE AND LEASE-BACK ETC: NEW PART 12A OF ITA 2007

1   ITA 2007 is amended as follows.

2   After section 681 insert—

"PART 12A

SALE AND LEASE-BACK ETC

CHAPTER 1

PAYMENTS CONNECTED WITH TRANSFERRED LAND

Overview

681A Overview

This Chapter provides that in certain circumstances where a transfer is made regarding land, and the transferor or an associate becomes liable to make a payment connected with the land, income tax relief for the payment is restricted.

Application of the Chapter

681AA Transferor or associate becomes liable for payment of rent

(1) Section 681AD has effect if—

    (a) land, or an estate or interest in land, is transferred,

    (b) the transferor, or a person associated with the transferor, becomes liable to make a payment of rent under a lease of the land or part of it, and

1150

Taxation (International and Other Provisions) Act 2010 (c. 8)
Schedule 4 — Sale and lease-back etc: new Part 12A of ITA 2007

    (c)   a deduction by way of relevant income tax relief (see section 681AC) is allowed for the payment.

(2)   Section 681AE has effect if —

    (a)   land, or an estate or interest in land, is transferred,

    (b)   the transferor, or a person associated with the transferor, becomes liable to make a payment of rent under a lease of the land or part of it, and

    (c)   a relevant deduction from earnings (see section 681AC) is allowed for the payment.

(3)   The reference in subsection (1)(a) or (2)(a) to a transfer of an estate or interest in land includes a reference to any of the following —

    (a)   the granting of a lease or another transaction involving the creation of a new estate or interest in the land,

    (b)   the transfer of the lessee's interest under a lease by surrender or forfeiture of the lease, and

    (c)   a transaction or series of transactions affecting land or an estate or interest in land, such that some person is the owner or one of the owners before and after the transaction or transactions but another person becomes or ceases to be one of the owners.

(4)   In relation to a transaction or series of transactions mentioned in subsection (3)(c), a person is to be regarded as a transferor for the purposes of this Chapter if the person —

    (a)   is an owner before the transaction or transactions, and

    (b)   is not the sole owner afterwards.

(5)   The liability mentioned in subsection (1)(b) or (2)(b) is one resulting from —

    (a)   a lease, of the land or part of it, granted (at the time of the transfer or later) by the transferee to the transferor, or

    (b)   another transaction or series of transactions affecting the land or an estate or interest in it.

(6)   The liability mentioned in subsection (1)(b) or (2)(b) is one arising at the time of the transfer or later.

(7)   The reference in subsection (1)(a) or (2)(a) to a transfer does not include a transfer on or before 14 April 1964.

681AB Transferor or associate becomes liable for payment other than rent

(1)   Section 681AD has effect if —

    (a)   land, or an estate or interest in land, is transferred,

    (b)   the transferor, or a person associated with the transferor, becomes liable to make a payment which is not rent under a lease but is otherwise connected with the land or part of it (whether it is a payment under a rentcharge or under some other transaction), and

    (c)   a deduction by way of relevant income tax relief (see section 681AC) is allowed for the payment.

(2)   Section 681AE has effect if —

    (a)   land, or an estate or interest in land, is transferred,

     (b)   the transferor, or a person associated with the transferor, becomes liable to make a payment which is not rent under a lease but is otherwise connected with the land or part of it (whether it is a payment under a rentcharge or under some other transaction), and

     (c)   a relevant deduction from earnings (see section 681AC) is allowed for the payment.

(3)   The reference in subsection (1)(a) or (2)(a) to a transfer of an estate or interest in land includes a reference to any of the following —

     (a)   the granting of a lease or another transaction involving the creation of a new estate or interest in the land,

     (b)   the transfer of the lessee's interest under a lease by surrender or forfeiture of the lease, and

     (c)   a transaction or series of transactions affecting land or an estate or interest in land, such that some person is the owner or one of the owners before and after the transaction or transactions but another person becomes or ceases to be one of the owners.

(4)   In relation to a transaction or series of transactions mentioned in subsection (3)(c), a person is to be regarded as a transferor for the purposes of this Chapter if the person —

     (a)   is an owner before the transaction or transactions, and

     (b)   is not the sole owner afterwards.

(5)   The liability mentioned in subsection (1)(b) or (2)(b) is one resulting from a transaction or series of transactions affecting the land or an estate or interest in it.

(6)   The liability mentioned in subsection (1)(b) or (2)(b) is one arising at the time of the transfer or later.

(7)   The reference in subsection (1)(a) or (2)(a) to a transfer does not include a transfer on or before 14 April 1964.

681AC Relevant income tax relief and relevant deduction from earnings

(1)   For the purposes of this Chapter each of the following is a deduction by way of relevant income tax relief —

     (a)   a deduction in calculating profits or losses of a trade, profession or vocation for income tax purposes,

     (b)   a deduction in calculating the profits of a UK property business for income tax purposes, and

     (c)   a deduction in calculating any loss for which relief is given under section 152 (losses from miscellaneous transactions), or in calculating profits or other income or gains chargeable to income tax under or by virtue of any provision to which section 1016 applies.

(2)   For the purposes of this Chapter each of the following is a relevant deduction from earnings —

     (a)   a deduction under section 336 of ITEPA 2003 (expenses), and

     (b)   a deduction from earnings in calculating losses in an employment for income tax purposes.

Relief: restriction and carrying forward

681AD Relevant income tax relief: deduction not to exceed commercial rent

(1) The rules in subsection (3) apply to the calculation of the deduction by way of relevant income tax relief allowed in a relevant period —

    (a) for the non-excluded element of the payment within section 681AA(1) or 681AB(1), or

    (b) if there are two or more such payments, for the non-excluded elements of those payments.

(2) For the purposes of this section —

    (a) in relation to a deduction within section 681AC(1)(a) "relevant period" means —

        (i) a period of account of the trade, profession or vocation concerned, or

        (ii) if no accounts of the trade, profession or vocation are drawn up for a period, the basis period of a tax year,

    (b) in relation to a deduction within section 681AC(1)(b) or (c) "relevant period" means —

        (i) a period of account of the business or person concerned, or

        (ii) if no accounts of the business are drawn up for a period or the person does not draw up accounts for a period, a tax year, and

    (c) the non-excluded element of a payment is the element of the payment not excluded under section 681AI (service charges etc).

(3) The rules are —

Rule 1 — meaning of amount E

For any relevant period, amount E (which may be nil) is the expense or total expenses to be brought, in accordance with generally accepted accounting practice, into account in the period in respect of —

    (a) the non-excluded element of the payment, or

    (b) the non-excluded elements of the payments.

Rule 2 — calculations

For every relevant period —

    (a) calculate the total of amount E for the period and amount E for every previous relevant period ending on or after the date of the transfer mentioned in section 681AA(1)(a) or 681AB(1)(a),

    (b) calculate the total of the deductions by way of relevant income tax relief for every previous relevant period ending on or after the date of that transfer, and

    (c) subtract the total at (b) from the total at (a) to give the cumulative unrelieved expenses for the period.

Rule 3 — meaning of post-spread period

A relevant period is a post-spread period if for that relevant period, and every later relevant period, there are no payments within section 681AA(1) or 681AB(1).

Rule 4 — the deduction allowed in a relevant period

Taxation (International and Other Provisions) Act 2010 (c. 8)
Schedule 4 — Sale and lease-back etc: new Part 12A of ITA 2007

1153

If a relevant period is not a post-spread period, the deduction allowed for the period is equal to the cumulative unrelieved expenses for the period, but is the commercial rent for the period if that is less (see section 681AJ or 681AK).

Rule 5 — relevant periods in which no deduction allowed

If a relevant period is a post-spread period, no deduction is allowed for the period.

Certain deductions from earnings: restriction and carrying forward of relief

681AE Deduction from earnings not to exceed commercial rent

(1) Subsection (3) applies to the calculation of the relevant deduction from earnings allowed for the non-excluded element of the payment within section 681AA(2) or 681AB(2).

(2) For the purposes of this section the non-excluded element of a payment is the element of the payment not excluded under section 681AI (service charges etc).

(3) The deduction must not exceed the commercial rent for the period for which the payment is made (see section 681AJ or 681AK).

681AF Carrying forward parts of payments

(1) This section applies if—
    (a) section 681AE has effect, and
    (b) conditions A and B are met.

(2) Condition A is that under section 681AE part of a payment which would otherwise be allowed as a relevant deduction from earnings is not allowed.

(3) Condition B is that one or more later payments are made, by the transferor or a person associated with the transferor, under—
    (a) the lease (if section 681AE has effect because of section 681AA(2)), or
    (b) the rentcharge or other transaction mentioned in section 681AB(2)(b) (if section 681AE has effect because of section 681AB(2)).

(4) The part of the payment mentioned in subsection (2) may be carried forward and treated for the purposes of a relevant deduction from earnings as if it were made—
    (a) when the next of the later payments is made, and
    (b) for the period for which that later payment is made.

(5) So far as a part of a payment carried forward under this section is not allowed as a relevant deduction from earnings, it may be carried forward again under this section.

681AG Aggregation and apportionment of payments

(1) This section applies for the purposes of section 681AE.

(2) If more than one payment is made for the same period, the payments must be taken together.

1154

Taxation (International and Other Provisions) Act 2010 (c. 8)
Schedule 4 — Sale and lease-back etc: new Part 12A of ITA 2007

(3)   If payments are made for periods which overlap—

    (a)   the payments must be apportioned, and

    (b)   the apportioned payments which belong to the common part of the overlapping periods must be taken together.

(4)   References in subsections (2) and (3) to payments include references to parts of payments which under section 681AF are treated as if made later than they were made.

681AH Payments made for later periods

(1)   This section applies for the purposes of sections 681AE to 681AG.

(2)   For the purposes of this section the relevant year, in relation to a payment, is the year which begins with the date it is made.

(3)   If a payment is made for a period all of which is after the relevant year, it must be treated as made for the relevant year.

(4)   If a payment is made for a period part of which is after the relevant year, it must be treated as if a corresponding part of it was made for the relevant year (and no part for a later period).

Interpretation etc

681AI Exclusion of service charges etc

(1)   This section applies for the purposes of sections 681AD and 681AE.

(2)   A payment must be excluded so far as it is in respect of any of the following—

    (a)   services,

    (b)   the use of relevant assets, and

    (c)   rates usually borne by the tenant.

(3)   The amount excluded must be just and reasonable.

(4)   If a lease or agreement contains provisions fixing the payments or parts of payments which are in respect of services or the use of assets, those provisions are not conclusive.

(5)   A relevant asset is any description of property or rights other than land or an interest in land.

681AJ Commercial rent: comparison with rent under a lease

(1)   Subsection (3) applies—

    (a)   for the purpose of making a comparison under rule 4 of section 681AD(3) if section 681AD has effect because of section 681AA(1), and

    (b)   for the purpose of making a comparison under section 681AE(3) if section 681AE has effect because of section 681AA(2).

(2)   In this section "the actual lease" means the lease mentioned in section 681AA(1)(b) or (2)(b).

Taxation (International and Other Provisions) Act 2010 (c. 8)
Schedule 4 — Sale and lease-back etc: new Part 12A of ITA 2007

1155

(3) The commercial rent is the rent which might be expected to be paid under a lease, of the land in respect of which the payment mentioned in section 681AA(1)(b) or (2)(b) is made, which—

  (a) was negotiated in the open market when the actual lease was created,

  (b) is of the same duration as the actual lease,

  (c) is subject to the terms and conditions of the actual lease as respects liability for maintenance and repairs, and

  (d) provides for rent payable at uniform intervals and at an appropriate rate.

(4) Rent is payable at an appropriate rate if—

  (a) it is payable at a uniform rate, or

  (b) in a case where the rent payable under the actual lease is rent at a progressive rate (and such that the amount of rent payable for a year is never less than the amount payable for a previous year), it progresses by gradations proportionate to those provided by the actual lease.

681AK Commercial rent: comparison with payments other than rent

(1) Subsection (2) applies—

  (a) for the purpose of making a comparison under rule 4 of section 681AD(3) if section 681AD has effect because of section 681AB(1), and

  (b) for the purpose of making a comparison under section 681AE(3) if section 681AE has effect because of section 681AB(2).

(2) The commercial rent is the rent which might be expected to be paid under a lease, of the land in respect of which the payment mentioned in section 681AB(1)(b) or (2)(b) is made, which—

  (a) was negotiated in the open market when the rentcharge or other transaction mentioned in section 681AB(1)(b) or (2)(b) was effected,

  (b) is a tenant's repairing lease, and

  (c) is of an appropriate duration.

(3) A tenant's repairing lease is a lease where the lessee is under an obligation to maintain and repair the whole (or substantially the whole) of the premises comprised in the lease.

(4) To see whether a lease is of an appropriate duration, take the period over which payments are to be made under the rentcharge or other transaction, and—

  (a) if that period is 200 years or more (or the obligation to make the payments is perpetual) an appropriate duration is 200 years, or

  (b) if that period is less than 200 years, an appropriate duration is the same duration as that period.

681AL Lease and rent

(1) This section applies for the purposes of this Chapter.

(2) A reference to a lease includes a reference to any of the following—

1156

Taxation (International and Other Provisions) Act 2010 (c. 8)
Schedule 4 — Sale and lease-back etc: new Part 12A of ITA 2007

    (a)   an underlease, sublease, tenancy or licence, and

    (b)   an agreement for a lease, underlease, sublease, tenancy or licence, and

    (c)   in the case of land outside the United Kingdom, an interest corresponding to a lease (as defined here).

(3)   A reference to rent includes a reference to any payment under a lease.

(4)   A reference to rent under a lease includes a reference to expenses which the tenant under the lease is treated as incurring in respect of the land subject to the lease under any of—

    (a)   sections 61 to 67 of ITTOIA 2005 (land occupied for trade purposes), and

    (b)   sections 292 to 297 of that Act (taxed leases).

(5)   Expenses within subsection (4) must be treated as having been paid as soon as they were incurred.

681AM Associated persons

(1)   This section applies for the purposes of this Chapter.

(2)   The following persons are associated with one another—

    (a)   the transferor in an affected transaction and the transferor in another affected transaction, if the two persons are acting in concert or if the two transactions are in any way reciprocal, and

    (b)   any person who is an associate of either of those associated transferors.

(3)   Two or more bodies corporate are associated with one another if they participate in, or are incorporated for the purposes of, a scheme—

    (a)   for the reconstruction of any body or bodies corporate, or

    (b)   for the amalgamation of any two or more bodies corporate.

(4)   Persons are associated with one another if they are associates as defined in section 681DL (relatives, settlements, persons controlling bodies, joint owners etc).

(5)   In subsection (2) "affected transaction" means a transaction within—

    (a)   section 681AA(1) or (2) or 681AB(1) or (2), or

    (b)   section 835(1) or (2) or 836(1) or (2) of CTA 2010.

681AN Land outside the UK

In the case of land outside the United Kingdom, expressions in this Chapter relating to interests in land and their disposition must be taken to relate to corresponding interests and dispositions."

3   After section 681AN insert—

"CHAPTER 2

NEW LEASE OF LAND AFTER ASSIGNMENT OR SURRENDER

Overview

681B Overview

(1)   This Chapter provides that in certain circumstances where a lease of land is assigned or surrendered and another lease is granted or assigned—

   (a)   consideration received for the assignment or surrender of the first lease is taxed as a receipt of a trade, profession or vocation or charged to income tax, and

   (b)   tax relief is allowed for rent under the other lease.

(2)   The Chapter provides that in certain circumstances where a lease is varied it is treated as surrendered and another lease is treated as granted.

Application of the Chapter

681BA New lease after assignment or surrender

(1)   This Chapter has effect if each of conditions A to E is met.

(2)   Condition A is that—

   (a)   a person ("L") is a lessee of land under a lease which has 50 years or less to run ("the original lease"), and

   (b)   L is entitled in respect of the rent under the original lease to a deduction by way of relevant income tax relief.

(3)   Condition B is that—

   (a)   L assigns the original lease to another person or surrenders it to L's landlord, and

   (b)   the consideration for the assignment or surrender would not (apart from this Chapter) be taxable except as capital in L's hands.

(4)   Condition C is that—

   (a)   another lease ("the new lease") is granted, or assigned, to L or a person linked to L, and

   (b)   the new lease is for a term of 15 years or less.

(5)   Condition D is that the new lease—

   (a)   is of all or part of the land which was the subject of the original lease, or

   (b)   includes all or part of the land which was the subject of the original lease.

(6)   Condition E is that neither L nor a person linked to L had, before 22 June 1971, a right enforceable at law or in equity to the grant of the new lease.

(7)   If each of conditions A to D is met but condition E is not met, see the relevant provisions in Schedule 2 to CTA 2010 and Schedule 9 to TIOPA 2010.

Taxation of consideration

681BB Taxation of consideration

(1)   An appropriate amount must be found under subsection (3) or (4) of —

     (a)   the consideration received by L for the assignment or surrender, or

     (b)   each instalment of the consideration (if it is paid in instalments).

(2)   For the purposes of the Income Tax Acts the appropriate amount must be treated in accordance with subsections (6) to (8) and not as a capital receipt.

(3)   If the term of the new lease is one year or less, the appropriate amount of the consideration or instalment is the whole of it.

(4)   If the term of the new lease is more than one year, the appropriate amount of the consideration or instalment is the proportion of it found by the formula —

$$\frac{16 - N}{15}$$

(5)   In subsection (4) N is the term of the new lease expressed in years (taking part of a year as an appropriate proportion of a year).

(6)   The way the appropriate amount must be treated depends on whether the following conditions are met —

     (a)   the consideration is received by L in the course of a trade, profession or vocation, and

     (b)   the rent payable by L, or a person linked to L, under the new lease is allowable as a deduction in calculating profits or losses of a trade, profession or vocation for tax purposes.

(7)   If the conditions are met the appropriate amount must be treated as a receipt of the trade, profession or vocation mentioned in subsection (6)(a).

(8)   If the conditions are not met the appropriate amount must be treated as an amount chargeable to income tax.

(9)   If income tax is charged under subsection (8) —

     (a)   it must be charged on the proportion of the appropriate amount arising in the tax year,

     (b)   the person liable for the tax is L, and

     (c)   the amount charged must be treated for income tax purposes as an amount of income.

681BC Position where new lease does not include all original property

(1) This section applies for the purposes of section 681BB if the property which is the subject of the new lease does not include all the property which was the subject of the original lease.

(2) The consideration received by L must be treated as reduced to the portion of it found under subsection (3).

(3) The portion is that which is reasonably attributable to such part of the original property as —
     (a) consists of the property which is the subject of the new lease, or
     (b) is included in the property which is the subject of the new lease.

(4) The original property is the property which was the subject of the original lease.

Relief for rent under new lease

681BD Relief for rent under new lease

(1) This section applies if the rent under the new lease is payable by a person within the charge to income tax.

(2) This section also applies if —
     (a) Chapter 2 of Part 19 of CTA 2010 (provision for corporation tax corresponding to this Chapter) has effect, and
     (b) the rent under the new lease is payable by a person within the charge to income tax.

(3) The provisions of ITTOIA 2005 providing for deductions or allowances by way of income tax relief in respect of payments of rent apply in relation to the rent under the new lease.

(4) In subsection (2), and in subsection (3) as applied by subsection (2), references to the new lease and rent are to be read as in Chapter 2 of Part 19 of CTA 2010.

New lease treated as ending

681BE New lease treated as ending

(1) Sections 681BF to 681BH treat the new lease as ending in certain circumstances for the purposes of this Chapter.

(2) If any of those provisions apply in a given case, and the new lease is treated as ending on different dates, it must be treated as ending on the earlier or earliest of them.

681BF Position where rent reduces

(1) If the rent for a relevant period exceeds the rent for the following comparable period, the term of the new lease must be treated as ending on the date when the relevant period ends.

(2) For the purposes of this section —

        (a)   a relevant period is a rental period of the new lease ending before its fifteenth anniversary,

        (b)   the following comparable period (in relation to a relevant period) is the rental period which is of the same duration as the relevant period and which begins on the day following the end of the relevant period,

        (c)   the rent for a period is the total rent payable under the new lease in respect of the period,

        (d)   a rental period is a period in respect of which a payment of rent is to be made, and

        (e)   the fifteenth anniversary of the new lease is the fifteenth anniversary of the date on which its term begins.

    (3)   For the purposes of this section—

        (a)   all rental periods of a quarter must be treated as being of the same duration, and

        (b)   all rental periods of a month must be treated as being of the same duration.

681BG Position where lease may be ended

    (1)   This section applies if under the new lease the lessor, or L or a person linked to L, has power to end the lease before the end of the term for which it was granted.

    (2)   The term of the lease must be treated as ending on the earliest date with effect from which the lessor, or L or a person linked to L, could end the lease by exercising the power.

681BH Position where lease may be varied

    (1)   This section applies if under the new lease L, or a person linked to L, has power to vary, in a manner beneficial to L or a person linked to L, obligations under the lease that are obligations of L or a person linked to L.

    (2)   The term of the lease must be treated as ending on the earliest date with effect from which L, or a person linked to L, could vary the obligations by exercising the power.

681BI Lease treated as ending: rentcharge

    (1)   Subsection (2) applies if a rentcharge payable by L, or a person linked to L, is secured on all or part of the property subject to the new lease.

    (2)   For the purposes of sections 681BF to 681BH the rent payable under the new lease must be treated as equal to the sum of the rentcharge and the rent payable under the lease.

Lease varied to provide for increased rent

681BJ Lease varied to provide for increased rent

    (1)   This section applies if each of conditions A to D is met.

    (2)   Condition A is that—

        (a)   a person ("the lessee") is a lessee of land under a lease which has 50 years or less to run ("the original lease"), and

    (b)   the lessee is entitled in respect of the rent under the original lease to a deduction by way of relevant income tax relief.

(3)   Condition B is that (by agreement with the landlord) the lessee varies the original lease.

(4)   Condition C is that under the variation—

    (a)   the lessee agrees to pay a rent greater than that payable under the original lease, and

    (b)   the lessee agrees to pay the greater rent in return for a consideration which would not (apart from this Chapter) be taxable except as capital in the lessee's hands.

(5)   Condition D is that under the variation the period during which the greater rent is to be paid ends 15 years or less after the date on which—

    (a)   the consideration is paid to the lessee, or

    (b)   the last instalment of the consideration is paid to the lessee (if it is paid in instalments).

(6)   If this section applies the lessee must be treated for the purposes of this Chapter—

    (a)   as having surrendered the original lease for the consideration mentioned in subsection (4)(b), and

    (b)   as having been granted a new lease for a term of 15 years or less but otherwise on the terms of the original lease varied as mentioned in subsection (3).

Interpretation

681BK Relevant income tax relief

For the purposes of this Chapter each of the following is a deduction by way of relevant income tax relief—

    (a)   a deduction in calculating profits or losses of a trade, profession or vocation for income tax purposes,

    (b)   a deduction in calculating the profits of a UK property business for income tax purposes,

    (c)   a deduction in calculating any loss for which relief is given under section 152 (losses from miscellaneous transactions), or in calculating profits or other income or gains chargeable to income tax under or by virtue of any provision to which section 1016 applies, and

    (d)   a deduction from earnings allowed under section 336 of ITEPA 2003 (expenses) or allowed in calculating losses in an employment for income tax purposes.

681BL Linked persons

(1)   In this Chapter references to a person linked to L are to a person who is—

    (a)   a partner of L,

    (b)   an associate of L, or

    (c)   an associate of a partner of L.

    (2)   "Associate" must be read in accordance with section 681DL (relatives, settlements, persons controlling bodies, joint owners etc).

681BM Lease, lessee, lessor and rent

    (1)   This section applies for the purposes of this Chapter.

    (2)   "Lease" includes—
        (a)   an agreement for a lease, and
        (b)   any tenancy.

    (3)   "Lease" does not include a mortgage.

    (4)   A reference to a lessee or lessor—
        (a)   is to be read in accordance with subsections (2) and (3), and
        (b)   includes a reference to the successors in title of a lessee or lessor.

    (5)   "Rent" includes a payment by a tenant for work to maintain or repair leased premises which the lease does not require the tenant to carry out; and "premises" here includes land.

    (6)   In the application of this section to Scotland "mortgage" means—
        (a)   a standard security, or
        (b)   a heritable security, as defined in the Conveyancing (Scotland) Act 1924, but including a security constituted by ex facie absolute disposition or assignation."

4   After section 681BM insert—

"Chapter 3

Leased trading assets

Overview

681C Overview

    This Chapter provides that, in certain circumstances where a payment is made under a lease of a trading asset, income tax relief for the payment is restricted.

Application of the Chapter

681CA Professions and vocations

    In this Chapter a reference to a trade includes a reference to a profession or vocation.

681CB Leased trading assets

    (1)   Section 681CC has effect if—
        (a)   condition A is met, and
        (b)   condition B or C is met.

    (2)   Condition A is that—
        (a)   a payment is made by a person under a lease of a relevant asset, and

Taxation (International and Other Provisions) Act 2010 (c. 8)
Schedule 4 — Sale and lease-back etc: new Part 12A of ITA 2007

1163

      (b)   a deduction is allowed for the payment in calculating the profits of a trade for income tax purposes.

  (3)   Condition B is that—

      (a)   at a time before the lease's creation the asset was used for the purposes of the trade, and

      (b)   when it was so used it was owned by the person then carrying on the trade.

  (4)   Condition C is that—

      (a)   at a time before the lease's creation the asset was used for the purposes of another trade,

      (b)   when it was so used it was owned by the person then carrying on the other trade, and

      (c)   when it was so used, or later, that person was carrying on the trade mentioned in subsection (2).

  (5)   The reference in subsection (2)(a) to a lease does not include a lease created on or before 14 April 1964.

  (6)   In this section references to a person carrying on a trade are to the person carrying on the trade for the time being.

Relief: restriction and carrying forward

681CC Tax deduction not to exceed commercial rent

  (1)   The rules in subsection (3) apply to the calculation of the deduction by way of relevant income tax relief allowed in a relevant period—

      (a)   for the non-excluded element of the payment within section 681CB(2), or

      (b)   if there are two or more such payments, for the non-excluded elements of those payments.

  (2)   For the purposes of this section—

      (a)   "relevant period" means—

          (i)   a period of account of the trade, or

         (ii)   if no accounts of the trade are drawn up for a period, the basis period of a tax year, and

      (b)   the non-excluded element of a payment is the element of the payment not excluded under section 681CD (long funding finance leases).

  (3)   The rules are—

Rule 1 — meaning of amount E

For any relevant period, amount E (which may be nil) is the expense or total expenses to be brought, in accordance with generally accepted accounting practice, into account in the period in respect of—

      (a)   the non-excluded element of the payment, or

      (b)   the non-excluded elements of the payments.

Rule 2 — calculations

For every relevant period—

   (a)   calculate the total of amount E for the period and amount E for every previous relevant period ending on or after the date of the creation of the lease mentioned in section 681CB(2)(a),

   (b)   calculate the total of the deductions by way of relevant income tax relief for every previous relevant period ending on or after that date, and

   (c)   subtract the total at (b) from the total at (a) to give the cumulative unrelieved expenses for the period.

Rule 3 — meaning of post-spread period

A relevant period is a post-spread period if for that relevant period, and every later relevant period, there are no payments within section 681CB(2).

Rule 4 — the deduction allowed in a relevant period

If a relevant period is not a post-spread period, the deduction allowed for the period is equal to the cumulative unrelieved expenses for the period, but is the commercial rent for the period if that is less (see section 681CE).

Rule 5 — relevant periods in which no deduction allowed

If a relevant period is a post-spread period, no deduction is allowed for the period.

681CD   Long funding finance leases

(1)   This section applies for the purposes of section 681CC.

(2)   A payment must be excluded so far as, in the case of the lessee, it is to be regarded in accordance with Chapter 6A of Part 2 of CAA 2001 as a payment under a lease which is a long funding finance lease for the purposes of that Part.

681CE   Commercial rent

(1)   Subsection (3) applies for the purpose of making a comparison under rule 4 of section 681CC(3).

(2)   In this section "the actual lease" means the lease mentioned in section 681CB(2)(a).

(3)   The commercial rent is the rent which might at the relevant time be expected to be paid under a lease of the asset if —

   (a)   the lease were for the rest of the asset's expected normal working life,

   (b)   the rent were payable at uniform intervals and at a uniform rate, and

   (c)   the rent gave a reasonable return for the asset's market value at the relevant time, taking account of the actual lease's terms and conditions.

(4)   The relevant time is the time when the actual lease was created.

(5)   An asset's expected normal working life is the period which might be expected, when it is first put into use, to pass before it is finally put out of use as being unfit for further use.

(6)   In applying subsection (5) it must be assumed that the asset will be used in the normal way, and to the normal extent, throughout the period.

(7) If the asset is used at the same time partly for the purposes of the trade mentioned in section 681CB(2)(b) and partly for other purposes, the commercial rent as defined in subsection (3) is to be determined by reference to what would be paid for such partial use.

Interpretation

681CF Lease

(1) This section applies for the purposes of this Chapter.

(2) A lease is (in relation to an asset) an agreement or arrangement under which payments are made for the use of or otherwise in respect of the asset.

(3) In particular it includes an agreement or arrangement under which the payments (or any of them) represent instalments of a purchase price or payments towards it.

681CG Relevant asset

For the purposes of this Chapter a relevant asset is any description of property or rights other than land or an interest in land."

5   After section 681CG insert—

"CHAPTER 4

LEASED ASSETS: CAPITAL SUMS

Overview

681D Overview

This Chapter provides that in certain circumstances where a payment is made under a lease of an asset, and a capital sum is obtained in respect of an interest in the asset, income tax is charged on an amount not greater than the capital sum.

Application of the Chapter

681DA Application of the Chapter

This Chapter applies if—
(a) condition A is met (see section 681DB), and
(b) condition B, C, D or E is met (see section 681DC).

681DB Payment under lease

(1) Condition A is that—
(a) a payment is made under a lease of a relevant asset, and
(b) the payment is one for which a deduction by way of relevant tax relief is allowed.

(2) Condition A is not met if section 681CC (leased trading assets: tax deductions)—
(a) applies to the payment, or

    (b)   would apply to it but for its being excluded under section 681CD (long funding finance leases).

(3)   Condition A is not met if section 865 of CTA 2010 (provision for corporation tax corresponding to section 681CC) —

    (a)   applies to the payment, or

    (b)   would apply to it but for its being excluded under section 866 of that Act (long funding finance leases).

(4)   The reference in subsection (1)(a) to a lease does not include a lease created on or before 14 April 1964.

681DC Sum obtained

(1)   Condition B is that the person making the payment —

    (a)   obtains a capital sum in respect of the lessee's interest in the lease, and

    (b)   is within the charge to income tax.

(2)   Condition C is that an associate of the person making the payment —

    (a)   obtains a capital sum by way of consideration in respect of the lessee's interest in the lease, and

    (b)   is within the charge to income tax.

(3)   Condition D is that —

    (a)   the lessor's interest in the lease, or any other interest in the asset, belongs to an associate of the person making the payment,

    (b)   the associate obtains a capital sum in respect of the interest, and

    (c)   the associate is within the charge to income tax.

(4)   Condition E is that —

    (a)   the lessor's interest in the lease, or any other interest in the asset, belongs to an associate of the person making the payment,

    (b)   an associate of that associate obtains a capital sum by way of consideration in respect of the interest, and

    (c)   the associate obtaining the sum is within the charge to income tax.

(5)   Condition B, C, D or E may be met before, at or after the time when the payment is made.

(6)   Condition B or C is not met if —

    (a)   the lease is a hire-purchase agreement for plant or machinery, and

    (b)   the capital sum is required to be brought into account as the whole or part of the disposal value of the plant or machinery under section 68 of CAA 2001.

(7)   Condition D or E is not met if —

    (a)   the capital sum is obtained in respect of the lessee's interest in the lease,

    (b)   the lease is a hire-purchase agreement for plant or machinery, and

    (c)   the capital sum is required to be brought into account as the whole or part of the disposal value of the plant or machinery under section 68 of CAA 2001.

Charge to income tax

681DD Charge to income tax

(1)   The person obtaining the capital sum is charged to income tax, for the tax year in which the sum is obtained, on the amount given by subsection (2).

(2)   That amount is —
    (a)   the amount of the payment for which a deduction by way of relevant tax relief is allowed, or
    (b)   the total amount of such payments (if more than one).

(3)   But subsections (1) and (2) have effect subject to —
    (a)   subsections (4) to (7), and
    (b)   section 681DE(3) (hire-purchase agreements).

(4)   The amount on which tax is charged under this section is not to exceed the capital sum obtained (but see section 681DE(4)).

(5)   Subsection (6) applies if —
    (a)   income tax is charged under this section in respect of a capital sum, and
    (b)   a payment or part of a payment is taken into account in deciding the amount on which the tax is charged.

(6)   The payment or part must be left out of account in deciding —
    (a)   whether income tax is to be charged under this section in respect of another capital sum, and
    (b)   the amount on which the tax is to be charged (if any is to be charged).

(7)   The order in which subsections (5) and (6) are applied is the order in which capital sums are obtained.

(8)   An amount on which income tax is charged under this section is treated for income tax purposes as an amount of income.

681DE Hire-purchase agreements

(1)   This section applies if —
    (a)   the lease is a hire-purchase agreement (as defined in section 998A), and
    (b)   the capital sum is obtained in respect of the lessee's interest in the lease (whether it is obtained by the person making the payment or by an associate).

(2)   Find the total of the following amounts —
    (a)   so much of any payment made under the lease by the person obtaining the capital sum as is not a payment for which a deduction by way of relevant tax relief is allowed, and

    (b)   if the lessee's interest was assigned to the person obtaining the capital sum, any capital payment made by that person as consideration for the assignment.

(3)   If the total of the amounts found under subsection (2) is equal to or greater than the capital sum, income tax is not charged under section 681DD in respect of the capital sum.

(4)   If the total of those amounts is less than the capital sum, in applying section 681DD(4) that total must be deducted from the capital sum.

(5)   If the capital sum is the consideration for part only of the lessee's interest in the lease —

    (a)   any amount found under subsection (2) (and still unallowed) must be reduced to a just and reasonable proportion of it, and

    (b)   in calculating that proportion account must be taken of the degree to which the payments mentioned in subsection (2) have contributed to the value of what is disposed of in return for the capital sum.

(6)   Subsection (7) applies if —

    (a)   more than one capital sum is (or is treated as) obtained by the same person in respect of the lessee's interest in the lease, and

    (b)   in arriving at a total under subsection (2) a payment is taken into account in respect of one of the capital sums.

(7)   So far as the payment is so taken into account it must not be taken into account in applying subsection (2) to another of the capital sums.

(8)   The order in which subsections (6) and (7) are applied is the order in which capital sums are obtained.

(9)   If the capital sum is obtained by the personal representatives of a deceased person, the reference in subsection (2)(a) to any payment made under the lease by the person obtaining the capital sum includes any payment made under the lease by the deceased.

681DF Adjustments where sum obtained before payment made

(1)   This section applies if a capital sum is obtained as mentioned in section 681DC and later a payment is made as mentioned in section 681DB.

(2)   Adjustments must be made if they are needed to give effect to a charge to income tax under section 681DD in respect of the capital sum.

(3)   An adjustment may be made within the period ending with the fifth anniversary of the 31 January following the tax year in which the payment is made.

(4)   Subsection (3) applies despite any time limit specified in the Income Tax Acts.

Obtaining of sum

681DG Sum obtained in respect of interest

A reference in this Chapter to a sum obtained in respect of an interest in an asset (whether the lessee's interest in a lease of the asset or the lessor's interest or any other interest) includes a reference to —

    (a) insurance money obtained in respect of the interest, and

    (b) sums representing money or money's worth obtained in respect of the interest by a transaction or series of transactions disposing of it.

681DH Sum obtained in respect of lessee's interest

(1) This section applies to a reference in this Chapter to a sum obtained in respect of the lessee's interest in a lease of an asset.

(2) The reference includes a reference to sums representing the consideration in money or money's worth obtained on any of the following occasions —

    (a) a surrender of the interest to the lessor,

    (b) an assignment of the lease, and

    (c) the creation of a sublease or another interest out of the lease.

(3) The reference also includes a reference to sums representing money or money's worth obtained in respect of the interest by a transaction or series of transactions under which the lessee's rights are merged in any way with the lessor's rights or with any other rights as respects the asset.

(4) Subsection (3) applies so far as the money or money's worth is attributable to the lessee's rights under the lease.

681DI Disposal of interest to associate

(1) This section applies for the purposes of this Chapter if a person disposes of an interest in an asset to a person who is the first person's associate (and the interest may be the lessee's interest in a lease of the asset or the lessor's interest or any other interest).

(2) The person disposing of the interest must be treated as obtaining in respect of it the greatest of —

    (a) the sum in fact obtained by the person,

    (b) the value of the interest in the open market, and

    (c) the value of the interest to the person to whom it is in effect transferred.

(3) The disposal —

    (a) may be direct or indirect, and

    (b) may be effected by a transaction or series of transactions described in section 681DG(b) or 681DH(3).

Apportionment

681DJ Apportionment of payments made and of sums obtained

(1) This section applies for the purposes of this Chapter.

(2) Subsection (3) applies if —

    (a) a payment is made,

    (b) it is one for which a deduction by way of relevant tax relief is allowed, and

    (c) it is made by persons carrying on a trade or profession in partnership.

(3) The payment must be apportioned in a manner which is just and reasonable.

(4) Subsection (5) applies if —

    (a) a sum is obtained in respect of an interest in an asset,

    (b) the sum is obtained by persons carrying on a trade or profession in partnership, and

    (c) the asset is and continues to be used for the purposes of the trade or profession.

(5) The sum must be apportioned between the partners in the shares in which they are entitled to the profits of the trade or profession at the time the sum is obtained.

(6) Subsection (7) applies if —

    (a) a sum is obtained in respect of an interest in an asset, and

    (b) the sum is obtained by persons jointly entitled to the interest.

(7) The sum must be apportioned according to their respective rights in the interest.

(8) Subsections (6) and (7) are subject to subsections (4) and (5).

681DK Manner of apportionment

(1) Subsections (2) and (3) apply if —

    (a) a payment or sum is to be apportioned under section 681DJ or under section 880 of CTA 2010,

    (b) at the time of the apportionment it appears that it is material to the liability to tax (whether income tax or corporation tax, and for whatever period) of two or more persons (in this section referred to collectively as "the set"),

    (c) a question arises as to the manner in which the payment or sum is to be apportioned, and

    (d) at the time of the apportionment, it appears that the apportionment is material to the income tax liability (for whatever period) of —

        (i) a person, or some two or more persons, in the set, or

        (ii) all the persons in the set.

(2) For the purposes of income tax of the person or persons mentioned in subsection (1)(d), the question is to be determined in the same way as an appeal.

(3) All the persons in the set are entitled to be a party to the proceedings.

Interpretation

681DL Associates

(1) This section applies for the purposes of this Chapter.

(2) Persons are associates if they are associated with each other.

(3) The following are associated with each other—
  (a) an individual and the individual's spouse or civil partner or relative,
  (b) an individual and a spouse or civil partner of a relative of the individual,
  (c) an individual and a relative of the individual's spouse or civil partner,
  (d) an individual and a spouse or civil partner of a relative of the individual's spouse or civil partner.

(4) The following are associated with each other—
  (a) a person as trustee of a settlement and an individual who (in relation to the settlement) is a settlor,
  (b) a person as trustee of a settlement and a person associated with an individual who (in relation to the settlement) is a settlor.

(5) The following are associated with each other—
  (a) a person and a body of persons of which the person has control,
  (b) a person and a body of persons of which persons associated with the person have control,
  (c) a person and a body of persons of which the person and persons associated with the person have control,
  (d) two or more bodies of persons associated with the same person under paragraphs (a) to (c).

(6) In relation to a disposal by joint owners, the joint owners and any person associated with any of them are associated with each other.

(7) For the purposes of this section—
  (a) a relative is a brother, sister, ancestor or lineal descendant,
  (b) a body of persons includes a partnership, and
  (c) "settlement" and "settlor" have the meanings given by section 620 of ITTOIA 2005.

681DM Capital sum

For the purposes of this Chapter a capital sum is any sum of money, or any money's worth, except so far as it or any part of it—
  (a) is to be treated for income tax purposes as a receipt to be taken into account in calculating the profits or losses of a trade, profession or vocation, or
  (b) is (apart from this Chapter) chargeable to income tax under or by virtue of any provision to which section 1016 applies.

681DN Lease

(1) This section applies for the purposes of this Chapter.

(2) A lease is (in relation to an asset) an agreement or arrangement under which payments are made for the use of or otherwise in respect of the asset.

(3) In particular it includes an agreement or arrangement under which the payments (or any of them) represent instalments of a purchase price or payments towards it.

681DO Relevant asset

For the purposes of this Chapter a relevant asset is any description of property or rights other than land or an interest in land.

681DP Relevant tax relief

For the purposes of this Chapter each of the following is a deduction by way of relevant tax relief —

    (a) a deduction in calculating profits or losses of a trade for corporation tax purposes,

    (b) a deduction in calculating any loss for which relief is given under section 91 of CTA 2010 (losses from miscellaneous transactions), or in calculating profits or gains chargeable to corporation tax under or by virtue of any provision to which section 1173 of CTA 2010 applies (miscellaneous charges),

    (c) a deduction under section 76 of ICTA (insurance companies),

    (d) a deduction under section 1219 of CTA 2009 (expenses of management of a company's investment business),

    (e) a deduction in calculating profits or losses of a trade, profession or vocation for income tax purposes,

    (f) a deduction in calculating any loss for which relief is allowed under section 152 (losses from miscellaneous transactions), or in calculating profits or other income or gains chargeable to income tax under or by virtue of any provision to which section 1016 applies, and

    (g) a deduction from earnings allowed under section 336 of ITEPA 2003 (expenses) or allowed in calculating losses in an employment for income tax purposes."

SCHEDULE 5   Section 369

FACTORING OF INCOME ETC: NEW CHAPTERS 5B AND 5C OF PART 13 OF ITA 2007

1   ITA 2007 is amended as follows.

Taxation (International and Other Provisions) Act 2010 (c. 8)
Schedule 5 — Factoring of income etc: new Chapters 5B and 5C of Part 13 of ITA 2007

1173

2   After section 809AZG insert—

"CHAPTER 5B

FINANCE ARRANGEMENTS

Type 1 arrangements

809BZA Type 1 finance arrangement defined

(1) For the purposes of this Chapter an arrangement is a type 1 finance arrangement if conditions A and B are met.

(2) Condition A is that under the arrangement—
   (a) a person ("the borrower") receives money or another asset ("the advance") from another person ("the lender"),
   (b) the borrower or a person connected with the borrower makes a disposal of an asset ("the security") to or for the benefit of the lender or a person connected with the lender, and
   (c) the lender or a person connected with the lender is entitled to payments in respect of the security.

(3) Condition B is that in accordance with generally accepted accounting practice—
   (a) the borrower's accounts for the period in which the advance is received record a financial liability in respect of it, and
   (b) the payments reduce the amount of the financial liability.

(4) If the borrower is a partnership the reference to the borrower's accounts includes a reference to the accounts of any member of the partnership.

(5) For the purposes of this section the borrower and the lender are not connected with one another.

809BZB Certain tax consequences not to have effect

(1) This section applies if a type 1 finance arrangement would have the relevant effect (ignoring this section).

(2) The arrangement is not to have that effect.

(3) The relevant effect is that—
   (a) an amount of income on which the borrower or a person connected with the borrower would otherwise have been charged to income tax is not so charged,
   (b) an amount which would otherwise have been brought into account in calculating for income tax purposes any income of the borrower or of a person connected with the borrower is not so brought into account, or
   (c) the borrower or a person connected with the borrower becomes entitled to an income deduction.

(4) But if the borrower is a partnership the relevant effect is that—
   (a) an amount of income on which a member of the partnership would otherwise have been charged to income tax is not so charged,

(b) an amount which would otherwise have been brought into account in calculating for income tax purposes any income of a member of the partnership is not so brought into account, or

(c) a member of the partnership becomes entitled to an income deduction.

(5) For the purposes of this section the borrower and the lender are not connected with one another.

(6) An income deduction is—

    (a) a deduction in calculating income for income tax purposes, or

    (b) a deduction from total income.

809BZC Payments treated as borrower's income

(1) This section applies if—

    (a) a type 1 finance arrangement would not have the relevant effect (ignoring section 809BZB(2)),

    (b) that arrangement would not have the corresponding corporation-tax effect (ignoring section 759(2) of CTA 2010), and

    (c) the borrower is—

        (i) within the charge to income tax, or

        (ii) a partnership at least one member of which is within the charge to income tax.

(2) The payments mentioned in section 809BZA(2)(c) must be treated for income tax purposes as income of the borrower payable in respect of the security.

(3) Subsection (2) applies whether or not the payments are also the income of another person for tax purposes.

(4) Subsections (3) to (6) of section 809BZB (meaning of relevant effect) apply for the purposes of this section as for those of that.

(5) In subsection (1)(b) "the corresponding corporation-tax effect" means the relevant effect as defined by section 759(3) to (6) of CTA 2010 (provision for corporation tax corresponding to section 809BZB(3) to (6)).

809BZD Deemed interest if borrower is not a partnership

(1) This section applies if—

    (a) there is a type 1 finance arrangement,

    (b) the borrower is not a partnership,

    (c) the arrangement is prevented by section 809BZB from having the relevant effect in relation to the borrower, or section 809BZC applies to the borrower, and

    (d) in accordance with generally accepted accounting practice the borrower's accounts record an amount as a finance charge in respect of the advance.

(2) For income tax purposes the borrower may treat the amount as interest payable on a loan.

(3)   If an amount is treated as interest ("deemed interest") under subsection (2), to find out when it is paid—

    (a)   treat the payments mentioned in section 809BZA(2)(c) as consisting of amounts for repaying the advance and amounts ("the interest elements") in respect of interest on the advance,

    (b)   treat the interest elements of the payments as paid when the payments are paid, and

    (c)   treat the deemed interest as paid at the times when the interest elements are treated as paid.

809BZE Deemed interest if borrower is a partnership

(1)   This section applies if each of conditions A to C is met.

(2)   Condition A is that—

    (a)   there is a type 1 finance arrangement, and

    (b)   the borrower is a partnership.

(3)   Condition B is that—

    (a)   the arrangement is prevented by section 809BZB from having the relevant effect in relation to a person who is a member of the partnership, or

    (b)   section 809BZC applies to the partnership (in which event "the person" in subsections (4) and (5) means the person within the charge to income tax who is a member of the partnership).

(4)   Condition C is that in accordance with generally accepted accounting practice the person's accounts, or the partnership's accounts, record an amount as a finance charge in respect of the advance.

(5)   For income tax purposes the person may treat the amount as interest payable by the partnership on a loan.

(6)   If an amount is treated as interest ("deemed interest") under subsection (5), to find out when it is paid—

    (a)   treat the payments mentioned in section 809BZA(2)(c) as consisting of amounts for repaying the advance and amounts ("the interest elements") in respect of interest on the advance,

    (b)   treat the interest elements of the payments as paid when the payments are paid, and

    (c)   treat the deemed interest as paid at the times when the interest elements are treated as paid."

3   After section 809BZE insert—

"Type 2 arrangements

809BZF Type 2 finance arrangement defined

(1)   For the purposes of this Chapter an arrangement is a type 2 finance arrangement if conditions A and B are met.

(2)   Condition A is that—

   (a)   under the arrangement a person ("the transferor") makes a disposal of an asset ("the security") to a partnership,

   (b)   the transferor is a member of the partnership immediately after the disposal (whether or not a member immediately before it),

   (c)   under the arrangement the partnership receives money or another asset ("the advance") from another person ("the lender"),

   (d)   there is a relevant change in relation to the partnership (see section 809BZG), and

   (e)   under the arrangement the share in the partnership's profits of the person involved in the change is determined by reference (wholly or partly) to payments in respect of the security.

(3)   Condition B is that in accordance with generally accepted accounting practice —

   (a)   the partnership's accounts for the period in which the advance is received record a financial liability in respect of it, and

   (b)   the payments reduce the amount of the financial liability.

(4)   The reference to the partnership's accounts includes a reference to the transferor's accounts.

809BZG Relevant change in relation to partnership

(1)   For the purposes of this Chapter there is a relevant change in relation to a partnership if condition A or condition B is met.

(2)   Condition A is that in connection with the arrangement the lender or a person connected with the lender becomes a member of the partnership at any time.

(3)   Condition B is that —

   (a)   in connection with the arrangement there is at any time a change in a member's share in the partnership's profits, and

   (b)   the member is the lender or a person connected with the lender or a person who in connection with the arrangement becomes at any time connected with the lender.

(4)   An event occurs in connection with the arrangement if it occurs directly or indirectly in consequence of it or otherwise in connection with it.

(5)   If there is a relevant change in relation to a partnership, a reference in this Chapter to the person involved in the change is —

   (a)   if it is condition A that is met, to the person who becomes a member of the partnership, and

   (b)   if it is condition B that is met, to the member of the partnership in whose share in the partnership's profits there is a change.

809BZH Certain tax consequences not to have effect

(1)   This section applies if —

   (a)   there is a type 2 finance arrangement, and

      (b)   any relevant change in relation to the partnership would have the relevant effect (ignoring this section).

(2)   In such a case—

      (a)   Part 9 of ITTOIA 2005 (partnerships) is to have effect in relation to the transferor as if the relevant change in relation to the partnership had not occurred, and

      (b)   accordingly the finance arrangement is not to have the relevant effect.

(3)   The relevant effect is that—

      (a)   an amount of income on which the transferor would otherwise have been charged to income tax is not so charged,

      (b)   an amount which would otherwise have been brought into account in calculating for income tax purposes any income of the transferor is not so brought into account, or

      (c)   the transferor becomes entitled to an income deduction.

(4)   In deciding whether subsection (1)(b) is met assume that amounts of income equal to the payments mentioned in section 809BZF(2)(e) were payable to the partnership before the relevant change in relation to it occurred.

(5)   An income deduction is—

      (a)   a deduction in calculating income for income tax purposes, or

      (b)   a deduction from total income.

809BZI Deemed interest

(1)   This section applies if—

      (a)   there is a type 2 finance arrangement,

      (b)   the transferor is a person within the charge to income tax, and

      (c)   in accordance with generally accepted accounting practice the partnership's accounts record an amount as a finance charge in respect of the advance.

(2)   For income tax purposes the transferor may treat the amount as interest payable by the transferor on a loan.

(3)   The reference in subsection (1) to the partnership's accounts includes a reference to the transferor's accounts.

(4)   If an amount is treated as interest ("deemed interest") under subsection (2), to find out when it is paid—

      (a)   treat the payments mentioned in section 809BZF(2)(e) as consisting of amounts for repaying the advance and amounts ("the interest elements") in respect of interest on the advance,

      (b)   treat the interest elements of the payments as paid when the payments are paid, and

      (c)   treat the deemed interest as paid at the times when the interest elements are treated as paid."

4   After section 809BZI insert—

"Type 3 arrangements

809BZJ Type 3 finance arrangement defined

(1)   For the purposes of this Chapter an arrangement is a type 3 finance arrangement if conditions A and B are met.

(2)   Condition A is that—

    (a)   a partnership holds an asset ("the security") as a partnership asset at any time before the arrangement is made,

    (b)   under the arrangement the partnership receives money or another asset ("the advance") from another person ("the lender"),

    (c)   there is a relevant change in relation to the partnership (see section 809BZG), and

    (d)   under the arrangement the share in the partnership's profits of the person involved in the change is determined by reference (wholly or partly) to payments in respect of the security.

(3)   Condition B is that in accordance with generally accepted accounting practice—

    (a)   the partnership's accounts for the period in which the advance is received record a financial liability in respect of it, and

    (b)   the payments reduce the amount of the financial liability.

(4)   The reference to the partnership's accounts includes a reference to the accounts of any person who is a member of the partnership immediately before the arrangement is made.

809BZK Certain tax consequences not to have effect

(1)   This section applies if—

    (a)   there is a type 3 finance arrangement, and

    (b)   any relevant change in relation to the partnership would have the relevant effect (ignoring this section).

(2)   The relevant effect is that—

    (a)   an amount of income on which a relevant member would otherwise have been charged to income tax is not so charged,

    (b)   an amount which would otherwise have been brought into account in calculating for income tax purposes any income of a relevant member is not so brought into account, or

    (c)   a relevant member becomes entitled to an income deduction.

(3)   A relevant member is a person who—

    (a)   was a member of the partnership immediately before the relevant change in relation to it occurred, and

    (b)   is not the lender.

(4)   If this section applies—

      (a)   Part 9 of ITTOIA 2005 (partnerships) is to have effect in relation to any relevant member as if the relevant change in relation to the partnership had not occurred, and

      (b)   accordingly the finance arrangement is not to have the relevant effect.

(5)   In deciding whether subsection (1)(b) is met assume that amounts of income equal to the payments mentioned in section 809BZJ(2)(d) were payable to the partnership before the relevant change in relation to it occurred.

(6)   An income deduction is —

      (a)   a deduction in calculating income for income tax purposes, or

      (b)   a deduction from total income.

809BZL Deemed interest

(1)   This section applies if —

      (a)   there is a type 3 finance arrangement,

      (b)   a relevant member is a person within the charge to income tax, and

      (c)   in accordance with generally accepted accounting practice the partnership's accounts record an amount as a finance charge in respect of the advance.

(2)   For income tax purposes the relevant member may treat the amount as interest payable by the partnership on a loan.

(3)   The reference in subsection (1) to the partnership's accounts includes a reference to the accounts of any relevant member.

(4)   If an amount is treated as interest ("deemed interest") under subsection (2), to find out when it is paid —

      (a)   treat the payments mentioned in section 809BZJ(2)(d) as consisting of amounts for repaying the advance and amounts ("the interest elements") in respect of interest on the advance,

      (b)   treat the interest elements of the payments as paid when the payments are paid, and

      (c)   treat the deemed interest as paid at the times when the interest elements are treated as paid.

(5)   A relevant member is a person who —

      (a)   was a member of the partnership immediately before the relevant change in relation to it occurred, and

      (b)   is not the lender."

5   After section 809BZL insert —

"Exceptions

809BZM Exceptions: preliminary

(1)   Sections 809BZN to 809BZP make provision for finance arrangement codes not to apply in certain circumstances.

(2)   For the purposes of those sections each of the following groups of provisions is a finance arrangement code —

    (a)   sections 809BZA to 809BZE (type 1 arrangements),

    (b)   sections 809BZF to 809BZI (type 2 arrangements), and

    (c)   sections 809BZJ to 809BZL (type 3 arrangements).

809BZN Exceptions

(1)   A finance arrangement code does not apply if the whole of the advance under the arrangement—

    (a)   is charged to tax on a relevant person as an amount of income,

    (b)   is brought into account in calculating for tax purposes any income of a relevant person, or

    (c)   is brought into account for the purposes of any provision of CAA 2001 as a disposal receipt, or proceeds from a balancing event or disposal event, of a relevant person.

(2)   Treat subsection (1)(c) as not met if—

    (a)   the receipt gives rise, or proceeds give rise, to a balancing charge, and

    (b)   the amount of the balancing charge is limited by any provision of CAA 2001.

(3)   A finance arrangement code does not apply if at all times the whole of the advance under the arrangement—

    (a)   is a debtor relationship of a relevant person for the purposes of Part 5 of CTA 2009 (loan relationships), or

    (b)   would be a debtor relationship of a relevant person for those purposes if that person were a company within the charge to corporation tax.

(4)   In subsection (3) references to a debtor relationship do not include references to a relationship to which Chapter 2 of Part 6 of CTA 2009 applies (relevant non-lending relationships).

(5)   A finance arrangement code does not apply so far as—

    (a)   section 263A of TCGA 1992 applies in relation to the arrangement (agreements for sale and repurchase of securities), or

    (b)   Schedule 13 to FA 2007 or Chapter 10 of Part 6 of CTA 2009 applies in relation to the arrangement (sale and repurchase of securities, and repos).

(6)   A finance arrangement code does not apply so far as Part 10A of this Act, Chapter 4 of Part 4 of TCGA 1992 or Chapter 6 of Part 6 of CTA 2009 has effect in relation to the arrangement (alternative finance arrangements).

(7)   A finance arrangement code does not apply so far as the security is plant or machinery which is the subject of a sale and finance leaseback.

(8)   For the purposes of subsection (7) apply section 221 of CAA 2001 to determine whether plant or machinery is the subject of a sale and finance leaseback.

(9)   A finance arrangement code does not apply so far as sections 228B and 228C of CAA 2001 (finance leaseback) apply in relation to the arrangement.

(10)   Section 809BZO defines a relevant person for the purposes of this section.

809BZO Exceptions: relevant person

(1)   This section defines a relevant person for the purposes of section 809BZN.

(2)   If (apart from sections 809BZN and 809BZP) sections 809BZA to 809BZE would apply, each of the following is a relevant person —
   (a)   the borrower, and
   (b)   a person connected with the borrower or (if the borrower is a partnership) a member of the partnership.

(3)   If (apart from sections 809BZN and 809BZP) sections 809BZF to 809BZI would apply, the transferor is a relevant person.

(4)   If (apart from sections 809BZN and 809BZP) sections 809BZJ to 809BZL would apply, a relevant member as there defined is a relevant person.

(5)   For the purposes of subsection (2)(b) the persons connected with the borrower include any persons who under section 993 (meaning of "connected") are connected with the borrower.

809BZP Power to make further exceptions

(1)   The Treasury may make regulations prescribing other circumstances in which a finance arrangement code is not to apply.

(2)   The regulations may amend sections 809BZN and 809BZO.

(3)   The power to make regulations includes —
   (a)   power to make provision that has effect in relation to times before the making of the regulations (but not times before 6 June 2006),
   (b)   power to make different provision for different cases or different purposes, and
   (c)   power to make incidental, supplemental, consequential and transitional provision and savings."

6   After section 809BZP insert —

"Supplementary

809BZQ Accounts

(1)   This section applies for the purposes of this Chapter.

(2)   A reference to the accounts of a person includes (if the person is a company) a reference to the consolidated group accounts of a group of companies of which it is a member.

(3)   In determining whether accounts record an amount as a financial liability in respect of an advance, assume that the period in which the

advance is received ended immediately after the receipt of the advance.

(4)   If a person does not draw up accounts in accordance with generally accepted accounting practice, assume that the person drew up the accounts in accordance with that practice.

809BZR   Arrangements

A reference in this Chapter to an arrangement includes a reference to an agreement or understanding (whether or not legally enforceable).

809BZS   Assets

(1)   This section applies for the purposes of this Chapter.

(2)   A reference to a person receiving an asset includes —
    (a)   a reference to the person obtaining (directly or indirectly) the value of an asset or otherwise deriving (directly or indirectly) a benefit from it, and
    (b)   a reference to the discharge (in whole or part) of a liability of the person.

(3)   A reference to a disposal of an asset includes a reference to anything constituting a disposal of it for the purposes of TCGA 1992.

(4)   A reference to payments in respect of an asset includes —
    (a)   a reference to payments in respect of another asset substituted for it under the arrangement, and
    (b)   a reference to obtaining (directly or indirectly) the value of an asset or otherwise deriving (directly or indirectly) a benefit from it."

7   After section 809BZS insert —

"CHAPTER 5C

LOAN OR CREDIT TRANSACTIONS

809CZA   Loan or credit transaction defined

(1)   This section defines a loan or credit transaction for the purposes of sections 809CZB and 809CZC.

(2)   A transaction is a loan or credit transaction if it is —
    (a)   effected with reference to the lending of money or the varying of the terms on which money is lent, or
    (b)   effected with a view to enabling or facilitating an arrangement concerning the lending of money or the varying of the terms on which money is lent.

(3)   A transaction is a loan or credit transaction if it is —
    (a)   effected with reference to the giving of credit or the varying of the terms on which credit is given, or
    (b)   effected with a view to enabling or facilitating an arrangement concerning the giving of credit or the varying of the terms on which credit is given.

(4)   Subsection (2) has effect whether the transaction is effected —
    (a)   between the lender and borrower,
    (b)   between either of them and a person connected with the other, or
    (c)   between a person connected with one and a person connected with the other.

(5)   Subsection (3) has effect whether the transaction is effected —
    (a)   between the creditor and debtor,
    (b)   between either of them and a person connected with the other, or
    (c)   between a person connected with one and a person connected with the other.

809CZB Certain payments treated as yearly interest

(1)   This section applies if a loan or credit transaction provides for a payment which is not interest but is —
    (a)   an annuity or other annual payment falling within Part 5 of ITTOIA 2005 and chargeable to income tax otherwise than as relevant foreign income, or
    (b)   an annuity or other annual payment which is from a source in the United Kingdom and chargeable to corporation tax under Chapter 5 of Part 10 of CTA 2009 (distributions from unauthorised unit trusts) or Chapter 7 of that Part (annual payments not otherwise charged).

(2)   The payment must be treated for the purposes of the Income Tax Acts as if it were a payment of yearly interest (see, in particular, section 874).

809CZC Tax charged on income transferred

(1)   This section applies if —
    (a)   under a loan or credit transaction a person transfers income arising from property,
    (b)   the person is not, as a result of Chapter 5B (finance arrangements), chargeable to income tax on the income transferred, and
    (c)   the person is within the charge to income tax.

(2)   In such a case —
    (a)   income tax is charged under this section,
    (b)   the tax is charged on an amount equal to the full amount of the income transferred,
    (c)   the tax is charged for the tax year in which the transfer takes place, and
    (d)   the person who transfers the income is liable for the tax.

(3)   This section does not prejudice the liability of any other person to tax.

(4)   For the purposes of this section a person transfers income if the person surrenders, waives or forgoes it.

(5)   Subsection (6) applies for the purposes of this section if —
    (a)   credit is given for the purchase price of property, and

(b)   the rights attaching to the property are such that the buyer's rights to income from the property are suspended or restricted during the life of the debt.

(6)   The buyer must be treated as surrendering income of an amount equal to the income the buyer in effect forgoes by obtaining the credit.

(7)   For the purposes of this section an amount of income payable subject to deduction of income tax must be taken as the amount before deduction of tax."

SCHEDULE 6   Section 370

UK REPRESENTATIVES OF NON-UK RESIDENTS

PART 1

NEW CHAPTERS 2B AND 2C OF PART 14 OF ITA 2007

1   After section 835B of ITA 2007 (which is inserted by Schedule 7) insert—

"CHAPTER 2B

UK REPRESENTATIVE OF NON-UK RESIDENT

Introduction

835C   Overview of Chapter

(1)   This Chapter provides for a branch or agency to be treated as the UK representative of a non-UK resident in respect of certain amounts chargeable to income tax.

(2)   For obligations and liabilities in relation to income tax imposed on a branch or agency which under this Chapter is treated as the UK representative of a non-UK resident, see Chapter 2C."

2   After section 835C insert—

"835D Income tax chargeable on company's income: application

This Chapter does not apply in relation to income tax chargeable on income of a company otherwise than as a trustee."

3   After section 835D insert—

"Branches and agencies

835E   Branch or agency treated as UK representative

(1)   This section applies if a non-UK resident carries on (alone or in partnership) any trade, profession or vocation through a branch or agency in the United Kingdom.

Taxation (International and Other Provisions) Act 2010 (c. 8)   **1185**
Schedule 6 – UK Representatives of non-UK residents
Part 1 – New Chapters 2B and 2C of Part 14 of ITA 2007

(2)   The branch or agency is the UK representative of the non-UK resident in relation to—

    (a)   the amount of any income from the trade, profession or vocation that arises (directly or indirectly) through or from the branch or agency, and

    (b)   the amount of any income from property or rights which are used by, or held by or for, the branch or agency.

(3)   The following rules are to be applied for the purposes of subsection (2) and Chapter 2C in relation to an amount within that subsection.

Rule 1

The UK representative continues to be the UK representative of the non-UK resident in relation to the amount even after ceasing to be a branch or agency through which the non-UK resident carries on the trade, profession or vocation concerned.

Rule 2

The UK representative is treated in relation to the amount as a distinct and separate person from the non-UK resident (if the representative would not otherwise be so treated).

Rule 3

If the branch or agency is carried on by persons in partnership, the partnership, as such, is treated in relation to the amount as the UK representative of the non-UK resident.

(4)   For further rules that apply where a trade or profession carried on by a non-UK resident in the United Kingdom is carried on in partnership, see section 835F.

(5)   This section needs to be read with sections 835G to 835K (which provide for descriptions of persons who are not to be regarded as the UK representative of a non-UK resident if certain conditions are met)."

4   After section 835E insert—

"835F Trade or profession carried on in partnership

(1)   Subsection (2) applies if a trade or profession carried on by a non-UK resident through a branch or agency in the United Kingdom is carried on by the non-UK resident in partnership.

(2)   The trade or profession carried on through the branch or agency is, for the purposes of section 835E and Chapter 2C, to be treated as including the notional trade or profession.

(3)   Subsection (4) applies (in addition to subsection (2) if that subsection also applies) if—

    (a)   a trade or profession carried on by a non-UK resident in the United Kingdom is carried on by the non-UK resident in partnership, and

    (b)   any member of the partnership is resident in the United Kingdom.

1186

Taxation (International and Other Provisions) Act 2010 (c. 8)
Schedule 6 — UK Representatives of non-UK residents
Part 1 — New Chapters 2B and 2C of Part 14 of ITA 2007

(4)   The notional trade or profession is, for the purposes of section 835E and Chapter 2C, to be treated as being a trade carried on in the United Kingdom through the partnership as such.

(5)   In this section "the notional trade or profession" means the notional trade from which the non-UK resident's share in the partnership's profits or losses is treated for the purposes of section 852 of ITTOIA 2005 as deriving."

5   After section 835F insert—

"Persons who are not UK representatives

835G Agents

(1)   This section applies if a non-UK resident carries on (alone or in partnership) a business through an agent in the United Kingdom.

(2)   The agent is not the UK representative of the non-UK resident in relation to an amount within section 835E(2) arising to the non-UK resident from—

(a)   so much of the non-UK resident's business as relates to disregarded transactions, or

(b)   property or rights which, as a result of disregarded transactions, are used by, or held by or for, the agent on behalf of the non-UK resident.

(3)   "Disregarded transactions" are transactions—

(a)   carried out through the agent in the United Kingdom, and

(b)   in respect of which the agent does not act in the course of carrying on a regular agency for the non-UK resident."

6   After section 835G insert—

"835H Brokers

(1)   This section applies if a non-UK resident carries on (alone or in partnership) a business through a broker in the United Kingdom.

(2)   The broker is not the UK representative of the non-UK resident in relation to an amount within section 835E(2) if—

(a)   the amount is transaction income in relation to a transaction carried out through the broker in the United Kingdom on behalf of the non-UK resident, and

(b)   the independent broker conditions are met in relation to the transaction (see section 835L).

(3)   In subsection (2) "transaction income", in relation to a transaction carried out through a broker in the United Kingdom on behalf of a non-UK resident, has the same meaning as in Chapter 1 (see section 814(5))."

Taxation (International and Other Provisions) Act 2010 (c. 8)
Schedule 6 — UK Representatives of non-UK residents
Part 1 — New Chapters 2B and 2C of Part 14 of ITA 2007

1187

7   After section 835H insert—

"835I Investment managers

(1)   This section applies if a non-UK resident carries on (alone or in partnership) a business through an investment manager in the United Kingdom.

(2)   The investment manager is not the UK representative of the non-UK resident in relation to an amount within section 835E(2) if—

     (a)   the amount is transaction income in relation to an investment transaction carried out through the investment manager in the United Kingdom on behalf of the non-UK resident, and

     (b)   the independent investment manager conditions are met in relation to the investment transaction (see section 835M).

(3)   In subsection (2) "transaction income", in relation to a transaction carried out through an investment manager in the United Kingdom on behalf of a non-UK resident, has the same meaning as in Chapter 1 (see section 814(5))."

8   After section 835I insert—

"835J Persons acting under alternative finance arrangements

(1)   Subsection (2) applies if an amount within section 835E(2) arising to a non-UK resident consists of alternative finance return.

(2)   Neither of the following is the UK representative of the non-UK resident in relation to the amount—

     (a)   the other party to the alternative finance arrangements,

     (b)   any other person acting for the non-UK resident in relation to the alternative finance arrangements.

(3)   In subsection (1) "alternative finance return" means alternative finance return within the application of section 564I, 564K or 564L(2) or (3).

(4)   In subsection (2) the reference to "the alternative finance arrangements" is a reference to the alternative finance arrangements under which the alternative finance return mentioned in subsection (1) arises."

9   After section 835J insert—

"835K Lloyd's agents

(1)   This section applies if—

     (a)   a non-UK resident ("X") is a member of Lloyd's, and

     (b)   an amount within section 835E(2) arises to X from X's underwriting business.

(2)   A person who has been X's members' agent or the managing agent of the syndicate in question is not the UK representative of X in relation to the amount or to matters connected with the amount.

(3)   For the purposes of this section—

     (a)   X is a member of Lloyd's if X is a member within the meaning of Chapter 3 of Part 2 of FA 1993, and

1188

Taxation (International and Other Provisions) Act 2010 (c. 8)
Schedule 6 – UK Representatives of non-UK residents
Part 1 – New Chapters 2B and 2C of Part 14 of ITA 2007

      (b)   "members' agent" and "managing agent" are to be construed in accordance with section 184 of that Act."

10   After section 835K insert—

"The independent broker conditions

835L   The independent broker conditions

    (1)   The independent broker conditions are met in relation to a transaction carried out on behalf of a non-UK resident by a broker in the United Kingdom if conditions A to D are met.

    (2)   Condition A is that at the time of the transaction the broker is carrying on the business of a broker.

    (3)   Condition B is that the transaction is carried out in the ordinary course of that business.

    (4)   Condition C is that the remuneration which the broker receives in respect of the transaction for the provision of the services of a broker to the non-UK resident is not less than is customary for that class of business.

    (5)   Condition D is that the broker does not fall (apart from this subsection) to be treated under this Chapter, or under Chapter 1 of Part 7A of TCGA 1992, as a UK representative of the non-UK resident in relation to any amounts that—

        (a)   are not included in transaction income in relation to the transaction (see section 835H(2) and (3)), and

        (b)   are chargeable to tax for the same tax year as that transaction income."

11   After section 835L insert—

"The independent investment manager conditions

835M The independent investment manager conditions

    (1)   The independent investment manager conditions are met in relation to an investment transaction carried out on behalf of a non-UK resident by an investment manager in the United Kingdom if conditions A to E are met.

    (2)   Condition A is that at the time of the transaction the investment manager is carrying on a business of providing investment management services.

    (3)   Condition B is that the transaction is carried out in the ordinary course of that business.

    (4)   Condition C is that, when the investment manager acts on behalf of the non-UK resident in relation to the transaction, the relationship between them, having regard to its legal, financial and commercial characteristics, is a relationship between persons carrying on independent businesses dealing with each other at arm's length.

Taxation (International and Other Provisions) Act 2010 (c. 8)
Schedule 6 — UK Representatives of non-UK residents
Part 1 — New Chapters 2B and 2C of Part 14 of ITA 2007

1189

(5) Condition D is that the requirements of the 20% rule are met (see section 835N).

(6) Condition E is that the remuneration which the investment manager receives in respect of the transaction for the provision of investment management services to the non-UK resident is not less than is customary for that class of business."

12 After section 835M insert—

"835N Investment managers: the 20% rule

(1) The requirements of the 20% rule are met if conditions A and B are met.

(2) Condition A is that, in relation to a qualifying period, it has been or is the intention of the investment manager and the persons connected with the investment manager that at least 80% of the non-UK resident's relevant disregarded income should consist of amounts to which none of them has a beneficial entitlement.

(3) Condition B is that, so far as there is a failure to fulfil that intention, that failure—

   (a) is attributable (directly or indirectly) to matters outside the control of the investment manager and persons connected with the investment manager, and

   (b) does not result from a failure by any of them to take such steps as may be reasonable for mitigating the effect of those matters in relation to the fulfilment of that intention."

13 After section 835N insert—

"835O Meaning of "qualifying period", "relevant disregarded income" and "beneficial entitlement"

(1) This section applies for the purposes of this Chapter.

(2) A "qualifying period" means—

   (a) the tax year in which the transaction income mentioned in section 835I(2) is chargeable to tax, or

   (b) a period of not more than 5 years comprising two or more tax years including that one.

(3) The "relevant disregarded income" of the non-UK resident for a qualifying period is the total of the non-UK resident's income for the tax years comprised in the qualifying period which derives from investment transactions—

   (a) carried out by the investment manager on the non-UK resident's behalf, and

   (b) in relation to which the independent investment manager conditions are met, ignoring the requirements of the 20% rule.

(4) A person has a "beneficial entitlement" to relevant disregarded income if the person has or may acquire a beneficial entitlement that is, or would be, attributable to the relevant disregarded income as a result of having an interest or other rights mentioned in subsection (5).

1190   *Taxation (International and Other Provisions) Act 2010 (c. 8)*
Schedule 6 — UK Representatives of non-UK residents
Part 1 — New Chapters 2B and 2C of Part 14 of ITA 2007

(5)   The interests and rights referred to in subsection (4) are —

        (a)   an interest (whether or not an interest giving a right to an immediate payment of a share in the profits or gains) in property in which the whole or any part of the relevant disregarded income is represented, or

        (b)   an interest in, or other rights in relation to, the non-UK resident."

14   After section 835O insert —

"835P Treatment of transactions where 20% rule not met

(1)   This section applies in the case of an investment transaction in relation to which the independent investment manager conditions are met, except for the requirements of the 20% rule.

(2)   This Chapter has effect as if the requirements of that rule were met in relation to the transaction, but only in relation to so much of the transaction income in relation to the transaction (see section 835I(2) and (3)) as does not represent an amount —

        (a)   which is relevant disregarded income of the non-UK resident, and

        (b)   to which the investment manager or a person connected with the investment manager has or has had any beneficial entitlement."

15   After section 835P insert —

"835Q Application of 20% rule to collective investment schemes

(1)   This section applies if amounts arise or accrue to the non-UK resident as a participant in a collective investment scheme.

(2)   It applies for the purposes of determining whether the requirements of the 20% rule are met in relation to a transaction carried out for the purposes of the scheme (so far as the transaction is one in respect of which amounts so arise or accrue).

(3)   In applying this section make the following assumptions —

        (a)   that all the transactions carried out for the purposes of the scheme are carried out on behalf of a company ("the assumed company") which is —

                (i)   constituted for the purposes of the scheme, and

                (ii)   non-UK resident, and

        (b)   that the participants do not have any rights in respect of the amounts arising or accruing in respect of those transactions, other than the rights which, if they held shares in the assumed company, would be their rights as shareholders.

(4)   If the scheme is such that the assumed company would not be regarded for tax purposes as carrying on a trade in the United Kingdom in relation to the tax year in which the transaction income mentioned in section 835I(2) is chargeable to tax, the requirements of the 20% rule are treated as met in relation to a transaction carried out for the purposes of the scheme.

Taxation (International and Other Provisions) Act 2010 (c. 8)   1191
Schedule 6 — UK Representatives of non-UK residents
Part 1 — New Chapters 2B and 2C of Part 14 of ITA 2007

(5)   If the scheme is such that the assumed company would be so regarded for tax purposes, sections 835N to 835P have effect in relation to a transaction carried out for the purposes of the scheme with the modifications in subsection (6).

(6)   The modifications are—

(a)   for references to the non-UK resident substitute references to the assumed company, and

(b)   for references to the non-UK resident's relevant disregarded income for a qualifying period substitute references to the sum of the amounts that would, for tax years comprised in the qualifying period, be chargeable to tax on the assumed company as profits deriving from the transactions—

(i)   carried out by the investment manager, and

(ii)   assumed to be carried out on behalf of the company.

(7)   In this section—

"collective investment scheme" has the meaning given by section 235 of FISMA 2000, and

"participant", in relation to a collective investment scheme, is construed in accordance with that section."

16   After section 835Q insert—

"Supplementary

835R Supplementary provision

(1)   For the purposes of this Chapter a person is to be regarded as carrying out a transaction on behalf of another if the person—

(a)   undertakes the transaction, whether on behalf of or to the account of the other, or

(b)   gives instructions for it to be so carried out by another.

(2)   In the case of a person who acts as a broker or investment manager as part only of a business, this Chapter has effect as if that part were a separate business."

17   After section 835R insert—

"835S Interpretation of Chapter

(1)   This section applies for the purposes of this Chapter.

(2)   "Branch or agency" means any factorship, agency, receivership, branch or management.

(3)   "Investment manager" has the same meaning as in Chapter 1 (see section 827).

(4)   "Investment transaction" means any transaction of a description specified for the purposes of this section in regulations made by the Commissioners for Her Majesty's Revenue and Customs.

(5)   Provision made in regulations under subsection (4) may, in particular, have effect in relation to the tax year current on the day on which the regulations are made."

1192

Taxation (International and Other Provisions) Act 2010 (c. 8)
Schedule 6 — UK Representatives of non-UK residents
Part 1 — New Chapters 2B and 2C of Part 14 of ITA 2007

18   After section 835S insert—

"CHAPTER 2C

INCOME TAX OBLIGATIONS AND LIABILITIES IMPOSED ON UK REPRESENTATIVES

835T   Introduction to Chapter

(1)   This Chapter applies to the enactments relating to income tax so far as they make provision for or in connection with the assessment, collection and recovery of tax, or of interest on tax.

(2)   Those enactments have effect in accordance with section 835U in relation to amounts in respect of which a branch or agency is to be treated as the UK representative of a non-UK resident under Chapter 2B.

(3)   In this section "enactment" includes an enactment contained in subordinate legislation within the meaning of the Interpretation Act 1978."

19   After section 835T insert—

"835U Obligations and liabilities of UK representative

(1)   The obligations and liabilities of a non-UK resident are to be treated, for the purposes of the enactments to which this Chapter applies, as if they were also the obligations and liabilities of the UK representative of the non-UK resident.

(2)   Subsection (3) applies if—
    (a)   the UK representative of a non-UK resident discharges an obligation or liability imposed by this section that corresponds to one to which the non-UK resident is subject, or
    (b)   a non-UK resident discharges an obligation or liability that corresponds to one to which the non-UK resident's UK representative is subject by virtue of this section.

(3)   The corresponding obligation or liability—
    (a)   of the non-UK resident (in a case within subsection (2)(a)), or
    (b)   of the UK representative (in a case within subsection (2)(b)),
    is discharged.

(4)   A non-UK resident is bound, as if they were the non-UK resident's own, by acts or omissions of the non-UK resident's UK representative in the discharge of the obligations and liabilities imposed on the representative by this section.

(5)   This section is subject to sections 835V and 835W."

20   After section 835U insert—

"835V Exceptions: notices and information

(1)   An obligation or liability attaching to a non-UK resident ("X") by reason of a notice or other document having been given or served on X does not also attach to the UK representative of X by virtue of

Taxation (International and Other Provisions) Act 2010 (c. 8)   **1193**
Schedule 6 — UK Representatives of non-UK residents
Part 1 — New Chapters 2B and 2C of Part 14 of ITA 2007

              section 835U unless the notice or other document (or a copy of it) has been given to or served on the representative.

(2)   An obligation or liability attaching to X by reason of a request or demand having been received by X does not also attach to the UK representative of X by virtue of section 835U unless the representative has been notified of the request or demand.

(3)   Subsection (4) applies to obligations relating to the provision of information that are imposed on the UK representative of X by section 835U in a case where the representative is X's independent agent.

(4)   The obligations do not require the UK representative to do anything except so far as it is practicable for the representative to do so.

(5)   For this purpose, the representative must act to the best of the representative's knowledge and belief after taking all reasonable steps to obtain the necessary information.

(6)   An obligation of X to provide information is not discharged by virtue of section 835U in a case where the UK representative of X has discharged the obligation only so far as required by subsection (4) of this section.

(7)   X is not bound by virtue of section 835U by mistakes in information provided by the UK representative of X in discharging, so far as required under subsection (4) of this section, an obligation imposed on the representative by section 835U unless—

    (a)   the mistake is the result of an act or omission of X, or

    (b)   the mistake is one to which X consented or in which X connived.

(8)   In this section "information" includes anything contained in a return, self-assessment, account, statement or report required to be provided to the Commissioners for Her Majesty's Revenue and Customs or to any officer of Revenue and Customs."

21   After section 835V insert—

"835W Exceptions: criminal offences and penalties etc

(1)   A person is not by virtue of section 835U liable to be proceeded against for a criminal offence unless the person—

    (a)   committed the offence, or

    (b)   consented to or connived in its commission.

(2)   An independent agent of a non-UK resident is not by virtue of section 835U liable to any civil penalty or surcharge in respect of an act or omission if conditions A and B are met.

(3)   Condition A is that the act or omission is not—

    (a)   an act or omission of the independent agent, or

    (b)   an act or omission to which the agent consented or in which the agent connived.

(4)   Condition B is that the independent agent is able to show that the amount of the penalty or surcharge will not be recoverable out of the

1194   *Taxation (International and Other Provisions) Act 2010 (c. 8)*
Schedule 6 — UK Representatives of non-UK residents
Part 1 — New Chapters 2B and 2C of Part 14 of ITA 2007

sums mentioned in section 835X(3) (after being indemnified for any other liabilities under section 835X)."

22   After section 835W insert—

"835X Indemnities

(1)   An independent agent of a non-UK resident is entitled to be indemnified for the amount of any liability of the non-UK resident which the agent has discharged by virtue of section 835U.

(2)   An independent agent of a non-UK resident is entitled to retain, from the sums mentioned in subsection (3), amounts sufficient to meet any liabilities which by virtue of section 835U the agent has discharged or to which the agent is subject.

(3)   The sums are those which—

     (a)   (ignoring subsection (2)) are due from the independent agent to the non-UK resident, or

     (b)   are received by the independent agent on behalf of the non-UK resident."

23   After section 835X insert—

"835Y Meaning of "independent agent"

(1)   In this Chapter "independent agent", in relation to a non-UK resident ("X"), means a person who is the UK representative of X in respect of any agency in which the person is acting on behalf of X in an independent capacity.

(2)   For this purpose a person does not act in an independent capacity on behalf of X unless the relationship between them, having regard to its legal, financial and commercial characteristics, is a relationship between persons carrying on independent businesses dealing with each other at arm's length."

Taxation (International and Other Provisions) Act 2010 (c. 8)
Schedule 6 — UK Representatives of non-UK residents
Part 2 — New Part 7A of TCGA 1992

1195

PART 2

NEW PART 7A OF TCGA 1992

24   After section 271 of TCGA 1992 insert—

"PART 7A

UK REPRESENTATIVES OF NON-UK RESIDENTS

CHAPTER 1

TREATMENT OF BRANCH OR AGENCY AS UK REPRESENTATIVE OF NON-UK RESIDENT

Introduction

271A   Overview of Chapter

(1)   This Chapter provides for a branch or agency to be treated as the UK representative of a non-UK resident in respect of certain amounts chargeable to capital gains tax.

(2)   For obligations and liabilities in relation to capital gains tax imposed on a branch or agency which under this Chapter is treated as the UK representative of a non-UK resident, see Chapter 2."

25   After section 271A insert—

"Branches and agencies

271B   Branch or agency treated as UK representative

(1)   This section applies if—
        (a)   a non-UK resident carries on (alone or in partnership) any trade, profession or vocation through a branch or agency in the United Kingdom, and
        (b)   the branch or agency is to be treated under Chapter 2B of Part 14 of ITA 2007 as the UK representative of the non-UK resident in relation to amounts within section 835E(2) of that Act.

(2)   The branch or agency is the UK representative of the non-UK resident in relation to amounts which, by reference to the branch or agency, are chargeable to capital gains tax under section 10 above.

(3)   The following rules are to be applied for the purposes of subsection (2) and Chapter 2 in relation to an amount within that subsection.

Rule 1
The UK representative continues to be the UK representative of the non-UK resident in relation to the amount even after ceasing to be a branch or agency through which the non-UK resident carries on the trade, profession or vocation concerned.

1196

Taxation (International and Other Provisions) Act 2010 (c. 8)
Schedule 6 — UK Representatives of non-UK residents
Part 2 — New Part 7A of TCGA 1992

Rule 2

The UK representative is treated in relation to the amount as a distinct and separate person from the non-UK resident (if the representative would not otherwise be so treated).

Rule 3

If the branch or agency is carried on by persons in partnership, the partnership, as such, is treated in relation to the amount as the UK representative of the non-UK resident.

(4) For further rules that apply where a trade or profession carried on by a non-UK resident in the United Kingdom is carried on in partnership, see section 271C."

26   After section 271B insert—

"271C Trade or profession carried on in partnership

(1) Subsection (2) applies if a trade or profession carried on by a non-UK resident through a branch or agency in the United Kingdom is carried on by the non-UK resident in partnership.

(2) The trade or profession carried on through the branch or agency is, for the purposes of section 271B and Chapter 2, to be treated as including the notional trade or profession.

(3) Subsection (4) applies (in addition to subsection (2) if that subsection also applies) if—

   (a) a trade or profession carried on by a non-UK resident in the United Kingdom is carried on by the non-UK resident in partnership, and

   (b) any member of the partnership is resident in the United Kingdom.

(4) The notional trade or profession is, for the purposes of section 271B and Chapter 2, to be treated as being a trade carried on in the United Kingdom through the partnership as such.

(5) In this section "the notional trade or profession" means the notional trade from which the non-UK resident's share in the partnership's profits or losses is treated for the purposes of section 852 of ITTOIA 2005 as deriving."

27   After section 271C insert—

"271D Interpretation of Chapter

In this Chapter—

   "branch or agency" means any factorship, agency, receivership, branch or management, and

   "non-UK resident" means a person who is not resident in the United Kingdom."

Taxation (International and Other Provisions) Act 2010 (c. 8) **1197**
Schedule 6 – UK Representatives of non-UK residents
Part 2 – New Part 7A of TCGA 1992

28   After section 271D insert—

"CHAPTER 2

CAPITAL GAINS TAX OBLIGATIONS AND LIABILITIES IMPOSED ON UK REPRESENTATIVES

271E   Introduction to Chapter

(1)   This Chapter applies to the enactments contained in—

    (a)   this Act,

    (b)   the Tax Acts, and

    (c)   subordinate legislation made under this Act or the Tax Acts,

so far as they make provision for or in connection with the assessment, collection and recovery of tax, or of interest on tax.

(2)   Those enactments have effect in accordance with section 271F in relation to amounts in respect of which a branch or agency is to be treated as the UK representative of a non-UK resident under Chapter 1.

(3)   In this section "subordinate legislation" has the same meaning as in the Interpretation Act 1978."

29   After section 271E insert—

"271F   Obligations and liabilities of UK representative

(1)   The obligations and liabilities of a non-UK resident are to be treated, for the purposes of the enactments to which this Chapter applies, as if they were also the obligations and liabilities of the UK representative of the non-UK resident.

(2)   Subsection (3) applies if—

    (a)   the UK representative of a non-UK resident discharges an obligation or liability imposed by this section that corresponds to one to which the non-UK resident is subject, or

    (b)   a non-UK resident discharges an obligation or liability that corresponds to one to which the non-UK resident's UK representative is subject by virtue of this section.

(3)   The corresponding obligation or liability—

    (a)   of the non-UK resident (in a case within subsection (2)(a)), or

    (b)   of the UK representative (in a case within subsection (2)(b)),

is discharged.

(4)   A non-UK resident is bound, as if they were the non-UK resident's own, by acts or omissions of the non-UK resident's UK representative in the discharge of the obligations and liabilities imposed on the representative by this section.

(5)   This section is subject to sections 271G and 271H."

1198

Taxation (International and Other Provisions) Act 2010 (c. 8)
Schedule 6 — UK Representatives of non-UK residents
Part 2 — New Part 7A of TCGA 1992

30   After section 271F insert—

"271G Exceptions: notices and information

(1)   An obligation or liability attaching to a non-UK resident ("X") by reason of a notice or other document having been given or served on X does not also attach to the UK representative of X by virtue of section 271F unless the notice or other document (or a copy of it) has been given to or served on the representative.

(2)   An obligation or liability attaching to X by reason of a request or demand having been received by X does not also attach to the UK representative of X by virtue of section 271F unless the representative has been notified of the request or demand.

(3)   Subsection (4) applies to obligations relating to the provision of information that are imposed on the UK representative of X by section 271F in a case where the representative is X's independent agent.

(4)   The obligations do not require the UK representative to do anything except so far as it is practicable for the representative to do so.

(5)   For this purpose, the representative must act to the best of the representative's knowledge and belief after taking all reasonable steps to obtain the necessary information.

(6)   An obligation of X to provide information is not discharged by virtue of section 271F in a case where the UK representative of X has discharged the obligation only so far as required by subsection (4) of this section.

(7)   X is not bound by virtue of section 271F by mistakes in information provided by the UK representative of X in discharging, so far as required under subsection (4) of this section, an obligation imposed on the representative by section 271F unless—

     (a)   the mistake is the result of an act or omission of X, or

     (b)   the mistake is one to which X consented or in which X connived.

(8)   In this section "information" includes anything contained in a return, self-assessment, account, statement or report required to be provided to the Commissioners for Her Majesty's Revenue and Customs or to any officer of Revenue and Customs."

31   After section 271G insert—

"271H Exceptions: criminal offences and penalties etc

(1)   A person is not by virtue of section 271F liable to be proceeded against for a criminal offence unless the person—

     (a)   committed the offence, or

     (b)   consented to or connived in its commission.

(2)   An independent agent of a non-UK resident is not by virtue of section 271F liable to any civil penalty or surcharge in respect of an act or omission if conditions A and B are met.

(3)   Condition A is that the act or omission is not—

Taxation (International and Other Provisions) Act 2010 (c. 8)
Schedule 6 — UK Representatives of non-UK residents
Part 2 — New Part 7A of TCGA 1992

1199

       (a)   an act or omission of the independent agent, or

       (b)   an act or omission to which the agent consented or in which the agent connived.

  (4)   Condition B is that the independent agent is able to show that the amount of the penalty or surcharge will not be recoverable out of the sums mentioned in section 271I(3) (after being indemnified for any other liabilities under section 271I)."

32   After section 271H insert—

"271I Indemnities

  (1)   An independent agent of a non-UK resident is entitled to be indemnified for the amount of any liability of the non-UK resident which the agent has discharged by virtue of section 271F.

  (2)   An independent agent of a non-UK resident is entitled to retain, from the sums mentioned in subsection (3), amounts sufficient to meet any liabilities which by virtue of section 271F the agent has discharged or to which the agent is subject.

  (3)   The sums are those which—

       (a)   (ignoring subsection (2)) are due from the independent agent to the non-UK resident, or

       (b)   are received by the independent agent on behalf of the non-UK resident."

33   After section 271I insert—

"271J Meaning of "non-UK resident" and "independent agent"

  (1)   In this Chapter "non-UK resident" means a person who is not resident in the United Kingdom.

  (2)   In this Chapter "independent agent", in relation to a non-UK resident ("X"), means a person who is the UK representative of X in respect of any agency in which the person is acting on behalf of X in an independent capacity.

  (3)   For this purpose a person does not act in an independent capacity on behalf of X unless the relationship between them, having regard to its legal, financial and commercial characteristics, is a relationship between persons carrying on independent businesses dealing with each other at arm's length."

1200   Taxation (International and Other Provisions) Act 2010 (c. 8)
                                    Schedule 7 — Miscellaneous relocations
                  Part 1 — Relocation of section 38 of, and Schedule 15 to, FA 1973

SCHEDULE 7   Section 371

MISCELLANEOUS RELOCATIONS

PART 1

RELOCATION OF SECTION 38 OF, AND SCHEDULE 15 TO, FA 1973

Taxes Management Act 1970 (c. 9)

1   TMA 1970 is amended as follows.

2   After Part 7 insert—

"PART 7A

HOLDERS OF LICENCES UNDER THE PETROLEUM ACT 1998

Licence-holders' liabilities for tax assessed on non-UK residents

77B   Pre-conditions for serving secondary-liability notice

(1)   Conditions A to E are the pre-conditions for the purposes of section 77C.

(2)   Condition A is that tax is assessed on a person not resident in the United Kingdom.

(3)   Condition B is that the tax is assessed in reliance on—
    (a)   section 276 of the 1992 Act,
    (b)   section 874 of ITTOIA 2005, or
    (c)   section 1313 of CTA 2009.

(4)   Condition C is that the tax assessed is not tax under ITEPA 2003.

(5)   Condition D is that—
    (a)   there is a licence to which the tax assessed is related (see section 77J for the meaning of tax related to a licence),
    (b)   there is more than one licence to which the tax assessed is related, or
    (c)   there is a licence, or more than one licence, to which part of the tax assessed is related but in addition part of the tax assessed is not related to any licence.

(6)   Condition E is that the tax is not paid in full within 30 days after it becomes due and payable.

(7)   In this Part "licence" means a licence under Part 1 of the Petroleum Act 1998.

77C   Secondary-liability notices

(1)   If each of the pre-conditions (see section 77B) is met, an officer of Revenue and Customs may serve on the holder of the licence concerned, or on the holder of any of the licences concerned, a notice—
    (a)   that states particulars of the assessment,

Taxation (International and Other Provisions) Act 2010 (c. 8) 1201
Schedule 7 — Miscellaneous relocations
Part 1 — Relocation of section 38 of, and Schedule 15 to, FA 1973

    (b)   that states the amount remaining unpaid and the date when it became payable,

    (c)   that requires the holder to pay, within 30 days of the service of the notice, the amount for which the holder is liable, and

    (d)   that, if the amount for which the holder is liable is given by subsection (3) or section 77G(7), gives particulars of how the amount was determined.

(2)   For the purposes of subsection (1), the amount for which the holder is liable is the amount remaining unpaid, together with any interest on it under sections 86 and 87A, but this is subject to subsection (3) and section 77G(7).

(3)   In a case within section 77B(5)(b) or (c), the amount for which the holder of the licence is liable is given by —

$$\frac{L}{T} \times (A + I)$$

(4)   In subsection (3) —

    A is the amount remaining unpaid,

    I is any interest due on that amount under sections 86 and 87A,

    T is the total amount of the profits or chargeable gains in respect of which the assessment is made, and

    L is so much of that total amount as is profits or chargeable gains related to the licence.

(5)   The power under subsection (1) is subject to section 77E (certain pre-1974 cases).

(6)   In this Part "secondary-liability notice" means a notice under subsection (1).

77D   Payments under secondary-liability notices

(1)   Any amount which a person is required to pay by a secondary-liability notice may be recovered from the person as if it were tax due and duly demanded from the person.

(2)   If a person ("H") pays any amount which a secondary-liability notice requires H to pay, H may recover the amount from the person on whom the assessment concerned was made.

(3)   A payment in pursuance of a secondary-liability notice is not allowed as a deduction in calculating any income, profits or losses for any tax purposes.

77E   Exception for certain pre-1974 cases

(1)   Section 77C(1) does not give power to serve a secondary-liability notice on the holder of a licence if the profits arose, or the chargeable gains accrued, to the assessed person in consequence of a contract made by the holder before 23 March 1973.

(2)   The exception under subsection (1) does not apply if —

    (a)   the assessed person is connected with the holder, or

    (b)   the contract was substantially varied on or after 23 March 1973.

1202   *Taxation (International and Other Provisions) Act 2010 (c. 8)*
Schedule 7 — Miscellaneous relocations
Part 1 — Relocation of section 38 of, and Schedule 15 to, FA 1973

(3)   For the purposes of subsection (2), whether a person is connected with another is determined in accordance with section 1122 of CTA 2010."

3   After section 77E insert—

"Exemption certificates

77F   Issue, cancellation and effect of exemption certificates

(1)   This section applies if there is a person ("T") who will or might become liable to tax which, if unpaid, could be recovered under this Part from a person ("H") who is the holder of a licence.

(2)   If an officer of Revenue and Customs, on an application made by T, is satisfied that T will comply with any obligations imposed on T by the Taxes Acts, the officer may issue to H a certificate exempting H from section 77C with respect to any tax payable by T.

(3)   If a certificate is issued to H under subsection (2), an officer of Revenue and Customs may, by notice in writing to H, cancel the certificate from the date specified in the notice.

(4)   The date specified in a notice under subsection (3) may not be earlier than 30 days after the service of the notice.

(5)   If a certificate is issued to H under subsection (2), section 77C does not apply to any tax payable by T which becomes due while the certificate is in force.

(6)   If a certificate is issued to H under subsection (2) but is subsequently cancelled under subsection (3), section 77C also does not apply to any tax payable by T which—

     (a)   becomes due after the certificate is cancelled, but

     (b)   is in respect of profits arising, or chargeable gains accruing, while the certificate is in force.

77G   Liabilities for assessments made after exemption certificate cancelled

(1)   Subsection (7) applies if—

     (a)   each of conditions A to C is met, and

     (b)   one of conditions D and E is met.

(2)   Condition A is that, after the cancellation under section 77F(3) of a certificate issued under section 77F(2) to a person ("H") who is the holder of a licence, tax related to the licence is assessed on the applicant for the certificate.

(3)   Condition B is that the tax is assessed in reliance on—

     (a)   section 276 of the 1992 Act,

     (b)   section 874 of ITTOIA 2005, or

     (c)   section 1313 of CTA 2009.

(4)   Condition C is that the tax assessed is not tax under ITEPA 2003.

(5)   Condition D is that—

Taxation (International and Other Provisions) Act 2010 (c. 8)   1203
Schedule 7 — Miscellaneous relocations
Part 1 — Relocation of section 38 of, and Schedule 15 to, FA 1973

(a) ignoring section 77F, H could be required by a secondary-liability notice to pay all of the tax remaining unpaid under the assessment, and

(b) the profits or chargeable gains in respect of which the assessment is made include (but are not limited to) profits arising, or chargeable gains accruing, while the certificate is in force.

(6) Condition E is that—

(a) as a result of section 77C(3), but ignoring section 77F, H could be required by a secondary-liability notice to pay some, but not all, of the tax remaining unpaid under the assessment, and

(b) the profits or chargeable gains that are—

(i) ones in respect of which the assessment is made, and

(ii) related to the licence,

include (but are not limited to) profits arising, or chargeable gains accruing, while the certificate is in force.

(7) If this subsection applies then, for the purposes of section 77C(1), the amount for which the holder of the licence is liable is the amount given by—

$$A \times \left(1 - \frac{CIF}{CIF + NIF}\right)$$

together with a corresponding proportion of any interest due under sections 86 and 87A on the amount remaining unpaid.

(8) In subsection (7)—

A is the amount that H could be required to pay as mentioned in paragraph (a) of whichever of conditions D and E is met ("the operative condition"),

CIF is the amount of the profits or chargeable gains mentioned in paragraph (b) of the operative condition that are ones arising, or accruing, while the certificate is in force, and

NIF is the amount of the profits or chargeable gains mentioned in paragraph (b) of the operative condition that are ones arising, or accruing, while the certificate is not in force."

4 After section 77G insert—

"Supplementary

77H Calculations under sections 77C(3) and 77G(7)

(1) Subsection (2) applies for the purposes of calculating any of the following amounts of profits or chargeable gains—

(a) L in a calculation under section 77C(3),

(b) CIF in a calculation under section 77G(7), and

(c) CIF + NIF in a calculation under section 77G(7) when it is condition E in section 77G that is met.

(2) The amount is to be calculated as if for the purposes of making a separate assessment in respect of those profits or chargeable gains on the person on whom the assessment was made.

1204   *Taxation (International and Other Provisions) Act 2010 (c. 8)*
Schedule 7 — Miscellaneous relocations
Part 1 — Relocation of section 38 of, and Schedule 15 to, FA 1973

(3)   An officer of Revenue and Customs applying subsection (2) is to make all such allocations and apportionments of receipts, expenses, allowances and deductions taken into account, or made, for the purposes of the actual assessment as appear to the officer to be just and reasonable in the circumstances.

77I   Information

(1)   The holder of a licence must, if required to do so by a notice served on the holder by an officer of Revenue and Customs, give to the officer within the time specified by the notice (which is not to be less than 30 days) such particulars as may be required by the notice of —

    (a)   licence-related transactions (see subsection (2)),

    (b)   licence-related payments (see subsection (3)), or

    (c)   persons to whom licence-related payments have been paid or are payable.

(2)   In subsection (1) "licence-related transaction" means a transaction in connection with activities authorised by the licence as a result of which any person is or might be liable to tax by virtue of —

    (a)   section 276 of the 1992 Act,

    (b)   section 874 of ITTOIA 2005, or

    (c)   section 1313 of CTA 2009.

(3)   In subsection (1) "licence-related payment" means —

    (a)   earnings which constitute employment income (see section 7(2)(a) of ITEPA 2003),

    (b)   amounts which are treated as earnings and constitute employment income (see section 7(2)(b) of ITEPA 2003), or

    (c)   other payments,

paid or payable in respect of duties or services performed in an area in which activities authorised by the licence may be carried on under the licence.

(4)   If a notice under subsection (1) is served on the holder of a licence, the holder must take reasonable steps to obtain the information necessary to enable the holder to comply with the notice.

77J   Meaning of "related to a licence" as respects tax, or profits or gains

(1)   Subsections (2) and (3) apply for the purposes of this Part.

(2)   An amount of tax is related to a licence if the tax is in respect of profits or chargeable gains related to the licence.

(3)   Profits or chargeable gains are related to a licence if they are —

    (a)   profits from activities authorised by the licence,

    (b)   profits from activities carried on in connection with activities authorised by the licence, or

    (c)   profits from, or chargeable gains accruing on the disposal of, exploration or exploitation rights connected with —

       (i)   activities authorised by the licence, or

       (ii)   activities carried on in connection with activities authorised by the licence.

(4)   In this section —

Taxation (International and Other Provisions) Act 2010 (c. 8)
Schedule 7 — Miscellaneous relocations
Part 1 — Relocation of section 38 of, and Schedule 15 to, FA 1973

1205

    (a)   "designated area" means an area designated by Order in Council under section 1(7) of the Continental Shelf Act 1964,

    (b)   "exploration or exploitation activities" means activities carried on in connection with the exploration or exploitation of so much of the seabed and subsoil and their natural resources as is situated in the United Kingdom or a designated area,

    (c)   "exploration or exploitation rights" means rights to—

        (i)   assets to be produced by exploration or exploitation activities,

        (ii)   interests in such assets, or

        (iii)   the benefit of such assets,

    (d)   any reference to the disposal of exploration or exploitation rights includes a reference to the disposal of unlisted shares deriving their value, or the greater part of their value, directly or indirectly from such rights,

    (e)   "shares" includes—

        (i)   stock, and

        (ii)   securities not creating or evidencing a charge on assets,

    (f)   "unlisted shares" means shares that are not listed on a recognised stock exchange, and

    (g)   "recognised stock exchange" has the meaning given by section 1005(1) and (2) of ITA 2007.

77K   Other definitions in Part 7A

(1)   This section applies for the purposes of this Part.

(2)   "Licence" has the meaning given by section 77B(7).

(3)   "Secondary-liability notice" has the meaning given by section 77C(6)."

5   (1)   Amend the first column of the Table in section 98 (special returns etc) as follows.

(2)   Omit the entry for paragraph 2 of Schedule 15 to FA 1973.

(3)   After the entry for regulations under section 59E of TMA 1970 insert—
        "Section 77I(1) of this Act."

Finance Act 1973 (c. 51)

6   FA 1973 is amended as follows.

7   Omit section 38 (which introduces and interprets Schedule 15).

8   Omit Schedule 15 (territorial extension of charge to tax: supplementary provisions).

Oil Taxation Act 1975 (c. 22)

9   The Oil Taxation Act 1975 is amended as follows.

10   In section 3(4) (expenditure not allowable under the section) for paragraph

1206   *Taxation (International and Other Provisions) Act 2010 (c. 8)*
Schedule 7 — Miscellaneous relocations
Part 1 — Relocation of section 38 of, and Schedule 15 to, FA 1973

     (f) (which refers to notices under paragraph 4 of Schedule 15 to FA 1973), and the "or" preceding it, substitute "or

    (f)   any payment made in pursuance of a notice under section 77C of the Taxes Management Act 1970 (notice requiring licence-holder to pay unpaid tax assessed on non-UK resident);".

PART 2

RELOCATION OF SECTION 24 OF FA 1974

Taxes Management Act 1970 (c. 9)

11   TMA 1970 is amended as follows.

12   In section 8 (personal return) after subsection (4) insert—

  "(4A)   Subsection (4B) applies if a notice under this section is given to a person within section 8ZA of this Act (certain persons employed etc by person not resident in United Kingdom who perform their duties for UK clients).

  (4B)   The notice may require a return of the person's income to include particulars of any general earnings (see section 7(3) of ITEPA 2003) paid to the person."

13   After section 8 insert—

"8ZA   Interpretation of section 8(4A)

   (1)   For the purposes of section 8(4A) of this Act, a person ("F") is within this section if each of conditions A to C is met.

   (2)   Condition A is that F performs in the United Kingdom, for a continuous period of 30 days or more, duties of an office or employment.

   (3)   Condition B is that the office or employment is under or with a person who—

     (a)   is not resident in the United Kingdom, but

     (b)   is resident outside the United Kingdom.

   (4)   Condition C is that the duties are performed for the benefit of a person who—

     (a)   is resident in the United Kingdom, or

     (b)   carries on a trade, profession or vocation in the United Kingdom."

14   After section 15 insert—

"15A   Non-resident's staff are UK client's employees for section 15 purposes

   (1)   Subsection (5) applies if each of conditions A to C is met.

   (2)   Condition A is that a person ("F") performs in the United Kingdom, for a continuous period of 30 days or more, duties of an office or employment.

Taxation (International and Other Provisions) Act 2010 (c. 8) 1207
Schedule 7 – Miscellaneous relocations
Part 2 – Relocation of section 24 of FA 1974

(3) Condition B is that the office or employment is under or with a person who —
    (a) is not resident in the United Kingdom, but
    (b) is resident outside the United Kingdom.

(4) Condition C is that the duties are performed for the benefit of a person ("P") who —
    (a) is resident in the United Kingdom, or
    (b) carries on a trade, profession or vocation in the United Kingdom.

(5) Section 15 of this Act applies as if P were F's employer, but only so as to enable P to be required to make a return of F's name and place of residence."

Finance Act 1974 (c. 30)

15   FA 1974 is amended as follows.

16   Omit section 24 (returns of persons treated as employees).

PART 3

RELOCATION OF SECTION 42 OF ICTA

Taxes Management Act 1970 (c. 9)

17   TMA 1970 is amended as follows.

18 (1) Amend the first column of the Table in section 98 (special returns etc) as follows.

    (2) Omit the entry for section 42 of ICTA.

    (3) Before the entry for section 647 of ITTOIA 2005 insert —
       "Section 302B of ITTOIA 2005."

Income and Corporation Taxes Act 1988 (c. 1)

19   ICTA is amended as follows.

20   Omit section 42 (appeals against determinations under Chapter 4 of Part 3 of ITTOIA 2005).

Income Tax (Trading and Other Income) Act 2005 (c. 5)

21   ITTOIA 2005 is amended as follows.

22   After section 302 insert —

"Determinations affecting liability of more than one person

302A Appeals against proposed determinations

    (1) Subsection (2) applies if it appears to an officer of Revenue and Customs that—

1208   *Taxation (International and Other Provisions) Act 2010 (c. 8)*
Schedule 7 — Miscellaneous relocations
Part 3 — Relocation of section 42 of ICTA

(a)   a determination is needed of an amount that is to be brought into account as a receipt under this Chapter in calculating the liability to tax of a person ("the first taxpayer"), and

(b)   the determination may affect the liability to income tax, corporation tax or capital gains tax of other persons.

(2)   The officer may give notice (a "provisional notice of determination") to the first taxpayer and the other persons of —

(a)   the determination the officer proposes to make, and

(b)   their rights under this section and section 302C.

(3)   A person to whom a provisional notice of determination is given may object to the proposed determination by giving notice (a "notice of objection") to the officer.

(4)   The notice of objection must be given within 30 days of the date on which the provisional notice of determination was given.

(5)   If an officer gives provisional notices of determination and no person gives a notice of objection —

(a)   a determination must be made by the officer as proposed in the provisional notices, and

(b)   the determination is not to be called in question in any proceedings.

302B   Section 302A: supplementary

(1)   A provisional notice of determination under section 302A(2) may include a statement of the grounds on which the officer proposes to make the determination.

(2)   Subsection (1) applies despite any obligation as to secrecy or other restriction on the disclosure of information.

(3)   An officer of Revenue and Customs may by notice ("a preliminary notice") require any person to give any information that appears to the officer to be needed for deciding whether to give any person a provisional notice of determination under section 302A(2).

(4)   The preliminary notice must state the time within which the information is to be given.

302C   Determination by tribunal

(1)   If a notice of objection is given under section 302A(3), the amount mentioned in section 302A(1) must be determined in the same way as an appeal.

(2)   All persons to whom provisional notices of determination have been given under section 302A(2) may be a party to —

(a)   any proceedings under subsection (1), and

(b)   any appeal arising out of those proceedings.

(3)   Those persons are bound by the determination made in the proceedings or on appeal, whether or not they have taken part in the proceedings.

(4)   Their successors in title are bound in the same way."

Taxation (International and Other Provisions) Act 2010 (c. 8)   **1209**
Schedule 7 — Miscellaneous relocations
Part 3 — Relocation of section 42 of ICTA

Corporation Tax Act 2009 (c. 4)

23   CTA 2009 is amended as follows.

24   In section 242(2) (determination by tribunal) for the words from "take part" to the end substitute "be a party to—
      (a)   any proceedings under subsection (1), and
      (b)   any appeal arising out of those proceedings."

PART 4

RELOCATION OF SECTION 84A OF ICTA

Income and Corporation Taxes Act 1988 (c. 1)

25   ICTA is amended as follows.

26   Omit section 84A (costs of establishing share option or profit sharing scheme: relief).

Income Tax (Trading and Other Income) Act 2005 (c. 5)

27   ITTOIA 2005 is amended as follows.

28   In Chapter 5 of Part 2, after section 94 insert—

"SAYE option schemes, CSOP schemes

94A   Costs of setting up SAYE option scheme or CSOP scheme

(1)   This section applies if—
      (a)   a company incurs expenses in setting up a scheme within subsection (2) that is approved by an officer of Revenue and Customs, and
      (b)   no employee or director acquires rights under the scheme before it is approved.

(2)   The schemes within this subsection are—
      (a)   SAYE option schemes within the meaning of the SAYE code (see section 516(4) of ITEPA 2003), and
      (b)   CSOP schemes within the meaning of the CSOP code (see section 521(4) of ITEPA 2003).
The references in subsection (1) to a scheme being approved are to it being approved under Schedule 3 or 4 to ITEPA 2003 (as the case may be).

(3)   A deduction for the expenses is to be made in calculating the profits of a trade carried on by the company.

(4)   If the approval is given more than 9 months after the end of the period of account in which the expenses are incurred, for the purposes of subsection (3) the deduction is to be made for the period of account in which the approval is given."

29   In section 272(2) (profits of property business: application of trading income

1210
Taxation (International and Other Provisions) Act 2010 (c. 8)
Schedule 7 — Miscellaneous relocations
Part 4 — Relocation of section 84A of ICTA

rules) at the appropriate place insert—

"section 94A	costs of setting up SAYE option scheme or CSOP scheme".

PART 5

RELOCATION OF SECTION 152 OF ICTA

Taxes Management Act 1970 (c. 9)

30   TMA 1970 is amended as follows.

31   (1) Amend section 48 (application of following provisions of Part 5) as follows.

(2) In subsection (2)(a) (application to appeals other than appeals against assessments) for "section 56" substitute "sections 54A to 54C and 56".

(3) In subsection (3) (meaning of "relevant provisions" for purpose of application to proceedings other than appeals) after "except sections 49A to 49I" insert "and 54A to 54C".

32   After section 54 insert—

"54A No questioning in appeal of amounts of certain social security income

(1) Subsection (2) applies if an amount is notified under section 54B(1) and—

    (a) no objection is made to the notification within 60 days after its date of issue, or such further period as may be allowed under section 54B(4) and (5), or

    (b) an objection is made but is withdrawn by the objector by notice.

(2) The amount is not to be questioned in any appeal against any assessment in respect of income including the amount.

(3) Subsection (4) applies if an amount is notified under section 54B(1) and—

    (a) an objection is made to the notification within 60 days after its date of issue, or such further period as may be allowed under section 54B(4) and (5),

    (b) the appropriate officer and the objector come to an agreement that the amount notified should be varied in a particular manner, and

    (c) the officer confirms that agreement in writing.

(4) The amount, as varied, is not to be questioned in any appeal against any assessment in respect of income including that amount.

(5) Subsection (4) does not apply if, within 60 days from the date when the agreement was come to, the objector gives to the appropriate officer notice that the objector wishes to repudiate or resile from the agreement.

Taxation (International and Other Provisions) Act 2010 (c. 8)
Schedule 7 — Miscellaneous relocations
Part 5 — Relocation of section 152 of ICTA

1211

54B   Notifications of taxable amounts of certain social security income

(1)   The appropriate officer may by notice notify a person who is liable to pay any income tax charged on any unemployment benefit, jobseeker's allowance or income support—

    (a)   of the amount on which the tax is charged, or

    (b)   of an alteration in an amount previously notified under paragraph (a) or this paragraph.

(2)   A notification under subsection (1) must—

    (a)   state its date of issue, and

    (b)   state that the person notified may object to the notification by notice given within 60 days after that date.

(3)   A notification under subsection (1)(b) cancels the previous notification concerned.

(4)   An objection to a notification under subsection (1) may be made later than 60 days after its date of issue if, on an application for the purpose—

    (a)   the appropriate officer is satisfied—

        (i)   that there was a reasonable excuse for not objecting before the end of the 60 days, and

        (ii)   that the application was made without unreasonable delay after the end of the 60 days, and

    (b)   the officer gives consent in writing.

(5)   If the officer is not so satisfied, the officer is to refer the application for determination by the tribunal.

54C   Interpretation of sections 54A and 54B: "appropriate officer" etc

(1)   In sections 54A and 54B "the appropriate officer" means the appropriate officer—

    (a)   in Great Britain, of the Department for Work and Pensions, and

    (b)   in Northern Ireland, of the Department for Social Development.

(2)   Section 48(1)(a) (meaning of "appeal" in the following provisions of Part 5) does not apply for the purposes of sections 54A and 54B."

Income and Corporation Taxes Act 1988 (c. 1)

33   ICTA is amended as follows.

34   Omit section 152 (notification of taxable amount of certain benefits).

PART 6

RELOCATION OF SECTION 337A(2) OF ICTA

Income and Corporation Taxes Act 1988

35   ICTA is amended as follows.

36   Omit section 6(5) (signpost to Part 8 of the Act).

1212

Taxation (International and Other Provisions) Act 2010 (c. 8)
Schedule 7 — Miscellaneous relocations
Part 6 — Relocation of section 337A(2) of ICTA

37   Omit section 337A(2) (in calculating a company's income, deductions in respect of interest to be made only under Part 5 of CTA 2009).

Corporation Tax Act 2009 (c. 4)

38   CTA 2009 is amended as follows.

39   After section 1301 insert—

"1301A Restriction of deductions for interest

In calculating a company's income from any source for corporation tax purposes, no deduction is allowed for interest otherwise than under Part 5 (loan relationships)."

PART 7

RELOCATION OF SECTION 475 OF ICTA

Income and Corporation Taxes Act 1988 (c. 1)

40   ICTA is amended as follows.

41   Omit section 475 (tax-free Treasury securities: exclusion of interest on borrowed money).

Income Tax (Trading and Other Income) Act 2005 (c. 5)

42   ITTOIA 2005 is amended as follows.

43   Before section 155 (before the italic cross-heading) insert—

"154A Certain non-UK residents with interest on 3½% War Loan 1952 Or After

(1)   This section applies if—
   (a)   in any tax year a person who is not ordinarily resident in the United Kingdom carries on a trade there—
      (i)   consisting of banking or insurance, or
      (ii)   consisting wholly or partly of dealing in securities, and
   (b)   in calculating the profits of the trade for the tax year any amount is disregarded as a result of section 714 (exemption of profits from FOTRA securities) because of a condition subject to which any 3½% War Loan 1952 Or After was issued.

(2)   Interest on money borrowed for the purposes of the trade is to be deducted in calculating the profits of the trade of that tax year only so far as it exceeds the ineligible amount.

(3)   The ineligible amount is found as follows—

Step 1

Add together all sums borrowed for the purposes of the trade and still owing in the basis period for the tax year.

Taxation (International and Other Provisions) Act 2010 (c. 8)
Schedule 7 — Miscellaneous relocations
Part 7 — Relocation of section 475 of ICTA

1213

Step 2

If the person carrying on the trade is a company, deduct any sums carrying interest which is not deducted in calculating the profits of the trade (otherwise than because of subsection (2)).

Step 3

If the amount found at Step 2 exceeds the total cost of the 3½% War Loan 1952 Or After held for the purposes of the trade in the basis period, deduct the excess from that amount.

Step 4

Calculate the average rate of interest in the basis period on money borrowed for the purposes of the trade.

Step 5

Calculate the amount of interest payable on the amount found at Step 3 at the rate found at Step 4 for the basis period.

The result is the ineligible amount.

(4) If the person's holding of 3½% War Loan 1952 Or After has fluctuated during the basis period, the total cost for the purposes of Step 3 is taken to be —

$$C \times \frac{AH}{TH}$$

where —

C is the cost of acquisition of the initial holding (if any) and any holdings acquired during the basis period,

AH is the average holding in that period, and

TH is the total of the initial holding (if any) and any holdings acquired during the basis period.

(5) In subsection (4) "initial holding" means the holding held by the person at the beginning of the basis period."

PART 8

RELOCATION OF SECTION 700 OF ICTA

Income and Corporation Taxes Act 1988 (c. 1)

44   ICTA is amended as follows.

45   Omit section 700 (adjustments and information).

Income Tax (Trading and Other Income) Act 2005 (c. 5)

46   ITTOIA 2005 is amended as follows.

47   After section 682 (assessments, adjustments and claims after the

1214

Taxation (International and Other Provisions) Act 2010 (c. 8)
Schedule 7 — Miscellaneous relocations
Part 8 — Relocation of section 700 of ICTA

administration period) insert—

"682A Statements relating to estate income

(1) If a person within subsection (2) requests it in writing, a personal representative of a deceased person must provide the person with a statement showing—

    (a) the amount treated as estate income arising from the person's interest in the whole or part of the deceased person's estate for which the person is liable to income tax for a tax year, and

    (b) the amount of any tax at the applicable rate which any such amount is treated as having borne.

(2) A person is within this subsection if—

    (a) the person has or has had an absolute or limited interest in the whole or part of the residue of the estate, or

    (b) estate income has arisen to the person from a discretionary interest the person has or has had in the whole or part of the residue of the estate.

(3) A statement under subsection (1) must be in writing.

(4) The duty to comply with a request under this section is enforceable by the person who made it."

PART 9

RELOCATION OF SECTION 787 OF ICTA

Income and Corporation Taxes Act 1988 (c. 1)

48   ICTA is amended as follows.

49   Omit section 787 (restriction of relief for payments of interest).

Income Tax Act 2007 (c. 3)

50   ITA 2007 is amended as follows.

51   In section 2(13) (overview of Part 13) after paragraph (h) (which is inserted by Schedule 8) insert—

        "(i)   leases of plant and machinery (Chapter 6), and

        (j)   tax relief for interest (Chapter 7)."

52   After section 809ZF (which is inserted by CTA 2010) insert—

"CHAPTER 7

AVOIDANCE INVOLVING OBTAINING TAX RELIEF FOR INTEREST

809ZG Tax relief schemes and arrangements

(1) Relief is not to be given under any provision of the Income Tax Acts to a person in respect of a payment of interest if a tax relief scheme has been effected, or tax relief arrangements have been made, in relation to the transaction under which the interest is paid.

Taxation (International and Other Provisions) Act 2010 (c. 8)   **1215**
Schedule 7 – Miscellaneous relocations
Part 9 – Relocation of section 787 of ICTA

(2) Subsection (1) applies whether the tax relief scheme is effected, or the tax relief arrangements are made, before or after the transaction.

(3) A scheme is a tax relief scheme in relation to a transaction for the purposes of subsection (1) if it is such that the sole or main benefit that might be expected to accrue to the person from the transaction is the obtaining of a reduction in tax liability by means of relief under the Income Tax Acts.

(4) Arrangements are tax relief arrangements in relation to a transaction for the purposes of subsection (1) if they are such that the sole or main benefit that might be expected to accrue to the person from the transaction is the obtaining of a reduction in tax liability by means of relief under the Income Tax Acts.

(5) In this section "relief" means relief by way of—
    (a) deduction in calculating profits or gains, or
    (b) deduction or set off against income."

PART 10

RELOCATION OF SECTIONS 130 TO 132 OF FA 1988

Taxes Management Act 1970 (c. 9)

53 TMA 1970 is amended as follows.

54 After section 109A insert—

"Companies ceasing to be UK resident

109B Provisions for securing payment by company of outstanding tax

(1) Each of conditions A to D must be met before a company ceases to be resident in the United Kingdom.

(2) Condition A is that the company gives to the Commissioners for Her Majesty's Revenue and Customs notice of its intention to cease to be resident in the United Kingdom.

(3) Condition B is that the notice specifies the time ("the migration time") when the company intends to cease to be resident in the United Kingdom.

(4) Condition C is that the company gives to the Commissioners—
    (a) a statement of the amount which, in its opinion, is the amount of the tax which is or will be payable by it in respect of periods beginning before the migration time, and
    (b) particulars of the arrangements which it proposes to make for securing the payment of that tax.

(5) Condition D is that—
    (a) arrangements are made by the company for securing the payment of the tax which is or will be payable by it in respect of periods beginning before the migration time, and
    (b) those arrangements, as made by the company, are approved for the purposes of this subsection by the Commissioners.

1216   *Taxation (International and Other Provisions) Act 2010 (c. 8)*
Schedule 7 – Miscellaneous relocations
Part 10 – Relocation of sections 130 to 132 of FA 1988

(6) If any question arises as to the amount which, for the purposes of subsection (5), should be regarded as the amount of tax which is or will be payable by the company in respect of periods beginning before the migration time, that question is to be referred to the tribunal.

(7) A decision of the tribunal under subsection (6) is final, despite sections 11 and 13 of the TCEA 2007 (appeals from tribunal decisions).

(8) If any information furnished by the company for the purpose of securing the Commissioners' approval under subsection (5) does not fully and accurately disclose all facts and considerations material for the Commissioners' decision under that subsection, any resulting approval is void.

109C Penalty for company's failure to comply with section 109B

If a company ceases to be resident in the United Kingdom at a time before each of conditions A to D in section 109B is met, the company is liable to a penalty not exceeding the amount of tax—

    (a) which is or will be payable by it in respect of periods beginning before that time, and

    (b) which has not been paid at that time.

109D Penalty for other persons if company fails to comply with section 109B

(1) Subsection (5) applies if—

    (a) condition E is met, and

    (b) either of conditions F and G is met.

(2) Condition E is that in relation to a company ("the migrating company") any person ("P") does or is party to the doing of any act which to P's knowledge amounts to or results in, or forms part of a series of acts which together amount to or result in, or will amount to or result in, the migrating company ceasing to be resident in the United Kingdom at a time before each of conditions A to D in section 109B is met.

(3) Condition F is that P is—

    (a) a director of the migrating company,

    (b) a company which has control of the migrating company, or

    (c) a director of a company which has control of the migrating company.

(4) Condition G is that the act mentioned in subsection (2) is a direction or instruction given—

    (a) to persons within subsection (3), but

    (b) otherwise than by way of advice given by a person acting in a professional capacity.

(5) If this subsection applies, P is liable to a penalty not exceeding the amount of tax—

    (a) which is or will be payable by the migrating company in respect of periods beginning before the time mentioned in subsection (2), and

    (b) which has not been paid at that time.

Taxation (International and Other Provisions) Act 2010 (c. 8)   **1217**
Schedule 7 — Miscellaneous relocations
Part 10 — Relocation of sections 130 to 132 of FA 1988

(6) Subsections (7) and (8) apply for the purposes of any proceedings against a person within subsection (3) for the recovery of a penalty under subsection (5).

(7) It is to be presumed that the person was party to every act of the migrating company unless the person proves that it was done without the person's consent or connivance.

(8) It is to be presumed, unless the contrary is proved, that any early-migration act was to the person's knowledge an early-migration act.

(9) In subsection (8) "early-migration act" means an act which in fact amounted to or resulted in, or formed part of a series of acts which together amounted to or resulted in, or would amount to or result in, the migrating company ceasing to be resident in the United Kingdom at a time before each of conditions A to D in section 109B is met.

109E Liability of other persons for unpaid tax

(1) This section applies if —
   (a) a company ("the migrating company") ceases to be resident in the United Kingdom at any time, and
   (b) any tax which is payable by the company in respect of periods beginning before that time is not paid within 6 months from the time when it becomes payable.

(2) The Commissioners for Her Majesty's Revenue and Customs may, at any time before the end of the period of 3 years beginning with the time when the amount of the tax is finally determined, serve on any person within subsection (3) a notice —
   (a) stating particulars of the tax payable, the amount remaining unpaid and the date when it became payable, and
   (b) requiring that person to pay that amount within 30 days of the service of the notice.

(3) The persons within this subsection are —
   (a) any company which is, or within the pre-migration year was, a member of the same group as the migrating company,
   (b) any person who is, or within the pre-migration year was, a controlling director of the migrating company, and
   (c) any person who is, or within the pre-migration year was, a controlling director of a company which has, or within the pre-migration year had, control over the migrating company.

(4) Any amount which a person is required to pay by a notice under this section may be recovered from the person as if it were tax due and duly demanded from the person.

(5) If a person ("P") pays any amount which a notice under this section requires P to pay, P may recover the amount from the migrating company.

(6) A payment in pursuance of a notice under this section is not allowed as a deduction in calculating any income, profits or losses for any tax purposes.

(7) In this section—

1218   *Taxation (International and Other Provisions) Act 2010 (c. 8)*
Schedule 7 — Miscellaneous relocations
Part 10 — Relocation of sections 130 to 132 of FA 1988

"controlling director", in relation to a company, means a director of the company who has control of the company,

"group" has the meaning which would be given by section 170 of the 1992 Act if in that section for references to 75 per cent subsidiaries there were substituted references to 51 per cent subsidiaries, and

"pre-migration year" means the period of 12 months ending with the time when the migrating company ceases to be resident in the United Kingdom.

109F   Interpretation of sections 109B to 109E

(1)   In sections 109B to 109E, any reference to the tax payable by a company includes a reference to—

    (a)   any amount which the company is liable to pay under section 77C (territorial extension of charge to tax),

    (b)   any amount of tax which the company is liable to pay under regulations made under section 684 of ITEPA 2003 (PAYE),

    (c)   any amount which the company is liable to pay under sections 61 and 62(1)(a) of the Finance Act 2004 (sub-contractors in the construction industry),

    (d)   any income tax which the company is liable to pay in respect of payments within section 946 of ITA 2007 (collection of tax: deposit-takers, building societies and certain companies), and

    (e)   any amount representing income tax which the company is liable to pay under section 966 of ITA 2007 (entertainers and sportsmen).

(2)   In sections 109B to 109E read in accordance with subsection (1), any reference to the tax payable by a company in respect of periods beginning before any particular time includes a reference to any interest—

    (a)   on the tax so payable, or

    (b)   on tax paid by the company in respect of such periods,

which the company is liable to pay in respect of periods beginning before or after that time.

(3)   In sections 109B to 109E "director", in relation to a company, is to be read in accordance with the following provisions—

    (a)   section 67(1) and (2) of ITEPA 2003, and

    (b)   section 452 of CTA 2010.

(4)   In sections 109B to 109E, any reference to a person having control of a company is to be read in accordance with sections 450 and 451 of CTA 2010."

Finance Act 1988 (c. 39)

55   FA 1988 is amended as follows.

56   Omit sections 130 to 132 (company migration).

Taxation (International and Other Provisions) Act 2010 (c. 8)
Schedule 7 — Miscellaneous relocations
Part 11 — Relocation of section 151 of FA 1989

1219

PART 11

RELOCATION OF SECTION 151 OF FA 1989

Taxes Management Act 1970 (c. 9)

57   TMA 1970 is amended as follows.

58   After section 30A insert—

"30AA Assessing income tax on trustees and personal representatives

(1)   Income tax charged on income arising to trustees of a settlement may be assessed and charged on, and in the name of, any one or more of the assessable trustees.

(2)   Income tax charged on income arising to the personal representatives of a deceased person may be assessed and charged on, and in the name of, any one or more of the assessable representatives.

(3)   In subsection (1) "the assessable trustees" means—
        (a)   the trustees of the settlement in the tax year in which the income arises, and
        (b)   any subsequent trustees of the settlement.

(4)   In subsection (2) "the assessable representatives" means—
        (a)   the persons who, in the tax year in which the income arises, are personal representatives of the deceased person, and
        (b)   any subsequent personal representatives of the deceased person."

Finance Act 1989 (c. 26)

59   FA 1989 is amended as follows.

60   Omit section 151 (assessment of trustees and personal representatives).

Income Tax (Trading and Other Income) Act 2005 (c. 5)

61   ITTOIA 2005 is amended as follows.

62   In Schedule 2 (transitionals and savings etc) omit paragraph 91 (interpretation of section 151(2) of FA 1989).

PART 12

RELOCATION OF SCHEDULE 12 TO F(NO.2)A 1992 SO FAR AS APPLYING FOR INCOME TAX PURPOSES

Finance (No.2) Act 1992 (c. 48)

63   F(No.2)A 1992 is amended as follows.

64   Omit section 66 (which introduces Schedule 12).

65   Omit Schedule 12 (banks etc in compulsory liquidation).

1220   *Taxation (International and Other Provisions) Act 2010 (c. 8)*
Schedule 7 — Miscellaneous relocations
Part 12 — Relocation of Schedule 12 to F(No.2)A 1992 so far as applying for income tax purposes

Income Tax (Trading and Other Income) Act 2005 (c. 5)

66   ITTOIA 2005 is amended as follows.

67   In section 369 (charge to tax on interest) after subsection (4) insert—

> "(5)   See also Chapter 3A of Part 14 of ITA 2007 (which provides for the receipts of certain types of company being wound up to be charged to income tax under that Chapter instead of under any other provision that would otherwise apply)."

Income Tax Act 2007 (c. 3)

68   ITA 2007 is amended as follows.

69   In section 2(14) (overview of Act: Part 14) after paragraph (c) insert ", and

> (d)   imposition of the charge to income tax on the receipts of certain types of company being wound up (Chapter 3A)."

70   In section 3(2) (overview of charges to income tax)—

> (a)   omit the "and" immediately before paragraph (e), and
> (b)   after paragraph (e) insert ", and
>
> > (f)   Chapter 3A of Part 14 of this Act (banks etc in compulsory liquidation)."

71   After section 837 insert—

"CHAPTER 3A

BANKS ETC IN COMPULSORY LIQUIDATION

837A Overview of Chapter

> (1)   This Chapter provides for the receipts of certain types of company being wound up to be charged to income tax.
>
> (2)   For provision charging the receipts of such companies to corporation tax, see Chapter 6 of Part 13 of CTA 2010.

837B Application of Chapter

> (1)   This Chapter applies if—
>
> > (a)   a company is being or has been wound up by the court in the United Kingdom, and
> > (b)   conditions A, B and C are met.
>
> (2)   Condition A is that the company was, at any time within the period mentioned in subsection (5), lawfully carrying on a business of accepting deposits as—
>
> > (a)   a person of the kind mentioned in paragraph (b) of the definition of "bank" in section 991(2) (persons with permission under Part 4 of FISMA 2000 to accept deposits), or
> > (b)   a permitted EEA credit institution.
>
> (3)   Condition B is that the company has permanently ceased to carry on the trade that included the business of accepting deposits (the "deposit-taking trade").

Taxation (International and Other Provisions) Act 2010 (c. 8)
Schedule 7 — Miscellaneous relocations
Part 12 — Relocation of Schedule 12 to F(No.2)A 1992 so far as applying for income tax purposes

1221

(4) Condition C is that the company is insolvent and —

    (a) was so when the winding up proceedings started, or

    (b) became so at any time in the period of 12 months following the day on which those proceedings started.

(5) The period referred to in subsection (2) is the period of 12 months ending with the earlier of —

    (a) the day on which the winding up proceedings started, and

    (b) the day on which the company permanently ceased to carry on the deposit-taking trade.

(6) In subsection (2)(b) a "permitted EEA credit institution" means an EEA firm of the kind mentioned in paragraph 5(b) of Schedule 3 to FISMA 2000 (credit institutions authorised by home state regulator) which has permission to accept deposits under paragraph 15 of that Schedule.

837C Charge to income tax on winding up receipts

(1) Winding up receipts arising from the deposit-taking trade are chargeable to income tax.

(2) Subsection (1) applies in relation to a winding up receipt only so far as its value was not brought into account in calculating the profits of the trade of any period before the permanent cessation of the trade.

(3) A "winding up receipt" means (subject to subsection (4)) a sum received by the company or its liquidator after —

    (a) the start of the winding up proceedings, or

    (b) if later, the permanent cessation of the deposit-taking trade.

(4) The following are not winding up receipts —

    (a) a sum received on behalf of a person entitled to the sum to the exclusion of the company and its liquidator, and

    (b) a sum realised by the transfer of an asset required to be valued under section 173 of ITTOIA 2005 (valuation of trading stock on cessation).

837D Transfer of rights to payment

(1) This section applies if —

    (a) the company or its liquidator transfers for value to another person the right to receive a sum arising from the deposit-taking trade, and

    (b) the sum is one which, if received by the company or its liquidator, would be a winding up receipt.

(2) If the transfer is at arm's length, this Chapter has effect as if the amount or value of the consideration for the transfer were a winding up receipt arising from the deposit-taking trade.

(3) If the transfer is not at arm's length, this Chapter has effect as if the value of the right transferred as between parties at arm's length were a winding up receipt arising from the deposit-taking trade.

1222   *Taxation (International and Other Provisions) Act 2010 (c. 8)*
Schedule 7 — Miscellaneous relocations
Part 12 — Relocation of Schedule 12 to F(No.2)A 1992 so far as applying for income tax purposes

837E Allowable deductions

(1) In calculating the amount on which income tax is charged under this Chapter for a tax year, deductions are allowed in accordance with this section from the amount which would otherwise be chargeable to income tax under this Chapter.

(2) A deduction is allowed for the total sum of all losses, expenses and debits within subsection (3) that are incurred during or before the tax year (but subject to subsections (4) and (5)).

(3) The losses, expenses and debits within this subsection are those which, if the company carrying on the deposit-taking trade had not permanently ceased to do so—

    (a) would have been deducted in calculating the profits of the trade for income or corporation tax purposes, or

    (b) would have been deducted from or set off against the profits of the trade for income or corporation tax purposes.

(4) No deduction is allowed if the loss, expense or debit arises directly or indirectly from the cessation itself.

(5) A loss, expense or debit is only within subsection (3) if incurred—

    (a) after the start of the winding up proceedings or, if later, the permanent cessation of the deposit-taking trade, or

    (b) in the case of a loss, at or before the permanent cessation of the deposit-taking trade.

(6) No deduction for an amount is allowed under this section if the amount has already been allowed (whether under this section or under any other provision of the Tax Acts).

837F Election to carry back

(1) This section applies if a winding up receipt arising from the deposit-taking trade is received in a tax year beginning no later than 6 years after the company permanently ceased to carry on the trade.

(2) The company or its liquidator may elect that the income tax chargeable under this Chapter in respect of the receipt is to be charged as if the receipt has been received on the date of the cessation.

(3) The election must be made before the end of the period of two years beginning immediately after the end of the tax year in which the receipt is received.

(4) If an election is made under this section an assessment to income tax must be made accordingly (regardless of anything in the Income Tax Acts).

837G Relationship of Chapter with other income tax provisions

If a winding up receipt arising from the deposit-taking trade is chargeable to income tax under this Chapter it is not chargeable to income tax under any other provision.

Taxation (International and Other Provisions) Act 2010 (c. 8)   **1223**
Schedule 7 — Miscellaneous relocations
Part 12 — Relocation of Schedule 12 to F(No.2)A 1992 so far as applying for income tax purposes

837H Interpretation of Chapter

(1) This section applies for the purposes of this Chapter.

(2) There is the permanent cessation of a company's trade if —
   (a) the company ceases to carry on the trade, or
   (b) the company ceases to be within the charge to corporation tax in respect of the trade,
whether or not the trade is in fact ceased.

(3) A company is insolvent at any time if at that time —
   (a) it is unable to pay its debts as they fall due, or
   (b) the value of its assets is less than the amount of its liabilities (including its contingent and prospective liabilities).

(4) "Company" means —
   (a) a company as defined in section 1(1) of the Companies Act 2006, or
   (b) an unregistered company as defined in section 220 of the Insolvency Act 1986 or Article 184 of the Insolvency (Northern Ireland) Order 1989 (S.I. 1989/2405 (N.I. 19)).

(5) For the meaning of "deposit-taking trade" and "winding up receipt", see sections 837B(3) and 837C(3) respectively."

72   In Schedule 4 (index of defined expressions) at the appropriate places insert —

"company (in Chapter 3A of Part 14)	section 837H(4)"
"deposit-taking trade (in Chapter 3A of Part 14)	section 837B(3)"
"winding up receipt (in Chapter 3A of Part 14)	section 837C(3)"

PART 13

RELOCATION OF SECTION 200 OF FA 1996 SO FAR AS APPLYING FOR INCOME TAX PURPOSES

Finance Act 1996 (c. 8)

73   FA 1996 is amended as follows.

74   (1) Amend section 200 (domicile for tax purposes of overseas electors) as follows.

(2) In subsection (1)(a) (determinations for purposes of inheritance tax, income tax or capital gains tax) omit ", income tax".

(3) In subsection (4)(a) (which refers to any of the taxes mentioned in subsection (1)(a)) for "any" substitute "either".

Income Tax Act 2007 (c. 3)

75   ITA 2007 is amended as follows.

1224   *Taxation (International and Other Provisions) Act 2010 (c. 8)*
Schedule 7 — Miscellaneous relocations
Part 13 — Relocation of section 200 of FA 1996 so far as applying for income tax purposes

76   In section 2(14)(b) (overview of Act: reference to Chapter 2 of Part 14) for "(Chapter 2)" substitute "and domicile (Chapters 2 and 2A)".

77   After section 835A insert—

"CHAPTER 2A

DOMICILE

835B   Domicile for income tax purposes of overseas electors

(1)   In determining for income tax purposes where a person is domiciled, disregard any relevant electoral action taken by the person (whether taken before, on or after the day on which TIOPA 2010 is passed).

(2)   For the purposes of this section, relevant electoral action is taken by a person if—

(a)   the person does anything with a view to, or in connection with, being registered as an overseas elector, or

(b)   the person, when registered as an overseas elector, votes in any election at which the person is entitled to vote as a result of being registered as an overseas elector.

(3)   For the purposes of this section, a person is registered as an overseas elector if the person is—

(a)   registered in any register of parliamentary electors in pursuance of such a declaration as is mentioned in section 1(1)(a) of the Representation of the People Act 1985 (extension of parliamentary franchise to certain non-resident British citizens), or

(b)   registered under section 3 of that Act (certain non-resident peers entitled to vote at European Parliamentary elections).

(4)   Subsection (1) does not prevent regard being had, in determining a person's domicile at any time, to any relevant electoral action taken by the person if—

(a)   the person's domicile at that time is being determined for the purpose of ascertaining that or any other person's liability to income tax, and

(b)   the person whose liability is being ascertained wishes regard to be had to that action.

(5)   If a person's domicile is determined in accordance with any such wishes, that domicile is to be regarded as having been determined for the purpose only of ascertaining the liability concerned."

PART 14

RELOCATION OF SECTION 36 OF FA 1998 AND SECTION 111 OF FA 2009

Taxes Management Act 1970 (c. 9)

78   TMA 1970 is amended as follows.

Taxation (International and Other Provisions) Act 2010 (c. 8)   **1225**
Schedule 7 — Miscellaneous relocations
Part 14 — Relocation of section 36 of FA 1998 and section 111 of FA 2009

79   In Part 5A (payment of tax) after section 59E insert—

"59F Arrangements for paying tax on behalf of group members

(1)   An officer of Revenue and Customs may enter into arrangements for the specified purpose with some or all of the members of a group.

(2)   For the purposes of subsection (1), arrangements entered into with some or all of the members of a group are for "the specified purpose" if they are arrangements for one of those members to discharge any liability of each of those members to pay corporation tax for the accounting periods to which the arrangements relate.

(3)   For the purposes of this section, a company and all its 51% subsidiaries form a group and, if any of those subsidiaries has 51% subsidiaries, the group includes them and their 51% subsidiaries, and so on.

(4)   Arrangements entered into under subsection (1) —
    (a)   may make provision in relation to cases where companies become or cease to be members of a group,
    (b)   may make provision in relation to the discharge of liability to pay interest or penalties,
    (c)   may make provision in relation to the discharge of liability to pay any amount within subsection (6),
    (d)   may make provision for or in connection with the termination of the arrangements, and
    (e)   may make such supplementary, incidental, consequential or transitional provision as is necessary for the purposes of the arrangements.

(5)   Arrangements entered into under subsection (1) —
    (a)   do not affect the liability to corporation tax, or to pay corporation tax, of any company to which the arrangements relate, and
    (b)   do not affect any other liability under the Tax Acts of any company to which the arrangements relate.

(6)   The following amounts are within this subsection—
    (a)   an amount due from a company under section 455 of CTA 2010 (charge to tax in case of loan to participator in close company) as if it were an amount of corporation tax chargeable on the company, and
    (b)   a sum chargeable on a company under section 747(4)(a) of the principal Act (controlled foreign companies) as if it were an amount of corporation tax."

80   In Part 5A after section 59F insert—

"59G Managed payment plans

(1)   This section applies if a person ("P") has entered into a managed payment plan in respect of —
    (a)   an amount on account of income tax which is to become payable in accordance with section 59A(2),
    (b)   an amount of income tax or capital gains tax which is to become payable in accordance with section 59B, or

1226

Taxation (International and Other Provisions) Act 2010 (c. 8)
Schedule 7 — Miscellaneous relocations
Part 14 — Relocation of section 36 of FA 1998 and section 111 of FA 2009

      (c)   an amount of corporation tax which is to become payable in accordance with section 59D.

(2)   P enters into a managed payment plan in respect of an amount if —

      (a)   P agrees to pay, and an officer of Revenue and Customs agrees to accept payment of, the amount by way of instalments,

      (b)   the instalments to be paid before the due date are balanced by the instalments to be paid after it (see section 59H), and

      (c)   the agreement meets such other requirements as may be specified in regulations made by the Commissioners for Her Majesty's Revenue and Customs.

(3)   But this section does not apply, in the case of an amount of corporation tax, if an arrangement under section 59F has been made in relation to the amount.

(4)   If P pays all of the instalments in accordance with the plan, P is to be treated as having paid, on the due date, the total of those instalments.

(5)   If P —

      (a)   pays one or more instalments in accordance with the plan, but

      (b)   fails to pay one or more later instalments in accordance with it,

P is to be treated as having paid, on the due date, the total of the instalments paid before the failure (but this is subject to subsection (6)).

(6)   If —

      (a)   subsection (5) applies in a case in which the first failure to pay an instalment occurs before the due date, and

      (b)   P would (in the absence of a managed payment plan) be entitled to be paid interest on any amount paid before that date,

then, despite that subsection, P is entitled to be paid that interest.

(7)   If —

      (a)   subsection (5) applies,

      (b)   P makes one or more payments after the due date (whether or not in accordance with the plan), and

      (c)   an officer of Revenue and Customs gives P a notice specifying any or all of those payments,

P is not liable to a penalty or surcharge for failing to pay the amount of the specified payments on or before the due date.

(8)   Regulations under this section may make different provision for different cases.

(9)   In this section "the due date", in relation to an amount mentioned in subsection (1), means the date on which it becomes payable.

59H   Balancing of instalments for the purposes of section 59G

(1)   Subsection (2) applies for the purposes of section 59G(2)(b).

Taxation (International and Other Provisions) Act 2010 (c. 8) 1227
Schedule 7 — Miscellaneous relocations
Part 14 — Relocation of section 36 of FA 1998 and section 111 of FA 2009

(2) The instalments to be paid before the due date are balanced by those to be paid after it if the time value of the instalments to be paid before that date is equal, or approximately equal, to the time value of the instalments to be paid after it.

(3) The time value of the instalments to be paid before the due date is the total of the time value of each of the instalments to be paid before that date (and the time value of the instalments to be paid after that date is to be read accordingly).

(4) The time value of an instalment is —

$$A \times T$$

where —

A is the amount of the instalment, and

T is the number of days before, or after, the due date that the instalment is to be paid.

(5) The Commissioners for Her Majesty's Revenue and Customs may by regulations make provision for the purpose of determining when an amount is approximately equal to another amount.

(6) Regulations under this section may make different provision for different cases."

Finance Act 1998 (c. 36)

81 FA 1998 is amended as follows.

82 Omit section 36 (arrangements with respect to payment of corporation tax).

Finance Act 2009 (c. 10)

83 FA 2009 is amended as follows.

84 Omit section 111 (managed payment plans).

PART 15

RELOCATION OF SECTION 118 OF FA 1998

Taxes Management Act 1970 (c. 9)

85 TMA 1970 is amended as follows.

86 In Part 4, after section 43D (which is inserted by Schedule 8) insert —

"43E Making of income tax claims by electronic communications etc

(1) The Commissioners for Her Majesty's Revenue and Customs may, by publishing them in a manner the Commissioners consider appropriate, give any claims directions that the Commissioners consider appropriate.

(2) In subsection (1) "claims directions" means general directions for the purposes of income tax relating to —

(a) the circumstances in which, and

(b) the conditions subject to which,

1228
Taxation (International and Other Provisions) Act 2010 (c. 8)
Schedule 7 — Miscellaneous relocations
Part 15 — Relocation of section 118 of FA 1998

claims by individuals under the Tax Acts may be made by the use of an electronic communications service or otherwise without producing a claim in writing.

(3) Directions under subsection (1) —

    (a) may not relate to the making of a claim by an individual in the individual's capacity as a trustee, partner or personal representative, but

    (b) subject to that, may relate to claims made by an individual through another person acting on the individual's behalf.

(4) Directions under subsection (1) may not relate to —

    (a) the making of a claim to which Schedule 1B to this Act applies, or

    (b) the making of a claim under any provision of the Capital Allowances Act 2001.

(5) Directions under subsection (1) —

    (a) cannot modify any requirement imposed by or under any enactment as to the period within which any claim is to be made or as to the contents of any claim, but

    (b) may include provision as to how any requirement as to the contents of a claim is to be met when the claim is not produced in writing.

(6) Directions under subsection (1) may make different provision in relation to the making of claims of different descriptions.

(7) A direction under subsection (1) may revoke or vary any previous direction given under that subsection.

(8) In subsection (2) "electronic communications service" has the same meaning as in the Communications Act 2003 (see section 32 of that Act).

(9) In subsections (1) to (6), references to the making of a claim include references to any of the following —

    (a) the making of an election,

    (b) the giving of a notification or notice,

    (c) the amendment of any return, claim, election, notification or notice, and

    (d) the withdrawal of any claim, election, notification or notice,

and in those subsections "claim" is to be read accordingly.

(10) For the purposes of subsection (9)(c) —

    (a) "return" includes any statement or declaration under the Income Tax Acts, and

    (b) the definition of "return" given by section 118(1) of this Act does not apply.

43F Effect of directions under section 43E

(1) If directions under section 43E(1) are in force in relation to the making of claims of any description to the Commissioners for Her Majesty's Revenue and Customs, claims of that description may be made to the Commissioners in accordance with the directions.

Taxation (International and Other Provisions) Act 2010 (c. 8)
Schedule 7 — Miscellaneous relocations
Part 15 — Relocation of section 118 of FA 1998

1229

(2) If directions under section 43E(1) are in force in relation to the making of claims of any description to an officer of Revenue and Customs, claims of that description may be made to an officer in accordance with the directions.

(3) Subsections (1) and (2) apply despite any enactment or subordinate legislation which requires claims of the description concerned to be made in writing or by notice.

(4) If directions under section 43E(1) are in force in relation to the making of claims of any description, claims of that description that are made without producing the claim in writing must be made in accordance with the directions.

(5) In subsection (3) "subordinate legislation" has the same meaning as in the Interpretation Act 1978.

(6) Section 43E(9) read with section 43E(10) (interpretation of references to making a claim, and meaning of "claim") applies for the purposes of subsections (1) to (4) (as well as for those of section 43E(1) to (6))."

Finance Act 1998 (c. 36)

87 FA 1998 is amended as follows.

88 Omit section 118 (claims for income tax purposes).

Income Tax (Trading and Other Income) Act 2005 (c. 5)

89 ITTOIA 2005 is amended as follows.

90 (1) Amend section 878 (other definitions) as follows.

(2) In subsection (3) (claims and elections) for "section 118 of FA 1998" substitute "section 43E(1) of TMA 1970".

(3) In subsection (4) for "(in" substitute "more generally (but in".

Income Tax Act 2007 (c. 3)

91 ITA 2007 is amended as follows.

92 In section 989 (interpretation of Income Tax Acts) in the definition of "notice" for "section 118 of FA 1998" substitute "section 43E(1) of TMA 1970".

93 (1) Amend section 1020 (claims and elections) as follows.

(2) In subsection (1) for "section 118 of FA 1998" substitute "section 43E(1) of TMA 1970".

(3) In subsection (2) for "(in" substitute "more generally (but in".

1230

Taxation (International and Other Provisions) Act 2010 (c. 8)
Schedule 7 — Miscellaneous relocations
Part 16 — Relocation of section 144 of FA 2000

PART 16

RELOCATION OF SECTION 144 OF FA 2000

Taxes Management Act 1970 (c. 9)

94   TMA 1970 is amended as follows.

95   After section 106 insert—

"Evasion

106A Offence of fraudulent evasion of income tax

(1)   A person commits an offence if that person is knowingly concerned in the fraudulent evasion of income tax by that or any other person.

(2)   A person guilty of an offence under this section is liable—

(a)   on summary conviction, to imprisonment for a term not exceeding 12 months or a fine not exceeding the statutory maximum, or both, or

(b)   on conviction on indictment, to imprisonment for a term not exceeding 7 years or a fine, or both.

(3)   In the application of subsection (2)(a)—

(a)   in England and Wales in relation to offences committed before the commencement of section 282(3) of the Criminal Justice Act 2003, and

(b)   in Northern Ireland,

for "12 months" substitute "6 months".

(4)   This section does not apply to things done or omitted before 1st January 2001."

Finance Act 2000 (c. 17)

96   FA 2000 is amended as follows.

97   Omit section 144 (offence of fraudulent evasion of income tax).

Serious Organised Crime and Police Act 2005 (c. 15)

98   The Serious Organised Crime and Police Act 2005 is amended as follows.

99   In section 76(3)(n) (offence under section 144 of FA 2000 is one for which a financial reporting order may be made) for "section 144 of the Finance Act 2000 (c. 17)" substitute "section 106A of the Taxes Management Act 1970".

Serious Crime Act 2007 (c. 27)

100   The Serious Crime Act 2007 is amended as follows.

101 (1) Amend Schedule 1 as follows.

(2)   In paragraph 8(3) (offence under section 144 of FA 2000 is a serious offence in England and Wales) for "section 144 of the Finance Act 2000 (c. 17)" substitute "section 106A of the Taxes Management Act 1970".

Taxation (International and Other Provisions) Act 2010 (c. 8)   **1231**
Schedule 7 — Miscellaneous relocations
Part 16 — Relocation of section 144 of FA 2000

(3) In paragraph 24(3) (offence under section 144 of FA 2000 is a serious offence in Northern Ireland) for "section 144 of the Finance Act 2000 (c. 17)" substitute "section 106A of the Taxes Management Act 1970".

PART 17

RELOCATION OF SECTION 199 OF FA 2003

Taxes Management Act 1970 (c. 9)

102   TMA 1970 is amended as follows.

103   After section 18A insert—

"18B Savings income: regulations about European and international aspects

(1)   The Treasury may make regulations for implementing and for dealing with matters arising out of or related to—

    (a)   any EU obligation created with a view to ensuring the effective taxation of savings income under the law of the United Kingdom and the laws of the other member States, and

    (b)   any arrangements made with a territory other than a member State with a view to ensuring the effective taxation of savings income under the law of the United Kingdom and the law of the other territory.

(2)   In this section "savings income" means—

    (a)   interest, apart from interest of a prescribed description, or

    (b)   other sums of a prescribed description.

(3)   The power to make regulations under this section is exercisable by statutory instrument.

(4)   A statutory instrument containing regulations under this section is subject to annulment in pursuance of a resolution of the House of Commons.

18C Regulations under section 18B: provision about "paying agents"

(1)   Regulations under section 18B may, in particular, require paying agents—

    (a)   to obtain and verify prescribed descriptions of information about the identity and residence of relevant payees to whom they make savings income payments, and

    (b)   to provide to the Commissioners for Her Majesty's Revenue and Customs, or an officer of Revenue and Customs, prescribed descriptions of information about relevant payees to whom they make savings income payments and about the savings income payments which they make to them.

(2)   Regulations under section 18B may include provision for the inspection on behalf of the Commissioners of books, documents and other records of persons who are, or appear to an officer to be, paying agents.

1232   *Taxation (International and Other Provisions) Act 2010 (c. 8)*
Schedule 7 – Miscellaneous relocations
Part 17 – Relocation of section 199 of FA 2003

(3)   In this section "paying agents" means persons of a prescribed description who make savings income payments to other persons.

(4)   In this section "relevant payees" means –

      (a)   persons of a prescribed description who are resident (within the meaning of regulations under section 18B) in a prescribed territory, and

      (b)   persons of any such other description as may be prescribed.

(5)   For the purposes of this section, a person makes savings income payments to another person if the person –

      (a)   makes payments of savings income to the other person, or

      (b)   secures the payment of savings income for the other person.

(6)   In this section "savings income" has the same meaning as in section 18B.

(7)   The descriptions of persons who may be prescribed under subsection (3) include, in particular, public officers and government departments.

(8)   The only territories which may be prescribed under subsection (4)(a) are –

      (a)   the other member States, and

      (b)   territories with which arrangements such as are mentioned in section 18B(1)(b) have been made.

18D   Content of regulations under section 18B: supplementary provision

(1)   Regulations under section 18B may include provision for notices under such regulations to be combined with notices under sections 17 and 18.

(2)   Regulations under section 18B may include provision about the time at or within which, and the manner in which, any requirement imposed by such regulations is to be complied with.

(3)   Regulations under section 18B may include provision for penalties for failure to comply with requirements imposed by such regulations, including provision applying any provision of this Act about the determination of penalties or any other matter relating to penalties.

(4)   Regulations under section 18B –

      (a)   may make different provision for different cases or descriptions of case, and

      (b)   may include incidental, supplemental, consequential and transitional provision and savings.

18E   Interpretation of sections 18B to 18D: "prescribed" etc

(1)   In sections 18B to 18D "prescribed" means prescribed by regulations under section 18B.

(2)   The following provisions do not apply for the purposes of sections 18B to 18D –

      (a)   section 118 of this Act (interpretation), and

Taxation (International and Other Provisions) Act 2010 (c. 8)   **1233**
Schedule 7 – Miscellaneous relocations
Part 17 – Relocation of section 199 of FA 2003

   (b)   section 18 of ITA 2007 (meaning of "savings income" in the Income Tax Acts)."

104 (1) Amend the first column of the Table in section 98 (special returns etc) as follows.

   (2)   Omit the entry for regulations under section 199 of the Finance Act 2003.

Finance Act 2003 (c. 14)

105   FA 2003 is amended as follows.

106   Omit section 199 (savings income: power to make regulations in connection with Community obligations and international arrangements).

PART 18

RELOCATION OF SECTION 61 OF F(NO.2)A 2005

Finance Act 1998 (c. 36)

107   FA 1998 is amended as follows.

108 (1) Amend Schedule 18 (company tax returns, assessments and related matters) as follows.

   (2)   After paragraph 87 insert—

"PART 10A

SEs

Company ceasing to be UK resident on formation of SE by merger

87A (1) Sub-paragraph (2) applies if at any time a company ceases to be resident in the United Kingdom in the course of the formation of an SE by merger, whether or not the company continues to exist after the formation of the SE.

   (2)   The other Parts of this Schedule apply after that time, but in relation to liabilities accruing and matters arising before that time—

      (a)   as if the company were still resident in the United Kingdom, and

      (b)   if the company has ceased to exist, as if the SE were the company.

SE ceasing to be UK resident

87B (1) Sub-paragraph (2) applies if at any time an SE—

      (a)   transfers its registered office from the United Kingdom, and

      (b)   ceases to be resident in the United Kingdom.

   (2)   The other Parts of this Schedule apply after that time, but in relation to liabilities accruing and matters arising before that time, as if the SE were still resident in the United Kingdom.

1234

Taxation (International and Other Provisions) Act 2010 (c. 8)
Schedule 7 — Miscellaneous relocations
Part 18 — Relocation of section 61 of F(No.2)A 2005

Meaning of SE

87C   In this Part "SE" means a European public limited-liability company (or Societas Europaea) within the meaning of Council Regulation (EC) No. 2157/2001 on the Statute for a European company."

(3) In the table in paragraph 98 (index of defined expressions) before the entry for "Self-assessment" insert—

"SE (in Part 10A)   paragraph 87C"

Finance (No. 2) Act 2005 (c. 22)

109   F(No.2) A 2005 is amended as follows.

110   Omit section 61 (continuity for transitional purposes in cases involving SEs).

PART 19

RELOCATION OF PARAGRAPH 13 OF SCHEDULE 13 TO FA 2007

Income Tax Act 2007 (c. 3)

111   ITA 2007 is amended as follows.

112   After section 925 insert—

"*Repos*

925A Creditor repos

(1) Subsection (2) applies if a company ("the lender") has a creditor repo for the purposes of Chapter 10 of Part 6 of CTA 2009 (see section 543 of that Act).

(2) Sections 918 to 925 have effect in relation to the lender while the arrangement is in force as if—
   (a) the lender paid the borrower amounts which are representative of the income payable on the securities that are initially sold,
   (b) the payments were made under requirements of the arrangement, and
   (c) the payments were made on the dates on which the income is payable.

(3) For the purposes of subsection (2), an arrangement is in force from the time when the securities are initially sold until the earlier of—
   (a) the time when the subsequent sale of the securities, or similar securities, takes place, and
   (b) the time when it becomes apparent that that sale will not take place.

Taxation (International and Other Provisions) Act 2010 (c. 8)
Schedule 7 – Miscellaneous relocations
Part 19 – Relocation of paragraph 13 of Schedule 13 to FA 2007

1235

925B Debtor repos

(1) Subsection (2) applies if a company ("the borrower") has a debtor repo for the purposes of Chapter 10 of Part 6 of CTA 2009 (see section 548 of that Act).

(2) The reverse charge provisions of this Chapter have effect in relation to the borrower while the arrangement is in force as if —

   (a) the lender paid the borrower amounts which are representative of the income payable on the securities that are initially sold,

   (b) the payments were made under requirements of the arrangement, and

   (c) the payments were made on the dates on which the income is payable.

(3) In subsection (2) "the reverse charge provisions of this Chapter" means —

   (a) regulations under section 918(4), and

   (b) sections 920 and 923.

(4) For the purposes of subsection (2), an arrangement is in force from the time when the securities are initially sold until the earlier of —

   (a) the time when the subsequent buying of the securities, or similar securities, takes place, and

   (b) the time when it becomes apparent that that buying will not take place.

925C Actual payments ignored if section 925A or 925B applies

If section 925A(2) or 925B(2) applies, any payment actually made under an arrangement which is representative of any income payable on any securities is to be treated for the purposes of sections 918 to 925 as if it had not been made.

925D Power to modify repo sections

(1) The Treasury may by regulations provide for all or any of the provisions of sections 925A to 925F to apply with modifications in relation to —

   (a) cases to which section 925E (non-standard repo cases) applies, or

   (b) cases involving redemption arrangements, or

   (c) both of those cases.

(2) A case involves redemption arrangements if —

   (a) arrangements, corresponding to those made in cases where a company has a repo, are made in relation to securities that are to be redeemed in the period after their sale, and

   (b) the arrangements are such that a person (instead of having the right or obligation to buy those securities, or similar or other securities, at any subsequent time) has a right or obligation in respect of the benefits which will result from the redemption.

1236

Taxation (International and Other Provisions) Act 2010 (c. 8)
Schedule 7 — Miscellaneous relocations
Part 19 — Relocation of paragraph 13 of Schedule 13 to FA 2007

(3) The regulations may make incidental, supplemental, consequential and transitional provision and savings.

(4) In this section "modifications" includes exceptions and omissions.

(5) For the purposes of subsection (2)(a) and section 925E(1), a company has a repo if —

    (a) for the purposes of Chapter 10 of Part 6 of CTA 2009 —

        (i) it has a creditor repo (see section 543 of that Act),

        (ii) it has a creditor quasi-repo (see section 544 of that Act),

        (iii) it has a debtor repo (see section 548 of that Act), or

        (iv) it has a debtor quasi-repo (see section 549 of that Act), or

    (b) as a result of section 547 of that Act, the company has a creditor repo for the purposes of section 546 of that Act.

925E Cases where section 925D applies: non-standard repos

(1) This section applies to a case if —

    (a) a company has a repo,

    (b) there has been a sale of the securities under the arrangement or arrangements by reference to which the company has the repo, and

    (c) any of conditions A to C is met.

(2) Condition A is that those securities, or similar or other securities, are not subsequently bought under the arrangement or arrangements.

(3) Condition B is that provision is made by or under an arrangement for different or additional securities to be treated as, or as included with, securities which, for the purposes of the subsequent purchase, are to represent those initially sold.

(4) Condition C is that provision is made by or under an arrangement for securities to be treated as not so included.

(5) Section 925D(5) interprets references in subsection (1) to a company having a repo.

925F Interpretation of the repo sections

(1) This section applies for the purposes of sections 925A to 925E and this section.

(2) "Arrangement" includes any agreement or understanding (whether or not legally enforceable).

(3) It does not matter whether or not provision of any arrangement conferring a right or imposing an obligation on any person to buy any securities is subject to any conditions.

(4) "Securities" means shares, stock or other securities issued by —

    (a) the government of the United Kingdom,

    (b) any public or local authority in the United Kingdom,

    (c) any UK resident company or other UK resident body,

Taxation (International and Other Provisions) Act 2010 (c. 8)   1237
Schedule 7 — Miscellaneous relocations
Part 19 — Relocation of paragraph 13 of Schedule 13 to FA 2007

    (d)   a government or public or local authority of a territory outside the United Kingdom, or

    (e)   any other body of persons not resident in the United Kingdom.

(5)   Securities are similar if they give their holders —

    (a)   the same rights against the same persons as to capital, interest and dividends, and

    (b)   the same remedies to enforce those rights.

(6)   Subsection (5) applies even if there is a difference in —

    (a)   the total nominal amounts of the securities,

    (b)   the form in which they are held, or

    (c)   the manner in which they can be transferred.

(7)   If —

    (a)   a person ("A") buys securities (or has a right or obligation to buy securities), but

    (b)   the securities are (or are to be) held for the benefit of another person ("B"),

B (not A) is treated as buying (or having the right or obligation to buy) the securities.

(8)   If —

    (a)   a person ("C") sells securities, but

    (b)   the proceeds of the sale are held for the benefit of another person ("D"),

D (not C) is treated as selling the securities."

113   In section 926 (interpretation of Chapter 9 of Part 15) after subsection (1) insert —

"(1A)   Subsection (1) applies subject to provision made in sections 925A to 925F about the interpretation of those sections or any part of them."

Finance Act 2007 (c. 11)

114   FA 2007 is amended as follows.

115   In Schedule 13 (sale and repurchase of securities) omit paragraph 13 (application of Chapter 9 of Part 15 of ITA 2007).

SCHEDULE 8   Section 374

MINOR AND CONSEQUENTIAL AMENDMENTS

PART 1

DOUBLE TAXATION RELIEF

Taxes Management Act 1970 (c. 9)

1   TMA 1970 is amended as follows.

1238   *Taxation (International and Other Provisions) Act 2010 (c. 8)*
                                              Schedule 8 — Minor and consequential amendments
                                                           Part 1 — Double taxation relief

2   In section 9A(4)(c) (scope of enquiries) for "section 804ZA of the principal Act (schemes and arrangements designed to increase relief)" substitute "section 81(2) of TIOPA 2010 (notice to counteract scheme or arrangement designed to increase double taxation relief)".

3   (1)   Amend section 12B (records to be kept for purposes of returns) as follows.

      (2)   In subsection (4A)(c) (records of foreign tax: not sufficient to preserve the information in them) for sub-paragraph (ii) substitute—

                      "(ii)   which would have been payable under the law of a territory outside the United Kingdom ("territory F") but for a development relief."

      (3)   After subsection (4A) insert—

            "(4B)   In subsection (4A)(c) "development relief" means a relief—

                      (a)   given under the law of territory F with a view to promoting industrial, commercial, scientific, educational or other development in a territory outside the United Kingdom, and

                      (b)   about which provision is made in arrangements that have effect under section 2(1) of TIOPA 2010 (double taxation relief by agreement with territories outside the United Kingdom)."

4   In section 24 (power to obtain information about income from securities) after subsection (3) insert—

            "(3ZA)   If—

                      (a)   a person beneficially entitled to income from any securities is resident in a territory outside the United Kingdom, and

                      (b)   there are double taxation arrangements with respect to income tax or corporation tax which relate to that territory,

                      subsection (3) does not exempt any bank from the duty of disclosing to the Board particulars relating to the income of that person.

            (3ZB)   In subsection (3ZA) "double taxation arrangements" means arrangements which have effect under section 2(1) of TIOPA 2010 (double taxation relief by agreement with territories outside the United Kingdom)."

5   In section 29(7A) (discovery assessments: relaxation of pre-conditions) for "section 804ZA of the principal Act" substitute "section 81(2) of TIOPA 2010 (notice to counteract scheme or arrangement designed to increase double taxation relief)".

6   In section 43C(5) (meaning of consequential claim) for "or 43A" substitute ", 43A or 43D(6)".

7   In Part 4, after section 43C insert—

       "43D Claims for double taxation relief in relation to petroleum revenue tax

            (1)   This section has effect in relation to a claim for relief under sections 2 to 6 of TIOPA 2010 in relation to petroleum revenue tax.

            (2)   The claim shall be for an amount which is quantified at the time when the claim is made.

Taxation (International and Other Provisions) Act 2010 (c. 8)
Schedule 8 – Minor and consequential amendments
Part 1 – Double taxation relief

1239

(3) If, after the claim has been made, the claimant discovers that an error or mistake has been made in the claim, the claimant may make a supplementary claim within the time allowed for making the original claim.

(4) Schedule 1A to this Act applies as respects the claim, but as if the reference in paragraph 2A(4) to a year of assessment included a reference to a chargeable period.

(5) The claim may not be made more than 4 years after the end of the chargeable period to which it relates, but this is subject to any provision of the Taxes Acts prescribing a longer or shorter period.

(6) If the claim or a supplementary claim could not have been allowed but for the making of an assessment to petroleum revenue tax after the end of the chargeable period to which the claim relates, the claim or supplementary claim may be made at any time before the end of the chargeable period following that in which the assessment is made.

(7) In this section "chargeable period" has the same meaning as in the Oil Taxation Act 1975 (see section 1(3) and (4) of that Act, under which a period that is a chargeable period ends with 30 June or 31 December and, apart from the first chargeable period in relation to an oil field, is a period of 6 months)."

Income and Corporation Taxes Act 1988 (c. 1)

8   ICTA is amended as follows.

9   In section 444BB(6) (meaning of "double taxation relief") –
   (a) in paragraph (b) for "unilateral relief under section 790(1)" substitute "relief under section 18(1)(b) and (2) of TIOPA 2010", and
   (b) for "having effect by virtue of section 788" substitute "which have effect under section 2(1) of that Act (double taxation relief by agreement with territories outside the United Kingdom)".

10 In section 750(3)(b) (disregard of certain double taxation relief) for "Part XVIII" substitute "Part 2 of TIOPA 2010 (double taxation relief)".

11 In section 751(6)(a) ("creditable tax" includes amounts of double taxation relief) for "Part XVIII" substitute "Part 2 of TIOPA 2010 (double taxation relief)".

12 In section 755A(4A)(b) (dividend paid by controlled foreign company to company carrying on life assurance business) for "subsection (4) of section 804B of this Act" substitute "subsection (5) of section 97 of TIOPA 2010".

13 Omit section 788 (giving effect to double taxation arrangements).

14 Omit section 789 (conversion of references to the profits tax in arrangements given effect under old law).

15 Omit section 790 (unilateral relief).

16 Omit section 791 (power to make regulations giving effect to section 788 and double taxation arrangements).

1240   *Taxation (International and Other Provisions) Act 2010 (c. 8)*
Schedule 8 — Minor and consequential amendments
Part 1 — Double taxation relief

17   Omit sections 792 to 798C (which contain rules about double taxation relief by way of credit).

18   Omit sections 799 and 801 to 801B (double taxation relief: dividends).

19   Omit sections 803 to 804E and 804G to 806 (further rules about credit relief).

20 (1) Amend section 806A as follows.

    (2) In subsection (2) —

        (a) in paragraph (c) for "section 801A" substitute "section 67(6) of TIOPA 2010",

        (b) in paragraph (c) for "subsection (1)(b) of that section" substitute "section 67(3) of that Act",

        (c) in paragraph (d) for "section 803" substitute "section 70(2) of TIOPA 2010",

        (d) in paragraph (d) for "subsection (1)(b) of that section" substitute "section 70(1)(d) of that Act", and

        (e) in paragraph (e) for "section 811" substitute "section 112 of TIOPA 2010".

    (3) In subsection (4)(a) for "section 797" substitute "section 42(2) of TIOPA 2010".

    (4) In subsection (5) —

        (a) for "section 799(1)" substitute "section 57(1) of TIOPA 2010",

        (b) for "section 801(2) or (3)" substitute "section 65(4) of TIOPA 2010", and

        (c) for "subsection (2) or (3) of section 801" substitute "section 65(4) of TIOPA 2010".

21 (1) Amend section 806B as follows.

    (2) In subsection (2)(b) for "section 797" substitute "section 42 of TIOPA 2010".

    (3) In subsection (3)(b) for "section 799(1)" substitute "section 57(1) of TIOPA 2010".

    (4) In subsection (4) —

        (a) in paragraph (a) for "section 799(1)" substitute "section 57(1) of TIOPA 2010",

        (b) in paragraph (b) for "section 799(1A)" substitute "Step 3 in section 58(1) of TIOPA 2010",

        (c) in paragraph (b) for "M%" substitute "M", and

        (d) in paragraph (b)(ii) for "U" substitute "PA".

    (5) In subsection (5) —

        (a) for "subsection (2) or (3) of section 801" substitute "section 65(4) of TIOPA 2010",

        (b) in each of paragraphs (a), (b)(ii) and (c)(ii) for "subsection (2) or (3), as the case may be, of section 801" substitute "section 65(4) of TIOPA 2010",

        (c) for "section 799(1A)" substitute "Step 3 in section 58(1) of TIOPA 2010",

        (d) for "M%" substitute "M", and

        (e) for "U" substitute "PA".

Taxation (International and Other Provisions) Act 2010 (c. 8)
Schedule 8 – Minor and consequential amendments
Part 1 – Double taxation relief

1241

(6) In subsection (7)(b) for "section 799(1)" substitute "section 59 of TIOPA 2010".

(7) In subsection (10) –

    (a) in the definition of "lower level dividend" for "section 801(2) or (3)" substitute "section 65(4) of TIOPA 2010",

    (b) in paragraph (a) of the definition of "the relevant tax" for "section 799(1)" substitute "section 57(1) of TIOPA 2010", and

    (c) in paragraph (b) of that definition for "section 801(2) or (3)" substitute "section 65(4) of TIOPA 2010".

22   In section 806C(3) and (4) for "this Part" substitute "Part 2 of TIOPA 2010".

23   In section 806D(3), (4) and (5) for "this Part" substitute "Part 2 of TIOPA 2010".

24   In section 806F(1) and (2) for "this Part" substitute "Part 2 of TIOPA 2010".

25   (1) Amend section 806J (interpretation of sections 806A to 806J) as follows.

   (2) In subsection (5)(b) for "subsection (6)(b) of section 790" substitute "section 15 or 16 of TIOPA 2010".

   (3) In subsection (5) for "subsection (10) of that section" substitute "section 12(3) of TIOPA 2010".

   (4) For subsection (6) substitute –

     "(6) For the purposes of the foreign dividend provisions of this Chapter a company is related to another company if that other company –

        (a) controls directly or indirectly, or

        (b) is a subsidiary of a company which controls directly or indirectly,

     at least 10% of the voting power in the first-mentioned company."

   (5) In subsection (7) in the definition of "the mixer cap" for "section 799(1)" substitute "Step 6 in section 58(1) of TIOPA 2010".

26   Omit sections 806L and 806M (unrelieved foreign tax).

27   Omit sections 807 and 807A (provision, in connection with relief, about accrued income profits and about loan relationships).

28   Omit sections 807B to 807G (provisions related to the Mergers Directive).

29   Omit sections 808A to 809 and 811 (provision, in connection with relief, about interest, royalties and discretionary trusts, and for deductions where no credit allowed).

30   In section 812(1)(b) for "section 788(1)" substitute "section 2(1) of TIOPA 2010".

31   In section 814(1)(a) for "section 788(1)" substitute "section 2(1) of TIOPA 2010".

32   Omit sections 815A to 815B and 816 (provision, in connection with relief, about transfer of non-UK trades, about foreign enterprises and about cases presented under arrangements, and provision about the Arbitration Convention and about disclosure of information).

1242   *Taxation (International and Other Provisions) Act 2010 (c. 8)*
Schedule 8 — Minor and consequential amendments
Part 1 — Double taxation relief

33   In section 828(4) (orders and regulations not subject to annulment) omit "791".

34   (1)   Amend Schedule 19ABA (modification of life assurance provisions of the Corporation Tax Acts in relation to BLAGAB group reinsurers) as follows.

       (2)   Omit paragraphs 9 to 11 (and their italic headings).

       (3)   After paragraph 25 insert—

"PART 4

MODIFICATION OF PART 2 OF TIOPA 2010 (DOUBLE TAXATION RELIEF)

26   TIOPA 2010 shall have effect with the following modifications.

Modification of section 102 (interpreting sections 99 to 101 for life assurance or gross roll-up business)

27   Omit section 102.

Modification of section 103 (interpreting sections 99 to 101 for other insurance business)

28   In section 103(1) omit the words from "if" to the end."

35   (1)   Amend Schedule 26 (reliefs against liability for tax in respect of chargeable profits of controlled foreign companies) as follows.

       (2)   In paragraph 3(5)(b) for "Part XVIII" substitute "Part 2 of TIOPA 2010".

       (3)   In paragraph 4(2) for "Part XVIII" substitute "Part 2 of TIOPA 2010 (double taxation relief)".

       (4)   In paragraph 4(4) for "section 796 or section 797" substitute "section 36, 40, 41 or 42 of TIOPA 2010".

       (5)   In paragraph 5(1) for paragraphs (a) and (b) substitute—

           "(a)   arrangements which have effect under section 2(1) of TIOPA 2010 (double taxation relief by agreement with territories outside the United Kingdom), or

           (b)   unilateral relief arrangements for a territory outside the United Kingdom (as defined by section 8 of that Act),".

       (6)   In paragraph 5(1) for "Part XVIII" substitute "Part 2 of TIOPA 2010".

       (7)   In paragraph 5(2) for "section 795(2)(b)" substitute "section 31(2)(b) and (3) of TIOPA 2010".

       (8)   In paragraph 6(1)(c) for "Part XVIII" substitute "Part 2 of TIOPA 2010".

36   Omit Schedule 28AB (prescribed schemes and arrangements for purposes of section 804ZA).

Finance Act 1989 (c. 26)

37   FA 1989 is amended as follows.

Taxation (International and Other Provisions) Act 2010 (c. 8) **1243**
Schedule 8 — Minor and consequential amendments
Part 1 — Double taxation relief

38   In section 115(1) (tax credits for dividends paid to non-residents by UK resident companies) for "having effect by virtue of section 788 of the Taxes Act 1988" substitute "which have effect under section 2(1) of the Taxation (International and Other Provisions) Act 2010".

39   In section 182A(6) (double taxation: disclosure of information: interpretation) for "section 815B(4) of the Taxes Act 1988" substitute "section 126 of the Taxation (International and Other Provisions) Act 2010".

Taxation of Chargeable Gains Act 1992 (c. 12)

40   TCGA 1992 is amended as follows.

41   In section 10(4) (persons exempt under Part 18 of ICTA) for "Part XVIII of the Taxes Act (double taxation relief agreements)" substitute "Part 2 of TIOPA 2010 (double taxation relief)".

42   In section 10B(3) (companies exempt under Part 18 of ICTA) for "Part 18 of the Taxes Act (double taxation relief agreements)" substitute "Part 2 of TIOPA 2010 (double taxation relief)".

43   In section 59(2)(b) (arrangements giving relief for partnership gains) for "falling within section 788 of the Taxes Act" substitute "that have effect under section 2(1) of TIOPA 2010".

44   In sections 140H(3), 140I(3) and 140J(3) (gains on which tax would have been charged but for the Mergers Directive) —
        (a)   for "Part 18 of the Taxes Act" substitute "Part 2 of TIOPA 2010", and
        (b)   for "arrangements having effect by virtue of section 788 of that Act (bilateral relief)" substitute "double taxation relief arrangements".

45   Omit section 277 (application to capital gains tax of provisions about double taxation relief).

46   Omit section 278 (deduction for foreign gains tax in respect of which double taxation relief by way of credit against UK tax not allowed).

47   In section 288(1) (interpretation) for the definition of "double taxation relief arrangements" substitute —
        ""double taxation relief arrangements" —
                (a)   in relation to a company means arrangements that have effect under section 2(1) of TIOPA 2010 except so far as they have effect in relation to petroleum revenue tax, and
                (b)   in relation to any other person means arrangements that have effect under section 2(1) of TIOPA 2010 but only so far as they have effect in relation to capital gains tax;".

Finance Act 1993 (c. 34)

48   FA 1993 is amended as follows.

49   Omit section 194 (application to petroleum revenue tax of provisions about double taxation relief).

50   In section 195(3) (interpretation of Part 3) omit ", other than section 194,".

1244   *Taxation (International and Other Provisions) Act 2010 (c. 8)*
Schedule 8 — Minor and consequential amendments
Part 1 — Double taxation relief

Finance (No. 2) Act 1997 (c. 58)

51   F(No.2) A 1997 is amended as follows.

52   (1)   Amend section 30 (tax credits) as follows.

       (2)   In subsection (9) for "section 788 of the Taxes Act 1988" substitute "section 2(1) of the Taxation (International and Other Provisions) Act 2010".

       (3)   In subsection (10)(a) for "by virtue of section 788 of the Taxes Act 1988" substitute "under section 2(1) of the Taxation (International and Other Provisions) Act 2010".

Finance Act 1998 (c. 36)

53   FA 1998 is amended as follows.

54   (1)   Amend Schedule 18 (company tax returns etc) as follows.

       (2)   In paragraph 8(1) (calculation of tax payable) —

         (a)   in paragraph 2 of the Second step for "section 788 or 790 of that Act" substitute "under sections 2 and 6 of TIOPA 2010 or under section 18(1)(b) and (2) of that Act", and

         (b)   in paragraph 3 of that step for "that Act" substitute "the Taxes Act 1988".

       (3)   In paragraph 22(3)(c) (records of foreign tax: not sufficient to preserve the information in them) for sub-paragraph (ii) substitute —

               "(ii)   which would have been payable under the law of a territory outside the United Kingdom ("territory F") but for a development relief."

       (4)   In paragraph 22 after sub-paragraph (3) insert —

         "(4)   In sub-paragraph (3)(c) "development relief" means a relief —

           (a)   given under the law of territory F with a view to promoting industrial, commercial, scientific, educational or other development in a territory outside the United Kingdom, and

           (b)   about which provision is made in arrangements which have effect under section 2(1) of TIOPA 2010 (double taxation relief by agreement with territories outside the United Kingdom)."

Finance Act 2000 (c. 17)

55   FA 2000 is amended as follows.

56   (1)   Amend Schedule 22 (tonnage tax) as follows.

       (2)   For paragraph 57(2)(a) ("relief" includes double taxation relief) substitute —

         "(a)   sections 2 and 6 of the Taxation (International and Other Provisions) Act 2010 (double taxation relief by agreement with territories outside the United Kingdom),

       (aa)   section 18(1)(b) and (2) of that Act (unilateral relief from double taxation), or".

Taxation (International and Other Provisions) Act 2010 (c. 8)
Schedule 8 — Minor and consequential amendments
Part 1 — Double taxation relief

1245

Capital Allowances Act 2001 (c. 2)

57   CAA 2001 is amended as follows.

58   In section 105(4) (meaning of "double taxation arrangements") for the words from "specified" to the end substitute "which have effect under section 2(1) of the Taxation (International and Other Provisions) Act 2010 (double taxation relief by agreement with territories outside the United Kingdom)".

Income Tax (Earnings and Pensions) Act 2003 (c. 1)

59   ITEPA 2003 is amended as follows.

60   In section 643(6) in the definition of "double taxation relief arrangements" for the words from "specified" to the end substitute "which have effect under section 2(1) of TIOPA 2010;".

Finance Act 2004 (c. 12)

61   FA 2004 is amended as follows.

62   In Chapter 7 of Part 3 (special withholding tax) omit—
        (a)   sections 107 to 111,
        (b)   sections 113 and 114, and
        (c)   section 115(4).

63   In section 189(3) (treatment of relevant UK earnings) for "by virtue of section 788 of ICTA" substitute "under section 2(1) of the Taxation (International and Other Provisions) Act 2010".

64   In Schedule 34 (non-UK pensions schemes: application of certain charges) in paragraph 20 (meaning of "double tax arrangements") for "by virtue of section 788 of ICTA" substitute "under section 2(1) of the Taxation (International and Other Provisions) Act 2010".

Income Tax (Trading and Other Income) Act 2005 (c. 5)

65   ITTOIA 2005 is amended as follows.

66   In section 397A(7) (interpretation of section) in the definition of "special withholding tax" for "section 107(3) of FA 2004" substitute "section 136(6) of TIOPA 2010".

67   For section 397BA(2)(a) (which refers to arrangements to which section 788 of ICTA applies) substitute—
        "(a)   arrangements made in relation to the territory have effect under section 2(1) of TIOPA 2010 ("double taxation relief arrangements"), and".

68   In section 763(3) (priority of double taxation arrangements) for "section 788 of ICTA" substitute "section 2(1) of TIOPA 2010".

69 (1) Section 764 (application of ICTA provisions about special relationships) is amended as follows.

     (2) In subsection (1), and in the title, for "ICTA" substitute "TIOPA 2010".

1246   *Taxation (International and Other Provisions) Act 2010 (c. 8)*
Schedule 8 — Minor and consequential amendments
Part 1 — Double taxation relief

(3) In subsection (1) for "special relationship provision" substitute "special relationship rule".

(4) In subsection (2) for "subsections (2) to (4) of section 808A of ICTA" substitute "section 131(3), (5) and (6) of TIOPA 2010".

(5) In subsection (3) for "subsections (2) to (7) and (9) of section 808B of ICTA" substitute "sections 132(3) to (5), (7) and (8) and 133 of TIOPA 2010".

70   In section 858(1)(b) (resident partners and double taxation agreements) for "section 788 of ICTA" substitute "section 2(1) of TIOPA 2010".

Income Tax Act 2007 (c. 3)

71   ITA 2007 is amended as follows.

72   In section 1(2)(a) (example of income tax provisions located outside ITA 2007) for "Part 18 of ICTA" substitute "Part 2 of TIOPA 2010".

73 (1) Amend section 26(1)(b) (provisions referred to at Step 6 of the calculation in section 23) as follows.

    (2) Omit the entries for sections 788 and 790 of ICTA.

    (3) Omit "and" before the entry for sections 677 and 678 of ITTOIA 2005.

    (4) After that entry insert—
            "sections 2 and 6 of TIOPA 2010 (double taxation relief: relief by agreement), and
            section 18(1)(b) and (2) of TIOPA 2010 (relief for foreign tax where no double taxation arrangements)."

74   In section 27(6) (tax reductions for individuals by way of double taxation relief)—
        (a) in paragraph (a) for "section 788 of ICTA" substitute "sections 2 and 6 of TIOPA 2010", and
        (b) in paragraph (b) for "section 790(1) of ICTA" substitute "section 18(1)(b) and (2) of TIOPA 2010".

75   In section 28(4) (tax reductions for non-individuals by way of double taxation relief)—
        (a) in paragraph (a) for "section 788 of ICTA" substitute "sections 2 and 6 of TIOPA 2010", and
        (b) in paragraph (b) for "section 790(1) of ICTA" substitute "section 18(1)(b) and (2) of TIOPA 2010".

76 (1) Amend section 29 (tax reductions: supplementary) as follows.

    (2) In subsection (4)(a) for "section 796(1), (2) and (3) of ICTA" substitute "sections 36(1) to (5) and (7) and 41 of TIOPA 2010".

    (3) In subsection (5) for "section 788 of ICTA" substitute "sections 2 and 6 of TIOPA 2010".

77 (1) Amend section 32 (liabilities not dealt with in calculation under section 23) as follows.

    (2) Omit the entry for section 804(5B)(a) of ICTA.

Taxation (International and Other Provisions) Act 2010 (c. 8)   **1247**
Schedule 8 — Minor and consequential amendments
Part 1 — Double taxation relief

(3) Omit the word "and" before the entry for section 682(4) of ITTOIA 2005.

(4) After that entry insert ", and

> under section 24(4) of TIOPA 2010 (recovery of excess credit for overseas tax)."

78   (1) Amend section 53 (transfer of unused relief: general) as follows.

     (2) In subsection (2) (tax reductions by way of double taxation relief) —

         (a) in paragraph (a) for "section 788 of ICTA" substitute "sections 2 and 6 of TIOPA 2010", and

         (b) in paragraph (b) for "section 790(1) of ICTA" substitute "section 18(1)(b) and (2) of TIOPA 2010".

     (3) In subsection (5) for "section 788 of ICTA" substitute "sections 2 and 6 of TIOPA 2010".

79   (1) In section 424(2) (gift aid: charge to tax: interpretation) amend paragraph (b) of the definition of "amount C" as follows.

     (2) In sub-paragraph (i) for "section 788 of ICTA" substitute "sections 2 and 6 of TIOPA 2010".

     (3) In sub-paragraph (ii) for "section 790(1) of ICTA" substitute "section 18(1)(b) and (2) of TIOPA 2010".

80   (1) Amend section 425 ("total amount of income tax" in sections 423 and 424) as follows.

     (2) In subsection (4) (tax reductions to be ignored) —

         (a) in paragraph (b) for "section 788 of ICTA" substitute "sections 2 and 6 of TIOPA 2010", and

         (b) in paragraph (c) for "section 790(1) of ICTA" substitute "section 18(1)(b) and (2) of TIOPA 2010".

     (3) In subsection (6) for "section 788 of ICTA" substitute "sections 2 and 6 of TIOPA 2010".

81   In section 527(2) omit paragraph (b) (subsection (1) does not apply to income chargeable to tax under section 804 of ICTA).

82   In section 582(2) (regulations may remove or reduce rights to claim double taxation relief) for "Part 18 of ICTA" substitute "Part 2 of TIOPA 2010".

83   In section 828C(4) (entitlement to double taxation relief) —

         (a) in paragraph (a) for "section 788 of ICTA" substitute "sections 2 and 6 of TIOPA 2010", and

         (b) in paragraph (b) for "section 790(1)" substitute "section 18(1)(b) and (2)".

84   In section 849(1) (interaction between Part 15 of ITA 2007 and regulations under section 791 of ICTA) for "section 791 of ICTA (double taxation relief: power to make regulations for carrying out section 788)" substitute "section 7 of TIOPA 2010 (double taxation arrangements: general regulations)".

85   In section 1023 (meaning in Act of "double taxation arrangements") for "section 788 of ICTA" substitute "section 2(1) of TIOPA 2010".

86   In section 1026 —

1248   *Taxation (International and Other Provisions) Act 2010 (c. 8)*
Schedule 8 — Minor and consequential amendments
Part 1 — Double taxation relief

    (a)   after paragraph (e) insert "or", and

    (b)   omit paragraph (g) ("non-qualifying income" in section 1025 includes deemed receipts under section 804(5B) of ICTA) and the "or" preceding it.

Finance Act 2008 (c. 9)

87   FA 2008 is amended as follows.

88   In Schedule 17 in paragraph 10(3) after paragraph (c) insert "and".

Corporation Tax Act 2009 (c. 4)

89   CTA 2009 is amended as follows.

90   In section 464(3) —

    (a)   in paragraph (f) for "section 795(4) of ICTA" substitute "section 31(5) of TIOPA 2010", and

    (b)   in paragraph (g) for "section 811(3) of ICTA" substitute "section 112(5) of TIOPA 2010".

91   In section 486(2) for "section 811 of ICTA" substitute "section 112 of TIOPA 2010".

92   In section 550(7) (meaning of "double taxation relief") for "Part 18 of ICTA" substitute "Part 2 of TIOPA 2010".

93   In section 697(3)(a) (exceptions to section 696) for "because of section 788 of ICTA" substitute "under section 2(1) of TIOPA 2010".

94   In section 782(1)(a) (intangible fixed assets transferred in the course of certain transfers of a business) —

    (a)   for "section 807B(2)(b)(iii) of ICTA" substitute "section 116(2)(b)(iii) of TIOPA 2010", and

    (b)   for "section 807C" substitute "section 117".

95   In section 793(3)(b) (when election under section 792 may be made) for "arrangements under Part 18 of ICTA" substitute "arrangements that have effect under section 2(1) of TIOPA 2010".

96   In section 827(7) (no claim under section if claim made under section 807B(6) of ICTA) —

    (a)   for "section 807B(6) of ICTA" substitute "section 116(6) of TIOPA 2010", and

    (b)   for "section 807C" substitute "section 117".

97   In section 906(3) —

    (a)   omit "and" after paragraph (a), and

    (b)   after paragraph (b) insert ", and

               (c)   section 112(5) of TIOPA 2010 (deduction for foreign tax where no credit available)."

98   For section 931C(1)(a) (which refers to arrangements to which section 788 of ICTA applies) substitute —

        "(a)   arrangements made in relation to the territory have effect under section 2(1) of TIOPA 2010 ("double taxation relief arrangements"), and".

Taxation (International and Other Provisions) Act 2010 (c. 8)   **1249**
Schedule 8 — Minor and consequential amendments
Part 1 — Double taxation relief

99   In section 931H(5) for "Part 18 of ICTA" substitute "Part 2 of TIOPA 2010".

100   In section 931J(7) for "Part 18 of ICTA" substitute "Part 2 of TIOPA 2010".

101   In section 1266(1)(b) (resident partners and double taxation agreements) for "section 788 of ICTA" substitute "section 2(1) of TIOPA 2010".

Finance Act 2009 (c. 10)

102   FA 2009 is amended as follows.

103   In section 56(1) (tax in respect of MEPs' pay) for "Part 18 of ICTA (double tax" substitute "Part 2 of TIOPA 2010 (double taxation".

104   In Schedule 16 in paragraph 7(2)(a) (purposes for which straddling accounting periods are split) after "Chapter 4 of Part 17, and Part 18, of ICTA" insert "and Part 2 of TIOPA 2010".

105   In Schedule 35 in paragraph 2(4)(b) for "section 788 of ICTA" substitute "sections 2 and 6 of TIOPA 2010".

PART 2

TRANSFER PRICING AND ADVANCE PRICING AGREEMENTS

Taxes Management Act 1970 (c. 9)

106   TMA 1970 is amended as follows.

107   In section 9A(4)(b) (scope of enquiries) for "paragraph 5C of Schedule 28AA to the principal Act" substitute "section 168(1) of TIOPA 2010".

108 (1)   Amend the second column of the Table in section 98 (special returns etc) as follows.

     (2)   Omit the entry for section 86(4) of FA 1999.

     (3)   At the appropriate place insert—
         "Section 228 of TIOPA 2010."

Income and Corporation Taxes Act 1988 (c. 1)

109   ICTA is amended as follows.

110   Omit section 770A (which introduces Schedule 28AA).

111   Omit Schedule 28AA (transfer pricing).

Finance Act 1998 (c. 36)

112   FA 1998 is amended as follows.

113   Omit section 110 (determinations requiring the sanction of the Commissioners for Her Majesty's Revenue and Customs).

114   Omit section 111 (duty to give notice to persons who may be able to make or amend a claim under paragraph 6 of Schedule 28AA or who may have rights to be heard in appeals under that Schedule).

1250

Taxation (International and Other Provisions) Act 2010 (c. 8)
Schedule 8 — Minor and consequential amendments
Part 2 — Transfer pricing and advance pricing agreements

Finance Act 1999 (c. 16)

115   FA 1999 is amended as follows.

116   Omit section 85 (advance pricing agreements).

117   Omit section 86(1) to (8) and (10) (provisions supplementary to section 85).

118   Omit section 87 (effect of advance pricing agreements on non-parties).

Finance Act 2000 (c. 17)

119 (1)   Schedule 22 to FA 2000 (tonnage tax) is amended as follows.

(2)   In paragraph 58(1) for the words after paragraph (b) substitute —
"Part 4 of the Taxation (International and Other Provisions) Act 2010 (transactions not at arm's length) has effect with the omission of sections 174 to 184, 187 to 189 and 191 to 196 (elimination of double counting etc)."

(3)   In paragraph 58(2) for "Schedule 28AA" substitute "Part 4 of the Taxation (International and Other Provisions) Act 2010".

(4)   In paragraph 59(1) for "Schedule 28AA to the Taxes Act 1988" substitute "Part 4 of the Taxation (International and Other Provisions) Act 2010".

(5)   For paragraph 59(2) substitute —

"(2)   As applied by sub-paragraph (1), Part 4 of the Taxation (International and Other Provisions) Act 2010 has effect with the omission of sections 174 to 184, 187 to 189 and 191 to 196 (elimination of double counting etc)."

(6)   In paragraph 59(3) for "Schedule 28AA" substitute "Part 4 of the Taxation (International and Other Provisions) Act 2010".

(7)   In paragraph 60(2) for "Schedule 28AA" substitute "Part 4 of the Taxation (International and Other Provisions) Act 2010".

Income Tax (Trading and Other Income) Act 2005 (c. 5)

120   ITTOIA 2005 is amended as follows.

121 (1)   Amend section 172F (transfer pricing rules to take precedence over sections 172D and 172E) as follows.

(2)   In subsection (1)(a) for "Schedule 28AA to ICTA" substitute "Part 4 of TIOPA 2010".

(3)   In subsection (1)(b) for "that Schedule" substitute "that Part".

(4)   In subsection (2) for "Schedule 28AA to ICTA without falling to be adjusted under that Schedule" substitute "Part 4 of TIOPA 2010 without falling to be adjusted under that Part".

(5)   For subsection (2)(a) and (b) substitute —
"(a)   the condition in section 147(1)(a) of TIOPA 2010 is met, and
(aa)   the participation condition is met (see subsection (2B)), but
(b)   either —

Taxation (International and Other Provisions) Act 2010 (c. 8)
Schedule 8 — Minor and consequential amendments
Part 2 — Transfer pricing and advance pricing agreements

1251

           (i)   one of the conditions in section 147(1)(c) and (d) of TIOPA 2010 is not met, or

           (ii)   one of the exceptions mentioned in subsection (2A) applies."

(6) After subsection (2) insert—

"(2A)   The exceptions are those in—

      (a)   section 447(5) of CTA 2009 (exchange gains or losses from loan relationships),

      (b)   section 694(8) of CTA 2009 (exchange gains or losses from derivative contracts),

      (c)   section 213 of TIOPA 2010 (saving for provisions relating to capital allowances), and

      (d)   section 214 of TIOPA 2010 (saving for provisions relating to chargeable gains).

(2B)   Section 148 of TIOPA 2010 (when the participation condition is met) applies for the purposes of subsection (2)(aa) as it applies for the purposes of section 147(1)(b) of TIOPA 2010."

122   In section 173(2) (trading stock not to be valued if paragraph 1(2) of Schedule 28AA to ICTA has effect) for "paragraph 1(2) of Schedule 28AA to ICTA" substitute "section 147(3) or (5) of TIOPA 2010".

Corporation Tax Act 2009 (c. 4)

123   CTA 2009 is amended as follows.

124 (1)   Amend section 161 (transfer pricing rules take precedence over rules about disposals and acquisitions of trading stock not made in course of the trade concerned) as follows.

(2) In subsection (1)(a) for "Schedule 28AA to ICTA" substitute "Part 4 of TIOPA 2010".

(3) In subsection (1)(b) for "that Schedule" substitute "that Part".

(4) For subsection (2) substitute—

"(2)   For the purposes of subsection (1)(b), the relevant consideration falls within Part 4 of TIOPA 2010 without falling to be adjusted under that Part if—

      (a)   the condition in section 147(1)(a) of TIOPA 2010 is met, and

      (b)   the participation condition is met (see subsection (3A)), but

      (c)   either—

           (i)   one of the conditions in section 147(1)(c) and (d) of TIOPA 2010 is not met, or

           (ii)   one of the exceptions mentioned in subsection (3) applies."

(5) In subsection (3) for paragraphs (c) and (d) substitute—

      "(c)   section 213 of TIOPA 2010 (saving for provisions relating to capital allowances), and

      (d)   section 214 of TIOPA 2010 (saving for provisions relating to chargeable gains)."

1252   *Taxation (International and Other Provisions) Act 2010 (c. 8)*
Schedule 8 – Minor and consequential amendments
Part 2 – Transfer pricing and advance pricing agreements

(6) After subsection (3) insert—

"(3A)   Section 148 of TIOPA 2010 (when the participation condition is met) applies for the purposes of subsection (2)(b) as it applies for the purposes of section 147(1)(b) of TIOPA 2010."

125   In section 162(2) (trading stock not to be valued if paragraph 1(2) of Schedule 28AA to ICTA has effect) for "paragraph 1(2) of Schedule 28AA to ICTA" substitute "section 147(3) or (5) of TIOPA 2010".

126   In section 340(7) (Schedule 28AA to ICTA does not apply to amounts accounted for under the section) for "Schedule 28AA to ICTA" substitute "Part 4 of TIOPA 2010".

127   In section 374(3)(a) (meaning of non-qualifying territory) for "paragraph 5E of Schedule 28AA to ICTA" substitute "section 173 of TIOPA 2010".

128 (1) Amend section 376(5) (interpretation of section 375) as follows.

(2) In the definition of "non-qualifying territory" for "paragraph 5E of Schedule 28AA to ICTA" substitute "section 173 of TIOPA 2010".

(3) In the definition of "small or medium-sized enterprise" for "paragraph 5D of that Schedule" substitute "section 172 of TIOPA 2010".

129   In section 377(3)(a) (meaning of non-qualifying territory) for "paragraph 5E of Schedule 28AA to ICTA" substitute "section 173 of TIOPA 2010".

130   In section 407(6)(a) (meaning of non-qualifying territory) for "paragraph 5E of Schedule 28AA to ICTA" substitute "section 173 of TIOPA 2010".

131 (1) Amend section 410(5) (interpretation of section) as follows.

(2) In the definition of "non-qualifying territory" for "paragraph 5E of Schedule 28AA to ICTA" substitute "section 173 of TIOPA 2010".

(3) In the definition of "small or medium-sized enterprise" for "paragraph 5D of that Schedule" substitute "section 172 of TIOPA 2010".

132   In section 444(3) (section is subject to section 445) for "Schedule 28AA to ICTA" substitute "Part 4 of TIOPA 2010".

133 (1) Amend section 445 (disapplication of section 444 where Schedule 28AA to ICTA applies) as follows.

(2) In subsection (1) for "Schedule 28AA to ICTA" substitute "Part 4 of TIOPA 2010".

(3) In each of paragraphs (a) and (b) of that subsection for "that Schedule" substitute "that Part".

(4) In subsection (2)(a) for "Schedule 28AA to ICTA" substitute "Part 4 of TIOPA 2010".

(5) In subsection (2)(b) for "that Schedule" substitute "that Part".

(6) In subsection (3) for "Schedule 28AA to ICTA" substitute "Part 4 of TIOPA 2010".

(7) For subsection (3)(a) substitute—

"(a)   the condition in section 147(1)(a) of TIOPA 2010 is met,

Taxation (International and Other Provisions) Act 2010 (c. 8)   **1253**
Schedule 8 – Minor and consequential amendments
Part 2 – Transfer pricing and advance pricing agreements

      (aa)   the participation condition is met (see subsection (3A)), and".

  (8) After subsection (3) insert —

      "(3A)   Section 148 of TIOPA 2010 (when the participation condition is met) applies for the purposes of subsection (3)(aa) as it applies for the purposes of section 147(1)(b) of TIOPA 2010."

  (9) In subsection (4) for "Schedule 28AA to ICTA," substitute "Part 4 of TIOPA 2010,".

  (10) In subsection (5) for "Schedule 28AA to ICTA (see paragraph 1 of that Schedule)" substitute "Part 4 of TIOPA 2010 (see sections 149 and 151 of that Act)".

  (11) In the title for "Schedule 28AA to ICTA" substitute "Part 4 of TIOPA 2010".

134 (1) Amend section 446 (bringing into account adjustments made under Schedule 28AA to ICTA) as follows.

  (2) In each of subsections (1), (2), (4) and (6), and in the title, for "Schedule 28AA to ICTA" substitute "Part 4 of TIOPA 2010".

135 (1) Amend section 447 (exchange gains and losses on debtor relationships: loans disregarded under Schedule 28AA to ICTA) as follows.

  (2) In subsection (1)(c) for "paragraph 1 of Schedule 28AA to ICTA" substitute "section 147(3) or (5) of TIOPA 2010".

  (3) In subsection (5) for "Schedule 28AA to ICTA" substitute "Part 4 of TIOPA 2010".

  (4) In subsection (7) for "Schedule 28AA to ICTA (see paragraph 1 of that Schedule)" substitute "Part 4 of TIOPA 2010 (see sections 149 and 151 of that Act)".

  (5) In the title for "Schedule 28AA to ICTA" substitute "Part 4 of TIOPA 2010".

136   In section 452(1)(a) and (3)(a) (exchange gains and losses where loan not on arm's length terms) for "paragraph 6D(2) of Schedule 28AA to ICTA" substitute "section 192(1) of TIOPA 2010".

137   In section 455(5) (section does not apply if paragraph 1(2) of Schedule 28AA to ICTA has effect) for "paragraph 1(2) of Schedule 28AA to ICTA" substitute "section 147(3) or (5) of TIOPA 2010".

138   In section 464(3)(a) (which refers to and describes section 445(2)) for "Schedule 28AA to ICTA" substitute "Part 4 of TIOPA 2010".

139   In section 484(1) (non-lending relationships treated as loan relationships: meaning of "interest") for "Schedule 28AA to ICTA" substitute "Part 4 of TIOPA 2010".

140   In section 508(2) (arrangements which are not alternative finance arrangements) —

      (a)   in paragraph (b) for "paragraph 1(2) of Schedule 28AA to ICTA" substitute "subsection (3) or (5) of section 147 of TIOPA 2010",

      (b)   in that paragraph for "in paragraph 1(2)(a) of that Schedule" substitute "in that subsection", and

1254   *Taxation (International and Other Provisions) Act 2010 (c. 8)*
Schedule 8 — Minor and consequential amendments
Part 2 — Transfer pricing and advance pricing agreements

        (c)   in paragraph (c) for "that Schedule" substitute "Part 4 of TIOPA 2010".

141   In section 625(7) (Schedule 28AA to ICTA does not apply to amounts if credits or debits in respect of those amounts are determined under the section), for "Schedule 28AA to ICTA" substitute "Part 4 of TIOPA 2010".

142 (1)   Amend section 693 (bringing into account adjustments under Schedule 28AA to ICTA) as follows.

       (2)   In subsections (1), (2) and (4), and the title, for "Schedule 28AA to ICTA" substitute "Part 4 of TIOPA 2010".

143 (1)   Amend section 694 (exchange gains and losses where derivative contracts not on arm's length terms) as follows.

       (2)   In subsections (2), (4) and (8) for "Schedule 28AA to ICTA" substitute "Part 4 of TIOPA 2010".

       (3)   In subsection (10) for "Schedule 28AA to ICTA (see paragraph 1 of that Schedule)" substitute "Part 4 of TIOPA 2010 (see sections 149 and 151 of that Act)".

144   In section 698(5) (section does not apply if paragraph 1(2) of Schedule 28AA to ICTA increases company's tax liability) for "paragraph 1(2) of Schedule 28AA to ICTA" substitute "section 147(3) or (5) of TIOPA 2010".

145 (1)   In the provisions mentioned in sub-paragraph (2) (provisions which relate to intangible fixed assets and refer to matters being subject to adjustments under Schedule 28AA to ICTA) for "Schedule 28AA to ICTA" substitute "Part 4 of TIOPA 2010".

       (2)   The provisions are —
            section 721(3),
            section 728(3),
            section 729(4),
            section 731(5),
            section 736(7),
            section 739(2),
            section 740(4),
            section 742(3), and
            section 743(3).

146   In section 775(3) (intangible fixed assets: transfers within a group) for "Schedule 28AA to ICTA" substitute "Part 4 of TIOPA 2010".

147 (1)   Amend section 846 (intangible fixed assets: transfers not at arm's length) as follows.

       (2)   In subsection (1)(a) for "Schedule 28AA to ICTA" substitute "Part 4 of TIOPA 2010".

       (3)   In subsection (1)(b) for "that Schedule" substitute "that Part".

       (4)   In subsection (2) for "within that Schedule" substitute "within that Part".

       (5)   For subsection (2)(a) substitute —
            "(a)   the condition in section 147(1)(a) of TIOPA 2010 is met,

Taxation (International and Other Provisions) Act 2010 (c. 8)   **1255**
Schedule 8 – Minor and consequential amendments
Part 2 – Transfer pricing and advance pricing agreements

        (aa)   the participation condition is met (see subsection (2A)), and".

    (6) After subsection (2) insert—

    "(2A)   Section 148 of TIOPA 2010 (when the participation condition is met) applies for the purposes of subsection (2)(aa) as it applies for the purposes of section 147(1)(b) of TIOPA 2010."

    (7) In subsection (3) for the words after "meaning" substitute "as in that Part (see, respectively, sections 149 and 151 of TIOPA 2010)".

148   In section 931P(4) (section does not apply if Schedule 28AA to ICTA applies) for "Schedule 28AA to ICTA" substitute "Part 4 of TIOPA 2010".

Finance Act 2009 (c. 10)

149   FA 2009 is amended as follows.

150   In Schedule 17 (international movement of capital) in paragraph 12(5) for "Paragraph 3 of Schedule 28AA to ICTA" substitute "Section 150 of TIOPA 2010".

PART 3

TAX ARBITRAGE

Finance (No. 2) Act 2005 (c. 22)

151   F(No.2)A 2005 is amended as follows.

152   Omit sections 24 to 28 (avoidance involving tax arbitrage).

153   Omit section 30 (interpretation of Chapter 4 of Part 2).

154   Omit section 31 (commencement of Chapter 4 of Part 2).

155   Omit Schedule 3 (qualifying schemes).

PART 4

TAX TREATMENT OF FINANCING COSTS AND INCOME

Taxes Management Act 1970 (c. 9)

156   TMA 1970 is amended as follows.

157 (1) Amend the first column of the Table in section 98 (special returns etc) as follows.

    (2) Omit the entry for regulations under Schedule 15 to FA 2009.

    (3) At the appropriate place insert—
          "Regulations under section 283, 284, 285, 295 or 297 of TIOPA 2010."

Finance Act 2009

158   FA 2009 is amended as follows.

1256

Taxation (International and Other Provisions) Act 2010 (c. 8)
Schedule 8 — Minor and consequential amendments
Part 4 — Tax treatment of financing costs and income

159   Omit section 35 (which introduces Schedule 15).

160   Omit paragraphs 1 to 94 and 97 to 99 of Schedule 15 (tax treatment of financing costs and income).

PART 5

OFFSHORE FUNDS

Inheritance Tax Act 1984 (c. 51)

161   The Inheritance Tax Act 1984 is amended as follows.

162   In section 174(1)(a) (income tax and unpaid inheritance tax) for "made under section 41(1) of the Finance Act 2008" substitute "under section 354(1) of the Taxation (International and Other Provisions) Act 2010".

Taxation of Chargeable Gains Act 1992 (c. 12)

163   TCGA 1992 is amended as follows.

164   In section 108(1)(c) (identification of relevant securities for corporation tax) for "made under section 41(1) of the Finance Act 2008" substitute "under section 354(1) of TIOPA 2010".

165   In section 212(1)(b) (annual deemed disposal of unit trusts etc) for "section 40A of the Finance Act 2008" substitute "section 355 of TIOPA 2010".

166   In Schedule 7AD (gains of insurance company from venture capital investment partnership) in paragraph 7(1) for "made under section 41(1) of the Finance Act 2008" substitute "under section 354(1) of TIOPA 2010".

Income Tax (Trading and Other Income) Act 2005 (c. 5)

167   ITTOIA 2005 is amended as follows.

168   In section 378A(7) (offshore fund distributions) for "section 40A of FA 2008" substitute "section 354 of TIOPA 2010 (see sections 355 to 363 of that Act)".

Finance Act 2008 (c. 9)

169   FA 2008 is amended as follows.

170   Omit sections 40A to 42A (offshore funds).

Corporation Tax Act 2009 (c. 4)

171   CTA 2009 is amended as follows.

172   In section 489 (meaning of "offshore fund etc") —
         (a)   for "Sections 40A to 40G of FA 2008" substitute "Sections 355 to 363 of TIOPA 2010", and
         (b)   for "sections 40A to 42A" substitute "Part 8".

Finance Act 2009 (c. 10)

173   FA 2009 is amended as follows.

Taxation (International and Other Provisions) Act 2010 (c. 8) **1257**
Schedule 8 — Minor and consequential amendments
Part 5 — Offshore funds

174   Omit paragraph 6 of Schedule 22 (restriction on regulation-making power under section 41 of FA 2008).

PART 6

OIL ACTIVITIES

Finance Act 1980 (c. 48)

175   FA 1980 is amended as follows.

176   In section 107(7) (transmedian fields) for "Chapter V of Part XII of the Taxes Act 1988" substitute "Chapter 16A of Part 2 of the Income Tax (Trading and Other Income) Act 2005".

Finance Act 1982 (c. 39)

177   FA 1982 is amended as follows.

178   In section 134(1) (alternative valuation of ethane used for petrochemical purposes) for "Chapter V of Part XII of the Taxes Act 1988" substitute "Chapter 16A of Part 2 of the Income Tax (Trading and Other Income) Act 2005".

179   In Schedule 19 (supplementary provisions relating to advance petroleum revenue tax) omit paragraph 10(7).

Income and Corporation Taxes Act 1988 (c. 1)

180   ICTA is amended as follows.

181   Omit section 493(1) to (6) (valuation of oil disposed of or appropriated in certain circumstances).

182   Omit section 495 (regional development grants).

183   Omit section 496 (tariff receipts and tax-exempt tariffing receipts).

184   Omit section 502(1) and (2) (interpretation of Chapter 5).

Finance Act 1991 (c. 31)

185   FA 1991 is amended as follows.

186   Omit sections 62 to 65 (abandonment guarantees and abandonment expenditure).

Finance Act 1999 (c. 16)

187   FA 1999 is amended as follows.

188   In section 98(7) (qualifying assets) for paragraphs (b) and (c) substitute —
          "(ba)   Chapter 16A of Part 2 of the Income Tax (Trading and Other Income) Act 2005 (oil activities)."

Income Tax (Trading and Other Income) Act 2005 (c. 5)

189   ITTOIA 2005 is amended as follows.

1258
Taxation (International and Other Provisions) Act 2010 (c. 8)
Schedule 8 — Minor and consequential amendments
Part 6 — Oil activities

190   In section 16(3) (oil extraction and related activities) for "section 502(1) of ICTA" substitute "sections 225A and 225B".

191   In Part 2 of Schedule 4 (index of defined expressions) at the appropriate places insert—

"abandonment guarantee (in Chapter 16A of Part 2)	section 225N(6)"
"chargeable period (in Chapter 16A of Part 2)	section 225E"
"contributing participator (in Chapter 16A of Part 2)	section 225R(3)"
"the defaulter (in Chapter 16A of Part 2)	section 225R(3)"
"default payment (in Chapter 16A of Part 2)	section 225R(3)"
"designated area (in Chapter 16A of Part 2)	section 225E"
"the guarantor (in Chapter 16A of Part 2)	section 225N(6)"
"oil (in Chapter 16A of Part 2)	section 225E"
"oil extraction activities (in Chapter 16A of Part 2)	section 225A"
"oil field (in Chapter 16A of Part 2)	section 225E"
"oil rights (in Chapter 16A of Part 2)	section 225B"
"OTA 1975 (in Chapter 16A of Part 2)	section 225E"
"participator (in Chapter 16A of Part 2)	section 225E"
"the relevant participator (in Chapter 16A of Part 2)	section 225N(6)"
"ring fence income (in Chapter 16A of Part 2)	section 225C"
"ring fence trade (in Chapter 16A of Part 2)	section 225D"

Income Tax Act 2007 (c. 3)

192   ITA 2007 is amended as follows.

193   In section 80(3) (ring fence income) for "same meaning as in Chapter 5 of Part 12 of ICTA (see section 502 of that Act)" substitute "meaning given by sections 225A and 225B of ITTOIA 2005".

PART 7

ALTERNATIVE FINANCE ARRANGEMENTS

Finance Act 1986 (c. 41)

194   FA 1986 is amended as follows.

Taxation (International and Other Provisions) Act 2010 (c. 8) 1259
Schedule 8 – Minor and consequential amendments
Part 7 – Alternative finance arrangements

195   In section 78(7)(d) (loan capital) –
        (a)   for "which fall within section 48A of the Finance Act 2005" substitute "to which section 564G of the Income Tax Act 2007", and
        (b)   after "bonds)" insert "applies".

196   In section 79 (loan capital: new provisions) –
        (a)   in subsection (6), as it has effect by virtue of subsection (8A)(a) of that section, for "section 48A(1) of the Finance Act 2005", in both places, substitute "section 564G(1) of the Income Tax Act 2007", and
        (b)   in subsection (8A)(b) for "section 48A of the Finance Act 2005" substitute "section 564G of the Income Tax Act 2007".

197   In section 99(9A) (interpretation) –
        (a)   for "falling within section 48A of the Finance Act 2005" substitute "to which section 564G of the Income Tax Act 2007", and
        (b)   after "bonds)" insert "applies".

Taxation of Chargeable Gains Act 1992 (c. 12)

198   TCGA 1992 is amended as follows.

199   In section 99(2) (application of Act to unit trust schemes) for "section 99A" substitute "sections 99A and 151W(a)".

200   In section 117 (meaning of "qualifying corporate bond") for subsection (6D) substitute –

        "(6D)   Section 151T provides for arrangements to which section 151N (alternative finance arrangements: investment bond arrangements) applies also to be a corporate bond for the purposes of this section."

201   Omit section 151F (treatment of alternative finance arrangements).

202   In the Table in section 288(8) (interpretation), in the entry for "unit trust scheme" and "unit holder", for "and 99A" substitute ", 99A and 151W(a)".

Income Tax (Earnings and Pensions) Act 2003 (c. 1)

203   ITEPA 2003 is amended as follows.

204   In section 420(1) (meaning of securities etc) for paragraph (h) and the "and" immediately preceding it substitute "and
        (h)   arrangements to which section 564G of ITA 2007 (alternative finance arrangements: investment bond arrangements) applies."

Finance Act 2003 (c. 14)

205   FA 2003 is amended as follows.

206   In section 71A(8) (alternative property finance: land sold to a financial institution and leased to individual) for "section 46 of the Finance Act 2005" substitute "section 564B of the Income Tax Act 2007".

207   In section 72(7) (alternative property finance in Scotland: land sold to a financial institution and leased to individual) for "section 46 of the Finance Act 2005" substitute "section 564B of the Income Tax Act 2007".

1260

Taxation (International and Other Provisions) Act 2010 (c. 8)
Schedule 8 — Minor and consequential amendments
Part 7 — Alternative finance arrangements

208   In section 72A(8) (alternative property finance in Scotland: land sold to a financial institution and individual in common) for "section 46 of the Finance Act 2005" substitute "section 564B of the Income Tax Act 2007".

209   In section 73(5)(a) (alternative property finance: land sold to a financial institution and resold to individual) for "section 46 of the Finance Act 2005" substitute "section 564B of the Income Tax Act 2007".

210   In section 73C (alternative finance investment bonds) for "falling within section 48A of the Finance Act 2005 (alternative finance investment bonds)" substitute "to which section 564G of the Income Tax Act 2007 or section 151N of the Taxation of Chargeable Gains Act 1992 (investment bond arrangements) applies".

Income Tax (Trading and Other Income) Act 2005 (c. 5)

211   ITTOIA 2005 is amended as follows.

212   In Part 2 of Schedule 4 (index of defined expressions) insert at the appropriate place —

"interest	section 564M of ITA 2007"

Finance Act 2005 (c. 7)

213   FA 2005 is amended as follows.

214   Omit sections 46 to 47A, 48(1), 48A, 48B(1) to (5) and (9) and 49 to 57 (alternative finance arrangements).

215   In Schedule 2 (alternative finance arrangements: further provisions) omit paragraphs 1, 8 and 10 to 13.

Finance Act 2006 (c. 25)

216   FA 2006 is amended as follows.

217   Omit section 97 (beneficial loans to employees).

218   Omit section 98 (orders amending Chapter 5 of Part 2 of FA 2005).

Income Tax Act 2007 (c. 3)

219   ITA 2007 is amended as follows.

220   In section 2 (overview of Act) after subsection (10) insert —

"(10A)   Part 10A is about alternative finance arrangements."

221   In section 383(6) (relief for interest payments) —
       (a)   for "section 51(2) of FA 2005" substitute "section 564O", and
       (b)   for "falling within section 47 of that Act" substitute "to which section 564C applies".

222   In section 849(4) (interaction with other Income Tax Acts provisions) for the words from the beginning to "make" substitute "Section 564Q (deduction of income tax at source under this Part) makes".

Taxation (International and Other Provisions) Act 2010 (c. 8)
Schedule 8 – Minor and consequential amendments
Part 7 – Alternative finance arrangements

1261

223   In Schedule 4 (index of expressions defined in that Act) insert at the appropriate place—

| "alternative finance arrangements (in Part 10A) | section 564A(2)" |
| "alternative finance return (in Part 10A) | sections 564I to 564L" |

Corporation Tax Act 2009 (c. 4)

224   CTA 2009 is amended as follows.

225   Omit section 521 (power to extend Chapter 6 of Part 6 of CTA 2009 etc to other arrangements).

226   Omit section 1310(5) (orders and regulations).

Finance Act 2009 (c. 10)

227   FA 2009 is amended as follows.

228   In section 123 (alternative finance investment bonds) for "falling within section 48A of FA 2005 (alternative finance investment bonds)" substitute "to which section 564G of ITA 2007 or section 151N of TCGA 1992 (investment bond arrangements) applies".

229 (1) Amend Schedule 61 (alternative finance investment bonds) as follows.

   (2) In paragraph 1(1) (interpretation) in the definition of "alternative finance investment bond" for "within section 48A of FA 2005 (alternative finance investment bond: introduction)" substitute "to which section 564G of ITA 2007 or section 151N of TCGA 1992 (investment bond arrangements) applies".

   (3) For paragraph 2 (issue, transfer and redemption of rights under bond not to be treated as chargeable transaction) substitute—

       "2   Section 564S of ITA 2007 (treatment of bond-holder and bond-issuer) applies for the purposes of any enactment about stamp duty land tax as it applies for the purposes of the Income Tax Acts."

   (4) In paragraph 4(1) for "section 48B(2) of FA 2005" substitute "section 564S of ITA 2007".

PART 8

LEASING ARRANGEMENTS: FINANCE LEASES AND LOANS

Taxation of Chargeable Gains Act 1992 (c. 12)

230   The Taxation of Chargeable Gains Act 1992 is amended as follows.

231   In section 37 (consideration chargeable to tax on income) at the end of

1262   *Taxation (International and Other Provisions) Act 2010 (c. 8)*
Schedule 8 – Minor and consequential amendments
Part 8 – Leasing arrangements: finance leases and loans

subsection (2) add—

"See also section 37A(4) and (5) (consideration on disposal of certain leases)."

Finance Act 1997 (c. 16)

232 (1) FA 1997 is amended as follows.

(2) Omit section 82 (finance leases and loans).

(3) In Schedule 12 (leasing arrangements: finance leases and loans) omit paragraphs 1 to 7, 9 to 17 and 20 to 30.

Capital Allowances Act 2001 (c. 2)

233   The Capital Allowances Act 2001 is amended as follows.

234   In section 60(1)(c) (meaning of "disposal receipt") for "paragraph 11" to "sum)" substitute "section 614BS of ITA 2007".

235   In section 420(b) (meaning of "disposal receipt") for "paragraph 11" to "sum)" substitute "section 614BS of ITA 2007".

236   In section 476(1)(b) (disposal value of patent rights) for "paragraph 11" to "sum)" substitute "section 614BS of ITA 2007".

Income Tax Act 2007 (c. 3)

237   The Income Tax Act 2007 is amended as follows.

238   In section 2 (overview of Act) after subsection (11) insert—

"(11A)   Part 11A is about leasing arrangements involving finance leases or loans."

239   In Schedule 4 (index of defined expressions) at the appropriate places insert—

"accountancy rental earnings (in Part 11A)	section 614AB(1)"
"accountancy rental excess (in Chapter 2 of Part 11A)	section 614BH(1) to (4)"
"accountancy rental excess (in Chapter 3 of Part 11A)	section 614BH(1) to (4), as it has effect as a result of section 614CD"
"asset (in Part 11A)	section 614DG"
"asset representing the leased asset (in Part 11A)	section 614DD"
"cumulative accountancy rental excess (in Chapter 2 of Part 11A)	section 614BH(5)"

Taxation (International and Other Provisions) Act 2010 (c. 8)
Schedule 8 — Minor and consequential amendments
Part 8 — Leasing arrangements: finance leases and loans

1263

"cumulative accountancy rental excess (in Chapter 3 of Part 11A)	section 614BH(5), as it has effect as a result of section 614CD"
"cumulative normal rental excess (in Chapter 2 of Part 11A)	section 614BJ(5)"
"cumulative normal rental excess (in Chapter 3 of Part 11A)	section 614BJ(5), as it has effect as a result of section 614CD"
"the current lessor (in Part 11A)	section 614DG"
"finance lessor (in Part 11A)	section 614DG"
"for accounting purposes (in Part 11A)	section 614DG"
"lease (in Part 11A)	section 614DG"
"the leasing arrangements (in Part 11A)	section 614DG"
"the lessee (in Part 11A)	section 614DG"
"the lessor (in Part 11A)	section 614DG"
"major lump sum (in Part 11A)	section 614BC(5)"
"normal rent (in Part 11A)	section 614AA"
"normal rental excess (in Chapter 2 of Part 11A)	section 614BJ(1) to (4)"
"normal rental excess (in Chapter 3 of Part 11A)	section 614BJ(1) to (4), as it has effect as a result of section 614CD"
"pay (in Part 11A)	section 614DG"
"period of account (in Part 11A)	section 614DB(1) to (3)"
"post-25 November 1996 scheme (in Part 11A)	section 614D(1)(b)"
"pre-26 November 1996 scheme (in Part 11A)	section 614D(1)(a)"
"related period of account (in Part 11A)	section 614DB(5)"
"related tax year (in Part 11A)	section 614DB(4)"
"rent (in Part 11A)	section 614DG"
"the rental earnings (in Part 11A)	section 614AC"
"sum (in Part 11A)	section 614DG"

1264

Taxation (International and Other Provisions) Act 2010 (c. 8)
Schedule 8 — Minor and consequential amendments
Part 9 — Sale and lease-back etc

PART 9

SALE AND LEASE-BACK ETC

Income and Corporation Taxes Act 1988 (c. 1)

240   ICTA is amended as follows.

241   Omit section 24 (which has come to apply only for the interpretation of section 780 of ICTA).

242   Omit sections 779 to 785 (sale and lease-back etc).

Taxation of Chargeable Gains Act 1992 (c. 12)

243   TCGA 1992 is amended as follows.

244   In Schedule 8 (leases) in paragraph 9(2) (gain reduced by amount on which income tax charged by reference to a capital sum) for "section 785 of the Taxes Act" substitute "section 681DM of ITA 2007".

Broadcasting Act 1996 (c. 55)

245   The Broadcasting Act 1996 is amended as follows.

246 (1) Amend Schedule 7 (transfer schemes: taxation provisions) as follows.

     (2) In paragraph 22(1) after "reliefs)" insert ", and sections 681AD and 681AE of the Income Tax Act 2007 (which make corresponding provision),".

     (3) In paragraph 22(2) —
          (a) before "and" insert "or section 681AA or 681AB of the Income Tax Act 2007", and
          (b) after the second occurrence of "2010" (which is inserted by CTA 2010) insert "or section 681AM of the Income Tax Act 2007".

     (4) In paragraph 23(1) after "consideration)" insert ", and Chapter 2 of Part 12A of the Income Tax Act 2007 (which makes corresponding provision),".

     (5) In paragraph 23(3) before "and sub-paragraph (2)" insert ", or section 681BA of the Income Tax Act 2007,".

     (6) In paragraph 24(1) after "others)" insert "and Chapter 4 of Part 12A of the Income Tax Act 2007 (which makes corresponding provision),".

     (7) In paragraph 24(2) for "leases: special cases)" substitute "lease of trading asset), and section 681CC of the Income Tax Act 2007 (which makes corresponding provision),".

     (8) For paragraph 24(3) substitute —

          "(3) In sub-paragraph (1) —
                    "lease" has the meaning given by section 884 of the Corporation Tax Act 2010 or section 681DN of the Income Tax Act 2007, and
                    "relevant asset" has the meaning given by section 885 of the Corporation Tax Act 2010 or section 681DO of the Income Tax Act 2007.

Taxation (International and Other Provisions) Act 2010 (c. 8)
Schedule 8 — Minor and consequential amendments
Part 9 — Sale and lease-back etc

1265

    (4) In sub-paragraph (2)—

"lease" has the meaning given by section 868 of the Corporation Tax Act 2010 or section 681CF of the Income Tax Act 2007, and

"relevant asset" has the meaning given by section 869 of the Corporation Tax Act 2010 or section 681CG of the Income Tax Act 2007."

Finance Act 1999 (c. 16)

247   FA 1999 is amended as follows.

248   In section 97(6), in the definition of "lease", for "sections 781 to 784 of the Taxes Act 1988" substitute "Chapter 3 of Part 19 of CTA 2010 (see section 868)".

Greater London Authority Act 1999 (c. 29)

249   The Greater London Authority Act 1999 is amended as follows.

250 (1) Amend paragraph 13 of Schedule 33 (taxation provisions: public-private partnership agreements: sale and leasebacks) as follows.

    (2) In sub-paragraph (1) before "shall" insert ", nor any of sections 681AD, 681AE and 681CC of the Income Tax Act 2007 (which make corresponding provision),".

    (3) In sub-paragraph (2) for "that Act" substitute "the Corporation Tax Act 2010 and Chapter 4 of Part 12A of the Income Tax Act 2007".

Transport Act 2000 (c. 38)

251   The Transport Act 2000 is amended as follows.

252   In paragraph 15 of Schedule 7 (transfer schemes: tax: leased assets)—
      (a) in sub-paragraph (1) before "(assets" insert "or Chapter 4 of Part 12A of the Income Tax Act 2007", and
      (b) in sub-paragraph (2) for "that Act" substitute "the Corporation Tax Act 2010 and section 681DI of the Income Tax Act 2007".

Income Tax (Trading and Other Income) Act 2005 (c. 5)

253   ITTOIA 2005 is amended as follows.

254 (1) Amend section 49 (car or motor cycle hire: supplementary) as follows.

    (2) In subsection (2)(a) omit "(see subsection (3))".

    (3) For subsections (3) to (5) substitute—

      "(3) For this purpose "hire-purchase agreement" has the meaning given by section 998A of ITA 2007."

255   In section 100(4) (meaning of sale and lease-back arrangement) after "as is described in" insert "section 681AA(1) or (2), 681AB(1) or (2) or 681BA of ITA 2007 or".

1266   *Taxation (International and Other Provisions) Act 2010 (c. 8)*
Schedule 8 — Minor and consequential amendments
Part 9 — Sale and lease-back etc

Income Tax Act 2007 (c. 3)

256   ITA 2007 is amended as follows.

257   In section 2 (overview of Act) after subsection (12) insert—

"(12A)   Part 12A is about sale and lease-back etc."

258   In section 989 at the appropriate place insert—
               ""hire-purchase agreement" is to be read in accordance with section 998A,".

259   After section 998 insert—

"998A Meaning of "hire-purchase agreement"

(1)   This section applies for the purposes of the provisions of the Income Tax Acts which apply this section.

(2)   A hire-purchase agreement is an agreement in whose case each of conditions A to C is met.

(3)   Condition A is that under the agreement goods are bailed (or in Scotland hired) in return for periodical payments by the person to whom they are bailed (or hired).

(4)   Condition B is that under the agreement the property in the goods will pass to the person to whom they are bailed (or hired) if the terms of the agreement are complied with and one or more of the following events occurs—

      (a)   the exercise of an option to purchase by that person,

      (b)   the doing of another specified act by any party to the agreement,

      (c)   the happening of another specified event.

(5)   Condition C is that the agreement is not a conditional sale agreement.

(6)   In subsection (5) "conditional sale agreement" means an agreement for the sale of goods under which—

      (a)   the purchase price or part of it is payable by instalments, and

      (b)   the property in the goods is to remain in the seller (even though they are to be in the possession of the buyer) until conditions specified in the agreement are met (whether as to the payment of instalments or otherwise)."

260 (1)   Amend section 1016(2) (table of provisions to which section applies) as follows.

(2)   In Part 2 of the table at the appropriate place insert—

"Section 681BB(8) and (9)	New lease after assignment or surrender"

Taxation (International and Other Provisions) Act 2010 (c. 8)
Schedule 8 — Minor and consequential amendments
Part 9 — Sale and lease-back etc

1267

(3) In Part 2 of the table at the appropriate place insert—

"Section 681DD	Leased assets: capital sums"

(4) In Part 3 of the table omit the entry for section 780(3A)(a) of ICTA.

(5) In Part 3 of the table omit the entry for section 781(1) of ICTA.

261   In Schedule 4 (index of defined expressions) at the appropriate places insert—

"associated (in Chapter 1 of Part 12A)	section 681AM"
"associates (in Chapter 4 of Part 12A)	section 681DL"
"capital sum (in Chapter 4 of Part 12A)	section 681DM"
"deduction by way of relevant income tax relief (in Chapter 1 of Part 12A)	section 681AC(1)"
"deduction by way of relevant income tax relief (in Chapter 2 of Part 12A)	section 681BK"
"deduction by way of relevant tax relief (in Chapter 4 of Part 12A)	section 681DP"
"dispositions of interests in land outside the United Kingdom (in Chapter 1 of Part 12A)	section 681AN"
"interests in land outside the United Kingdom (in Chapter 1 of Part 12A)	section 681AN"
"lease (in Chapter 1 of Part 12A)	section 681AL(2)"
"lease (in Chapter 2 of Part 12A)	section 681BM(2), (3)"
"lease (in Chapter 3 of Part 12A)	section 681CF"
"lease (in Chapter 4 of Part 12A)	section 681DN"
"lessee (in Chapter 2 of Part 12A)	section 681BM(4)"
"lessor (in Chapter 2 of Part 12A)	section 681BM(4)"
"linked (in relation to a person) (in Chapter 2 of Part 12A)	section 681BL"
"relevant asset (in Chapter 3 of Part 12A)	section 681CG"
"relevant asset (in Chapter 4 of Part 12A)	section 681DO"
"relevant deduction from earnings (in Chapter 1 of Part 12A)	section 681AC(2)"
"rent (in Chapter 1 of Part 12A)	section 681AL(3), (4)"
"rent (in Chapter 2 of Part 12A)	section 681BM(5)"

1268

Taxation (International and Other Provisions) Act 2010 (c. 8)
Schedule 8 — Minor and consequential amendments
Part 9 — Sale and lease-back etc

"sum obtained in respect of an interest in an asset (in Chapter 4 of Part 12A)	section 681DG"
"sum obtained in respect of the lessee's interest in a lease of an asset (in Chapter 4 of Part 12A)	section 681DH".

Corporation Tax Act 2009 (c. 4)

262   CTA 2009 is amended as follows.

263   In section 97(4) (meaning of sale and lease-back arrangement) after "as is described in" insert "section 681AA(1) or (2) or 681AB(1) or (2) of ITA 2007 or".

PART 10

FACTORING OF INCOME ETC

Income and Corporation Taxes Act 1988 (c. 1)

264   ICTA is amended as follows.

265   Omit sections 774A to 774G (factoring of income receipts etc).

266   Omit section 786 (transactions associated with loans or credit).

Taxation of Chargeable Gains Act 1992 (c. 12)

267   TCGA 1992 is amended as follows.

268 (1) Amend section 263E (structured finance arrangements) as follows.

     (2) In subsection (1)(a) for "section 774B of the Taxes Act" substitute "section 809BZB or 809BZC of ITA 2007".

     (3) In subsection (6) in the definition of "the borrower" for "section 774A of the Taxes Act" substitute "the defining section".

     (4) In subsection (6) after the definition of "the borrower" insert—
              ""the defining section" in relation to a structured finance arrangement—
                 (a) means section 809BZA of ITA 2007 if it is section 809BZB or 809BZC of ITA 2007 that applies in relation to the arrangement, and
                 (b) means section 758 of CTA 2010 if it is section 759 or 760 of CTA 2010 that applies in relation to the arrangement,".

     (5) In subsection (6) in the definition of "the lender" for "that section" substitute "the defining section".

     (6) In subsection (6) in the definition of "security" for "subsection (2)(c) and (d) of that section" substitute "subsection (2)(b) and (c) of the defining section".

Taxation (International and Other Provisions) Act 2010 (c. 8)   **1269**
Schedule 8 — Minor and consequential amendments
Part 10 — Factoring of income etc

Income Tax (Trading and Other Income) Act 2005 (c. 5)

269   ITTOIA 2005 is amended as follows.

270   After section 281 insert—

"281A Sums to which sections 277 to 281 do not apply

   (1)   This section applies if a grant of a lease constitutes a disposal of an asset for the purposes of section 809BZA(2)(b) or 809BZF(2)(a) of ITA 2007 (disposals under finance arrangements).

   (2)   Sections 277 to 281 do not apply in relation to a premium paid in respect of the grant."

Income Tax Act 2007 (c. 3)

271   ITA 2007 is amended as follows.

272   In section 2(13) (overview of Part 13) omit the "or" after paragraph (e), and after paragraph (f) insert—
            "(g)   finance arrangements (Chapter 5B),
            (h)   loan or credit transactions (Chapter 5C),".

273   For section 809AZE (transfers of income streams: exception for transfer by way of security) substitute—

"809AZE Exception: transfer by way of security

   (1)   This Chapter does not apply if—
         (a)   the consideration for the transfer is the advance under a type 1 finance arrangement, and
         (b)   the transferor is, or is a member of a partnership which is, the borrower in relation to the arrangement.

   (2)   This Chapter does not apply if—
         (a)   the consideration for the transfer is the advance under a type 2 finance arrangement or a type 3 finance arrangement, and
         (b)   the transferor is a member of the partnership which receives that advance under the arrangement.

   (3)   In this section—
         "type 1 finance arrangement" has the meaning given for the purposes of Chapter 5B by section 809BZA,
         "type 2 finance arrangement" has the meaning given for the purposes of Chapter 5B by section 809BZF, and
         "type 3 finance arrangement" has the meaning given for the purposes of Chapter 5B by section 809BZJ."

274 (1)   Amend section 1016(2) (table of provisions to which section applies) as follows.

1270
Taxation (International and Other Provisions) Act 2010 (c. 8)
Schedule 8 — Minor and consequential amendments
Part 10 — Factoring of income etc

(2) In Part 2 of the table at the appropriate place insert—

"Section 809CZC(2)	Income transferred under a loan or credit transaction"

(3) In Part 3 of the table omit the entry for section 786(5)(a) of ICTA.

275   In Schedule 4 (index of defined expressions) at the appropriate places insert—

"accounts (in Chapter 5B of Part 13)	section 809BZQ"
"arrangements (in Chapter 5B of Part 13)	section 809BZR"
"disposal of an asset (in Chapter 5B of Part 13)	section 809BZS(3)"
"payments in respect of an asset (in Chapter 5B of Part 13)	section 809BZS(4)"
"person involved in a relevant change (in Chapter 5B of Part 13)	section 809BZG(5)"
"person receiving an asset (in Chapter 5B of Part 13)	section 809BZS(2)"
"relevant change in relation to a partnership (in Chapter 5B of Part 13)	section 809BZG"
"type 1 finance arrangement (in Chapter 5B of Part 13)	section 809BZA"
"type 2 finance arrangement (in Chapter 5B of Part 13)	section 809BZF"
"type 3 finance arrangement (in Chapter 5B of Part 13)	section 809BZJ".

PART 11

UK REPRESENTATIVES OF NON-UK RESIDENTS

Finance Act 1995 (c. 4)

276   FA 1995 is amended as follows.

277   Omit section 126 (UK representatives of non-residents).

278   Omit section 127 (persons not treated as UK representatives).

279   Omit Schedule 23 (obligations etc imposed on UK representatives).

Taxation (International and Other Provisions) Act 2010 (c. 8)
Schedule 8 – Minor and consequential amendments
Part 11 – UK representatives of non-UK residents

1271

Income Tax Act 2007 (c. 3)

280   ITA 2007 is amended as follows.

281   In section 2(14) (overview of Act) —

  (a)   omit the "and" immediately after paragraph (b), and

  (b)   after paragraph (b) insert —

      "(ba)   rules about UK representatives of non-UK residents (Chapters 2B and 2C),".

282   In section 813(2) (meaning of "disregarded income") for "section 126 of, and Schedule 23 to, FA 1995 (UK representatives of non-UK residents)" substitute "Chapter 2B".

283 (1) Amend section 817 (independent broker conditions) as follows.

  (2) In subsection (3) omit "by the broker".

  (3) In subsection (5) for "section 126 of, and Schedule 23 to, FA 1995" substitute "Chapter 2B of this Part, or of Chapter 1 of Part 7A of TCGA 1992,".

284   In section 824 (application of 20% rule to collective investment schemes) at the end of subsection (2) insert "(so far as the transaction is one in respect of which such amounts so arise or accrue)".

285 (1) Amend section 1014(2) (orders and regulations to which section does not apply) as follows.

  (2) Omit paragraph (ba).

  (3) In paragraph (g) —

  (a)   omit the word "and" at the end of sub-paragraph (iib), and

  (b)   after that sub-paragraph insert —

      "(iic)   section 835S(4) (meaning of "investment transaction"), and".

286   In Schedule 4 (index of defined expressions) at the appropriate places insert —

"beneficial entitlement (in Chapter 2B of Part 14)	section 835O(4)"
"branch or agency (in Chapter 2B of Part 14)	section 835S(2)"
"independent agent (in Chapter 2C of Part 14)	section 835Y"
"the independent broker conditions (in Chapter 2B of Part 14)	section 835L"
"the independent investment manager conditions (in Chapter 2B of Part 14)	section 835M"
"investment manager (in Chapter 2B of Part 14)	section 835S(3)"

1272   *Taxation (International and Other Provisions) Act 2010 (c. 8)*
Schedule 8 − Minor and consequential amendments
Part 11 − UK representatives of non-UK residents

"investment transaction (in Chapter 2B of Part 14)	section 835S(4)"
"qualifying period (in Chapter 2B of Part 14)	section 835O(2)"
"relevant disregarded income (in Chapter 2B of Part 14)	section 835O(3)"

PART 12

AMENDMENTS FOR PURPOSES CONNECTED WITH OTHER TAX LAW REWRITE ACTS

Solicitors (Northern Ireland) Order 1976 (S.I. 1976/582 (N.I. 12))

287   The Solicitors (Northern Ireland) Order 1976 is amended as follows.

288   In paragraph 38(3) of Schedule 1A for the words from the beginning to "1988" substitute "In sections 748(4), 749 and 771(5) and (6) of the Income Tax Act 2007".

Administration of Justice Act 1985 (c. 61)

289   The Administration of Justice Act 1985 is amended as follows.

290   In paragraph 36(3) of Schedule 2 for "749," substitute "748(4), 749 and".

Income and Corporation Taxes Act 1988 (c. 1)

291   ICTA is amended as follows.

292   Omit section 59(3) and (4) (person answerable for tax charged in accordance with section 12 of ITTOIA 2005 on profits of markets or fairs, or on tolls, fisheries or other profits not distrainable).

Broadcasting Act 1996 (c. 55)

293   The Broadcasting Act 1996 is amended as follows.

294 (1)   Amend paragraph 19 of Schedule 7 (no profit or loss by reason of a direct disposal transfer) as follows.

(2)   For the words from the beginning of the paragraph to "accrue to the BBC" substitute "In determining for the purposes of Part 3 of the Corporation Tax Act 2009 the profits or losses of a trade or part of a trade carried on by the BBC wholly or partly in the United Kingdom, it is to be assumed that no profits or losses arise to the BBC".

(3)   In sub-paragraph (a) for "section 100 of the Taxes Act 1988" substitute "section 163 of the Corporation Tax Act 2009".

(4)   In the italic heading preceding the paragraph for "Case I of Schedule D" substitute "Part 3 of the Corporation Tax Act 2009".

Greater London Authority Act 1999 (c. 29)

295   The Greater London Authority Act 1999 is amended as follows.

Taxation (International and Other Provisions) Act 2010 (c. 8) 1273
Schedule 8 — Minor and consequential amendments
Part 12 — Amendments for purposes connected with other tax law rewrite Acts

296 In paragraph 7 of Schedule 33 (taxation provisions: revenue nature of payments under public-private partnership agreements) —
  (a) in sub-paragraph (a) for "Case I of Schedule D" substitute "Part 3 of the Corporation Tax Act 2009", and
  (b) in sub-paragraph (b) for "Case I of Schedule D" substitute "Part 3 of the Corporation Tax Act 2009".

Income Tax (Earnings and Pensions) Act 2003 (c. 1)

297 ITEPA 2003 is amended as follows.

298 In section 211(2) (which refers to section 215, which in turn now refers to section 776(1) of ITTOIA 2005 in place of section 331(1) of ICTA) for "section 331 of ICTA" substitute "section 776(1) of ITTOIA 2005".

299 In section 215 (which now refers to section 776(1) of ITTOIA 2005 in place of section 331(1) of ICTA) in the title for "section 331 of ICTA" substitute "section 776(1) of ITTOIA 2005".

300 In section 331(1) (Part 5 is to be read with section 835(3) and (4) of ICTA) for "section 835(3) and (4) of ICTA" substitute "section 25(1) to (3) of ITA 2007".

Finance Act 2004 (c. 12)

301 FA 2004 is amended as follows.

302 (1) Amend section 318 (interpretation of Part 7) as follows.

  (2) In subsection (1) —
    (a) after the definition of "arrangements" insert —
      ""company" has the meaning given by section 1121 of the Corporation Tax Act 2010;", and
    (b) after the definition of "tax" insert —
      ""trade" includes every venture in the nature of trade."

  (3) Omit subsection (2).

Finance Act 2005 (c. 7)

303 FA 2005 is amended as follows.

304 Omit section 48B(6) to (8) (alternative finance arrangements: alternative finance investment bonds).

305 In Schedule 2 (alternative finance arrangements: further provisions) omit paragraph 9.

Income Tax Act 2007 (c. 3)

306 ITA 2007 is amended as follows.

307 In section 887(4) (industrial and provident society payments) for "section 486(7) of ICTA" substitute "section 500(2) of CTA 2009".

Corporation Tax Act 2009 (c. 4)

308 CTA 2009 is amended as follows.

1274   *Taxation (International and Other Provisions) Act 2010 (c. 8)*
Schedule 8 — Minor and consequential amendments
Part 12 — Amendments for purposes connected with other tax law rewrite Acts

309   Before section 1 insert—

"A1   Overview of the Corporation Tax Acts

(1)   The main Acts relating to corporation tax are—

     (a)   this Act (which covers the ground described in section 1),

     (b)   CTA 2010 (which covers the ground described in section 1 of that Act), and

     (c)   TCGA 1992 (so far as relating to chargeable gains accruing to a company in respect of which the company is chargeable to corporation tax).

(2)   Enactments relating to corporation tax are also contained in other Acts: see in particular—

     (a)   Chapter 1 of Part 12 of ICTA (insurance companies),

     (b)   Chapter 4 of Part 17 of that Act (controlled foreign companies),

     (c)   Schedule 18 to FA 1998 (company tax returns, assessments and related matters),

     (d)   Schedule 22 to FA 2000 (tonnage tax),

     (e)   CAA 2001 (allowances for capital expenditure),

     (f)   Part 2 of TIOPA 2010 (double taxation relief),

     (g)   Parts 4 and 5 of that Act (transfer pricing and advance pricing agreements),

     (h)   Part 6 of that Act (tax arbitrage),

     (i)   Part 7 of that Act (tax treatment of financing costs and income), and

     (j)   Part 8 of that Act (offshore funds).

(3)   Schedule 1 to the Interpretation Act 1978 defines "the Corporation Tax Acts" as the enactments relating to the taxation of the income and chargeable gains of companies and of company distributions (including provisions relating to income tax)."

310   In section 39(2) (profits of mines, quarries and other concerns) for "clause" substitute "section".

311   In section 1269 (interpretation of sections 1267 and 1268) in the title for "clauses" substitute "sections".

312   In paragraph 75 of Schedule 2 (transitional provision and savings: investment bond arrangements) at the end insert—

     "(5)   So far as section 519(2) has effect for income tax or capital gains tax purposes in relation to the disposal after 6 April 2007 of investment bond arrangements (whenever entered into), it is treated as always having had effect."

PART 13

GENERAL

Taxes Management Act 1970 (c. 9)

313   TMA 1970 is amended as follows.

Taxation (International and Other Provisions) Act 2010 (c. 8)   **1275**
Schedule 8 — Minor and consequential amendments
Part 13 — General

314   In section 118(1) after the definition of "the 1992 Act" insert—

         ""TIOPA 2010" means the Taxation (International and Other Provisions) Act 2010,".

Income and Corporation Taxes Act 1988 (c. 1)

315   ICTA is amended as follows.

316   In section 831(3) (interpretation of ICTA) after the definition of "the Management Act" insert—

         ""TIOPA 2010" means the Taxation (International and Other Provisions) Act 2010;".

Taxation of Chargeable Gains Act 1992 (c. 12)

317   TCGA 1992 is amended as follows.

318 (1)   Amend section 287 (powers to make orders or regulations under enactments relating to the taxation of chargeable gains) as follows.

     (2)   In subsection (1) (powers to be exercisable by statutory instrument) for "subsection (2)" substitute "subsections (2) and (2A)".

     (3)   After subsection (2) insert—

         "(2A)   Subsection (1) above shall not apply in relation to any power conferred by TIOPA 2010 (see instead section 372 of that Act)."

319   In section 288(1) (interpretation) after the definition of "the Taxes Act" insert—

         ""TIOPA 2010" means the Taxation (International and Other Provisions) Act 2010;".

Finance Act 1998 (c. 36)

320   FA 1998 is amended as follows.

321 (1)   Amend Schedule 18 (company tax returns etc) as follows.

     (2)   In paragraph 25(1) (scope of enquiries) for the words from "a transfer pricing notice" to "arbitrage)" substitute "a notice within sub-paragraph (3)".

     (3)   In paragraph 25 after sub-paragraph (2) insert—

         "(3)   A notice is within this sub-paragraph if it is—

         (a)   a notice under section 184G or 184H of the Taxation of Chargeable Gains Act 1992 (avoidance involving capital losses),

         (b)   a notice under section 81(2) of TIOPA 2010 (schemes and arrangements designed to increase relief),

         (c)   a transfer pricing notice under section 168(1) of TIOPA 2010 (provision not at arm's length: medium-sized enterprise), or

         (d)   a notice under section 232 or 249 of TIOPA 2010 (avoidance involving tax arbitrage)."

1276

Taxation (International and Other Provisions) Act 2010 (c. 8)
Schedule 8 — Minor and consequential amendments
Part 13 — General

(4) In paragraph 42(2A) (disapplication of restrictions on power to make discovery assessment or determination) for the words after "return, a notice" substitute "within sub-paragraph (4)."

(5) In paragraph 42 after sub-paragraph (3) insert—

"(4) A notice is within this sub-paragraph if it is—

(a) a notice under section 184G or 184H of the Taxation of Chargeable Gains Act 1992 (avoidance involving capital losses),

(b) a notice under section 81(2) of TIOPA 2010 (schemes and arrangements designed to increase relief), or

(c) a notice under section 232 or 249 of TIOPA 2010 (avoidance involving tax arbitrage)."

(6) After paragraph 97 insert—

"Meaning of TIOPA 2010

97A In this Schedule "TIOPA 2010" means the Taxation (International and Other Provisions) Act 2010."

(7) In the list in paragraph 98 after the entry for "tax payable" insert—

"TIOPA 2010	paragraph 97A".

Income Tax (Earnings and Pensions) Act 2003 (c. 1)

322 ITEPA 2003 is amended as follows.

323 In Part 1 of Schedule 1 (abbreviations of Acts etc) after the entry for CTA 2010 (which is inserted by CTA 2010) insert—

"TIOPA 2010	The Taxation (International and Other Provisions) Act 2010".

Income Tax (Trading and Other Income) Act 2005 (c. 5)

324 ITTOIA 2005 is amended as follows.

325 In Part 1 of Schedule 4 (abbreviations of Acts) after the entry for CTA 2010 (which is inserted by CTA 2010) insert—

"TIOPA 2010	The Taxation (International and Other Provisions) Act 2010".

Income Tax Act 2007 (c. 3)

326 ITA 2007 is amended as follows.

327 In section 1014(2) (orders and regulations under the Income Tax Acts to

Taxation (International and Other Provisions) Act 2010 (c. 8)
Schedule 8 — Minor and consequential amendments
Part 13 — General

1277

which the section does not apply) for "and" after paragraph (f) substitute—
>"(fa)   TIOPA 2010 (see instead section 372 of that Act), and".

328   In section 1017 (abbreviated references to Acts) for the "and" at the end of the definition of "TCGA 1992" substitute—
>""TIOPA 2010" means the Taxation (International and Other Provisions) Act 2010, and".

Corporation Tax Act 2009 (c. 4)

329   CTA 2009 is amended as follows.

330   In section 1312 (abbreviated references to Acts) after the definition of "TCGA 1992" insert—
>""TIOPA 2010" means the Taxation (International and Other Provisions) Act 2010,".

Finance Act 2009 (c. 10)

331   FA 2009 is amended as follows.

332   In section 126(1) (abbreviated references to Acts) after the entry for TCGA 1992 insert—
>""TIOPA 2010" means the Taxation (International and Other Provisions) Act 2010,".

SCHEDULE 9

Section 377

TRANSITIONALS AND SAVINGS ETC

PART 1

GENERAL PROVISIONS

Continuity of the law: general

1   The repeal of provisions and their enactment in a rewritten form by this Act does not affect the continuity of the law.

2   Paragraph 1 does not apply to any change made by this Act in the effect of the law.

3   Any subordinate legislation or other thing which—
>(a)   has been made or done, or has effect as if made or done, under or for the purposes of a superseded enactment so far as it applied for relevant tax purposes, and
>(b)   is in force or effective immediately before the commencement of the corresponding rewritten provision,

has effect after that commencement as if made or done under or for the purposes of the rewritten provision.

4   (1) Any reference (express or implied) in this Act, another enactment or an instrument or document to a rewritten provision is to be read as including, in relation to times, circumstances or purposes in relation to which any

1278   *Taxation (International and Other Provisions) Act 2010 (c. 8)*
Schedule 9 — Transitionals and savings etc
Part 1 — General provisions

corresponding superseded enactment had effect for relevant tax purposes, a reference to the superseded enactment so far as applying for those relevant tax purposes.

(2) Any reference (express or implied) in this Act, another enactment or an instrument or document to—

(a) things done under or for the purposes of a rewritten provision, or

(b) things falling to be done under or for the purposes of a rewritten provision,

is to be read as including, in relation to times, circumstances or purposes in relation to which any corresponding superseded enactment had effect for relevant tax purposes, a reference to things done or falling to be done under or for the purposes of the superseded enactment so far as applying for those relevant tax purposes.

5 (1) Any reference (express or implied) in any enactment, instrument or document to a superseded enactment in its application for relevant tax purposes is to be read, so far as is required for those relevant tax purposes, as including, in relation to times, circumstances or purposes in relation to which any corresponding rewritten provision has effect, a reference to the rewritten provision.

(2) Any reference (express or implied) in any enactment, instrument or document to—

(a) things done under or for the purposes of a superseded enactment in its application for relevant tax purposes, or

(b) things falling to be done under or for the purposes of a superseded enactment in its application for relevant tax purposes,

is to be read, so far as is required for those relevant tax purposes, as including, in relation to times, circumstances or purposes in relation to which any corresponding rewritten provision has effect, a reference to things done or falling to be done under or for the purposes of the rewritten provision.

6 Paragraphs 1 to 5 have effect instead of section 17(2) of the Interpretation Act 1978 (but are without prejudice to any other provision of that Act).

7 Paragraphs 4 and 5 apply only so far as the context permits.

General saving for old transitional provisions and savings

8 (1) The repeal by this Act of a transitional or saving provision relating to the coming into force of a provision rewritten in this Act does not affect the operation of the transitional or saving provision, so far as it is not specifically rewritten in this Act but remains capable of having effect in relation to the corresponding provision of this Act.

(2) The repeal by this Act of an enactment previously repealed subject to savings does not affect the continued operation of those savings.

(3) The repeal by this Act of a saving on the previous repeal of an enactment does not affect the operation of the saving so far as it is not specifically rewritten in this Act but remains capable of having effect.

Taxation (International and Other Provisions) Act 2010 (c. 8)
Schedule 9 — Transitionals and savings etc
Part 1 — General provisions

1279

Interpretation

9 (1) In this Part—

"enactment" includes subordinate legislation (within the meaning of the Interpretation Act 1978),

"relevant tax purposes" means, in relation to a superseded enactment, tax purposes for which the enactment has been rewritten by this Act, and

"superseded enactment" means an earlier enactment which has been rewritten by this Act for certain tax purposes (whether it applied only for those purposes or for those and other tax purposes).

(2) References in this Part to the repeal of a provision include references to its revocation and to its express or implied disapplication for particular tax purposes.

PART 2

CHANGES IN THE LAW

10 (1) This paragraph applies if, in the case of any person—

(a) a thing is done or an event occurs before 1 April 2010, and

(b) because of a change in the law made by this Act, the corporation tax consequences of that thing or event for the relevant period are different from what they would otherwise have been.

(2) This paragraph also applies if, in the case of any person—

(a) a thing is done or an event occurs before 6 April 2010, and

(b) because of a change in the law made by this Act, the income tax consequences of that thing or event for the relevant period are different from what they would otherwise have been.

(3) If the person so elects, this Act applies with such modifications as may be necessary to secure that the consequences for that tax for that period are the same as they would have been if the change in the law had not been made.

(4) In sub-paragraphs (1) and (2) "the relevant period" means—

(a) for corporation tax purposes, any accounting period beginning before and ending on or after 1 April 2010, and

(b) for income tax purposes, any period of account beginning before and ending on or after 6 April 2010.

(5) If this paragraph applies in the case of two or more persons in relation to the same thing or event, an election made under this paragraph by any one of those persons is of no effect unless a corresponding election is made by the other or each of the others.

(6) An election under this paragraph must be made—

(a) for corporation tax purposes, not later than 2 years after the end of the accounting period, and

(b) for income tax purposes, on or before the first anniversary of the 31 January following the tax year in which the period of account ends.

1280

Taxation (International and Other Provisions) Act 2010 (c. 8)
Schedule 9 — Transitionals and savings etc
Part 3 — Double taxation relief

PART 3

DOUBLE TAXATION RELIEF

Conversion of references to the profits tax in old arrangements

11   (1) Sub-paragraph (2) applies to any arrangements —
            (a) made in relation to the profits tax (which was abolished by section 46(3) of FA 1965), and
            (b) specified in an Order in Council made —
                  (i) under section 347 of the Income Tax Act 1952, or
                  (ii) under any earlier enactment corresponding to that section.

      (2) The arrangements have effect —
            (a) in relation to corporation tax as they are expressed to have effect in relation to the profits tax (and not as they had effect in relation to income tax), and
            (b) in relation to income to which the charge to corporation tax on income applies, and in relation to gains to which the charge to corporation tax on chargeable gains applies, as they are expressed to have effect in relation to profits chargeable to the profits tax,
            but with the substitution of accounting periods for chargeable accounting periods.

      (3) Sub-paragraph (2) applies subject to any contrary provision contained in arrangements —
            (a) made after the passing of FA 1965 (which was passed on 5 August 1965), and
            (b) specified in an Order in Council made —
                  (i) under section 347 of the Income Tax Act 1952, or
                  (ii) under any later enactment corresponding to that section.

      (4) Sub-paragraph (2) applies despite section 18(5) of this Act.

Effect in relation to capital gains tax of arrangements given effect before introduction of that tax

12   Any arrangements specified in an Order in Council made under section 347 of the Income Tax Act 1952 before 5 August 1965, so far as they provide (in whatever terms) for relief from tax chargeable in the United Kingdom on capital gains, have effect in relation to capital gains tax.

Double taxation arrangements to which section 11(3) applies

13   Section 11(3) does not have effect in relation to arrangements made before 21 March 2000.

Unilateral relief for underlying tax on dividends

14   (1) Condition C in section 15 (credit for underlying tax on dividend paid to sub-10% associate) is not met if the reduction below the 10% limit took place before 1 April 1972.

      (2) Condition C in section 16 (credit for underlying tax on dividend paid by exchanged associate) is not met if the exchange took place before 1 April 1972.

Taxation (International and Other Provisions) Act 2010 (c. 8)   **1281**
Schedule 9 — Transitionals and savings etc
Part 3 — Double taxation relief

Time limits for claims for relief

15   (1)   If article 10 of the 2009 Order applies—

     (a)   section 19(2)(a) (claims for relief under section 18(2) in relation to income tax or capital gains to be made by fourth anniversary of end of tax year) has effect at times before 1 April 2012 as if for "fourth anniversary of the end of" there were substituted "fifth anniversary of the 31 January next following",

     (b)   section 19(3)(a) (claims for relief under section 18(2) in relation to corporation tax to be made within 4 years) has effect at times before 1 April 2012 as if for "4" there were substituted "6",

     (c)   section 77(3)(a) (claims for relief under section 73(1) to be made within 4 years) has effect at times before 1 April 2012 as if for "four" there were substituted "6", and

     (d)   section 43D(5) of TMA 1970 (which is inserted by Part 1 of Schedule 8 and is about claims for relief under sections 2 to 6 in relation to petroleum revenue tax) has effect at times before 1 April 2012 as if for "4 years after the end of" there were substituted "5 years after the 31 January next following".

   (2)   In sub-paragraph (1) "the 2009 Order" means the Finance Act 2008, Schedule 39 (Appointed Day, Transitional Provision and Savings) Order 2009 (S.I. 2009/403).

Taking account of underlying tax

16   In relation to distributions paid before 1 July 2009, the amount of any income or gain is not to be increased under section 31(2)(b) by so much of any underlying tax within section 31(3)(a) as represents relievable underlying tax, within the meaning of sections 806A to 806J of ICTA, arising in respect of another dividend and treated as underlying tax under those sections.

Reduction in credit: payment by reference to foreign tax

17   Section 34 does not have effect in relation to payments made before 22 April 2009.

Credit against corporation tax on trade income: anti-avoidance

18   Section 45(2) has effect in relation to a credit for foreign tax only if the credit relates to—

     (a)   a payment of foreign tax on or after 22 April 2009, or

     (b)   income received on or after that date in respect of which foreign tax has been deducted at source.

Credit against corporation tax on trade income: banks

19   Section 49 has effect in relation to a credit for foreign tax only if the credit relates to—

     (a)   a payment of foreign tax on or after 22 April 2009, or

     (b)   income received on or after that date in respect of which foreign tax has been deducted at source.

1282   *Taxation (International and Other Provisions) Act 2010 (c. 8)*
Schedule 9 — Transitionals and savings etc
Part 3 — Double taxation relief

Meaning of "relevant profits" in section 58

20   In relation to dividends paid before 1 July 2009, section 59 has effect with the following modifications —

    (a)   the omission of subsections (2) and (3),

    (b)   in subsection (4), the omission of "is not within subsection (3) but", and

    (c)   in subsection (5), the omission of "is not within subsection (3) and".

Conditions for relief for underlying tax paid by company lower in dividend-paying chain

21   Section 65(3)(a) applies with the omission of sub-paragraph (ii) if the dividend paid by the second company to the first company is paid before 22 April 2009.

Application of sections 109 and 110 in relation to pre-1 October 2007 cases

22   (1)   Section 109 does not apply in the case of a debtor repo, within the meaning given by section 548 of CTA 2009, if the arrangement mentioned in that section of that Act came into force before 1 October 2007.

    (2)   Section 110 does not apply in the case of a stock lending arrangement, within the meaning given by section 263B of TCGA 1992, under which the lender transfers securities to the borrower otherwise than by way of sale before 1 October 2007.

    (3)   This Act has effect with the modifications set out in sub-paragraphs (4) and (5), but those modifications —

        (a)   do not apply in the case of a debtor repo, within the meaning given by section 548 of CTA 2009, if the arrangement mentioned in that section comes into force on or after 1 October 2007, and

        (b)   do not apply in the case of a stock lending arrangement, within the meaning given by section 263B of TCGA 1992, under which the lender transfers securities to the borrower otherwise than by way of sale on or after 1 October 2007.

    (4)   In section 108(3) for "section 109 or 110" substitute "section 109A".

    (5)   For sections 109 and 110 substitute —

"109A Repo or stock-lending cases in which no disregard under section 108

    (1)   Tax attributable to interest accruing to a company under a loan relationship is within this section if —

        (a)   at the time when the interest accrues, the company has ceased to be a party to the relationship as a result of having made the initial transfer under or in accordance with any repo or stock-lending arrangements relating to the relationship, and

        (b)   that time is in the period for which those arrangements have effect.

    (2)   In this section "repo or stock-lending arrangements", in relation to a loan relationship, means (subject to subsection (3)) any arrangements consisting in or involving an agreement or series of agreements under which provision is made —

Taxation (International and Other Provisions) Act 2010 (c. 8)
Schedule 9 – Transitionals and savings etc
Part 3 – Double taxation relief

1283

> > (a) for the transfer from one person ("A") to another of any rights under the relationship, and
> >
> > (b) for A subsequently to be or become entitled, or required –
> >
> > > (i) to have the same or equivalent rights transferred to A, or
> > >
> > > (ii) to have rights in respect of benefits accruing in respect of the relationship on redemption.
>
> (3) Arrangements are not repo or stock-lending arrangements for the purposes of this section if they are excluded from section 730A of ICTA by section 730A(8) of ICTA.
>
> (4) For the purposes of subsection (2) rights under a loan relationship are equivalent to rights under another loan relationship if they entitle the holder of an asset representing the relationship –
>
> > (a) to the same rights against the same persons as to capital, interest and dividends, and
> >
> > (b) to the same remedies for the enforcement of those rights,
>
> despite any difference in the total nominal amounts of the assets, in the form in which they are held or in the manner in which they can be transferred.
>
> (5) In this section –
>
> > (a) "the initial transfer", in relation to any repo or stock-lending arrangements, is a reference to the transfer mentioned in subsection (2)(a), and
> >
> > (b) a reference to the period for which repo or stock-lending arrangements have effect is a reference to the period from the making of the initial transfer until whichever is the earlier of the following –
> >
> > > (i) the discharge of the obligations arising by virtue of the entitlement or requirement mentioned in subsection (2)(b), or
> > >
> > > (ii) the time when it becomes apparent that the discharge of those obligations will not take place."

Income increased by amounts paid by reference to foreign tax for which deduction allowed

23   Section 112(3) does not have effect in relation to payments made before 22 April 2009.

Offshore fund treated after 1 December 2009 as distributing fund under repealed Chapter 5 of Part 17 of ICTA

24   In paragraph 5(4)(b) of Schedule 27 to ICTA (offshore funds: distributing funds) as it has effect as a result of paragraph 3 of Schedule 1 to the Offshore Funds (Tax) Regulations 2009 (S.I. 2009/3001), the reference to section 811 of ICTA is to be treated as a reference to section 112 of this Act.

Limited effect of amendments of sections 806A to 806J of ICTA

25   The amendments in sections 806A to 806J of ICTA that are made by Part 1 of Schedule 8 have effect only in relation to distributions paid before 1 July 2009.

1284   *Taxation (International and Other Provisions) Act 2010 (c. 8)*
Schedule 9 — Transitionals and savings etc
Part 3 — Double taxation relief

Interpretative rules saved for the purposes of applying sections 806A to 806K of ICTA to distributions paid before 1 July 2009

26   (1)   Despite their repeal by this Act, the saved rules have effect for the purposes of applying sections 806A to 806K of ICTA in relation to distributions paid —

      (a)   before 1st July 2009, but

      (b)   in accounting periods ending on or after 1st April 2010.

   (2)   In this paragraph "the saved rules" means the following provisions of ICTA —

      (a)   section 788(4),

      (b)   in section 788(5), the first two sentences,

      (c)   section 790(12), and

      (d)   section 792.

   (3)   The saved rules, so far as having effect as mentioned in sub-paragraph (1), have effect with the following modifications.

   (4)   Section 788(4) of ICTA has effect as if for "by virtue of this section" there were substituted "under section 2(1) of TIOPA 2010".

   (5)   In section 788(5) of ICTA the first sentence has effect as if for the words before "any amount of tax" there were substituted "For the purposes of Chapter 2 of this Part in its application to relief under sections 2 and 6 of TIOPA 2010, but subject to section 31(4) of TIOPA 2010,".

   (6)   Section 790(12) of ICTA has effect as if for the words from the beginning to "unilateral relief," there were substituted "In Chapter 2 of this Part in its application to relief under section 18(1)(b) and (2) of TIOPA 2010,".

   (7)   Section 792(1) of ICTA has effect as if —

      (a)   for "by virtue of section 788" (in both places) there were substituted "under section 2(1) of TIOPA 2010",

      (b)   for "Chapter 7 of Part 3 of the Finance Act 2004" there were substituted "Part 3 of TIOPA 2010", and

      (c)   for "section 790" there were substituted "section 18(1)(b) and (2) of TIOPA 2010".

   (8)   Section 792 of ICTA has effect as if after subsection (3) there were (by way of relocation of provisions of section 790(3) of ICTA) inserted —

      "(4)   Any expression in this Chapter which imports a reference to relief under arrangements for the time being having effect under section 2(1) of TIOPA 2010 shall be deemed to import also a reference to unilateral relief."

Repealed references to Part 18 of ICTA saved for purposes of sections 806A to 806K of ICTA

27   (1)   Sub-paragraph (2) has effect for the purposes of applying sections 806A to 806K of ICTA in relation to distributions paid —

      (a)   before 1st July 2009, but

      (b)   in accounting periods ending on or after 1st April 2010.

   (2)   The reference to Part 2 of this Act contained in each of the provisions mentioned in sub-paragraph (3) is to be treated as including a reference to Part 18 of ICTA.

Taxation (International and Other Provisions) Act 2010 (c. 8)
Schedule 9 — Transitionals and savings etc
Part 3 — Double taxation relief

1285

(3) The provisions are —

    (a) paragraph 4(2) of Schedule 26 to ICTA (controlled foreign companies: dividends), and

    (b) sections 140H(3), 140I(3) and 140J(3) of TCGA 1992 (foreign tax not charged as a result of Mergers Directive to be treated as charged).

Part 4

Transfer pricing

Transfer pricing: meaning of potential advantage

28   Section 155(6)(b) does not have effect in relation to distributions paid before 1 July 2009.

Part 5

Advance pricing agreements

29   (1) An agreement made before 27 July 1999 cannot have effect as an advance pricing agreement for the purposes of Part 5.

    (2) Section 218(1)(c) (agreement must contain declaration that it is made for the purposes of section 218) applies in relation to an agreement made before 1 April 2010 as if after "this section" there were inserted "or a declaration that it is made for the purposes of section 85 of FA 1999".

Part 6

Tax avoidance (arbitrage)

Arbitrage: contributions to capital of UK resident companies before 16 March 2005

30   Sections 249 to 254 (tax arbitrage: receipt notices) do not apply in relation to any contribution to the capital of a UK resident company made before 16 March 2005.

Part 7

Tax treatment of financing costs and income

Periods of account in relation to which Part 7 does not have effect

31   (1) Part 7 of this Act does not have effect in relation to periods of account of the worldwide group that begin before 1 January 2010 (but see also sub-paragraphs (2) and (3)).

    (2) Sub-paragraph (3) applies in relation to a period of account of the worldwide group ("the relevant period of account") if —

        (a) the ultimate parent of the group changes the date to which financial statements of the group are drawn up,

        (b) as a result of the change, the relevant period of account —

            (i) begins before 1 January 2010, and

1286

Taxation (International and Other Provisions) Act 2010 (c. 8)
Schedule 9 — Transitionals and savings etc
Part 7 — Tax treatment of financing costs and income

    (ii)   includes a period that would, if the change had not been made, have fallen within a period of account beginning on or after that date, and

    (c)   the main purpose, or one of the main purposes, of the ultimate parent of the group in making the change is to secure that the first period of account in relation to which Part 7 has effect does not include any period falling within the relevant period of account.

(3)   The relevant period of account is treated for the purposes of sub-paragraph (1) as not beginning before 1 January 2010.

Exclusion of certain debits and credits

32   (1)   An amount that would, apart from this paragraph, meet condition A, B or C in section 313 (definition of "financing expense amount") does not meet that condition if it is a debit that, but for a relevant enactment, would be brought into account for corporation tax purposes in an accounting period beginning before 1 January 2010.

(2)   For this purpose the following are "relevant enactments" —

    (a)   section 373 of CTA 2009 (late interest treated as not accruing until paid in some cases),

    (b)   section 407 of that Act (postponement until redemption of debits for connected companies' deeply discounted securities),

    (c)   section 409 of that Act (postponement until redemption of debits for close companies' deeply discounted securities), and

    (d)   regulation 3A of the Loan Relationships and Derivative Contracts (Change of Accounting Practice) Regulations 2004 (S.I. 2004/3271) (prescribed debits and credits brought into account over prescribed period).

(3)   An amount that would, apart from this paragraph, meet condition A, B or C in section 314 (definition of "financing income amount") does not meet that condition if it is a credit that, but for the regulation mentioned in sub-paragraph (2)(d), would be brought into account for corporation tax purposes in an accounting period beginning before 1 January 2010.

PART 8

OFFSHORE FUNDS

Restriction on regulation-making power under section 354

33   (1)   Regulations under section 354 may not make provision about the treatment of a person in respect of any rights in an affected offshore fund that are acquired by the person—

    (a)   before 1 December 2009, or

    (b)   in accordance with sub-paragraph (3).

(2)   Sub-paragraph (1) is subject to paragraph 34.

(3)   Rights are acquired by a person in accordance with this sub-paragraph if—

    (a)   the rights are acquired by the person in accordance with a legally enforceable agreement in writing that was entered into by the person before 30 April 2009,

Taxation (International and Other Provisions) Act 2010 (c. 8)   1287
Schedule 9 – Transitionals and savings etc
Part 8 – Offshore funds

      (b)   in the case of a conditional agreement, the conditions are satisfied before that date, and

      (c)   the agreement is not varied on or after that date.

  (4) For the purposes of this paragraph rights of a person in a fund are rights in an affected offshore fund if—

      (a)   the fund is an offshore fund within the meaning of section 354, but

      (b)   on the date on which the person acquired them, the fund was not an offshore fund within the meaning of Chapter 5 of Part 17 of ICTA.

34   Paragraph 33 does not prevent regulations under section 354 making—

      (a)   provision for a person to elect to be treated in accordance with the regulations in respect of rights referred to in that paragraph, or

      (b)   provision that does not increase the person's liability to tax in respect of such rights.

PART 9

OIL ACTIVITIES

Regional development grants

35   In relation to periods of account (within the meaning given by section 6 of CAA 2001) beginning before 6 April 2011—

      (a)   section 225K(3)(b) of ITTOIA 2005 has effect as if—

         (i)   ", 3" were inserted after "Part 2", and

         (ii)   ", industrial buildings" were inserted after "machinery", and

      (b)   section 225L(3) and (7) of that Act have effect as if ", 3" were inserted after "Part 2".

Reimbursement by defaulter in respect of certain abandonment expenditure

36 (1) If article 10 of the 2009 Order applies, section 225T(5) of ITTOIA 2005 has effect at times before 1 April 2012 as if for "4" there were substituted "6".

  (2) In sub-paragraph (1) "the 2009 Order" means the Finance Act 2008, Schedule 39 (Appointed Day, Transitional Provision and Savings) Order 2009 (S.I. 2009/403).

PART 10

ALTERNATIVE FINANCE ARRANGEMENTS

Alternative finance arrangements entered into before certain dates etc

37 (1) The alternative finance provisions do not apply to purchase and resale arrangements entered into before 6 April 2005 or diminishing shared ownership arrangements entered into before the relevant date.

  (2) If deposit arrangements, profit share agency arrangements or investment bond arrangements were entered into before the relevant date, the alternative finance provisions only apply if alternative finance return is payable under the arrangements on or after the relevant date and then—

      (a)   apply for the purposes of income tax in relation to payments of alternative finance return under the arrangements to a person other

1288

Taxation (International and Other Provisions) Act 2010 (c. 8)
Schedule 9 — Transitionals and savings etc
Part 10 — Alternative finance arrangements

than a company on or after the relevant date (so far as relevant to the tax year 2010-11 and subsequent tax years), and

(b) if a company is a party to the arrangements, apply in relation to the company in respect of the arrangements with effect from the relevant date (so far as relevant to those tax years or, as the case may be, any accounting period ending on or after 1 April 2010).

(3) Sub-paragraph (2) is subject to sub-paragraph (4).

(4) For the purposes of income tax and capital gains tax in relation to the disposal after 6 April 2007 of investment bond arrangements (whenever entered into), the relevant provisions are treated as always having had effect.

(5) An order made under section 1005 of ITA 2007 (recognised stock exchanges: designation) that includes such provision as is mentioned in section 1005(2A) may be expressed as respects that provision —

(a) to have had effect as from 1 April 2007 for the purposes of arrangements entered into on or after that date, and

(b) for the purposes mentioned in sub-paragraph (4) as always having had effect.

(6) In this paragraph —

"alternative finance provisions" means —

(a) section 367A of ICTA 1988,

(b) Chapter 4 of Part 4 of TCGA 1992, and

(c) Part 10A and section 1005(2A) of ITA 2007,

"alternative finance return" has the same meaning as in Chapter 4 of Part 4 of TCGA 1992 (see section 151S of that Act) or Chapter 10A of ITA 2007 (see section 564L of that Act),

"deposit arrangements", "diminishing shared ownership arrangements", "investment bond arrangements", "profit share agency arrangements" and "purchase and resale arrangements" have the same meaning as in Chapter 4 of Part 4 of TCGA 1992 (see section 151H(3) of that Act) or Chapter 10A of ITA 2007 (see section 564A(3) of that Act),

"the relevant date" means —

(a) in the case of deposit arrangements, 6 April 2005,

(b) in the case of diminishing shared ownership arrangements or profit share agency arrangements, for income tax purposes 6 April 2006, and

(c) in the case of investment bond arrangements, for corporation tax purposes 1 April 2007 and for income tax and capital gains tax purposes 6 April 2007, and

"the relevant provisions" means —

(a) for income tax purposes, sections 564G, 564L(3) to (5), and 564S to 564U of ITA 2007 and section 1005(2A) of that Act so far as it relates to section 564G of that Act, and

(b) for capital gains tax purposes, sections 151N, 151S(3) and (4) and 151T to 151W of TCGA 1992 and section 1005(2A) of ITA 2007 so far as it relates to section 151N of TCGA 1992.

Taxation (International and Other Provisions) Act 2010 (c. 8)
Schedule 9 — Transitionals and savings etc
Part 10 — Alternative finance arrangements

1289

Alternative finance arrangements not offshore funds

38   So far as Chapter 5 of Part 17 of ICTA continues to apply for any purpose, references to section 354 of this Act in section 151W(b) of TCGA 1992, section 564U(b) of ITA 2007 and section 519(4)(b) of CTA 2009 are to be read for that purpose as references to that Chapter.

Alternative finance arrangements entered into before 15 October 2009

39   (1) In relation to arrangements entered into before 15 October 2009, Part 10A of ITA 2007 (alternative finance arrangements) applies with the following modifications.

        (2) In section 564B(1) (meaning of "financial institution") —
            (a)   in paragraph (e) for ", diminishing shared ownership arrangements or profit share agency arrangements" substitute "or diminishing shared ownership arrangements",
            (b)   at the end of that paragraph insert "or",
            (c)   omit paragraph (g) and "or" at the end of that paragraph, and
            (d)   omit paragraph (h).

        (3) In section 564F(1) (profit share agency arrangements) —
            (a)   in paragraph (a) for "an agent" substitute "a financial institution as agent", and
            (b)   omit paragraph (b).

40   (1) In relation to arrangements entered into before 15 October 2009, Chapter 4 of Part 4 of TCGA 1992 (alternative finance arrangements) applies with the following modifications.

        (2) In section 151I(1) (meaning of "financial institution") —
            (a)   in paragraph (e) for ", diminishing shared ownership arrangements or profit share agency arrangements" substitute "or diminishing shared ownership arrangements",
            (b)   at the end of that paragraph insert "or",
            (c)   omit paragraph (g) and "or" at the end of that paragraph, and
            (d)   omit paragraph (h).

        (3) In section 151M(1) (profit share agency arrangements) —
            (a)   in paragraph (a) for "an agent" substitute "a financial institution as agent", and
            (b)   omit paragraph (b).

PART 11

SALE AND LEASE-BACK ETC

New lease of land after assignment or surrender: right to new lease existed pre-22 June 1971

41   (1) Sub-paragraphs (2) and (3) apply if —
            (a)   each of conditions A to D in section 681BA of ITA 2007, or each of conditions A to D in section 850 of CTA 2010, is met (new lease granted to, or to person linked with, lessee under assigned or surrendered lease),

1290

Taxation (International and Other Provisions) Act 2010 (c. 8)
Schedule 9 – Transitionals and savings etc
Part 11 – Sale and lease-back etc

     (b)   condition E in that section is not met (condition that no right to new lease existed before 22 June 1971), and

     (c)   the rent under the new lease is payable by a person within the charge to income tax.

(2) No part of the rent paid under the new lease is to be treated as a payment of capital.

(3) The provisions of ITTOIA 2005 providing for deductions or allowances by way of income tax relief in respect of payments of rent apply in relation to the rent under the new lease.

(4) Section 681BM of ITA 2007 (meaning of "rent" etc) applies for the purposes of this paragraph.

PART 12

FACTORING OF INCOME ETC

Application of Chapter 5B of Part 13 of ITA 2007 (finance arrangements) to pre-6 June 2006 arrangements

42   Chapter 5B of Part 13 of ITA 2007 (which is inserted by Schedule 5 to this Act) has no effect in relation to an arrangement made before 6 June 2006 so far as section 43B or 43D of ICTA applies to the arrangement (sections 43B and 43D of ICTA contain provision about rent factoring: their repeal by paragraph 1 of Schedule 6 to FA 2006 does not apply in relation to pre-6 June 2006 transactions).

Application of section 809BZN of ITA 2007 (finance arrangements: exceptions)

43 (1) In relation to a transfer before 22 April 2009, section 809BZN of ITA 2007 (which is inserted by Schedule 5 to this Act) has effect as if after subsection (1) there were inserted—

    "(1A)   For the purposes of subsection (1) the effect of section 785A of ICTA (rent factoring of leases of plant or machinery) is to be disregarded."

(2) If the arrangement mentioned in section 809BZN of ITA 2007 came into force before 1 October 2007, subsection (5)(b) of that section applies as if for "Schedule 13 to FA 2007 or Chapter 10 of Part 6 of CTA 2009" there were substituted "paragraph 15 of Schedule 9 to FA 1996".

(3) Paragraph 14(6) of Schedule 13 to FA 2007 (when an arrangement is in force) applies for the purposes of sub-paragraph (2) of this paragraph as for those of that Schedule.

(4) In the case of plant or machinery which is the subject of a sale and finance leaseback (as defined in section 221 of CAA 2001) where the date of the transaction (within the meaning of that section) is before 9 October 2007, section 809BZN(8) of ITA 2007 has effect as if at the end there were inserted ", but in applying that section it is to be assumed that the words "and which are not a long funding lease in the case of the lessor" were omitted from section 219(1)(b) of that Act (meaning of "finance lease")".

(5) In relation to transactions referred to in section 228A(2)(a) of CAA 2001 (as substituted by paragraph 12 of Schedule 20 to FA 2008) and entered into before 9 October 2007, section 809BZN(9) of ITA 2007 has effect as if at the

Taxation (International and Other Provisions) Act 2010 (c. 8)
Schedule 9 — Transitionals and savings etc
Part 12 — Factoring of income etc

1291

end there were inserted "with the modifications contained in section 228F of that Act".

Application of section 809CZC of ITA 2007 (income-transfer under loan or credit transaction)

44   In relation to a transfer before 22 April 2009, section 809CZC(4) of ITA 2007 (which is inserted by Schedule 5 to this Act) has effect as if—

    (a)   after "the person" there were inserted "assigns," and

    (b)   after "it" there were inserted "(without a sale or transfer of the property)".

PART 13

MISCELLANEOUS RELOCATIONS

Application of sections 925A to 925F of ITA 2007 (repos)

45   (1)   Sections 925A to 925F and 926(1A) of ITA 2007 (which are inserted by Part 19 of Schedule 7 to this Act) do not have effect in relation to an arrangement that comes into force before 1 October 2007.

    (2)   Paragraph 14(6) of Schedule 13 to FA 2007 (when an arrangement is in force) applies for the purposes of sub-paragraph (1) of this paragraph as for those of that Schedule.

SCHEDULE 10

Section 378

REPEALS AND REVOCATIONS

PART 1

DOUBLE TAXATION RELIEF

Reference	*Extent of repeal or revocation*
Income and Corporation Taxes Act 1988 (c. 1)	Sections 788 to 799. Sections 801 to 801B. Sections 803 to 804E. Sections 804G to 806. Sections 806L to 807G. Sections 808A to 809. Section 811. Sections 815A to 815B. Section 816. In section 828(4), "791". In Schedule 19ABA, paragraphs 9 to 11. Schedule 28AB.
Finance Act 1990 (c. 29)	In Schedule 7, paragraph 5.
Taxation of Chargeable Gains Act 1992 (c. 12)	Sections 277 and 278.
Finance (No. 2) Act 1992 (c. 48)	Section 50. Section 51(1) and (2). Section 52.

1292

Taxation (International and Other Provisions) Act 2010 (c. 8)
Schedule 10 – Repeals and revocations
Part 1 – Double taxation relief

Reference	Extent of repeal or revocation
Finance Act 1993 (c. 34)	Section 194. In section 195(3), the words ", other than section 194,".
Finance Act 1994 (c. 9)	Section 217. In Schedule 8, paragraph 12.
Finance Act 1996 (c. 8)	In Schedule 14, paragraphs 41 to 47. In Schedule 20, paragraph 39. In Schedule 21, paragraphs 22 and 23.
Finance Act 1997 (c. 16)	Sections 90 and 91.
Finance Act 1998 (c. 36)	Section 82(2). Sections 106 and 107.
Finance Act 2000 (c. 17)	In Schedule 30, paragraphs 1, 2, 3, 4(1) to (12), 5 to 9, 11, 12, 15 to 17, 18(1), 20, 23 to 25, 27, 28 and 30.
Finance Act 2001 (c. 9)	In Schedule 27, paragraphs 1, 2 and 6.
Finance Act 2002 (c. 23)	In section 88 — (a) subsection (1), (b) in subsection (2)(a), the references to sections 788(7)(a), 790(3), (5)(b), (10A)(d) and (10C), 792(1) and (3), 793A(1)(a) and (3), 795A(1)(b) and 815AA(1) of ICTA, and (c) subsection (2)(b), (c) and (f). In Schedule 25, paragraphs 54 and 55. In Schedule 27, paragraph 12(2) and (3). In Schedule 30, paragraph 5.
Income Tax (Earnings and Pensions) Act 2003 (c. 1)	In Schedule 6, paragraph 103.
Finance Act 2003 (c. 14)	In section 153 — (a) in subsection (1)(a), "790(6A)(b), 801(1A)(b), 804A(1)(a), 806L(1), (2), (4) and (5), 806M(2) to (5) and 815A(6)", and (b) in subsection (2)(a), "794(2)(bb),". Section 154. In Schedule 27, paragraph 1(3). In Schedule 33, paragraph 11.
Finance Act 2004 (c. 12)	Sections 107 to 115. In Schedule 7, paragraph 7.
Finance Act 2004, Sections 38 to 40 and 45 and Schedule 6 (Consequential Amendment of Enactments) Order 2004 (S.I. 2004/2310)	In the Schedule, paragraph 34.
Income Tax (Trading and Other Income) Act 2005 (c. 5)	In Schedule 1, paragraphs 321 to 323 and 325.
Finance Act 2005 (c. 7)	Section 85. Section 86(1) and (2)(a). Section 87.

Taxation (International and Other Provisions) Act 2010 (c. 8)
Schedule 10 — Repeals and revocations
Part 1 — Double taxation relief

1293

Reference	Extent of repeal or revocation
Finance Act 2005 (c. 7) — *cont.*	Section 88(3). Section 91(5). In Schedule 4, paragraph 7. Schedule 5.
Commissioners for Revenue and Customs Act 2005 (c. 11)	In Schedule 4, paragraph 37.
Finance (No. 2) Act 2005 (c. 22)	Section 43. Section 59(1).
Finance Act 2006 (c. 25)	Section 176. In Schedule 13, paragraph 24.

Income Tax Act 2007 (c. 3)	In section 26(1)(b) —
	  (a) the entries for sections 788 and 790 of ICTA, and
	  (b) the word "and" before the entry for sections 677 and 678 of ITTOIA 2005.
	In section 32 —
	  (a) the entry for section 804(5B)(a) of ICTA, and
	  (b) the word "and" before the entry for section 682(4) of ITTOIA 2005.
	Section 527(2)(b).
	In section 1026, paragraph (g) and the "or" preceding it.
	In Schedule 1, paragraphs 192 to 196, 197(2), 198(2), (3), (4)(a) and (5) to (7), 199, 200(a) and 202(a).

Finance Act 2007 (c. 11)	Section 35. In Schedule 7, paragraphs 48 to 53. In Schedule 14, paragraph 10.
Income Tax Act 2007 (Amendment) (No. 3) Order 2007 (S.I. 2007/3506)	Article 3(5).
Finance Act 2008 (c. 9)	Section 57. Section 59. In Schedule 17, in paragraph 10(3), paragraph (e) and the "and" preceding it. In Schedule 39, paragraphs 24 and 26.
Transfer of Tribunal Functions and Revenue and Customs Appeals Order 2009 (S.I. 2009/56)	In Schedule 1, paragraph 422(3).
Corporation Tax Act 2009 (c. 4)	In section 906(3), the word "and" after paragraph (a). In Schedule 1, paragraphs 245, 246, 247(2), (3)(a) and (4) to (8), 248 to 251, 255 to 264 and 282(2) and (3).
Finance Act 2009 (c. 10)	Sections 57, 59 and 60. In Schedule 14, paragraph 8.

1294

Taxation (International and Other Provisions) Act 2010 (c. 8)
Schedule 10 — Repeals and revocations
Part 1 — Double taxation relief

Reference	*Extent of repeal or revocation*
Income Tax Act 2007 (Amendment) (No. 2) Order 2009 (S.I. 2009/2859)	Article 4(6).

PART 2

TRANSFER PRICING AND ADVANCE PRICING AGREEMENTS

Reference	*Extent of repeal or revocation*
Taxes Management Act 1970 (c. 9)	In the second column of the Table in section 98, the entry for section 86(4) of FA 1999.
Income and Corporation Taxes Act 1988 (c. 1)	Section 770A. Schedule 28AA.
Finance Act 1998 (c. 36)	Section 108(1) and (2). Sections 110 and 111. Schedule 16.
Finance Act 1999 (c. 16)	Sections 85 to 87.
Capital Allowances Act 2001 (c. 2)	In Schedule 2, paragraph 68.
Finance Act 2001 (c. 9)	In Schedule 29, paragraphs 35 and 38(1) to (3).
Finance Act 2002 (c. 23)	In Schedule 23, paragraph 21. In Schedule 27, paragraph 15.
Finance Act 2004 (c. 12)	Sections 30 to 32. Section 34(2) and (3). Sections 35 and 36. In Schedule 5, paragraphs 11 to 13.
Income Tax (Trading and Other Income) Act 2005 (c. 5)	In Schedule 1, paragraphs 351 and 508.
Finance (No. 2) Act 2005 (c. 22)	In Schedule 8, paragraph 1.
Finance Act 2006 (c. 25)	In Schedule 13, paragraph 26.
Income Tax Act 2007 (c. 3)	In Schedule 1, paragraph 239.
Income Tax Act 2007 (Amendment) (No. 3) Order 2007 (S.I. 2007/3506)	Article 2(4).
Transfer of Tribunal Functions and Revenue and Customs Appeals Order 2009 (S.I. 2009/56)	In Schedule 1, paragraphs 162(2) and (4) and 252.
Corporation Tax Act 2009 (c. 4)	In Schedule 1, paragraph 291(2) to (4), (5)(b), (6) and (8).
Finance Act 2009 (c. 10)	In Schedule 14, paragraph 14. In Schedule 15, paragraph 96.

Taxation (International and Other Provisions) Act 2010 (c. 8)
Schedule 10 — Repeals and revocations
Part 3 — Tax arbitrage

1295

PART 3

TAX ARBITRAGE

Reference	Extent of repeal
Finance (No. 2) Act 2005 (c. 22)	Sections 24 to 31 and Schedule 3.
Corporation Tax Act 2009 (c. 4)	In Schedule 1, paragraphs 670 and 671.
Finance Act 2009 (c. 10)	In Schedule 24, paragraph 6.

PART 4

TAX TREATMENT OF FINANCING COSTS AND INCOME

Reference	Extent of repeal
Taxes Management Act 1970 (c. 9)	In the first column of the Table in section 98, the entry for regulations under Schedule 15 to FA 2009.
Finance Act 2009	Section 35. In Schedule 15, paragraphs 1 to 95 and 97 to 99.

PART 5

OFFSHORE FUNDS

Reference	Extent of repeal
Finance Act 2008 (c. 9)	Sections 40A to 42A.
Finance Act 2009	In section 44, the words from "Part 1" to "funds), and". In Schedule 22, Part 1.

PART 6

OIL ACTIVITIES

Reference	Extent of repeal
Finance Act 1982 (c. 39)	In Schedule 19, paragraph 10(7).
Income and Corporation Taxes Act 1988 (c. 1)	Section 493(1) to (6). Sections 495 and 496. Section 502(1) and (2).
Finance Act 1990 (c. 29)	Section 62(3).
Finance Act 1991 (c. 31)	Sections 62 to 65.
Finance (No. 2) Act 1992 (c. 48)	Section 55.
Petroleum Act 1998 (c. 17)	In Schedule 4, paragraph 25.
Finance Act 1998 (c. 36)	Section 152(3).
Capital Allowances Act 2001 (c. 2)	In Schedule 2, paragraphs 42 and 73.
Finance Act 2004 (c. 12)	Section 285(7).

1296

Taxation (International and Other Provisions) Act 2010 (c. 8)
Schedule 10 — Repeals and revocations
Part 6 — Oil activities

Reference	Extent of repeal
Finance Act 2004 (c. 12) —*cont.*	In Schedule 37, paragraphs 10 and 11.
Income Tax (Trading and Other Income) Act 2005 (c. 5)	In Schedule 1, paragraphs 192 to 194.
Finance Act 2006 (c. 25)	Section 151. In Schedule 18, paragraph 12(3)(b) and (7).
Finance Act 2008 (c. 9)	Section 104. In Schedule 27, paragraph 21. In Schedule 39, paragraph 27.
Corporation Tax Act 2009 (c. 4)	In Schedule 1, paragraph 356.

PART 7

ALTERNATIVE FINANCE ARRANGEMENTS

Reference	Extent of repeal or revocation
Taxation of Chargeable Gains Act 1992 (c. 12)	Section 151F.
Finance Act 2005 (c. 7)	Sections 46 to 47A, 48(1), 48A, 48B(1) to (5) and (9) and 49 to 57. In Schedule 2, paragraphs 1, 8 and 10 to 13.
Finance Act 2006	Section 95(1) to (8) and (11). Sections 96 to 98.
Income Tax Act 2007 (c. 3)	In Schedule 1, paragraphs 597 to 599.
Finance Act 2007 (c. 11)	Section 53(1) to (10), (13) and (14). Section 54.
Employment Income (Meaning of Securities) Order 2007 (S.I. 2007/2130)	The whole Order.
Finance Act 2008	Section 156.
Alternative Finance Arrangements (Community Investment Tax Relief) Order 2008 (S.I. 2008/1821)	The whole Order.
Corporation Tax Act 2009	Section 521. Section 1310(5). In Schedule 1, paragraphs 649 to 661 and 683.
Finance Act 2009 (c. 10)	In Schedule 61, paragraph 27.

PART 8

LEASING ARRANGEMENTS: FINANCE LEASES AND LOANS

Reference	Extent of repeal
Finance Act 1997 (c. 16)	Section 82. In Schedule 12, paragraphs 1 to 7, 9 to 17 and 20 to 30.

Taxation (International and Other Provisions) Act 2010 (c. 8)   1297
Schedule 10 — Repeals and revocations
Part 8 — Leasing arrangements: finance leases and loans

Reference	Extent of repeal
Finance Act 1998 (c. 36)	In Schedule 7, paragraph 12.
Capital Allowances Act 2001 (c. 2)	In Schedule 2, paragraph 98.
Finance Act 2002 (c. 23)	Section 103(4)(e).
Income Tax (Trading and Other Income) Act 2005 (c. 5)	In Schedule 1, paragraph 494.
Finance Act 2006 (c. 25)	In Schedule 9, paragraph 7.
Finance Act 2008 (c. 9)	In Schedule 2, paragraph 69(3).
Corporation Tax Act 2009 (c. 4)	In Schedule 1, paragraphs 447 and 448.

PART 9

SALE AND LEASE-BACK ETC

Reference	Extent of repeal or revocation
Income and Corporation Taxes Act 1988 (c. 1)	Section 24. Sections 779 to 785.
Finance Act 1996 (c. 8)	In Schedule 21, paragraph 21.
Finance Act 1998	In Schedule 7, in paragraph 1, the entries for provisions of sections 779, 780, 781, 782 and 785 of ICTA.
Capital Allowances Act 2001	In Schedule 2, paragraph 57.
Income Tax (Earnings and Pensions) Act 2003 (c. 1)	In Schedule 6, paragraphs 101 and 102.
Finance Act 2004, Sections 38 to 40 and 45 and Schedule 6 (Consequential Amendment of Enactments) Order 2004 (S.I. 2004/2310)	In the Schedule, paragraphs 32 and 33.
Income Tax (Trading and Other Income) Act 2005	In section 49(2)(a), the words "(see subsection (3))". In Schedule 1, paragraphs 314 to 319.
Tax and Civil Partnership Regulations 2005 (S.I. 2005/3229)	Regulation 98.
Finance Act 2006	In Schedule 9, paragraph 3.
Income Tax Act 2007 (c. 3)	In section 1016(2), in Part 3 of the table, the entries for sections 780(3A)(a) and 781(1) of ICTA. In Schedule 1, paragraphs 187 to 190.
Transfer of Tribunal Functions and Revenue and Customs Appeals Order 2009 (S.I. 2009/56)	In Schedule 1, paragraph 156(2).

1298

Taxation (International and Other Provisions) Act 2010 (c. 8)
Schedule 10 — Repeals and revocations
Part 9 — Sale and lease-back etc

Reference	Extent of repeal or revocation
Corporation Tax Act 2009 (c. 4)	In Schedule 1, paragraphs 13(2)(a), 232(2) and (3)(b) and (d), 233, 234(3) and (4)(a) and (c) and 236.

Part 10

FACTORING OF INCOME ETC

Reference	Extent of repeal
Income and Corporation Taxes Act 1988 (c. 1)	Sections 774A to 774G. Section 786.
Income Tax (Trading and Other Income) Act 2005 (c. 5)	In Schedule 1, paragraph 320.
Finance Act 2006 (c. 25)	In Schedule 6, paragraphs 6 and 8.
Income Tax Act 2007 (c. 3)	In section 2(13)(e), the word "or" at the end. In section 1016(2), in Part 3 of the table, the entry for section 786(5)(a) of ICTA.
Finance Act 2007 (c. 11)	In Schedule 5, paragraphs 3 to 7 and 17(4). In Schedule 14, paragraph 9.
Corporation Tax Act 2009	In Schedule 1, paragraphs 226 to 229 and 241.

Part 11

UK REPRESENTATIVES OF NON-UK RESIDENTS

Reference	Extent of repeal or revocation
Finance Act 1995 (c. 4)	Sections 126 and 127. Schedule 23.
Finance Act 1998 (c. 36)	In Schedule 7, paragraph 10.
Financial Services and Markets Act 2000 (Consequential Amendments) (Taxes) Order 2001 (S.I. 2001/3629)	Article 89.
Finance Act 2003 (c. 14)	In Schedule 27, paragraphs 4 and 5.
Income Tax (Trading and Other Income) Act 2005	In Schedule 1, paragraph 479.
Finance Act 2005 (c. 7)	Section 48(3).
Finance Act 2006	Section 95(10).
Income Tax Act 2007	In section 2(14), the word "and" immediately after paragraph (b). In section 817(3), the words "by the broker". In section 1014(2), paragraph (ba) and, in paragraph (g), the word "and" at the end of sub-paragraph (iib). In Schedule 1, paragraph 367.
Finance Act 2007	Section 53(11).

Taxation (International and Other Provisions) Act 2010 (c. 8) 1299
Schedule 10 — Repeals and revocations
Part 11 — UK representatives of non-UK residents

Reference	Extent of repeal or revocation
Finance Act 2008 (c. 9)	In Schedule 16, paragraphs 1, 2 and 11(1).
Corporation Tax Act 2009 (c. 4)	In Schedule 1, paragraph 401(a).

PART 12

MISCELLANEOUS RELOCATIONS

Reference	Extent of repeal or revocation
Taxes Management Act 1970 (c. 9)	In the first column of the Table in section 98 — (a) the entry for paragraph 2 of Schedule 15 to FA 1973, (b) the entry for section 42 of ICTA, and (c) the entry for regulations under section 199 of FA 2003.
Finance Act 1973 (c. 51)	Section 38. Schedule 15.
Finance Act 1974 (c. 30)	Section 24.
Finance Act 1976 (c. 40)	In Schedule 9, paragraph 5.
Finance Act 1978 (c. 42)	Section 29(3).
Finance Act 1984 (c. 43)	Section 124.
Finance (No. 2) Act 1987 (c. 51)	Section 86(3)(b).
Income and Corporation Taxes Act 1988 (c. 1)	Section 6(5). Section 42. Section 84A. Section 152. Section 337A(2). Section 475. Section 700. Section 787. In Schedule 29, in the Table in paragraph 32, the entries relating to Schedule 15 to FA 1973.
Finance Act 1988 (c. 39)	Sections 130 to 132.
Finance Act 1989 (c. 26)	Section 151. Section 164(5)(b).
Finance Act 1991 (c. 31)	Section 42.
Taxation of Chargeable Gains Act 1992 (c. 12)	In Schedule 10, paragraphs 3 and 16(6).
Finance (No. 2) Act 1992 (c. 48)	Section 66. Schedule 12.
Finance Act 1995 (c. 4)	In Schedule 18, paragraph 6.
Jobseekers Act 1995 (c. 18)	In Schedule 2, paragraph 13.
Finance Act 1996 (c. 8)	In section 200(1)(a), the words ", income tax". In Schedule 14, paragraph 27.

1300

Taxation (International and Other Provisions) Act 2010 (c. 8)
Schedule 10 — Repeals and revocations
Part 12 — Miscellaneous relocations

Reference	*Extent of repeal or revocation*
Finance Act 1996 (c. 8) — *cont.*	In Schedule 28, in paragraph 3 — (a) in sub-paragraph (1), the words from "for subsection (1)" to the end, and (b) sub-paragraph (2). In Schedule 38, paragraph 1.
Petroleum Act 1998 (c. 17)	In Schedule 4, paragraph 5.
Finance Act 1998 (c. 36)	Section 36. Section 118. In Schedule 7 — (a) in paragraph 1, the word "84A(2)(a)," and (b) in paragraph 8 the words from "and Schedule 12" to the end. In Schedule 14, paragraphs 6 and 7(3) and, in paragraph 7(5), the words "Except as provided by the preceding provisions of this paragraph,".
Finance Act 2000 (c. 17)	Section 144.
Capital Allowances Act 2001 (c. 2)	In Schedule 2, paragraph 101.
Finance Act 2002 (c. 23)	Section 107.
Secretaries of State for Education and Skills and for Work and Pensions Order 2002 (S.I. 2002/1397)	In the Schedule, paragraph 6.
Income Tax (Earnings and Pensions) Act 2003 (c. 1)	In Schedule 6, paragraphs 11, 23 and 144 to 147.
Finance Act 2003 (c. 14)	Section 199.
Communications Act 2003 (c. 21)	In Schedule 17, paragraph 152.
Finance Act 2004 (c. 12)	In Schedule 12, paragraph 12.
Finance Act 2004, Sections 38 to 40 and 45 and Schedule 6 (Consequential Amendment of Enactments) Order 2004 (S.I. 2004/2310)	In the Schedule, paragraph 4.
Income Tax (Trading and Other Income) Act 2005 (c. 5)	In Schedule 1, paragraphs 24, 59, 291, 387 and 388. In Schedule 2, paragraph 91.
Finance (No. 2) Act 2005 (c. 22)	Section 61.
Finance Act 2006 (c. 25)	Section 71(2) and (3). In Schedule 13, paragraph 29.
Income Tax Act 2007 (c. 3)	In section 3(2), the word "and" immediately before paragraph (e). In Schedule 1, paragraph 275.
Finance Act 2007 (c. 11)	In Schedule 13, paragraph 13.

Taxation (International and Other Provisions) Act 2010 (c. 8)
Schedule 10 — Repeals and revocations
Part 12 — Miscellaneous relocations

1301

Reference	Extent of repeal or revocation
Transfer of Tribunal Functions and Revenue and Customs Appeals Order 2009 (S.I. 2009/56)	In Schedule 1, paragraphs 133(3), 135(2) and 164.
Corporation Tax Act 2009 (c. 4)	In Schedule 1, paragraphs 104(3)(a), 160(a), 209(c) and (d), 242(2), 311, 312, 389 and 390.
Finance Act 2009 (c. 10)	Section 111.

PART 13

REPEALS FOR PURPOSES CONNECTED WITH OTHER TAX LAW REWRITE ACTS

Reference	Extent of repeal
Income and Corporation Taxes Act 1988 (c. 1)	Section 59(3) and (4).
Finance Act 1988 (c. 39)	In Schedule 3, paragraph 21.
Finance Act 1991 (c. 31)	In Schedule 11, paragraph 2(1) and (3).
Finance Act 1993 (c. 34)	Section 72. Section 107(2)(a). In Schedule 6, paragraph 10.
Finance Act 1994 (c. 9)	In Schedule 19, paragraph 37.
Finance (No. 2) Act 1997 (c. 58)	In Schedule 4, paragraph 21.
Finance Act 1998 (c. 36)	Section 27(1)(b). Section 79(2). Section 119. In Schedule 7 — (a) in paragraph 1, the words "109A(2)(d), (4) and (4A),", the words "117(1), (3)(b) and (4),", the word "160(1C)(b),", the word "368(3),", the word "526(1)(b)," and the words "830(4) in the second place,", and (b) in paragraph 3, the words "and 112(1)".
Finance Act 1999 (c. 16)	In Schedule 4, paragraphs 1(2) and 3(3).
Finance Act 2000 (c. 17)	Section 78.
Regulation of Care (Scotland) Act 2001 (asp 8)	In Schedule 3, paragraph 14(d) and (e).
Finance Act 2004 (c. 12)	Section 318(2).
Income Tax (Trading and Other Income) Act 2005 (c. 5)	In Schedule 1, paragraphs 35(3)(a) and (4) and 401.
Finance Act 2005 (c. 7)	Section 48B(6) to (8). In Schedule 2, paragraph 9.
Finance (No. 2) Act 2005 (c. 22)	In Schedule 8, paragraphs 2 and 3.

In relation to the repeal in F(No.2)A 1997, see paragraph 171 of Schedule 2 to ITA 2007.

1302

Taxation (International and Other Provisions) Act 2010 (c. 8)
Schedule 11 – Index of defined expressions used in Parts 2 to 8
Part 1 – Double taxation relief: index of defined expressions used in Parts 2 and 3

SCHEDULE 11

Section 379

Index of defined expressions used in Parts 2 to 8

Part 1

Double taxation relief: index of defined expressions used in Parts 2 and 3

the arrangements (in Chapter 2 of Part 2)	section 21(1)
chargeable gain (in Part 2 so far as relating to capital gains tax)	section 105
double taxation arrangements (in Part 2)	section 2(4)
double taxation arrangements (in Part 3)	section 136(2)
foreign tax (in Chapter 2 of Part 2)	section 21(1)
international arrangements (in Part 3)	section 136(3)
the non-UK territory (in Chapter 2 of Part 2)	section 21(1)
the Savings Directive (in Part 3)	section 136(4)
savings income (in Part 3)	section 136(5)
special withholding tax (in Part 3)	section 136(6)
tax not chargeable directly or by deduction (in Chapter 2 of Part 2)	sections 17(3) and 20(4)
tax payable or chargeable (in Chapter 2 of Part 2)	sections 17(3) and 20(4)
tax payable or paid under the law of a territory outside the United Kingdom (in Chapter 2 of Part 2, except section 29, in its application to relief under unilateral relief arrangements)	section 8(2)
underlying tax (in Chapter 2 of Part 2)	section 21(1)
unilateral relief arrangements (in Part 2)	section 8(1)

Part 2

Transfer pricing: index of defined expressions used in Part 4

the actual provision (in Part 4)	section 149
the advantaged person (in Chapter 4 of Part 4)	section 174(1)
the affected persons (in Part 4)	section 149(1), (2)
the arm's length provision (in Part 4)	section 151

Taxation (International and Other Provisions) Act 2010 (c. 8)
Schedule 11 — Index of defined expressions used in Parts 2 to 8
Part 2 — Transfer pricing: index of defined expressions used in Part 4

1303

control (of a body corporate or firm) (in Part 4)	section 217
the disadvantaged person (in Chapter 4 of Part 4)	section 174(1)
firm (in Part 4)	section 217(8)
the guarantor company (in Chapter 5 of Part 4)	section 191(5)
the issuing company (in Chapter 5 of Part 4)	section 191(5)
losses (in Part 4)	section 156(1)
medium-sized enterprise (in Chapter 3 of Part 4)	section 172
participation (direct or indirect) in the management, control or capital of another person (in Part 4)	Chapter 2 of Part 4
potential advantage in relation to United Kingdom taxation (in Part 4)	section 155(2)
profits (in Part 4)	section 156(2)
the relevant activities (in Part 4)	section 216
relevant notice (in Chapter 4 of Part 4)	section 190
section 182 claim (in Part 4)	section 181(3)
the security (in Chapter 5 of Part 4)	section 191(5)
small enterprise (in Chapter 3 of Part 4)	section 172
transaction, and series of transactions (in Part 4)	section 150
transfer pricing notice (in Chapter 3 of Part 4)	section 168(2)

PART 3

ADVANCE PRICING AGREEMENTS: INDEX OF DEFINED EXPRESSIONS USED IN PART 5

advance pricing agreement (in Part 5)	section 218(1)
the Commissioners (in Part 5)	section 230
officer (in Part 5)	section 230

PART 4

TAX ARBITRAGE: INDEX OF DEFINED EXPRESSIONS USED IN PART 6

closure notice (in Part 6)	section 259(1)
company tax return (in Part 6)	section 259(1)

1304

Taxation (International and Other Provisions) Act 2010 (c. 8)
Schedule 11 — Index of defined expressions used in Parts 2 to 8
Part 4 — Tax arbitrage: index of defined expressions used in Part 6

connected (in Part 6)	section 259(2)
deduction notice (in Part 6)	section 232(2)
the deduction scheme conditions (in Part 6)	section 232(2)
discovery assessment (in Part 6)	section 259(1)
notice of enquiry (in Part 6)	section 259(1)
receipt notice (in Part 6)	section 249(2)
the receipt scheme conditions (in Part 6)	section 249(2)
scheme (in Part 6)	section 258
security (in Part 6)	section 259(1)
series of transactions (in Part 6)	section 258(2), (3)

PART 5

TAX TREATMENT OF FINANCING COSTS AND INCOME: INDEX OF DEFINED EXPRESSIONS USED IN PART 7

amount disclosed in financial statements for a period (in Part 7 except Chapter 2)	section 350
amounts disclosed in financial statements (in Part 7)	section 349
available amount (in Part 7)	section 332
the Commissioners (in Part 7)	section 353
company to which Chapter 3 applies (in Chapter 3 of Part 7)	section 275
company to which Chapter 4 applies (in Chapter 4 of Part 7)	section 287
corporate entity (in Part 7)	section 340
EEA territory (in Chapter 5 of Part 7)	section 301(2)
effective interest method (in Part 7)	section 351
the end date (in Chapter 2 of Part 7)	section 262(8)
entity (in Part 7)	section 351
excluded scheme (in Chapter 6 of Part 7)	section 312(2), (3)
financial instrument (in Chapter 2 of Part 7)	section 270(1)
financial statements of the worldwide group (in Part 7)	section 346(2)

Taxation (International and Other Provisions) Act 2010 (c. 8)
Schedule 11 — Index of defined expressions used in Parts 2 to 8
Part 5 — Tax treatment of financing costs and income: index of defined expressions used in Part 7

1305

financing expense amount (in Part 7)	section 313
financing income amount (in Chapter 5 of Part 7 and section 311)	section 305
financing income amount (in the rest of Part 7)	section 314
FISMA 2000 (in Part 7)	section 353
FSA Handbook (in Part 7)	section 353
group (in Part 7)	section 338
HMRC (in Part 7)	section 353
insurance activities (in Chapter 2 of Part 7)	section 269
insurance-related activities (in Chapter 2 of Part 7)	section 269
large in relation to a group (in Part 7)	section 344
lending activities (in Chapter 2 of Part 7)	section 268
net financing deduction (in Part 7)	section 329
parent (in Part 7)	section 351
period of account of the worldwide group (in Part 7)	section 346(3)
qualifying activities (in Chapter 2 of Part 7)	section 267
relevant accounting period (in Part 7)	section 352
relevant associate (in Chapter 5 of Part 7)	section 300
relevant dealing (in Chapter 2 of Part 7)	section 270(2), (3)
relevant group company (in Part 7)	section 345
relevant non-corporate entity (in Part 7)	section 341
the relevant period of account (in Chapter 3 of Part 7)	section 274(1)
the relevant period of account (in Chapter 4 of Part 7)	section 286(1)
the reporting body (in Chapter 3 of Part 7)	section 277
the reporting body (in Chapter 4 of Part 7)	section 289
scheme (in Chapter 6 of Part 7)	section 312(1)
the start date (in Chapter 2 of Part 7)	section 262(8)
subsidiary (in Part 7)	section 351
tax of a territory outside the United Kingdom (in Chapter 5 of Part 7)	section 304(2), (3)

1306   *Taxation (International and Other Provisions) Act 2010 (c. 8)*
Schedule 11 — Index of defined expressions used in Parts 2 to 8
Part 5 — Tax treatment of financing costs and income: index of defined expressions used in Part 7

tax of the United Kingdom (in Chapter 5 of Part 7)	section 304(1)
tax-resident (in Chapter 5 of Part 7)	section 301(1)
tested expense amount (in Part 7)	section 329
tested income amount (in Part 7)	section 330
total disallowed amount (in Chapter 3 of Part 7)	section 274(2)
total disallowed amount (in Chapter 4 of Part 7)	section 286(2)
UK group company (in Part 7)	section 345
UK trading income (in Chapter 2 of Part 7)	section 266(3)
ultimate parent (in Part 7)	section 339
the worldwide group (in Part 7)	section 337
worldwide trading income (in Chapter 2 of Part 7)	section 266(3)

PART 6

OFFSHORE FUNDS: INDEX OF DEFINED EXPRESSIONS USED IN PART 8

participant (in Part 8)	section 362(1)
participation (in Part 8)	section 362(2)
part of umbrella arrangements (in Part 8)	section 363(2)
umbrella arrangements (in Part 8)	section 363(1)

Child Poverty Act 2010

CHAPTER 9

CONTENTS

PART 1

NATIONAL TARGETS, STRATEGIES AND REPORTS

Child Poverty Act 2010

2010 CHAPTER 9

An Act to set targets relating to the eradication of child poverty, and to make other provision about child poverty.   [25th March 2010]

B E IT ENACTED by the Queen's most Excellent Majesty, by and with the advice and consent of the Lords Spiritual and Temporal, and Commons, in this present Parliament assembled, and by the authority of the same, as follows:—

PART 1

NATIONAL TARGETS, STRATEGIES AND REPORTS

Targets relating to child poverty

1   The 2010 target

(1)   The Secretary of State must, as soon as reasonably practicable after the end of the 2010 target year and in any event not later than 30 June 2012, lay before Parliament a report on whether the 2010 target has been met.

(2)   The 2010 target is that in the financial year beginning with 1 April 2010, 1.7 million children or fewer live in qualifying households in the United Kingdom that fell within the relevant income group for the purposes of section 3 (the relative low income target).

(3)   The report must be based on statistics that the Statistics Board has designated under section 12 of the Statistics and Registration Service Act 2007 (assessment) as National Statistics.

(4)   Whether the target has been met in relation to the 2010 target year is to be determined by reference to the statistics.

(5)   If the target has not been met, the report must explain why it has not been met.

(6)   The 2010 target year is the financial year beginning with 1 April 2010.

2   Duty of Secretary of State to ensure that targets in sections 3 to 6 are met

(1)   It is the duty of the Secretary of State to ensure that the following targets are met in relation to the United Kingdom in relation to the target year —

(a)   the relative low income target in section 3,

(b)   the combined low income and material deprivation target in section 4,

(c)   the absolute low income target in section 5, and

(d)   the persistent poverty target in section 6.

(2)   The target year is the financial year beginning with 1 April 2020.

3   The relative low income target

(1)   The relative low income target is that less than 10% of children who live in qualifying households live in households that fall within the relevant income group.

(2)   For the purposes of this section, a household falls within the relevant income group, in relation to a financial year, if its equivalised net income for the financial year is less than 60% of median equivalised net household income for the financial year.

4   The combined low income and material deprivation target

(1)   The combined low income and material deprivation target is that less than 5% of children who live in qualifying households—

(a)   live in households that fall within the relevant income group, and

(b)   experience material deprivation.

(2)   For the purposes of subsection (1)(a), a household falls within the relevant income group, in relation to a financial year, if its equivalised net income for the financial year is less than 70% of median equivalised net household income for the financial year.

(3)   Regulations must specify the circumstances in which a child is to be regarded for the purposes of subsection (1)(b) as experiencing material deprivation in a financial year.

5   The absolute low income target

(1)   The absolute low income target is that less than 5% of children who live in qualifying households live in households falling within the relevant income group.

(2)   For the purposes of this section, a household falls within the relevant income group, in relation to a financial year, if its equivalised net income for the financial year is less than 60% of the adjusted base amount.

(3)   "The adjusted base amount", in relation to a financial year, is the base amount adjusted in a prescribed manner to take account of changes in the value of money since the base year.

(4)   In this section —

"the base amount" means the amount of median equivalised net household income for the base year;

"the base year" means the financial year beginning with 1 April 2010.

6   The persistent poverty target

(1)   In relation to a financial year ("the relevant financial year"), the persistent poverty target is that less than the target percentage of children who have lived in qualifying households during each of the survey years have lived in households that have been within the relevant income group in at least 3 of the survey years.

(2)   The survey years are—

    (a)   the calendar year that ends in the relevant financial year, and

    (b)   the 3 previous calendar years.

(3)   For the purposes of this section, the target percentage is a percentage to be prescribed by regulations made before 2015.

(4)   For the purposes of this section, a household falls within the relevant income group, in relation to a calendar year, if its equivalised net income for the year is less than 60% of median equivalised net household income for the year.

(5)   Instead of exercising the power conferred by subsection (3), the Secretary of State may by regulations amend this section so as to substitute a different persistent poverty target for that set out in subsections (1) to (4).

(6)   Regulations under subsection (5) may only be made—

    (a)   before 2015, and

    (b)   with the consent of the Commission.

7   Interpretation of terms used in relation to targets

(1)   Regulations may for the purposes of this Part make provision about the following—

    (a)   what is a qualifying household;

    (b)   the circumstances in which a child is or is not to be regarded as living in a qualifying household;

    (c)   what is to be regarded as the income of a household for a financial year;

    (d)   what deductions are to be made in calculating the net income of a household;

    (e)   how net household income is to be equivalised.

(2)   The deductions prescribed under subsection (1)(d) are not to include housing costs, but regulations under that provision may provide that specified expenses are not to be treated as housing costs.

(3)   In this Part "equivalised", in relation to household income, means adjusted to take account of variations in household size and composition.

(4)   In making regulations under subsection (1)(a), the Secretary of State must have regard to the desirability of ensuring that the targets in sections 3 to 6 have as wide an application as is reasonably practicable, having regard to the statistical surveys that are being or can reasonably be expected to be undertaken.

The Child Poverty Commission

8 The Child Poverty Commission

(1) There is to be a body called the Child Poverty Commission (in this Act referred to as "the Commission").

(2) The Commission's functions are those conferred on it by or under this Act.

(3) Schedule 1 contains further provisions about the Commission.

(4) The Secretary of State may by order provide for the Commission to cease to exist on a day —

   (a) specified in or determined in accordance with the order, and

   (b) falling after the target year.

(5) An order under subsection (4) may contain such transitional or consequential provision as the Secretary of State considers necessary or expedient in connection with the abolition of the Commission.

(6) That provision may include provision amending, repealing or revoking —

   (a) the provisions of this Act so far as relating to the Commission;

   (b) any provision of any other Act (whenever passed);

   (c) any provision of any instrument made under an Act (whenever made).

Strategies: duties of Secretary of State

9 UK strategies

(1) The Secretary of State must, before the end of the period of 12 months beginning with the day on which this Act is passed, publish and lay before Parliament the first UK strategy.

(2) A "UK strategy" is a strategy under this section setting out the measures that the Secretary of State proposes to take —

   (a) for the purpose of complying with section 2 (duty to ensure that targets are met), and

   (b) for the purpose of ensuring as far as possible that children in the United Kingdom do not experience socio-economic disadvantage.

(3) A UK strategy may also refer to proposals of the Scottish Ministers, the Welsh Ministers or the relevant Northern Ireland department.

(4) Before the end of the period to which a UK strategy relates, the Secretary of State must review the strategy and publish and lay before Parliament a revised UK strategy, but this subsection does not apply after the beginning of the target year.

(5) In preparing a UK strategy, the Secretary of State must consider what (if any) measures ought to be taken in each of the following areas —

   (a) the promotion and facilitation of the employment of parents or of the development of the skills of parents,

   (b) the provision of financial support for children and parents,

   (c) the provision of information, advice and assistance to parents and the promotion of parenting skills,

    (d)   physical and mental health, education, childcare and social services, and

    (e)   housing, the built or natural environment and the promotion of social inclusion.

(6)   When considering for the purpose of a UK strategy what measures ought to be taken in relation to each of those areas, the Secretary of State —

    (a)   must consider which groups of children in the United Kingdom appear to be disproportionately affected by socio-economic disadvantage, and

    (b)   must consider the likely impact of each measure on children within each of those groups.

(7)   A UK strategy must —

    (a)   where it relates to a period ending before the end of the target year —

        (i)   describe the progress that the Secretary of State considers needs to be made by the end of the period to which the strategy relates if the targets in sections 3 to 6 are to be met in relation to the United Kingdom in relation to the target year, and

        (ii)   describe the other progress that the Secretary of State intends to make by the end of the period to which the strategy relates in achieving the purpose mentioned in subsection (2)(b), and

    (b)   describe the progress that the Secretary of State intends to make by the end of the target year in achieving the purpose mentioned in subsection (2)(b), otherwise than by ensuring that the targets are met.

(8)   A UK strategy other than the first must also —

    (a)   describe the measures taken in accordance with the previous UK strategy and the measures taken in accordance with a Scottish strategy, a Welsh strategy or a Northern Ireland strategy,

    (b)   describe the effect of those measures on progress towards meeting the targets in sections 3 to 6, and

    (c)   describe other effects of those measures that contribute to the achievement of the purpose mentioned in subsection (2)(b).

(9)   References in this section to the period to which a UK strategy relates are references to the period beginning with the date on which the UK strategy is laid before Parliament and —

    (a)   except in the case of a UK strategy laid before Parliament less than 3 years before the beginning of the target year, ending 3 years later, and

    (b)   in that excepted case, ending with the target year.

10   Provision of advice by Commission and consultation with others

(1)   In preparing a UK strategy, the Secretary of State must request the advice of the Commission, and specify in the request the date by which the advice is to be given.

(2)   The Secretary of State may at any time request the Commission to give advice, by a specified date, on any matter connected with —

    (a)   a UK strategy, or

    (b)   the targets in sections 3 to 6.

(3)   The Secretary of State must have regard to any advice given by the Commission under this section.

(4) In preparing a UK strategy, the Secretary of State—

    (a) must consult such local authorities and associations of local authorities in England as the Secretary of State thinks fit,

    (b) must consult the Scottish Ministers, the Welsh Ministers and the relevant Northern Ireland department,

    (c) must consult such children, and organisations working with or representing children, as the Secretary of State thinks fit,

    (d) must consult such parents, and organisations working with or representing parents, as the Secretary of State thinks fit, and

    (e) may consult such other persons as the Secretary of State thinks fit.

(5) In preparing a UK strategy, the Secretary of State must have regard to any Scottish strategy, Welsh strategy or Northern Ireland strategy.

Strategies: duties of Scottish Ministers and relevant Northern Ireland department

11 Scottish strategies

(1) The Scottish Ministers must, before the end of the period of 12 months beginning with the day on which this Act is passed, publish and lay before the Scottish Parliament the first Scottish strategy.

(2) A "Scottish strategy" is a strategy under this section setting out the measures that the Scottish Ministers propose to take—

    (a) for the purpose of contributing to the compliance by the Secretary of State with section 2 (duty to ensure that targets are met), and

    (b) for the purpose of ensuring as far as possible that children in Scotland do not experience socio-economic disadvantage.

(3) Before the end of the period to which a Scottish strategy relates, the Scottish Ministers must review the strategy and publish and lay before the Scottish Parliament a revised Scottish strategy, but this subsection does not apply after the beginning of the target year.

(4) A Scottish strategy must—

    (a) where it relates to a period ending before the end of the target year—

        (i) describe the progress that the Scottish Ministers intend to make in Scotland by the end of the period to which the strategy relates in contributing to the meeting of the targets in sections 3 to 6 in relation to the target year,

        (ii) describe the other progress that the Scottish Ministers intend to make by the end of the period to which the strategy relates in achieving the purpose mentioned in subsection (2)(b), and

    (b) describe the progress that the Scottish Ministers intend to make by the end of the target year in achieving the purpose mentioned in subsection (2)(b), otherwise than by contributing to the meeting of the targets.

(5) A Scottish strategy other than the first must also—

    (a) describe the measures taken by the Scottish Ministers in accordance with the previous Scottish strategy,

    (b) describe the effect of those measures in contributing to the meeting of the targets in sections 3 to 6, and

    (c) describe other effects of those measures that contribute to the achievement of the purpose mentioned in subsection (2)(b).

(6)   A Scottish strategy may not include proposals that relate to reserved matters, within the meaning of the Scotland Act 1998.

(7)   The Scottish Ministers must, on or before each report date relating to a Scottish strategy, lay before the Scottish Parliament a report which—

   (a)   describes the measures taken by the Scottish Ministers in accordance with the Scottish strategy,

   (b)   describes the effect of those measures in contributing to the meeting of the targets in sections 3 to 6, and

   (c)   describes other effects of those measures that contribute to the achievement of the purpose mentioned in subsection (2)(b).

(8)   The report dates relating to a Scottish strategy are each anniversary of the day on which it was laid before the Scottish Parliament, other than an anniversary which falls—

   (a)   on or after the date on which a subsequent Scottish strategy is so laid, or

   (b)   after the end of the target year.

(9)   References in this section to the period to which a Scottish strategy relates are references to the period beginning with the date on which the Scottish strategy is laid before the Scottish Parliament and—

   (a)   except in the case of a Scottish strategy laid before that Parliament less than 3 years before the beginning of the target year, ending 3 years later, and

   (b)   in that excepted case, ending with the target year.

12   Northern Ireland strategies

(1)   The relevant Northern Ireland department must, before the end of the period of 12 months beginning with the day on which this Act is passed, publish and lay before the Northern Ireland Assembly the first Northern Ireland strategy.

(2)   A "Northern Ireland strategy" is a strategy under this section setting out the measures that the Northern Ireland departments propose to take—

   (a)   for the purpose of contributing to the compliance by the Secretary of State with section 2 (duty to ensure that targets are met), and

   (b)   for the purpose of ensuring as far as possible that children in Northern Ireland do not experience socio-economic disadvantage.

(3)   Before the end of the period to which a Northern Ireland strategy relates, the relevant Northern Ireland department must review the strategy and publish and lay before the Northern Ireland Assembly a revised Northern Ireland strategy, but this subsection does not apply after the beginning of the target year.

(4)   A Northern Ireland strategy must—

   (a)   where it relates to a period ending before the end of the target year—

      (i)   describe the progress that the Northern Ireland departments intend to make in Northern Ireland by the end of the period to which the strategy relates in contributing to the meeting of the targets in sections 3 to 6 in relation to the target year,

      (ii)   describe the other progress that the Northern Ireland departments intend to make by the end of the period to which the strategy relates in achieving the purpose mentioned in subsection (2)(b), and

(b)   describe the progress that the Northern Ireland departments intend to make by the end of the target year in achieving the purpose mentioned in subsection (2)(b), otherwise than by contributing to the meeting of the targets.

(5)   A Northern Ireland strategy other than the first must also —

(a)   describe the measures taken by the Northern Ireland departments in accordance with the previous Northern Ireland strategy,

(b)   describe the effect of those measures in contributing to the meeting of the targets in sections 3 to 6, and

(c)   describe other effects of those measures that contribute to the achievement of the purpose mentioned in subsection (2)(b).

(6)   A Northern Ireland strategy may not include proposals that relate to excepted or reserved matters, within the meaning of the Northern Ireland Act 1998.

(7)   The relevant Northern Ireland department must, on or before each report date relating to a Northern Ireland strategy, lay before the Northern Ireland Assembly a report which —

(a)   describes the measures taken by the Northern Ireland departments in accordance with the Northern Ireland strategy,

(b)   describes the effect of those measures in contributing to the meeting of the targets in sections 3 to 6, and

(c)   describes other effects of those measures that contribute to the achievement of the purpose mentioned in subsection (2)(b).

(8)   The report dates relating to a Northern Ireland strategy are each anniversary of the day on which it was laid before the Northern Ireland Assembly, other than an anniversary which falls —

(a)   on or after the date on which a subsequent Northern Ireland strategy is so laid, or

(b)   after the end of the target year.

(9)   References in this section to the period to which a Northern Ireland strategy relates are references to the period beginning with the date on which the Northern Ireland strategy is laid before the Northern Ireland Assembly and —

(a)   except in the case of a Northern Ireland strategy laid before the Assembly less than 3 years before the beginning of the target year, ending 3 years later, and

(b)   in that excepted case, ending with the target year.

13   Advice and consultation: Scotland and Northern Ireland

(1)   In preparing a Scottish strategy or a Northern Ireland strategy, the devolved administration must request the advice of the Commission, and specify in the request the date by which the advice is to be given.

(2)   The devolved administration must have regard to any advice given by the Commission under this section.

(3)   In preparing a Scottish strategy or a Northern Ireland strategy, the devolved administration —

(a)   in the case of a Scottish strategy, must consult such local authorities or associations of local authorities in Scotland as the devolved administration thinks fit,

      (b)   must consult the Secretary of State,

      (c)   must consult such children, and organisations working with or representing children, as the devolved administration thinks fit,

      (d)   must consult such parents, and organisations working with or representing parents, as the devolved administration thinks fit, and

      (e)   may consult such other persons as the devolved administration thinks fit.

(4)   In this section "the devolved administration" means—

      (a)   in relation to a Scottish strategy, the Scottish Ministers, and

      (b)   in relation to a Northern Ireland strategy, the relevant Northern Ireland department.

Reports by Secretary of State

14   Reports by Secretary of State

(1)   The Secretary of State must, on or before each report date relating to a UK strategy, lay before Parliament a report on the progress made—

      (a)   towards meeting the targets in sections 3 to 6, and

      (b)   in implementing the UK strategy.

(2)   The report dates relating to a UK strategy are each anniversary of the day on which it was laid before Parliament, other than an anniversary which falls—

      (a)   on or after the date on which a subsequent UK strategy is so laid, or

      (b)   after the end of the target year.

(3)   The Secretary of State must, as soon as reasonably practicable after the end of the target year, lay before Parliament a report on the progress made in implementing the most recent UK strategy.

(4)   A report under subsection (1) or (3) must in particular—

      (a)   describe the measures taken by the Secretary of State in accordance with the UK strategy,

      (b)   describe the measures taken by the Scottish Ministers, the Welsh Ministers and the Northern Ireland departments in accordance with a Scottish strategy, a Welsh strategy or a Northern Ireland strategy,

      (c)   in the case of a report under subsection (1), describe the effect of all those measures on progress towards the targets and on progress in achieving the purpose mentioned in section 9(2)(b).

(5)   If the UK strategy has not been implemented in full, the report must describe the respects in which it has not been implemented and the reasons for this.

(6)   Before preparing a report under subsection (1) or (3), the Secretary of State must consult the Scottish Ministers, the Welsh Ministers and the relevant Northern Ireland department.

15   Statement required in relation to target year

(1)   The report under section 14(3) must include a statement of—

      (a)   the percentage of children living in qualifying households in the United Kingdom in the target year who were living in households that fell within the relevant income group for the purposes of section 3 (the relative low income target);

    (b)   the percentage of children living in qualifying households in the United Kingdom in the target year who were for the purposes of section 4 (the combined low income and material deprivation target) living in households that fell within the relevant income group and experiencing material deprivation;

    (c)   the percentage of children living in qualifying households in the United Kingdom in the target year who were living in households that fell within the relevant income group for the purposes of section 5 (the absolute low income target);

    (d)   the percentage of children who have lived in qualifying households during the survey years (as defined by section 6(2)) which relate to the target year who have lived in households that fell within the relevant income group for the purposes of section 6 (the persistent poverty target) in at least 3 of the survey years.

(2)   The statement must be based on statistics that the Statistics Board has designated under section 12 of the Statistics and Registration Service Act 2007 (assessment) as National Statistics.

(3)   Whether the targets in sections 3 to 6 have been met in relation to the target year is to be determined by reference to the percentages given in the statement.

(4)   If any of the targets in sections 3 to 6 has not been met, the report under section 14(3) must explain why it has not been met.

Economic and fiscal circumstances

16   Economic and fiscal circumstances

(1)   The matters mentioned in subsection (2) must be taken into account —

    (a)   by the Secretary of State in preparing a UK strategy;

    (b)   by the Commission in considering any advice to be given to the Secretary of State, the Scottish Ministers or the relevant Northern Ireland department.

(2)   Those matters are —

    (a)   economic circumstances and in particular the likely impact of any measure on the economy;

    (b)   fiscal circumstances and in particular the likely impact of any measure on taxation, public spending and public borrowing.

(3)   In preparing a Scottish strategy or a Northern Ireland strategy, the Scottish Ministers or the relevant Northern Ireland department must have regard to —

    (a)   the resources that are or may be available to the Scottish Ministers or, as the case may be, to the Northern Ireland departments, and

    (b)   the effect of the implementation of the strategy on those resources.

Continuing effect of targets after target year

17   Continuing effect of targets after target year

Schedule 2 contains provision about the effect of the targets in sections 3 to 6 in relation to financial years after the target year.

Supplementary

18   Interpretation of Part 1

(1)   In this Part—

"the Commission" means the Child Poverty Commission;

"financial year" means the 12 months ending with 31 March;

"Northern Ireland strategy" has the meaning given by section 12(2);

"the relevant Northern Ireland department" means the Office of the First Minister and deputy First Minister;

"Scottish strategy" has the meaning given by section 11(2);

"target year" (except in the expression "renewed target year") has the meaning given by section 2(2);

"UK strategy" has the meaning given by section 9(2);

"Welsh strategy" means a strategy prepared by the Welsh Ministers under Part 1 of the Children and Families (Wales) Measure 2010.

(2)   In this Part "qualifying household" and other terms relating to households are to be read in accordance with section 7.

PART 2

DUTIES OF LOCAL AUTHORITIES AND OTHER BODIES IN ENGLAND

19   Responsible local authorities

For the purposes of this Part, each of the following is a responsible local authority—

(a)   a county council in England;

(b)   a district council in England, other than a council for a district in a county for which there is a county council;

(c)   a London borough council;

(d)   the Council of the Isles of Scilly;

(e)   the Common Council of the City of London in its capacity as a local authority.

20   Partner authorities

(1)   For the purposes of this Part, each of the following is a partner authority in relation to a responsible local authority—

(a)   any person mentioned in subsection (2) who acts or is established for an area which, or any part of which, coincides with or falls within the responsible local authority's area;

(b)   the person mentioned in subsection (3).

(2) The persons referred to in subsection (1)(a) are—

    (a) any district council which is not a responsible local authority;

    (b) a police authority;

    (c) a chief officer of police;

    (d) an Integrated Transport Authority for an integrated transport area in England;

    (e) Transport for London;

    (f) a Strategic Health Authority;

    (g) a Primary Care Trust;

    (h) a youth offending team established under section 39 of the Crime and Disorder Act 1998.

(3) The person referred to in subsection (1)(b) is the Secretary of State, but only in relation to—

    (a) the Secretary of State's functions under section 2 of the Employment and Training Act 1973 (arrangements with respect to obtaining etc. employment or employees);

    (b) the Secretary of State's functions under sections 2 and 3 of the Offender Management Act 2007 (responsibility for ensuring provision of probation services throughout England and Wales).

(4) The Secretary of State's functions under this Part as a partner authority of a local authority in relation to the functions referred to in subsection (3)(b) are functions to which section 2(1)(c) of the Offender Management Act 2007 (functions to be performed through arrangements under section 3 of that Act) applies.

(5) In subsection (1)(a), references to the area for which a person acts or is established are references—

    (a) in the case of the Commissioner of Police of the Metropolis, to the metropolitan police district (within the meaning of the Police Act 1996);

    (b) in the case of the Commissioner of the City of London Police, to the City of London police area (within the meaning of that Act);

    (c) in the case of any other chief officer of police, to the police area listed in Schedule 1 to that Act for which the chief officer's police force is maintained;

    (d) in the case of Transport for London, to Greater London.

(6) The Secretary of State may by order—

    (a) amend subsection (2) or (3) by—

        (i) adding to it any person who has functions of a public nature;

        (ii) removing from it any person for the time being mentioned in it; or

        (iii) adding to subsection (3) any function of the Secretary of State or removing from it any function for the time being mentioned in it; and

    (b) make such other amendments of this section as appear to the Secretary of State to be necessary or expedient in consequence of provision made under paragraph (a).

(7) Before making an order under subsection (6) the Secretary of State must consult such representatives of local government and such other persons (if any) as the Secretary of State thinks fit.

21   Co-operation to reduce child poverty in local area

(1)   Each responsible local authority must make arrangements to promote co-operation between –

    (a)   the authority;

    (b)   each of its partner authorities; and

    (c)   such other persons or bodies as the authority thinks fit.

(2)   The arrangements are to be made with a view to reducing, and mitigating the effects of, child poverty in the responsible local authority's area.

(3)   Each partner authority must co-operate with the responsible local authority in the making of arrangements under this section.

(4)   The responsible local authority and each partner authority must, in exercising their functions under this section, have regard to any guidance given to them for the purpose by the Secretary of State.

(5)   A responsible local authority and any partner authority may for the purposes of arrangements under this section –

    (a)   provide staff, goods, services, accommodation or other resources;

    (b)   establish and maintain a pooled fund.

(6)   A pooled fund is a fund –

    (a)   which is made up of contributions by the responsible local authority and the partner authority or authorities concerned, and

    (b)   out of which payments may be made towards expenditure incurred in the discharge of functions of the responsible local authority and functions of the partner authority or authorities.

22   Local child poverty needs assessment

(1)   The arrangements made by a responsible local authority under section 21 must include arrangements to prepare and publish an assessment of the needs of children living in poverty in its area ("a local child poverty needs assessment").

(2)   The Secretary of State may by regulations make provision about local child poverty needs assessments.

(3)   Those regulations may in particular include provision as to –

    (a)   matters that must be considered in a local child poverty needs assessment;

    (b)   when and how an assessment must be published;

    (c)   keeping an assessment under review;

    (d)   when and how an assessment must be revised;

    (e)   consultation to be carried out during the preparation or revision of an assessment;

    (f)   other steps required or permitted to be taken in connection with the preparation or revision of an assessment.

(4)   The responsible local authority and each partner authority must, in exercising their functions under this section, have regard to any guidance given to them for the purpose by the Secretary of State.

23   Joint child poverty strategy for local area

(1)   The arrangements made by a responsible local authority under section 21 must include arrangements to prepare a joint child poverty strategy in relation to its area and to modify it in accordance with this section.

(2)   The joint child poverty strategy must set out the measures that the responsible local authority and each partner authority propose to take for the purpose of reducing, and mitigating the effects of, child poverty in the responsible local authority's area.

(3)   Those measures—
   (a)   must include measures relating to matters identified in a local child poverty needs assessment;
   (b)   may include measures relating to other matters identified by the responsible local authority or a partner authority in connection with child poverty in the responsible local authority's area.

(4)   The responsible local authority may at any time modify the joint child poverty strategy.

(5)   When a responsible local authority revises a local child poverty needs assessment it must consider whether any modification of the joint child poverty strategy is required.

(6)   In preparing or modifying the joint child poverty strategy, the responsible local authority—
   (a)   must consult such children, and organisations working with or representing children, as the authority thinks fit,
   (b)   must consult such parents, and organisations working with or representing parents, as the authority thinks fit, and
   (c)   may consult such other persons or bodies as the authority thinks fit.

(7)   The responsible local authority and each partner authority must, in exercising their functions under this section, have regard to any guidance given to them for the purpose by the Secretary of State.

(8)   The responsible local authority and each partner authority must have regard to the joint child poverty strategy in exercising their functions.

(9)   References in this section to a local child poverty needs assessment are to a local child poverty needs assessment prepared by the responsible local authority under section 22.

24   Sustainable community strategy

In section 4 of the Local Government Act 2000 (strategies for promoting well-being), in subsection (3)—
   (a)   omit the word "and" immediately after sub-paragraph (ii) of paragraph (a), and
   (b)   after paragraph (a) insert—
   "(aa)   must, if it is a local authority in England, have regard to the following, so far as they relate to the authority's area—

(i) any arrangements made under section 21 of the Child Poverty Act 2010 (co-operation to reduce child poverty in local area);

(ii) any local child poverty needs assessment prepared under section 22 of that Act (local child poverty needs assessment);

(iii) any joint child poverty strategy prepared under section 23 of that Act (joint child poverty strategy for local area), and".

25 Meaning of "child poverty" in Part 2

(1) This section has effect for the interpretation of this Part.

(2) A child is to be taken to be living in poverty if the child experiences socio-economic disadvantage, and references to "child poverty" have a corresponding meaning.

(3) Without limiting subsection (2), a child is to be taken to experience socio-economic disadvantage during any period in which—

(a) the child lives in a household that falls within the relevant income group for the purposes of section 3 (the relative low income target) or section 5 (the absolute low income target), or

(b) the child lives in a household that falls within the relevant income group for the purposes of subsection (1)(a) of section 4 (combined low income and material deprivation target) and is regarded for the purposes of subsection (1)(b) of that section as experiencing material deprivation.

(4) Expressions used in subsection (3) and in Part 1 of this Act have the same meaning in that subsection as in that Part.

PART 3

MISCELLANEOUS AND GENERAL

Free school lunches and milk

26 Free school lunches and milk

(1) In section 512ZB of the Education Act 1996 (provision of free school lunches and milk), in subsection (4)—

(a) after "A person" insert "("C")",

(b) in paragraph (a)—

(i) for "his parent" substitute "C's parent",

(ii) at the end of sub-paragraph (iia), insert "or", and

(iii) omit sub-paragraph (iv) (including the "or" immediately following it),

(c) after paragraph (a) insert—

"(aa) C meets any conditions prescribed for the purposes of this paragraph and C's parent is, in such circumstances as may be so prescribed—

      (i)   in receipt of any benefit or allowance not falling within paragraph (a) that is so prescribed, or

      (ii)   entitled to any tax credit under the Tax Credits Act 2002 or element of such a tax credit, that is so prescribed, or",

(d)   in paragraph (b)—

    (i)   for "he, himself, is—" substitute "C is—",

    (ii)   at the end of sub-paragraph (ii), insert "or", and

    (iii) omit sub-paragraph (iii), and

(e)   at the end insert—

    "(c)   C meets any conditions prescribed for the purposes of this paragraph and is—

      (i)   in receipt of any benefit or allowance not falling within paragraph (b) that is so prescribed, or

      (ii)   entitled to any tax credit under the Tax Credits Act 2002 or element of such a tax credit, that is so prescribed."

(2)   Any regulations made under paragraph (a)(iv) of subsection (4) of section 512ZB of the Education Act 1996 and in force immediately before the coming into force of this section are to have effect as if made under paragraph (aa) of that subsection.

(3)   Any regulations made under paragraph (b)(iii) of subsection (4) of section 512ZB of the Education Act 1996 and in force immediately before the coming into force of this section are to have effect as if made under paragraph (c) of that subsection.

General

27   General interpretation

(1)   In this Act—

"child" means—

(a)   a person under the age of 16, or

(b)   a person who is a qualifying young person for the purposes of Part 9 of the Social Security Contributions and Benefits Act 1992 or Part 9 of the Social Security Contributions and Benefits (Northern Ireland) Act 1992 (child benefit);

"parent" means—

(a)   any individual who has parental responsibility for a child, or

(b)   any other individual with whom a child resides and who has care of the child;

"prescribed" means prescribed by regulations;

"regulations" means regulations made by the Secretary of State under this Act.

(2)   In paragraph (a) of the definition of "parent" in subsection (1), the reference to "parental responsibility"—

(a)   in relation to England and Wales, is to be read in accordance with the Children Act 1989,

    (b)   in relation to Northern Ireland, is to be read in accordance with the Children (Northern Ireland) Order 1995, and

    (c)   in relation to Scotland, is to be read as a reference to parental responsibilities within the meaning of the Children (Scotland) Act 1995.

28 Regulations and orders

(1) Any power to make regulations or an order under this Act is exercisable by statutory instrument.

(2) Any regulations or order under this Act may –

    (a)   make different provision for different cases,

    (b)   include supplementary, incidental and consequential provision, and

    (c)   make transitional provisions and savings.

(3) A power conferred by any provision of this Act to make regulations or an order includes power to provide for a person to exercise a discretion in dealing with any matter.

(4) A statutory instrument containing –

    (a)   regulations under any provision of this Act, other than regulations made only under section 5(3) or 22(2), or

    (b)   an order under section 8(4),

may not be made unless a draft of the instrument has been laid before, and approved by a resolution of, each House of Parliament.

(5) A statutory instrument containing –

    (a)   regulations made only under section 5(3) or 22(2), or

    (b)   an order under section 20(6),

is subject to annulment in pursuance of a resolution of either House of Parliament.

29 Financial provisions

There is to be paid out of money provided by Parliament –

    (a)   any expenditure incurred under or by virtue of this Act by a Minister of the Crown, and

    (b)   any increase attributable to this Act in the sums payable under any other Act out of money so provided.

30 Extent

(1) Except as provided by subsections (2) to (4), the provisions of this Act extend to England and Wales, Scotland and Northern Ireland.

(2) Section 11 extends to Scotland only.

(3) Section 12 extends to Northern Ireland only.

(4) Part 2 and section 26 extend to England and Wales only.

31 Commencement

(1) This Act, except Part 2 and section 26, comes into force on the day on which this Act is passed.

(2) Part 2 and section 26 come into force at the end of the period of 2 months beginning with the day on which this Act is passed.

32   Short title

This Act may be cited as the Child Poverty Act 2010.

SCHEDULES

SCHEDULE 1

Section 8

THE CHILD POVERTY COMMISSION

Membership, chair and deputy chair

1   (1)   The members of the Commission are to be —
     (a)   a chair appointed by the Secretary of State,
     (b)   a member appointed by the Scottish Ministers,
     (c)   a member appointed by the Welsh Ministers,
     (d)   a member appointed by the relevant Northern Ireland department, and
     (e)   such number of other members appointed by the Secretary of State as the Secretary of State may determine.

   (2)   Before appointing a member under sub-paragraph (1)(e), the Secretary of State must consult —
     (a)   the chair, and
     (b)   the Scottish Ministers, the Welsh Ministers and the relevant Northern Ireland department.

   (3)   The Commission may appoint one of the members as the deputy chair.

   (4)   The Secretary of State must have regard to the desirability of securing that the Commission (taken as a whole) has experience in or knowledge of —
     (a)   the formulation, implementation and evaluation of policy relating to child poverty;
     (b)   research in connection with child poverty;
     (c)   work with children and families experiencing poverty.

Term of office

2   Members are to hold and vacate office in accordance with the terms of their appointment, subject to the following provisions.

3   Members must be appointed for a term of not more than 5 years.

4   The consent of the Secretary of State is required for the terms of an appointment made under paragraph 1(1)(b) to (d).

5   A member may resign by giving notice in writing to the Secretary of State.

6   The Secretary of State may remove a member if —
     (a)   the person has been absent from 3 or more consecutive meetings of the Commission, without its permission,

(b) the person has become bankrupt or has made an arrangement with creditors,

(c) the person's estate has been sequestrated in Scotland or the person, under Scots law, has made a composition or arrangement with, or granted a trust deed for, creditors, or

(d) the Secretary of State is satisfied that the person is otherwise unable or unfit to perform the duties of the office.

7   A person ceases to be the chair or the deputy chair if the person—

(a) resigns that office by giving notice in writing to the Secretary of State, or

(b) ceases to be a member.

8   A person who holds or has held office as the chair, or as the deputy chair or other member, may be reappointed, whether or not to the same office.

Staff and facilities

9   The Secretary of State may provide the Commission with—

(a) such staff,

(b) such accommodation, equipment and other facilities, and

(c) such sums,

as the Secretary of State may determine are required by the Commission in the exercise of its functions.

Research

10   (1) The Commission may at any time request the Secretary of State to carry out, or commission others to carry out, such research on behalf of the Commission for the purpose of the carrying out of the Commission's functions as the Commission may specify in the request.

(2) If the Secretary of State decides not to comply with the request, the Secretary of State must notify the Commission of the reasons for the decision.

Payments to members

11   The Secretary of State may pay to or in respect of the members of the Commission such remuneration, allowances and expenses as the Secretary of State may determine.

Status

12   The Commission is not to be regarded—

(a) as the servant or agent of the Crown, or

(b) as enjoying any status, privilege or immunity of the Crown.

Sub-committees

13   The Commission may establish sub-committees.

Validity of proceedings

14   The Commission may regulate—

        (a)   its own procedure (including quorum), and

        (b)   the procedure of any sub-committee (including quorum).

15   The validity of anything done by the Commission or any sub-committee is not affected by —

        (a)   any vacancy in the membership of the Commission or sub-committee, or

        (b)   any defect in the appointment of any member of the Commission or sub-committee.

Discharge of functions

16   The Commission may authorise a sub-committee or member to exercise any of the Commission's functions.

Provision of advice by Commission

17 (1)   The Commission must comply with any request made by the Secretary of State under section 10 or by the Scottish Ministers or the relevant Northern Ireland department under section 13.

    (2)   Advice given by the Commission under either of those sections must contain the reasons for the advice.

    (3)   As soon as reasonably practicable after giving advice under either of those sections, the Commission must publish the advice in such manner as it thinks fit.

Public records

18   In Schedule 1 to the Public Records Act 1958 (definition of public records) in Part 2 of the Table at the end of paragraph 3 at the appropriate place insert —
       "The Child Poverty Commission."

Parliamentary Commissioner

19   In Schedule 2 to the Parliamentary Commissioner Act 1967 (departments etc subject to investigation) at the appropriate place insert —
       "The Child Poverty Commission."

Disqualification

20 (1)   In Part 2 of Schedule 1 to the House of Commons Disqualification Act 1975 (bodies of which all members are disqualified) at the appropriate place insert —
       "The Child Poverty Commission."

    (2)   In Part 2 of Schedule 1 to the Northern Ireland Assembly Disqualification Act 1975 (bodies of which all members are disqualified) at the appropriate place insert —
       "The Child Poverty Commission."

Freedom of information

21   In Part 6 of Schedule 1 to the Freedom of Information Act 2000 (other public

bodies and offices: general) at the appropriate place insert —
"The Child Poverty Commission."

SCHEDULE 2

CONTINUING EFFECT OF TARGETS AFTER TARGET YEAR

Interpretation of Schedule

1   In this Schedule —
       "renewed target year" means —
          (a)   a financial year in relation to which the Secretary of State is
                required by paragraph 2 to ensure that the targets are met, or
          (b)   a financial year specified under paragraph 3(a);
       "the targets" means the targets in sections 3, 4 and 6 and, subject to
          paragraph 9, the target in section 5;
       "target statement" —
          (a)   in relation to the target year, means the report required by
                section 14(3), and
          (b)   in relation to a renewed target year, means the statement
                required by paragraph 8.

Duty to maintain targets

2   If the target statement relating to the target year or a renewed target year
       indicates that the targets have been met in relation to that financial year, the
       Secretary of State must ensure that they are also met in relation to the
       financial year following that in which that target statement is laid before
       Parliament.

Duty to make regulations requiring targets to be met in specified financial year

3   If the target statement relating to the target year or a renewed target year
       indicates that any of the targets has not been met in relation to that financial
       year, the Secretary of State must make regulations under this paragraph —
          (a)   requiring the Secretary of State to ensure that the targets are met in
                relation to a later financial year specified in the regulations,
          (b)   requiring the Secretary of State, the Scottish Ministers and the
                relevant Northern Ireland department to publish strategies,
          (c)   requiring consultation by the Secretary of State, in relation to any
                strategy prepared by the Secretary of State, with the persons
                mentioned in section 10(4)(a) to (d) and consultation by the Scottish
                Ministers and the relevant Northern Ireland department, in relation
                to strategies prepared by them, with the persons whom they are
                required to consult under section 13(3)(a) to (d), and
          (d)   requiring the Secretary of State to publish annual reports on the
                implementation of any strategy prepared by the Secretary of State.

4   Regulations under paragraph 3 must be made as soon as reasonably
       practicable after the time when the target statement referred to in that
       paragraph is laid before Parliament.

5   Regulations under paragraph 3 may confer or impose functions on the Commission.

6   The provision that may be made by regulations under paragraph 3 includes provision corresponding to that made (in relation to financial years not later than the target year) by any of the following—

   (a)   sections 9 and 10 (UK strategies);
   (b)   sections 11, 12 and 13 (Scottish and Northern Ireland strategies);
   (c)   section 14 (reports);
   (d)   paragraph 17 of Schedule 1 (provision of advice by Commission).

Economic and fiscal circumstances

7   (1)   The matters mentioned in section 16(2) must be taken into account—

      (a)   by the Secretary of State in preparing a strategy under regulations under paragraph 3;
      (b)   by the Commission in considering any advice to be given under any such regulations.

   (2)   In preparing a strategy under regulations under paragraph 3, the Scottish Ministers or the relevant Northern Ireland department must have regard to the matters mentioned in section 16(3)(a) and (b).

Statement as to whether targets are met in relation to renewed target year

8   (1)   The Secretary of State must, as soon as reasonably practicable after the end of each renewed target year, lay before Parliament a statement of—

      (a)   the percentage of children living in qualifying households in the United Kingdom in the renewed target year who were living in households that fell within the relevant income group for the purposes of section 3 (the relative low income target);
      (b)   the percentage of children living in qualifying households in the United Kingdom in the renewed target year who were for the purposes of section 4 (the combined low income and material deprivation target) living in households that fell within the relevant income group and experiencing material deprivation;
      (c)   if the absolute low income target in section 5 applies in relation to the renewed target year, the percentage of children living in qualifying households in the United Kingdom in the renewed target year who were living in households that fell within the relevant income group for the purposes of that section;
      (d)   the percentage of children who have lived in qualifying households during the survey years (as defined by section 6(2)) which relate to the renewed target year who have lived in households that fell within the relevant income group for the purposes of section 6 (the persistent poverty target) in at least 3 of the survey years.

   (2)   The statement must be based on statistics that the Statistics Board has designated under section 12 of the Statistics and Registration Service Act 2007 (assessment) as National Statistics.

   (3)   Whether the targets have been met in relation to a renewed target year is to be determined by reference to the percentages given in the statement.

(4) If any of the targets has not been met, the statement must explain why it has not been met.

Power to exclude or modify absolute low income target

9   (1) Regulations may—

    (a) amend the percentage specified in subsection (1) of section 5 (the absolute low income target) or the base year specified in subsection (4) of that section in their application in relation to any financial year later than the target year, or

    (b) repeal section 5, and the reference to that section in section 25(3)(a).

   (2) Regulations made by virtue of sub-paragraph (1)(b) do not affect the application of section 5 in relation to the target year or any other financial year before the regulations are made.

Third Parties (Rights against Insurers) Act 2010

CHAPTER 10

CONTENTS

Third Parties (Rights against Insurers) Act 2010

2010 CHAPTER 10

An Act to make provision about the rights of third parties against insurers of liabilities to third parties in the case where the insured is insolvent, and in certain other cases. [25th March 2010]

B E IT ENACTED by the Queen's most Excellent Majesty, by and with the advice and consent of the Lords Spiritual and Temporal, and Commons, in this present Parliament assembled, and by the authority of the same, as follows: —

Transfer of rights to third parties

1   Rights against insurer of insolvent person etc

(1)   This section applies if —
   (a)   a relevant person incurs a liability against which that person is insured under a contract of insurance, or
   (b)   a person who is subject to such a liability becomes a relevant person.

(2)   The rights of the relevant person under the contract against the insurer in respect of the liability are transferred to and vest in the person to whom the liability is or was incurred (the "third party").

(3)   The third party may bring proceedings to enforce the rights against the insurer without having established the relevant person's liability; but the third party may not enforce those rights without having established that liability.

(4)   For the purposes of this Act, a liability is established only if its existence and amount are established; and, for that purpose, "establish" means establish —
   (a)   by virtue of a declaration under section 2 or a declarator under section 3,
   (b)   by a judgment or decree,

      (c)   by an award in arbitral proceedings or by an arbitration, or

      (d)   by an enforceable agreement.

(5)   In this Act—

      (a)   references to an "insured" are to a person who incurs or who is subject to a liability to a third party against which that person is insured under a contract of insurance;

      (b)   references to a "relevant person" are to a person within sections 4 to 7;

      (c)   references to a "third party" are to be construed in accordance with subsection (2);

      (d)   references to "transferred rights" are to rights under a contract of insurance which are transferred under this section.

2   Establishing liability in England and Wales and Northern Ireland

(1)   This section applies where a person (P)—

      (a)   claims to have rights under a contract of insurance by virtue of a transfer under section 1, but

      (b)   has not yet established the insured's liability which is insured under that contract.

(2)   P may bring proceedings against the insurer for either or both of the following—

      (a)   a declaration as to the insured's liability to P;

      (b)   a declaration as to the insurer's potential liability to P.

(3)   In such proceedings P is entitled, subject to any defence on which the insurer may rely, to a declaration under subsection (2)(a) or (b) on proof of the insured's liability to P or (as the case may be) the insurer's potential liability to P.

(4)   Where proceedings are brought under subsection (2)(a) the insurer may rely on any defence on which the insured could rely if those proceedings were proceedings brought against the insured in respect of the insured's liability to P.

(5)   Subsection (4) is subject to section 12(1).

(6)   Where the court makes a declaration under this section, the effect of which is that the insurer is liable to P, the court may give the appropriate judgment against the insurer.

(7)   Where a person applying for a declaration under subsection (2)(b) is entitled or required, by virtue of the contract of insurance, to do so in arbitral proceedings, that person may also apply in the same proceedings for a declaration under subsection (2)(a).

(8)   In the application of this section to arbitral proceedings, subsection (6) is to be read as if "tribunal" were substituted for "court" and "make the appropriate award" for "give the appropriate judgment".

(9)   When bringing proceedings under subsection (2)(a), P may also make the insured a defendant to those proceedings.

(10)   If (but only if) the insured is a defendant to proceedings under this section (whether by virtue of subsection (9) or otherwise), a declaration under subsection (2) binds the insured as well as the insurer.

(11)　In this section, references to the insurer's potential liability to P are references to the insurer's liability in respect of the insured's liability to P, if established.

3　Establishing liability in Scotland

(1)　This section applies where a person (P) —

　　(a)　claims to have rights under a contract of insurance by virtue of a transfer under section 1, but

　　(b)　has not yet established the insured's liability which is insured under that contract.

(2)　P may bring proceedings against the insurer for either or both of the following —

　　(a)　a declarator as to the insured's liability to P;

　　(b)　a declarator as to the insurer's potential liability to P.

(3)　Where proceedings are brought under subsection (2)(a) the insurer may rely on any defence on which the insured could rely if those proceedings were proceedings brought against the insured in respect of the insured's liability to P.

(4)　Subsection (3) is subject to section 12(1).

(5)　Where the court grants a declarator under this section, the effect of which is that the insurer is liable to P, the court may grant the appropriate decree against the insurer.

(6)　Where a person applying for a declarator under subsection (2)(b) is entitled or required, by virtue of the contract of insurance, to do so in an arbitration, that person may also apply in the same arbitration for a declarator under subsection (2)(a).

(7)　In the application of this section to an arbitration, subsection (5) is to be read as if "tribunal" were substituted for "court" and "make the appropriate award" for "grant the appropriate decree".

(8)　When bringing proceedings under subsection (2)(a), P may also make the insured a defender to those proceedings.

(9)　If (but only if) the insured is a defender to proceedings under this section (whether by virtue of subsection (8) or otherwise), a declarator under subsection (2) binds the insured as well as the insurer.

(10)　In this section, the reference to the insurer's potential liability to P is a reference to the insurer's liability in respect of the insured's liability to P, if established.

Relevant persons

4　Individuals

(1)　An individual is a relevant person if any of the following is in force in respect of that individual in England and Wales —

　　(a)　a deed of arrangement registered in accordance with the Deeds of Arrangement Act 1914,

　　(b)　an administration order made under Part 6 of the County Courts Act 1984,

(c) an enforcement restriction order made under Part 6A of that Act,

(d) subject to subsection (4), a debt relief order made under Part 7A of the Insolvency Act 1986,

(e) a voluntary arrangement approved in accordance with Part 8 of that Act, or

(f) a bankruptcy order made under Part 9 of that Act.

(2) An individual is a relevant person if any of the following is in force in respect of that individual (or, in the case of paragraph (a) or (b), that individual's estate) in Scotland —

(a) an award of sequestration made under section 5 of the Bankruptcy (Scotland) Act 1985,

(b) a protected trust deed within the meaning of that Act, or

(c) a composition approved in accordance with Schedule 4 to that Act.

(3) An individual is a relevant person if any of the following is in force in respect of that individual in Northern Ireland —

(a) an administration order made under Part 6 of the Judgments Enforcement (Northern Ireland) Order 1981 (S.I. 1981/226 (N.I. 6)),

(b) a deed of arrangement registered in accordance with Chapter 1 of Part 8 of the Insolvency (Northern Ireland) Order 1989 (S.I. 1989/2405 (N.I. 19)),

(c) a voluntary arrangement approved under Chapter 2 of Part 8 of that Order, or

(d) a bankruptcy order made under Part 9 of that Order.

(4) If an individual is a relevant person by virtue of subsection (1)(d), that person is a relevant person for the purposes of section 1(1)(b) only.

(5) Where an award of sequestration made under section 5 of the Bankruptcy (Scotland) Act 1985 is recalled or reduced, any rights which were transferred under section 1 as a result of that award are re-transferred to and vest in the person who became a relevant person as a result of the award.

(6) Where an order discharging an individual from an award of sequestration made under section 5 of the Bankruptcy (Scotland) Act 1985 is recalled or reduced under paragraph 17 or 18 of Schedule 4 to that Act, the order is to be treated for the purposes of this section as never having been made.

5 Individuals who die insolvent

(1) An individual who dies insolvent is a relevant person for the purposes of section 1(1)(b) only.

(2) For the purposes of this section an individual (D) is to be regarded as having died insolvent if, following D's death —

(a) D's estate falls to be administered in accordance with an order under section 421 of the Insolvency Act 1986 or Article 365 of the Insolvency (Northern Ireland) Order 1989 (S.I. 1989/2405 (N. I. 19)),

(b) an award of sequestration is made under section 5 of the Bankruptcy (Scotland) Act 1985 in respect of D's estate and the award is not recalled or reduced, or

(c) a judicial factor is appointed under section 11A of the Judicial Factors (Scotland) Act 1889 in respect of D's estate and the judicial factor certifies that the estate is absolutely insolvent within the meaning of the Bankruptcy (Scotland) Act 1985.

(3) Where a transfer of rights under section 1 takes place as a result of an insured person being a relevant person by virtue of this section, references in this Act to an insured are, where the context so requires, to be read as references to the insured's estate.

6   Corporate bodies etc

(1) A body corporate or an unincorporated body is a relevant person if —

     (a) a compromise or arrangement between the body and its creditors (or a class of them) is in force, having been sanctioned in accordance with section 899 of the Companies Act 2006, or

     (b) the body has been dissolved under section 1000, 1001 or 1003 of that Act, and the body has not been —

         (i) restored to the register by virtue of section 1025 of that Act, or

         (ii) ordered to be restored to the register by virtue of section 1031 of that Act.

(2) A body corporate or an unincorporated body is a relevant person if, in England and Wales or Scotland —

     (a) a voluntary arrangement approved in accordance with Part 1 of the Insolvency Act 1986 is in force in respect of it,

     (b) an administration order made under Part 2 of that Act is in force in respect of it,

     (c) there is a person appointed in accordance with Part 3 of that Act who is acting as receiver or manager of the body's property (or there would be such a person so acting but for a temporary vacancy),

     (d) the body is, or is being, wound up voluntarily in accordance with Chapter 2 of Part 4 of that Act,

     (e) there is a person appointed under section 135 of that Act who is acting as provisional liquidator in respect of the body (or there would be such a person so acting but for a temporary vacancy), or

     (f) the body is, or is being, wound up by the court following the making of a winding-up order under Chapter 6 of Part 4 of that Act or Part 5 of that Act.

(3) A body corporate or an unincorporated body is a relevant person if, in Scotland —

     (a) an award of sequestration has been made under section 6 of the Bankruptcy (Scotland) Act 1985 in respect of the body's estate, and the body has not been discharged under that Act,

     (b) the body has been dissolved and an award of sequestration has been made under that section in respect of its estate,

     (c) a protected trust deed within the meaning of the Bankruptcy (Scotland) Act 1985 is in force in respect of the body's estate, or

     (d) a composition approved in accordance with Schedule 4 to that Act is in force in respect of the body.

(4) A body corporate or an unincorporated body is a relevant person if, in Northern Ireland —

    (a)   a voluntary arrangement approved in accordance with Part 2 of the Insolvency (Northern Ireland) Order 1989 (S.I. 1989/2405 (N. I. 19)) is in force in respect of the body,

    (b)   an administration order made under Part 3 of that Order is in force in respect of the body,

    (c)   there is a person appointed in accordance with Part 4 of that Order who is acting as receiver or manager of the body's property (or there would be such a person so acting but for a temporary vacancy),

    (d)   the body is, or is being, wound up voluntarily in accordance with Chapter 2 of Part 5 of that Order,

    (e)   there is a person appointed under Article 115 of that Order who is acting as provisional liquidator in respect of the body (or there would be such a person so acting but for a temporary vacancy), or

    (f)   the body is, or is being, wound up by the court following the making of a winding-up order under Chapter 6 of Part 5 of that Order or Part 6 of that Order.

(5)   A body within subsection (1)(a) is not a relevant person in relation to a liability that is transferred to another body by the order sanctioning the compromise or arrangement.

(6)   Where a body is a relevant person by virtue of subsection (1)(a), section 1 has effect to transfer rights only to a person on whom the compromise or arrangement is binding.

(7)   Where an award of sequestration made under section 6 of the Bankruptcy (Scotland) Act 1985 is recalled or reduced, any rights which were transferred under section 1 as a result of that award are re-transferred to and vest in the person who became a relevant person as a result of the award.

(8)   Where an order discharging a body from an award of sequestration made under section 6 of the Bankruptcy (Scotland) Act 1985 is recalled or reduced under paragraph 17 or 18 of Schedule 4 to that Act, the order is to be treated for the purposes of this section as never having been made.

(9)   In this section—

    (a)   a reference to a person appointed in accordance with Part 3 of the Insolvency Act 1986 includes a reference to a person appointed under section 101 of the Law of Property Act 1925;

    (b)   a reference to a receiver or manager of a body's property includes a reference to a receiver or manager of part only of the property and to a receiver only of the income arising from the property or from part of it;

    (c)   for the purposes of subsection (3) "body corporate or unincorporated body" includes any entity, other than a trust, the estate of which may be sequestrated under section 6 of the Bankruptcy (Scotland) Act 1985;

    (d)   a reference to a person appointed in accordance with Part 4 of the Insolvency (Northern Ireland) Order 1989 (S.I. 1989/2405 (N. I. 19)) includes a reference to a person appointed under section 19 of the Conveyancing Act 1881.

7   Scottish trusts

(1)   A trustee of a Scottish trust is, in respect of a liability of that trustee that falls to be met out of the trust estate, a relevant person if—

(a)   an award of sequestration has been made under section 6 of the Bankruptcy (Scotland) Act 1985 in respect of the trust estate, and the trust has not been discharged under that Act,

(b)   a protected trust deed within the meaning of that Act is in force in respect of the trust estate, or

(c)   a composition approved in accordance with Schedule 4 to that Act is in force in respect of the trust estate.

(2)   Where an award of sequestration made under section 6 of the Bankruptcy (Scotland) Act 1985 is recalled or reduced any rights which were transferred under section 1 as a result of that award are re-transferred to and vest in the person who became a relevant person as a result of the award.

(3)   Where an order discharging an individual, body or trust from an award of sequestration made under section 6 of the Bankruptcy (Scotland) Act 1985 is recalled or reduced under paragraph 17 or 18 of Schedule 4 to that Act, the order is to be treated for the purposes of this section as never having been made.

(4)   In this section "Scottish trust" means a trust the estate of which may be sequestrated under section 6 of the Bankruptcy (Scotland) Act 1985.

Transferred rights: supplemental

8   Limit on rights transferred

Where the liability of an insured to a third party is less than the liability of the insurer to the insured (ignoring the effect of section 1), no rights are transferred under that section in respect of the difference.

9   Conditions affecting transferred rights

(1)   This section applies where transferred rights are subject to a condition (whether under the contract of insurance from which the transferred rights are derived or otherwise) that the insured has to fulfil.

(2)   Anything done by the third party which, if done by the insured, would have amounted to or contributed to fulfilment of the condition is to be treated as if done by the insured.

(3)   The transferred rights are not subject to a condition requiring the insured to provide information or assistance to the insurer if that condition cannot be fulfilled because the insured is—

(a)   an individual who has died, or

(b)   a body corporate that has been dissolved.

(4)   A condition requiring the insured to provide information or assistance to the insurer does not include a condition requiring the insured to notify the insurer of the existence of a claim under the contract of insurance.

(5)   The transferred rights are not subject to a condition requiring the prior discharge by the insured of the insured's liability to the third party.

(6)   In the case of a contract of marine insurance, subsection (5) applies only to the extent that the liability of the insured is a liability in respect of death or personal injury.

(7)   In this section—

"contract of marine insurance" has the meaning given by section 1 of the Marine Insurance Act 1906;

"dissolved" means dissolved under—

    (a)   Chapter 9 of Part 4 of the Insolvency Act 1986,

    (b)   section 1000, 1001 or 1003 of the Companies Act 2006, or

    (c)   Chapter 9 of Part 5 of the Insolvency (Northern Ireland) Order 1989 (S.I. 1989/2405 (N. I. 19));

"personal injury" includes any disease and any impairment of a person's physical or mental condition.

10   Insurer's right of set off

(1)   This section applies if—

    (a)   rights of an insured under a contract of insurance have been transferred to a third party under section 1,

    (b)   the insured is under a liability to the insurer under the contract ("the insured's liability"), and

    (c)   if there had been no transfer, the insurer would have been entitled to set off the amount of the insured's liability against the amount of the insurer's own liability to the insured.

(2)   The insurer is entitled to set off the amount of the insured's liability against the amount of the insurer's own liability to the third party in relation to the transferred rights.

Provision of information etc

11   Information and disclosure for third parties

Schedule 1 (information and disclosure for third parties) has effect.

Enforcement of transferred rights

12   Limitation and prescription

(1)   Subsection (2) applies where a person brings proceedings for a declaration under section 2(2)(a), or for a declarator under section 3(2)(a), and the proceedings are started or, in Scotland, commenced—

    (a)   after the expiry of a period of limitation applicable to an action against the insured to enforce the insured's liability, or of a period of prescription applicable to that liability, but

    (b)   while such an action is in progress.

(2)   The insurer may not rely on the expiry of that period as a defence unless the insured is able to rely on it in the action against the insured.

(3)   For the purposes of subsection (1), an action is to be treated as no longer in progress if it has been concluded by a judgment or decree, or by an award, even if there is an appeal or a right of appeal.

(4) Where a person who has already established an insured's liability to that person brings proceedings under this Act against the insurer, nothing in this Act is to be read as meaning—

    (a) that, for the purposes of the law of limitation in England and Wales, that person's cause of action against the insurer arose otherwise than at the time when that person established the liability of the insured,

    (b) that, for the purposes of the law of prescription in Scotland, the obligation in respect of which the proceedings are brought became enforceable against the insurer otherwise than at that time, or

    (c) that, for the purposes of the law of limitation in Northern Ireland, that person's cause of action against the insurer arose otherwise than at the time when that person established the liability of the insured.

13 Jurisdiction within the United Kingdom

(1) Where a person (P) domiciled in a part of the United Kingdom is entitled to bring proceedings under this Act against an insurer domiciled in another part, P may do so in the part where P is domiciled or in the part where the insurer is domiciled (whatever the contract of insurance may stipulate as to where proceedings are to be brought).

(2) The following provisions of the Civil Jurisdiction and Judgments Act 1982 (relating to determination of domicile) apply for the purposes of subsection (1)—

    (a) section 41(2), (3), (5) and (6) (individuals);

    (b) section 42(1), (3), (4) and (8) (corporations and associations);

    (c) section 45(2) and (3) (trusts);

    (d) section 46(1), (3) and (7) (the Crown).

(3) In Schedule 5 to that Act (proceedings excluded from general provisions as to allocation of jurisdiction within the United Kingdom) at the end add—

"Proceedings by third parties against insurers

    11   Proceedings under the Third Parties (Rights against Insurers) Act 2010."

Enforcement of insured's liability

14 Effect of transfer on insured's liability

(1) Where rights in respect of an insured's liability to a third party are transferred under section 1, the third party may enforce that liability against the insured only to the extent (if any) that it exceeds the amount recoverable from the insurer by virtue of the transfer.

(2) Subsection (3) applies if a transfer of rights under section 1 occurs because the insured person is a relevant person by virtue of—

    (a) section 4(1)(a) or (e), (2)(b) or (3)(b) or (c),

    (b) section 6(1)(a), (2)(a), (3)(c) or (4)(a), or

    (c) section 7(1)(b).

(3) If the liability is subject to the arrangement, trust deed or compromise by virtue of which the insured is a relevant person, the liability is to be treated as subject

to that arrangement, trust deed or compromise only to the extent that the liability exceeds the amount recoverable from the insurer by virtue of the transfer.

(4) Subsection (5) applies if a transfer of rights under section 1 occurs in respect of a liability which, after the transfer, becomes one that is subject to a composition approved in accordance with Schedule 4 to the Bankruptcy (Scotland) Act 1985.

(5) The liability is to be treated as subject to the composition only to the extent that the liability exceeds the amount recoverable from the insurer by virtue of the transfer.

(6) For the purposes of this section the amount recoverable from the insurer does not include any amount that the third party is unable to recover as a result of —

    (a) a shortage of assets on the insurer's part, in a case where the insurer is a relevant person, or

    (b) a limit set by the contract of insurance on the fund available to meet claims in respect of a particular description of liability of the insured.

(7) Where a third party is eligible to make a claim in respect of the insurer's liability under or by virtue of rules made under Part 15 of the Financial Services and Markets Act 2000 (the Financial Services Compensation Scheme) —

    (a) subsection (6)(a) applies only if the third party has made such a claim, and

    (b) the third party is to be treated as being able to recover from the insurer any amount paid to, or due to, the third party as a result of the claim.

Application of Act

15   Reinsurance

This Act does not apply to a case where the liability referred to in section 1(1) is itself a liability incurred by an insurer under a contract of insurance.

16   Voluntarily-incurred liabilities

It is irrelevant for the purposes of section 1 whether or not the liability of the insured is or was incurred voluntarily.

17   Avoidance

(1) A contract of insurance to which this section applies is of no effect in so far as it purports, whether directly or indirectly, to avoid or terminate the contract or alter the rights of the parties under it in the event of the insured —

    (a) becoming a relevant person, or

    (b) dying insolvent (within the meaning given by section 5(2)).

(2) A contract of insurance is one to which this section applies if the insured's rights under it are capable of being transferred under section 1.

18   Cases with a foreign element

Except as expressly provided, the application of this Act does not depend on whether there is a connection with a part of the United Kingdom; and in particular it does not depend on —

(a)   whether or not the liability (or the alleged liability) of the insured to the third party was incurred in, or under the law of, England and Wales, Scotland or Northern Ireland;

(b)   the place of residence or domicile of any of the parties;

(c)   whether or not the contract of insurance (or a part of it) is governed by the law of England and Wales, Scotland or Northern Ireland;

(d)   the place where sums due under the contract of insurance are payable.

Supplemental

19   Power to amend Act

(1)   The Secretary of State may by order made by statutory instrument amend section 4, 5 or 6 so as to —

(a)   substitute a reference to a provision of Northern Ireland legislation with a reference to a different provision of Northern Ireland legislation, or

(b)   add a reference to a provision of a description within subsection (2).

(2)   A provision is within this subsection if —

(a)   it is made by or under Northern Ireland legislation, and

(b)   in the opinion of the Secretary of State, it corresponds with a provision under the law of England and Wales or the law of Scotland that is referred to in the section being amended.

(3)   An order under this section may include consequential, incidental, supplementary, transitional, transitory or saving provision.

(4)   An order under this section may not be made unless a draft of the statutory instrument containing the order has been laid before, and approved by a resolution of, each House of Parliament.

20   Amendments, transitionals, repeals, etc

(1)   Schedule 2 (amendments) has effect.

(2)   Schedule 3 (transitory, transitional and saving provisions) has effect.

(3)   Schedule 4 (repeals and revocations) has effect.

21   Short title, commencement and extent

(1)   This Act may be cited as the Third Parties (Rights against Insurers) Act 2010.

(2)   This Act comes into force on such day as the Secretary of State may by order made by statutory instrument appoint.

(3)   This Act extends to England and Wales, Scotland and Northern Ireland, subject as follows.

(4)   Section 2 and paragraphs 3 and 4 of Schedule 1 do not extend to Scotland.

(5)   Section 3 extends to Scotland only.

(6)   Any amendment, repeal or revocation made by this Act has the same extent as the provision to which it relates.

*Third Parties (Rights against Insurers) Act 2010 (c. **10**)*
Schedule 1 — Information and disclosure for third parties

1347

SCHEDULES

SCHEDULE 1

Section 11

INFORMATION AND DISCLOSURE FOR THIRD PARTIES

Notices requesting information

1   (1) If a person (A) reasonably believes that —
   - (a) another person (B) has incurred a liability to A, and
   - (b) B is a relevant person,

   A may, by notice in writing, request from B such information falling within sub-paragraph (3) as the notice specifies.

   (2) If a person (A) reasonably believes that —
   - (a) a liability has been incurred to A,
   - (b) the person who incurred the liability is insured against it under a contract of insurance,
   - (c) rights of that person under the contract have been transferred to A under section 1, and
   - (d) there is a person (C) who is able to provide information falling within sub-paragraph (3),

   A may, by notice in writing, request from C such information falling within that sub-paragraph as the notice specifies.

   (3) The following is the information that falls within this sub-paragraph —
   - (a) whether there is a contract of insurance that covers the supposed liability or might reasonably be regarded as covering it;
   - (b) if there is such a contract —
      - (i) who the insurer is;
      - (ii) what the terms of the contract are;
      - (iii) whether the insured has been informed that the insurer has claimed not to be liable under the contract in respect of the supposed liability;
      - (iv) whether there are or have been any proceedings between the insurer and the insured in respect of the supposed liability and, if so, relevant details of those proceedings;
      - (v) in a case where the contract sets a limit on the fund available to meet claims in respect of the supposed liability and other liabilities, how much of it (if any) has been paid out in respect of other liabilities;
      - (vi) whether there is a fixed charge to which any sums paid out under the contract in respect of the supposed liability would be subject.

(4) For the purpose of sub-paragraph (3)(b)(iv), relevant details of proceedings are—

    (a) in the case of court proceedings—

        (i) the name of the court;

        (ii) the case number;

        (iii) the contents of all documents served in the proceedings in accordance with rules of court or orders made in the proceedings, and the contents of any such orders;

    (b) in the case of arbitral proceedings or, in Scotland, an arbitration—

        (i) the name of the arbitrator;

        (ii) information corresponding with that mentioned in paragraph (a)(iii).

(5) In sub-paragraph (3)(b)(vi), in its application to Scotland, "fixed charge" means a fixed security within the meaning given by section 47(1) of the Bankruptcy and Diligence etc (Scotland) Act 2007 (asp 3).

(6) A notice given by a person under this paragraph must include particulars of the facts on which that person relies as entitlement to give the notice.

Provision of information where notice given under paragraph 1

2 (1) A person (R) who receives a notice under paragraph 1 must, within the period of 28 days beginning with the day of receipt of the notice—

    (a) provide to the person who gave the notice any information specified in it that R is able to provide;

    (b) in relation to any such information that R is not able to provide, notify that person why R is not able to provide it.

(2) Where—

    (a) a person (R) receives a notice under paragraph 1,

    (b) there is information specified in the notice that R is not able to provide because it is contained in a document that is not in R's control,

    (c) the document was at one time in R's control, and

    (d) R knows or believes that it is now in another person's control,

R must, within the period of 28 days beginning with the day of receipt of the notice, provide the person who gave the notice with whatever particulars R can as to the nature of the information and the identity of that other person.

(3) If R fails to comply with a duty imposed on R by this paragraph, the person who gave R the notice may apply to court for an order requiring R to comply with the duty.

(4) No duty arises by virtue of this paragraph in respect of information as to which a claim to legal professional privilege or, in Scotland, to confidentiality as between client and professional legal adviser could be maintained in legal proceedings.

Notices requiring disclosure: defunct bodies

3 (1) If—

    (a)   a person (P) has started proceedings under this Act against an insurer in respect of a liability that P claims has been incurred to P by a body corporate, and

    (b)   the body is defunct,

P may by notice in writing require a person to whom sub-paragraph (2) applies to disclose to P any documents that are relevant to that liability.

(2) This sub-paragraph applies to a person if —

    (a)   immediately before the time of the alleged transfer under section 1, that person was an officer or employee of the body, or

    (b)   immediately before the body became defunct, that person was —

        (i)   acting as an insolvency practitioner in relation to the body (within the meaning given by section 388(1) of the Insolvency Act 1986 or Article 3 of the Insolvency (Northern Ireland) Order 1989 (S.I. 1989/2405 N.I. 19)), or

        (ii) acting as the official receiver in relation to the winding up of the body.

(3) A notice under this paragraph must be accompanied by —

    (a)   a copy of the particulars of claim required to be served in connection with the proceedings mentioned in sub-paragraph (1), or

    (b)   where those proceedings are arbitral proceedings, the particulars of claim that would be required to be so served if they were court proceedings.

(4) For the purposes of this paragraph a body corporate is defunct if, subject to sub-paragraph (5), it has been dissolved under —

    (a)   Chapter 9 of Part 4 of the Insolvency Act 1986,

    (b)   Chapter 9 of Part 5 of the Insolvency (Northern Ireland) Order 1989 (S.I. 1989/2405 N.I. 19)), or

    (c)   section 1000, 1001 or 1003 of the Companies Act 2006.

(5) But a body corporate is not defunct for the purposes of this paragraph if the body has been —

    (a)   restored to the register by virtue of section 1025 of the Companies Act 2006, or

    (b)   ordered to be restored to the register by virtue of section 1031 of that Act.

Disclosure and inspection where notice given under paragraph 3

4   (1) Subject to the provisions of this paragraph and to any necessary modifications —

    (a)   the duties of disclosure of a person who receives a notice under paragraph 3, and

    (b)   the rights of inspection of the person giving the notice,

are the same as the corresponding duties and rights under Civil Procedure Rules of parties to court proceedings in which an order for standard disclosure has been made.

(2) In sub-paragraph (1), in its application to Northern Ireland —

    (a)   the reference to Civil Procedure Rules is —

(i)   in the case of proceedings in the High Court, to be read as a reference to the Rules of the Court of Judicature (Northern Ireland) 1980 (S.R. 1980 No. 346), and

(ii) in the case of proceedings in the county court, to be read as a reference to the County Court Rules (Northern Ireland) 1981 (S.R. 1981 No. 225), and

(b)   the reference to an order for standard disclosure is to be read as a reference to an order for discovery.

(3)   A person who by virtue of sub-paragraph (1) or (2) has to serve a list of documents must do so within the period of 28 days beginning with the day of receipt of the notice.

(4)   A person who has received a notice under paragraph 3 and has served a list of documents in response to it is not under a duty of disclosure by reason of that notice in relation to documents that the person did not have when the list was served.

Avoidance

5   A contract of insurance is of no effect in so far as it purports, whether directly or indirectly —

(a)   to avoid or terminate the contract or alter the rights of the parties under it in the event of a person providing information, or giving disclosure, that the person is required to provide or give by virtue of a notice under paragraph 1 or 3, or

(b)   otherwise to prohibit, prevent or restrict a person from providing such information or giving such disclosure.

Other rights to information etc

6   Rights to information, or to inspection of documents, that a person has by virtue of paragraph 1 or 3 are in addition to any such rights as the person has apart from that paragraph.

Interpretation

7   For the purposes of this Schedule —

(a)   a person is able to provide information only if —

(i)   that person can obtain it without undue difficulty from a document that is in that person's control, or

(ii) where that person is an individual, the information is within that person's knowledge;

(b)   a document is in a person's control if it is in that person's possession or if that person has a right to possession of it or to inspect or take copies of it.

SCHEDULE 2

AMENDMENTS

Road Traffic (Northern Ireland) Order 1981 (S.I. 1981/154 (N.I. 1))

1   In Article 100 of the Road Traffic (Northern Ireland) Order 1981 (bankruptcy etc of insured persons not to affect certain claims by third-parties) —
   (a)   for "such event as is mentioned in section 1(1) of the Third Parties (Rights against Insurers) Act (Northern Ireland) 1930" substitute "event which results in that person being a relevant person for the purposes of the Third Parties (Rights against Insurers) Act 2010", and
   (b)   for "the said Act of 1930" substitute "that Act".

Road Traffic Act 1988 (c. 52)

2   In section 153 of the Road Traffic Act 1988 (bankruptcy etc of insured or secured persons not to affect claims by third parties) —
   (a)   in subsection (1), for "any of the events mentioned in subsection (2) below" substitute "an event which results in that person being a relevant person for the purposes of the Third Parties (Rights against Insurers) Act 2010",
   (b)   in that subsection, for "Third Parties (Rights against Insurers) Act 1930" substitute "that Act",
   (c)   omit subsection (2), and
   (d)   in subsection (3), for "Third Parties (Rights against Insurers) Act 1930" substitute "Third Parties (Rights against Insurers) Act 2010".

Merchant Shipping Act 1995 (c. 21)

3   In section 165 of the Merchant Shipping Act 1995 (rights of third parties against insurers), in subsection (5), for "Third Parties (Rights against Insurers) Act 1930 and the Third Parties (Rights against Insurers) Act (Northern Ireland) 1930" substitute "Third Parties (Rights against Insurers) Act 2010".

Cross-Border Insolvency Regulations 2006 (S.I. 2006/1030)

4   In paragraph 5 of Schedule 1 to the Cross-Border Insolvency Regulations 2006 (scope of Article 1), for "Third Parties (Rights against Insurers) Act 1930" substitute "Third Parties (Rights against Insurers) Act 2010".

Cross-Border Insolvency Regulations (Northern Ireland) 2007 (S.R. 2007/115)

5   In paragraph 5 of Schedule 1 to the Cross-Border Insolvency Regulations (Northern Ireland) 2007 (scope of Article 1), for "Third Parties (Rights against Insurers) Act (Northern Ireland) 1930" substitute "Third Parties (Rights against Insurers) Act 2010".

SCHEDULE 3

Section 20

TRANSITORY, TRANSITIONAL AND SAVING PROVISIONS

1   (1) Section 1(1)(a) applies where the insured became a relevant person before, as well as when the insured becomes such a person on or after, commencement day.

        (2) Section 1(1)(b) applies where the liability was incurred before, as well as where it is incurred on or after, commencement day.

2   Until the coming into force of section 47(1) of the Bankruptcy and Diligence etc (Scotland) Act 2007 (asp 3), the reference to that provision in paragraph 1(5) of Schedule 1 is to be read as a reference to section 486(1) of the Companies Act 1985.

3   Despite its repeal by this Act, the Third Parties (Rights against Insurers) Act 1930 continues to apply in relation to—

        (a) cases where the event referred to in subsection (1) of section 1 of that Act and the incurring of the liability referred to in that subsection both happened before commencement day;

        (b) cases where the death of the deceased person referred to in subsection (2) of that section happened before that day.

4   Despite its repeal by this Act, the Third Parties (Rights against Insurers) Act (Northern Ireland) 1930 continues to apply in relation to—

        (a) cases where the event referred to in subsection (1) of section 1 of that Act and the incurring of the liability referred to in that subsection both happened before commencement day;

        (b) cases where the death of the deceased person referred to in subsection (2) of that section happened before that day.

5   In this Schedule "commencement day" means the day on which this Act comes into force.

SCHEDULE 4

Section 20

REPEALS AND REVOCATIONS

Title	Extent of repeal or revocation
Third Parties (Rights Against Insurers) Act (Northern Ireland) 1930 (c. 19)	The whole Act.
Third Parties (Rights against Insurers) Act 1930 (c. 25)	The whole Act.
Insolvency Act 1985 (c. 65)	In Schedule 8, paragraph 7 and the cross heading preceding it.
Bankruptcy (Scotland) Act 1985 (c. 66)	In Schedule 7, paragraph 6 and the cross heading preceding it.
Insolvency Act 1986 (c. 45)	In Schedule 14, the entries relating to the Third Parties (Rights against Insurers) Act 1930.

Title	Extent of repeal or revocation
Road Traffic Act 1988 (c. 52)	Section 153(2).
Insolvency (Northern Ireland) Order 1989 (S.I. 1989/2405 (N.I. 19))	In Schedule 9, paragraphs 63 to 65 and the cross heading preceding paragraph 63.
Limited Liability Partnerships Regulations 2001 (S.I. 2001/1090)	In Schedule 5, paragraph 2 and the cross heading preceding it.
Enterprise Act 2002 (Insolvency) Order 2003 (S.I. 2003/2096)	In the Schedule, paragraphs 1 to 3 and the cross heading preceding paragraph 1.
Limited Liability Partnership Regulations (Northern Ireland) 2004 (S.R. 2004 No. 307)	In Schedule 4, paragraph 2 and the cross heading preceding it.
Insolvency (Northern Ireland) Order 2005 (S.I. 2005/1455 (N.I. 10))	In Schedule 2, paragraphs 2 to 4 and the cross heading preceding paragraph 2.

1354

Cluster Munitions (Prohibitions) Act 2010

CHAPTER 11

CONTENTS

Cluster Munitions (Prohibitions) Act 2010

2010 CHAPTER 11

An Act to make provision for giving effect to the Convention on Cluster Munitions. [25th March 2010]

B E IT ENACTED by the Queen's most Excellent Majesty, by and with the advice and consent of the Lords Spiritual and Temporal, and Commons, in this present Parliament assembled, and by the authority of the same, as follows:—

Munitions to which Act applies

1 Munitions to which Act applies

(1) This section applies for the purposes of this Act.

(2) "The Convention" means the Convention on Cluster Munitions, signed by the United Kingdom at Oslo on 3 December 2008.

(3) "Prohibited munition" means—
   (a) a cluster munition, or
   (b) an explosive bomblet that is specifically designed to be dispersed or released from dispensers affixed to aircraft ("a relevant explosive bomblet").

(4) "Prohibited munition" does not include a mine.

(5) "Cluster munition", "explosive bomblet", "dispenser" and "mine" have the same meaning as in the Convention.

(6) Schedule 1 sets out the definitions of "cluster munition", "explosive bomblet", "dispenser" and "mine" given by Article 2 of the Convention (together with definitions of related terms).

Offences

2   Offences

(1)   It is an offence for a person to—
  (a)   use a prohibited munition,
  (b)   develop or produce a prohibited munition,
  (c)   acquire a prohibited munition,
  (d)   make arrangements under which another person acquires a prohibited munition,
  (e)   have a prohibited munition in the person's possession,
  (f)   transfer a prohibited munition, or
  (g)   make arrangements under which another person transfers a prohibited munition.

(2)   It is an offence for a person to assist, encourage or induce any other person to engage in any conduct mentioned in paragraphs (a) to (g) of subsection (1).

(3)   A person guilty of an offence under this section is liable, on conviction on indictment, to imprisonment for a term not exceeding 14 years or to a fine, or to both.

3   Meaning of acquisition and transfer

(1)   This section applies for the purposes of this Act.

(2)   A person acquires a prohibited munition if the person acquires it or enters into a contract to acquire it.

(3)   A person transfers a prohibited munition if the person—
  (a)   disposes of it,
  (b)   moves it into or from the United Kingdom, or
  (c)   enters into a contract to do anything mentioned in paragraph (a) or (b).

(4)   "Acquire" means buy, hire, borrow or accept as a gift, and "dispose" means sell, let on hire, lend or give.

(5)   A person is not to be taken to acquire or dispose of a prohibited munition by reason only of the person's acquisition or disposal of an interest in or right over land containing cluster munition remnants.

(6)   "Cluster munition remnants" has the same meaning as in the Convention.

(7)   Schedule 1 sets out the definition of "cluster munition remnants" given by Article 2 of the Convention (together with definitions of related terms).

4   Application of section 2

(1)   Section 2(1) applies to conduct in the United Kingdom or elsewhere.

(2)   Section 2(2) applies to assistance, encouragement and inducements in the United Kingdom or elsewhere.

(3)   But in their application to conduct, and to assistance, encouragement and inducements, outside the United Kingdom, subsections (1) and (2) of section 2 apply only to—

        (a)   United Kingdom nationals,

        (b)   Scottish partnerships, and

        (c)   bodies incorporated under the law of any part of the United Kingdom.

(4)   Section 2(2) applies whether or not the conduct assisted, encouraged or induced takes place, or (if it takes place) will take place, in the United Kingdom or elsewhere.

(5)   Her Majesty may by Order in Council provide that this section is to have effect as if the list of persons in subsection (3) included bodies incorporated under the law of any of the Channel Islands, the Isle of Man or any British overseas territory.

(6)   For the purposes of this section a United Kingdom national is an individual who is—

        (a)   a British citizen, a British overseas territories citizen, a British National (Overseas) or a British Overseas citizen,

        (b)   a person who under the British Nationality Act 1981 is a British subject, or

        (c)   a British protected person within the meaning of that Act.

(7)   Proceedings for an offence under section 2 committed outside the United Kingdom may be taken, and the offence may for incidental purposes be treated as having been committed, in any place in the United Kingdom.

(8)   In the application of subsection (7) to Scotland, any such proceedings against a person may be taken—

        (a)   in any sheriff court district in which the person is apprehended or is in custody, or

        (b)   in such sheriff court district as the Lord Advocate may determine.

(9)   In subsection (8) "sheriff court district" is to be construed in accordance with the Criminal Procedure (Scotland) Act 1995 (see section 307(1) of that Act).

Defences

5   Enabling destruction

(1)   It is a defence for a person (P) charged with an offence under section 2(1)(e) to show that P had the prohibited munition in P's possession for the purpose of enabling it to be destroyed.

(2)   It is a defence for a person (P) charged with an offence under section 2(1)(f) to show that P transferred the prohibited munition for the purpose of enabling it to be destroyed.

(3)   It is a defence for a person (P) charged with an offence under section 2(1)(g) to show that P made the arrangements for the transfer of the prohibited munition for the purpose of enabling it to be destroyed.

(4)   It is a defence for a person (P) charged with an offence under section 2(1)(c) to show that—

        (a)   the acquisition of the prohibited munition was by means of a transfer made for the purpose of enabling it to be destroyed, and

        (b)   P acquired the prohibited munition for that purpose.

(5) It is a defence for a person (P) charged with an offence under section 2(1)(d) to show that —

  (a) at the time when P made the arrangements for the acquisition of the prohibited munition, P had reasonable cause to believe that the acquisition would be by means of a transfer made for the purpose of enabling it to be destroyed, and

  (b) P made the arrangements for that purpose.

(6) It is a defence for a person (P) charged with an offence under section 2(2) of assisting, encouraging or inducing any other person to engage in any conduct to show that, at the time of the assistance, encouragement or inducement, P had reasonable cause to believe that the other person would have a defence in respect of the conduct by virtue of any of subsections (1) to (5).

6 Other purposes permitted by Convention

(1) It is a defence for a person (P) charged with an offence under section 2(1)(e) to show that—

  (a) P had the prohibited munition in P's possession with the intention that it would be used only for permitted purposes, and

  (b) P's possession of the prohibited munition was in accordance with the terms of an authorisation given to P by the Secretary of State.

(2) It is a defence for a person (P) charged with an offence under section 2(1)(f) to show that—

  (a) P transferred the prohibited munition with the intention that it would be used only for permitted purposes, and

  (b) the transfer was in accordance with the terms of an authorisation given to P by the Secretary of State.

(3) It is a defence for a person (P) charged with an offence under section 2(1)(g) to show that—

  (a) P made the arrangements for the transfer of the prohibited munition with the intention that it would be used only for permitted purposes, and

  (b) the Secretary of State had authorised the transfer.

(4) It is a defence for a person (P) charged with an offence under section 2(1)(c) to show that—

  (a) the acquisition of the prohibited munition was by means of a transfer which had been authorised by the Secretary of State, and

  (b) P acquired the prohibited munition with the intention that it would be used only for permitted purposes.

(5) It is a defence for a person (P) charged with an offence under section 2(1)(d) to show that—

  (a) at the time when P made the arrangements for the acquisition of the prohibited munition, P had reasonable cause to believe that the acquisition would be by means of a transfer which had been authorised by the Secretary of State, and

  (b) P made the arrangements with the intention that the prohibited munition would be used only for permitted purposes.

(6) It is a defence for a person (P) charged with an offence under section 2(2) of assisting, encouraging or inducing any other person to engage in any conduct

to show that, at the time of the assistance, encouragement or inducement, P had reasonable cause to believe that the other person would have a defence in respect of the conduct by virtue of any of subsections (1) to (5).

(7) The Secretary of State may not, for the purposes of this section, authorise the possession or transfer of prohibited munitions in numbers in excess of what is necessary for permitted purposes.

(8) For the purposes of this section the following are "permitted purposes" —
   (a) the development of, and training in, techniques for the detection, clearance or destruction of cluster munitions, explosive submunitions and relevant explosive bomblets,
   (b) the development of counter-measures in respect of cluster munitions, explosive submunitions and relevant explosive bomblets, and
   (c) the purposes of any proceedings under this Act, or of any criminal investigation or other criminal proceedings (whether in the United Kingdom or elsewhere), in which the prohibited munition is or may be evidence.

(9) In subsection (8) "explosive submunition" has the same meaning as in the Convention.

(10) Schedule 1 sets out the definition of "explosive submunition" given by Article 2 of the Convention (as a term related to the definition of "cluster munition").

7 Defences relating to state of mind of defendant etc.

(1) It is a defence for a person (P) charged with an offence under section 2(1)(a) or (c) to (g) to show that, at the time of the conduct constituting the offence, P neither knew nor suspected, nor had reason to suspect, that the object in question was a prohibited munition.

(2) It is a defence for a person (P) charged with an offence under section 2(1)(e) to show that, having come to know or suspect while the object in question was in P's possession that it was a prohibited munition, P took all reasonable steps, as soon as reasonably practicable after P first had that knowledge or suspicion, to inform the Secretary of State, or a constable or member of a service police force, of P's knowledge or suspicion.

(3) It is a defence for a person (P) charged with an offence under section 2(1)(e) to show that P did not have any knowledge or suspicion that the object in question was a prohibited munition, nor any reason for such a suspicion, until P became aware of the Secretary of State's exercise in the case of that object of a power conferred on the Secretary of State by this Act.

(4) It is a defence for a person (P) charged with an offence under section 2(2) to show that, at the time of the assistance, encouragement or inducement, P neither knew nor suspected, nor had reason to suspect, that the conduct assisted, encouraged or induced related, or might relate, to a prohibited munition.

(5) In subsection (2), "service police force" means —
   (a) the Royal Navy Police,
   (b) the Royal Military Police, or
   (c) the Royal Air Force Police.

8   Visiting forces

(1)   It is a defence for a person (P) charged with an offence under section 2(1)(e) to show that—

    (a)   at the time when P had possession of the prohibited munition, P was a member of a visiting force of a State that was not a party to the Convention or was working with such a force, and

    (b)   P's possession of the prohibited munition was in accordance with the terms of an authorisation given to that State by the Secretary of State.

(2)   It is a defence for a person (P) charged with an offence under section 2(1)(f), which is alleged to have been committed by moving a prohibited munition into or from the United Kingdom or entering into a contract to move a prohibited munition into or from the United Kingdom, to show that—

    (a)   at the time when P moved the prohibited munition or entered into the contract to move it, P was a member of a visiting force of a State that was not a party to the Convention, and

    (b)   the movement was or (as the case may be) would be in accordance with the terms of an authorisation given to that State by the Secretary of State.

(3)   It is a defence for a person (P) charged with an offence under section 2(1)(g), which is alleged to have been committed by making arrangements under which a member of a visiting force of a State that was not a party to the Convention moves a prohibited munition into or from the United Kingdom or enters into a contract to move a prohibited munition into or from the United Kingdom, to show that at the time when P made the arrangements—

    (a)   P was a member of a visiting force of a State that was not a party to the Convention or was working with such a force, and

    (b)   P had reasonable cause to believe that the movement would be in accordance with the terms of an authorisation given to that State by the Secretary of State.

(4)   It is a defence for a person (P) charged with an offence under section 2(2) of assisting, encouraging or inducing any other person to engage in any conduct to show that at the time of the assistance, encouragement or inducement—

    (a)   P was a member of a visiting force of a State that was not a party to the Convention or was working with such a force, and

    (b)   P had reasonable cause to believe that the other person would have a defence in respect of the conduct by virtue of any of subsections (1) to (3).

(5)   For the purposes of this section, a person is working with a visiting force at any time when the person is providing a service to the force under a contract or helping it in any other way.

(6)   In this section—

    (a)   "visiting force" means any such body, contingent or detachment of the forces of any country as is a visiting force for the purposes of any of the provisions of Part 1 of the Visiting Forces Act 1952, and

    (b)   "member", in relation to a visiting force, has the meaning given by section 12(1) of that Act.

9 International military operations and activities

(1) It is a defence for a person charged with an offence specified in any of paragraphs 1 to 6 of Schedule 2 to show that the person's conduct took place in the course of, or for the purposes of, an international military operation or an international military co-operation activity.

(2) A military operation is an international military operation if—

    (a) both members of Her Majesty's armed forces and members of the armed forces of one or more States other than the United Kingdom participate in the operation,

    (b) at least one of the other States is not a party to the Convention, and

    (c) the operation involves or might involve conduct by members of the armed forces of a State that is not a party to the Convention, or by other persons acting under the authority of such a State, which would be in contravention of the Convention if it were conduct by members of the armed forces of a State that is a party to the Convention or by other persons acting under the authority of such a State.

(3) An activity is an international military co-operation activity if—

    (a) it is an activity, other than a military operation, undertaken in pursuance of co-operation between the government of the United Kingdom and the government of one or more States other than the United Kingdom for any purpose related to—

        (i) the defence of the United Kingdom or any of those States, or

        (ii) Her Majesty's armed forces or the armed forces of any of those States,

    (b) at least one of the other States is not a party to the Convention, and

    (c) the activity involves or might involve conduct by members of the armed forces of a State that is not a party to the Convention, or by other persons acting under the authority of such a State, which would be in contravention of the Convention if it were conduct by members of the armed forces of a State that is a party to the Convention or by other persons acting under the authority of such a State.

(4) Subsection (5) applies if a question arises in any proceedings as to whether—

    (a) subsection (2)(a) applies in relation to a military operation, or

    (b) subsection (3)(a) applies in relation to an activity.

(5) A certificate issued by or under the authority of the Secretary of State stating any fact relating to that question is conclusive evidence of that fact.

(6) Paragraphs 7 and 8 of Schedule 2 make further provision about the application of the defence under subsection (1) in relation to particular offences specified in that Schedule.

(7) In this section—

    "Her Majesty's armed forces" means any of Her Majesty's forces within the meaning of the Armed Forces Act 2006;

    "military operation" includes any naval or air force operation.

10 Supplementary provision: evidential burden and authorisations

(1) Subsection (2) applies where a person relies on a defence under this Act.

(2)   If evidence is adduced which is sufficient to raise an issue with respect to the defence, the court must assume that the defence is satisfied unless the prosecution proves beyond reasonable doubt that it is not.

(3)   For the purposes of sections 6 and 8, an authorisation given before the coming into force of this Act has the same effect as one given on or after its coming into force.

Securing destruction of prohibited munitions

11   Suspicious objects

(1)   This section applies where—

   (a)   the Secretary of State has grounds to suspect that an object is a prohibited munition, and

   (b)   it does not appear to the Secretary of State that the only persons in possession of the object (assuming it is a prohibited munition) are persons who, if charged with an offence under section 2(1)(e), would have a defence under section 5 or 6.

(2)   The Secretary of State may serve a notice on—

   (a)   any person who appears to the Secretary of State to have possession of the object;

   (b)   any other person who appears to the Secretary of State to have an interest which the Secretary of State believes would be materially affected if the object were to be destroyed.

(3)   The notice must—

   (a)   describe the object and state its location,

   (b)   state that the Secretary of State suspects that the object is a prohibited munition and give the reasons for that suspicion,

   (c)   state that the Secretary of State is considering whether to secure the destruction of the object under sections 14 to 16,

   (d)   refer to the obligation imposed by subsection (4) and specify a date for the purposes of that subsection, and

   (e)   refer to the right conferred by subsection (5).

(4)   A person on whom a notice is served under this section and who, at the time the notice is served, has possession of the object must not relinquish possession before the date specified in the notice.

(5)   A person on whom a notice is served under this section may make representations to the Secretary of State that—

   (a)   the object is not a prohibited munition;

   (b)   the only persons in possession of the object (assuming it is a prohibited munition) are persons who, if charged with an offence under section 2(1)(e), would have a defence under section 5 or 6.

12   Power to enter premises and search for prohibited munitions

(1)   The Secretary of State may authorise a person to enter and search premises if the Secretary of State has reasonable cause to believe that conditions A to C are satisfied.

(2) A justice of the peace may issue a warrant authorising a person acting under the authority of the Secretary of State to enter and search premises if the justice of the peace is satisfied, on information on oath, that there is reasonable cause to believe that conditions A and B are satisfied.

(3) Condition A is that there is an object on the premises that is a prohibited munition.

(4) Condition B is that the case is not one where the only persons in possession of the object (assuming it is a prohibited munition) are persons who, if charged with an offence under section 2(1)(e), would have a defence under section 5 or 6.

(5) Condition C is that—
  (a) the public has access to the premises, or
  (b) the premises are occupied by a person who consents to the premises being entered and searched.

(6) Subsections (1) and (2) apply whether or not a notice has been served under section 11.

(7) An application for a warrant under subsection (2)—
  (a) may be made by any person acting under the authority of the Secretary of State, and
  (b) must specify the premises in respect of which the application is made.

(8) A warrant issued under subsection (2) may authorise entry on one occasion only.

(9) A warrant issued under subsection (2)—
  (a) continues in force for the period of one month beginning with the date on which it was issued, and
  (b) may be executed by any person acting under the authority of the Secretary of State.

(10) In the application of subsection (2) to Scotland—
  (a) the references to a justice of the peace are to be read as including references to the sheriff, and
  (b) the reference to information on oath is to be read as a reference to evidence on oath.

13 Removal or immobilisation of prohibited munitions

(1) A person authorised by a warrant issued under section 12(2) to enter premises may, if necessary, use force to enter the premises.

(2) A person who enters premises under an authorisation given under section 12(1) or a warrant issued under section 12(2) may take such other persons and such equipment on to the premises as appear to that person to be necessary.

(3) If a person enters premises under such an authorisation or warrant and a prohibited munition is found on the premises, the person may make the prohibited munition safe.

(4) Where subsection (3) applies, the person may also—
  (a) if it is reasonably practicable to do so, seize and remove the prohibited munition, or

       (b)   in any other case, affix a warning to the prohibited munition, or in a conspicuous position to something near the prohibited munition, stating that the prohibited munition is not to be moved or interfered with before the date specified in the warning and that the warning is not to be interfered with before that date.

(5)   But a person may not exercise the powers under subsections (3) and (4) if satisfied that—

       (a)   the prohibited munition is in the possession of one or more persons, and

       (b)   that person, or each of those persons, is a person who, if charged with an offence under section 2(1)(e), would have a defence under section 5 or 6.

(6)   An authorisation given under section 12(1) or a warrant issued under section 12(2) may provide that the person who exercises the powers conferred by the authorisation or the warrant may, if that person is not a constable, do so only in the presence of a constable.

(7)   For the purposes of subsection (3) a prohibited munition is made safe if, without being destroyed, it is prevented from being an immediate danger.

14   Power to destroy removed prohibited munitions

(1)   This section applies if a prohibited munition is removed from premises under section 13(4)(a).

(2)   Before the end of the first six-month period, the Secretary of State must serve a notice on—

       (a)   any person who appears to the Secretary of State to have had possession of the prohibited munition immediately before its removal, and

       (b)   any other person who appears to the Secretary of State to have an interest which the Secretary of State believes would be materially affected by the destruction of the prohibited munition.

(3)   The notice must—

       (a)   describe the prohibited munition and state its location,

       (b)   state that the Secretary of State proposes to secure its destruction and give the reasons for this proposal,

       (c)   refer to the right of objection conferred by subsection (4), and

       (d)   refer to the conditions to which the exercise of that right is subject by virtue of subsection (5) and specify a date for the purposes of that subsection.

(4)   A person on whom a notice is served under subsection (2) may object to the Secretary of State's proposal to secure the destruction of the prohibited munition.

(5)   Any objection made under subsection (4) must—

       (a)   be made in writing to the Secretary of State before such date as is specified in the notice, and

       (b)   state why the prohibited munition should not be destroyed.

(6) The Secretary of State may, at any time during the second six-month period, decide that the prohibited munition should be destroyed, and if the Secretary of State so decides the Secretary of State may authorise a person to destroy it.

(7) Before reaching a decision under subsection (6) the Secretary of State must—

    (a) allow any person on whom a notice has been served under subsection (2) time to respond, and

    (b) take into account any objections to the proposed destruction of the prohibited munition (whether made in response to a notice or otherwise).

(8) If a prohibited munition is destroyed under this section the Secretary of State may recover from any person who had possession of the prohibited munition immediately before its removal any costs reasonably incurred by the Secretary of State in connection with the removal and destruction.

(9) Subsection (10) applies where—

    (a) the Secretary of State has not, by the end of the second six-month period, authorised the destruction of the prohibited munition, and

    (b) a person had possession of the prohibited munition immediately before its removal.

(10) The Secretary of State must return the prohibited munition to the person mentioned in subsection (9)(b) or, if there is more than one such person, to such of them as the Secretary of State thinks appropriate.

(11) For the purposes of this section—

    (a) the "first six-month period" is the period of six months beginning with the day after the removal of the prohibited munition, and

    (b) the "second six-month period" is the period of six months beginning with the day after the first six-month period ends.

15 Destruction of immobilised prohibited munitions

(1) This section applies if a warning relating to a prohibited munition has been affixed under section 13(4)(b).

(2) Before the end of the first six-month period, the Secretary of State must serve a notice on—

    (a) any person who appears to the Secretary of State to have had possession of the prohibited munition immediately before the warning was affixed, and

    (b) any other person who appears to the Secretary of State to have an interest which the Secretary of State believes would be materially affected by the destruction of the prohibited munition.

(3) The notice must—

    (a) describe the prohibited munition and state its location,

    (b) state that the Secretary of State proposes to secure its destruction and give the reasons for this proposal,

    (c) refer to the right of objection conferred by subsection (4), and

    (d) refer to the conditions to which the exercise of that right is subject by virtue of subsection (5) and specify a date for the purposes of that subsection.

(4) A person on whom a notice is served under subsection (2) may object to the Secretary of State's proposal to secure the destruction of the prohibited munition.

(5) Any objection made under subsection (4) must—

    (a) be made in writing to the Secretary of State before such date as is specified in the notice, and

    (b) state why the prohibited munition should not be destroyed.

(6) The Secretary of State may, at any time during the second six-month period, decide that the prohibited munition should be destroyed, and if the Secretary of State so decides the prohibited munition may be destroyed in accordance with section 16.

(7) Before reaching a decision under subsection (6) the Secretary of State must—

    (a) allow any person on whom a notice has been served under subsection (2) time to respond, and

    (b) take into account any objections to the proposed destruction of the prohibited munition (whether made in response to a notice or otherwise).

(8) If a prohibited munition is destroyed in pursuance of a decision taken under subsection (6) the Secretary of State may recover from any person who had possession of the prohibited munition immediately before the warning was affixed any costs reasonably incurred by the Secretary of State in connection with the destruction.

(9) For the purposes of this section—

    (a) the "first six-month period" is the period of six months beginning with the day after the warning was affixed, and

    (b) the "second six-month period" is the period of six months beginning with the day after the first six-month period ends.

16 Power to enter premises and destroy immobilised prohibited munitions

(1) Subsection (2) applies where—

    (a) the Secretary of State decides under section 15(6) that a prohibited munition should be destroyed, and

    (b) the prohibited munition is on premises to which the public has access or on premises which are occupied by a person who consents to action being taken under subsection (2).

(2) The Secretary of State may authorise a person to enter the premises and destroy the prohibited munition if it is found there.

(3) Subsection (4) applies where a justice of the peace is satisfied, on information on oath, that—

    (a) the Secretary of State has decided under section 15(6) that a prohibited munition should be destroyed, and

    (b) the prohibited munition is on premises where a warning relating to that prohibited munition was affixed under section 13(4)(b).

(4) The justice of the peace may issue a warrant authorising a person acting under the authority of the Secretary of State to enter the premises and destroy the prohibited munition if it is found there.

(5)   An application for a warrant under subsection (4)—

    (a)   may be made by any person acting under the authority of the Secretary of State, and

    (b)   must specify the premises in respect of which the application is made.

(6)   A warrant issued under subsection (4) may authorise entry on one occasion only.

(7)   A warrant issued under subsection (4)—

    (a)   continues in force for the period of one month beginning with the date on which it was issued, and

    (b)   may be executed by any person acting under the authority of the Secretary of State.

(8)   A person authorised by a warrant issued under subsection (4) to enter premises may, if necessary, use force to enter the premises.

(9)   A person who enters premises under an authorisation given under subsection (2) or a warrant issued under subsection (4) may take such other persons and such equipment on to the premises as appear to that person to be necessary.

(10)   An authorisation given under subsection (2) or a warrant issued under subsection (4) may provide that the person who exercises the powers conferred by the authorisation or the warrant may, if that person is not a constable, do so only in the presence of a constable.

(11)   In the application of subsections (3) and (4) to Scotland—

    (a)   the references to a justice of the peace are to be read as including references to the sheriff, and

    (b)   the reference to information on oath is to be read as a reference to evidence on oath.

17   Compensation for destruction

(1)   This section applies if a person (P) claims that—

    (a)   a prohibited munition has been destroyed under section 14 or 16,

    (b)   P had an interest which was materially affected by the destruction,

    (c)   P sustained loss as a result of the destruction, and

    (d)   no notice was served on P under section 14 or (as the case may be) section 15 (whether or not one was served on any other person).

(2)   P may make an application for compensation to the High Court or, in Scotland, the Court of Session.

(3)   If the Court finds that P's claim is justified, the Court may order the Secretary of State to pay to P such amount (if any) by way of compensation as the Court considers just.

(4)   If the Court believes that the prohibited munition would have been destroyed even if a notice had been served on P under the section concerned, the Court must not order compensation to be paid under this section.

18   Offences relating to destruction etc.

(1)   A person (P) is guilty of an offence if, without reasonable excuse, P contravenes section 11(4) (relinquishing possession of suspicious object).

(2)   A person (P) is guilty of an offence if P wilfully obstructs another person in the doing by that other person of any of the following—

 (a)   entering or searching premises under an authorisation given or warrant issued under section 12(1) or (2);

 (b)   making a prohibited munition safe, seizing or removing a prohibited munition, or affixing a warning, under section 13(3) or (4);

 (c)   destroying a prohibited munition under an authorisation given under section 14(6);

 (d)   entering premises under an authorisation given or warrant issued under section 16(2) or (4);

 (e)   destroying a prohibited munition under an authorisation given or warrant issued under section 16(2) or (4);

 (f)   attempting to do anything mentioned in any of paragraphs (a) to (e).

(3)   A person (P) is guilty of an offence if—

 (a)   a warning relating to a prohibited munition has been affixed under section 13(4)(b),

 (b)   before the date specified in the warning, P moves or interferes with the prohibited munition or interferes with the warning, and

 (c)   P has no reasonable excuse for doing so.

(4)   A person guilty of an offence under any of subsections (1) to (3) is liable—

 (a)   on summary conviction, to a fine not exceeding the statutory maximum, or

 (b)   on conviction on indictment, to a fine.

(5)   A person who knowingly makes a false or misleading statement in response to a notice served under section 11, 14 or 15 is guilty of an offence and liable—

 (a)   on summary conviction, to a fine not exceeding the statutory maximum, or

 (b)   on conviction on indictment, to imprisonment for a term not exceeding two years or to a fine, or to both.

19   Securing destruction of prohibited munitions: supplementary

The powers conferred by sections 11 to 16 are in addition to, and do not affect, any power exercisable in relation to an object otherwise than by virtue of those sections.

Information and records

20   Information and records for Convention purposes

(1)   The Secretary of State may serve a notice on any person requiring the person to give such information as is described in the notice.

(2)   The information required to be given by a notice served under subsection (1)—

 (a)   must be information that the Secretary of State has reasonable cause to believe is or will be needed in connection with anything to be done for the purposes of the Convention;

 (b)   may relate to a state of affairs subsisting before the coming into force of this Act or the entry into force of the Convention.

(3)   A notice served under subsection (1) may specify —
   (a)   the form in which the information must be given;
   (b)   the period within which the information must be given.

(4)   The Secretary of State may also serve a notice on any person requiring the person to keep such records as are specified in the notice.

(5)   The records required to be kept by a notice served under subsection (4) must be records that the Secretary of State has reasonable cause to believe will facilitate the giving of information which that person may at any time be required to give under subsection (1).

(6)   The power conferred by subsection (1) may not be exercised so as to require a person to give information which might incriminate the person or, if that person is married or a civil partner, the person's spouse or civil partner.

(7)   The power conferred by subsection (1) may not be exercised so as to require a person to give information in respect of which a claim to legal professional privilege (or, in Scotland, to confidentiality of communications) could be maintained in legal proceedings.

(8)   A person who without reasonable excuse fails to comply with a notice served under subsection (1) or (4) is guilty of an offence and liable —
   (a)   on summary conviction, to a fine not exceeding the statutory maximum, or
   (b)   on conviction on indictment, to a fine.

(9)   A person on whom a notice is served under subsection (1) and who knowingly makes a false or misleading statement in response to it is guilty of an offence and liable —
   (a)   on summary conviction, to a fine not exceeding the statutory maximum, or
   (b)   on conviction on indictment, to imprisonment for a term not exceeding two years or to a fine, or to both.

21   Power to search and obtain evidence: issue of warrant

(1)   A justice of the peace may issue a warrant authorising a person acting under the authority of the Secretary of State to enter and search premises if the justice of the peace is satisfied, on information on oath, that either condition A or condition B is satisfied in relation to those premises.

(2)   Condition A is that there are reasonable grounds for suspecting that an offence under this Act is being, has been or is about to be committed on the premises.

(3)   Condition B is that there are reasonable grounds for suspecting that evidence of the commission of an offence under this Act is to be found on the premises.

(4)   An application for a warrant under this section —
   (a)   may be made by any person acting under the authority of the Secretary of State, and
   (b)   must specify the premises in respect of which the application is made.

(5)   A warrant issued under this section may authorise entry on one occasion only.

(6)   A warrant issued under this section —

      (a)   continues in force for the period of one month beginning with the date on which it was issued, and

      (b)   may be executed by any person acting under the authority of the Secretary of State.

(7)   In the application of subsection (1) to Scotland —

      (a)   the references to a justice of the peace are to be read as including references to the sheriff, and

      (b)   the reference to information on oath is to be read as a reference to evidence on oath.

22   Power to search and obtain evidence: supplementary

(1)   A person authorised by a warrant issued under section 21 to enter premises may, if necessary, use force to enter the premises.

(2)   A person who enters premises under a warrant issued under section 21 may —

      (a)   take such other persons and such equipment on to the premises as appear to that person to be necessary;

      (b)   inspect any document found on the premises which the person has reasonable cause to believe may be required as evidence for the purposes of proceedings in respect of an offence under this Act;

      (c)   take copies of, or seize and remove, any such document;

      (d)   require information which is stored in an electronic form and is accessible from the premises to be produced in a form in which it can be taken away and in which it is visible and legible (or from which it can readily be produced in a visible and legible form);

      (e)   take copies of, or seize and remove, anything produced in pursuance of paragraph (d) which the person has reasonable cause to believe may be required as evidence for the purposes of proceedings in respect of an offence under this Act;

      (f)   inspect, seize and remove any device or equipment found on the premises which the person has reasonable cause to believe may be required as such evidence;

      (g)   inspect, sample, seize and remove any substance found on the premises which the person has reasonable cause to believe may be required as such evidence.

(3)   Anything seized under subsection (2) may be retained for so long as is necessary in all the circumstances.

(4)   A person who seizes anything under subsection (2) must, if requested to do so by a person who occupied the premises at the time of the seizure or who had possession or control of the thing immediately before it was seized, provide a record of its seizure.

(5)   Subsection (2) does not authorise a person to take action in relation to anything in respect of which a claim to legal professional privilege (or, in Scotland, to confidentiality of communications) could be maintained in legal proceedings.

(6)   Subsection (7) applies where a constable enters premises —

      (a)   under a warrant issued under section 21, or

      (b)   by virtue of subsection (2)(a) of this section.

(7) The constable may search any person found on the premises whom the constable has reasonable cause to believe to be in possession of any document, device, equipment or substance which may be required as evidence for the purposes of proceedings in respect of an offence under this Act.

(8) No constable may, by virtue of subsection (7), search a person of the opposite sex.

(9) A warrant issued under section 21 may provide that the person who exercises the powers conferred by the warrant may, if that person is not a constable, do so only in the presence of a constable.

(10) A person who wilfully obstructs another in the exercise of any power under this section is guilty of an offence and liable—

    (a) on summary conviction, to a fine not exceeding the statutory maximum, or

    (b) on conviction on indictment, to a fine.

23 Disclosure of information

(1) This section applies to information if—

    (a) it was obtained under, or in connection with anything done under, this Act or the Convention, and

    (b) it relates to a particular business or other activity carried on by any person.

(2) So long as the business or activity continues to be carried on, the information must not be disclosed except—

    (a) with the consent of the person for the time being carrying on the business or activity,

    (b) in connection with anything done for the purposes of the Convention,

    (c) in connection with anything done for the purposes of this Act,

    (d) for any of the purposes specified in section 17(2)(a) to (d) of the Anti-terrorism, Crime and Security Act 2001 (disclosure related to criminal investigation or criminal proceedings),

    (e) in connection with the enforcement of any restriction on imports or exports, or

    (f) with a view to ensuring the security of the United Kingdom.

(3) Section 18 of the Anti-terrorism, Crime and Security Act 2001 (restriction on disclosure of information for overseas purposes) has effect in relation to a disclosure authorised by subsection (2)(d) as it has effect in relation to a disclosure authorised by any of the provisions to which section 17 of that Act applies.

(4) A person who discloses information in contravention of this section is guilty of an offence and liable—

    (a) on summary conviction, to a fine not exceeding the statutory maximum, or

    (b) on conviction on indictment, to imprisonment for a term not exceeding two years or to a fine, or to both.

(5) Where any of paragraphs (b) to (f) of subsection (2) applies, the information may be disclosed notwithstanding any obligation not to disclose it that would otherwise apply.

Criminal proceedings

24   Consent to prosecution

Proceedings for an offence under this Act may not be instituted —

(a)   in England and Wales, except by or with the consent of the Attorney General;

(b)   in Northern Ireland, except by or with the consent of the Attorney General for Northern Ireland.

25   Forfeiture in case of conviction

(1)   This section applies if a person is convicted of an offence under this Act.

(2)   The court by or before which the person is convicted may order that anything that is shown to the court's satisfaction to relate to the offence is to be —

(a)   forfeited, and

(b)   destroyed, or otherwise dealt with, in the manner specified in the order.

(3)   The court may order under subsection (2) that the forfeited item is to be dealt with as the Secretary of State sees fit.

(4)   If the court so orders, the powers of the Secretary of State include —

(a)   the power to direct the destruction of the forfeited item, and

(b)   the power to secure the disposal of the forfeited item in any other way that appears to the Secretary of State to be appropriate.

(5)   Subsection (6) applies where —

(a)   the court proposes to order under subsection (2) that a thing be forfeited, and

(b)   a person claiming to have an interest in it applies to be heard by the court.

(6)   The court must not make the order unless the person has been given an opportunity to show why it should not be made.

26   Offences by bodies corporate etc.

(1)   Where an offence under this Act is committed by a body corporate and the offence is proved —

(a)   to have been committed with the consent or connivance of an officer of the body corporate, or

(b)   to be attributable to any neglect on the part of an officer of the body corporate,

the officer (as well as the body corporate) is guilty of the offence and is liable to be proceeded against and punished accordingly.

(2)   Where an offence under this Act is committed by a Scottish partnership and the offence is proved —

(a)   to have been committed with the consent or connivance of a partner of the partnership, or

(b)   to be attributable to any neglect on the part of a partner of the partnership, the partner (as well as the partnership) is guilty of the offence and is liable to be proceeded against and punished accordingly.

(3) In this section—

"officer", in relation to a body corporate, means—

(a) a director, manager, secretary or other similar officer of the body corporate, or

(b) any person who was purporting to act in any such capacity;

"partner", in relation to a Scottish partnership, includes any person who was purporting to act as a partner of the partnership.

(4) In subsection (3) "director", in relation to a body corporate whose affairs are managed by its members, means a member of the body corporate.

General

27 Safeguards etc. in connection with exercise of powers of entry

(1) A person who enters premises under an authorisation given under section 12(1) or 16(2) ("the authorised person") must, if requested to do so by a person on the premises, produce evidence of the authorised person's identity and entitlement to exercise the power.

(2) Subsections (3) to (5) apply where a person ("the authorised person") enters premises under a warrant issued under section 12(2), 16(4) or 21(1).

(3) If the occupier of the premises is present, the authorised person must—

(a) produce evidence of the authorised person's identity,

(b) produce a copy of the warrant, and

(c) supply the occupier with a copy.

(4) If the occupier of the premises is not present, but another person appearing to the authorised person to be in charge of the premises is, subsection (3) applies as if any reference to the occupier were a reference to the person in charge of the premises.

(5) If neither the occupier nor any other person appearing to the authorised person to be in charge of the premises is present, the authorised person must leave a copy of the warrant in a prominent place on the premises.

(6) A person who enters premises under an authorisation given or warrant issued under section 12(1) or (2), 16(2) or (4) or 21(1) must do so at a reasonable hour unless it appears to the person that the purpose of entry would be frustrated by entry at a reasonable hour.

(7) A person who enters premises which are unoccupied under an authorisation given or warrant issued under section 12(1) or (2), 16(2) or (4) or 21(1) must take all reasonable steps to ensure that the premises are left as secure against entry as they were when the person found them.

(8) Subsections (2) to (6) do not apply where the authorised person is a constable who enters the premises under a warrant issued under section 12(2), 16(4) or 21(1).

28   Service of notices

(1)   A notice required or authorised by this Act to be served on a person other than a Scottish partnership or a body corporate may be served by—

    (a)   delivering it to the person, or

    (b)   sending it by post to the person at the person's usual or last-known residence, or usual or last-known place of business, in the United Kingdom.

(2)   A notice required or authorised by this Act to be served on a Scottish partnership may be served by—

    (a)   delivering it to a partner of the partnership, or a person having control or management of the partnership business, at the principal office of the partnership, or

    (b)   sending it by post to such a partner or person at that office.

(3)   A notice required or authorised by this Act to be served on a body corporate may be served by—

    (a)   delivering it to the secretary or clerk of the body corporate at its registered or principal office, or

    (b)   sending it by post to the secretary or clerk at the registered or principal office.

(4)   In the application of subsection (3) to a company registered outside the United Kingdom, the references to its principal office include references to its principal office within the United Kingdom (if any).

29   Power to modify Act

(1)   The Secretary of State may by order made by statutory instrument make such modifications of this Act as the Secretary of State considers necessary or desirable to give effect to any amendment of the Convention made in pursuance of the provisions of the Convention.

(2)   An order under subsection (1) may also make such modifications of any other enactment (whenever passed or made) as the Secretary of State considers necessary or desirable in consequence of the modifications of this Act made by that order.

(3)   A statutory instrument containing an order under subsection (1) may not be made unless a draft of the statutory instrument has been laid before and approved by resolution of each House of Parliament.

(4)   In this section—

    "enactment" means a provision contained in, or in an instrument made under—

        (a)   an Act of Parliament,

        (b)   an Act of the Scottish Parliament,

        (c)   a Measure or Act of the National Assembly for Wales, or

        (d)   Northern Ireland legislation;

    a "modification" includes an addition, repeal or revocation.

30   Interpretation

(1)   In this Act—

"acquisition", "disposal" (except in clause 25(4)(b)), "transfer", and related expressions, are to be construed in accordance with section 3;

"cluster munition", "prohibited munition" and "relevant explosive bomblet" have the meanings given by section 1;

"the Convention" has the meaning given by section 1(2);

"premises" includes land, moveable structures, vehicles, vessels, aircraft and hovercraft.

(2) For the purposes of this Act a cluster munition or a relevant explosive bomblet is to be taken to be destroyed if it is permanently prevented (by dismantling or any other means) from being used as a cluster munition or a relevant explosive bomblet.

(3) For the purposes of this Act a State is a party to the Convention if it has ratified, accepted or approved the Convention, or has acceded to it, and either—

(a) the Convention is in force in relation to the State, or

(b) the State is applying Article 1 of the Convention on a provisional basis in accordance with Article 18 of the Convention.

31 Amendments of other Acts

Schedule 3 contains minor and consequential amendments of other Acts.

32 Crown application

(1) This Act binds the Crown.

(2) No contravention by the Crown of a provision of this Act makes the Crown criminally liable.

(3) Subsection (2) does not affect the criminal liability of persons in the service of the Crown.

(4) The High Court or, in Scotland, the Court of Session may, on the application of a person appearing to the Court to have an interest, declare unlawful an act or omission of the Crown which constitutes a contravention of a provision of this Act.

(5) Nothing in this section affects Her Majesty in her private capacity.

(6) Subsection (5) is to be read as if section 38(3) of the Crown Proceedings Act 1947 (references to Her Majesty in her private capacity) were contained in this Act.

33 Extent

(1) Subject to the following provisions of this section, this Act extends to England and Wales, Scotland and Northern Ireland.

(2) An amendment made by this Act has the same extent as that of the provision amended.

(3) Her Majesty may by Order in Council provide for any of the provisions of this Act to extend, with modifications (including additions or omissions) or without modifications, to any of the Channel Islands, the Isle of Man or any British overseas territory.

34   Commencement and short title

(1)   This Act comes into force on the day on which it is passed.

(2)   This Act may be cited as the Cluster Munitions (Prohibitions) Act 2010.

*Cluster Munitions (Prohibitions) Act 2010 (c. **11**)*
Schedule 1 — Definitions of cluster munition, explosive bomblet etc.

1379

SCHEDULES

SCHEDULE 1 Sections 1(6), 3(7) and 6(10)

DEFINITIONS OF CLUSTER MUNITION, EXPLOSIVE BOMBLET ETC.

Definition of cluster munition and related terms

Article 2.2. "Cluster munition" means a conventional munition that is designed to disperse or release explosive submunitions each weighing less than 20 kilograms, and includes those explosive submunitions. It does not mean the following:

(a) A munition or submunition designed to dispense flares, smoke, pyrotechnics or chaff; or a munition designed exclusively for an air defence role;

(b) A munition or submunition designed to produce electrical or electronic effects;

(c) A munition that, in order to avoid indiscriminate area effects and the risks posed by unexploded submunitions, has all of the following characteristics:

    (i) Each munition contains fewer than ten explosive submunitions;

    (ii) Each explosive submunition weighs more than four kilograms;

    (iii) Each explosive submunition is designed to detect and engage a single target object;

    (iv) Each explosive submunition is equipped with an electronic self-destruction mechanism;

    (v) Each explosive submunition is equipped with an electronic self-deactivating feature.

Article 2.3. "Explosive submunition" means a conventional munition that in order to perform its task is dispersed or released by a cluster munition and is designed to function by detonating an explosive charge prior to, on or after impact.

Article 2.5. "Unexploded submunition" means an explosive submunition that has been dispersed or released by, or otherwise separated from, a cluster munition and has failed to explode as intended.

Article 2.9. "Self-destruction mechanism" means an incorporated automatically-functioning mechanism which is in addition to the primary initiating mechanism of the munition and which secures the destruction of the munition into which it is incorporated.

Article 2.10. "Self-deactivating" means automatically rendering a munition inoperable by means of the irreversible exhaustion of a component, for example a battery, that is essential to the operation of the munition.

Definition of explosive bomblet

Article 2.13. "Explosive bomblet" means a conventional munition, weighing less than 20 kilograms, which is not self-propelled and which, in order to perform its task, is dispersed or released by a dispenser, and is designed to function by detonating an explosive charge prior to, on or after impact.

Definition of dispenser

Article 2.14. "Dispenser" means a container that is designed to disperse or release explosive bomblets and which is affixed to an aircraft at the time of dispersal or release.

Definition of mine

Article 2.12. "Mine" means a munition designed to be placed under, on or near the ground or other surface area and to be exploded by the presence, proximity or contact of a person or a vehicle.

Definition of cluster munition remnants and related terms

Article 2.7. "Cluster munition remnants" means failed cluster munitions, abandoned cluster munitions, unexploded submunitions and unexploded bomblets.

Article 2.4. "Failed cluster munition" means a cluster munition that has been fired, dropped, launched, projected or otherwise delivered and which should have dispersed or released its explosive submunitions but failed to do so.

Article 2.5. "Unexploded submunition" means an explosive submunition that has been dispersed or released by, or otherwise separated from, a cluster munition and has failed to explode as intended.

Article 2.6. "Abandoned cluster munitions" means cluster munitions or explosive submunitions that have not been used and that have been left behind or dumped, and that are no longer under the control of the party that left them behind or dumped them. They may or may not have been prepared for use.

Article 2.15. "Unexploded bomblet" means an explosive bomblet that has been dispersed, released or otherwise separated from a dispenser and has failed to explode as intended.

SCHEDULE 2

Section 9(1) and (6)

OFFENCES TO WHICH SECTION 9 APPLIES

Specified offences

1   An offence under section 2(1)(e) or (g).

2   An offence under subsection (2) of section 2 of assisting, encouraging or inducing another person to engage in any conduct mentioned in paragraphs (a) or (e) to (g) of subsection (1) of that section.

3   An offence under Part 2 of the Serious Crime Act 2007 in relation to —
        (a)   an offence under section 2(1)(a) or (f), or
        (b)   an offence specified in this Schedule.

4   An offence committed by inciting the commission of —
        (a)   an offence under section 2(1)(a) or (f), or
        (b)   an offence specified in this Schedule.

5   An offence committed by aiding, abetting, counselling or procuring the commission of —
        (a)   an offence under section 2(1)(a) or (f), or
        (b)   an offence specified in this Schedule.

6   An offence of attempting to commit or conspiring to commit an offence specified in this Schedule.

Application of defence under section 9(1): offences relating to use or transfer

7   (1)   This paragraph applies where a person is charged with —
        (a)   an offence under section 2(1)(g) (making arrangements under which another person transfers a prohibited munition),
        (b)   an offence specified in any of paragraphs 2 to 5 where the conduct constituting the offence relates to the use or transfer of a prohibited munition, or
        (c)   an offence specified in paragraph 6 where the conduct constituting the offence consists of attempting or conspiring to commit an offence mentioned in paragraph (a) or (b).

    (2)   The defence under section 9(1) applies in relation to the offence only if the person also shows that —
        (a)   the use or transfer was (or was to be) only by members of the armed forces of a State that was not a party to the Convention or by other persons acting under the authority of such a State, or
        (b)   the person had reasonable cause to believe that the use or transfer was (or was to be) only as mentioned in paragraph (a).

Application of defence under section 9(1): offences relating to conduct by visiting forces etc.

8   (1)   The defence under section 9(1) does not apply where a person is charged with an offence under section 2(1)(e) if it is proved that, at the time of the conduct constituting the offence, the person was a member of a visiting force of a State that was not a party to the Convention or was working with such a force.

(2) The defence under section 9(1) does not apply where a person is charged with an offence under section 2(1)(g) if it is proved that—

    (a) at the time of the conduct constituting the offence, the person was a member of a visiting force of a State that was not a party to the Convention or was working with such a force, and

    (b) the conduct consisted of the person making arrangements under which a member of such a visiting force moves a prohibited munition into or from the United Kingdom or enters into a contract to move a prohibited munition into or from the United Kingdom.

(3) The defence under section 9(1) does not apply where a person is charged with an offence specified in paragraphs 2 to 6 if it is proved that—

    (a) at the time of the conduct constituting the offence, the person was a member of a visiting force of a State that was not a party to the Convention or was working with such a force, and

    (b) the conduct was related to anything to which sub-paragraph (4) applies.

(4) This sub-paragraph applies to—

    (a) the possession of a prohibited munition by a member of a visiting force of a State that was not a party to the Convention or a person working with such a force,

    (b) the movement of a prohibited munition into or from the United Kingdom by a member of such a visiting force,

    (c) the entering into a contract by a member of such a visiting force to move a prohibited munition into or from the United Kingdom,

    (d) the making of arrangements by a member of such a visiting force or a person working with such a force under which a member of such a force—

        (i) moves a prohibited munition into or from the United Kingdom, or

        (ii) enters into a contract to move a prohibited munition into or from the United Kingdom.

(5) In this paragraph "member of a visiting force" and "person working with such a force" are to be construed in accordance with section 8.

SCHEDULE 3 Section 31

AMENDMENTS OF OTHER ACTS

Criminal Justice and Police Act 2001 (c. 16)

1   In Schedule 1 to the Criminal Justice and Police Act 2001 (powers of seizure), at the end of Part 1 (powers to which section 50 applies) insert—

"Cluster Munitions (Prohibitions) Act 2010 (c. 11)

    73M   Each of the powers of seizure conferred by the provisions of section 22(2)(c), (e), (f) and (g) of the Cluster Munitions (Prohibitions) Act 2010 (seizure of evidence of offences under that Act)."

Serious Crime Act 2007 (c. 27)

2 In Schedule 3 to the Serious Crime Act 2007 (listed offences that are to be disregarded), at the end of Part 1 (offences common to England and Wales and Northern Ireland) insert—

  "*Cluster Munitions (Prohibitions) Act 2010 (c. 11)*

  24A An offence under section 2(2) of the Cluster Munitions (Prohibitions) Act 2010 (assisting, encouraging or inducing another to engage in conduct mentioned in section 2(1) of that

1384

Appropriation (No. 2) Act 2010

2010 CHAPTER 12

CONTENTS

Appropriation (No. 2) Act 2010

2010 CHAPTER 12

An Act to Appropriate the supply authorised in this Session of Parliament for the service of the year ending with 31 March 2011.   [8th April 2010]

WHEREAS the Commons of the United Kingdom in Parliament assembled have resolved to authorise the use of resources and the issue of sums out of the Consolidated Fund towards making good the supply which they have granted to Her Majesty in this Session of Parliament: —

Be it therefore enacted by the Queen's most Excellent Majesty, by and with the advice and consent of the Lords Spiritual and Temporal, and Commons, in this present Parliament assembled, and by the authority of the same, as follows: —

1   Appropriation of amounts and sums voted for supply services

(1)   All the amounts and sums authorised by the Consolidated Fund Act 2009 for the service of the year ending with 31 March 2011, totalling, as is shown in Schedule 1, £,218,175,405,000 in amounts of resources authorised for use and £219,011,739,000 in sums authorised for issue from the Consolidated Fund, are appropriated, and shall be deemed to have been appropriated as from the date of the passing of that Act, to the Estimates and Requests for Resources specified in Schedule 2 to this Act.

(2)   The abstracts of Schedule 1 and of Schedule 2 which are annexed to this Act shall have effect as part of this Act.

2   Short title

This Act may be cited as the Appropriation (No. 2) Act 2010.

ABSTRACT OF SCHEDULE 1

(RESOURCES AUTHORISED FOR USE AND GRANTS OUT OF THE CONSOLIDATED FUND)

Resources authorised for use £218,175,405,000

Grants out of the Consolidated Fund £219,011,739,000

ABSTRACT OF SCHEDULE 2

(APPROPRIATION OF AMOUNTS AND SUMS VOTED FOR SUPPLY SERVICES)

Part		Net resources authorised for use	Grants out of the Consolidated Fund
		£	£
2010–11			
Part 1.	Department for Children, Schools and Families	24,867,328,000	24,891,014,000
Part 2.	Teachers' Pension Scheme (England & Wales)	4,655,862,000	990,221,000
Part 3.	Office for Standards in Education, Children's Services and Skills	80,273,000	81,067,000
Part 4.	Office of Qualifications and Examinations Regulation	9,000,000	9,000,000
Part 5.	Department of Health	36,930,935,000	36,719,318,000
Part 6.	National Health Service Pension Scheme	5,636,990,000	0
Part 7.	Food Standards Agency	60,466,000	59,540,000
Part 8.	Department for Transport	7,033,541,000	5,966,392,000
Part 9.	Office of Rail Regulation	0	0
Part 10.	Department for Communities and Local Government	17,434,832,000	17,433,673,000
Part 11.	Department for Business, Innovation and Skills	9,653,466,000	11,071,732,000
Part 12.	UK Trade & Investment	53,011,000	53,352,000
Part 13.	Export Credits Guarantee Department	13,308,000	0
Part 14.	Office of Fair Trading	29,731,000	29,156,000
Part 15.	Postal Services Commission	0	0
Part 16.	Home Office	4,839,675,000	4,907,782,000
Part 17.	Charity Commission	13,598,000	13,418,000
Part 18.	Ministry of Justice	21,725,401,000	21,681,964,000
Part 19.	Ministry of Justice: Judicial Pensions Scheme	30,166,000	0
Part 20.	United Kingdom Supreme Court	1,593,000	1,317,000
Part 21.	Northern Ireland Court Service	70,000,000	70,000,000
Part 22.	The National Archives	21,928,000	17,585,000
Part 23.	Crown Prosecution Service	303,329,000	302,635,000
Part 24.	Serious Fraud Office	17,519,000	18,354,000
Part 25.	HM Procurator General and Treasury Solicitor	6,133,000	6,905,000
Part 26.	Ministry of Defence	17,877,873,000	16,985,773,000
Part 27.	Armed Forces retired pay, pensions etc	2,565,141,000	898,235,000

Part 28.	Foreign and Commonwealth Office	948,684,000	938,652,000
Part 29.	Department for International Development	2,608,705,000	2,518,156,000
Part 30.	Department for International Development: Overseas Superannuation	32,136,000	49,497,000
Part 31.	Department of Energy and Climate Change	1,295,470,000	1,451,972,000
Part 32.	UK Atomic Energy Authority Pension Schemes	118,408,000	100,908,000
Part 33.	Office of Gas and Electricity Markets	315,000	4,570,000
Part 34.	Department for Environment, Food and Rural Affairs	2,407,050,000	2,356,293,000
Part 35.	Water Services Regulation Authority	27,000	52,000
Part 36.	Department for Culture, Media and Sport	2,317,239,000	2,313,019,000
Part 37.	Department for Work and Pensions	35,459,096,000	35,608,217,000
Part 38.	Government Equalities Office	38,612,000	38,611,000
Part 39.	Northern Ireland Office	6,076,752,000	6,104,895,000
Part 40.	HM Treasury	847,640,000	15,861,987,000
Part 41.	HM Revenue and Customs	7,279,971,000	7,244,655,000
Part 42.	National Savings and Investments	70,698,000	70,824,000
Part 43.	The Statistics Board	104,711,000	102,461,000
Part 44.	Government Actuary's Department	264,000	122,000
Part 45.	Crown Estate Office	1,064,000	1,060,000
Part 46.	Cabinet Office	178,601,000	163,687,000
Part 47.	Security and Intelligence Agencies	836,037,000	825,651,000
Part 48.	Cabinet Office: Civil Superannuation	3,213,450,000	655,425,000
Part 49.	National School of Government	177,000	146,000
Part 50.	Central Office of Information	306,000	299,000
Part 51.	Office of the Parliamentary Commissioner for Administration and the Health Service Commissioner for England	15,401,000	15,437,000
Part 52.	House of Lords	52,803,000	44,130,000
Part 53.	House of Commons: Members	73,374,000	86,231,000
Part 54.	House of Commons: Administration	116,100,000	95,400,000
Part 55.	National Audit Office	35,685,000	35,145,000
Part 56.	The Electoral Commission	10,741,000	10,926,000
Part 57.	Independent Parliamentary Standards Authority	103,509,000	103,536,000
Part 58.	The Local Government Boundary Commission for England	1,280,000	1,342,000
	GRAND TOTAL...................	218,175,405,000	219,011,739,000

Appropriation (No.2) Act 2010 (c.12)
Schedule 1 – Resources authorised for use and Grants out of the Consolidated Fund

1393

SCHEDULE 1

Section 1

RESOURCES AUTHORISED FOR USE AND GRANTS OUT OF THE CONSOLIDATED FUND

	Resources authorised for use	Grants out of the Consolidated Fund
	£	£
For the service of the year ending 31 March 2011 — Under the Consolidated Fund Act 2009	218,175,405,000	219,011,739,000
TOTAL	218,175,405,000	219,011,739,000

1394

Appropriation (No.2) Act 2010 (c.12)
Schedule 2 – Appropriation of amounts and sums voted for supply services
Part 1 – Department for Children, Schools and Families, 2010–11

SCHEDULE 2   Section 1

APPROPRIATION OF AMOUNTS AND SUMS VOTED FOR SUPPLY SERVICES

PART 1

DEPARTMENT FOR CHILDREN, SCHOOLS AND FAMILIES, 2010–11

Table of —

(a) the resources authorised for use, on account, to meet the costs of the Estimate and Requests for Resources which are specified in the first column of the Table for the year ending with 31 March 2011; and

(b) the sums authorised for issue out of the Consolidated Fund, on account, to meet those costs.

Estimate/ Request for Resources	Net Resources authorised for use	Grants out of the Consolidated Fund
	£	£
DEPARTMENT FOR CHILDREN, SCHOOLS AND FAMILIES		24,891,014,000
1. To help build a competitive economy and inclusive society by: creating opportunities for everyone to develop their learning; releasing potential in people to make the most of themselves; and achieving excellence in standards of education and levels of skills	24,040,357,000	
2. Promoting the physical, intellectual and social development of babies and young children through Sure Start, Early Years Provision and Childcare	826,971,000	
TOTAL, 2010-11	24,867,328,000	24,891,014,000

Appropriation (No.2) Act 2010 (c. 12)
Schedule 2 – Appropriation of amounts and sums voted for supply services
Part 2 – Teachers' Pension Scheme (England & Wales), 2010–11

1395

PART 2

TEACHERS' PENSION SCHEME (ENGLAND & WALES), 2010–11

Table of —

(c) the resources authorised for use, on account, to meet the costs of the Estimate and Requests for Resources which are specified in the first column of the Table for the year ending with 31 March 2011; and

(d) the sums authorised for issue out of the Consolidated Fund, on account, to meet those costs.

Estimate/ Request for Resources	Net Resources authorised for use £	Grants out of the Consolidated Fund £
TEACHERS' PENSION SCHEME (ENGLAND & WALES)		990,221,000
1. Teachers' pensions	4,655,862,000	
TOTAL, 2010–11	4,655,862,000	990,221,000

1396

Appropriation (No.2) Act 2010 (c.12)
Schedule 2 – Appropriation of amounts and sums voted for supply services
Part 3 – Office for Standards in Education, Children's Services and Skills, 2010–11

PART 3

OFFICE FOR STANDARDS IN EDUCATION, CHILDREN'S SERVICES AND SKILLS, 2010–11

Table of—

(a) the resources authorised for use, on account, to meet the costs of the Estimate and Requests for Resources which are specified in the first column of the Table for the year ending with 31 March 2011; and

(b) the sums authorised for issue out of the Consolidated Fund, on account, to meet those costs.

Estimate/ Request for Resources	Net Resources authorised for use £	Grants out of the Consolidated Fund £
OFFICE FOR STANDARDS IN EDUCATION, CHILDREN'S SERVICES AND SKILLS **1. Serving the interests of children and young people, parents, adult learners, employers and the wider community in England by promoting improvement in the quality of education, skills and young people's care through independent inspection, regulation and reporting**	80,273,000	81,067,000
TOTAL, 2010–11	80,273,000	81,067,000

Appropriation (No.2) Act 2010 (c.12)
Schedule 2 – Appropriation of amounts and sums voted for supply services
Part 4 – Office of Qualifications and Examinations Regulation, 2010–11

1397

PART 4

OFFICE OF QUALIFICATIONS AND EXAMINATIONS REGULATION, 2010–11

Table of –

(c) the resources authorised for use, on account, to meet the costs of the Estimate and Requests for Resources which are specified in the first column of the Table for the year ending with 31 March 2011; and

(d) the sums authorised for issue out of the Consolidated Fund, on account, to meet those costs.

Estimate/ Request for Resources	Net Resources authorised for use £	Grants out of the Consolidated Fund £
OFFICE OF QUALIFICATIONS AND EXAMINATIONS REGULATION		9,000,000
1. To be an independent regulator of qualifications and statutory assessments, in order to safeguard the standards of those qualifications and assessments, improve public confidence in those standards, raise awareness of qualifications and the system for regulating them, and to secure that qualifications are provided efficiently and represent value for money	9,000,000	
TOTAL, 2010–11	9,000,000	9,000,000

1398

Appropriation (No.2) Act 2010 (c.12)
Schedule 2 – Appropriation of amounts and sums voted for supply services
Part 5 – Department of Health, 2010–11

PART 5

DEPARTMENT OF HEALTH, 2010–11

Table of —

(a) the resources authorised for use, on account, to meet the costs of the Estimate and Requests for Resources which are specified in the first column of the Table for the year ending with 31 March 2011; and

(b) the sums authorised for issue out of the Consolidated Fund, on account, to meet those costs.

Estimate/ Request for Resources	Net Resources authorised for use £	Grants out of the Consolidated Fund £
DEPARTMENT OF HEALTH		36,719,318,000
1. Securing health care for those who need it	35,441,016,000	
2. Securing social care for adults who need it and, at national level, protecting, promoting and improving the nation's health	1,482,676,000	
3. Office of the Independent Regulator for NHS Foundation Trusts	7,243,000	
TOTAL, 2010–11	36,930,935,000	36,719,318,000

Appropriation (No.2) Act 2010 (c.12)
Schedule 2 – Appropriation of amounts and sums voted for supply services
Part 6 – National Health Service Pension Scheme, 2010–11

1399

PART 6

NATIONAL HEALTH SERVICE PENSION SCHEME, 2010–11

Table of —

(a) the resources authorised for use, on account, to meet the costs of the Estimate and Requests for Resources which are specified in the first column of the Table for the year ending with 31 March 2011; and

(b) the sums authorised for issue out of the Consolidated Fund, on account, to meet those costs.

Estimate/ *Request for Resources*	*Net Resources authorised for use*	*Grants out of the Consolidated Fund*
	£	£
NATIONAL HEALTH SERVICE PENSION SCHEME		0
1. National Health Service Pension Scheme	5,636,990,000	
TOTAL, 2010–11	5,636,990,000	0

1400

Appropriation (No.2) Act 2010 (c.12)
Schedule 2 – Appropriation of amounts and sums voted for supply services
Part 7 – Food Standards Agency, 2010–11

PART 7

FOOD STANDARDS AGENCY, 2010–11

Table of—

(a) the resources authorised for use, on account, to meet the costs of the Estimate and Requests for Resources which are specified in the first column of the Table for the year ending with 31 March 2011; and

(b) the sums authorised for issue out of the Consolidated Fund, on account, to meet those costs.

Estimate/ Request for Resources	Net Resources authorised for use	Grants out of the Consolidated Fund
	£	£
FOOD STANDARDS AGENCY **1. Protecting and promoting public health in relation to food**	60,466,000	59,540,000
TOTAL, 2010–11	60,466,000	59,540,000

Appropriation (No.2) Act 2010 (c.12)
Schedule 2 – Appropriation of amounts and sums voted for supply services
Part 8 – Department for Transport, 2010–11

1401

PART 8

DEPARTMENT FOR TRANSPORT, 2010–11

Table of —

(a) the resources authorised for use, on account, to meet the costs of the Estimate and Requests for Resources which are specified in the first column of the Table for the year ending with 31 March 2011; and

(b) the sums authorised for issue out of the Consolidated Fund, on account, to meet those costs.

Estimate/ Request for Resources	Net Resources authorised for use £	Grants out of the Consolidated Fund £
DEPARTMENT FOR TRANSPORT **1. Transport that works for everyone**	7,033,541,000	5,966,392,000
TOTAL, 2010–11	7,033,541,000	5,966,392,000

1402

Appropriation (No.2) Act 2010 (c.12)
Schedule 2 – Appropriation of amounts and sums voted for supply services
Part 9 – Office of Rail Regulation, 2010–11

PART 9

OFFICE OF RAIL REGULATION, 2010–11

Table of —

(a) the resources authorised for use, on account, to meet the costs of the Estimate and Requests for Resources which are specified in the first column of the Table for the year ending with 31 March 2011; and

(b) the sums authorised for issue out of the Consolidated Fund, on account, to meet those costs.

Estimate/ Request for Resources	Net Resources authorised for use £	Grants out of the Consolidated Fund £
OFFICE OF RAIL REGULATION 1. To create a better railway for passengers and freight, and better value for public funding authorities though independent, fair and effective regulation	0	0
TOTAL, 2010–11	0	0

Appropriation (No.2) Act 2010 (c.12)
Schedule 2 – Appropriation of amounts and sums voted for supply services
Part 10 – Department for Communities and Local Government, 2010–11

1403

PART 10

DEPARTMENT FOR COMMUNITIES AND LOCAL GOVERNMENT, 2010–11

Table of—

(a) the resources authorised for use, on account, to meet the costs of the Estimate and Requests for Resources which are specified in the first column of the Table for the year ending with 31 March 2011; and

(b) the sums authorised for issue out of the Consolidated Fund, on account, to meet those costs.

Estimate/ *Request for Resources*	*Net Resources* *authorised for use* £	*Grants out of the* *Consolidated Fund* £
DEPARTMENT FOR COMMUNITIES AND LOCAL GOVERNMENT		17,433,673,000
1. Improving the quality of life by creating thriving, inclusive and sustainable communities in all regions	5,698,733,000	
2. Providing for effective devolved decision making within a national framework	11,736,099,000	
TOTAL, 2010-11	17,434,832,000	17,433,673,000

1404

Appropriation (No.2) Act 2010 (c. 12)
Schedule 2 – Appropriation of amounts and sums voted for supply services
Part 11 – Department for Business, Innovation and Skills, 2010–11

PART 11

DEPARTMENT FOR BUSINESS, INNOVATION AND SKILLS, 2010–11

Table of —

(a) the resources authorised for use, on account, to meet the costs of the Estimate and Requests for Resources which are specified in the first column of the Table for the year ending with 31 March 2011; and

(b) the sums authorised for issue out of the Consolidated Fund, on account, to meet those costs.

Estimate/ Request for Resources	Net Resources authorised for use £	Grants out of the Consolidated Fund £
DEPARTMENT FOR BUSINESS, INNOVATION AND SKILLS		11,071,732,000
1. To help ensure business success in an increasingly competitive world	1,137,181,000	
2. Increasing Scientific excellence in the UK and maximising its contribution to society	1,612,867,000	
3. To help build a competitive economy by creating opportunities for everyone to develop their learning and skills	6,903,418,000	
TOTAL, 2010–11	9,653,466,000	11,071,732,000

Appropriation (No.2) Act 2010 (c.12)
Schedule 2 – Appropriation of amounts and sums voted for supply services
Part 12 – UK Trade & Investment, 2010–11

1405

PART 12

UK TRADE & INVESTMENT, 2010–11

Table of—

(a) the resources authorised for use, on account, to meet the costs of the Estimate and Requests for Resources which are specified in the first column of the Table for the year ending with 31 March 2011; and

(b) the sums authorised for issue out of the Consolidated Fund, on account, to meet those costs.

Estimate/ Request for Resources	Net Resources authorised for use	Grants out of the Consolidated Fund
	£	£
UK TRADE & INVESTMENT **1. To enhance the competitiveness of companies in the UK through overseas trade and investments; and attract a continuing high level of quality foreign direct investment**	53,011,000	53,352,000
TOTAL, 2010–11	53,011,000	53,352,000

1406

Appropriation (No.2) Act 2010 (c.12)
Schedule 2 – Appropriation of amounts and sums voted for supply services
Part 13 – Export Credits Guarantee Department, 2010–11

PART 13

EXPORT CREDITS GUARANTEE DEPARTMENT, 2010–11

Table of —

(a) the resources authorised for use, on account, to meet the costs of the Estimate and Requests for Resources which are specified in the first column of the Table for the year ending with 31 March 2011; and

(b) the sums authorised for issue out of the Consolidated Fund, on account, to meet those costs.

Estimate/ *Request for Resources*	*Net Resources* *authorised for use* £	*Grants out of the* *Consolidated Fund* £
EXPORT CREDITS GUARANTEE DEPARTMENT **1. To provide export finance assistance through interest support to benefit the UK economy by facilitating exports**	13,308,000	0
2. To provide export credit guarantees and investment insurance to benefit the UK economy by facilitating exports	0	
TOTAL, 2010–11	13,308,000	0

Appropriation (No.2) Act 2010 (c.12)
Schedule 2 – Appropriation of amounts and sums voted for supply services
Part 14 – Office of Fair Trading, 2010–11

1407

PART 14

OFFICE OF FAIR TRADING, 2010–11

Table of —

(a) the resources authorised for use, on account, to meet the costs of the Estimate and Requests for Resources which are specified in the first column of the Table for the year ending with 31 March 2011; and

(b) the sums authorised for issue out of the Consolidated Fund, on account, to meet those costs.

Estimate/ *Request for Resources*	*Net Resources authorised for use* £	*Grants out of the Consolidated Fund* £
OFFICE OF FAIR TRADING **1. Advancing and safeguarding the economic interests of UK consumers**	29,731,000	29,156,000
TOTAL, 2010–11	29,731,000	29,156,000

1408

Appropriation (No.2) Act 2010 (c.12)
Schedule 2 – Appropriation of amounts and sums voted for supply services
Part 15 – Postal Services Commission, 2010–11

PART 15

POSTAL SERVICES COMMISSION, 2010–11

Table of —

(a) the resources authorised for use, on account, to meet the costs of the Estimate and Requests for Resources which are specified in the first column of the Table for the year ending with 31 March 2011; and

(b) the sums authorised for issue out of the Consolidated Fund, on account, to meet those costs.

Estimate/ Request for Resources	Net Resources authorised for use £	Grants out of the Consolidated Fund £
POSTAL SERVICES COMMISSION **1. Ensuring the provision of a universal postal service at a uniform tariff, protecting consumers and promoting competition**	0	0
TOTAL, 2010–11	0	0

Appropriation (No.2) Act 2010 (c.12)
Schedule 2 – Appropriation of amounts and sums voted for supply services
Part 16 – Home Office, 2010–11

1409

PART 16

HOME OFFICE, 2010–11

Table of —

(a) the resources authorised for use, on account, to meet the costs of the Estimate and Requests for Resources which are specified in the first column of the Table for the year ending with 31 March 2011; and

(b) the sums authorised for issue out of the Consolidated Fund, on account, to meet those costs.

Estimate/ Request for Resources	Net Resources authorised for use	Grants out of the Consolidated Fund
	£	£
HOME OFFICE		4,907,782,000
1. Working together to protect the public	4,839,675,000	
TOTAL, 2010–11	4,839,675,000	4,907,782,000

1410

Appropriation (No. 2) Act 2010 (c. 12)
Schedule 2 – Appropriation of amounts and sums voted for supply services
Part 17 – Charity Commission, 2010–11

PART 17

CHARITY COMMISSION, 2010–11

Table of —

(a) the resources authorised for use, on account, to meet the costs of the Estimate and Requests for Resources which are specified in the first column of the Table for the year ending with 31 March 2011; and

(b) the sums authorised for issue out of the Consolidated Fund, on account, to meet those costs.

Estimate/ Request for Resources	Net Resources authorised for use	Grants out of the Consolidated Fund
	£	£
CHARITY COMMISSION 1. Giving the public confidence in the integrity of charity	13,598,000	13,418,000
TOTAL, 2010–11	13,598,000	13,418,000

Appropriation (No.2) Act 2010 (c.12)
Schedule 2 – Appropriation of amounts and sums voted for supply services
Part 18 – Ministry of Justice, 2010–11

1411

PART 18

MINISTRY OF JUSTICE, 2010–11

Table of —

(a) the resources authorised for use, on account, to meet the costs of the Estimate and Requests for Resources which are specified in the first column of the Table for the year ending with 31 March 2011; and

(b) the sums authorised for issue out of the Consolidated Fund, on account, to meet those costs.

Estimate/ Request for Resources	Net Resources authorised for use £	Grants out of the Consolidated Fund £
MINISTRY OF JUSTICE		21,681,964,000
1. To promote the development of a modern, fair, cost effective and efficient system of justice for all	4,131,185,000	
2.Overseeing the effective operation of the devolution settlement in Scotland and representing the interests of Scotland within the UK Government	11,841,146,000	
3. To support the Secretary of State in discharging his role of representing Wales in the UK Government, representing the UK Government in Wales and ensuring the smooth working of the devolution settlement in Wales	5,753,070,000	
TOTAL, 2010–11	21,725,401,000	21,681,964,000

1412

Appropriation (No.2) Act 2010 (c.12)
Schedule 2 – Appropriation of amounts and sums voted for supply services
Part 19 – Ministry of Justice: Judicial Pensions Scheme, 2010–11

PART 19

MINISTRY OF JUSTICE: JUDICIAL PENSIONS SCHEME, 2010–11

Table of —

(a) the resources authorised for use, on account, to meet the costs of the Estimate and Requests for Resources which are specified in the first column of the Table for the year ending with 31 March 2011; and

(b) the sums authorised for issue out of the Consolidated Fund, on account, to meet those costs.

Estimate/ Request for Resources	Net Resources authorised for use	Grants out of the Consolidated Fund
	£	£
MINISTRY OF JUSTICE: JUDICIAL PENSIONS SCHEME		0
1. Judicial Pensions Scheme	30,166,000	
TOTAL, 2010–11	30,166,000	0

Appropriation (No.2) Act 2010 (c.12)
Schedule 2 – Appropriation of amounts and sums voted for supply services
Part 20 – United Kingdom Supreme Court, 2010–11

1413

PART 20

UNITED KINGDOM SUPREME COURT, 2010–11

Table of –

(a) the resources authorised for use, on account, to meet the costs of the Estimate and Requests for Resources which are specified in the first column of the Table for the year ending with 31 March 2011; and

(b) the sums authorised for issue out of the Consolidated Fund, on account, to meet those costs.

Estimate/ Request for Resources	Net Resources authorised for use	Grants out of the Consolidated Fund
	£	£
UNITED KINGDOM SUPREME COURT		1,317,000
1. To support the efficient and effective administration of the UK Supreme Court and the provision of appropriate support to the Judicial Committee of the Privy Council	1,593,000	
TOTAL, 2010–11	1,593,000	1,317,000

1414

Appropriation (No.2) Act 2010 (c.12)
Schedule 2 – Appropriation of amounts and sums voted for supply services
Part 21 – Northern Ireland Court Service, 2010–11

PART 21

NORTHERN IRELAND COURT SERVICE, 2010–11

Table of —

(a) the resources authorised for use, on account, to meet the costs of the Estimate and Requests for Resources which are specified in the first column of the Table for the year ending with 31 March 2011; and

(b) the sums authorised for issue out of the Consolidated Fund, on account, to meet those costs.

Estimate/ Request for Resources	Net Resources authorised for use £	Grants out of the Consolidated Fund £
NORTHERN IRELAND COURT SERVICE **1. Supporting the effective and efficient administration of justice in Northern Ireland**	70,000,000	70,000,000
TOTAL, 2010–11	70,000,000	70,000,000

Appropriation (No.2) Act 2010 (c.12)
Schedule 2 – Appropriation of amounts and sums voted for supply services
Part 22 – The National Archives, 2010–11

1415

PART 22

THE NATIONAL ARCHIVES, 2010–11

Table of —

(a) the resources authorised for use, on account, to meet the costs of the Estimate and Requests for Resources which are specified in the first column of the Table for the year ending with 31 March 2011; and

(b) the sums authorised for issue out of the Consolidated Fund, on account, to meet those costs.

Estimate/ Request for Resources	Net Resources authorised for use £	Grants out of the Consolidated Fund £
THE NATIONAL ARCHIVES **1. Promoting the study of the past in order to inform the present and the future by selecting, preserving and making publicly available public records of historical value and by encouraging high standards of care and public access for archives of historical value outside the public records and leading on UK information management re-use policy, spreading best practice, setting standards and ensuring compliance across the public sector and managing Crown and Parliamentary copyright and delivering cost effective publishing services and advice across government**	21,928.000	17,585,000
TOTAL, 2010–11	21,928,000	17,585,000

1416

Appropriation (No.2) Act 2010 (c.12)
Schedule 2 – Appropriation of amounts and sums voted for supply services
Part 23 – Crown Prosecution Service, 2010–11

PART 23

CROWN PROSECUTION SERVICE, 2010–11

Table of —

(a) the resources authorised for use, on account, to meet the costs of the Estimate and Requests for Resources which are specified in the first column of the Table for the year ending with 31 March 2011; and

(b) the sums authorised for issue out of the Consolidated Fund, on account, to meet those costs.

Estimate/ Request for Resources	Net Resources authorised for use £	Grants out of the Consolidated Fund £
CROWN PROSECUTION SERVICE **1. To bring offenders to justice, recover proceeds of crime, improve services to victims and witnesses and promote confidence by firm and fair decision making and presentation of cases in court.**	303,329,000	302,635,000
TOTAL, 2010–11	303,329,000	302,635,000

Appropriation (No.2) Act 2010 (c.12)
Schedule 2 – Appropriation of amounts and sums voted for supply services
Part 24 – Serious Fraud Office, 2010–11

1417

PART 24

SERIOUS FRAUD OFFICE, 2010–11

Table of —

(a) the resources authorised for use, on account, to meet the costs of the Estimate and Requests for Resources which are specified in the first column of the Table for the year ending with 31 March 2011; and

(b) the sums authorised for issue out of the Consolidated Fund, on account, to meet those costs.

Estimate/ Request for Resources	Net Resources authorised for use £	Grants out of the Consolidated Fund £
SERIOUS FRAUD OFFICE		18,354,000
1. Reducing fraud and the cost of fraud and delivering justice and the rule of law	17,519,000	
TOTAL, 2010–11	17,519,000	18,354,000

1418

Appropriation (No. 2) Act 2010 (c.12)
Schedule 2 – Appropriation of amounts and sums voted for supply services
Part 25 – HM Procurator General and Treasury Solicitor, 2010–11

PART 25

HM PROCURATOR GENERAL AND TREASURY SOLICITOR, 2010–11

Table of —

(a) the resources authorised for use, on account, to meet the costs of the Estimate and Requests for Resources which are specified in the first column of the Table for the year ending with 31 March 2011; and

(b) the sums authorised for issue out of the Consolidated Fund, on account, to meet those costs.

Estimate/ Request for Resources	Net Resources authorised for use £	Grants out of the Consolidated Fund £
HM PROCURATOR GENERAL AND TREASURY SOLICITOR **1. Providing comprehensive and competitive legal services to government departments and publicly funded bodies**	6,133,000	6,905,000
TOTAL, 2010–11	6,133,000	6,905,000

Appropriation (No.2) Act 2010 (c.12)
Schedule 2 – Appropriation of amounts and sums voted for supply services
 – Ministry of Defence, 2010–11

1419

PART 26

MINISTRY OF DEFENCE, 2010–11

Table of—

(a) the resources authorised for use, on account, to meet the costs of the Estimate and Requests for Resources which are specified in the first column of the Table for the year ending with 31 March 2011; and

(b) the sums authorised for issue out of the Consolidated Fund, on account, to meet those costs.

Estimate/ *Request for Resources*	*Net Resources authorised for use* £	*Grants out of the Consolidated Fund* £
MINISTRY OF DEFENCE		16,985,773,000
1. Provision of defence capability (including provision for Naval Service to a number not exceeding 42,550; provision for Army Service to a number not exceeding 124,030; provision for Air Force Service to a number not exceeding 47,400; and provision for officers and men in the Reserve Forces not exceeding the numbers specified in respect of each of the Reserve Forces for the purposes of Parts 1, 3, 4 and 5 of the Reserve Forces Act 1996 in House of Commons Paper No.304 of Session 2009–10)	16,124,766,000	
2. Operations and Peace-Keeping	1,292,440,000	
3. War Pensions and Allowances, etc	460,667,000	
TOTAL, 2010–11	17,877,873,000	16,985,773,000

1420

Appropriation (No.2) Act 2010 (c.12)
Schedule 2 – Appropriation of amounts and sums voted for supply services
Part 27 – Armed Forces retired pay, pensions etc, 2010–11

PART 27

ARMED FORCES RETIRED PAY, PENSIONS ETC, 2010–11

Table of —

(a) the resources authorised for use, on account, to meet the costs of the Estimate and Requests for Resources which are specified in the first column of the Table for the year ending with 31 March 2011; and

(b) the sums authorised for issue out of the Consolidated Fund, on account, to meet those costs.

Estimate/ *Request for Resources*	*Net Resources* *authorised for use* £	*Grants out of the* *Consolidated Fund* £
ARMED FORCES RETIRED PAY, PENSIONS ETC **1. Armed Forces retired pay, pensions etc**	 2,565,141,000	898,235,000
TOTAL, 2010–11	2,565,141,000	898,235,000

Appropriation (No.2) Act 2010 (c.12)
Schedule 2 – Appropriation of amounts and sums voted for supply services
Part 28 – Foreign and Commonwealth Office, 2010–11

1421

PART 28

FOREIGN AND COMMONWEALTH OFFICE, 2010–11

Table of —

(a) the resources authorised for use, on account, to meet the costs of the Estimate and Requests for Resources which are specified in the first column of the Table for the year ending with 31 March 2011; and

(b) the sums authorised for issue out of the Consolidated Fund, on account, to meet those costs.

Estimate/ Request for Resources	*Net Resources authorised for use* £	*Grants out cf the Consolidated Fund* £
FOREIGN AND COMMONWEALTH OFFICE		938,652,000
1. Promoting internationally the interests of the UK and contributing to a strong world community	760,584,000	
2. Conflict prevention	188,100,000	
TOTAL, 2010–11	948,684,000	938,652,000

1422

Appropriation (No.2) Act 2010 (c. 12)
Schedule 2 – Appropriation of amounts and sums voted for supply services
Part 29 – Department for International Development, 2010–11

PART 29

DEPARTMENT FOR INTERNATIONAL DEVELOPMENT, 2010–11

Table of —

(a) the resources authorised for use, on account, to meet the costs of the Estimate and Requests for Resources which are specified in the first column of the Table for the year ending with 31 March 2011; and

(b) the sums authorised for issue out of the Consolidated Fund, on account, to meet those costs.

Estimate/ Request for Resources	Net Resources authorised for use £	Grants out of the Consolidated Fund £
DEPARTMENT FOR INTERNATIONAL DEVELOPMENT		2,518,156,000
1. Eliminating poverty in poorer countries	2,596,465,000	
2. Conflict prevention	12,240,000	
TOTAL, 2010–11	2,608,705,000	2,518,156,000

Appropriation (No.2) Act 2010 (c. 12)
Schedule 2 – Appropriation of amounts and sums voted for supply services
Part 30 – Department for International Development: Overseas Superannuation, 2010–11

1423

PART 30

DEPARTMENT FOR INTERNATIONAL DEVELOPMENT: OVERSEAS SUPERANNUATION, 2010–11

Table of —

(a) the resources authorised for use, on account, to meet the costs of the Estimate and Requests for Resources which are specified in the first column of the Table for the year ending with 31 March 2011; and

(b) the sums authorised for issue out of the Consolidated Fund, on account, to meet those costs.

Estimate/ Request for Resources	Net Resources authorised for use £	Grants out of the Consolidated Fund £
DEPARTMENT FOR INTERNATIONAL DEVELOPMENT: OVERSEAS SUPERANNUATION		49,497,000
1. Overseas superannuation	32,136,000	
TOTAL, 2010–11	32,136,000	49,497,000

1424

Appropriation (No.2) Act 2010 (c.12)
Schedule 2 – Appropriation of amounts and sums voted for supply services
Part 31 – Department of Energy and Climate Change, 2010–11

PART 31

DEPARTMENT OF ENERGY AND CLIMATE CHANGE, 2010–11

Table of —

(a) the resources authorised for use, on account, to meet the costs of the Estimate and Requests for Resources which are specified in the first column of the Table for the year ending with 31 March 2011; and

(b) the sums authorised for issue out of the Consolidated Fund, on account, to meet those costs.

Estimate/ *Request for Resources*	Net Resources *authorised for use* £	Grants out of the Consolidated Fund £
DEPARTMENT OF ENERGY AND CLIMATE CHANGE **1. Supporting the provision of energy that is affordable, secure and sustainable; bringing about a low carbon UK; securing an international agreement on climate change; promoting low carbon technologies at home and in developing countries; managing historic energy liabilities effectively and responsibly.**	1,295,470,000	1,451,972,000
TOTAL, 2010–11	1,295,470,000	1,451,972,000

Appropriation (No.2) Act 2010 (c.12)
Schedule 2 – Appropriation of amounts and sums voted for supply services
Part 32 – UK Atomic Energy Authority Pension Schemes, 2010–11

1425

PART 32

UK ATOMIC ENERGY AUTHORITY PENSION SCHEMES, 2010–11

Table of –

(a) the resources authorised for use, on account, to meet the costs of the Estimate and Requests for Resources which are specified in the first column of the Table for the year ending with 31 March 2011; and

(b) the sums authorised for issue out of the Consolidated Fund, on account, to meet those costs.

Estimate/ *Request for Resources*	*Net Resources* *authorised for use* £	*Grants out of the* *Consolidated Fund* £
UK ATOMIC ENERGY AUTHORITY PENSION SCHEMES **1. Effective management of UKAEA pension schemes**	 118,408,000	100,908,000
TOTAL, 2010–11	118,408,000	100,908,000

1426

Appropriation (No.2) Act 2010 (c.12)
Schedule 2 – Appropriation of amounts and sums voted for supply services
Part 33 – Office of Gas and Electricity Markets, 2010–11

PART 33

OFFICE OF GAS AND ELECTRICITY MARKETS, 2010–11

Table of —

(a) the resources authorised for use, on account, to meet the costs of the Estimate and Requests for Resources which are specified in the first column of the Table for the year ending with 31 March 2011; and

(b) the sums authorised for issue out of the Consolidated Fund, on account, to meet those costs.

Estimate/ *Request for Resources*	*Net Resources* *authorised for use* £	*Grants out of the* *Consolidated Fund* £
OFFICE OF GAS AND ELECTRICITY MARKETS **1. Protecting consumers by regulating monopolies and promoting competition in the electricity and gas industry, and expenditure in connection with environmental programmes**	315,000	4,570,000
TOTAL, 2010–11	315,000	4,570,000

Appropriation (No.2) Act 2010 (c.12)
Schedule 2 – Appropriation of amounts and sums voted for supply services
  – Department for Environment, Food and Rural Affairs, 2010–11

1427

PART 34

DEPARTMENT FOR ENVIRONMENT, FOOD AND RURAL AFFAIRS, 2010–11

Table of —

(a) the resources authorised for use, on account, to meet the costs of the Estimate and Requests for Resources which are specified in the first column of the Table for the year ending with 31 March 2011; and

(b) the sums authorised for issue out of the Consolidated Fund, on account, to meet those costs.

Estimate/ Request for Resources	Net Resources authorised for use £	Grants out of the Consolidated Fund £
DEPARTMENT FOR ENVIRONMENT, FOOD AND RURAL AFFAIRS		2,356,293,000
1. Ensuring that consumers benefit from competitively priced food, produced to high standards of safety; environmental care and animal welfare from a sustainable, efficient food chain, to contribute to the well being of rural and coastal communities and funding aspects of the Common Agricultural Policy and Rural Development Programme for England Guarantee Section as economically, efficiently and effectively as possible	2,373,219,000	
2. Direction of the delivery of the Government's Strategy for Trees, Woods and Forests in England and taking the lead in development and promotion of sustainable forest management across Great Britain	33,831,000	
TOTAL, 2010–11	2,407,050,000	2,356,293,000

1428

Appropriation (No.2) Act 2010 (c.12)
Schedule 2 – Appropriation of amounts and sums voted for supply services
Part 35 – Water Services Regulation Authority, 2010–11

PART 35

WATER SERVICES REGULATION AUTHORITY, 2010–11

Table of —

(a) the resources authorised for use, on account, to meet the costs of the Estimate and Requests for Resources which are specified in the first column of the Table for the year ending with 31 March 2011; and

(b) the sums authorised for issue out of the Consolidated Fund, on account, to meet those costs.

Estimate/ Request for Resources	*Net Resources authorised for use*	*Grants out of the Consolidated Fund*
	£	£
WATER SERVICES REGULATION AUTHORITY		52,000
1. Regulation of the Water Industry	27,000	
TOTAL, 2010–11	27,000	52,000

Appropriation (No.2) Act 2010 (c.12)   **1429**
Schedule 2 – Appropriation of amounts and sums voted for supply services
Part 36 – Department for Culture, Media and Sport, 2010–11

PART 36

DEPARTMENT FOR CULTURE, MEDIA AND SPORT, 2010–11

Table of —

(a) the resources authorised for use, on account, to meet the costs of the Estimate and Requests for Resources which are specified in the first column of the Table for the year ending with 31 March 2011; and

(b) the sums authorised for issue out of the Consolidated Fund, on account, to meet those costs.

Estimate/ Request for Resources	Net Resources authorised for use £	Grants out of the Consolidated Fund £
DEPARTMENT FOR CULTURE, MEDIA AND SPORT		2,313,019,000
1. Improving the quality of life through cultural and sporting activities	938,439,000	
2. Broadening access to a rich and varied cultural and sporting life through broadcasting and other services and activities	1,378,800,000	
TOTAL, 2010–11	2,317,239,000	2,313,019,000

1430

Appropriation (No.2) Act 2010 (c.12)
Schedule 2 – Appropriation of amounts and sums voted for supply services
– Department for Work and Pensions, 2010–11

Part 37

DEPARTMENT FOR WORK AND PENSIONS, 2010–11

Table of —

(a) the resources authorised for use, on account, to meet the costs of the Estimate and Requests for Resources which are specified in the first column of the Table for the year ending with 31 March 2011; and

(b) the sums authorised for issue out of the Consolidated Fund, on account, to meet those costs.

Estimate/ Request for Resources	Net Resources authorised for use £	Grants out of the Consolidated Fund £
DEPARTMENT FOR WORK AND PENSIONS		35,608,217,000
1. Ensuring the best start for all children and ending child poverty in 20 years	304,164,000	
2. Promote work as the best form of welfare for people of working age, whilst protecting the position of those in greatest need	20,608,323,000	
3. Combat poverty and promote security and independence in retirement for today's and tomorrow's pensioners	5,502,320,000	
4. Improve the rights and opportunities for disabled people in a fair and inclusive society	8,214,722,000	
5. Corporate contracts and support services	829,567,000	
TOTAL, 2010–11	35,459,096,000	35,608,217,000

Appropriation (No.2) Act 2010 (c.12)
Schedule 2 – Appropriation of amounts and sums voted for supply services
Part 38 – Government Equalities Office, 2010–11

1431

PART 38

GOVERNMENT EQUALITIES OFFICE, 2010–11

Table of —

(a) the resources authorised for use, on account, to meet the costs of the Estimate and Requests for Resources which are specified in the first column of the Table for the year ending with 31 March 2011; and

(b) the sums authorised for issue out of the Consolidated Fund, on account, to meet those costs.

Estimate/ *Request for Resources*	*Net Resources* *authorised for use* £	*Grants out of the* *Consolidated Fund* £
GOVERNMENT EQUALITIES OFFICE **1. Promoting a fair and equal society where everyone has the opportunity to prosper and reach their full potential**	38,612,000	38,611,000
TOTAL, 2010–11	38,612,000	38,611,000

1432

Appropriation (No.2) Act 2010 (c.12)
Schedule 2 – Appropriation of amounts and sums voted for supply services
Part 39 – Northern Ireland Office, 2010–11

PART 39

NORTHERN IRELAND OFFICE, 2010–11

Table of —

(a) the resources authorised for use, on account, to meet the costs of the Estimate and Requests for Resources which are specified in the first column of the Table for the year ending with 31 March 2011; and

(b) the sums authorised for issue out of the Consolidated Fund, on account, to meet those costs.

Estimate/ *Request for Resources*	*Net Resources* *authorised for use* £	*Grants out of the* *Consolidated Fund* £
NORTHERN IRELAND OFFICE		6,104,895,000
1. Playing a full part in implementing the Good Friday Agreement and representing the interests of Northern Ireland in the UK Government; supporting and developing an efficient, effective and responsive Criminal Justice System; upholding and sustaining the rule of law and preventing crime; maintaining a secure and humane prison service and reducing the risks of re-offending	559,302,000	
2. Providing appropriate funding to the Northern Ireland Consolidated Fund for the delivery of transferred public services as defined by the Northern Ireland Act 1998 and the Northern Ireland Act 2000	5,517,450,000	
TOTAL, 2010–11	6,076,752,000	6,104,895,000

*Appropriation (No.2) Act 2010 (c.**12**)*
Schedule 2 – Appropriation of amounts and sums voted for supply services
  Part 40 – HM Treasury, 2010–11

1433

PART 40

HM TREASURY, 2010–11

Table of—

(a) the resources authorised for use, on account, to meet the costs of the Estimate and Requests for Resources which are specified in the first column of the Table for the year ending with 31 March 2011; and

(b) the sums authorised for issue out of the Consolidated Fund, on account, to meet those costs.

Estimate/ Request for Resources	Net Resources authorised for use £	Grants out of the Consolidated Fund £
HM TREASURY		15,861,987,000
1. Maintain sound public finances and ensure high and sustainable growth, well being and prosperity for all	146,608,000	
2. Cost-effective management of the supply of coins and actions to protect the integrity of coinage	23,625,000	
3. Promoting a stable financial system and offering protection to ordinary savers, depositors, businesses and borrowers	677,407,000	
TOTAL, 2010–11	847,640,000	15,861,987,000

1434

Appropriation (No. 2) Act 2010 (c. 12)
Schedule 2 – Appropriation of amounts and sums voted for supply services
Part 41 – HM Revenue and Customs, 2010–11

PART 41

HM REVENUE AND CUSTOMS, 2010–11

Table of —

(a) the resources authorised for use, on account, to meet the costs of the Estimate and Requests for Resources which are specified in the first column of the Table for the year ending with 31 March 2011; and

(b) the sums authorised for issue out of the Consolidated Fund, on account, to meet those costs.

Estimate/ Request for Resources	Net Resources authorised for use £	Grants out of the Consolidated Fund £
HM REVENUE AND CUSTOMS		7,244,655,000
1. Administering the tax and customs control systems fairly and efficiently and making it as easy as possible for individuals and businesses to understand and comply with their obligations and receive their tax credit and other entitlements	1,653,871,000	
2. Undertaking rating and council tax valuation work in England and Wales and providing valuation and property management services to central government and other bodies where public funds are involved	0	
3. Providing payments in lieu of tax relief to certain bodies	69,885,000	
4. Making payments of rates to Local Authorities on behalf of certain bodies	27,965,000	
5. Payments of Child Benefit, Health in Pregnancy Grant and Child Trust Fund endowments	5,528,250,000	
TOTAL, 2010–11	7,279,971,000	7,244,655,000

Appropriation (No.2) Act 2010 (c.12)
Schedule 2 – Appropriation of amounts and sums voted for supply services
Part 42 – National Savings and Investments, 2010–11

1435

PART 42

NATIONAL SAVINGS AND INVESTMENTS, 2010–11

Table of —

(a) the resources authorised for use, on account, to meet the costs of the Estimate and Requests for Resources which are specified in the first column of the Table for the year ending with 31 March 2011; and

(b) the sums authorised for issue out of the Consolidated Fund, on account, to meet those costs.

Estimate/ Request for Resources	Net Resources authorised for use £	Grants out of the Consolidated Fund £
NATIONAL SAVINGS AND INVESTMENTS		70,824,000
1. Reducing the costs to the taxpayer of government borrowing now and in the future	70,698,000	
TOTAL, 2010–11	70,698,000	70,824,000

1436

Appropriation (No.2) Act 2010 (c.12)
Schedule 2 – Appropriation of amounts and sums voted for supply services
Part 43 – The Statistics Board, 2010–11

PART 43

THE STATISTICS BOARD, 2010–11

Table of—

(a) the resources authorised for use, on account, to meet the costs of the Estimate and Requests for Resources which are specified in the first column of the Table for the year ending with 31 March 2011; and

(b) the sums authorised for issue out of the Consolidated Fund, on account, to meet those costs.

Estimate/ Request for Resources	Net Resources authorised for use £	Grants out of the Consolidated Fund £
THE STATISTICS BOARD **1. To promote and safeguard the production and publication of official statistics that serve the public good**	104,711,000	102,461,000
TOTAL, 2010–11	104,711,000	102,461,000

Appropriation (No.2) Act 2010 (c.12)
Schedule 2 – Appropriation of amounts and sums voted for supply services
Part 44 – Government Actuary's Department, 2010–11

1437 ﹀

PART 44

GOVERNMENT ACTUARY'S DEPARTMENT, 2010–11

Table of—

(a) the resources authorised for use, on account, to meet the costs of the Estimate and Requests for Resources which are specified in the first column of the Table for the year ending with 31 March 2011; and

(b) the sums authorised for issue out of the Consolidated Fund, on account, to meet those costs.

Estimate/ *Request for Resources*	*Net Resources authorised for use* £	*Grants out of the Consolidated Fund* £
GOVERNMENT ACTUARY'S DEPARTMENT		122,000
1. Providing an actuarial consultancy service	264,000	
TOTAL, 2010–11	264,000	122,000

1438

Appropriation (No. 2) Act 2010 (c.12)
Schedule 2 – Appropriation of amounts and sums voted for supply services
Part 45 – Crown Estate Office, 2010–11

PART 45

CROWN ESTATE OFFICE, 2010–11

Table of —

(a) the resources authorised for use, on account, to meet the costs of the Estimate and Requests for Resources which are specified in the first column of the Table for the year ending with 31 March 2011; and

(b) the sums authorised for issue out of the Consolidated Fund, on account, to meet those costs.

Estimate/ *Request for Resources*	*Net Resources* *authorised for use* £	*Grants out of the* *Consolidated Fund* £
CROWN ESTATE OFFICE **1. To maintain and enhance the value of The Crown Estate and the return obtained from it**	1,064,000	1,060,000
TOTAL, 2010–11	1,064,000	1,060,000

Appropriation (No.2) Act 2010 (c.12)
Schedule 2 – Appropriation of amounts and sums voted for supply services
Part 46 – Cabinet Office, 2010–11

1439

PART 46

CABINET OFFICE, 2010–11

Table of –

(a) the resources authorised for use, on account, to meet the costs of the Estimate and Requests for Resources which are specified in the first column of the Table for the year ending with 31 March 2011; and

(b) the sums authorised for issue out of the Consolidated Fund, on account, to meet those costs.

Estimate/ *Request for Resources*	*Net Resources authorised for use* £	*Grants out of the Consolidated Fund* £
CABINET OFFICE		163,687,000
1. Supporting the Prime Minister's Office closely in ensuring the delivery of Government objectives	178,601,000	
TOTAL, 2010–11	178,601,000	163,687,000

1440

Appropriation (No.2) Act 2010 (c. 12)
Schedule 2 – Appropriation of amounts and sums voted for supply services
Part 47 – Security and Intelligence Agencies, 2010–11

PART 47

SECURITY AND INTELLIGENCE AGENCIES, 2010–11

Table of —

(a) the resources authorised for use, on account, to meet the costs of the Estimate and Requests for Resources which are specified in the first column of the Table for the year ending with 31 March 2011; and

(b) the sums authorised for issue out of the Consolidated Fund, on account, to meet those costs.

Estimate/ Request for Resources	Net Resources authorised for use	Grants out of the Consolidated Fund
	£	£
SECURITY AND INTELLIGENCE AGENCIES **1. Protecting and promoting the national security and economic well being of the UK**	836,037,000	825,651,000
TOTAL, 2010–11	836,037,000	825,651,000

Appropriation (No.2) Act 2010 (c.12)
Schedule 2 – Appropriation of amounts and sums voted for supply services
Part 48 – Cabinet Office: Civil Superannuation, 2010–11

1441

PART 48

CABINET OFFICE: CIVIL SUPERANNUATION, 2010–11

Table of —

(a) the resources authorised for use, on account, to meet the costs of the Estimate and Requests for Resources which are specified in the first column of the Table for the year ending with 31 March 2011; and

(b) the sums authorised for issue out of the Consolidated Fund, on account, to meet those costs.

Estimate/ Request for Resources	Net Resources authorised for use £	Grants out of the Consolidated Fund £
CABINET OFFICE: CIVIL SUPERANNUATION		655,425,000
1. Civil superannuation	3,213,450,000	
TOTAL, 2010–11	3,213,450,000	655,425,000

1442

Appropriation (No.2) Act 2010 (c.12)
Schedule 2 – Appropriation of amounts and sums voted for supply services
Part 49 – National School of Government, 2010–11

PART 49

NATIONAL SCHOOL OF GOVERNMENT, 2010–11

Table of—

(a) the resources authorised for use, on account, to meet the costs of the Estimate and Requests for Resources which are specified in the first column of the Table for the year ending with 31 March 2011; and

(b) the sums authorised for issue out of the Consolidated Fund, on account, to meet those costs.

Estimate/ Request for Resources	Net Resources authorised for use £	Grants out of the Consolidated Fund £
NATIONAL SCHOOL OF GOVERNMENT **1. To provide a centre of excellence for learning and development in support of the strategic business priorities of Government**	177,000	146,000
TOTAL, 2010–11	177,000	146,000

Appropriation (No.2) Act 2010 (c.12)
Schedule 2 – Appropriation of amounts and sums voted for supply services
Part 50 – Central Office of Information, 2010–11

1443

PART 50

CENTRAL OFFICE OF INFORMATION, 2010–11

Table of —

(a) the resources authorised for use, on account, to meet the costs of the Estimate and Requests for Resources which are specified in the first column of the Table for the year ending with 31 March 2011; and

(b) the sums authorised for issue out of the Consolidated Fund, on account, to meet those costs.

Estimate/ Request for Resources	Net Resources authorised for use £	Grants out of the Consolidated Fund £
CENTRAL OFFICE OF INFORMATION **1. Achieving maximum communication effectiveness with best value for money**	306,000	299,000
TOTAL, 2010–11	306,000	299,000

1444

Appropriation (No.2) Act 2010 (c.12)
Schedule 2 – Appropriation of amounts and sums voted for supply services
Part 51 – Office of the Parliamentary Commissioner for Administration and the Health Service Commissioner
for England, 2010–11

PART 51

OFFICE OF THE PARLIAMENTARY COMMISSIONER FOR ADMINISTRATION AND THE HEALTH SERVICE COMMISSIONER FOR ENGLAND, 2010–11

Table of —

(a) the resources authorised for use, on account, to meet the costs of the Estimate and Requests for Resources which are specified in the first column of the Table for the year ending with 31 March 2011; and

(b) the sums authorised for issue out of the Consolidated Fund, on account, to meet those costs.

Estimate/ *Request for Resources*	*Net Resources authorised for use* £	*Grants out of the Consolidated Fund* £
OFFICE OF THE PARLIAMENTARY COMMISSIONER FOR ADMINISTRATION AND THE HEALTH SERVICE COMMISSIONER FOR ENGLAND **1. To undertake the work of the Parliamentary Commissioner for Administration and the Health Service Commissioner for England**	15,401,000	15,437,000
TOTAL, 2010–11	15,401,000	15,437,000

Appropriation (No.2) Act 2010 (c.12)
Schedule 2 – Appropriation of amounts and sums voted for supply services
Part 52 – House of Lords, 2010–11

1445

PART 52

HOUSE OF LORDS, 2010–11

Table of —

(a) the resources authorised for use, on account, to meet the costs of the Estimate and Requests for Resources which are specified in the first column of the Table for the year ending with 31 March 2011; and

(b) the sums authorised for issue out of the Consolidated Fund, on account, to meet those costs.

Estimate/ Request for Resources	Net Resources authorised for use £	Grants out of the Consolidated Fund £
HOUSE OF LORDS **1. Members' expenses and administration, etc.**	 52,803,000	44,130,000
TOTAL, 2010–11	52,803,000	44,130,000

1446

Appropriation (No.2) Act 2010 (c.12)
Schedule 2 – Appropriation of amounts and sums voted for supply services
Part 53 – House of Commons: Members, 2010–11

PART 53

HOUSE OF COMMONS: MEMBERS, 2010–11

Table of —

(a) the resources authorised for use, on account, to meet the costs of the Estimate and Requests for Resources which are specified in the first column of the Table for the year ending with 31 March 2011; and

(b) the sums authorised for issue out of the Consolidated Fund, on account, to meet those costs.

Estimate/ Request for Resources	Net Resources authorised for use	Grants out of the Consolidated Fund
	£	£
HOUSE OF COMMONS MEMBERS 1. Members' salaries, allowances and other costs	73,374,000	86,231,000
TOTAL, 2010–11	73,374,000	86,231,000

Appropriation (No.2) Act 2010 (c.12)
Schedule 2 – Appropriation of amounts and sums voted for supply services
Part 54 – House of Commons: Administration, 2010–11

1447

PART 54

HOUSE OF COMMONS: ADMINISTRATION, 2010–11

Table of —

(a) the resources authorised for use, on account, to meet the costs of the Estimate and Requests for Resources which are specified in the first column of the Table for the year ending with 31 March 2011; and

(b) the sums authorised for issue out of the Consolidated Fund, on account, to meet those costs.

Estimate/ *Request for Resources*	*Net Resources* *authorised for use* £	*Grants out of the* *Consolidated Fund* £
HOUSE OF COMMONS: ADMINISTRATION		95,400,000
1. House of Commons: Administrative Expenditure	114,400,000	
2. Grants to other bodies	1,700,000	
TOTAL, 2010–11	116,100,000	95,400,000

1448

Appropriation (No.2) Act 2010 (c.12)
Schedule 2 – Appropriation of amounts and sums voted for supply services
Part 55 – National Audit Office, 2010–11

PART 55

NATIONAL AUDIT OFFICE, 2010–11

Table of —

(a) the resources authorised for use, on account, to meet the costs of the Estimate and Requests for Resources which are specified in the first column of the Table for the year ending with 31 March 2011; and

(b) the sums authorised for issue out of the Consolidated Fund, on account, to meet those costs.

Estimate/ Request for Resources	Net Resources authorised for use £	Grants out of the Consolidated Fund £
NATIONAL AUDIT OFFICE **1. Providing independent assurance to Parliament and other organisations on the management of public resources**	35,685,000	35,145,000
TOTAL, 2010–11	35,685,000	35,145,000

Appropriation (No.2) Act 2010 (c.12)
Schedule 2 – Appropriation of amounts and sums voted for supply services
  Part 56 – The Electoral Commission, 2010–11

1449

PART 56

THE ELECTORAL COMMISSION, 2010–11

Table of—

(a) the resources authorised for use, on account, to meet the costs of the Estimate and Requests for Resources which are specified in the first column of the Table for the year ending with 31 March 2011; and

(b) the sums authorised for issue out of the Consolidated Fund, on account, to meet those costs.

Estimate/ Request for Resources	Net Resources authorised for use	Grants out of the Consolidated Fund
	£	£
THE ELECTORAL COMMISSION		10,926,000
1. The Electoral Commission	10,741,000	
TOTAL, 2010–11	10,741,000	10,926,000

1450

Appropriation (No.2) Act 2010 (c.12)
Schedule 2 – Appropriation of amounts and sums voted for supply services
Part 57 – Independent Parliamentary Standards Authority, 2010–11

PART 57

INDEPENDENT PARLIAMENTARY STANDARDS AUTHORITY, 2010–11

Table of —

(c) the resources authorised for use, on account, to meet the costs of the Estimate and Requests for Resources which are specified in the first column of the Table for the year ending with 31 March 2011; and

(d) the sums authorised for issue out of the Consolidated Fund, on account, to meet those costs.

Estimate/ Request for Resources	Net Resources authorised for use £	Grants out of the Consolidated Fund £
INDEPENDENT PARLIAMENTARY STANDARDS AUTHORITY **1. IPSA**	 103,509,000	103,536,000
TOTAL, 2010–11	103,509,000	103,536,000

Appropriation (No.2) Act 2010 (c. 12)
Schedule 2 – Appropriation of amounts and sums voted for supply services
Part 58 – The Local Government Boundary Commission for England, 2010–11

1451

PART 58

THE LOCAL GOVERNMENT BOUNDARY COMMISSION FOR ENGLAND, 2010–11

Table of –

(e) the resources authorised for use, on account, to meet the costs of the Estimate and Requests for Resources which are specified in the first column of the Table for the year ending with 31 March 2011; and

(f) the sums authorised for issue out of the Consolidated Fund, on account, to meet those costs.

Estimate/ *Request for Resources*	*Net Resources* *authorised for use* £	*Grants out of the* *Consolidated Fund* £
THE LOCAL GOVERNMENT BOUNDARY COMMISSION FOR ENGLAND		1,342,000
1. The Local Government Boundary Commission for England	1,280,000	
TOTAL, 2010–11	1,280,000	1,342,000

Finance Act 2010

CHAPTER 13

CONTENTS

PART 1

CHARGES, RATES ETC

Income tax

Corporation tax

Capital gains tax

Capital allowances

Stamp duty land tax

Inheritance tax

Alcohol and tobacco

PART 2

ANTI-AVOIDANCE AND REVENUE PROTECTION

PART 3

OTHER PROVISIONS

1458

Finance Act 2010

2010 CHAPTER 13

An Act to grant certain duties, to alter other duties, and to amend the law relating to the National Debt and the Public Revenue, and to make further provision in connection with finance. [8th April 2010]

Most Gracious Sovereign

WE, Your Majesty's most dutiful and loyal subjects, the Commons of the United Kingdom in Parliament assembled, towards raising the necessary supplies to defray Your Majesty's public expenses, and making an addition to the public revenue, have freely and voluntarily resolved to give and to grant unto Your Majesty the several duties hereinafter mentioned; and do therefore most humbly beseech Your Majesty that it may be enacted, and be it enacted by the Queen's most Excellent Majesty, by and with the advice and consent of the Lords Spiritual and Temporal, and Commons, in this present Parliament assembled, and by the authority of the same, as follows: —

PART 1

CHARGES, RATES ETC

Income tax

1 Charge, main rates, thresholds and allowances etc for 2010-11

(1) Income tax is charged for the tax year 2010-11.

(2) For that tax year —

    (a) the basic rate is 20%,

    (b) the higher rate is 40%, and

    (c) the additional rate is 50%.

(3) The amounts specified in the following provisions of ITA 2007 are the same for the tax year 2010-11 as for the tax year 2009-10—

    (a) sections 10(5) and 12(3) (basic rate limit and starting rate limit for savings),

    (b) sections 35, 36(1), 37(1) and 38(1) (personal allowances and blind person's allowance),

    (c) sections 43, 45(3)(a) and (b) and 46(3)(a) and (b) (tax reductions for married couples and civil partners), and

    (d) sections 36(2), 37(2), 45(4) and 46(4) (adjusted net income limit).

Corporation tax

2 Charge and main rate for financial year 2011

(1) Corporation tax is charged for the financial year 2011.

(2) For that year the rate of corporation tax is—

    (a) 28% on profits of companies other than ring fence profits, and

    (b) 30% on ring fence profits of companies.

(3) In subsection (2) "ring fence profits" has the same meaning as in Part 8 of CTA 2010 (see section 276 of that Act).

3 Small profits rates and fractions for financial year 2010

(1) For the financial year 2010 the small profits rate is—

    (a) 21% on profits of companies other than ring fence profits, and

    (b) 19% on ring fence profits of companies.

(2) For the purposes of Part 3 of CTA 2010, for that year—

    (a) the standard fraction is 7/400ths, and

    (b) the ring fence fraction is 11/400ths.

(3) In subsection (1) "ring fence profits" has the same meaning as in Part 8 of CTA 2010 (see section 276 of that Act).

Capital gains tax

4 Increase in entrepreneurs' relief

(1) In section 169N(3) of TCGA 1992 (limit on entrepreneurs' relief)—

    (a) for "£1 million" (in both places) substitute "£2 million", and

    (b) in paragraph (b), after "total of" insert "so much of" and insert at the end "as was subject to reduction under subsection (2)".

(2) The amendments made by subsection (1) have effect in relation to qualifying business disposals occurring on or after 6 April 2010.

Capital allowances

5   Annual investment allowance

(1)   In section 51A(5) of CAA 2001 (entitlement to annual investment allowance: maximum allowance), for "£50,000" substitute "£100,000".

(2)   The amendment made by subsection (1) has effect in relation to expenditure incurred on or after the relevant date.

(3)   Subsections (4) and (5) apply in relation to a chargeable period ("the actual chargeable period") which—

    (a)   begins before the relevant date, and

    (b)   ends on or after that date.

(4)   The maximum allowance under section 51A of CAA 2001 for the actual chargeable period is the sum of each maximum allowance that would be found if—

    (a)   the period beginning with the first day of the chargeable period and ending with the day before the relevant date, and

    (b)   the period beginning with the relevant date and ending with the last day of the chargeable period,

were treated as separate chargeable periods.

(5)   But, so far as concerns expenditure incurred before the relevant date, the maximum allowance under section 51A of that Act for the actual chargeable period is to be calculated as if the amendment made by subsection (1) had not been made.

(6)   In this section "the relevant date" means—

    (a)   for corporation tax purposes, 1 April 2010, and

    (b)   for income tax purposes, 6 April 2010.

Stamp duty land tax

6   Relief for first-time buyers

(1)   Part 4 of FA 2003 (stamp duty land tax) is amended as follows.

(2)   After section 57A insert—

"57AA First-time buyers

(1)   A land transaction is exempt from charge under section 55 if—

    (a)   it is a relevant acquisition of a major interest in land,

    (b)   the land consists entirely of residential property,

    (c)   the relevant consideration (see section 55) for the transaction (other than any consisting of rent) is more than £125,000 but not more than £250,000,

    (d)   the purchaser, or (if more than one) each of the purchasers, is a first-time buyer who intends to occupy the residential property as the purchaser's only or main residence, and

    (e)   (subject to subsection (4)) the transaction is not one of a number of linked transactions.

(2)   In this section "first-time buyer" means a person who—

   (a)   has not previously been a purchaser in relation to a relevant acquisition of a major interest in land which consisted of or included residential property,

   (b)   has not previously acquired an equivalent interest in such land under the law of a territory outside the United Kingdom,

   (c)   has not previously been, or been one of the persons who was, "the person" for the purposes of section 71A, 72, 72A or 73 in a case where the first transaction within the meaning of the section concerned was a relevant acquisition of a major interest in land which consisted of or included residential property, and

   (d)   would not have been such a person for those purposes in such a case if the provisions mentioned in paragraph (c) had been in force, and had had effect in the territory concerned, at all material times (subject, where required, to appropriate modifications).

(3)   In this section "relevant acquisition of a major interest in land" means an acquisition of a major interest in land other than—

   (a)   the grant of a lease for a term of less than 21 years, or

   (b)   the assignment of a lease which has less than 21 years to run.

(4)   Subsection (1)(e) does not prevent a transaction being exempt from charge under section 55 if each of the linked transactions is one the subject-matter of which is land, or an interest in or right over land, which falls within section 116(1)(a), (b) or (c) by reason of its connection with the same building."

(3)   After section 73C insert—

"73CA Sections 71A to 73: first-time buyers

(1)   Where section 71A, 72, 72A or 73 applies, the first transaction within the meaning of the section concerned is exempt from charge under section 55 if—

   (a)   the transaction is a relevant acquisition of a major interest in land,

   (b)   the land consists entirely of residential property,

   (c)   the relevant consideration (see section 55) for the transaction (other than any consisting of rent) is more than £125,000 but not more than £250,000,

   (d)   the person (within the meaning of the section concerned), or (if more than one) each of them, is a first-time buyer who intends to occupy the residential property as the person's only or main residence, and

   (e)   (subject to subsection (3)) the transaction is not one of a number of linked transactions.

(2)   In subsection (1)—

   "first-time buyer", and

   "relevant acquisition of a major interest in land",

have the same meaning as in section 57AA.

(3)   Subsection (4) of section 57AA applies for the purposes of this section."

(4) In section 110 (approval of regulations under general power), insert at the end—

"(6) This section does not apply to regulations containing only provision varying section 57AA or 73CA, or paragraph 15 of Schedule 9, which does not increase any person's liability to tax."

(5) In Schedule 9 (right to buy, shared ownership leases etc), insert at the end—

"First-time buyers

15 (1) This paragraph applies where—

    (a) a lease is granted as mentioned in sub-paragraph (1)(a) of paragraph 2 and the conditions in sub-paragraph (2) of that paragraph are met but no election is made for tax to be charged in accordance with that paragraph,

    (b) a lease is granted as mentioned in sub-paragraph (1)(a) of paragraph 4 and the conditions in sub-paragraph (2) of that paragraph are met but no election is made for tax to be charged in accordance with that paragraph,

    (c) paragraph 4A applies in relation to the acquisition of an interest (but the acquisition is not exempt from charge by virtue of sub-paragraph (2) of that paragraph),

    (d) a shared ownership trust is declared but no election is made for tax to be charged in accordance with paragraph 9, or

    (e) an equity-acquisition payment is made under a shared ownership trust (but the equity-acquisition payment, and the consequential increase in the purchaser's beneficial interest, are not exempt from charge by virtue of paragraph 10).

(2) Neither section 57AA nor section 73CA applies in relation to—

    (a) the acquisition of the lease,

    (b) the acquisition of the interest,

    (c) the declaration of the shared ownership trust, or

    (d) the equity-acquisition payment and the consequential increase in the purchaser's beneficial interest."

(6) The amendments made by this section have effect in relation to any land transaction of which the effective date is on or after 25 March 2010 but before 25 March 2012.

7 Rate in respect of residential property where consideration over £1m

(1) In section 55(2) of FA 2003 (amount of SDLT chargeable), in Table A (bands and percentages for residential property), for the final entry (cases where relevant consideration is more than £500,000 to be chargeable at 4%) substitute—

"More than £500,000 but not more than £1,000,000	4%
More than £1,000,000	5%".

(2) The amendment made by subsection (1) has effect in relation to any land transaction of which the effective date is on or after 6 April 2011.

(3) But that amendment does not have effect in relation to any transaction—

    (a) effected in pursuance of a contract entered into and substantially performed before 25 March 2010, or

    (b) effected in pursuance of a contract entered into before that date and not excluded by subsection (4).

(4) A transaction effected in pursuance of a contract entered into before 25 March 2010 is excluded by this subsection if—

    (a) there is any variation of the contract, or assignment (or assignation) of rights under the contract, on or after 25 March 2010,

    (b) the transaction is effected in consequence of the exercise on or after that date of any option, right of pre-emption or similar right, or

    (c) on or after that date there is an assignment (or assignation), subsale or other transaction relating to the whole or part of the subject-matter of the contract as a result of which a person other than the purchaser under the contract becomes entitled to call for a conveyance.

Inheritance tax

8 Rate bands

(1) The Table substituted in Schedule 1 to IHTA 1984 by section 155(1)(b) and (4) of FA 2006 (which provides for a rate of nil per cent on such portion of the value concerned as does not exceed £325,000 and a rate of 40 per cent on such portion as exceeds that amount) has effect in relation to chargeable transfers made on or after 6 April 2010.

(2) Accordingly, omit—

    (a) in IHTA 1984, the Table substituted in Schedule 1 in relation to chargeable transfers made on or after that date (which provided for a rate of nil per cent on such portion of the value concerned as does not exceed £350,000 and a rate of 40 per cent on such portion as exceeds that amount), and

    (b) in FA 2007, section 4 (which substituted it).

(3) Section 8 of IHTA 1984 (indexation) does not have effect by virtue of any difference between the retail prices index for the month of September in 2010, 2011, 2012 or 2013 and the previous September.

Alcohol and tobacco

9 Rates of alcoholic liquor duties

(1) ALDA 1979 is amended as follows.

(2) In section 5 (rate of duty on spirits), for "£22.64" substitute "£23.80".

(3) In section 36(1AA)(a) (standard rate of duty on beer), for "£16.47" substitute "£17.32".

(4) In section 62(1A) (rates of duty on cider)—

    (a) in paragraph (a) (rate of duty per hectolitre in the case of sparkling cider of a strength exceeding 5.5 per cent), for "£207.20" substitute "£217.83",

      (b)   in paragraph (b) (rate of duty per hectolitre in the case of cider of a strength exceeding 7.5 per cent which is not sparkling cider), for "£47.77" substitute "£54.04", and

      (c)   in paragraph (c) (rate of duty per hectolitre in any other case), for "£31.83" substitute "£36.01".

(5)   In section 62(1A) (as amended by subsection (4)) –

      (a)   in paragraph (b), for "£54.04" substitute "£50.22", and

      (b)   in paragraph (c), for "£36.01" substitute "£33.46".

(6)   For the table in Schedule 1 substitute –

"TABLE OF RATES OF DUTY ON WINE AND MADE-WINE

PART 1

WINE OR MADE-WINE OF A STRENGTH NOT EXCEEDING 22 PER CENT

Description of wine or made-wine	Rates of duty per hectolitre £
Wine or made-wine of a strength not exceeding 4 per cent	69.32
Wine or made-wine of a strength exceeding 4 per cent but not exceeding 5.5 per cent	95.33
Wine or made-wine of a strength exceeding 5.5 per cent but not exceeding 15 per cent and not being sparkling	225.00
Sparkling wine or sparkling made-wine of a strength exceeding 5.5 per cent but less than 8.5 per cent	217.83
Sparkling wine or sparkling made-wine of a strength of 8.5 per cent or of a strength exceeding 8.5 per cent but not exceeding 15 per cent	288.20
Wine or made-wine of a strength exceeding 15 per cent but not exceeding 22 per cent	299.97

PART 2

WINE OR MADE-WINE OF A STRENGTH EXCEEDING 22 PER CENT

Description of wine or made-wine	Rates of duty per litre of alcohol in wine or made-wine £
Wine or made-wine of a strength exceeding 22 per cent	23.80".

(7) The amendments made by subsections (2) to (4) and (6) are treated as having come into force on 29 March 2010.

(8) The amendments made by subsection (5) come into force on 30 June 2010.

10 Rates of tobacco products duty

(1) For the table in Schedule 1 to TPDA 1979 substitute—

"TABLE

1. Cigarettes	An amount equal to 24 per cent of the retail price plus £119.03 per thousand cigarettes
2. Cigars	£180.28 per kilogram
3. Hand-rolling tobacco	£129.59 per kilogram
4. Other smoking tobacco and chewing tobacco	£79.26 per kilogram".

(2) The amendment made by subsection (1) is treated as having come into force at 6 pm on 24 March 2010.

Vehicle excise duty

11 Rates for motorcycles

(1) In paragraph 2(1) of Schedule 1 to VERA 1994 (annual rates of duty: motorcycles)—

    (a) in paragraph (c) (motorbicycle which has engine with cylinder capacity exceeding 400cc but not exceeding 600cc), for "£48" substitute "£50", and

    (b) in paragraph (d) (motorcycle not within any of paragraphs (a) to (c)), for "£66" substitute "£70".

(2) The amendments made by subsection (1) have effect in relation to licences taken out on or after 1 April 2010.

Fuel duties

12 Fuel duties: rates and rebates from April 2010

(1) HODA 1979 is amended as follows.

(2) In section 6(1A) (main rates)—

    (a) in paragraph (a) (unleaded petrol), for "£0.5619" substitute "£0.5719",

    (b) in paragraph (aa) (aviation gasoline), for "£0.3457" substitute "£0.3835",

    (c) in paragraph (b) (light oil other than unleaded petrol or aviation gasoline), for "£0.6591" substitute "£0.6691", and

    (d) in paragraph (c) (heavy oil), for "£0.5619" substitute "£0.5719".

(3) In section 6AA(3) (rate of duty on biodiesel), for "shall be £0.3619 a litre" substitute "is the same as that in the case of heavy oil".

(4) In section 6AB (rate of duty on bioblend) —
  (a) in subsection (3), for the words after "is the" substitute "same as that in the case of heavy oil.", and
  (b) omit subsections (4) and (5).

(5) In section 6AD(3) (rate of duty on bioethanol), for "shall be £0.3619 a litre." substitute "is the same as that in the case of unleaded petrol."

(6) In section 6AE (rate of duty on blends of bioethanol and hydrocarbon oil) —
  (a) in subsection (3), for the words after "bioethanol blend" substitute "is the same as that in the case of unleaded petrol.", and
  (b) omit subsections (4) and (5).

(7) In section 8(3) (road fuel gas) —
  (a) in paragraph (a) (natural road fuel gas), for "£0.2216" substitute "£0.2360", and
  (b) in paragraph (b) (other road fuel gas), for "£0.2767" substitute "£0.3053".

(8) In section 11(1) (rebate on heavy oil) —
  (a) in paragraph (a) (fuel oil), for "£0.1037" substitute "£0.1055", and
  (b) in paragraph (b) (gas oil), for "£0.1080" substitute "£0.1099".

(9) In section 14(1) (rebate on light oil for use as furnace fuel), for "£0.1037" substitute "£0.1055".

(10) In section 14A(2) (rebate on certain biodiesel), for "£0.1080" substitute "£0.1099".

(11) The following are revoked —
  (a) the Hydrocarbon Oil Duties (Hydrogenation of Biomass) (Reliefs) Regulations 2006 (S.I. 2006/3426),
  (b) the Hydrocarbon Oil Duties (Sulphur-free Diesel) (Hydrogenation of Biomass) (Reliefs) (Amendment) Regulations 2007 (S.I. 2007/2406), and
  (c) regulation 11 of the Hydrocarbon Oil, Biofuels and Other Fuel Substitutes (Determination of Composition of a Substance and Miscellaneous Amendments) Regulations 2008 (S.I. 2008/753).

(12) The amendments made by this section are treated as having come into force on 1 April 2010.

13 Fuel duties: further changes in rates and rebates

(1) HODA 1979 is amended as follows.

(2) In section 6(1A) (main rates) —
  (a) in paragraph (a) (unleaded petrol) —
      (i) on 1 October 2010, for "£0.5719" substitute "£0.5819", and
      (ii) on 1 January 2011, for "£0.5819" substitute "£0.5895",
  (b) in paragraph (b) (light oil other than unleaded petrol or aviation gasoline) —
      (i) on 1 October 2010, for "£0.6691" substitute "£0.6791", and

      (ii)   on 1 January 2011, for "£0.6791" substitute "£0.6867", and

    (c)   in paragraph (c) (heavy oil) —

      (i)   on 1 October 2010, for "£0.5719" substitute "£0.5819", and

      (ii)   on 1 January 2011, for "£0.5819" substitute "£0.5895".

(3)   In section 8(3) (road fuel gas) —

    (a)   in paragraph (a) (natural road fuel gas) —

      (i)   on 1 October 2010, for "£0.2360" substitute "£0.2505", and

      (ii)   on 1 January 2011, for "£0.2505" substitute "£0.2615", and

    (b)   in paragraph (b) (other road fuel gas) —

      (i)   on 1 October 2010, for "£0.3053" substitute "£0.3195", and

      (ii)   on 1 January 2011, for "£0.3195" substitute "£0.3304".

(4)   In section 11(1) (rebate on heavy oil) —

    (a)   in paragraph (a) (fuel oil) —

      (i)   on 1 October 2010, for "£0.1055" substitute "£0.1074", and

      (ii)   on 1 January 2011, for "£0.1074" substitute "£0.1088", and

    (b)   in paragraph (b) (gas oil) —

      (i)   on 1 October 2010, for "£0.1099" substitute "£0.1118", and

      (ii)   on 1 January 2011, for "£0.1118" substitute "£0.1133".

(5)   In section 14(1) (rebate on light oil for use as furnace fuel)

    (a)   on 1 October 2010, for "£0.1055" substitute "£0.1074", and

    (b)   on 1 January 2011, for "£0.1074" substitute "£0.1088".

(6)   In section 14A(2) (rebate on certain biodiesel) —

    (a)   on 1 October 2010, for "£0.1099" substitute "£0.1118", and

    (b)   on 1 January 2011, for "£0.1118" substitute "£0.1133".

Other environmental taxes

14   Rates of air passenger duty

(1)   In section 30 of FA 1994 (air passenger duty: rates) —

    (a)   in subsection (2) (journeys ending in UK or Part 1 territory), for "£11" substitute "£12" and for "£22" substitute "£24",

    (b)   in subsection (3) (journeys ending in Part 2 territory), for "£45" substitute "£60" and for "£90" substitute "£120",

    (c)   in subsection (4) (journeys ending in Part 3 territory), for "£50" substitute "£75" and for "£100" substitute "£150", and

    (d)   in subsection (4A) (other journeys), for "£55" substitute "£85" and for "£110" substitute "£170".

(2)   The amendments made by subsection (1) have effect in relation to the carriage of passengers beginning on or after 1 November 2010.

15   Standard rate of landfill tax

(1)   In section 42(1) and (2) of FA 1996 (standard amount of landfill tax), for "£48" substitute "£56".

(2) The amendments made by subsection (1) have effect in relation to disposals made (or treated as made) on or after 1 April 2011.

16 Rate of aggregates levy

(1) In section 16(4) of FA 2001 (rate of aggregates levy), for "£2" substitute "£2.10".

(2) The amendment made by subsection (1) has effect in relation to aggregate subjected to commercial exploitation on or after 1 April 2011.

17 Rates of climate change levy

(1) In Schedule 6 to FA 2000 (climate change levy), for the table in paragraph 42(1) substitute—

"TABLE

Taxable commodity supplied	Rate at which levy payable if supply is not a reduced-rate supply
Electricity	£0.00485 per kilowatt hour
Gas supplied by a gas utility or any gas supplied in a gaseous state that is of a kind supplied by a gas utility	£0.00169 per kilowatt hour
Any petroleum gas, or other gaseous hydrocarbon, supplied in a liquid state	£0.01083 per kilogram
Any other taxable commodity	£0.01321 per kilogram".

(2) The amendment made by subsection (1) has effect in relation to supplies treated as taking place on or after 1 April 2011.

18 Climate change levy: reduced-rate supplies

(1) In Schedule 6 to FA 2000 (climate change levy), in paragraph 42(1)(c) (reduced-rate supplies), for "20 per cent." substitute "35 per cent.".

(2) The amendment made by subsection (1) has effect in relation to supplies treated as taking place on or after 1 April 2011.

Gambling

19 Rate of bingo duty

(1) In section 17(1)(b) of BGDA 1981 (bingo duty chargeable at 22 per cent of bingo promotion profits), for "22" substitute "20".

(2) The amendment made by subsection (1) has effect in relation to accounting periods beginning on or after 29 March 2010.

20   Rates of gaming duty

(1)   In section 11(2) of FA 1997 (rates of gaming duty), for the table substitute—

"TABLE

Part of gross gaming yield	*Rate*
The first £1,975,000	15 per cent
The next £1,361,500	20 per cent
The next £2,385,000	30 per cent
The next £5,033,500	40 per cent
The remainder	50 per cent".

(2)   The amendment made by subsection (1) has effect in relation to accounting periods beginning on or after 1 April 2010.

21   Amusement machine licence duty

(1)   In section 23(2) of BGDA 1981 (amount of duty payable on amusement machine licence), for the table substitute—

"TABLE

Months for which licence granted	*Category A* £	*Category B1* £	*Category B2* £	*Category B3* £	*Category B4* £	*Category C* £
1	520	265	210	210	190	85
2	1015	505	395	395	360	150
3	1520	760	605	605	545	225
4	2025	1015	800	800	725	300
5	2540	1270	1000	1000	900	375
6	3050	1520	1195	1195	1085	450
7	3555	1775	1395	1395	1265	520
8	4060	2025	1600	1600	1450	600
9	4570	2285	1800	1800	1630	675
10	5075	2540	1995	1995	1810	750
11	5580	2795	2195	2195	1990	820
12	5805	2905	2285	2285	2075	860".

(2) The amendment made by subsection (1) has effect in relation to cases where the application for the amusement machine licence is received by the Commissioners for Her Majesty's Revenue and Customs after 4 pm on 26 March 2010.

New taxes

22 Bank payroll tax

Schedule 1 contains provision for and in connection with bank payroll tax.

23 Pensions: high income excess relief charge

Schedule 2 contains provision for and in connection with high income excess relief charge.

PART 2

ANTI-AVOIDANCE AND REVENUE PROTECTION

Losses, capital allowances etc

24 Sideways relief etc

Schedule 3 contains provision about sideways relief etc.

25 Property loss relief

(1) Chapter 4 of Part 4 of ITA 2007 (losses from property businesses) is amended as follows.

(2) In section 117 (overview of Chapter), after subsection (2) insert —

"(3) This Chapter also contains provision restricting relief under this Chapter (see section 127A)."

(3) In section 120 (deduction of property losses from general income), after subsection (6) insert —

"(7) See also section 127A (no relief for tax-generated losses attributable to annual investment allowance)."

(4) After section 127 insert —

"Restrictions on relief

127A No relief for tax-generated losses attributable to annual investment allowance

(1) This section applies if —
    (a) in a tax year a person makes a loss in a UK property business or overseas property business (whether carried on alone or in partnership),
    (b) the loss has a capital allowances connection (see section 123(2)), and

    (c)   the loss arises directly or indirectly in consequence of, or otherwise in connection with, relevant tax avoidance arrangements.

(2)   No property loss relief against general income may be given to the person for so much of the applicable amount of the loss as is attributable to an annual investment allowance.

(3)   For the purposes of subsection (2), the applicable amount of the loss is to be treated as attributable to capital allowances before anything else and to an annual investment allowance before any other capital allowance.

(4)   In subsection (1) "relevant tax avoidance arrangements" means arrangements—

    (a)   to which the person is a party, and

    (b)   the main purpose, or one of the main purposes, of which is being in a position to make use of an annual investment allowance in the obtaining of a reduction in tax liability by means of property loss relief against general income.

(5)   In subsection (4) "arrangements" includes any agreement, understanding, scheme, transaction or series of transactions (whether or not legally enforceable).

(6)   In this section "the applicable amount of the loss" has the meaning given by section 122."

(5)   The amendments made by this section have effect in relation to a loss if it arises directly or indirectly in consequence of, or otherwise in connection with—

    (a)   arrangements which are entered into on or after 24 March 2010, or

    (b)   any transaction forming part of arrangements which is entered into on or after that date.

(6)   But those amendments do not have effect where the arrangements are, or any such transaction is, entered into pursuant to an unconditional obligation in a contract made before that date.

(7)   "An unconditional obligation" means an obligation which may not be varied or extinguished by the exercise of a right (whether or not under the contract).

26   Capital allowance buying

Schedule 4 contains provisions about capital allowance buying.

27   Leased assets

Schedule 5 contains provisions about leased assets.

28   Cushion gas

(1)   Part 2 of CAA 2001 (plant and machinery allowances) is amended as follows.

(2)   Section 70J (meaning of "funding lease") is amended as follows.

(3) After subsection (1) insert—

"(1A) A plant or machinery lease is also a "funding lease" if the plant or machinery is cushion gas."

(4) In subsection (2), for "Subsection (1) is" substitute "Subsections (1) and (1A) are".

(5) After subsection (6) insert—

"(7) In this section "cushion gas" means gas that functions or is intended to function as plant in a particular gas storage facility."

(6) In section 104A(1) (special rate expenditure)—
   (a) omit the "and" at the end of paragraph (d), and
   (b) after paragraph (e) insert "and
        (f) expenditure incurred on or after 1 April 2010 on the provision of cushion gas (within the meaning given by section 70J(7))."

(7) After section 104F insert—

"104G Disposal events in respect of cushion gas

(1) This section applies if expenditure incurred by a person on the provision of cushion gas used in a particular gas storage facility includes both new expenditure and old expenditure.

(2) Any disposal event which concerns any of that cushion gas is to be treated for the purposes of this Part as relating to cushion gas which is the subject of the new expenditure before cushion gas which is the subject of the old expenditure.

(3) The result of subsection (2) (including any further application of that subsection) is that a disposal event may be treated as relating—
   (a) only to cushion gas which is the subject of the new expenditure,
   (b) both to—
        (i) cushion gas which is the subject of the new expenditure, and
        (ii) cushion gas which is the subject of the old expenditure, or
   (c) only to cushion gas which is the subject of the old expenditure.

(4) If a disposal event is treated, as a result of subsection (2), as relating both to—
   (a) cushion gas which is the subject of the new expenditure, and
   (b) cushion gas which is the subject of the old expenditure,
   it is to be treated for the purposes of this Part as two separate disposal events, the first relating to cushion gas within paragraph (a) and the second relating to cushion gas within paragraph (b).

(5) In this section—
        "cushion gas" has the meaning given by section 70J(7),
        "new expenditure" means expenditure incurred on or after 1 April 2010, and
        "old expenditure" means expenditure incurred before that date."

(8) The amendments made by subsections (2) to (5) have effect in relation to leases whose inception (within the meaning given by section 70YI(1) of CAA 2001) is on or after 1 April 2010.

(9) The amendments made by subsection (6) have effect in relation to expenditure incurred on or after 1 April 2010.

(10) The amendment made by subsection (7) has effect in relation to disposal events on or after 1 April 2010.

29   Sale of lessors: consortium relationships

(1) Chapters 3 and 4 of Part 9 of CTA 2010 (sales of lessors) are amended as follows.

(2) In section 393(7) (qualifying 75% subsidiaries), omit "or 90%".

(3) In section 394 (consortium relationships) −
   (a) in subsections (1)(b), (4) and (5)(b), for "90%" substitute "75%", and
   (b) in subsection (9)(b), omit "or 90%".

(4) In section 398 (qualifying 75% or 90% subsidiary), omit −
   (a) subsections (5) and (6), and
   (b) in subsection (7)(b), "and "90% subsidiary"",
   and, in the heading, omit "**or 90%**".

(5) In section 405(2)(b) and (6) (adjustments to basic amount), for "90%" substitute "75%".

(6) In sections 408(5)(b) and 430(4)(b) (associated company), for "90%" substitute "75%".

(7) In Schedule 4 to CTA 2010, omit the entry relating to "qualifying 90% subsidiary (in Chapters 3 to 6 of Part 9)".

(8) The amendments made by this section have effect where the relevant day is on or after 9 December 2009.

(9) Corresponding amendments, having effect where the relevant day is on or after that date, are to be treated as having been made in Schedule 10 to FA 2006.

Charities etc

30   Charities and community amateur sports clubs: definitions

Schedule 6 contains provision about the meaning of "charity" (and related expressions) and "community amateur sports club".

31   Gifts of shares etc to charities

Schedule 7 contains provision about schemes to obtain or increase relief in respect of certain gifts to charities.

32 Miscellaneous amendments

Schedule 8 contains miscellaneous amendments of provisions relating to charities.

Remittance basis

33 "Relevant person"

(1) Section 809M of ITA 2007 (remittance basis: meaning of "relevant person") is amended as follows.

(2) In subsection (2)(f), insert at the end "or a company which is a 51% subsidiary of such a company,".

(3) In subsection (3)(ca), for "Act)," substitute "Act) and, in relation to a company that would be a close company if it were resident in the United Kingdom, means a person who would be such a participator if it were a close company,".

(4) The amendments made by this section are treated as having come into force on 6 April 2010.

34 Foreign currency bank accounts

Schedule 9 contains provision about foreign currency bank accounts.

Other international matters

35 Penalties: offshore income etc

(1) Schedule 10 contains provision about penalties in respect of offshore income etc.

(2) Schedule 10 comes into force on such day as the Treasury may by order appoint.

(3) An order under subsection (2) —
   (a) may make different provision for different purposes, and
   (b) may include transitional provisions and savings.

(4) The Treasury may by order make any incidental, supplemental, consequential, transitional or transitory provision or saving that appears appropriate in consequence of, or otherwise in connection with, Schedule 10.

(5) An order under subsection (4) may —
   (a) make different provision for different purposes, and
   (b) make provision amending, repealing or revoking an enactment or instrument (whenever passed or made).

(6) An order under this section is to be made by statutory instrument.

(7) A statutory instrument containing an order under subsection (4) is subject to annulment in pursuance of a resolution of the House of Commons.

36   Reliefs and reductions for foreign tax

Schedule 11 contains provision about activities designed to increase the amount allowed by way of credit or reduction in respect of foreign tax.

37   Asset transfer to non-resident company: recovery of postponed charge

(1)   In section 140 of TCGA 1992 (postponement of charge on transfer of assets to non-resident company) —

    (a)   in subsection (4), for "the consideration received by it on the disposal shall be treated as increased by" substitute "there shall be deemed to accrue to the transferor company as a chargeable gain on that occasion", and

    (b)   after that subsection insert —

      "(4A)   A chargeable gain which is deemed to accrue under subsection (4) is in addition to any gain or loss that actually accrues to the transferor company on the disposal of the securities."

(2)   In Schedule 7AC to that Act (exemption for disposals by companies with substantial shareholding), omit paragraph 35 (recovery of charge postponed on transfer of asset to non-resident company).

(3)   The amendments made by this section have effect in relation to disposals of securities on or after 6 January 2010.

Securities etc

38   Transactions in securities

Schedule 12 contains provision about transactions in securities.

39   Approved CSOP schemes: eligible shares

(1)   In Part 4 of Schedule 4 to ITEPA 2003 (shares to which approved CSOP schemes can apply), omit paragraph 17(1)(c) (shares in a company which is under the control of a listed company).

(2)   Accordingly, in that Schedule —

    (a)   in paragraph 17 —

      (i)   after sub-paragraph (1)(a) insert "or",

      (ii)   omit "or" at the end of sub-paragraph (1)(b), and

      (iii)   omit sub-paragraph (2), and

    (b)   omit paragraph 20(3)(c) (and the "or" before it).

(3)   The amendments made by this section —

    (a)   come into force on 24 September 2010, and

    (b)   have effect in relation to options granted on or after that day.

(4)   If —

    (a)   during the period beginning with 24 March 2010 and ending with 23 September 2010 ("the transitional period"), a share option is granted to an individual in accordance with the provisions of an approved CSOP scheme, and

    (b)   the shares which may be acquired by the exercise of the option are shares in a company which is under the control of a listed company, other than shares of a class listed on a recognised stock exchange,

the share option is to be treated for the purposes of the CSOP code as not having been granted in accordance with the provisions of an approved CSOP scheme.

(5)   An alteration made to a scheme during the transitional period in order to meet the amended paragraph 17 requirement is to be regarded as an alteration made in a key feature of the scheme for the purposes of paragraph 30 of Schedule 4 to ITEPA 2003 (withdrawal of approval).

(6)   Where the amended paragraph 17 requirement is not met in respect of an approved CSOP scheme at the end of the transitional period, the requirement is to be treated for the purposes of paragraph 30(2)(a) of that Schedule (disqualifying events) as ceasing to be met immediately after that time.

(7)   Where, by virtue of subsection (6), approval is withdrawn from a scheme under Part 7 of that Schedule, that withdrawal has effect (from the time determined in accordance with paragraph 30(1) of that Schedule) in relation to options granted on or after 24 September 2010 only.

(8)   In subsections (3) to (7) references to options having been granted include new share options granted under the terms of a provision included in a scheme under paragraph 26 of Schedule 4 to ITEPA 2003 (exchange of shares on company reorganisation); but paragraph 27(5) of that Schedule (new share options treated as granted at same time as old share options) does not apply for the purposes of those subsections.

(9)   In this section—

    "the amended paragraph 17 requirement" means the requirement of paragraph 17 of Schedule 4 to ITEPA 2003 as amended by this section;

    "approved" and "CSOP scheme" have the meaning given by section 521 of that Act;

    "control" and "listed company" have the same meaning as in paragraph 17 of Schedule 4 to that Act.

40   Unauthorised unit trusts

Schedule 13 contains provision about unauthorised unit trusts.

41   Index-linked gilt-edged securities

Schedule 14 contains provision about index-linked gilt-edged securities.

42   Approved share incentive plans

(1)   Paragraph 84(1) of Schedule 2 to ITEPA 2003 (approved share incentive plans) is amended as follows.

(2)   For paragraph (d) substitute—

    "(d)   an alteration being made—

        (i)   in the share capital of a company any of whose shares are subject to the plan trust, or

          (ii)   in the rights attaching to any shares of such a company,

        that materially affects the value of shares that are subject to the plan trust;".

(3) In paragraph (e), for "have been awarded to participants" substitute "are subject to the plan trust".

(4) Section 989 of CTA 2009 (deduction for contribution to plan trust) is amended as follows.

(5) In subsection (1), after paragraph (a) insert—

    "(aa)   the payment is not made pursuant to tax avoidance arrangements,".

(6) After subsection (6) insert—

   "(6A)   For the purposes of this section the payment mentioned in subsection (1)(a) is made pursuant to tax avoidance arrangements if—

      (a)   it is made pursuant to arrangements entered into by the paying company, and

      (b)   the main purpose, or one of the main purposes, of the paying company in entering into the arrangements was to obtain a deduction or an increased deduction.

   (6B)   In subsection (6A) "arrangements" includes any arrangements, scheme or understanding of any kind, whether or not legally enforceable, involving a single transaction or two or more transactions."

(7) The amendments made by subsections (1) to (3) have effect in relation to events taking place on or after 24 March 2010.

(8) The amendments made by subsections (4) to (6) have effect in relation to payments made on or after that day.

Loan relationships and derivative contracts

43   Close companies: release of loans to participators etc

(1) In CTA 2009, after section 321 insert—

"321A Restriction on debits resulting from release of loans to participators etc

   (1)   This section applies if—

      (a)   a loan gives rise to a charge to tax under section 455 of CTA 2010 (including a charge by virtue of section 459 or 460 of that Act), and

      (b)   the whole or a part of the debt in respect of the loan is released or written off.

   (2)   No debit is to be brought into account for the purposes of this Part in respect of the release or writing off."

(2) The amendment made by subsection (1) has effect in relation to debts (or parts of debts) released or written off on or after 24 March 2010.

44   Connected companies: releases of debts

Schedule 15 contains provision about releases of debts in cases involving connected companies.

45   Relationships treated as loan relationships etc: repos

(1)   In paragraph 4 of Schedule 13 to FA 2007 (ignoring effect on borrower of sale of securities), in sub-paragraph (4) omit the "and" at the end of paragraph (a) and after that paragraph insert—

"(aa)   an amount representative of income payable in respect of the securities is not to be ignored as a result of sub-paragraph (3)(b) if it is, in accordance with generally accepted accounting practice, so recognised or taken into account, and".

(2)   In section 550 of CTA 2009 (ignoring effect on borrower of sale of securities)—

(a)   in subsection (4), for "and (6)" substitute "to (6)", and

(b)   after subsection (5) insert—

"(5A)   For the purposes of the charge to corporation tax, an amount representative of income payable in respect of the securities is not to be ignored as a result of subsection (3)(b) if—

(a)   it is, in accordance with generally accepted accounting practice, recognised in determining the borrower's profit or loss for that or any other period, or

(b)   it is taken into account in calculating the amounts which are so recognised."

(3)   The amendments made by this section are treated as always having had effect.

46   Risk transfer schemes

Schedule 16 contains provision about risk transfer schemes.

Insurance companies

47   Apportionment of asset value increases

(1)   In Chapter 1 of Part 12 of ICTA (insurance companies etc), after section 432C insert—

"432CA Apportionment of asset value increase where line 51 amount decreases

(1)   This section applies where—

(a)   an insurance company is not a non-profit company in relation to a period of account ("the current period of account"),

(b)   in the case of any business with which an account of the company for the current period of account is concerned ("the relevant business"), an amount is a relevant brought into account amount for that period of account (see subsection (2)),

(c)   section 432C applies for determining the extent to which the relevant brought into account amount is referable to life assurance business or to gross roll-up business, and

(d)   the line 51 reduction condition is met (see subsection (3)).

(2)   An amount is a relevant brought into account amount for a period of account if—

    (a)   it is brought into account as mentioned in subsection (2)(b) of section 83 of the Finance Act 1989 (increases in value of non-linked assets) for that period,

    (b)   it is deemed to be brought into account for that period by subsection (2B) of that section in consequence of the transfer of non-linked assets, or

    (c)   it is taken into account under subsection (2) of that section for that period by virtue of section 444AB as being the relevant amount in relation to non-linked assets.

(3)   The line 51 reduction condition is met if—

    (a)   the amount shown in column 1 of line 51 of Form 14 of the company's periodical return in respect of the relevant business for the current period of account, is less than

    (b)   the amount so shown for the period of account immediately before it;

and the amount of the difference is "the relevant reduction".

(4)   Section 432C applies in relation to so much of the relevant brought into account amount as does not exceed the relevant reduction ("the affected amount") as if it were brought into account as an increase in the value of assets in the case of the relevant business for the applicable appropriate period of account of the company.

(5)   A period of account is an "appropriate period of account" if it ended before the current period of account and—

    (a)   the amount shown in column 1 of line 51 of Form 14 of the company's periodical return in respect of the relevant business for it, was more than

    (b)   the amount so shown for the period of account immediately before it;

and the amount of the difference is "the relevant increase."

(6)   The "applicable" appropriate period of account is the one which ended most recently ("the most recent appropriate period of account").

(7)   But if the relevant increase in the case of the most recent appropriate period of account is less than the affected amount, the most recent appropriate period of account is the applicable appropriate period of account in relation to only so much of the affected amount as does not exceed that relevant increase.

(8)   In that case, the appropriate period of account which ended most recently before the most recent appropriate period of account is the applicable appropriate period of account in relation to so much of the remainder as does not exceed the relevant increase in the case of that appropriate period of account (and, where necessary, so on until the applicable appropriate period of account is established in relation to all of the affected amount or there are no more appropriate periods of account).

(9)   If the current period of account is not the first in relation to which this section has applied in the case of the business concerned, the amount of the relevant increase in the case of any appropriate period of account

("the period in question") is to be treated as reduced by the relevant aggregate.

(10) The "relevant aggregate" is the aggregate of so much of the affected amount for any period or periods of account earlier than the current period of account as was an amount to which section 432C applied as if it were brought into account as mentioned in subsection (4) for the period in question.

(11) For the purposes of this section an insurance company which has elected under section 83YA(9) of the Finance Act 1989 (changes in value of assets brought into account: non-profit companies) to be treated as a non-profit company in relation to a period of account is to be regarded as a non-profit company in relation to the period of account."

(2) The amendment made by subsection (1) has effect if the current period of account is a period of account beginning on or after 9 December 2009.

(3) No period of account beginning before that date counts as an appropriate period of account for the purposes of section 432CA of ICTA.

(4) But where the operation of that section does not establish the applicable appropriate period of account in relation to all or any of the affected amount ("the unallocated amount"), section 432C of ICTA applies in relation to the unallocated amount as if it were brought into account as an increase in the value of assets in the case of the relevant business for the last period of account beginning before 9 December 2009.

Pensions

48 Extension of special annual allowance charge

(1) Schedule 35 to FA 2009 (special annual allowance charge) is amended as follows.

(2) In paragraph 1(2) (high-income individual) —
   (a) in the first sentence, for "£150,000" substitute "£130,000", and
   (b) insert at the end —
      "Paragraph 16A makes special provision about cases in which the individual's relevant income for the tax year 2009-10 is less than £150,000."

(3) In paragraph 2 (calculation of relevant income) —
   (a) in the last sentence of sub-paragraph (1),
   (b) in sub-paragraph (2) (in each place), and
   (c) in sub-paragraph (3) (in both places),
   for "£150,000" substitute "£130,000".

(4) After sub-paragraph (5) of that paragraph insert —

   "(5A) If —
      (a) the individual's relevant income for the tax year (whether that is the tax year 2009-10 or a later tax year) would (apart from this sub-paragraph) be less than £130,000 if the reference in sub-paragraph (5) to a scheme made on or after

22 April 2009 were to a scheme made on or after 9 December 2009, and

(b) the individual's relevant income for the tax year 2009-10 is less than £150,000,

the individual's relevant income for the tax year is to be assumed to be less than £130,000."

(5) In paragraph 11(3)(b), after "22 April" insert "2009".

(6) After paragraph 16 insert—

"Individuals with relevant income below £150,000 in 2009-10

16A (1) This paragraph has effect if the individual's relevant income for the tax year 2009-10 is less than £150,000.

(2) References in this Schedule to a pre-22 April 2009 pension input amount are to a pre-9 December 2009 pension input amount.

(3) References in this Schedule to noon on 22 April 2009 are to 9 December 2009.

(4) Other references in this Schedule to 22 April 2009 (except in paragraph 2) are to 9 December 2009.

(5) The reference in paragraph 16(2) to 21 April 2009 is to 8 December 2009.

(6) If the amount arrived at in the case of the individual under sub-paragraph (1) of paragraph 2 for the tax year 2009-10 is less than £150,000, take the steps in that sub-paragraph in relation to the tax year 2007-08 and the tax year 2008-09.

If the result is £150,000 or more for either or both of those earlier tax years the individual's relevant income for the tax year 2009-10 is to be assumed for the purposes of sub-paragraph (1) to be £150,000.

(7) If there is a scheme the main purpose, or one of the main purposes, of which is to secure that the individual's relevant income for the tax year 2009-10 is less than £150,000, it is to be assumed for the purposes of sub-paragraph (1) to be £150,000."

(7) The amendments made by this section have effect for the tax year 2009-10 and subsequent tax years (but see paragraph 21(2) of Schedule 35 to FA 2009).

49   Information

In section 251(5) of FA 2004 (persons who can be required to provide information to scheme administrators etc), after paragraph (a) insert—
"(aa)   employers of members of a registered pension scheme,".

Value added tax and insurance premium tax

50   Extension of reverse charge provisions to supplies of services

(1) In section 55A of VATA 1994 (customers to account for tax on supplies of goods of a kind used in missing trader intra-community fraud), after "goods" (in each place, including the heading) insert "or services".

   (2)   In paragraph 2(3B) of Schedule 11 to that Act (power to require notifications relating to supplies to which section 55A(6) applies), after "goods" insert "or services".

51 Insurance premium tax: separate contracts

   (1)   Part 3 of FA 1994 (insurance premium tax) is amended as follows.

   (2)   Section 72 (meaning of "premium") is amended as follows.

   (3)   After subsection (1A) insert—

   "(1AA) A contract ("the relevant contract") is not to be regarded as a separate contract for the purposes of subsection (1A) above if conditions A to D are met.

   (1AB) Condition A is that the insured is an individual ("I") and enters into the taxable insurance contract in a personal capacity.

   (1AC) Condition B is that I—
      (a)   is required to enter into the relevant contract by, or as a condition of entering into, the taxable insurance contract, or
      (b)   would be unlikely to enter into the relevant contract without also entering into the taxable insurance contract.

   (1AD) Condition C is that—
      (a)   the amount charged to I under the relevant contract in respect of any particular services is not open to negotiation by I, or
      (b)   the other terms on which particular services are to be provided to I under the relevant contract are not open to such negotiation.

   (1AE) Condition D is that the amount charged to I under the taxable insurance contract is arrived at without a comprehensive assessment having been undertaken of the individual circumstances of I which might affect the level of risk."

   (4)   After subsection (9) insert—

   "(9A) Provision may be made by order amending subsections (1AA) to (1AE) above."

   (5)   In section 74(4) and (6) (orders which need to be approved by House of Commons), for "or 71" substitute ", 71 or 72".

   (6)   The amendment made by subsection (3) has effect in relation to payments made on or after 24 March 2010.

Inheritance tax

52 Reversionary interests of purchaser or settlor etc in relevant property

   (1)   In IHTA 1984, after section 81 insert—

"81A Reversionary interests in relevant property

   (1)   Where a reversionary interest in relevant property to which—
      (a)   a person who acquired it for a consideration in money or money's worth, or

       (b)   the settlor or the spouse or civil partner of the settlor,

(a "relevant reversioner") is beneficially entitled comes to an end by reason of the relevant reversioner becoming entitled to an interest in possession in the relevant property, the relevant reversioner is to be treated as having made a disposition of the reversionary interest at that time.

   (2)   A transfer of value of a reversionary interest in relevant property to which a relevant reversioner is beneficially entitled is to be taken to be a transfer which is not a potentially exempt transfer."

  (2) The amendment made by subsection (1) has effect in relation to reversionary interests to which a relevant reversioner becomes beneficially entitled on or after 9 December 2009.

53   Interests in possession

  (1) IHTA 1984 is amended as follows.

  (2) In section 3A (potentially exempt transfers) —
     (a)   in subsection (6), omit "other than section 52", and
     (b)   after that subsection insert —

       "(6A) The reference in subsection (6) above to any provision of this Act does not include section 52 below except where the transfer of value treated as made by that section is one treated as made on the coming to an end of an interest which falls within section 5(1B) below."

  (3) In section 5 (meaning of estate) —
     (a)   in subsection (1)(a)(ii), after "below" insert "unless it falls within subsection (1B) below", and
     (b)   after subsection (1A) insert —

       "(1B) An interest in possession falls within this subsection if the person —
          (a)   was domiciled in the United Kingdom on becoming beneficially entitled to it, and
          (b)   became beneficially entitled to it by virtue of a disposition which was prevented from being a transfer of value by section 10 below."

  (4) In —
     (a)   section 49(1A) (treatment of interests in possession),
     (b)   section 51(1A) (disposal of interest in possession), and
     (c)   section 52(2A) and (3A) (charge on termination of interest in possession),
insert at the end (not as part of paragraph (c)) —
    "or falls within section 5(1B) above."

  (5) In section 57A(1A) (relief where property enters maintenance fund), insert at the end (not as part of paragraph (c)) —
    "or fell within section 5(1B) above."

  (6) In section 100(1A) (alterations of capital etc where participators are trustees),

insert at the end (not as part of paragraph (c)) —
  "or falls within section 5(1B) above."

(7) In section 101(1A) (companies' interests in settled property), insert at the end (not as part of paragraph (b)) —
  "or falls within section 5(1B) above."

(8) In section 102ZA(1)(b)(ii) of FA 1986 (gifts with reservation: termination of interests in possession), after "serial interest" insert "or falls within section 5(1B) of the 1984 Act".

(9) In F(No.2)A 1987, omit section 96(2)(c).

(10) The amendments made by this section have effect in relation to an interest in possession to which a person is beneficially entitled if the person becomes beneficially entitled to it on or after 9 December 2009.

Stamp taxes

54 SDRT: depositary receipt systems and clearance services systems

(1) Part 4 of FA 1986 (stamp duty reserve tax) is amended as follows.

(2) In section 95(1) (depositary receipts: exceptions), before "there shall be" insert "subject to section 97C,".

(3) In section 97(1) (clearance services: exceptions), before "there shall be" insert "subject to section 97C,".

(4) In section 97B (transfer between depositary receipt system and clearance system), after subsection (1) insert —

"(1A) Subsection (1) is subject to section 97C."

(5) After that section insert —

  "97C Transfers to non-EU depositary receipt and clearance services systems

  (1) This section applies where arrangements are made in accordance with which chargeable securities are —
    (a) issued to an EU system, and
    (b) subsequently transferred from an EU system to a non-EU system.

  (2) Nothing in section 95(1), 97(1) or 97B(1) disapplies a charge to tax under section 93 or 96 in respect of that transfer if —
    (a) the chargeable securities have not previously been transferred, or
    (b) where they have previously been transferred, the transfer (or, if more than one, each of them) was an exempt transfer.

  (3) For the purposes of subsection (1)(a) chargeable securities are issued to an EU system if —
    (a) pursuant to an arrangement of the kind mentioned in section 93(1), they are issued to a nominee in respect of an EU depositary receipt issuer, or

(b)   pursuant to an arrangement of the kind mentioned in section 96(1), they are issued to a nominee in respect of an EU clearance service operator.

(4)   For the purposes of subsection (1)(b) —

(a)   a transfer is from an EU system if it is from a company which is incorporated under the law of a member State and at the time of the transfer falls within section 67(6) or 70(6), and

(b)   a transfer is to a non-EU system if it is to a company which is not incorporated under the law of a member State and at the time of the transfer falls within section 67(6) or 70(6).

(5)   In this section —

"arrangements" includes any agreement, understanding, scheme, transaction or series of transactions (whether or not legally enforceable);

"EU clearance service operator" means a person —

(a)   whose business is or includes the provision of clearance services for the purchase and sale of chargeable securities, and

(b)   who —

(i)   if it is a company, is incorporated under the law of a member State, and

(ii)   in any other case, is resident in a member State;

"EU depositary receipt issuer" means a person —

(a)   whose business is or includes issuing depositary receipts for chargeable securities, and

(b)   who —

(i)   if it is a company, is incorporated under the law of a member State, and

(ii)   in any other case, is resident in a member State;

"exempt transfer" means a transfer in respect of which, by reason of section 90(5), 95(1), 97(1) or 97B(1), no charge to stamp duty reserve tax arises;

"nominee" —

(a)   in respect of an EU clearance service operator, means a person whose business is or includes holding chargeable securities as nominee for the EU clearance service operator, and

(b)   in respect of an EU depositary receipt issuer, means a person whose business is or includes holding chargeable securities as nominee or agent for the EU depositary receipt issuer."

(6)   The amendments made by this section have effect in relation to transfers of chargeable securities on or after 1 October 2009.

55   SDLT: partnerships

(1)   In section 75C of FA 2003 (SDLT anti-avoidance: supplemental) —

(a)   in subsection (8), omit paragraph (b) (and the "and" before it), and

(b) after that subsection insert —

"(8A) Nothing in Part 3 of Schedule 15 applies to the notional transaction under section 75A."

(2) The amendments made by subsection (1) have effect in relation to any notional transaction of which the effective date is on or after 24 March 2010.

(3) But those amendments do not have effect in relation to a notional transaction if any scheme transaction is —

    (a) completed before that date,

    (b) effected in pursuance of a contract entered into and substantially performed before that date, or

    (c) effected in pursuance of a contract entered into before that date and not excluded by subsection (4).

(4) A scheme transaction effected in pursuance of a contract entered into before 24 March 2010 is excluded by this subsection if —

    (a) there is any variation of the contract, or assignment (or assignation) of rights under the contract, on or after 24 March 2010,

    (b) the transaction is effected in consequence of the exercise on or after that date of any option, right of pre-emption or similar right, or

    (c) it is a land transaction and on or after that date there is an assignment (or assignation), subsale or other transaction relating to the whole or part of the subject-matter of the contract as a result of which a person other than the purchaser under the contract becomes entitled to call for a conveyance.

Administration

56 Disclosure of tax avoidance schemes

Schedule 17 contains amendments of the provisions relating to the disclosure of tax avoidance schemes.

57 Opening of postal packets

(1) Section 106 of the Postal Services Act 2000 (power to detain postal packets containing contraband) is amended as follows.

(2) In subsection (4), for paragraphs (a) and (b) substitute "in the presence of a representative of the postal operator".

(3) Omit subsection (5).

(4) In subsection (7)(b), omit "if he is absent".

PART 3

OTHER PROVISIONS

Income tax: benefits in kind

58   Zero and low emission vehicles

(1)   Chapter 6 of Part 3 of ITEPA 2003 (taxable benefits: cars, vans and related benefits) is amended as follows.

(2)   Section 139 (cars first registered in 1998 or later with emissions figure) is amended as follows.

(3)   For subsection (1A) substitute—

"(1A)   A car is a qualifying low emissions car for any year if it has a low CO_2 emissions figure for that year."

(4)   In subsection (1B), for "10%" substitute—

"(a)   in a case where the car's CO_2 emissions figure for the year does not exceed 75 grams per kilometre driven, 5%, and

(b)   otherwise, 10%."

(5)   In subsection (5), for "this section" substitute "subsections (2)(b) and (3)(a)".

(6)   Omit subsection (5A).

(7)   Section 140 (cars first registered in 1998 or later without emissions figure) is amended as follows.

(8)   In subsection (3), for the words after "year is" substitute—

"(a)   the special percentage if the car cannot in any circumstances emit CO_2 by being driven, and

(b)   35% in any other case."

(9)   After that subsection insert—

"(3A)   The special percentage is—

(a)   for the tax years 2010-11 to 2014-15, 0%, and

(b)   for the tax year 2015-16 and subsequent tax years, 9%."

(10)   Omit subsection (4).

(11)   In section 149(4) (car fuel benefit), for "for an electrically propelled vehicle" substitute "or any energy for a car which cannot in any circumstances emit CO_2 by being driven."

(12)   In section 155 (vans), for subsections (1) to (3) substitute—

"(1)   The cash equivalent of the benefit of a van for a tax year is—

(a)   nil in a case to which subsection (2) applies, and

(b)   £3,000 in any other case.

(2)   This subsection applies if—

(a)   the restricted private use condition is met in relation to the van for the tax year, or

    (b)   the van cannot in any circumstances emit CO_2 by being driven and the tax year is any of the tax years 2010-11 to 2014-15."

(13)   In —

    (a)   section 156(1) (reduction for periods when van unavailable), and

    (b)   section 158(1) (reduction for payments for private use),

for "155(2)(a) or (b)" substitute "155(1)".

(14)   In section 160 (van fuel benefit) —

    (a)   in subsection (1), for "155(2)(b)" substitute "155(1)(b)", and

    (b)   omit subsection (4).

(15)   In section 170(1A) (power to amend section 155(2)(a) and (3)(b)) —

    (a)   in paragraph (a), for "155(2)(a)" substitute "155(1)(a)" and after "employee" insert "or a zero-emission van", and

    (b)   in paragraph (b), for "155(3)(b)" substitute "155(1)(b)".

(16)   In FA 2006, in section 59, omit subsection (7).

(17)   In FA 2009, in Schedule 28, omit paragraph 7.

(18)   The amendments made by subsections (2) to (16) have effect for the tax year 2010-11 and subsequent tax years.

(19)   The amendment made by subsection (17) is treated as always having had effect.

(20)   The amendment of section 142 of ITEPA 2003 made by paragraph 8 of Schedule 28 to FA 2009 has effect for the tax year 2010-11 (as well as for the tax year 2011-12 and subsequent tax years).

59   Cars with CO_2 emissions figure

(1)   Chapter 6 of Part 3 of ITEPA 2003 (taxable benefits: cars, vans and related benefits) is further amended as follows.

(2)   For section 139 substitute —

"139   Cars with a CO_2 emissions figure: the appropriate percentage

    (1)   The appropriate percentage for a year for a car with a CO_2 emissions figure depends on the car's CO_2 emissions figure.

    (2)   If the car's CO_2 emissions figure is less than the relevant threshold for the year, the appropriate percentage for the year is —

        (a)   if the year is 2012-13, 2013-14 or 2014-15 and the car's CO_2 emissions figure for the year does not exceed 75 grams per kilometre driven, 5%, and

        (b)   otherwise, 10%.

    (3)   If the car's CO_2 emissions figure is equal to the relevant threshold for the year, the appropriate percentage for the year is 11% ("the threshold percentage").

    (4)   If the car's CO_2 emissions figure exceeds the relevant threshold for the year, the appropriate percentage for the year is whichever is the lesser of —

      (a)   the threshold percentage increased by one percentage point for each 5 grams per kilometre driven by which the CO_2 emissions figure exceeds the relevant threshold for the year, and

      (b)   35%.

  (5)   The relevant threshold is 100 grams per kilometre driven.

  (6)   If the car's CO_2 emissions figure is not a multiple of 5, it is to be rounded down to the nearest multiple of 5 for the purposes of subsections (3) and (4)(a).

  (7)   This section is subject to—

      (a)   section 141 (diesel cars), and

      (b)   any regulations made by the Treasury under section 170(4) (power to reduce the appropriate percentage)."

  (3)   In section 170 (Treasury orders and regulations varying various amounts)—

      (a)   omit subsection (2A) (power to vary limit in section 139(3A)), and

      (b)   in subsection (3)—

          (i)   for ""lower" substitute ""relevant",

          (ii)   for "the Table in section 139(4)" substitute "section 139(5)", and

          (iii)   for "2006" substitute "2013".

  (4)   In consequence of the amendments made by subsections (2) and (3), omit—

      (a)   in FA 2006, section 59,

      (b)   in FA 2009, in Schedule 28, paragraphs 6, 9 and 10(1), and

      (c)   in this Act, section 58(2) to (5).

  (5)   The amendments made by this section have effect for the tax year 2012-13 and subsequent tax years.

60   Subsidised meals for employees: salary sacrifice etc

  (1)   Section 317 of ITEPA 2003 (exemption from income tax in respect of provision for employees by employer of free or subsidised meals) is amended as follows.

  (2)   In subsection (1), for "C" substitute "D".

  (3)   After subsection (4) insert—

    "(4A)   Condition D is that the provision is not pursuant to—

      (a)   relevant salary sacrifice arrangements, or

      (b)   relevant flexible remuneration arrangements."

  (4)   After subsection (5) insert—

    "(5A)   In this section—

          "relevant salary sacrifice arrangements" means arrangements (whenever made, whether before or after the employment began) under which the employee gives up the right to receive an amount of general earnings or specific employment income in return for the provision of free or subsidised meals;

          "relevant flexible remuneration arrangements" means arrangements (whenever made, whether before or after the employment began) under which the employee and employer agree that the employee is to be provided with free or subsidised meals rather than receive some other description of employment income."

(5) The amendments made by this section have effect for the tax year 2011-12 and subsequent tax years.

Corporation tax

61 Sale of lessors: election out of charge

Schedule 18 contains provision amending Chapter 3 of Part 9 of CTA 2010 (and corresponding earlier provision) to introduce a system for electing out of the charge on a qualifying change.

62 Accounting standards: loan relationships and derivative contracts

Schedule 19 contains provision conferring powers on the Treasury to make regulations about cases where, in consequence of a change in accounting standards in relation to loan relationships or derivative contracts, there is a change in the way in which a company is permitted or required for accounting purposes to recognise amounts.

Miscellaneous

63 Champions League final

Schedule 20 contains provision exempting certain persons from income tax in respect of certain income arising in connection with the 2011 Champions League final.

64 FSCS intervention in relation to insurance contracts

(1) The Treasury may by regulations make provision for and in connection with the application of the relevant taxes in relation to circumstances in which there is relevant intervention under the FSCS.

(2) "Relevant intervention" means—

    (a) anything done under, or while seeking to make, arrangements for securing continuity of insurance in connection with protected contracts of insurance,

    (b) anything done as part of measures for safeguarding policyholders in connection with protected contracts of insurance, or

    (c) the payment of compensation in connection with protected contracts of insurance.

(3) In this section—

    "the FSCS" means the Financial Services Compensation Scheme (established under Part 15 of FISMA 2000);

    "protected contracts of insurance" has the same meaning as in the Handbook made by the Financial Services Authority under that Act as it has effect from time to time.

(4) The provision that may be made by regulations under this section includes provision imposing any of the relevant taxes (as well as provisions for exemptions or reliefs).

(5) The relevant taxes are—

    (a) income tax,

    (b) capital gains tax,

    (c) corporation tax,

    (d) inheritance tax,

    (e) stamp duty land tax,

    (f) stamp duty,

    (g) stamp duty reserve tax, and

    (h) insurance premium tax.

(6) Regulations under this section may include provision having effect in relation to any time before they are made if the provision does not increase any person's liability to tax.

(7) The provision made by regulations under this section may be framed as provision modifying, or applying with appropriate modifications, provisions having effect in relation to protected contracts of insurance.

(8) Regulations under this section may, in particular—

    (a) amend, repeal or revoke or otherwise modify any enactment or instrument (whenever passed or made),

    (b) make different provision for different cases or otherwise for different purposes, and

    (c) make incidental, consequential, supplementary or transitional provision.

(9) Regulations under this section are to be made by statutory instrument.

(10) A statutory instrument containing regulations under this section is subject to annulment in pursuance of a resolution of the House of Commons.

65 Stamp duty and SDRT: clearing houses

(1) In sections 116(1)(b) and 117(1)(b) of FA 1991 (investment exchanges and clearing houses: stamp duty and SDRT), for the words after "description) of such an exchange" substitute "or clearing house, or a nominee (or nominee of a prescribed description) of a member of such an exchange or clearing house, and".

(2) The amendments made by subsection (1) are treated as always having had effect.

66 Alcoholic liquor duties: power to amend definition of "cider"

In section 1 of ALDA 1979 (dutiable alcoholic liquors), after subsection (6) insert—

    "(6A) The Treasury may by order made by statutory instrument amend subsection (6) above.

    (6B) An order under subsection (6A) above may make—

        (a) consequential amendments in this Act or any other enactment,

(b) other consequential provision, and

(c) supplementary, incidental and transitional provision.

(6C) A statutory instrument containing an order under subsection (6A) above is to be laid before the House of Commons after being made; and, unless it is approved by that House before the end of the period of 28 days beginning with the date on which it is made, ceases to have effect at the end of that period (but without that affecting anything previously done under it or the making of a new order).

(6D) In reckoning that period no account is to be taken of any time —

(a) during which Parliament is dissolved or prorogued, or

(b) during which the House of Commons is adjourned for more than 4 days."

67 Climate change levy: compatible state aid

In paragraph 42 of Schedule 6 to FA 2000 (amount payable by way of levy), after sub-paragraph (2) insert —

"(3) If a reduced-rate supply is part of an aid scheme within Article 25 of Commission Regulation (EC) No. 800/2008, sub-paragraph (4) cites the title and publication reference of that Regulation for the purpose of complying with Article 3(1) of that Regulation.

(4) That citation is Commission Regulation (EC) No. 800/2008 of 6 August 2008 declaring certain categories of aid compatible with the common market in application of Articles 87 and 88 of the Treaty (General block exemption Regulation) (O.J. 2008 No. L214/3) (with the reference to Articles 87 and 88 being read, as a result of the Treaty of Lisbon, as a reference to Articles 107 and 108 of the Treaty on the Functioning of the European Union)."

68 Pensions: minor corrections

(1) Section 280(2) of FA 2004 (Part 4: index) is amended as follows.

(2) After the definition of "active membership period (in sections 221 to 223)" insert —

"additional rate	section 6(2) of ITA 2007 (as applied by section 989 of that Act)".

(3) In the definition of "basic rate limit", for "20(2)" substitute "10".

(4) After the entry relating to "higher rate" insert —

"higher rate limit	section 10 of ITA 2007".

(5) The amendments made by subsections (2) and (4) have effect for the tax year 2010-11 and subsequent tax years.

(6)   The amendment made by subsection (3) has effect for the tax year 2008-09 and subsequent tax years.

Final provisions

69   Interpretation

(1)   In this Act—

"ALDA 1979" means the Alcoholic Liquor Duties Act 1979;

"BGDA 1981" means the Betting and Gaming Duties Act 1981;

"CAA 2001" means the Capital Allowances Act 2001;

"CTA 2009" means the Corporation Tax Act 2009;

"CTA 2010" means the Corporation Tax Act 2010;

"FISMA 2000" means the Financial Services and Markets Act 2000;

"HODA 1979" means the Hydrocarbon Oil Duties Act 1979;

"ICTA" means the Income and Corporation Taxes Act 1988;

"IHTA 1984" means the Inheritance Tax Act 1984;

"ITA 2007" means the Income Tax Act 2007;

"ITEPA 2003" means the Income Tax (Earnings and Pensions) Act 2003;

"ITTOIA 2005" means the Income Tax (Trading and Other Income) Act 2005;

"TCGA 1992" means the Taxation of Chargeable Gains Act 1992;

"TIOPA 2010" means the Taxation (International and Other Provisions) Act 2010;

"TMA 1970" means the Taxes Management Act 1970;

"TPDA 1979" means the Tobacco Products Duty Act 1979;

"VATA 1994" means the Value Added Tax Act 1994;

"VERA 1994" means the Vehicle Excise and Registration Act 1994.

(2)   In this Act—

"FA", followed by a year, means the Finance Act of that year;

"F(No.2)A", followed by a year, means the Finance (No.2) Act of that year.

70   Short title

This Act may be cited as the Finance Act 2010.

SCHEDULES

SCHEDULE 1

BANK PAYROLL TAX

PART 1

THE TAX

The tax

1 (1) This Schedule makes provision for taxable companies to be charged to a tax to be known as "bank payroll tax".

   (2) Bank payroll tax is chargeable on the aggregate of the amounts of chargeable relevant remuneration awarded during the chargeable period to or in respect of relevant banking employees of a taxable company by reason of their employment as relevant banking employees.

   (3) Relevant remuneration awarded during the chargeable period to or in respect of a relevant banking employee of a taxable company by reason of the employee's employment as a relevant banking employee is "chargeable" relevant remuneration only if and to the extent that its amount exceeds £25,000.

Rate

2 Bank payroll tax is charged at the rate of 50%.

"Taxable company"

3 "Taxable company" means a company which—
   (a) is a UK resident bank or a relevant foreign bank,
   (b) is a company not within paragraph (a) which is a member of a banking group and—
      (i) is a UK resident investment company or a UK resident financial trading company, or
      (ii) is a relevant foreign financial trading company, or
   (c) is a building society or is a UK resident investment company, or a UK resident financial trading company, which is a member of the same group as a building society.

"Relevant remuneration"

4 (1) "Relevant remuneration", in relation to a relevant banking employee of a taxable company, means anything that—

(a) constitutes earnings (within the meaning of section 62 of ITEPA 2003) in relation to the employee's employment by the taxable company as a relevant banking employee, or

(b) while not constituting earnings, constitutes a benefit provided by reason of that employment.

(2) Whether or not the relevant banking employee is chargeable to income tax in respect of anything is irrelevant in determining whether or not it is relevant remuneration.

(3) Excluded remuneration is not relevant remuneration.

"Excluded remuneration"

5 (1) "Excluded remuneration" means —

(a) anything which is regular salary or wages or a regular benefit,

(b) anything in the case of which a contractual obligation to pay or provide it to or in respect of the employee concerned arose before the beginning of the chargeable period,

(c) any shares awarded under an approved share incentive plan (within the meaning of section 488 of ITEPA 2003), or

(d) any share option granted under an approved SAYE option scheme (within the meaning of section 516 of that Act).

(2) In sub-paragraph (1)(a) "regular", in relation to salary or wages or a benefit, means so much of the amount of the salary or wages or benefit as cannot vary according to —

(a) the performance of, or of any part of —

(i) any business of the taxable company concerned, or

(ii) any business of a person connected with the taxable company,

(b) the contribution made by the employee concerned to the performance of, or of any part of, any business within paragraph (a)(i) or (ii),

(c) the performance by the employee of any of the duties of the employment, or

(d) any similar considerations.

(3) For the purposes of sub-paragraph (1)(b) a contractual obligation to pay or provide something to or in respect of the employee does not arise until —

(a) the amount to be paid or provided is fixed or is capable of becoming fixed without the exercise of discretion by any person, or

(b) the total amount of things to be paid or provided to or in respect of a number of employees including the employee is fixed or is capable of becoming fixed without the exercise of discretion by any person.

(4) A contractual obligation to pay or provide something is taken to arise for those purposes even if payment or provision of it is dependent on compliance by the employee with any conditions.

"Awarded"

6 (1) Relevant remuneration is "awarded" during the chargeable period if —

(a)   a contractual obligation to pay or provide it arises during the chargeable period, or

(b)   the relevant remuneration is paid or provided during the chargeable period without any such obligation having arisen during the chargeable period,

but subject to sub-paragraph (3).

(2)   Sub-paragraph (3)(a) of paragraph 5 applies for the purposes of sub-paragraph (1) as for the purposes of sub-paragraph (1)(b) of that paragraph.

(3)   Relevant remuneration is not to be taken to be awarded during the chargeable period by virtue of sub-paragraph (1)(a) if —

(a)   it is required to be paid or provided at intervals,

(b)   it is to be paid or provided in respect of contribution, performance or similar considerations only for times after the end of the chargeable period, and

(c)   the reduction or elimination of a liability to bank payroll tax is not the main purpose or one of the main purposes of any person in assuming the obligation to pay or provide it.

(4)   Sub-paragraph (4) of paragraph 5 applies for the purposes of this paragraph as for the purposes of sub-paragraph (1)(b) of that paragraph.

"Amount" of remuneration

7   (1)   Subject to sub-paragraphs (2) to (4), the amount of any relevant remuneration is —

(a)   if it is money, its amount when awarded,

(b)   if it is money's worth, the amount of the money's worth when awarded, or

(c)   if it is a benefit not constituting earnings, the cost of providing it.

(2)   Where relevant remuneration is awarded to or in respect of an employee by virtue of paragraph 6(1)(a) and its amount is not fixed when it is awarded, its amount is such as it is reasonable at that time to assume would be its amount (in accordance with sub-paragraph (1)) if and when paid or provided.

(3)   Where the market value of any relevant remuneration at the time it is awarded exceeds, or would exceed, what would otherwise be its amount, its amount is that market value.

(4)   Where anything constituting relevant remuneration is or would be, when awarded, subject to any restriction or restrictions, the restriction is, or restrictions are, to be ignored in arriving at its amount.

(5)   For this purpose "restriction" means any condition, restriction or other similar provision which causes the value of the relevant remuneration to be less than it otherwise would be.

"The chargeable period"

8   "The chargeable period" is the period —

(a)   beginning at 12.30 pm on 9 December 2009, and

(b)   ending with 5 April 2010.

"Relevant banking employee"

9   (1) An employee of a taxable company is a relevant banking employee of the taxable company if —

   (a) the employment in which the employee is employed by the taxable company is a banking employment, and

   (b) either —

      (i) the employee is resident in the United Kingdom in the tax year 2009-10, or

      (ii) the duties of the banking employment are at any time in that tax year performed wholly or partly in the United Kingdom.

   (2) "Banking employment" means an employment the duties of which are wholly or mainly concerned (whether directly or indirectly) with activities to which sub-paragraph (3) applies.

   (3) This sub-paragraph applies to activities which are —

   (a) listed regulated activities, or

   (b) activities which are not listed regulated activities but consist of the lending of money or of dealing in currency or commodities as principal.

   (4) "Listed regulated activity" means an activity which is a regulated activity for the purposes of FISMA 2000 by virtue of any of the following provisions of the Financial Services and Markets Act 2000 (Regulated Activities) Order 2001 (S.I. 2001/544) —

   (a) article 5 (accepting deposits),

   (b) article 14 (dealing in investments as principal),

   (c) article 21 (dealing in investments as agent),

   (d) article 25 (arranging deals in investments),

   (e) article 40 (safeguarding and administering investments),

   (f) article 53 (advising on investments), and

   (g) article 61 (entering into regulated mortgage contracts).

   (5) But an activity is not a listed regulated activity in relation to an employee of a taxable company if —

   (a) the taxable company is an insurance company, or a member of the same group as an insurance company, and the activity is carried on wholly on behalf of the insurance company, or

   (b) it —

      (i) is either of the activities described in the provisions mentioned in sub-paragraph (4)(c) and (d), and

      (ii) is carried on as part of, or wholly in support of, activities of the taxable company, or of a company which is a member of the same group as the taxable company, and the activities consist of acting as discretionary investment manager for clients none of which is a linked entity.

   (6) An employee of a taxable company who spends no more than 60 days in the United Kingdom in the tax year 2009-10 is to be treated as not being a relevant banking employee of the taxable company.

   (7) In determining for the purposes of sub-paragraph (6) whether an individual spends no more than 60 days in the United Kingdom treat a day as a day

spent by the individual in the United Kingdom if (and only if) the individual is present in the United Kingdom at the end of the day.

(8) But in determining that issue for those purposes do not treat as a day spent by the individual in the United Kingdom any day on which the individual arrives in the United Kingdom as a passenger if—

　(a) the individual departs from the United Kingdom on the next day, and

　(b) during the time between arrival and departure the individual does not engage in activities which are to a substantial extent unrelated to the individual's passage through the United Kingdom.

Multiple employments

10 (1) The threshold of £25,000 in paragraph 1(3) applies whether or not an employee has more than one employment as a relevant banking employee with a taxable company.

(2) If relevant remuneration is awarded during the chargeable period to or in respect of a relevant banking employee by reason of the employee's employment as such by a number of associated taxable companies, the threshold in paragraph 1(3) in relation to each of the taxable companies is £25,000 divided by the number of the taxable companies.

(3) For this purpose taxable companies are associated if—

　(a) one of them is under the control of the other, or

　(b) one of them is under the control of a third person who controls or is under the control of the other.

Payments etc to intermediaries

11 (1) This paragraph applies where—

　(a) an individual personally performs banking services for a taxable company,

　(b) the banking services are provided not under a contract directly between the individual and the taxable company but under arrangements involving any other person ("the intermediary"), and

　(c) the circumstances are such that, if the banking services were provided under a contract directly between the taxable company and the individual, the individual would be a relevant banking employee of the taxable company.

(2) The individual is to be regarded as a relevant banking employee of the taxable company.

(3) Anything done by the intermediary in relation to the individual which, if the banking services were provided under a contract directly between the taxable company and the individual, would be regarded as the award of relevant remuneration during the chargeable period to or in respect of the individual (as a relevant banking employee) by reason of the employee's employment as a relevant banking employee is to be so regarded.

(4) "Banking services" means services which are wholly or mainly concerned (whether directly or indirectly) with activities which are activities to which paragraph 9(3) applies.

Arrangements for future payments etc

12   (1)   This paragraph applies where —

   (a)   arrangements are made during the chargeable period by reason of an employee's employment as a relevant banking employee of a taxable company,

   (b)   the arrangements make provision under which money may be paid, or any money's worth or other benefit provided, to or in respect of the employee in accordance with the arrangements, and

   (c)   were the money so paid, or the money's worth or other benefit so provided, during the chargeable period, it would be relevant remuneration awarded to or in respect of the employee during the chargeable period.

   (2)   The making of the arrangements is to be regarded as the awarding of relevant remuneration to or in respect of the relevant banking employee by reason of the employment; and the amount of the relevant remuneration is to regarded as the amount of any money which it is reasonable to assume will be paid, and any money's worth or other benefit which it is reasonable to assume will be provided, as mentioned in sub-paragraph (1).

Loans

13   (1)   This paragraph applies where —

   (a)   at any time during the chargeable period a relevant loan is provided to or in respect of a relevant banking employee of a taxable company by reason of the employee's employment as a relevant banking employee otherwise than pursuant to a contractual obligation arising before the chargeable period, or

   (b)   at any time during the chargeable period there arises a contractual obligation to provide a relevant loan to or in respect of the employee by reason of the employee's employment as a relevant banking employee of the taxable company.

   (2)   A loan is a "relevant" loan if the main purpose, or one of the main purposes, of providing it, or undertaking to provide it, is the reduction or elimination of a liability to bank payroll tax or any other tax or national insurance contributions.

   (3)   The loan is to be regarded as relevant remuneration awarded during the chargeable period to or in respect of the relevant banking employee by reason of the employee's employment as a relevant banking employee; and the amount of the relevant remuneration is to be regarded as the amount which is loaned or (where the amount of the loan is not fixed) the amount which it is reasonable to assume will be loaned.

   (4)   A contractual obligation to provide a relevant loan is taken to arise for the purposes of this paragraph even if provision of it is dependent on compliance by the relevant banking employee with any conditions.

Anti-avoidance

14   (1)   This paragraph applies where —

   (a)   relevant arrangements are entered into by one or more persons during the chargeable period, and

    (b)   the main purpose, or one of the main purposes, of the person, or any of the persons, in entering into the relevant arrangements is a relevant tax avoidance purpose.

(2) "Relevant arrangements" means arrangements involving either or both of the following—

    (a)   the making of a payment of money, or the provision of any money's worth or other benefit, otherwise than during the chargeable period, and

    (b)   the giving otherwise than in the form of relevant remuneration of any reward which equates in substance to relevant remuneration.

(3) A "relevant tax avoidance purpose" is the reduction or elimination of a liability to bank payroll tax which would exist if—

    (a)   in a case within paragraph (a) of sub-paragraph (2), the money were paid, or the money's worth or other benefit provided, during the chargeable period, or

    (b)   in a case within paragraph (b) of that sub-paragraph, the reward were given in the form of relevant remuneration.

(4) Liability to bank payroll tax is to be determined as it would have been if—

    (a)   in a case within paragraph (a) of sub-paragraph (2), the money were paid, or the money's worth or other benefit provided, during the chargeable period, or

    (b)   in a case within paragraph (b) of that sub-paragraph, the reward were given in the form of relevant remuneration.

No deduction in computing profits

15   No amount of bank payroll tax is to be taken into account in calculating profits or losses for the purposes of income tax or corporation tax.

PART 2

COLLECTION AND MANAGEMENT OF TAX

Responsibility for collection and management

16   The Commissioners are responsible for the collection and management of bank payroll tax.

Due date for payment

17   Bank payroll tax is payable by taxable companies on or before 31 August 2010.

Obligation to deliver return

18 (1) In order to establish the amount of bank payroll tax payable by it, every taxable company must deliver a return to HMRC.

    (2) The return must be delivered on or before 31 August 2010.

    (3) A return under this paragraph is referred to as a bank payroll tax return.

1502

Finance Act 2010 (c. 13)
Schedule 1 — Bank payroll tax
Part 2 — Collection and management of tax

Content etc of return

19 (1) HMRC may publish requirements as to—

    (a) the information to be contained in bank payroll tax returns,

    (b) the form in which they must be made,

    (c) the manner in which they must be delivered, and

    (d) the documents to be delivered with them.

(2) A bank payroll tax return must include—

    (a) an assessment (a "self-assessment") of the amount of bank payroll tax payable by the taxable company on the basis of the information contained in it, and

    (b) a declaration by the person making it that, to the best of that person's knowledge, it is correct and complete.

Failure to include self-assessment

20 (1) If a taxable company delivers a bank payroll tax return but fails to include a self-assessment, HMRC may make the assessment on the company's behalf on the basis of the information contained in it.

(2) The assessment is treated for the purposes of this Schedule as a self-assessment and as included in the return.

Amendment of return by company

21 (1) A taxable company may amend its bank payroll tax return.

(2) An amendment under this paragraph is made by notice to HMRC in such form, and accompanied by such information, as HMRC may reasonably require.

(3) No such amendment may be made after 31 August 2011.

(4) Nothing in sub-paragraph (1) permits a taxable company to amend its return to revise an amount determined under paragraph 7(2), 12(2) or 13(3) merely because the amount determined under that provision differs from the amount which is actually paid or provided (or loaned).

Correction of return by HMRC

22 (1) HMRC may amend a bank payroll tax return so as to correct obvious errors or omissions in it (whether errors of principle, arithmetical mistakes or otherwise).

(2) A correction under this paragraph is made by notice to the taxable company concerned.

(3) No such correction may be made more than 9 months after—

    (a) the day on which the return was delivered, or

    (b) if the correction is required in consequence of an amendment made under paragraph 21, the day on which that amendment was made.

(4) A correction under this paragraph is of no effect if the taxable company gives notice rejecting it.

(5) Notice of rejection must be given—

Finance Act 2010 (c. 13)
Schedule 1 — Bank payroll tax
Part 2 — Collection and management of tax

1503

(a) to the officer of Revenue and Customs by whom the correction notice was given, and

(b) before the end of the period of 30 days beginning with the date on which the correction notice was given.

Enquiry into return

23 (1) HMRC may enquire into a bank payroll tax return if they give notice to the taxable company of their intention to do so within the time allowed.

(2) If the return was delivered on or before 31 August 2010, notice of enquiry may be given at any time on or before 31 August 2011.

(3) If the return was delivered after 31 August 2010, notice of enquiry may be given at any time up to and including whichever of 31 January, 30 April, 31 July or 31 October next follows the first anniversary of the day on which the return was delivered.

(4) An enquiry extends to anything contained in the return or required to be contained in the return.

(5) The following provisions of Schedule 18 to FA 1998 apply to an enquiry into a bank payroll tax return under this Schedule as they apply to an enquiry into a company tax return under that Schedule —
   (a) paragraph 24(4) to (5) (notice of enquiry),
   (b) paragraph 25(2) (enquiry following amendment by company) (but as if the reference there to paragraph 24(2) or (3) were to sub-paragraph (2) or (3) of this paragraph),
   (c) paragraph 31 (amendment of return by company during enquiry),
   (d) paragraphs 31A to 31D (referral of questions to the tribunal during enquiry),
   (e) paragraph 32(1) (completion of enquiry),
   (f) paragraph 33 (direction to complete enquiry), and
   (g) paragraph 34 (amendment of return after enquiry).

Determination by HMRC

24 (1) HMRC may determine to the best of their knowledge and belief the amount of bank payroll tax payable by a taxable company if the company has not delivered a bank payroll tax return on or before 31 August 2010.

(2) Notice of the determination —
   (a) must be served on the company, and
   (b) must state the date on which it is given.

(3) The amount determined by HMRC is taken to be the amount payable by the company (in the same way as if it were an assessment) unless and until the determination is superseded by a relevant assessment.

(4) A relevant assessment is an assessment —
   (a) included in a bank payroll tax return delivered by the company within the period of 12 months beginning with the date on which notice of the determination was given, or
   (b) made by HMRC under paragraph 20 following delivery of such a return.

1504

Finance Act 2010 (c. 13)
Schedule 1 — Bank payroll tax
Part 2 — Collection and management of tax

(5) If —

    (a)   proceedings have been commenced for the recovery of an amount determined by HMRC under this paragraph, and

    (b)   before the proceedings are concluded, the determination is superseded by a relevant assessment,

the proceedings may be continued as if they were proceedings for the recovery of so much of the tax shown in the assessment as has not been paid.

(6) No determination may be made under this paragraph after 31 August 2013.

Discovery assessment by HMRC

25   (1) This paragraph applies if HMRC discover, with respect to a taxable company, any of the following situations —

    (a)   an amount which ought to have been assessed to bank payroll tax has not been assessed,

    (b)   an assessment to bank payroll tax is insufficient, or

    (c)   an amount of bank payroll tax has been repaid which ought not to have been repaid.

(2) HMRC may make an assessment (a "discovery assessment") in the amount or further amount which ought in their opinion to be charged or recovered in order to make good to the Crown the loss of bank payroll tax.

(3) If the company has delivered a bank payroll tax return, HMRC may only make a discovery assessment if condition A or condition B is met.

(4) Condition A is that the situation discovered by HMRC was brought about carelessly or deliberately by the company or a person acting on its behalf.

(5) Condition B is that HMRC could not reasonably have been expected to be aware of the situation at the time when they —

    (a)   ceased to be entitled to give notice of enquiry into the return, or

    (b)   completed their enquiries into the return.

26   Notice of a discovery assessment —

    (a)   must be served on the taxable company, and

    (b)   must state the date on which it is given and the time by which an appeal may be brought against it.

27   (1) No discovery assessment may be made after the relevant deadline.

(2) The relevant deadline is 5 April 2030 if the situation —

    (a)   was brought about deliberately by the taxable company, or

    (b)   was attributable to the taxable company's careless failure to deliver a bank payroll tax return on or before 31 August 2010.

(3) Subject to sub-paragraph (2)(b), the relevant deadline is 5 April 2016 if the situation was brought about carelessly by the taxable company.

(4) In all other cases, the relevant deadline is 5 April 2014.

(5) In this paragraph —

    (a)   references to the situation are to the one discovered by HMRC, and

    (b)   references to the taxable company include a person acting on the company's behalf.

Finance Act 2010 (c. 13)
Schedule 1 — Bank payroll tax
Part 2 — Collection and management of tax

1505

28 (1) If a discovery assessment is made with respect to a taxable company, the company may appeal against it.

(2) Notice of appeal must be given—

    (a) in writing,

    (b) within the period of 30 days beginning with the date on which notice of the assessment was given, and

    (c) to the officer of Revenue and Customs by whom notice of the assessment was given.

(3) Any objection to a discovery assessment on the ground that paragraph 25, 26 or 27 was not complied with can only be made on an appeal against the assessment under this paragraph.

Collection and recovery

29 (1) HMRC may publish requirements as to the method or methods of payment to be used by taxable companies for paying bank payroll tax.

(2) Part 6 of TMA 1970 (collection and recovery) applies in relation to a charge to bank payroll tax as it applies in relation to a charge to corporation tax.

(3) See also Chapter 5 of Part 7 of FA 2008 (which makes general provision about payment and enforcement).

Interest on late payments and repayments

30 (1) This paragraph applies if an order is made under section 104(3) of FA 2009 appointing a day on which sections 101 to 103 of that Act are to come into force for the purposes of bank payroll tax.

(2) Part 2 of Schedule 53 to that Act (which makes special provision about the late payment interest start date) has effect for those purposes as if—

    (a) the reference in paragraph 4(1) to income tax or capital gains tax included a reference to bank payroll tax, and

    (b) the Part included a provision that the late payment interest start date in respect of an amount of bank payroll tax assessed and recoverable under paragraph 25(1)(c) of this Schedule is 31 August 2010.

(3) Interest charged under section 101 of FA 2009 on an amount of bank payroll tax may be enforced as if it were an amount of bank payroll tax payable by the taxable company.

Overpaid tax etc

31 (1) Paragraphs 50 to 51G of Schedule 18 to FA 1998 (overpaid tax etc) apply (so far as relevant) to bank payroll tax assessable for the chargeable period as they apply to corporation tax assessable for an accounting period, subject to the following modifications.

(2) With respect to bank payroll tax, a claim under paragraph 51 may not be made after 31 August 2014.

(3) For the purposes of paragraph 51E, the relevant restrictions for making a discovery assessment under this Schedule are—

    (a) the conditions mentioned in paragraph 25(3), and

    (b) expiry of the relevant deadline as defined in paragraph 27.

1506

Finance Act 2010 (c. 13)
Schedule 1 — Bank payroll tax
Part 2 — Collection and management of tax

(4) Nothing in sub-paragraph (1) permits a taxable company to make a claim under paragraph 51 of Schedule 18 to FA 1998 with respect to bank payroll tax merely because an amount determined under paragraph 7(2), 12(2) or 13(3) differs from the amount which is actually paid or provided (or loaned).

Appeals and other proceedings

32 (1) Part 5 of TMA 1970 (appeals and other proceedings) applies in relation to an appeal against a discovery assessment to bank payroll tax as it applies in relation to an appeal against an assessment to corporation tax.

(2) References in that Part to tax are to be read accordingly.

33 (1) Where a provision of FA 1998 is applied by this Part of this Schedule, a reference in section 46D of TMA 1970 (questions to be determined by the relevant tribunal) to that provision includes a reference to that provision as so applied.

(2) A reference in section 48 of TMA 1970 (application to appeals and other proceedings) to the Taxes Acts includes a reference to those Acts as applied by this Part of this Schedule.

(3) Where a provision of FA 1998 is applied by this Part of this Schedule —
    (a) a reference in section 55 of TMA 1970 (recovery of tax not postponed) to that provision includes a reference to that provision as so applied, and
    (b) references in that section to tax are to be read accordingly.

Obligation to preserve records

34 (1) Each taxable company must —
    (a) keep such records as may be needed to enable it to establish and verify the amount of bank payroll tax payable by it and to deliver a correct and complete bank payroll tax return, and
    (b) preserve those records, and any other relevant records, until the end of 31 August 2016.

(2) Other relevant records are records that —
    (a) may be needed for a purpose mentioned in sub-paragraph (1)(a), and
    (b) are in the company's possession or power immediately before the commencement of this Schedule.

(3) The obligation under sub-paragraph (1)(b) may be discharged by —
    (a) preserving the records in any form and by any means, or
    (b) preserving the information contained in them in any form and by any means.

(4) The obligation under sub-paragraph (1)(b) includes an obligation to preserve supporting documents (such as contracts, accounts and correspondence).

35 (1) A taxable company which fails to comply with paragraph 34 is liable to a penalty of an amount not exceeding £3,000.

(2) Sections 100 to 102 of TMA 1970 apply to a penalty under this paragraph as they apply to a penalty under section 12B(5) of that Act.

Finance Act 2010 (c. 13)
Schedule 1 — Bank payroll tax
Part 2 — Collection and management of tax

1507

Information powers

36 (1) Schedule 36 to FA 2008 (information and inspection powers) has effect as if the definition of tax in paragraph 63(1) included bank payroll tax.

   (2) Paragraph 21 of that Schedule (taxpayer notices) applies where a taxable company has made a bank payroll tax return as it applies where a person has made a company tax return and, in relation to bank payroll tax —

   (a) a reference in that paragraph to a chargeable period is to the chargeable period within the meaning of this Schedule, and

   (b) a reference in that paragraph to a notice of enquiry is to a notice of enquiry under paragraph 23 of this Schedule.

Penalties

37 (1) Schedule 24 to FA 2007 (penalties for errors) has effect as if in the Table in paragraph 1 —

   (a) the list of taxes included bank payroll tax, and

   (b) the list of documents included a bank payroll tax return.

   (2) In relation to bank payroll tax, any reference in that Schedule to a tax period is to the chargeable period within the meaning of this Schedule.

38 (1) Schedule 55 to FA 2009 (penalties for failure to make returns etc) has effect as if —

   (a) a bank payroll tax return were specified in the Table in paragraph 1 (and bank payroll tax were specified in relation to it), and

   (b) the reference in paragraph 2 to a return falling within certain items in the Table included a reference to a bank payroll tax return.

   (2) Schedule 55 to FA 2009 has effect for the purposes of bank payroll tax in accordance with this paragraph whether or not it has come into force for other purposes.

39 (1) Schedule 56 to FA 2009 (penalties for failure to make payments on time etc) has effect for the purposes of bank payroll tax as follows.

   (2) The part of the Table in paragraph 1 headed "Principal amounts" has effect as if bank payroll tax were specified in column 2 and, in relation to that tax —

   (a) an amount shown (or treated as shown) in a bank payroll tax return were specified in column 3, and

   (b) 31 August 2010 were specified in column 4.

   (3) The part of that Table headed "Amounts payable in default of a return being made" has effect as if bank payroll tax were specified in column 2 and, in relation to that tax —

   (a) an amount shown in a determination under paragraph 24 of this Schedule were specified in column 3, and

   (b) 31 August 2010 were specified in column 4.

   (4) The part of that Table headed "Amount shown to be due in other assessments, determinations, etc" has effect as if —

   (a) bank payroll tax were a tax falling within any of items 1 to 6, 9 or 10, and

   (b) an amount shown (or treated as shown) in a bank payroll tax return were an amount falling within any of those items.

1508

Finance Act 2010 (c. 13)
Schedule 1 — Bank payroll tax
Part 2 — Collection and management of tax

(5) Paragraph 2 (assessments and determinations in default of return) has effect as if the reference in paragraph (a) to a return falling within any item in the Table in Schedule 55 included a reference to a bank payroll tax return.

(6) Paragraph 3 (amount of penalty) has effect as if sub-paragraph (1)(a) included a reference to a payment of bank payroll tax.

(7) Schedule 56 to FA 2009 has effect for the purposes of bank payroll tax in accordance with this paragraph whether or not it has come into force for other purposes.

Miscellaneous

40 (1) The following provisions of TMA 1970 apply for the purposes of bank payroll tax and this Schedule as they apply for the purposes of corporation tax and the Taxes Acts—
    (a) section 108 (responsibility of company officers),
    (b) section 112 (loss, destruction or damage to assessments, returns etc),
    (c) section 114 (want of form), and
    (d) section 115 (delivery and service of documents).

(2) The application of section 115 of TMA 1970 in relation to the delivery of bank payroll tax returns is subject to any requirements published under paragraph 19(1) of this Schedule.

41 Chapter 6 of Part 22 of CTA 2010 (collection etc of tax from UK representatives of non-UK resident companies) applies to this Part of this Schedule as it applies to enactments relating to corporation tax.

42 Section 118(5) to (7) of TMA 1970 (meaning of carelessly etc) applies for the interpretation of this Part of this Schedule, with references to tax being read as references to bank payroll tax.

PART 3

DEFINITIONS

"UK resident bank" and "relevant foreign bank"

43 (1) "UK resident bank" means a company which—
    (a) is resident in the United Kingdom,
    (b) is an authorised person for the purposes of FISMA 2000 (see section 31 of that Act),
    (c) is a person—
        (i) whose activities include the relevant regulated activity described in the provision mentioned in paragraph 44(1)(a), or
        (ii) which is both a BIPRU 730k firm and a full scope BIPRU investment firm, whose activities consist wholly or mainly of any of the relevant regulated activities described in the provisions mentioned in paragraph 44(1)(b) to (f) and which meets the capital resources condition,
    (d) carries on that relevant regulated activity, or those relevant regulated activities, wholly or mainly in the course of trade, and
    (e) is not an excluded company.

(2) "UK resident bank" also includes a company which—

    (a) meets the conditions in sub-paragraph (1)(a) and (e), and

    (b) is a member of a partnership which meets the conditions in sub-paragraph (1)(b) to (d).

(3) "Relevant foreign bank" means a company which—

    (a) is not resident in the United Kingdom,

    (b) is an authorised person for the purposes of FISMA 2000 (see section 31 of that Act),

    (c) is a person which carries on a trade in the United Kingdom through a permanent establishment in the United Kingdom and—

        (i) whose activities include the relevant regulated activity described in the provision mentioned in paragraph 44(1)(a), or

        (ii) which is both a BIPRU 730k firm and a full scope BIPRU investment firm, whose activities consist wholly or mainly of any of the relevant regulated activities described in the provisions mentioned in paragraph 44(1)(b) to (f) and which meets the capital resources condition,

    (d) carries on that relevant regulated activity, or those relevant regulated activities, wholly or mainly in the course of that trade, and

    (e) is not an excluded company.

(4) "Relevant foreign bank" also includes a company which—

    (a) meets the conditions in sub-paragraph (3)(a) and (e), and

    (b) is a member of a partnership which meets the conditions in sub-paragraph (1)(b) to (d).

"Relevant regulated activity", "capital resources condition", "excluded company", "asset management activities", "linked entity" etc

44 (1) "Relevant regulated activity" means an activity which is a regulated activity for the purposes of FISMA 2000 by virtue of any of the following provisions of the Financial Services and Markets Act 2000 (Regulated Activities) Order 2001 (S.I. 2001/544)—

    (a) article 5 (accepting deposits),

    (b) article 14 (dealing in investments as principal),

    (c) article 21 (dealing in investments as agent),

    (d) article 25 (arranging deals in investments),

    (e) article 40 (safeguarding and administering investments), and

    (f) article 61 (entering into regulated mortgage contracts).

(2) "The capital resources condition" is that the company has a capital resources requirement of at least £100 million.

(3) But if the company is a member of a group, "the capital resources condition" is that the company and—

    (a) any other companies which—

        (i) are members of the group,

        (ii) meet either of the conditions in sub-paragraph (4),

        (iii) are not excluded companies, and

        (iv) are not members of any partnership within paragraph (b), and

    (b)   any partnership—

        (i)   the members of which are or include one or more companies that are members of the group and not excluded companies, and

        (ii)   which meets either of those conditions,

have (in aggregate) capital resources requirements of at least that amount.

(4)   The conditions referred to in sub-paragraph (3) are that the company or partnership—

    (a)   is both a BIPRU 730k firm and a full scope BIPRU investment firm, or

    (b)   is a company or partnership which carries on in the United Kingdom activities including the relevant regulated activity described in the provision mentioned in sub-paragraph (1)(a).

(5)   For the purposes of sub-paragraphs (2) and (3) the capital resources requirement of a company or a partnership is that as at the end of the last period of account of the company or partnership ending no later than the end of the chargeable period.

(6)   In determining whether the company is a UK resident bank or a relevant foreign bank by virtue of paragraph 43(2) or (4), the references in sub-paragraph (2) to the company are to the partnership.

(7)   If any company or partnership whose capital resources may be material for the purposes of sub-paragraph (2) or (3) prepares its accounts in a currency other than sterling, the amount of its capital resources at the end of the period of account mentioned in that sub-paragraph is to be translated into its sterling equivalent by reference to the average spot rate of exchange on the day on which that period ends.

(8)   If any company whose capital resources may be material for the purposes of sub-paragraph (2) or (3) carries on a trade in the United Kingdom through a permanent establishment in the United Kingdom, its capital resources are to be determined as they would be for the purposes of corporation tax (see Chapter 4 of Part 2 of CTA 2009).

(9)   "Excluded company" means a company which is—

    (a)   an insurance company or an insurance special purpose vehicle,

    (b)   a company which is a member of a group and does not carry on any relevant regulated activities otherwise than on behalf of an insurance company or insurance special purpose vehicle which is a member of the same group,

    (c)   a company which does not carry on any relevant regulated activities otherwise than as the manager of a pension scheme,

    (d)   an investment trust (within the meaning given by section 1158 of CTA 2010),

    (e)   a company which does not carry on any relevant regulated activities other than asset management activities,

    (f)   an exempt BIPRU commodities firm,

    (g)   a company which does not carry on any relevant regulated activities otherwise than for the purpose of trading in commodities or commodity derivatives,

    (h)   a company which does not carry on any relevant regulated activities otherwise than for the purpose of dealing in contracts for differences as principal with persons all or all but an insignificant proportion of whom are retail clients or of dealing in contracts for differences with another person to enable the company or other person to deal in contracts for differences as principal with such persons,

(i) a society incorporated under the Friendly Societies Act 1992,

(j) a society registered as a credit union under the Industrial and Provident Societies Act 1965 or the Credit Unions (Northern Ireland) Order 1985 (S.I. 1985/1205 (NI 12)), or

(k) a building society.

(10) "Asset management activities" means activities which consist (or, if they were carried on in the United Kingdom, would consist) of any or all of the following—

(a) acting as the operator of a collective investment scheme (within the meaning of Part 17 of FISMA 2000: see sections 235 and 237 of that Act),

(b) acting as a discretionary investment manager for clients none of which is a linked entity, and

(c) acting as an authorised corporate director.

(11) "Linked entity", in relation to a company ("C"), means—

(a) a member of the same group as C,

(b) a company in which a company which is a member of the same group as C has a major interest (within the meaning of Part 5 of CTA 2009: see section 473 of that Act), or

(c) a partnership the members of which include a company—

(i) which is a member of the same group as C, and

(ii) whose share of the profits or losses of a trade carried on by the partnership for an accounting period of the partnership any part of which falls within the chargeable period is at least a 40% share (see Part 17 of CTA 2009 for provisions about shares of partnership profits and losses).

(12) The following have the meanings given in the Handbook of Rules and Guidance made by the Financial Services Authority (as that Handbook has effect from time to time)—

"authorised corporate director",

"BIPRU 730k firm",

"capital resources requirement",

"contracts for differences",

"discretionary investment manager",

"exempt BIPRU commodities firm",

"full scope BIPRU investment firm",

"pension scheme",

"principal", and

"retail clients".

(13) A company which would be a BIPRU 730k firm and a full scope BIPRU investment firm by virtue of activities carried on in the United Kingdom but for the fact that its registered office (or, if it does not have a registered office, its head office) is not in the United Kingdom is to be treated as being one.

(14) The Treasury may by order amend this paragraph.

(15) An order under this paragraph may be made so as to have effect in relation to any time after the beginning of the chargeable period.

(16) An order under this paragraph is to be made by statutory instrument.

(17) An order under this paragraph may not be made unless a draft of the instrument containing it has been laid before, and approved by a resolution of, the House of Commons.

"Member of a banking group"

45 (1) A company is a "member of a banking group" at any time if—
    (a) it is within sub-paragraph (2) at that time, or
    (b) it was within that sub-paragraph immediately before the chargeable period.

(2) A company is within this sub-paragraph if—
    (a) it is a member of a group,
    (b) any of conditions A to C is met, and
    (c) the group does not meet the exempt activities test.

(3) Condition A is that the principal company of the group is a UK resident bank or a relevant foreign bank.

(4) Condition B is that—
    (a) the principal company of the group is a company which is not resident in the United Kingdom but which (if it were so resident) would be a UK resident bank, or
    (b) the principal company of the group is a company which is not resident in the United Kingdom, and is a member of a partnership which is not so resident, but which (if both the company and the partnership were so resident) would be a UK resident bank,
    and (in either case) any member of the group is a UK resident bank or a relevant foreign bank.

(5) Condition C is that—
    (a) the principal company is the holding company of another company, and
    (b) if that other company were the principal company of the group, condition A or B would be met.

(6) For the purposes of condition C a company ("H") is a "holding company" of another company ("S") if—
    (a) H is an investment company, and
    (b) S is—
        (i) an effective 51% subsidiary of H, and
        (ii) not an effective 51% subsidiary of any company which is not an investment company.

(7) A group meets the exempt activities test if at least 90% of the trading income of the group for the relevant period is derived from exempt activities.

(8) For this purpose—
    "exempt activities" means—

    (a)   insurance activities, asset management activities and related activities, and

    (b)   activities carried on by a company which is not a financial trading company (or a company which would be a financial trading company if it were resident in the United Kingdom) other than lending activities or dealing on own account,

"the relevant period", in relation to a group, means the last period of account of the group ending no later than the end of the chargeable period, and

"the trading income of the group" for the relevant period is to be calculated in accordance with paragraph 46.

(9) In sub-paragraph (8) —

"insurance activities" means —

    (a)   the effecting or carrying out of contracts of insurance by a regulated insurer, and

    (b)   investment business that arises directly from activities falling within paragraph (a);

"lending activities" means —

    (a)   acceptance of deposits or other repayable funds,

    (b)   lending of money, including consumer credit, mortgage credit, factoring (with or without recourse) and financing of commercial transactions (including forfeiting),

    (c)   finance leasing (as lessor),

    (d)   issuing and administering means of payment,

    (e)   provision of guarantees or commitments to provide money,

    (f)   money transmission services,

    (g)   provision of alternative finance arrangements, and

    (h)   other activities carried on in connection with activities falling within any of paragraphs (a) to (g);

"related activities" means —

    (a)   activities which are ancillary to insurance activities or asset management activities of any company which is a member of the group (whether or not the company carrying on the insurance activities or asset management activities), and

    (b)   activities which would not be carried on but for such insurance activities or asset management activities being carried on,

but does not include dealing on own account.

(10) In sub-paragraph (9) —

"activities" includes buying, holding, managing and selling assets;

"regulated insurer", in relation to a group, means a member of the group that —

    (a)   is authorised under the law of any territory to carry on insurance business, or

    (b)   is a member of a body or organisation which is so authorised.

(11) A company which is a member of a banking group ceases to be a member of a banking group when it ceases to be within sub-paragraph (2), but only if it ceases to be within that provision as a result of —

      (a)   an arm's length transaction undertaken for wholly commercial purposes, or

      (b)   following a recommendation of a relevant regulatory body.

(12)   For the purposes of sub-paragraph (11) obtaining a tax advantage is not a commercial purpose.

(13)   "Tax advantage" means—

      (a)   a relief from tax or increased relief from tax (relief here including a tax credit),

      (b)   a repayment of tax or increased repayment of tax,

      (c)   the avoidance or reduction of a charge to tax or an assessment to tax (obtained in any way), or

      (d)   the avoidance of a possible assessment to tax (so obtained),

    and, for this purpose, "tax" includes bank payroll tax and any other tax.

(14)   In sub-paragraph (11) "relevant regulatory body" means—

      (a)   the Financial Services Authority, or

      (b)   a body discharging functions under the law of a country or territory outside the United Kingdom corresponding to functions discharged by the Financial Services Authority.

(15)   In this paragraph "dealing on own account" has the same meaning as in Directive 2004/39/EC of the European Parliament and of the Council of 21 April 2004 on markets in financial instruments (see Article 4(1)(6)).

"The trading income of the group" for the relevant period

46   (1)   This paragraph applies for calculating the "trading income of the group" for the relevant period for the purposes of paragraph 45.

    (2)   The trading income for the group for the relevant period is the aggregate of—

      (a)   the gross income calculated in accordance with sub-paragraph (3), and

      (b)   the net income calculated in accordance with sub-paragraph (4).

    (3)   The income referred to in sub-paragraph (2)(a) is the gross income—

      (a)   arising from the activities of the group (other than net-basis activities), and

      (b)   disclosed as such in the financial statements of the group,

    without taking account of any deductions (whether for expenses or otherwise).

    (4)   The income referred to in sub-paragraph (2)(b) is the net income arising from the net-basis activities of the group that—

      (a)   is accounted for as such under international accounting standards or in accordance with practice which is generally accepted accounting practice in the territory in which the principal company of the group is resident, or

      (b)   would be accounted for as such if income arising from such activities were accounted for under such standards or in accordance with such practice.

(5) In this paragraph "net-basis activities" means activities normally reported on a net basis in financial statements prepared in accordance with such standards or practice.

"Investment company" etc

47 (1) "Investment company"—

  (a) means a company whose business consists wholly or mainly of, and the principal part of whose income is derived from, the making of investments, and

  (b) also includes any savings bank or other bank for savings.

  (2) "UK resident investment company" means an investment company which is resident in the United Kingdom.

"Financial trading company" etc

48 (1) "Financial trading company" means a company which—

  (a) is an authorised person for the purposes of FISMA 2000 (see section 31 of that Act), or

  (b) is not within paragraph (a) but carries on a trade consisting wholly or partly in dealing in securities.

  (2) "UK resident financial trading company" means a financial trading company which is resident in the United Kingdom.

  (3) "Relevant foreign financial trading company" means a company which meets conditions A and B.

  (4) Condition A is that the company—

  (a) is not resident in the United Kingdom, and

  (b) carries on a trade in the United Kingdom through a permanent establishment in the United Kingdom.

  (5) Condition B is that, disregarding any activities of the company other than those carried on through that permanent establishment, the company is a financial trading company.

  (6) In this paragraph "securities" includes—

  (a) shares,

  (b) rights of unit holders in unit trust schemes to which TCGA 1992 applies as a result of section 99 of that Act, and

  (c) in the case of a company with no share capital, interests in the company possessed by members of the company.

Other interpretative provisions

49 (1) In this Schedule—

  "arrangements" includes any agreement, understanding, scheme, transaction or series of transactions (whether or not legally enforceable);

  "benefit" includes a facility of any kind;

  "building society" means a building society within the meaning of the Building Societies Act 1986;

"the Commissioners" means the Commissioners of Her Majesty's Revenue and Customs;

"contract of insurance" has the meaning given by section 431(2) of ICTA;

"control" has the meaning given by section 995 of ITA 2007;

"employment", "employee" and "employer" have the same meaning as in the employment income Parts of ITEPA 2003 (see sections 4 and 5 of that Act);

"enactment" includes an enactment or instrument (whenever passed or made);

"HMRC" means Her Majesty's Revenue and Customs;

"insurance company" and "insurance special purpose vehicle" have the meaning given by section 431(2) of ICTA;

"market value" has the same meaning it has for the purposes of TCGA 1992 by virtue of Part 8 of that Act;

"money's worth" has the meaning given by section 62(3) of ITEPA 2003;

"partnership" includes—

(a) a limited liability partnership, and

(b) an entity established under the law of a territory outside the United Kingdom of a similar character to a partnership (and "member", in relation to a partnership, is to be read accordingly);

"period of account" and "permanent establishment" have the meaning given by section 1119 of CTA 2010;

"the tax year 2009-10" has the same meaning as in the Income Tax Acts (see section 989 of ITA 2007).

(2) Section 170(2) to (11) of TCGA 1992 ("group", "principal company", "effective 51% subsidiary", "company" etc) has effect for the interpretation of this Schedule as for the interpretation of sections 171 to 181 of that Act.

(3) Section 993 of ITA 2007 (meaning of "connected" persons) applies for the purposes of this Schedule.

(4) For the purposes of this Schedule the territory in which a company is resident is to be determined as for the purposes of the Corporation Tax Acts.

SCHEDULE 2   Section 23

PENSIONS: HIGH INCOME EXCESS RELIEF CHARGE

1   Part 4 of FA 2004 (pension schemes etc) is amended as follows.

2   After section 213 insert—

"High income excess relief charge

213A High income excess relief charge

(1) A charge to income tax, to be known as the high income excess relief charge, arises where—

> > > (a) an individual who is a member of one or more registered pension schemes has a high income for a tax year, and
> > >
> > > (b) there is a total pension savings amount in the case of the individual for the tax year.
> >
> > (2) The person liable to the high income excess relief charge is the individual.
> >
> > (3) The individual is liable to the high income excess relief charge whether or not—
> >
> > > (a) the individual, and
> > >
> > > (b) the scheme administrator of the pension scheme or schemes concerned,
> >
> > are UK resident, ordinarily UK resident or domiciled in the United Kingdom.
> >
> > (4) The high income excess relief charge is a charge at the appropriate rate in respect of the total pension savings amount.
> >
> > (5) The total pension savings amount is not to be treated as income for any purpose of the Tax Acts apart from this Part.
> >
> > (6) In calculating the individual's liability to income tax for the tax year the amount of any income tax to which the individual is liable under this section is to be added at Step 7 of the calculation in section 23 of ITA 2007 (which applies as if this section were a provision listed in section 30 of that Act).
> >
> > (7) The following sections make further provision about the high income excess relief charge—
> >
> > > (a) sections 213B to 213D (high income),
> > >
> > > (b) section 213E (the appropriate rate),
> > >
> > > (c) sections 213F to 213N (total pension savings amount),
> > >
> > > (d) section 213O (anti-avoidance), and
> > >
> > > (e) section 213P (power to amend).

213B High income

> An individual has a high income for a tax year if—
>
> > (a) the individual's gross income for the tax year is £150,000 or more, and
> >
> > (b) the individual's relevant income for the tax year is not less than £130,000.

213C Gross income

> To find the individual's gross income for a tax year take the following steps—
>
> *Step 1*
>
> Identify the individual's total income for the tax year.
>
> *Step 2*
>
> Add the amount of any deductions made from any employment income of the individual for the tax year under Part 12 of ITEPA 2003 (payroll giving), under section 193(2) of this Act or under Chapter 2 of Part 5 of ITEPA 2003 (employee's expenses) in accordance with paragraph 51 of Schedule 36 to this Act.

Step 3

Deduct the amount of any relief under the provisions listed in section 24 of ITA 2007, other than Chapter 3 of Part 8 of that Act (gifts of shares, securities or real property to charity) and sections 193(4) and 194(1) of this Act, to which the individual is entitled for the tax year.

Step 4

Add so much of the amount that is the total pension savings amount in the case of the individual for the tax year as remains after deducting from it the amount of any relievable pension contributions paid by or on behalf of the individual during the tax year.

The result is the individual's gross income for the tax year.

213D Relevant income

(1) To find the individual's relevant income for a tax year take the following steps —

Step 1

Identify the individual's total income for the tax year.

Step 2

Add the amount of any deductions made from any employment income of the individual for the tax year under Part 12 of ITEPA 2003 (payroll giving), under section 193(2) of this Act or under Chapter 2 of Part 5 of ITEPA 2003 (employee's expenses) in accordance with paragraph 51 of Schedule 36 to this Act.

Step 3

Deduct the amount of any relief under the provisions listed in section 24 of ITA 2007, other than Chapter 3 of Part 8 of that Act (gifts of shares, securities or real property to charity) and sections 193(4) and 194(1) of this Act, to which the individual is entitled for the tax year.

Step 4

Add any amount by which what would otherwise be general earnings or specific employment income of the individual for the tax year has been reduced by relevant salary sacrifice arrangements or relevant flexible remuneration arrangements.

The result is the individual's relevant income for the tax year.

(2) In subsection (1) —

"relevant salary sacrifice arrangements" means arrangements under which the individual gives up the right to receive general earnings or specific employment income in return for the making of relevant pension provision and which are made on or after 22 April 2009 (whether before or after the employment in question began);

"relevant flexible remuneration arrangements" means arrangements under which the individual and an employer of the individual agree that relevant pension provision is to be made rather than the individual receive some description of employment income and which are made on or after 22 April 2009 (whether before or after the employment in question began).

(3) In subsection (2) "relevant pension provision" means the payment of contributions (or additional contributions) to a pension scheme in

respect of the individual or otherwise (by an employer of the individual or any other person) to secure an increase in the amount of benefits to which the individual or any person who is a dependant of, or is connected with, the individual is actually or prospectively entitled under a pension scheme.

(4) Section 993 of ITA 2007 (meaning of "connected" persons) applies for the purposes of subsection (3).

213E The appropriate rate

(1) "The appropriate rate", in relation to the total pension savings amount in the case of the individual for a tax year, is —

    (a) 0% in relation to so much (if any) of that amount as, when added to the individual's reduced net income for the tax year, does not exceed the basic rate limit,

    (b) 20% in relation to so much (if any) of that amount as, when so added, exceeds the basic rate limit but does not exceed the higher rate limit, and

    (c) 30% in relation to so much (if any) of that amount as, when so added, exceeds the higher rate limit.

(2) But where the individual's gross income for the tax year is less than £180,000, the percentages in subsection (1)(b) and (c) are each reduced (but to no less than 0%) by 1 percentage point for every £1,000 by which it is less than £180,000.

(3) The individual's reduced net income for the tax year is the amount after taking step 3 in section 23 of ITA 2007 in the case of the individual for the tax year.

(4) Where the basic rate limit or the higher rate limit for the tax year is (in accordance with section 192 of this Act and section 414 of ITA 2007) increased in the case of the individual, the references to the limit in subsection (1) are to the limit as so increased.

213F Total pension savings amount

(1) The total pension savings amount in the case of an individual for a tax year is arrived at by aggregating the pension savings amounts in respect of each arrangement relating to the individual under a registered pension scheme of which the individual is a member.

(2) The pension savings amount in respect of an arrangement —

    (a) is the amount arrived at under section 213G if it is a money purchase arrangement other than a cash balance arrangement,

    (b) is the amount arrived at under section 213H if it is a cash balance arrangement,

    (c) is the amount arrived at under section 213J if it is a defined benefits arrangement, and

    (d) is the amount arrived at under section 213N if it is a hybrid arrangement.

(3) Where the pension savings amount in respect of an arrangement would otherwise be a negative amount it is to be taken to be nil.

(4) Where —

      (a)   the total pension input amount in the case of the individual under section 229 for the tax year, exceeds

      (b)   the amount of the annual allowance for the tax year,

the total pension savings amount in the case of the individual for the tax year is reduced by the amount of the excess.

(5)   The Treasury may by regulations make provision —

      (a)   for an arrangement relating to the individual to be left out of account in arriving at the total pension savings amount in the case of the individual for a tax year if the individual meets the condition in subsection (6) throughout the tax year and such conditions as are prescribed by the regulations are met, and

      (b)   for modifying the operation of any of the provisions relating to the high income excess relief charge in relation to an arrangement relating to the individual for a tax year if the individual meets the condition in subsection (6) for only part of the tax year and such conditions as are prescribed by the regulations are met.

(6)   The condition in this subsection, in relation to the individual and an arrangement under a pension scheme, is that the individual is a deferred member of the pension scheme (or would be if it were the only arrangement under the pension scheme relating to the individual).

213G Money purchase arrangements other than cash balance arrangements

(1)   The pension savings amount in respect of a money purchase arrangement other than a cash balance arrangement is the total of —

      (a)   any relievable pension contributions paid by or on behalf of the individual under the arrangement, and

      (b)   contributions paid in respect of the individual under the arrangement by an employer of the individual,

during the tax year.

(2)   The references to contributions in subsection (1)(a) and (b) do not include minimum payments under —

      (a)   section 8 of the Pension Schemes Act 1993, or

      (b)   section 4 of the Pension Schemes (Northern Ireland) Act 1993,

or any amount recovered under regulations made under subsection (3) of either of those sections.

(3)   When at any time contributions paid under a pension scheme by an employer otherwise than in respect of any individual become held for the purposes of the provision under an arrangement under the pension scheme of benefits to or in respect of an individual, they are to be treated as being contributions paid at that time in respect of the individual under the arrangement.

(4)   If during the tax year the individual becomes entitled to a serious ill-health lump sum under the arrangement or dies, the pension savings amount in the case of the individual in respect of the arrangement is nil.

213H Cash balance arrangements

(1) The pension savings amount in respect of a cash balance arrangement is the appropriate increase.

(2) The appropriate increase is —
$$(ACR \times CARARF) - (UOR \times OARARF)$$
where —

ACR is the amount of the closing rights (see subsection (3)), adjusted in accordance with section 213I,

CARARF is the factor which is the appropriate age-related factor (see section 213L) in relation to the closing rights,

UOR is the amount of the opening rights (see subsection (4)), uprated in accordance with section 213M, and

OARARF is the factor which is the appropriate age-related factor (see section 213L) in relation to the opening rights.

(3) The amount of the closing rights is the amount which would, on the relevant assumptions, be available for the provision of benefits to or in respect of the individual under the arrangement if the individual became entitled to the benefits at the end of the tax year.

(4) The amount of the opening rights is the amount which would, on the relevant assumptions, be available for the provision of benefits to or in respect of the individual under the arrangement if the individual became entitled to the benefits at the end of the preceding tax year.

(5) If, during the tax year, minimum payments are made under —
  (a) section 8 of the Pension Schemes Act 1993, or
  (b) section 4 of the Pension Schemes (Northern Ireland) Act 1993,
in relation to the individual in connection with a cash balance arrangement, the amount is to be subtracted from what would otherwise be the pension savings amount in the case of the individual in respect of the arrangement.

(6) If during the tax year the individual becomes entitled to a serious ill-health lump sum under the arrangement or dies, the pension savings amount in the case of the individual in respect of the arrangement is nil.

(7) In this section and section 213J "the relevant assumptions" means —
  (a) the valuation assumptions (see section 277) as modified by regulations made by the Treasury, and
  (b) such other assumptions as the Treasury may by regulations prescribe.

213I Adjustment of closing rights

(1) This section applies for adjusting ACR under section 213H.

(2) If, during the tax year, the rights of the individual under the arrangement have been reduced by having become subject to a pension debit, the amount of the reduction is to be added to ACR.

(3) If, during the tax year, the rights of the individual under the arrangement have been increased by the individual having become entitled to a pension credit deriving from the same or another

registered pension scheme, the amount of the increase is to be subtracted from ACR.

(4) If, during the tax year, the rights of the individual under the arrangement have been reduced by reason of a transfer relating to the individual of any sums or assets held for the purposes of, or representing accrued rights under, the arrangement so as to become held for the purposes of, or to represent rights under, any other pension scheme that is—

(a) a registered pension scheme, or

(b) a qualifying recognised overseas pension scheme,

the amount of the reduction is to be added to ACR.

(5) If, during the tax year, the rights of the individual under the arrangement have been increased by reason of a transfer relating to the individual of any sums or assets held for the purposes of, or representing accrued rights under, any pension scheme so as to become held for the purposes of, or to represent rights under, the arrangement, the amount of the increase is to be subtracted from ACR.

(6) If, during the tax year, the rights of the individual under the arrangement have been reduced by any surrender made, or similar action taken, pursuant to an option available to the individual under the arrangement, the amount of the reduction is to be added to ACR.

(7) If, during the tax year—

(a) benefit crystallisation event 1, 2, 3, or 4 occurs in relation to the individual and the arrangement,

(b) benefit crystallisation event 6 so occurs by virtue of the individual becoming entitled to a pension commencement lump sum or a lifetime allowance excess lump sum, or

(c) there is an allocation of rights of the individual under the arrangement (not falling within paragraph (a)),

the amount of the reduction in the amount of the rights available for the provision of benefits to or in respect of the individual occurring by reason of the event or allocation is to be added to ACR.

213J Defined benefits arrangements

(1) The pension savings amount in respect of a defined benefits arrangement is the aggregate of—

(a) the appropriate pension increase (see subsection (2)), and

(b) the appropriate lump sum increase (see subsection (5)).

(2) The appropriate pension increase is—

$$(ACP \times CAPARF) - (UOP \times OAPARF)$$

where—

ACP is the amount of the closing pension (see subsection (3)), adjusted in accordance with section 213K,

CAPARF is the factor which is the appropriate age-related factor (see section 213L) in relation to the closing pension,

UOP is the amount of the opening pension (see subsection (4)), uprated in accordance with section 213M, and

OAPARF is the factor which is the appropriate age-related factor (see section 213L) in relation to the opening pension.

(3) The amount of the closing pension is the annual rate of the pension to which the individual would, on the relevant assumptions, be entitled under the arrangement if the individual became entitled to it at the end of the tax year.

(4) The amount of the opening pension is the annual rate of the pension to which the individual would, on the relevant assumptions, be entitled under the arrangement if the individual became entitled to it at the end of the preceding tax year.

(5) The appropriate lump sum increase is —

$$(ACLS \times CALSARF) - (UOLS \times OALSARF)$$

where —

ACLS is the amount of the closing lump sum (see subsection (6)), adjusted in accordance with section 213K,

CALSARF is the factor which is the appropriate age-related factor (see section 213L) in relation to the closing lump sum,

UOLS is the amount of the opening lump sum (see subsection (7)), uprated in accordance with section 213M, and

OALSARF is the factor which is the appropriate age-related factor (see section 213L) in relation to the opening lump sum.

(6) The amount of the closing lump sum is the amount of the lump sum to which the individual would, on the relevant assumptions, be entitled under the arrangement if the individual became entitled to it at the end of the tax year.

(7) The amount of the opening lump sum is the amount of the lump sum to which the individual would, on the relevant assumptions, be entitled under the arrangement if the individual became entitled to it at the end of the preceding tax year.

(8) If, during the tax year, minimum payments are made under —

(a) section 8 of the Pension Schemes Act 1993, or

(b) section 4 of the Pension Schemes (Northern Ireland) Act 1993,

in relation to the individual in connection with a defined benefits arrangement, the amount is to be subtracted from what would otherwise be the pension savings amount in the case of the individual in respect of the arrangement.

(9) If during the tax year the individual becomes entitled to a serious ill-health lump sum under the arrangement or dies, the pension savings amount in the case of the individual in respect of the arrangement is nil.

213K Adjustment of closing pension and lump sum

(1) This section applies for adjusting ACP and ACLS under section 213J.

(2) If, during the tax year, the annual rate of the pension, or the amount of the lump sum, to which the individual would be entitled under the arrangement has been reduced by having become subject to a pension debit, the amount of the reduction is to be added to ACP or ACLS.

(3) If, during the tax year, the annual rate of the pension, or the amount of the lump sum, to which the individual would be entitled under the arrangement has been increased by the individual having become entitled to a pension credit deriving from the same or another registered pension scheme, the amount of the increase is to be subtracted from ACP or ACLS.

(4) If, during the tax year, the annual rate of the pension, or the amount of the lump sum, to which the individual would be entitled under the arrangement has been reduced by reason of a transfer relating to the individual of any sums or assets held for the purposes of, or representing accrued rights under, the arrangement so as to become held for the purposes of, or to represent rights under, any other pension scheme that is—

(a) a registered pension scheme, or

(b) a qualifying recognised overseas pension scheme,

the amount of the reduction is to be added to ACP or ACLS.

(5) If, during the tax year, the annual rate of the pension, or the amount of the lump sum, to which the individual would be entitled under the arrangement has been increased by reason of a transfer relating to the individual of any sums or assets held for the purposes of, or representing accrued rights under, any pension scheme so as to become held for the purposes of, or to represent rights under, the arrangement, the amount of the increase is to be subtracted from ACP or ACLS.

(6) If, during the tax year, the annual rate of the pension, or the amount of the lump sum, to which the individual would be entitled under the arrangement has been reduced by any commutation, allocation or surrender made, or similar action taken, pursuant to an option available to the individual under the arrangement, the amount of the reduction is to be added to ACP or ACLS.

(7) If, during the tax year—

(a) benefit crystallisation event 2 or 3 occurs in relation to the individual and the arrangement, or

(b) benefit crystallisation event 6 occurs in relation to the individual and the arrangement by virtue of the individual becoming entitled to a pension commencement lump sum or a lifetime allowance excess lump sum,

the annual rate of the pension, or the amount of the lump sum, to which the individual became entitled (otherwise than by commutation of lump sum or of pension) is to be added to ACP or ACLS.

213L Age-related factors

(1) The Treasury must make regulations about age-related factors.

(2) Different provision may be made in relation to rights age-related factors and lump sum age-related factors, on the one hand, and pension age-related factors on the other.

(3) For the purposes of sections 213H and 213J the "appropriate" age-related factor is the age-related factor which applies in the case of the

individual, and the amount of the rights or lump sum, or rate of the pension, in accordance with the regulations.

(4) Regulations under subsection (1) must make provision for the age-related factor or factors applying in the case of the individual to be arrived at by reference to —

    (a)   the age of the individual, and

    (b)   the relevant normal pension age,

at the relevant time.

(5) The relevant time, in relation to factors for a tax year, is the end of the tax year unless the case is one in which there is a change in the relevant normal pension age during the tax year.

(6) In that case, the relevant time, in relation to the relevant normal pension age and the opening rights, opening pension or opening lump sum for the tax year, is the end of the previous tax year.

(7) Regulations under subsection (1) may make provision for the age-related factor or factors applying in the case of an individual and an arrangement to vary according to the nature and extent of the benefits which may be provided to or in respect of the individual under the arrangement.

(8) Before making the first regulations under subsection (1) the Treasury must seek advice from the Government Actuary or the Deputy Government Actuary.

(9) Before making any other regulations under subsection (1) the Treasury must carry out a review of the provision made by the regulations for the time being in force under this section; and when conducting such a review the Treasury must seek advice from the Government Actuary or the Deputy Government Actuary.

(10) The Treasury must carry out a review of the provision made by the regulations for the time being in force under subsection (1) —

    (a)   no later than the end of the period of 5 years beginning with the day on which the first regulations are made under this section, and

    (b)   no later than the end of the period of 5 years beginning with the last review of the provision made by the regulations for the time being in force under this section.

(11) In this section "the relevant normal pension age", in relation to an individual and an arrangement, means the age at which the individual would be unconditionally entitled to benefits under the arrangement without any reduction on account of age (assuming that the individual were a deferred member of the pension scheme under which it is an arrangement and it were the only arrangement under the pension scheme relating to the individual).

(12) But the Treasury may by regulations make provision for the relevant normal pension age to be the age specified in, or determined in accordance with, the regulations in cases of such descriptions as are specified in the regulations.

(13) The Treasury may by regulations make provision modifying the operation of sections 213H to 213K in relation to cases where the

relevant normal pension age in relation to an individual and an arrangement is not the same in relation to all the rights or benefits under the arrangement.

213M Uprating of opening rights, pension and lump sum

(1) This section applies for uprating UOR under section 213H and UOP and UOLS under section 213J.

(2) Each is to be increased by the appropriate percentage.

(3) The appropriate percentage for a tax year is the percentage arrived at for the tax year in accordance with provision made by order made by the Treasury.

(4) An order under subsection (3) —

   (a) must make provision for securing that the appropriate percentage for a tax year reflects any decrease in the value of money over a specified period, and

   (b) may do so by reference to any movement in a specified index, or an average of any movements in specified indices, over a specified period.

(5) If an order is made under subsection (3) which amends any provision included in an order by virtue of subsection (4)(b), the Treasury must as soon as reasonably practicable after the making of the order carry out a review of the provision made by the regulations for the time being in force under section 213L(1).

213N Hybrid arrangements

(1) The pension savings amount in respect of a hybrid arrangement is the greater or greatest of such of amounts A, B and C as are relevant amounts.

(2) An amount is a relevant amount in the case of a hybrid arrangement if, in any circumstances, the benefits that may be provided to or in respect of the individual under the arrangement may be benefits of the variety mentioned in the definition of that amount.

(3) Amount A is what would be the pension savings amount under section 213G if the benefits provided to or in respect of the individual under the arrangement were money purchase benefits other than cash balance benefits.

(4) Amount B is what would be the pension savings amount under section 213H if the benefits provided to or in respect of the individual under the arrangement were cash balance benefits.

(5) Amount C is what would be the pension savings amount under section 213J if the benefits provided to or in respect of the individual under the arrangement were defined benefits.

213O Anti-avoidance

(1) This section applies if a high income excess relief charge scheme applies in the case of the individual for the tax year.

(2) A scheme is a high income excess relief charge scheme if in the case of the individual for the tax year conditions A to C are met.

(3) Condition A is that it is reasonable to assume that the main purpose, or one of the main purposes, of the scheme is to avoid the whole or any part of the liability of the individual to the high income excess relief charge for the tax year.

(4) Condition B is that the scheme involves either or both of the following—

(a) reducing the individual's gross income or relevant income for the tax year, and

(b) reducing the total pension savings amount in the case of the individual for the tax year.

(5) Condition C is that the scheme involves the reduction, or any of the reductions, being redressed by—

(a) an increase in the individual's gross income or relevant income, or the total pension savings amount in the case of the individual, for a different tax year, or

(b) the provision at any time of some other benefit to or for the benefit of the individual or any person who is a dependant of, or is connected with, the individual.

(6) The individual is to be treated for the purposes of the high income excess relief charge as if—

(a) the individual's gross income and relevant income for the tax year, and

(b) the total pension savings amount in the case of the individual for the tax year,

were what they would be apart from the scheme.

(7) In this section "scheme" includes any arrangement, agreement, understanding, transaction or series of transactions (whether or not legally enforceable).

(8) Section 993 of ITA 2007 (meaning of "connected" persons) applies for the purposes of subsection (5).

213P Power to make regulations about charge

(1) The Treasury may by regulations make provision about the high income excess relief charge.

(2) The provision may include modifications of any provision made in sections 213A to 213O.

(3) The provision may include provision consequential on, or supplementary or incidental to, the provision made by those sections and transitional provisions (including provision making modifications of enactments).

(4) The provision may not include provision increasing any person's liability to tax.

(5) "Modifications" includes amendments."

3 (1) Section 282 (orders and regulations) is amended as follows.

(2) After subsection (1) insert—

"(1A)   The first regulations under section 213L(1) may not be made unless a draft of the instrument containing them has been laid before, and approved by a resolution of, the House of Commons."

(3)   In subsection (2), after "Part" insert "(other than one of which a draft has been approved by a resolution of the House of Commons)".

4   In Schedule 34 (non-UK schemes: application of certain charges), after paragraph 7A insert—

"High income excess relief charge

7B   (1)   The Commissioners for Her Majesty's Revenue and Customs may by regulations make provision for the provisions of this Part of this Act relating to the high income excess relief charge to apply in relation to individuals who are or have been members of a currently-relieved non-UK pension scheme subject to modifications contained in the regulations.

(2)   Regulations under sub-paragraph (1) may—
      (a)   include provision having effect in relation to times before they are made,
      (b)   confer discretion on the Commissioners for Her Majesty's Revenue and Customs or officers of Revenue and Customs, and
      (c)   make different provision for different cases."

5   The amendments made by this Schedule have effect for the tax year 2011-12 and subsequent tax years.

SCHEDULE 3   Section 24

SIDEWAYS RELIEF ETC

Amendments of Chapter 2 of Part 4 of ITA 2007

1   Chapter 2 of Part 4 of ITA 2007 (trade losses) is amended as follows.

2   In section 60(1)(c) (overview of Chapter), for "(see sections 75" substitute "and capital gains relief (see sections 74ZA".

3   In section 64(8) (deduction of losses from general income)—
      (a)   in paragraph (ba), for "74A" substitute "74ZA",
      (b)   at the end of paragraph (c), insert "and", and
      (c)   omit paragraph (e).

4   In section 72(5) (relief for individuals for losses in first 4 years of trade)—
      (a)   in paragraph (ba), for "74A" substitute "74ZA",
      (b)   at the end of paragraph (c), insert "and", and
      (c)   omit paragraph (e).

5   Before section 74A insert—

"74ZA No relief for tax-generated losses

(1) This section applies if —

    (a) during a tax year a person carries on (alone or in partnership) a trade, profession or vocation ("the relevant activity"),

    (b) the person makes a loss in the relevant activity in that tax year, and

    (c) the loss arises directly or indirectly in consequence of, or otherwise in connection with, relevant tax avoidance arrangements.

(2) No sideways relief or capital gains relief may be given to the person for the loss (but subject to subsection (5)).

(3) In subsection (1) "relevant tax avoidance arrangements" means arrangements —

    (a) to which the person is a party, and

    (b) the main purpose, or one of the main purposes, of which is the obtaining of a reduction in tax liability by means of sideways relief or capital gains relief.

(4) In subsection (3) "arrangements" includes any agreement, understanding, scheme, transaction or series of transactions (whether or not legally enforceable).

(5) This section has no effect in relation to any loss that derives wholly from qualifying film expenditure (see section 74D).

(6) For the purposes of this section —

    (a) capital gains relief is, in relation to a loss, the treatment of a loss as an allowable loss by virtue of section 261B of TCGA 1992 (use of trading loss as a CGT loss), and

    (b) capital gains relief is given for a loss when it is so treated."

6   Omit section 74B (no relief for tax-generated losses in case of non-active individuals carrying on trade).

7   (1) Section 74C (meaning of "non-active capacity" for purposes of sections 74A and 74B etc) is amended as follows.

    (2) In subsection (1), for "sections 74A and 74B" substitute "section 74A".

    (3) In the heading, for "**sections 74A and 74B**" substitute "**section 74A**".

8   (1) Section 74D (meaning of "qualifying film expenditure" for purposes of sections 74A and 74B) is amended as follows.

    (2) In subsections (1) and (4), for "74A and 74B" substitute "74ZA and 74A".

    (3) In the heading, for "**74A and 74B**" substitute "**74ZA and 74A**".

9   Omit section 81 (dealings in commodity futures).

Other amendments

10   In FA 2009, in Schedule 6, in paragraph 1(11) —

    (a) in paragraph (b), for "74B" substitute "74ZA",

    (b) at the end of paragraph (c), insert "and", and

    (c)   omit paragraph (e) (and the "and" before it).

Commencement

11   (1) The amendments made by this Schedule have effect in relation to a loss if it arises directly or indirectly in consequence of, or otherwise in connection with —

    (a)   arrangements which are entered into on or after 21 October 2009, or

    (b)   any transaction forming part of arrangements which is entered into on or after that date.

    (2) But those amendments do not have effect where the arrangements are, or any such transaction is, entered into pursuant to an unconditional obligation in a contract made before that date.

    (3) "An unconditional obligation" means an obligation which may not be varied or extinguished by the exercise of a right (whether or not under the contract).

SCHEDULE 4

Section 26

CAPITAL ALLOWANCE BUYING

1   Part 2 of CAA 2001 (plant and machinery allowances) is amended as follows.

2   After Chapter 16 insert —

"CHAPTER 16A

AVOIDANCE INVOLVING ALLOWANCE BUYING

Introduction

212A Scope of Chapter

    This Chapter provides for restrictions on the ways in which effect may be given to an allowance in certain circumstances where there has been a qualifying change in relation to a company ("C").

212B Where Chapter applies

    (1) This Chapter applies where —

    (a)   C carries on a trade ("the relevant trade") (whether or not in partnership with another person or other persons),

    (b)   there is a qualifying change in relation to C on any day ("the relevant day"),

    (c)   C, or (where the relevant trade is carried on in partnership) the partnership ("P"), has a relevant excess of allowances in relation to the relevant trade, and

    (d)   the qualifying change has an unallowable purpose.

    (2) Sections 212C to 212I specify when there is a qualifying change in relation to C on the relevant day.

    (3) Sections 212J to 212L specify when C or P has a relevant excess of allowances in relation to the relevant trade.

(4) Section 212M specifies when the qualifying change has an unallowable purpose.

(5) Sections 212N to 212S make provision about what happens when this Chapter applies.

Qualifying change

212C When there is qualifying change in relation to C

(1) There is a qualifying change in relation to C on the relevant day if one or more of conditions A to D is met.

(2) Condition A is that—

    (a) the principal company or companies of C at the beginning of the relevant day is not, or are not, the same as at the end of that day, or

    (b) there is no principal company of C at the beginning of the relevant day but there is one, or are more than one, at the end of the relevant day.

(3) Condition B is that—

    (a) any principal company of C is a consortium principal company ("CPC"), and

    (b) CPC's ownership proportion at the end of the relevant day is more than at the beginning of the relevant day.

(4) Condition C is that on the relevant day —

    (a) C ceases to carry on the whole or part of the relevant trade, and

    (b) it begins to be carried on in partnership by two or more companies,

in circumstances in which Chapter 1 of Part 22 of CTA 2010 (transfers of trade without change of ownership) applies in relation to the transfer of the relevant trade.

(5) Condition D is that—

    (a) the relevant trade is, at the beginning of the relevant day, carried on by C in partnership, and

    (b) C's relevant percentage share in the relevant trade at the end of the relevant day is less than at the beginning of the relevant day (or is nil).

212D Guide to sections explaining section 212C

(1) Section 212E explains—

    (a) what are principal companies of C, and

    (b) which are consortium principal companies of C,

for the purposes of section 212C(2) and (3).

(2) Section 212F explains—

    (a) when a company is owned by a consortium, and

    (b) who are the members of the consortium,

for the purposes of section 212E.

(3)   Section 212G explains the meaning of "qualifying 75% subsidiary" for the purposes of sections 212E and 212F.

(4)   Section 212H explains the meaning of "ownership proportion" in section 212C(3).

(5)   Section 212I explains the meaning of "relevant percentage share" in section 212C(5).

212E Principal companies

(1)   A company ("U") is a principal company of C if—
  (a)   C is a qualifying 75% subsidiary of U, and
  (b)   U is not a qualifying 75% subsidiary of another company.

(2)   A company ("V") is a principal company of C if—
  (a)   C is a qualifying 75% subsidiary of U,
  (b)   U is a qualifying 75% subsidiary of V, and
  (c)   V is not a qualifying 75% subsidiary of another company.

(3)   If V is a qualifying 75% subsidiary of another company ("W"), W is a principal company of C unless W is a qualifying 75% subsidiary of another company, and so on.

(4)   A company ("X") is a principal company of C if—
  (a)   C is owned by a consortium of which X is a member, or
  (b)   C is a qualifying 75% subsidiary of a company owned by a consortium of which X is a member,
and X is not a qualifying 75% subsidiary of another company.

(5)   A company ("Y") is a principal company of C if—
  (a)   C is owned by a consortium of which X is a member, or
  (b)   C is a qualifying 75% subsidiary of a company owned by a consortium of which X is a member,
and X is a qualifying 75% subsidiary of Y but Y is not a qualifying 75% subsidiary of another company.

(6)   If Y is a qualifying 75% subsidiary of another company ("Z"), Z is a principal company of C unless Z is a qualifying 75% subsidiary of another company, and so on.

(7)   A company that is a principal company of C by virtue of any of subsections (4) to (6) is a consortium principal company of C.

212F When company is owned by consortium and consortium members

(1)   This section defines what a company being owned by, or a member of, a consortium means for the purposes of section 212E.

(2)   A company is owned by a consortium if—
  (a)   it is not a qualifying 75% subsidiary of another company,
  (b)   at least 75% of its ordinary share capital is beneficially owned between them by other companies, and
  (c)   none of those other companies owns less than 5% of that capital.

(3)   Those other companies are the members of the consortium.

212G Qualifying 75% subsidiaries

(1) For the purposes of sections 212E and 212F a company ("the subsidiary company") is a qualifying 75% subsidiary of another company ("the parent company") if condition 1 or 2 is met and condition 3 is met.

(2) Condition 1 is that —
   (a) the subsidiary company has ordinary share capital, and
   (b) the subsidiary company is a 75% subsidiary of the parent company (see section 1154(3) of CTA 2010).

(3) Condition 2 is that —
   (a) the subsidiary company does not have ordinary share capital, and
   (b) the parent company has control of the subsidiary company.

(4) Condition 3 is that the parent company —
   (a) is beneficially entitled to at least 75% of any profits available for distribution to equity holders of the subsidiary company, and
   (b) would be beneficially entitled to at least 75% of any assets of the subsidiary company available for distribution to its equity holders on a winding-up.

(5) Chapter 6 of Part 5 of CTA 2010 (equity holders and profits or assets available for distribution) applies for the purposes of subsection (4) as that Chapter applies for the purposes of section 151(4)(a) and (b) of that Act (meaning of "75% subsidiary").

(6) But in a case where the subsidiary company does not have ordinary share capital, Chapter 6 of Part 5 of that Act applies for those purposes as if the members of that company were equity holders of that company for the purposes of that Chapter.

212H Ownership proportion

(1) For the purposes of section 212C(3) CPC's "ownership proportion" is the lowest of —
   (a) the percentage of the ordinary share capital of C that is beneficially owned by CPC,
   (b) the percentage to which CPC is beneficially entitled of any profits available for distribution to equity holders of C, and
   (c) the percentage to which CPC would be beneficially entitled of any assets of C available for distribution to its equity holders on a winding-up.

(2) Chapter 6 of Part 5 of CTA 2010 applies for the purposes of subsection (1) as that Chapter applies for the purposes of section 143(3)(b) and (c) (condition 1: surrendering company owned by consortium) and section 144(3)(b) and (c) (condition 1: claimant company owned by consortium) of that Act.

(3) But in a case where the subsidiary company does not have ordinary share capital, Chapter 6 of Part 5 of that Act applies for those purposes as if the members of that company were equity holders of that company for the purposes of that Chapter.

212I Relevant percentage share

(1) For the purposes of section 212C(5) C's "relevant percentage share" is C's percentage share in the profits or losses of the trade.

(2) For this purpose C's percentage share in the profits or losses of a trade at any time is determined on a just and reasonable basis.

(3) In making that determination regard must be had, in particular, to any matter that would be taken into account in determining under section 1262 of CTA 2009 (but without regard to sections 1263 and 1264 of that Act) the company's share at that time in the profits or losses of the trade.

Relevant excess of allowances

212J Relevant excess of allowances

(1) C or P has a relevant excess of allowances in relation to the relevant trade if —

$$RTWDV > BSV$$

(2) Section 212K defines RTWDV and section 212L defines BSV.

(3) References in this Chapter to plant and machinery do not include excluded plant and machinery.

(4) Plant and machinery is "excluded plant and machinery" if —

(a) expenditure incurred on the provision of it is not, as a result of section 34A, qualifying expenditure for the purposes of this Part, or

(b) it is, as a result of section 67, treated for the purposes of this Part as owned otherwise than by C or P.

212K Relevant tax written-down value

(1) RTWDV is the relevant tax written-down value and is to be found by adding together amounts 1 and 2.

(2) Amount 1 is the total amount of any unrelieved qualifying expenditure in respect of plant and machinery contained in —

(a) single asset pools,

(b) class pools, or

(c) the main pool,

which is available to be carried forward (in accordance with section 59) from the old period and used in calculating the profits of the relevant trade.

(3) Amount 2 is the total of any qualifying expenditure incurred on the provision of a ship for the purposes of the relevant trade which, at the end of the old period, is unrelieved by virtue of notice having been given under section 130.

(4) For the purposes of this Part the amount of unrelieved qualifying expenditure contained in any pool which is available to be carried forward (in accordance with section 59) from the old period and used in calculating the profits of the relevant trade is to be calculated on the assumptions —

    (a)   that any qualifying expenditure that could have been (but was not) allocated to the pool before the end of the old period had been so allocated at the end of the old period,

    (b)   that any qualifying expenditure prevented from being allocated to the pool by section 58(5) had been so allocated at the end of the old period, and

    (c)   that any transaction taking place on the relevant day that has the effect of reducing the amount of unrelieved qualifying expenditure in the pool had not taken place.

(5)   Where condition C in section 212C is met—

    (a)   references in subsection (2) to any unrelieved qualifying expenditure in respect of plant and machinery contained in a pool which is available to be carried forward (in accordance with section 59) from the old period and used in calculating the profits of the relevant trade, and

    (b)   the reference in subsection (3) to any qualifying expenditure incurred on the provision of a ship for the purposes of the relevant trade which, at the end of the old period, is unrelieved by virtue of notice having been given under section 130,

are to what it would have been but for the qualifying change.

(6)   In this section "the old period" means the period which is the old period for the purposes of section 212O (or would be if this Chapter applied): see section 212N(3).

(7)   The plant and machinery in respect of which there is unrelieved qualifying expenditure such as is mentioned in subsection (2), or qualifying expenditure such as is mentioned in subsection (3), is referred to in the following provisions as "the relevant plant and machinery".

212L Balance sheet value

(1)   BSV is the balance sheet value of the relevant plant and machinery and is to be found by adding together the amounts (if any) which would be shown in respect of it in the appropriate balance sheet of C or P.

(2)   For this purpose the amounts shown in the appropriate balance sheet in respect of the relevant plant or machinery are—

    (a)   the amounts shown in that balance sheet as the net book value (or carrying amount) in respect of it, and

    (b)   the amounts shown in that balance sheet as the net investment in respect of finance leases of it.

(3)   If—

    (a)   any of the relevant plant or machinery is a fixture in any land, and

    (b)   the amount which falls (or would fall) to be shown in the appropriate balance sheet as the net book value (or carrying amount) of the land would include an amount in respect of the fixture,

the amount of the net book value (or carrying amount) in respect of the fixture is determined on a just and reasonable basis.

(4) If—

    (a) any of the relevant plant or machinery is subject to a finance lease, and

    (b) any land or asset which is not plant or machinery is subject to that lease,

the amount of the net investment in respect of the finance lease of that plant or machinery is determined on a just and reasonable basis.

(5) In this section any reference to any amount shown in the appropriate balance sheet of C or P is the amount which, assuming that a balance sheet of C or P were drawn up in accordance with subsection (6), would fall to be shown in that balance sheet.

(6) A balance sheet is drawn up in accordance with this subsection if it is drawn up in accordance with generally accepted accounting practice so as to reflect the position as at the beginning of the relevant day but adjusted to reflect the disposal of any of the relevant plant or machinery which is disposed of on the relevant day.

(7) In this section—

    "finance lease" means a lease which, in accordance with generally accepted accounting practice, falls (or would fall) to be treated as a finance lease or loan in accounts of C or P;

    "fixture"—

        (a) means any plant or machinery that is so installed or otherwise fixed in or to a building or other description of land as to become, in law, part of that building or other land, and

        (b) includes any boiler or water-filled radiator installed in a building as part of a space or water heating system.

Unallowable purpose

212M Unallowable purpose

(1) The qualifying change has an unallowable purpose if the main purpose, or one of the main purposes, of change arrangements is to obtain a relevant tax advantage (for any person).

(2) "Change arrangements" means any arrangements made to bring about, or otherwise connected with, the qualifying change; and "arrangements" includes any agreement, understanding, scheme, transaction or series of transactions (whether or not legally enforceable).

(3) "Obtain a relevant tax advantage" means become entitled to a reduction in profits, or an increase in losses, for the purposes of corporation tax in consequence of a claim to allowances in respect of qualifying expenditure in respect of the relevant plant and machinery or qualifying expenditure within section 212K(3).

What happens when Chapter applies

212N Old and new accounting periods

(1) The accounting period of C which is current on the relevant day ends with that day and a new accounting period of C begins with the following day (but subject to subsection (2)).

(2) In a case in which condition A, B or D in section 212C is met and the relevant trade was, at the beginning of the relevant day, carried on by C in partnership with another company or other companies subsection (1) does not apply but —

    (a) the period which, for the purposes of Part 17 of CTA 2009, is the accounting period of the partnership current on the relevant day ends with that day, and

    (b) there begins with the following day a new accounting period —

        (i) of the partnership, or

        (ii) where condition D is met and C's relevant percentage share in the relevant trade is nil after the qualifying change, of the company or partnership by which the relevant trade is carried on after the relevant change.

(3) For the purposes of section 212O "the old period" means the accounting period of C or the partnership in which C carries on the relevant trade which ends with the relevant day.

(4) For the purposes of section 212P "the new period" means the accounting period —

    (a) of C or that partnership, or

    (b) where condition D is met and C's relevant percentage share in the relevant trade is nil after the qualifying change, of the company or partnership by which the relevant trade is carried on after the relevant change,

which begins with the following day.

212O When there is excess of allowances in pool: amount of excess

(1) Section 212P has effect where C or P has an excess of allowances in any single asset pool, any class pool or the main pool at the end of the old period; and a pool in the case of which there is an excess of allowances is referred to in this section and section 212P as a "relevant pool".

(2) For the purposes of this section C or P has an excess of allowances in a pool if —

$$PA > BSVP$$

(3) In this section and section 212Q —

    PA, in relation to a pool, is the amount specified in section 212K(2) in relation to the pool, and

    BSVP, in relation to a pool, is so much of BSV as, on a just and reasonable apportionment, it is appropriate to attribute to the pool.

(4) For the purposes of section 212P the amount of the excess of allowances in relation to any relevant pool ("the relevant pool in question") is the difference between PA and BSVP.

(5) But if, in relation to any other pool—

$$BSVP > PA$$

what would otherwise be the amount of the excess of allowances in relation to the relevant pool in question for the purposes of section 212P is reduced by so much of the difference between BSVP and PA as is not taken into account under this subsection in relation to another relevant pool or under section 212Q(8).

212P Effect of excess of allowances on pools

(1) The unrelieved qualifying expenditure in each relevant pool is to be taken to be reduced at the beginning of the new period by the amount of the excess of allowances in relation to the pool.

(2) The amount of the excess of allowances is to be treated from the beginning of the new period as if it were qualifying expenditure in a new pool of the same description as the relevant pool (and so subject to the same provisions of this Part, other than this Chapter).

(3) Where, following the qualifying change, a person ceases to carry on a trade (or part of a trade) and C begins to carry on (whether or not in partnership) the activities of that trade (or part of a trade) as part of its trade, for the purposes of claiming any allowance in respect of qualifying expenditure in the new pool the carrying on of those activities by C is to be regarded as the carrying on of a separate trade.

(4) A loss attributable to an allowance claimed in respect of qualifying expenditure in the new pool may not be set off under section 37 of CTA 2010 (trade loss relief against total profits of same or earlier accounting period) otherwise than against the profits of a qualifying activity carried on by C, or any company that is a member of P, at the beginning of the relevant day.

(5) And the amount of such a loss which may be so set off by any person is not to exceed the amount of the loss which would have been available for such set off by the person but for the qualifying change.

(6) A loss attributable to an allowance claimed in respect of qualifying expenditure in the new pool may not be set off by way of group relief in accordance with Part 5 of CTA 2010 (surrender of losses by way of group relief) by a company ("the claimant company") unless it would have been available for such set off but for the qualifying change.

(7) And the amount of such a loss which is available for such set off by the claimant company is not to exceed the amount of the loss which would have been available for such set off by the claimant company but for the qualifying change.

(8) Where any activity not carried on by C, or a company that is a member of P, at the beginning of the relevant day would otherwise be regarded for the purposes of corporation tax as forming part of a qualifying activity carried on by C or the member of P at that time it is not to be so regarded for the purposes of subsection (4).

(9) In a case in which condition C in section 212C is met, the references in subsections (1) and (2) to the beginning of the new period are to the time of the qualifying change (and section 948 of CTA 2010 has effect subject to this section).

212Q When there are postponed capital allowances

(1) This section has effect where C or P has relevant postponed capital allowances.

(2) C or P has relevant postponed capital allowances if amount 2 in section 212K(3) is an amount other than nil.

(3) Where, following the qualifying change, a person ceases to carry on a trade (or part of a trade) and C begins to carry on (whether or not in partnership) the activities of that trade (or part of a trade) as part of its trade, for the purposes of claiming any allowance in respect of qualifying expenditure such as is mentioned in section 212K(3) the carrying on of those activities by C is to be regarded as the carrying on of a separate trade.

(4) A loss attributable to an allowance claimed in respect of qualifying expenditure such as is mentioned in section 212K(3) may not be set off under section 37 of CTA 2010 otherwise than against the profits of a qualifying activity carried on by C, or any company that is a member of P, at the beginning of the relevant day.

(5) And the amount of such a loss which may be so set off by any person is not to exceed the amount of the loss which would have been available for such set off by the person but for the qualifying change.

(6) A loss attributable to an allowance claimed in respect of qualifying expenditure such as is mentioned in section 212K(3) may not be set off by way of group relief in accordance with Part 5 of CTA 2010 by a company ("the claimant company") unless it would have been available for such set off but for the qualifying change.

(7) And the amount of such a loss which is available for such set off by the claimant company is not to exceed the amount of the loss which would have been available for such set off by the claimant company but for the qualifying change.

(8) If, in relation to any pool—
$$BSVP > PA$$
what would otherwise be the amount of qualifying expenditure such as is mentioned in section 212K(3) is to be treated for the purposes of this section as reduced by so much of the difference between BSVP and PA in relation to the pool as is not taken into account under section 212O(5) in relation to a relevant pool.

(9) Where any activity not carried on by C, or a company that is a member of P, at the beginning of the relevant day would otherwise be regarded for the purposes of corporation tax as forming part of a qualifying activity carried on by C or the member of P at that time it is not to be so regarded for the purposes of subsection (4).

212R Apportionment of proceeds of disposal of relevant plant and machinery

Any amount required to be brought into account in connection with a disposal event in respect of any relevant plant and machinery is to be apportioned between the new pool and the relevant pool concerned on a just and reasonable basis.

212S Transactions on relevant day

(1) This section applies if any plant and machinery is transferred on the relevant day and (apart from subsection (4)(c) of section 212K) the transfer would have the effect of reducing RTWDV (as determined in accordance with that section).

(2) No person other than C or P is entitled to claim an allowance in respect of the plant or machinery after the transfer."

3   For the heading of Chapter 17 substitute "OTHER ANTI-AVOIDANCE".

4   Section 247 (giving effect to allowances and charges: trades) is renumbered as subsection (1) of that section; and after that subsection insert—

"(2) See Chapter 16A for provision restricting in certain circumstances the ways in which effect may be given to an allowance by virtue of subsection (1)(a)."

5   The amendments made by this Schedule have effect where the relevant day is on or after 21 July 2009.

6   But in relation to cases where the relevant day is before 9 December 2009 the amendment made by paragraph 2 has effect—

(a)   with the omission of section 212C(2)(b),

(b)   as if in section 212K(1) "which is amount 1" were substituted for "and is to be found by adding together amounts 1 and 2",

(c)   with the omission of section 212K(3) and (4)(c),

(d)   with the omission from section 212O(5) of the words "or under section 212Q(8)",

(e)   with the omission of section 212Q, and

(f)   with the omission of section 212S.

SCHEDULE 5

LEASED ASSETS

Restriction of qualifying expenditure

1   (1) In Chapter 17 of Part 2 of CAA 2001 (plant and machinery: anti-avoidance), after section 228M insert—

"Restriction of qualifying expenditure in case of certain leased assets

228MA Restriction of qualifying expenditure

(1) This section applies where capital expenditure is incurred on the provision of plant or machinery ("the asset") and at the time the expenditure is incurred —

    (a) the asset is leased or arrangements exist under which it is to be leased, and

    (b) arrangements have been entered into in relation to payments under the lease that have the effect of reducing the value of the asset to the lessor ("V").

(2) For the purposes of capital allowances the lessor's qualifying expenditure on the asset is restricted to V.

(3) The value of the asset to the lessor is given by —

$$V = VI + VR$$

where —

    VI is the present value of the lessor's income from the asset, and
    VR is the present value of the residual value of the asset reduced by the amount of any rental rebate.

(4) For this purpose —

    (a) the lessor's income from the asset is the total of all the amounts that —

        (i) have been received by the lessor, or it is reasonable to expect the lessor will receive, in connection with the lease, and

        (ii) have been brought into account by the lessor, or it is reasonable to expect the lessor will bring into account, as income in computing profits chargeable to tax, and

    (b) the residual value of the asset is what it is reasonable to expect will be the market value of the lessor's interest in the asset immediately after the termination of the lease.

(5) In determining the lessor's income from the asset, exclude —

    (a) disposal receipts brought, or to be brought, into account under Part 2, and

    (b) so much of any amount as represents charges for services or qualifying UK or foreign tax (within the meaning of section 70YE) to be paid by the lessor.

(6) Where capital expenditure has previously been incurred by the lessor on the provision of the asset, the reference in subsection (2) to the lessor's qualifying expenditure on the asset is to be read as a reference to the total amount of the lessor's qualifying expenditure on the asset.

(7) The following provisions supplement this section —

    (a) section 228MB provides for the calculation of "present value", and

    (b) section 228MC defines what is meant by a rental rebate.

(8) In this section and sections 228MB and 228MC "lease" includes any arrangements which provide for plant or machinery to be leased or otherwise made available by a person ("the lessor") to another person ("the lessee").

228MB Calculation of present value

(1) For the purposes of section 228MA the "present value" of an amount is to be calculated by using the interest rate implicit in the lease.

(2) The general rule is that the interest rate implicit in the lease is the interest rate that would apply in accordance with normal commercial criteria, including, in particular, generally accepted accounting practice (where applicable).

(3) If the interest rate implicit in the lease cannot be determined in accordance with subsection (2), it is taken to be 1% above LIBOR.

(4) For this purpose —
  (a) LIBOR means the London interbank offered rate on the relevant day for deposits for a term of 12 months in the relevant currency,
  (b) the relevant day is the day on which the lease was entered into (or if that was not a business day, the first business day after that day), and
  (c) the relevant currency is the currency in which rentals under the lease are payable.

228MC Rental rebate

(1) For the purposes of section 228MA "rental rebate" means any sum payable to the lessee that is calculated by reference to the termination value of the asset.

(2) The general rule is that the termination value of an asset is the value of the asset at or about the time when the lease terminates.

(3) Calculation by reference to the termination value includes calculation by reference to any one or more of —
  (a) the proceeds of sale, if the asset is sold,
  (b) any insurance proceeds, compensation or similar sums in respect of the asset, and
  (c) an estimate of the market value of the asset.

(4) Calculation by reference to the termination value also includes —
  (a) determination in a way which, or by reference to factors or criteria which, might reasonably be expected to produce a broadly similar result to calculation by reference to the termination value, or
  (b) any other form of calculation indirectly by reference to the termination value."

(2) The amendment made by sub-paragraph (1) has effect in relation to capital expenditure incurred on or after 9 December 2009.

Restriction of deduction for rental rebate

2   (1) In Chapter 4 of Part 2 of ITTOIA 2005 (trading income: rules restricting deductions), after section 55A insert—

"Rental rebates

55B   Rental rebates

    (1) Where plant or machinery ("the asset") is leased and a rental rebate is payable by the lessor, the amount of the deduction allowable in respect of the rebate is limited to—

        (a) the amount of the lessor's income from the lease, or

        (b) in the case of a finance lease, that amount excluding the finance charge.

    (2) "Rental rebate" means any sum payable to the lessee that is calculated by reference to the termination value of the asset.

    (3) For this purpose—

        (a) the termination value of an asset is the value of the asset at or about the time when the lease terminates,

        (b) calculation by reference to the termination value includes calculation by reference to any one or more of—

            (i) the proceeds of sale, if the asset is sold,

            (ii) any insurance proceeds, compensation or similar sums in respect of the asset,

            (iii) an estimate of the market value of the asset, and

        (c) calculation by reference to the termination value also includes—

            (i) determination in a way which, or by reference to factors or criteria which, might reasonably be expected to produce a broadly similar result to calculation by reference to the termination value, or

            (ii) any other form of calculation indirectly by reference to the termination value.

    (4) For the purposes of this section—

        (a) the income of the lessor from the lease is the total of all the amounts receivable in connection with the lease that have been brought into account in calculating the lessor's income for income tax purposes, excluding—

            (i) disposal receipts brought into account under Part 2 of CAA 2001 (see section 60(1) of that Act), and

            (ii) so much of any amount as represents charges for services or qualifying UK or foreign tax (within the meaning of section 70YE of that Act) to be paid by the lessor, and

        (b) the finance charge, in relation to a finance lease, is—

            (i) if the lease is one that, under generally accepted accounting practice, falls (or would fall) to be treated as a loan, so much of the rentals under the lease as fall (or would fall) to be treated as interest, or

          (ii)   in any other case, the amount that, in accordance with generally accepted accounting practice, falls (or would fall) to be treated as the gross return on investment.

  (5)   Where the asset is acquired by the lessor in a transaction in relation to which an election is made under section 266 of CAA 2001 (election where predecessor and successor are connected persons), this section applies as if the successor had been the lessor at all material times and everything done to or by the predecessor had been done to or by the successor.

  (6)   Where the whole or part of a rental rebate is disallowed under this section as a deduction in computing profits —

      (a)   the amount disallowed, or

      (b)   if less, the amount by which the rental rebate exceeds the amount of capital expenditure incurred by the lessor,

may be treated for the purposes of capital gains tax as an allowable loss accruing to the lessor on the termination of the lease.

That allowable loss is deductible only from chargeable gains accruing to the lessor on the disposal of the asset.

  (7)   This section does not apply to a long funding finance lease (see section 148C)."

(2) In Chapter 4 of Part 3 of CTA 2009 (trading income: rules restricting deductions), after section 60 insert —

"60A Rental rebates

  (1)   Where plant or machinery ("the asset") is leased and a rental rebate is payable by the lessor, the amount of the deduction allowable in respect of the rebate is limited to —

      (a)   the amount of the lessor's income from the lease, or

      (b)   in the case of a finance lease, that amount excluding the finance charge.

  (2)   "Rental rebate" means any sum payable to the lessee that is calculated by reference to the termination value of the asset.

  (3)   For this purpose —

      (a)   the termination value of an asset is the value of the asset at or about the time when the lease terminates,

      (b)   calculation by reference to the termination value includes calculation by reference to any one or more of —

          (i)   the proceeds of sale, if the asset is sold,

          (ii)   any insurance proceeds, compensation or similar sums in respect of the asset, and

          (iii)   an estimate of the market value of the asset, and

      (c)   calculation by reference to the termination value also includes —

          (i)   determination in a way which, or by reference to factors or criteria which, might reasonably be expected to produce a broadly similar result to calculation by reference to the termination value, or

Finance Act 2010 (c. 13) **1547**
Schedule 6 – Charities and community amateur sports clubs: definitions
Part 1 – Definition of "charity", "charitable company" and "charitable trust"

(3) Sub-paragraphs (1) and (2) are subject to any express provision to the contrary.

(4) For the meaning of "charitable purpose", see section 2 of the Charities Act 2006 (which—

    (a) applies regardless of where the body of persons or trust in question is established, and

    (b) for this purpose forms part of the law of each part of the United Kingdom (see section 80(3) to (6) of that Act)).

Jurisdiction condition

2 (1) A body of persons or trust meets the jurisdiction condition if it falls to be subject to the control of—

    (a) a relevant UK court in the exercise of its jurisdiction with respect to charities, or

    (b) any other court in the exercise of a corresponding jurisdiction under the law of a relevant territory.

(2) In sub-paragraph (1)(a) "a relevant UK court" means—

    (a) the High Court,

    (b) the Court of Session, or

    (c) the High Court in Northern Ireland.

(3) In sub-paragraph (1)(b) "a relevant territory" means—

    (a) a member State other than the United Kingdom, or

    (b) a territory specified in regulations made by the Commissioners for Her Majesty's Revenue and Customs.

(4) Regulations under this paragraph are to be made by statutory instrument.

(5) A statutory instrument containing regulations under this paragraph is subject to annulment in pursuance of a resolution of the House of Commons.

Registration condition

3 (1) A body of persons or trust meets the registration condition if—

    (a) in the case of a body of persons or trust that is a charity within the meaning of the Charities Act 1993, condition A is met, and

    (b) in the case of any other body of persons or trust, condition B is met.

(2) Condition A is that the body of persons or trust has complied with any requirement to be registered in the register of charities kept under section 3 of the Charities Act 1993.

(3) Condition B is that the body of persons or trust has complied with any requirement under the law of a territory outside England and Wales to be registered in a register corresponding to that mentioned in sub-paragraph (2).

Management condition

4 (1) A body of persons or trust meets the management condition if its managers are fit and proper persons to be managers of the body or trust.

1548

Finance Act 2010 (c. 13)
Schedule 6 — Charities and community amateur sports clubs: definitions
Part 1 — Definition of "charity", "charitable company" and "charitable trust"

(2) In this paragraph "managers", in relation to a body of persons or trust, means the persons having the general control and management of the administration of the body or trust.

Periods over which management condition treated as met

5 (1) This paragraph applies in relation to any period throughout which the management condition is not met.

(2) The management condition is treated as met throughout the period if the Commissioners for Her Majesty's Revenue and Customs consider that—

(a) the failure to meet the management condition has not prejudiced the charitable purposes of the body or trust, or

(b) it is just and reasonable in all the circumstances for the condition to be treated as met throughout the period.

Publication of names and addresses of bodies or trusts regarded by HMRC as charities

6 Her Majesty's Revenue and Customs may publish the name and address of any body of persons or trust that appears to them to meet, or at any time to have met, the definition of a charity in paragraph 1.

Enactments to which this Part applies

7 The enactments to which this Part applies are the enactments relating to—

(a) income tax

(b) capital gains tax,

(c) corporation tax,

(d) value added tax,

(e) inheritance tax,

(f) stamp duty,

(g) stamp duty land tax, and

(h) stamp duty reserve tax.

PART 2

REPEALS OF SUPERSEDED DEFINITIONS AND OTHER CONSEQUENTIAL AMENDMENTS

FA 1982

8 In section 129(1) of FA 1982 (stamp duty: exemption from duty on grants, transfers to charities etc), for "a body of persons established for charitable purposes only or to the trustees of a trust so established" substitute "a charitable company or to the trustees of a charitable trust".

FA 1983

9 In section 46(3) of FA 1983 (Historic Buildings and Monuments Commission for England) for "a body of persons established for charitable purposes only" substitute "a charitable company".

IHTA 1984

10   In section 272 of IHTA 1984 (general interpretation), omit the definitions of "charity" and "charitable".

FA 1986

11   In section 90(7) of FA 1986 (stamp duty reserve tax: exceptions from principal charge) —

    (a)   in paragraph (a), for "a body of persons established for charitable purposes only" substitute "a charitable company", and

    (b)   in paragraph (b), for "a trust so established" substitute "a charitable trust".

FA 1989

12   In paragraph 4 of Schedule 5 to FA 1989 (employee share ownership trusts), omit sub-paragraph (10).

TCGA 1992

13   (1)   TCGA 1992 is amended as follows.

    (2)   In section 222(8B)(b)(iii) (relief on disposal of private residence), for "established for charitable purposes only" substitute "a charitable company".

    (3)   In section 256 (charities), omit subsections (6) and (8).

    (4)   In section 256C (attributing gains to the non-exempt amount: charitable companies), omit subsection (6).

    (5)   In section 256D (how gains are attributed to the non-exempt amount: charitable companies), omit subsection (7).

F(No.2)A 1997

14   In section 35(3)(a) of F(No.2)A 1997 (transitional relief for charities) omit "(as defined in section 506(1) of the Taxes Act 1988)".

FA 1999

15   (1)   Schedule 19 to FA 1999 (stamp duty and stamp duty reserve tax: unit trusts) is amended as follows.

    (2)   In paragraph 6(3) —

    (a)   in paragraph (a), for "a body of persons established for charitable purposes only" substitute "a charitable company", and

    (b)   in paragraph (b), for "a trust established for those purposes only" substitute "a charitable trust".

    (3)   In paragraph 15(c), for "bodies of persons established for charitable purposes only or trustees of trusts so established" substitute "charitable companies or trustees of charitable trusts".

1550   *Finance Act 2010 (c. 13)*
Schedule 6 — Charities and community amateur sports clubs: definitions
Part 2 — Repeals of superseded definitions and other consequential amendments

CAA 2001

16   In section 63(2) of CAA 2001 (cases in which disposal value is nil) —

    (a)   in paragraph (a), omit "within the meaning of Part 10 of ITA 2007 (see section 519 of that Act)", and

    (b)   in paragraph (aa), omit "within the meaning of Part 11 of CTA 2010 (see section 467 of that Act)".

ITEPA 2003

17   (1)   ITEPA 2003 is amended as follows.

    (2)   In section 99(3)(b)(ii) (accommodation provided for performance of duties), for "established for charitable purposes only" substitute "a charitable company".

    (3)   In section 216(3)(b) (provisions not applicable to lower-paid employments) for "established for charitable purposes only" substitute "a charitable company".

    (4)   In section 223(7)(b)(ii) (payments on account of director's tax other than by the director), for "established for charitable purposes only" substitute "a charitable company".

    (5)   In section 290(5) (accommodation benefits of ministers of religion), omit the definition of "charity".

    (6)   In section 351 (expenses of ministers of religion), omit subsection (5).

    (7)   In section 714(2) (payroll giving: meaning of "donation"), in the definition of "charity", omit "means any body of persons or trust established for charitable purposes only and".

FA 2003

18   Schedule 8 to FA 2003 (SDLT: charities relief) is amended as follows.

19   In paragraph 1 (charities relief), omit sub-paragraph (4).

20   In paragraph 4 (charitable trusts), in sub-paragraph (2), omit "and "charity" has the same meaning as in paragraph 1".

ITTOIA 2005

21   (1)   ITTOIA 2005 is amended as follows.

    (2)   In section 410(3)(b) (when stock dividend income arises), for "trust established for charitable purposes only" substitute "charitable trust".

    (3)   In section 545(1) (definitions for Chapter 9 of Part 4), omit the definition of "charitable trust".

    (4)   In section 568(3) (special rule for certain income of trustees), for "trust established for charitable purposes" substitute "charitable trust".

    (5)   In Part 2 of Schedule 4 (index of defined expressions) —

        (a)   in the entry for "charitable trust (in Chapter 9 of Part 4)" —

            (i)   omit "(in Chapter 9 of Part 4)", and

Finance Act 2010 (c. 13)   1551
Schedule 6 — Charities and community amateur sports clubs: definitions
Part 2 — Repeals of superseded definitions and other consequential amendments

             (ii)   for "section 545(1)" substitute "paragraph 1 of Schedule 6 to FA 2010", and

     (b)   in the entry for "charity", for "section 989 of ITA 2007" substitute "paragraph 1 of Schedule 6 to FA 2010".

F(No.2)A 2005

22   In section 18(3)(b)(i) of F(No.2)A 2005 (authorised unit trusts and OEICS: specific powers) omit "(within the meaning of section 989 of ITA 2007)".

ITA 2007

23   (1) ITA 2007 is amended as follows.

     (2) In section 479(1)(b) (special rates for trustees' income), for "trust established for charitable purposes only" substitute "charitable trust".

     (3) In section 481(1)(c) (other special rates for trustees), for "trust established for charitable purposes only" substitute "charitable trust".

     (4) Omit section 519 (meaning of "charitable trust").

     (5) In section 873(2) (discretionary or accumulation settlements), in paragraphs (a) and (b), for "trust established for charitable purposes only" substitute "charitable trust".

     (6) In section 989 (definitions), omit the definition of "charity".

     (7) In Schedule 4 (index of defined expressions) —
       (a)   in the entry for "charitable trust (in Part 10)" —
             (i)   omit "(in Part 10)", and
             (ii)   for "section 519" substitute "paragraph 1 of Schedule 6 to FA 2010", and
       (b)   in the entries for "charity", "charity (in Chapter 2 of Part 8)" and "charity (in Chapter 3 of Part 8)", for "section 989" substitute "paragraph 1 of Schedule 6 to FA 2010".

FA 2008

24   In paragraph 60(2) of Schedule 36 to FA 2008 (references to carrying on a business), omit the definition of "charity".

CTA 2009

25   (1) CTA 2009 is amended as follows.

     (2) In section 1319 (other definitions), omit the definition of "charity".

     (3) In Schedule 4 (index of defined expressions), in the entry for "charity", for "section 1319" substitute "paragraph 1 of Schedule 6 to FA 2010".

FA 2009

26   In paragraph 8 of Schedule 49 to FA 2009 (general interpretation), omit the definition of "charity".

1552

Finance Act 2010 (c. 13)
Schedule 6 — Charities and community amateur sports clubs: definitions
Part 2 — Repeals of superseded definitions and other consequential amendments

CTA 2010

27 (1) CTA 2010 is amended as follows.

(2) In section 202 (meaning of "charity" in Chapter 2 of Part 6) —
   (a) for "means" substitute "includes", and
   (b) omit paragraph (a).

(3) In section 217 (meaning of "charity" in Chapter 3 of Part 6) —
   (a) for "means" substitute "includes", and
   (b) omit paragraph (a).

(4) Omit section 467 (meaning of "charitable company" in Part 11).

(5) In section 610(2)(a) (discretionary payments by trustees to companies), omit "as defined in section 467".

(6) In section 1119 (definitions), omit the definition of "charity".

(7) In Schedule 4 (index of defined expressions) —
   (a) in the entry for "charitable company (in Part 11)" —
       (i)   omit "(in Part 11)", and
       (ii) for "section 467" substitute "paragraph 1 of Schedule 6 to FA 2010",
   (b) in the entry for "charity (except in Chapters 2 and 3 of Part 6)" for "section 1119" substitute "paragraph 1 of Schedule 6 to FA 2010",
   (c) in the entry for "charity (in Chapter 2 of Part 6)", for "section 202" substitute "paragraph 1 of Schedule 6 to FA 2010 (and see section 202 of this Act)", and
   (d) in the entry for "charity (in Chapter 3 of Part 6)", for "section 217" substitute "paragraph 1 of Schedule 6 to FA 2010 (and see section 217 of this Act)".

TIOPA 2010

28   In section 326(3) of TIOPA 2010 (charities), omit the definition of "charity" and the "and" immediately after it.

Power to make further consequential provision

29 (1) The Commissioners for Her Majesty's Revenue and Customs may by order make such further consequential, incidental, supplemental, transitional or transitory provision or saving as appears appropriate in consequence of, or otherwise in connection with, Part 1.

(2) An order under this paragraph may —
   (a) make different provision for different purposes, and
   (b) make provision repealing, revoking or otherwise amending any enactment or instrument (whenever passed or made).

(3) An order under this paragraph is to be made by statutory instrument.

(4) A statutory instrument containing an order under this paragraph is subject to annulment in pursuance of an order of the House of Commons.

Finance Act 2010 (c. 13) 1553
Schedule 6 — Charities and community amateur sports clubs: definitions
Part 2 — Repeals of superseded definitions and other consequential amendments

PART 3

MEANING OF "COMMUNITY AMATEUR SPORTS CLUB"

30   Chapter 9 of Part 13 of CTA 2010 (community amateur sports clubs) is amended as follows.

31   In section 658(1) (meaning) omit the "and" at the end of paragraph (b) and after paragraph (c) insert—

>   "(d)   meets the location condition (see section 661A), and
>
>   (e)   meets the management condition (see section 661B)."

32   After section 661 insert—

"661A The location condition

(1)   A club meets the location condition for the purposes of section 658 if—

(a)   it is established in a member State or a relevant territory, and

(b)   the facilities that it provides for eligible sports are all located in a single member State or relevant territory.

(2)   In this section "relevant territory" means a territory specified in regulations under paragraph 2(3)(b) of Schedule 6 to FA 2010 (definition of "charity" etc).

661B   The management condition

(1)   A club meets the management condition for the purposes of section 658 if its managers are fit and proper persons to be managers of the club.

(2)   In this paragraph "managers", in relation to a club, means the persons having the general control and management of the administration of the club.

661C   Periods over which management condition treated as met

(1)   This paragraph applies in relation to any period throughout which the management condition is not met.

(2)   The management condition is treated as met throughout the period if the Commissioners for Her Majesty's Revenue and Customs consider that—

(a)   the failure to meet the management condition has not prejudiced the purposes of the club, or

(b)   it is just and reasonable in all the circumstances for the condition to be treated as met throughout the period."

PART 4

COMMENCEMENT

Commencement of Part 1

33   (1)   Part 1 is treated as having come into force on 6 April 2010.

1554

*Finance Act 2010 (c. **13**)*
Schedule 6 — Charities and community amateur sports clubs: definitions
Part 4 — Commencement

(2) But the definitions of "charity", "charitable company" and "charitable trust" in that Part do not apply for the purposes of an enactment in relation to which, on that date, another definition applies until such time as that other definition ceases to have effect on the coming into force of provision made by or under Part 2.

(3) For provision about the coming into force of provision made by that Part, see paragraph 34.

Commencement of Part 2

34 (1) The repeal of the definition of "charity" in section 989 of ITA 2007 made by paragraph 23(6) above has effect—

(a) so far as it applies for the purposes of Chapter 2 of Part 8 of that Act (gift aid), in relation to gifts made on or after 6 April 2010, and

(b) so far as it applies for other purposes, in accordance with such provision as the Treasury may make by order.

(2) The other amendments made by Part 2 come into force in accordance with such provision as the Treasury may make by order.

(3) An order under this paragraph may—

(a) make different provision for different purposes, and

(b) include transitional provision and savings.

(4) An order under this paragraph is to be made by statutory instrument.

Commencement of Part 3

35 The amendments made by Part 3 are treated as having come into force on 6 April 2010.

SCHEDULE 7

Section 31

GIFTS OF SHARES ETC TO CHARITIES

Gifts by individuals

1 Chapter 3 of Part 8 of ITA 2007 (relief for gifts by individuals of shares, securities and real property to charities etc) is amended as follows.

2 (1) Section 437 (value of net benefit to charity) is amended as follows.

(2) In subsection (1), for "market" (in both places) substitute "relevant".

(3) After that subsection insert—

"(1A) In subsection (1) "relevant value" means—

(a) where subsection (1B) applies, the lower of the market value and the acquisition value, and

(b) otherwise, the market value.

(1B) This subsection applies where—

(a) the qualifying investment, or anything from which it derives or which it represents (whether in whole or in part and whether directly or indirectly), was acquired by the individual making the disposal within the period of 4 years ending with the day on which the disposal is made,

    (b)   the acquisition was made as part of a scheme, and

    (c)   the main purpose, or one of the main purposes, of the individual in entering into the scheme was to obtain relief, or an increased amount of relief, under this Chapter.

    (1C)   In subsection (1B) "scheme" includes any scheme, arrangement or understanding of any kind, whether or not legally enforceable, involving a single transaction or two or more transactions."

    (4) In subsection (2), after the entry relating to section 438 insert—

        "section 438A (acquisition value of qualifying investments),".

3   After section 438 insert—

"438A Acquisition value of qualifying investments

    (1)   For the purposes of this Chapter the acquisition value of a qualifying investment disposed of by an individual is—

    (a)   where the qualifying investment was acquired by the individual within the period of 4 years ending with the day on which the disposal is made, the cost to the individual of acquiring it, or

    (b)   where something from which the qualifying investment derives or which it represents was so acquired, such proportion of the cost to the individual of acquiring that thing as is just and reasonable to attribute to the qualifying investment.

    (2)   A reference in subsection (1) to the cost to the individual of an acquisition is to—

    (a)   the consideration given by the individual for the acquisition, less

    (b)   any amount that is received in connection with the acquisition, by the individual or a person connected with the individual, as part of the scheme in question."

4   In Schedule 4 to ITA 2007 (index of defined expressions), after the entry relating to accumulated or discretionary income insert—

"acquisition value of a qualifying investment (in Chapter 3 of Part 8)	section 438A".

Gifts by companies

5   Chapter 3 of Part 6 of CTA 2010 (charitable donations relief: amounts treated as qualifying charitable donations) is amended as follows.

6   (1) Section 209 (value of net benefit to charity) is amended as follows.

    (2) In subsection (1), for "market" (in both places) substitute "relevant".

    (3) After that subsection insert—

"(1A) In subsection (1) "relevant value" means—

    (a) where subsection (1B) applies, the lower of the market value and the acquisition value, and

    (b) otherwise, the market value.

(1B) This subsection applies where—

    (a) the qualifying investment, or anything from which it derives or which it represents (whether in whole or in part and whether directly or indirectly), was acquired by the company making the disposal within the period of 4 years ending with the day on which the disposal is made,

    (b) the acquisition was made as part of a scheme, and

    (c) the main purpose, or one of the main purposes, of the company in entering into the scheme was to obtain relief, or an increased amount of relief, as a result of this Chapter.

(1C) In subsection (1B) "scheme" includes any scheme, arrangement or understanding of any kind, whether or not legally enforceable, involving a single transaction or two or more transactions."

(4) In subsection (2), after paragraph (a) insert—

    "(aa) section 210A (acquisition value of qualifying investments),".

7   After section 210 insert—

"210A Acquisition value of qualifying investments

(1) For the purposes of this Chapter the acquisition value of a qualifying investment disposed of by a company is—

    (a) where the qualifying investment was acquired by the company within the period of 4 years ending with the day on which the disposal is made, the cost to the company of acquiring it, or

    (b) where something from which the qualifying investment derives or which it represents was so acquired, such proportion of the cost to the company of acquiring that thing as is just and reasonable to attribute to the qualifying investment.

(2) A reference in subsection (1) to the cost to the company of an acquisition is to—

    (a) the consideration given by the company for the acquisition, less

    (b) any amount that is received in connection with the acquisition, by the company or a person connected with it, as part of the scheme in question."

8   In Schedule 4 to CTA 2010 (index of defined expressions), after the entry relating to accounts (in Chapter 2 of Part 16) insert—

"acquisition value of a qualifying investment (in Chapter 3 of Part 6)	section 210A".

Commencement and corresponding ICTA amendments

9   The amendments made by this Schedule have effect in relation to any disposal made to a charity on or after 15 December 2009.

10   Amendments corresponding to the ones made by paragraphs 6 and 7, having effect in relation to any such disposal, are to be treated as having been made in section 587B of ICTA.

SCHEDULE 8

Section 32

CHARITIES: MISCELLANEOUS AMENDMENTS

Payroll giving

1   (1) In ITA 2007, after section 521 insert—

"521A Gifts under payroll deduction schemes: income tax liability and exemption

   (1)   This section applies if gifts are made to charitable trusts by individuals and the gifts are donations for the purposes of Part 12 of ITEPA 2003 (payroll giving).

   (2)   Income tax is charged on the gifts under this section.

   (3)   It is charged on the full amount of the gifts arising in the tax year.

   (4)   But a gift is not taken into account in calculating total income so far as it is applied to charitable purposes only.

   (5)   The trustees of the charitable trust are liable for any tax charged under this section."

   (2) In CTA 2010, after section 472 insert—

"472A Gifts under payroll deduction schemes: corporation tax liability and exemption

   (1)   If a charitable company receives a gift from an individual and the gift is a donation for the purposes of Part 12 of ITEPA 2003 (payroll giving), the gift is treated as an amount in respect of which the charitable company is chargeable to corporation tax, under the charge to corporation tax on income.

   (2)   But the gift is not taken into account in calculating total profits so far as it is applied to charitable purposes only.

   (3)   The exemption under subsection (2) requires a claim."

Payments to bodies outside the UK: non-charitable expenditure

2   (1) In section 547(b) of ITA 2007 (payments by charitable trusts to bodies outside the UK), after "such steps as" insert "the Commissioners for Her Majesty's Revenue and Customs consider".

(2) In section 500(b) of CTA 2010 (payments by charitable companies to bodies outside the UK), after "such steps as" insert "the Commissioners for Her Majesty's Revenue and Customs consider".

Gift aid: disqualified overseas gifts

3   (1) Chapter 2 of Part 8 of ITA 2007 (gift aid) is amended as follows.

(2) In section 416 (meaning of "qualifying donation") —
  (a)   in subsection (1)(a) for "G" substitute "F", and
  (b)   omit subsection (8).

(3) Omit section 422 (disqualified overseas gifts).

(4) In section 429(3) (giving through self-assessment return), for "G" substitute "F".

Gift aid administration: charitable trusts

4   (1) Section 42 of TMA 1970 (procedure for making claims etc) is amended as follows.

(2) In subsection (2), for "(3A)" substitute "(3ZA)".

(3) After subsection (3) insert —

  "(3ZA)   Subsection (2) above shall not apply in relation to any claim by the trustees of a charitable trust for an amount to be exempt from tax by virtue of section 521(4) of ITA 2007 (gifts entitling donor to gift aid relief: charitable trusts)."

5   (1) ITA 2007 is amended as follows.

(2) In section 518(4) (overview of Part 10), for "section 538" substitute "sections 538 and 538A".

(3) After section 538 insert —

"538A Claims in relation to gift aid relief

  (1)   This section applies to claims for amounts to be exempt from tax by virtue of section 521(4) (gifts entitling donor to gift aid relief: charitable trusts).

  (2)   A claim to which this section applies may be made —
    (a)   to an officer of Revenue and Customs, or
    (b)   by being included in a return under section 8A of TMA 1970 (trustee's self-assessment return).

  (3)   In this section —
      "free-standing claim" means a claim made as mentioned in subsection (2)(a), and
      "tax return claim" means a claim made as mentioned in subsection (2)(b).

  (4)   The Commissioners for Her Majesty's Revenue and Customs may by regulations make provision —
    (a)   limiting the number of free-standing claims that may be made by a person in a tax year, or

    (b) requiring a claim for an amount below an amount specified in the regulations to be made as a tax return claim.

  (5) The regulations may make different provision for different cases or purposes."

Gift aid administration: charitable companies

6   (1) Schedule 18 to FA 1998 (company tax returns, assessments and related matters) is amended as follows.

  (2) In paragraph 9 (claims that cannot be made without a return), after sub-paragraph (2) insert —

     "(2A) But this paragraph does not apply to a claim by a company for an amount to be exempt from tax by virtue of —

       (a) section 472 of CTA 2010 (gifts qualifying for gift aid relief: charitable companies), or

       (b) section 475 of that Act (gifts qualifying for gift aid relief: eligible bodies)."

  (3) In paragraph 57 (claims or elections affecting a single accounting period), after sub-paragraph (1) insert —

     "(1A) But this paragraph does not apply to a claim by a company for an amount to be exempt from tax by virtue of —

       (a) section 472 of CTA 2010 (gifts qualifying for gift aid relief: charitable companies), or

       (b) section 475 of that Act (gifts qualifying for gift aid relief: eligible bodies)."

7   In CTA 2010, after section 477 insert —

"Claims

477A Claims in relation to gift aid relief

  (1) This section applies to claims for amounts to be exempt from tax by virtue of —

    (a) section 472 (gifts qualifying for gift aid relief: charitable companies), or

    (b) section 475 (gifts qualifying for gift aid relief: eligible bodies).

  (2) A claim to which this section applies may be made —

    (a) to an officer of Revenue and Customs, or

    (b) where the claimant is a company, by being included in the claimant's company tax return.

  (3) In this section —

    "free-standing claim" means a claim made as mentioned in subsection (2)(a), and

    "tax return claim" means a claim made as mentioned in subsection (2)(b).

  (4) The Commissioners for Her Majesty's Revenue and Customs may by regulations make provision —

(a) limiting the number of free-standing claims that may be made by a person in a tax year, or

(b) requiring a claim for an amount below an amount specified in the regulations to be made as a tax return claim.

(5) The regulations may make different provision for different cases or purposes."

Commencement

8 (1) The amendments made by paragraph 1 have effect in relation to gifts made on or after 24 March 2010.

(2) An amendment corresponding to that made by paragraph 1(2), having effect in relation to gifts made on or after that date, is to be treated as having been made in ICTA.

(3) The amendments made by paragraph 2 have effect in relation to payments representing expenditure incurred on or after 24 March.

(4) An amendment corresponding to that made by paragraph 2(2), having effect in relation to payments representing expenditure incurred on or after that date, is to be treated as having been made in ICTA.

(5) The amendments made by paragraph 3 have effect in relation to gifts made on or after 6 April 2010.

(6) The amendments made by paragraphs 4 and 6 have effect in relation to claims whenever made.

SCHEDULE 9

Section 34

FOREIGN CURRENCY BANK ACCOUNTS

1 In TCGA 1992, after section 252 insert—

"252A Foreign currency bank accounts and the remittance basis

Schedule 8A contains provision about the calculation of chargeable gains on disposals of debts to which section 252(1) applies which are not situated in the United Kingdom."

2 In that Act, after Schedule 8 insert—

"SCHEDULE 8A

FOREIGN CURRENCY BANK ACCOUNTS

Introductory

1 (1) This Schedule applies where—

(a) an individual makes a disposal of a debt to which section 252(1) applies ("the relevant disposal"),

(b) the debt ("the section 252 debt") is not situated in the United Kingdom, and

     (c)   money or money's worth which is remitted foreign income ("the section 37 amount") is excluded under section 37 from the consideration for the relevant disposal.

    (2) For this purpose "remitted foreign income" means income of the individual which is chargeable to income tax on the alternative basis of charge set out in Chapter A1 of Part 14 of ITA 2007 (remittance basis).

    (3) In determining whether the condition in sub-paragraph (1)(c) is met, the following provisions of this Schedule are to be ignored.

Section 37 operates to exclude the whole consideration

2   (1) This paragraph applies where the section 37 amount constitutes the whole of the unreduced consideration.

    (2) If the relevant disposal is a part disposal of the section 252 debt, section 42 applies as if the reference in subsection (2)(a) of that section to the consideration for the disposal were a reference to the unreduced consideration for the disposal.

    (3) Any loss accruing to the individual on the relevant disposal is not an allowable loss.

Section 37 operates to exclude part of the consideration

3   (1) This paragraph applies where the section 37 amount constitutes part of the unreduced consideration.

    (2) For the purposes of this Act the relevant disposal is to be treated as if it were —
       (a)   a disposal of so much of the section 252 debt as is represented by the section 37 proportion of the sum mentioned in sub-paragraph (3) ("debt A"), and
       (b)   a separate disposal of so much of the section 252 debt as is represented by the remainder of that sum ("debt B").

    (3) That sum is —
       (a)   if the relevant disposal is a disposal of the whole of the section 252 debt, the sum referred to in section 252(1), and
       (b)   if the relevant disposal is a part disposal of that debt, the proportion of the sum referred to in section 252(1) to which that part disposal relates.

    (4) Sub-paragraphs (5) to (9) apply for the purposes of —
       (a)   the computation of the gain accruing on the disposals under sub-paragraph (2), and
       (b)   the application of Chapter 3 of Part 2 of this Act in relation to the part of the debt (if any) which remains undisposed of.

    (5) The consideration for the disposal (before any exclusion under section 37) is —
       (a)   in the case of debt A, the section 37 amount, and

      (b)   in the case of debt B, the remainder of the unreduced consideration.

  (6) If the relevant disposal is not a part disposal of the section 252 debt —

      (a)   the section 37 proportion of the debt costs and the disposal costs is to be attributed to debt A, and

      (b)   the remaining debt costs and disposal costs are to be attributed to debt B.

  (7) Sub-paragraphs (8) and (9) apply if the relevant disposal is a part disposal of the section 252 debt.

  (8) Section 42(2) applies as if it provided for the debt costs to be apportioned between debt A, debt B and the remainder of the section 252 debt in the proportions which those parts of the section 252 debt bear to one another.

  (9) The section 37 proportion of the disposal costs is to be attributed to debt A and the remaining disposal costs are to be attributed to debt B.

  (10) Any loss accruing to the individual on the disposal of debt A is not an allowable loss.

Interpretation

4   In this Schedule —

      "debt costs" means the sums which under section 38(1)(a) and (b) are attributable to the section 252 debt;

      "disposal costs" means the costs within section 38(1)(c) in relation to the relevant disposal;

      "the section 252 debt", "the relevant disposal" and "the section 37 amount" are to be construed in accordance with paragraph 1;

      "the section 37 proportion" means the proportion of the unreduced consideration which constitutes the section 37 amount;

      "the unreduced consideration" means the consideration for the relevant disposal ignoring the exclusion of the section 37 amount."

3   The amendments made by this Schedule have effect in relation to disposals on or after 16 December 2009.

SCHEDULE 10

PENALTIES: OFFSHORE INCOME ETC

Schedule 24 to FA 2007

1   Schedule 24 to FA 2007 (penalties for errors) is amended as follows.

2   For paragraph 4 substitute —

"4   (1) This paragraph sets out the penalty payable under paragraph 1.

(2) If the inaccuracy is in category 1, the penalty is —

    (a) for careless action, 30% of the potential lost revenue,

    (b) for deliberate but not concealed action, 70% of the potential lost revenue, and

    (c) for deliberate and concealed action, 100% of the potential lost revenue.

(3) If the inaccuracy is in category 2, the penalty is —

    (a) for careless action, 45% of the potential lost revenue,

    (b) for deliberate but not concealed action, 105% of the potential lost revenue, and

    (c) for deliberate and concealed action, 150% of the potential lost revenue.

(4) If the inaccuracy is in category 3, the penalty is —

    (a) for careless action, 60% of the potential lost revenue,

    (b) for deliberate but not concealed action, 140% of the potential lost revenue, and

    (c) for deliberate and concealed action, 200% of the potential lost revenue.

(5) Paragraph 4A explains the 3 categories of inaccuracy.

4A   (1) An inaccuracy is in category 1 if —

    (a) it involves a domestic matter, or

    (b) it involves an offshore matter and —

        (i) the territory in question is a category 1 territory, or

        (ii) the tax at stake is a tax other than income tax or capital gains tax.

(2) An inaccuracy is in category 2 if —

    (a) it involves an offshore matter,

    (b) the territory in question is a category 2 territory, and

    (c) the tax at stake is income tax or capital gains tax.

(3) An inaccuracy is in category 3 if —

    (a) it involves an offshore matter,

    (b) the territory in question is a category 3 territory, and

    (c) the tax at stake is income tax or capital gains tax.

(4) An inaccuracy "involves an offshore matter" if it results in a potential loss of revenue that is charged on or by reference to —

    (a) income arising from a source in a territory outside the UK,

    (b) assets situated or held in a territory outside the UK,

    (c) activities carried on wholly or mainly in a territory outside the UK, or

    (d) anything having effect as if it were income, assets or activities of a kind described above.

(5) An inaccuracy "involves a domestic matter" if it results in a potential loss of revenue that is charged on or by reference to anything not mentioned in sub-paragraph (4)(a) to (d).

(6) If a single inaccuracy is in more than one category (each referred to as a "relevant category") —

    (a) it is to be treated for the purposes of this Schedule as if it were separate inaccuracies, one in each relevant category according to the matters that it involves, and

    (b) the potential lost revenue is to be calculated separately in respect of each separate inaccuracy.

(7) "Category 1 territory", "category 2 territory" and "category 3 territory" are defined in paragraph 21A.

(8) "Assets" has the meaning given in section 21(1) of TCGA 1992, but also includes sterling.

4B   The penalty payable under paragraph 1A is 100% of the potential lost revenue.

4C   The penalty payable under paragraph 2 is 30% of the potential lost revenue.

4D   Paragraphs 5 to 8 define "potential lost revenue"."

3   For paragraph 10 substitute—

"10 (1) If a person who would otherwise be liable to a penalty of a percentage shown in column 1 of the Table (a "standard percentage") has made a disclosure, HMRC must reduce the standard percentage to one that reflects the quality of the disclosure.

(2) But the standard percentage may not be reduced to a percentage that is below the minimum shown for it—

    (a) in the case of a prompted disclosure, in column 2 of the Table, and

    (b) in the case of an unprompted disclosure, in column 3 of the Table.

Standard %	Minimum % for prompted disclosure	Minimum % for unprompted disclosure
30%	15%	0%
45%	22.5%	0%
60%	30%	0%
70%	35%	20%
105%	52.5%	30%
140%	70%	40%
100%	50%	30%
150%	75%	45%

Standard %	Minimum % for prompted disclosure	Minimum % for unprompted disclosure
200%	100%	60%".

4   In paragraph 12 (interaction with other penalties), for sub-paragraph (4) substitute –

"(4) Where penalties are imposed under paragraphs 1 and 1A in respect of the same inaccuracy, the aggregate of the amounts of the penalties must not exceed the relevant percentage of the potential lost revenue.

(5) The relevant percentage is –
  (a) if the penalty imposed under paragraph 1 is for an inaccuracy in category 1, 100%,
  (b) if the penalty imposed under paragraph 1 is for an inaccuracy in category 2, 150%, and
  (c) if the penalty imposed under paragraph 1 is for an inaccuracy in category 3, 200%."

5   In Part 5 (general), before the heading "*Interpretation*" insert –

"*Classification of territories*

21A (1) A category 1 territory is a territory designated as a category 1 territory by order made by the Treasury.

(2) A category 2 territory is a territory that is neither –
  (a) a category 1 territory, nor
  (b) a category 3 territory.

(3) A category 3 territory is a territory designated as a category 3 territory by order made by the Treasury.

(4) In considering how to classify a territory for the purposes of this paragraph, the Treasury must have regard to –
  (a) the existence of any arrangements between the UK and that territory for the exchange of information for tax enforcement purposes,
  (b) the quality of any such arrangements (in particular, whether they provide for information to be exchanged automatically or on request), and
  (c) the benefit that the UK would be likely to obtain from receiving information from that territory, were such arrangements to exist with it.

(5) An order under this paragraph is to be made by statutory instrument.

(6) Subject to sub-paragraph (7), an instrument containing an order under this paragraph is subject to annulment in pursuance of a resolution of the House of Commons.

(7) If the order is –

    (a)   the first order to be made under sub-paragraph (1), or

    (b)   the first order to be made under sub-paragraph (3),

it may not be made unless a draft of the instrument containing it has been laid before, and approved by a resolution of, the House of Commons.

(8) An order under this paragraph does not apply to inaccuracies in a document given to HMRC (or, in a case within paragraph 3(2), inaccuracies discovered by P) before the date on which the order comes into force.

Location of assets etc

21B (1) The Treasury may by regulations make provision for determining for the purposes of paragraph 4A where—

    (a)   a source of income is located,

    (b)   an asset is situated or held, or

    (c)   activities are wholly or mainly carried on.

(2) Different provision may be made for different cases and for income tax and capital gains tax.

(3) Regulations under this paragraph are to be made by statutory instrument.

(4) An instrument containing regulations under this paragraph is subject to annulment in pursuance of a resolution of the House of Commons."

6   After paragraph 23A insert—

"23B   "UK" means the United Kingdom, including the territorial sea of the United Kingdom."

Schedule 41 to FA 2008

7   Schedule 41 to FA 2008 (penalties: failure to notify and certain VAT and excise wrongdoing) is amended as follows.

8   For paragraph 6 substitute—

"6   (1) This paragraph sets out the penalty payable under paragraph 1.

(2) If the failure is in category 1, the penalty is—

    (a)   for a deliberate and concealed failure, 100% of the potential lost revenue,

    (b)   for a deliberate but not concealed failure, 70% of the potential lost revenue, and

    (c)   for any other case, 30% of the potential lost revenue.

(3) If the failure is in category 2, the penalty is—

    (a)   for a deliberate and concealed failure, 150% of the potential lost revenue,

    (b)   for a deliberate but not concealed failure, 105% of the potential lost revenue, and

    (c)   for any other case, 45% of the potential lost revenue.

    (4) If the failure is in category 3, the penalty is—

        (a) for a deliberate and concealed failure, 200% of the potential lost revenue,

        (b) for a deliberate but not concealed failure, 140% of the potential lost revenue, and

        (c) for any other case, 60% of the potential lost revenue.

    (5) Paragraph 6A explains the 3 categories of failure.

6A (1) A failure is in category 1 if—

        (a) it involves a domestic matter, or

        (b) it involves an offshore matter and—

              (i) the territory in question is a category 1 territory, or

             (ii) the tax at stake is a tax other than income tax or capital gains tax.

    (2) A failure is in category 2 if—

        (a) it involves an offshore matter,

        (b) the territory in question is a category 2 territory, and

        (c) the tax at stake is income tax or capital gains tax.

    (3) A failure is in category 3 if—

        (a) it involves an offshore matter,

        (b) the territory in question is a category 3 territory, and

        (c) the tax at stake is income tax or capital gains tax.

    (4) A failure "involves an offshore matter" if it results in a potential loss of revenue that is charged on or by reference to—

        (a) income arising from a source in a territory outside the UK,

        (b) assets situated or held in a territory outside the UK,

        (c) activities carried on wholly or mainly in a territory outside the UK, or

        (d) anything having effect as if it were income, assets or activities of a kind described above.

    (5) A failure "involves a domestic matter" if it results in a potential loss of revenue that is charged on or by reference to anything not mentioned in sub-paragraph (4)(a) to (d).

    (6) If a single failure is in more than one category (each referred to as a "relevant category")—

        (a) it is to be treated for the purposes of this Schedule as if it were separate failures, one in each relevant category according to the matters that it involves, and

        (b) the potential lost revenue in respect of each separate failure is taken to be such share of the potential lost revenue in respect of the single failure (see paragraphs 7 and 11) as is just and reasonable.

    (7) For the purposes of this Schedule—

        (a) paragraph 21A of Schedule 24 to FA 2007 (classification of territories) has effect, but

     (b)   an order under that paragraph does not apply to relevant obligations that are to be complied with by a date before the date on which the order comes into force.

   (8) Regulations under paragraph 21B of Schedule 24 to FA 2007 (location of assets etc) apply for the purposes of paragraph 6A of this Schedule as they apply for the purposes of paragraph 4A of that Schedule.

   (9) In this paragraph—

     "assets" has the meaning given in section 21(1) of TCGA 1992, but also includes sterling;

     "UK" means the United Kingdom, including the territorial sea of the United Kingdom.

6B   The penalty payable under any of paragraphs 2, 3(1) and 4 is—

     (a)   for a deliberate and concealed act or failure, 100% of the potential lost revenue,

     (b)   for a deliberate but not concealed act or failure, 70% of the potential lost revenue, and

     (c)   for any other case, 30% of the potential lost revenue.

6C   The penalty payable under paragraph 3(2) is 100% of the potential lost revenue.

6D   Paragraphs 7 to 11 define "potential lost revenue"."

9   For paragraph 13 substitute—

   "13 (1) If a person who would otherwise be liable to a penalty of a percentage shown in column 1 of the Table (a "standard percentage") has made a disclosure, HMRC must reduce the standard percentage to one that reflects the quality of the disclosure.

   (2) But the standard percentage may not be reduced to a percentage that is below the minimum shown for it—

     (a)   for a prompted disclosure, in column 2 of the Table, and

     (b)   for an unprompted disclosure, in column 3 of the Table.

   (3) Where the Table shows a different minimum for case A and case B—

     (a)   the case A minimum applies if—

       (i)   the penalty is one under paragraph 1, and

       (ii)   HMRC become aware of the failure less than 12 months after the time when the tax first becomes unpaid by reason of the failure, and

     (b)   otherwise, the case B minimum applies.

Standard %	Minimum % for prompted disclosure	Minimum % for unprompted disclosure
30%	case A: 10% case B: 20%	case A: 0% case B: 10%
45%	case A: 15% case B: 30%	case A: 0% case B: 15%
60%	case A: 20% case B: 40%	case A: 0% case B: 20%
70%	35%	20%
105%	52.5%	30%
140%	70%	40%
100%	50%	30%
150%	75%	45%
200%	100%	60%".

Schedule 55 to FA 2009

10   Schedule 55 to FA 2009 (penalties for failure to make returns etc) is amended as follows.

11   (1) Paragraph 6 (amount of penalty if failure continues more than 12 months) is amended as follows.

(2) In sub-paragraph (3)(a), for "100%" substitute "the relevant percentage".

(3) After sub-paragraph (3) insert—

"(3A)   For the purposes of sub-paragraph (3)(a), the relevant percentage is—

(a)   for the withholding of category 1 information, 100%,

(b)   for the withholding of category 2 information, 150%, and

(c)   for the withholding of category 3 information, 200%."

(4) In sub-paragraph (4)(a), for "70%" substitute "the relevant percentage".

(5) After sub-paragraph (4) insert—

"(4A)   For the purposes of sub-paragraph (4)(a), the relevant percentage is—

(a)   for the withholding of category 1 information, 70%,

(b)   for the withholding of category 2 information, 105%, and

(c)   for the withholding of category 3 information, 140%."

(6) After sub-paragraph (5) insert—

"(6)   Paragraph 6A explains the 3 categories of information."

12   After paragraph 6 insert—

"6A (1) Information is category 1 information if—

   (a) it involves a domestic matter, or

   (b) it involves an offshore matter and—

      (i) the territory in question is a category 1 territory, or

      (ii) it is information which would enable or assist HMRC to assess P's liability to a tax other than income tax or capital gains tax.

(2) Information is category 2 information if—

   (a) it involves an offshore matter,

   (b) the territory in question is a category 2 territory, and

   (c) it is information which would enable or assist HMRC to assess P's liability to income tax or capital gains tax.

(3) Information is category 3 information if—

   (a) it involves an offshore matter,

   (b) the territory in question is a category 3 territory, and

   (c) it is information which would enable or assist HMRC to assess P's liability to income tax or capital gains tax.

(4) Information "involves an offshore matter" if the liability to tax which would have been shown in the return includes a liability to tax charged on or by reference to—

   (a) income arising from a source in a territory outside the UK,

   (b) assets situated or held in a territory outside the UK,

   (c) activities carried on wholly or mainly in a territory outside the UK, or

   (d) anything having effect as if it were income, assets or activities of a kind described above.

(5) Information "involves a domestic matter" if the liability to tax which would have been shown in the return includes a liability to tax charged on or by reference to anything not mentioned in sub-paragraph (4)(a) to (d).

(6) If the information which P withholds falls into more than one category—

   (a) P's failure to make the return is to be treated for the purposes of this Schedule as if it were separate failures, one for each category of information according to the matters which the information involves, and

   (b) for each separate failure, the liability to tax which would have been shown in the return in question is taken to be such share of the liability to tax which would have been shown in the return mentioned in paragraph (a) as is just and reasonable.

(7) For the purposes of this Schedule—

   (a) paragraph 21A of Schedule 24 to FA 2007 (classification of territories) has effect, but

      (b)   an order under that paragraph does not apply to a failure if the filing date is before the date on which the order comes into force.

   (8) Regulations under paragraph 21B of Schedule 24 to FA 2007 (location of assets etc) apply for the purposes of paragraph 6A of this Schedule as they apply for the purposes of paragraph 4A of that Schedule.

   (9) In this paragraph—

      "assets" has the meaning given in section 21(1) of TCGA 1992, but also includes sterling;

      "UK" means the United Kingdom, including the territorial sea of the United Kingdom."

13   (1) Paragraph 15 (reductions for disclosure) is amended as follows.

   (2) For sub-paragraphs (1) and (2) substitute—

     "(1) If a person who would otherwise be liable to a penalty of a percentage shown in column 1 of the Table (a "standard percentage") has made a disclosure, HMRC must reduce the standard percentage to one that reflects the quality of the disclosure.

     (2) But the standard percentage may not be reduced to a percentage that is below the minimum shown for it—

        (a) in the case of a prompted disclosure, in column 2 of the Table, and

        (b) in the case of an unprompted disclosure, in column 3 of the Table.

Standard %	Minimum % for prompted disclosure	Minimum % for unprompted disclosure
70%	35%	20%
105%	52.5%	30%
140%	70%	40%
100%	50%	30%
150%	75%	45%
200%	100%	60%".

   (3) Omit sub-paragraphs (3) and (4).

14   In paragraph 17 (interaction with other penalties)—

      (a) in sub-paragraph (3), for "100%" substitute "the relevant percentage", and

      (b) after that sub-paragraph insert—

     "(4) The relevant percentage is—

    (a)   if one of the penalties is a penalty under paragraph 6(3) or (4) and the information withheld is category 3 information, 200%,

    (b)   if one of the penalties is a penalty under paragraph 6(3) or (4) and the information withheld is category 2 information, 150%, and

    (c)   in all other cases, 100%."

SCHEDULE 11

RELIEFS AND REDUCTIONS FOR FOREIGN TAX

Effect of foreign tax becoming payable

1   (1) Paragraph 3 of Schedule 28AB to ICTA (schemes about effect of paying foreign tax) is amended as follows.

    (2) In sub-paragraph (2)—

        (a)   in paragraph (a), after "paid" insert "or payable", and

        (b)   in paragraph (b), for "of the payment of that amount of foreign tax on the foreign tax total" substitute "on the foreign tax total of that amount being so paid or payable".

    (3) In sub-paragraph (3)(b), for "the payment by the claimant of that amount of foreign tax" substitute "that amount of foreign tax being paid or payable by the claimant".

2   (1) Section 85 of TIOPA 2010 (schemes about effect of paying foreign tax) is amended as follows.

    (2) In subsection (2)—

        (a)   for paragraph (a) substitute—

            "(a)   an amount of foreign tax ("the FT amount") is paid or payable by C, and", and

        (b)   in paragraph (b), for "of the payment of the FT amount on the foreign-tax total" substitute "on the foreign-tax total of the FT amount being so paid or payable".

    (3) In subsection (3), in paragraph (b) of the definition of "the foreign-tax total", for "the payment by C of the FT amount" substitute "the FT amount being paid or payable by C".

3   (1) The amendments made by paragraphs 1 and 2 have effect in relation to amounts of foreign tax payable on or after 21 October 2009.

    (2) But see paragraph 5 for amounts of foreign tax payable on or after 1 April 2010 (as regards corporation tax) or 6 April 2010 (as regards income tax or capital gains tax).

Schemes about deemed foreign tax

4   (1) In TIOPA 2010, after section 85 insert—

"85A Section 83(2) and (4): schemes involving deemed foreign tax

(1)   This section applies to a scheme or arrangement if in relation to a claimant—

    (a)   an amount ("amount X") is treated by virtue of a provision of the Tax Acts as if it were an amount of foreign tax paid or payable by the claimant in respect of a source of income, and

    (b)   condition A or B is met.

(2)   Condition A is met if, when the claimant entered into the scheme or arrangement, it could reasonably be expected that, under the scheme or arrangement, no real foreign tax would be paid or payable by a participant.

(3)   Condition B is met if, when the claimant entered into the scheme or arrangement, it could reasonably be expected that, under the scheme or arrangement—

    (a)   an amount of real foreign tax ("the RFT amount") would be paid or payable by a participant, but

    (b)   the effect on the foreign-tax total of the RFT amount being so paid or payable would be to increase the foreign-tax total by less than the amount allowable to the claimant as a credit in respect of amount X.

(4)   In this section—

    "claimant" means a person who for a chargeable period has claimed, or is in a position to claim, for any credit that under the arrangements is to be allowed for foreign tax;

    "the foreign-tax total" has the meaning given by section 85(3), except that the reference to "the FT amount being paid or payable by C" must be read as a reference to "the RFT amount being paid or payable by any of them";

    "income" includes a chargeable gain;

    "participant" means a person who is party to, or concerned in, the scheme or arrangement;

    "real foreign tax" means—

    (a)   in a case involving section 10 (accrued income profits), the foreign tax chargeable in respect of the interest on the securities, as mentioned in subsection (1)(c) of that section,

    (b)   in a case involving section 792 or 794 of CTA 2010 (manufactured overseas dividends), the foreign tax chargeable in respect of the overseas dividend of which the manufactured overseas dividend is representative, as mentioned in section 790 of that Act, and

    (c)   in any other case, the foreign tax chargeable in respect of the source of income of which the source mentioned in subsection (1)(a) is representative."

(2)   The amendment made by this paragraph has effect in relation to amounts treated as if they were amounts of foreign tax paid or payable on or after 21 October 2009.

(3) A corresponding amendment, having effect in relation to such amounts, is to be treated as having been made in Schedule 28AB to ICTA.

Foreign tax payable by other participants

5 (1) In section 85 of TIOPA 2010 (schemes about effect of paying foreign tax) as amended by paragraph 2 —

    (a) in subsection (1), for "for foreign tax" substitute "in respect of the payment of an amount of foreign tax ("the FT amount")",

    (b) for subsection (2) substitute —

        "(2) The condition is that, when C entered into the scheme or arrangement, it could reasonably be expected that the effect on the foreign-tax total of the FT amount being paid or payable would be to increase that total by less than amount X.", and

    (c) in subsection (3) —

        (i) for "subsection (2)(b)" substitute "subsection (2)", and

        (ii) in paragraph (b) of the definition of "the foreign-tax total", omit "by C".

(2) In section 85A of TIOPA 2010 (schemes involving deemed foreign tax) as inserted by paragraph 4 —

    (a) in subsection (1)(a), omit "by the claimant", and

    (b) in subsection (4), in the definition of "the foreign-tax total", omit "by C".

(3) The amendments made by this paragraph have effect in relation to amounts of foreign tax, or amounts treated as if they were amounts of foreign tax, payable —

    (a) as regards corporation tax, on or after 1 April 2010, and

    (b) as regards income tax or capital gains tax, on or after 6 April 2010.

Claims etc made before scheme or arrangement made

6 (1) In section 86 of TIOPA 2010 (schemes about claims or elections etc) —

    (a) in subsection (1), omit "under the scheme or arrangement", and

    (b) after subsection (3) insert —

        "(3A) Reference in subsection (1) to a step that is taken or not taken by a participant includes one that was taken or not taken by a participant before the scheme or arrangement was made.

        (3B) The reason for taking or not taking a step does not matter so long as it has the effect mentioned in subsection (1)."

(2) The amendments made by this paragraph have effect in relation to amounts of foreign tax payable —

    (a) as regards corporation tax, on or after 1 April 2010, and

    (b) as regards income tax or capital gains tax, on or after 6 April 2010.

Limit on reduction for foreign tax

7 (1) In section 112 of TIOPA 2010 (deduction from income for foreign tax), after subsection (2) insert —

"(2A)   But if X is less than Y, an amount equal to the difference between X and Y must be subtracted from the amount by which any income of a person ("the relevant income") is reduced under subsection (1)(a).

(2B)   In subsection (2A)—

X is the amount of the relevant income that the person would (disregarding this section) be required to bring into account for income tax or corporation tax purposes, less any deduction that the person would be allowed to make for the amount paid in respect of non-UK tax, and

Y is the amount of the relevant income (that is to say, the amount on which the amount in respect of non-UK tax is paid)."

(2)   The amendment made by this paragraph has effect in relation to amounts in respect of non-UK tax that are paid—

(a)   as regards corporation tax, on or after 1 April 2010, and

(b)   as regards income tax, on or after 6 April 2010.

SCHEDULE 12

Section 58

TRANSACTIONS IN SECURITIES

Income tax

1   Chapter 1 of Part 13 of ITA 2007 (transactions in securities: income tax advantages) is amended as follows.

2   For sections 682 to 694 substitute—

"Introduction

682   Overview of Chapter

This Chapter makes provision for counteracting income tax advantages from transactions in securities.

683   Provisions of Chapter

(1)   Sections 684 to 687 specify when a person is liable to counteraction of income tax advantages from transactions in securities.

(2)   Sections 695 to 700 make provision about the procedure for counteraction of such income tax advantages.

(3)   Sections 701 and 702 make provision for a clearance procedure.

(4)   Section 705 makes provision for appeals against counteraction notices.

(5)   Sections 712 deals with cases in which a person liable to counteraction dies.

(6)   Section 713 contains interpretative provisions.

Person liable to counteraction of income tax advantages

684   **Person liable to counteraction of income tax advantage**

(1)   This section applies to a person where—

    (a)   the person is a party to a transaction in securities or two or more transactions in securities (see subsection (2)),

    (b)   the circumstances are covered by section 685 and not excluded by section 686,

    (c)   the main purpose, or one of the main purposes, of the person in being a party to the transaction in securities, or any of the transactions in securities, is to obtain an income tax advantage, and

    (d)   the person obtains an income tax advantage in consequence of the transaction or the combined effect of the transactions.

(2)   In this Chapter "transaction in securities" means a transaction, of whatever description, relating to securities, and includes in particular—

    (a)   the purchase, sale or exchange of securities,

    (b)   issuing or securing the issue of new securities,

    (c)   applying or subscribing for new securities, and

    (d)   altering or securing the alteration of the rights attached to securities.

(3)   Section 687 defines "income tax advantage".

(4)   This section is subject to—

    section 696(3) (disapplication of this section where person receiving preliminary notification that section 684 may apply makes statutory declaration and relevant officer of Revenue and Customs sees no reason to take further action), and

    section 697(5) (determination by tribunal that there is no prima facie case that section 684 applies).

685   **Receipt of consideration in connection with distribution by or assets of close company**

(1)   The circumstances covered by this section are circumstances where condition A or condition B is met.

(2)   Condition A is that, as a result of the transaction in securities or any one or more of the transactions in securities, the person receives relevant consideration in connection with—

    (a)   the distribution, transfer or realisation of assets of a close company,

    (b)   the application of assets of a close company in discharge of liabilities, or

    (c)   the direct or indirect transfer of assets of one close company to another close company,

and does not pay or bear income tax on the consideration (apart from this Chapter).

(3)   Condition B is that—

      (a)   the person receives relevant consideration in connection with the transaction in securities or any one or more of the transactions in securities,

      (b)   two or more close companies are concerned in the transaction or transactions in securities concerned, and

      (c)   the person does not pay or bear income tax on the consideration (apart from this Chapter).

(4)   In a case within subsection (2)(a) or (b) "relevant consideration" means consideration which—

      (a)   is or represents the value of—

          (i)   assets which are available for distribution by way of dividend by the company, or

          (ii)   assets which would have been so available apart from anything done by the company,

      (b)   is received in respect of future receipts of the company, or

      (c)   is or represents the value of trading stock of the company.

(5)   In a case within subsection (2)(c) or (3) "relevant consideration" means consideration which consists of any share capital or any security issued by a close company and which is or represents the value of assets which—

      (a)   are available for distribution by way of dividend by the company,

      (b)   would have been so available apart from anything done by the company, or

      (c)   are trading stock of the company.

(6)   The references in subsection (2)(a) and (b) to assets do not include assets which are shown to represent a return of sums paid by subscribers on the issue of securities, despite the fact that under the law of the country in which the company is incorporated assets of that description are available for distribution by way of dividend.

(7)   So far as subsection (2)(c) or (3) relates to share capital other than redeemable share capital, it applies only so far as the share capital is repaid (on a winding up or otherwise); and for this purpose any distribution made in respect of any shares on a winding up or dissolution of the company is to be treated as a repayment of share capital.

(8)   References in this section to the receipt of consideration include references to the receipt of any money or money's worth.

(9)   In this section—

      "security" includes securities not creating or evidencing a charge on assets;

      "share" includes stock and any other interest of a member in a company.

686   Excluded circumstances: fundamental change of ownership

(1)   Circumstances are excluded by this section if—

      (a)   immediately before the transaction in securities (or the first of the transactions in securities) the person (referred to in this section as "the party") holds shares or an interest in shares in the close company, and

(b) there is a fundamental change of ownership of the close company.

(2) There is a fundamental change of ownership of the close company if —

(a) as a result of the transaction or transactions in securities, conditions A, B and C are met, and

(b) those conditions continue to be met for a period of 2 years.

(3) Condition A is that at least 75% of the ordinary share capital of the close company is held beneficially by —

(a) a person who is not connected with the party and has not been so connected within the period of 2 years ending with the day on which the transaction in securities (or the first of the transactions in securities) takes place, or

(b) persons none of whom is so connected or has been so connected within that period.

(4) Condition B is that shares in the close company held by that person or those persons carry an entitlement to at least 75% of the distributions which may be made by the company.

(5) Condition C is that shares so held carry at least 75% of the total voting rights in the close company.

687 Income tax advantage

(1) For the purposes of this Chapter the person obtains an income tax advantage if —

(a) the amount of any income tax which would be payable by the person in respect of the relevant consideration if it constituted a qualifying distribution exceeds the amount of any capital gains tax payable in respect of it, or

(b) income tax would be payable by the person in respect of the relevant consideration if it constituted a qualifying distribution and no capital gains tax is payable in respect of it.

(2) So much of the relevant consideration as exceeds the maximum amount that could in any circumstances have been paid to the person by way of a qualifying distribution at the time when the relevant consideration is received is to be left out of account for the purposes of subsection (1).

(3) The amount of the income tax advantage is the amount of the excess or (if no capital gains tax is payable) the amount of the income tax which would be payable.

(4) In this section "relevant consideration" has the same meaning as in section 685."

3 In section 698(6) (counteraction notices), omit —

(a) the entry relating to section 699, and

(b) in the entry relating to section 700, "in section 690 cases".

4 Omit section 699 (limit on amount assessed in section 689 and 690 cases).

5   In section 700 (timing of assessments in section 690 cases) —

    (a)   in subsection (1), for "690 (receipt of relevant company assets (circumstance E))" substitute "685(2)(c) or (3)", and

    (b)   in the heading, omit "**in section 690 cases**".

6   In the heading before section 701, omit "*and information powers*".

7   (1) Section 713 (interpretation) is amended as follows.

    (2) Before the definition of "company" insert —

        ""close company" includes a company that would be a close company if it were resident in the United Kingdom,".

    (3) Omit the definition of "transaction in securities".

Corporation tax

8   Part 15 of CTA 2010 (transactions in securities: corporation tax advantages) is amended as follows.

9   In section 733(2) (company liable to counteraction of corporation tax advantage), omit the entry relating to section 735.

10   Omit section 735 (abnormal dividends used for exemptions or reliefs).

Consequential amendments

11   In section 809S of ITA 2007 (remittance basis: anti-avoidance provisions relating to transfers of mixed funds), for subsection (4) substitute —

    "(4)   "Income tax advantage" means —

      (a)   a relief from income tax or increased relief from income tax,

      (b)   a repayment of income tax or increased repayment of income tax,

      (c)   the avoidance or reduction of a charge to income tax or an assessment to income tax, or

      (d)   the avoidance of a possible assessment to income tax;

    and for this purpose "relief from income tax" includes a tax credit.

    (4A) For the purposes of subsection (4)(c) and (d) it does not matter whether the avoidance or reduction is effected —

      (a)   by receipts accruing in such a way that the recipient does not pay or bear income tax on them, or

      (b)   by a deduction in calculating profits or gains."

12   (1) Schedule 4 to that Act (index of defined expressions) is amended as follows.

    (2) After the definition of "close company" insert —

"close company (in Chapter 1 of Part 13)	section 713".

    (3) In the entry relating to "income tax advantage (in Chapter 1 of Part 13)", for "683(1)" substitute "687".

(4) In the entry relating to "transaction in securities (in Chapter 1 of Part 13)", for "713" substitute "684(2)".

13   In FA 2007, in Schedule 26, omit paragraph 12(11).

14   In CTA 2010, in Schedule 1, omit paragraphs 545 and 546.

Commencement

15   (1) The amendments made by paragraphs 2 to 5, 7 and 11 to 13 (and paragraph 1 so far as relating to them) have effect in relation to income tax advantages obtained on or after 24 March 2010.

(2) The amendment made by paragraph 6 (and paragraph 1 so far as relating to it) are treated as having come into force on 1 April 2009.

(3) The amendments made by paragraphs 8 to 10 have effect in relation to corporation tax advantages obtained on or after 1 April 2010.

(4) The repeals made by paragraph 14 are treated as having come into force on 1 April 2010.

SCHEDULE 13   Section 40

UNAUTHORISED UNIT TRUSTS

Amendments of Chapter 13 of Part 15 of ITA 2007

1   (1) Chapter 13 of Part 15 of ITA 2007 (deduction of income tax at source: unauthorised unit trusts) is amended as follows.

(2) In section 941(6) (deemed payments to unit holders and deemed deductions of income tax), after the definition of "deemed deduction", insert—
    ""deemed income" means the gross amount of income treated as received as mentioned in subsection (1),".

(3) In section 942 (income tax to be collected from trustees) after subsection (5) insert—

    "(6)   No relief under—
        (a)   sections 2 and 6 of TIOPA 2010 (double taxation arrangements: relief by agreement), or
        (b)   section 18(1)(b) and (2) of that Act (relief for foreign tax where no double taxation arrangements),
    is allowed in relation to income tax to be collected by virtue of this section."

(4) After section 943 (calculation of trustees' income pool) insert—

"943A Treatment of cases involving double tax relief

    (1)   This section applies where—
        (a)   the trustees of an unauthorised unit trust are treated as making deemed payments to unit holders in a tax year ("the current tax year"),

    (b)   there is a reduction in the income pool in the current tax year, and

    (c)   the amount of the trustees' double tax relief pool as at the start of the current tax year is greater than zero.

(2)   Section 848 (income tax deducted at source treated as income tax paid by recipient) does not apply to the foreign element of the deemed deduction treated as made from any of the deemed payments.

(3)   Instead, for the purposes of the Tax Acts —

    (a)   the foreign element of the deemed deduction is treated as if it were tax payable under the law of a territory outside the United Kingdom with which there are not in force any arrangements under section 2(1) of TIOPA 2010 (double taxation relief by agreement), and

    (b)   the foreign element of the deemed income represented by the deemed payment is treated as if it were income that —

        (i)   arises in a territory of the kind mentioned in paragraph (a), and

        (ii)   is income by reference to which the tax treated under paragraph (a) as payable was computed.

(4)   A reference in this Chapter to a reduction in the income pool in a tax year is to the amount (if any) by which —

    (a)   the amount of the income pool at the start of the tax year, exceeds

    (b)   the amount of the income pool at the start of the following tax year.

(5)   See —

        section 943B for provision about references to the "foreign element" of a deemed deduction or deemed income, and

        section 943C for provision about the calculation of the trustees' double tax relief pool as at the beginning of a tax year.

943B The "foreign element" of a deemed deduction or deemed income

(1)   References in this Chapter to the "foreign element" of —

    (a)   a deemed deduction treated as made in a tax year, or

    (b)   deemed income treated as received in a tax year,

are to the deemed deduction or deemed income multiplied by the relevant fraction.

(2)   For this purpose "the relevant fraction" means —

$$\frac{A}{B}$$

where —

    A is —

        (a)   the reduction in the income pool in the tax year multiplied by the basic rate for the year, or

        (b)   if lower, the amount of the trustees' double tax relief pool as at the start of the tax year;

B is the total of the deemed deductions treated as made in the tax year.

943C Calculation of trustees' double tax relief pool

(1)   This is how the amount of the trustees' double tax relief pool as at the start of a tax year ("the current tax year") is calculated.

(2)   The trustees' double tax relief pool as at the start of the current tax year is—

$$A + B - C$$

where—

A is—

   (a)   the amount of the trustees' double tax relief pool as at the start of the previous tax year, or

   (b)   if the current tax year is the tax year during which the unauthorised unit trust is established, or the trustees have been UK resident for no tax year prior to the current tax year, nil;

B is the amount of the reduction, if any, in the liability of the trustees to income tax in the previous tax year under—

   (a)   sections 2 and 6 of TIOPA 2010 (double taxation arrangements: relief by agreement), or

   (b)   section 18(1)(b) and (2) of TIOPA 2010 (relief for foreign tax where no double taxation arrangements);

C is the sum of the foreign elements (if any) of deemed deductions from deemed payments treated as made in the previous tax year.

(3)   If the trustees were non-UK resident for the previous tax year, references in subsection (2) to the previous tax year are to be read as references to the last tax year prior to the current tax year for which the trustees were UK resident.

943D Annual statements

(1)   This section applies in relation to any tax year in which the trustees of an unauthorised unit trust are treated as making a deemed payment to a unit holder.

(2)   The trustees must, as soon as reasonably practicable after the end of the tax year, give the unit holder a statement (an "annual statement").

(3)   The annual statement must include the following information in relation to each deemed payment treated as made by the trustees to the unit holder in the tax year—

   (a)   the date on which the deemed payment was treated as made,

   (b)   the gross amount of the deemed payment,

   (c)   the foreign element (if any) of the deemed income represented by the deemed payment,

   (d)   the deemed deduction made from the deemed payment, and

   (e)   the foreign element (if any) of that deemed deduction.

(4) The duties imposed by this section are enforceable by the unit holder."

Consequential amendments

2 (1) In section 550 of ITTOIA 2005 (distributions from unauthorised unit trusts: income tax treated as paid), after "is" insert ", subject to section 943A of that Act (treatment of cases involving double tax relief),".

(2) In section 848 of ITA 2007 (income tax deducted at source treated as income tax paid by the recipient), at the end insert—

"(4) In relation to income tax deducted at source under section 941 (unauthorised unit trusts), this section is subject to section 943A (treatment of cases involving double tax relief)."

(3) In Schedule 4 to that Act (index of defined expressions), insert at the appropriate places—

| "deemed income (in Chapter 13 of Part 15) | section 941(6)" |
| "foreign element (in Chapter 13 of Part 15) | section 943B". |

(4) In section 971 of CTA 2009 (distributions from unauthorised unit trusts: overview of Chapter), in subsection (2)(a), after "is" insert ", subject to section 943A of that Act (treatment of cases involving double tax relief),".

Commencement

3 The amendments made by this Schedule have effect in relation to payments treated under section 941(2) of ITA 2007 as made on or after 21 October 2009.

Transitional provision: opening value of trustees' double tax relief pool

4 (1) This paragraph applies, and section 943C of ITA 2007 does not apply, in relation to the determination of the amount of the trustees' double tax relief pool as at the start of the tax year 2009-10.

(2) That amount is—
 (a) if amounts A and B are both greater than £20,000, the lower of those amounts, and
 (b) in any other case, nil.

(3) Amount A is the sum of—
 (a) any amount by which the liability of the trustees to income tax for the tax year 2007-08 is reduced under—
  (i) sections 2 and 6 of TIOPA 2010 (double taxation arrangements: relief by agreement), or
  (ii) section 18(1)(b) and (2) of that Act (relief for foreign tax where no double taxation arrangements), and
 (b) any amount by which the liability of the trustees to income tax for the following tax year is so reduced.

(4) Amount B is 20% of the amount (if any) of the trustees' income pool as at the start of the tax year 2009-10 (calculated in accordance with section 943 of ITA 2007).

SCHEDULE 14

Section 41

INDEX-LINKED GILT-EDGED SECURITIES

Amendments of Chapter 12 of Part 5 of CTA 2009

1   Chapter 12 of Part 5 of CTA 2009 (loan relationships: special rules for particular kinds of securities) is amended as follows.

2   In section 398(2) (overview of Chapter), for paragraph (a) substitute—
> "(a)   sections 399 to 400C (index-linked gilt-edged securities),
> (aa)   sections 401 to 405 (other gilt-edged securities),".

3   For the heading before section 399 substitute—

"Index-linked gilt-edged securities".

4   (1) Section 399 (index-linked gilt-edged securities: basic rules) is amended as follows.

     (2) For the heading substitute "**Basic rules**".

     (3) For subsection (3) substitute—

> "(3)   For provision requiring adjustments to be made to amounts determined under subsection (2), see sections 400 to 400C (adjustments for changes in index)."

     (4) In subsection (4), for "section 400" substitute "sections 400 to 400C".

5   (1) Section 400 (index-linked gilt-edged securities: adjustments for changes in index) is amended as follows.

     (2) For the heading substitute "**Adjustments for changes in index**".

     (3) In subsection (1)(a)—
> (a)   for "the amounts" substitute "an amount", and
> (b)   for "fall" substitute "falls".

     (4) After subsection (2) insert—

> "(2A)   Subsection (2) is subject to sections 400A to 400C (relevant hedging schemes)."

6   After section 400 insert—

"400A Adjustments for changes in index: relevant hedging schemes

     (1) This section applies where—
> (a)   section 400 applies in relation to an amount to be brought into account for an accounting period of a company ("company A") in respect of a security, and
> (b)   conditions 1 to 3 are met.

(2) Condition 1 is that company A is a party to a relevant hedging scheme at any time in the accounting period.

(3) Condition 2 is that there is an increase in the retail prices index between the times mentioned in subsection (1) of section 400.

(4) Condition 3 is that the index-linked capital return on the security in the accounting period, or a proportion of it, is hedged.

(5) Where this section applies, any increase in the carrying value of the security at the earlier of the times mentioned in subsection (1) of section 400 that would, apart from this section, be made under subsection (2) of that section is reduced —

   (a) in a case in which the index-linked capital return on the security in the accounting period is wholly hedged, to nil, and

   (b) in a case in which only a proportion of that return is hedged, by the same proportion.

(6) For the purposes of this section "a relevant hedging scheme" means a scheme the purpose, or one of the main purposes, of any party to which, on entering into the scheme, is to secure that the index-linked capital return on the security, or a proportion of it, is hedged.

(7) For the purposes of this section the "index-linked capital return" of the security is so much of the return on the security as —

   (a) would, disregarding section 400, result in an increase in the carrying value of the security between the times mentioned in subsection (1) of that section, and

   (b) is attributable to an increase in the retail prices index.

(8) For the purposes of this section the index-linked capital return on the security, or any proportion of that return, is "hedged" if (whether because of the operation of a swap or otherwise) the pre-tax economic profit or loss made by the relevant group or company in the accounting period is unaffected by it.

(9) In subsection (8) "the relevant group or company" means —

   (a) company A and every other company that is at any time in the accounting period —

      (i) associated with company A, and

      (ii) a party to the relevant hedging scheme, or

   (b) if there is no such other company, company A.

(10) In this section "scheme" includes any scheme, arrangements or understanding of any kind whatever, whether or not legally enforceable, involving a single transaction or two or more transactions.

400B Interpretation of section 400A: economic profits and losses

(1) A reference in section 400A to an "economic" profit or loss made by any person in a period is to a profit or loss made by that person in that period, computed taking into account unrealised (as well as realised) profits and losses.

(2) For the purposes of section 400A an economic profit or loss is made by a group of companies if it is made by the members of the group considered together.

(3) In determining for the purposes of section 400A the amount of an economic profit or loss made by a group of companies in any period, the economic profits and losses of each member of the group are to be computed over that period (whether or not that period is an accounting period of the member).

(4) A reference in section 400A to a "pre-tax" economic profit or loss is a reference to an economic profit or loss determined disregarding any gain or loss made as a result of the operation of any provision of the Corporation Tax Acts.

400C Meaning of "associated with"

(1) For the purposes of section 400A, a company ("company B") is associated with company A at a time ("the relevant time") during an accounting period of company A ("the accounting period") if any of the following five conditions is met.

(2) The first condition is that the financial results of company A and company B, for a period that includes the relevant time, meet the consolidation condition.

(3) The second condition is that there is a connection between company A and company B for the accounting period.

(4) The third condition is that, at the relevant time, company A has a major interest in company B or company B has a major interest in company A.

(5) The fourth condition is that—
  (a) the financial results of company A and a third company, for a period that includes the relevant time, meet the consolidation condition, and
  (b) at the relevant time the third company has a major interest in company B.

(6) The fifth condition is that—
  (a) there is a connection between company A and a third company for the accounting period, and
  (b) at the relevant time the third company has a major interest in company B.

(7) In this paragraph the financial results of any two companies for any period meet "the consolidation condition" if—
  (a) they are required to be comprised in group accounts prepared under section 399 of the Companies Act 2006 (duty of certain parent companies to prepare group accounts), or
  (b) they would be required to be comprised in such accounts but for the application of an exemption mentioned in subsection (3) of that section.

(8) Section 466 (companies connected for an accounting period) applies for the purposes of this section.

(9) In this section "scheme" includes any scheme, arrangements or understanding of any kind whatever, whether or not legally enforceable, involving a single transaction or two or more transactions.

Other gilt-edged securities".

Consequential amendment

7   In section 317(5)(g) of CTA 2009 (carrying value), for "and 400" substitute "to 400C".

Commencement

8   The amendments made by this Schedule have effect in relation to adjustments made under section 400(2) of CTA 2009 in respect of increases in the retail prices index over periods beginning on or after 9 December 2009.

Transitional provision

9   (1) This paragraph applies in relation to an accounting period of a company beginning before 9 December 2009 if, apart from this paragraph—

(a) an amount to be brought into account for the purposes of Part 5 of CTA 2009 in respect of an index-linked gilt-edged security falls to be determined by reference to its value at two different times, and

(b) the earlier time is before 9 December 2009 and the later time is on or after that date.

(2) Instead of bringing into account the amount determined as mentioned in sub-paragraph (1)(a), the company is to bring into account the amounts that it would have brought into account for—

(a) that part of the accounting period that falls before 9 December 2009, and

(b) that part of the accounting period that falls on or after that date,

had those parts been separate periods of account (and so separate accounting periods).

SCHEDULE 15   Section 44

CONNECTED COMPANIES: RELEASES OF DEBTS

Amendments of section 322 of CTA 2009

1   (1) Section 322 of CTA 2009 (release of debts: cases where credits not required to be brought into account) is amended as follows.

(2) In subsection (4), after "release is" insert "not a release of relevant rights and is".

(3) After that subsection insert—

"(4A)   "Relevant rights" has the same meaning for the purposes of this section as it has for the purposes of section 358."

Amendments of Chapter 6 of Part 5 of CTA 2009

2　(1)　Chapter 6 of Part 5 of CTA 2009 (connected companies relationships: release of debts etc) is amended as follows.

(2)　In section 353(2)(b) (introduction to Chapter), for "except where the release is a deemed release under section 361 or 362" substitute "subject to some exceptions".

(3)　In section 358 (exclusion of credits on release of connected companies debts: general) —

(a)　in subsection (1)(a), for "a company's debtor relationship is released," substitute "a debtor relationship of a company ("D") is released, and",

(b)　in subsection (2), for "The company" substitute "D" and for "it is a deemed release" substitute "—

(a)　it is a deemed release, or

(b)　it is a release of relevant rights.", and

(c)　at the end insert—

"(4)　For the purposes of this section "relevant rights" means rights of a company ("C") that—

(a)　were acquired by C in circumstances that, but for the application of the corporate rescue exception or the debt-for-debt exception, would have resulted in a deemed release under section 361(3), or

(b)　were acquired by another company in such circumstances and transferred to C by way of an assignment or assignments.

(5)　The amount of the credit that D is required to bring into account in respect of a release of relevant rights is—

(a)　the amount of the discount received on the acquisition, less

(b)　the sum of any credits brought into account in respect of that amount (whether in the accounting period in which the release takes place or in a previous accounting period) by C or, in a case within subsection (4)(b), by the company that acquired the rights or any company to which the rights were subsequently assigned.

(6)　A reference in subsection (5) to the amount of the discount received on the acquisition is to the amount that would have been treated as released under section 361(4) on the acquisition, but for the application of the corporate rescue exception or the debt-for-debt exception."

(4)　In section 361 (acquisition of creditor rights by connected company at undervalue) —

(a)　in subsection (1), for paragraph (f) substitute—

"(f)　no relevant exception applies.", and

(b)　for subsection (2) substitute—

"(2)　In subsection (1) "relevant exception" means—

   (a)   the corporate rescue exception (see section 361A),

   (b)   the debt-for-debt exception (see section 361B), or

   (c)   the equity-for-debt exception (see section 361C)."

(5) After section 361 insert—

"361A The corporate rescue exception

(1)   For the purposes of section 361, the "corporate rescue exception" applies if—

   (a)   the acquisition is an arm's length transaction,

   (b)   there has been a change in the ownership of D at any time in the period beginning one year before, and ending 60 days after, the date of the acquisition,

   (c)   it is reasonable to assume that, but for the change in ownership, D would, within one year of the date of the change of ownership, have met one of the insolvency conditions, and

   (d)   it is reasonable to assume that, but for the change in ownership, the acquisition would not have been made.

(2)   Subject to subsection (3), section 769 of ICTA (rules for ascertaining change in ownership of company) applies for the purpose of construing a reference in this section to a change in the ownership of a company.

(3)   A reference in this section to a change in the ownership of a company, in the case of a company that is a building society, is a reference to—

   (a)   an amalgamation of two or more building societies under section 93 of the Building Societies Act 1986,

   (b)   a transfer of all the engagements of one building society to another under section 94 of that Act, or

   (c)   a transfer of the whole of the business of a building society to a company under section 97 of that Act.

(4)   Sections 322(6) and 323 (insolvency conditions) apply for the purposes of this section.

361B The debt-for-debt exception

(1)   For the purposes of section 361, the "debt-for-debt exception" applies if condition 1 or 2 is met.

(2)   Condition 1 is that—

   (a)   the acquisition is an arm's length transaction,

   (b)   the rights that are acquired are rights under a loan relationship that is represented by a security ("the old security"),

   (c)   the consideration given by C for the acquisition consists only of a security ("the new security") representing a loan relationship to which C is a party as debtor, and

   (d)   the new security—

      (i)   has the same nominal value as the old security, and

      (ii)   at the time of the acquisition, has substantially the same market value as the old security.

    (3)   Condition 2 is that—

        (a)   the acquisition is an arm's length transaction,

        (b)   the rights that are acquired are rights under a loan relationship that is represented by an asset other than a security ("the old unsecured loan"),

        (c)   the consideration given by C for the acquisition consists only of an asset other than a security ("the new unsecured loan") representing a loan relationship to which C is a party as debtor, and

        (d)   the amount of the new unsecured loan, and its terms, are substantially the same as those of the old unsecured loan.

    (4)   In this section "market value" has the same meaning as in TCGA 1992 (see sections 272 and 273 of that Act).

    (5)   In determining for the purposes of this section the market value of a security in a case in which the security represents a loan relationship to which section 415 (loan relationships with embedded derivatives) applies, rights or liabilities within subsection (1)(b) of that section are to be treated as comprised in the loan relationship.

361C The equity-for-debt exception

    (1)   For the purposes of section 361 the "equity-for-debt exception" applies if the following two conditions are met.

    (2)   The first condition is that the acquisition is an arm's length transaction.

    (3)   The second condition is that the consideration given by C for the acquisition consists only of—

        (a)   shares forming part of the ordinary share capital of C,

        (b)   shares forming part of the ordinary share capital of a company connected with C, or

        (c)   an entitlement to shares within paragraph (a) or (b)."

  (6) In section 363—

      (a)   in the heading, for "and" substitute "to", and

      (b)   in subsections (1) and (4), for "and" substitute "to".

Commencement

3   (1)   The amendments made by paragraph 1 have effect in relation to a release of rights that takes place on or after 9 November 2009.

    (2)   The amendments made by paragraph 2(2) and (4) to (6) have effect in relation to a relevant acquisition that is made on or after 14 October 2009.

    (3)   The amendments made by paragraph 2(3) have effect in relation to a release of rights that takes place on or after 14 October 2009.

    (4)   Sub-paragraphs (1) to (3) are subject to paragraph 4.

    (5)   In this paragraph and paragraph 4 "relevant acquisition" means an acquisition of rights within subsection (1)(a) to (e) of section 361 of CTA 2009 (acquisition of creditor rights by connected company at an undervalue).

Transitional provision

4 (1) The amendments made by this Schedule do not have effect in relation to a relevant acquisition that is made on or after 14 October 2009, or to a release of rights acquired by way of such an acquisition, if—

(a) the acquisition is made pursuant to an agreement entered into before 14 October 2009, or

(b) the acquisition is made during the transitional period and condition A, B or C is met.

(2) Condition A is that, before 14 October 2009—

(a) the original creditor received a proposal from the new creditor that the acquisition should be made, or

(b) the new creditor received a proposal from the original creditor that the acquisition should be made.

(3) Condition B is that—

(a) the acquisition is of rights under a loan relationship that is represented by a security,

(b) during the transitional period the new creditor acquires rights under other loan relationships represented by securities, and

(c) before 14 October 2009, either—

(i) persons together holding more than 50% by value of the securities referred to in paragraphs (a) and (b) ("the bought-back securities") received proposals from the new creditor that the acquisitions should be made, or

(ii) the new creditor received proposals from persons together holding more than 50% by value of the bought-back securities that the acquisitions should be made.

(4) In sub-paragraphs (2) and (3)—

(a) a reference to the original creditor includes any person acting on behalf of, or who controls, the original creditor,

(b) a reference to the new creditor includes any person acting on behalf of, or who controls, the new creditor, and

(c) a reference to a person holding a security includes any person acting on behalf of, or who controls, the person holding the security.

(5) Condition C is that—

(a) before 14 October 2009, the Financial Services Authority gave its agreement ("the FSA agreement") to the acquisition being made (and had not withdrawn that agreement),

(b) if the FSA agreement was given subject to the agreement of any other person, the agreement of that other person was also given (and not withdrawn) before that date, and

(c) condition A or B would have been met but for the compliance by the original creditor or the new creditor with any other term on which the FSA agreement was given.

(6) In this paragraph—

(a) "the original creditor", in relation to a relevant acquisition, means the person from whom the rights are acquired, and

(b) "the new creditor", in relation to a relevant acquisition, means the person who acquires the rights.

(7) In this paragraph "the transitional period" means the period—

    (a) beginning with 14 October 2009, and

    (b) ending with 31 January 2010.

(8) Section 472 of CTA 2009 (meaning of "control") applies for the purposes of this paragraph.

SCHEDULE 16   _{Section 46}

RISK TRANSFER SCHEMES

Amendments

1   CTA 2010 is amended as follows.

2   In section 1(4) (overview of Act) omit the "and" at the end of paragraph (g), insert ", and" at the end of paragraph (h) and after that paragraph insert—

       "(i) risk transfer schemes (see Part 21A)."

3   After Part 21 insert—

"PART 21A

RISK TRANSFER SCHEMES

Introduction

937A Overview

     This Part contains rules about the treatment of certain losses made by companies as a result of risk transfer schemes.

937B Group schemes and single company schemes

(1) A risk transfer scheme may be—

    (a) a group scheme, or

    (b) a risk transfer scheme other than a group scheme (a "single-company scheme").

(2) A risk transfer scheme to which a company ("company A") is a party is a "group scheme" if at least one company other than company A is at any time both—

    (a) associated with company A, and

    (b) a party to the scheme.

(3) In this Part "the relevant group" means—

    (a) company A, and

    (b) each company other than company A in relation to which the condition in subsection (2) is met.

(4) In its application in relation to single company schemes, this Part applies subject to the following modifications.

(5) The modifications are that—

    (a)   references to the relevant group, a member of the relevant group, or the members of the relevant group, are treated as references to company A, and

    (b)   sections 937E(2) and 937L(2) are treated as omitted.

Basic definitions

937C Meaning of "risk transfer scheme"

(1)   A scheme to which a company ("company A") is a party is a "risk transfer scheme" if conditions 1 to 3 are met.

(2)   Condition 1 is that the purpose, or one of the main purposes, of any member of the relevant group on entering into the scheme is to obtain a financial advantage for the relevant group that it is reasonable to assume could not otherwise have been obtained without the relevant group becoming subject to (or incurring the cost of avoiding) a relevant risk.

(3)   In subsection (2) "a relevant risk" means a risk that the relevant group would make economic losses in one or more accounting periods of company A as a result of fluctuations in —

    (a)   the rate of exchange between any two currencies,

    (b)   the retail prices index (or any similar general index of prices) or any other index, or

    (c)   any price or other value.

(4)   Condition 2 is that, as a result of the scheme, and disregarding the effect of this Part, the relevant group —

    (a)   is not subject to the relevant risk, or

    (b)   is subject only to a negligible proportion of that risk.

(5)   Condition 3 is that, disregarding the effect of the provisions of the Corporation Tax Acts, condition 2 would not be met.

(6)   For the purposes of this section the relevant group obtains a "financial advantage" from a scheme if, taking into account the effect of the scheme on each member of the group, the scheme —

    (a)   increases the return on any investment,

    (b)   reduces the costs of any borrowing, or

    (c)   has an effect economically equivalent to that mentioned in paragraph (a) or (b).

937D Meaning of "the scheme rate, index or value"

In this Part "the scheme rate, index or value", in relation to a risk transfer scheme, means the rate, index or value mentioned in section 937C(3)(a), (b) or (c) in relation to the relevant risk for the scheme.

937E Scheme losses and scheme profits

(1)   A loss or profit made by a company in an accounting period is a "scheme loss" or "scheme profit" in relation to a risk transfer scheme to which the company is a party at any time in the period if the loss or profit —

    (a)   is from a loan relationship, or derivative contract, that is part of the scheme,

    (b)   would, apart from this Part, be brought into account in determining a debit or credit for the purposes of Part 5 of CTA 2009 (loan relationships) or Part 7 of that Act (derivative contracts), and

    (c)   arises as a result of fluctuations in the scheme rate, index or value.

(2)   References in this Part to a scheme loss or scheme profit made by a company in a period that is not an accounting period of that company are to the scheme loss or scheme profit that the company would have made in the period from the loan relationship or derivative contract in question if the period had been an accounting period of the company.

(3)   References in this section to a loss or profit from a loan relationship or a derivative contract include —

    (a)   a loss or profit from a related transaction, and

    (b)   a loss or profit of a capital nature.

(4)   In subsection (3)(a) "related transaction" has the meaning given by —

    (a)   section 304 of CTA 2009 (in relation to a loan relationship), or

    (b)   section 596 of that Act (in relation to a derivative contract).

937F Ring-fenced scheme losses and relevant scheme profits

(1)   Subsection (2) applies if —

    (a)   a company makes one or more scheme losses in an accounting period in relation to a risk transfer scheme, and

    (b)   disregarding any profits or losses made otherwise than as a result of the scheme, the relevant group makes a pre-tax economic loss in the period as a result of fluctuations in the scheme rate, index or value.

(2)   The relevant proportion of each scheme loss made by the company in the accounting period is a "ring-fenced scheme loss".

(3)   For this purpose "the relevant proportion" means —

$$\frac{A - B - C}{A}$$

where —

    A is the total of the scheme losses made in the period in relation to the scheme by the members of the relevant group,

    B is the total of the scheme profits made in the period in relation to the scheme by the members of the relevant group, and

    C is the pre-tax economic loss referred to in subsection (1)(b).

(4)   Subsection (5) applies if —

    (a)   a company makes one or more scheme profits in an accounting period in relation to a risk transfer scheme, and

    (b)   disregarding any profits or losses made otherwise than as a result of the scheme, the relevant group makes a pre-tax economic profit in the period as a result of fluctuations in the scheme rate, index or value.

(5) The relevant proportion of each scheme profit made by the company in the accounting period is a "relevant scheme profit".

(6) For this purpose "the relevant proportion" means —

$$\frac{A - B - C}{A}$$

where —

  A is the total of the scheme profits made in the period in relation to the scheme by the members of the relevant group,

  B is the total of the scheme losses made in the period in relation to the scheme by the members of the relevant group, and

  C is the pre-tax economic profit referred to in subsection (4)(b).

Treatment of ring-fenced scheme losses

937G Ring-fenced scheme loss: treatment in period in which made

(1) This section applies for the purpose of determining the amount (if any) of a ring-fenced scheme loss that may be brought into account by a company in the accounting period in which it is made.

(2) If the amount of the company's profits pool for the scheme as at the beginning of the period is nil, the ring-fenced scheme loss may not be brought into account.

(3) If the amount of the company's profits pool for the scheme as at the beginning of the period is —

  (a) greater than nil, and

  (b) less than the total of the ring-fenced scheme losses made in the period in relation to the scheme by the company,

only the relevant proportion of the ring-fenced scheme loss may be brought into account.

(4) For this purpose "the relevant proportion" means —

$$\frac{A}{B}$$

where —

  A is the amount of the company's profits pool as at the beginning of the period, and

  B is the total of the ring-fenced scheme losses made in the period in relation to the scheme by the company.

(5) If the amount of the company's profits pool for the scheme as at the beginning of the period is equal to or greater than the total of the ring-fenced scheme losses made in the period in relation to the scheme by the company, the ring-fenced scheme loss may be brought into account in full.

(6) A reference in this paragraph to bringing a ring-fenced scheme loss into account is to bringing it into account in determining a debit or credit for the purposes of Part 5 of CTA 2009 (loan relationships) or Part 7 of that Act (derivative contracts).

937H Ring-fenced scheme loss: treatment in subsequent periods

(1) This section applies where —

    (a) a company makes one or more scheme profits in an accounting period in relation to a risk transfer scheme,

    (b) disregarding any profits or losses made otherwise than as a result of the scheme, the relevant group makes a pre-tax economic profit in the period as a result of fluctuations in the scheme rate, index or value, and

    (c) the amount of the company's losses pool for the scheme as at the beginning of the period is greater than nil.

(2) The company may bring into account, as if it were a loss made in the period from a loan relationship —

$$A \times B$$

where —

    A is so much of the amount of the company's losses pool as at the beginning of the period as does not exceed the total of the relevant scheme profits made in the period in relation to the scheme by the company, and

    B is the proportion of the total of the relevant scheme profits made in the period in relation to the scheme by the company that consists of profits made from its loan relationships.

(3) The company may bring into account, as if it were a loss made in the period from a derivative contract —

$$A \times C$$

where —

    A has the same meaning as in subsection (2), and

    C is the proportion of the total of the relevant scheme profits made in the period in relation to the scheme by the company that consists of profits made from its derivative contracts.

(4) A reference in this section to bringing an amount into account is to bringing it into account in determining a debit or credit for the purposes of Part 5 of CTA 2009 (loan relationships) or Part 7 of that Act (derivative contracts).

A company's losses pool and profits pool

937I A company's losses pool and profits pool

(1) The amount of a company's losses pool for a risk transfer scheme as at the beginning of an accounting period ("the current accounting period") is —

$$A + B - C$$

where —

    A is —

        (a) the amount of the pool as at the beginning of the previous accounting period, or

        (b) if the risk transfer scheme began in the current accounting period, nil,

B is the total amount, if any, of ring-fenced scheme losses made in the previous accounting period in relation to the scheme by the company that, as a result of the application of section 937G(2) or (3), are not brought into account in that period, and

C is the total amount (if any) that, as a result of the application of section 937H(2) or (3), is brought into account in the previous accounting period in relation to the scheme by the company.

(2) The amount of a company's profits pool for a risk transfer scheme as at the beginning of an accounting period ("the current accounting period") is—

$$A + B - C$$

where—

A is—

   (a) the amount of the pool as at the beginning of the previous accounting period, or

   (b) if the risk transfer scheme began in the current accounting period, nil,

B is—

   (a) the total of any relevant scheme profits made in the previous accounting period in relation to the scheme by the company, less

   (b) the total amount (if any) that, as a result of the application of section 937H(2) or (3), is brought into account in that accounting period in relation to the scheme by the company, and

C is the total amount (if any) of ring-fenced scheme losses made in the previous accounting period in relation to the scheme by the company that, as a result of the application of section 937G(3) or (5), are brought into account in that period.

General

937J Tax capacity assumption

(1) This section applies for the purpose of determining whether condition 2 in section 937C is met.

(2) Where a member of the relevant group ("the company") makes a scheme loss in an accounting period, the economic profits and losses made by the relevant group in the period must be calculated on the assumption that the company obtained the full tax benefit of the loss.

(3) The "full tax benefit" of the loss is the reduction in the corporation tax liability of the company that would result if—

   (a) the loss were brought into account, and

   (b) the company's profits chargeable to corporation tax, before doing so, were equal to the debit (or the reduction in any credit) determined by reference to the loss.

(4) A reference in this section to bringing a loss into account is to bringing it into account in determining a debit or credit for the

purposes of Part 5 of CTA 2009 (loan relationships) or Part 7 of that Act (derivative contracts).

937K Meaning of "associated with"

(1) For the purposes of this Part a company ("company B") is associated with another company ("company A") at a time ("the relevant time") if any of the following five conditions is met.

(2) The first condition is that the financial results of company A and company B, for a period that includes the relevant time, meet the consolidation condition.

(3) The second condition is that there is a connection between company A and company B for the accounting period of company A in which the relevant time falls.

(4) The third condition is that, at the relevant time, company A has a major interest in company B or company B has a major interest in company A.

(5) The fourth condition is that—
  (a) the financial results of company A and a third company, for a period that includes the relevant time, meet the consolidation condition, and
  (b) at the relevant time the third company has a major interest in company B.

(6) The fifth condition is that—
  (a) there is a connection between company A and a third company for the accounting period of company A in which the relevant time falls, and
  (b) at the relevant time the third company has a major interest in company B.

(7) In this section the financial results of any two companies for any period meet "the consolidation condition" if—
  (a) they are required to be comprised in group accounts prepared under section 399 of the Companies Act 2006 (duty of certain parent companies to prepare group accounts), or
  (b) they would be required to be comprised in such accounts but for the application of an exemption mentioned in subsection (3) of that section.

(8) The following provisions apply for the purposes of this section—
  sections 466 to 471 of CTA 2009 (companies connected for accounting period), and
  sections 473 and 474 of CTA 2009 (meaning of "major interest").

937L Interpretation of references to economic losses and profits

(1) A reference in this Part to an "economic" loss or profit made by any person in a period is to a loss or profit made by that person in that period, computed taking into account unrealised (as well as realised) losses and profits.

(2) For the purposes of this Part an economic loss or profit is made "by the relevant group" if it is made by the members of the relevant group considered together.

(3) Where—

    (a) any member of the relevant group makes a scheme loss or profit in an accounting period, and

    (b) that scheme loss or profit is, under generally accepted accounting practice, calculated by reference to fluctuations in the scheme rate, index or value over a longer period,

the economic loss or profit made by the group in the accounting period as a result of those fluctuations is, so far as it relates to that scheme loss or profit, to be computed over that longer period.

(4) In determining for the purposes of this Part the amount of an economic loss or profit made by the relevant group in any period, the economic losses and profits of each member of the relevant group—

    (a) are (subject to subsection (3)) to be computed over that period (whether or not that period is an accounting period of the member), but

    (b) are only to be taken into account to the extent that they are attributable to times at which the member is a party to the risk transfer scheme in question.

(5) A reference in this Part to a "pre-tax" economic loss or profit is a reference to an economic loss or profit determined disregarding any loss or gain made as a result of the operation of any provision of the Corporation Tax Acts.

937M Foreign currency accounting

(1) In determining under this Part amounts that a company may or may not bring into account in an accounting period, economic losses and profits are to be computed in the tax calculation currency of that company in that accounting period.

(2) Section 17(5) of CTA 2010 (meaning of references to the tax calculation currency of a company) applies for the purposes of this section.

937N Meaning of "scheme"

In this Part "scheme" includes any scheme, arrangements or understanding of any kind whatever, whether or not legally enforceable, involving a single transaction or two or more transactions.

Power to amend this Part

937O Power to amend this Part in its application to dealers in securities

(1) The Treasury may by order amend any enactment contained in this Part so as to apply (with or without modifications) the rules in this Part about scheme losses and scheme profits to losses and profits made in a trade.

    (2)   The power conferred by subsection (1) may only be exercised in relation to losses and profits made by a company that carries on a banking business, an insurance business or a business consisting wholly or partly of dealing in securities.

    (3)   In this section "securities" includes—

        (a)   shares,

        (b)   rights of unit holders in unit trust schemes to which TCGA 1992 applies as a result of section 99 of that Act, and

        (c)   in the case of a company with no share capital, interests in the company possessed by members of the company.

    (4)   An order under this section—

        (a)   may make different provision for different cases or purposes, and

        (b)   may include incidental, consequential, supplementary or transitional provision."

4   In Schedule 4 (index of defined expressions), insert at the appropriate places—

"associated with (in Part 21A)	section 937K"
"economic loss (in Part 21A)	section 937L"
"economic profit (in Part 21A)	section 937L"
"the relevant group (in Part 21A)	section 937B(3)"
"relevant scheme profit (in Part 21A)	section 937F"
"ring-fenced scheme loss (in Part 21A)	section 937F"
"risk transfer scheme (in Part 21A)	section 937C"
"scheme (in Part 21A)	section 937N"
"scheme loss (in Part 21A)	section 937E"
"scheme profit (in Part 21A)	section 937E"
"the scheme rate, index or value (in Part 21A)	section 937D".

Commencement and transitional provision

5   (1)   The amendments made by this Schedule have effect in relation to accounting periods that begin on or after 1 April 2010 ("the commencement date").

    (2)   Where a company has an accounting period ("the straddling accounting period") that—

        (a)   begins before the commencement date, and

        (b)   ends on or after that date,

    the straddling accounting period is to be treated as split.

    (3)   Where this paragraph provides that the straddling accounting period is to be treated as split, that part of the straddling accounting period that falls

before the commencement date and that part of the straddling accounting period that falls on or after that date are to be treated for the purposes of the amendments made by this Schedule as separate accounting periods.

(4) In relation to the first accounting period of a company in relation to which the amendments made by this Schedule have effect—

    (a) section 937I of CTA 2010 (as inserted by paragraph 3 above) does not apply, and

    (b) as at the beginning of the period, the amounts of the company's losses pool and profits pool for any risk transfer scheme to which the company is a party is nil.

SCHEDULE 17   Section 56

DISCLOSURE OF TAX AVOIDANCE SCHEMES

Introduction

1   Part 7 of FA 2004 (disclosure of tax avoidance schemes) is amended as follows.

Initial marketing

2   (1) Section 307 (meaning of "promoter") is amended as follows.

  (2) In paragraph (a) of subsection (1), for the words from "business" to "makes" substitute "business, the person ("P")—

        (i) is to any extent responsible for the design of the proposed arrangements,

        (ii) makes a firm approach to another person ("C") in relation to the notifiable proposal with a view to P making the notifiable proposal available for implementation by C or any other person, or

       (iii) makes".

  (3) In paragraph (b) of that subsection, after "(a)(ii)" insert "or (iii)".

  (4) After subsection (1) insert—

    "(1A) For the purposes of this Part a person is an introducer in relation to a notifiable proposal if the person makes a marketing contact with another person in relation to the notifiable proposal."

  (5) After subsection (4) insert—

    "(4A) For the purposes of this Part a person makes a firm approach to another person in relation to a notifiable proposal if the person makes a marketing contact with the other person in relation to the notifiable proposal at a time when the proposed arrangements have been substantially designed.

    (4B) For the purposes of this Part a person makes a marketing contact with another person in relation to a notifiable proposal if—

        (a) the person communicates information about the notifiable proposal to the other person,

      (b) the communication is made with a view to that other person, or any other person, entering into transactions forming part of the proposed arrangements, and

      (c) the information communicated includes an explanation of the advantage in relation to any tax that might be expected to be obtained from the proposed arrangements.

  (4C) For the purposes of subsection (4A) proposed arrangements have been substantially designed at any time if by that time the nature of the transactions to form part of them has been sufficiently developed for it to be reasonable to believe that a person who wished to obtain the advantage mentioned in subsection (4B)(c) might enter into—

      (a) transactions of the nature developed, or

      (b) transactions not substantially different from transactions of that nature."

  (6) In subsection (5), after "promoter" insert "or introducer".

  (7) In subsection (6), after "promoter" (in both places) insert "or introducer".

3   (1) Section 308(2) (duties of promoter) is amended as follows.

  (2) For "earlier" substitute "earliest".

  (3) Before paragraph (a) insert—

    "(za) the date on which the promoter first makes a firm approach to another person in relation to a notifiable proposal,".

4   In section 313A(1) (pre-disclosure enquiry), for "of a proposal or arrangements" substitute "or introducer of a proposal, or the promoter of arrangements,".

5   In section 318(1) (interpretation), after the definition of "HMRC" insert—

      ""introducer", in relation to a notifiable proposal, has the meaning given by section 307;

      "make a firm approach" has the meaning given by section 307(4A);

      "make a marketing contact" has the meaning given by section 307(4B);".

Promoters to provide client lists

6   After section 313 insert—

"313ZA Duty to provide details of clients

  (1) This section applies where a person who is a promoter in relation to notifiable arrangements is providing (or has provided) services to any person ("the client") in connection with the notifiable arrangements and either—

      (a) the promoter is subject to the reference number information requirement, or

      (b) the promoter has failed to comply with section 308(1) or (3) in relation to the notifiable arrangements (or the notifiable proposal for them) but would be subject to the reference number information requirement if a reference number had been allocated to the notifiable arrangements.

(2) For the purposes of this section "the reference number information requirement" is the requirement under section 312(2) to provide to the client prescribed information relating to the reference number allocated to the notifiable arrangements.

(3) The promoter must, within the prescribed period after the end of the relevant period, provide HMRC with prescribed information in relation to the client.

(4) In subsection (3) "the relevant period" means such period during which the promoter is or would be subject to the reference number information requirement as is prescribed.

(5) The promoter need not comply with subsection (3) in relation to any notifiable arrangements at any time after HMRC have given notice under section 312(6) in relation to the notifiable arrangements."

7   In section 316 (information to be provided in manner and form specified by HMRC), for "and 313(1) and (3)" substitute ", 313(1) and (3) and 313ZA(3)".

8   In section 317(2) (regulations), after "may" insert "make different provision for different cases and may".

Information provided to introducers

9   After section 313B insert —

"313C Information provided to introducers

(1) Where HMRC suspect —
   (a) that a person ("P") is an introducer in relation to a proposal, and
   (b) that the proposal may be notifiable,
   they may by written notice require P to provide HMRC with prescribed information in relation to each person who has provided P with any information relating to the proposal.

(2) A notice must specify the proposal to which it relates.

(3) P must comply with a requirement under or by virtue of subsection (1) within —
   (a) the prescribed period, or
   (b) such longer period as HMRC may direct."

Penalties

10   (1) Section 98C of TMA 1970 (penalties for failures to comply with duties relating to disclosure of tax avoidance schemes) is amended as follows.

(2) In subsection (1)(a) (initial penalty for failing to comply with duties), for "£5,000" substitute —
   "(i) in the case of a provision mentioned in paragraph (a), (b) or (c) of that subsection, £600 for each day during the initial period (but see also subsections (2A), (2B) and (2ZC) below), and
   (ii) in any other case, £5,000."

(3) In subsection (2) —

    (a)   omit the "and" at the end of paragraph (da),

    (b)   after that paragraph insert—

> "(db)   section 313ZA (duty of promoter to provide details of clients),", and

    (c)   insert at the end "and

> (f)   section 313C (duty of introducer to give details of persons who have provided information)."

(4) After that subsection insert—

"(2ZA) In this section "the initial period" means the period—

    (a)   beginning with the relevant day, and

    (b)   ending with the earlier of the day on which the penalty under subsection (1)(a)(i) is determined and the last day before the failure ceases;

and for this purpose "the relevant day" is the day specified in relation to the failure in the following table.

TABLE

Failure	Relevant day
A failure to comply with subsection (1) or (3) of section 308 in so far as the subsection applies by virtue of an order under section 306A	The first day after the end of the period prescribed under section 306A(6)
A failure to comply with subsection (1) or (3) of section 308 in so far as the subsection applies by virtue of an order under section 308A(2)	The first day after the end of the period prescribed under subsections (5) and (6)(a) of section 308A (as it may have been extended by a direction under subsection (6)(b) of that section)
Any other failure to comply with subsection (1) of section 308	The first day after the end of the period prescribed under that subsection
Any other failure to comply with subsection (3) of section 308	The first day after the end of the period prescribed under that subsection
A failure to comply with subsection (1) of section 309	The first day after the end of the period prescribed under that subsection
A failure to comply with section 310	The first day after the latest time by which section 310 must be complied with in the case concerned

(2ZB) The amount of a penalty under subsection (1)(a)(i) is to be arrived at after taking account of all relevant considerations, including the desirability of its being set at a level which appears appropriate for deterring the person, or other persons, from similar failures to comply on future occasions having regard (in particular)—

    (a)   in the case of a penalty for a person's failure to comply with section 308(1) or (3), to the amount of any fees received, or likely to have been received, by the person in connection with the notifiable proposal (or arrangements implementing the notifiable proposal), or with the notifiable arrangements, and

   (b)   in the case of a penalty for a person's failure to comply with section 309(1) or 310, to the amount of any advantage gained, or sought to be gained, by the person in relation to any tax prescribed under section 306(1)(b) in relation to the notifiable arrangements.

(2ZC)   If the maximum penalty under subsection (1)(a)(i) above appears inappropriately low after taking account of those considerations, the penalty is to be of such amount not exceeding £1 million as appears appropriate having regard to those considerations.

(2ZD)   Where it appears to an officer of Revenue and Customs that a penalty under subsection (1)(a)(i) above has been determined on the basis that the initial period begins with a day later than that which the officer considers to be the relevant day, an officer of Revenue and Customs may commence proceedings for a re-determination of the penalty.

(2ZE)   The Treasury may by regulations vary —

   (a)   any of the sums for the time being specified in subsection (1) above, and

   (b)   the sum specified in subsection (2ZC) above."

(5)   In subsection (2A), for "amount specified in subsection (1)(b) above shall be increased to the prescribed sum" substitute "amounts specified in subsection (1)(a)(i) and (b) above shall be increased to the prescribed sum in relation to days falling after the prescribed period".

(6)   In subsection (2B), for "amount specified in subsection (1)(b)" substitute "amounts specified in subsection (1)(a)(i) and (b)".

(7)   In subsection (2C)(b), after "section" insert "306A or".

(8)   In subsection (2D), after "under section" insert "306A or".

(9)   In subsection (2E), after "under section" insert "306A or".

(10)   In subsection (2F) —

   (a)   in the opening words, for "subsection (2C)" substitute "this section", and

   (b)   in paragraph (c), after "subsection" insert "(2ZE) or".

Commencement

11   (1)   The amendments made by this Schedule come into force on such day as the Treasury may by order made by statutory instrument appoint.

   (2)   An order may appoint different days for different provisions or for different purposes.

SCHEDULE 18

Section 61

SALE OF LESSORS: ELECTION OUT OF CHARGE

Main changes

1   Chapter 3 of Part 9 of CTA 2010 (sale of lessors: leasing business carried on by company alone) is amended as follows.

2   (1) Section 382 (introduction to Chapter) is amended as follows.

    (2) In subsection (1)—

        (a) for "qualifying change of ownership in relation to" substitute "relevant change in the relationship between", and

        (b) insert at the end "and a principal company of the company."

    (3) In subsection (3), for ""qualifying change of ownership", see sections 392 to 398." substitute ""relevant change in the relationship between a company and a principal company of the company", see sections 392 to 394."

3   In section 383 (income and matching expense in different accounting periods), after subsection (1) insert—

    "(1A) For the meaning of "qualifying change of ownership", see sections 394A to 398A"

4   For section 392 (and the italic heading before it) substitute—

""Relevant change in relationship"

392   "Relevant change in relationship"

    For the purposes of the sales of lessors Chapters there is a relevant change in the relationship between a company ("A") and a principal company of A on any day in any of the circumstances in section 393 or 394 (qualifying 75% subsidiaries and consortium relationships)."

5   After section 394 insert—

""Qualifying change of ownership"

394A "Qualifying change of ownership"

    For the purposes of the sales of lessors Chapters there is a qualifying change of ownership in relation to a company ("A") on any day if there is a relevant change in the relationship on that day between A and a principal company of A unless any of the following apply—

        (a) section 395(2),

        (b) section 396(2), or

        (c) section 398A(2) or (5)."

6   After section 398 insert—

"Election out of qualifying change of ownership

398A Election out of qualifying change of ownership

(1) This section applies if—

    (a) on any day ("the relevant day") a company ("A") carries on a business of leasing plant or machinery otherwise than in partnership,

    (b) there is a relevant change in the relationship between A and a principal company of A ("P") on the relevant day, and

    (c) an election that this section is to apply is made by A.

(2) For the purposes of the sales of lessors Chapters, there is no qualifying change of ownership in relation to A on the relevant day as a result of the change in the relationship but—

    (a) subsections (2)(b) and (4)(b) of section 383 nevertheless apply,

    (b) section 398D (and section 398C so far as relating to it) has effect during the relevant period, and

    (c) sections 398E to 398G (and section 398C so far as relating to section 398E) have effect on the relevant day and during the relevant period.

(3) "The relevant period" is the period—

    (a) beginning with the day after the relevant day, and

    (b) ending with the day on which there is next a relevant change in the relationship between A and a principal company of A falling within subsection (4) (or continuing indefinitely if there is not another such relevant change).

(4) A relevant change in the relationship between A and a principal company of A falls within this subsection if, as a result of it, the (unadjusted) basic amount (see section 399) is (or, but for a further election, would be) treated as a receipt of the business of leasing plant or machinery carried on by A.

(5) Where during the relevant period there is a relevant change in the relationship between A and a principal company of A but the relevant period is not brought to an end by it, for the purposes of the sales of lessors Chapters there is no qualifying change of ownership in relation to A as a result of the change in the relationship.

398B The election

(1) The election under section 398A must state the date of the relevant day.

(2) The election must be made—

    (a) by notice to an officer of Revenue and Customs, and

    (b) during the period of two years beginning with the relevant day.

(3) The election is irrevocable.

(4) All such assessments and adjustments of assessments are to be made as are necessary to give effect to the election.

398C Special treatment of A's trade or business that includes leasing

(1) Sections 398D and 398E make special provision about the trade or property business consisting of or including A's business of leasing plant or machinery.

(2) In those sections "the relevant activity" means —

    (a) if A's business of leasing plant or machinery constitutes or forms part of a trade, that trade, and

    (b) if it forms part of a property business, that property business.

398D Restrictions on use of losses etc

(1) No loss may be deducted under —

    (a) Chapter 2 of Part 4,

    (b) section 62, or

    (c) section 189,

from so much of the total profits of A as are attributable to the carrying on of the relevant activity except to the extent that the loss or charge is attributable to the carrying on of the relevant activity.

(2) Group relief is not to be given under Part 5 against so much of the total profits of A as are attributable to the carrying on of the relevant activity.

(3) No deficit may be set off under section 461 of CTA 2009 (non-trading deficit from loan relationship) against profits attributable to the carrying on of the relevant activity except to the extent that the deficit is attributable to the carrying on of the relevant activity.

(4) No loss may be set off under section 753 of CTA 2009 (non-trading loss on intangible fixed assets) against so much of the total profits of A as are attributable to the carrying on of the relevant activity except to the extent that the loss or charge is attributable to the carrying on of the relevant activity.

(5) No deduction is to be allowed under section 1219 of CTA 2009 (expenses of management of investment business) from so much of the total profits of A as are attributable to the carrying on of the relevant activity except to the extent that the expenses concerned are attributable to the carrying on of the relevant activity.

(6) If A is a controlled foreign company within the meaning of Chapter 4 of Part 17 of ICTA in relation to which an apportionment falls to be made under section 747(3) of that Act in respect of the accounting period ending with the relevant day, no sum may be set off under paragraph 1 of Schedule 26 to ICTA by any person in respect of so much of the chargeable profits of A as are apportioned to the person and are attributable to the carrying on of the relevant activity.

(7) If A would otherwise be a tonnage tax company under Schedule 22 to FA 2000 (tonnage tax) it is to be treated as not being such a company.

398E Restriction on artificial losses or reductions in profits

(1) This section applies if any expenditure incurred by A in carrying on the relevant activity has an unallowable purpose.

(2) In calculating the profits or losses of A for any accounting period for the purposes of corporation tax so much of the expenditure as, on a just and reasonable apportionment, is attributable to the unallowable purpose is to be left out of account.

(3) Expenditure has an unallowable purpose if the main purpose, or one of the main purposes, of A in incurring it is to obtain a relevant tax advantage ("the unallowable purpose").

(4) A "relevant tax advantage" is—

(a) a reduction in the profits which, for the purposes of corporation tax, are attributable to the carrying on of the relevant activity by A,

(b) the creation of a loss which, for those purposes, is so attributable, or

(c) an increase in losses which, for those purposes, are so attributable.

398F Limit on availability of capital allowances to A

(1) Expenditure incurred by A in providing plant or machinery is not qualifying expenditure for the purposes of Part 2 of CAA 2001 if the expenditure is incurred on the acquisition or creation of an independent asset.

(2) An asset is an "independent" asset if, in the normal course of business—

(a) it could be used individually (whether or not it could also be used in conjunction with another asset or other assets as a constituent part of a single asset consisting of more than one asset (a "combined asset")), or

(b) it could be used (at different times) as a constituent part of different combined assets.

398G Transfers into and out of A

(1) Section 948 does not apply where A is the predecessor or the successor.

(2) Where section 948 does not apply as a result of subsection (1), the plant or machinery belonging to the trade is to be treated for the purposes of the Corporation Tax Acts as sold by the predecessor to the successor on the day of cessation for an amount equal to its market value on that day.

(3) Where A is the predecessor, section 265(2)(b) of CAA 2001 (successions) applies—

(a) even if the relevant property has been sold to the successor, and

(b) as if the reference to market value were to market value as determined in accordance with section 437(9)."

Interpretation

7   In section 437 of CTA 2010 (interpretation of the sales of lessors Chapters), after subsection (8) insert—

"(8A)   "Property business" means a UK property business or an overseas property business."

8   In Schedule 4 to that Act (index of defined expressions), insert at the appropriate places —

"property business (in Chapters 3 to 6 of Part 9)	section 437(8A)"
"relevant change in relationship (in Chapters 3 to 6 of Part 9)	section 392",

and in the entry relating to "qualifying change of ownership in relation to a company (in Chapters 3 to 6 of Part 9)" for "392 to 398" substitute "394A to 398A").

Commencement etc

9   The amendments made by this Schedule have effect where the relevant day is on or after 9 December 2009.

10   Amendments corresponding to those made by this Schedule, having effect where the relevant day is on or after that date, are to be treated as having been made in Schedule 10 to FA 2006.

11   Neither section 398F of CTA 2010 (inserted by paragraph 6) nor the corresponding provision treated as inserted by paragraph 10 apply in relation to expenditure incurred in pursuance of a written contract which is finalised by A before 9 December 2009; and for this purpose a contract is finalised on the earliest date on which —

(a)   it is unconditional or (if conditional) the conditions are met, and

(b)   no terms remain to be agreed.

12   Section 398A of CTA 2010 (as inserted by paragraph 6) has effect in relation to a relevant change in the relationship between A and a principal company of A in the case of which the relevant day is before 24 March 2010 as if —

(a)   in subsection (3)(b), the words "falling within subsection (4)", and

(b)   subsections (4) and (5),

were omitted.

13   Section 398D of CTA 2010 (as inserted by paragraph 6) —

(a)   has effect with the omission of subsection (6) in relation to accounting periods beginning before 24 March 2010, and

(b)   has effect with the omission of subsection (7) until that date.

SCHEDULE 19

ACCOUNTING STANDARDS: LOAN RELATIONSHIPS AND DERIVATIVE CONTRACTS

Loan relationships

1   In Chapter 18 of Part 5 of CTA 2009 (loan relationships: general and supplementary provision), before section 466 (and the heading before it) insert —

"Changes in accounting standards

465A Power to make regulations where accounting standards change

(1)   The Treasury may by regulations make provision for cases where, in consequence of a change in accounting standards, there is a relevant accounting change.

(2)   "Change in accounting standards" means the issue, revocation, amendment or recognition of, or withdrawal of recognition from, an accounting standard by an accounting body.

(3)   "Relevant accounting change" means a change in the way in which a company is permitted or required, for accounting purposes, to recognise amounts which —
    (a)   are brought into account by the company as credits or debits for any period for the purposes of this Part, or
    (b)   would be so brought into account but for any provision made by or under this Part.

(4)   Regulations under subsection (1) may amend this Part (apart from this section).

(5)   Regulations under subsection (1) may —
    (a)   make different provision for different cases,
    (b)   make incidental, supplemental, consequential and transitional provision and savings, and
    (c)   make provision subject to an election or other specified circumstances.

(6)   Regulations making consequential provision by virtue of subsection (5)(b) may, in particular, include provision amending a provision of the Corporation Tax Acts.

(7)   Regulations under subsection (1) may apply to a pre-commencement period if they make provision in relation to a relevant accounting change which may or must be adopted, for accounting purposes, for a period of account, or part of a period of account, which coincides with that pre-commencement period.

(8)   In this section —
        "accounting body" means the International Accounting Standards Board or the Accounting Standards Board, or a successor body to either of those Boards;
        "accounting standard" includes any statement of practice, guidance or other similar document;

> "pre-commencement period", in relation to regulations, means an accounting period, or part of an accounting period, which begins before the regulations are made."

Derivative contracts

2   In Chapter 13 of Part 7 of CTA 2009 (derivative contracts: general and supplementary provision), after section 701 insert—

"Changes to accounting standards

701A Power to make regulations where accounting standards change

(1) The Treasury may by regulations make provision for cases where, in consequence of a change in accounting standards, there is a relevant accounting change.

(2) "Change in accounting standards" means the issue, revocation, amendment or recognition of, or withdrawal of recognition from, an accounting standard by an accounting body.

(3) "Relevant accounting change" means a change in the way in which a company is permitted or required, for accounting purposes, to recognise amounts which—

    (a) are brought into account by the company as credits or debits for any period for the purposes of this Part, or

    (b) would be so brought into account but for any provision made by or under this Part.

(4) Regulations under subsection (1) may amend this Part (apart from this section).

(5) Regulations under subsection (1) may—

    (a) make different provision for different cases,

    (b) make incidental, supplemental, consequential and transitional provision and savings, and

    (c) make provision subject to an election or other specified circumstances.

(6) Regulations making consequential provision by virtue of subsection (5)(b) may, in particular, include provision amending a provision of the Corporation Tax Acts.

(7) Regulations under subsection (1) may apply to a pre-commencement period if they make provision in relation to a relevant accounting change which may or must be adopted, for accounting purposes, for a period of account (or part of a period of account) which coincides with that pre-commencement period.

(8) In this section—

    "accounting body" means the International Accounting Standards Board or the Accounting Standards Board, or a successor body to either of those Boards;

    "accounting standard" includes any statement of practice, guidance or other similar document;

"pre-commencement period", in relation to regulations, means an accounting period (or part of an accounting period) which begins before the regulations are made."

Affirmative resolution procedure

3   In section 1310(4) of CTA 2009 (orders and regulations subject to affirmative resolution of House of Commons), before paragraph (za) insert—

"(zza)   section 465A or 701A (powers to make regulations where accounting standards change),".

SCHEDULE 20

Section 63

CHAMPIONS LEAGUE FINAL

Exemption from income tax

1   (1) This paragraph applies if an employee or contractor of an overseas team which competes in the 2011 Champions League final ("the final") is neither UK resident nor ordinarily UK resident at the time of the final.

     (2) That person is not liable to income tax in respect of any income arising to the person which is related to duties or services performed by the person in the United Kingdom in connection with the final.

     (3) This paragraph is subject to paragraphs 2 and 3.

     (4) For the meaning of some expressions used in this paragraph, see paragraphs 5 and 6.

Exclusion of certain income

2   Paragraph 1(2) does not apply to income which arises as a result of—
         (a)   a contract entered into after the final, or
         (b)   any amendment, after the final, of a contract entered into before the end of the final.

Tax avoidance

3   (1) This paragraph applies if conditions A and B are met.

     (2) Condition A is that arrangements have been made which, but for this paragraph, would result in a person obtaining exemption under paragraph 1 in respect of particular income.

     (3) Condition B is that those arrangements have, or form part of arrangements which have, as their main purpose, or one of their main purposes, the obtaining of that exemption.

     (4) Paragraph 1(2) does not apply to that income.

Disapplication of section 966 of ITA 2007

4   Section 966 of ITA 2007 (duty to deduct and account for sums representing income tax) does not apply to any payment or transfer which gives rise to income within paragraph 1(2).

Interpretation

5   References in this Schedule to income are to be read as references to—

   (a)   income that would be employment income but for the provisions of paragraph 1, and

   (b)   profits of a trade, profession or vocation (including profits treated as arising as a result of provision made by or under sections 13 and 14 of ITTOIA 2005).

6   In this Schedule—

   "the 2011 Champions League final" means the final of the UEFA Champions League 2010/2011 competition held in England in 2011;

   "contractor", in relation to an overseas team, means an individual who is not an employee of the team but who performs services for the team—

      (a)   under the terms of a contract with the team, or

      (b)   under the terms of a contract, or that individual's employment, with a company which is a member of the same group of companies as the team (within the meaning given by section 152 of CTA 2010);

   "employee" and "employment" are to be read in accordance with section 4 of ITEPA 2003;

   "overseas team" means a football club which is not a member of the Football Association, the Scottish Football Association, the Football Association of Wales or the Irish Football Association.

Anti-Slavery Day Act 2010

CHAPTER 14

CONTENTS

Anti-Slavery Day Act 2010

2010 CHAPTER 14

An Act to introduce a national day to raise awareness of the need to eradicate all forms of slavery, human trafficking and exploitation; and for connected purposes. [8th April 2010]

B E IT ENACTED by the Queen's most Excellent Majesty, by and with the advice and consent of the Lords Spiritual and Temporal, and Commons, in this present Parliament assembled, and by the authority of the same, as follows:—

1 Anti-Slavery Day

(1) The Secretary of State shall by order made by statutory instrument specify a date which shall be observed each year as Anti-Slavery Day.

(2) The purpose of Anti-Slavery Day shall be to—
   (a) acknowledge that millions of men, women and children continue to be victims of slavery, depriving them of basic human dignity and freedom;
   (b) raise awareness amongst young people and others of the dangers and consequences of slavery, human trafficking and exploitation and encourage them to be proactive in the fight against it;
   (c) draw attention to—
      (i) the progress made by government and those working to combat all forms of slavery, human trafficking and exploitation, and
      (ii) what more needs to be done.

(3) In this Act "slavery" includes—
   (a) trafficking for sexual exploitation,
   (b) child trafficking,
   (c) trafficking for forced labour, and
   (d) domestic servitude.

2 Short title and extent

(1) This Act may be cited as the Anti-Slavery Day Act 2010.

(2) This Act extends to England and Wales.

Equality Act 2010

CHAPTER 15

CONTENTS

PART 3

SERVICES AND PUBLIC FUNCTIONS

Preliminary

Provision of services, etc.

Supplementary

PART 4

PREMISES

Preliminary

Disposal and management

CHAPTER 4

SUPPLEMENTARY

PART 6

EDUCATION

CHAPTER 1

SCHOOLS

CHAPTER 2

FURTHER AND HIGHER EDUCATION

CHAPTER 3

GENERAL QUALIFICATIONS BODIES

CHAPTER 4

MISCELLANEOUS

PART 7

ASSOCIATIONS

Preliminary

Membership, etc.

Special provision for political parties

Supplementary

PART 8

PROHIBITED CONDUCT: ANCILLARY

PART 9

ENFORCEMENT

CHAPTER 1

INTRODUCTORY

CHAPTER 2

CIVIL COURTS

CHAPTER 3

EMPLOYMENT TRIBUNALS

CHAPTER 4

EQUALITY OF TERMS

CHAPTER 5

MISCELLANEOUS

PART 10

CONTRACTS, ETC.

Contracts and other agreements

Collective agreements and rules of undertakings

CHAPTER 2

PUBLIC SERVICE VEHICLES

CHAPTER 3

RAIL VEHICLES

CHAPTER 4

SUPPLEMENTARY

PART 13

DISABILITY: MISCELLANEOUS

PART 14

GENERAL EXCEPTIONS

PART 15

FAMILY PROPERTY

PART 16

GENERAL AND MISCELLANEOUS

Civil partnerships

EU obligations

Application

Subordinate legislation

Amendments, etc.

Interpretation

Final provisions

Equality Act 2010

2010 CHAPTER 15

An Act to make provision to require Ministers of the Crown and others when making strategic decisions about the exercise of their functions to have regard to the desirability of reducing socio-economic inequalities; to reform and harmonise equality law and restate the greater part of the enactments relating to discrimination and harassment related to certain personal characteristics; to enable certain employers to be required to publish information about the differences in pay between male and female employees; to prohibit victimisation in certain circumstances; to require the exercise of certain functions to be with regard to the need to eliminate discrimination and other prohibited conduct; to enable duties to be imposed in relation to the exercise of public procurement functions; to increase equality of opportunity; to amend the law relating to rights and responsibilities in family relationships; and for connected purposes. [8th April 2010]

B E IT ENACTED by the Queen's most Excellent Majesty, by and with the advice and consent of the Lords Spiritual and Temporal, and Commons, in this present Parliament assembled, and by the authority of the same, as follows:—

PART 1

SOCIO-ECONOMIC INEQUALITIES

1   Public sector duty regarding socio-economic inequalities

(1)   An authority to which this section applies must, when making decisions of a strategic nature about how to exercise its functions, have due regard to the desirability of exercising them in a way that is designed to reduce the inequalities of outcome which result from socio-economic disadvantage.

(2)   In deciding how to fulfil a duty to which it is subject under subsection (1), an authority must take into account any guidance issued by a Minister of the Crown.

(3)   The authorities to which this section applies are —

    (a)   a Minister of the Crown;

    (b)   a government department other than the Security Service, the Secret Intelligence Service or the Government Communications Head-quarters;

    (c)   a county council or district council in England;

    (d)   the Greater London Authority;

    (e)   a London borough council;

    (f)   the Common Council of the City of London in its capacity as a local authority;

    (g)   the Council of the Isles of Scilly;

    (h)   a Strategic Health Authority established under section 13 of the National Health Service Act 2006, or continued in existence by virtue of that section;

    (i)   a Primary Care Trust established under section 18 of that Act, or continued in existence by virtue of that section;

    (j)   a regional development agency established by the Regional Development Agencies Act 1998;

    (k)   a police authority established for an area in England.

(4)   This section also applies to an authority that —

    (a)   is a partner authority in relation to a responsible local authority, and

    (b)   does not fall within subsection (3),

but only in relation to its participation in the preparation or modification of a sustainable community strategy.

(5)   In subsection (4) —

"partner authority" has the meaning given by section 104 of the Local Government and Public Involvement in Health Act 2007;

"responsible local authority" has the meaning given by section 103 of that Act;

"sustainable community strategy" means a strategy prepared under section 4 of the Local Government Act 2000.

(6)   The reference to inequalities in subsection (1) does not include any inequalities experienced by a person as a result of being a person subject to immigration control within the meaning given by section 115(9) of the Immigration and Asylum Act 1999.

2   Power to amend section 1

(1)   A Minister of the Crown may by regulations amend section 1 so as to —

    (a)   add a public authority to the authorities that are subject to the duty under subsection (1) of that section;

    (b)   remove an authority from those that are subject to the duty;

    (c)   make the duty apply, in the case of a particular authority, only in relation to certain functions that it has;

    (d)   in the case of an authority to which the application of the duty is already restricted to certain functions, remove or alter the restriction.

(2)   In subsection (1) "public authority" means an authority that has functions of a public nature.

(3)   Provision made under subsection (1) may not impose a duty on an authority in relation to any devolved Scottish functions or devolved Welsh functions.

(4)   The Scottish Ministers or the Welsh Ministers may by regulations amend section 1 so as to—

    (a)   add a relevant authority to the authorities that are subject to the duty under subsection (1) of that section;

    (b)   remove a relevant authority from those that are subject to the duty;

    (c)   make the duty apply, in the case of a particular relevant authority, only in relation to certain functions that it has;

    (d)   in the case of a relevant authority to which the application of the duty is already restricted to certain functions, remove or alter the restriction.

(5)   For the purposes of the power conferred by subsection (4) on the Scottish Ministers, "relevant authority" means an authority whose functions—

    (a)   are exercisable only in or as regards Scotland,

    (b)   are wholly or mainly devolved Scottish functions, and

    (c)   correspond or are similar to those of an authority for the time being specified in section 1(3).

(6)   For the purposes of the power conferred by subsection (4) on the Welsh Ministers, "relevant authority" means an authority whose functions—

    (a)   are exercisable only in or as regards Wales,

    (b)   are wholly or mainly devolved Welsh functions, and

    (c)   correspond or are similar to those of an authority for the time being specified in subsection (3) of section 1 or referred to in subsection (4) of that section.

(7)   Before making regulations under this section, the Scottish Ministers or the Welsh Ministers must consult a Minister of the Crown.

(8)   Regulations under this section may make any amendments of section 1 that appear to the Minister or Ministers to be necessary or expedient in consequence of provision made under subsection (1) or (as the case may be) subsection (4).

(9)   Provision made by the Scottish Ministers or the Welsh Ministers in reliance on subsection (8) may, in particular, amend section 1 so as to—

    (a)   confer on the Ministers a power to issue guidance;

    (b)   require a relevant authority to take into account any guidance issued under a power conferred by virtue of paragraph (a);

    (c)   disapply section 1(2) in consequence of the imposition of a requirement by virtue of paragraph (b).

(10)   Before issuing guidance under a power conferred by virtue of subsection (9)(a), the Ministers must—

    (a)   take into account any guidance issued by a Minister of the Crown under section 1;

    (b)   consult a Minister of the Crown.

(11)   For the purposes of this section—

    (a)   a function is a devolved Scottish function if it is exercisable in or as regards Scotland and it does not relate to reserved matters (within the meaning of the Scotland Act 1998);

    (b)   a function is a devolved Welsh function if it relates to a matter in respect of which functions are exercisable by the Welsh Ministers, the First

Minister for Wales or the Counsel General to the Welsh Assembly Government, or to a matter within the legislative competence of the National Assembly for Wales.

3 Enforcement

A failure in respect of a performance of a duty under section 1 does not confer a cause of action at private law.

PART 2

EQUALITY: KEY CONCEPTS

CHAPTER 1

PROTECTED CHARACTERISTICS

4 The protected characteristics

The following characteristics are protected characteristics —
> age;
> disability;
> gender reassignment;
> marriage and civil partnership;
> pregnancy and maternity;
> race;
> religion or belief;
> sex;
> sexual orientation.

5 Age

(1) In relation to the protected characteristic of age —
  (a) a reference to a person who has a particular protected characteristic is a reference to a person of a particular age group;
  (b) a reference to persons who share a protected characteristic is a reference to persons of the same age group.

(2) A reference to an age group is a reference to a group of persons defined by reference to age, whether by reference to a particular age or to a range of ages.

6 Disability

(1) A person (P) has a disability if —
  (a) P has a physical or mental impairment, and
  (b) the impairment has a substantial and long-term adverse effect on P's ability to carry out normal day-to-day activities.

(2) A reference to a disabled person is a reference to a person who has a disability.

(3) In relation to the protected characteristic of disability —
  (a) a reference to a person who has a particular protected characteristic is a reference to a person who has a particular disability;

    (b)   a reference to persons who share a protected characteristic is a reference to persons who have the same disability.

(4)   This Act (except Part 12 and section 190) applies in relation to a person who has had a disability as it applies in relation to a person who has the disability; accordingly (except in that Part and that section) —

    (a)   a reference (however expressed) to a person who has a disability includes a reference to a person who has had the disability, and

    (b)   a reference (however expressed) to a person who does not have a disability includes a reference to a person who has not had the disability.

(5)   A Minister of the Crown may issue guidance about matters to be taken into account in deciding any question for the purposes of subsection (1).

(6)   Schedule 1 (disability: supplementary provision) has effect.

7   Gender reassignment

(1)   A person has the protected characteristic of gender reassignment if the person is proposing to undergo, is undergoing or has undergone a process (or part of a process) for the purpose of reassigning the person's sex by changing physiological or other attributes of sex.

(2)   A reference to a transsexual person is a reference to a person who has the protected characteristic of gender reassignment.

(3)   In relation to the protected characteristic of gender reassignment —

    (a)   a reference to a person who has a particular protected characteristic is a reference to a transsexual person;

    (b)   a reference to persons who share a protected characteristic is a reference to transsexual persons.

8   Marriage and civil partnership

(1)   A person has the protected characteristic of marriage and civil partnership if the person is married or is a civil partner.

(2)   In relation to the protected characteristic of marriage and civil partnership —

    (a)   a reference to a person who has a particular protected characteristic is a reference to a person who is married or is a civil partner;

    (b)   a reference to persons who share a protected characteristic is a reference to persons who are married or are civil partners.

9   Race

(1)   Race includes —

    (a)   colour;

    (b)   nationality;

    (c)   ethnic or national origins.

(2)   In relation to the protected characteristic of race —

    (a)   a reference to a person who has a particular protected characteristic is a reference to a person of a particular racial group;

    (b)   a reference to persons who share a protected characteristic is a reference to persons of the same racial group.

(3)   A racial group is a group of persons defined by reference to race; and a reference to a person's racial group is a reference to a racial group into which the person falls.

(4)   The fact that a racial group comprises two or more distinct racial groups does not prevent it from constituting a particular racial group.

(5)   A Minister of the Crown may by order—

    (a)   amend this section so as to provide for caste to be an aspect of race;

    (b)   amend this Act so as to provide for an exception to a provision of this Act to apply, or not to apply, to caste or to apply, or not to apply, to caste in specified circumstances.

(6)   The power under section 207(4)(b), in its application to subsection (5), includes power to amend this Act.

10   Religion or belief

(1)   Religion means any religion and a reference to religion includes a reference to a lack of religion.

(2)   Belief means any religious or philosophical belief and a reference to belief includes a reference to a lack of belief.

(3)   In relation to the protected characteristic of religion or belief—

    (a)   a reference to a person who has a particular protected characteristic is a reference to a person of a particular religion or belief;

    (b)   a reference to persons who share a protected characteristic is a reference to persons who are of the same religion or belief.

11   Sex

In relation to the protected characteristic of sex—

    (a)   a reference to a person who has a particular protected characteristic is a reference to a man or to a woman;

    (b)   a reference to persons who share a protected characteristic is a reference to persons of the same sex.

12   Sexual orientation

(1)   Sexual orientation means a person's sexual orientation towards—

    (a)   persons of the same sex,

    (b)   persons of the opposite sex, or

    (c)   persons of either sex.

(2)   In relation to the protected characteristic of sexual orientation—

    (a)   a reference to a person who has a particular protected characteristic is a reference to a person who is of a particular sexual orientation;

    (b)   a reference to persons who share a protected characteristic is a reference to persons who are of the same sexual orientation.

CHAPTER 2

PROHIBITED CONDUCT

Discrimination

13   Direct discrimination

(1)   A person (A) discriminates against another (B) if, because of a protected characteristic, A treats B less favourably than A treats or would treat others.

(2)   If the protected characteristic is age, A does not discriminate against B if A can show A's treatment of B to be a proportionate means of achieving a legitimate aim.

(3)   If the protected characteristic is disability, and B is not a disabled person, A does not discriminate against B only because A treats or would treat disabled persons more favourably than A treats B.

(4)   If the protected characteristic is marriage and civil partnership, this section applies to a contravention of Part 5 (work) only if the treatment is because it is B who is married or a civil partner.

(5)   If the protected characteristic is race, less favourable treatment includes segregating B from others.

(6)   If the protected characteristic is sex —
    (a)   less favourable treatment of a woman includes less favourable treatment of her because she is breast-feeding;
    (b)   in a case where B is a man, no account is to be taken of special treatment afforded to a woman in connection with pregnancy or childbirth.

(7)   Subsection (6)(a) does not apply for the purposes of Part 5 (work).

(8)   This section is subject to sections 17(6) and 18(7).

14   Combined discrimination: dual characteristics

(1)   A person (A) discriminates against another (B) if, because of a combination of two relevant protected characteristics, A treats B less favourably than A treats or would treat a person who does not share either of those characteristics.

(2)   The relevant protected characteristics are —
    (a)   age;
    (b)   disability;
    (c)   gender reassignment;
    (d)   race
    (e)   religion or belief;
    (f)   sex;
    (g)   sexual orientation.

(3)   For the purposes of establishing a contravention of this Act by virtue of subsection (1), B need not show that A's treatment of B is direct discrimination because of each of the characteristics in the combination (taken separately).

(4) But B cannot establish a contravention of this Act by virtue of subsection (1) if, in reliance on another provision of this Act or any other enactment, A shows that A's treatment of B is not direct discrimination because of either or both of the characteristics in the combination.

(5) Subsection (1) does not apply to a combination of characteristics that includes disability in circumstances where, if a claim of direct discrimination because of disability were to be brought, it would come within section 116 (special educational needs).

(6) A Minister of the Crown may by order amend this section so as to—

(a) make further provision about circumstances in which B can, or in which B cannot, establish a contravention of this Act by virtue of subsection (1);

(b) specify other circumstances in which subsection (1) does not apply.

(7) The references to direct discrimination are to a contravention of this Act by virtue of section 13.

15   Discrimination arising from disability

(1) A person (A) discriminates against a disabled person (B) if—

(a) A treats B unfavourably because of something arising in consequence of B's disability, and

(b) A cannot show that the treatment is a proportionate means of achieving a legitimate aim.

(2) Subsection (1) does not apply if A shows that A did not know, and could not reasonably have been expected to know, that B had the disability.

16   Gender reassignment discrimination: cases of absence from work

(1) This section has effect for the purposes of the application of Part 5 (work) to the protected characteristic of gender reassignment.

(2) A person (A) discriminates against a transsexual person (B) if, in relation to an absence of B's that is because of gender reassignment, A treats B less favourably than A would treat B if—

(a) B's absence was because of sickness or injury, or

(b) B's absence was for some other reason and it is not reasonable for B to be treated less favourably.

(3) A person's absence is because of gender reassignment if it is because the person is proposing to undergo, is undergoing or has undergone the process (or part of the process) mentioned in section 7(1).

17   Pregnancy and maternity discrimination: non-work cases

(1) This section has effect for the purposes of the application to the protected characteristic of pregnancy and maternity of—

(a) Part 3 (services and public functions);

(b) Part 4 (premises);

(c) Part 6 (education);

(d) Part 7 (associations).

(2) A person (A) discriminates against a woman if A treats her unfavourably because of a pregnancy of hers.

(3) A person (A) discriminates against a woman if, in the period of 26 weeks beginning with the day on which she gives birth, A treats her unfavourably because she has given birth.

(4) The reference in subsection (3) to treating a woman unfavourably because she has given birth includes, in particular, a reference to treating her unfavourably because she is breast-feeding.

(5) For the purposes of this section, the day on which a woman gives birth is the day on which —

   (a) she gives birth to a living child, or

   (b) she gives birth to a dead child (more than 24 weeks of the pregnancy having passed).

(6) Section 13, so far as relating to sex discrimination, does not apply to anything done in relation to a woman in so far as —

   (a) it is for the reason mentioned in subsection (2), or

   (b) it is in the period, and for the reason, mentioned in subsection (3).

18 Pregnancy and maternity discrimination: work cases

(1) This section has effect for the purposes of the application of Part 5 (work) to the protected characteristic of pregnancy and maternity.

(2) A person (A) discriminates against a woman if, in the protected period in relation to a pregnancy of hers, A treats her unfavourably —

   (a) because of the pregnancy, or

   (b) because of illness suffered by her as a result of it.

(3) A person (A) discriminates against a woman if A treats her unfavourably because she is on compulsory maternity leave.

(4) A person (A) discriminates against a woman if A treats her unfavourably because she is exercising or seeking to exercise, or has exercised or sought to exercise, the right to ordinary or additional maternity leave.

(5) For the purposes of subsection (2), if the treatment of a woman is in implementation of a decision taken in the protected period, the treatment is to be regarded as occurring in that period (even if the implementation is not until after the end of that period).

(6) The protected period, in relation to a woman's pregnancy, begins when the pregnancy begins, and ends —

   (a) if she has the right to ordinary and additional maternity leave, at the end of the additional maternity leave period or (if earlier) when she returns to work after the pregnancy;

   (b) if she does not have that right, at the end of the period of 2 weeks beginning with the end of the pregnancy.

(7) Section 13, so far as relating to sex discrimination, does not apply to treatment of a woman in so far as —

   (a) it is in the protected period in relation to her and is for a reason mentioned in paragraph (a) or (b) of subsection (2), or

   (b) it is for a reason mentioned in subsection (3) or (4).

19 Indirect discrimination

(1) A person (A) discriminates against another (B) if A applies to B a provision, criterion or practice which is discriminatory in relation to a relevant protected characteristic of B's.

(2) For the purposes of subsection (1), a provision, criterion or practice is discriminatory in relation to a relevant protected characteristic of B's if —

   (a) A applies, or would apply, it to persons with whom B does not share the characteristic,

   (b) it puts, or would put, persons with whom B shares the characteristic at a particular disadvantage when compared with persons with whom B does not share it,

   (c) it puts, or would put, B at that disadvantage, and

   (d) A cannot show it to be a proportionate means of achieving a legitimate aim.

(3) The relevant protected characteristics are —

   age;
   disability;
   gender reassignment;
   marriage and civil partnership;
   race;
   religion or belief;
   sex;
   sexual orientation.

Adjustments for disabled persons

20 Duty to make adjustments

(1) Where this Act imposes a duty to make reasonable adjustments on a person, this section, sections 21 and 22 and the applicable Schedule apply; and for those purposes, a person on whom the duty is imposed is referred to as A.

(2) The duty comprises the following three requirements.

(3) The first requirement is a requirement, where a provision, criterion or practice of A's puts a disabled person at a substantial disadvantage in relation to a relevant matter in comparison with persons who are not disabled, to take such steps as it is reasonable to have to take to avoid the disadvantage.

(4) The second requirement is a requirement, where a physical feature puts a disabled person at a substantial disadvantage in relation to a relevant matter in comparison with persons who are not disabled, to take such steps as it is reasonable to have to take to avoid the disadvantage.

(5) The third requirement is a requirement, where a disabled person would, but for the provision of an auxiliary aid, be put at a substantial disadvantage in relation to a relevant matter in comparison with persons who are not disabled, to take such steps as it is reasonable to have to take to provide the auxiliary aid.

(6) Where the first or third requirement relates to the provision of information, the steps which it is reasonable for A to have to take include steps for ensuring that

in the circumstances concerned the information is provided in an accessible format.

(7)   A person (A) who is subject to a duty to make reasonable adjustments is not (subject to express provision to the contrary) entitled to require a disabled person, in relation to whom A is required to comply with the duty, to pay to any extent A's costs of complying with the duty.

(8)   A reference in section 21 or 22 or an applicable Schedule to the first, second or third requirement is to be construed in accordance with this section.

(9)   In relation to the second requirement, a reference in this section or an applicable Schedule to avoiding a substantial disadvantage includes a reference to—

(a)   removing the physical feature in question,

(b)   altering it, or

(c)   providing a reasonable means of avoiding it.

(10)   A reference in this section, section 21 or 22 or an applicable Schedule (apart from paragraphs 2 to 4 of Schedule 4) to a physical feature is a reference to—

(a)   a feature arising from the design or construction of a building,

(b)   a feature of an approach to, exit from or access to a building,

(c)   a fixture or fitting, or furniture, furnishings, materials, equipment or other chattels, in or on premises, or

(d)   any other physical element or quality.

(11)   A reference in this section, section 21 or 22 or an applicable Schedule to an auxiliary aid includes a reference to an auxiliary service.

(12)   A reference in this section or an applicable Schedule to chattels is to be read, in relation to Scotland, as a reference to moveable property.

(13)   The applicable Schedule is, in relation to the Part of this Act specified in the first column of the Table, the Schedule specified in the second column.

Part of this Act	*Applicable Schedule*
Part 3 (services and public functions)	Schedule 2
Part 4 (premises)	Schedule 4
Part 5 (work)	Schedule 8
Part 6 (education)	Schedule 13
Part 7 (associations)	Schedule 15
Each of the Parts mentioned above	Schedule 21

21   Failure to comply with duty

(1)   A failure to comply with the first, second or third requirement is a failure to comply with a duty to make reasonable adjustments.

(2)   A discriminates against a disabled person if A fails to comply with that duty in relation to that person.

(3)   A provision of an applicable Schedule which imposes a duty to comply with the first, second or third requirement applies only for the purpose of establishing whether A has contravened this Act by virtue of subsection (2); a failure to comply is, accordingly, not actionable by virtue of another provision of this Act or otherwise.

22   Regulations

(1)   Regulations may prescribe—

   (a)   matters to be taken into account in deciding whether it is reasonable for A to take a step for the purposes of a prescribed provision of an applicable Schedule;

   (b)   descriptions of persons to whom the first, second or third requirement does not apply.

(2)   Regulations may make provision as to—

   (a)   circumstances in which it is, or in which it is not, reasonable for a person of a prescribed description to have to take steps of a prescribed description;

   (b)   what is, or what is not, a provision, criterion or practice;

   (c)   things which are, or which are not, to be treated as physical features;

   (d)   things which are, or which are not, to be treated as alterations of physical features;

   (e)   things which are, or which are not, to be treated as auxiliary aids.

(3)   Provision made by virtue of this section may amend an applicable Schedule.

Discrimination: supplementary

23   Comparison by reference to circumstances

(1)   On a comparison of cases for the purposes of section 13, 14, or 19 there must be no material difference between the circumstances relating to each case.

(2)   The circumstances relating to a case include a person's abilities if—

   (a)   on a comparison for the purposes of section 13, the protected characteristic is disability;

   (b)   on a comparison for the purposes of section 14, one of the protected characteristics in the combination is disability.

(3)   If the protected characteristic is sexual orientation, the fact that one person (whether or not the person referred to as B) is a civil partner while another is married is not a material difference between the circumstances relating to each case.

24   Irrelevance of alleged discriminator's characteristics

(1)   For the purpose of establishing a contravention of this Act by virtue of section 13(1), it does not matter whether A has the protected characteristic.

(2)   For the purpose of establishing a contravention of this Act by virtue of section 14(1), it does not matter—

   (a)   whether A has one of the protected characteristics in the combination;

   (b)   whether A has both.

25 References to particular strands of discrimination

(1) Age discrimination is —

    (a) discrimination within section 13 because of age;

    (b) discrimination within section 19 where the relevant protected characteristic is age.

(2) Disability discrimination is —

    (a) discrimination within section 13 because of disability;

    (b) discrimination within section 15;

    (c) discrimination within section 19 where the relevant protected characteristic is disability;

    (d) discrimination within section 21.

(3) Gender reassignment discrimination is —

    (a) discrimination within section 13 because of gender reassignment;

    (b) discrimination within section 16;

    (c) discrimination within section 19 where the relevant protected characteristic is gender reassignment.

(4) Marriage and civil partnership discrimination is —

    (a) discrimination within section 13 because of marriage and civil partnership;

    (b) discrimination within section 19 where the relevant protected characteristic is marriage and civil partnership.

(5) Pregnancy and maternity discrimination is discrimination within section 17 or 18.

(6) Race discrimination is —

    (a) discrimination within section 13 because of race;

    (b) discrimination within section 19 where the relevant protected characteristic is race.

(7) Religious or belief-related discrimination is —

    (a) discrimination within section 13 because of religion or belief;

    (b) discrimination within section 19 where the relevant protected characteristic is religion or belief.

(8) Sex discrimination is —

    (a) discrimination within section 13 because of sex;

    (b) discrimination within section 19 where the relevant protected characteristic is sex.

(9) Sexual orientation discrimination is —

    (a) discrimination within section 13 because of sexual orientation;

    (b) discrimination within section 19 where the relevant protected characteristic is sexual orientation.

Other prohibited conduct

26 Harassment

(1) A person (A) harasses another (B) if—

    (a)   A engages in unwanted conduct related to a relevant protected characteristic, and

    (b)   the conduct has the purpose or effect of –

        (i)   violating B's dignity, or

        (ii)   creating an intimidating, hostile, degrading, humiliating or offensive environment for B.

(2)   A also harasses B if –

    (a)   A engages in unwanted conduct of a sexual nature, and

    (b)   the conduct has the purpose or effect referred to in subsection (1)(b).

(3)   A also harasses B if –

    (a)   A or another person engages in unwanted conduct of a sexual nature or that is related to gender reassignment or sex,

    (b)   the conduct has the purpose or effect referred to in subsection (1)(b), and

    (c)   because of B's rejection of or submission to the conduct, A treats B less favourably than A would treat B if B had not rejected or submitted to the conduct.

(4)   In deciding whether conduct has the effect referred to in subsection (1)(b), each of the following must be taken into account –

    (a)   the perception of B;

    (b)   the other circumstances of the case;

    (c)   whether it is reasonable for the conduct to have that effect.

(5)   The relevant protected characteristics are –

        age;

        disability;

        gender reassignment;

        race;

        religion or belief;

        sex;

        sexual orientation.

27   Victimisation

(1)   A person (A) victimises another person (B) if A subjects B to a detriment because –

    (a)   B does a protected act, or

    (b)   A believes that B has done, or may do, a protected act.

(2)   Each of the following is a protected act –

    (a)   bringing proceedings under this Act;

    (b)   giving evidence or information in connection with proceedings under this Act;

    (c)   doing any other thing for the purposes of or in connection with this Act;

    (d)   making an allegation (whether or not express) that A or another person has contravened this Act.

(3)   Giving false evidence or information, or making a false allegation, is not a protected act if the evidence or information is given, or the allegation is made, in bad faith.

(4) This section applies only where the person subjected to a detriment is an individual.

(5) The reference to contravening this Act includes a reference to committing a breach of an equality clause or rule.

PART 3

SERVICES AND PUBLIC FUNCTIONS

Preliminary

28 Application of this Part

(1) This Part does not apply to the protected characteristic of —
    (a) age, so far as relating to persons who have not attained the age of 18;
    (b) marriage and civil partnership.

(2) This Part does not apply to discrimination, harassment or victimisation —
    (a) that is prohibited by Part 4 (premises), 5 (work) or 6 (education), or
    (b) that would be so prohibited but for an express exception.

(3) This Part does not apply to —
    (a) a breach of an equality clause or rule;
    (b) anything that would be a breach of an equality clause or rule but for section 69 or Part 2 of Schedule 7;
    (c) a breach of a non-discrimination rule.

Provision of services, etc.

29 Provision of services, etc.

(1) A person (a "service-provider") concerned with the provision of a service to the public or a section of the public (for payment or not) must not discriminate against a person requiring the service by not providing the person with the service.

(2) A service-provider (A) must not, in providing the service, discriminate against a person (B) —
    (a) as to the terms on which A provides the service to B;
    (b) by terminating the provision of the service to B;
    (c) by subjecting B to any other detriment.

(3) A service-provider must not, in relation to the provision of the service, harass —
    (a) a person requiring the service, or
    (b) a person to whom the service-provider provides the service.

(4) A service-provider must not victimise a person requiring the service by not providing the person with the service.

(5) A service-provider (A) must not, in providing the service, victimise a person (B) —
    (a) as to the terms on which A provides the service to B;

      (b)   by terminating the provision of the service to B;

      (c)   by subjecting B to any other detriment.

(6)   A person must not, in the exercise of a public function that is not the provision of a service to the public or a section of the public, do anything that constitutes discrimination, harassment or victimisation.

(7)   A duty to make reasonable adjustments applies to —

      (a)   a service-provider (and see also section 55(7));

      (b)   a person who exercises a public function that is not the provision of a service to the public or a section of the public.

(8)   In the application of section 26 for the purposes of subsection (3), and subsection (6) as it relates to harassment, neither of the following is a relevant protected characteristic —

      (a)   religion or belief;

      (b)   sexual orientation.

(9)   In the application of this section, so far as relating to race or religion or belief, to the granting of entry clearance (within the meaning of the Immigration Act 1971), it does not matter whether an act is done within or outside the United Kingdom.

(10)   Subsection (9) does not affect the application of any other provision of this Act to conduct outside England and Wales or Scotland.

Supplementary

30   Ships and hovercraft

(1)   This Part (subject to subsection (2)) applies only in such circumstances as are prescribed in relation to —

      (a)   transporting people by ship or hovercraft;

      (b)   a service provided on a ship or hovercraft.

(2)   Section 29(6) applies in relation to the matters referred to in paragraphs (a) and (b) of subsection (1); but in so far as it relates to disability discrimination, section 29(6) applies to those matters only in such circumstances as are prescribed.

(3)   It does not matter whether the ship or hovercraft is within or outside the United Kingdom.

(4)   "Ship" has the same meaning as in the Merchant Shipping Act 1995.

(5)   "Hovercraft" has the same meaning as in the Hovercraft Act 1968.

(6)   Nothing in this section affects the application of any other provision of this Act to conduct outside England and Wales or Scotland.

31   Interpretation and exceptions

(1)   This section applies for the purposes of this Part.

(2)   A reference to the provision of a service includes a reference to the provision of goods or facilities.

(3) A reference to the provision of a service includes a reference to the provision of a service in the exercise of a public function.

(4) A public function is a function that is a function of a public nature for the purposes of the Human Rights Act 1998.

(5) Where an employer arranges for another person to provide a service only to the employer's employees —

    (a) the employer is not to be regarded as the service-provider, but

    (b) the employees are to be regarded as a section of the public.

(6) A reference to a person requiring a service includes a reference to a person who is seeking to obtain or use the service.

(7) A reference to a service-provider not providing a person with a service includes a reference to —

    (a) the service-provider not providing the person with a service of the quality that the service-provider usually provides to the public (or the section of it which includes the person), or

    (b) the service-provider not providing the person with the service in the manner in which, or on the terms on which, the service-provider usually provides the service to the public (or the section of it which includes the person).

(8) In relation to the provision of a service by either House of Parliament, the service-provider is the Corporate Officer of the House concerned; and if the service involves access to, or use of, a place in the Palace of Westminster which members of the public are allowed to enter, both Corporate Officers are jointly the service-provider.

(9) Schedule 2 (reasonable adjustments) has effect.

(10) Schedule 3 (exceptions) has effect.

PART 4

PREMISES

Preliminary

32 Application of this Part

(1) This Part does not apply to the following protected characteristics —

    (a) age;

    (b) marriage and civil partnership.

(2) This Part does not apply to discrimination, harassment or victimisation —

    (a) that is prohibited by Part 5 (work) or Part 6 (education), or

    (b) that would be so prohibited but for an express exception.

(3) This Part does not apply to the provision of accommodation if the provision —

    (a) is generally for the purpose of short stays by individuals who live elsewhere, or

    (b) is for the purpose only of exercising a public function or providing a service to the public or a section of the public.

(4) The reference to the exercise of a public function, and the reference to the provision of a service, are to be construed in accordance with Part 3.

(5) This Part does not apply to —

    (a) a breach of an equality clause or rule;

    (b) anything that would be a breach of an equality clause or rule but for section 69 or Part 2 of Schedule 7;

    (c) a breach of a non-discrimination rule.

Disposal and management

33 Disposals, etc.

(1) A person (A) who has the right to dispose of premises must not discriminate against another (B) —

    (a) as to the terms on which A offers to dispose of the premises to B;

    (b) by not disposing of the premises to B;

    (c) in A's treatment of B with respect to things done in relation to persons seeking premises.

(2) Where an interest in a commonhold unit cannot be disposed of unless a particular person is a party to the disposal, that person must not discriminate against a person by not being a party to the disposal.

(3) A person who has the right to dispose of premises must not, in connection with anything done in relation to their occupation or disposal, harass —

    (a) a person who occupies them;

    (b) a person who applies for them.

(4) A person (A) who has the right to dispose of premises must not victimise another (B) —

    (a) as to the terms on which A offers to dispose of the premises to B;

    (b) by not disposing of the premises to B;

    (c) in A's treatment of B with respect to things done in relation to persons seeking premises.

(5) Where an interest in a commonhold unit cannot be disposed of unless a particular person is a party to the disposal, that person must not victimise a person by not being a party to the disposal.

(6) In the application of section 26 for the purposes of subsection (3), neither of the following is a relevant protected characteristic —

    (a) religion or belief;

    (b) sexual orientation.

34 Permission for disposal

(1) A person whose permission is required for the disposal of premises must not discriminate against another by not giving permission for the disposal of the premises to the other.

(2) A person whose permission is required for the disposal of premises must not, in relation to an application for permission to dispose of the premises, harass a person —

> (a) who applies for permission to dispose of the premises, or
>
> (b) to whom the disposal would be made if permission were given.

(3) A person whose permission is required for the disposal of premises must not victimise another by not giving permission for the disposal of the premises to the other.

(4) In the application of section 26 for the purposes of subsection (2), neither of the following is a relevant protected characteristic —

> (a) religion or belief;
>
> (b) sexual orientation.

(5) This section does not apply to anything done in the exercise of a judicial function.

35 Management

(1) A person (A) who manages premises must not discriminate against a person (B) who occupies the premises —

> (a) in the way in which A allows B, or by not allowing B, to make use of a benefit or facility;
>
> (b) by evicting B (or taking steps for the purpose of securing B's eviction);
>
> (c) by subjecting B to any other detriment.

(2) A person who manages premises must not, in relation to their management, harass —

> (a) a person who occupies them;
>
> (b) a person who applies for them.

(3) A person (A) who manages premises must not victimise a person (B) who occupies the premises —

> (a) in the way in which A allows B, or by not allowing B, to make use of a benefit or facility;
>
> (b) by evicting B (or taking steps for the purpose of securing B's eviction);
>
> (c) by subjecting B to any other detriment.

(4) In the application of section 26 for the purposes of subsection (2), neither of the following is a relevant protected characteristic —

> (a) religion or belief;
>
> (b) sexual orientation.

Reasonable adjustments

36 Leasehold and commonhold premises and common parts

(1) A duty to make reasonable adjustments applies to —

> (a) a controller of let premises;
>
> (b) a controller of premises to let;
>
> (c) a commonhold association;
>
> (d) a responsible person in relation to common parts.

(2) A controller of let premises is —

> (a) a person by whom premises are let, or

      (b)   a person who manages them.

(3)   A controller of premises to let is—

      (a)   a person who has premises to let, or

      (b)   a person who manages them.

(4)   The reference in subsection (1)(c) to a commonhold association is a reference to the association in its capacity as the person who manages a commonhold unit.

(5)   A responsible person in relation to common parts is—

      (a)   where the premises to which the common parts relate are let (and are not part of commonhold land or in Scotland), a person by whom the premises are let;

      (b)   where the premises to which the common parts relate are part of commonhold land, the commonhold association.

(6)   Common parts are—

      (a)   in relation to let premises (which are not part of commonhold land or in Scotland), the structure and exterior of, and any common facilities within or used in connection with, the building or part of a building which includes the premises;

      (b)   in relation to commonhold land, every part of the commonhold which is not for the time being a commonhold unit in accordance with the commonhold community statement.

(7)   A reference to letting includes a reference to sub-letting; and for the purposes of subsection (1)(a) and (b), a reference to let premises includes premises subject to a right to occupy.

(8)   This section does not apply to premises of such description as may be prescribed.

37   Adjustments to common parts in Scotland

(1)   The Scottish Ministers may by regulations provide that a disabled person is entitled to make relevant adjustments to common parts in relation to premises in Scotland.

(2)   The reference in subsection (1) to a disabled person is a reference to a disabled person who—

      (a)   is a tenant of the premises,

      (b)   is an owner of the premises, or

      (c)   is otherwise entitled to occupy the premises,

and uses or intends to use the premises as the person's only or main home.

(3)   Before making regulations under subsection (1), the Scottish Ministers must consult a Minister of the Crown.

(4)   Regulations under subsection (1) may, in particular—

      (a)   prescribe things which are, or which are not, to be treated as relevant adjustments;

      (b)   prescribe circumstances in which the consent of an owner of the common parts is required before a disabled person may make an adjustment;

      (c)   provide that the consent to adjustments is not to be withheld unreasonably;

(d)   prescribe matters to be taken into account, or to be disregarded, in deciding whether it is reasonable to consent to adjustments;

(e)   prescribe circumstances in which consent to adjustments is to be taken to be withheld;

(f)   make provision about the imposition of conditions on consent to adjustments;

(g)   make provision as to circumstances in which the sheriff may make an order authorising a disabled person to carry out adjustments;

(h)   make provision about the responsibility for costs arising (directly or indirectly) from an adjustment;

(i)   make provision about the reinstatement of the common parts to the condition they were in before an adjustment was made;

(j)   make provision about the giving of notice to the owners of the common parts and other persons;

(k)   make provision about agreements between a disabled person and an owner of the common parts;

(l)   make provision about the registration of information in the Land Register of Scotland or the recording of documents in the Register of Sasines relating to an entitlement of a disabled person or an obligation on an owner of the common parts;

(m)   make provision about the effect of such registration or recording;

(n)   make provision about who is to be treated as being, or as not being, a person entitled to occupy premises otherwise than as tenant or owner.

(5)   In this section—

"common parts" means, in relation to premises, the structure and exterior of, and any common facilities within or used in connection with, the building or part of a building which includes the premises but only in so far as the structure, exterior and common facilities are not solely owned by the owner of the premises;

"relevant adjustments" means, in relation to a disabled person, alterations or additions which are likely to avoid a substantial disadvantage to which the disabled person is put in using the common parts in comparison with persons who are not disabled.

Supplementary

38   Interpretation and exceptions

(1)   This section applies for the purposes of this Part.

(2)   A reference to premises is a reference to the whole or part of the premises.

(3)   A reference to disposing of premises includes, in the case of premises subject to a tenancy, a reference to—

(a)   assigning the premises,

(b)   sub-letting them, or

(c)   parting with possession of them.

(4)   A reference to disposing of premises also includes a reference to granting a right to occupy them.

(5)   A reference to disposing of an interest in a commonhold unit includes a reference to creating an interest in a commonhold unit.

(6) A reference to a tenancy is to a tenancy created (whether before or after the passing of this Act)—

   (a)   by a lease or sub-lease,

   (b)   by an agreement for a lease or sub-lease,

   (c)   by a tenancy agreement, or

   (d)   in pursuance of an enactment,

and a reference to a tenant is to be construed accordingly.

(7) A reference to commonhold land, a commonhold association, a commonhold community statement, a commonhold unit or a unit-holder is to be construed in accordance with the Commonhold and Leasehold Reform Act 2002.

(8) Schedule 4 (reasonable adjustments) has effect.

(9) Schedule 5 (exceptions) has effect.

PART 5

WORK

CHAPTER 1

EMPLOYMENT, ETC.

Employees

39   Employees and applicants

(1) An employer (A) must not discriminate against a person (B)—

   (a)   in the arrangements A makes for deciding to whom to offer employment;

   (b)   as to the terms on which A offers B employment;

   (c)   by not offering B employment.

(2) An employer (A) must not discriminate against an employee of A's (B)—

   (a)   as to B's terms of employment;

   (b)   in the way A affords B access, or by not affording B access, to opportunities for promotion, transfer or training or for receiving any other benefit, facility or service;

   (c)   by dismissing B;

   (d)   by subjecting B to any other detriment.

(3) An employer (A) must not victimise a person (B)—

   (a)   in the arrangements A makes for deciding to whom to offer employment;

   (b)   as to the terms on which A offers B employment;

   (c)   by not offering B employment.

(4) An employer (A) must not victimise an employee of A's (B)—

   (a)   as to B's terms of employment;

   (b)   in the way A affords B access, or by not affording B access, to opportunities for promotion, transfer or training or for any other benefit, facility or service;

Equality Act 2010 (c. 15)
Part 5 — Work
Chapter 1 — Employment, etc.

1653

      (c)   by dismissing B;

      (d)   by subjecting B to any other detriment.

(5)   A duty to make reasonable adjustments applies to an employer.

(6)   Subsection (1)(b), so far as relating to sex or pregnancy and maternity, does not apply to a term that relates to pay —

      (a)   unless, were B to accept the offer, an equality clause or rule would have effect in relation to the term, or

      (b)   if paragraph (a) does not apply, except in so far as making an offer on terms including that term amounts to a contravention of subsection (1)(b) by virtue of section 13, 14 or 18.

(7)   In subsections (2)(c) and (4)(c), the reference to dismissing B includes a reference to the termination of B's employment —

      (a)   by the expiry of a period (including a period expiring by reference to an event or circumstance);

      (b)   by an act of B's (including giving notice) in circumstances such that B is entitled, because of A's conduct, to terminate the employment without notice.

(8)   Subsection (7)(a) does not apply if, immediately after the termination, the employment is renewed on the same terms.

40   Employees and applicants: harassment

(1)   An employer (A) must not, in relation to employment by A, harass a person (B) —

      (a)   who is an employee of A's;

      (b)   who has applied to A for employment.

(2)   The circumstances in which A is to be treated as harassing B under subsection (1) include those where —

      (a)   a third party harasses B in the course of B's employment, and

      (b)   A failed to take such steps as would have been reasonably practicable to prevent the third party from doing so.

(3)   Subsection (2) does not apply unless A knows that B has been harassed in the course of B's employment on at least two other occasions by a third party; and it does not matter whether the third party is the same or a different person on each occasion.

(4)   A third party is a person other than —

      (a)   A, or

      (b)   an employee of A's.

41   Contract workers

(1)   A principal must not discriminate against a contract worker —

      (a)   as to the terms on which the principal allows the worker to do the work;

      (b)   by not allowing the worker to do, or to continue to do, the work;

      (c)   in the way the principal affords the worker access, or by not affording the worker access, to opportunities for receiving a benefit, facility or service;

      (d)   by subjecting the worker to any other detriment.

(2) A principal must not, in relation to contract work, harass a contract worker.

(3) A principal must not victimise a contract worker —
   (a) as to the terms on which the principal allows the worker to do the work;
   (b) by not allowing the worker to do, or to continue to do, the work;
   (c) in the way the principal affords the worker access, or by not affording the worker access, to opportunities for receiving a benefit, facility or service;
   (d) by subjecting the worker to any other detriment.

(4) A duty to make reasonable adjustments applies to a principal (as well as to the employer of a contract worker).

(5) A "principal" is a person who makes work available for an individual who is —
   (a) employed by another person, and
   (b) supplied by that other person in furtherance of a contract to which the principal is a party (whether or not that other person is a party to it).

(6) "Contract work" is work such as is mentioned in subsection (5).

(7) A "contract worker" is an individual supplied to a principal in furtherance of a contract such as is mentioned in subsection (5)(b).

Police officers

42   Identity of employer

(1) For the purposes of this Part, holding the office of constable is to be treated as employment —
   (a) by the chief officer, in respect of any act done by the chief officer in relation to a constable or appointment to the office of constable;
   (b) by the responsible authority, in respect of any act done by the authority in relation to a constable or appointment to the office of constable.

(2) For the purposes of this Part, holding an appointment as a police cadet is to be treated as employment —
   (a) by the chief officer, in respect of any act done by the chief officer in relation to a police cadet or appointment as one;
   (b) by the responsible authority, in respect of any act done by the authority in relation to a police cadet or appointment as one.

(3) Subsection (1) does not apply to service with the Civil Nuclear Constabulary (as to which, see section 55(2) of the Energy Act 2004).

(4) Subsection (1) does not apply to a constable at SOCA, SPSA or SCDEA.

(5) A constable at SOCA or SPSA is to be treated as employed by it, in respect of any act done by it in relation to the constable.

(6) A constable at SCDEA is to be treated as employed by the Director General of SCDEA, in respect of any act done by the Director General in relation to the constable.

43   Interpretation

(1) This section applies for the purposes of section 42.

(2) "Chief officer" means —

    (a) in relation to an appointment under a relevant Act, the chief officer of police for the police force to which the appointment relates;

    (b) in relation to any other appointment, the person under whose direction and control the body of constables or other persons to which the appointment relates is;

    (c) in relation to a constable or other person under the direction and control of a chief officer of police, that chief officer of police;

    (d) in relation to any other constable or any other person, the person under whose direction and control the constable or other person is.

(3) "Responsible authority" means —

    (a) in relation to an appointment under a relevant Act, the police authority that maintains the police force to which the appointment relates;

    (b) in relation to any other appointment, the person by whom a person would (if appointed) be paid;

    (c) in relation to a constable or other person under the direction and control of a chief officer of police, the police authority that maintains the police force for which that chief officer is the chief officer of police;

    (d) in relation to any other constable or any other person, the person by whom the constable or other person is paid.

(4) "Police cadet" means a person appointed to undergo training with a view to becoming a constable.

(5) "SOCA" means the Serious Organised Crime Agency; and a reference to a constable at SOCA is a reference to a constable seconded to it to serve as a member of its staff.

(6) "SPSA" means the Scottish Police Services Authority; and a reference to a constable at SPSA is a reference to a constable —

    (a) seconded to it to serve as a member of its staff, and

    (b) not at SCDEA.

(7) "SCDEA" means the Scottish Crime and Drugs Enforcement Agency; and a reference to a constable at SCDEA is a reference to a constable who is a police member of it by virtue of paragraph 7(2)(a) or (b) of Schedule 2 to the Police, Public Order and Criminal Justice (Scotland) Act 2006 (asp 10) (secondment).

(8) For the purposes of this section, the relevant Acts are —

    (a) the Metropolitan Police Act 1829;

    (b) the City of London Police Act 1839;

    (c) the Police (Scotland) Act 1967;

    (d) the Police Act 1996.

(9) A reference in subsection (2) or (3) to a chief officer of police includes, in relation to Scotland, a reference to a chief constable.

Partners

44 Partnerships

(1) A firm or proposed firm must not discriminate against a person —

(a) in the arrangements it makes for deciding to whom to offer a position as a partner;

(b) as to the terms on which it offers the person a position as a partner;

(c) by not offering the person a position as a partner.

(2) A firm (A) must not discriminate against a partner (B) –

(a) as to the terms on which B is a partner;

(b) in the way A affords B access, or by not affording B access, to opportunities for promotion, transfer or training or for receiving any other benefit, facility or service;

(c) by expelling B;

(d) by subjecting B to any other detriment.

(3) A firm must not, in relation to a position as a partner, harass –

(a) a partner;

(b) a person who has applied for the position.

(4) A proposed firm must not, in relation to a position as a partner, harass a person who has applied for the position.

(5) A firm or proposed firm must not victimise a person –

(a) in the arrangements it makes for deciding to whom to offer a position as a partner;

(b) as to the terms on which it offers the person a position as a partner;

(c) by not offering the person a position as a partner.

(6) A firm (A) must not victimise a partner (B) –

(a) as to the terms on which B is a partner;

(b) in the way A affords B access, or by not affording B access, to opportunities for promotion, transfer or training or for receiving any other benefit, facility or service;

(c) by expelling B;

(d) by subjecting B to any other detriment.

(7) A duty to make reasonable adjustments applies to –

(a) a firm;

(b) a proposed firm.

(8) In the application of this section to a limited partnership within the meaning of the Limited Partnerships Act 1907, "partner" means a general partner within the meaning of that Act.

45 Limited liability partnerships

(1) An LLP or proposed LLP must not discriminate against a person –

(a) in the arrangements it makes for deciding to whom to offer a position as a member;

(b) as to the terms on which it offers the person a position as a member;

(c) by not offering the person a position as a member.

(2) An LLP (A) must not discriminate against a member (B) –

(a) as to the terms on which B is a member;

Equality Act 2010 (c. 15)
Part 5 – Work
Chapter 1 – Employment, etc.

1657

(b)   in the way A affords B access, or by not affording B access, to opportunities for promotion, transfer or training or for receiving any other benefit, facility or service;

(c)   by expelling B;

(d)   by subjecting B to any other detriment.

(3)   An LLP must not, in relation to a position as a member, harass—

(a)   a member;

(b)   a person who has applied for the position.

(4)   A proposed LLP must not, in relation to a position as a member, harass a person who has applied for the position.

(5)   An LLP or proposed LLP must not victimise a person—

(a)   in the arrangements it makes for deciding to whom to offer a position as a member;

(b)   as to the terms on which it offers the person a position as a member;

(c)   by not offering the person a position as a member.

(6)   An LLP (A) must not victimise a member (B)—

(a)   as to the terms on which B is a member;

(b)   in the way A affords B access, or by not affording B access, to opportunities for promotion, transfer or training or for receiving any other benefit, facility or service;

(c)   by expelling B;

(d)   by subjecting B to any other detriment.

(7)   A duty to make reasonable adjustments applies to—

(a)   an LLP;

(b)   a proposed LLP.

46   Interpretation

(1)   This section applies for the purposes of sections 44 and 45.

(2)   "Partnership" and "firm" have the same meaning as in the Partnership Act 1890.

(3)   "Proposed firm" means persons proposing to form themselves into a partnership.

(4)   "LLP" means a limited liability partnership (within the meaning of the Limited Liability Partnerships Act 2000).

(5)   "Proposed LLP" means persons proposing to incorporate an LLP with themselves as members.

(6)   A reference to expelling a partner of a firm or a member of an LLP includes a reference to the termination of the person's position as such—

(a)   by the expiry of a period (including a period expiring by reference to an event or circumstance);

(b)   by an act of the person (including giving notice) in circumstances such that the person is entitled, because of the conduct of other partners or members, to terminate the position without notice;

(c)   (in the case of a partner of a firm) as a result of the dissolution of the partnership.

(7)   Subsection (6)(a) and (c) does not apply if, immediately after the termination, the position is renewed on the same terms.

The Bar

47   Barristers

(1)   A barrister (A) must not discriminate against a person (B) —

    (a)   in the arrangements A makes for deciding to whom to offer a pupillage or tenancy;

    (b)   as to the terms on which A offers B a pupillage or tenancy;

    (c)   by not offering B a pupillage or tenancy.

(2)   A barrister (A) must not discriminate against a person (B) who is a pupil or tenant —

    (a)   as to the terms on which B is a pupil or tenant;

    (b)   in the way A affords B access, or by not affording B access, to opportunities for training or gaining experience or for receiving any other benefit, facility or service;

    (c)   by terminating the pupillage;

    (d)   by subjecting B to pressure to leave chambers;

    (e)   by subjecting B to any other detriment.

(3)   A barrister must not, in relation to a pupillage or tenancy, harass —

    (a)   the pupil or tenant;

    (b)   a person who has applied for the pupillage or tenancy.

(4)   A barrister (A) must not victimise a person (B) —

    (a)   in the arrangements A makes for deciding to whom to offer a pupillage or tenancy;

    (b)   as to the terms on which A offers B a pupillage or tenancy;

    (c)   by not offering B a pupillage or tenancy.

(5)   A barrister (A) must not victimise a person (B) who is a pupil or tenant —

    (a)   as to the terms on which B is a pupil or tenant;

    (b)   in the way A affords B access, or by not affording B access, to opportunities for training or gaining experience or for receiving any other benefit, facility or service;

    (c)   by terminating the pupillage;

    (d)   by subjecting B to pressure to leave chambers;

    (e)   by subjecting B to any other detriment.

(6)   A person must not, in relation to instructing a barrister —

    (a)   discriminate against a barrister by subjecting the barrister to a detriment;

    (b)   harass the barrister;

    (c)   victimise the barrister.

(7)   A duty to make reasonable adjustments applies to a barrister.

(8)   The preceding provisions of this section (apart from subsection (6)) apply in relation to a barrister's clerk as they apply in relation to a barrister; and for that

purpose the reference to a barrister's clerk includes a reference to a person who carries out the functions of a barrister's clerk.

(9) A reference to a tenant includes a reference to a barrister who is permitted to work in chambers (including as a squatter or door tenant); and a reference to a tenancy is to be construed accordingly.

48 Advocates

(1) An advocate (A) must not discriminate against a person (B) —

    (a) in the arrangements A makes for deciding who to take as A's devil or to whom to offer membership of a stable;

    (b) as to the terms on which A offers to take B as A's devil or offers B membership of a stable;

    (c) by not offering to take B as A's devil or not offering B membership of a stable.

(2) An advocate (A) must not discriminate against a person (B) who is a devil or a member of a stable —

    (a) as to the terms on which B is a devil or a member of the stable;

    (b) in the way A affords B access, or by not affording B access, to opportunities for training or gaining experience or for receiving any other benefit, facility or service;

    (c) by terminating A's relationship with B (where B is a devil);

    (d) by subjecting B to pressure to leave the stable;

    (e) by subjecting B to any other detriment.

(3) An advocate must not, in relation to a relationship with a devil or membership of a stable, harass —

    (a) a devil or member;

    (b) a person who has applied to be taken as the advocate's devil or to become a member of the stable.

(4) An advocate (A) must not victimise a person (B) —

    (a) in the arrangements A makes for deciding who to take as A's devil or to whom to offer membership of a stable;

    (b) as to the terms on which A offers to take B as A's devil or offers B membership of a stable;

    (c) by not offering to take B as A's devil or not offering B membership of a stable.

(5) An advocate (A) must not victimise a person (B) who is a devil or a member of a stable —

    (a) as to the terms on which B is a devil or a member of the stable;

    (b) in the way A affords B access, or by not affording B access, to opportunities for training or gaining experience or for receiving any other benefit, facility or service;

    (c) by terminating A's relationship with B (where B is a devil);

    (d) by subjecting B to pressure to leave the stable;

    (e) by subjecting B to any other detriment.

(6) A person must not, in relation to instructing an advocate —

    (a) discriminate against the advocate by subjecting the advocate to a detriment;

      (b)   harass the advocate;

      (c)   victimise the advocate.

(7)   A duty to make reasonable adjustments applies to an advocate.

(8)   This section (apart from subsection (6)) applies in relation to an advocate's clerk as it applies in relation to an advocate; and for that purpose the reference to an advocate's clerk includes a reference to a person who carries out the functions of an advocate's clerk.

(9)   "Advocate" means a practising member of the Faculty of Advocates.

Office-holders

49 Personal offices: appointments, etc.

(1)   This section applies in relation to personal offices.

(2)   A personal office is an office or post—

      (a)   to which a person is appointed to discharge a function personally under the direction of another person, and

      (b)   in respect of which an appointed person is entitled to remuneration.

(3)   A person (A) who has the power to make an appointment to a personal office must not discriminate against a person (B)—

      (a)   in the arrangements A makes for deciding to whom to offer the appointment;

      (b)   as to the terms on which A offers B the appointment;

      (c)   by not offering B the appointment.

(4)   A person who has the power to make an appointment to a personal office must not, in relation to the office, harass a person seeking, or being considered for, the appointment.

(5)   A person (A) who has the power to make an appointment to a personal office must not victimise a person (B)—

      (a)   in the arrangements A makes for deciding to whom to offer the appointment;

      (b)   as to the terms on which A offers B the appointment;

      (c)   by not offering B the appointment.

(6)   A person (A) who is a relevant person in relation to a personal office must not discriminate against a person (B) appointed to the office—

      (a)   as to the terms of B's appointment;

      (b)   in the way A affords B access, or by not affording B access, to opportunities for promotion, transfer or training or for receiving any other benefit, facility or service;

      (c)   by terminating B's appointment;

      (d)   by subjecting B to any other detriment.

(7)   A relevant person in relation to a personal office must not, in relation to that office, harass a person appointed to it.

(8)   A person (A) who is a relevant person in relation to a personal office must not victimise a person (B) appointed to the office—

Equality Act 2010 (c. 15)
Part 5 — Work
Chapter 1 — Employment, etc.

1661

    (a)   as to the terms of B's appointment;

    (b)   in the way A affords B access, or by not affording B access, to opportunities for promotion, transfer or training or for receiving any other benefit, facility or service;

    (c)   by terminating B's appointment;

    (d)   by subjecting B to any other detriment.

(9)   A duty to make reasonable adjustments applies to —

    (a)   a person who has the power to make an appointment to a personal office;

    (b)   a relevant person in relation to a personal office.

(10)   For the purposes of subsection (2)(a), a person is to be regarded as discharging functions personally under the direction of another person if that other person is entitled to direct the person as to when and where to discharge the functions.

(11)   For the purposes of subsection (2)(b), a person is not to be regarded as entitled to remuneration merely because the person is entitled to payments —

    (a)   in respect of expenses incurred by the person in discharging the functions of the office or post, or

    (b)   by way of compensation for the loss of income or benefits the person would or might have received had the person not been discharging the functions of the office or post.

(12)   Subsection (3)(b), so far as relating to sex or pregnancy and maternity, does not apply to a term that relates to pay —

    (a)   unless, were B to accept the offer, an equality clause or rule would have effect in relation to the term, or

    (b)   if paragraph (a) does not apply, except in so far as making an offer on terms including that term amounts to a contravention of subsection (3)(b) by virtue of section 13, 14 or 18.

50   Public offices: appointments, etc.

(1)   This section and section 51 apply in relation to public offices.

(2)   A public office is —

    (a)   an office or post, appointment to which is made by a member of the executive;

    (b)   an office or post, appointment to which is made on the recommendation of, or subject to the approval of, a member of the executive;

    (c)   an office or post, appointment to which is made on the recommendation of, or subject to the approval of, the House of Commons, the House of Lords, the National Assembly for Wales or the Scottish Parliament.

(3)   A person (A) who has the power to make an appointment to a public office within subsection (2)(a) or (b) must not discriminate against a person (B) —

    (a)   in the arrangements A makes for deciding to whom to offer the appointment;

    (b)   as to the terms on which A offers B the appointment;

    (c)   by not offering B the appointment.

1662

Equality Act 2010 (c. **15**)
Part 5 — Work
Chapter 1 — Employment, etc.

(4) A person who has the power to make an appointment to a public office within subsection (2)(a) or (b) must not, in relation to the office, harass a person seeking, or being considered for, the appointment.

(5) A person (A) who has the power to make an appointment to a public office within subsection (2)(a) or (b) must not victimise a person (B) —

    (a) in the arrangements A makes for deciding to whom to offer the appointment;

    (b) as to the terms on which A offers B the appointment;

    (c) by not offering B the appointment.

(6) A person (A) who is a relevant person in relation to a public office within subsection (2)(a) or (b) must not discriminate against a person (B) appointed to the office —

    (a) as to B's terms of appointment;

    (b) in the way A affords B access, or by not affording B access, to opportunities for promotion, transfer or training or for receiving any other benefit, facility or service;

    (c) by terminating the appointment;

    (d) by subjecting B to any other detriment.

(7) A person (A) who is a relevant person in relation to a public office within subsection (2)(c) must not discriminate against a person (B) appointed to the office —

    (a) as to B's terms of appointment;

    (b) in the way A affords B access, or by not affording B access, to opportunities for promotion, transfer or training or for receiving any other benefit, facility or service;

    (c) by subjecting B to any other detriment (other than by terminating the appointment).

(8) A relevant person in relation to a public office must not, in relation to that office, harass a person appointed to it.

(9) A person (A) who is a relevant person in relation to a public office within subsection (2)(a) or (b) must not victimise a person (B) appointed to the office —

    (a) as to B's terms of appointment;

    (b) in the way A affords B access, or by not affording B access, to opportunities for promotion, transfer or training or for receiving any other benefit, facility or service;

    (c) by terminating the appointment;

    (d) by subjecting B to any other detriment.

(10) A person (A) who is a relevant person in relation to a public office within subsection (2)(c) must not victimise a person (B) appointed to the office —

    (a) as to B's terms of appointment;

    (b) in the way A affords B access, or by not affording B access, to opportunities for promotion, transfer or training or for receiving any other benefit, facility or service;

    (c) by subjecting B to any other detriment (other than by terminating the appointment).

(11) A duty to make reasonable adjustments applies to —

    (a) a relevant person in relation to a public office;

     (b)   a person who has the power to make an appointment to a public office within subsection (2)(a) or (b).

(12)   Subsection (3)(b), so far as relating to sex or pregnancy and maternity, does not apply to a term that relates to pay —

     (a)   unless, were B to accept the offer, an equality clause or rule would have effect in relation to the term, or

     (b)   if paragraph (a) does not apply, except in so far as making an offer on terms including that term amounts to a contravention of subsection (3)(b) by virtue of section 13, 14 or 18.

51   Public offices: recommendations for appointments, etc.

(1)   A person (A) who has the power to make a recommendation for or give approval to an appointment to a public office within section 50(2)(a) or (b), must not discriminate against a person (B) —

     (a)   in the arrangements A makes for deciding who to recommend for appointment or to whose appointment to give approval;

     (b)   by not recommending B for appointment to the office;

     (c)   by making a negative recommendation of B for appointment to the office;

     (d)   by not giving approval to the appointment of B to the office.

(2)   A person who has the power to make a recommendation for or give approval to an appointment to a public office within section 50(2)(a) or (b) must not, in relation to the office, harass a person seeking or being considered for the recommendation or approval.

(3)   A person (A) who has the power to make a recommendation for or give approval to an appointment to a public office within section 50(2)(a) or (b), must not victimise a person (B) —

     (a)   in the arrangements A makes for deciding who to recommend for appointment or to whose appointment to give approval;

     (b)   by not recommending B for appointment to the office;

     (c)   by making a negative recommendation of B for appointment to the office;

     (d)   by not giving approval to the appointment of B to the office.

(4)   A duty to make reasonable adjustments applies to a person who has the power to make a recommendation for or give approval to an appointment to a public office within section 50(2)(a) or (b).

(5)   A reference in this section to a person who has the power to make a recommendation for or give approval to an appointment to a public office within section 50(2)(a) is a reference only to a relevant body which has that power; and for that purpose "relevant body" means a body established —

     (a)   by or in pursuance of an enactment, or

     (b)   by a member of the executive.

52   Interpretation and exceptions

(1)   This section applies for the purposes of sections 49 to 51.

(2)   "Personal office" has the meaning given in section 49.

(3)   "Public office" has the meaning given in section 50.

(4)   An office or post which is both a personal office and a public office is to be treated as being a public office only.

(5)   Appointment to an office or post does not include election to it.

(6)   "Relevant person", in relation to an office, means the person who, in relation to a matter specified in the first column of the table, is specified in the second column (but a reference to a relevant person does not in any case include the House of Commons, the House of Lords, the National Assembly for Wales or the Scottish Parliament).

Matter	*Relevant person*
A term of appointment	The person who has the power to set the term.
Access to an opportunity	The person who has the power to afford access to the opportunity (or, if there is no such person, the person who has the power to make the appointment).
Terminating an appointment	The person who has the power to terminate the appointment.
Subjecting an appointee to any other detriment	The person who has the power in relation to the matter to which the conduct in question relates (or, if there is no such person, the person who has the power to make the appointment).
Harassing an appointee	The person who has the power in relation to the matter to which the conduct in question relates.

(7)   A reference to terminating a person's appointment includes a reference to termination of the appointment—

    (a)   by the expiry of a period (including a period expiring by reference to an event or circumstance);

    (b)   by an act of the person (including giving notice) in circumstances such that the person is entitled, because of the relevant person's conduct, to terminate the appointment without notice.

(8)   Subsection (7)(a) does not apply if, immediately after the termination, the appointment is renewed on the same terms.

(9)   Schedule 6 (excluded offices) has effect.

Qualifications

53   Qualifications bodies

(1)   A qualifications body (A) must not discriminate against a person (B)—

Equality Act 2010 (c. 15)
Part 5 — Work
Chapter 1 — Employment, etc.

1665

    (a) in the arrangements A makes for deciding upon whom to confer a relevant qualification;

    (b) as to the terms on which it is prepared to confer a relevant qualification on B;

    (c) by not conferring a relevant qualification on B.

(2) A qualifications body (A) must not discriminate against a person (B) upon whom A has conferred a relevant qualification—

    (a) by withdrawing the qualification from B;

    (b) by varying the terms on which B holds the qualification;

    (c) by subjecting B to any other detriment.

(3) A qualifications body must not, in relation to conferment by it of a relevant qualification, harass—

    (a) a person who holds the qualification, or

    (b) a person who applies for it.

(4) A qualifications body (A) must not victimise a person (B)—

    (a) in the arrangements A makes for deciding upon whom to confer a relevant qualification;

    (b) as to the terms on which it is prepared to confer a relevant qualification on B;

    (c) by not conferring a relevant qualification on B.

(5) A qualifications body (A) must not victimise a person (B) upon whom A has conferred a relevant qualification—

    (a) by withdrawing the qualification from B;

    (b) by varying the terms on which B holds the qualification;

    (c) by subjecting B to any other detriment.

(6) A duty to make reasonable adjustments applies to a qualifications body.

(7) The application by a qualifications body of a competence standard to a disabled person is not disability discrimination unless it is discrimination by virtue of section 19.

54 Interpretation

(1) This section applies for the purposes of section 53.

(2) A qualifications body is an authority or body which can confer a relevant qualification.

(3) A relevant qualification is an authorisation, qualification, recognition, registration, enrolment, approval or certification which is needed for, or facilitates engagement in, a particular trade or profession.

(4) An authority or body is not a qualifications body in so far as—

    (a) it can confer a qualification to which section 96 applies,

    (b) it is the responsible body of a school to which section 85 applies,

    (c) it is the governing body of an institution to which section 91 applies,

    (d) it exercises functions under the Education Acts, or

    (e) it exercises functions under the Education (Scotland) Act 1980.

(5) A reference to conferring a relevant qualification includes a reference to renewing or extending the conferment of a relevant qualification.

(6) A competence standard is an academic, medical or other standard applied for the purpose of determining whether or not a person has a particular level of competence or ability.

Employment services

55 Employment service-providers

(1) A person (an "employment service-provider") concerned with the provision of an employment service must not discriminate against a person—

    (a) in the arrangements the service-provider makes for selecting persons to whom to provide, or to whom to offer to provide, the service;

    (b) as to the terms on which the service-provider offers to provide the service to the person;

    (c) by not offering to provide the service to the person.

(2) An employment service-provider (A) must not, in relation to the provision of an employment service, discriminate against a person (B)—

    (a) as to the terms on which A provides the service to B;

    (b) by not providing the service to B;

    (c) by terminating the provision of the service to B;

    (d) by subjecting B to any other detriment.

(3) An employment service-provider must not, in relation to the provision of an employment service, harass—

    (a) a person who asks the service-provider to provide the service;

    (b) a person for whom the service-provider provides the service.

(4) An employment service-provider (A) must not victimise a person (B)—

    (a) in the arrangements A makes for selecting persons to whom to provide, or to whom to offer to provide, the service;

    (b) as to the terms on which A offers to provide the service to B;

    (c) by not offering to provide the service to B.

(5) An employment service-provider (A) must not, in relation to the provision of an employment service, victimise a person (B)—

    (a) as to the terms on which A provides the service to B;

    (b) by not providing the service to B;

    (c) by terminating the provision of the service to B;

    (d) by subjecting B to any other detriment.

(6) A duty to make reasonable adjustments applies to an employment service-provider, except in relation to the provision of a vocational service.

(7) The duty imposed by section 29(7)(a) applies to a person concerned with the provision of a vocational service; but a failure to comply with that duty in relation to the provision of a vocational service is a contravention of this Part for the purposes of Part 9 (enforcement).

56   Interpretation

(1)   This section applies for the purposes of section 55.

(2)   The provision of an employment service includes—

    (a)   the provision of vocational training;

    (b)   the provision of vocational guidance;

    (c)   making arrangements for the provision of vocational training or vocational guidance;

    (d)   the provision of a service for finding employment for persons;

    (e)   the provision of a service for supplying employers with persons to do work;

    (f)   the provision of a service in pursuance of arrangements made under section 2 of the Employment and Training Act 1973 (functions of the Secretary of State relating to employment);

    (g)   the provision of a service in pursuance of arrangements made or a direction given under section 10 of that Act (careers services);

    (h)   the exercise of a function in pursuance of arrangements made under section 2(3) of the Enterprise and New Towns (Scotland) Act 1990 (functions of Scottish Enterprise, etc. relating to employment);

    (i)   an assessment related to the conferment of a relevant qualification within the meaning of section 53 above (except in so far as the assessment is by the qualifications body which confers the qualification).

(3)   This section does not apply in relation to training or guidance in so far as it is training or guidance in relation to which another provision of this Part applies.

(4)   This section does not apply in relation to training or guidance for pupils of a school to which section 85 applies in so far as it is training or guidance to which the responsible body of the school has power to afford access (whether as the responsible body of that school or as the responsible body of any other school at which the training or guidance is provided).

(5)   This section does not apply in relation to training or guidance for students of an institution to which section 91 applies in so far as it is training or guidance to which the governing body of the institution has power to afford access.

(6)   "Vocational training" means—

    (a)   training for employment, or

    (b)   work experience (including work experience the duration of which is not agreed until after it begins).

(7)   A reference to the provision of a vocational service is a reference to the provision of an employment service within subsection (2)(a) to (d) (or an employment service within subsection (2)(f) or (g) in so far as it is also an employment service within subsection (2)(a) to (d)); and for that purpose—

    (a)   the references to an employment service within subsection (2)(a) do not include a reference to vocational training within the meaning given by subsection (6)(b), and

    (b)   the references to an employment service within subsection (2)(d) also include a reference to a service for assisting persons to retain employment.

(8)   A reference to training includes a reference to facilities for training.

1668

Equality Act 2010 (c. 15)
Part 5 — Work
Chapter 1 — Employment, etc.

Trade organisations

57 Trade organisations

(1) A trade organisation (A) must not discriminate against a person (B) —

    (a) in the arrangements A makes for deciding to whom to offer membership of the organisation;

    (b) as to the terms on which it is prepared to admit B as a member;

    (c) by not accepting B's application for membership.

(2) A trade organisation (A) must not discriminate against a member (B) —

    (a) in the way it affords B access, or by not affording B access, to opportunities for receiving a benefit, facility or service;

    (b) by depriving B of membership;

    (c) by varying the terms on which B is a member;

    (d) by subjecting B to any other detriment.

(3) A trade organisation must not, in relation to membership of it, harass —

    (a) a member, or

    (b) an applicant for membership.

(4) A trade organisation (A) must not victimise a person (B) —

    (a) in the arrangements A makes for deciding to whom to offer membership of the organisation;

    (b) as to the terms on which it is prepared to admit B as a member;

    (c) by not accepting B's application for membership.

(5) A trade organisation (A) must not victimise a member (B) —

    (a) in the way it affords B access, or by not affording B access, to opportunities for receiving a benefit, facility or service;

    (b) by depriving B of membership;

    (c) by varying the terms on which B is a member;

    (d) by subjecting B to any other detriment.

(6) A duty to make reasonable adjustments applies to a trade organisation.

(7) A trade organisation is —

    (a) an organisation of workers,

    (b) an organisation of employers, or

    (c) any other organisation whose members carry on a particular trade or profession for the purposes of which the organisation exists.

Local authority members

58 Official business of members

(1) A local authority must not discriminate against a member of the authority in relation to the member's carrying out of official business —

    (a) in the way the authority affords the member access, or by not affording the member access, to opportunities for training or for receiving any other facility;

    (b) by subjecting the member to any other detriment.

(2) A local authority must not, in relation to a member's carrying out of official business, harass the member.

(3) A local authority must not victimise a member of the authority in relation to the member's carrying out of official business —
   (a) in the way the authority affords the member access, or by not affording the member access, to opportunities for training or for receiving any other facility;
   (b) by subjecting the member to any other detriment.

(4) A member of a local authority is not subjected to a detriment for the purposes of subsection (1)(b) or (3)(b) only because the member is —
   (a) not appointed or elected to an office of the authority,
   (b) not appointed or elected to, or to an office of, a committee or sub-committee of the authority, or
   (c) not appointed or nominated in exercise of an appointment power of the authority.

(5) In subsection (4)(c), an appointment power of a local authority is a power of the authority, or of a group of bodies including the authority, to make —
   (a) appointments to a body;
   (b) nominations for appointment to a body.

(6) A duty to make reasonable adjustments applies to a local authority.

59 Interpretation

(1) This section applies for the purposes of section 58.

(2) "Local authority" means —
   (a) a county council in England;
   (b) a district council in England;
   (c) the Greater London Authority;
   (d) a London borough council;
   (e) the Common Council of the City of London;
   (f) the Council of the Isles of Scilly;
   (g) a parish council in England;
   (h) a county council in Wales;
   (i) a community council in Wales;
   (j) a county borough council in Wales;
   (k) a council constituted under section 2 of the Local Government etc. (Scotland) Act 1994;
   (l) a community council in Scotland.

(3) A Minister of the Crown may by order amend subsection (2) so as to add, vary or omit a reference to a body which exercises functions that have been conferred on a local authority within paragraph (a) to (l).

(4) A reference to the carrying-out of official business by a person who is a member of a local authority is a reference to the doing of anything by the person —
   (a) as a member of the authority,

(b) as a member of a body to which the person is appointed by, or appointed following nomination by, the authority or a group of bodies including the authority, or

(c) as a member of any other public body.

(5) "Member", in relation to the Greater London Authority, means —

(a) the Mayor of London;

(b) a member of the London Assembly.

Recruitment

60   Enquiries about disability and health

(1) A person (A) to whom an application for work is made must not ask about the health of the applicant (B) —

(a) before offering work to B, or

(b) where A is not in a position to offer work to B, before including B in a pool of applicants from whom A intends (when in a position to do so) to select a person to whom to offer work.

(2) A contravention of subsection (1) (or a contravention of section 111 or 112 that relates to a contravention of subsection (1)) is enforceable as an unlawful act under Part 1 of the Equality Act 2006 (and, by virtue of section 120(8), is enforceable only by the Commission under that Part).

(3) A does not contravene a relevant disability provision merely by asking about B's health; but A's conduct in reliance on information given in response may be a contravention of a relevant disability provision.

(4) Subsection (5) applies if B brings proceedings before an employment tribunal on a complaint that A's conduct in reliance on information given in response to a question about B's health is a contravention of a relevant disability provision.

(5) In the application of section 136 to the proceedings, the particulars of the complaint are to be treated for the purposes of subsection (2) of that section as facts from which the tribunal could decide that A contravened the provision.

(6) This section does not apply to a question that A asks in so far as asking the question is necessary for the purpose of —

(a) establishing whether B will be able to comply with a requirement to undergo an assessment or establishing whether a duty to make reasonable adjustments is or will be imposed on A in relation to B in connection with a requirement to undergo an assessment,

(b) establishing whether B will be able to carry out a function that is intrinsic to the work concerned,

(c) monitoring diversity in the range of persons applying to A for work,

(d) taking action to which section 158 would apply if references in that section to persons who share (or do not share) a protected characteristic were references to disabled persons (or persons who are not disabled) and the reference to the characteristic were a reference to disability, or

(e) if A applies in relation to the work a requirement to have a particular disability, establishing whether B has that disability.

Equality Act 2010 (c. 15)
Part 5 — Work
Chapter 1 — Employment, etc.

1671

(7) In subsection (6)(b), where A reasonably believes that a duty to make reasonable adjustments would be imposed on A in relation to B in connection with the work, the reference to a function that is intrinsic to the work is to be read as a reference to a function that would be intrinsic to the work once A complied with the duty.

(8) Subsection (6)(e) applies only if A shows that, having regard to the nature or context of the work —

   (a) the requirement is an occupational requirement, and

   (b) the application of the requirement is a proportionate means of achieving a legitimate aim.

(9) "Work" means employment, contract work, a position as a partner, a position as a member of an LLP, a pupillage or tenancy, being taken as a devil, membership of a stable, an appointment to a personal or public office, or the provision of an employment service; and the references in subsection (1) to offering a person work are, in relation to contract work, to be read as references to allowing a person to do the work.

(10) A reference to offering work is a reference to making a conditional or unconditional offer of work (and, in relation to contract work, is a reference to allowing a person to do the work subject to fulfilment of one or more conditions).

(11) The following, so far as relating to discrimination within section 13 because of disability, are relevant disability provisions —

   (a) section 39(1)(a) or (c);

   (b) section 41(1)(b);

   (c) section 44(1)(a) or (c);

   (d) section 45(1)(a) or (c);

   (e) section 47(1)(a) or (c);

   (f) section 48(1)(a) or (c);

   (g) section 49(3)(a) or (c);

   (h) section 50(3)(a) or (c);

   (i) section 51(1);

   (j) section 55(1)(a) or (c).

(12) An assessment is an interview or other process designed to give an indication of a person's suitability for the work concerned.

(13) For the purposes of this section, whether or not a person has a disability is to be regarded as an aspect of that person's health.

(14) This section does not apply to anything done for the purpose of vetting applicants for work for reasons of national security.

CHAPTER 2

OCCUPATIONAL PENSION SCHEMES

61 Non-discrimination rule

(1) An occupational pension scheme must be taken to include a non-discrimination rule.

(2) A non-discrimination rule is a provision by virtue of which a responsible person (A) —

    (a) must not discriminate against another person (B) in carrying out any of A's functions in relation to the scheme;

    (b) must not, in relation to the scheme, harass B;

    (c) must not, in relation to the scheme, victimise B.

(3) The provisions of an occupational pension scheme have effect subject to the non-discrimination rule.

(4) The following are responsible persons —

    (a) the trustees or managers of the scheme;

    (b) an employer whose employees are, or may be, members of the scheme;

    (c) a person exercising an appointing function in relation to an office the holder of which is, or may be, a member of the scheme.

(5) A non-discrimination rule does not apply in relation to a person who is a pension credit member of a scheme.

(6) An appointing function is any of the following —

    (a) the function of appointing a person;

    (b) the function of terminating a person's appointment;

    (c) the function of recommending a person for appointment;

    (d) the function of approving an appointment.

(7) A breach of a non-discrimination rule is a contravention of this Part for the purposes of Part 9 (enforcement).

(8) It is not a breach of a non-discrimination rule for the employer or the trustees or managers of a scheme to maintain or use in relation to the scheme rules, practices, actions or decisions relating to age which are of a description specified by order by a Minister of the Crown.

(9) An order authorising the use of rules, practices, actions or decisions which are not in use before the order comes into force must not be made unless the Minister consults such persons as the Minister thinks appropriate.

(10) A non-discrimination rule does not have effect in relation to an occupational pension scheme in so far as an equality rule has effect in relation to it (or would have effect in relation to it but for Part 2 of Schedule 7).

(11) A duty to make reasonable adjustments applies to a responsible person.

62 Non-discrimination alterations

(1) This section applies if the trustees or managers of an occupational pension scheme do not have power to make non-discrimination alterations to the scheme.

(2) This section also applies if the trustees or managers of an occupational pension scheme have power to make non-discrimination alterations to the scheme but the procedure for doing so —

    (a) is liable to be unduly complex or protracted, or

    (b) involves obtaining consents which cannot be obtained or which can be obtained only with undue delay or difficulty.

(3) The trustees or managers may by resolution make non-discrimination alterations to the scheme.

(4) Non-discrimination alterations may have effect in relation to a period before the date on which they are made.

(5) Non-discrimination alterations to an occupational pension scheme are such alterations to the scheme as may be required for the provisions of the scheme to have the effect that they have in consequence of section 61(3).

63 Communications

(1) In their application to communications the following provisions apply in relation to a disabled person who is a pension credit member of an occupational pension scheme as they apply in relation to a disabled person who is a deferred member or pensioner member of the scheme—

    (a) section 61;

    (b) section 120;

    (c) section 126;

    (d) paragraph 19 of Schedule 8 (and such other provisions of that Schedule as apply for the purposes of that paragraph).

(2) Communications include—

    (a) the provision of information;

    (b) the operation of a dispute resolution procedure.

CHAPTER 3

EQUALITY OF TERMS

Sex equality

64 Relevant types of work

(1) Sections 66 to 70 apply where—

    (a) a person (A) is employed on work that is equal to the work that a comparator of the opposite sex (B) does;

    (b) a person (A) holding a personal or public office does work that is equal to the work that a comparator of the opposite sex (B) does.

(2) The references in subsection (1) to the work that B does are not restricted to work done contemporaneously with the work done by A.

65 Equal work

(1) For the purposes of this Chapter, A's work is equal to that of B if it is—

    (a) like B's work,

    (b) rated as equivalent to B's work, or

    (c) of equal value to B's work.

(2) A's work is like B's work if—

    (a) A's work and B's work are the same or broadly similar, and

    (b)   such differences as there are between their work are not of practical importance in relation to the terms of their work.

(3)   So on a comparison of one person's work with another's for the purposes of subsection (2), it is necessary to have regard to—

    (a)   the frequency with which differences between their work occur in practice, and

    (b)   the nature and extent of the differences.

(4)   A's work is rated as equivalent to B's work if a job evaluation study—

    (a)   gives an equal value to A's job and B's job in terms of the demands made on a worker, or

    (b)   would give an equal value to A's job and B's job in those terms were the evaluation not made on a sex-specific system.

(5)   A system is sex-specific if, for the purposes of one or more of the demands made on a worker, it sets values for men different from those it sets for women.

(6)   A's work is of equal value to B's work if it is—

    (a)   neither like B's work nor rated as equivalent to B's work, but

    (b)   nevertheless equal to B's work in terms of the demands made on A by reference to factors such as effort, skill and decision-making.

66   Sex equality clause

(1)   If the terms of A's work do not (by whatever means) include a sex equality clause, they are to be treated as including one.

(2)   A sex equality clause is a provision that has the following effect—

    (a)   if a term of A's is less favourable to A than a corresponding term of B's is to B, A's term is modified so as not to be less favourable;

    (b)   if A does not have a term which corresponds to a term of B's that benefits B, A's terms are modified so as to include such a term.

(3)   Subsection (2)(a) applies to a term of A's relating to membership of or rights under an occupational pension scheme only in so far as a sex equality rule would have effect in relation to the term.

(4)   In the case of work within section 65(1)(b), a reference in subsection (2) above to a term includes a reference to such terms (if any) as have not been determined by the rating of the work (as well as those that have).

67   Sex equality rule

(1)   If an occupational pension scheme does not include a sex equality rule, it is to be treated as including one.

(2)   A sex equality rule is a provision that has the following effect—

    (a)   if a relevant term is less favourable to A than it is to B, the term is modified so as not to be less favourable;

    (b)   if a term confers a relevant discretion capable of being exercised in a way that would be less favourable to A than to B, the term is modified so as to prevent the exercise of the discretion in that way.

(3)   A term is relevant if it is—

    (a)   a term on which persons become members of the scheme, or

(b)   a term on which members of the scheme are treated.

(4)   A discretion is relevant if its exercise in relation to the scheme is capable of affecting –
    (a)   the way in which persons become members of the scheme, or
    (b)   the way in which members of the scheme are treated.

(5)   The reference in subsection (3)(b) to a term on which members of a scheme are treated includes a reference to the term as it has effect for the benefit of dependants of members.

(6)   The reference in subsection (4)(b) to the way in which members of a scheme are treated includes a reference to the way in which they are treated as the scheme has effect for the benefit of dependants of members.

(7)   If the effect of a relevant matter on persons of the same sex differs according to their family, marital or civil partnership status, a comparison for the purposes of this section of the effect of that matter on persons of the opposite sex must be with persons who have the same status.

(8)   A relevant matter is –
    (a)   a relevant term;
    (b)   a term conferring a relevant discretion;
    (c)   the exercise of a relevant discretion in relation to an occupational pension scheme.

(9)   This section, so far as relating to the terms on which persons become members of an occupational pension scheme, does not have effect in relation to pensionable service before 8 April 1976.

(10)   This section, so far as relating to the terms on which members of an occupational pension scheme are treated, does not have effect in relation to pensionable service before 17 May 1990.

68   Sex equality rule: consequential alteration of schemes

(1)   This section applies if the trustees or managers of an occupational pension scheme do not have power to make sex equality alterations to the scheme.

(2)   This section also applies if the trustees or managers of an occupational pension scheme have power to make sex equality alterations to the scheme but the procedure for doing so –
    (a)   is liable to be unduly complex or protracted, or
    (b)   involves obtaining consents which cannot be obtained or which can be obtained only with undue delay or difficulty.

(3)   The trustees or managers may by resolution make sex equality alterations to the scheme.

(4)   Sex equality alterations may have effect in relation to a period before the date on which they are made.

(5)   Sex equality alterations to an occupational pension scheme are such alterations to the scheme as may be required to secure conformity with a sex equality rule.

69 Defence of material factor

(1) The sex equality clause in A's terms has no effect in relation to a difference between A's terms and B's terms if the responsible person shows that the difference is because of a material factor reliance on which—

    (a) does not involve treating A less favourably because of A's sex than the responsible person treats B, and

    (b) if the factor is within subsection (2), is a proportionate means of achieving a legitimate aim.

(2) A factor is within this subsection if A shows that, as a result of the factor, A and persons of the same sex doing work equal to A's are put at a particular disadvantage when compared with persons of the opposite sex doing work equal to A's.

(3) For the purposes of subsection (1), the long-term objective of reducing inequality between men's and women's terms of work is always to be regarded as a legitimate aim.

(4) A sex equality rule has no effect in relation to a difference between A and B in the effect of a relevant matter if the trustees or managers of the scheme in question show that the difference is because of a material factor which is not the difference of sex.

(5) "Relevant matter" has the meaning given in section 67.

(6) For the purposes of this section, a factor is not material unless it is a material difference between A's case and B's.

70 Exclusion of sex discrimination provisions

(1) The relevant sex discrimination provision has no effect in relation to a term of A's that—

    (a) is modified by, or included by virtue of, a sex equality clause or rule, or

    (b) would be so modified or included but for section 69 or Part 2 of Schedule 7.

(2) Neither of the following is sex discrimination for the purposes of the relevant sex discrimination provision—

    (a) the inclusion in A's terms of a term that is less favourable as referred to in section 66(2)(a);

    (b) the failure to include in A's terms a corresponding term as referred to in section 66(2)(b).

(3) The relevant sex discrimination provision is, in relation to work of a description given in the first column of the table, the provision referred to in the second column so far as relating to sex.

Description of work	Provision
Employment	Section 39(2)
Appointment to a personal office	Section 49(6)
Appointment to a public office	Section 50(6)

71   Sex discrimination in relation to contractual pay

(1)   This section applies in relation to a term of a person's work —
    (a)   that relates to pay, but
    (b)   in relation to which a sex equality clause or rule has no effect.

(2)   The relevant sex discrimination provision (as defined by section 70) has no effect in relation to the term except in so far as treatment of the person amounts to a contravention of the provision by virtue of section 13 or 14.

Pregnancy and maternity equality

72   Relevant types of work

Sections 73 to 76 apply where a woman —
    (a)   is employed, or
    (b)   holds a personal or public office.

73   Maternity equality clause

(1)   If the terms of the woman's work do not (by whatever means) include a maternity equality clause, they are to be treated as including one.

(2)   A maternity equality clause is a provision that, in relation to the terms of the woman's work, has the effect referred to in section 74(1), (6) and (8).

(3)   In the case of a term relating to membership of or rights under an occupational pension scheme, a maternity equality clause has only such effect as a maternity equality rule would have.

74   Maternity equality clause: pay

(1)   A term of the woman's work that provides for maternity-related pay to be calculated by reference to her pay at a particular time is, if each of the following three conditions is satisfied, modified as mentioned in subsection (5).

(2)   The first condition is that, after the time referred to in subsection (1) but before the end of the protected period —
    (a)   her pay increases, or
    (b)   it would have increased had she not been on maternity leave.

(3)   The second condition is that the maternity-related pay is not —
    (a)   what her pay would have been had she not been on maternity leave, or
    (b)   the difference between the amount of statutory maternity pay to which she is entitled and what her pay would have been had she not been on maternity leave.

(4)   The third condition is that the terms of her work do not provide for the maternity-related pay to be subject to —
    (a)   an increase as mentioned in subsection (2)(a), or
    (b)   an increase that would have occurred as mentioned in subsection (2)(b).

(5)   The modification referred to in subsection (1) is a modification to provide for the maternity-related pay to be subject to —
    (a)   any increase as mentioned in subsection (2)(a), or

    (b)   any increase that would have occurred as mentioned in subsection (2)(b).

(6)   A term of her work that—

    (a)   provides for pay within subsection (7), but

    (b)   does not provide for her to be given the pay in circumstances in which she would have been given it had she not been on maternity leave,

is modified so as to provide for her to be given it in circumstances in which it would normally be given.

(7)   Pay is within this subsection if it is—

    (a)   pay (including pay by way of bonus) in respect of times before the woman is on maternity leave,

    (b)   pay by way of bonus in respect of times when she is on compulsory maternity leave, or

    (c)   pay by way of bonus in respect of times after the end of the protected period.

(8)   A term of the woman's work that—

    (a)   provides for pay after the end of the protected period, but

    (b)   does not provide for it to be subject to an increase to which it would have been subject had she not been on maternity leave,

is modified so as to provide for it to be subject to the increase.

(9)   Maternity-related pay is pay (other than statutory maternity pay) to which a woman is entitled—

    (a)   as a result of being pregnant, or

    (b)   in respect of times when she is on maternity leave.

(10)   A reference to the protected period is to be construed in accordance with section 18.

75   Maternity equality rule

(1)   If an occupational pension scheme does not include a maternity equality rule, it is to be treated as including one.

(2)   A maternity equality rule is a provision that has the effect set out in subsections (3) and (4).

(3)   If a relevant term does not treat time when the woman is on maternity leave as it treats time when she is not, the term is modified so as to treat time when she is on maternity leave as time when she is not.

(4)   If a term confers a relevant discretion capable of being exercised so that time when she is on maternity leave is treated differently from time when she is not, the term is modified so as not to allow the discretion to be exercised in that way.

(5)   A term is relevant if it is—

    (a)   a term relating to membership of the scheme,

    (b)   a term relating to the accrual of rights under the scheme, or

    (c)   a term providing for the determination of the amount of a benefit payable under the scheme.

(6)   A discretion is relevant if its exercise is capable of affecting—

    (a)   membership of the scheme,

    (b)   the accrual of rights under the scheme, or

    (c)   the determination of the amount of a benefit payable under the scheme.

(7)   This section does not require the woman's contributions to the scheme in respect of time when she is on maternity leave to be determined otherwise than by reference to the amount she is paid in respect of that time.

(8)   This section, so far as relating to time when she is on ordinary maternity leave but is not being paid by her employer, applies only in a case where the expected week of childbirth began on or after 6 April 2003.

(9)   This section, so far as relating to time when she is on additional maternity leave but is not being paid by her employer —

    (a)   does not apply to the accrual of rights under the scheme in any case;

    (b)   applies for other purposes only in a case where the expected week of childbirth began on or after 5 October 2008.

(10)   In this section —

    (a)   a reference to being on maternity leave includes a reference to having been on maternity leave, and

    (b)   a reference to being paid by the employer includes a reference to receiving statutory maternity pay from the employer.

76   Exclusion of pregnancy and maternity discrimination provisions

(1)   The relevant pregnancy and maternity discrimination provision has no effect in relation to a term of the woman's work that is modified by a maternity equality clause or rule.

(2)   The inclusion in the woman's terms of a term that requires modification by virtue of section 73(2) or (3) is not pregnancy and maternity discrimination for the purposes of the relevant pregnancy and maternity discrimination provision.

(3)   The relevant pregnancy and maternity discrimination provision is, in relation to a description of work given in the first column of the table, the provision referred to in the second column so far as relating to pregnancy and maternity.

Description of work	Provision
Employment	Section 39(2)
Appointment to a personal office	Section 49(6)
Appointment to a public office	Section 50(6)

Disclosure of information

77   Discussions about pay

(1)   A term of a person's work that purports to prevent or restrict the person (P) from disclosing or seeking to disclose information about the terms of P's work

is unenforceable against P in so far as P makes or seeks to make a relevant pay disclosure.

(2) A term of a person's work that purports to prevent or restrict the person (P) from seeking disclosure of information from a colleague about the terms of the colleague's work is unenforceable against P in so far as P seeks a relevant pay disclosure from the colleague; and "colleague" includes a former colleague in relation to the work in question.

(3) A disclosure is a relevant pay disclosure if made for the purpose of enabling the person who makes it, or the person to whom it is made, to find out whether or to what extent there is, in relation to the work in question, a connection between pay and having (or not having) a particular protected characteristic.

(4) The following are to be treated as protected acts for the purposes of the relevant victimisation provision—

    (a) seeking a disclosure that would be a relevant pay disclosure;

    (b) making or seeking to make a relevant pay disclosure;

    (c) receiving information disclosed in a relevant pay disclosure.

(5) The relevant victimisation provision is, in relation to a description of work specified in the first column of the table, section 27 so far as it applies for the purposes of a provision mentioned in the second column.

Description of work	*Provision by virtue of which section 27 has effect*
Employment	Section 39(3) or (4)
Appointment to a personal office	Section 49(5) or (8)
Appointment to a public office	Section 50(5) or (9)

78 Gender pay gap information

(1) Regulations may require employers to publish information relating to the pay of employees for the purpose of showing whether, by reference to factors of such description as is prescribed, there are differences in the pay of male and female employees.

(2) This section does not apply to—

    (a) an employer who has fewer than 250 employees;

    (b) a person specified in Schedule 19;

    (c) a government department or part of the armed forces not specified in that Schedule.

(3) The regulations may prescribe—

    (a) descriptions of employer;

    (b) descriptions of employee;

    (c) how to calculate the number of employees that an employer has;

    (d) descriptions of information;

    (e) the time at which information is to be published;

    (f) the form and manner in which it is to be published.

(4) Regulations under subsection (3)(e) may not require an employer, after the first publication of information, to publish information more frequently than at intervals of 12 months.

(5) The regulations may make provision for a failure to comply with the regulations—

    (a) to be an offence punishable on summary conviction by a fine not exceeding level 5 on the standard scale;

    (b) to be enforced, otherwise than as an offence, by such means as are prescribed.

(6) The reference to a failure to comply with the regulations includes a reference to a failure by a person acting on behalf of an employer.

Supplementary

79 Comparators

(1) This section applies for the purposes of this Chapter.

(2) If A is employed, B is a comparator if subsection (3) or (4) applies.

(3) This subsection applies if—

    (a) B is employed by A's employer or by an associate of A's employer, and

    (b) A and B work at the same establishment.

(4) This subsection applies if—

    (a) B is employed by A's employer or an associate of A's employer,

    (b) B works at an establishment other than the one at which A works, and

    (c) common terms apply at the establishments (either generally or as between A and B).

(5) If A holds a personal or public office, B is a comparator if—

    (a) B holds a personal or public office, and

    (b) the person responsible for paying A is also responsible for paying B.

(6) If A is a relevant member of the House of Commons staff, B is a comparator if—

    (a) B is employed by the person who is A's employer under subsection (6) of section 195 of the Employment Rights Act 1996, or

    (b) if subsection (7) of that section applies in A's case, B is employed by the person who is A's employer under that subsection.

(7) If A is a relevant member of the House of Lords staff, B is a comparator if B is also a relevant member of the House of Lords staff.

(8) Section 42 does not apply to this Chapter; accordingly, for the purposes of this Chapter only, holding the office of constable is to be treated as holding a personal office.

(9) For the purposes of this section, employers are associated if—

    (a) one is a company of which the other (directly or indirectly) has control, or

    (b) both are companies of which a third person (directly or indirectly) has control.

80   Interpretation and exceptions

(1)   This section applies for the purposes of this Chapter.

(2)   The terms of a person's work are—
   (a)   if the person is employed, the terms of the person's employment that are in the person's contract of employment, contract of apprenticeship or contract to do work personally;
   (b)   if the person holds a personal or public office, the terms of the person's appointment to the office.

(3)   If work is not done at an establishment, it is to be treated as done at the establishment with which it has the closest connection.

(4)   A person (P) is the responsible person in relation to another person if—
   (a)   P is the other's employer;
   (b)   P is responsible for paying remuneration in respect of a personal or public office that the other holds.

(5)   A job evaluation study is a study undertaken with a view to evaluating, in terms of the demands made on a person by reference to factors such as effort, skill and decision-making, the jobs to be done—
   (a)   by some or all of the workers in an undertaking or group of undertakings, or
   (b)   in the case of the armed forces, by some or all of the members of the armed forces.

(6)   In the case of Crown employment, the reference in subsection (5)(a) to an undertaking is to be construed in accordance with section 191(4) of the Employment Rights Act 1996.

(7)   "Civil partnership status" has the meaning given in section 124(1) of the Pensions Act 1995.

(8)   Schedule 7 (exceptions) has effect.

CHAPTER 4

SUPPLEMENTARY

81   Ships and hovercraft

(1)   This Part applies in relation to—
   (a)   work on ships,
   (b)   work on hovercraft, and
   (c)   seafarers,
only in such circumstances as are prescribed.

(2)   For the purposes of this section, it does not matter whether employment arises or work is carried out within or outside the United Kingdom.

(3)   "Ship" has the same meaning as in the Merchant Shipping Act 1995.

(4)   "Hovercraft" has the same meaning as in the Hovercraft Act 1968.

(5)   "Seafarer" means a person employed or engaged in any capacity on board a ship or hovercraft.

(6) Nothing in this section affects the application of any other provision of this Act to conduct outside England and Wales or Scotland.

82 Offshore work

(1) Her Majesty may by Order in Council provide that in the case of persons in offshore work—

    (a) specified provisions of this Part apply (with or without modification);

    (b) Northern Ireland legislation making provision for purposes corresponding to any of the purposes of this Part applies (with or without modification).

(2) The Order may—

    (a) provide for these provisions, as applied by the Order, to apply to individuals (whether or not British citizens) and bodies corporate (whether or not incorporated under the law of a part of the United Kingdom), whether or not such application affects activities outside the United Kingdom;

    (b) make provision for conferring jurisdiction on a specified court or class of court or on employment tribunals in respect of offences, causes of action or other matters arising in connection with offshore work;

    (c) exclude from the operation of section 3 of the Territorial Waters Jurisdiction Act 1878 (consents required for prosecutions) proceedings for offences under the provisions mentioned in subsection (1) in connection with offshore work;

    (d) provide that such proceedings must not be brought without such consent as may be required by the Order.

(3) "Offshore work" is work for the purposes of—

    (a) activities in the territorial sea adjacent to the United Kingdom,

    (b) activities such as are mentioned in subsection (2) of section 11 of the Petroleum Act 1998 in waters within subsection (8)(b) or (c) of that section, or

    (c) activities mentioned in paragraphs (a) and (b) of section 87(1) of the Energy Act 2004 in waters to which that section applies.

(4) Work includes employment, contract work, a position as a partner or as a member of an LLP, or an appointment to a personal or public office.

(5) Northern Ireland legislation includes an enactment contained in, or in an instrument under, an Act that forms part of the law of Northern Ireland.

(6) In the application to Northern Ireland of subsection (2)(b), the reference to employment tribunals is to be read as a reference to industrial tribunals.

(7) Nothing in this section affects the application of any other provision of this Act to conduct outside England and Wales or Scotland.

83 Interpretation and exceptions

(1) This section applies for the purposes of this Part.

(2) "Employment" means—

    (a) employment under a contract of employment, a contract of apprenticeship or a contract personally to do work;

(b)   Crown employment;

(c)   employment as a relevant member of the House of Commons staff;

(d)   employment as a relevant member of the House of Lords staff.

(3)   This Part applies to service in the armed forces as it applies to employment by a private person; and for that purpose —

(a)   references to terms of employment, or to a contract of employment, are to be read as including references to terms of service;

(b)   references to associated employers are to be ignored.

(4)   A reference to an employer or an employee, or to employing or being employed, is (subject to section 212(11)) to be read with subsections (2) and (3); and a reference to an employer also includes a reference to a person who has no employees but is seeking to employ one or more other persons.

(5)   "Relevant member of the House of Commons staff" has the meaning given in section 195 of the Employment Rights Act 1996; and such a member of staff is an employee of —

(a)   the person who is the employer of that member under subsection (6) of that section, or

(b)   if subsection (7) of that section applies in the case of that member, the person who is the employer of that member under that subsection.

(6)   "Relevant member of the House of Lords staff" has the meaning given in section 194 of that Act (which provides that such a member of staff is an employee of the Corporate Officer of the House of Lords).

(7)   In the case of a person in Crown employment, or in employment as a relevant member of the House of Commons staff, a reference to the person's dismissal is a reference to the termination of the person's employment.

(8)   A reference to a personal or public office, or to an appointment to a personal or public office, is to be construed in accordance with section 52.

(9)   "Crown employment" has the meaning given in section 191 of the Employment Rights Act 1996.

(10)   Schedule 8 (reasonable adjustments) has effect.

(11)   Schedule 9 (exceptions) has effect.

PART 6

EDUCATION

CHAPTER 1

SCHOOLS

84   Application of this Chapter

This Chapter does not apply to the following protected characteristics —

(a)   age;

(b)   marriage and civil partnership.

85   Pupils: admission and treatment, etc.

(1)   The responsible body of a school to which this section applies must not discriminate against a person—

    (a)   in the arrangements it makes for deciding who is offered admission as a pupil;

    (b)   as to the terms on which it offers to admit the person as a pupil;

    (c)   by not admitting the person as a pupil.

(2)   The responsible body of such a school must not discriminate against a pupil—

    (a)   in the way it provides education for the pupil;

    (b)   in the way it affords the pupil access to a benefit, facility or service;

    (c)   by not providing education for the pupil;

    (d)   by not affording the pupil access to a benefit, facility or service;

    (e)   by excluding the pupil from the school;

    (f)   by subjecting the pupil to any other detriment.

(3)   The responsible body of such a school must not harass—

    (a)   a pupil;

    (b)   a person who has applied for admission as a pupil.

(4)   The responsible body of such a school must not victimise a person—

    (a)   in the arrangements it makes for deciding who is offered admission as a pupil;

    (b)   as to the terms on which it offers to admit the person as a pupil;

    (c)   by not admitting the person as a pupil.

(5)   The responsible body of such a school must not victimise a pupil—

    (a)   in the way it provides education for the pupil;

    (b)   in the way it affords the pupil access to a benefit, facility or service;

    (c)   by not providing education for the pupil;

    (d)   by not affording the pupil access to a benefit, facility or service;

    (e)   by excluding the pupil from the school;

    (f)   by subjecting the pupil to any other detriment.

(6)   A duty to make reasonable adjustments applies to the responsible body of such a school.

(7)   In relation to England and Wales, this section applies to—

    (a)   a school maintained by a local authority;

    (b)   an independent educational institution (other than a special school);

    (c)   a special school (not maintained by a local authority).

(8)   In relation to Scotland, this section applies to—

    (a)   a school managed by an education authority;

    (b)   an independent school;

    (c)   a school in respect of which the managers are for the time being receiving grants under section 73(c) or (d) of the Education (Scotland) Act 1980.

(9)   The responsible body of a school to which this section applies is—

    (a)   if the school is within subsection (7)(a), the local authority or governing body;

(b)   if it is within subsection (7)(b) or (c), the proprietor;

(c)   if it is within subsection (8)(a), the education authority;

(d)   if it is within subsection (8)(b), the proprietor;

(e)   if it is within subsection (8)(c), the managers.

(10)   In the application of section 26 for the purposes of subsection (3), none of the following is a relevant protected characteristic—

(a)   gender reassignment;

(b)   religion or belief;

(c)   sexual orientation.

86   Victimisation of pupils, etc. for conduct of parents, etc.

(1)   This section applies for the purposes of section 27 in its application to section 85(4) or (5).

(2)   The references to B in paragraphs (a) and (b) of subsection (1) of section 27 include a reference to a parent or sibling of the child in question.

(3)   Giving false evidence or information, or making a false allegation, in good faith is not a protected act in a case where—

(a)   the evidence or information is given, or the allegation is made, by a parent or sibling of the child, and

(b)   the child has acted in bad faith.

(4)   Giving false evidence or information, or making a false allegation, in bad faith, is a protected act in a case where—

(a)   the evidence or information is given, or the allegation is made, by a parent or sibling of the child, and

(b)   the child has acted in good faith.

(5)   In this section—

"child" means a person who has not attained the age of 18;

"sibling" means a brother or sister, a half-brother or half-sister, or a stepbrother or stepsister.

87   Application of certain powers under Education Act 1996

(1)   Sections 496 and 497 of the Education Act 1996 (powers to give directions where responsible body of school in default of obligations, etc.) apply to the performance of a duty under section 85.

(2)   But neither of sections 496 and 497 of that Act applies to the performance of a duty under that section by the proprietor of an independent educational institution (other than a special school).

88   Disabled pupils: accessibility

Schedule 10 (accessibility) has effect.

89   Interpretation and exceptions

(1)   This section applies for the purposes of this Chapter.

(2) Nothing in this Chapter applies to anything done in connection with the content of the curriculum.

(3) "Pupil"—
  (a) in relation to England and Wales, has the meaning given in section 3(1) of the Education Act 1996;
  (b) in relation to Scotland, has the meaning given in section 135(1) of the Education (Scotland) Act 1980.

(4) "Proprietor"—
  (a) in relation to a school in England and Wales, has the meaning given in section 579(1) of the Education Act 1996;
  (b) in relation to a school in Scotland, has the meaning given in section 135(1) of the Education (Scotland) Act 1980.

(5) "School"—
  (a) in relation to England and Wales, has the meaning given in section 4 cf the Education Act 1996;
  (b) in relation to Scotland, has the meaning given in section 135(1) of the Education (Scotland) Act 1980.

(6) A reference to a school includes a reference to an independent educational institution in England; and a reference to an independent educational institution in England is to be construed in accordance with Chapter 1 of Part 4 of the Education and Skills Act 2008.

(7) A reference to an independent educational institution is a reference to—
  (a) an independent educational institution in England, or
  (b) an independent school in Wales.

(8) "Independent school"—
  (a) in relation to Wales, has the meaning given in section 463 of the Education Act 1996;
  (b) in relation to Scotland, has the meaning given in section 135(1) of the Education (Scotland) Act 1980.

(9) "Special school" has the meaning given in section 337 of the Education Act 1996.

(10) "Local authority" means—
  (a) in relation to England, an English local authority within the meaning of section 162 of the Education and Inspections Act 2006;
  (b) in relation to Wales, a Welsh local authority within the meaning of that section.

(11) "Education authority", in relation to Scotland, has the meaning given in section 135(1) of the Education (Scotland) Act 1980.

(12) Schedule 11 (exceptions) has effect.

CHAPTER 2

FURTHER AND HIGHER EDUCATION

90 Application of this Chapter

This Chapter does not apply to the protected characteristic of marriage and civil partnership.

91 Students: admission and treatment, etc.

(1) The responsible body of an institution to which this section applies must not discriminate against a person—

    (a) in the arrangements it makes for deciding who is offered admission as a student;

    (b) as to the terms on which it offers to admit the person as a student;

    (c) by not admitting the person as a student.

(2) The responsible body of such an institution must not discriminate against a student—

    (a) in the way it provides education for the student;

    (b) in the way it affords the student access to a benefit, facility or service;

    (c) by not providing education for the student;

    (d) by not affording the student access to a benefit, facility or service;

    (e) by excluding the student;

    (f) by subjecting the student to any other detriment.

(3) The responsible body of such an institution must not discriminate against a disabled person—

    (a) in the arrangements it makes for deciding upon whom to confer a qualification;

    (b) as to the terms on which it is prepared to confer a qualification on the person;

    (c) by not conferring a qualification on the person;

    (d) by withdrawing a qualification from the person or varying the terms on which the person holds it.

(4) Subsection (3) applies only to disability discrimination.

(5) The responsible body of such an institution must not harass—

    (a) a student;

    (b) a person who has applied for admission as a student;

    (c) a disabled person who holds or has applied for a qualification conferred by the institution.

(6) The responsible body of such an institution must not victimise a person—

    (a) in the arrangements it makes for deciding who is offered admission as a student;

    (b) as to the terms on which it offers to admit the person as a student;

    (c) by not admitting the person as a student.

(7) The responsible body of such an institution must not victimise a student—

    (a) in the way it provides education for the student;

   (b)   in the way it affords the student access to a benefit, facility or service;
   (c)   by not providing education for the student;
   (d)   by not affording the student access to a benefit, facility or service;
   (e)   by excluding the student;
   (f)   by subjecting the student to any other detriment.

(8)   The responsible body of such an institution must not victimise a disabled person—
   (a)   in the arrangements it makes for deciding upon whom to confer a qualification;
   (b)   as to the terms on which it is prepared to confer a qualification on the person;
   (c)   by not conferring a qualification on the person;
   (d)   by withdrawing a qualification from the person or varying the terms on which the person holds it.

(9)   A duty to make reasonable adjustments applies to the responsible body of such an institution.

(10)   In relation to England and Wales, this section applies to—
   (a)   a university;
   (b)   any other institution within the higher education sector;
   (c)   an institution within the further education sector.

(11)   In relation to Scotland, this section applies to—
   (a)   a university;
   (b)   a designated institution;
   (c)   a college of further education.

(12)   A responsible body is—
   (a)   in the case of an institution within subsection (10)(a), (b) or (c), the governing body;
   (b)   in the case of an institution within subsection (11)(a) or (b), the governing body;
   (c)   in the case of a college of further education under the management of a board of management, the board of management;
   (d)   in the case of any other college of further education, any board of governors of the college or any person responsible for the management of the college, whether or not formally constituted as a governing body or board of governors.

92   Further and higher education courses

(1)   The responsible body in relation to a course to which this section applies must not discriminate against a person—
   (a)   in the arrangements it makes for deciding who is enrolled on the course;
   (b)   as to the terms on which it offers to enrol the person on the course;
   (c)   by not accepting the person's application for enrolment.

(2)   The responsible body in relation to such a course must not discriminate against a person who is enrolled on the course in the services it provides or offers to provide.

(3) The responsible body in relation to such a course must not harass a person who—

    (a) seeks enrolment on the course;

    (b) is enrolled on the course;

    (c) is a user of services provided by the body in relation to the course.

(4) The responsible body in relation to such a course must not victimise a person—

    (a) in the arrangements it makes for deciding who is enrolled on the course;

    (b) as to the terms on which it offers to enrol the person on the course;

    (c) by not accepting the person's application for enrolment.

(5) The responsible body in relation to such a course must not victimise a person who is enrolled on the course in the services it provides or offers to provide.

(6) A duty to make reasonable adjustments applies to the responsible body.

(7) This section applies to—

    (a) a course of further or higher education secured by a responsible body in England or Wales;

    (b) a course of education provided by the governing body of a maintained school under section 80 of the School Standards and Framework Act 1998;

    (c) a course of further education secured by an education authority in Scotland.

(8) A responsible body is—

    (a) a local authority in England or Wales, for the purposes of subsection (7)(a);

    (b) the governing body of a maintained school, for the purposes of subsection (7)(b);

    (c) an education authority in Scotland, for the purposes of subsection (7)(c).

(9) In this section—

    "course", in relation to further education, includes each component part of a course if there is no requirement imposed on persons registered for a component part of the course to register for another component part of the course;

    "enrolment" includes registration for a component part of a course;

    "maintained school" has the meaning given in section 20(7) of the School Standards and Framework Act 1998;

    "services" means services of any description which are provided wholly or mainly for persons enrolled on a course to which this section applies.

93 Recreational or training facilities

(1) The responsible body in relation to facilities to which this section applies must not discriminate against a person—

    (a) in the arrangements it makes for deciding who is provided with the facilities;

    (b) as to the terms on which it offers to provide the facilities to the person;

    (c) by not accepting the person's application for provision of the facilities.

(2) The responsible body in relation to such facilities must not discriminate against a person who is provided with the facilities in the services it provides or offers to provide.

(3) The responsible body in relation to such facilities must not harass a person who —

    (a) seeks to have the facilities provided;

    (b) is provided with the facilities;

    (c) is a user of services provided by the body in relation to the facilities.

(4) The responsible body in relation to such facilities must not victimise a person —

    (a) in the arrangements it makes for deciding who is provided with the facilities;

    (b) as to the terms on which it offers to provide the facilities to the person;

    (c) by not accepting the person's application for provision of the facilities.

(5) The responsible body in relation to such facilities must not victimise a person who is provided with the facilities in the services it provides or offers to provide.

(6) A duty to make reasonable adjustments applies to the responsible body.

(7) This section applies to —

    (a) facilities secured by a local authority in England under section 507A or 507B of the Education Act 1996;

    (b) facilities secured by a local authority in Wales under section 508 of that Act;

    (c) recreational or training facilities provided by an education authority in Scotland.

(8) A responsible body is —

    (a) a local authority in England, for the purposes of subsection (7)(a);

    (b) a local authority in Wales, for the purposes of subsection (7)(b);

    (c) an education authority in Scotland, for the purposes of subsection (7)(c).

(9) This section does not apply to the protected characteristic of age, so far as relating to persons who have not attained the age of 18.

94 Interpretation and exceptions

(1) This section applies for the purposes of this Chapter.

(2) Nothing in this Chapter applies to anything done in connection with the content of the curriculum.

(3) A reference to a student, in relation to an institution, is a reference to a person for whom education is provided by the institution.

(4) A reference to a university includes a reference to a university college and a college, school or hall of a university.

(5) A reference to an institution within the further or higher education sector is to be construed in accordance with section 91 of the Further and Higher Education Act 1992.

(6) "Further education" —

      (a)   in relation to England and Wales, has the meaning given in section 2 of the Education Act 1996;

      (b)   in relation to Scotland, has the meaning given in section 1(3) of the Further and Higher Education (Scotland) Act 1992.

(7)   "Higher education" –

      (a)   in relation to England and Wales, means education provided by means of a course of a description mentioned in Schedule 6 to the Education Reform Act 1988;

      (b)   in relation to Scotland, has the meaning given in section 38 of the Further and Higher Education (Scotland) Act 1992.

(8)   "College of further education" has the meaning given in section 36 of the Further and Higher Education (Scotland) Act 1992.

(9)   "Designated institution" has the meaning given in section 44 of that Act.

(10)   "Local authority" means –

      (a)   in relation to England, an English local authority within the meaning of section 162 of the Education and Inspections Act 2006;

      (b)   in relation to Wales, a Welsh local authority within the meaning of that section.

(11)   "Education authority" has the meaning given by section 135(1) of the Education (Scotland) Act 1980.

(12)   Schedule 12 (exceptions) has effect.

CHAPTER 3

GENERAL QUALIFICATIONS BODIES

95   Application of this Chapter

This Chapter does not apply to the protected characteristic of marriage and civil partnership.

96   Qualifications bodies

(1)   A qualifications body (A) must not discriminate against a person (B) –

      (a)   in the arrangements A makes for deciding upon whom to confer a relevant qualification;

      (b)   as to the terms on which it is prepared to confer a relevant qualification on B;

      (c)   by not conferring a relevant qualification on B.

(2)   A qualifications body (A) must not discriminate against a person (B) upon whom A has conferred a relevant qualification –

      (a)   by withdrawing the qualification from B;

      (b)   by varying the terms on which B holds the qualification;

      (c)   by subjecting B to any other detriment.

(3)   A qualifications body must not, in relation to conferment by it of a relevant qualification, harass –

      (a)   a person who holds the qualification, or

    (b)   a person who applies for it.

(4)   A qualifications body (A) must not victimise a person (B) –

    (a)   in the arrangements A makes for deciding upon whom to confer a relevant qualification;

    (b)   as to the terms on which it is prepared to confer a relevant qualification on B;

    (c)   by not conferring a relevant qualification on B.

(5)   A qualifications body (A) must not victimise a person (B) upon whom A has conferred a relevant qualification –

    (a)   by withdrawing the qualification from B;

    (b)   by varying the terms on which B holds the qualification;

    (c)   by subjecting B to any other detriment.

(6)   A duty to make reasonable adjustments applies to a qualifications body.

(7)   Subsection (6) does not apply to the body in so far as the appropriate regulator specifies provisions, criteria or practices in relation to which the body –

    (a)   is not subject to a duty to make reasonable adjustments;

    (b)   is subject to a duty to make reasonable adjustments, but in relation to which such adjustments as the regulator specifies should not be made.

(8)   For the purposes of subsection (7) the appropriate regulator must have regard to –

    (a)   the need to minimise the extent to which disabled persons are disadvantaged in attaining the qualification because of their disabilities;

    (b)   the need to secure that the qualification gives a reliable indication of the knowledge, skills and understanding of a person upon whom it is conferred;

    (c)   the need to maintain public confidence in the qualification.

(9)   The appropriate regulator –

    (a)   must not specify any matter for the purposes of subsection (7) unless it has consulted such persons as it thinks appropriate;

    (b)   must publish matters so specified (including the date from which they are to have effect) in such manner as is prescribed.

(10)   The appropriate regulator is –

    (a)   in relation to a qualifications body that confers qualifications in England, a person prescribed by a Minister of the Crown;

    (b)   in relation to a qualifications body that confers qualifications in Wales, a person prescribed by the Welsh Ministers;

    (c)   in relation to a qualifications body that confers qualifications in Scotland, a person prescribed by the Scottish Ministers.

(11)   For the purposes of subsection (10), a qualification is conferred in a part of Great Britain if there are, or may reasonably be expected to be, persons seeking to obtain the qualification who are or will be assessed for those purposes wholly or mainly in that part.

97   Interpretation

(1)   This section applies for the purposes of section 96.

(2) A qualifications body is an authority or body which can confer a relevant qualification.

(3) A relevant qualification is an authorisation, qualification, approval or certification of such description as may be prescribed—

    (a) in relation to conferments in England, by a Minister of the Crown;

    (b) in relation to conferments in Wales, by the Welsh Ministers;

    (c) in relation to conferments in Scotland, by the Scottish Ministers.

(4) An authority or body is not a qualifications body in so far as—

    (a) it is the responsible body of a school to which section 85 applies,

    (b) it is the governing body of an institution to which section 91 applies,

    (c) it exercises functions under the Education Acts, or

    (d) it exercises functions under the Education (Scotland) Act 1980.

(5) A qualifications body does not include an authority or body of such description, or in such circumstances, as may be prescribed.

(6) A reference to conferring a relevant qualification includes a reference—

    (a) to renewing or extending the conferment of a relevant qualification;

    (b) to authenticating a relevant qualification conferred by another person.

(7) A reference in section 96(8), (10) or (11) to a qualification is a reference to a relevant qualification.

(8) Subsection (11) of section 96 applies for the purposes of subsection (3) of this section as it applies for the purposes of subsection (10) of that section.

CHAPTER 4

MISCELLANEOUS

98 Reasonable adjustments

Schedule 13 (reasonable adjustments) has effect.

99 Educational charities and endowments

Schedule 14 (educational charities and endowments) has effect.

PART 7

ASSOCIATIONS

Preliminary

100 Application of this Part

(1) This Part does not apply to the protected characteristic of marriage and civil partnership.

(2) This Part does not apply to discrimination, harassment or victimisation—

    (a) that is prohibited by Part 3 (services and public functions), Part 4 (premises), Part 5 (work) or Part 6 (education), or

(b)   that would be so prohibited but for an express exception.

Membership, etc.

101   Members and associates

(1)   An association (A) must not discriminate against a person (B) —
  (a)   in the arrangements A makes for deciding who to admit to membership;
  (b)   as to the terms on which A is prepared to admit B to membership;
  (c)   by not accepting B's application for membership.

(2)   An association (A) must not discriminate against a member (B) —
  (a)   in the way A affords B access, or by not affording B access, to a benefit, facility or service;
  (b)   by depriving B of membership;
  (c)   by varying B's terms of membership;
  (d)   by subjecting B to any other detriment.

(3)   An association (A) must not discriminate against an associate (B) —
  (a)   in the way A affords B access, or by not affording B access, to a benefit, facility or service;
  (b)   by depriving B of B's rights as an associate;
  (c)   by varying B's rights as an associate;
  (d)   by subjecting B to any other detriment.

(4)   An association must not harass —
  (a)   a member;
  (b)   a person seeking to become a member;
  (c)   an associate.

(5)   An association (A) must not victimise a person (B) —
  (a)   in the arrangements A makes for deciding who to admit to membership;
  (b)   as to the terms on which A is prepared to admit B to membership;
  (c)   by not accepting B's application for membership.

(6)   An association (A) must not victimise a member (B) —
  (a)   in the way A affords B access, or by not affording B access, to a benefit, facility or service;
  (b)   by depriving B of membership;
  (c)   by varying B's terms of membership;
  (d)   by subjecting B to any other detriment.

(7)   An association (A) must not victimise an associate (B) —
  (a)   in the way A affords B access, or by not affording B access, to a benefit, facility or service;
  (b)   by depriving B of B's rights as an associate;
  (c)   by varying B's rights as an associate;
  (d)   by subjecting B to any other detriment.

102 Guests

(1) An association (A) must not discriminate against a person (B) –

    (a) in the arrangements A makes for deciding who to invite, or who to permit to be invited, as a guest;

    (b) as to the terms on which A is prepared to invite B, or to permit B to be invited, as a guest;

    (c) by not inviting B, or not permitting B to be invited, as a guest.

(2) An association (A) must not discriminate against a guest (B) invited by A or with A's permission (whether express or implied) –

    (a) in the way A affords B access, or by not affording B access, to a benefit, facility or service;

    (b) by subjecting B to any other detriment.

(3) An association must not harass –

    (a) a guest;

    (b) a person seeking to be a guest.

(4) An association (A) must not victimise a person (B) –

    (a) in the arrangements A makes for deciding who to invite, or who to permit to be invited, as a guest;

    (b) as to the terms on which A is prepared to invite B, or to permit B to be invited, as a guest;

    (c) by not inviting B, or not permitting B to be invited, as a guest.

(5) An association (A) must not victimise a guest (B) invited by A or with A's permission (whether express or implied) –

    (a) in the way A affords B access, or by not affording B access, to a benefit, facility or service;

    (b) by subjecting B to any other detriment.

103 Sections 101 and 102: further provision

(1) A duty to make reasonable adjustments applies to an association.

(2) In the application of section 26 for the purposes of section 101(4) or 102(3), neither of the following is a relevant protected characteristic –

    (a) religion or belief;

    (b) sexual orientation.

Special provision for political parties

104 Selection of candidates

(1) This section applies to an association which is a registered political party.

(2) A person does not contravene this Part only by acting in accordance with selection arrangements.

(3) Selection arrangements are arrangements –

    (a) which the party makes for regulating the selection of its candidates in a relevant election,

    (b)   the purpose of which is to reduce inequality in the party's representation in the body concerned, and

    (c)   which, subject to subsection (7), are a proportionate means of achieving that purpose.

(4)   The reference in subsection (3)(b) to inequality in a party's representation in a body is a reference to inequality between—

    (a)   the number of the party's candidates elected to be members of the body who share a protected characteristic, and

    (b)   the number of the party's candidates so elected who do not share that characteristic.

(5)   For the purposes of subsection (4), persons share the protected characteristic of disability if they are disabled persons (and section 6(3)(b) is accordingly to be ignored).

(6)   Selection arrangements do not include short-listing only such persons as have a particular protected characteristic.

(7)   But subsection (6) does not apply to the protected characteristic of sex; and subsection (3)(c) does not apply to short-listing in reliance on this subsection.

(8)   The following elections are relevant elections—

    (a)   Parliamentary Elections;

    (b)   elections to the European Parliament;

    (c)   elections to the Scottish Parliament;

    (d)   elections to the National Assembly for Wales;

    (e)   local government elections within the meaning of section 191, 203 or 204 of the Representation of the People Act 1983 (excluding elections for the Mayor of London).

105   Time-limited provision

(1)   Section 104(7) and the words ", subject to subsection (7)," in section 104(3)(c) are repealed at the end of 2030 unless an order is made under subsection (2).

(2)   At any time before the end of 2030, a Minister of the Crown may by order provide that subsection (1) is to have effect with the substitution of a later time for that for the time being specified there.

(3)   In section 3 of the Sex Discrimination (Election Candidates) Act 2002 (expiry of that Act), in subsection (1) for "2015" substitute "2030".

(4)   The substitution made by subsection (3) does not affect the power to substitute a later time by order under section 3 of that Act.

106   Information about diversity in range of candidates, etc.

(1)   This section applies to an association which is a registered political party.

(2)   If the party had candidates at a relevant election, the party must, in accordance with regulations, publish information relating to protected characteristics of persons who come within a description prescribed in the regulations in accordance with subsection (3).

(3)   One or more of the following descriptions may be prescribed for the purposes of subsection (2)—

    (a)   successful applicants for nomination as a candidate at the relevant election;

    (b)   unsuccessful applicants for nomination as a candidate at that election;

    (c)   candidates elected at that election;

    (d)   candidates who are not elected at that election.

(4)   The duty imposed by subsection (2) applies only in so far as it is possible to publish information in a manner that ensures that no person to whom the information relates can be identified from that information.

(5)   The following elections are relevant elections —

    (a)   Parliamentary Elections;

    (b)   elections to the European Parliament;

    (c)   elections to the Scottish Parliament;

    (d)   elections to the National Assembly for Wales.

(6)   This section does not apply to the following protected characteristics —

    (a)   marriage and civil partnership;

    (b)   pregnancy and maternity.

(7)   The regulations may provide that the information to be published —

    (a)   must (subject to subsection (6)) relate to all protected characteristics or only to such as are prescribed;

    (b)   must include a statement, in respect of each protected characteristic to which the information relates, of the proportion that the number of persons who provided the information to the party bears to the number of persons who were asked to provide it.

(8)   Regulations under this section may prescribe —

    (a)   descriptions of information;

    (b)   descriptions of political party to which the duty is to apply;

    (c)   the time at which information is to be published;

    (d)   the form and manner in which information is to be published;

    (e)   the period for which information is to be published.

(9)   Provision by virtue of subsection (8)(b) may, in particular, provide that the duty imposed by subsection (2) does not apply to a party which had candidates in fewer constituencies in the election concerned than a prescribed number.

(10)   Regulations under this section —

    (a)   may provide that the duty imposed by subsection (2) applies only to such relevant elections as are prescribed;

    (b)   may provide that a by-election or other election to fill a vacancy is not to be treated as a relevant election or is to be so treated only to a prescribed extent;

    (c)   may amend this section so as to provide for the duty imposed by subsection (2) to apply in the case of additional descriptions of election.

(11)   Nothing in this section authorises a political party to require a person to provide information to it.

Supplementary

107   Interpretation and exceptions

(1)   This section applies for the purposes of this Part.

(2)   An "association" is an association of persons —
  - (a)   which has at least 25 members, and
  - (b)   admission to membership of which is regulated by the association's rules and involves a process of selection.

(3)   A Minister of the Crown may by order amend subsection (2)(a) so as to substitute a different number for that for the time being specified there.

(4)   It does not matter —
  - (a)   whether an association is incorporated;
  - (b)   whether its activities are carried on for profit.

(5)   Membership is membership of any description; and a reference to a member is to be construed accordingly.

(6)   A person is an "associate", in relation to an association, if the person —
  - (a)   is not a member of the association, but
  - (b)   in accordance with the association's rules, has some or all of the rights as a member as a result of being a member of another association.

(7)   A reference to a registered political party is a reference to a party registered in the Great Britain register under Part 2 of the Political Parties, Elections and Referendums Act 2000.

(8)   Schedule 15 (reasonable adjustments) has effect.

(9)   Schedule 16 (exceptions) has effect.

PART 8

PROHIBITED CONDUCT: ANCILLARY

108   Relationships that have ended

(1)   A person (A) must not discriminate against another (B) if —
  - (a)   the discrimination arises out of and is closely connected to a relationship which used to exist between them, and
  - (b)   conduct of a description constituting the discrimination would, if it occurred during the relationship, contravene this Act.

(2)   A person (A) must not harass another (B) if —
  - (a)   the harassment arises out of and is closely connected to a relationship which used to exist between them, and
  - (b)   conduct of a description constituting the harassment would, if it occurred during the relationship, contravene this Act.

(3)   It does not matter whether the relationship ends before or after the commencement of this section.

(4)   A duty to make reasonable adjustments applies to A in so far as B continues to be placed at a substantial disadvantage as mentioned in section 20.

(5) For the purposes of subsection (4), sections 20, 21 and 22 and the applicable Schedules are to be construed as if the relationship had not ended.

(6) For the purposes of Part 9 (enforcement), a contravention of this section relates to the Part of this Act that would have been contravened if the relationship had not ended.

(7) But conduct is not a contravention of this section in so far as it also amounts to victimisation of B by A.

109 Liability of employers and principals

(1) Anything done by a person (A) in the course of A's employment must be treated as also done by the employer.

(2) Anything done by an agent for a principal, with the authority of the principal, must be treated as also done by the principal.

(3) It does not matter whether that thing is done with the employer's or principal's knowledge or approval.

(4) In proceedings against A's employer (B) in respect of anything alleged to have been done by A in the course of A's employment it is a defence for B to show that B took all reasonable steps to prevent A —

    (a) from doing that thing, or

    (b) from doing anything of that description.

(5) This section does not apply to offences under this Act (other than offences under Part 12 (disabled persons: transport)).

110 Liability of employees and agents

(1) A person (A) contravenes this section if —

    (a) A is an employee or agent,

    (b) A does something which, by virtue of section 109(1) or (2), is treated as having been done by A's employer or principal (as the case may be), and

    (c) the doing of that thing by A amounts to a contravention of this Act by the employer or principal (as the case may be).

(2) It does not matter whether, in any proceedings, the employer is found not to have contravened this Act by virtue of section 109(4).

(3) A does not contravene this section if —

    (a) A relies on a statement by the employer or principal that doing that thing is not a contravention of this Act, and

    (b) it is reasonable for A to do so.

(4) A person (B) commits an offence if B knowingly or recklessly makes a statement mentioned in subsection (3)(a) which is false or misleading in a material respect.

(5) A person guilty of an offence under subsection (4) is liable on summary conviction to a fine not exceeding level 5 on the standard scale.

(6) Part 9 (enforcement) applies to a contravention of this section by A as if it were the contravention mentioned in subsection (1)(c).

(7) The reference in subsection (1)(c) to a contravention of this Act does not include a reference to disability discrimination in contravention of Chapter 1 of Part 6 (schools).

111 Instructing, causing or inducing contraventions

(1) A person (A) must not instruct another (B) to do in relation to a third person (C) anything which contravenes Part 3, 4, 5, 6 or 7 or section 108(1) or (2) or 112(1) (a basic contravention).

(2) A person (A) must not cause another (B) to do in relation to a third person (C) anything which is a basic contravention.

(3) A person (A) must not induce another (B) to do in relation to a third person (C) anything which is a basic contravention.

(4) For the purposes of subsection (3), inducement may be direct or indirect.

(5) Proceedings for a contravention of this section may be brought —
   (a) by B, if B is subjected to a detriment as a result of A's conduct;
   (b) by C, if C is subjected to a detriment as a result of A's conduct;
   (c) by the Commission.

(6) For the purposes of subsection (5), it does not matter whether —
   (a) the basic contravention occurs;
   (b) any other proceedings are, or may be, brought in relation to A's conduct.

(7) This section does not apply unless the relationship between A and B is such that A is in a position to commit a basic contravention in relation to B.

(8) A reference in this section to causing or inducing a person to do something includes a reference to attempting to cause or induce the person to do it.

(9) For the purposes of Part 9 (enforcement), a contravention of this section is to be treated as relating —
   (a) in a case within subsection (5)(a), to the Part of this Act which, because of the relationship between A and B, A is in a position to contravene in relation to B;
   (b) in a case within subsection (5)(b), to the Part of this Act which, because of the relationship between B and C, B is in a position to contravene in relation to C.

112 Aiding contraventions

(1) A person (A) must not knowingly help another (B) to do anything which contravenes Part 3, 4, 5, 6 or 7 or section 108(1) or (2) or 111 (a basic contravention).

(2) It is not a contravention of subsection (1) if —
   (a) A relies on a statement by B that the act for which the help is given does not contravene this Act, and
   (b) it is reasonable for A to do so.

(3) B commits an offence if B knowingly or recklessly makes a statement mentioned in subsection (2)(a) which is false or misleading in a material respect.

(4)   A person guilty of an offence under subsection (3) is liable on summary conviction to a fine not exceeding level 5 on the standard scale.

(5)   For the purposes of Part 9 (enforcement), a contravention of this section is to be treated as relating to the provision of this Act to which the basic contravention relates.

(6)   The reference in subsection (1) to a basic contravention does not include a reference to disability discrimination in contravention of Chapter 1 of Part 6 (schools).

PART 9

ENFORCEMENT

CHAPTER 1

INTRODUCTORY

113   Proceedings

(1)   Proceedings relating to a contravention of this Act must be brought in accordance with this Part.

(2)   Subsection (1) does not apply to proceedings under Part 1 of the Equality Act 2006.

(3)   Subsection (1) does not prevent —
  (a)   a claim for judicial review;
  (b)   proceedings under the Immigration Acts;
  (c)   proceedings under the Special Immigration Appeals Commission Act 1997;
  (d)   in Scotland, an application to the supervisory jurisdiction of the Court of Session.

(4)   This section is subject to any express provision of this Act conferring jurisdiction on a court or tribunal.

(5)   The reference to a contravention of this Act includes a reference to a breach of an equality clause or rule.

(6)   Chapters 2 and 3 do not apply to proceedings relating to an equality clause or rule except in so far as Chapter 4 provides for that.

(7)   This section does not apply to —
  (a)   proceedings for an offence under this Act;
  (b)   proceedings relating to a penalty under Part 12 (disabled persons: transport).

CHAPTER 2

CIVIL COURTS

114   Jurisdiction

(1)   A county court or, in Scotland, the sheriff has jurisdiction to determine a claim relating to —

    (a)   a contravention of Part 3 (services and public functions);

    (b)   a contravention of Part 4 (premises);

    (c)   a contravention of Part 6 (education);

    (d)   a contravention of Part 7 (associations);

    (e)   a contravention of section 108, 111 or 112 that relates to Part 3, 4, 6 or 7.

(2)   Subsection (1)(a) does not apply to a claim within section 115.

(3)   Subsection (1)(c) does not apply to a claim within section 116.

(4)   Subsection (1)(d) does not apply to a contravention of section 106.

(5)   For the purposes of proceedings on a claim within subsection (1)(a) —

    (a)   a decision in proceedings on a claim mentioned in section 115(1) that an act is a contravention of Part 3 is binding;

    (b)   it does not matter whether the act occurs outside the United Kingdom.

(6)   The county court or sheriff —

    (a)   must not grant an interim injunction or interdict unless satisfied that no criminal matter would be prejudiced by doing so;

    (b)   must grant an application to stay or sist proceedings under subsection (1) on grounds of prejudice to a criminal matter unless satisfied the matter will not be prejudiced.

(7)   In proceedings in England and Wales on a claim within subsection (1), the power under section 63(1) of the County Courts Act 1984 (appointment of assessors) must be exercised unless the judge is satisfied that there are good reasons for not doing so.

(8)   In proceedings in Scotland on a claim within subsection (1), the power under rule 44.3 of Schedule 1 to the Sheriff Court (Scotland) Act 1907 (appointment of assessors) must be exercised unless the sheriff is satisfied that there are good reasons for not doing so.

(9)   The remuneration of an assessor appointed by virtue of subsection (8) is to be at a rate determined by the Lord President of the Court of Session.

115   Immigration cases

(1)   A claim is within this section if it relates to the act of an immigration authority in taking a relevant decision and —

    (a)   the question whether the act is a contravention of Part 3 has been or could be raised on an appeal which is pending, or could be brought, under the immigration provisions, or

    (b)   it has been decided on an appeal under those provisions that the act is not a contravention of Part 3.

(2)   The relevant decision is not —

    (a)   subject to challenge in proceedings on a claim within section 114(1)(a), or

    (b)   affected by the decision of a court in such proceedings.

(3)   For the purposes of subsection (1)(a) a power to grant permission to appeal out of time must be ignored.

(4)   Each of the following is an immigration authority –

    (a)   the Secretary of State;

    (b)   an immigration officer;

    (c)   a person responsible for the grant or refusal of entry clearance (within the meaning of section 33(1) of the Immigration Act 1971).

(5)   The immigration provisions are –

    (a)   the Special Immigration Appeals Commission Act 1997, or

    (b)   Part 5 of the Nationality, Immigration and Asylum Act 2002.

(6)   A relevant decision is –

    (a)   a decision under the Immigration Acts relating to the entitlement of a person to enter or remain in the United Kingdom;

    (b)   a decision on an appeal under the immigration provisions relating to a decision within paragraph (a).

(7)   An appeal is pending if it is pending for the purposes of section 104 of the Nationality, Immigration and Asylum Act 2002 or (as the case may be) for the purposes of that section as it is applied by section 2(2)(j) of the Special Immigration Appeals Commission Act 1997.

116 Education cases

(1)   A claim is within this section if it may be made to –

    (a)   the First-tier Tribunal in accordance with Part 2 of Schedule 17,

    (b)   the Special Educational Needs Tribunal for Wales in accordance with Part 2 of that Schedule, or

    (c)   an Additional Support Needs Tribunal for Scotland in accordance with Part 3 of that Schedule.

(2)   A claim is also within this section if it must be made in accordance with appeal arrangements within the meaning of Part 4 of that Schedule.

(3)   Schedule 17 (disabled pupils: enforcement) has effect.

117 National security

(1)   Rules of court may, in relation to proceedings on a claim within section 114, confer power as mentioned in subsections (2) to (4); but a power so conferred is exercisable only if the court thinks it expedient to do so in the interests of national security.

(2)   The rules may confer power to exclude from all or part of the proceedings –

    (a)   the claimant or pursuer;

    (b)   a representative of the claimant or pursuer;

    (c)   an assessor.

(3) The rules may confer power to permit a claimant, pursuer or representative who has been excluded to make a statement to the court before the commencement of the proceedings, or part of the proceedings, to which the exclusion relates.

(4) The rules may confer power to take steps to keep secret all or part of the reasons for the court's decision.

(5) The Attorney General or, in Scotland, the Advocate General for Scotland may appoint a person to represent the interests of a claimant or pursuer in, or in any part of, proceedings to which an exclusion by virtue of subsection (2)(a) or (b) relates.

(6) A person (P) may be appointed under subsection (5) only if —

    (a) in relation to proceedings in England and Wales, P is a person who, for the purposes of the Legal Services Act 2007, is an authorised person in relation to an activity which constitutes the exercise of a right of audience or the conduct of litigation;

    (b) in relation to proceedings in Scotland, P is an advocate or qualified to practise as a solicitor in Scotland.

(7) P is not responsible to the person whose interests P is appointed to represent.

118 Time limits

(1) Proceedings on a claim within section 114 may not be brought after the end of —

    (a) the period of 6 months starting with the date of the act to which the claim relates, or

    (b) such other period as the county court or sheriff thinks just and equitable.

(2) If subsection (3) or (4) applies, subsection (1)(a) has effect as if for "6 months" there were substituted "9 months".

(3) This subsection applies if —

    (a) the claim relates to the act of a qualifying institution, and

    (b) a complaint relating to the act is referred under the student complaints scheme before the end of the period of 6 months starting with the date of the act.

(4) This subsection applies if —

    (a) the claim relates to a dispute referred for conciliation in pursuance of arrangements under section 27 of the Equality Act 2006, and

    (b) subsection (3) does not apply.

(5) If it has been decided under the immigration provisions that the act of an immigration authority in taking a relevant decision is a contravention of Part 3 (services and public functions), subsection (1) has effect as if for paragraph (a) there were substituted —

    "(a) the period of 6 months starting with the day after the expiry of the period during which, as a result of section 114(2), proceedings could not be brought in reliance on section 114(1)(a);".

(6) For the purposes of this section —

    (a)   conduct extending over a period is to be treated as done at the end of the period;

    (b)   failure to do something is to be treated as occurring when the person in question decided on it.

(7)   In the absence of evidence to the contrary, a person (P) is to be taken to decide on failure to do something —

    (a)   when P does an act inconsistent with doing it, or

    (b)   if P does no inconsistent act, on the expiry of the period in which P might reasonably have been expected to do it.

(8)   In this section —

    "immigration authority", "immigration provisions" and "relevant decision" each have the meaning given in section 115;

    "qualifying institution" has the meaning given in section 11 of the Higher Education Act 2004;

    "the student complaints scheme" means a scheme for the review of qualifying complaints (within the meaning of section 12 of that Act) that is provided by the designated operator (within the meaning of section 13(5)(b) of that Act).

119   Remedies

(1)   This section applies if a county court or the sheriff finds that there has been a contravention of a provision referred to in section 114(1).

(2)   The county court has power to grant any remedy which could be granted by the High Court —

    (a)   in proceedings in tort;

    (b)   on a claim for judicial review.

(3)   The sheriff has power to make any order which could be made by the Court of Session —

    (a)   in proceedings for reparation;

    (b)   on a petition for judicial review.

(4)   An award of damages may include compensation for injured feelings (whether or not it includes compensation on any other basis).

(5)   Subsection (6) applies if the county court or sheriff —

    (a)   finds that a contravention of a provision referred to in section 114(1) is established by virtue of section 19, but

    (b)   is satisfied that the provision, criterion or practice was not applied with the intention of discriminating against the claimant or pursuer.

(6)   The county court or sheriff must not make an award of damages unless it first considers whether to make any other disposal.

(7)   The county court or sheriff must not grant a remedy other than an award of damages or the making of a declaration unless satisfied that no criminal matter would be prejudiced by doing so.

CHAPTER 3

EMPLOYMENT TRIBUNALS

120 Jurisdiction

(1) An employment tribunal has, subject to section 121, jurisdiction to determine a complaint relating to—

    (a) a contravention of Part 5 (work);

    (b) a contravention of section 108, 111 or 112 that relates to Part 5.

(2) An employment tribunal has jurisdiction to determine an application by a responsible person (as defined by section 61) for a declaration as to the rights of that person and a worker in relation to a dispute about the effect of a non-discrimination rule.

(3) An employment tribunal also has jurisdiction to determine an application by the trustees or managers of an occupational pension scheme for a declaration as to their rights and those of a member in relation to a dispute about the effect of a non-discrimination rule.

(4) An employment tribunal also has jurisdiction to determine a question that—

    (a) relates to a non-discrimination rule, and

    (b) is referred to the tribunal by virtue of section 122.

(5) In proceedings before an employment tribunal on a complaint relating to a breach of a non-discrimination rule, the employer—

    (a) is to be treated as a party, and

    (b) is accordingly entitled to appear and be heard.

(6) Nothing in this section affects such jurisdiction as the High Court, a county court, the Court of Session or the sheriff has in relation to a non-discrimination rule.

(7) Subsection (1)(a) does not apply to a contravention of section 53 in so far as the act complained of may, by virtue of an enactment, be subject to an appeal or proceedings in the nature of an appeal.

(8) In subsection (1), the references to Part 5 do not include a reference to section 60(1).

121 Armed forces cases

(1) Section 120(1) does not apply to a complaint relating to an act done when the complainant was serving as a member of the armed forces unless—

    (a) the complainant has made a service complaint about the matter, and

    (b) the complaint has not been withdrawn.

(2) If the complaint is made under the service complaint procedures, it is to be treated for the purposes of subsection (1)(b) as withdrawn if—

    (a) neither the officer to whom it is made nor a superior officer refers it to the Defence Council, and

    (b) the complainant does not apply for it to be referred to the Defence Council.

(3) If the complaint is made under the old service redress procedures, it is to be treated for the purposes of subsection (1)(b) as withdrawn if the complainant does not submit it to the Defence Council under those procedures.

(4) The reference in subsection (3) to the old service redress procedures is a reference to the procedures (other than those relating to the making of a report on a complaint to Her Majesty) referred to in—

   (a) section 180 of the Army Act 1955,

   (b) section 180 of the Air Force Act 1955, or

   (c) section 130 of the Naval Discipline Act 1957.

(5) The making of a complaint to an employment tribunal in reliance on subsection (1) does not affect the continuation of the service complaint procedures or (as the case may be) the old service redress procedures.

122 References by court to tribunal, etc.

(1) If it appears to a court in which proceedings are pending that a claim or counter-claim relating to a non-discrimination rule could more conveniently be determined by an employment tribunal, the court may strike out the claim or counter-claim.

(2) If in proceedings before a court a question arises about a non-discrimination rule, the court may (whether or not on an application by a party to the proceedings)—

   (a) refer the question, or direct that it be referred by a party to the proceedings, to an employment tribunal for determination, and

   (b) stay or sist the proceedings in the meantime.

123 Time limits

(1) Proceedings on a complaint within section 120 may not be brought after the end of—

   (a) the period of 3 months starting with the date of the act to which the complaint relates, or

   (b) such other period as the employment tribunal thinks just and equitable.

(2) Proceedings may not be brought in reliance on section 121(1) after the end of—

   (a) the period of 6 months starting with the date of the act to which the proceedings relate, or

   (b) such other period as the employment tribunal thinks just and equitable.

(3) For the purposes of this section—

   (a) conduct extending over a period is to be treated as done at the end of the period;

   (b) failure to do something is to be treated as occurring when the person in question decided on it.

(4) In the absence of evidence to the contrary, a person (P) is to be taken to decide on failure to do something—

   (a) when P does an act inconsistent with doing it, or

   (b) if P does no inconsistent act, on the expiry of the period in which P might reasonably have been expected to do it.

124   Remedies: general

(1)   This section applies if an employment tribunal finds that there has been a contravention of a provision referred to in section 120(1).

(2)   The tribunal may —
   (a)   make a declaration as to the rights of the complainant and the respondent in relation to the matters to which the proceedings relate;
   (b)   order the respondent to pay compensation to the complainant;
   (c)   make an appropriate recommendation.

(3)   An appropriate recommendation is a recommendation that within a specified period the respondent takes specified steps for the purpose of obviating or reducing the adverse effect of any matter to which the proceedings relate —
   (a)   on the complainant;
   (b)   on any other person.

(4)   Subsection (5) applies if the tribunal —
   (a)   finds that a contravention is established by virtue of section 19, but
   (b)   is satisfied that the provision, criterion or practice was not applied with the intention of discriminating against the complainant.

(5)   It must not make an order under subsection (2)(b) unless it first considers whether to act under subsection (2)(a) or (c).

(6)   The amount of compensation which may be awarded under subsection (2)(b) corresponds to the amount which could be awarded by a county court or the sheriff under section 119.

(7)   If a respondent fails, without reasonable excuse, to comply with an appropriate recommendation in so far as it relates to the complainant, the tribunal may —
   (a)   if an order was made under subsection (2)(b), increase the amount of compensation to be paid;
   (b)   if no such order was made, make one.

125   Remedies: national security

(1)   In national security proceedings, an appropriate recommendation (as defined by section 124) must not be made in relation to a person other than the complainant if the recommendation would affect anything done by —
   (a)   the Security Service,
   (b)   the Secret Intelligence Service,
   (c)   the Government Communications Headquarters, or
   (d)   a part of the armed forces which is, in accordance with a requirement of the Secretary of State, assisting the Government Communications Headquarters.

(2)   National security proceedings are —
   (a)   proceedings to which a direction under section 10(3) of the Employment Tribunals Act 1996 (national security) relates;
   (b)   proceedings to which an order under section 10(4) of that Act relates;
   (c)   proceedings (or the part of proceedings) to which a direction pursuant to regulations made under section 10(5) of that Act relates;

(d) proceedings (or the part of proceedings) in relation to which an employment tribunal acts pursuant to regulations made under section 10(6) of that Act.

126 Remedies: occupational pension schemes

(1) This section applies if an employment tribunal finds that there has been a contravention of a provision referred to in section 120(1) in relation to —

(a) the terms on which persons become members of an occupational pension scheme, or

(b) the terms on which members of an occupational pension scheme are treated.

(2) In addition to anything which may be done by the tribunal under section 124 the tribunal may also by order declare —

(a) if the complaint relates to the terms on which persons become members of a scheme, that the complainant has a right to be admitted to the scheme;

(b) if the complaint relates to the terms on which members of the scheme are treated, that the complainant has a right to membership of the scheme without discrimination.

(3) The tribunal may not make an order under subsection (2)(b) of section 124 unless —

(a) the compensation is for injured feelings, or

(b) the order is made by virtue of subsection (7) of that section.

(4) An order under subsection (2) —

(a) may make provision as to the terms on which or the capacity in which the claimant is to enjoy the admission or membership;

(b) may have effect in relation to a period before the order is made.

CHAPTER 4

EQUALITY OF TERMS

127 Jurisdiction

(1) An employment tribunal has, subject to subsection (6), jurisdiction to determine a complaint relating to a breach of an equality clause or rule.

(2) The jurisdiction conferred by subsection (1) includes jurisdiction to determine a complaint arising out of a breach of an equality clause or rule; and a reference in this Chapter to a complaint relating to such a breach is to be read accordingly.

(3) An employment tribunal also has jurisdiction to determine an application by a responsible person for a declaration as to the rights of that person and a worker in relation to a dispute about the effect of an equality clause or rule.

(4) An employment tribunal also has jurisdiction to determine an application by the trustees or managers of an occupational pension scheme for a declaration as to their rights and those of a member in relation to a dispute about the effect of an equality rule.

(5) An employment tribunal also has jurisdiction to determine a question that—

    (a) relates to an equality clause or rule, and

    (b) is referred to the tribunal by virtue of section 128(2).

(6) This section does not apply to a complaint relating to an act done when the complainant was serving as a member of the armed forces unless—

    (a) the complainant has made a service complaint about the matter, and

    (b) the complaint has not been withdrawn.

(7) Subsections (2) to (5) of section 121 apply for the purposes of subsection (6) of this section as they apply for the purposes of subsection (1) of that section.

(8) In proceedings before an employment tribunal on a complaint relating to a breach of an equality rule, the employer—

    (a) is to be treated as a party, and

    (b) is accordingly entitled to appear and be heard.

(9) Nothing in this section affects such jurisdiction as the High Court, a county court, the Court of Session or the sheriff has in relation to an equality clause or rule.

128 References by court to tribunal, etc.

(1) If it appears to a court in which proceedings are pending that a claim or counter-claim relating to an equality clause or rule could more conveniently be determined by an employment tribunal, the court may strike out the claim or counter-claim.

(2) If in proceedings before a court a question arises about an equality clause or rule, the court may (whether or not on an application by a party to the proceedings)—

    (a) refer the question, or direct that it be referred by a party to the proceedings, to an employment tribunal for determination, and

    (b) stay or sist the proceedings in the meantime.

129 Time limits

(1) This section applies to—

    (a) a complaint relating to a breach of an equality clause or rule;

    (b) an application for a declaration referred to in section 127(3) or (4).

(2) Proceedings on the complaint or application may not be brought in an employment tribunal after the end of the qualifying period.

(3) If the complaint or application relates to terms of work other than terms of service in the armed forces, the qualifying period is, in a case mentioned in the first column of the table, the period mentioned in the second column.

Case	Qualifying period
A standard case	The period of 6 months beginning with the last day of the employment or appointment.

Case	*Qualifying period*
A stable work case (but not if it is also a concealment or incapacity case (or both))	The period of 6 months beginning with the day on which the stable working relationship ended.
A concealment case (but not if it is also an incapacity case)	The period of 6 months beginning with the day on which the worker discovered (or could with reasonable diligence have discovered) the qualifying fact.
An incapacity case (but not if it is also a concealment case)	The period of 6 months beginning with the day on which the worker ceased to have the incapacity.
A case which is a concealment case and an incapacity case.	The period of 6 months beginning with the later of the days on which the period would begin if the case were merely a concealment or incapacity case.

(4) If the complaint or application relates to terms of service in the armed forces, the qualifying period is, in a case mentioned in the first column of the table, the period mentioned in the second column.

Case	*Qualifying period*
A standard case	The period of 9 months beginning with the last day of the period of service during which the complaint arose.
A concealment case (but not if it is also an incapacity case)	The period of 9 months beginning with the day on which the worker discovered (or could with reasonable diligence have discovered) the qualifying fact.
An incapacity case (but not if it is also a concealment case)	The period of 9 months beginning with the day on which the worker ceased to have the incapacity.
A case which is a concealment case and an incapacity case.	The period of 9 months beginning with the later of the days on which the period would begin if the case were merely a concealment or incapacity case.

130 Section 129: supplementary

(1) This section applies for the purposes of section 129.

(2) A standard case is a case which is not —

    (a) a stable work case,

    (b) a concealment case,

    (c) an incapacity case, or

    (d) a concealment case and an incapacity case.

(3)   A stable work case is a case where the proceedings relate to a period during which there was a stable working relationship between the worker and the responsible person (including any time after the terms of work had expired).

(4)   A concealment case in proceedings relating to an equality clause is a case where —

(a)   the responsible person deliberately concealed a qualifying fact from the worker, and

(b)   the worker did not discover (or could not with reasonable diligence have discovered) the qualifying fact until after the relevant day.

(5)   A concealment case in proceedings relating to an equality rule is a case where —

(a)   the employer or the trustees or managers of the occupational pension scheme in question deliberately concealed a qualifying fact from the member, and

(b)   the member did not discover (or could not with reasonable diligence have discovered) the qualifying fact until after the relevant day.

(6)   A qualifying fact for the purposes of subsection (4) or (5) is a fact —

(a)   which is relevant to the complaint, and

(b)   without knowledge of which the worker or member could not reasonably have been expected to bring the proceedings.

(7)   An incapacity case in proceedings relating to an equality clause with respect to terms of work other than terms of service in the armed forces is a case where the worker had an incapacity during the period of 6 months beginning with the later of —

(a)   the relevant day, or

(b)   the day on which the worker discovered (or could with reasonable diligence have discovered) the qualifying fact deliberately concealed from the worker by the responsible person.

(8)   An incapacity case in proceedings relating to an equality clause with respect to terms of service in the armed forces is a case where the worker had an incapacity during the period of 9 months beginning with the later of —

(a)   the last day of the period of service during which the complaint arose, or

(b)   the day on which the worker discovered (or could with reasonable diligence have discovered) the qualifying fact deliberately concealed from the worker by the responsible person.

(9)   An incapacity case in proceedings relating to an equality rule is a case where the member of the occupational pension scheme in question had an incapacity during the period of 6 months beginning with the later of —

(a)   the relevant day, or

(b)   the day on which the member discovered (or could with reasonable diligence have discovered) the qualifying fact deliberately concealed from the member by the employer or the trustees or managers of the scheme.

(10)   The relevant day for the purposes of this section is —

(a)   the last day of the employment or appointment, or

(b)   the day on which the stable working relationship between the worker and the responsible person ended.

131   Assessment of whether work is of equal value

(1)   This section applies to proceedings before an employment tribunal on—

    (a)   a complaint relating to a breach of an equality clause or rule, or

    (b)   a question referred to the tribunal by virtue of section 128(2).

(2)   Where a question arises in the proceedings as to whether one person's work is of equal value to another's, the tribunal may, before determining the question, require a member of the panel of independent experts to prepare a report on the question.

(3)   The tribunal may withdraw a requirement that it makes under subsection (2); and, if it does so, it may—

    (a)   request the panel member to provide it with specified documentation;

    (b)   make such other requests to that member as are connected with the withdrawal of the requirement.

(4)   If the tribunal requires the preparation of a report under subsection (2) (and does not withdraw the requirement), it must not determine the question unless it has received the report.

(5)   Subsection (6) applies where—

    (a)   a question arises in the proceedings as to whether the work of one person (A) is of equal value to the work of another (B), and

    (b)   A's work and B's work have been given different values by a job evaluation study.

(6)   The tribunal must determine that A's work is not of equal value to B's work unless it has reasonable grounds for suspecting that the evaluation contained in the study—

    (a)   was based on a system that discriminates because of sex, or

    (b)   is otherwise unreliable.

(7)   For the purposes of subsection (6)(a), a system discriminates because of sex if a difference (or coincidence) between values that the system sets on different demands is not justifiable regardless of the sex of the person on whom the demands are made.

(8)   A reference to a member of the panel of independent experts is a reference to a person—

    (a)   who is for the time being designated as such by the Advisory, Conciliation and Arbitration Service (ACAS) for the purposes of this section, and

    (b)   who is neither a member of the Council of ACAS nor one of its officers or members of staff.

(9)   "Job evaluation study" has the meaning given in section 80(5).

132   Remedies in non-pensions cases

(1)   This section applies to proceedings before a court or employment tribunal on a complaint relating to a breach of an equality clause, other than a breach with respect to membership of or rights under an occupational pension scheme.

(2)   If the court or tribunal finds that there has been a breach of the equality clause, it may—

      (a)   make a declaration as to the rights of the parties in relation to the matters to which the proceedings relate;

      (b)   order an award by way of arrears of pay or damages in relation to the complainant.

(3)   The court or tribunal may not order a payment under subsection (2)(b) in respect of a time before the arrears day.

(4)   In relation to proceedings in England and Wales, the arrears day is, in a case mentioned in the first column of the table, the day mentioned in the second column.

Case	Arrears day
A standard case	The day falling 6 years before the day on which the proceedings were instituted.
A concealment case or an incapacity case (or a case which is both).	The day on which the breach first occurred.

(5)   In relation to proceedings in Scotland, the arrears day is the first day of –

      (a)   the period of 5 years ending with the day on which the proceedings were commenced, or

      (b)   if the case involves a relevant incapacity, or a relevant fraud or error, the period of 20 years ending with that day.

133   Remedies in pensions cases

(1)   This section applies to proceedings before a court or employment tribunal on a complaint relating to –

      (a)   a breach of an equality rule, or

      (b)   a breach of an equality clause with respect to membership of, or rights under, an occupational pension scheme.

(2)   If the court or tribunal finds that there has been a breach as referred to in subsection (1) –

      (a)   it may make a declaration as to the rights of the parties in relation to the matters to which the proceedings relate;

      (b)   it must not order arrears of benefits or damages or any other amount to be paid to the complainant.

(3)   Subsection (2)(b) does not apply if the proceedings are proceedings to which section 134 applies.

(4)   If the breach relates to a term on which persons become members of the scheme, the court or tribunal may declare that the complainant is entitled to be admitted to the scheme with effect from a specified date.

(5)   A date specified for the purposes of subsection (4) must not be before 8 April 1976.

(6)   If the breach relates to a term on which members of the scheme are treated, the court or tribunal may declare that the complainant is, in respect of a specified

period, entitled to secure the rights that would have accrued if the breach had not occurred.

(7) A period specified for the purposes of subsection (6) must not begin before 17 May 1990.

(8) If the court or tribunal makes a declaration under subsection (6), the employer must provide such resources to the scheme as are necessary to secure for the complainant (without contribution or further contribution by the complainant or other members) the rights referred to in that subsection.

134 Remedies in claims for arrears brought by pensioner members

(1) This section applies to proceedings before a court or employment tribunal on a complaint by a pensioner member of an occupational pension scheme relating to a breach of an equality clause or rule with respect to a term on which the member is treated.

(2) If the court or tribunal finds that there has been a breach referred to in subsection (1), it may —

    (a) make a declaration as to the rights of the complainant and the respondent in relation to the matters to which the proceedings relate;

    (b) order an award by way of arrears of benefits or damages or of any other amount in relation to the complainant.

(3) The court or tribunal must not order an award under subsection (2)(b) in respect of a time before the arrears day.

(4) If the court or tribunal orders an award under subsection (2)(b), the employer must provide such resources to the scheme as are necessary to secure for the complainant (without contribution or further contribution by the complainant or other members) the amount of the award.

(5) In relation to proceedings in England and Wales, the arrears day is, in a case mentioned in the first column of the table, the day mentioned in the second column.

Case	*Arrears day*
A standard case	The day falling 6 years before the day on which the proceedings were commenced.
A concealment case or an incapacity case (or a case which is both).	The day on which the breach first occurred.

(6) In relation to proceedings in Scotland, the arrears day is the first day of —

    (a) the period of 5 years ending with the day on which the proceedings were commenced, or

    (b) if the case involves a relevant incapacity, or a relevant fraud or error, the period of 20 years ending with that day.

135 Supplementary

(1) This section applies for the purposes of sections 132 to 134.

(2)   A standard case is a case which is not—

    (a)   a concealment case,

    (b)   an incapacity case, or

    (c)   a concealment case and an incapacity case.

(3)   A concealment case in relation to an equality clause is a case where—

    (a)   the responsible person deliberately concealed a qualifying fact (as defined by section 130) from the worker, and

    (b)   the worker commenced the proceedings before the end of the period of 6 years beginning with the day on which the worker discovered (or could with reasonable diligence have discovered) the qualifying fact.

(4)   A concealment case in relation to an equality rule is a case where—

    (a)   the employer or the trustees or managers of the occupational pension scheme in question deliberately concealed a qualifying fact (as defined by section 130) from the member, and

    (b)   the member commenced the proceedings before the end of the period of 6 years beginning with the day on which the member discovered (or could with reasonable diligence have discovered) the qualifying fact.

(5)   An incapacity case is a case where the worker or member—

    (a)   had an incapacity when the breach first occurred, and

    (b)   commenced the proceedings before the end of the period of 6 years beginning with the day on which the worker or member ceased to have the incapacity.

(6)   A case involves a relevant incapacity or a relevant fraud or error if the period of 5 years referred to in section 132(5)(a) is, as a result of subsection (7) below, reckoned as a period of more than 20 years.

(7)   For the purposes of the reckoning referred to in subsection (6), no account is to be taken of time when the worker or member—

    (a)   had an incapacity, or

    (b)   was induced by a relevant fraud or error to refrain from commencing proceedings (not being a time after the worker or member could with reasonable diligence have discovered the fraud or error).

(8)   For the purposes of subsection (7)—

    (a)   a fraud is relevant in relation to an equality clause if it is a fraud on the part of the responsible person;

    (b)   an error is relevant in relation to an equality clause if it is induced by the words or conduct of the responsible person;

    (c)   a fraud is relevant in relation to an equality rule if it is a fraud on the part of the employer or the trustees or managers of the scheme;

    (d)   an error is relevant in relation to an equality rule if it is induced by the words or conduct of the employer or the trustees or managers of the scheme.

(9)   A reference in subsection (8) to the responsible person, the employer or the trustees or managers includes a reference to a person acting on behalf of the person or persons concerned.

(10)   In relation to terms of service, a reference in section 132(5) or subsection (3) or (5)(b) of this section to commencing proceedings is to be read as a reference to making a service complaint.

(11) A reference to a pensioner member of a scheme includes a reference to a person who is entitled to the present payment of pension or other benefits derived through a member.

(12) In relation to proceedings before a court—
    (a) a reference to a complaint is to be read as a reference to a claim, and
    (b) a reference to a complainant is to be read as a reference to a claimant.

CHAPTER 5

MISCELLANEOUS

136 Burden of proof

(1) This section applies to any proceedings relating to a contravention of this Act.

(2) If there are facts from which the court could decide, in the absence of any other explanation, that a person (A) contravened the provision concerned, the court must hold that the contravention occurred.

(3) But subsection (2) does not apply if A shows that A did not contravene the provision.

(4) The reference to a contravention of this Act includes a reference to a breach of an equality clause or rule.

(5) This section does not apply to proceedings for an offence under this Act.

(6) A reference to the court includes a reference to—
    (a) an employment tribunal;
    (b) the Asylum and Immigration Tribunal;
    (c) the Special Immigration Appeals Commission;
    (d) the First-tier Tribunal;
    (e) the Special Educational Needs Tribunal for Wales;
    (f) an Additional Support Needs Tribunal for Scotland.

137 Previous findings

(1) A finding in relevant proceedings in respect of an act which has become final is to be treated as conclusive in proceedings under this Act.

(2) Relevant proceedings are proceedings before a court or employment tribunal under any of the following—
    (a) section 19 or 20 of the Race Relations Act 1968;
    (b) the Equal Pay Act 1970;
    (c) the Sex Discrimination Act 1975;
    (d) the Race Relations Act 1976;
    (e) section 6(4A) of the Sex Discrimination Act 1986;
    (f) the Disability Discrimination Act 1995;
    (g) Part 2 of the Equality Act 2006;
    (h) the Employment Equality (Religion and Belief) Regulations 2003 (S.I. 2003/1660);
    (i) the Employment Equality (Sexual Orientation) Regulations 2003 (S.I. 2003/1661);

(j)   the Employment Equality (Age) Regulations 2006 (S.I. 2006/1031);

(k)   the Equality Act (Sexual Orientation) Regulations 2007 (S.I. 2007/1263).

(3)   A finding becomes final—

(a)   when an appeal against the finding is dismissed, withdrawn or abandoned, or

(b)   when the time for appealing expires without an appeal having been brought.

138   Obtaining information, etc.

(1)   In this section—

(a)   P is a person who thinks that a contravention of this Act has occurred in relation to P;

(b)   R is a person who P thinks has contravened this Act.

(2)   A Minister of the Crown must by order prescribe—

(a)   forms by which P may question R on any matter which is or may be relevant;

(b)   forms by which R may answer questions by P.

(3)   A question by P or an answer by R is admissible as evidence in proceedings under this Act (whether or not the question or answer is contained in a prescribed form).

(4)   A court or tribunal may draw an inference from—

(a)   a failure by R to answer a question by P before the end of the period of 8 weeks beginning with the day on which the question is served;

(b)   an evasive or equivocal answer.

(5)   Subsection (4) does not apply if—

(a)   R reasonably asserts that to have answered differently or at all might have prejudiced a criminal matter;

(b)   R reasonably asserts that to have answered differently or at all would have revealed the reason for not commencing or not continuing criminal proceedings;

(c)   R's answer is of a kind specified for the purposes of this paragraph by order of a Minister of the Crown;

(d)   R's answer is given in circumstances specified for the purposes of this paragraph by order of a Minister of the Crown;

(e)   R's failure to answer occurs in circumstances specified for the purposes of this paragraph by order of a Minister of the Crown.

(6)   The reference to a contravention of this Act includes a reference to a breach of an equality clause or rule.

(7)   A Minister of the Crown may by order—

(a)   prescribe the period within which a question must be served to be admissible under subsection (3);

(b)   prescribe the manner in which a question by P, or an answer by R, may be served.

(8)   This section—

    (a)   does not affect any other enactment or rule of law relating to interim or preliminary matters in proceedings before a county court, the sheriff or an employment tribunal, and

    (b)   has effect subject to any enactment or rule of law regulating the admissibility of evidence in such proceedings.

139 Interest

(1)   Regulations may make provision—

    (a)   for enabling an employment tribunal to include interest on an amount awarded by it in proceedings under this Act;

    (b)   specifying the manner in which, and the periods and rate by reference to which, the interest is to be determined.

(2)   Regulations may modify the operation of an order made under section 14 of the Employment Tribunals Act 1996 (power to make provision as to interest on awards) in so far as it relates to an award in proceedings under this Act.

140 Conduct giving rise to separate proceedings

(1)   This section applies in relation to conduct which has given rise to two or more separate proceedings under this Act, with at least one being for a contravention of section 111 (instructing, causing or inducing contraventions).

(2)   A court may transfer proceedings to an employment tribunal.

(3)   An employment tribunal may transfer proceedings to a court.

(4)   A court or employment tribunal is to be taken for the purposes of this Part to have jurisdiction to determine a claim or complaint transferred to it under this section; accordingly—

    (a)   a reference to a claim within section 114(1) includes a reference to a claim transferred to a court under this section, and

    (b)   a reference to a complaint within section 120(1) includes a reference to a complaint transferred to an employment tribunal under this section.

(5)   A court or employment tribunal may not make a decision that is inconsistent with an earlier decision in proceedings arising out of the conduct.

(6)   "Court" means—

    (a)   in relation to proceedings in England and Wales, a county court;

    (b)   in relation to proceedings in Scotland, the sheriff.

141 Interpretation, etc.

(1)   This section applies for the purposes of this Part.

(2)   A reference to the responsible person, in relation to an equality clause or rule, is to be construed in accordance with Chapter 3 of Part 5.

(3)   A reference to a worker is a reference to the person to the terms of whose work the proceedings in question relate; and, for the purposes of proceedings relating to an equality rule or a non-discrimination rule, a reference to a worker includes a reference to a member of the occupational pension scheme in question.

(4)   A reference to the terms of a person's work is to be construed in accordance with Chapter 3 of Part 5.

(5)   A reference to a member of an occupational pension scheme includes a reference to a prospective member.

(6)   In relation to proceedings in England and Wales, a person has an incapacity if the person —

    (a)   has not attained the age of 18, or

    (b)   lacks capacity (within the meaning of the Mental Capacity Act 2005).

(7)   In relation to proceedings in Scotland, a person has an incapacity if the person —

    (a)   has not attained the age of 16, or

    (b)   is incapable (within the meaning of the Adults with Incapacity (Scotland) Act 2000 (asp 4)).

(8)   "Service complaint" means a complaint under section 334 of the Armed Forces Act 2006; and "service complaint procedures" means the procedures prescribed by regulations under that section (except in so far as relating to references under section 337 of that Act).

(9)   "Criminal matter" means —

    (a)   an investigation into the commission of an alleged offence;

    (b)   a decision whether to commence criminal proceedings;

    (c)   criminal proceedings.

PART 10

CONTRACTS, ETC.

Contracts and other agreements

142   Unenforceable terms

(1)   A term of a contract is unenforceable against a person in so far as it constitutes, promotes or provides for treatment of that or another person that is of a description prohibited by this Act.

(2)   A relevant non-contractual term is unenforceable against a person in so far as it constitutes, promotes or provides for treatment of that or another person that is of a description prohibited by this Act, in so far as this Act relates to disability.

(3)   A relevant non-contractual term is a term which —

    (a)   is a term of an agreement that is not a contract, and

    (b)   relates to the provision of an employment service within section 56(2)(a) to (e) or to the provision under a group insurance arrangement of facilities by way of insurance.

(4)   A reference in subsection (1) or (2) to treatment of a description prohibited by this Act does not include —

    (a)   a reference to the inclusion of a term in a contract referred to in section 70(2)(a) or 76(2), or

    (b)   a reference to the failure to include a term in a contract as referred to in section 70(2)(b).

(5)   Subsection (4) does not affect the application of section 148(2) to this section.

143 Removal or modification of unenforceable terms

(1)   A county court or the sheriff may, on an application by a person who has an interest in a contract or other agreement which includes a term that is unenforceable as a result of section 142, make an order for the term to be removed or modified.

(2)   An order under this section must not be made unless every person who would be affected by it—

    (a)   has been given notice of the application (except where notice is dispensed with in accordance with rules of court), and

    (b)   has been afforded an opportunity to make representations to the county court or sheriff.

(3)   An order under this section may include provision in respect of a period before the making of the order.

144 Contracting out

(1)   A term of a contract is unenforceable by a person in whose favour it would operate in so far as it purports to exclude or limit a provision of or made under this Act.

(2)   A relevant non-contractual term (as defined by section 142) is unenforceable by a person in whose favour it would operate in so far as it purports to exclude or limit a provision of or made under this Act, in so far as the provision relates to disability.

(3)   This section does not apply to a contract which settles a claim within section 114.

(4)   This section does not apply to a contract which settles a complaint within section 120 if the contract—

    (a)   is made with the assistance of a conciliation officer, or

    (b)   is a qualifying compromise contract.

(5)   A contract within subsection (4) includes a contract which settles a complaint relating to a breach of an equality clause or rule or of a non-discrimination rule.

(6)   A contract within subsection (4) includes an agreement by the parties to a dispute to submit the dispute to arbitration if—

    (a)   the dispute is covered by a scheme having effect by virtue of an order under section 212A of the Trade Union and Labour Relations (Consolidation) Act 1992, and

    (b)   the agreement is to submit the dispute to arbitration in accordance with the scheme.

Collective agreements and rules of undertakings

145 Void and unenforceable terms

(1) A term of a collective agreement is void in so far as it constitutes, promotes or provides for treatment of a description prohibited by this Act.

(2) A rule of an undertaking is unenforceable against a person in so far as it constitutes, promotes or provides for treatment of the person that is of a description prohibited by this Act.

146 Declaration in respect of void term, etc.

(1) A qualifying person (P) may make a complaint to an employment tribunal that a term is void, or that a rule is unenforceable, as a result of section 145.

(2) But subsection (1) applies only if —

   (a) the term or rule may in the future have effect in relation to P, and

   (b) where the complaint alleges that the term or rule provides for treatment of a description prohibited by this Act, P may in the future be subjected to treatment that would (if P were subjected to it in present circumstances) be of that description.

(3) If the tribunal finds that the complaint is well-founded, it must make an order declaring that the term is void or the rule is unenforceable.

(4) An order under this section may include provision in respect of a period before the making of the order.

(5) In the case of a complaint about a term of a collective agreement, where the term is one made by or on behalf of a person of a description specified in the first column of the table, a qualifying person is a person of a description specified in the second column.

Description of person who made collective agreement	*Qualifying person*
Employer	A person who is, or is seeking to be, an employee of that employer
Organisation of employers	A person who is, or is seeking to be, an employee of an employer who is a member of that organisation
Association of organisations of employers	A person who is, or is seeking to be, an employee of an employer who is a member of an organisation in that association

(6) In the case of a complaint about a rule of an undertaking, where the rule is one made by or on behalf of a person of a description specified in the first column of the table, a qualifying person is a person of a description specified in the second column.

Description of person who made rule of undertaking	Qualifying person
Employer	A person who is, or is seeking to be, an employee of that employer
Trade organisation or qualifications body	A person who is, or is seeking to be, a member of the organisation or body
	A person upon whom the body has conferred a relevant qualification
	A person seeking conferment by the body of a relevant qualification

Supplementary

147   Meaning of "qualifying compromise contract"

(1)   This section applies for the purposes of this Part.

(2)   A qualifying compromise contract is a contract in relation to which each of the conditions in subsection (3) is met.

(3)   Those conditions are that—

    (a)   the contract is in writing,

    (b)   the contract relates to the particular complaint,

    (c)   the complainant has, before entering into the contract, received advice from an independent adviser about its terms and effect (including, in particular, its effect on the complainant's ability to pursue the complaint before an employment tribunal),

    (d)   on the date of the giving of the advice, there is in force a contract of insurance, or an indemnity provided for members of a profession or professional body, covering the risk of a claim by the complainant in respect of loss arising from the advice,

    (e)   the contract identifies the adviser, and

    (f)   the contract states that the conditions in paragraphs (c) and (d) are met.

(4)   Each of the following is an independent adviser—

    (a)   a qualified lawyer;

    (b)   an officer, official, employee or member of an independent trade union certified in writing by the trade union as competent to give advice and as authorised to do so on its behalf;

    (c)   a worker at an advice centre (whether as an employee or a volunteer) certified in writing by the centre as competent to give advice and as authorised to do so on its behalf;

    (d)   a person of such description as may be specified by order.

(5)   Despite subsection (4), none of the following is an independent adviser in relation to a qualifying compromise contract—

    (a)   a person who is a party to the contract or the complaint;

    (b)   a person who is connected to a person within paragraph (a);

(c)   a person who is employed by a person within paragraph (a) or (b);

(d)   a person who is acting for a person within paragraph (a) or (b) in relation to the contract or the complaint;

(e)   a person within subsection (4)(b) or (c), if the trade union or advice centre is a person within paragraph (a) or (b);

(f)   a person within subsection (4)(c) to whom the complainant makes a payment for the advice.

(6)   A "qualified lawyer", for the purposes of subsection (4)(a), is —

    (a)   in relation to England and Wales, a person who, for the purposes of the Legal Services Act 2007, is an authorised person in relation to an activity which constitutes the exercise of a right of audience or the conduct of litigation;

    (b)   in relation to Scotland, an advocate (whether in practice as such or employed to give legal advice) or a solicitor who holds a practising certificate.

(7)   "Independent trade union" has the meaning given in section 5 of the Trade Union and Labour Relations (Consolidation) Act 1992.

(8)   Two persons are connected for the purposes of subsection (5) if —

    (a)   one is a company of which the other (directly or indirectly) has control, or

    (b)   both are companies of which a third person (directly or indirectly) has control.

(9)   Two persons are also connected for the purposes of subsection (5) in so far as a connection between them gives rise to a conflict of interest in relation to the contract or the complaint.

148   Interpretation

(1)   This section applies for the purposes of this Part.

(2)   A reference to treatment of a description prohibited by this Act does not include treatment in so far as it is treatment that would contravene —

    (a)   Part 1 (public sector duty regarding socio-economic inequalities), or

    (b)   Chapter 1 of Part 11 (public sector equality duty).

(3)   "Group insurance arrangement" means an arrangement between an employer and another person for the provision by that other person of facilities by way of insurance to the employer's employees (or a class of those employees).

(4)   "Collective agreement" has the meaning given in section 178 of the Trade Union and Labour Relations (Consolidation) Act 1992.

(5)   A rule of an undertaking is a rule within subsection (6) or (7).

(6)   A rule within this subsection is a rule made by a trade organisation or a qualifications body for application to —

    (a)   its members or prospective members,

    (b)   persons on whom it has conferred a relevant qualification, or

    (c)   persons seeking conferment by it of a relevant qualification.

(7)   A rule within this subsection is a rule made by an employer for application to —

    (a)   employees,

    (b)   persons who apply for employment, or

    (c)   persons the employer considers for employment.

(8)   "Trade organisation", "qualifications body" and "relevant qualification" each have the meaning given in Part 5 (work).

PART 11

ADVANCEMENT OF EQUALITY

CHAPTER 1

PUBLIC SECTOR EQUALITY DUTY

149   Public sector equality duty

(1)   A public authority must, in the exercise of its functions, have due regard to the need to—

    (a)   eliminate discrimination, harassment, victimisation and any other conduct that is prohibited by or under this Act;

    (b)   advance equality of opportunity between persons who share a relevant protected characteristic and persons who do not share it;

    (c)   foster good relations between persons who share a relevant protected characteristic and persons who do not share it.

(2)   A person who is not a public authority but who exercises public functions must, in the exercise of those functions, have due regard to the matters mentioned in subsection (1).

(3)   Having due regard to the need to advance equality of opportunity between persons who share a relevant protected characteristic and persons who do not share it involves having due regard, in particular, to the need to—

    (a)   remove or minimise disadvantages suffered by persons who share a relevant protected characteristic that are connected to that characteristic;

    (b)   take steps to meet the needs of persons who share a relevant protected characteristic that are different from the needs of persons who do not share it;

    (c)   encourage persons who share a relevant protected characteristic to participate in public life or in any other activity in which participation by such persons is disproportionately low.

(4)   The steps involved in meeting the needs of disabled persons that are different from the needs of persons who are not disabled include, in particular, steps to take account of disabled persons' disabilities.

(5)   Having due regard to the need to foster good relations between persons who share a relevant protected characteristic and persons who do not share it involves having due regard, in particular, to the need to—

    (a)   tackle prejudice, and

    (b)   promote understanding.

(6)   Compliance with the duties in this section may involve treating some persons more favourably than others; but that is not to be taken as permitting conduct that would otherwise be prohibited by or under this Act.

Equality Act 2010 (c. 15)
Part 11 – Advancement of equality
Chapter 1 – Public sector equality duty

1727

(7)   The relevant protected characteristics are—

age;

disability;

gender reassignment;

pregnancy and maternity;

race;

religion or belief;

sex;

sexual orientation.

(8)   A reference to conduct that is prohibited by or under this Act includes a reference to—

(a)   a breach of an equality clause or rule;

(b)   a breach of a non-discrimination rule.

(9)   Schedule 18 (exceptions) has effect.

150   Public authorities and public functions

(1)   A public authority is a person who is specified in Schedule 19.

(2)   In that Schedule—

Part 1 specifies public authorities generally;

Part 2 specifies relevant Welsh authorities;

Part 3 specifies relevant Scottish authorities.

(3)   A public authority specified in Schedule 19 is subject to the duty imposed by section 149(1) in relation to the exercise of all of its functions unless subsection (4) applies.

(4)   A public authority specified in that Schedule in respect of certain specified functions is subject to that duty only in respect of the exercise of those functions.

(5)   A public function is a function that is a function of a public nature for the purposes of the Human Rights Act 1998.

151   Power to specify public authorities

(1)   A Minister of the Crown may by order amend Part 1, 2 or 3 of Schedule 19.

(2)   The Welsh Ministers may by order amend Part 2 of Schedule 19.

(3)   The Scottish Ministers may by order amend Part 3 of Schedule 19.

(4)   The power under subsection (1), (2) or (3) may not be exercised so as to—

(a)   add an entry to Part 1 relating to a relevant Welsh or Scottish authority or a cross-border Welsh or Scottish authority;

(b)   add an entry to Part 2 relating to a person who is not a relevant Welsh authority;

(c)   add an entry to Part 3 relating to a person who is not a relevant Scottish authority.

(5)   A Minister of the Crown may by order amend Schedule 19 so as to make provision relating to a cross-border Welsh or Scottish authority.

1728

Equality Act 2010 (c. 15)
Part 11 — Advancement of equality
Chapter 1 — Public sector equality duty

(6) On the first exercise of the power under subsection (5) to add an entry relating to a cross-border Welsh or Scottish authority to Schedule 19, a Minister of the Crown must—

   (a) add a Part 4 to the Schedule for cross-border authorities, and

   (b) add the cross-border Welsh or Scottish authority to that Part.

(7) Any subsequent exercise of the power under subsection (5) to add an entry relating to a cross-border Welsh or Scottish authority to Schedule 19 must add that entry to Part 4 of the Schedule.

(8) An order may not be made under this section so as to extend the application of section 149 unless the person making it considers that the extension relates to a person by whom a public function is exercisable.

(9) An order may not be made under this section so as to extend the application of section 149 to—

   (a) the exercise of a function referred to in paragraph 3 of Schedule 18 (judicial functions, etc);

   (b) a person listed in paragraph 4(2)(a) to (e) of that Schedule (Parliament, devolved legislatures and General Synod);

   (c) the exercise of a function listed in paragraph 4(3) of that Schedule (proceedings in Parliament or devolved legislatures).

152   Power to specify public authorities: consultation and consent

(1) Before making an order under a provision specified in the first column of the Table, a Minister of the Crown must consult the person or persons specified in the second column.

Provision	*Consultees*
Section 151(1)	The Commission
Section 151(1), so far as relating to a relevant Welsh authority	The Welsh Ministers
Section 151(1), so far as relating to a relevant Scottish authority	The Scottish Ministers
Section 151(5)	The Commission
Section 151(5), so far as relating to a cross-border Welsh authority	The Welsh Ministers
Section 151(5), so far as relating to a cross-border Scottish authority	The Scottish Ministers

(2) Before making an order under section 151(2), the Welsh Ministers must—

   (a) obtain the consent of a Minister of the Crown, and

   (b) consult the Commission.

(3) Before making an order under section 151(3), the Scottish Ministers must—

   (a) obtain the consent of a Minister of the Crown, and

   (b) consult the Commission.

Equality Act 2010 (c. 15)
Part 11 — Advancement of equality
Chapter 1 — Public sector equality duty

1729

153 Power to impose specific duties

(1) A Minister of the Crown may by regulations impose duties on a public authority specified in Part 1 of Schedule 19 for the purpose of enabling the better performance by the authority of the duty imposed by section 149(1).

(2) The Welsh Ministers may by regulations impose duties on a public authority specified in Part 2 of Schedule 19 for that purpose.

(3) The Scottish Ministers may by regulations impose duties on a public authority specified in Part 3 of Schedule 19 for that purpose.

(4) Before making regulations under this section, the person making them must consult the Commission.

154 Power to impose specific duties: cross-border authorities

(1) If a Minister of the Crown exercises the power in section 151(5) to add an entry for a public authority to Part 4 of Schedule 19, the Minister must include after the entry a letter specified in the first column of the Table in subsection (3).

(2) Where a letter specified in the first column of the Table in subsection (3) is included after an entry for a public authority in Part 4 of Schedule 19, the person specified in the second column of the Table—

    (a) may by regulations impose duties on the authority for the purpose of enabling the better performance by the authority of the duty imposed by section 149(1), subject to such limitations as are specified in that column;

    (b) must in making the regulations comply with the procedural requirement specified in that column.

(3) This is the Table—

Letter	Person by whom regulations may be made and procedural requirements
A	Regulations may be made by a Minister of the Crown in relation to the authority's functions that are not devolved Welsh functions.
	The Minister of the Crown must consult the Welsh Ministers before making the regulations.
	Regulations may be made by the Welsh Ministers in relation to the authority's devolved Welsh functions.
	The Welsh Ministers must consult a Minister of the Crown before making the regulations.
B	Regulations may be made by a Minister of the Crown in relation to the authority's functions that are not devolved Scottish functions.
	The Minister of the Crown must consult the Scottish Ministers before making the regulations.

1730

Equality Act 2010 (c. 15)
Part 11 — Advancement of equality
Chapter 1 — Public sector equality duty

Letter	Person by whom regulations may be made and procedural requirements
	Regulations may be made by the Scottish Ministers in relation to the authority's devolved Scottish functions.
	The Scottish Ministers must consult a Minister of the Crown before making the regulations.
C	Regulations may be made by a Minister of the Crown in relation to the authority's functions that are neither devolved Welsh functions nor devolved Scottish functions.
	The Minister of the Crown must consult the Welsh Ministers and the Scottish Ministers before making the regulations.
	Regulations may be made by the Welsh Ministers in relation to the authority's devolved Welsh functions.
	The Welsh Ministers must consult a Minister of the Crown before making the regulations.
	Regulations may be made by the Scottish Ministers in relation to the authority's devolved Scottish functions.
	The Scottish Ministers must consult a Minister of the Crown before making the regulations.
D	The regulations may be made by a Minister of the Crown.
	The Minister of the Crown must consult the Welsh Ministers before making the regulations.

(4) Before making regulations under subsection (2), the person making them must consult the Commission.

155 Power to impose specific duties: supplementary

(1) Regulations under section 153 or 154 may require a public authority to consider such matters as may be specified from time to time by —

    (a) a Minister of the Crown, where the regulations are made by a Minister of the Crown;

    (b) the Welsh Ministers, where the regulations are made by the Welsh Ministers;

    (c) the Scottish Ministers, where the regulations are made by the Scottish Ministers.

(2) Regulations under section 153 or 154 may impose duties on a public authority that is a contracting authority within the meaning of the Public Sector Directive in connection with its public procurement functions.

(3) In subsection (2) —

Equality Act 2010 (c. 15)
Part 11 — Advancement of equality
Chapter 1 — Public sector equality duty

1731

"public procurement functions" means functions the exercise of which is regulated by the Public Sector Directive;

"the Public Sector Directive" means Directive 2004/18/EC of the European Parliament and of the Council of 31 March 2004 on the coordination of procedures for the award of public works contracts, public supply contracts and public service contracts, as amended from time to time.

(4) Subsections (1) and (2) do not affect the generality of section 153 or 154(2)(a).

(5) A duty imposed on a public authority under section 153 or 154 may be modified or removed by regulations made by —

    (a) a Minister of the Crown, where the original duty was imposed by regulations made by a Minister of the Crown;

    (b) the Welsh Ministers, where the original duty was imposed by regulations made by the Welsh Ministers;

    (c) the Scottish Ministers, where the original duty was imposed by regulations made by the Scottish Ministers.

156 Enforcement

A failure in respect of a performance of a duty imposed by or under this Chapter does not confer a cause of action at private law.

157 Interpretation

(1) This section applies for the purposes of this Chapter.

(2) A relevant Welsh authority is a person (other than the Assembly Commission) whose functions —

    (a) are exercisable only in or as regards Wales, and

    (b) are wholly or mainly devolved Welsh functions.

(3) A cross-border Welsh authority is a person other than a relevant Welsh authority (or the Assembly Commission) who has any function that —

    (a) is exercisable in or as regards Wales, and

    (b) is a devolved Welsh function.

(4) The Assembly Commission has the same meaning as in the Government of Wales Act 2006.

(5) A function is a devolved Welsh function if it relates to —

    (a) a matter in respect of which functions are exercisable by the Welsh Ministers, the First Minister for Wales or the Counsel General to the Welsh Assembly Government, or

    (b) a matter within the legislative competence of the National Assembly for Wales.

(6) A relevant Scottish authority is a public body, public office or holder of a public office —

    (a) which is not a cross-border Scottish authority or the Scottish Parliamentary Corporate Body,

    (b) whose functions are exercisable only in or as regards Scotland, and

    (c) at least some of whose functions do not relate to reserved matters.

1732

Equality Act 2010 (c. 15)
Part 11 — Advancement of equality
Chapter 1 — Public sector equality duty

   (7)   A cross-border Scottish authority is a cross-border public authority within the meaning given by section 88(5) of the Scotland Act 1998.

   (8)   A function is a devolved Scottish function if it —

       (a)   is exercisable in or as regards Scotland, and

       (b)   does not relate to reserved matters.

   (9)   Reserved matters has the same meaning as in the Scotland Act 1998.

CHAPTER 2

POSITIVE ACTION

158 Positive action: general

   (1)   This section applies if a person (P) reasonably thinks that —

       (a)   persons who share a protected characteristic suffer a disadvantage connected to the characteristic,

       (b)   persons who share a protected characteristic have needs that are different from the needs of persons who do not share it, or

       (c)   participation in an activity by persons who share a protected characteristic is disproportionately low.

   (2)   This Act does not prohibit P from taking any action which is a proportionate means of achieving the aim of —

       (a)   enabling or encouraging persons who share the protected characteristic to overcome or minimise that disadvantage,

       (b)   meeting those needs, or

       (c)   enabling or encouraging persons who share the protected characteristic to participate in that activity.

   (3)   Regulations may specify action, or descriptions of action, to which subsection (2) does not apply.

   (4)   This section does not apply to —

       (a)   action within section 159(3), or

       (b)   anything that is permitted by virtue of section 104.

   (5)   If section 104(7) is repealed by virtue of section 105, this section will not apply to anything that would have been so permitted but for the repeal.

   (6)   This section does not enable P to do anything that is prohibited by or under an enactment other than this Act.

159 Positive action: recruitment and promotion

   (1)   This section applies if a person (P) reasonably thinks that —

       (a)   persons who share a protected characteristic suffer a disadvantage connected to the characteristic, or

       (b)   participation in an activity by persons who share a protected characteristic is disproportionately low.

   (2)   Part 5 (work) does not prohibit P from taking action within subsection (3) with the aim of enabling or encouraging persons who share the protected characteristic to —

    (a)   overcome or minimise that disadvantage, or

    (b)   participate in that activity.

(3)   That action is treating a person (A) more favourably in connection with recruitment or promotion than another person (B) because A has the protected characteristic but B does not.

(4)   But subsection (2) applies only if—

    (a)   A is as qualified as B to be recruited or promoted,

    (b)   P does not have a policy of treating persons who share the protected characteristic more favourably in connection with recruitment or promotion than persons who do not share it, and

    (c)   taking the action in question is a proportionate means of achieving the aim referred to in subsection (2).

(5)   "Recruitment" means a process for deciding whether to—

    (a)   offer employment to a person,

    (b)   make contract work available to a contract worker,

    (c)   offer a person a position as a partner in a firm or proposed firm,

    (d)   offer a person a position as a member of an LLP or proposed LLP,

    (e)   offer a person a pupillage or tenancy in barristers' chambers,

    (f)   take a person as an advocate's devil or offer a person membership of an advocate's stable,

    (g)   offer a person an appointment to a personal office,

    (h)   offer a person an appointment to a public office, recommend a person for such an appointment or approve a person's appointment to a public office, or

    (i)   offer a person a service for finding employment.

(6)   This section does not enable P to do anything that is prohibited by or under an enactment other than this Act.

PART 12

DISABLED PERSONS: TRANSPORT

CHAPTER 1

TAXIS, ETC.

160   Taxi accessibility regulations

(1)   The Secretary of State may make regulations (in this Chapter referred to as "taxi accessibility regulations") for securing that it is possible for disabled persons—

    (a)   to get into and out of taxis in safety;

    (b)   to do so while in wheelchairs;

    (c)   to travel in taxis in safety and reasonable comfort;

    (d)   to do so while in wheelchairs.

(2)   The regulations may, in particular, require a regulated taxi to conform with provision as to—

    (a)   the size of a door opening for the use of passengers;

    (b)   the floor area of the passenger compartment;

    (c)   the amount of headroom in the passenger compartment;

    (d)   the fitting of restraining devices designed to ensure the stability of a wheelchair while the taxi is moving.

(3)   The regulations may also —

    (a)   require the driver of a regulated taxi which is plying for hire, or which has been hired, to comply with provisions as to the carrying of ramps or other devices designed to facilitate the loading and unloading of wheelchairs;

    (b)   require the driver of a regulated taxi in which a disabled person is being carried while in a wheelchair to comply with provisions as to the position in which the wheelchair is to be secured.

(4)   The driver of a regulated taxi which is plying for hire or has been hired commits an offence —

    (a)   by failing to comply with a requirement of the regulations, or

    (b)   if the taxi fails to conform with any provision of the regulations with which it is required to conform.

(5)   A person guilty of an offence under subsection (4) is liable on summary conviction to a fine not exceeding level 3 on the standard scale.

(6)   In this section —

        "passenger compartment" has such meaning as is specified in taxi accessibility regulations;

        "regulated taxi" means a taxi to which taxi accessibility regulations are expressed to apply.

161 Control of numbers of licensed taxis: exception

(1)   This section applies if —

    (a)   an application for a licence in respect of a vehicle is made under section 37 of the Town Police Clauses Act 1847,

    (b)   it is possible for a disabled person —

        (i)   to get into and out of the vehicle in safety,

        (ii)   to travel in the vehicle in safety and reasonable comfort, and

        (iii)   to do the things mentioned in sub-paragraphs (i) and (ii) while in a wheelchair of a size prescribed by the Secretary of State, and

    (c)   the proportion of taxis licensed in respect of the area to which the licence would (if granted) apply that conform to the requirement in paragraph (b) is less than the proportion that is prescribed by the Secretary of State.

(2)   Section 16 of the Transport Act 1985 (which modifies the provisions of the Town Police Clauses Act 1847 about hackney carriages to allow a licence to ply for hire to be refused in order to limit the number of licensed carriages) does not apply in relation to the vehicle; and those provisions of the Town Police Clauses Act 1847 are to have effect subject to this section.

(3)   In section 16 of the Transport Act 1985, after "shall" insert "(subject to section 161 of the Equality Act 2010)".

Equality Act 2010 (c. 15)
Part 12 — Disabled persons: transport
Chapter 1 — Taxis, etc.

1735

162 Designated transport facilities

(1) The appropriate authority may by regulations provide for the application of any taxi provision (with or without modification) to—

    (a) vehicles used for the provision of services under a franchise agreement, or

    (b) drivers of such vehicles.

(2) A franchise agreement is a contract entered into by the operator of a designated transport facility for the provision, by the other party to the contract, of hire car services—

    (a) for members of the public using any part of the facility, and

    (b) which involve vehicles entering any part of the facility.

(3) In this section—

    "appropriate authority" means—

        (a) in relation to transport facilities in England and Wales, the Secretary of State;

        (b) in relation to transport facilities in Scotland, the Scottish Ministers;

    "designated" means designated by order made by the appropriate authority;

    "hire car" has such meaning as is prescribed by the appropriate authority;

    "operator", in relation to a transport facility, means a person who is concerned with the management or operation of the facility;

    "taxi provision" means a provision of—

        (a) this Chapter, or

        (b) regulations made in pursuance of section 20(2A) of the Civic Government (Scotland) Act 1982,

    which applies in relation to taxis or drivers of taxis;

    "transport facility" means premises which form part of a port, airport, railway station or bus station.

(4) For the purposes of section 2(2) of the European Communities Act 1972 (implementation of EU obligations), the Secretary of State may exercise a power conferred by this section on the Scottish Ministers.

163 Taxi licence conditional on compliance with taxi accessibility regulations

(1) A licence for a taxi to ply for hire must not be granted unless the vehicle conforms with the provisions of taxi accessibility regulations with which a vehicle is required to conform if it is licensed.

(2) Subsection (1) does not apply if a licence is in force in relation to the vehicle at any time during the period of 28 days immediately before the day on which the licence is granted.

(3) The Secretary of State may by order provide for subsection (2) to cease to have effect on a specified date.

(4) The power under subsection (3) may be exercised differently for different areas or localities.

164 Exemption from taxi accessibility regulations

(1) The Secretary of State may by regulations provide for a relevant licensing authority to apply for an order (an "exemption order") exempting the authority from the requirements of section 163.

(2) Regulations under subsection (1) may, in particular, make provision requiring an authority proposing to apply for an exemption order—

    (a) to carry out such consultation as is specified;

    (b) to publish its proposals in the specified manner;

    (c) before applying for the order, to consider representations made about the proposal;

    (d) to make the application in the specified form.

In this subsection "specified" means specified in the regulations.

(3) An authority may apply for an exemption order only if it is satisfied—

    (a) that, having regard to the circumstances in its area, it is inappropriate for section 163 to apply, and

    (b) that the application of that section would result in an unacceptable reduction in the number of taxis in its area.

(4) After consulting the Disabled Persons Transport Advisory Committee and such other persons as the Secretary of State thinks appropriate, the Secretary of State may—

    (a) make an exemption order in the terms of the application for the order;

    (b) make an exemption order in such other terms as the Secretary of State thinks appropriate;

    (c) refuse to make an exemption order.

(5) The Secretary of State may by regulations make provision requiring a taxi plying for hire in an area in respect of which an exemption order is in force to conform with provisions of the regulations as to the fitting and use of swivel seats.

(6) Regulations under subsection (5) may make provision corresponding to section 163.

(7) In this section—

    "relevant licensing authority" means an authority responsible for licensing taxis in any area of England and Wales other than the area to which the Metropolitan Public Carriage Act 1869 applies;

    "swivel seats" has such meaning as is specified in regulations under subsection (5).

165 Passengers in wheelchairs

(1) This section imposes duties on the driver of a designated taxi which has been hired—

    (a) by or for a disabled person who is in a wheelchair, or

    (b) by another person who wishes to be accompanied by a disabled person who is in a wheelchair.

(2) This section also imposes duties on the driver of a designated private hire vehicle, if a person within paragraph (a) or (b) of subsection (1) has indicated to the driver that the person wishes to travel in the vehicle.

(3) For the purposes of this section —

    (a) a taxi or private hire vehicle is "designated" if it appears on a list maintained under section 167;

    (b) "the passenger" means the disabled person concerned.

(4) The duties are —

    (a) to carry the passenger while in the wheelchair;

    (b) not to make any additional charge for doing so;

    (c) if the passenger chooses to sit in a passenger seat, to carry the wheelchair;

    (d) to take such steps as are necessary to ensure that the passenger is carried in safety and reasonable comfort;

    (e) to give the passenger such mobility assistance as is reasonably required.

(5) Mobility assistance is assistance —

    (a) to enable the passenger to get into or out of the vehicle;

    (b) if the passenger wishes to remain in the wheelchair, to enable the passenger to get into and out of the vehicle while in the wheelchair;

    (c) to load the passenger's luggage into or out of the vehicle;

    (d) if the passenger does not wish to remain in the wheelchair, to load the wheelchair into or out of the vehicle.

(6) This section does not require the driver —

    (a) unless the vehicle is of a description prescribed by the Secretary of State, to carry more than one person in a wheelchair, or more than one wheelchair, on any one journey;

    (b) to carry a person in circumstances in which it would otherwise be lawful for the driver to refuse to carry the person.

(7) A driver of a designated taxi or designated private hire vehicle commits an offence by failing to comply with a duty imposed on the driver by this section.

(8) A person guilty of an offence under subsection (7) is liable on summary conviction to a fine not exceeding level 3 on the standard scale.

(9) It is a defence for a person charged with the offence to show that at the time of the alleged offence —

    (a) the vehicle conformed to the accessibility requirements which applied to it, but

    (b) it would not have been possible for the wheelchair to be carried safely in the vehicle.

(10) In this section and sections 166 and 167 "private hire vehicle" means —

    (a) a vehicle licensed under section 48 of the Local Government (Miscellaneous Provisions) Act 1976;

    (b) a vehicle licensed under section 7 of the Private Hire Vehicles (London) Act 1998;

    (c) a vehicle licensed under an equivalent provision of a local enactment;

    (d) a private hire car licensed under section 10 of the Civic Government (Scotland) Act 1982.

166   Passengers in wheelchairs: exemption certificates

(1)   A licensing authority must issue a person with a certificate exempting the person from the duties imposed by section 165 (an "exemption certificate") if satisfied that it is appropriate to do so —

    (a)   on medical grounds, or

    (b)   on the ground that the person's physical condition makes it impossible or unreasonably difficult for the person to comply with those duties.

(2)   An exemption certificate is valid for such period as is specified in the certificate.

(3)   The driver of a designated taxi is exempt from the duties imposed by section 165 if —

    (a)   an exemption certificate issued to the driver is in force, and

    (b)   the prescribed notice of the exemption is exhibited on the taxi in the prescribed manner.

(4)   The driver of a designated private hire vehicle is exempt from the duties imposed by section 165 if —

    (a)   an exemption certificate issued to the driver is in force, and

    (b)   the prescribed notice of the exemption is exhibited on the vehicle in the prescribed manner.

(5)   For the purposes of this section, a taxi or private hire vehicle is "designated" if it appears on a list maintained under section 167.

(6)   In this section and section 167 "licensing authority", in relation to any area, means the authority responsible for licensing taxis or, as the case may be, private hire vehicles in that area.

167   Lists of wheelchair-accessible vehicles

(1)   For the purposes of section 165, a licensing authority may maintain a list of vehicles falling within subsection (2).

(2)   A vehicle falls within this subsection if —

    (a)   it is either a taxi or a private hire vehicle, and

    (b)   it conforms to such accessibility requirements as the licensing authority thinks fit.

(3)   A licensing authority may, if it thinks fit, decide that a vehicle may be included on a list maintained under this section only if it is being used, or is to be used, by the holder of a special licence under that licence.

(4)   In subsection (3) "special licence" has the meaning given by section 12 of the Transport Act 1985 (use of taxis or hire cars in providing local services).

(5)   "Accessibility requirements" are requirements for securing that it is possible for disabled persons in wheelchairs —

    (a)   to get into and out of vehicles in safety, and

    (b)   to travel in vehicles in safety and reasonable comfort,

either staying in their wheelchairs or not (depending on which they prefer).

(6)   The Secretary of State may issue guidance to licensing authorities as to —

    (a)   the accessibility requirements which they should apply for the purposes of this section;

Equality Act 2010 (c. 15)
Part 12 — Disabled persons: transport
Chapter 1 — Taxis, etc.

1739

    (b)   any other aspect of their functions under or by virtue of this section.

(7)   A licensing authority which maintains a list under subsection (1) must have regard to any guidance issued under subsection (6).

168   Assistance dogs in taxis

(1)   This section imposes duties on the driver of a taxi which has been hired —
    (a)   by or for a disabled person who is accompanied by an assistance dog, or
    (b)   by another person who wishes to be accompanied by a disabled person with an assistance dog.

(2)   The driver must —
    (a)   carry the disabled person's dog and allow it to remain with that person;
    (b)   not make any additional charge for doing so.

(3)   The driver of a taxi commits an offence by failing to comply with a duty imposed by this section.

(4)   A person guilty of an offence under this section is liable on summary conviction to a fine not exceeding level 3 on the standard scale.

169   Assistance dogs in taxis: exemption certificates

(1)   A licensing authority must issue a person with a certificate exempting the person from the duties imposed by section 168 (an "exemption certificate") if satisfied that it is appropriate to do so on medical grounds.

(2)   In deciding whether to issue an exemption certificate the authority must have regard, in particular, to the physical characteristics of the taxi which the person drives or those of any kind of taxi in relation to which the person requires the certificate.

(3)   An exemption certificate is valid —
    (a)   in respect of a specified taxi or a specified kind of taxi;
    (b)   for such period as is specified in the certificate.

(4)   The driver of a taxi is exempt from the duties imposed by section 168 if —
    (a)   an exemption certificate issued to the driver is in force with respect to the taxi, and
    (b)   the prescribed notice of the exemption is exhibited on the taxi in the prescribed manner.
    The power to make regulations under paragraph (b) is exercisable by the Secretary of State.

(5)   In this section "licensing authority" means —
    (a)   in relation to the area to which the Metropolitan Public Carriage Act 1869 applies, Transport for London;
    (b)   in relation to any other area in England and Wales, the authority responsible for licensing taxis in that area.

170   Assistance dogs in private hire vehicles

(1)   The operator of a private hire vehicle commits an offence by failing or refusing to accept a booking for the vehicle —

    (a)   if the booking is requested by or on behalf of a disabled person or a person who wishes to be accompanied by a disabled person, and

    (b)   the reason for the failure or refusal is that the disabled person will be accompanied by an assistance dog.

(2)   The operator commits an offence by making an additional charge for carrying an assistance dog which is accompanying a disabled person.

(3)   The driver of a private hire vehicle commits an offence by failing or refusing to carry out a booking accepted by the operator –

    (a)   if the booking is made by or on behalf of a disabled person or a person who wishes to be accompanied by a disabled person, and

    (b)   the reason for the failure or refusal is that the disabled person is accompanied by an assistance dog.

(4)   A person guilty of an offence under this section is liable on summary conviction to a fine not exceeding level 3 on the standard scale.

(5)   In this section –

    "driver" means a person who holds a licence under –

        (a)   section 13 of the Private Hire Vehicles (London) Act 1998 ("the 1998 Act"),

        (b)   section 51 of the Local Government (Miscellaneous Provisions) Act 1976 ("the 1976 Act"), or

        (c)   an equivalent provision of a local enactment;

    "licensing authority", in relation to any area in England and Wales, means the authority responsible for licensing private hire vehicles in that area;

    "operator" means a person who holds a licence under –

        (a)   section 3 of the 1998 Act,

        (b)   section 55 of the 1976 Act, or

        (c)   an equivalent provision of a local enactment;

    "private hire vehicle" means a vehicle licensed under –

        (a)   section 6 of the 1998 Act,

        (b)   section 48 of the 1976 Act, or

        (c)   an equivalent provision of a local enactment.

171   Assistance dogs in private hire vehicles: exemption certificates

(1)   A licensing authority must issue a driver with a certificate exempting the driver from the offence under section 170(3) (an "exemption certificate") if satisfied that it is appropriate to do so on medical grounds.

(2)   In deciding whether to issue an exemption certificate the authority must have regard, in particular, to the physical characteristics of the private hire vehicle which the person drives or those of any kind of private hire vehicle in relation to which the person requires the certificate.

(3)   An exemption certificate is valid –

    (a)   in respect of a specified private hire vehicle or a specified kind of private hire vehicle;

    (b)   for such period as is specified in the certificate.

(4)   A driver does not commit an offence under section 170(3) if –

(a) an exemption certificate issued to the driver is in force with respect to the private hire vehicle, and

(b) the prescribed notice of the exemption is exhibited on the vehicle in the prescribed manner.

The power to make regulations under paragraph (b) is exercisable by the Secretary of State.

(5) In this section "driver", "licensing authority" and "private hire vehicle" have the same meaning as in section 170.

172 Appeals

(1) A person who is aggrieved by the refusal of a licensing authority in England and Wales to issue an exemption certificate under section 166, 169 or 171 may appeal to a magistrates' court before the end of the period of 28 days beginning with the date of the refusal.

(2) A person who is aggrieved by the refusal of a licensing authority in Scotland to issue an exemption certificate under section 166 may appeal to the sheriff before the end of the period of 28 days beginning with the date of the refusal.

(3) On an appeal under subsection (1) or (2), the magistrates' court or sheriff may direct the licensing authority to issue the exemption certificate to have effect for such period as is specified in the direction.

(4) A person who is aggrieved by the decision of a licensing authority to include a vehicle on a list maintained under section 167 may appeal to a magistrates' court or, in Scotland, the sheriff before the end of the period of 28 days beginning with the date of the inclusion.

173 Interpretation

(1) In this Chapter—

"accessibility requirements" has the meaning given in section 167(5);

"assistance dog" means—

(a) a dog which has been trained to guide a blind person;

(b) a dog which has been trained to assist a deaf person;

(c) a dog which has been trained by a prescribed charity to assist a disabled person who has a disability that consists of epilepsy or otherwise affects the person's mobility, manual dexterity, physical co-ordination or ability to lift, carry or otherwise move everyday objects;

(d) a dog of a prescribed category which has been trained to assist a disabled person who has a disability (other than one falling within paragraph (c)) of a prescribed kind;

"taxi"—

(a) means a vehicle which is licensed under section 37 of the Town Police Clauses Act 1847 or section 6 of the Metropolitan Public Carriage Act 1869, and

(b) in sections 162 and 165 to 167, also includes a taxi licensed under section 10 of the Civic Government (Scotland) Act 1982,

but does not include a vehicle drawn by a horse or other animal;

"taxi accessibility regulations" has the meaning given by section 160(1).

(2)   A power to make regulations under paragraph (c) or (d) of the definition of "assistance dog" in subsection (1) is exercisable by the Secretary of State.

CHAPTER 2

PUBLIC SERVICE VEHICLES

174   PSV accessibility regulations

(1)   The Secretary of State may make regulations (in this Chapter referred to as "PSV accessibility regulations") for securing that it is possible for disabled persons —

    (a)   to get on to and off regulated public service vehicles in safety and without unreasonable difficulty (and, in the case of disabled persons in wheelchairs, to do so while remaining in their wheelchairs), and

    (b)   to travel in such vehicles in safety and reasonable comfort.

(2)   The regulations may, in particular, make provision as to the construction, use and maintenance of regulated public service vehicles, including provision as to —

    (a)   the fitting of equipment to vehicles;

    (b)   equipment to be carried by vehicles;

    (c)   the design of equipment to be fitted to, or carried by, vehicles;

    (d)   the fitting and use of restraining devices designed to ensure the stability of wheelchairs while vehicles are moving;

    (e)   the position in which wheelchairs are to be secured while vehicles are moving.

(3)   In this section "public service vehicle" means a vehicle which is —

    (a)   adapted to carry more than 8 passengers, and

    (b)   a public service vehicle for the purposes of the Public Passenger Vehicles Act 1981;

and in this Chapter "regulated public service vehicle" means a public service vehicle to which PSV accessibility regulations are expressed to apply.

(4)   The regulations may make different provision —

    (a)   as respects different classes or descriptions of vehicle;

    (b)   as respects the same class or description of vehicle in different circumstances.

(5)   The Secretary of State must not make regulations under this section or section 176 or 177 without consulting —

    (a)   the Disabled Persons Transport Advisory Committee, and

    (b)   such other representative organisations as the Secretary of State thinks fit.

175   Offence of contravening PSV accessibility regulations

(1)   A person commits an offence by —

    (a)   contravening a provision of PSV accessibility regulations;

    (b)   using on a road a regulated public service vehicle which does not conform with a provision of the regulations with which it is required to conform;

Equality Act 2010 (c. 15)
Part 12 — Disabled persons: transport
Chapter 2 — Public service vehicles

1743

    (c)   causing or permitting such a regulated public service vehicle to be used on a road.

(2)   A person guilty of an offence under this section is liable on summary conviction to a fine not exceeding level 4 on the standard scale.

(3)   If an offence under this section committed by a body corporate is committed with the consent or connivance of, or is attributable to neglect on the part of, a responsible person, the responsible person as well as the body corporate is guilty of the offence.

(4)   In subsection (3) a responsible person, in relation to a body corporate, is —
    (a)   a director, manager, secretary or similar officer;
    (b)   a person purporting to act in the capacity of a person mentioned in paragraph (a);
    (c)   in the case of a body corporate whose affairs are managed by its members, a member.

(5)   If, in Scotland, an offence committed by a partnership or an unincorporated association is committed with the consent or connivance of, or is attributable to neglect on the part of, a partner or person concerned in the management of the association, the partner or person as well as the partnership or association is guilty of the offence.

176   Accessibility certificates

(1)   A regulated public service vehicle must not be used on a road unless —
    (a)   a vehicle examiner has issued a certificate (an "accessibility certificate") that such provisions of PSV accessibility regulations as are prescribed are satisfied in respect of the vehicle, or
    (b)   an approval certificate has been issued under section 177 in respect of the vehicle.

(2)   Regulations may make provision —
    (a)   with respect to applications for, and the issue of, accessibility certificates;
    (b)   providing for the examination of vehicles in respect of which applications have been made;
    (c)   with respect to the issue of copies of accessibility certificates which have been lost or destroyed.

(3)   The operator of a regulated public service vehicle commits an offence if the vehicle is used in contravention of this section.

(4)   A person guilty of an offence under this section is liable on summary conviction to a fine not exceeding level 4 on the standard scale.

(5)   A power to make regulations under this section is exercisable by the Secretary of State.

(6)   In this section "operator" has the same meaning as in the Public Passenger Vehicles Act 1981.

1744

Equality Act 2010 (c. 15)
Part 12 — Disabled persons: transport
Chapter 2 — Public service vehicles

177 Approval certificates

(1) The Secretary of State may approve a vehicle for the purposes of this section if satisfied that such provisions of PSV accessibility regulations as are prescribed for the purposes of section 176 are satisfied in respect of the vehicle.

(2) A vehicle which is so approved is referred to in this section as a "type vehicle".

(3) Subsection (4) applies if a declaration in the prescribed form is made by an authorised person that a particular vehicle conforms in design, construction and equipment with a type vehicle.

(4) A vehicle examiner may issue a certificate in the prescribed form (an "approval certificate") that it conforms to the type vehicle.

(5) Regulations may make provision—
   (a) with respect to applications for, and grants of, approval under subsection (1);
   (b) with respect to applications for, and the issue of, approval certificates;
   (c) providing for the examination of vehicles in respect of which applications have been made;
   (d) with respect to the issue of copies of approval certificates in place of certificates which have been lost or destroyed.

(6) The Secretary of State may at any time withdraw approval of a type vehicle.

(7) If an approval is withdrawn—
   (a) no further approval certificates are to be issued by reference to the type vehicle; but
   (b) an approval certificate issued by reference to the type vehicle before the withdrawal continues to have effect for the purposes of section 176.

(8) A power to make regulations under this section is exercisable by the Secretary of State.

(9) In subsection (3) "authorised person" means a person authorised by the Secretary of State for the purposes of that subsection.

178 Special authorisations

(1) The Secretary of State may by order authorise the use on roads of—
   (a) a regulated public service vehicle of a class or description specified by the order, or
   (b) a regulated public service vehicle which is so specified.

(2) Nothing in sections 174 to 177 prevents the use of a vehicle in accordance with the order.

(3) The Secretary of State may by order make provision for securing that provisions of PSV accessibility regulations apply to regulated public service vehicles of a description specified by the order, subject to any modifications or exceptions specified by the order.

(4) An order under subsection (1) or (3) may make the authorisation or provision (as the case may be) subject to such restrictions and conditions as are specified by or under the order.

Equality Act 2010 (c. 15)
Part 12 — Disabled persons: transport
Chapter 2 — Public service vehicles

1745

(5) Section 207(2) does not require an order under this section that applies only to a specified vehicle, or to vehicles of a specified person, to be made by statutory instrument; but such an order is as capable of being amended or revoked as an order made by statutory instrument.

179 Reviews and appeals

(1) Subsection (2) applies if the Secretary of State refuses an application for the approval of a vehicle under section 177(1) and, before the end of the prescribed period, the applicant—

    (a) asks the Secretary of State to review the decision, and

    (b) pays any fee fixed under section 180.

(2) The Secretary of State must—

    (a) review the decision, and

    (b) in doing so, consider any representations made in writing by the applicant before the end of the prescribed period.

(3) A person applying for an accessibility certificate or an approval certificate may appeal to the Secretary of State against the refusal of a vehicle examiner to issue the certificate.

(4) An appeal must be made within the prescribed time and in the prescribed manner.

(5) Regulations may make provision as to the procedure to be followed in connection with appeals.

(6) On the determination of an appeal, the Secretary of State may—

    (a) confirm, vary or reverse the decision appealed against;

    (b) give directions to the vehicle examiner for giving effect to the Secretary of State's decision.

(7) A power to make regulations under this section is exercisable by the Secretary of State.

180 Fees

(1) The Secretary of State may charge such fees, payable at such times, as are prescribed in respect of—

    (a) applications for, and grants of, approval under section 177(1);

    (b) applications for, and the issue of, accessibility certificates and approval certificates;

    (c) copies of such certificates;

    (d) reviews and appeals under section 179.

(2) Fees received by the Secretary of State must be paid into the Consolidated Fund.

(3) The power to make regulations under subsection (1) is exercisable by the Secretary of State.

(4) The regulations may make provision for the repayment of fees, in whole or in part, in such circumstances as are prescribed.

1746

Equality Act 2010 (c. 15)
Part 12 – Disabled persons: transport
Chapter 2 – Public service vehicles

(5) Before making the regulations the Secretary of State must consult such representative organisations as the Secretary of State thinks fit.

181 Interpretation

In this Chapter –

"accessibility certificate" has the meaning given in section 176(1);

"approval certificate" has the meaning given in section 177(4);

"PSV accessibility regulations" has the meaning given in section 174(1);

"regulated public service vehicle" has the meaning given in section 174(3).

CHAPTER 3

RAIL VEHICLES

182 Rail vehicle accessibility regulations

(1) The Secretary of State may make regulations (in this Chapter referred to as "rail vehicle accessibility regulations") for securing that it is possible for disabled persons –

   (a) to get on to and off regulated rail vehicles in safety and without unreasonable difficulty;

   (b) to do so while in wheelchairs;

   (c) to travel in such vehicles in safety and reasonable comfort;

   (d) to do so while in wheelchairs.

(2) The regulations may, in particular, make provision as to the construction, use and maintenance of regulated rail vehicles including provision as to –

   (a) the fitting of equipment to vehicles;

   (b) equipment to be carried by vehicles;

   (c) the design of equipment to be fitted to, or carried by, vehicles;

   (d) the use of equipment fitted to, or carried by, vehicles;

   (e) the toilet facilities to be provided in vehicles;

   (f) the location and floor area of the wheelchair accommodation to be provided in vehicles;

   (g) assistance to be given to disabled persons.

(3) The regulations may contain different provision –

   (a) as respects different classes or descriptions of rail vehicle;

   (b) as respects the same class or description of rail vehicle in different circumstances;

   (c) as respects different networks.

(4) In this section –

"network" means any permanent way or other means of guiding or supporting rail vehicles, or any section of it;

"rail vehicle" means a vehicle constructed or adapted to carry passengers on a railway, tramway or prescribed system other than a vehicle used in the provision of a service for the carriage of passengers on the high-speed rail system or the conventional TEN rail system;

"regulated rail vehicle" means a rail vehicle to which provisions of rail vehicle accessibility regulations are expressed to apply.

(5) In subsection (4) —

"conventional TEN rail system" and "high-speed rail system" have the meaning given in regulation 2(3) of the Railways (Interoperability) Regulations 2006 (S.I. 2006/397);

"prescribed system" means a system using a mode of guided transport ("guided transport" having the same meaning as in the Transport and Works Act 1992) that is specified in rail vehicle accessibility regulations;

"railway" and "tramway" have the same meaning as in the Transport and Works Act 1992.

(6) The Secretary of State must exercise the power to make rail vehicle accessibility regulations so as to secure that on and after 1 January 2020 every rail vehicle is a regulated rail vehicle.

(7) Subsection (6) does not affect subsection (3), section 183(1) or section 207(4)(a).

(8) Before making regulations under subsection (1) or section 183, the Secretary of State must consult —

(a) the Disabled Persons Transport Advisory Committee, and

(b) such other representative organisations as the Secretary of State thinks fit.

183 Exemptions from rail vehicle accessibility regulations

(1) The Secretary of State may by order (an "exemption order") —

(a) authorise the use for carriage of a regulated rail vehicle even though the vehicle does not conform with the provisions of rail vehicle accessibility regulations with which it is required to conform;

(b) authorise a regulated rail vehicle to be used for carriage otherwise than in conformity with the provisions of rail vehicle accessibility regulations with which use of the vehicle is required to conform.

(2) Authority under subsection (1)(a) or (b) may be for —

(a) a regulated rail vehicle that is specified or of a specified description,

(b) use in specified circumstances of a regulated rail vehicle, or

(c) use in specified circumstances of a regulated rail vehicle that is specified or of a specified description.

(3) The Secretary of State may by regulations make provision as to exemption orders including, in particular, provision as to —

(a) the persons by whom applications for exemption orders may be made;

(b) the form in which applications are to be made;

(c) information to be supplied in connection with applications;

(d) the period for which exemption orders are to continue in force;

(e) the revocation of exemption orders.

(4) After consulting the Disabled Persons Transport Advisory Committee and such other persons as the Secretary of State thinks appropriate, the Secretary of State may —

(a) make an exemption order in the terms of the application for the order;

(b) make an exemption order in such other terms as the Secretary of State thinks appropriate;

(c) refuse to make an exemption order.

(5) The Secretary of State may make an exemption order subject to such conditions and restrictions as are specified.

(6) "Specified" means specified in an exemption order.

184 Procedure for making exemption orders

(1) A statutory instrument that contains an order under section 183(1), if made without a draft having been laid before and approved by a resolution of each House of Parliament, is subject to annulment in pursuance of a resolution of either House.

(2) The Secretary of State must consult the Disabled Persons Transport Advisory Committee before deciding which of the parliamentary procedures available under subsection (1) is to be adopted in connection with the making of any particular order under section 183(1).

(3) An order under section 183(1) may be made without a draft of the instrument that contains it having been laid before and approved by a resolution of each House of Parliament only if —
    (a) regulations under subsection (4) are in force; and
    (b) the making of the order without such laying and approval is in accordance with the regulations.

(4) The Secretary of State may by regulations set out the basis on which the Secretary of State, when making an order under section 183(1), will decide which of the parliamentary procedures available under subsection (1) is to be adopted in connection with the making of the order.

(5) Before making regulations under subsection (4), the Secretary of State must consult —
    (a) the Disabled Persons Transport Advisory Committee; and
    (b) such other persons as the Secretary of State considers appropriate.

185 Annual report on exemption orders

(1) After the end of each calendar year the Secretary of State must prepare a report on —
    (a) the exercise in that year of the power to make orders under section 183(1);
    (b) the exercise in that year of the discretion under section 184(1).

(2) A report under subsection (1) must (in particular) contain —
    (a) details of each order made under section 183(1) in the year in question;
    (b) details of consultation carried out under sections 183(4) and 184(2) in connection with orders made in that year under section 183(1).

(3) The Secretary of State must lay before Parliament each report prepared under this section.

186 Rail vehicle accessibility: compliance

(1) Schedule 20 (rail vehicle accessibility: compliance) has effect.

(2)   This section and that Schedule are repealed at the end of 2010 if the Schedule is not brought into force (either fully or to any extent) before the end of that year.

187   Interpretation

(1)   In this Chapter —

   "rail vehicle" and "regulated rail vehicle" have the meaning given in section 182(4);

   "rail vehicle accessibility regulations" has the meaning given in section 182(1).

(2)   For the purposes of this Chapter a vehicle is used "for carriage" if it is used for the carriage of passengers.

CHAPTER 4

SUPPLEMENTARY

188   Forgery, etc.

(1)   In this section "relevant document" means —

   (a)   an exemption certificate issued under section 166, 169 or 171;

   (b)   a notice of a kind mentioned in section 166(3)(b), 169(4)(b) or 171(4)(b);

   (c)   an accessibility certificate (see section 176);

   (d)   an approval certificate (see section 177).

(2)   A person commits an offence if, with intent to deceive, the person —

   (a)   forges, alters or uses a relevant document;

   (b)   lends a relevant document to another person;

   (c)   allows a relevant document to be used by another person;

   (d)   makes or has possession of a document which closely resembles a relevant document.

(3)   A person guilty of an offence under subsection (2) is liable —

   (a)   on summary conviction, to a fine not exceeding the statutory maximum;

   (b)   on conviction on indictment, to imprisonment for a term not exceeding 2 years or to a fine or to both.

(4)   A person commits an offence by knowingly making a false statement for the purpose of obtaining an accessibility certificate or an approval certificate.

(5)   A person guilty of an offence under subsection (4) is liable on summary conviction to a fine not exceeding level 4 on the standard scale.

PART 13

DISABILITY: MISCELLANEOUS

189   Reasonable adjustments

Schedule 21 (reasonable adjustments: supplementary) has effect.

190   Improvements to let dwelling houses

(1)   This section applies in relation to a lease of a dwelling house if each of the following applies—

(a)   the tenancy is not a protected tenancy, a statutory tenancy or a secure tenancy;

(b)   the tenant or another person occupying or intending to occupy the premises is a disabled person;

(c)   the disabled person occupies or intends to occupy the premises as that person's only or main home;

(d)   the tenant is entitled, with the consent of the landlord, to make improvements to the premises;

(e)   the tenant applies to the landlord for consent to make a relevant improvement.

(2)   Where the tenant applies in writing for the consent—

(a)   if the landlord refuses to give consent, the landlord must give the tenant a written statement of the reason why the consent was withheld;

(b)   if the landlord neither gives nor refuses to give consent within a reasonable time, consent must be taken to have been unreasonably withheld.

(3)   If the landlord gives consent subject to a condition which is unreasonable, the consent must be taken to have been unreasonably withheld.

(4)   If the landlord's consent is unreasonably withheld, it must be taken to have been given.

(5)   On any question as to whether—

(a)   consent was unreasonably withheld, or

(b)   a condition imposed was unreasonable,

it is for the landlord to show that it was not.

(6)   If the tenant fails to comply with a reasonable condition imposed by the landlord on the making of a relevant improvement, the failure is to be treated as a breach by the tenant of an obligation of the tenancy.

(7)   An improvement to premises is a relevant improvement if, having regard to the disabled peron's disability, it is likely to facilitate that person's enjoyment of the premises.

(8)   Subsections (2) to (7) apply only in so far as provision of a like nature is not made by the lease.

(9)   In this section—

"improvement" means an alteration in or addition to the premises and includes—

(a)   an addition to or alteration in the landlord's fittings and fixtures;

(b)   an addition or alteration connected with the provision of services to the premises;

(c)   the erection of a wireless or television aerial;

(d)   carrying out external decoration;

"lease" includes a sub-lease or other tenancy, and "landlord" and "tenant" are to be construed accordingly;

"protected tenancy" has the same meaning as in section 1 of the Rent Act 1977;

"statutory tenancy" is to be construed in accordance with section 2 of that Act;

"secure tenancy" has the same meaning as in section 79 of the Housing Act 1985.

PART 14

GENERAL EXCEPTIONS

191 Statutory provisions

Schedule 22 (statutory provisions) has effect.

192 National security

A person does not contravene this Act only by doing, for the purpose of safeguarding national security, anything it is proportionate to do for that purpose.

193 Charities

(1) A person does not contravene this Act only by restricting the provision of benefits to persons who share a protected characteristic if —

    (a) the person acts in pursuance of a charitable instrument, and

    (b) the provision of the benefits is within subsection (2).

(2) The provision of benefits is within this subsection if it is —

    (a) a proportionate means of achieving a legitimate aim, or

    (b) for the purpose of preventing or compensating for a disadvantage linked to the protected characteristic.

(3) It is not a contravention of this Act for —

    (a) a person who provides supported employment to treat persons who have the same disability or a disability of a prescribed description more favourably than those who do not have that disability or a disability of such a description in providing such employment;

    (b) a Minister of the Crown to agree to arrangements for the provision of supported employment which will, or may, have that effect.

(4) If a charitable instrument enables the provision of benefits to persons of a class defined by reference to colour, it has effect for all purposes as if it enabled the provision of such benefits —

    (a) to persons of the class which results if the reference to colour is ignored, or

    (b) if the original class is defined by reference only to colour, to persons generally.

(5) It is not a contravention of this Act for a charity to require members, or persons wishing to become members, to make a statement which asserts or implies membership or acceptance of a religion or belief; and for this purpose restricting the access by members to a benefit, facility or service to those who make such a statement is to be treated as imposing such a requirement.

(6) Subsection (5) applies only if—

    (a) the charity, or an organisation of which it is part, first imposed such a requirement before 18 May 2005, and

    (b) the charity or organisation has not ceased since that date to impose such a requirement.

(7) It is not a contravention of section 29 for a person, in relation to an activity which is carried on for the purpose of promoting or supporting a charity, to restrict participation in the activity to persons of one sex.

(8) A charity regulator does not contravene this Act only by exercising a function in relation to a charity in a manner which the regulator thinks is expedient in the interests of the charity, having regard to the charitable instrument.

(9) Subsection (1) does not apply to a contravention of—

    (a) section 39;

    (b) section 40;

    (c) section 41;

    (d) section 55, so far as relating to the provision of vocational training.

(10) Subsection (9) does not apply in relation to disability.

194 Charities: supplementary

(1) This section applies for the purposes of section 193.

(2) That section does not apply to race, so far as relating to colour.

(3) "Charity"—

    (a) in relation to England and Wales, has the meaning given by section 1(1) of the Charities Act 2006;

    (b) in relation to Scotland, means a body entered in the Scottish Charity Register.

(4) "Charitable instrument" means an instrument establishing or governing a charity (including an instrument made or having effect before the commencement of this section).

(5) The charity regulators are—

    (a) the Charity Commission for England and Wales;

    (b) the Scottish Charity Regulator.

(6) Section 107(5) applies to references in subsection (5) of section 193 to members, or persons wishing to become members, of a charity.

(7) "Supported employment" means facilities provided, or in respect of which payments are made, under section 15 of the Disabled Persons (Employment) Act 1944.

195 Sport

(1) A person does not contravene this Act, so far as relating to sex, only by doing anything in relation to the participation of another as a competitor in a gender-affected activity.

(2) A person does not contravene section 29, 33, 34 or 35, so far as relating to gender reassignment, only by doing anything in relation to the participation of

a transsexual person as a competitor in a gender-affected activity if it is necessary to do so to secure in relation to the activity –

    (a)   fair competition, or

    (b)   the safety of competitors.

(3)   A gender-affected activity is a sport, game or other activity of a competitive nature in circumstances in which the physical strength, stamina or physique of average persons of one sex would put them at a disadvantage compared to average persons of the other sex as competitors in events involving the activity.

(4)   In considering whether a sport, game or other activity is gender-affected in relation to children, it is appropriate to take account of the age and stage of development of children who are likely to be competitors.

(5)   A person who does anything to which subsection (6) applies does not contravene this Act only because of the nationality or place of birth of another or because of the length of time the other has been resident in a particular area or place.

(6)   This subsection applies to –

    (a)   selecting one or more persons to represent a country, place or area or a related association, in a sport or game or other activity of a competitive nature;

    (b)   doing anything in pursuance of the rules of a competition so far as relating to eligibility to compete in a sport or game or other such activity.

196   General

Schedule 23 (general exceptions) has effect.

197   Age

(1)   A Minister of the Crown may by order amend this Act to provide that any of the following does not contravene this Act so far as relating to age –

    (a)   specified conduct;

    (b)   anything done for a specified purpose;

    (c)   anything done in pursuance of arrangements of a specified description.

(2)   Specified conduct is conduct –

    (a)   of a specified description,

    (b)   carried out in specified circumstances, or

    (c)   by or in relation to a person of a specified description.

(3)   An order under this section may –

    (a)   confer on a Minister of the Crown or the Treasury a power to issue guidance about the operation of the order (including, in particular, guidance about the steps that may be taken by persons wishing to rely on an exception provided for by the order);

    (b)   require the Minister or the Treasury to carry out consultation before issuing guidance under a power conferred by virtue of paragraph (a);

    (c)   make provision (including provision to impose a requirement) that refers to guidance issued under a power conferred by virtue of paragraph (a).

(4)   Guidance given by a Minister of the Crown or the Treasury in anticipation of the making of an order under this section is, on the making of the order, to be treated as if it has been issued in accordance with the order.

(5)   For the purposes of satisfying a requirement imposed by virtue of subsection (3)(b), the Minister or the Treasury may rely on consultation carried out before the making of the order that imposes the requirement (including consultation carried out before the commencement of this section).

(6)   Provision by virtue of subsection (3)(c) may, in particular, refer to provisions of the guidance that themselves refer to a document specified in the guidance.

(7)   Guidance issued (or treated as issued) under a power conferred by virtue of subsection (3)(a) comes into force on such day as the person who issues the guidance may by order appoint; and an order under this subsection may include the text of the guidance or of extracts from it.

(8)   This section is not affected by any provision of this Act which makes special provision in relation to age.

(9)   The references to this Act in subsection (1) do not include references to—

    (a)   Part 5 (work);

    (b)   Chapter 2 of Part 6 (further and higher education).

PART 15

FAMILY PROPERTY

198   Abolition of husband's duty to maintain wife

The rule of common law that a husband must maintain his wife is abolished.

199   Abolition of presumption of advancement

(1)   The presumption of advancement (by which, for example, a husband is presumed to be making a gift to his wife if he transfers property to her, or purchases property in her name) is abolished.

(2)   The abolition by subsection (1) of the presumption of advancement does not have effect in relation to—

    (a)   anything done before the commencement of this section, or

    (b)   anything done pursuant to any obligation incurred before the commencement of this section.

200   Amendment of Married Women's Property Act 1964

(1)   In section 1 of the Married Women's Property Act 1964 (money and property derived from housekeeping allowance made by husband to be treated as belonging to husband and wife in equal shares)—

    (a)   for "the husband for" substitute "either of them for", and

    (b)   for "the husband and the wife" substitute "them".

(2)   Accordingly, that Act may be cited as the Matrimonial Property Act 1964.

(3)   The amendments made by this section do not have effect in relation to any allowance made before the commencement of this section.

201 Civil partners: housekeeping allowance

(1) After section 70 of the Civil Partnership Act 2004 insert—

"70A Money and property derived from housekeeping allowance

Section 1 of the Matrimonial Property Act 1964 (money and property derived from housekeeping allowance to be treated as belonging to husband and wife in equal shares) applies in relation to—

    (a) money derived from any allowance made by a civil partner for the expenses of the civil partnership home or for similar purposes, and

    (b) any property acquired out of such money,

as it applies in relation to money derived from any allowance made by a husband or wife for the expenses of the matrimonial home or for similar purposes, and any property acquired out of such money."

(2) The amendment made by this section does not have effect in relation to any allowance made before the commencement of this section.

PART 16

GENERAL AND MISCELLANEOUS

Civil partnerships

202 Civil partnerships on religious premises

(1) The Civil Partnership Act 2004 is amended as follows.

(2) Omit section 6(1)(b) and (2) (prohibition on use of religious premises for registration of civil partnership).

(3) In section 6A (power to approve premises for registration of civil partnership), after subsection (2), insert—

"(2A) Regulations under this section may provide that premises approved for the registration of civil partnerships may differ from those premises approved for the registration of civil marriages.

(2B) Provision by virtue of subsection (2)(b) may, in particular, provide that applications for approval of premises may only be made with the consent (whether general or specific) of a person specified, or a person of a description specified, in the provision.

(2C) The power conferred by section 258(2), in its application to the power conferred by this section, includes in particular—

    (a) power to make provision in relation to religious premises that differs from provision in relation to other premises;

    (b) power to make different provision for different kinds of religious premises."

(4) In that section, after subsection (3), insert—

"(3A) For the avoidance of doubt, nothing in this Act places an obligation on religious organisations to host civil partnerships if they do not wish to do so.

    (3B)   "Civil marriage" means marriage solemnised otherwise than according to the rites of the Church of England or any other religious usages.

    (3C)   "Religious premises" means premises which—

        (a)   are used solely or mainly for religious purposes, or

        (b)   have been so used and have not subsequently been used solely or mainly for other purposes."

EU obligations

203 Harmonisation

(1)   This section applies if—

    (a)   there is a Community obligation of the United Kingdom which a Minister of the Crown thinks relates to the subject matter of the Equality Acts,

    (b)   the obligation is to be implemented by the exercise of the power under section 2(2) of the European Communities Act 1972 (the implementing power), and

    (c)   the Minister thinks that it is appropriate to make harmonising provision in the Equality Acts.

(2)   The Minister may by order make the harmonising provision.

(3)   If the Minister proposes to make an order under this section, the Minister must consult persons and organisations the Minister thinks are likely to be affected by the harmonising provision.

(4)   If, as a result of the consultation under subsection (3), the Minister thinks it appropriate to change the whole or part of the proposal, the Minister must carry out such further consultation with respect to the changes as the Minister thinks appropriate.

(5)   The Equality Acts are the Equality Act 2006 and this Act.

(6)   Harmonising provision is provision made in relation to relevant subject matter of the Equality Acts—

    (a)   which corresponds to the implementing provision, or

    (b)   which the Minister thinks is necessary or expedient in consequence of or related to provision made in pursuance of paragraph (a) or the implementing provision.

(7)   The implementing provision is provision made or to be made in exercise of the implementing power in relation to so much of the subject matter of the Equality Acts as implements a Community obligation.

(8)   Relevant subject matter of the Equality Acts is so much of the subject matter of those Acts as does not implement a Community obligation.

(9)   A harmonising provision may amend a provision of the Equality Acts.

(10)   The reference to this Act does not include a reference to this section or Schedule 24 or to a provision specified in that Schedule.

(11)   A Minister of the Crown must report to Parliament on the exercise of the power under subsection (2)—

(a)   at the end of the period of 2 years starting on the day this section comes into force;

(b)   at the end of each succeeding period of 2 years.

204 Harmonisation: procedure

(1)   If, after the conclusion of the consultation required under section 203, the Minister thinks it appropriate to proceed with the making of an order under that section, the Minister must lay before Parliament—

    (a)   a draft of a statutory instrument containing the order, together with

    (b)   an explanatory document.

(2)   The explanatory document must—

    (a)   introduce and give reasons for the harmonising provision;

    (b)   explain why the Minister thinks that the conditions in subsection (1) of section 203 are satisfied;

    (c)   give details of the consultation carried out under that section;

    (d)   give details of the representations received as a result of the consultation;

    (e)   give details of such changes as were made as a result of the representations.

(3)   Where a person making representations in response to the consultation has requested the Minister not to disclose them, the Minister must not disclose them under subsection (2)(d) if, or to the extent that, to do so would (disregarding any connection with proceedings in Parliament) constitute an actionable breach of confidence.

(4)   If information in representations made by a person in response to consultation under section 203 relates to another person, the Minister need not disclose the information under subsection (2)(d) if or to the extent that—

    (a)   the Minister thinks that the disclosure of information could adversely affect the interests of that other person, and

    (b)   the Minister has been unable to obtain the consent of that other person to the disclosure.

(5)   The Minister may not act under subsection (1) before the end of the period of 12 weeks beginning with the day on which the consultation under section 203(3) begins.

(6)   Laying a draft of a statutory instrument in accordance with subsection (1) satisfies the condition as to laying imposed by subsection (8) of section 208, in so far as that subsection applies in relation to orders under section 203.

Application

205 Crown application

(1)   The following provisions of this Act bind the Crown—

    (a)   Part 1 (public sector duty regarding socio-economic inequalities);

    (b)   Part 3 (services and public functions), so far as relating to the exercise of public functions;

    (c)   Chapter 1 of Part 11 (public sector equality duty).

(2) Part 5 (work) binds the Crown as provided for by that Part.

(3) The remainder of this Act applies to Crown acts as it applies to acts done by a private person.

(4) For the purposes of subsection (3), an act is a Crown act if (and only if) it is done—

    (a) by or on behalf of a member of the executive,

    (b) by a statutory body acting on behalf of the Crown, or

    (c) by or on behalf of the holder of a statutory office acting on behalf of the Crown.

(5) A statutory body or office is a body or office established by an enactment.

(6) The provisions of Parts 2 to 4 of the Crown Proceedings Act 1947 apply to proceedings against the Crown under this Act as they apply to proceedings in England and Wales which, as a result of section 23 of that Act, are treated for the purposes of Part 2 of that Act as civil proceedings by or against the Crown.

(7) The provisions of Part 5 of that Act apply to proceedings against the Crown under this Act as they apply to proceedings in Scotland which, as a result of that Part, are treated as civil proceedings by or against the Crown.

(8) But the proviso to section 44 of that Act (removal of proceedings from the sheriff to the Court of Session) does not apply to proceedings under this Act.

206 Information society services

Schedule 25 (information society services) has effect.

Subordinate legislation

207 Exercise of power

(1) A power to make an order or regulations under this Act is exercisable by a Minister of the Crown, unless there is express provision to the contrary.

(2) Orders, regulations or rules under this Act must be made by statutory instrument.

(3) Subsection (2) does not apply to—

    (a) a transitional exemption order under Part 1 of Schedule 11,

    (b) a transitional exemption order under Part 1 of Schedule 12, or

    (c) an order under paragraph 1(3) of Schedule 14 that does not modify an enactment.

(4) Orders or regulations under this Act—

    (a) may make different provision for different purposes;

    (b) may include consequential, incidental, supplementary, transitional, transitory or saving provision.

(5) Nothing in section 163(4), 174(4) or 182(3) affects the generality of the power under subsection (4)(a).

(6) The power under subsection (4)(b), in its application to section 37, 153, 154(2), 155(5), 197 or 216 or to paragraph 7(1) of Schedule 11 or paragraph 1(3) or 2(3)

of Schedule 14, includes power to amend an enactment (including, in the case of section 197 or 216, this Act).

(7)   In the case of section 216 (commencement), provision by virtue of subsection (4)(b) may be included in a separate order from the order that provides for the commencement to which the provision relates; and, for that purpose, it does not matter—

    (a)   whether the order providing for the commencement includes provision by virtue of subsection (4)(b);

    (b)   whether the commencement has taken place.

(8)   A statutory instrument containing an Order in Council under section 82 (offshore work) is subject to annulment in pursuance of a resolution of either House of Parliament.

208   Ministers of the Crown, etc.

(1)   This section applies where the power to make an order or regulations under this Act is exercisable by a Minister of the Crown or the Treasury.

(2)   A statutory instrument containing (whether alone or with other provision) an order or regulations that amend this Act or another Act of Parliament, or an Act of the Scottish Parliament or an Act or Measure of the National Assembly for Wales, is subject to the affirmative procedure.

(3)   But a statutory instrument is not subject to the affirmative procedure by virtue of subsection (2) merely because it contains—

    (a)   an order under section 59 (local authority functions);

    (b)   an order under section 151 (power to amend list of public authorities for the purposes of the public sector equality duty) that provides for the omission of an entry where the authority concerned has ceased to exist or the variation of an entry where the authority concerned has changed its name;

    (c)   an order under paragraph 1(3) of Schedule 14 (educational charities and endowments) that modifies an enactment.

(4)   A statutory instrument containing (whether alone or with other provision) an order or regulations mentioned in subsection (5) is subject to the affirmative procedure.

(5)   The orders and regulations referred to in subsection (4) are—

    (a)   regulations under section 30 (services: ships and hovercraft);

    (b)   regulations under section 78 (gender pay gap information);

    (c)   regulations under section 81 (work: ships and hovercraft);

    (d)   an order under section 105 (election candidates: expiry of provision);

    (e)   regulations under section 106 (election candidates: diversity information);

    (f)   regulations under section 153 or 154(2) (public sector equality duty: powers to impose specific duties);

    (g)   regulations under section 184(4) (rail vehicle accessibility: procedure for exemption orders);

    (h)   an order under section 203 (EU obligations: harmonisation);

    (i)   regulations under paragraph 9(3) of Schedule 20 (rail vehicle accessibility: determination of turnover for purposes of penalties).

(6) A statutory instrument that is not subject to the affirmative procedure by virtue of subsection (2) or (4) is subject to the negative procedure.

(7) But a statutory instrument is not subject to the negative procedure by virtue of subsection (6) merely because it contains—

(a) an order under section 183(1) (rail vehicle accessibility: exemptions);

(b) an order under section 216 (commencement) that—

(i) does not amend an Act of Parliament, an Act of the Scottish Parliament or an Act or Measure of the National Assembly for Wales, and

(ii) is not made in reliance on section 207(7).

(8) If a statutory instrument is subject to the affirmative procedure, the order or regulations contained in it must not be made unless a draft of the instrument is laid before and approved by a resolution of each House of Parliament.

(9) If a statutory instrument is subject to the negative procedure, it is subject to annulment in pursuance of a resolution of either House of Parliament.

(10) If a draft of a statutory instrument containing an order or regulations under section 2, 151, 153, 154(2) or 155(5) would, apart from this subsection, be treated for the purposes of the Standing Orders of either House of Parliament as a hybrid instrument, it is to proceed in that House as if it were not a hybrid instrument.

209 The Welsh Ministers

(1) This section applies where the power to make an order or regulations under this Act is exercisable by the Welsh Ministers.

(2) A statutory instrument containing (whether alone or with other provision) an order or regulations mentioned in subsection (3) is subject to the affirmative procedure.

(3) The orders and regulations referred to in subsection (2) are—

(a) regulations under section 2 (socio-economic inequalities);

(b) an order under section 151 (power to amend list of public authorities for the purposes of the public sector equality duty);

(c) regulations under section 153 or 154(2) (public sector equality duty: powers to impose specific duties);

(d) regulations under section 155(5) that amend an Act of Parliament or an Act or Measure of the National Assembly for Wales (public sector equality duty: power to modify or remove specific duties).

(4) But a statutory instrument is not subject to the affirmative procedure by virtue of subsection (2) merely because it contains an order under section 151 that provides for—

(a) the omission of an entry where the authority concerned has ceased to exist, or

(b) the variation of an entry where the authority concerned has changed its name.

(5) A statutory instrument that is not subject to the affirmative procedure by virtue of subsection (2) is subject to the negative procedure.

(6) If a statutory instrument is subject to the affirmative procedure, the order or regulations contained in it must not be made unless a draft of the instrument is laid before and approved by a resolution of the National Assembly for Wales.

(7) If a statutory instrument is subject to the negative procedure, it is subject to annulment in pursuance of a resolution of the National Assembly for Wales.

210 The Scottish Ministers

(1) This section applies where the power to make an order, regulations or rules under this Act is exercisable by the Scottish Ministers.

(2) A statutory instrument containing (whether alone or with other provision) an order or regulations mentioned in subsection (3) is subject to the affirmative procedure.

(3) The orders and regulations referred to in subsection (2) are—
 (a) regulations under section 2 (socio-economic inequalities);
 (b) regulations under section 37 (power to make provision about adjustments to common parts in Scotland);
 (c) an order under section 151 (power to amend list of public authorities for the purposes of the public sector equality duty);
 (d) regulations under section 153 or 154(2) (public sector equality duty: powers to impose specific duties);
 (e) regulations under section 155(5) that amend an Act of Parliament or an Act of the Scottish Parliament (public sector equality duty: power to modify or remove specific duties).

(4) But a statutory instrument is not subject to the affirmative procedure by virtue of subsection (2) merely because it contains an order under section 151 that provides for—
 (a) the omission of an entry where the authority concerned has ceased to exist, or
 (b) the variation of an entry where the authority concerned has changed its name.

(5) A statutory instrument that is not subject to the affirmative procedure by virtue of subsection (2) is subject to the negative procedure.

(6) If a statutory instrument is subject to the affirmative procedure, the order or regulations contained in it must not be made unless a draft of the instrument is laid before and approved by a resolution of the Scottish Parliament.

(7) If a statutory instrument is subject to the negative procedure, it is subject to annulment in pursuance of a resolution of the Scottish Parliament.

Amendments, etc.

211 Amendments, repeals and revocations

(1) Schedule 26 (amendments) has effect.

(2) Schedule 27 (repeals and revocations) has effect.

Interpretation

212   General interpretation

(1)   In this Act—

"armed forces" means any of the naval, military or air forces of the Crown;

"the Commission" means the Commission for Equality and Human Rights;

"detriment" does not, subject to subsection (5), include conduct which amounts to harassment;

"the Education Acts" has the meaning given in section 578 of the Education Act 1996;

"employment" and related expressions are (subject to subsection (11)) to be read with section 83;

"enactment" means an enactment contained in—

    (a)   an Act of Parliament,

    (b)   an Act of the Scottish Parliament,

    (c)   an Act or Measure of the National Assembly for Wales, or

    (d)   subordinate legislation;

"equality clause" means a sex equality clause or maternity equality clause;

"equality rule" means a sex equality rule or maternity equality rule;

"man" means a male of any age;

"maternity equality clause" has the meaning given in section 73;

"maternity equality rule" has the meaning given in section 75;

"non-discrimination rule" has the meaning given in section 61;

"occupational pension scheme" has the meaning given in section 1 of the Pension Schemes Act 1993;

"parent" has the same meaning as in—

    (a)   the Education Act 1996 (in relation to England and Wales);

    (b)   the Education (Scotland) Act 1980 (in relation to Scotland);

"prescribed" means prescribed by regulations;

"profession" includes a vocation or occupation;

"sex equality clause" has the meaning given in section 66;

"sex equality rule" has the meaning given in section 67;

"subordinate legislation" means—

    (a)   subordinate legislation within the meaning of the Interpretation Act 1978, or

    (b)   an instrument made under an Act of the Scottish Parliament or an Act or Measure of the National Assembly for Wales;

"substantial" means more than minor or trivial;

"trade" includes any business;

"woman" means a female of any age.

(2)   A reference (however expressed) to an act includes a reference to an omission.

(3)   A reference (however expressed) to an omission includes (unless there is express provision to the contrary) a reference to—

    (a)   a deliberate omission to do something;

    (b)   a refusal to do it;

    (c)   a failure to do it.

(4) A reference (however expressed) to providing or affording access to a benefit, facility or service includes a reference to facilitating access to the benefit, facility or service.

(5) Where this Act disapplies a prohibition on harassment in relation to a specified protected characteristic, the disapplication does not prevent conduct relating to that characteristic from amounting to a detriment for the purposes of discrimination within section 13 because of that characteristic.

(6) A reference to occupation, in relation to premises, is a reference to lawful occupation.

(7) The following are members of the executive —
   (a)   a Minister of the Crown;
   (b)   a government department;
   (c)   the Welsh Ministers, the First Minister for Wales or the Counsel General to the Welsh Assembly Government;
   (d)   any part of the Scottish Administration.

(8) A reference to a breach of an equality clause or rule is a reference to a breach of a term modified by, or included by virtue of, an equality clause or rule.

(9) A reference to a contravention of this Act does not include a reference to a breach of an equality clause or rule, unless there is express provision to the contrary.

(10) "Member", in relation to an occupational pension scheme, means an active member, a deferred member or a pensioner member (within the meaning, in each case, given by section 124 of the Pensions Act 1995).

(11) "Employer", "deferred member", "pension credit member", "pensionable service", "pensioner member" and "trustees or managers" each have, in relation to an occupational pension scheme, the meaning given by section 124 of the Pensions Act 1995.

(12) A reference to the accrual of rights under an occupational pension scheme is to be construed in accordance with that section.

(13) Nothing in section 28, 32, 84, 90, 95 or 100 is to be regarded as an express exception.

213 References to maternity leave, etc.

(1) This section applies for the purposes of this Act.

(2) A reference to a woman on maternity leave is a reference to a woman on —
   (a)   compulsory maternity leave,
   (b)   ordinary maternity leave, or
   (c)   additional maternity leave.

(3) A reference to a woman on compulsory maternity leave is a reference to a woman absent from work because she satisfies the conditions prescribed for the purposes of section 72(1) of the Employment Rights Act 1996.

(4) A reference to a woman on ordinary maternity leave is a reference to a woman absent from work because she is exercising the right to ordinary maternity leave.

(5) A reference to the right to ordinary maternity leave is a reference to the right conferred by section 71(1) of the Employment Rights Act 1996.

(6) A reference to a woman on additional maternity leave is a reference to a woman absent from work because she is exercising the right to additional maternity leave.

(7) A reference to the right to additional maternity leave is a reference to the right conferred by section 73(1) of the Employment Rights Act 1996.

(8) "Additional maternity leave period" has the meaning given in section 73(2) of that Act.

214 Index of defined expressions

Schedule 28 lists the places where expressions used in this Act are defined or otherwise explained.

Final provisions

215 Money

There is to be paid out of money provided by Parliament any increase attributable to this Act in the expenses of a Minister of the Crown.

216 Commencement

(1) The following provisions come into force on the day on which this Act is passed—
   (a) section 186(2) (rail vehicle accessibility: compliance);
   (b) this Part (except sections 202 (civil partnerships on religious premises), 206 (information society services) and 211 (amendments, etc)).

(2) Part 15 (family property) comes into force on such day as the Lord Chancellor may by order appoint.

(3) The other provisions of this Act come into force on such day as a Minister of the Crown may by order appoint.

217 Extent

(1) This Act forms part of the law of England and Wales.

(2) This Act, apart from section 190 (improvements to let dwelling houses) and Part 15 (family property), forms part of the law of Scotland.

(3) Each of the following also forms part of the law of Northern Ireland—
   (a) section 82 (offshore work);
   (b) section 105(3) and (4) (expiry of Sex Discrimination (Election Candidates) Act 2002);
   (c) section 199 (abolition of presumption of advancement).

218 Short title

This Act may be cited as the Equality Act 2010.

SCHEDULES

SCHEDULE 1

Section 6

DISABILITY: SUPPLEMENTARY PROVISION

PART 1

DETERMINATION OF DISABILITY

Impairment

1   Regulations may make provision for a condition of a prescribed description to be, or not to be, an impairment.

Long-term effects

2   (1) The effect of an impairment is long-term if—
 (a) it has lasted for at least 12 months,
 (b) it is likely to last for at least 12 months, or
 (c) it is likely to last for the rest of the life of the person affected.

 (2) If an impairment ceases to have a substantial adverse effect on a person's ability to carry out normal day-to-day activities, it is to be treated as continuing to have that effect if that effect is likely to recur.

 (3) For the purposes of sub-paragraph (2), the likelihood of an effect recurring is to be disregarded in such circumstances as may be prescribed.

 (4) Regulations may prescribe circumstances in which, despite sub-paragraph (1), an effect is to be treated as being, or as not being, long-term.

Severe disfigurement

3   (1) An impairment which consists of a severe disfigurement is to be treated as having a substantial adverse effect on the ability of the person concerned to carry out normal day-to-day activities.

 (2) Regulations may provide that in prescribed circumstances a severe disfigurement is not to be treated as having that effect.

 (3) The regulations may, in particular, make provision in relation to deliberately acquired disfigurement.

Substantial adverse effects

4   Regulations may make provision for an effect of a prescribed description on the ability of a person to carry out normal day-to-day activities to be treated as being, or as not being, a substantial adverse effect.

1766

Equality Act 2010 (c. 15)
Schedule 1 — Disability: supplementary provision
Part 1 — Determination of disability

Effect of medical treatment

5   (1) An impairment is to be treated as having a substantial adverse effect on the ability of the person concerned to carry out normal day-to-day activities if —

      (a) measures are being taken to treat or correct it, and

      (b) but for that, it would be likely to have that effect.

    (2) "Measures" includes, in particular, medical treatment and the use of a prosthesis or other aid.

    (3) Sub-paragraph (1) does not apply —

      (a) in relation to the impairment of a person's sight, to the extent that the impairment is, in the person's case, correctable by spectacles or contact lenses or in such other ways as may be prescribed;

      (b) in relation to such other impairments as may be prescribed, in such circumstances as are prescribed.

Certain medical conditions

6   (1) Cancer, HIV infection and multiple sclerosis are each a disability.

    (2) HIV infection is infection by a virus capable of causing the Acquired Immune Deficiency Syndrome.

Deemed disability

7   (1) Regulations may provide for persons of prescribed descriptions to be treated as having disabilities.

    (2) The regulations may prescribe circumstances in which a person who has a disability is to be treated as no longer having the disability.

    (3) This paragraph does not affect the other provisions of this Schedule.

Progressive conditions

8   (1) This paragraph applies to a person (P) if —

      (a) P has a progressive condition,

      (b) as a result of that condition P has an impairment which has (or had) an effect on P's ability to carry out normal day-to-day activities, but

      (c) the effect is not (or was not) a substantial adverse effect.

    (2) P is to be taken to have an impairment which has a substantial adverse effect if the condition is likely to result in P having such an impairment.

    (3) Regulations may make provision for a condition of a prescribed description to be treated as being, or as not being, progressive.

Past disabilities

9   (1) A question as to whether a person had a disability at a particular time ("the relevant time") is to be determined, for the purposes of section 6, as if the provisions of, or made under, this Act were in force when the act complained of was done had been in force at the relevant time.

    (2) The relevant time may be a time before the coming into force of the provision of this Act to which the question relates.

PART 2

GUIDANCE

Preliminary

10   This Part of this Schedule applies in relation to guidance referred to in section 6(5).

Examples

11   The guidance may give examples of —
    (a)   effects which it would, or would not, be reasonable, in relation to particular activities, to regard as substantial adverse effects;
    (b)   substantial adverse effects which it would, or would not, be reasonable to regard as long-term.

Adjudicating bodies

12   (1)   In determining whether a person is a disabled person, an adjudicating body must take account of such guidance as it thinks is relevant.

    (2)   An adjudicating body is —
        (a)   a court;
        (b)   a tribunal;
        (c)   a person (other than a court or tribunal) who may decide a claim relating to a contravention of Part 6 (education).

Representations

13   Before issuing the guidance, the Minister must —
    (a)   publish a draft of it;
    (b)   consider any representations made to the Minister about the draft;
    (c)   make such modifications as the Minister thinks appropriate in the light of the representations.

Parliamentary procedure

14   (1)   If the Minister decides to proceed with proposed guidance, a draft of it must be laid before Parliament.

    (2)   If, before the end of the 40-day period, either House resolves not to approve the draft, the Minister must take no further steps in relation to the proposed guidance.

    (3)   If no such resolution is made before the end of that period, the Minister must issue the guidance in the form of the draft.

    (4)   Sub-paragraph (2) does not prevent a new draft of proposed guidance being laid before Parliament.

    (5)   The 40-day period —
        (a)   begins on the date on which the draft is laid before both Houses (or, if laid before each House on a different date, on the later date);

> (b) does not include a period during which Parliament is prorogued or dissolved;
>
> (c) does not include a period during which both Houses are adjourned for more than 4 days.

Commencement

15   The guidance comes into force on the day appointed by order by the Minister.

Revision and revocation

16   (1) The Minister may—

> (a) revise the whole or part of guidance and re-issue it;
> (b) by order revoke guidance.

(2) A reference to guidance includes a reference to guidance which has been revised and re-issued.

SCHEDULE 2

Section 31

SERVICES AND PUBLIC FUNCTIONS: REASONABLE ADJUSTMENTS

Preliminary

1   This Schedule applies where a duty to make reasonable adjustments is imposed on A by this Part.

The duty

2   (1) A must comply with the first, second and third requirements.

(2) For the purposes of this paragraph, the reference in section 20(3), (4) or (5) to a disabled person is to disabled persons generally.

(3) Section 20 has effect as if, in subsection (4), for "to avoid the disadvantage" there were substituted—

> "(a) to avoid the disadvantage, or
> (b) to adopt a reasonable alternative method of providing the service or exercising the function."

(4) In relation to each requirement, the relevant matter is the provision of the service, or the exercise of the function, by A.

(5) Being placed at a substantial disadvantage in relation to the exercise of a function means—

> (a) if a benefit is or may be conferred in the exercise of the function, being placed at a substantial disadvantage in relation to the conferment of the benefit, or
> (b) if a person is or may be subjected to a detriment in the exercise of the function, suffering an unreasonably adverse experience when being subjected to the detriment.

(6) In relation to the second requirement, a physical feature includes a physical feature brought by or on behalf of A, in the course of providing the service or exercising the function, on to premises other than those that A occupies (as well as including a physical feature in or on premises that A occupies).

(7) If A is a service-provider, nothing in this paragraph requires A to take a step which would fundamentally alter—

(a) the nature of the service, or

(b) the nature of A's trade or profession.

(8) If A exercises a public function, nothing in this paragraph requires A to take a step which A has no power to take.

Special provision about transport

3 (1) This paragraph applies where A is concerned with the provision of a service which involves transporting people by land, air or water.

(2) It is never reasonable for A to have to take a step which would—

(a) involve the alteration or removal of a physical feature of a vehicle used in providing the service;

(b) affect whether vehicles are provided;

(c) affect what vehicles are provided;

(d) affect what happens in the vehicle while someone is travelling in it.

(3) But, for the purpose of complying with the first or third requirement, A may not rely on sub-paragraph (2)(b), (c) or (d) if the vehicle concerned is—

(a) a hire-vehicle designed and constructed for the carriage of passengers, comprising more than 8 seats in addition to the driver's seat and having a maximum mass not exceeding 5 tonnes,

(b) a hire-vehicle designed and constructed for the carriage of goods and having a maximum mass not exceeding 3.5 tonnes,

(c) a vehicle licensed under section 48 of the Local Government (Miscellaneous Provisions) Act 1976 or section 7 of the Private Hire Vehicles (London) Act 1998 (or under a provision of a local Act corresponding to either of those provisions),

(d) a private hire car (within the meaning of section 23 of the Civic Government (Scotland) Act 1982),

(e) a public service vehicle (within the meaning given by section 1 of the Public Passenger Vehicles Act 1981),

(f) a vehicle built or adapted to carry passengers on a railway or tramway (within the meaning, in each case, of the Transport and Works Act 1992),

(g) a taxi,

(h) a vehicle deployed to transport the driver and passengers of a vehicle that has broken down or is involved in an accident, or

(i) a vehicle deployed on a system using a mode of guided transport (within the meaning of the Transport and Works Act 1992).

(4) In so far as the second requirement requires A to adopt a reasonable alternative method of providing the service to disabled persons, A may not, for the purpose of complying with the requirement, rely on sub-paragraph (2)(b), (c) or (d) if the vehicle is within sub-paragraph (3)(h).

(5) A may not, for the purpose of complying with the first, second or third requirement rely on sub-paragraph (2) of this paragraph if A provides the service by way of a hire-vehicle built to carry no more than 8 passengers.

(6) For the purposes of sub-paragraph (5) in its application to the second requirement, a part of a vehicle is to be regarded as a physical feature if it requires alteration in order to facilitate the provision of—

    (a) hand controls to enable a disabled person to operate braking and accelerator systems in the vehicle, or

    (b) facilities for the stowage of a wheelchair.

(7) For the purposes of sub-paragraph (6)(a), fixed seating and in-built electrical systems are not physical features; and for the purposes of sub-paragraph (6)(b), fixed seating is not a physical feature.

(8) In the case of a vehicle within sub-paragraph (3), a relevant device is not an auxiliary aid for the purposes of the third requirement.

(9) A relevant device is a device or structure, or equipment, the installation, operation or maintenance of which would necessitate making a permanent alteration to, or which would have a permanent effect on, the internal or external fabric of the vehicle.

(10) Regulations may amend this paragraph so as to provide for sub-paragraph (2) not to apply, or to apply only so far as is prescribed, in relation to vehicles of a prescribed description.

Interpretation

4   (1) This paragraph applies for the purposes of paragraph 3.

    (2) A "hire-vehicle" is a vehicle hired (by way of a trade) under a hiring agreement to which section 66 of the Road Traffic Offenders Act 1988 applies.

    (3) A "taxi", in England and Wales, is a vehicle—

        (a) licensed under section 37 of the Town Police Clauses Act 1847,

        (b) licensed under section 6 of the Metropolitan Public Carriage Act 1869, or

        (c) drawn by one or more persons or animals.

    (4) A "taxi", in Scotland, is—

        (a) a hire car engaged, by arrangements made in a public place between the person to be transported (or a person acting on that person's behalf) and the driver, for a journey starting there and then, or

        (b) a vehicle drawn by one or more persons or animals.

SCHEDULE 3

SERVICES AND PUBLIC FUNCTIONS: EXCEPTIONS

PART 1

CONSTITUTIONAL MATTERS

Parliament

1   (1) Section 29 does not apply to the exercise of —
       (a)   a function of Parliament;
       (b)   a function exercisable in connection with proceedings in Parliament.

       (2) Sub-paragraph (1) does not permit anything to be done to or in relation to an individual unless it is done by or in pursuance of a resolution or other deliberation of either House or of a Committee of either House.

Legislation

2   (1) Section 29 does not apply to preparing, making or considering —
       (a)   an Act of Parliament;
       (b)   a Bill for an Act of Parliament;
       (c)   an Act of the Scottish Parliament;
       (d)   a Bill for an Act of the Scottish Parliament;
       (e)   an Act of the National Assembly for Wales;
       (f)   a Bill for an Act of the National Assembly for Wales.

       (2) Section 29 does not apply to preparing, making, approving or considering —
       (a)   a Measure of the National Assembly for Wales;
       (b)   a proposed Measure of the National Assembly for Wales.

       (3) Section 29 does not apply to preparing, making, confirming, approving or considering an instrument which is made under an enactment by —
       (a)   a Minister of the Crown;
       (b)   the Scottish Ministers or a member of the Scottish Executive;
       (c)   the Welsh Ministers, the First Minister for Wales or the Counsel General to the Welsh Assembly Government.

       (4) Section 29 does not apply to preparing, making, confirming, approving or considering an instrument to which paragraph 6(a) of Schedule 2 to the Synodical Government Measure 1969 (1969 No. 2) (Measures, Canons, Acts of Synod, orders, etc.) applies.

       (5) Section 29 does not apply to anything done in connection with the preparation, making, consideration, approval or confirmation of an instrument made by —
       (a)   Her Majesty in Council;
       (b)   the Privy Council.

       (6) Section 29 does not apply to anything done in connection with the imposition of a requirement or condition which comes within Schedule 22 (statutory provisions).

Judicial functions

3 (1) Section 29 does not apply to—

   (a) a judicial function;

   (b) anything done on behalf of, or on the instructions of, a person exercising a judicial function;

   (c) a decision not to commence or continue criminal proceedings;

   (d) anything done for the purpose of reaching, or in pursuance of, a decision not to commence or continue criminal proceedings.

   (2) A reference in sub-paragraph (1) to a judicial function includes a reference to a judicial function conferred on a person other than a court or tribunal.

Armed forces

4 (1) Section 29(6), so far as relating to relevant discrimination, does not apply to anything done for the purpose of ensuring the combat effectiveness of the armed forces.

   (2) "Relevant discrimination" is—

   (a) age discrimination;

   (b) disability discrimination;

   (c) gender reassignment discrimination;

   (d) sex discrimination.

Security services, etc.

5 Section 29 does not apply to—

   (a) the Security Service;

   (b) the Secret Intelligence Service;

   (c) the Government Communications Headquarters;

   (d) a part of the armed forces which is, in accordance with a requirement of the Secretary of State, assisting the Government Communications Headquarters.

PART 2

EDUCATION

6 In its application to a local authority in England and Wales, section 29, so far as relating to age discrimination or religious or belief-related discrimination, does not apply to—

   (a) the exercise of the authority's functions under section 14 of the Education Act 1996 (provision of schools);

   (b) the exercise of its function under section 13 of that Act in so far as it relates to a function of its under section 14 of that Act.

7 In its application to an education authority, section 29, so far as relating to age discrimination or religious or belief-related discrimination, does not apply to—

   (a) the exercise of the authority's functions under section 17 of the Education (Scotland) Act 1980 (provision of schools);

    (b)   the exercise of its functions under section 1 of that Act, section 2 of the Standards in Scotland's Schools etc. Act 2000 (asp 6) or section 4 or 5 of the Education (Additional Support for Learning) (Scotland) Act 2004 (asp 4) (general responsibility for education) in so far as it relates to a matter specified in paragraph (a);

    (c)   the exercise of its functions under subsection (1) of section 50 of the Education (Scotland) Act 1980 (education of pupils in exceptional circumstances) in so far as it consists of making arrangements of the description referred to in subsection (2) of that section.

8   (1)   In its application to a local authority in England and Wales or an education authority, section 29, so far as relating to sex discrimination, does not apply to the exercise of the authority's functions in relation to the establishment of a school.

    (2)   But nothing in sub-paragraph (1) is to be taken as disapplying section 29 in relation to the exercise of the authority's functions under section 14 of the Education Act 1996 or section 17 of the Education (Scotland) Act 1980.

9   Section 29, so far as relating to age discrimination, does not apply in relation to anything done in connection with—

    (a)   the curriculum of a school,

    (b)   admission to a school,

    (c)   transport to or from a school, or

    (d)   the establishment, alteration or closure of schools.

10   (1)   Section 29, so far as relating to disability discrimination, does not require a local authority in England or Wales exercising functions under the Education Acts or an education authority exercising relevant functions to remove or alter a physical feature.

    (2)   Relevant functions are functions under—

    (a)   the Education (Scotland) Act 1980,

    (b)   the Education (Scotland) Act 1996,

    (c)   the Standards in Scotland's Schools etc. Act 2000, or

    (d)   the Education (Additional Support for Learning) (Scotland) Act 2004.

11   Section 29, so far as relating to religious or belief-related discrimination, does not apply in relation to anything done in connection with—

    (a)   the curriculum of a school;

    (b)   admission to a school which has a religious ethos;

    (c)   acts of worship or other religious observance organised by or on behalf of a school (whether or not forming part of the curriculum);

    (d)   the responsible body of a school which has a religious ethos;

    (e)   transport to or from a school;

    (f)   the establishment, alteration or closure of schools.

12   This Part of this Schedule is to be construed in accordance with Chapter 1 of Part 6.

1774

Equality Act 2010 (c. 15)
Schedule 3 — Services and public functions: exceptions
Part 3 — Health and care

PART 3

HEALTH AND CARE

Blood services

13 (1) A person operating a blood service does not contravene section 29 only by refusing to accept a donation of an individual's blood if —

    (a) the refusal is because of an assessment of the risk to the public, or to the individual, based on clinical, epidemiological or other data obtained from a source on which it is reasonable to rely, and

    (b) the refusal is reasonable.

  (2) A blood service is a service for the collection and distribution of human blood for the purposes of medical services.

  (3) "Blood" includes blood components.

Health and safety

14 (1) A service-provider (A) who refuses to provide the service to a pregnant woman does not discriminate against her in contravention of section 29 because she is pregnant if —

    (a) A reasonably believes that providing her with the service would, because she is pregnant, create a risk to her health or safety,

    (b) A refuses to provide the service to persons with other physical conditions, and

    (c) the reason for that refusal is that A reasonably believes that providing the service to such persons would create a risk to their health or safety.

  (2) A service-provider (A) who provides, or offers to provide, the service to a pregnant woman on conditions does not discriminate against her in contravention of section 29 because she is pregnant if —

    (a) the conditions are intended to remove or reduce a risk to her health or safety,

    (b) A reasonably believes that the provision of the service without the conditions would create a risk to her health or safety,

    (c) A imposes conditions on the provision of the service to persons with other physical conditions, and

    (d) the reason for the imposition of those conditions is that A reasonably believes that the provision of the service to such persons without those conditions would create a risk to their health or safety.

Care within the family

15 A person (A) does not contravene section 29 only by participating in arrangements under which (whether or not for reward) A takes into A's home, and treats as members of A's family, persons requiring particular care and attention.

PART 4

IMMIGRATION

Disability

16 (1) This paragraph applies in relation to disability discrimination.

    (2) Section 29 does not apply to—

        (a) a decision within sub-paragraph (3);

        (b) anything done for the purposes of or in pursuance of a decision within that sub-paragraph.

    (3) A decision is within this sub-paragraph if it is a decision (whether or not taken in accordance with immigration rules) to do any of the following on the ground that doing so is necessary for the public good—

        (a) to refuse entry clearance;

        (b) to refuse leave to enter or remain in the United Kingdom;

        (c) to cancel leave to enter or remain in the United Kingdom;

        (d) to vary leave to enter or remain in the United Kingdom;

        (e) to refuse an application to vary leave to enter or remain in the United Kingdom.

    (4) Section 29 does not apply to—

        (a) a decision taken, or guidance given, by the Secretary of State in connection with a decision within sub-paragraph (3);

        (b) a decision taken in accordance with guidance given by the Secretary of State in connection with a decision within that sub-paragraph.

Nationality and ethnic or national origins

17 (1) This paragraph applies in relation to race discrimination so far as relating to—

        (a) nationality, or

        (b) ethnic or national origins.

    (2) Section 29 does not apply to anything done by a relevant person in the exercise of functions exercisable by virtue of a relevant enactment.

    (3) A relevant person is—

        (a) a Minister of the Crown acting personally, or

        (b) a person acting in accordance with a relevant authorisation.

    (4) A relevant authorisation is a requirement imposed or express authorisation given—

        (a) with respect to a particular case or class of case, by a Minister of the Crown acting personally;

        (b) with respect to a particular class of case, by a relevant enactment or by an instrument made under or by virtue of a relevant enactment.

    (5) The relevant enactments are—

        (a) the Immigration Acts,

        (b) the Special Immigration Appeals Commission Act 1997,

    (c)   a provision made under section 2(2) of the European Communities Act 1972 which relates to immigration or asylum, and

    (d)   a provision of Community law which relates to immigration or asylum.

(6) The reference in sub-paragraph (5)(a) to the Immigration Acts does not include a reference to—

    (a)   sections 28A to 28K of the Immigration Act 1971 (powers of arrest, entry and search, etc.), or

    (b)   section 14 of the Asylum and Immigration (Treatment of Claimants, etc.) Act 2004 (power of arrest).

Religion or belief

18 (1) This paragraph applies in relation to religious or belief-related discrimination.

(2) Section 29 does not apply to a decision within sub-paragraph (3) or anything done for the purposes of or in pursuance of a decision within that sub-paragraph.

(3) A decision is within this sub-paragraph if it is a decision taken in accordance with immigration rules—

    (a)   to refuse entry clearance or leave to enter the United Kingdom, or to cancel leave to enter or remain in the United Kingdom, on the grounds that the exclusion of the person from the United Kingdom is conducive to the public good, or

    (b)   to vary leave to enter or remain in the United Kingdom, or to refuse an application to vary leave to enter or remain in the United Kingdom, on the grounds that it is undesirable to permit the person to remain in the United Kingdom.

(4) Section 29 does not apply to a decision within sub-paragraph (5), or anything done for the purposes of or in pursuance of a decision within that sub-paragraph, if the decision is taken on grounds mentioned in sub-paragraph (6).

(5) A decision is within this sub-paragraph if it is a decision (whether or not taken in accordance with immigration rules) in connection with an application for entry clearance or for leave to enter or remain in the United Kingdom.

(6) The grounds referred to in sub-paragraph (4) are—

    (a)   the grounds that a person holds an office or post in connection with a religion or belief or provides a service in connection with a religion or belief,

    (b)   the grounds that a religion or belief is not to be treated in the same way as certain other religions or beliefs, or

    (c)   the grounds that the exclusion from the United Kingdom of a person to whom paragraph (a) applies is conducive to the public good.

(7) Section 29 does not apply to—

    (a)   a decision taken, or guidance given, by the Secretary of State in connection with a decision within sub-paragraph (3) or (5);

> (b) a decision taken in accordance with guidance given by the Secretary of State in connection with a decision within either of those sub-paragraphs.

Interpretation

19   A reference to entry clearance, leave to enter or remain or immigration rules is to be construed in accordance with the Immigration Act 1971.

PART 5

INSURANCE, ETC.

Services arranged by employer

20   (1) Section 29 does not apply to the provision of a relevant financial service if the provision is in pursuance of arrangements made by an employer for the service-provider to provide the service to the employer's employees, and other persons, as a consequence of the employment.

    (2) "Relevant financial service" means —

> (a) insurance or a related financial service, or
> (b) a service relating to membership of or benefits under a personal pension scheme (within the meaning given by section 1 of the Pension Schemes Act 1993).

Disability

21   (1) It is not a contravention of section 29, so far as relating to disability discrimination, to do anything in connection with insurance business if —

> (a) that thing is done by reference to information that is both relevant to the assessment of the risk to be insured and from a source on which it is reasonable to rely, and
> (b) it is reasonable to do that thing.

    (2) "Insurance business" means business which consists of effecting or carrying out contracts of insurance; and that definition is to be read with —

> (a) section 22 of the Financial Services and Markets Act 2000,
> (b) any relevant order under that Act, and
> (c) Schedule 2 to that Act.

Sex, gender reassignment, pregnancy and maternity

22   (1) It is not a contravention of section 29, so far as relating to relevant discrimination, to do anything in relation to an annuity, life insurance policy, accident insurance policy or similar matter involving the assessment of risk if —

> (a) that thing is done by reference to actuarial or other data from a source on which it is reasonable to rely, and
> (b) it is reasonable to do that thing.

    (2) In the case of a contract of insurance, or a contract for related financial services, entered into before 6 April 2008, sub-paragraph (1) applies only in relation to differences in premiums and benefits that are applicable to a person under the contract.

(3) In the case of a contract of insurance, or a contract for related financial services, entered into on or after 6 April 2008, sub-paragraph (1) applies only in relation to differences in premiums and benefits if —

    (a) the use of sex as a factor in the assessment of risk is based on relevant and accurate actuarial and statistical data,

    (b) the data are compiled, published (whether in full or in summary form) and regularly updated in accordance with guidance issued by the Treasury,

    (c) the differences are proportionate having regard to the data, and

    (d) the differences do not result from costs related to pregnancy or to a woman's having given birth in the period of 26 weeks ending on the day on which the thing in question is done.

(4) "Relevant discrimination" is —

    (a) gender reassignment discrimination;

    (b) pregnancy and maternity discrimination;

    (c) sex discrimination.

(5) For the purposes of the application of sub-paragraph (3) to gender reassignment discrimination by virtue of section 13, that section has effect as if in subsection (1), after "others" there were inserted "of B's sex".

(6) In the application of sub-paragraph (3) to a contract entered into before 22 December 2008, paragraph (d) is to be ignored.

Existing insurance policies

23 (1) It is not a contravention of section 29, so far as relating to relevant discrimination, to do anything in connection with insurance business in relation to an existing insurance policy.

(2) "Relevant discrimination" is —

    (a) age discrimination;

    (b) disability discrimination;

    (c) gender reassignment discrimination;

    (d) pregnancy and maternity discrimination;

    (e) race discrimination;

    (f) religious or belief-related discrimination;

    (g) sex discrimination;

    (h) sexual orientation discrimination.

(3) An existing insurance policy is a policy of insurance entered into before the date on which this paragraph comes into force.

(4) Sub-paragraph (1) does not apply where an existing insurance policy was renewed, or the terms of such a policy were reviewed, on or after the date on which this paragraph comes into force.

(5) A review of an existing insurance policy which was part of, or incidental to, a general reassessment by the service-provider of the pricing structure for a group of policies is not a review for the purposes of sub-paragraph (4).

(6) "Insurance business" has the meaning given in paragraph 21.

PART 6

MARRIAGE

Gender reassignment: England and Wales

24 (1) A person does not contravene section 29, so far as relating to gender reassignment discrimination, only because of anything done in reliance on section 5B of the Marriage Act 1949 (solemnisation of marriages involving person of acquired gender).

   (2) A person (A) whose consent to the solemnisation of the marriage of a person (B) is required under section 44(1) of the Marriage Act 1949 (solemnisation in registered building) does not contravene section 29, so far as relating to gender reassignment discrimination, by refusing to consent if A reasonably believes that B's gender has become the acquired gender under the Gender Recognition Act 2004.

   (3) Sub-paragraph (4) applies to a person (A) who may, in a case that comes within the Marriage Act 1949 (other than the case mentioned in sub-paragraph (1)), solemnise marriages according to a form, rite or ceremony of a body of persons who meet for religious worship.

   (4) A does not contravene section 29, so far as relating to gender reassignment discrimination, by refusing to solemnise, in accordance with a form, rite or ceremony as described in sub-paragraph (3), the marriage of a person (B) if A reasonably believes that B's gender has become the acquired gender under the Gender Recognition Act 2004.

Gender reassignment: Scotland

25 (1) An approved celebrant (A) does not contravene section 29, so far as relating to gender reassignment discrimination, only by refusing to solemnise the marriage of a person (B) if A reasonably believes that B's gender has become the acquired gender under the Gender Recognition Act 2004.

   (2) In sub-paragraph (1) "approved celebrant" has the meaning given in section 8(2)(a) of the Marriage (Scotland) Act 1977 (persons who may solemnise marriage).

PART 7

SEPARATE AND SINGLE SERVICES

Separate services for the sexes

26 (1) A person does not contravene section 29, so far as relating to sex discrimination, by providing separate services for persons of each sex if —
   (a) a joint service for persons of both sexes would be less effective, and
   (b) the limited provision is a proportionate means of achieving a legitimate aim.

   (2) A person does not contravene section 29, so far as relating to sex discrimination, by providing separate services differently for persons of each sex if —
   (a) a joint service for persons of both sexes would be less effective,

1780

Equality Act 2010 (c. 15)
Schedule 3 — Services and public functions: exceptions
Part 7 — Separate and single services

        (b)   the extent to which the service is required by one sex makes it not reasonably practicable to provide the service otherwise than as a separate service provided differently for each sex, and

        (c)   the limited provision is a proportionate means of achieving a legitimate aim.

(3) This paragraph applies to a person exercising a public function in relation to the provision of a service as it applies to the person providing the service.

Single-sex services

27   (1) A person does not contravene section 29, so far as relating to sex discrimination, by providing a service only to persons of one sex if —

        (a)   any of the conditions in sub-paragraphs (2) to (7) is satisfied, and

        (b)   the limited provision is a proportionate means of achieving a legitimate aim.

(2) The condition is that only persons of that sex have need of the service.

(3) The condition is that —

        (a)   the service is also provided jointly for persons of both sexes, and

        (b)   the service would be insufficiently effective were it only to be provided jointly.

(4) The condition is that —

        (a)   a joint service for persons of both sexes would be less effective, and

        (b)   the extent to which the service is required by persons of each sex makes it not reasonably practicable to provide separate services.

(5) The condition is that the service is provided at a place which is, or is part of —

        (a)   a hospital, or

        (b)   another establishment for persons requiring special care, supervision or attention.

(6) The condition is that —

        (a)   the service is provided for, or is likely to be used by, two or more persons at the same time, and

        (b)   the circumstances are such that a person of one sex might reasonably object to the presence of a person of the opposite sex.

(7) The condition is that —

        (a)   there is likely to be physical contact between a person (A) to whom the service is provided and another person (B), and

        (b)   B might reasonably object if A were not of the same sex as B.

(8) This paragraph applies to a person exercising a public function in relation to the provision of a service as it applies to the person providing the service.

Gender reassignment

28   (1) A person does not contravene section 29, so far as relating to gender reassignment discrimination, only because of anything done in relation to a matter within sub-paragraph (2) if the conduct in question is a proportionate means of achieving a legitimate aim.

Equality Act 2010 (c. 15)
Schedule 3 — Services and public functions: exceptions
Part 7 — Separate and single services

1781

(2) The matters are—

    (a)   the provision of separate services for persons of each sex;

    (b)   the provision of separate services differently for persons of each sex;

    (c)   the provision of a service only to persons of one sex.

Services relating to religion

29   (1)   A minister does not contravene section 29, so far as relating to sex discrimination, by providing a service only to persons of one sex or separate services for persons of each sex, if—

    (a)   the service is provided for the purposes of an organised religion,

    (b)   it is provided at a place which is (permanently or for the time being) occupied or used for those purposes, and

    (c)   the limited provision of the service is necessary in order to comply with the doctrines of the religion or is for the purpose of avoiding conflict with the strongly held religious convictions of a significant number of the religion's followers.

    (2)   The reference to a minister is a reference to a minister of religion, or other person, who—

    (a)   performs functions in connection with the religion, and

    (b)   holds an office or appointment in, or is accredited, approved or recognised for purposes of, a relevant organisation in relation to the religion.

    (3)   An organisation is a relevant organisation in relation to a religion if its purpose is—

    (a)   to practise the religion,

    (b)   to advance the religion,

    (c)   to teach the practice or principles of the religion,

    (d)   to enable persons of the religion to receive benefits, or to engage in activities, within the framework of that religion, or

    (e)   to foster or maintain good relations between persons of different religions.

    (4)   But an organisation is not a relevant organisation in relation to a religion if its sole or main purpose is commercial.

Services generally provided only for persons who share a protected characteristic

30   If a service is generally provided only for persons who share a protected characteristic, a person (A) who normally provides the service for persons who share that characteristic does not contravene section 29(1) or (2)—

    (a)   by insisting on providing the service in the way A normally provides it, or

    (b)   if A reasonably thinks it is impracticable to provide the service to persons who do not share that characteristic, by refusing to provide the service.

1782

Equality Act 2010 (c. 15)
Schedule 3 — Services and public functions: exceptions
Part 8 — Television, radio and on-line broadcasting and distribution

PART 8

TELEVISION, RADIO AND ON-LINE BROADCASTING AND DISTRIBUTION

31 (1) Section 29 does not apply to the provision of a content service (within the meaning given by section 32(7) of the Communications Act 2003).

    (2) Sub-paragraph (1) does not apply to the provision of an electronic communications network, electronic communications service or associated facility (each of which has the same meaning as in that Act).

PART 9

TRANSPORT

Application to disability

32   This Part of this Schedule applies in relation to disability discrimination.

Transport by air

33 (1) Section 29 does not apply to—
        (a) transporting people by air;
        (b) a service provided on a vehicle for transporting people by air.

    (2) Section 29 does not apply to anything governed by Regulation (EC) No 1107/2006 of the European Parliament and of the Council of 5 July 2006 concerning the rights of disabled persons and persons with reduced mobility when travelling by air.

Transport by land

34 (1) Section 29 does not apply to transporting people by land, unless the vehicle concerned is—
        (a) a hire-vehicle designed and constructed for the carriage of passengers and comprising no more than 8 seats in addition to the driver's seat,
        (b) a hire-vehicle designed and constructed for the carriage of passengers, comprising more than 8 seats in addition to the driver's seat and having a maximum mass not exceeding 5 tonnes,
        (c) a hire-vehicle designed and constructed for the carriage of goods and having a maximum mass not exceeding 3.5 tonnes,
        (d) a vehicle licensed under section 48 of the Local Government (Miscellaneous Provisions) Act 1976 or section 7 of the Private Hire Vehicles (London) Act 1998 (or under a provision of a local Act corresponding to either of those provisions),
        (e) a private hire car (within the meaning of section 23 of the Civic Government (Scotland) Act 1982),
        (f) a public service vehicle (within the meaning given by section 1 of the Public Passenger Vehicles Act 1981),
        (g) a vehicle built or adapted to carry passengers on a railway or tramway (within the meaning, in each case, of the Transport and Works Act 1992),
        (h) a taxi,

(i) a vehicle deployed to transport the driver and passengers of a vehicle that has broken down or is involved in an accident, or

(j) a vehicle deployed on a system using a mode of guided transport (within the meaning of the Transport and Works Act 1992).

(2) Paragraph 4 of Schedule 2 applies for the purposes of this paragraph as it applies for the purposes of paragraph 3 of that Schedule.

PART 10

SUPPLEMENTARY

Power to amend

35 (1) A Minister of the Crown may by order amend this Schedule—

(a) so as to add, vary or omit an exception to section 29, so far as relating to disability, religion or belief or sexual orientation;

(b) so as to add, vary or omit an exception to section 29(6), so far as relating to gender reassignment, pregnancy and maternity, race or sex.

(2) But provision by virtue of sub-paragraph (1) may not amend this Schedule—

(a) so as to omit an exception in paragraph 1, 2 or 3;

(b) so as to reduce the extent to which an exception in paragraph 1, 2 or 3 applies.

(3) For the purposes of an order under sub-paragraph (1)(a), so far as relating to disability, which makes provision in relation to transport by air, it does not matter whether the transport is within or outside the United Kingdom.

(4) Before making an order under this paragraph the Minister must consult the Commission.

(5) Nothing in this paragraph affects the application of any other provision of this Act to conduct outside England and Wales or Scotland.

SCHEDULE 4

Section 38

PREMISES: REASONABLE ADJUSTMENTS

Preliminary

1 This Schedule applies where a duty to make reasonable adjustments is imposed on A by this Part.

The duty in relation to let premises

2 (1) This paragraph applies where A is a controller of let premises.

(2) A must comply with the first and third requirements.

(3) For the purposes of this paragraph, the reference in section 20(3) to a provision, criterion or practice of A's includes a reference to a term of the letting.

(4) For those purposes, the reference in section 20(3) or (5) to a disabled person is a reference to a disabled person who—

    (a) is a tenant of the premises, or

    (b) is otherwise entitled to occupy them.

(5) In relation to each requirement, the relevant matters are—

    (a) the enjoyment of the premises;

    (b) the use of a benefit or facility, entitlement to which arises as a result of the letting.

(6) Sub-paragraph (2) applies only if A receives a request from or on behalf of the tenant or a person entitled to occupy the premises to take steps to avoid the disadvantage or provide the auxiliary aid.

(7) If a term of the letting that prohibits the tenant from making alterations puts the disabled person at the disadvantage referred to in the first requirement, A is required to change the term only so far as is necessary to enable the tenant to make alterations to the let premises so as to avoid the disadvantage.

(8) It is never reasonable for A to have to take a step which would involve the removal or alteration of a physical feature.

(9) For the purposes of this paragraph, physical features do not include furniture, furnishings, materials, equipment or other chattels in or on the premises; and none of the following is an alteration of a physical feature—

    (a) the replacement or provision of a sign or notice;

    (b) the replacement of a tap or door handle;

    (c) the replacement, provision or adaptation of a door bell or door entry system;

    (d) changes to the colour of a wall, door or any other surface.

(10) The terms of a letting include the terms of an agreement relating to it.

The duty in relation to premises to let

3 (1) This paragraph applies where A is a controller of premises to let.

(2) A must comply with the first and third requirements.

(3) For the purposes of this paragraph, the reference in section 20(3) or (5) to a disabled person is a reference to a disabled person who is considering taking a letting of the premises.

(4) In relation to each requirement, the relevant matter is becoming a tenant of the premises.

(5) Sub-paragraph (2) applies only if A receives a request by or on behalf of a disabled person within sub-paragraph (3) for A to take steps to avoid the disadvantage or provide the auxiliary aid.

(6) Nothing in this paragraph requires A to take a step which would involve the removal or alteration of a physical feature.

(7) Sub-paragraph (9) of paragraph 2 applies for the purposes of this paragraph as it applies for the purposes of that paragraph.

The duty in relation to commonhold units

4   (1) This paragraph applies where A is a commonhold association; and the reference to a commonhold association is a reference to the association in its capacity as the person who manages a commonhold unit.

       (2) A must comply with the first and third requirements.

       (3) For the purposes of this paragraph, the reference in section 20(3) to a provision, criterion or practice of A's includes a reference to —

          (a) a term of the commonhold community statement, or

          (b) any other term applicable by virtue of the transfer of the unit to the unit-holder.

       (4) For those purposes, the reference in section 20(3) or (5) to a disabled person is a reference to a disabled person who —

          (a) is the unit-holder, or

          (b) is otherwise entitled to occupy the unit.

       (5) In relation to each requirement, the relevant matters are —

          (a) the enjoyment of the unit;

          (b) the use of a benefit or facility, entitlement to which arises as a result of a term within sub-paragraph (3)(a) or (b).

       (6) Sub-paragraph (2) applies only if A receives a request from or on behalf of the unit-holder or a person entitled to occupy the unit to take steps to avoid the disadvantage or provide the auxiliary aid.

       (7) If a term within sub-paragraph (3)(a) or (b) that prohibits the unit-holder from making alterations puts the disabled person at the disadvantage referred to in the first requirement, A is required to change the term only so far as is necessary to enable the unit-holder to make alterations to the unit so as to avoid the disadvantage.

       (8) It is never reasonable for A to have to take a step which would involve the removal or alteration of a physical feature; and sub-paragraph (9) of paragraph 2 applies in relation to a commonhold unit as it applies in relation to let premises.

The duty in relation to common parts

5   (1) This paragraph applies where A is a responsible person in relation to common parts.

       (2) A must comply with the second requirement.

       (3) For the purposes of this paragraph, the reference in section 20(4) to a physical feature is a reference to a physical feature of the common parts.

       (4) For those purposes, the reference in section 20(4) to a disabled person is a reference to a disabled person who —

          (a) is a tenant of the premises,

          (b) is a unit-holder, or

          (c) is otherwise entitled to occupy the premises,

       and uses or intends to use the premises as the person's only or main home.

(5) In relation to the second requirement, the relevant matter is the use of the common parts.

(6) Sub-paragraph (2) applies only if—

    (a) A receives a request by or on behalf of a disabled person within sub-paragraph (4) for A to take steps to avoid the disadvantage, and

    (b) the steps requested are likely to avoid or reduce the disadvantage.

Consultation on adjustments relating to common parts

6   (1) In deciding whether it is reasonable to take a step for the purposes of paragraph 5, A must consult all persons A thinks would be affected by the step.

    (2) The consultation must be carried out within a reasonable period of the request being made.

    (3) A is not required to have regard to a view expressed against taking a step in so far as A reasonably believes that the view is expressed because of the disabled person's disability.

    (4) Nothing in this paragraph affects anything a commonhold association is required to do pursuant to Part 1 of the Commonhold and Leasehold Reform Act 2002.

Agreement on adjustments relating to common parts

7   (1) If A decides that it is reasonable to take a step for the purposes of paragraph 5, A and the disabled person must agree in writing the rights and responsibilities of each of them in relation to the step.

    (2) An agreement under this paragraph must, in particular, make provision as to the responsibilities of the parties in relation to—

    (a) the costs of any work to be undertaken;

    (b) other costs arising from the work;

    (c) the restoration of the common parts to their former condition if the relevant disabled person stops living in the premises.

    (3) It is always reasonable before the agreement is made for A to insist that the agreement should require the disabled person to pay—

    (a) the costs referred to in paragraphs (a) and (b) of sub-paragraph (2), and

    (b) the costs of the restoration referred to in paragraph (c) of that sub-paragraph.

    (4) If an agreement under this paragraph is made, A's obligations under the agreement become part of A's interest in the common parts and pass on subsequent disposals accordingly.

    (5) Regulations may require a party to an agreement under this paragraph to provide, in prescribed circumstances, prescribed information about the agreement to persons of a prescribed description.

    (6) The regulations may require the information to be provided in a prescribed form.

(7) Regulations may make provision as to circumstances in which an agreement under this paragraph is to cease to have effect, in so far as the agreement does not itself make provision for termination.

Victimisation

8 (1) This paragraph applies where the relevant disabled person comes within paragraph 2(4)(b), 4(4)(b) or 5(4)(c).

(2) A must not, because of costs incurred in connection with taking steps to comply with a requirement imposed for the purposes of paragraph 2, 4 or 5, subject to a detriment —
   (a) a tenant of the premises, or
   (b) the unit-holder.

Regulations

9 (1) This paragraph applies for the purposes of section 36 and this Schedule.

(2) Regulations may make provision as to —
   (a) circumstances in which premises are to be treated as let, or as not let, to a person;
   (b) circumstances in which premises are to be treated as being, or as not being, to let;
   (c) who is to be treated as being, or as not being, a person entitled to occupy premises otherwise than as tenant or unit-holder;
   (d) who is to be treated as being, or as not being, a person by whom premises are let;
   (e) who is to be treated as having, or as not having, premises to let;
   (f) who is to be treated as being, or as not being, a manager of premises.

(3) Provision made by virtue of this paragraph may amend this Schedule.

SCHEDULE 5

Section 38

PREMISES: EXCEPTIONS

Owner-occupier

1 (1) This paragraph applies to the private disposal of premises by an owner-occupier.

(2) A disposal is a private disposal only if the owner-occupier does not —
   (a) use the services of an estate agent for the purpose of disposing of the premises, or
   (b) publish (or cause to be published) an advertisement in connection with their disposal.

(3) Section 33(1) applies only in so far as it relates to race.

(4) Section 34(1) does not apply in so far as it relates to —
   (a) religion or belief, or
   (b) sexual orientation.

(5) In this paragraph—

"estate agent" means a person who, by way of profession or trade, provides services for the purpose of—

    (a)   finding premises for persons seeking them, or

    (b)   assisting in the disposal of premises;

"owner-occupier" means a person who—

    (a)   owns an estate or interest in premises, and

    (b)   occupies the whole of them.

2   (1) Section 36(1)(a) does not apply if—

    (a)   the premises are, or have been, the only or main home of a person by whom they are let, and

    (b)   since entering into the letting, neither that person nor any other by whom they are let has used a manager for managing the premises.

(2) A manager is a person who, by profession or trade, manages let premises.

(3) Section 36(1)(b) does not apply if—

    (a)   the premises are, or have been, the only or main home of a person who has them to let, and

    (b)   neither that person nor any other who has the premises to let uses the services of an estate agent for letting the premises.

(4) "Estate agent" has the meaning given in paragraph 1.

Small premises

3   (1) This paragraph applies to anything done by a person in relation to the disposal, occupation or management of part of small premises if—

    (a)   the person or a relative of that person resides, and intends to continue to reside, in another part of the premises, and

    (b)   the premises include parts (other than storage areas and means of access) shared with residents of the premises who are not members of the same household as the resident mentioned in paragraph (a).

(2) Sections 33(1), 34(1) and 35(1) apply only in so far as they relate to race.

(3) Premises are small if—

    (a)   the only other persons occupying the accommodation occupied by the resident mentioned in sub-paragraph (1)(a) are members of the same household,

    (b)   the premises also include accommodation for at least one other household,

    (c)   the accommodation for each of those other households is let, or available for letting, on a separate tenancy or similar agreement, and

    (d)   the premises are not normally sufficient to accommodate more than two other households.

(4) Premises are also small if they are not normally sufficient to provide residential accommodation for more than six persons (in addition to the resident mentioned in sub-paragraph (1)(a) and members of the same household).

(5) In this paragraph, "relative" means—

    (a)   spouse or civil partner,

    (b)   unmarried partner,

    (c)   parent or grandparent,

    (d)   child or grandchild (whether or not legitimate),

    (e)   the spouse, civil partner or unmarried partner of a child or grandchild,

    (f)   brother or sister (whether of full blood or half-blood), or

    (g)   a relative within paragraph (c), (d), (e) or (f) whose relationship arises as a result of marriage or civil partnership.

(6) In sub-paragraph (5), a reference to an unmarried partner is a reference to the other member of a couple consisting of —

    (a)   a man and a woman who are not married to each other but are living together as husband and wife, or

    (b)   two people of the same sex who are not civil partners of each other but are living together as if they were.

4   (1) Section 36(1) does not apply if —

    (a)   the premises in question are small premises,

    (b)   the relevant person or a relative of that person resides, and intends to continue to reside, in another part of the premises, and

    (c)   the premises include parts (other than storage areas and means of access) shared with residents of the premises who are not members of the same household as the resident mentioned in paragraph (b).

(2) The relevant person is the person who, for the purposes of section 36(1), is —

    (a)   the controller of the premises, or

    (b)   the responsible person in relation to the common parts to which the premises relate.

(3) "Small premises" and "relative" have the same meaning as in paragraph 3.

5   A Minister of the Crown may by order amend paragraph 3 or 4.

SCHEDULE 6

Section 52

OFFICE-HOLDERS: EXCLUDED OFFICES

Work to which other provisions apply

1   (1) An office or post is not a personal or public office in so far as one or more of the provisions mentioned in sub-paragraph (2) —

    (a)   applies in relation to the office or post, or

    (b)   would apply in relation to the office or post but for the operation of some other provision of this Act.

(2) Those provisions are —

    (a)   section 39 (employment);

    (b)   section 41 (contract work);

    (c)   section 44 (partnerships).

    (d)   section 45 (LLPs);

    (e)   section 47 (barristers);

    (f)   section 48 (advocates);

(g) section 55 (employment services) so far as applying to the provision of work experience within section 56(2)(a) or arrangements within section 56(2)(c) for such provision.

Political offices

2 (1) An office or post is not a personal or public office if it is a political office.

(2) A political office is an office or post set out in the second column of the following Table —

Political setting	*Office or post*
Houses of Parliament	An office of the House of Commons held by a member of that House
	An office of the House of Lords held by a member of that House
	A Ministerial office within the meaning of section 2 of the House of Commons Disqualification Act 1975
	The office of the Leader of the Opposition within the meaning of the Ministerial and other Salaries Act 1975
	The office of the Chief Opposition Whip, or of an Assistant Opposition Whip, within the meaning of that Act
Scottish Parliament	An office of the Scottish Parliament held by a member of the Parliament
	The office of a member of the Scottish Executive
	The office of a junior Scottish Minister
National Assembly for Wales	An office of the National Assembly for Wales held by a member of the Assembly
	The office of a member of the Welsh Assembly Government
Local government in England (outside London)	An office of a county council, district council or parish council in England held by a member of the council
	An office of the Council of the Isles of Scilly held by a member of the Council
Local government in London	An office of the Greater London Authority held by the Mayor of London or a member of the London Assembly

Political setting	Office or post
	An office of a London borough council held by a member of the council
	An office of the Common Council of the City of London held by a member of the Council
Local government in Wales	An office of a county council, county borough council or community council in Wales held by a member of the council
Local government in Scotland	An office of a council constituted under section 2 of the Local Government etc. (Scotland) Act 1994 held by a member of the council
	An office of a council established under section 51 of the Local Government (Scotland) Act 1973 held by a member of the council
Political parties	An office of a registered political party

(3) The reference to a registered political party is a reference to a party registered in the Great Britain register under Part 2 of the Political Parties, Elections and Referendums Act 2000.

Honours etc.

3   A life peerage (within the meaning of the Life Peerages Act 1958), or any other dignity or honour conferred by the Crown, is not a personal or public office.

SCHEDULE 7   Section 80

EQUALITY OF TERMS: EXCEPTIONS

PART 1

TERMS OF WORK

Compliance with laws regulating employment of women, etc.

1   Neither a sex equality clause nor a maternity equality clause has effect in relation to terms of work affected by compliance with laws regulating —
  (a) the employment of women;
  (b) the appointment of women to personal or public offices.

1792

Equality Act 2010 (c. 15)
Schedule 7 — Equality of terms: exceptions
Part 1 — Terms of work

Pregnancy, etc.

2   A sex equality clause does not have effect in relation to terms of work affording special treatment to women in connection with pregnancy or childbirth.

PART 2

OCCUPATIONAL PENSION SCHEMES

Preliminary

3   (1)   A sex equality rule does not have effect in relation to a difference as between men and women in the effect of a relevant matter if the difference is permitted by or by virtue of this Part of this Schedule.

       (2)   "Relevant matter" has the meaning given in section 67.

State retirement pensions

4   (1)   This paragraph applies where a man and a woman are eligible, in such circumstances as may be prescribed, to receive different amounts by way of pension.

       (2)   The difference is permitted if, in prescribed circumstances, it is attributable only to differences between men and women in the retirement benefits to which, in prescribed circumstances, the man and woman are or would be entitled.

       (3)   "Retirement benefits" are benefits under sections 43 to 55 of the Social Security Contributions and Benefits Act 1992 (state retirement pensions).

Actuarial factors

5   (1)   A difference as between men and women is permitted if it consists of applying to the calculation of the employer's contributions to an occupational pension scheme actuarial factors which—

             (a)   differ for men and women, and

             (b)   are of such description as may be prescribed.

       (2)   A difference as between men and women is permitted if it consists of applying to the determination of benefits of such description as may be prescribed actuarial factors which differ for men and women.

Power to amend

6   (1)   Regulations may amend this Part of this Schedule so as to add, vary or omit provision about cases where a difference as between men and women in the effect of a relevant matter is permitted.

       (2)   The regulations may make provision about pensionable service before the date on which they come into force (but not about pensionable service before 17 May 1990).

SCHEDULE 8

Section 83

WORK: REASONABLE ADJUSTMENTS

PART 1

INTRODUCTORY

Preliminary

1   This Schedule applies where a duty to make reasonable adjustments is imposed on A by this Part of this Act.

The duty

2   (1)   A must comply with the first, second and third requirements.

     (2)   For the purposes of this paragraph—
       (a)   the reference in section 20(3) to a provision, criterion or practice is a reference to a provision, criterion or practice applied by or on behalf of A;
       (b)   the reference in section 20(4) to a physical feature is a reference to a physical feature of premises occupied by A;
       (c)   the reference in section 20(3), (4) or (5) to a disabled person is to an interested disabled person.

     (3)   In relation to the first and third requirements, a relevant matter is any matter specified in the first column of the applicable table in Part 2 of this Schedule.

     (4)   In relation to the second requirement, a relevant matter is—
       (a)   a matter specified in the second entry of the first column of the applicable table in Part 2 of this Schedule, or
       (b)   where there is only one entry in a column, a matter specified there.

     (5)   If two or more persons are subject to a duty to make reasonable adjustments in relation to the same interested disabled person, each of them must comply with the duty so far as it is reasonable for each of them to do so.

3   (1)   This paragraph applies if a duty to make reasonable adjustments is imposed on A by section 55 (except where the employment service which A provides is the provision of vocational training within the meaning given by section 56(6)(b)).

     (2)   The reference in section 20(3), (4) and (5) to a disabled person is a reference to an interested disabled person.

     (3)   In relation to each requirement, the relevant matter is the employment service which A provides.

     (4)   Sub-paragraph (5) of paragraph 2 applies for the purposes of this paragraph as it applies for the purposes of that paragraph.

1794

Equality Act 2010 (c. 15)
Schedule 8 — Work: reasonable adjustments
Part 2 — Interested disabled person

PART 2

INTERESTED DISABLED PERSON

Preliminary

4   An interested disabled person is a disabled person who, in relation to a relevant matter, is of a description specified in the second column of the applicable table in this Part of this Schedule.

Employers (see section 39)

5   (1) This paragraph applies where A is an employer.

Relevant matter	*Description of disabled person*
Deciding to whom to offer employment.	A person who is, or has notified A that the person may be, an applicant for the employment.
Employment by A.	An applicant for employment by A.
	An employee of A's.

(2) Where A is the employer of a disabled contract worker (B), A must comply with the first, second and third requirements on each occasion when B is supplied to a principal to do contract work.

(3) In relation to the first requirement (as it applies for the purposes of sub-paragraph (2)) —
  (a) the reference in section 20(3) to a provision, criterion or practice is a reference to a provision, criterion or practice applied by or on behalf of all or most of the principals to whom B is or might be supplied,
  (b) the reference to being put at a substantial disadvantage is a reference to being likely to be put at a substantial disadvantage that is the same or similar in the case of each of the principals referred to in paragraph (a), and
  (c) the requirement imposed on A is a requirement to take such steps as it would be reasonable for A to have to take if the provision, criterion or practice were applied by or on behalf of A.

(4) In relation to the second requirement (as it applies for the purposes of sub-paragraph (2)) —
  (a) the reference in section 20(4) to a physical feature is a reference to a physical feature of premises occupied by each of the principals referred to in sub-paragraph (3)(a),
  (b) the reference to being put at a substantial disadvantage is a reference to being likely to be put at a substantial disadvantage that is the same or similar in the case of each of those principals, and
  (c) the requirement imposed on A is a requirement to take such steps as it would be reasonable for A to have to take if the premises were occupied by A.

Equality Act 2010 (c. 15)
Schedule 8 — Work: reasonable adjustments
Part 2 — Interested disabled person

1795

(5) In relation to the third requirement (as it applies for the purposes of sub-paragraph (2)) —

    (a) the reference in section 20(5) to being put at a substantial disadvantage is a reference to being likely to be put at a substantial disadvantage that is the same or similar in the case of each of the principals referred to in sub-paragraph (3)(a), and

    (b) the requirement imposed on A is a requirement to take such steps as it would be reasonable for A to have to take if A were the person to whom B was supplied.

Principals in contract work (see section 41)

6   (1) This paragraph applies where A is a principal.

Relevant matter	*Description of disabled person*
Contract work that A may make available.	A person who is, or has notified A that the person may be, an applicant to do the work.
Contract work that A makes available.	A person who is supplied to do the work.

(2) A is not required to do anything that a disabled person's employer is required to do by virtue of paragraph 5.

Partnerships (see section 44)

7   (1) This paragraph applies where A is a firm or a proposed firm.

Relevant matter	*Description of disabled person*
Deciding to whom to offer a position as a partner.	A person who is, or has notified A that the person may be, a candidate for the position.
A position as a partner.	A candidate for the position.
	The partner who holds the position.

(2) Where a firm or proposed firm (A) is required by this Schedule to take a step in relation to an interested disabled person (B) —

    (a) the cost of taking the step is to be treated as an expense of A;

    (b) the extent to which B should (if B is or becomes a partner) bear the cost is not to exceed such amount as is reasonable (having regard in particular to B's entitlement to share in A's profits).

LLPs (see section 45)

8   (1) This paragraph applies where A is an LLP or a proposed LLP.

1796

Equality Act 2010 (c. 15)
Schedule 8 — Work: reasonable adjustments
Part 2 — Interested disabled person

Relevant matter	*Description of disabled person*
Deciding to whom to offer a position as a member.	A person who is, or has notified A that the person may be, a candidate for the position.
A position as a member.	A candidate for the position.
	The member who holds the position.

(2) Where an LLP or proposed LLP (A) is required by this Schedule to take a step in relation to an interested disabled person (B) —

    (a) the cost of taking the step is to be treated as an expense of A;

    (b) the extent to which B should (if B is or becomes a member) bear the cost is not to exceed such amount as is reasonable (having regard in particular to B's entitlement to share in A's profits).

Barristers and their clerks (see section 47)

9   This paragraph applies where A is a barrister or barrister's clerk.

Relevant matter	*Description of disabled person*
Deciding to whom to offer a pupillage or tenancy.	A person who is, or has notified A that the person may be, an applicant for the pupillage or tenancy.
A pupillage or tenancy.	An applicant for the pupillage or tenancy.
	The pupil or tenant.

Advocates and their clerks (see section 48)

10   This paragraph applies where A is an advocate or advocate's clerk.

Relevant matter	*Description of disabled person*
Deciding who to offer to take as a devil or to whom to offer membership of a stable.	A person who applies, or has notified A that the person may apply, to be taken as a devil or to become a member of the stable.
The relationship with a devil or membership of a stable.	An applicant to be taken as a devil or to become a member of the stable.
	The devil or member.

Equality Act 2010 (c. 15)
Schedule 8 – Work: reasonable adjustments
Part 2 – Interested disabled person

1797

Persons making appointments to offices etc. (see sections 49 to 51)

11   This paragraph applies where A is a person who has the power to make an appointment to a personal or public office.

Relevant matter	*Description of disabled person*
Deciding to whom to offer the appointment.	A person who is, or has notified A that the person may be, seeking the appointment.
	A person who is being considered for the appointment.
Appointment to the office.	A person who is seeking, or being considered for, appointment to the office.

12   This paragraph applies where A is a relevant person in relation to a personal or public office.

Relevant matter	*Description of disabled person*
Appointment to the office.	A person appointed to the office.

13   This paragraph applies where A is a person who has the power to make a recommendation for, or give approval to, an appointment to a public office.

Relevant matter	*Description of disabled person*
Deciding who to recommend or approve for appointment to the office.	A person who is, or has notified A that the person may be, seeking recommendation or approval for appointment to the office.
	A person who is being considered for recommendation or approval for appointment to the office.
An appointment to the office.	A person who is seeking, or being considered for, appointment to the office in question.

14   In relation to the second requirement in a case within paragraph 11, 12 or 13, the reference in paragraph 2(2)(b) to premises occupied by A is to be read as a reference to premises—
    (a)   under the control of A, and
    (b)   at or from which the functions of the office concerned are performed.

1798
Equality Act 2010 (c. 15)
Schedule 8 – Work: reasonable adjustments
Part 2 – Interested disabled person

Qualifications bodies (see section 53)

15 (1) This paragraph applies where A is a qualifications body.

Relevant matter	Description of disabled person
Deciding upon whom to confer a relevant qualification.	A person who is, or has notified A that the person may be, an applicant for the conferment of the qualification.
Conferment by the body of a relevant qualification.	An applicant for the conferment of the qualification.
	A person who holds the qualification.

(2) A provision, criterion or practice does not include the application of a competence standard.

Employment service-providers (see section 55)

16 This paragraph applies where—

   (a) A is an employment service-provider, and

   (b) the employment service which A provides is vocational training within the meaning given by section 56(6)(b).

Relevant matter	Description of disabled person
Deciding to whom to offer to provide the service.	A person who is, or has notified A that the person may be, an applicant for the provision of the service.
Provision by A of the service.	A person who applies to A for the provision of the service.
	A person to whom A provides the service.

Trade organisations (see section 57)

17 This paragraph applies where A is a trade organisation.

Relevant matter	Description of disabled person
Deciding to whom to offer membership of the organisation.	A person who is, or has notified A that the person may be, an applicant for membership.
Membership of the organisation.	An applicant for membership.
	A member.

Equality Act 2010 (c. 15)
Schedule 8 — Work: reasonable adjustments
Part 2 — Interested disabled person

1799

Local authorities (see section 58)

18   (1) This paragraph applies where A is a local authority.

Relevant matter	Description of disabled person
A member's carrying-out of official business.	The member.

    (2) Regulations may, for the purposes of a case within this paragraph, make provision —

        (a) as to circumstances in which a provision, criterion or practice is, or is not, to be taken to put a disabled person at the disadvantage referred to in the first requirement;

        (b) as to circumstances in which a physical feature is, or is not, to be taken to put a disabled person at the disadvantage referred to in the second requirement;

        (c) as to circumstances in which it is, or in which it is not, reasonable for a local authority to be required to take steps of a prescribed description;

        (d) as to steps which it is always, or which it is never, reasonable for a local authority to take.

Occupational pensions (see section 61)

19   This paragraph applies where A is, in relation to an occupational pension scheme, a responsible person within the meaning of section 61.

Relevant matter	Description of disabled person
Carrying out A's functions in relation to the scheme.	A person who is or may be a member of the scheme.

PART 3

LIMITATIONS ON THE DUTY

Lack of knowledge of disability, etc.

20   (1) A is not subject to a duty to make reasonable adjustments if A does not know, and could not reasonably be expected to know —

        (a) in the case of an applicant or potential applicant, that an interested disabled person is or may be an applicant for the work in question;

        (b) in any other case referred to in this Part of this Schedule, that an interested disabled person has a disability and is likely to be placed at the disadvantage referred to in the first, second or third requirement.

    (2) An applicant is, in relation to the description of A specified in the first column of the table, a person of a description specified in the second column (and the reference to a potential applicant is to be construed accordingly).

1800

Equality Act 2010 (c. 15)
Schedule 8 – Work: reasonable adjustments
Part 3 – Limitations on the duty

Description of A	Applicant
An employer	An applicant for employment
A firm or proposed firm	A candidate for a position as a partner
An LLP or proposed LLP	A candidate for a position as a member
A barrister or barrister's clerk	An applicant for a pupillage or tenancy
An advocate or advocate's clerk	An applicant for being taken as an advocate's devil or for becoming a member of a stable
A relevant person in relation to a personal or public office	A person who is seeking appointment to, or recommendation or approval for appointment to, the office
A qualifications body	An applicant for the conferment of a relevant qualification
An employment service-provider	An applicant for the provision of an employment service
A trade organisation	An applicant for membership

(3) If the duty to make reasonable adjustments is imposed on A by section 55, this paragraph applies only in so far as the employment service which A provides is vocational training within the meaning given by section 56(6)(b).

SCHEDULE 9

Section 83

WORK: EXCEPTIONS

PART 1

OCCUPATIONAL REQUIREMENTS

General

1 (1) A person (A) does not contravene a provision mentioned in sub-paragraph (2) by applying in relation to work a requirement to have a particular protected characteristic, if A shows that, having regard to the nature or context of the work—

    (a) it is an occupational requirement,

    (b) the application of the requirement is a proportionate means of achieving a legitimate aim, and

    (c) the person to whom A applies the requirement does not meet it (or A has reasonable grounds for not being satisfied that the person meets it).

(2) The provisions are—

      (a)   section 39(1)(a) or (c) or (2)(b) or (c);

      (b)   section 41(1)(b);

      (c)   section 44(1)(a) or (c) or (2)(b) or (c);

      (d)   section 45(1)(a) or (c) or (2)(b) or (c);

      (e)   section 49(3)(a) or (c) or (6)(b) or (c);

      (f)   section 50(3)(a) or (c) or (6)(b) or (c);

      (g)   section 51(1).

(3) The references in sub-paragraph (1) to a requirement to have a protected characteristic are to be read—

      (a)   in the case of gender reassignment, as references to a requirement not to be a transsexual person (and section 7(3) is accordingly to be ignored);

      (b)   in the case of marriage and civil partnership, as references to a requirement not to be married or a civil partner (and section 8(2) is accordingly to be ignored).

(4) In the case of a requirement to be of a particular sex, sub-paragraph (1) has effect as if in paragraph (c), the words from "(or" to the end were omitted.

Religious requirements relating to sex, marriage etc., sexual orientation

2   (1) A person (A) does not contravene a provision mentioned in sub-paragraph (2) by applying in relation to employment a requirement to which sub-paragraph (4) applies if A shows that—

      (a)   the employment is for the purposes of an organised religion,

      (b)   the application of the requirement engages the compliance or non-conflict principle, and

      (c)   the person to whom A applies the requirement does not meet it (or A has reasonable grounds for not being satisfied that the person meets it).

(2) The provisions are—

      (a)   section 39(1)(a) or (c) or (2)(b) or (c);

      (b)   section 49(3)(a) or (c) or (6)(b) or (c);

      (c)   section 50(3)(a) or (c) or (6)(b) or (c);

      (d)   section 51(1).

(3) A person does not contravene section 53(1) or (2)(a) or (b) by applying in relation to a relevant qualification (within the meaning of that section) a requirement to which sub-paragraph (4) applies if the person shows that—

      (a)   the qualification is for the purposes of employment mentioned in sub-paragraph (1)(a), and

      (b)   the application of the requirement engages the compliance or non-conflict principle.

(4) This sub-paragraph applies to—

      (a)   a requirement to be of a particular sex;

      (b)   a requirement not to be a transsexual person;

      (c)   a requirement not to be married or a civil partner;

      (d)   a requirement not to be married to, or the civil partner of, a person who has a living former spouse or civil partner;

(e)   a requirement relating to circumstances in which a marriage or civil partnership came to an end;

(f)   a requirement related to sexual orientation.

(5) The application of a requirement engages the compliance principle if the requirement is applied so as to comply with the doctrines of the religion.

(6) The application of a requirement engages the non-conflict principle if, because of the nature or context of the employment, the requirement is applied so as to avoid conflicting with the strongly held religious convictions of a significant number of the religion's followers.

(7) A reference to employment includes a reference to an appointment to a personal or public office.

(8) In the case of a requirement within sub-paragraph (4)(a), sub-paragraph (1) has effect as if in paragraph (c) the words from "(or" to the end were omitted.

Other requirements relating to religion or belief

3   A person (A) with an ethos based on religion or belief does not contravene a provision mentioned in paragraph 1(2) by applying in relation to work a requirement to be of a particular religion or belief if A shows that, having regard to that ethos and to the nature or context of the work—

(a)   it is an occupational requirement,

(b)   the application of the requirement is a proportionate means of achieving a legitimate aim, and

(c)   the person to whom A applies the requirement does not meet it (or A has reasonable grounds for not being satisfied that the person meets it).

Armed forces

4   (1) A person does not contravene section 39(1)(a) or (c) or (2)(b) by applying in relation to service in the armed forces a relevant requirement if the person shows that the application is a proportionate means of ensuring the combat effectiveness of the armed forces.

(2) A relevant requirement is—

(a)   a requirement to be a man;

(b)   a requirement not to be a transsexual person.

(3) This Part of this Act, so far as relating to age or disability, does not apply to service in the armed forces; and section 55, so far as relating to disability, does not apply to work experience in the armed forces.

Employment services

5   (1) A person (A) does not contravene section 55(1) or (2) if A shows that A's treatment of another person relates only to work the offer of which could be refused to that other person in reliance on paragraph 1, 2, 3 or 4.

(2) A person (A) does not contravene section 55(1) or (2) if A shows that A's treatment of another person relates only to training for work of a description mentioned in sub-paragraph (1).

(3) A person (A) does not contravene section 55(1) or (2) if A shows that—

> (a) A acted in reliance on a statement made to A by a person with the power to offer the work in question to the effect that, by virtue of sub-paragraph (1) or (2), A's action would be lawful, and
>
> (b) it was reasonable for A to rely on the statement.

(4) A person commits an offence by knowingly or recklessly making a statement such as is mentioned in sub-paragraph (3)(a) which in a material respect is false or misleading.

(5) A person guilty of an offence under sub-paragraph (4) is liable on summary conviction to a fine not exceeding level 5 on the standard scale.

Interpretation

6 (1) This paragraph applies for the purposes of this Part of this Schedule.

(2) A reference to contravening a provision of this Act is a reference to contravening that provision by virtue of section 13.

(3) A reference to work is a reference to employment, contract work, a position as a partner or as a member of an LLP, or an appointment to a personal or public office.

(4) A reference to a person includes a reference to an organisation.

(5) A reference to section 39(2)(b), 44(2)(b), 45(2)(b), 49(6)(b) or 50(6)(b) is to be read as a reference to that provision with the omission of the words "or for receiving any other benefit, facility or service".

(6) A reference to section 39(2)(c), 44(2)(c), 45(2)(c), 49(6)(c), 50(6)(c), 53(2)(a) or 55(2)(c) (dismissal, etc.) does not include a reference to that provision so far as relating to sex.

(7) The reference to paragraph (b) of section 41(1), so far as relating to sex, is to be read as if that paragraph read—
> "(b) by not allowing the worker to do the work."

PART 2

EXCEPTIONS RELATING TO AGE

Preliminary

7 For the purposes of this Part of this Schedule, a reference to an age contravention is a reference to a contravention of this Part of this Act, so far as relating to age.

Retirement

8 (1) It is not an age contravention to dismiss a relevant worker at or over the age of 65 if the reason for the dismissal is retirement.

(2) Each of the following is a relevant worker—
> (a) an employee within the meaning of section 230(1) of the Employment Rights Act 1996;
>
> (b) a person in Crown employment;
>
> (c) a relevant member of the House of Commons staff;

(d)   a relevant member of the House of Lords staff.

(3)   Retirement is a reason for dismissal only if it is a reason for dismissal by virtue of Part 10 of the Employment Rights Act 1996.

Applicants at or approaching retirement age

9   (1)   A person does not contravene section 39(1)(a) or (c), so far as relating to age, in a case where the other person—

(a)   has attained the age limit, or would have attained it before the end of six months beginning with the date on which the application for the employment had to be made, and

(b)   would, if recruited for the employment, be a relevant worker within the meaning of paragraph 8.

(2)   The age limit is whichever is the greater of—

(a)   the age of 65, and

(b)   the normal retirement age in the case of the employment concerned.

(3)   The reference to the normal retirement age is to be construed in accordance with section 98ZH of the Employment Rights Act 1996.

Benefits based on length of service

10   (1)   It is not an age contravention for a person (A) to put a person (B) at a disadvantage when compared with another (C), in relation to the provision of a benefit, facility or service in so far as the disadvantage is because B has a shorter period of service than C.

(2)   If B's period of service exceeds 5 years, A may rely on sub-paragraph (1) only if A reasonably believes that doing so fulfils a business need.

(3)   A person's period of service is whichever of the following A chooses—

(a)   the period for which the person has been working for A at or above a level (assessed by reference to the demands made on the person) that A reasonably regards as appropriate for the purposes of this paragraph, or

(b)   the period for which the person has been working for A at any level.

(4)   The period for which a person has been working for A must be based on the number of weeks during the whole or part of which the person has worked for A.

(5)   But for that purpose A may, so far as is reasonable, discount—

(a)   periods of absence;

(b)   periods that A reasonably regards as related to periods of absence.

(6)   For the purposes of sub-paragraph (3)(b), a person is to be treated as having worked for A during any period in which the person worked for a person other than A if—

(a)   that period counts as a period of employment with A as a result of section 218 of the Employment Rights Act 1996, or

(b)   if sub-paragraph (a) does not apply, that period is treated as a period of employment by an enactment pursuant to which the person's employment was transferred to A.

(7) For the purposes of this paragraph, the reference to a benefit, facility or service does not include a reference to a benefit, facility or service which may be provided only by virtue of a person's ceasing to work.

The national minimum wage: young workers

11 (1) It is not an age contravention for a person to pay a young worker (A) at a lower rate than that at which the person pays an older worker (B) if—

    (a) the hourly rate for the national minimum wage for a person of A's age is lower than that for a person of B's age, and

    (b) the rate at which A is paid is below the single hourly rate.

(2) A young worker is a person who qualifies for the national minimum wage at a lower rate than the single hourly rate; and an older worker is a person who qualifies for the national minimum wage at a higher rate than that at which the young worker qualifies for it.

(3) The single hourly rate is the rate prescribed under section 1(3) of the National Minimum Wage Act 1998.

The national minimum wage: apprentices

12 (1) It is not an age contravention for a person to pay an apprentice who does not qualify for the national minimum wage at a lower rate than the person pays an apprentice who does.

(2) An apprentice is a person who—

    (a) is employed under a contract of apprenticeship, or

    (b) as a result of provision made by virtue of section 3(2)(a) of the National Minimum Wage Act 1998 (persons not qualifying), is treated as employed under a contract of apprenticeship.

Redundancy

13 (1) It is not an age contravention for a person to give a qualifying employee an enhanced redundancy payment of an amount less than that of an enhanced redundancy payment which the person gives to another qualifying employee, if each amount is calculated on the same basis.

(2) It is not an age contravention to give enhanced redundancy payments only to those who are qualifying employees by virtue of sub-paragraph (3)(a) or (b).

(3) A person is a qualifying employee if the person—

    (a) is entitled to a redundancy payment as a result of section 135 of the Employment Rights Act 1996,

    (b) agrees to the termination of the employment in circumstances where the person would, if dismissed, have been so entitled,

    (c) would have been so entitled but for section 155 of that Act (requirement for two years' continuous employment), or

    (d) agrees to the termination of the employment in circumstances where the person would, if dismissed, have been so entitled but for that section.

(4) An enhanced redundancy payment is a payment the amount of which is, subject to sub-paragraphs (5) and (6), calculated in accordance with section 162(1) to (3) of the Employment Rights Act 1996.

(5) A person making a calculation for the purposes of sub-paragraph (4) –

    (a) may treat a week's pay as not being subject to a maximum amount;

    (b) may treat a week's pay as being subject to a maximum amount above that for the time being specified in section 227(1) of the Employment Rights Act 1996;

    (c) may multiply the appropriate amount for each year of employment by a figure of more than one.

(6) Having made a calculation for the purposes of sub-paragraph (4) (whether or not in reliance on sub-paragraph (5)), a person may multiply the amount calculated by a figure of more than one.

(7) In sub-paragraph (5), "the appropriate amount" has the meaning given in section 162 of the Employment Rights Act 1996, and "a week's pay" is to be read with Chapter 2 of Part 14 of that Act.

(8) For the purposes of sub-paragraphs (4) to (6), the reference to "the relevant date" in subsection (1)(a) of section 162 of that Act is, in the case of a person who is a qualifying employee by virtue of sub-paragraph (3)(b) or (d), to be read as reference to the date of the termination of the employment.

Life assurance

14 (1) This paragraph applies if a person (A) takes early retirement because of ill health.

(2) It is not an age contravention to provide A with life assurance cover for the period starting when A retires and ending –

    (a) if there is a normal retirement age, when A attains the normal retirement age;

    (b) in any other case, when A attains the age of 65.

(3) The normal retirement age in relation to A is the age at which, when A retires, persons holding comparable positions in the same undertaking are normally required to retire.

Child care

15 (1) A person does not contravene a relevant provision, so far as relating to age, only by providing, or making arrangements for or facilitating the provision of, care for children of a particular age group.

(2) The relevant provisions are –

    (a) section 39(2)(b);

    (b) section 41(1)(c);

    (c) section 44(2)(b);

    (d) section 45(2)(b);

    (e) section 47(2)(b);

    (f) section 48(2)(b);

    (g) section 49(6)(b);

    (h) section 50(6)(b);

      (i)   section 57(2)(a);

      (j)   section 58(3)(a).

(3) Facilitating the provision of care for a child includes —

      (a)   paying for some or all of the cost of the provision;

      (b)   helping a parent of the child to find a suitable person to provide care for the child;

      (c)   enabling a parent of the child to spend more time providing care for the child or otherwise assisting the parent with respect to the care that the parent provides for the child.

(4) A child is a person who has not attained the age of 17.

(5) A reference to care includes a reference to supervision.

Contributions to personal pension schemes

16 (1) A Minister of the Crown may by order provide that it is not an age contravention for an employer to maintain or use, with respect to contributions to personal pension schemes, practices, actions or decisions relating to age which are of a specified description.

    (2) An order authorising the use of practices, actions or decisions which are not in use before the order comes into force must not be made unless the Minister consults such persons as the Minister thinks appropriate.

    (3) "Personal pension scheme" has the meaning given in section 1 of the Pension Schemes Act 1993; and "employer", in relation to a personal pension scheme, has the meaning given in section 318(1) of the Pensions Act 2004.

PART 3

OTHER EXCEPTIONS

Non-contractual payments to women on maternity leave

17 (1) A person does not contravene section 39(1)(b) or (2), so far as relating to pregnancy and maternity, by depriving a woman who is on maternity leave of any benefit from the terms of her employment relating to pay.

    (2) The reference in sub-paragraph (1) to benefit from the terms of a woman's employment relating to pay does not include a reference to —

      (a)   maternity-related pay (including maternity-related pay that is increase-related),

      (b)   pay (including increase-related pay) in respect of times when she is not on maternity leave, or

      (c)   pay by way of bonus in respect of times when she is on compulsory maternity leave.

    (3) For the purposes of sub-paragraph (2), pay is increase-related in so far as it is to be calculated by reference to increases in pay that the woman would have received had she not been on maternity leave.

    (4) A reference to terms of her employment is a reference to terms of her employment that are not in her contract of employment, her contract of apprenticeship or her contract to do work personally.

(5) "Pay" means benefits —

  (a) that consist of the payment of money to an employee by way of wages or salary, and

  (b) that are not benefits whose provision is regulated by the contract referred to in sub-paragraph (4).

(6) "Maternity-related pay" means pay to which a woman is entitled —

  (a) as a result of being pregnant, or

  (b) in respect of times when she is on maternity leave.

Benefits dependent on marital status, etc.

18 (1) A person does not contravene this Part of this Act, so far as relating to sexual orientation, by doing anything which prevents or restricts a person who is not married from having access to a benefit, facility or service —

  (a) the right to which accrued before 5 December 2005 (the day on which section 1 of the Civil Partnership Act 2004 came into force), or

  (b) which is payable in respect of periods of service before that date.

(2) A person does not contravene this Part of this Act, so far as relating to sexual orientation, by providing married persons and civil partners (to the exclusion of all other persons) with access to a benefit, facility or service.

Provision of services etc. to the public

19 (1) A does not contravene a provision mentioned in sub-paragraph (2) in relation to the provision of a benefit, facility or service to B if A is concerned with the provision (for payment or not) of a benefit, facility or service of the same description to the public.

(2) The provisions are —

  (a) section 39(2) and (4);

  (b) section 41(1) and (3);

  (c) sections 44(2) and (6) and 45(2) and (6);

  (d) sections 49(6) and (8) and 50(6), (7), (9) and (10).

(3) Sub-paragraph (1) does not apply if —

  (a) the provision by A to the public differs in a material respect from the provision by A to comparable persons,

  (b) the provision to B is regulated by B's terms, or

  (c) the benefit, facility or service relates to training.

(4) "Comparable persons" means —

  (a) in relation to section 39(2) or (4), the other employees;

  (b) in relation to section 41(1) or (3), the other contract workers supplied to the principal;

  (c) in relation to section 44(2) or (6), the other partners of the firm;

  (d) in relation to section 45(2) or (6), the other members of the LLP;

  (e) in relation to section 49(6) or (8) or 50(6), (7), (9) or (10), persons holding offices or posts not materially different from that held by B.

(5) "B's terms" means —

  (a) the terms of B's employment,

  (b) the terms on which the principal allows B to do the contract work,

      (c)   the terms on which B has the position as a partner or member, or

      (d)   the terms of B's appointment to the office.

  (6) A reference to the public includes a reference to a section of the public which includes B.

Insurance contracts, etc.

20 (1) It is not a contravention of this Part of this Act, so far as relating to relevant discrimination, to do anything in relation to an annuity, life insurance policy, accident insurance policy or similar matter involving the assessment of risk if —

      (a)   that thing is done by reference to actuarial or other data from a source on which it is reasonable to rely, and

      (b)   it is reasonable to do it.

  (2) "Relevant discrimination" is —

      (a)   gender reassignment discrimination;

      (b)   marriage and civil partnership discrimination;

      (c)   pregnancy and maternity discrimination;

      (d)   sex discrimination.

SCHEDULE 10   Section 88

ACCESSIBILITY FOR DISABLED PUPILS

Accessibility strategies

1 (1) A local authority in England and Wales must, in relation to schools for which it is the responsible body, prepare —

      (a)   an accessibility strategy;

      (b)   further such strategies at such times as may be prescribed.

  (2) An accessibility strategy is a strategy for, over a prescribed period —

      (a)   increasing the extent to which disabled pupils can participate in the schools' curriculums;

      (b)   improving the physical environment of the schools for the purpose of increasing the extent to which disabled pupils are able to take advantage of education and benefits, facilities or services provided or offered by the schools;

      (c)   improving the delivery to disabled pupils of information which is readily accessible to pupils who are not disabled.

  (3) The delivery in sub-paragraph (2)(c) must be —

      (a)   within a reasonable time;

      (b)   in ways which are determined after taking account of the pupils' disabilities and any preferences expressed by them or their parents.

  (4) An accessibility strategy must be in writing.

  (5) A local authority must keep its accessibility strategy under review during the period to which it relates and, if necessary, revise it.

(6) A local authority must implement its accessibility strategy.

2 (1) In preparing its accessibility strategy, a local authority must have regard to—

    (a) the need to allocate adequate resources for implementing the strategy;

    (b) guidance as to the matters mentioned in sub-paragraph (3).

(2) The authority must also have regard to guidance as to compliance with paragraph 1(5).

(3) The matters are—

    (a) the content of an accessibility strategy;

    (b) the form in which it is to be produced;

    (c) persons to be consulted in its preparation.

(4) Guidance may be issued—

    (a) for England, by a Minister of the Crown;

    (b) for Wales, by the Welsh Ministers.

(5) A local authority must, if asked, make a copy of its accessibility strategy available for inspection at such reasonable times as it decides.

(6) A local authority in England must, if asked by a Minister of the Crown, give the Minister a copy of its accessibility strategy.

(7) A local authority in Wales must, if asked by the Welsh Ministers, give them a copy of its accessibility strategy.

Accessibility plans

3 (1) The responsible body of a school in England and Wales must prepare—

    (a) an accessibility plan;

    (b) further such plans at such times as may be prescribed.

(2) An accessibility plan is a plan for, over a prescribed period—

    (a) increasing the extent to which disabled pupils can participate in the school's curriculum,

    (b) improving the physical environment of the school for the purpose of increasing the extent to which disabled pupils are able to take advantage of education and benefits, facilities or services provided or offered by the school, and

    (c) improving the delivery to disabled pupils of information which is readily accessible to pupils who are not disabled.

(3) The delivery in sub-paragraph (2)(c) must be—

    (a) within a reasonable time;

    (b) in ways which are determined after taking account of the pupils' disabilities and any preferences expressed by them or their parents.

(4) An accessibility plan must be in writing.

(5) The responsible body must keep its accessibility plan under review during the period to which it relates and, if necessary, revise it.

(6) The responsible body must implement its accessibility plan.

(7) A relevant inspection may extend to the performance by the responsible body of its functions in relation to the preparation, publication, review, revision and implementation of its accessibility plan.

(8) A relevant inspection is an inspection under —

    (a) Part 1 of the Education Act 2005, or

    (b) Chapter 1 of Part 4 of the Education and Skills Act 2008 (regulation and inspection of independent education provision in England).

4   (1) In preparing an accessibility plan, the responsible body must have regard to the need to allocate adequate resources for implementing the plan.

    (2) The proprietor of an independent educational institution (other than an Academy) must, if asked, make a copy of the school's accessibility plan available for inspection at such reasonable times as the proprietor decides.

    (3) The proprietor of an independent educational institution in England (other than an Academy) must, if asked by a Minister of the Crown, give the Minister a copy of the school's accessibility plan.

    (4) The proprietor of an independent school in Wales (other than an Academy) must, if asked by the Welsh Ministers, give them a copy of the school's accessibility plan.

Power of direction

5   (1) This sub-paragraph applies if the appropriate authority is satisfied (whether or not on a complaint) that a responsible body —

    (a) has acted or is proposing to act unreasonably in the discharge of a duty under this Schedule, or

    (b) has failed to discharge such a duty.

    (2) This sub-paragraph applies if the appropriate authority is satisfied (whether or not on a complaint) that a responsible body of a school specified in sub-paragraph (3) —

    (a) has acted or is proposing to act unreasonably in the discharge of a duty the body has in relation to the provision to the authority of copies of the body's accessibility plan or the inspection of that plan, or

    (b) has failed to discharge the duty.

    (3) The schools are —

    (a) schools approved under section 342 of the Education Act 1996 (non-maintained special schools);

    (b) Academies.

    (4) This sub-paragraph applies if a Tribunal has made an order under paragraph 5 of Schedule 17 and the appropriate authority is satisfied (whether or not on a complaint) that the responsible body concerned —

    (a) has acted or is proposing to act unreasonably in complying with the order, or

    (b) has failed to comply with the order.

    (5) If sub-paragraph (1), (2) or (4) applies, the appropriate authority may give a responsible body such directions as the authority thinks expedient as to —

    (a) the discharge by the body of the duty, or

    (b)   compliance by the body with the order.

(6) A direction may be given in relation to sub-paragraph (1) or (2) even if the performance of the duty is contingent on the opinion of the responsible body.

(7) A direction may not, unless sub-paragraph (8) applies, be given to the responsible body of a school in England in respect of a matter —

    (a)   that has been complained about to a Local Commissioner in accordance with Chapter 2 of Part 10 of the Apprenticeships, Skills, Children and Learning Act 2009 (parental complaints against governing bodies etc.), or

    (b)   that the appropriate authority thinks could have been so complained about.

(8) This sub-paragraph applies if —

    (a)   the Local Commissioner has made a recommendation to the responsible body under section 211(4) of the Apprenticeships, Skills, Children and Learning Act 2009 (statement following investigation) in respect of the matter, and

    (b)   the responsible body has not complied with the recommendation.

(9) A direction —

    (a)   may be varied or revoked by the appropriate authority;

    (b)   may be enforced, on the application of the appropriate authority, by a mandatory order obtained in accordance with section 31 of the Senior Courts Act 1981.

(10) The appropriate authority is —

    (a)   in relation to the responsible body of a school in England, the Secretary of State;

    (b)   in relation to the responsible body of a school in Wales, the Welsh Ministers.

Supplementary

6   (1) This paragraph applies for the purposes of this Schedule.

(2) Regulations may prescribe services which are, or are not, to be regarded as being —

    (a)   education;

    (b)   a benefit, facility or service.

(3) The power to make regulations is exercisable by —

    (a)   in relation to England, a Minister of the Crown;

    (b)   in relation to Wales, the Welsh Ministers.

(4) "Disabled pupil" includes a disabled person who may be admitted to the school as a pupil.

(5) "Responsible body" means —

    (a)   in relation to a maintained school or a maintained nursery school, the local authority or governing body;

    (b)   in relation to a pupil referral unit, the local authority;

    (c)   in relation to an independent educational institution, the proprietor;

(d) in relation to a special school not maintained by a local authority, the proprietor.

(6) "Governing body", in relation to a maintained school, means the body corporate (constituted in accordance with regulations under section 19 of the Education Act 2002) which the school has as a result of that section.

(7) "Maintained school" has the meaning given in section 20 of the School Standards and Framework Act 1998; and "maintained nursery school" has the meaning given in section 22 of that Act.

SCHEDULE 11   Section 89

SCHOOLS: EXCEPTIONS

PART 1

SEX DISCRIMINATION

Admission to single-sex schools

1   (1) Section 85(1), so far as relating to sex, does not apply in relation to a single-sex school.

(2) A single-sex school is a school which—
   (a) admits pupils of one sex only, or
   (b) on the basis of the assumption in sub-paragraph (3), would be taken to admit pupils of one sex only.

(3) That assumption is that pupils of the opposite sex are to be disregarded if—
   (a) their admission to the school is exceptional, or
   (b) their numbers are comparatively small and their admission is confined to particular courses or classes.

(4) In the case of a school which is a single-sex school by virtue of sub-paragraph (3)(b), section 85(2)(a) to (d), so far as relating to sex, does not prohibit confining pupils of the same sex to particular courses or classes.

Single-sex boarding at schools

2   (1) Section 85(1), so far as relating to sex, does not apply in relation to admission as a boarder to a school to which this paragraph applies.

(2) Section 85(2)(a) to (d), so far as relating to sex, does not apply in relation to boarding facilities at a school to which this paragraph applies.

(3) This paragraph applies to a school (other than a single-sex school) which has some pupils as boarders and others as non-boarders and which—
   (a) admits as boarders pupils of one sex only, or
   (b) on the basis of the assumption in sub-paragraph (4), would be taken to admit as boarders pupils of one sex only.

(4) That assumption is that pupils of the opposite sex admitted as boarders are to be disregarded if their numbers are small compared to the numbers of other pupils admitted as boarders.

Single-sex schools turning co-educational

3   (1) If the responsible body of a single-sex school decides to alter its admissions arrangements so that the school will cease to be a single-sex school, the body may apply for a transitional exemption order in relation to the school.

      (2) If the responsible body of a school to which paragraph 2 applies decides to alter its admissions arrangements so that the school will cease to be one to which that paragraph applies, the body may apply for a transitional exemption order in relation to the school.

      (3) A transitional exemption order in relation to a school is an order which, during the period specified in the order as the transitional period, authorises —

          (a) sex discrimination by the responsible body of the school in the arrangements it makes for deciding who is offered admission as a pupil;

          (b) the responsible body, in the circumstances specified in the order, not to admit a person as a pupil because of the person's sex.

      (4) Paragraph 4 applies in relation to the making of transitional exemption orders.

      (5) The responsible body of a school does not contravene this Act, so far as relating to sex discrimination, if —

          (a) in accordance with a transitional exemption order, or

          (b) pending the determination of an application for a transitional exemption order in relation to the school,

      it does not admit a person as a pupil because of the person's sex.

4   (1) In the case of a maintained school within the meaning given by section 32 of the Education and Inspections Act 2006, a transitional exemption order may be made in accordance with such provision as is made in regulations under section 21 of that Act (orders made by local authority or adjudicator in relation to schools in England).

      (2) In the case of a school in Wales maintained by a local authority, a transitional exemption order may be made in accordance with paragraph 22 of Schedule 6, or paragraph 17 of Schedule 7, to the School Standards and Framework Act 1998 (orders made by Welsh Ministers).

      (3) In the case of a school in Scotland managed by an education authority or in respect of which the managers are for the time being receiving grants under section 73(c) or (d) of the Education (Scotland) Act 1980 —

          (a) the responsible body may submit to the Scottish Ministers an application for the making of a transitional exemption order, and

          (b) the Scottish Ministers may make the order.

      (4) Where, under section 113A of the Learning and Skills Act 2000, the Learning and Skills Council for England make proposals to the Secretary of State for an alteration in the admissions arrangements of a single-sex school or a school to which paragraph 2 applies —

          (a) the making of the proposals is to be treated as an application to the Secretary of State for the making of a transitional exemption order, and

          (b) the Secretary of State may make the order.

(5) Where proposals are made to the Welsh Ministers under section 113A of the Learning and Skills Act 2000 for an alteration in the admissions arrangements of a single-sex school or a school to which paragraph 2 applies—

    (a) the making of the proposals is to be treated as an application to the Welsh Ministers for the making of a transitional exemption order, and

    (b) the Welsh Ministers may make the order.

(6) In the case of a school in England or Wales not coming within sub-paragraph (1), (2), (4) or (5) or an independent school in Scotland—

    (a) the responsible body may submit to the Commission an application for the making of a transitional exemption order, and

    (b) the Commission may make the order.

(7) An application under sub-paragraph (6) must specify—

    (a) the period proposed by the responsible body as the transitional period to be specified in the order,

    (b) the stages within that period by which the body proposes to move to the position where section 85(1)(a) and (c), so far as relating to sex, is complied with, and

    (c) any other matters relevant to the terms and operation of the order applied for.

(8) The Commission must not make an order on an application under sub-paragraph (6) unless satisfied that the terms of the application are reasonable, having regard to—

    (a) the nature of the school's premises,

    (b) the accommodation, equipment and facilities available, and

    (c) the responsible body's financial resources.

PART 2

RELIGIOUS OR BELIEF-RELATED DISCRIMINATION

School with religious character etc.

5   Section 85(1) and (2)(a) to (d), so far as relating to religion or belief, does not apply in relation to—

    (a) a school designated under section 69(3) of the School Standards and Framework Act 1998 (foundation or voluntary school with religious character);

    (b) a school listed in the register of independent schools for England or for Wales, if the school's entry in the register records that the school has a religious ethos;

    (c) a school transferred to an education authority under section 16 of the Education (Scotland) Act 1980 (transfer of certain schools to education authorities) which is conducted in the interest of a church or denominational body;

    (d) a school provided by an education authority under section 17(2) of that Act (denominational schools);

    (e) a grant-aided school (within the meaning of that Act) which is conducted in the interest of a church or denominational body;

(f) a school registered in the register of independent schools for Scotland if the school admits only pupils who belong, or whose parents belong, to one or more particular denominations;

(g) a school registered in that register if the school is conducted in the interest of a church or denominational body.

Curriculum, worship, etc.

6   Section 85(2)(a) to (d), so far as relating to religion or belief, does not apply in relation to anything done in connection with acts of worship or other religious observance organised by or on behalf of a school (whether or not forming part of the curriculum).

Power to amend

7   (1) A Minister of the Crown may by order amend this Part of this Schedule—

(a) so as to add, vary or omit an exception to section 85;

(b) so as to make provision about the construction or application of section 19(2)(d) in relation to section 85.

(2) The power under sub-paragraph (1) is exercisable only in relation to religious or belief-related discrimination.

(3) Before making an order under this paragraph the Minister must consult—

(a) the Welsh Ministers,

(b) the Scottish Ministers, and

(c) such other persons as the Minister thinks appropriate.

PART 3

DISABILITY DISCRIMINATION

Permitted form of selection

8   (1) A person does not contravene section 85(1), so far as relating to disability, only by applying a permitted form of selection.

(2) In relation to England and Wales, a permitted form of selection is—

(a) in the case of a maintained school which is not designated as a grammar school under section 104 of the School Standards and Framework Act 1998, a form of selection mentioned in section 99(2) or (4) of that Act;

(b) in the case of a maintained school which is so designated, its selective admission arrangements (within the meaning of section 104 of that Act);

(c) in the case of an independent educational institution, arrangements which provide for some or all of its pupils to be selected by reference to general or special ability or aptitude, with a view to admitting only pupils of high ability or aptitude.

(3) In relation to Scotland, a permitted form of selection is—

(a) in the case of a school managed by an education authority, arrangements approved by the Scottish Ministers for the selection of pupils for admission;

(b) in the case of an independent school, arrangements which provide for some or all of its pupils to be selected by reference to general or special ability or aptitude, with a view to admitting only pupils of high ability or aptitude.

(4) "Maintained school" has the meaning given in section 22 of the School Standards and Framework Act 1998.

SCHEDULE 12   Section 94

FURTHER AND HIGHER EDUCATION EXCEPTIONS

PART 1

SINGLE-SEX INSTITUTIONS, ETC.

Admission to single-sex institutions

1   (1) Section 91(1), so far as relating to sex, does not apply in relation to a single-sex institution.

(2) A single-sex institution is an institution to which section 91 applies, which—
     (a) admits students of one sex only, or
     (b) on the basis of the assumption in sub-paragraph (3), would be taken to admit students of one sex only.

(3) That assumption is that students of the opposite sex are to be disregarded if—
     (a) their admission to the institution is exceptional, or
     (b) their numbers are comparatively small and their admission is confined to particular courses or classes.

(4) In the case of an institution which is a single-sex institution by virtue of sub-paragraph (3)(b), section 91(2)(a) to (d), so far as relating to sex, does not prohibit confining students of the same sex to particular courses or classes.

Single-sex institutions turning co-educational

2   (1) If the responsible body of a single-sex institution decides to alter its admissions arrangements so that the institution will cease to be a single-sex institution, the body may apply for a transitional exemption order in relation to the institution.

(2) A transitional exemption order relating to an institution is an order which, during the period specified in the order as the transitional period, authorises—
     (a) sex discrimination by the responsible body of the institution in the arrangements it makes for deciding who is offered admission as a student;
     (b) the responsible body, in the circumstances specified in the order, not to admit a person as a student because of the person's sex.

(3) Paragraph 3 applies in relation to the making of a transitional exemption order.

1818

Equality Act 2010 (c. 15)
Schedule 12 — Further and higher education exceptions
Part 1 — Single-sex institutions, etc.

(4) The responsible body of an institution does not contravene this Act, so far as relating to sex discrimination, if —

    (a) in accordance with a transitional exemption order, or

    (b) pending the determination of an application for a transitional exemption order in relation to the institution,

it does not admit a person as a student because of the person's sex.

(5) The responsible body of an institution does not contravene this Act, so far as relating to sex discrimination, if —

    (a) in accordance with a transitional exemption order, or

    (b) pending the determination of an application for a transitional exemption order in relation to the institution,

it discriminates in the arrangements it makes for deciding who is offered admission as a student.

3   (1) In the case of a single-sex institution —

    (a) its responsible body may submit to the Commission an application for the making of a transitional exemption order, and

    (b) the Commission may make the order.

(2) An application under sub-paragraph (1) must specify —

    (a) the period proposed by the responsible body as the transitional period to be specified in the order,

    (b) the stages, within that period, by which the body proposes to move to the position where section 91(1)(a) and (c), so far as relating to sex, is complied with, and

    (c) any other matters relevant to the terms and operation of the order applied for.

(3) The Commission must not make an order on an application under sub-paragraph (1) unless satisfied that the terms of the application are reasonable, having regard to —

    (a) the nature of the institution's premises,

    (b) the accommodation, equipment and facilities available, and

    (c) the responsible body's financial resources.

PART 2

OTHER EXCEPTIONS

Occupational requirements

4   A person (P) does not contravene section 91(1) or (2) if P shows that P's treatment of another person relates only to training that would help fit that other person for work the offer of which the other person could be refused in reliance on Part 1 of Schedule 9.

Institutions with a religious ethos

5   (1) The responsible body of an institution which is designated for the purposes of this paragraph does not contravene section 91(1), so far as relating to religion or belief, if, in the admission of students to a course at the institution —

    (a) it gives preference to persons of a particular religion or belief,

> (b) it does so to preserve the institution's religious ethos, and
>
> (c) the course is not a course of vocational training.

(2) A Minister of the Crown may by order designate an institution if satisfied that the institution has a religious ethos.

Benefits dependent on marital status, etc.

6   A person does not contravene section 91, so far as relating to sexual orientation, by providing married persons and civil partners (to the exclusion of all other persons) with access to a benefit, facility or service.

Child care

7   (1) A person does not contravene section 91(2)(b) or (d), so far as relating to age, only by providing, or making arrangements for or facilitating the provision of, care for children of a particular age group.

(2) Facilitating the provision of care for a child includes—

> (a) paying for some or all of the cost of the provision;
>
> (b) helping a parent of the child to find a suitable person to provide care for the child;
>
> (c) enabling a parent of the child to spend more time providing care for the child or otherwise assisting the parent with respect to the care that the parent provides for the child.

(3) A child is a person who has not attained the age of 17.

(4) A reference to care includes a reference to supervision.

SCHEDULE 13

Section 98

EDUCATION: REASONABLE ADJUSTMENTS

Preliminary

1   This Schedule applies where a duty to make reasonable adjustments is imposed on A by this Part.

The duty for schools

2   (1) This paragraph applies where A is the responsible body of a school to which section 85 applies.

(2) A must comply with the first and third requirements.

(3) For the purposes of this paragraph—

> (a) the reference in section 20(3) to a provision, criterion or practice is a reference to a provision, criterion or practice applied by or on behalf of A;
>
> (b) the reference in section 20(3) or (5) to a disabled person is—
>
> > (i) in relation to a relevant matter within sub-paragraph (4)(a), a reference to disabled persons generally;

> > (ii) in relation to a relevant matter within sub-paragraph (4)(b), a reference to disabled pupils generally.

> (4) In relation to each requirement, the relevant matters are—
> > (a) deciding who is offered admission as a pupil;
> > (b) provision of education or access to a benefit, facility or service.

The duty for further or higher education institutions

3 (1) This paragraph applies where A is the responsible body of an institution to which section 91 applies.

> (2) A must comply with the first, second and third requirements.

> (3) For the purposes of this paragraph—
> > (a) the reference in section 20(3) to a provision, criterion or practice is a reference to a provision, criterion or practice applied by or on behalf of A;
> > (b) the reference in section 20(4) to a physical feature is a reference to a physical feature of premises occupied by A;
> > (c) the reference in section 20(3), (4) or (5) to a disabled person is—
> > > (i) in relation to a relevant matter within sub-paragraph (4)(a), a reference to disabled persons generally;
> > > (ii) in relation to a relevant matter within sub-paragraph (4)(b) or (c), a reference to disabled students generally;
> > > (iii) in relation to a relevant matter within sub-paragraph (4)(d) or (e) below, a reference to an interested disabled person.

> (4) In relation to each requirement, the relevant matters are—
> > (a) deciding who is offered admission as a student;
> > (b) provision of education;
> > (c) access to a benefit, facility or service;
> > (d) deciding on whom a qualification is conferred;
> > (e) a qualification that A confers.

4 (1) An interested disabled person is a disabled person who, in relation to a relevant matter specified in the first column of the table, is of a description specified in the second column.

Case	*Description of disabled person*
Deciding upon whom to confer a qualification.	A person who is, or has notified A that the person may be, an applicant for the conferment of the qualification.
A qualification that A confers.	An applicant for the conferment by A of the qualification.
	A person on whom A confers the qualification.

> (2) A provision, criterion or practice does not include the application of a competence standard.

(3) A competence standard is an academic, medical or other standard applied for the purpose of determining whether or not a person has a particular level of competence or ability.

The duty relating to certain other further or higher education courses

5   (1) This paragraph applies where A is the responsible body in relation to a course to which section 92 applies.

(2) A must comply with the first, second and third requirements; but if A is the governing body of a maintained school (within the meaning given by that section), A is not required to comply with the second requirement.

(3) For the purposes of this paragraph —
    (a) the reference in section 20(3) to a provision, criterion or practice is a reference to a provision, criterion or practice applied by or on behalf of A;
    (b) the reference in section 20(4) to a physical feature is a reference to a physical feature of premises occupied by A;
    (c) the reference in section 20(3), (4) or (5) to a disabled person is —
        (i) in relation to a relevant matter within sub-paragraph (4)(a), a reference to disabled persons generally;
        (ii) in relation to a relevant matter within sub-paragraph (4)(b), a reference to disabled persons generally who are enrolled on the course.

(4) In relation to each requirement, the relevant matters are —
    (a) arrangements for enrolling persons on a course of further or higher education secured by A;
    (b) services provided by A for persons enrolled on the course.

The duty relating to recreational or training facilities

6   (1) This paragraph applies where A is the responsible body in relation to facilities to which section 93 applies.

(2) A must comply with the first, second and third requirements.

(3) For the purposes of this paragraph —
    (a) the reference in section 20(3) to a provision, criterion or practice is a reference to a provision, criterion or practice applied by or on behalf of A;
    (b) the reference in section 20(4) to a physical feature is a reference to a physical feature of premises occupied by A;
    (c) the reference in section 20(3), (4) or (5) to a disabled person is a reference to disabled persons generally.

(4) In relation to each requirement, the relevant matter is A's arrangements for providing the recreational or training facilities.

Code of practice

7   In deciding whether it is reasonable for A to have to take a step for the purpose of complying with the first, second or third requirement, A must

have regard to relevant provisions of a code of practice issued under section 14 of the Equality Act 2006.

Confidentiality requests

8   (1) This paragraph applies if a person has made a confidentiality request of which A is aware.

     (2) In deciding whether it is reasonable for A to have to take a step in relation to that person so as to comply with the first, second or third requirement, A must have regard to the extent to which taking the step is consistent with the request.

     (3) In a case within paragraph 2, a "confidentiality request" is a request —
          (a) that the nature or existence of a disabled person's disability be treated as confidential, and
          (b) which satisfies either of the following conditions.

     (4) The first condition is that the request is made by the person's parent.

     (5) The second condition is that —
          (a) it is made by the person, and
          (b) A reasonably believes that the person has sufficient understanding of the nature and effect of the request.

     (6) In a case within paragraph 3, a "confidentiality request" is a request by a disabled person that the nature or existence of the person's disability be treated as confidential.

The duty for general qualifications bodies

9   (1) This paragraph applies where A is a qualifications body for the purposes of section 96.

     (2) Paragraphs 3 and 4(1), so far as relating to qualifications, apply to a qualifications body as they apply to a responsible body.

     (3) This paragraph is subject to section 96(7).

SCHEDULE 14   Section 99

EDUCATIONAL CHARITIES AND ENDOWMENTS

Educational charities

1   (1) This paragraph applies to a trust deed or other instrument —
          (a) which concerns property applicable for or in connection with the provision of education in an establishment in England and Wales to which section 85 or 91 applies, and
          (b) which in any way restricts the benefits available under the instrument to persons of one sex.

     (2) Sub-paragraph (3) applies if, on the application of the trustees or the responsible body (within the meaning of that section), a Minister of the

Crown is satisfied that the removal or modification of the restriction would be conducive to the advancement of education without sex discrimination.

(3) The Minister may by order make such modifications of the instrument as appear to the Minister expedient for removing or modifying the restriction.

(4) If the trust was created by a gift or bequest, an order must not be made until the end of the period of 25 years after the date when the gift or bequest took effect.

(5) Sub-paragraph (4) does not apply if the donor or the personal representatives of the donor or testator consent in writing to making the application for the order.

(6) The Minister must require the applicant to publish a notice —
   (a) containing particulars of the proposed order;
   (b) stating that representations may be made to the Minister within a period specified in the notice.

(7) The period must be not less than one month beginning with the day after the date of the notice.

(8) The applicant must publish the notice in the manner specified by the Minister.

(9) The cost of publication may be paid out of the property of the trust.

(10) Before making the order, the Minister must take account of representations made in accordance with the notice.

Educational endowments

2   (1) This paragraph applies to an educational endowment —
   (a) to which section 104 of the Education (Scotland) Act 1980 applies, and
   (b) which in any way restricts the benefit of the endowment to persons of one sex.

(2) Sub-paragraph (3) applies if, on the application of the governing body of an educational endowment, the Scottish Ministers are satisfied that the removal or modification of the provision which restricts the benefit of the endowment to persons of one sex would be conducive to the advancement of education without sex discrimination.

(3) The Scottish Ministers may by order make such provision as they think expedient for removing or modifying the restriction.

(4) If the Scottish Ministers propose to make such an order they must publish a notice in such manner as they think sufficient for giving information to persons they think may be interested in the endowment —
   (a) containing particulars of the proposed order;
   (b) stating that representations may be made with respect to the proposal within such period as is specified in the notice.

(5) The period must be not less than one month beginning with the day after the date of publication of the notice.

(6) The cost of publication is to be paid out of the funds of the endowment to which the notice relates.

(7) Before making an order, the Scottish Ministers —

  (a) must consider representations made in accordance with the notice;

  (b) may cause a local inquiry to be held into the representations under section 67 of the Education (Scotland) Act 1980.

(8) A reference to an educational endowment includes a reference to —

  (a) a scheme made or approved for the endowment under Part 6 of the Education (Scotland) Act 1980;

  (b) in the case of an endowment the governing body of which is entered in the Scottish Charity Register, a scheme approved for the endowment under section 39 or 40 of the Charities and Trustee Investment (Scotland) Act 2005 (asp 10);

  (c) an endowment which is, by virtue of section 108(1) of the Education (Scotland) Act 1980, treated as if it were an educational endowment (or which would, but for the disapplication of that section by section 122(4) of that Act, be so treated);

  (d) a university endowment, the Carnegie Trust, a theological endowment and a new endowment.

(9) Expressions used in this paragraph and in Part 6 of the Education (Scotland) Act 1980 have the same meaning in this paragraph as in that Part.

SCHEDULE 15   Section 107

ASSOCIATIONS: REASONABLE ADJUSTMENTS

Preliminary

1   This Schedule applies where a duty to make reasonable adjustments is imposed on an association (A) by this Part.

The duty

2   (1) A must comply with the first, second and third requirements.

  (2) For the purposes of this paragraph, the reference in section 20(3), (4) or (5) to a disabled person is a reference to disabled persons who —

    (a) are, or are seeking to become or might wish to become, members,

    (b) are associates, or

    (c) are, or are likely to become, guests.

  (3) Section 20 has effect as if, in subsection (4), for "to avoid the disadvantage" there were substituted —

      "(a) to avoid the disadvantage, or

      (b) to adopt a reasonable alternative method of affording access to the benefit, facility or service or of admitting persons to membership or inviting persons as guests."

  (4) In relation to the first and third requirements, the relevant matters are —

    (a) access to a benefit, facility or service;

    (b)   members' or associates' retaining their rights as such or avoiding having them varied;

    (c)   being admitted to membership or invited as a guest.

(5)   In relation to the second requirement, the relevant matters are—

    (a)   access to a benefit, facility or service;

    (b)   being admitted to membership or invited as a guest.

(6)   In relation to the second requirement, a physical feature includes a physical feature brought by or on behalf of A, in the course of or for the purpose of providing a benefit, facility or service, on to premises other than those that A occupies (as well as including a physical feature in or on premises that A occupies).

(7)   Nothing in this paragraph requires A to take a step which would fundamentally alter—

    (a)   the nature of the benefit, facility or service concerned, or

    (b)   the nature of the association.

(8)   Nor does anything in this paragraph require a member or associate in whose house meetings of the association take place to make adjustments to a physical feature of the house.

SCHEDULE 16

Section 107

ASSOCIATIONS: EXCEPTIONS

Single characteristic associations

1   (1)   An association does not contravene section 101(1) by restricting membership to persons who share a protected characteristic.

    (2)   An association that restricts membership to persons who share a protected characteristic does not breach section 101(3) by restricting the access by associates to a benefit, facility or service to such persons as share the characteristic.

    (3)   An association that restricts membership to persons who share a protected characteristic does not breach section 102(1) by inviting as guests, or by permitting to be invited as guests, only such persons as share the characteristic.

    (4)   Sub-paragraphs (1) to (3), so far as relating to race, do not apply in relation to colour.

    (5)   This paragraph does not apply to an association that is a registered political party.

Health and safety

2   (1)   An association (A) does not discriminate against a pregnant woman in contravention of section 101(1)(b) because she is pregnant if—

    (a)   the terms on which A is prepared to admit her to membership include a term intended to remove or reduce a risk to her health or safety,

    (b)   A reasonably believes that admitting her to membership on terms which do not include that term would create a risk to her health or safety,

    (c)   the terms on which A is prepared to admit persons with other physical conditions to membership include a term intended to remove or reduce a risk to their health or safety, and

    (d)   A reasonably believes that admitting them to membership on terms which do not include that term would create a risk to their health or safety.

(2) Sub-paragraph (1) applies to section 102(1)(b) as it applies to section 101(1)(b); and for that purpose a reference to admitting a person to membership is to be read as a reference to inviting the person as a guest or permitting the person to be invited as a guest.

(3) An association (A) does not discriminate against a pregnant woman in contravention of section 101(2)(a) or (3)(a) or 102(2)(a) because she is pregnant if —

    (a)   the way in which A affords her access to a benefit, facility or service is intended to remove or reduce a risk to her health or safety,

    (b)   A reasonably believes that affording her access to the benefit, facility or service otherwise than in that way would create a risk to her health or safety,

    (c)   A affords persons with other physical conditions access to the benefit, facility or service in a way that is intended to remove or reduce a risk to their health or safety, and

    (d)   A reasonably believes that affording them access to the benefit, facility or service otherwise than in that way would create a risk to their health or safety.

(4) An association (A) which does not afford a pregnant woman access to a benefit, facility or service does not discriminate against her in contravention of section 101(2)(a) or (3)(a) or 102(2)(a) because she is pregnant if —

    (a)   A reasonably believes that affording her access to the benefit, facility or service would, because she is pregnant, create a risk to her health or safety,

    (b)   A does not afford persons with other physical conditions access to the benefit, facility or service, and

    (c)   the reason for not doing so is that A reasonably believes that affording them access to the benefit, facility or service would create a risk to their health or safety.

(5) An association (A) does not discriminate against a pregnant woman under section 101(2)(c) or (3)(c) because she is pregnant if —

    (a)   the variation of A's terms of membership, or rights as an associate, is intended to remove or reduce a risk to her health or safety,

    (b)   A reasonably believes that not making the variation to A's terms or rights would create a risk to her health or safety,

    (c)   A varies the terms of membership, or rights as an associate, of persons with other physical conditions,

    (d)   the variation of their terms or rights is intended to remove or reduce a risk to their health or safety, and

    (e)   A reasonably believes that not making the variation to their terms or rights would create a risk to their health or safety.

SCHEDULE 17

Section 116

DISABLED PUPILS: ENFORCEMENT

PART 1

INTRODUCTORY

1   In this Schedule —
      "the Tribunal" means —
          (a)   in relation to a school in England, the First-tier Tribunal;
          (b)   in relation to a school in Wales, the Special Educational Needs Tribunal for Wales;
          (c)   in relation to a school in Scotland, an Additional Support Needs Tribunal for Scotland;
      "the English Tribunal" means the First-tier Tribunal;
      "the Welsh Tribunal" means the Special Educational Needs Tribunal for Wales;
      "the Scottish Tribunal" means an Additional Support Needs Tribunal for Scotland;
      "responsible body" is to be construed in accordance with section 85.

PART 2

TRIBUNALS IN ENGLAND AND WALES

Introductory

2   This Part of this Schedule applies in relation to the English Tribunal and the Welsh Tribunal.

Jurisdiction

3   A claim that a responsible body has contravened Chapter 1 of Part 6 because of a person's disability may be made to the Tribunal by the person's parent.

Time for bringing proceedings

4   (1) Proceedings on a claim may not be brought after the end of the period of 6 months starting with the date when the conduct complained of occurred.

    (2) If, in relation to proceedings or prospective proceedings under section 27 of the Equality Act 2006, the dispute is referred for conciliation in pursuance of arrangements under that section before the end of that period, the period is extended by 3 months.

    (3) The Tribunal may consider a claim which is out of time.

    (4) Sub-paragraph (3) does not apply if the Tribunal has previously decided under that sub-paragraph not to consider a claim.

    (5) For the purposes of sub-paragraph (1) —
          (a)   if the contravention is attributable to a term in a contract, the conduct is to be treated as extending throughout the duration of the contract;

1828

Equality Act 2010 (c. 15)
Schedule 17 — Disabled pupils: enforcement
Part 2 — Tribunals in England and Wales

   (b) conduct extending over a period is to be treated as occurring at the end of the period;

   (c) failure to do something is to be treated as occurring when the person in question decided on it.

 (6) In the absence of evidence to the contrary, a person (P) is to be taken to decide on failure to do something —

   (a) when P acts inconsistently with doing it, or

   (b) if P does not act inconsistently, on the expiry of the period in which P might reasonably have been expected to do it.

Powers

5 (1) This paragraph applies if the Tribunal finds that the contravention has occurred.

 (2) The Tribunal may make such order as it thinks fit.

 (3) The power under sub-paragraph (2) —

   (a) may, in particular, be exercised with a view to obviating or reducing the adverse effect on the person of any matter to which the claim relates;

   (b) does not include power to order the payment of compensation.

Procedure

6 (1) This paragraph applies in relation to the Welsh Tribunal.

 (2) The Welsh Ministers may by regulations make provision as to —

   (a) the proceedings on a claim under paragraph 3;

   (b) the making of a claim.

 (3) The regulations may, in particular, include provision —

   (a) as to the manner in which a claim must be made;

   (b) for enabling functions relating to preliminary or incidental matters (including in particular a decision under paragraph 4(3) to be performed by the President or by the person occupying the chair);

   (c) enabling hearings to be conducted in the absence of a member other than the person occupying the chair;

   (d) as to persons who may appear on behalf of the parties;

   (e) for granting such rights to disclosure or inspection of documents or to further particulars as may be granted by the county court;

   (f) requiring persons to attend to give evidence and produce documents;

   (g) for authorising the administration of oaths to witnesses;

   (h) for deciding claims without a hearing in prescribed circumstances;

   (i) as to the withdrawal of claims;

   (j) for enabling the Tribunal to stay proceedings;

   (k) for the award of costs or expenses;

   (l) for settling costs or expenses (and, in particular, for enabling costs to be assessed in the county court);

   (m) for the registration and proof of decisions and orders;

Equality Act 2010 (c. 15)
Schedule 17 — Disabled pupils: enforcement
Part 2 — Tribunals in England and Wales

1829

(n)   for enabling prescribed decisions to be reviewed, or prescribed orders to be varied or revoked, in such circumstances as may be decided in accordance with the regulations.

(4)   Proceedings must be held in private, except in prescribed circumstances.

(5)   The Welsh Ministers may pay such allowances for the purpose of or in connection with the attendance of persons at the Tribunal as they may decide.

(6)   Part 1 of the Arbitration Act 1996 does not apply to the proceedings, but regulations may make provision in relation to such proceedings that corresponds to a provision of that Part.

(7)   The regulations may make provision for a claim to be heard, in prescribed circumstances, with an appeal under Part 4 of the Education Act 1996 (special educational needs).

(8)   A person commits an offence by failing to comply with—

(a)   a requirement in respect of the disclosure or inspection of documents imposed by virtue of sub-paragraph (3)(e), or

(b)   a requirement imposed by virtue of sub-paragraph (3)(f).

(9)   A person guilty of the offence is liable on summary conviction to a fine not exceeding level 3 on the standard scale.

PART 3

TRIBUNALS IN SCOTLAND

Introductory

7   This Part of this Schedule applies in relation to the Scottish Tribunal.

Jurisdiction

8   A claim that a responsible body has contravened Chapter 1 of Part 6 because of a person's disability may be made to the Tribunal by—

(a)   the person's parent;

(b)   where the person has capacity to make the claim, the person.

Powers

9   (1)   This paragraph applies if the Tribunal finds the contravention has occurred.

(2)   The Tribunal may make such order as it thinks fit.

(3)   The power under sub-paragraph (2)—

(a)   may, in particular, be exercised with a view to obviating or reducing the adverse effect on the person of any matter to which the claim relates;

(b)   does not include power to order the payment of compensation.

Procedure etc.

10   (1)   The Scottish Ministers may make rules as to—

(a)   the proceedings on a claim under paragraph 8;

(b)   the making of a claim.

(2)   The rules may, in particular, include provision for or in connection with—

   (a)   the form and manner in which a claim must be made;

   (b)   the time within which a claim is to be made;

   (c)   the withdrawal of claims;

   (d)   the recovery and inspection of documents;

   (e)   the persons who may appear on behalf of the parties;

   (f)   the persons who may be present at proceedings alongside any party or witness to support the party or witness;

   (g)   enabling specified persons other than the parties to appear or be represented in specified circumstances;

   (h)   requiring specified persons to give notice to other specified persons of specified matters;

   (i)   the time within which any such notice must be given;

   (j)   enabling Tribunal proceedings to be conducted in the absence of any member of a Tribunal other than the convener;

   (k)   enabling any matters that are preliminary or incidental to the determination of proceedings to be determined by the convenor of a Tribunal alone or with such other members of the Tribunal as may be specified;

   (l)   enabling Tribunals to be held in private;

   (m)   enabling a Tribunal to exclude any person from attending all or part of Tribunal proceedings;

   (n)   enabling a Tribunal to impose reporting restrictions in relation to all or part of Tribunal proceedings;

   (o)   enabling a Tribunal to determine specified matters without holding a hearing;

   (p)   the recording and publication of decisions and orders of a Tribunal;

   (q)   enabling a Tribunal to commission medical and other reports in specified circumstances;

   (r)   requiring a Tribunal to take specified actions, or to determine specified proceedings, within specified periods;

   (s)   enabling a Tribunal to make an award of expenses;

   (t)   the taxation or assessment of such expenses;

   (u)   enabling a Tribunal, in specified circumstances, to review, or to vary or revoke, any of its decisions, orders or awards;

   (v)   enabling a Tribunal, in specified circumstances, to review the decisions, orders or awards of another Tribunal and take such action (including variation and revocation) in respect of those decisions, orders or awards as it thinks fit.

Appeals

11   (1)   Either of the persons specified in sub-paragraph (2) may appeal on a point of law to the Court of Session against a decision of a Tribunal relating to a claim under this Schedule.

   (2)   Those persons are—

      (a)   the person who made the claim;

      (b)   the responsible body.

(3) Where the Court of Session allows an appeal under sub-paragraph (1) it may —

    (a) remit the reference back to the Tribunal or to a differently constituted Tribunal to be considered again and give the Tribunal such directions about the consideration of the case as the Court thinks fit;

    (b) make such ancillary orders as it considers necessary or appropriate.

Amendment of Education (Additional Support for Learning) (Scotland) Act 2004

12   The Education (Additional Support for Learning) (Scotland) Act 2004 (asp 4) is amended as follows —

    (a) in section 17(1), omit "to exercise the functions which are conferred on a Tribunal by virtue of this Act";

    (b) after section 17(1), insert —

        "(1A) Tribunals are to exercise the functions which are conferred on them by virtue of —

            (a) this Act, and

            (b) the Equality Act 2010";

    (c) in the definition of "Tribunal functions" in paragraph 1 of Schedule 1, after "Act" insert "or the Equality Act 2010".

PART 4

ADMISSIONS AND EXCLUSIONS

Admissions

13 (1) This paragraph applies if appeal arrangements have been made in relation to admissions decisions.

    (2) A claim that a responsible body has, because of a person's disability, contravened Chapter 1 of Part 6 in respect of an admissions decision must be made under the appeal arrangements.

    (3) The body hearing the claim has the powers it has in relation to an appeal under the appeal arrangements.

    (4) Appeal arrangements are arrangements under —

        (a) section 94 of the School Standards and Framework Act 1998, or

        (b) an agreement between the responsible body for an Academy and the Secretary of State under section 482 of the Education Act 1996,

enabling an appeal to be made by the person's parent against the decision.

    (5) An admissions decision is —

        (a) a decision of a kind mentioned in section 94(1) or (2) of the School Standards and Framework Act 1998;

        (b) a decision as to the admission of a person to an Academy taken by the responsible body or on its behalf.

Exclusions

14 (1) This paragraph applies if appeal arrangements have been made in relation to exclusion decisions.

1832

Equality Act 2010 (c. 15)
Schedule 17 — Disabled pupils: enforcement
Part 4 — Admissions and exclusions

(2) A claim that a responsible body has, because of a person's disability, contravened Chapter 1 of Part 6 in respect of an exclusion decision must be made under the appeal arrangements.

(3) The body hearing the claim has the powers it has in relation to an appeal under the appeal arrangements.

(4) Appeal arrangements are arrangements under—
    (a) section 52(3) of the Education Act 2002, or
    (b) an agreement between the responsible body for an Academy and the Secretary of State under section 482 of the Education Act 1996,
enabling an appeal to be made by the person's parent against the decision.

(5) An exclusion decision is—
    (a) a decision of a kind mentioned in 52(3) of the Education Act 2002;
    (b) a decision taken by the responsible body or on its behalf not to reinstate a pupil who has been permanently excluded from an Academy by its head teacher.

(6) "Responsible body", in relation to a maintained school, includes the discipline committee of the governing body if that committee is required to be established as a result of regulations made under section 19 of the Education Act 2002.

(7) "Maintained school" has the meaning given in section 20(7) of the School Standards and Framework Act 1998.

SCHEDULE 18   Section 149

PUBLIC SECTOR EQUALITY DUTY: EXCEPTIONS

Children

1 (1) Section 149, so far as relating to age, does not apply to the exercise of a function relating to—
    (a) the provision of education to pupils in schools;
    (b) the provision of benefits, facilities or services to pupils in schools;
    (c) the provision of accommodation, benefits, facilities or services in community homes pursuant to section 53(1) of the Children Act 1989;
    (d) the provision of accommodation, benefits, facilities or services pursuant to arrangements under section 82(5) of that Act (arrangements by the Secretary of State relating to the accommodation of children);
    (e) the provision of accommodation, benefits, facilities or services in residential establishments pursuant to section 26(1)(b) of the Children (Scotland) Act 1995.

(2) "Pupil" and "school" each have the same meaning as in Chapter 1 of Part 6.

Immigration

2   (1) In relation to the exercise of immigration and nationality functions, section 149 has effect as if subsection (1)(b) did not apply to the protected characteristics of age, race or religion or belief; but for that purpose "race" means race so far as relating to —

        (a) nationality, or

        (b) ethnic or national origins.

    (2) "Immigration and nationality functions" means functions exercisable by virtue of —

        (a) the Immigration Acts (excluding sections 28A to 28K of the Immigration Act 1971 so far as they relate to criminal offences),

        (b) the British Nationality Act 1981,

        (c) the British Nationality (Falkland Islands) Act 1983,

        (d) the British Nationality (Hong Kong) Act 1990,

        (e) the Hong Kong (War Wives and Widows) Act 1996,

        (f) the British Nationality (Hong Kong) Act 1997,

        (g) the Special Immigration Appeals Commission Act 1997, or

        (h) a provision made under section 2(2) of the European Communities Act 1972, or of Community law, which relates to the subject matter of an enactment within paragraphs (a) to (g).

Judicial functions, etc.

3   (1) Section 149 does not apply to the exercise of —

        (a) a judicial function;

        (b) a function exercised on behalf of, or on the instructions of, a person exercising a judicial function.

    (2) The references to a judicial function include a reference to a judicial function conferred on a person other than a court or tribunal.

Exceptions that are specific to section 149(2)

4   (1) Section 149(2) (application of section 149(1) to persons who are not public authorities but by whom public functions are exercisable) does not apply to —

        (a) a person listed in sub-paragraph (2);

        (b) the exercise of a function listed in sub-paragraph (3).

    (2) Those persons are —

        (a) the House of Commons;

        (b) the House of Lords;

        (c) the Scottish Parliament;

        (d) the National Assembly for Wales;

        (e) the General Synod of the Church of England;

        (f) the Security Service;

        (g) the Secret Intelligence Service;

        (h) the Government Communications Headquarters;

     (i)   a part of the armed forces which is, in accordance with a requirement of the Secretary of State, assisting the Government Communications Headquarters.

(3) Those functions are—

    (a)   a function in connection with proceedings in the House of Commons or the House of Lords;

    (b)   a function in connection with proceedings in the Scottish Parliament (other than a function of the Scottish Parliamentary Corporate Body);

    (c)   a function in connection with proceedings in the National Assembly for Wales (other than a function of the Assembly Commission).

Power to amend Schedule

5   (1)   A Minister of the Crown may by order amend this Schedule so as to add, vary or omit an exception to section 149.

    (2)   But provision by virtue of sub-paragraph (1) may not amend this Schedule—

    (a)   so as to omit an exception in paragraph 3;

    (b)   so as to omit an exception in paragraph 4(1) so far as applying for the purposes of paragraph 4(2)(a) to (e) or (3);

    (c)   so as to reduce the extent to which an exception referred to in paragraph (a) or (b) applies.

SCHEDULE 19

Section 150

PUBLIC AUTHORITIES

PART 1

PUBLIC AUTHORITIES: GENERAL

Ministers of the Crown and government departments

A Minister of the Crown.

A government department other than the Security Service, the Secret Intelligence Service or the Government Communications Headquarters.

Armed forces

Any of the armed forces other than any part of the armed forces which is, in accordance with a requirement of the Secretary of State, assisting the Government Communications Headquarters.

National Health Service

A Strategic Health Authority established under section 13 of the National Health Service Act 2006, or continued in existence by virtue of that section.

A Primary Care Trust established under section 18 of that Act, or continued in existence by virtue of that section.

Equality Act 2010 (c. 15)   **1835**
Schedule 19 — Public authorities
Part 1 — Public authorities: general

An NHS trust established under section 25 of that Act.

A Special Health Authority established under section 28 of that Act other than NHS Blood and Transplant and the NHS Business Services Authority.

An NHS foundation trust within the meaning given by section 30 of that Act.

Local government

A county council, district council or parish council in England.

A parish meeting constituted under section 13 of the Local Government Act 1972.

Charter trustees constituted under section 246 of that Act for an area in England.

The Greater London Authority.

A London borough council.

The Common Council of the City of London in its capacity as a local authority or port health authority.

The Sub-Treasurer of the Inner Temple or the Under-Treasurer of the Middle Temple, in that person's capacity as a local authority.

The London Development Agency.

The London Fire and Emergency Planning Authority.

Transport for London.

The Council of the Isles of Scilly.

The Broads Authority established by section 1 of the Norfolk and Suffolk Broads Act 1988.

A regional development agency established by the Regional Development Agencies Act 1998 (other than the London Development Agency).

A fire and rescue authority constituted by a scheme under section 2 of the Fire and Rescue Services Act 2004, or a scheme to which section 4 of that Act applies, for an area in England.

An internal drainage board which is continued in being by virtue of section 1 of the Land Drainage Act 1991 for an area in England.

A National Park authority established by an order under section 63 of the Environment Act 1995 for an area in England.

A Passenger Transport Executive for an integrated transport area in England (within the meaning of Part 2 of the Transport Act 1968).

A port health authority constituted by an order under section 2 of the Public Health (Control of Disease) Act 1984 for an area in England.

A waste disposal authority established by virtue of an order under section 10(1) of the Local Government Act 1985.

A joint authority established under Part 4 of that Act for an area in England (including, by virtue of section 77(9) of the Local Transport Act 2008, an Integrated Transport Authority established under Part 5 of that Act of 2008).

A body corporate established pursuant to an order under section 67 of the Local Government Act 1985.

A joint committee constituted in accordance with section 102(1)(b) of the Local Government Act 1972 for an area in England.

A joint board which is continued in being by virtue of section 263(1) of that Act for an area in England.

Other educational bodies

The governing body of an educational establishment maintained by an English local authority (within the meaning of section 162 of the Education and Inspections Act 2006).

The governing body of an institution in England within the further education sector (within the meaning of section 91(3) of the Further and Higher Education Act 1992).

The governing body of an institution in England within the higher education sector (within the meaning of section 91(5) of that Act).

Police

A police authority established under section 3 of the Police Act 1996.

The Metropolitan Police Authority established under section 5B of that Act.

The Common Council of the City of London in its capacity as a police authority.

PART 2

PUBLIC AUTHORITIES: RELEVANT WELSH AUTHORITIES

Welsh Assembly Government, etc.

The Welsh Ministers.

The First Minister for Wales.

The Counsel General to the Welsh Assembly Government.

A subsidiary of the Welsh Ministers (within the meaning given by section 134(4) of the Government of Wales Act 2006).

National Health Service

A Local Health Board established under section 11 of the National Health Service (Wales) Act 2006.

An NHS trust established under section 18 of that Act.

A Special Health Authority established under section 22 of that Act other than NHS Blood and Transplant and the NHS Business Services Authority.

A Community Health Council in Wales.

Local government

A county council, county borough council or community council in Wales.

Charter trustees constituted under section 246 of the Local Government Act 1972 for an area in Wales.

A fire and rescue authority constituted by a scheme under section 2 of the Fire and Rescue Services Act 2004, or a scheme to which section 4 of that Act applies, for an area in Wales.

An internal drainage board which is continued in being by virtue of section 1 of the Land Drainage Act 1991 for an area in Wales.

A National Park authority established by an order under section 63 of the Environment Act 1995 for an area in Wales.

A port health authority constituted by an order under section 2 of the Public Health (Control of Disease) Act 1984 for an area in Wales.

A joint authority established under Part 4 of the Local Government Act 1985 for an area in Wales.

A joint committee constituted in accordance with section 102(1)(b) of the Local Government Act 1972 for an area in Wales.

A joint board which is continued in being by virtue of section 263(1) of that Act for an area in Wales.

Other educational bodies

The governing body of an educational establishment maintained by a Welsh local authority (within the meaning of section 162 of the Education and Inspections Act 2006).

The governing body of an institution in Wales within the further education sector (within the meaning of section 91(3) of the Further and Higher Education Act 1992).

The governing body of an institution in Wales within the higher education sector (within the meaning of section 91(5) of that Act).

PART 3

PUBLIC AUTHORITIES: RELEVANT SCOTTISH AUTHORITIES

Scottish Administration

An office-holder in the Scottish Administration (within the meaning given by section 126(7)(a) of the Scotland Act 1998).

National Health Service

A Health Board constituted under section 2 of the National Health Service (Scotland) Act 1978.

A Special Health Board constituted under that section.

Local government

A council constituted under section 2 of the Local Government etc. (Scotland) Act 1994.

A community council established under section 51 of the Local Government (Scotland) Act 1973.

A joint board within the meaning of section 235(1) of that Act.

A joint fire and rescue board constituted by a scheme under section 2(1) of the Fire (Scotland) Act 2005.

A licensing board established under section 5 of the Licensing (Scotland) Act 2005, or continued in being by virtue of that section.

A National Park authority established by a designation order made under section 6 of the National Parks (Scotland) Act 2000.

1838

Equality Act 2010 (c. 15)
Schedule 19 — Public authorities
Part 3 — Public authorities: relevant Scottish authorities

Scottish Enterprise and Highlands and Islands Enterprise, established under the Enterprise and New Towns (Scotland) Act 1990.

Other educational bodies

An education authority in Scotland (within the meaning of section 135(1) of the Education (Scotland) Act 1980).

The managers of a grant-aided school (within the meaning of that section).

The board of management of a college of further education (within the meaning of section 36(1) of the Further and Higher Education (Scotland) Act 1992).

In the case of such a college of further education not under the management of a board of management, the board of governors of the college or any person responsible for the management of the college, whether or not formally constituted as a governing body or board of governors.

The governing body of an institution within the higher education sector (within the meaning of Part 2 of the Further and Higher Education (Scotland) Act 1992).

Police

A police authority established under section 2 of the Police (Scotland) Act 1967.

SCHEDULE 20

Section 186

RAIL VEHICLE ACCESSIBILITY: COMPLIANCE

Rail vehicle accessibility compliance certificates

1   (1) A regulated rail vehicle which is prescribed, or is of a prescribed class or description, must not be used for carriage unless a compliance certificate is in force for the vehicle.

    (2) A "compliance certificate" is a certificate that the Secretary of State is satisfied that the regulated rail vehicle conforms with the provisions of rail vehicle accessibility regulations with which it is required to conform.

    (3) A compliance certificate is subject to such conditions as are specified in it.

    (4) A compliance certificate may not be issued for a rail vehicle unless the Secretary of State has been provided with a report of a compliance assessment of the vehicle.

    (5) A "compliance assessment" is an assessment of a rail vehicle against provisions of rail vehicle accessibility regulations with which the vehicle is required to conform.

    (6) If a regulated rail vehicle is used for carriage in contravention of sub-paragraph (1), the Secretary of State may require the operator of the vehicle to pay a penalty.

(7) The Secretary of State must review a decision not to issue a compliance certificate if before the end of the prescribed period the applicant—

    (a)   asks the Secretary of State to review the decision, and

    (b)   pays any fee fixed under paragraph 4.

(8) For the purposes of the review, the Secretary of State must consider any representations made by the applicant in writing before the end of the prescribed period.

Regulations as to compliance certificates

2   (1) Regulations may make provision as to compliance certificates.

    (2) The regulations may (in particular) include provision—

        (a)   as to applications for and issue of certificates;

        (b)   specifying conditions to which certificates are subject;

        (c)   as to the period for which a certificate is in force;

        (d)   as to circumstances in which a certificate ceases to be in force;

        (e)   dealing with failure to comply with a specified condition;

        (f)   for the examination of rail vehicles in respect of which applications have been made;

        (g)   with respect to the issue of copies of certificates in place of those which have been lost or destroyed.

Regulations as to compliance assessments

3   (1) Regulations may make provision as to compliance assessments.

    (2) The regulations—

        (a)   may make provision as to the person who has to have carried out the assessment;

        (b)   may (in particular) require that the assessment be one carried out by a person who has been appointed by the Secretary of State to carry out compliance assessments (an "appointed assessor").

    (3) For the purposes of any provisions in the regulations made by virtue of sub-paragraph (2)(b), the regulations—

        (a)   may make provision about appointments of appointed assessors, including (in particular)—

            (i)   provision for an appointment to be on application or otherwise than on application;

            (ii)   provision as to who may be appointed;

            (iii)   provision as to the form of applications for appointment;

            (iv)   provision as to information to be supplied with applications for appointment;

            (v)   provision as to terms and conditions, or the period or termination, of an appointment;

            (vi)   provision for terms and conditions of an appointment, including any as to its period or termination, to be as agreed by the Secretary of State when making the appointment;

        (b)   may make provision authorising an appointed assessor to charge fees in connection with, or incidental to, the carrying out of a compliance assessment, including (in particular)—

(i) provision restricting the amount of a fee;

(ii) provision authorising fees that contain a profit element;

(iii) provision for advance payment of fees;

(c) may make provision requiring an appointed assessor to carry out a compliance assessment, and to do so in accordance with any procedures that may be prescribed, if prescribed conditions (which may include conditions as to the payment of fees to the assessor) are satisfied;

(d) must make provision for the referral to the Secretary of State of disputes between —

(i) an appointed assessor carrying out a compliance assessment, and

(ii) the person who requested the assessment,

relating to which provisions of rail vehicle accessibility regulations the vehicle is to be assessed against or to what amounts to conformity with any of those provisions.

(4) For the purposes of sub-paragraph (3)(b) to (d) a compliance assessment includes pre-assessment activities (for example, a consideration of how the outcome of a compliance assessment would be affected by the carrying out of particular proposed work).

Fees in respect of compliance certificates

4 (1) The Secretary of State may charge such fees, payable at such times, as are prescribed in respect of —

(a) applications for, and the issue of, compliance certificates;

(b) copies of compliance certificates;

(c) reviews under paragraph 1(7);

(d) referrals of disputes under provision made by virtue of paragraph 3(3)(d).

(2) Fees received by the Secretary of State must be paid into the Consolidated Fund.

(3) Regulations under this paragraph may make provision for the repayment of fees, in whole or in part, in such circumstances as are prescribed.

(4) Before making regulations under this paragraph the Secretary of State must consult such representative organisations as the Secretary of State thinks fit.

Penalty for using rail vehicle that does not conform with accessibility regulations

5 (1) If the Secretary of State thinks that a regulated rail vehicle does not conform with a provision of rail vehicle accessibility regulations with which it is required to conform, the Secretary of State may give the operator of the vehicle a notice —

(a) identifying the vehicle, the provision and how the vehicle fails to conform;

(b) specifying the improvement deadline.

(2) The improvement deadline may not be earlier than the end of the prescribed period beginning with the day the notice is given.

(3) Sub-paragraph (4) applies if —

    (a)   the Secretary of State has given a notice under sub-paragraph (1),

    (b)   the improvement deadline specified in the notice has passed, and

    (c)   the Secretary of State thinks that the vehicle still does not conform with the provision identified in the notice.

(4) The Secretary of State may give the operator a further notice —

    (a)   identifying the vehicle, the provision and how the vehicle fails to conform;

    (b)   specifying the final deadline.

(5) The final deadline may not be earlier than the end of the prescribed period beginning with the day the further notice is given.

(6) The Secretary of State may require the operator to pay a penalty if —

    (a)   the Secretary of State has given notice under sub-paragraph (4), and

    (b)   the vehicle is used for carriage at a time after the final deadline when the vehicle does not conform with the provision identified in the notice.

Penalty for using rail vehicle otherwise than in conformity with accessibility regulations

6   (1) If the Secretary of State thinks that a regulated rail vehicle has been used for carriage otherwise than in conformity with a provision of rail vehicle accessibility regulations with which the use of the vehicle is required to conform, the Secretary of State may give the operator of the vehicle a notice —

    (a)   identifying the provision and how it was breached;

    (b)   identifying each vehicle operated by the operator that is covered by the notice;

    (c)   specifying the improvement deadline.

(2) The improvement deadline may not be earlier than the end of the prescribed period beginning with the day the notice is given.

(3) Sub-paragraph (4) applies if —

    (a)   the Secretary of State has given a notice under sub-paragraph (1),

    (b)   the improvement deadline specified in the notice has passed, and

    (c)   the Secretary of State thinks that a vehicle covered by the notice has after that deadline been used for carriage otherwise than in conformity with the provision identified in the notice.

(4) The Secretary of State may give the operator a further notice —

    (a)   identifying the provision and how it was breached;

    (b)   identifying each vehicle operated by the operator that is covered by the further notice;

    (c)   specifying the final deadline.

(5) The final deadline may not be earlier than the end of the prescribed period beginning with the day the further notice is given.

(6) The Secretary of State may require the operator to pay a penalty if —

    (a)   the Secretary of State has given notice under sub-paragraph (4), and

    (b)   a vehicle covered by the notice is at a time after the final deadline used for carriage otherwise than in conformity with the provision identified in the notice.

Inspection of rail vehicles

7   (1) If the condition in sub-paragraph (2) is satisfied, a person authorised by the Secretary of State (an "inspector") may inspect a regulated rail vehicle for conformity with provisions of the accessibility regulations with which it is required to conform.

(2) The condition is that the Secretary of State —
  (a) has reasonable grounds for suspecting that the vehicle does not conform with such provisions, or
  (b) has given a notice under paragraph 5(1) or (4) relating to the vehicle.

(3) For the purpose of exercising the power under sub-paragraph (1) an inspector may —
  (a) enter premises if the inspector has reasonable grounds for suspecting that the vehicle is at the premises;
  (b) enter the vehicle;
  (c) require any person to afford such facilities and assistance with respect to matters under the person's control as are necessary to enable the inspector to exercise the power.

(4) An inspector must, if required to do so, produce evidence of the Secretary of State's authorisation.

(5) For the purposes of paragraph 5(1) the Secretary of State may draw such inferences as appear proper from any obstruction of the exercise of the power under sub-paragraph (1).

(6) Sub-paragraphs (7) and (8) apply if the power under sub-paragraph (1) is exercisable by virtue of sub-paragraph (2)(b).

(7) The Secretary of State may treat paragraph 5(3)(c) as satisfied in relation to a vehicle if —
  (a) the inspector takes steps to exercise the power after a notice is given under paragraph 5(1) but before a notice is given under paragraph 5(4), and
  (b) a person obstructs the exercise of the power.

(8) The Secretary of State may require the operator of a vehicle to pay a penalty if —
  (a) the operator, or a person acting on the operator's behalf, intentionally obstructs the exercise of the power, and
  (b) the obstruction occurs after a notice has been given under paragraph 5(4) in respect of the vehicle.

(9) In this paragraph "inspect" includes test.

Supplementary powers

8   (1) For the purposes of paragraph 5 the Secretary of State may give notice to a person requiring the person to supply the Secretary of State by a time specified in the notice with a vehicle number or other identifier for a rail vehicle —
  (a) of which the person is the operator, and
  (b) which is specified in the notice.

(2) The time specified may not be earlier than the end of the period of 14 days beginning with the day the notice is given.

(3) If the person does not comply with the notice, the Secretary of State may require the person to pay a penalty.

(4) If the Secretary of State has given a notice to a person under paragraph 5(1) or 6(1), the Secretary of State may request the person to supply the Secretary of State, by a time specified in the request, with a statement detailing the steps taken in response to the notice.

(5) The time specified may not be earlier than the improvement deadline.

(6) The Secretary of State may treat paragraph 5(3)(c) or (as the case may be) paragraph 6(3)(c) as being satisfied in relation to a vehicle if a request under sub-paragraph (4) is not complied with by the time specified.

Penalties: amount, due date and recovery

9   (1) In this paragraph and paragraphs 10 to 12 "penalty" means a penalty under this Schedule.

(2) The amount of a penalty must not exceed whichever is the lesser of —
   (a)   the maximum prescribed for the purposes of this sub-paragraph;
   (b)   10% of the turnover of the person on whom it is imposed.

(3) Turnover is to be determined by such means as are prescribed.

(4) A penalty must be paid to the Secretary of State before the end of the prescribed period.

(5) A sum payable as a penalty may be recovered as a debt due to the Secretary of State.

(6) In proceedings for recovery of a penalty no question may be raised as to —
   (a)   liability to the penalty;
   (b)   its amount.

(7) Sums paid to the Secretary of State as a penalty must be paid into the Consolidated Fund.

Penalties: code of practice

10   (1) The Secretary of State must issue a code of practice specifying matters to be considered in determining the amount of a penalty.

(2) The Secretary of State may —
   (a)   revise the whole or part of the code;
   (b)   issue the code as revised.

(3) Before issuing the code the Secretary of State must lay a draft of it before Parliament.

(4) After laying the draft before Parliament, the Secretary of State may bring the code into operation by order.

(5) The Secretary of State must have regard to the code and any other relevant matter —
   (a)   when imposing a penalty;

> (b)   when considering an objection under paragraph 11.

(6)   In sub-paragraphs (3) to (5) a reference to the code includes a reference to the code as revised.

Penalties: procedure

11   (1)   If the Secretary of State decides that a person is liable to a penalty the Secretary of State must notify the person.

(2)   The notification must—
   (a)   state the Secretary of State's reasons for the decision;
   (b)   state the amount of the penalty;
   (c)   specify the date by which and manner in which the penalty must be paid;
   (d)   explain how the person may object to the penalty.

(3)   The person may give the Secretary of State notice of objection to the penalty on the ground that—
   (a)   the person is not liable to the penalty, or
   (b)   the amount of the penalty is too high.

(4)   A notice of objection must—
   (a)   be in writing;
   (b)   give the reasons for the objection;
   (c)   be given before the end of the period prescribed for the purposes of this sub-paragraph.

(5)   On considering a notice of objection the Secretary of State may—
   (a)   cancel the penalty;
   (b)   reduce the amount of the penalty;
   (c)   do neither of those things.

(6)   The Secretary of State must inform the objector of the decision under sub-paragraph (5) before the end of the period prescribed for the purposes of this sub-paragraph (or such longer period as is agreed with the objector).

Penalties: appeals

12   (1)   A person may appeal to the court against a penalty on the ground that—
   (a)   the person is not liable to the penalty;
   (b)   the amount of the penalty is too high.

(2)   The court may—
   (a)   allow the appeal and cancel the penalty;
   (b)   allow the appeal and reduce the amount of the penalty;
   (c)   dismiss the appeal.

(3)   An appeal under this section is a re-hearing of the Secretary of State's decision and is to be determined having regard to—
   (a)   any code of practice under paragraph 10 which has effect at the time of the appeal;
   (b)   any other matter which the court thinks is relevant (whether or not the Secretary of State was aware of it).

(4) An appeal may be brought under this section whether or not—

    (a) the person has given notice of objection under paragraph 11(3);

    (b) the penalty has been reduced under paragraph 11(5).

(5) In this section "the court" is—

    (a) in England and Wales, a county court;

    (b) in Scotland, the sheriff.

(6) The sheriff may transfer the proceedings to the Court of Session.

(7) If the sheriff makes a determination under sub-paragraph (2), a party to the proceedings may appeal against the determination on a point of law to—

    (a) the Sheriff Principal, or

    (b) the Court of Session.

Forgery, etc.

13   (1) Section 188 has effect—

    (a) as if a compliance certificate were a "relevant document";

    (b) as if subsection (4) included a reference to a compliance certificate.

(2) A person commits an offence by pretending, with intent to deceive, to be a person authorised to exercise a power under paragraph 7.

(3) A person guilty of an offence under sub-paragraph (2) is liable on summary conviction to a fine not exceeding level 4 on the standard scale.

Regulations

14   A power to make regulations under this Schedule is exercisable by the Secretary of State.

Interpretation

15   (1) In this Schedule—

    "compliance assessment" has the meaning given in paragraph 1(5);

    "compliance certificate" has the meaning given in paragraph 1(2);

    "operator", in relation to a rail vehicle, means the person having the management of the vehicle.

(2) If an exemption order under section 183 authorises the use of a rail vehicle even though the vehicle does not conform with a provision of rail vehicle accessibility regulations, a reference in this Schedule to provisions of rail vehicle accessibility regulations with which the vehicle is required to conform does not, in relation to the vehicle, include a reference to that provision.

SCHEDULE 21

REASONABLE ADJUSTMENTS: SUPPLEMENTARY

Preliminary

1   This Schedule applies for the purposes of Schedules 2, 4, 8, 13 and 15.

Binding obligations, etc.

2   (1) This paragraph applies if —

(a) a binding obligation requires A to obtain the consent of another person to an alteration of premises which A occupies,

(b) where A is a controller of let premises, a binding obligation requires A to obtain the consent of another person to a variation of a term of the tenancy, or

(c) where A is a responsible person in relation to common parts, a binding obligation requires A to obtain the consent of another person to an alteration of the common parts.

(2) For the purpose of discharging a duty to make reasonable adjustments —

(a) it is always reasonable for A to have to take steps to obtain the consent, but

(b) it is never reasonable for A to have to make the alteration before the consent is obtained.

(3) In this Schedule, a binding obligation is a legally binding obligation in relation to premises, however arising; but the reference to a binding obligation in sub-paragraph (1)(a) or (c) does not include a reference to an obligation imposed by a tenancy.

(4) The steps referred to in sub-paragraph (2)(a) do not include applying to a court or tribunal.

Landlord's consent

3   (1) This paragraph applies if —

(a) A occupies premises under a tenancy,

(b) A is proposing to make an alteration to the premises so as to comply with a duty to make reasonable adjustments, and

(c) but for this paragraph, A would not be entitled to make the alteration.

(2) This paragraph also applies if —

(a) A is a responsible person in relation to common parts,

(b) A is proposing to make an alteration to the common parts so as to comply with a duty to make reasonable adjustments,

(c) A is the tenant of property which includes the common parts, and

(d) but for this paragraph, A would not be entitled to make the alteration.

(3) The tenancy has effect as if it provided —

(a) for A to be entitled to make the alteration with the written consent of the landlord,

(b) for A to have to make a written application for that consent,

(c) for the landlord not to withhold the consent unreasonably, and

(d) for the landlord to be able to give the consent subject to reasonable conditions.

(4) If a question arises as to whether A has made the alteration (and, accordingly, complied with a duty to make reasonable adjustments), any constraint attributable to the tenancy must be ignored unless A has applied to the landlord in writing for consent to the alteration.

(5) For the purposes of sub-paragraph (1) or (2), A must be treated as not entitled to make the alteration if the tenancy —

(a) imposes conditions which are to apply if A makes an alteration, or

(b) entitles the landlord to attach conditions to a consent to the alteration.

Proceedings before county court or sheriff

4 (1) This paragraph applies if, in a case within Part 3, 4, 6 or 7 of this Act —

(a) A has applied in writing to the landlord for consent to the alteration, and

(b) the landlord has refused to give consent or has given consent subject to a condition.

(2) A (or a disabled person with an interest in the alteration being made) may refer the matter to a county court or, in Scotland, the sheriff.

(3) The county court or sheriff must determine whether the refusal or condition is unreasonable.

(4) If the county court or sheriff finds that the refusal or condition is unreasonable, the county court or sheriff —

(a) may make such declaration as it thinks appropriate;

(b) may make an order authorising A to make the alteration specified in the order (and requiring A to comply with such conditions as are so specified).

Joining landlord as party to proceedings

5 (1) This paragraph applies to proceedings relating to a contravention of this Act by virtue of section 20.

(2) A party to the proceedings may request the employment tribunal, county court or sheriff ("the judicial authority") to direct that the landlord is joined or sisted as a party to the proceedings.

(3) The judicial authority —

(a) must grant the request if it is made before the hearing of the complaint or claim begins;

(b) may refuse the request if it is made after the hearing begins;

(c) must refuse the request if it is made after the complaint or claim has been determined.

(4) If the landlord is joined or sisted as a party to the proceedings, the judicial authority may determine whether —

(a) the landlord has refused to consent to the alteration;

    (b)   the landlord has consented subject to a condition;

    (c)   the refusal or condition was unreasonable.

(5)   If the judicial authority finds that the refusal or condition was unreasonable, it—

    (a)   may make such declaration as it thinks appropriate;

    (b)   may make an order authorising A to make the alteration specified in the order (and requiring A to comply with such conditions as are so specified);

    (c)   may order the landlord to pay compensation to the complainant or claimant.

(6)   An employment tribunal may act in reliance on sub-paragraph (5)(c) instead of, or in addition to, acting in reliance on section 124(2); but if it orders the landlord to pay compensation it must not do so in reliance on section 124(2).

(7)   If a county court or the sheriff orders the landlord to pay compensation, it may not order A to do so.

Regulations

6   (1)   Regulations may make provision as to circumstances in which a landlord is taken for the purposes of this Schedule to have—

    (a)   withheld consent;

    (b)   withheld consent reasonably;

    (c)   withheld consent unreasonably.

(2)   Regulations may make provision as to circumstances in which a condition subject to which a landlord gives consent is taken—

    (a)   to be reasonable;

    (b)   to be unreasonable.

(3)   Regulations may make provision supplementing or modifying the preceding paragraphs of this Schedule, or provision made under this paragraph, in relation to a case where A's tenancy is a sub-tenancy.

(4)   Provision made by virtue of this paragraph may amend the preceding paragraphs of this Schedule.

Interpretation

7   An expression used in this Schedule and in Schedule 2, 4, 8, 13 or 15 has the same meaning in this Schedule as in that Schedule.

SCHEDULE 22

Section 191

STATUTORY PROVISIONS

Statutory authority

1   (1)   A person (P) does not contravene a provision specified in the first column of the table, so far as relating to the protected characteristic specified in the second column in respect of that provision, if P does anything P must do pursuant to a requirement specified in the third column.

Specified provision	Protected characteristic	Requirement
Parts 3 to 7	Age	A requirement of an enactment
Parts 3 to 7 and 12	Disability	A requirement of an enactment
		A relevant requirement or condition imposed by virtue of an enactment
Parts 3 to 7	Religion or belief	A requirement of an enactment
		A relevant requirement or condition imposed by virtue of an enactment
Section 29(6) and Parts 6 and 7	Sex	A requirement of an enactment
Parts 3, 4, 6 and 7	Sexual orientation	A requirement of an enactment
		A relevant requirement or condition imposed by virtue of an enactment

(2) A reference in the table to Part 6 does not include a reference to that Part so far as relating to vocational training.

(3) In this paragraph a reference to an enactment includes a reference to—

  (a) a Measure of the General Synod of the Church of England;

  (b) an enactment passed or made on or after the date on which this Act is passed.

(4) In the table, a relevant requirement or condition is a requirement or condition imposed (whether before or after the passing of this Act) by—

  (a) a Minister of the Crown;

  (b) a member of the Scottish Executive;

  (c) the National Assembly for Wales (constituted by the Government of Wales Act 1998);

  (d) the Welsh Ministers, the First Minister for Wales or the Counsel General to the Welsh Assembly Government.

Protection of women

2 (1) A person (P) does not contravene a specified provision only by doing in relation to a woman (W) anything P is required to do to comply with—

  (a) a pre-1975 Act enactment concerning the protection of women;

  (b) a relevant statutory provision (within the meaning of Part 1 of the Health and Safety at Work etc. Act 1974) if it is done for the purpose of the protection of W (or a description of women which includes W);

    (c)   a requirement of a provision specified in Schedule 1 to the Employment Act 1989 (provisions concerned with protection of women at work).

(2)   The references to the protection of women are references to protecting women in relation to —

    (a)   pregnancy or maternity, or

    (b)   any other circumstances giving rise to risks specifically affecting women.

(3)   It does not matter whether the protection is restricted to women.

(4)   These are the specified provisions —

    (a)   Part 5 (work);

    (b)   Part 6 (education), so far as relating to vocational training.

(5)   A pre-1975 Act enactment is an enactment contained in —

    (a)   an Act passed before the Sex Discrimination Act 1975;

    (b)   an instrument approved or made by or under such an Act (including one approved or made after the passing of the 1975 Act).

(6)   If an Act repeals and re-enacts (with or without modification) a pre-1975 enactment then the provision re-enacted must be treated as being in a pre-1975 enactment.

(7)   For the purposes of sub-paragraph (1)(c), a reference to a provision in Schedule 1 to the Employment Act 1989 includes a reference to a provision for the time being having effect in place of it.

(8)   This paragraph applies only to the following protected characteristics —

    (a)   pregnancy and maternity;

    (b)   sex.

Educational appointments, etc: religious belief

3   (1)   A person does not contravene Part 5 (work) only by doing a relevant act in connection with the employment of another in a relevant position.

(2)   A relevant position is —

    (a)   the head teacher or principal of an educational establishment;

    (b)   the head, a fellow or other member of the academic staff of a college, or institution in the nature of a college, in a university;

    (c)   a professorship of a university which is a canon professorship or one to which a canonry is annexed.

(3)   A relevant act is anything it is necessary to do to comply with —

    (a)   a requirement of an instrument relating to the establishment that the head teacher or principal must be a member of a particular religious order;

    (b)   a requirement of an instrument relating to the college or institution that the holder of the position must be a woman;

    (c)   an Act or instrument in accordance with which the professorship is a canon professorship or one to which a canonry is annexed.

(4) Sub-paragraph (3)(b) does not apply to an instrument taking effect on or after 16 January 1990 (the day on which section 5(3) of the Employment Act 1989 came into force).

(5) A Minister of the Crown may by order provide that anything in sub-paragraphs (1) to (3) does not have effect in relation to —

    (a) a specified educational establishment or university;

    (b) a specified description of educational establishments.

(6) An educational establishment is —

    (a) a school within the meaning of the Education Act 1996 or the Education (Scotland) Act 1980;

    (b) a college, or institution in the nature of a college, in a university;

    (c) an institution designated by order made, or having effect as if made, under section 129 of the Education Reform Act 1988;

    (d) a college of further education within the meaning of section 36 of the Further and Higher Education (Scotland) Act 1992;

    (e) a university in Scotland;

    (f) an institution designated by order under section 28 of the Further and Higher Education Act 1992 or section 44 of the Further and Higher Education (Scotland) Act 1992.

(7) This paragraph does not affect paragraph 2 of Schedule 9.

4   A person does not contravene this Act only by doing anything which is permitted for the purposes of —

    (a) section 58(6) or (7) of the School Standards and Framework Act 1998 (dismissal of teachers because of failure to give religious education efficiently);

    (b) section 60(4) and (5) of that Act (religious considerations relating to certain appointments);

    (c) section 124A of that Act (preference for certain teachers at independent schools of a religious character).

Crown employment, etc.

5   (1) A person does not contravene this Act —

    (a) by making or continuing in force rules mentioned in sub-paragraph (2);

    (b) by publishing, displaying or implementing such rules;

    (c) by publishing the gist of such rules.

(2) The rules are rules restricting to persons of particular birth, nationality, descent or residence —

    (a) employment in the service of the Crown;

    (b) employment by a prescribed public body;

    (c) holding a public office (within the meaning of section 50).

(3) The power to make regulations for the purpose of sub-paragraph (2)(b) is exercisable by the Minister for the Civil Service.

(4) In this paragraph "public body" means a body (whether corporate or unincorporated) exercising public functions (within the meaning given by section 31(4)).

SCHEDULE 23   Section 196

GENERAL EXCEPTIONS

Acts authorised by statute or the executive

1   (1) This paragraph applies to anything done —

   (a) in pursuance of an enactment;

   (b) in pursuance of an instrument made by a member of the executive under an enactment;

   (c) to comply with a requirement imposed (whether before or after the passing of this Act) by a member of the executive by virtue of an enactment;

   (d) in pursuance of arrangements made (whether before or after the passing of this Act) by or with the approval of, or for the time being approved by, a Minister of the Crown;

   (e) to comply with a condition imposed (whether before or after the passing of this Act) by a Minister of the Crown.

   (2) A person does not contravene Part 3, 4, 5 or 6 by doing anything to which this paragraph applies which discriminates against another because of the other's nationality.

   (3) A person (A) does not contravene Part 3, 4, 5 or 6 if, by doing anything to which this paragraph applies, A discriminates against another (B) by applying to B a provision, criterion or practice which relates to —

   (a) B's place of ordinary residence;

   (b) the length of time B has been present or resident in or outside the United Kingdom or an area within it.

Organisations relating to religion or belief

2   (1) This paragraph applies to an organisation the purpose of which is —

   (a) to practise a religion or belief,

   (b) to advance a religion or belief,

   (c) to teach the practice or principles of a religion or belief,

   (d) to enable persons of a religion or belief to receive any benefit, or to engage in any activity, within the framework of that religion or belief, or

   (e) to foster or maintain good relations between persons of different religions or beliefs.

   (2) This paragraph does not apply to an organisation whose sole or main purpose is commercial.

   (3) The organisation does not contravene Part 3, 4 or 7, so far as relating to religion or belief or sexual orientation, only by restricting —

   (a) membership of the organisation;

   (b) participation in activities undertaken by the organisation or on its behalf or under its auspices;

   (c) the provision of goods, facilities or services in the course of activities undertaken by the organisation or on its behalf or under its auspices;

   (d) the use or disposal of premises owned or controlled by the organisation.

(4) A person does not contravene Part 3, 4 or 7, so far as relating to religion or belief or sexual orientation, only by doing anything mentioned in sub-paragraph (3) on behalf of or under the auspices of the organisation.

(5) A minister does not contravene Part 3, 4 or 7, so far as relating to religion or belief or sexual orientation, only by restricting —
  (a) participation in activities carried on in the performance of the minister's functions in connection with or in respect of the organisation;
  (b) the provision of goods, facilities or services in the course of activities carried on in the performance of the minister's functions in connection with or in respect of the organisation.

(6) Sub-paragraphs (3) to (5) permit a restriction relating to religion or belief only if it is imposed —
  (a) because of the purpose of the organisation, or
  (b) to avoid causing offence, on grounds of the religion or belief to which the organisation relates, to persons of that religion or belief.

(7) Sub-paragraphs (3) to (5) permit a restriction relating to sexual orientation only if it is imposed —
  (a) because it is necessary to comply with the doctrine of the organisation, or
  (b) to avoid conflict with strongly held convictions within sub-paragraph (9).

(8) In sub-paragraph (5), the reference to a minister is a reference to a minister of religion, or other person, who —
  (a) performs functions in connection with a religion or belief to which the organisation relates, and
  (b) holds an office or appointment in, or is accredited, approved or recognised for the purposes of the organisation.

(9) The strongly held convictions are —
  (a) in the case of a religion, the strongly held religious convictions of a significant number of the religion's followers;
  (b) in the case of a belief, the strongly held convictions relating to the belief of a significant number of the belief's followers.

(10) This paragraph does not permit anything which is prohibited by section 29, so far as relating to sexual orientation, if it is done —
  (a) on behalf of a public authority, and
  (b) under the terms of a contract between the organisation and the public authority.

(11) In the application of this paragraph in relation to sexual orientation, sub-paragraph (1)(e) must be ignored.

(12) In the application of this paragraph in relation to sexual orientation, in sub-paragraph (3)(d), "disposal" does not include disposal of an interest in premises by way of sale if the interest being disposed of is —
  (a) the entirety of the organisation's interest in the premises, or
  (b) the entirety of the interest in respect of which the organisation has power of disposal.

(13) In this paragraph —

    (a)   "disposal" is to be construed in accordance with section 38;

    (b)   "public authority" has the meaning given in section 150(1).

Communal accommodation

3   (1)   A person does not contravene this Act, so far as relating to sex discrimination or gender reassignment discrimination, only because of anything done in relation to —

    (a)   the admission of persons to communal accommodation;

    (b)   the provision of a benefit, facility or service linked to the accommodation.

    (2)   Sub-paragraph (1)(a) does not apply unless the accommodation is managed in a way which is as fair as possible to both men and women.

    (3)   In applying sub-paragraph (1)(a), account must be taken of —

    (a)   whether and how far it is reasonable to expect that the accommodation should be altered or extended or that further accommodation should be provided, and

    (b)   the frequency of the demand or need for use of the accommodation by persons of one sex as compared with those of the other.

    (4)   In applying sub-paragraph (1)(a) in relation to gender reassignment, account must also be taken of whether and how far the conduct in question is a proportionate means of achieving a legitimate aim.

    (5)   Communal accommodation is residential accommodation which includes dormitories or other shared sleeping accommodation which for reasons of privacy should be used only by persons of the same sex.

    (6)   Communal accommodation may include —

    (a)   shared sleeping accommodation for men and for women;

    (b)   ordinary sleeping accommodation;

    (c)   residential accommodation all or part of which should be used only by persons of the same sex because of the nature of the sanitary facilities serving the accommodation.

    (7)   A benefit, facility or service is linked to communal accommodation if —

    (a)   it cannot properly and effectively be provided except for those using the accommodation, and

    (b)   a person could be refused use of the accommodation in reliance on sub-paragraph (1)(a).

    (8)   This paragraph does not apply for the purposes of Part 5 (work) unless such arrangements as are reasonably practicable are made to compensate for —

    (a)   in a case where sub-paragraph (1)(a) applies, the refusal of use of the accommodation;

    (b)   in a case where sub-paragraph (1)(b) applies, the refusal of provision of the benefit, facility or service.

Training provided to non-EEA residents, etc.

4   (1)   A person (A) does not contravene this Act, so far as relating to nationality, only by providing a non-resident (B) with training, if A thinks that B does not intend to exercise in Great Britain skills B obtains as a result.

(2) A non-resident is a person who is not ordinarily resident in an EEA state.

(3) The reference to providing B with training is—

    (a) if A employs B in relevant employment, a reference to doing anything in or in connection with the employment;

    (b) if A as a principal allows B to do relevant contract work, a reference to doing anything in or in connection with allowing B to do the work;

    (c) in a case within paragraph (a) or (b) or any other case, a reference to affording B access to facilities for education or training or ancillary benefits.

(4) Employment or contract work is relevant if its sole or main purpose is the provision of training in skills.

(5) In the case of training provided by the armed forces or Secretary of State for purposes relating to defence, sub-paragraph (1) has effect as if—

    (a) the reference in sub-paragraph (2) to an EEA state were a reference to Great Britain, and

    (b) in sub-paragraph (4), for "its sole or main purpose is" there were substituted "it is for purposes including".

(6) "Contract work" and "principal" each have the meaning given in section 41.

SCHEDULE 24

Section 203

HARMONISATION: EXCEPTIONS

Part 1 (public sector duty regarding socio-economic inequalities)

Chapter 2 of Part 5 (occupational pensions)

Section 78 (gender pay gap)

Section 106 (election candidates: diversity information)

Chapters 1 to 3 and 5 of Part 9 (enforcement), except section 136

Sections 142 and 146 (unenforceable terms, declaration in respect of void terms)

Chapter 1 of Part 11 (public sector equality duty)

Part 12 (disabled persons: transport)

Part 13 (disability: miscellaneous)

Section 197 (power to specify age exceptions)

Part 15 (family property)

Part 16 (general and miscellaneous)

Schedule 1 (disability: supplementary provision)

In Schedule 3 (services and public functions: exceptions) —

   (a)   in Part 3 (health and care), paragraphs 13 and 14;

   (b)   Part 4 (immigration);

   (c)   Part 5 (insurance);

   (d)   Part 6 (marriage);

   (e)   Part 7 (separate and single services), except paragraph 30;

   (f)   Part 8 (television, radio and on-line broadcasting and distribution);

   (g)   Part 9 (transport);

   (h)   Part 10 (supplementary)

Schedule 4 (premises: reasonable adjustments)

Schedule 5 (premises: exceptions), except paragraph 1

Schedule 6 (office-holders: excluded offices), except so far as relating to colour or nationality or marriage and civil partnership

Schedule 8 (work: reasonable adjustments)

In Schedule 9 (work: exceptions) —

   (a)   Part 1 (general), except so far as relating to colour or nationality;

   (b)   Part 2 (exceptions relating to age);

   (c)   Part 3 (other exceptions), except paragraph 19 so far as relating to colour or nationality

Schedule 10 (education: accessibility for disabled pupils)

Schedule 13 (education: reasonable adjustments), except paragraphs 2, 5, 6 and 9

Schedule 17 (education: disabled pupils: enforcement)

Schedule 18 (public sector equality duty: exceptions)

Schedule 19 (list of public authorities)

Schedule 20 (rail vehicle accessibility: compliance)

Schedule 21 (reasonable adjustments: supplementary)

In Schedule 22 (exceptions: statutory provisions), paragraphs 2 and 5

Schedule 23 (general exceptions), except paragraph 2

Schedule 25 (information society services)

SCHEDULE 25

Section 206

INFORMATION SOCIETY SERVICES

Service providers

1   (1) This paragraph applies where a person concerned with the provision of an information society service (an "information society service provider") is established in Great Britain.

   (2) This Act applies to anything done by the person in an EEA state (other than the United Kingdom) in providing the service as this Act would apply if the act in question were done by the person in Great Britain.

2   (1) This paragraph applies where an information society service provider is established in an EEA state (other than the United Kingdom).

   (2) This Act does not apply to anything done by the person in providing the service.

Exceptions for mere conduits

3   (1) An information society service provider does not contravene this Act only by providing so much of an information society service as consists in —
      (a) the provision of access to a communication network, or
      (b) the transmission in a communication network of information provided by the recipient of the service.

   (2) But sub-paragraph (1) applies only if the service provider does not —
      (a) initiate the transmission,
      (b) select the recipient of the transmission, or
      (c) select or modify the information contained in the transmission.

   (3) For the purposes of sub-paragraph (1), the provision of access to a communication network, and the transmission of information in a communication network, includes the automatic, intermediate and transient storage of the information transmitted so far as the storage is solely for the purpose of carrying out the transmission in the network.

   (4) Sub-paragraph (3) does not apply if the information is stored for longer than is reasonably necessary for the transmission.

Exception for caching

4   (1) This paragraph applies where an information society service consists in the transmission in a communication network of information provided by a recipient of the service.

   (2) The information society service provider does not contravene this Act only by doing anything in connection with the automatic, intermediate and temporary storage of information so provided if —
      (a) the storage of the information is solely for the purpose of making more efficient the onward transmission of the information to other recipients of the service at their request, and
      (b) the condition in sub-paragraph (3) is satisfied.

   (3) The condition is that the service-provider —

(a)   does not modify the information,

(b)   complies with such conditions as are attached to having access to the information, and

(c)   (where sub-paragraph (4) applies) expeditiously removes the information or disables access to it.

(4)   This sub-paragraph applies if the service-provider obtains actual knowledge that—

(a)   the information at the initial source of the transmission has been removed from the network,

(b)   access to it has been disabled, or

(c)   a court or administrative authority has required the removal from the network of, or the disablement of access to, the information.

Exception for hosting

5   (1)   An information society service provider does not contravene this Act only by doing anything in providing so much of an information society service as consists in the storage of information provided by a recipient of the service, if—

(a)   the service provider had no actual knowledge when the information was provided that its provision amounted to a contravention of this Act, or

(b)   on obtaining actual knowledge that the provision of the information amounted to a contravention of that section, the service provider expeditiously removed the information or disabled access to it.

(2)   Sub-paragraph (1) does not apply if the recipient of the service is acting under the authority of the control of the service provider.

Monitoring obligations

6   An injunction or interdict under Part 1 of the Equality Act 2006 may not impose on a person concerned with the provision of a service of a description given in paragraph 3(1), 4(1) or 5(1)—

(a)   a liability the imposition of which would contravene Article 12, 13 or 14 of the E-Commerce Directive;

(b)   a general obligation of the description given in Article 15 of that Directive.

Interpretation

7   (1)   This paragraph applies for the purposes of this Schedule.

(2)   "Information society service"—

(a)   has the meaning given in Article 2(a) of the E-Commerce Directive (which refers to Article 1(2) of Directive 98/34/EC of the European Parliament and of the Council of 22 June 1998 laying down a procedure for the provision of information in the field of technical standards and regulations), and

(b)   is summarised in recital 17 of the E-Commerce Directive as covering "any service normally provided for remuneration, at a distance, by means of electronic equipment for the processing (including digital compression) and storage of data, and at the individual request of a recipient of a service".

(3) "The E-Commerce Directive" means Directive 2000/31/EC of the European Parliament and of the Council of 8 June 2000 on certain legal aspects of information society services, in particular electronic commerce, in the Internal Market (Directive on electronic commerce).

(4) "Recipient" means a person who (whether for professional purposes or not) uses an information society service, in particular for seeking information or making it accessible.

(5) An information society service-provider is "established" in a country or territory if the service-provider —
   (a) effectively pursues an economic activity using a fixed establishment in that country or territory for an indefinite period, and
   (b) is a national of an EEA state or a body mentioned in Article 48 of the EEC treaty.

(6) The presence or use in a particular place of equipment or other technical means of providing an information society service is not itself sufficient to constitute the establishment of a service-provider.

(7) Where it cannot be decided from which of a number of establishments an information society service is provided, the service is to be regarded as provided from the establishment at the centre of the information society service provider's activities relating to that service.

(8) Section 212(4) does not apply to references to providing a service.

SCHEDULE 26

AMENDMENTS

Section 211

Local Government Act 1988

1   Part 2 of the Local Government Act 1988 (public supply or works contracts) is amended as follows.

2   In section 17 (local and other public authority contracts: exclusion of non-commercial considerations) —
   (a) omit subsection (9), and
   (b) after that subsection insert —

   "(10) This section does not prevent a public authority to which it applies from exercising any function regulated by this section with reference to a non-commercial matter to the extent that the authority considers it necessary or expedient to do so to enable or facilitate compliance with —
      (a) the duty imposed on it by section 149 of the Equality Act 2010 (public sector equality duty), or
      (b) any duty imposed on it by regulations under section 153 or 154 of that Act (powers to impose specific duties)."

3   Omit section 18 (exceptions to section 17 relating to race relations matters).

4   In section 19 (provisions supplementary to or consequential on section 17) omit subsection (10).

Employment Act 1989

5   (1) Section 12 of the Employment Act 1989 (Sikhs: requirements as to safety helmets) is amended as follows.

     (2) In subsection (1), for "requirement or condition", in the first three places, substitute "provision, criterion or practice".

     (3) In that subsection, for the words from "section 1(1)(b)" to the end substitute "section 19 of the Equality Act 2010 (indirect discrimination), the provision, criterion or practice is to be taken as one in relation to which the condition in subsection (2)(d) of that section (proportionate means of achieving a legitimate aim) is satisfied".

     (4) In subsection (2), for the words from "the Race Relations Act" to the end substitute "section 13 of the Equality Act 2010 as giving rise to discrimination against any other person".

Equality Act 2006

6   The Equality Act 2006 is amended as follows.

7   (1) Section 8 (equality and diversity) is amended as follows.

     (2) In subsection (1)—
          (a) in paragraph (d) for "equality enactments" substitute "Equality Act 2010", and
          (b) in paragraph (e) for "the equality enactments" substitute "that Act".

     (3) In subsection (4) for "Disability Discrimination Act 1995 (c. 50)" substitute "Equality Act 2010".

8   In section 10(2) (meaning of group) for paragraph (d) substitute—
               "(d)   gender reassignment (within the meaning of section 7 of the Equality Act 2010),".

9   For section 11(3)(c) (interpretation) substitute—
               "(c)   a reference to the equality and human rights enactments is a reference to the Human Rights Act 1998, this Act and the Equality Act 2010."

10   (1) Section 14 (codes of practice) is amended as follows.

     (2) For subsection (1) substitute—

               "(1)   The Commission may issue a code of practice in connection with any matter addressed by the Equality Act 2010."

     (3) In subsection (2)(a) for "a provision or enactment listed in subsection (1)" substitute "the Equality Act 2010 or an enactment made under that Act".

     (4) In subsection (3)—

    (a)   in paragraph (a) for "section 49G(7) of the Disability Discrimination Act 1995 (c. 50)" substitute "section 190(7) of the Equality Act 2010", and

    (b)   for paragraph (c)(iv) substitute—

        "(iv)   section 190 of the Equality Act 2010."

  (5) In subsection (5)(a) for "listed in subsection (1)" substitute "a matter addressed by the Equality Act 2010".

  (6) In subsection (9) for "section 76A" to "duties)" substitute "section 149, 153 or 154 of the Equality Act 2010 (public sector equality duty)".

11   In section 16(4) (inquiries: matters which the Commission may consider and report on) for "equality enactments" substitute "Equality Act 2010".

12   In section 21(2)(b) (unlawful act notice: specification of legislative provision) for "equality enactments" substitute "Equality Act 2010".

13   After section 24 insert—

"24A Enforcement powers: supplemental

  (1) This section has effect in relation to—

    (a)   an act which is unlawful because, by virtue of any of sections 13 to 18 of the Equality Act 2010, it amounts to a contravention of any of Parts 3, 4, 5, 6 or 7 of that Act,

    (b)   an act which is unlawful because it amounts to a contravention of section 60(1) of that Act (or to a contravention of section 111 or 112 of that Act that relates to a contravention of section 60(1) of that Act) (enquiries about disability and health),

    (c)   an act which is unlawful because it amounts to a contravention of section 106 of that Act (information about diversity in range of election candidates etc.),

    (d)   an act which is unlawful because, by virtue of section 108(1) of that Act, it amounts to a contravention of any of Parts 3, 4, 5, 6 or 7 of that Act, or

    (e)   the application of a provision, criterion or practice which, by virtue of section 19 of that Act, amounts to a contravention of that Act.

  (2) For the purposes of sections 20 to 24 of this Act, it is immaterial whether the Commission knows or suspects that a person has been or may be affected by the unlawful act or application.

  (3) For those purposes, an unlawful act includes making arrangements to act in a particular way which would, if applied to an individual, amount to a contravention mentioned in subsection (1)(a).

  (4) Nothing in this Act affects the entitlement of a person to bring proceedings under the Equality Act 2010 in respect of a contravention mentioned in subsection (1)."

14   Omit section 25 (restraint of unlawful advertising etc.).

15   Omit section 26 (supplemental).

16 (1) Section 27 (conciliation) is amended as follows.

(2) For subsection (1) (disputes in relation to which the Commission may make arrangements for the provision of conciliation services) substitute—

"(1) The Commission may make arrangements for the provision of conciliation services for disputes in respect of which proceedings have been or could be determined by virtue of section 114 of the Equality Act 2010."

17 (1) Section 28 (legal assistance) is amended as follows.

(2) In subsection (1)—

(a) in paragraph (a) for "equality enactments" substitute "Equality Act 2010", and

(b) in paragraph (b) for "the equality enactments" substitute "that Act".

(3) In subsection (5) for "Part V of the Disability Discrimination Act 1995 (c. 50) (public" substitute "Part 12 of the Equality Act 2010 (disabled persons:".

(4) In subsection (6)—

(a) for "the equality enactments", on the first occasion it appears, substitute "the Equality Act 2010", and

(b) for "the equality enactments", on each other occasion it appears, substitute "that Act".

(5) In subsection (7)—

(a) in paragraph (a) for "equality enactments" substitute "Equality Act 2010", and

(b) in paragraph (b) for "the equality enactments" substitute "that Act".

(6) In subsection (8) for "Part V of the Disability Discrimination Act 1995 (c. 50)" substitute "Part 12 of the Equality Act 2010".

(7) In subsection (9) for "equality enactments" substitute "Equality Act 2010".

(8) In subsection (12)—

(a) for "A reference in" to "includes a reference" substitute "This section applies", and

(b) after paragraph (b) add "as it applies to the Equality Act 2010."

18 For section 31(1) (duties in respect of which Commission may assess compliance) substitute—

"(1) The Commission may assess the extent to which or the manner in which a person has complied with a duty under or by virtue of section 149, 153 or 154 of the Equality Act 2010 (public sector equality duty)."

19 (1) Section 32 (public sector duties: compliance notice) is amended as follows.

(2) For subsection (1) substitute—

"(1) This section applies where the Commission thinks that a person has failed to comply with a duty under or by virtue of section 149, 153 or 154 of the Equality Act 2010 (public sector equality duty)."

(3) In subsection (4) for "section 76A" to "Disability Discrimination Act 1995" substitute "section 149 of the Equality Act 2010".

(4) In subsection (9)(a) for "section 76A" to "Disability Discrimination Act 1995 (c. 50)" substitute "section 149 of the Equality Act 2010".

(5) In subsection (9)(b) for "in any other case" substitute "where the notice related to a duty by virtue of section 153 or 154 of that Act".

(6) In subsection (11) for "section 76B" to "Disability Discrimination Act 1995" substitute "section 153 or 154 of the Equality Act 2010".

20 Omit section 33 (equality and human rights enactments).

21 (1) Section 34 (meaning of unlawful) is amended as follows.

(2) In subsection (1) for "equality enactments" substitute "Equality Act 2010".

(3) In subsection (2) —
   (a) after "virtue of" insert "any of the following provisions of the Equality Act 2010", and
   (b) for paragraphs (a) to (c) substitute —
      "(a) section 1 (public sector duty regarding socio-economic inequalities),
       (b) section 149, 153 or 154 (public sector equality duty),
       (c) Part 12 (disabled persons: transport), or
       (d) section 190 (disability: improvements to let dwelling houses)."

22 (1) Section 35 (general: definitions) is amended as follows.

(2) In the definition of "religion or belief", for "Part 2 (as defined by section 44)" substitute "section 10 of the Equality Act 2010".

(3) For the definition of "sexual orientation" substitute —
      ""sexual orientation" has the same meaning as in section 12 of the Equality Act 2010."

23 In section 39(4) (orders subject to affirmative resolution procedure) for ", 27(10) or 33(3)" substitute "or 27(10)".

24 Omit section 43 (transitional: rented housing in Scotland).

25 Omit Part 2 (discrimination on grounds of religion or belief).

26 Omit section 81 (regulations).

27 Omit Part 4 (public functions).

28 In section 94(3) (extent: Northern Ireland) —
   (a) omit "and 41 to 56", and
   (b) omit "and the Disability Discrimination Act 1995 (c. 50)".

29 (1) Schedule 1 (the Commission: constitution, etc.) is amended as follows.

(2) In paragraph 52(3)(a) for "Parts 1, 3, 4, 5 and 5B of the Disability Discrimination Act 1995 (c. 50)" substitute "Parts 2, 3, 4, 6, 7, 12 and 13 of the Equality Act 2010, in so far as they relate to disability".

(3) In paragraph 53 for "Part 2 of the Disability Discrimination Act 1995 (c. 50)" substitute "Part 5 of the Equality Act 2010".

(4) In paragraph 54 for "Part 2 of the Disability Discrimination Act 1995" substitute "Part 5 of the Equality Act 2010".

30   In Schedule 3 (consequential amendments), omit paragraphs 6 to 35 and 41 to 56.

SCHEDULE 27   Section 211

REPEALS AND REVOCATIONS

PART 1

REPEALS

Short title	Extent of repeal
Equal Pay Act 1970	The whole Act.
Sex Discrimination Act 1975	The whole Act.
Race Relations Act 1976	The whole Act.
Sex Discrimination Act 1986	The whole Act.
Local Government Act 1988	Section 17(9). Section 18. Section 19(10).
Employment Act 1989	Sections 1 to 7. Section 9.
Social Security Act 1989	In Schedule 5, paragraph 5.
Disability Discrimination Act 1995	The whole Act.
Pensions Act 1995	Sections 62 to 65.
Greater London Authority Act 1999	Section 404.
Sex Discrimination (Election Candidates) Act 2002	Section 1.
Civil Partnership Act 2004	Section 6(1)(b) and (2).
Education (Additional Support for Learning) (Scotland) Act 2004	In section 17(1) "to exercise the functions which are conferred on a Tribunal by virtue of this Act".
Equality Act 2006	Section 25. Section 26. Section 33. Section 43. Part 2. Section 81. Part 4. In section 94(3) "and 41 to 56" and "and the Disability Discrimination Act 1995 (c. 50)". In Schedule 3 — (a) paragraphs 6 to 35; (b) paragraphs 41 to 56.

PART 2

REVOCATIONS

Title	Extent of revocation
Occupational Pension Schemes (Equal Treatment) Regulations 1995 (S.I. 1995/3183)	The whole Regulations.
Employment Equality (Religion or Belief) Regulations 2003 (S.I. 2003/1660)	The whole Regulations.
Employment Equality (Sexual Orientation) Regulations 2003 (S.I. 2003/1661)	The whole Regulations.
Disability Discrimination Act 1995 (Pensions) Regulations 2003 (S.I. 2003/2770)	The whole Regulations.
Occupational Pension Schemes (Equal Treatment) (Amendment) Regulations 2005 (S.I. 2005/1923)	The whole Regulations.
Employment Equality (Age) Regulations 2006 (S.I. 2006/1031)	The whole Regulations (other than Schedules 6 and 8).
Equality Act (Sexual Orientation) Regulations 2007 (S.I. 2007/1263)	The whole Regulations.
Sex Discrimination (Amendment of Legislation) Regulations 2008 (S.I. 2008/963)	The whole Regulations.

SCHEDULE 28

Section 214

INDEX OF DEFINED EXPRESSIONS

Expression	Provision
Accrual of rights, in relation to an occupational pension scheme	Section 212(12)
Additional maternity leave	Section 213(6) and (7)
Additional maternity leave period	Section 213(8)
Age discrimination	Section 25(1)

Expression	Provision
Age group	Section 5(2)
Armed forces	Section 212(1)
Association	Section 107(2)
Auxiliary aid	Section 20(11)
Belief	Section 10(2)
Breach of an equality clause or rule	Section 212(8)
The Commission	Section 212(1)
Commonhold	Section 38(7)
Compulsory maternity leave	Section 213(3)
Contract work	Section 41(6)
Contract worker	Section 41(7)
Contravention of this Act	Section 212(9)
Crown employment	Section 83(9)
Detriment	Section 212(1) and (5)
Disability	Section 6(1)
Disability discrimination	Section 25(2)
Disabled person	Section 6(2) and (4)
Discrimination	Sections 13 to 19, 21 and 108
Disposal, in relation to premises	Section 38(3) to (5)
Education Acts	Section 212(1)
Employer, in relation to an occupational pension scheme	Section 212(11)
Employment	Section 212(1)
Enactment	Section 212(1)
Equality clause	Section 212(1)
Equality rule	Section 212(1)
Firm	Section 46(2)
Gender reassignment	Section 7(1)
Gender reassignment discrimination	Section 25(3)
Harassment	Section 26(1)

Expression	Provision
Independent educational institution	Section 89(7)
LLP	Section 46(4)
Man	Section 212(1)
Marriage and civil partnership	Section 8
Marriage and civil partnership discrimination	Section 25(4)
Maternity equality clause	Section 212(1)
Maternity equality rule	Section 212(1)
Maternity leave	Section 213(2)
Member, in relation to an occupational pension scheme	Section 212(10)
Member of the executive	Section 212(7)
Non-discrimination rule	Section 212(1)
Occupation, in relation to premises	Section 212(6)
Occupational pension scheme	Section 212(1)
Offshore work	Section 82(3)
Ordinary maternity leave	Section 213(4) and (5)
Parent	Section 212(1)
Pension credit member	Section 212(11)
Pensionable service	Section 212(11)
Pensioner member	Section 212(11)
Personal office	Section 49(2)
Physical feature	Section 20(10)
Pregnancy and maternity discrimination	Section 25(5)
Premises	Section 38(2)
Prescribed	Section 212(1)
Profession	Section 212(1)
Proposed firm	Section 46(3)
Proposed LLP	Section 46(5)
Proprietor, in relation to a school	Section 89(4)

Expression	*Provision*
Protected characteristics	Section 4
Protected period, in relation to pregnancy	Section 18(6)
Provision of a service	Sections 31 and 212(4)
Public function	Sections 31(4) and 150(5)
Public office	Sections 50(2) and 52(4)
Pupil	Section 89(3)
Race	Section 9(1)
Race discrimination	Section 25(6)
Reasonable adjustments, duty to make	Section 20
Relevant member of the House of Commons staff	Section 83(5)
Relevant member of the House of Lords staff	Section 83(6)
Relevant person, in relation to a personal or public office	Section 52(6)
Religion	Section 10(1)
Religious or belief-related discrimination	Section 25(7)
Requirement, the first, second or third	Section 20
Responsible body, in relation to a further or higher education institution	Section 91(12)
Responsible body, in relation to a school	Section 85(9)
School	Section 89(5) and (6)
Service-provider	Section 29(1)
Sex	Section 11
Sex discrimination	Section 25(8)
Sex equality clause	Section 212(1)
Sex equality rule	Section 212(1)
Sexual orientation	Section 12(1)
Sexual orientation discrimination	Section 25(9)

Expression	Provision
Student	Section 94(3)
Subordinate legislation	Section 212(1)
Substantial	Section 212(1)
Taxi, for the purposes of Part 3 (services and public functions)	Schedule 2, paragraph 4
Taxi, for the purposes of Chapter 1 of Part 12 (disabled persons: transport)	Section 173(1)
Tenancy	Section 38(6)
Trade	Section 212(1)
Transsexual person	Section 7(2)
Trustees or managers, in relation to an occupational pension scheme	Section 212(11)
University	Section 94(4)
Victimisation	Section 27(1)
Vocational training	Section 56(6)
Woman	Section 212(1)